AN OXFORD COMPANION TO

THE ROMANTIC AGE

BRITISH CULTURE 1776–1832

IN MEMORY OF

PATSY HARDY

(1941–1994)

AN OXFORD COMPANION TO

THE ROMANTIC AGE

British Culture 1776–1832

GENERAL EDITOR

IAIN McCALMAN

ASSOCIATE EDITORS

Jon Mee   Gillian Russell   Clara Tuite

ASSISTANT EDITORS

Kate Fullagar   Patsy Hardy

OXFORD

UNIVERSITY PRESS

OXFORD

UNIVERSITY PRESS

Great Clarendon Street, Oxford OX2 6DP

Oxford University Press is a department of the University of Oxford.
It furthers the University's objective of excellence in research, scholarship,
and education by publishing worldwide in

Oxford New York

Athens Auckland Bangkok Bogotá Buenos Aires Calcutta
Cape Town Chennai Dar es Salaam Delhi Florence Hong Kong Istanbul
Karachi Kuala Lumpur Madrid Melbourne Mexico City Mumbai
Nairobi Paris São Paulo Singapore Taipei Tokyo Toronto Warsaw

with associated companies in Berlin Ibadan

Oxford is a registered trade mark of Oxford University Press
in the UK and in certain other countries

Published in the United States
by Oxford University Press Inc., New York

British Library Cataloguing in Publication Data

Data available

Library of Congress Cataloging in Publication Data

Data available

ISBN 0–19–812297–7

1 3 5 7 9 10 8 6 4 2

Typeset in Bulmer
by Jayvee, Trivandrum, India
Printed in Great Britain
on acid-free paper by
Bookcraft Ltd.,
Midsomer Norton, Somerset

PREFACE

Our *Companion* has unashamedly borrowed many of its aspirations and principles of organization from the insights and achievements of mighty predecessors in our period, 1776–1832—from the 'Presbyterian' encyclopedias, Romantic cultural miscellanies and histories, and fledgeling companions which I discuss in my historical introduction, 'A Romantic Age *Companion*'.

An undertaking as large as this accrues many debts, more than we can hope to acknowledge. However we would like to extend our particular thanks to Professor Paul Bourke and the Division of Historical Studies, Research School of the Social Sciences, Australian National University, who provided us with research assistance and encouragement to launch the enterprise; to the staff of the Humanities Research Centre, ANU, who have had to live with the untoward demands of the *Companion* for several years; to the Australian Research Council Special Research Centre for Cross-Cultural Research, ANU, for helping to provide editorial assistance in the crucial closing stages; to the Australian Research Council for providing a large grant to Professor McCalman, and small grants to Drs Mee and Russell, without which we would not have had the time or resources to undertake the project; and to All Souls College, Oxford, for providing Professor McCalman with a Visiting Fellowship in 1997–8 during which the editing was completed. Oxford University Press have been model publishers: encouraging, patient, rigorous, and constructively critical throughout, especially Jason Freeman, Andrew Lockett, and Frances Whistler, whose skills and friendship we have come to appreciate greatly. A number of our contributors have helped in various aspects of the editing process, over and above their formal commitments: Judith Barbour, Marilyn Butler, Deirdre Coleman, Martin Fitzpatrick, Jerome J. McGann, Mark Philp, and R. K. Webb deserve special mention in this regard. We would also like to extend warm thanks to our music advisers, Cyril Erlich, Simon McVeigh, and Philip Olleson, who gathered together a splendid network of music contributors for us. Good companions, all.

Readers will detect an inevitable antipodean inflection in our *Companion*: while this may carry some disadvantages, it also squares with our belief that much of the stunning vitality of the Romantic age derived from exchanges between margins and metropole.

IAIN MCCALMAN
JON MEE, GILLIAN RUSSELL, CLARA TUITE

CONTENTS

IV. EMERGING KNOWLEDGES

· PART TWO ·
ALPHABETICAL ENTRIES

NOTES TO READERS

This *Companion* divides into two separate, but interconnected, parts: major essays, followed by alphabetical entries. A network of cross-references, described below, links all elements of the book. In Part One we offer a series of long essays on key topics by leading experts, which aspire to combine general synthesis and leading-edge revisionist research. There are forty-two of these essays (counting the historical introduction), each of around 5,000 words. Though we have avoided any overall interpretative theory that would artificially integrate the whole, we have organized the essays under four broad conceptual headings: Transforming Polity and Nation; Reordering Social and Private Worlds; Culture, Consumption, and the Arts; and Emerging Knowledges. They can thus be read singly, in conceptual clusters, or systematically as a broad cultural history of the period. The index to Part One will further enable the reader to track incidents, events, individuals, or ideas across the full range of these essays.

Cross-references are of two kinds, to distinguish references to the two parts. In referring to the long essays in Part One, the title and essay number are given in bold, for example ***Enlightenment [32]**; running headlines in Part One will assist in locating the relevant essay. For references to the alphabetically organized entries in Part Two (and for cross-references between articles in that part), a simple asterisk is used before the word under which the article is ordered, for example Edmund *Burke.

The Part Two entries can be used to amplify the long essays or can function, encyclopedia-like, as a freestanding study aid or reference tool for rapid consultation. These shorter entries cover individual and group biographies, cultural and political movements, important incidents and events, influential ideas and discourses, and technical terms or definitions (titles of works do not have separate entries but are discussed under their authors). The criteria for inclusion are as follows: all subjects viewed by the editors as intrinsically and self-evidently important to the cultural history of the period; and, in addition, subjects which have been referred to—often more than once—by the essay contributors in Part One, and on which readers may seek further information. In some cases entries have been included for major figures, such as Locke, Hume, and Rousseau, who preceded our chronological period or who lived outside Britain, because we judge them to have exercised a major intellectual impact on the Romantic age: they are discussed mainly as conduits of ideas rather than as biographical figures.

Our aim in adopting this binary structure has been to accommodate the general reader, the enquiring student, and the scholarly specialist (appreciating that they can sometimes be the same person operating in different modes). By working the different parts of our *Companion* together, readers of all stamps can, we hope, gain fresh and multiple perspectives on this formative modern period and its cultural movements. And if the process of selection has been, and must always be, in some measure arbitrary, this *Companion* does at least reflect the choices of a great many specialists, as well as team of editors and editorial advisers. But there is deliberately no uniform voice or ideological line here. Like many of our protagonists in 'the Romantic age', we have given more emphasis to informed plurality than to homogeneity of outlook and style; and we have tried to retain that interest in marginality and idiosyncrasy which so illuminated the cultural miscellanies and histories of the Romantic age.

In Part Two headwords are arranged alphabetically, with Mc or M' ordered as though they were spelled Mac. Various one-line cross-references direct readers to appropriate sections. Bold capitals have been used for the names of people; bold upper and lower case have been used for all other words. Where people have two or more names, we have aimed to list them under the one most commonly used, though we have generally also provided a one-line cross-reference accommodating the alternative version. Thus, Frances Burney is found under Burney, not D'Arblay, and Henry Dundas is located under Dundas, not Melville. Figures who were known by various pseudonyms have mainly been ordered under their real names: 'Christopher North' is listed as John Wilson, 'Anthony Pasquin' is listed as John Williams. Welsh bards have been arranged according to their English names, though the corresponding Welsh name is included in the entry. In some cases individuals are discussed not as separate biographical entries but within their broader social, political, or cultural contexts: information on George 'Beau' Brummell, for example, is found in dandyism, on John Wilkes in Wilkites. One-line entries beside their names signal where the relevant entry is located.

Footnotes have not been used in either part. Instead, each essay in Part One is accompanied by a list of some dozen suggestions for further reading. Collectively these constitute a useful general bibliography for the period as a whole. Capitalization of titles of works—whether of our period or contemporary, whether English or non-English—has been standardized to modern conventions. Spelling has been modernized where appropriate.

We have relied heavily on certain publications to guide our style and accuracy, including the *Dictionary of National Biography*, *The Oxford Companion to English Literature*, and *The Feminist Companion to Literature in English*. For consistency in reference to architectural matters, we have deferred to H. M. Colvin's *A Biographical Dictionary of British Architects 1660–1840* (1995).

Last-mentioned but not least, the pictures form an integral part of the conception of the *Companion*. There are well over a hundred, chosen not merely to illustrate but also to amplify the information supplied in the essays and entries that they accompany. On many occasions an illustration is relevant to more than one part of the book, and here marginal cross-references draw the reader's attention to the figure-number in question. The aim has been to enhance both text and context, to reflect the fascination with visual culture—with new styles and subject-matter in painting, with print-making and caricature, fashion and design—of the Romantic epoch.

ESSAY CONTRIBUTORS

Assistant Professor Daniel Abramson, Connecticut College, Connecticut

Professor G. J. Barker-Benfield, University at Albany, State University of New York

Professor David Bindman, University College, London

Professor John Brewer, European University Institute, Florence

Dr Ian Britain, Monash University

Dr Robert Brown, Australian National University

Professor Marilyn Butler, Exeter College, Oxford

Professor Barbara Caine, Monash University

Professor James Chandler, University of Chicago

Professor Gregory Claeys, Royal Holloway and Bedford New College, London

Dr J. E. Cookson, University of Canterbury, Christchurch

Professor H. T. Dickinson, University of Edinburgh

Emeritus Professor Cyril Ehrlich, Queen's University, Belfast

Dr Martin Fitzpatrick, University of Wales, Aberystwyth

Dr Celina Fox, London

Dr John Gascoigne, University of New South Wales

Dr Mark Hallett, University of York

Dr Anne Janowitz, University of Warwick

Associate Professor Jon Klancher, Boston University

Dr Nigel Leask, Queens' College, Cambridge

Dr David Lemmings, University of Newcastle, New South Wales

Dr Sarah Lloyd, Australian National University

Professor Iain McCalman, Australian National University

Professor Jerome J. McGann, University of Virginia

Dr Simon McVeigh, Goldsmiths College, London

Dr C. Suzanne Matheson, University of Windsor, Ontario

Dr Jon Mee, University College, Oxford

Dr Peter Otto, University of Melbourne

Dr Maureen Perkins, University of Western Australia

Associate Professor David Philips, University of Melbourne

Dr Mark Philp, Oriel College, Oxford

Professor Roy Porter, Wellcome Institute for the History of Medicine, London

Dr Fiona Robertson, University of Durham

Dr Gillian Russell, Australian National University

Dr John Stevenson, Worcester College, Oxford

Professor Nicholas Thomas, Australian National University

Dr Clara Tuite, University of Melbourne

Professor James Walvin, University of York

Professor R. K. Webb, University of Maryland, Baltimore County

Professor Donald Winch, University of Sussex

Dr Eileen Yeo, University of Sussex

Dr Richard Yeo, Griffith University, Queensland

ENTRY CONTRIBUTORS

This list is alphabetical by contributor's surname, followed by the abbreviation used to identify his or her entries in Part Two. These abbreviations are usually the initial letters of the contributor's first-name and surname (sometimes, to avoid confusion, a contraction of the surname is used). Readers using this list to identify a contributor are thus advised to seek under the *last* element of the abbreviation.

Contributor	Abbreviation	Contributor	Abbreviation
William J. Ashworth	WJA	Trevor Herbert	TH
Simon Bainbridge	SB	Elisabeth Jay	EJ
Judith Barbour	JB	Geraint H. Jenkins	GHJ
George Biddlecombe	GB	Phyllis Kinney	PK
George A. Boeck	GAB	Jon Klancher	JK
Peter Borsay	PB	Jonathan Lamb	JL
Robert Brown	RB	Claire Lamont	CL
Janet Browne	JBR	Leanne Langley	LL
Andrew R. Buck	ARB	Fred Langman	FL
Miranda Burgess	MB	Nigel Leask	NL
Simon Burrows	SBU	David Lemmings	DL
Rosemary Campbell	RCA	Sarah Lloyd	SL
Malcolm Chase	MC	Sarah Lodge	SLO
William Christie	WC	Peter Lord	PL
Gregory Claeys	GC	Iain McCalman	IMCC
Deirdre Coleman	DC	Kirsten McCue	KMCC
Susan Conley	SC	Oliver MacDonagh	OMACD
Victoria L. Cooper	VLC	Alastair MacLachlan	AMACL
Ian Copland	IC	Christine MacLeod	CMACL
Rachel Cowgill	RC	Maureen McNeil	MMCN
Michael Davis	MD	Simon McVeigh	SMCV
R. W. Davis	RWD	Javed Majeed	JMA
Dorothy De Val	DDEV	C. Suzanne Matheson	CSM
Harry Dickinson	HD	Jon Mee	JM
Brian P. Dolan	BPD	Anne Mellor	AM
Detlef W. Dörrbecker	DWD	Prys Morgan	PM
David Duff	DD	John Morrow	JMO
Michael Durey	MDU	Timothy B. Morton	TBM
Paul Duro	PD	Iwan R. Morus	IRM
Gavin Edwards	GE	Andrew Noble	AN
Patricia Fara	PF	Peter B. Nockles	PBN
Martin Fitzpatrick	MF	Ruan O'Donnell	RO'D
Jonathan Fulcher	JF	Philip Olleson	PO
Kate Fullagar	KF	Peter Otto	POT
John Gascoigne	JGA	Fiona M. Palmer	FMP
Paula Gillett	PG	Benjamin Penny	BP
Kevin Gilmartin	KG	Maureen Perkins	MP
Jane Girdham	JG	Seamus Perry	SPP
Robbie Goh	RG	David Philips	DP
Knud Haakonssen	KH	Mark Philp	MPH
Lisbeth Haakonssen	LH	Stephanie R. Pratt	SRP
Jocelyn Hackforth-Jones	JH-J	Stephen Prickett	SP
Iain Hampsher-Monk	IH-M	Suzanne Rickard	SR
Christopher W. Hart	CWH	Nicholas Roe	NR
Judith Hawley	JH	Fred Rosen	FR
Andrew Hemingway	AH	Michael Rosenthal	MR

Gillian Russell	GR	Simon Ville	SV
Sean Sawyer	SS	James Walvin	JWA
James A. Secord	JAS	R. K. Webb	RKW
Michael Shortland	MSH	William Weber	WW
Samuel Smiles	SSM	Roger Wells	RW
Jane Stabler	JS	Shearer West	SW
Mark Storey	MS	R. S. White	RSW
Lee Taylor	LT	Lisa Wilson	LW
Udo Thiel	UT	John Wiltshire	JW
D. O. Thomas	DOT	Marcus Wood	MW
Nicholas Thomas	NT	Ian Woodfield	IW
Neil L. Tranter	NLT	David Worrall	DW
Clara Tuite	CT	Alison W. Yarrington	AWY
Paul Turnbull	PT	Richard Yeo	RY

A ROMANTIC AGE *COMPANION*

IAIN McCALMAN

When we first contemplated producing an *Oxford Companion* to British culture in the Romantic age, a shrewd early consultant dramatized the difficulties ahead by listing some of the subjects traversed in a cultural history source-book that had been compiled within the period itself. The *Omniana*, edited jointly by Robert *Southey and S. T. *Coleridge in 1812, covered such subjects as Methodist Camp meetings; Catholic devotion to the Virgin; ships' names; criticism; the Cap of Liberty; circulation of the blood; party passion; sects in Egypt; Toleration; beer and ale; dancing; the opinions of the *Edinburgh Review* concerning war; burial-grounds; young prodigies; and the universe. This was surely relevant material for the kind of work we were proposing, yet how on earth were we to draw our boundaries? Did we even know precisely what we meant by 'the Romantic period'? Was 'Romantic' in fact the most suitable label with which to frame the broad-based cultural history project that we had in mind? And how, practically, would we organize and control within a single, realistically sized volume the plethora of individuals, events, and ideas that should feature in such an ambitious undertaking? As cultural historians we intended to follow the published advice of editorial adviser and contributor Jerome McGann: to distinguish between Romanticism as a set of cultural/aesthetic formations and 'the Romantic period' as a particular historical epoch; but this approach also opened a Pandora's box of its own.

*Romanticism is a notoriously slippery concept of modern history. As early as 1801, in his *Neology, or Vocabulary of New Words*, the French radical littérateur L. S. Mercier had written of the word 'romantic' that one could certainly feel but should not define it. Most modern scholars feel similarly that Europe experienced a sweeping cultural transformation during the late eighteenth and early nineteenth centuries; few, however, can agree on its precise character or time period. It is a historical truism that the idea of Romanticism as a distinct, self-labelled cultural movement and aesthetic practice originated in late-eighteenth-century Germany, where a group of young patriotic artists and intellectuals headed by Friedrich Schlegel (1772–1829) fashioned a fighting programme that opposed both the revolutionary war and the dominant aesthetic values of their enemy, the French. Against the formal, mimetic style of French classicism, Schlegel and his comrades extolled the expressive, imaginative role of the artist; against the mechanistic Enlightenment materialism of the French *philosophes*, the German Romantics revered religion and feeling; against the universalist abstractions of French rationalism, they valued the organic, the particular, and the historical. Yet, as another of our editorial advisers and contributors, Marilyn Butler, has long argued, the anti-classical and anti-Gallic project of German Romanticism, however influential elsewhere in Europe, was not simply replicated in Britain. No wonder Louis Mercier had difficulty defining the neologism 'romantic' in 1801, for how was he to categorize his British relative by marriage, Thomas *Holcroft, who wrote 'Romantic' novels steeped in sensibility yet was as obsessively rationalist, Francophile, and revolutionary as Mercier himself? What, too, do we make of that archetypal young British Romantic, Percy *Shelley, who professed a closer affinity with the rational Enlightenment theories of *philosophes* like Voltaire, *Volney, and Holbach than with those of German Romantics like Schlegel and Novalis, whom he regarded as reactionaries? In his essay on **poetry [29]** Jerome McGann points out that the most canonical of all British Romantics, William *Wordsworth, in that most canonical of all manifestos, the Preface to the *Lyrical Ballads* (1800), levelled his fire not against classicism but against its opposite, attacking the extravagance, excess, and 'outrageous stimulation' engendered by *Gothic novels and *Della Cruscan poems of radical sensibility.

This contrast between Shelley and Wordsworth, men of different generations and opposite political persuasions, is a reminder of another of McGann's central points: unless we are careful, the label 'Romantic' can encourage us to overlook major conflicts and differences between even the most representative of its adherents. William *Blake, the spiky London artisan who espoused revolution, antinomianism, and excess, or Lord *Byron, the urbane Whig aristocrat, libertine, and satirist, both shared *some* but emphatically not *other* poetic and social aspirations with Wordsworth, whose introverted rural 'mythos' of landscape and common life has done so much to shape modern conceptions of British Romanticism. What these three disparate figures undoubtedly did share, McGann has elsewhere argued, was a 'Romantic ideology'. Crudely we may define this as a displacing ideal forged by artists, writers, and intellectuals as they struggled at the turn of the century to cope with commercial and professional changes in the arts and letters, as well as with the ferment of national war and revolution. Of course British Romanticism cannot be reduced simply to ideology: nevertheless it was nourished by the biographical myth that insecure intellectuals erected for themselves, a transcendent ideal that elevated creative *imagination, individual *genius, and the inward self over the prosaic requirements of scribbling for a living.

However much we might admire the work of great poets like Wordsworth and Coleridge, we do them and the British culture of their day a disservice by glossing over this ideological aspect of Romanticism. Isolating a narrow set of typical aesthetic features which we label 'Romantic' and then link to a precise temporal period—usually 1789–1832—can be a frustratingly circular and self-limiting process. Over the years it has led some critics to equate Romanticism with a tiny, exclusive, and diminishing band of poetic geniuses. The rich plurality of voices that featured in a standard late-nineteenth-century Romantic primer such as C. H. Herford's *The Age of Wordsworth* (1897) had, until relatively recently, become unfamiliar to most late-twentieth-century students and scholars. Herford, as a matter of course, analysed women writers like Amelia *Opie, Sydney *Owenson, and Charlotte *Smith; Irish, Scots, and other provincial novelists like Gerald *Griffin, William *Carleton, and Jane *Porter; dramatists like Joanna *Baillie; poets like Mary *Robinson and Felicia *Hemans; scientists like Thomas *Beddoes and Mary *Somerville; and historians like Catharine *Macaulay and William *Roscoe. Many of these now feature amongst the rich spectrum of writers discussed by Fiona Robertson in the **novel [31]**, and some are part of the lost pleiad that McGann would reinstate in a new cultural history of Romantic poetry.

Such a restoration must do more than simply recruit Wordsworth's obscurer friends or Jane *Austen's relatives. The rediscovery of neglected historical figures and events does not mean, either, that we must abandon the great Romantic canon. Rather, historical recovery enables us to recontextualize and enlarge this canon by shifting our angles of vision. Writers like Wordsworth and Coleridge can be freshly illuminated within the context of the fiery debates, crushing commercial pressures, and chance events of a historical period that was felt to be seething with conflict. Theirs was a time when world revolution featured as largely as the quest for inward consciousness. The 'Romantic age' must be capacious enough, for example, to encompass the sentimental and ardently libertarian Della Cruscan literary school of the 1780s. Otherwise we would simply be confirming the brilliant ideological work of professional *anti-Jacobins like William *Gifford who deliberately set about to extinguish the literary achievements of Della Cruscan radicals like Robert *Merry, Mary Robinson, and their legatee, John *Keats. We must appreciate that British Romanticism was not always introspective, rural, and quietistic. Some of its enthusiasms began and remained overtly political, public, and satirical (see *prints [22], David Bindman), as well as civic, classical, *millenarian, and *utopian [9] (Gregory Claeys). As often as not Romantics were deeply indebted, even when hostile, to the precursor cult of *sensibility [11] (G. J. Barker-Benfield) or to *Enlightenment [32] (Martin Fitzpatrick) missions of cultural discovery manifested in studies of *language [40] (Jon Mee), *mythology [36] (Nigel Leask), and *exploration [37] (Nicholas Thomas). And although we cannot hope within a single volume to do full justice to the powerful decentralist energies generated within our period—particularly in Ireland, which has rightly been given an *Oxford Companion* of its own, we must heed England's geographical and social peripheries. They ranged from the growing external *empire [5] (John Gascoigne) of Canada, Africa, Asia, and the Pacific to what some contemporaries felt were the internal 'colonies' of Scotland, Wales, and Ireland.

Under the rubric of 'the Romantic age' we must somehow find room for counterspirits— supposed misfits, throwbacks, and resisters such as the poet George *Crabbe, the philosopher-novelist William *Godwin, the utilitarian jurist Jeremy *Bentham, and the Scots orator Henry *Brougham, all of whom make it into William *Hazlitt's *Spirit of the Age* (1825) but are found rarely in the pages of modern surveys. Herford's primer took care to include many who stood to Romanticism 'in a relationship often of antagonism or disdain, of imperfect sympathy or half-hearted recoil'. Among these were some of the greatest writers of the eighteenth century; they included Adam *Smith and the early disciples of *political economy [33] (Donald Winch); Mary *Wollstonecraft and other marginalized *women [4] (Barbara Caine), thinkers said to lack the Romantic capacity of 'genius'; the neglected band of Dissenters, *Evangelicals, or pious rationalists (see *religion [10], R. K. Webb) who threw their creative energies into campaigns associated with *poverty [12] (Sarah Lloyd), *policing [7] (David Philips), and *slavery [6] (James Walvin). Because few of the canonical Romantics managed to have their plays staged, for example, does not alter the immense cultural significance of *theatre [24] (Gillian Russell) during our period. Because architecturally *neoclassicism was as fertile as Gothic Revival does not make *architecture [28] (Daniel Abramson) any the less important for students of Romanticism. Neither are we bound to accept without question Romanticism's most cherished given of all—the supremacy of the literary. At the very least we might ask how it is that literature became the dominant and often exclusive marker of 'the Romantic age' when the lens of cultural history reveals a vast field of other signs and symbolic systems in energetic circulation. These include vital expressions of *popular culture [23] (Iain McCalman and Maureen Perkins) such as songs, toasts, prints, parades, protests, and performances.

Given the morass of difficulties associated with the term 'Romantic', we were tempted to opt for the alternative period label often favoured by historians—'the age of Revolution'. Usually treated as synonymous with the rise of democracy, the revolutionary age seemed at least to possess clear-cut and symbolically freighted boundary markers. The American Declaration of Independence of 1776 signalled the opening of the period and the Great *Reform Act of 1832 closed it. There was no disputing, either, the powerful eighteenth-century resonance of the term 'revolution'. Though the word was already familiar in political discussion, it was the *French Revolution, and especially Edmund *Burke's version of it, which decisively overrode its earlier associations with an astronomical-like return to states of lawful virtue. Burke's *Reflections* of 1790 established the new idea of 'revolution' as a radical and decisive break with the past that overthrew an old order. Yet we soon found that the dominant political connotations of the term 'revolution' produced a fresh series of period ambiguities and exclusions. Even had politics been our sole concern, it is not clear that such a label would adequately have captured the *fin de siècle* peculiarities of the British case. H. T. Dickinson detects popular *democracy [3] in Britain well before both the American and French revolutions. He, Mark Philp, and J. E. Cookson also imply that a more appropriate label for our period might actually be 'the age of counter-revolution'. They point out that government and *loyalist opposition to France's export of *revolution [1] and *war [2] generated unintentionally convergent and transformative forces within Britain. Paradoxically, counter-revolution hastened the trend towards democracy, stimulated the state's centralizing fiscal, administrative, and welfare functions, and went a long way towards forging a new brand of British nationalism.

True, the word 'revolution' also began in the late eighteenth century to carry some association with the idea of change in the social as well as political order, but this has only produced a fresh crop of problems for modern scholars. When historians in the nineteenth century extended the term 'revolution' from the political to the economic sphere by coining the neologisms 'agricultural revolution' and 'industrial revolution', they instigated what we now know to be a false trail. The connotation of revolution as swift and total transformation made it a deeply inappropriate label for Britain's much more gradual and uneven process of *industrialization [14] (John Stevenson) and agricultural modernization (see *land [16], Anne Janowitz). To encompass these economic dimensions of revolution we would need to extend our period backwards and forwards by at least a century. Moreover, historians are only now beginning to appreciate the economic and cultural significance of *consumerism [19] (Roy Porter) in our period. Porter sees Romanticism and consumerism as linked movements, common outgrowths of a new epistemology and aesthetics of sensory experience and subjectivity that derived from the empiricism of *Locke.

Other contributors also register key cultural transformations: in *class [15] perceptions, conflicts, and languages (Eileen Yeo); in gender ideologies and expectations (see *domesticity [13], Clara Tuite); in the functioning of the ancient common *law [8] (David Lemmings) which had so long undergirded England's legal system; in the conceptions and practices of *natural philosophy [34] (Richard Yeo), now breaking into specialized, professionally tended science disciplines; in the mapping and understanding of human *psychology [39] (Robert Brown) and mental behaviour; and in the profession and practice of *medicine [18] (Roy Porter). Moreover, cultural change is of its nature less easy than politics to confine within strict and synchronous temporal boundaries. Cyril Ehrlich and Simon McVeigh argue, for example, that the real revolution in British *music [26] occurred in the 1830s, right at the end of our period. Conversely, one of Britain's most portentous transformations—the rise of new opinion-making cultural publics—seems to have begun around the mid-eighteenth century. Changes in the professions, institutions, and markets of *publishing [21] (John Brewer and Iain McCalman), *prose [30] (Jon Klancher), *painting [27] (Mark Hallett), *viewing [20] (Suzanne Matheson), and *design [25] (Celina Fox) reflected the growth of new leisured and sociable reading, reasoning, and buying publics. Such publics (for there were more than one) included a mix of commercial, professional, and middling sorts—women and men, provincials and metropolitans. Often unenfranchised and socially marginalized, these groups saw themselves as 'patriots' deploying a constellation of nativist, puritan, and civic humanist or 'country' traditions of thought to criticize Britain's morally decadent aristocratic élites. Their collective cultural project and products can be seen as a *Kulturkampf*, a new cultural consciousness that demanded moral regeneration through national rebirth.

This last idea returns us to the starting-point of our discussion—what to call our period? It also suggests, on balance, that 'Romantic age' is the best available label, provided we understand it to signify an age of self-conscious and diverse cultural revolution that takes its name from the canonical group of writers who crystallized many of its key changes and who became ideologically ascendant in the process. Ultimately this phrase best encompasses our conception of British cultural transformation over a temporal period roughly bounded by the 1770s and the 1830s. True, the period must necessarily remain a little fuzzy, extending forwards and backwards where appropriate, but, as McGann has argued in *The New Oxford Book of Romantic Period Verse* (1994), that very fuzziness can be productive. To adapt a phrase from the cultural historian Robert Darnton, Romanticism is 'good to think' because it highlights ambiguities and complexities. Despite the fact that 'Romantic' was not a consistently used self-label of late Georgian and *Regency British intellectuals, and despite the many differences and conflicts between the men and women writers, musicians, scientists, and painters who occupy these pages, they seem to have shared a sense of participating in a massive movement of cultural revisionism. This awareness pervades Hazlitt's *Spirit of the Age* from beginning to end. In almost every biography, including those of such super-rational spirits as Bentham and Godwin, he also finds occasion to use the word 'romantic', as if groping for some unifying label to contain his diverse and conflicting cast. And if the impact of political revolution greatly complicated and sometimes fractured the forms of this revisionist cultural project, in no case did it altogether eclipse the original ideal.

Our protagonists shared a sense of living in and being shaped by a revolutionary historical time. James Chandler shows that poets from *Barbauld to Shelley and novelists from *Scott to *Bulwer-Lytton experienced a new and exhilarating sense of *history [38]. They believed themselves to be participating in a common temporal period moved by its own characteristic energies. The rapidity of social change and communication made them feel that human relations were being transformed under their very eyes. Never before, John Stuart *Mill observed in the *Examiner* in 1831, had the notion of comparing one's own time with earlier epochs been *the* dominant idea of an age. Contemporaries sensed, and often said, that they were part of a second cultural Renaissance. This was a common aspiration whether or not one questioned the chances of surpassing the achievements of mighty predecessors like *Shakespeare and *Milton. Fittingly, their project for cultural regeneration often entailed novel efforts to recover, understand, and map the character of culture itself, deploying in the process new forms of *literary theory [41] (Peter Otto), interdisciplinarity, and comparativism.

Moreover, the challenge of how to frame a cultural history that adequately captured the multiplicity of human experience rang just as loudly two centuries ago in the ears of the editors of a contemporary guidebook like the *Omniana*. Compiling works of this kind confronted Coleridge and Southey repeatedly with what they had early come to view as a crisis of their own age—the problem of whether it was possible to retain or recover the unity of knowledge in the face of unprecedented tendencies towards diversity and fragmentation. Following Michel Foucault, the eighteenth century is often seen as the 'age of classification' in which Enlightenment *philosophes* tried to exercise dominion over the world by ordering, classifying, and controlling all knowledge within a rational system. Nowhere was this taxonomic mission better exemplified than in D'Alembert's *Encyclopédie* (1751–72) and Smellie's *Encyclopaedia Britannica* (1768–71). Yet Coleridge, for one, believed that the massive *encyclopedias of his own day had already abandoned the great Renaissance ideal of representing the unity of the arts and sciences according to a systematic plan. 'What a strange abuse has been made of the word encyclopaedia!' he wrote to Southey in 1803. 'It signifies, properly, grammar, logic, rhetoric, and ethics and metaphysics, which . . . formed a circle of knowledge . . . To call a huge unconnected miscellany of the *omne scibile*, in an arrangement determined by the accident of initial letters, an encyclopaedia, is an impudent ignorance of your Presbyterian bookmakers.'

By 1817, when he was himself approached to edit the *Encyclopaedia Metropolitana*, Coleridge had an even clearer sense of what a betrayal of the great Western encyclopedic enterprise had been perpetrated by 'Presbyterian bookmakers'. By the latter he meant the string of editors and publishers who had produced various versions of *Chambers's Cyclopaedia* (1728) and its vast successor, the *Encyclopaedia Britannica*. Coleridge criticized men like Ephraim Chambers (*c*.1680–1740), James 'Balloon' Tytler (?1747–1805), Abraham Rees (1743–1825), George Gleig (1753–1840), and William Smellie (1740–95), along with their textual enterprises, on several scores. These men and their books were for the most part products of the *Scottish Enlightenment—Dissenters, rationalists, or sceptics whom Coleridge saw as British counterparts of the encyclopedists in France. The French *philosophes* Diderot and D'Alembert had notoriously used their encyclopedia to lop religion off a reorganized tree of knowledge. If the French Revolution had been ushered in by the efforts of a conspiracy of atheistical *philosophes*, the *Encyclopédie* had been their *machine de guerre*.

In the Britain of 1817 the evidence of a similarly radicalized encyclopedism was everywhere to be seen, many of its products coming from Coleridge's former political colleagues. There were litanies of ruling-class corruption like P. F. McCallum's *Red Book* of 1810 (modelled on France's infamous *Livre Rouge* of 1790), subversive radical dictionaries like Charles *Pigott's notorious *Political Dictionary* (1795), infidel periodicals like George Cannon's *Theological Inquirer* (1815) claiming to be a condensed *Collectanea Sceptica* of all the ages, and influential radical knowledge miscellanies like H. D. Symonds's *Universal Magazine* (1804–15). By abandoning systematic method in favour of alphabetical organization, the Scottish encyclopedists had, Coleridge believed, hastened the democratization, fragmentation, and trivialization of knowledge. Responsibility for shaping and purveying the system of learning had been wrenched from a learned and enlightened author and given over to an ignorant reader who would either raid the encyclopedia indiscriminately or read its miscellaneous contents from beginning to end with the mindless alphabetical logic of the autodidact. Coleridge could glimpse a trend towards the manufacturing of cheap condensations of knowledge for a mass market that would in the 1830s overturn élite *education [17] (Ian Britain) through the penny cyclopedias of Henry Brougham's Society for the Diffusion of Useful Knowledge. Where encyclopedias still aimed to reach the learned reader, it was no longer a rounded scholar like Coleridge himself that they sought but a narrow expert interested only in the coverage of specialized subjects.

Coleridge believed that the Scottish encyclopedists had profoundly misread their historical age. Their ragbag methods, he wrote in 1817, had failed to deliver a coherent philosophical response to the 'scientific and moral revolutions' of recent times, and they had overlooked a 'manifest tendency' in arts and sciences to move towards unity rather than fragmentation, 'to lose their former insulated character and organize themselves as one harmonious body of knowledge'. German *Naturphilosophie* pointed the way, and Coleridge drew on such foreign theory when outlining a 'methodical compendium' of knowledge to lead his projected reader in logical steps up an ascending chain of knowledge. This would comprise eight interconnected 'classes' which progressed by organic linkages through pure, mixed, and applied philosophical principles towards a universal idea. His ambitious schema was destined, however, never to be tried. Practicalities of time, cost, and reader accessibility forced the publisher to make an immediate modification, then eventually to reconstruct the encyclopedia altogether. Coleridge's contribution was confined largely to the *Prospectus* (1817) and a *General Introduction* published in January 1818. His grand pedagogic vision had been reduced, he fumed, to a 'topsy-turvied' farce, 'an infamous catchpenny'.

Coleridge's old friend Southey was not surprised. He himself had withdrawn from editing a vast *Bibliotheca Britannica* proposed by Longmans in 1803, tactfully resisting an extraordinary nine-volume outline supplied by Coleridge because 'your plan is too good, too gigantic, quite beyond my powers'. Actually, Southey was being perfectly candid. He knew that he lacked a philosophic cast of mind, and had half-hoped (he told a Bristol correspondent in July 1803) that such a project would give 'present focus' to 'stray reading', perhaps 'sprouting out like potato-rinds to an uncalculated return'. Coleridge's grandiose vision had crystallized what Southey and many of his friends already sensed: an eighteenth-century information explosion powered by new print technologies and an accelerating popular literacy had ended the possibility of total knowledge. Indeed, systematic encyclopedism had long been satirized as a quixotic and futile exercise by Laurence Sterne, one of Southey's favourite novelists. Sterne's *Tristram Shandy* (1759) encapsulated the encyclopedic personality in its portrait of the eccen-

1. Portrait of Robert Southey (1795), painted by Peter Van Dyke during Southey's radical years and initial friendship with Coleridge.

tric scholar-pedant Slawkenbergius, compiler of the folio *De Nasis*. Our contributor Judith Hawley has elsewhere shown how Sterne's fiction anticipated Bakhtinian multivocality by shadowing and parodying the Enlightenment encyclopedic mission, consciously using its forms to celebrate fragmentation, heterogeneity, and even incoherence. Hack counterparts of Slawkenbergius can also be found in a succession of satirical verse ethnographies, from Pope's *Dunciad* (1728), through *Mathias's *Pursuits of Literature* (1795) and Byron's *English Bards and Scotch Reviewers* (1809), to W. H. *Ireland's paradoxically encyclopedic *Scribblomania* of 1815. When, in the same year, Thomas Love *Peacock wrote *Headlong Hall*, he inevitably chose Coleridge as a model for the eccentric Mr Panscope, 'who had run through the whole circle of sciences, and understood them all equally well', and who spent his spare moments feverishly reading Abraham Rees's edition of the *Cyclopaedia*.

Yet, though they might be sceptical of Panscopic aspirations to restore encyclopedic unity to the circle of the arts and sciences, many of Coleridge's colleagues seemed to have worked towards a similar end—only in different ways—by embracing the very principles of miscellany and subjectivity that he so abhorred. Whether or not consciously, they seem to have replaced the lost mission of encyclopedism with a new, early-nineteenth-century derivative—the Romantic cultural history laid out in commonplace books, table books, everyday books, conversation books, and *essay collections. No one illustrates this new trajectory better than William Hazlitt, who abandoned his early Coleridge-like aspiration of becoming a famous systematizer when his philosophical works of 1805 and 1812 flopped. By 1817, when Coleridge was penning his mammoth *Prospectus*, Hazlitt had found a new forte and purpose as a writer of miscellaneous essays. Building on the inspiration of Renaissance forebears such as Montaigne and Rabelais, as well as the comically learned and haphazard ramblings of Thomas Amory's *John Buncle* (1766), Hazlitt fashioned an alternative to Coleridge's ideal of universal knowledge. He used the impressionistic personal essay written in 'familiar' but not 'random' style to impose meaning and coherence on the chaos of contemporary knowledge. It aimed to evoke the spirit of the age by interpreting the actions of the subjective mind operating in history, and in doing so foreshadowed the eclectic mode of writing that was to become so characteristic of its successor, the Victorian age. Hazlitt had already told Henry Crabb *Robinson in 1810 that he lacked the necessary talents for encyclopedia writing: these were to condense a comprehensive and authoritative survey of facts and theories 'already known or advanced'. Where an encyclopedia finished, he liked to begin, by adding 'an idle speculation or two of my own'. True, the Edinburgh lawyer and editor of the *Supplement* to the *Encyclopaedia Britannica* (1815–45), Macvey Napier (1776–1847), did manage to recruit Hazlitt to write a major essay on 'Fine Arts'. However, Napier—in Coleridge's terms an archetypal 'Presbyterian bookmaker'—was deeply disconcerted by the result, criticizing Hazlitt's idiosyncratic assertions, free informal tone, and liberal use of literary tropes and figures. Hazlitt's real answer to such systematic encyclopedism was to produce a brilliant series of miscellaneous, personal, and discursive works which blended the *lecture, the sociable conversation, and the learned reference book—*Round Table* (1818), *Table Talk* (1821–2), *Spirit of the Age* (1825), *The Plain Speaker* (1826), and *Conversations with James Northcote* (1830). Significantly, his poetic counterpart, Lord Byron, was launching a similar project at a similar time. Soon after the publication of *Round Table*, Byron began fashioning his medley epic *Don Juan* (1819–24), a reply to the philosophical pretensions of Coleridge's *Biographia Literaria*.

   Southey's cultural histories of his own times, also written in the early decades of the nineteenth century, rested still more centrally on the principles and methods of miscellany. They included a documentary-fictive collection of *Letters from England* (1807), a Shandyesque encyclopedia novel, *The Doctor* (1834–47), a conversation book with the dead, *Sir Thomas More; or Colloquies on the Prospects of Society* (1829), and, of course, the collaborative compilation *Omniana* (1812). All these miscellany-histories were built on the same recondite foundations: several shrewd contemporary critics noted that the commonplace book stood at the heart of Southey's method as a prose writer, *reviewer, essayist, and historian. Surprisingly, though, none seems to have recognized his innovative adaptation of the commonplace principle. For centuries the commonplace book had been a standard authorial tool, used primarily as an *aide-mémoire* arranged under systematic heads for retrieving stock aphorisms and information in order to enhance conversation, formal rhetoric, and *sermons. *Companion* contributor Richard Yeo has argued recently that the commonplace book thus played an important, if complex, role in the evolution of the late-eighteenth-century encyclopedia. But Southey's commonplace books differed from the conventional encyclopedic ideal, and from those of many predecessors, in having a definite and original interpretative purpose. While some commonplace collectors might vaguely gather information illustrative of the universal virtues and vices of mankind, Southey was obsessed, as Crabb Robinson noted in an 1812 review of *Omniana*, with the curiosities, queer things, and 'perversities and whims' within the culture of his day. On one level we can see Southey engaged in the pervasive quest of Romantic *antiquarianism [35] (Marilyn Butler) to chart and recover folk cultures threatened with extinction by the rapidity of social and industrial change. His commonplace books bear a close resemblance, for example, to the successful 'kaleidoscope' folk miscellanies which the radical publisher William *Hone began producing in the late 1820s under such titles as *The Everyday Book* and *The Table Book*.

Southey's second, related preoccupation in these commonplace books was with the under-world currents of popular enthusiasm, irrationality, *quackery, occult science, and superstition which still ran strongly in the Britain of his day, notwithstanding all the forces of rational modernity working towards their demise. He viewed such phenomena with a mixture of fear and fascination, but he frequently warned his readers not to despise the imaginative, creative, and often prescient energies of such ancient folk ways. Few Romantic contemporaries charted this terrain better, as he skilfully deployed the rich bric-à-brac of a lifetime of prodigious reading and notation. Motley and miscellany were thus mobilized in the interests of cultural history: visual counterparts can be seen in a proliferation of British rebuses, collectors' cabinets, and capriccio pictograms. At his best Southey anticipated both Walter Benjamin's modern utopian project to build a history purely from the bricolage of other people's writings and E. P. Thompson's great mission to rescue the culture of the common peoples from posterity's enormous condescension.

Surprisingly Coleridge himself, that inveterate foe of encyclopedic miscellany, pioneered a related Romantic cultural genre of 'table talk'. In a letter of 1810 Southey noted ironically that his old friend's fetish for rational system went hand in hand with 'rambling' habits of reading, organizing, and talking. Few contemporaries disputed Hazlitt's judgement that Coleridge was the greatest talker of his age: the polymathic range and randomness of his discourse was legendary. In a letter of April 1819 John Keats recalled a two-mile walk on Hampstead Heath during which Coleridge 'broached a thousand things', ranging over such topics as nightingales, metaphysics, different genera and species of dreams, nightmares, monsters, the Kraken, and mermaids. Contemporaries were divided, however, as to whether any unifying principle underlay such barrages of discourse. Thomas *Carlyle claimed acerbically in 1824 that Coleridge had 'no method in his talk; he wanders like a man sailing among many currents.' But those who knew Coleridge better thought they saw something deeper. Wordsworth observed in 1830 that 'there was always a train, a stream in Coleridge's discourse . . . a connection between its parts in his own mind'. Thomas *De Quincey, writing in *Blackwood's Magazine* in 1845, identified a principle in operation which he defined as 'the vast power of combination'. He believed that Coleridge could gather 'into focal concentration the largest body of objects, apparently disconnected, that any man ever yet, by any magic could assemble, or, having assembled, could manage'.

Certainly Coleridge had very definite ideas on the character and purpose of table talk as a literary genre. Drawing inspiration from the published conversation of Martin Luther (1652), as well, no doubt, as that of the great talker Samuel *Johnson, Coleridge asserted that table talk was a vital form of pedagogy. As such, it needed to establish a mean between the strictly private and the public subject, between spontaneity and systematic exposition. But it was emphatically not, he stressed, a democratic form like the wretched Scottish popular encyclopedias. Rather, its provenance was firmly linked to his ideal of clerisy: it should comprise learned discourse which addressed all the personal, intellectual, and civic contexts of educated hearers (and readers). Despite its Edinburgh origins, Coleridge would thus probably not have disputed the definition of table talk outlined in the preface to *Constable's Miscellany* of 1827. Borrowing from classical and oriental models, this called for a judicious blending of 'moral apophthegms', critical remarks, comic and serious incidents, and scientific or literary information 'more or less modified by natural habits and the state of human knowledge'.

As this suggests—though Coleridge would have been the last person to concede it—the Scottish encyclopedists of his day had been no less conscious than he of the need to grapple on many fronts with the problem of unity and diversity within an exploding and fissiparous world of knowledge. Chambers, like Southey, had been keenly aware of the emergence of a general, as well as of a specialized, brand of reader, and had sought to reach both these publics. Like Southey, too, he had believed that miscellany could work in intellectually creative and serendipitous ways. He noted in his Preface to the *Cyclopaedia* that in 'the promiscuous system' of alphabetical ordering, 'where numbers of things are thrown precariously together, we sometimes discover relations among them'. But, above all, the alphabetical system facilitated easy retrieval of information for the reader, especially for the non-scholar whose needs might be occasional and particular. Moreover, Chambers had, like Coleridge, attempted to retain or recover the possibility of systematic reading by publishing a map of knowledge at the front of his *Cyclopaedia*. In theory, this chart could enable the reader to reassemble the scattered alphabetical parts into a coherent, systematic whole. And if the editors of the subsequent *Encyclopaedia Britannica* abandoned such a plan, they nevertheless worked to institute new forms of intellectual coherence by other means. One of these was to rely on the Scottish Enlightenment principle of historicity. Dugald *Stewart thought that the defects of D'Alembert's *Encyclopédie* might partially be remedied by tracing the genealogy and evolution of ideas, as well as their relations. The controversial introduction of biography in later editions of the *Britannica* amplified this emphasis on the historicity of knowledge. By commissioning long essays from experts in each of the newly emerging disciplines within the arts and sciences, the *Encyclopaedia Britannica* also worked to achieve systematic interpretation and analysis within, if not between, its parts. In the process it moved the large-scale eighteenth-century encyclopedia from being primarily a synthesizer and condenser of second-hand knowledge to a potential source of leading-edge analysis by the disciplinary experts of the day. Thus at one level the *Britannica* had achieved what Coleridge could only have approved: it had shaped itself to speak solely to the learned, leaving general readers to appease their magpie appetites by using cheaper, abbreviated dictionaries of terms.

Somewhere between the massive encyclopedias of the 'Presbyterian bookmakers' and the idiosyncratic cultural miscellanies of Southey and his ilk, another genre made a quiet entry onto the publishing scene during the Romantic period. This was the '*Companion*'. Books of this title had appeared intermittently since at least the seventeenth century, but there is a marked increase from the mid- to late eighteenth century, continuing steadily into the Victorian age. What was a *Companion*? Nobody, including its authors, seems to have been sure; throughout our period the genre manifests a particularly unstable and uncertain identity. One of its oldest and most consistent incarnations seems to have been as a form of commonplace book or anthology providing religious homilies and consolatory advice to the sick, sad, or confused. Here the word '*Companion*' presumably aimed to instil a sense of comfort and solace. Another sub-genre of *Companion* clearly saw itself as a source of friendly entertainment: there are a plethora of 'cheerful', 'jovial', 'recreative', and 'agreeable' early-nineteenth-century *Companions* mostly retailing *glees, songs, jokes, toasts, enigmas, charades, rebuses, customs, and sayings. By contrast, we also find highly specialist scientific *Companions* on such subjects as astronomical globes or the sidereal hemispheres of the solar system. These combine encyclopedia-like condensations of information with shorter definitions of terms. Finally, a multitude of literary and philosophical *Companions*, many of them anthologies of poems, tales, fables, and essays have been broken into extracts or summarized to serve as portable, cheap substitutes for expensive scholarly libraries. What seems to link all such diverse sub-genres seems to be an aspiration towards what today would be called 'reader-friendliness'. They stress the possible pleasure, ease, and sociability entailed in acquiring knowledge.

This, too, was powerfully in the mind of Leigh *Hunt when in 1828 he launched a generically related miscellaneous literary and political magazine which he called *The Companion*. He hoped it would blend Baconian knowledge, 'the pleasures of the imagination and the advantages of moral truth', 'the common talk of life', and the irresistible solvent of freely expressed political opinion. Following in the footsteps of his earlier, varyingly successful magazines such as *The Examiner* (1808), *The Reflector* (1810–12), and *The Liberal* (1822–3), he aimed to produce a middlebrow miscellany which reflected the personal viewpoints and talents of a group of like-minded literary companions. In the past these had included his brother John Hunt (1775–1848), as well as his friends *Lamb, Hazlitt, Byron, and Shelley. Although personal differences among this group had been a major source of the failure of his previous enterprises, Hunt was determined to try again. His *Companion* contributors, he stressed, would not express a unified view of the world, but generate a collision and comparison of opinions from which truth would emerge. Finally, he hoped to present the work in a form that was always entertaining and personable, so as to generate a real friendship between his periodical and the reader.

When, after only a year of operation, Leigh Hunt wrote 'the Companion's farewell to his readers', he blamed the demise of the enterprise on isolation and personal difficulties in what had been one of the most painful periods of his life. Deprived of key friendships through the death of Shelley and Byron, unable to pay his contributors, distracted by family demands, the *Companion* had, he observed, become too much a reflection of his single personality, too dependent on his personal strengths and weaknesses. While this *Companion* to the Romantic age certainly has its quota of the last, I cannot similarly complain about working in isolation. When I contemplate the efforts and achievements of the small editorial circle of Gillian Russell, Jon Mee, Clara Tuite, Kate Fullagar, and, until her untimely death, Patsy Hardy, it is clear that the term 'Companion' has never been more appropriate.

Armour, R. W., & Howes, R. F., *Coleridge the Talker: A Series of Contemporary Descriptions and Comments*, New York, 1969; Butler, M., *Romantics, Rebels, and Reactionaries: English Literature and Its Background 1760–1830*, Oxford, 1981; Foucault, M., *The Order of Things: An Archaeology of the Human Sciences*, New York, 1970; Hawley, J., 'Laurence Sterne and the Circle of Arts and Sciences: A Study of *Tristram Shandy* and Its Relation to Encyclopaedias', D.Phil., Oxford, 1990; Kafker, F. A., 'Notable Encyclopaedias of the Late Eighteenth Century: Eleven Successors of the *Encyclopédie*', *Studies on Voltaire and the Eighteenth Century*, 315 (Oxford, 1994); McGann, J. J., *The Romantic Ideology: A Critical Investigation*, Chicago, 1983; (ed.), *The New Oxford Book of Romantic Period Verse*, Oxford, 1994; Newman, G., *The Rise of English Nationalism: A Cultural History 1740–1830*, London, 1987; Stafford, B. M., 'The Eighteenth Century: Towards an Interdisciplinary Model', *Art Bulletin*, 70 (1988), 6–24; Yeo, R., 'Ephraim Chambers's *Cyclopaedia* (1728) and the Tradition of Commonplaces', *Journal of the History of Ideas*, 57 (1996), 157–75; 'Reading Encyclopaedias: Science and the Organization of Knowledge in British Dictionaries of Arts and Sciences, 1730–1850', *Isis*, 82 (1991), 24–49.

· PART ONE ·

· I ·

TRANSFORMING
POLITY AND NATION

1 · REVOLUTION MARK PHILP

The sense of the term 'revolution' changes dramatically between the first shots of *American Revolution in the spring of 1775 through to the year of European revolutions in 1848. It changes in three ways: in the growing sense that revolutionary change might be progressive, rather than merely restoring a political system or constitution to some historically prior and uncorrupt state; in broadening its scope to move from a restoration of the political domain to encapsulate a sense of social and economic, as well as political, restructuring; and in the independent role which the common people come to play in the dynamics of the revolutionary process. Indeed, as the meaning of revolution changes, so do revolutionaries' sense of their natural allies and enemies: in 1789 the unitarian divine Richard *Price called on friends and defenders of freedom; fifty years later Karl Marx issued his clarion call for workers of the world to unite. And, as the lexicon and the meanings change, so too do the parameters of political intentionality and possibility—revolutions cease to be understood as fortuitous upheavals, or as the outcome of developing *Enlightenment [32]. They come to be seen as a function of revolutionary will and organization. Thomas *Paine's account of the mechanism of revolution was optimistic: 'If systems of government can be introduced, less expensive, and more productive of general happiness, than those which have existed, all attempts to oppose their progress will in the end be fruitless. Reason, like time, will make its own way, and prejudice will fall in its combat with interest.' By the beginning of the nineteenth century only utopians were as sanguine, and events both in Britain and France during the 1790s taught that organization was an inevitable component of radical political reform and revolutionary change [see *utopianism, 9].

There should be little doubt that France played the major role in transforming the meaning of revolution. The French case peppers the works of Marx and Lenin and underlies their understanding of the revolutionary process. But there is a distinctive story to be told of the way that the events of the 1790s translated the *French Revolution into a dual challenge to the authority of the British state—from domestic reformers on the one hand, and from the strains of fighting arguably the most extensive and demanding *war [2] in British history (the loss of life among servicemen was proportionately higher than in the First World War). This story details how the language of political conflict in Britain is transformed as French events bring to British political discourse both the universalism of 1776 and 1789 and, increasingly, a set of broader social demands; how the reactions of the government and the political élite encouraged the development of an extensive extra-parliamentary reform movement, parts of which, by the end of the decade, learnt that the language of reform had become indistinguishable from that of *insurrection and revolution; and how the British state, in mobilizing its resources for the war with France and reacting to the threat of domestic disorder, was able to draw on a language of *patriotism reinvested with meaning by the war and rooted in a series of practical initiatives and institutions.

Many believed that the American Revolution had helped prepare the way for the French. In the closing passages of his *Discourse on the Love of our Country* (1789), written in commemoration of a still earlier revolution, the *Glorious Revolution of 1688, Richard Price looked to the future in the light of the recent past:

After sharing in the benefits of one Revolution, I have been spared to be a witness to two other

Revolutions, both glorious. And now, methinks, I see the ardor for liberty catching and spreading, a general amendment beginning in human affairs, the dominion of kings changed for the dominion of laws, and the dominion of priests giving way to the dominion of reason and conscience. Be encouraged all ye friends of freedom and writers in its defence . . . Behold the light you have struck out, after setting America free, reflected to France and there kindled into a blaze that lays despotism in ashes and warms and illuminates Europe!

The history of this 'blaze' is a complex one, in which Price's own text plays a part. His uncharacteristic hyperbole was seized upon by Edmund *Burke, in *Reflections on the Revolution in France* (1790), and denounced as celebrating not the Glorious Revolution of 1688 but the revolution of 1642–8 and, thereby, the execution of Charles I. Arguably Burke's early and extreme revulsion also owed much to his scorching experience during the *Gordon riots of June 1780. As well as being vilified by Protestant Association propaganda, he had been personally threatened by the mob and—in a retreat from *Whig principles—had welcomed the armed military intervention which had been personally instigated by George III. To celebrate events in France was, for Burke, to celebrate civil war and mob violence. To advance the claims of *natural

2. Detail of *The Riot in Broad Street, 7 June 1780*, engraving by J. Heath after Francis Wheatley (1790), depicting the mob pillage of the Gordon riots and intimating their eventual repression.

rights and liberty against the order of society, and to see the right of reform as inherent in the sovereignty of the people, was to threaten the fundamental laws of nature.

Burke's reaction to events in France was seen as extreme by many of his contemporaries— some took it as a sign of madness. Yet his *Reflections* marked out a position for a conservative ideology, and a celebration of the distinctive character of the English inheritance which came to exert a powerful influence over this and subsequent decades. Burke characterized the choice in stark terms: either to accept the status quo, or to jeopardize the Englishman's liberties, his culture, and his civilization. If few saw the choice so bleakly when the *Reflections* were published in November 1790, many were persuaded to do so by the second half of the decade. One factor in their thinking was, without doubt, the way that events in France seemed pantomimically to fulfil Burke's worst fears. The widespread massacre of prisoners in Paris in September 1792, the outbursts of insurrection and civil war within France, the construction of the Terror, and the internationalization of the revolution through conquest made Burke's version of 1789 seem powerfully prescient. Few were inclined to ask how far these developments might themselves have been prompted by the war launched on the French by the combined European powers; still fewer asked how far Burke's work might itself have played a role in promoting this military challenge to the legitimacy of France's revolution.

Events in Britain were equally important in swinging support behind Burke's interpretation. Between November 1790 and December 1792, popular support for reform in Britain was seen by many of the political élite as having reached epidemic proportions. Burke was not entirely innocent here. The *Reflections* prompted a pamphlet debate on an unprecedented scale (and of an unprecedentedly high quality: several of its contributions—by Paine, Mary *Wollstonecraft, William *Godwin, and James *Mackintosh—remain widely read today). The debate served, in its initial stages, to introduce into the generally favourable response to events in France, and the sense that they were following the pattern of 1688, a division between those who were prepared to welcome its proclamation of natural rights and formal equality and those who distrusted such 'French principles' and were willing to find some accommodation with Burke. Initially, there was little sense of a tension between the common assumption of the rights of the freeborn Englishman, which were firmly fixed in the language of *Wilkite parliamentary opposition of the 1770s, and the opposition to the war with America, as well as the more abstract rights associated with France. But with the publication of Paine's *Rights of Man* (1791), especially the second part in the spring of 1792, the republican implications of the natural rights doctrines canvassed by the supporters of France became unmistakable. This did not make reformers republicans, but it made the language of *republicanism readily available, and in doing so combined with Burke's *Reflections* to raise the stakes of the controversy. By setting the poles of the political continuum at such odds, the more conciliatory loyal and reformist positions became less stable and the political choices starker. In each successive year of the decade it required an ever greater degree of commitment to remain true to one's reformist principles; but while this discouraged some, for others the greater commitment resulted in greater radicalism. At the same time, even *loyalists found that the status quo was not an unalloyed blessing. Paine's republican writings, and a whole spate of popular pamphlets, squibs, **prints [22]**, and broadsheets, provided insistent satirical puncturing of the political élite, laughing at their titles and pretensions and finding nothing but corruption and self-interest beneath their protestations of public service and civic virtue. This debunking of the élite was deeply corrosive, both because it threw into question claims to the natural character of political and social authority and because it articulated a set of doubts about aristocratic culture and its influence which could be held even by otherwise conservative members of the middle classes. Hence the tendency of loyalist pamphlets, such as those by Hannah *More, to concentrate on the virtues of the industrious middle classes, rather than on defending aristocratic privilege.

The paper war of the 1790s is important not simply for the issues it raised but also because of the character and extent of the audience it reached. Burke's *Reflections* sold some 30,000 copies in the first two years after its publication; it drew over 100 replies, and probably over 200 works in support. But the volume of items is overshadowed by the extent of circulation achieved by some of the contributions. Paine's *Rights of Man*, on the most conservative estimate, probably sold between 100,000 and 200,000 copies in the first three years after its publication, and with the procedures available to ensure multiple readerships and the 'bridging mechanisms' which brought the text even to illiterate and semi-literate people, it seems likely that a substantial proportion of all classes would have had some acquaintance with Paine. In addition, the ephemera of the debate—the *street literature, the *ballads, the chalked graffiti, the parodies and caricatures—kept these issues in the public domain, maintained their salience, and sustained, both for the reformers and for the common people who looked on, a *frisson* of delight from their satirical subversion of a discomfited élite. The innovative character of many works in the debate, their rhetorical inventiveness and power, their sheer volume and mass circulation, ensured that the controversy over France and reform pervaded British society in one form or other. This 'mass' popular character to the debate was deliberately sought by reformers, but from the winter of 1792–3 the common people also became the target for loyalist tracts, ballads, and broadsides. The task of addressing the people was subsequently taken up in 1794–5 by Hannah More and others concerned with the moral reformation of **popular culture [23]** by means of the mass production and distribution of the *Cheap Repository Tracts. By the height of the *invasion scare in 1803 the mass dissemination of loyalist ballads and broadsides had become an unquestioned part of government strategy.

3. Detail from *Contrasted Opinions of Paine's Pamphlet* (1791), attributed to F. G. Byron, an amateur painter and distant cousin of the poet. The figures of Burke on the left and Fox on the right reflect the 'infernal nature' of the debate over Thomas Paine's *Rights of Man* which swept through the country in the 1790s.

One effect, then, of the revolution controversy and the war with France was the further extension, well beyond the radical movements generated by opposition to the American war, of a popular political culture conversant with a national political agenda. The vehicles for the dissemination of politically reformist literature were the metropolitan and provincial *corresponding societies which sprang into life in the first two or three years of the decade. The London-based *Society for Constitutional Information (originally founded in 1780, but in abeyance by the end of the decade) recommenced activities in 1790 in company with the *London Revolution Society and the Manchester Constitutional Society. But the real spate of activity occurred later: from the end of 1791 and the beginning of 1792 societies were formed in Liverpool, Stockport, Warrington, Leeds, Wakefield, Halifax, Newcastle upon Tyne, Cambridge, Norwich, Great Yarmouth, Ipswich, Chester, Derby, Belper, Birmingham,

Walsall, Coventry, and Wolverhampton. Sheffield alone had eight societies. The newest phenomenon in all this was the London Corresponding Society, founded by Thomas *Hardy, which catered specifically for the working man and which, consequently, marked a major departure from the older societies, which were dominated by minor gentry and professional men.

In response to the spread of this extra-parliamentary reform movement, the wide dissemination of Paine's work, and the proliferation of reforming handbills, chap-books, poems, songs, and squibs being pumped out by radical presses both in London and in the provinces, the government issued a Royal Proclamation Against Seditious Writings and Publications in May 1792 and inaugurated a prosecution for libel against Paine for *Rights of Man: Part the Second*. But while several hundred county and borough meetings sent in loyal addresses to the king through the summer of 1792, the government's confidence was not helped by a spate of food *riots, or by the fierce rhetoric which peppered the societies' correspondence with France, expressing support and admiration for their revolution and sometimes the wish to emulate it. Local magistrates also found evidence of potential insurgence in handbills and verses, Dissenting *sermons and casual conversations, strikes, riots, murmurings in the army, and finally in rumours of the wholesale production of arms. To add to government concern, Scotland greeted each new French victory in its war with the counter-revolutionary coalition with toasts, bells, and lighted windows; Henry *Dundas (Lord Melville), the home secretary, was regularly burnt in effigy, there was a spate of violent rioting towards the end of the year, and in December a general convention of reformers was held in Edinburgh. Ireland faced corn riots from the summer of 1792, and a swelling of republican agitation in the north; there was the prospect of further attempts to remove the disabilities of the Catholics at the end of the year.

The events of the autumn of 1792 raised the spectre of mass organized and centrally directed radical political activity, in a context of increasing international tension and a likelihood of war. In December 1792 the government, seeming to believe that insurrection was imminent, embodied the militia, fortified the Tower, brought hundreds of troops into London, and issued a further Proclamation Against Seditious Writings.

There was some consolation for the government late in November 1792 in the form of the *Association for the Preservation of Liberty and Property against Republicans and Levellers, an independent initiative by John *Reeves, a London magistrate. Reeves published a series of loyal resolutions in several of the London papers, and suggested that meetings to pass similar resolutions might be held throughout the country, to which there was a widespread favourable response. Local associations played an active role in initiating prosecutions of radical printers, booksellers, and activists, and in the circulation of loyalist tracts. Although supported by the traditional political élite, the associations undoubtedly attracted the involvement of many men (and occasionally women) of lesser social standing, who eagerly grasped the opportunities offered for political participation. Loyalist meetings, collection of signatures for petitions, endorsement of declarations of principles, public meetings, dinners, ritualized Paine burnings, and loyalist marches all extended participation beyond local élites to members of the middling orders and the respectable artisan classes. In this sense the associations served to broaden the political nation while insisting on the sanctity of the status quo.

From the publications of the loyalist associations it is clear that the semblance of reasoned political debate which first marked the earlier pamphlets on the Revolution had been completely abandoned. Political argument had become a war of words, and this in turn had developed into an increasingly violent portrayal of the horrors of French and British radicalism. Most significantly, the British reformers were commonly represented as demanding an equalization of property, not just an equalization of political rights. Although this was partly a rhetorical device, the example of France after 1789 added a powerful element of anxiety to such claims.

From the early summer of 1792, when the first Royal Proclamation Against Seditious Writings was issued and prosecution against Paine's *Rights of Man: Part the Second* was inaugurated, the establishment suffered recurrent bouts of anxiety about the prospect of a political and social revolution. These anxieties were not groundless, nor should we dismiss the loyalists' campaign as mere rhetoric. Many experienced the spread of popular radical literature as deeply threatening, and feared that social equality was firmly on the agenda for many radical sympathizers. Indeed, for those who did not read too carefully, Paine was himself advocating this. In the second part of *Rights of Man*, he included an extended section arguing for support for the destitute, infirm, and aged, financed from current taxation and a progressive property tax. His proposals were sufficiently radical (although in line with most modern welfare states) to convey to his opponents a more general sense that the right of property would not be sanctified in the event of a major political change. Moreover, his *Agrarian Justice* (1796), written after having escaped execution under Maximilien Robespierre and in the wake of the proto-socialist 'Conspiracy of Equals' led by François Babeuf in March 1796, provided a still more radical and principled case for redistribution to meet the requirements of egalitarian justice. From a doctrine demanding a political revolution for the defence of rights and liberties, Paine came to advance demands for something much closer to a social revolution. Nor was he alone; in Britain he was attacked by radicals such as Thomas *Spence for failing to go far enough in his critique of private property, and *Spenceans became and remained prominent members of the radical societies well into the nineteenth century.

It is not surprising that the issue of political reform should come to be portrayed in highly polarized and polemicized terms, even though early radicalism was without doubt reformist rather than revolutionary in character. Although their rhetoric could at times be florid, the constitutional societies for the most part concentrated on fairly traditional activities; *petitioning, circulating resolutions, corresponding, and *debating. Indeed, when tarred with the brush of murderous French extremism and insurrectionary disloyalty by the loyalists, many people with sympathies for reform felt it both appropriate and prudent to sign loyalist declarations. At the same time, the onset of hostilities with France, the obvious intransigence of the government, and the prosecution of radical publishers and booksellers forced many radicals to recognize that they could not rely on traditional methods for achieving reform but would have to find new tactics to advance their cause.

Again, Paine's work offered a ready solution, and one again drawn from his American experience. In his *Letter Addressed to the Addressers of the Late Proclamation* (September 1792), he argued that the proper means of reform would be the calling of a British convention, whose authority would, by deriving from the sovereignty of the people, supersede that of Parliament. There were relatively unthreatening precedents for such conventions, as in the *Wyvill movement of the early 1780s, but such a movement, developed during the onset of the war with France and possibly animated by a desire to usurp the legitimacy of Parliament, inevitably aroused government unease. The British Convention in Scotland in November and December 1793 led to the Scottish Treason Trials in January and March 1794, and the transportation of the central participants. In May of the same year leading English radicals were arrested and, following further arrests in October, were arraigned on charges of High Treason [see *Treason Trials]. They were accused of attempting to usurp parliamentary powers by summoning another British Convention. Although they were eventually acquitted, the reform movement suffered a major setback. The Society for Constitutional Information closed down, reopening only briefly in November 1795, and the London Corresponding Society did not recover from internal factions, often arising from accusations of *spying for the government, until the summer of 1795. It was then able to use the widespread unrest over the war, and the rioting against food shortages and recruitment practices, as an opportunity to organize mass public meetings to call for peace and demand reform. The government responded with the *gagging acts which forbade public meetings of more than a specified number, amended the conditions under which the law of treason could be applied, and increased the penalties for sedition. For a brief period there was a flurry of opposition activity, with Charles James *Fox leading the movement against the bills, but without success.

In the last four years of the decade the British government came under considerable strain: the war with France was going badly; the country was under constant threat of invasion from 1797; and it had major difficulties financing the war, resulting in a banking crisis in early 1797 and the suspension of specie payments (maintained until 1821). At the end of 1797 William *Pitt was forced to introduce a bill trebling assessed taxes, and a scheme of voluntary contributions to aid war funding was also established; but neither proved adequate to meet needs, and the following year he was forced to introduce an *income tax—leading some to accuse him of sharing the Jacobins' disregard for the sanctity of private property. The government also faced widespread if sporadic popular protest. Food rioting was extensive from 1794 to 1796 and again from 1799 to 1801 [see *famine], and from 1795 there were riots as new regulations for registering for the militia were put into practice. When the first Scottish Militia Act (1797) was implemented, widespread protest flared up throughout Scotland. In 1797 there were *naval mutinies in Nore and Spithead, allegedly fuelled by London Corresponding Society literature, and there was an agreed policy of subversion of the army among some cells of the United Englishmen—the English counterpart to the United Irishmen. There was a brief French landing in Wales in February 1797 and an abortive rebellion in Ireland, with a mistimed French landing in Ireland in 1798.

Faced with these strains, the government took more draconian measures against the radical organizations. In 1799–1800 the London Corresponding Society and the British and Irish *United societies were outlawed. Habeas corpus remained suspended from January 1795 to the end of 1801—with the exception of a few months in 1795—and in the last year of the decade there was widespread arrest and detention of suspected radicals. Broadly, the picture is one of a decreasing number of radicals, more and more tightly constrained in their activities by the law, their sense of persecution compounded by frequent betrayals by government spies, being driven either into silence or into more covert forms of activity. Even those whose political principles did not become more extreme found that they were pressed into more extreme methods to achieve their ends. And, although the egalitarianism which their opponents foisted upon them was never a central plank for most radicals, it did become an important plank of the Spenceans. Small in number and often dismissed as cranks, these formed an important bridge between the movements of the 1790s and the *Chartists of the 1840s. But the categories of radical discourse remained predominantly political rather than social. Some concern with the poor and the destitute was a feature of the radical movement (as among conservative *Evangelicals and others), but this never amounted, in the 1790s, to a broader sense of *class [15] interests and class conflict. Indeed, throughout the decade and well into the nineteenth century, whether in England, Scotland, or Ireland, there was considerable cross-class mixing in organizations for reform, accentuated by the eccentric distribution of the franchise and the impact of religious Dissent. This meant that for several generations British radicalism would take a broadly popular rather than a class form, and that it could forge significant temporary links with populist parliamentarians such as Sir Francis *Burdett and Henry *Hunt.

Indeed, the most striking example of this co-operative activity was the resurgence of organized political radicalism in the years 1817–19, during which extra-parliamentary politics was dominated first by petitions and 'remonstrances' and subsequently by the spread of mass meetings (culminating in the *Peterloo massacre in August 1819), ending in a satirical frenzy prompted by the *Queen Caroline affair (when George IV attempted to divorce his wife) and in a new series of acts against workers' organizations and the popular press. Throughout this period, as in the earlier part of the decade (notably with the *Luddites and a spate of *agrarian rioting in 1816), there were insurrectionary tendencies within working-class and artisan communities, registered by frequent panics among the political élite that the people were arming. But, as in the 1790s, the major part of the organized political activity of this period relied on traditional methods of protest and took political reform as its sole objective. Social reform and a reduction in taxation were often seen as the inevitable consequences of political reform, but it was the latter which served to unite local discontents into a national movement. As in the 1790s it remains a matter of debate how far revolutionary and insurrectionary ambitions had spread among the people, influenced by Spenceans and ultra-radicals, but there is no doubt that in so far as there was a national movement between 1817 and 1820 it was one united under a political leadership, notably Henry Hunt and John *Cartwright, and with a political press, notably William *Cobbett, T. J. *Wooler, and William *Hone, dedicated to a narrow agenda of *parliamentary reform.

The British governing class and administrative state survived both the ideological and practical onslaught from radicalism and the drain on its resources caused by the war with France, but it did not do so unchanged. In some respects it came to resemble its principal antagonist. It was forced to conduct a mass mobilization, trebling the number of men in its armed forces from the highest total of the American war. It was also forced to expand the militia and to endorse the creation of a *volunteer force throughout the country. In 1803–4 something like 20 per cent of the adult male populations of the rural counties and 35 per cent of the more industrial and urban counties were enlisted in the volunteers. The result was a country in arms, with a substantial proportion of the British male public holding weapons, something which Pitt had refused to countenance in the winter of 1792-3. Women also were mobilized, in the buying and sending of uniforms for the troops, in the making of flags and banners for the volunteers, and in the raising of public subscriptions. The government found it necessary to introduce mechanisms for the support of the families of its soldiers and sailors, and for those of the militia sent to Ireland, thereby extending the role of the administration into forms of welfare provision which would have warmed Paine's heart! And the state developed for the first time a substantial domestic intelligence network, which had its greatest impact in the last years of the decade, when the suspension of habeas corpus allowed the government to take preventative action by detaining radicals on rather doubtful evidence. A good deal of this activity is continuous with the traditional, post-1688 role of the state as a fiscal-military apparatus, designed to raise money and fight wars. From the 1790s to 1815 it achieved this on an unprecedented scale, but most of its activities were similar in kind to those it had undertaken throughout the century. One major difference, however, was that it had to secure exponential increases in taxation and popular mobilization in a period in which the legitimacy of the established order was continually challenged by extra-parliamentary movements. To do this required a recasting of the traditional relationship between a patrician governing élite and its subject people.

The war with France, while increasing the strains on the state, also allowed the government to present the alternatives in stark terms, as it did in 1792–6. But such a strategy became increasingly inadequate after 1796 as the threat of invasion loomed. The government needed to know that it could rely on the people, to finance it and to fight for it, and on neither count could the people be bullied into compliance on a mass scale. They needed to be carried along from conviction—especially once the government had agreed to the creation of an armed volunteer force.

There has been considerable controversy over the question whether Britain came close to a revolution in the 1790s. The account given here suggests that this is not necessarily the most apt question. What Pitt's government faced was certainly not an organized domestic revolutionary movement. Rather, it faced (and had helped to bring about) a situation in which the financial, manpower, and logistic strains on the nation were such that it became unclear whether the will to resist a French invasion or to continue the fight with the French could be sustained. The radicals, by the end of the decade, for the most part saw things in these terms. They had to rely on there being such widespread anti-government feeling that an invasion would not be resisted; and they had therefore to plan, not on a ground-swell of revolutionary fervour sufficient to topple the government, but on a successful French landing facing minimal popular resistance. Since there was no sizeable French landing on the mainland, it is difficult to know whether the revolutionaries' hopes were wholly illusory, but the extent of the volunteering which took place does suggest that by the end of the decade there was a significant strain of loyalism which the government could rely on in the event of such a crisis. This loyalism was not for the most part natural or inherent, nor was it an entailed inheritance with landed property. In fact, it was more common among the manufacturing and urban counties than among propertied interests, despite these having to gain from parliamentary reform. This intensification arises in part from the process of élite and popular mobilization for domestic defence and the associated spread of popular propaganda suffused with nationalist and loyalist rhetoric. But in using these means to draw men and women into an identification with their nation, the government had to extend to them an unprecedented degree of trust and participation. The explosion of popular print culture in the 1790s, the mass mobilization of the armed forces, the militia, and the volunteers, and the measures undertaken to finance the war and defend the realm all ensured that the government and its agenda touched almost every British citizen. Moreover, in doing so it was soliciting their involvement, whether in the singing of loyal songs, participation in patriotic pageants, or practical involvement in matters of local defence.

This does not mean that those who participated were die-hard loyalists. On the contrary, while there may have been a genuine and deep fear of a French invasion amongst some, it is equally likely that the compliance of these men and women was conditional. They probably valued their participation more than the loyalty which others inferred from it, and to this extent the government inevitably aroused expectations of popular involvement which it would find embarrassing after the end of the war. Moreover, it provided a language of patriotism, national interest, and *constitutionalism which, if not quite the universalist set of rights that Paine offered, could none the less mobilize powerful lobbies against the government in times of peace. On this account, however, what insured the government against collapse, in a period of acute domestic and international stresses, was its capacity to generate through participation a degree of national identity and unity. This allowed the government to sustain sufficient credit with the people to ensure popular support of its policy. By the end of the Napoleonic wars the British state had pulled through the crisis, but in large part it had done so by helping to bring into being something like a national political culture with a national political agenda. And in this sense we might say that the revolution in France helped produce its counterpart in Britain. It did so by extending the activities of the fiscal-military state beyond the bounds of its traditional patrician political culture, by emphasizing the national character of the political crisis, and by appealing to the national identity of the citizens without whose support it would collapse.

The legacy of this state involvement is a complex one. Although some have claimed that it made the people significant agents of change, this understates the extent to which the state was driven, in the wake of its enormous expansion during the French wars, to retrench across the board. In the decades after *Waterloo, despite a buoyant and demanding popular politics, the state was forced by pressure from the financial and landed élites of the country to move towards a diminution of state involvement within society and the economy—a pressure deriving from a widespread concern that the British war machine was unacceptably wasteful and expensive. It is precisely because of the extensiveness of state activities during the revolutionary period, and the associated weight of wartime taxation and spiralling *national debt, that a popular politics demanding a more egalitarian state was bound to fail. Hence in part we find the paradox of unprecedented widespread popular political activity coupled with no substantial social or political reform. Popular politics and agitation had become a central feature of British politics; but it was not until the 1840s and the rise of Chartism that it began to build the organizational structures it required to support its demands, and it was not until considerably later that its social agenda became a viable political platform.

Bayley, C. A., *Imperial Meridian: The British Empire and the World 1780–1830*, London, 1989; Brewer, J., *The Sinews of Power: War, Money and the English State 1688–1783*, London, 1983; Butler, M., *Burke, Paine, Godwin and the Revolution Controversy*, Cambridge, 1984; Colley, L., *Britons: Forging the Nation 1707–1837*, New Haven, Conn., 1992; Dickinson, H. T., *British Radicalism and the French Revolution 1785–1815*, Oxford, 1985; Good- win, A., *The Friends of Liberty: The English Democratic Movement in the Age of the French Revolution*, London, 1979; McCalman, I., *Radical Underworld: Prophets, Revolutionaries and Pornographers in London, 1795–1840*, Cambridge, 1988; Philp, M. (ed.), *The French Revolution and British Popular Politics*, Cambridge, 1991; Thompson, E. P., *The Making of the English Working Class* (1963), Harmondsworth, 1968.

2 · WAR   J. E. COOKSON

'Limited' and 'total' war have been terms used to indicate the massive escalation of European war that occurred between the eighteenth and twentieth centuries. As descriptive categories 'limited' and 'total' war may serve well enough, but to conceptualize them is exceedingly difficult, if not impossible. One problem is that there is no absolute against which to measure 'totality'. What is a 'total' threat to a society? What is 'total' mobilization? What is 'total' victory or defeat? Another problem is that war and preparation for war, modern war at least, is dynamic rather than stable, as states constantly seek to repair their disadvantage and extend their advantage over their enemies or potential enemies. For this reason, 'military revolutions' have arguably occurred in every century since the sixteenth. Many European states in the eighteenth century created militias in an attempt to increase their military manpower, foreshadowing the huge mobilizations of armed civilians in the Napoleonic period. Changes in military tactics based on the increased use of light infantry, the increased mobility and amount of artillery, the adoption of the column as an attacking formation, and the separation of armies into all-arms divisions for greater operational flexibility are said to have constituted a 'tactical revolution' which *Napoleon, in particular, perfected later. Developments of this significance challenge the view that eighteenth-century warfare was resistant to innovation—like so much else in the *ancien régime*—until *revolution [1] destroyed the authority of the past and introduced new conditions and new possibilities.

Eighteenth-century war, therefore, cannot be said to have been 'limited' by its practitioners, who displayed the same urge as their successors to find security—even to the point of preparing ambitious war plans or of attacking the enemy's resource base, as Marlborough did when he laid waste Bavarian territory in his 1704 Blenheim campaign. War in the age of Marlborough and Frederick the Great was, however, 'limited' by the enormous constraints imposed by poor communications, small industrial sectors, and labour-intensive production which were not lifted until the emergence of industrial societies in the nineteenth century.

4. *The Death of Major Pierson* by John Singleton Copley (1783), his most celebrated and consciously heroic history painting.

There is much irony in this, because the **Enlightenment [32]** encouraged the view that war would become increasingly anachronistic with the spread of commercial civilization. Commerce was seen to be permanently prosperous only when the exchange was mutually beneficial, and it was found possible to imagine the whole world so enmeshed by ties of interdependence, fair dealing, and tolerance of others that war would become pointless. Such ideas were reinforced for British liberal opinion by a rapidly commercializing society. On the Continent the *philosophes* argued that war, like the religious fanaticism of earlier centuries with which it was closely associated, would be eclipsed by the 'age of reason'. Both views thus held that pacific tendencies in societies were on the rise and that war was becoming inconsequential. In Britain the Enlightenment view of war as the trivial and increasingly anachronistic pursuit of rulers was articulated by Thomas *Paine in *Rights of Man* (1791). He blamed war on monarchical governments encouraged by equally self-interested, parasitical aristocracies who were concerned only for power and reputation. On the other hand, claimed Paine, a democratic future would also be a warless future. Only establish representative governments and the real interests of populations would be asserted against the unnecessary waste and misery of war.

However, although anti-war argument was strongly advanced on occasions, it had little effect on British policy and public attitudes, which were profoundly shaped by the long struggle with powerful France from 1689, sometimes called the 'Second Hundred Years War'. Even deeper roots stretched back to the sixteenth century and a Protestant nationalism ever fearful of a Catholic supremacy being established on the Continent. To see the Anglo-French wars of the eighteenth century simply as wars for trade and colonies is to miss a key point: the French state, larger in territory and population, militarily superior, and strategically placed to launch an *invasion, was always conceived as a gigantic threat to Britain itself. Trade, furthermore, was considered vital to national security, since it provided the wealth that narrowed the disparity of power between Britain and France. War rhetoric in eighteenth-century Britain

consistently presented France as the country's 'natural' enemy, and stressed the theme of national danger to the extent that it is unrecognizable as the language of 'limited' war. Britain, in fact, was a bellicose society; its national consciousness shaped by competition with France, its exposure to invasion not infrequent, the interests it had to defend numerous and far-flung.

Global rivalry with France was a significant factor in the first major conflict of our period—the *American Revolution. The American colonies were believed to be integral to Britain's world position. To relinquish them meant that a large and vital part of the British trading system would be lost, doing infinite damage to Britain's power and standing everywhere and renewing opportunities for French expansion after the defeats France had incurred in the Seven Years War (1756–63). Although the American war remained contentious in British politics, the Bourbon alliance with the Americans in 1778 indicated that the chief threat now came from the French, whose navy achieved great freedom of operation in the Caribbean and western Atlantic.

Priorities in the conflict became the defence of the national base and the exposed territories overseas. As it happened, French naval power failed to effect an invasion of Britain, and elsewhere was mostly successfully contained. When the costs of the war came to be counted, Britain's position in the Caribbean and India was still secure; and even the loss of the American colonies proved to have little impact on the continued expansion of British trade.

Nevertheless, the American war provoked a pessimistic assessment of Britain's economic progress (and, by implication, of its future as a great power) which held considerable authority until about the turn of the century. Richard *Price was the most notable proponent of these pessimistic views, addressing in particular the problem of taxation and the *national debt. His claim that both were reaching insupportable levels was construed as an attack on the warfare state, since war was the obvious cause. His case was underpinned by the economic ideas of Adam *Smith, which treated taxation and military recruitment as channelling capital and labour resources away from productive use; but Price also argued stoutly that England's population was declining, a key indicator of economic malaise. However, his claims were challenged after 1798, when authoritative estimates of the national income began to be prepared and the first census, with accompanying work, settled the debate about *population. While it continued to be possible to make the theoretical point that war was growth-retarding, the mass of available data showed that in Britain impressive growth had occurred in spite of the country having to fight the greatest war in its history.

The American conflict influenced attitudes to war in one other significant respect. From the beginning of the crisis the advocates of peace and conciliation, led by Edmund *Burke, warned that Britain was dealing with the protest of a people and that a people could not be easily coerced. They argued that even if a military solution prevailed, the colonies would be ungovernable because their publics would be alienated and hostile. The opposition to 'Pitt's war' in the 1790s made much the same case. Charles James *Fox and his supporters regarded the *French Revolution as a tremendous assertion of the popular will against corrupt and oppressive government, arguing that the attempt to conquer the revolution by military force only had the effect of creating an 'armed nation' which then developed into an invincible military system. Napoleon's rise to power and subsequent career fitted very easily into this analysis. As late as 1815 the *Whig opposition in parliament demurred against attacking the restored Napoleon on the grounds that the ease with which he had overthrown the Bourbon monarchy indicated the public strength of his regime.

There was some understanding here of the intensity war would assume once whole societies were engaged. Yet whatever Britain's experience of mass mobilization and popular *patriotism during the wars between 1793 and 1815, anti-war opinion in the early nineteenth century never offered an interpretation of the age as one of increasing militarism or xenophobia. The Peace Society formed in 1816 was even slow to accept that the problem of war was, in part at least, the problem of relations between governments, and that practical measures like arbitration might defuse tension in the international system. Instead, its pacifism revealed the enduring influence of older traditions. One was that of the Protestant sectaries—most notably, of course, the *Quakers—emphasizing the moral autonomy of the individual. The other, not necessarily separate from the first, can be associated with *Evangelical reform which had taken up the *millenarianism inspired by providential beliefs. In Britain the outcome of the war was interpreted as evidence of God's plan. The excitement increased rather than diminished as the country claimed the title of 'saviour of Europe', and as the expansion of its territories and power around the globe accelerated after 1810. The world position Britain assumed as a result of the Napoleonic wars renewed the vision of a warless world, with commerce having an important part in its making.

Such views can seem to indicate a society that was complacent about its institutions, confidently insular against foreign states, and not conspicuously militaristic—though it felt an imperial destiny. On the other hand, the 'Great War' (as the nineteenth century named it) was not solely responsible for shaping this ethos, for the same attitudes were beginning to receive ample expression from about the end of the Seven Years War. According to Linda Colley's analysis, if war with revolutionary and Napoleonic France shaped British society in any way, it was in its nation-making effect. This could be said to reinforce the conventional view that the Napoleonic wars were the 'wars of the nations': that once organized mass resistance became the price of state survival, wars became struggles between peoples whose fighting spirit depended on appeals to save the *patrie* and the ideals and values it was made to enshrine. In the case of Britain the 'new totality' of war in fact had manifold implications. At their peak strength the armed forces comprised over three-quarters of a million men, nearly half of whom were locally trained civilian *volunteers but who offered service in any part of the country in the event of invasion. However, civilian participation in national defence went far beyond the volunteers: rural workers were enrolled to assist the army and to 'drive' districts by removing or destroying anything of use to the enemy; women formed 'committees of clothing' to provide for the troops, or featured in patriotic ceremonies to underline the point that the whole of society was under threat; patriotic subscriptions, which were numerous, organized down to the parish level, and solicitous for the pennies of the poor, were made equally symbolic of 'patriotic union'. The patriotic crowd also became an important physical manifestation of national resolve. In London the numbers could be truly enormous—200,000 watched the King review the volunteers in Hyde Park in 1803. But the crowds were proportionately just as large in the provinces: 60,000 were said to have attended the Leeds 'military festival' in 1795; in Wiltshire 20,000 came to see colours presented to the local yeomanry regiment in 1798. The sheer volume of counter-invasion propaganda, most of it directed at the lower orders, itself indicates the strength of the drive for mass mobilization. Moreover, the language and imagery of these broadsides were those of 'total' war; Napoleon was depicted as a tyrant who would consign the population to slavery, and his army as a raping, murdering, plundering horde.

It is much more difficult to determine whether this national mobilization, quite unprecedented in its scale and intensity, significantly altered British society. By continental standards Britain was an exceptionally cohesive and nationalistic state, with a national parliament, the success of the Anglo-Scottish Union, linguistic unity, flourishing print culture, and well-developed communications. A Protestant and francophobic nationalism existed above class and sectional differences, articulated by both the élite and those outside the formal political system. Another source of cohesion was the *monarchy. From the 1780s, partly by George III's own efforts, this became the object of increasing public interest until it stood forth as the pre-eminent symbol of national unity. National defence in the Napoleonic period was undoubtedly a unique, nation-forming experience in that huge numbers were brought into actual national service, in a situation when the highest possible value was placed on that service. The effect of this was reinforced by the tide of rhetoric praising, exhorting, and frightening the lower orders, as the possessing classes worried about the consequences of depending on an armed populace. But it is still possible to be sceptical about whether war worked on the mass psyche to produce a markedly different postwar society. Indeed, caution seems good advice in view of the disagreement that continues among historians over the amount of social change attributable to Britain's participation in 'total' war in the twentieth century.

If it is claimed that mass involvement in war created a nationalistic and militarized populace, it does not necessarily follow that this was also a loyal populace. Early nineteenth-century Britain was characterized by the growth of popular radicalism, *trade unions, and non-Anglican religion which at times converted into huge popular movements presenting a formidable challenge to the old order. Even during the war itself the patriotic crowd did not completely displace its protesting counterpart. One example is the 'loyalist reaction' to popular radicalism in 1792–3 in which the lower orders were bombarded with propaganda and encouraged to make anti-radical demonstrations, only to be followed in 1795 by widespread 'hunger disorders' and renewed radical activity [see *famine and *loyalism]. The prominence of the militia in the protests of 1795 ought also to be a reminder that militarization and loyalty did not necessarily go hand in hand. During the next food crisis, in 1800, numerous volunteers took the side of the populace they were meant to control, though two years earlier they had enlisted under their officers for the defence of the country. Confronted by a local magistrate, some volunteers in the Wolverhampton area told him that they had enrolled 'to protect their King and Constitution and that they hold such offers sacred; but that it was never intended by them to give security to the inhuman oppressor, whilst the Poor are starving in the midst of plenty.' Clearly, national defence patriotism coexisted with other loyalties, invariably superseding these when the threat of invasion was very real but at other times having to accommodate and even submit to them. Popular patriotism had an episodic character reminiscent of popular radicalism, which flared spectacularly into mass mobilizations given the right conditions. And insofar as it defined any loyalty, it was loyalty to the monarch, who was rapidly becoming a symbol above political and social contentions. Similarly, the Union flag and the national anthem and some other songs became affirmations of British identity appropriated by all and sundry.

It is possible to examine popular attitudes more closely to test the depth of patriotic commitment during the war when, for obvious reasons, it can be expected to have been maximized. In spite of the nation's military effort, the popular image of the soldier as one who relinquished the freedoms of civilian existence for slavery, exile, and (very likely) horrible death remained firmly fixed. Much opposition to service in the home forces resulted from fear that men would be drafted into the army; but the key evidence is provided by recruiting figures which year after year failed to rise, whatever the army's needs or the Duke of *Wellington's victories. The main home defence force, the militia, raised by ballot, was the nearest Britain came to conscription. Its recruitment caused serious disorders in England in 1796 and Scotland in 1797. However, resistance to the ballot was contained by allowing volunteers exemption and by filling the ranks of the militia with substitutes whose permanent service kept down the ballot's use.

The local volunteers, the third component of the country's military force, belie the patriotism traditionally associated with them because the service they offered was limited and conditional in so many ways. With some difficulty most volunteer corps were persuaded to serve outside their localities if invasion occurred, but it proved quite impossible to amalgamate the smaller ones into the battalions that the army required. It is no exaggeration to say that the greatest armed challenge the British state had faced up to this time was met by a populace

5. *Recruits* (*c.*1780), by William
Henry Bunbury. A sceptical view,
long-standing in eighteenth-
century Britain, of the qualities
of recruits and of the officers
recruiting them.

whose service coincided with their interests and 'rights' rather than with the needs of the state.
There can be no doubt that, had the French invaded, the volunteers, along with others, would
have fought a war of national resistance, much as happened in the less cohesive societies of
France in 1792–3, Spain in 1808–13, and Germany in 1812–13 in response to foreign invasion or
occupation. But in the event this was not Britain's fate, and volunteers tended to stay in their
corps only so long as the pay and other benefits made it worth their while, or until the need to
earn a livelihood took them away, or until the militia exemption was no longer required. To
study the volunteer rank and file, especially the rank and file of the great proletarian mobilization of 1803, is to come face to face with the opportunistic, improvised, survivalist existence of
the poor. There were occasions when the collective protest of the men resembled any crowd
action of the time, as a conflict of popular beliefs and expectations against the demands of
social superiors. Without the backing of the Mutiny Act, volunteer officers depended on their
social authority and force of personality to impose military order. The volunteers never managed to span the yawning gulf in British society between the military and the civilian. Neither
the army nor the militia drew more than a tiny proportion of recruits from this source.

   The nineteenth century's 'Great War', then, like the next Great War, does not appear to have
significantly militarized British society. After 1815 the army at home retired to its barracks (now
abundantly provided thanks to the war), where its separateness from civilian life was reinforced. Meanwhile the auxiliary forces were disbanded at the first opportunity by a government anxious to economize and even more anxious to be rid of an armed population. The
remnants of the 'armed nation' that were saved were the yeomanry, the cavalry arm of the volunteers, who were reliable under the gentry and who made a valuable addition to very limited
*police resources. They, however, cannot really stand in the way of a further proposition con-
cerning the impact of the war mobilization: that the addition of mass numbers to war was
related to the addition of mass numbers to politics, specifically the great early-nineteenth-
century *petitioning campaigns on the issues of *parliamentary reform, *Catholic emancipation, and *abolitionism.

The idea that war helped to politicize the populace to the extent of producing truly national movements is at odds with that view of British society which continues to insist on the inherent localism of its politics and government. Local élites, often quite broad-based, controlled an expanding area of public authority as they sought to promote development and to cope with urban growth and popular disorder, something done in the absence—rather than with the intervention—of national policy and central regulation. Much of the cohesiveness of the British state came from the way parliament was used by local communities to settle their disputes and back their actions with statutory authority; indeed, most of parliament's business was concerned with these matters until well into the nineteenth century. During the war the degree of local autonomy was demonstrated in the abject failure of the provisional cavalry in 1797 and of Pitt's Additional Force in 1804–5, and in the way communities protected themselves against militia 'conscription'. Volunteer corps were to a significant degree organized and financed, and had their officers chosen, without reference to the state. Their localism, in defiance of the army and the county lieutenancies, could be pronounced. Britain had yet to become a modern state, if only because too much independent military authority remained within its boundaries and compulsory military service was still incompletely enforced. National defence, the most important matter of all to the state, was a loosely articulated system which linked the counties only weakly and depended heavily on local initiative and compliance. One might even argue that during the war the British state was recognizable in its medieval form as an imperfect federation of local communities complete with magnate-led forces (the militia) and raw levies (the volunteers).

All this may be said by way of claiming that war nationalism did not supplant but rather coexisted with local concerns and still quite fierce local loyalties. Early-nineteenth-century popular movements can be described similarly as weak national alliances which occurred at particular times: they were locally organized with little help from outside, they were often locally specific in their demands, and they were maintained for only a short period. Britain undoubtedly was, by contemporary standards, a nationalistic society, but its nationalism mostly existed as sentiment, and thus was far removed from the more organized and ideological versions that later developed.

Where, then, did national defence patriotism and the associated mobilization have their greatest social effect? First, on Scotland, where the home force fencibles of 1793 and the militia of 1797 placed the defence of Scotland in predominantly Scottish hands for the first time since the Union. Secondly, on the middling people, especially urban élites, who are now recognized as the main progenitors of patriotism, quick to appreciate its possibilities as a community-building force in an age of unparalleled urban growth and disorder. In the towns, patriotism, while the war lasted, was added to *philanthropy as a mode of government, the means by which towns could define themselves and town populations could be unified and ordered. As in Scotland, patriotism in its urban setting was used to secure identities that were seen to need reinforcement: that of Scotland because of England's dominance within the Union, and that of towns because they were often in conflict with county rulers or seemed inchoate communities.

Scotland's search for national identity in the eighteenth century has been shown to have increasingly invoked Scotland's pre-Union past—the country's existence as an ancient, independent kingdom with a proud military tradition against its more powerful neighbours. Prior to the Napoleonic wars, the militia issue—the question of whether Scotland should provide for its own defence—had focused feeling about national self-respect and the disappearance of that Scotland which had negotiated the Union as a free and equal party. The army recruited heavily in Scotland for both the Seven Years War and the American War, and turned immediately to this resource on the outbreak of war in 1793. This was only the beginning of a massive military effort in which militia and volunteers gave Scots the satisfaction of providing for their own defence as well as offering their contribution to the defence of the southern kingdom. They could also point to the Scottish regiments in the army, whose identity by the end of the war was protected. The cult of the Highland soldier was one product of this heightened sense of national identity; regimental history as a genre originated in Scotland with Colonel David Stewart's (1772–1829) *Sketches of . . . the Highlanders* (1822), a work initially conceived as a history of the 42nd regiment, the famous Black Watch. Another product of Scottish militarism was the planned National Monument on Edinburgh's Calton Hill, which, though never completed, was to be built by public subscription and, at one time at least, was intended to be 'a hallowed place of record' detailing the service of all Scots in the war down to the volunteer rank and file. The continuation of the Scottish regiments after the war, maintained from 1825 by permanent depots in the country, played a vital role in the development of Scottish national consciousness. Such regiments enabled Scots to take pride in imperial victories and conquests as their own achievements as much as England's, at the same time as they confirmed the survival of Scots national 'spirit' and that version of Scotland's past built around this national identity.

While Scottish militarism went from strength to strength in the nineteenth century, the urban militarism of the Napoleonic period dwindled with the disbandment of the auxiliary forces. (It is not clear how much a war literature based on reminiscences and campaign histories, and with a predominantly middle-class readership, became a substitute for actual military involvement.) As long as the war continued, however, urban interest in military service was unabated, and the patriotic crowd became a particular feature of urban life. Patriotic 'festivals' in the towns were always conspicuous and splendid, if only because towns could raise larger volunteer corps and produce grander spectacles. These occasions reached a climax with the celebration of the royal jubilee in 1809 and the end of the war in 1814. Over the next twenty years patriotic celebration on a similar scale occurred only for the coronations of 1821 and 1831. The earlier emphasis on patriotism as a state ideology, employed by the aristocratic élite in control of the state to dissipate and divert popular opposition, has given way to a focus on the prominence of patriotism in urban societies and middle class life in general. As a ruling device, patriotism is seen operating to best effect in the towns, where incumbent élites, interested in developing civic cultures and often faced with the problems of controlling large, disparate populations, readily appreciated how it could be used to unify their communities and secure their authority.

National defence and the concerns of urban rulers meshed perfectly. For one thing, patriotic activity mostly suppressed divisions within local élites, including the enmities usually present in corporate towns where an 'outsider' group challenged an entrenched municipal oligarchy. By arming the populace, volunteering particularly provided incentives for élite co-operation lest the élite be assailed by a monster of its own making. On the other hand, the armed populace of towns, like the patriotic crowds, could be presented as powerful physical manifestations of communal unity and harmony. For two decades of war, patriotism in its urban setting was pre-eminently a town-making force. While the growth and change taking place in urban societies often proved to be beyond the effective control of urban rulers, all kinds of patriotic endeavour were kept very much in the hands of the latter, and their civic ideals never received better advertisement.

Town-making and the assertion of Scottish nationhood were particular features of the British state which should remind us that there continued to be strong resemblances between Britain's political structure and those found in continental Europe. Despite years of large-scale war, bureaucratic centralization in Britain amounted to very little, so that an impressive show of authority and power at the centre, rather like a Georgian mansion and household, turns out to have depended largely on what was actually done by a scarcely visible army of functionaries, each engaged in his local task. Comparatively little conflict took place in central politics between the small governing élite and those outside, simply because the power that mattered most, the power to control local communities, was found elsewhere. In 1813–14 two great public campaigns, especially identifiable with middle-class opinion, occurred: petitions to open India to Christian missionaries and petitions for the abolition of the slave trade by the European powers—over 500 addressed the latter issue. In 1816 the government's intention to prolong the property or *income tax was beaten down by over 200 representations. Yet it cannot be said that such huge mobilizations indicated a shift from middle-class localism to middle-class centralist ambitions. As with other popular actions of this kind, these movements on closer inspection are shown to have depended on local initiative with minimal outside direction. They also were typically reactive to events (and even removed from domestic issues), and did not constitute an attempt to build a sustained opposition. In short, Britain in the structure of its public life was still an *ancien régime*. National defence patriotism, which was the nationalism of the age, was inevitably localized because that was the world it encountered.

Brewer, J., *The Sinews of Power: War, Money and the English State 1688–1783*, London, 1989; Colley, L., 'The Apotheosis of George III: Loyalty, Royalty and the British Nation 1760–1820', *Past and Present*, 102 (1984), 94–129; *Britons: Forging the Nation 1707–1837*, New Haven, Conn., 1992; Cookson, J. E., *The Friends of Peace: Anti-War Liberalism in England 1793–1815*, Cambridge, 1983; 'The English Volunteer Movement of the French Wars 1793–1815: Some Contexts', *Historical Journal*, 32 (1989), 867–91; Cottrell, S., 'The Devil on Two Sticks: Franco- phobia in 1803', in R. Samuel, ed., *Patriotism: the Making and Unmaking of British National Identity*, London, 1989; Dickinson, H. T., ed., *Britain and the French Revolution*, London, 1989; Dinwiddy, J., 'England' in O. Dann and J. Dinwiddy, eds., *Nationalism in the Age of the French Revolution*, Ronceverte, 1988; Emsley, C., *British Society and the French Wars 1793–1815*, London, 1979; 'The Military and Popular Disorder in England 1790–1801', *Journal of the Society for Army Historical Research*, 61 (1983), 10–21, 96–112.

3 · DEMOCRACY   H. T. DICKINSON

Britain in the late eighteenth and early nineteenth centuries remained an aristocratically dominated society in which a propertied, mainly landowning élite dominated the formal institutions of the political system: the court, the executive offices of state, parliament, and the institutions of local administration and justice. Although the Crown lost some of its power over this period, it remained a major force in political life. Most of those in positions of power believed that political authority should be in the hands of men with substantial property, and expected the middling and lower classes to remain deferential to their superiors. Despite the threats posed to the established political and social order during the age of revolution, the propertied élite remained ascendant. The *Reform Bill of 1832 did not significantly diminish their power and did not hand power over to the middle classes, still less to the working classes. Indeed, in some ways it consolidated traditional political influence.

None the less, while a small group of mainly landed nobles and gentry dominated the formal institutions of power and Britain successfully avoided any revolutionary upheaval (unlike most other countries in Europe), it did develop a political system during this period in which the middling and lower orders exerted considerable influence. In the urban centres, these classes developed a complex and sophisticated political and social culture that enabled them to influence elections to parliament and town councils, to propagate their views across the country, to associate together in a whole range of voluntary and independent societies, and to form pressure groups capable of influencing the political decisions taken by the propertied ruling class.

This was a period of dramatic social and economic change. The *population of Britain doubled between 1776 and 1832, and the proportion of the population living in towns and engaging in commerce and industry increased significantly. The ruling élite faced few problems in governing the rural areas of Britain, but the political culture of the towns of Britain was very different. Towns provided a wider range of occupations, skills, and earnings, greater religious diversity, and more competition. They also offered a greater range of opportunities for the ambitious and industrious to advance themselves. High literacy rates in urban areas and a flourishing provincial press played a major role in stimulating new ideas and facilitating political discussion [see *publishing, 21]. In most towns the middle and lower classes developed a wide variety of clubs and societies able to provide social, educational, and economic benefits. Members made their own rules, appointed their own officials, provided fellowship, and tried to offer assistance and support to each other, often refusing the patronage of the mighty, freeing themselves from the constraints of the client economy, and insisting on the equal standing of members. These voluntary associations displayed a commitment to intellectual innovation and social improvement, a readiness to support local schools, hospitals, libraries, and other amenities, and a growing eagerness to participate in public life. There were clubs to promote knowledge and education, reading and *debating, and to protect the interests of small employers and working men. By the 1820s, a few 'labour exchanges' even existed where workers exchanged the products they had made, and there were also a few co-operative communities where families shared possessions and worked together as a unit. The most popular and widespread voluntary associations were the working-class *friendly societies. *Trade unions (illegal from 1800 to 1824) often flourished under the guise of these societies, while, in periods of crisis, educational and debating clubs frequently discussed issues of public concern. Urban radicalism was to find in such institutions a ready-made foundation for the creation of overtly political societies.

The extent of direct participation in the parliamentary and local political process in the late eighteenth century is sometimes underestimated by modern scholars. About 15 per cent of adult males had the vote, while after the Reform Bill of 1832 (with a much increased population) this rose to about 18 per cent of adult males. Although there were a few 'rotten boroughs' with minute electorates, most voters lived in the most populous counties or in the larger towns, where they were often simply too numerous to be bullied or bribed by rich candidates. Instead, candidates were expected to be local men who would show some kind of concern for the interests and wishes of the electorate, and even for those who did not possess the vote. When voters organized themselves effectively, they often elected notably radical representatives. Middlesex as well as the City of London, Westminster, Norwich, and other large towns were able to elect reformers to parliament, and it should not be forgotten that it was under the *unreformed* electoral system that the *Whigs secured a substantial majority in favour of *parliamentary reform in the general election of 1831.

National issues often did not interest townsfolk as much as the need to solve the various local problems associated with urbanization, such as regulating markets and shops, building roads, bridges, and docks, disposing of sewage, providing a clean water supply, cleaning and policing the streets, and tackling crime, disease, and poverty. In addressing these problems, local authorities had to raise revenue through taxation as well as from their control of local properties, charities, and amenities. Not surprisingly, the exercise of these extensive powers led to much public debate and vigorous disputation. In the process, people learned to organize so as to bring pressure to bear upon the local or national government, upon the propertied élite in the local community, or upon parliament. Local committees and even national societies coordinated the activities of a welter of pressure groups, printed and distributed propaganda, organized public meetings, lobbied individual MPs, initiated massive *petitioning campaigns, hired lawyers to draft legislation, and paid to send witnesses to parliament to support their case. Some campaigns were conducted on a massive scale and enlisted the support of hundreds of thousands of people, such as those for greater religious equality organized by the Protestant Dissenters in 1787–90 and the Irish Catholics in the 1820s, and the huge campaign to abolish the slave trade in 1788–92 and to abolish *slavery [6] itself in the early 1830s. There were also dozens of smaller and less well-organized campaigns in support of temperance, factory reforms, and educational reforms, as well as in defence of particular economic interests. As in public meetings, women often participated prominently in these lobbying groups.

Members of the working classes could not afford to mount such expensive and sophisticated lobbying campaigns, but they had their own ways of bringing pressure to bear. Trade unions were capable of sustaining well-organized industrial disputes, even though they were illegal, throughout this period. A less well-organized, but even more common, form of popular agitation was the exercise of the collective strength of the people in crowds and demonstrations, both peaceful and violent, which could impress and sometimes even alarm the governing élite at a local and national level [see *class, 15]. Crowds could actually improve integration and social order on festive, ceremonial, and celebratory occasions, but during periods of heightened tension they could be more hostile and aggressive in support of economic protests and political demands. During the *Gordon riots of June 1780 London was out of control for several days, and the same thing happened in Birmingham in 1791 and in Bristol and Merthyr Tydfil in 1831. In 1795–6 and 1800–1 Britain experienced the most serious and widespread food riots in its history, several counties experienced severe industrial disorder during the worst *Luddite protests of 1811–13, while in 1830 thousands of agricultural labourers across the southern counties took part in the alarming Swing riots. Since there was no adequate professional police force and no large army to call upon, those in power could never afford to ignore the violent protests of the common people [see *riots and *policing, 7].

Violent protests and radical political agitation were most likely to occur in periods of crisis created by economic depression at home and revolution abroad. Bad harvests and industrial depression were particularly severe in the mid- and late-1790s, 1810–13, 1816–20, and 1829–32, while the American and French *wars [2] produced high taxes, inflation, financial instability, and an economy distorted by wartime demands and commercial warfare. Soon after the end of the Napoleonic war in 1815 the economy went into recession, and stayed depressed until the early 1820s. The country was burdened by an enormous *national debt, the labour market was flooded with 300,000 men released from the army and navy, and the government no longer gave contracts for a wide variety of military and naval supplies. With foreign countries raising tariff barriers to protect their own domestic industries, the export of British manufactured goods slumped. The result was widespread social unrest and political agitation. However, it was not just economic hardship which drove these movements. The *American Revolution and the *French Revolutions of 1789 and 1830 stimulated political discussion and agitation in Britain, so that reformers of all shades of opinion were galvanized into political action and generated major campaigns for parliamentary reform on a national scale.

By the late eighteenth century the people of Britain were confident that they had defeated royal tyranny (if not royal patronage) and convinced that they were blessed with more liberties than almost any other people on earth. They appreciated that they lived under the rule of *law [8] and that these laws applied to both rich and poor. There was no system of torture and no arbitrary imprisonment (except for a short period during the French revolutionary crisis). No citizen could be executed or imprisoned for a long period unless convicted by a jury of fellow citizens. All citizens also enjoyed considerable freedom of expression and possessed the right to petition Crown or parliament for the redress of grievances, and all citizens were free to express their views in print, because there was no pre-publication censorship (aside from *theatre [24]), though, of course, they might risk a charge of treason, sedition, or libel after they had published. The various religious groups in the country differed in their political rights, but *toleration meant that they could all worship freely. *Freedom of the press was rightly regarded as one of the great liberties of the British people, and government efforts to increase the price of *newspapers, magazines, and pamphlets in order to keep them out of the hands of the ordinary people were unsuccessful. Possessed of a well-developed sense of justice and an awareness of their own rights and liberties, they were prepared to take direct action or to agitate in a variety of ways to redress their grievances.

These rights and civil liberties had been won after many struggles, but many political theorists and propagandists argued that the people had a claim to even greater political rights. The intellectual supports for these arguments were informed by three basic traditions: the idea of an ancient Anglo-Saxon *constitution, enshrining the genuine liberties of Englishmen lost at the Norman Conquest; a Lockean tradition of *natural rights theory which was given a radical and democratic thrust in Thomas *Paine's *Rights of Man* (1791); and an emerging tradition of philosophical radicalism associated with Jeremy *Bentham and early *utilitarianism. The first informed demands for a reinstitution of long-usurped rights of popular participation, the second was developed into an insistence on an implied contractual agreement between government and governed and the existence of a set of indefeasible natural rights, and the third provided a cogent critique of the inefficiencies of the patronage system. But to many political philosophers and propagandists these were less philosophical foundations for their arguments and more a set of lexicons upon which they drew, often promiscuously, in their writings—intermingled with rhetorical flourishes drawn from classical *republicanism and its demands for a virtuous and active citizenry, as well as from the work of continental thinkers such as Voltaire, Montesquieu, and *Rousseau. The result was an immensely fertile intellectual context for political argument and debate, generating some of Britain's finest political writing.

Those radicals who demanded political reform were not only influenced by different intellectual traditions; they also advocated a variety of different reform programmes. Some were convinced that it was Crown patronage and aristocratic influence which posed the main dangers to the rights of the people. To defeat this insidious threat the people must be encouraged to prize their liberties: voters were urged to reject courtiers, placemen, and moneyed men as their representatives, and advised to elect honest, independent country gentlemen in their stead. There were also proposals to exclude placemen from parliament, eliminate bribery and corruption in *elections, secure more frequent general elections, and redistribute parliamentary seats from small rotten boroughs to the larger counties and the more populous urban centres [see *Wyvillites]. The more radical reformers were prepared to go much further and empower all men with positive political rights. As early as 1780 the Westminster Association was advancing the six main points of parliamentary reform: universal manhood suffrage, equal constituencies, annual general elections, the secret ballot, the abolition of property qualifications for parliamentary candidates, and the payment of MPs. Initially this programme had very little support, but it was widely adopted by the radicals of the early 1790s and by the revived radical movement after 1815. There was increasing agreement among the leading spokesmen for radical reform that the right to vote should be attached to the person and not to the property of man. To deny any man the franchise was to cast a slur on his moral character and to assert that he was less than a man. The possession or lack of wealth or property was no proof of moral worth or civic virtue. Radicals frequently condemned all hereditary honours, titles, and privileges, yet still only a tiny minority of them wanted to abolish the House of Lords and fewer still the *monarchy. Moreover, in the struggle for the rights of man, most radicals were concerned quite literally with only the liberty of adult males and regarded *women [4], like children, as weak, dependent creatures incapable of exercising independent judgement. No more than a handful of radicals contemplated demanding the franchise for women.

Most radicals were convinced that parliamentary reform was essential not only to ensure that all men would enjoy the same political rights but also to redress the social and economic grievances of the poor. *Poverty [12] was seen as the creation of the crippling tax burden which had to support an extravagant monarchy and a corrupt parliament as well as finance a series of pointless foreign wars. Parliamentary reform would result in cheaper government and much lower taxes, the abolition of tithes, the repeal of the game laws, and changes to the laws which put so many small debtors in prison. Paine believed that the rich should be taxed to fund a range of social welfare reforms, and that a democratic political system would save huge amounts of money by reducing corruption, waste, and the size of the civil administration and the military establishment. His critique became a part of radical polemic in the succeeding decades. William *Cobbett, for instance, regularly denounced the government's vast patronage system which corrupted politicians, city financiers, government contractors, civil servants, officers in the armed services, and even clergymen of the Church of England. Horrified by the size of the national debt and by the burden of taxation on the poor, he blamed this system of 'Old Corruption' for enriching the few while impoverishing the many.

A still more radical group of thinkers rejected Paine's political critique and saw the major

6. This anti-government print by T. French (1795) reflects the view of many radicals in the 1790s that new restrictions on freedom of speech, and the onerous burdens of wartime taxation, were obliterating traditional English civil and political liberties.

A FREEBORN ENGLISHMAN,
the Admiration of the World; the Envy of Surrounding Nations;
&c &c.

source of poverty as the grossly unequal distribution of wealth. They regarded the landed élite as the main economic tyrants, and sought a more equal distribution of land. In the late eighteenth century, for instance, Thomas *Spence advanced his Land Plan, which called for the destruction of all private property. His admirers, the *Spenceans, continued to spread his message well into the nineteenth century, but by the 1820s some early utopian *socialists were linking inequality and economic oppression with rapid *industrialization [14] and unrestrained capitalism. In the view of such writers as Charles Hall (c.1745–c.1845), Robert *Owen, William *Thompson, and Thomas Hodgskin (1787–1869), most of the wealth produced by labour in Britain's newly industrial society was wrongfully appropriated by the idle rich because they controlled capital, land, and political power. This unjust and unequal society was wasteful, blindly competitive, and oppressive. Political reform alone would not do enough to improve the lives of the labouring poor. The unregulated competition of capitalism must also be abolished and workers given the just reward for their labour. These critics of capitalism did not claim, however, that capital and labour must always be class enemies or that industrial society could be transformed only by class conflict and violent revolution. In their view, class harmony was a realizable goal.

There were four periods of political and economic crisis in which popular radicalism flourished: in 1765–85 during the American Revolution, in 1789–98 during the French Revolution, in 1815–21 during the years of severe postwar distress, and in 1829–32 during the crisis over the Great Reform Bill. Yet these years saw no truly mass movements, for popular protest was inclined to be parochial, and, when it did become nationally orchestrated, radicalism tended to work through existing urban institutions. Most of the leaders of the reform movements during these years (including Thomas Attwood (1765–1838), Christopher Wyvill (1740–1822), John *Cartwright, Francis *Burdett, and Henry *Hunt) were middle- rather than working-class. A significant number were professional men, publishers, writers, or small landowners. Only a few leading radicals, such as Thomas *Hardy, Francis *Place, and Cobbett, were born poor, but many of these also rose to become professional agitators for political reform. Initially, most of the supporters of parliamentary reform also came from the urban middle classes, but by the 1790s significant numbers of skilled artisans had been recruited and after 1815 the majority of rank-and-file reformers were workers in industry and commerce. Only intermittently did radicalism extend into a popular movement. Throughout all periods the reform movement received its greatest support from the major urban and commercial or industrial areas of the country: from in and around London, the industrial areas of the east and west midlands, south Lancashire and west Yorkshire, regional centres such as Norwich and Bristol, Tyneside, Clydeside, and the industrial areas of south Wales. When the working classes joined the reform movement, it was dominated principally by the skilled craftsmen and semi-skilled artisans in the textile and metal industries, and those workers in mining and transportation. Few rural workers or domestic servants enrolled in the radical cause, and yet these were still the two largest groups of workers in the country. At no period did a majority of the labouring poor support political radicalism, though, in the grim years after 1815, several hundred thousand workers were recruited to the cause of reform.

No unified, national organization existed to pull together all the different strands and groups interested in the campaign for parliamentary reform. Instead, each stage in the radical campaign had several leading spokesmen, often virtually in competition with each other. These worked with a leading society, such as (at different times) the Yorkshire Association, the London Corresponding Society (see *corresponding societies), the Hampden Club, the National Union of the Working Classes, or the Birmingham Political Union, trying with only partial success to give a clear lead to dozens, even hundreds, of other reform societies. The Yorkshire Association had attracted the support of about 8,000 men in the county on its launch in 1779, the London Corresponding Society had over 3,000 active members at one stage and could attract many more supporters for some of its activities, while the Birmingham Political Union had over 10,000 members in 1832. Most radical clubs adopted similar practices: they elected officials (usually a president, secretary, and treasurer); arranged speeches, *lectures, and debates; disseminated propaganda; prepared addresses and petitions to king and parliament; and sometimes organized marches, open-air meetings, and crowd demonstrations. Some efforts were made to co-ordinate the activities of these clubs and associations on a national scale. The Yorkshire Association gave a lead in organizing reform petitions across the country in the early 1780s, and an effort was made by the corresponding societies in 1793 to hold a convention in Edinburgh of delegates from radical societies across Britain. The former campaign failed to draw in all supporters of reform and the latter project ended in disaster, with the leaders condemned for sedition and transported. At no stage did the radical movement unite all reformers in the country behind a national campaign or a specific programme: many radicals found additional or alternative satisfaction in the conviviality and fellowship of their local debating club or *tavern.

During the periods of active radical campaigning for parliamentary reform two tactics in particular were employed by the popular reform organizations: an attempt to educate public opinion through the printed and spoken word and an effort to support the demand for reform by massive petitioning campaigns. Most clubs and societies debated political questions and organized lectures and speeches, but they relied even more on the printed word. Radicals both exploited the opportunity provided by existing newspapers and periodicals and found the money and the customers to produce their own propaganda. The *Society for Constitutional Information freely distributed over 88,000 pieces of printed propaganda between 1780 and 1783. William Cobbett's radical weekly journal, the *Political Register*, which he restarted in November 1818, sold one million copies in the first six months of its existence, while the *Poor Man's Guardian* sold about 16,000 copies of every issue during the crisis of the Great Reform Bill in the early 1830s. Until the government reduced the tax on newspapers in 1836, the sales of illegal newspapers, many of which supported the radical cause, were greater than the sales of all the legitimate newspapers in the country added together. In addition to newspapers, radicals produced a huge number of individual tracts and pamphlets. Some sold tens of thousands of copies, while perhaps as many as 200,000 copies of Paine's *Rights of Man* were distributed, and an amazing two million copies of Queen Caroline's *Answer to the King* were distributed from London alone in 1820, as well as being widely reprinted elsewhere. The radicals also tried on occasion to prove to government and parliament that they had massive popular support by organizing nationwide petitioning campaigns. In 1780 the reformers sent in petitions signed by about 60,000 people. A radical petitioning campaign organized by John Cartwright secured 130,000 signatures, while in 1817 over 700 petitions were supported by over 1,500,000 people in over 350 towns across the country. Hundreds of petitions were also organized in 1830–2. Impressive as such figures are, none of these petitioning campaigns attracted as much public support as did those for the abolition of slavery and the slave trade.

At three separate points in the development of radicalism, the movement resorted to mass meetings—sometimes known as the radical platform. In 1795, in 1816–21, and in 1831 radicals organized huge public rallies in the open air, which attracted tens of thousands of people and, on occasion, over 100,000 people. A charismatic orator such as Henry Hunt could attract, instruct, inspire, and entertain vast crowds. Hunt was the main speaker at some of the largest radical meetings in London in November and December 1816, February 1817, September 1818, and July 1819. On these public platforms Hunt adopted an independent, uncompromising, and resolutely democratic tone, and promoted a common sense of purpose among his listeners. Probably the largest, most effective, and most sophisticated single publicity campaign mounted by the radicals in these years, however, was the *Queen Caroline affair of 1820–1. When the unpopular George IV sought to divorce the queen, the radicals of London and tens of thousands of ordinary Londoners rallied to her cause and gave a lead to the whole nation. The amount of printed propaganda generated was staggering. For several months the newspapers were full of little else, and hundreds of individual pamphlets and graphic *satires, many of them bestsellers, appeared in support of the queen. Never was a reigning monarch so savagely and coarsely attacked in the public prints as was George IV. In addition, over 800 petitions and addresses were presented to the queen. There were also many popular celebrations, public processions, crowd demonstrations, and loyal deputations. The metropolis revelled in a welter of pageantry, with many activities accompanied by bands, banners, slogans, and symbols, and with buildings, streets, and even ships on the Thames illuminated. When the queen died in August 1821 throngs insisted that her cortège should pass through the streets of London on its way to Brunswick so that the people could pay their last respects. In a clash with troops two men were killed, and some 70,000 people later attended the funeral of these 'martyrs'. The prestige of the monarchy and the stability of the Tory government were both badly shaken: the radicals were able to restore the freedom of open political agitation despite the repressive legislation of 1819.

The vast majority of radicals and reformers used constitutional means and peaceful tactics. This does not mean, however, that all radicals opposed the use of force or that there was no prospect of revolution in Britain during this period. There were a number of occasions when economic distress, industrial disorder, and popular radicalism might have led to armed *insurrection or even revolution. The Luddite industrial disorder of 1811–13, the widespread distress and radical protests of 1816–20, and the agrarian revolt, industrial protests, and political riots of 1830–1 might all have sparked off an insurrection if the ruling authorities had lost their nerve or had reacted in a different way. Revolutionary conspirators did exist and did plan violent action in 1796–8 and in 1816–17, but at no stage were they well organized, well led, well armed, or well supported. And at no point did the government or local authorities panic. Indeed, the government responded with repressive legislation, the arrest of leading radicals, and a firm clamp-down on public agitation.

The defeat of all the radical campaigns before 1830–2 owed much to the failures of the radical leadership and the repressive policies of the government. It must also be conceded that only a minority of the people were ever converted into radical activists campaigning for parliamentary reform. Indeed, many of the people held decidedly conservative views on such issues as religion and social change. Popular hostility was aroused against Catholics in 1780 and 1829 and Protestant Dissenters in the early 1790s, and against American rebels in the 1770s and French revolutionaries in the 1790s. Although the élite sometimes encouraged popular antipathy to religious minorities and foreign enemies, it is clear that many ordinary people shared these prejudices and needed little encouragement to take action. Such manifestations of popular conservatism were the result of deep-rooted prejudices and widely held opinions in favour of the existing constitution in church and state. What an examination of popular conservatism shows is that the ruling class themselves did not always believe that political opinions and public action should be restricted to a narrow, propertied oligarchy. They were quite prepared to countenance and even encourage mass involvement in political questions so long as this agitation served to buttress rather than challenge the existing political order. While fearing the activities of radical critics, the élite welcomed demonstrations of support for the existing power structure. In doing so, they had to accept that the British people could and did fulfil an increasingly democratic political role.

Some historians represent the passing of a parliamentary reform bill in 1832 solely as the product of forces at work within high politics. This interpretation underestimates the influence of popular pressure in the political system. The passing of *Catholic emancipation in 1829, which had such disastrous consequences on Tory unity, owed much to the efforts of Daniel *O'Connell's leadership of the Catholic Association. The depressed state of the economy led to the agrarian revolt of 1830 and to massive industrial protests in south Wales in 1831. Middle-class voters greatly increased Whig representation in the House of Commons at the crucial general election of 1831. Prolonged parliamentary debates on the Reform Bill led to the creation of a host of new political societies, the political unions especially, across the country, and to a revival of many moribund reform clubs. The radicals produced a torrent of propaganda in favour of reform, presented several thousand petitions, and held huge open-air meetings and public demonstrations in cities and towns such as London and Birmingham. The political temperature was so high that serious rioting broke out in Derby, Nottingham, and Bristol in October 1831 after the defeat of the Reform Bill.

The Reform Act which was finally passed in 1832 was far more limited than most radicals had wanted or expected. The worst rotten boroughs were abolished and the largest unrepresented towns were given direct representation, but the distribution of seats was far from equal. The franchise was given to many of the rural and urban middle classes, but not to the poor. Nothing was done about the frequency of general elections, the secret ballot, the property qualifications of candidates, or the payment of MPs. The radical campaign for a democratic reform of parliament had clearly failed. Yet it would be wrong to say that the British people were not free or that those without a vote were powerless to influence government or parliament. The people had long demonstrated that they were a political force in British society: they had successfully defended their civil liberties, developed a radical ideology, created effective pressure groups, and proved that they could recruit hundreds of thousands of ordinary people in support of political reform. The Great Reform Act of 1832 proved that concessions could be forced from the ruling élite, the constitution could be reformed, and the franchise could be extended, if well-organized popular campaigns were mounted. It was a lesson that was learned by the leaders of both *Chartism and the Anti-Corn Law League in the years ahead.

Brock, M., *The Great Reform Act*, London, 1973; Cannon, J., *Parliamentary Reform 1640–1832*, Cambridge, 1973; Dickinson, H. T., *British Radicalism and the French Revolution 1789–1815*, Oxford, 1985; Dinwiddy, J. R., *From Luddism to the First Reform Bill*, Oxford, 1986; Goodwin, A., *The Friends of Liberty: The English Democratic Movement in the Age of the French Revolution*, London, 1979; McCalman, I., *Radical Underworld: Prophets, Revolutionaries, and Pornographers in London, 1795–1840*, Cambridge, 1988; Royle, E., & Walvin, J., *English Radicals and Reformers 1760–1848*, Brighton, 1982; Stevenson, J., *Popular Disturbances in England 1700–1870*, London, 1979; Thompson, E. P., *The Making of the English Working Class* (1963), Harmondsworth, 1968; Veitch, G. S., *The Genesis of Parliamentary Reform*, London, 1965.

4 · WOMEN   BARBARA CAINE

The French Declaration of the Rights of Man and the Citizen of 1789 gave rise immediately to the question of whether there were comparable rights for women. The French feminist and revolutionary Olympe de Gouges (1748–93) and Mary *Wollstonecraft were but two of the women who began, during the *French Revolution, to demand independent legal and political rights for women and hence initiated modern feminism. But the question of women's rights was always complex. Women were rarely overt reference-points in discussing the rights of man, the issue rather being the assertion of the rights of all men as against the privileges of a small group of men. By contrast, all discussions of the rights of women necessarily involved a demand that at least some of the rights of men be extended to women. Thus men were set up as the standard, and debate centred on the extent to which women resembled or differed from them intellectually and morally. Inevitably, this meant that while women could demand some specific rights, the term 'man' remained synonymous with the term 'human'. Women could demand a recognition of their own rationality and entitlement to citizenship, but within the prevailing terms of political discourse they could hardly even find the words with which to demand other rights and privileges which went with the full humanity claimed by men. It was impossible for women to demand the right to be seen as sexual subjects rather than as sexual objects, for example, and equally difficult for them to claim the capacity of *genius.

The *Enlightenment [32] insistence on human rationality and the *natural rights of man, like the attacks on hereditary and caste privileges, all inevitably suggested possible avenues and freedoms for women. But increasingly historians and literary scholars have commented on the lack of interest in the rights or wrongs of women evident amongst those very philosophers who argued most ardently for the rights of men. Recently, many scholars have extended the discussion of women and the Enlightenment beyond political and philosophical texts and into medical and scientific ones. These latter works exhibited a growing emphasis on the differences between men and women—in anatomy and physiology, in intellect, emotions, and moral capacities—providing an extensive set of arguments to show why the rights of men were seen as sex-specific ones, inappropriate to women.

The emphasis on sexual difference which became so marked in the eighteenth century was closely connected with the equally marked emphasis on the contrast between public and private spheres: the expanding masculine public sphere of political, civic, and intellectual life, and of industry and commerce, formed a counterpoint to the feminine private sphere, which centred on family life and on the care and early education of children. This whole process also meant that womanliness and femininity, like manliness and masculinity, underwent extensive discussion and redefinition [see *sensibility, 11].

Much attention has been paid recently to the transformation of womanhood at this time, and especially to the importance of *Evangelicalism, with its insistence on the home as the centre of moral and religious life. For the Evangelicals, women's domestic piety became a necessary counterpart to the rationalism and even brutality of the commercial world [see *domesticity, 13]. In the view of many Evangelicals, middle-class men would only retain their religious beliefs and their moral centre if persuaded to do so by their pious and beloved womenfolk. Within this framework, women faced an extraordinarily paradoxical situation. They were expected to be the religious and moral guides and leaders of men, to whom they were in every other way subordinate. Similarly, they were to raise the moral and religious tone of their family and household, and through this of the wider social world—a world to which they were denied direct access, at least in terms of political rights.

While new emphasis was being placed on the importance of women as the anchors of both domestic and public life, it is also necessary to look at the problems posed for women by the extensive redefinition of manliness and masculinity which occurred particularly amongst middle-class men at the same time. This redefinition involved not only the claiming by men of rationality, humanity, and genius as masculine qualities, but also, as in the discourse of *political economy [33], the appropriation into the masculine realm of those activities like productive labour once thought of as belonging to both men and women. As Mary *Shelley illustrated in *Frankenstein* (1818), even capacities once thought of as necessarily female— the ability to give birth, or to create life—were being appropriated by masculinist *natural philosophy [34].

The changing role of men within the family has recently become a subject of extensive historical interest as scholars have begun to look at the eighteenth-century emphasis on the importance of the home as the site of education and civic virtue. It is by now almost an axiom within the history of the family that the eighteenth century brought a decline in patriarchal authority, as an older, authoritarian family gave way to a closer-knit unit enshrining the value of affective individualism. John *Locke's psychological and educational theories were important here; they stressed the need for parents to understand and care for their children, and to ensure obedience by inculcating senses of filial obligation, respect, and loyalty. Mary Wollstonecraft was one of many who greatly approved of Locke's educational ideas. 'A slavish bondage to parents cramps every faculty of the mind,' she wrote, 'and Mr Locke very judiciously observes that, "if the mind be curbed and humbled too much in children; or their spirits be abased and broken by too strict a hand over them; they lose all vigour and industry".' Wollstonecraft believed that excessively strict parental rule might itself account for the weakness of women, who were subjected to it more rigorously than boys.

However, Locke's demand that fathers become less concerned with discipline and more involved in the education of their children made patriarchy gentler, while ensuring that fathers retained all their power. Although Locke's plan assumed that parents would work together, in fact the father assumed the dominant educational role, with the mother's role being purely ancillary. The mother acted as intermediary between father and child, but had no acknow-ledged voice of her own. Because of her perception of the disproportionate status of the father in a domestic setting, a young girl would be particularly susceptible to such impressions when her father undertook her tutelage. This transformation of fatherhood served to make the father the central and most important figure, not only in the home but also in the emotional lives of children. Women's maternal and domestic activities provided necessary services, but offered nothing comparable to the knowledge or education offered by men. This educational approach has been seen as the reason that educated women, including Frances *Burney, Hannah *More, and Maria *Edgeworth, were so extraordinarily docile and dutiful, identify-ing closely with their fathers, subordinating their work to paternal demands, and sharing their fathers' concern about the need to control female sexuality and disorder.

One cannot help wondering whether it was not perhaps the fact that Mary Wollstonecraft's father was a drunken, violent, and dissolute man, concerned neither about the physical well-being nor about the education of his children, that gave Wollstonecraft the critical perspective on masculinity which is so fundamental to her assertion of women's rights, even while it co-exists so clearly with her sense of the importance of manly virtue. More clearly than anyone else, Wollstonecraft herself shows the complex consequences for women of this increasing valorization of the masculine, as she veered between identifying herself strongly with the new ideal of manliness and the power of masculine reason on the one hand and feeling intense anger at the exclusion of women from the concept of rationality and humanity on the other.

Like other women of her time, Wollstonecraft's intellectual development consisted of encounters with philosophers whose work she admired and found inspiring, but who denied to women intellectual capacities, education and independence, and even, in some cases, any direct connection with human nature. What differentiated Wollstonecraft from her contem-poraries was her anger at such views. She greatly admired the educational ideals in *Rousseau's *Émile* (1762), but was appalled at the contrast between Émile's broad education and Sophie's narrow training, devised explicitly to render her docile and obedient.

Inevitably, Wollstonecraft was powerfully influenced by the valorization of men in all she read. So great was male pre-eminence in moral matters, as well as in political and philosoph-ical ones, that it made it very difficult even to find a language with which to praise women. As a radical democrat, Wollstonecraft adopted the practice common amongst radical writers, such as Thomas *Paine, of using as the ultimate measure of praise or condemnation terms derived from manliness or from femininity respectively. Even in her major work, *A Vindication of* *the Rights of Woman* (1792), dissolute aristocrats, like members of standing armies, were all described as emasculated or effeminate—lacking in the nobility of the common man.

This framework enabled Wollstonecraft to show that women's weaknesses were not inherent in their physical or mental make-up, but rather were shared by other groups who lacked proper employment or independence and who were part of hierarchical structures. Yet at the very moment that Wollstonecraft was insisting that much of the weakness of women, like that of standing armies and aristocrats, resulted from their lack of education or of employment, her language inevitably served both to connect these dissolute beings with women and to reinforce the idea that strength, nobility, and rationality are concomitants of certain forms of masculinity.

While accepting and using this masculinist language herself, Wollstonecraft was nevertheless acutely aware of the ways in which sexual stereotyping functioned in her own day—politically, socially, and aesthetically. In the attack on Edmund *Burke which makes up so much of her work *A Vindication of the Rights of Men* (1790), she singled out for particular comment the sexual attitudes behind some of Burke's 'empty rhetorical flourishes'. To Burke's notorious description in *Reflections on the Revolution in France* (1790) of the women who met the French royal family on their return to Paris as 'the furies of hell, in the abused shape of the vilest of women', she acidly responded: 'Probably you mean women who gained a livelihood by selling vegetables or fish . . . who never had any advantages of education.'

While criticizing Burke, Wollstonecraft herself was often scathing in her comments on women. Many historians have commented on what certainly appears sometimes to be extreme misogyny, but we need to reiterate the lack of adequate terminology available for her to praise women. This issue is made particularly clear in the case of one contemporary woman writer whom she truly admired, Catharine *Macaulay. She regarded Macaulay's *Letters on Education* (1790) as an exceptional work, displaying 'a degree of sound reason and profound thought which either through defective organs, or a mistaken education, seldom appears in female productions'. Yet she seemed only able to pay tribute to Macaulay by describing her as a 'masculine and fervid writer'. Two years later, in writing *A Vindication of the Rights of Woman*, Wollstonecraft was extremely troubled by the implications of her earlier article, refusing to call Macaulay's understanding 'masculine', 'because I admit not of such an arrogant assumption of reason'. She wanted now to claim Macaulay as a model of what women could be; she argued that Macaulay's judgement, 'the matured fruit of profound thinking, was a proof that a woman can acquire judgement in the full extent of that word'.

This 'arrogant assumption of reason' by men was the main focus of Wollstonecraft's *Vindication of the Rights of Woman*, now widely regarded as the founding text in modern British feminism. Written in a few weeks of furious activity in 1792, the book was inspired by her indignation at the fact that women were explicitly being excluded from the compulsory schooling offered to men in France. French legislators, Wollstonecraft argued, demanded freedom and the right to judge for themselves as men respecting their own happiness, but they were quite happy to subjugate women. 'Who made man the exclusive judge,' she asked, 'if woman partake with him the gift of reason?' In arguing that they were acting to promote the happiness of women, the men of the French Constituent Assembly were following the model of all tyrants.

In the *Vindication*, Wollstonecraft set out her arguments about the fundamental rights which followed the assertion that women, like men, were rational creatures. From her point of view there were two aspects to this question: first, it involved rethinking conventional ideas about women's conduct and moral qualities, taking as the first principle that there was only one standard of human virtue which must be the same for men and women. She criticized, for example, the gendering of qualities, whereby in men the term 'modesty' referred to 'that soberness of mind which teaches a man not to think more highly of himself than he ought to think' while in women the term referred only to sexual demeanour. This had to give way, she asserted, to a single set of human virtues with the same meanings for men and women.

Second, alongside the discussion of moral questions, Wollstonecraft argued for the institutional and legal changes which would follow from the recognition of women's rationality and moral autonomy. These included the need for an *education [17] based on rational principles which combined intellectual training with useful skills; the need for an end to the sexual double standard, whereby women were held to account for standards of sexual morality that men themselves did not practise; the need for the reform of marriage; and the need for the admission of women to fields of study and of paid employment, which would allow them economic independence. Wollstonecraft specified the study of medicine and business as possible professional pursuits, and of politics and history for intellectual and moral improvement. Such activities would allow women a much-needed alternative to marriage. Wollstonecraft saw women's education not only as extending their rationality but also as the necessary basis for their autonomy, and she believed that their duties as mothers provided the basis of their claims to be independent citizens.

In the *Vindication*, Wollstonecraft's discussion focuses strongly on questions of *female education and autonomy, the issues of greatest concern to many late-eighteenth- and nineteenth-century feminists. But it omits two other questions which were central to her own life (and harder to deal with than those she discussed directly): women's right to sexual subjectivity, and their right to intellectual creativity.

The initially favourable reception of Wollstonecraft's *Vindication* demonstrates the extent to which some of her views were accepted by her contemporaries. The importance of improving women's education, for example—of emphasizing their minds and souls rather than their bodies—and of redirecting that education away from accomplishments towards a training of the intellect along rational lines, had long been advocated as a way of improving the situation of women. By the late eighteenth century, an improved education was demanded even by those who did not see the social, legal, or economic position of women as a problem. Wollstonecraft's educational ideas were shared not only by Catharine Macaulay and Mary *Hays, with whom Wollstonecraft was closely identified, but also by others like Maria Edgeworth who rejected any notion of championing the rights of woman. Wollstonecraft's theories were equally supported by those concerned to reassert women's subordinate position, like Hannah More and Jane *West. The presentation of women as rational and educable, and the importance of education as a basis of prudent and successful marriage and wise motherhood, were, moreover, the subjects of much late-eighteenth- and early-nineteenth-century fiction. Several of the novels of Jane *Austen, as well as Susan *Ferrier's *Marriage* (1818), stress the connection between rational education and the training and control of feeling; they contrast education and wise marriage on the one hand with ignorance, frivolity, and destructive imprudence on the other.

While Wollstonecraft's ideas on education reflected the broad progressive current of her day, her view of the relationship between the specific duties of women, such as between their independence from men and their claim to citizenship, did not achieve the same general acceptance. For her, the question of female citizenship remained central, connected in the *Vindication* with every discussion of women's education, work, and motherhood. In order to render women's 'private virtue a public benefit', she argued, women needed 'a civil existence in the state', whether they were married or single, both as a means of improving their private circumstances and as a way of contributing to the common good.

Wollstonecraft hinted at her belief 'that women ought to have representatives, instead of being arbitrarily governed without having any direct share allowed them in the deliberations of government', but she did not pursue this idea thoroughly. She could only discuss political representation for women in the context of the limitations of the franchise for some classes of men: thus women were 'as well represented as a numerous class of hard-working mechanics, who pay for the support of royalty when they can hardly stop their children's mouths with bread'.

The question of women's citizenship was a difficult one for Wollstonecraft. While rejecting the idea that sexual difference applied to intellectual or moral faculties, she accepted that there was a natural division of labour between the sexes and that women's proper location was in the home. Like many of her contemporaries, she supported Rousseau's insistence on the importance of direct maternal care, including breastfeeding, and of the role of mothers in the education of young children. She saw these activities as elevating the status of motherhood, but differed from Rousseau in her insistence that the maternal activities of women in themselves required education and independence from men, and that they provided the basis for a distinct form of citizenship. Ironically, this bound her to a view of women's duties which was as narrow and uniform as that which she protested against—and one which did not, in fact, allow for all her own aspirations for women. As she explained herself,

to avoid misconstruction, though I consider that women in the common walks of life are called to fulfil the duties of wives and mothers, by religion and reason, I cannot help lamenting that women of a superior cast have not a road open by which they can pursue more extensive plans of usefulness and independence.

Wollstonecraft was trapped here in an insoluble dilemma. In seeking to recognize the importance of sexual difference in terms which did not demean women, and to explore their conditions and needs, she focused necessarily on mothers. Yet in so doing she reduced all women to a single function—something not so very different from that levelling of all women to a single standard of meekness and docility of which she was so critical. At the same time, there was no other way for her to insist both on a re-evaluation of sexual difference and on the need for women to have a form of citizenship that incorporated or recognized that difference. She sought to make motherhood as much as possible like a profession—hence her insistence on the active engagement of mothers in the nursing, educating, and training of their children. She also sought to separate motherhood from the sexual relationship of husband and wife; unless women were able to be psychologically independent of men, she argued, it was impossible for them to develop virtue, to follow their own sense of duty, or properly to meet the needs of their children. She could not demand this, though, without confining women in some way to a narrowly defined familial and domestic sphere.

While Wollstonecraft paid little attention to the question of women's political representation, this question became a central one by the 1820s and 1830s. It was the major issue in the most important feminist text of the early nineteenth century, William *Thompson's *Appeal of One-Half the Human Race* (1825). Thompson's work was specifically intended as a response to James *Mill, who in his 'Essay on Government' (1820) argued that neither women nor working-class men needed to be granted political rights in a representative system. Women did not need political rights, Mill claimed, as the interests of almost all them were involved either in those of their fathers or in those of their husbands. Similarly, working-class men did not require separate representation, as their interests would be looked after by the group that Mill regarded as the most wise and virtuous part of the community: the middle rank. Thompson, whose ideas had been influenced by his friendship with the Irish *Saint-Simonian feminist Anna *Wheeler, saw the denial to women of citizenship and political rights as being directly connected with their abject sexual and domestic slavery. He argued that all women were in need of political rights, most particularly married women. 'Having been reduced, by the want of political rights, to a state of helplessness, slavery, and of consequent unequal enjoyments, pains, and privations', married women, he claimed, 'are *more in need* of political rights than any other portion of human beings, to gain some emergence from this state.'

Thompson was more outspoken than Wollstonecraft both in his discussion of political representation and in his treatment of women's sexuality. Like Wollstonecraft, he emphasized the role of male sexual licence and profligacy in the degradation of women within marriage and within society generally. He expressed outrage at the way in which every aspect of women's lives was directed towards the gratification of men's animal appetites. And he discussed at length the ways in which existing sexual morality gave pre-eminence to male desire while refusing even to recognize the existence of women's sexuality. One of the greatest injustices women suffered, especially once married, he argued, arose from the fact that under present norms and circumstances, a 'woman is more the slave of man for the gratification of her desires than man is of woman'. Where men could seek sexual pleasure and gratification outside marriage, existing moral codes made this impossible for women—indeed, there was no recognition even of women's entitlement to sexual activity or fulfilment in marriage. In marriage, man was the master and commander; woman obeyed. Woman consequently is 'not permitted to appear to feel, or desire. The whole of what is called her education training her to be the obedient instrument of man's sensual gratification, she is not permitted even to wish for any gratification for herself.'

While Thompson discussed this question openly, Wollstonecraft shied away from it. The *Vindication* offered an acute analysis of sensibility and pleasure as instruments of patriarchal control, showing how women's sexuality and dependency were constructed. But rather than demanding women's right to control of their own sexuality, Wollstonecraft insisted on a puritan sexual ethic for women, even in the more experimental realm of fiction. Although in her novels she emphasized the ways in which marriage imprisoned women, denying them all rights not only to their property but also to their children and their own bodies, she did not suggest any alternatives. She highlighted the issue of rape in marriage, seeing it as almost institutionalized since women were conventionally required to make themselves attractive to their husbands while men had never even to think about how they appeared to their wives. But while women's desire and the need to find forms of relationships which did not impose the burdens of marriage was a concern in Wollstonecraft's own life, it was not an issue directly addressed in her writings.

This is all the more notable because her life came to represent for many, both in our period and in the twentieth century, the sexual revolution implicit in the demand for women's rights. In her rejection of existing codes of sexual and marital conduct, Wollstonecraft unquestionably claimed the right to active sexual desire. Moreover, her life, as depicted in William *Godwin's *Memoirs of the Author of a Vindication of the Rights of Woman* (1798), consisted largely of emotional involvements carried out in complete disregard for conventional moral and sexual codes. Her pursuit of Henry *Fuseli, her fraught liaison with the American adventurer Gilbert Imlay (1752–1828), and her relationship and marriage with Godwin himself were decidedly unconventional. The story of her life provided for those who opposed the rights of woman, in particular anti-Jacobin writers such as William *Gifford and Richard *Polwhele, a perfect illustration of the connection between women's rights and unrestrained female passion, proving that both not only were destructive of family life and social stability but also led to despair, attempted suicides, and a complete breakdown of any semblance of orderly life.

Godwin's *Memoirs* of Wollstonecraft destroyed her reputation. This work has been the subject of much critical comment since its first publication, and it certainly does stress Wollstonecraft's emotional life while denying her any serious intellectual or political interests. But what is of particular significance here is the impossibility for Godwin to depict Wollstonecraft's emotional and sexual history in any way that did not render them ludicrous, pitiable, and contemptible. This was so not simply because of Godwin and Wollstonecraft's personal vagaries, but rather because the idea that women were properly the objects of male desire was so deeply ingrained in eighteenth-century thinking as to make it impossible even to address women as sexual and desiring subjects.

The question of women's active desire was dealt with in fiction at this time by Mary Hays and, after Wollstonecraft's death, by Frances Burney. But their work simply helps to show how difficult an issue it was. Mary Hays's novel *Memoirs of Emma Courtney* (1796), which centres

7. *Mrs. Godwin*, a portrait of Mary
Wollstonecraft engraved by J. Chapman
after an unattributed painting dating from
after her marriage to William Godwin
in 1797: the masculine dress, hairstyle,
and features of this engraving echo
widespread conservative attacks on her
unwomanly or 'unsexed' character.

on a woman's unrequited love, helps perhaps to explain why Wollstonecraft herself did not
address this question. For while revealing the sufferings women faced through being expected
to respond only to male desire, never daring to speak their own, it serves also to emphasize
women's enslavement to their own sensibility and emotions. Hays's quivering heroine seems
to have no existence but in her feelings—hence her novel replicated precisely that narrowly
constrained idea of femininity which Wollstonecraft protested against most strongly.

   Although dressed in a comic vein, Frances Burney's discussion of women's desire in her last
novel, *The Wanderer, or Female Difficulties* (1814), is also problematic. Elinor Joddrel, the
woman who demands the right to love and to speak her love, is a comic character who, in the
very act of declaiming her feelings, forfeits both her dignity and her self-respect. After a series
of histrionic outbursts to the man who has rejected her love, accompanied by various attempts
at suicide, Elinor tries to explain the motives behind her pursuit of a man who clearly does not
return her affections. Her conduct, she insists, was guided by reason, not mere passion. But an
explanation of her motives

may lead you to a subject which you have long, in common with every man that breathes, wished
exploded, the Rights of Woman: Rights, however, which all your sex, with all its arbitrary assumption
of superiority, can never disprove, for they are the Rights of Human nature; to which the two sexes
equally and unalienably belong.

The particular right with which she is concerned is that of a woman 'if endowed with senses to
make use of them'. Why, Elinor demands,

not alone, is woman to be excluded from the exertions of courage, the field of glory, the immortal death
of honour? . . . must even her heart be circumscribed by boundaries as narrow as her sphere of action in
life? Must she be taught to subdue all its native emotions? To hide them as sin, and to deny them
as shame? Must her affections be bestowed but as the recompense of flattery received; not of merit

discriminated? Must everything that she does be prescribed by rule? . . . Must nothing that is spontaneous, generous, intuitive, spring from her soul to her lips?

Elinor's questions do not persuade the man she loves to do anything but pity her. Certainly they do not cause him to transfer his affections from the docile Juliet—herself the victim of much social and sexual prejudice. Elinor's demands remain unanswered in the novel; moreover, the comic form in which they are presented serves to remove from them any sense of urgency.

The assumption that sexual desire and, indeed, all forms of active sexuality were embodied in men affected not only questions of sexual behaviour, morality, and decorum but also discussions about aesthetics and artistic creativity [see *literary theory, 41]. Here, too, Wollstonecraft was clearly aware of the ways in which contemporary views, values, and structures of discourse excluded and denigrated women and denied them their rightful position in society. But she was unable to establish a form in which to articulate women's claim to creativity or genius. She showed her outrage at the gendering of aesthetic values most clearly in her attack on Edmund Burke's use of the language of sexual difference in his contrast between the *sublime and the beautiful. Burke's gendering of the sublime as masculine, in his influential *A Philosophical Enquiry into the Origin of our Ideas on the Sublime and Beautiful* (1757), she argued, denied women both creative power and moral virtue, while encouraging them to cultivate weakness to gain male approval. It thus provided a comprehensive illustration of the ways in which existing ideas about sexual qualities limited women in every aspect of their lives. She charged Burke with having convinced women

that *littleness* and *weakness* are the very essence of beauty; and that the Supreme being, in giving women beauty in the most supereminent degree, seemed to command them, by the powerful voice of Nature, not to cultivate the moral virtues that chance to excite respect, and interfere with the pleasing sensations they were created to inspire.

But while venting her anger at Burke for his demeaning representation of women, and for his endorsement of the idea that women should never exert themselves, Wollstonecraft was herself constrained by masculine traditions and genres. The fact that by the end of the eighteenth century the idea of genius was transformed from being regarded as a kind of talent into a superior type of person who walked a 'sublime' path between 'sanity' and 'madness', between the 'monstrous' and the 'superhuman', reinforced the view that the driving force of Romantic genius came from male sexual energies. There was almost no way of connecting it with female emotions and sensitivity. As this suggests, the question of genius and the question of women's sexual subjectivity were very closely linked. Wollstonecraft herself made the connection when, in talking about the transience of sexual feeling, she contrasted ordinary sexual feeling with 'the romantic passion that is the concomitant of genius'. Creative power and genius required male physical strength and stamina, and often also the appropriation by men of the female qualities of feeling and intuition. While Wollstonecraft, like Hays, frequently insisted on the need for women to train their intellectual capacities and to have access to the whole intellectual spectrum, neither of them could find a way to negotiate women's access to this ultimate creative realm.

The process by which genius was gendered serves to underline the problems women faced in asserting their full humanity. The connection between masculinity and genius was never argued out, but rather assumed in many different texts and forms, becoming gradually established as a dominant belief. It relied not simply on the assertion of a male right to creative power, which could be rebutted, but rather on the ways in which men controlled all forms of discourse, assuming at the same time an unbreakable connection between the sex of writers and the kind of work they could do. The power of this connection is shown clearly in regard to Wollstonecraft herself in the comments of her husband, William Godwin. Godwin asserted that Mary Wollstonecraft was a genius, but the very form of this assertion raised questions about its meaning. While claiming the *Vindication of the Rights of Woman* as a work of genius, Godwin insisted that it could scarcely maintain a place in the first class of human productions. It would always be found wanting 'when tried by the hoary and long-established laws of literary composition'. These laws ultimately centred on a gendered idea of style, a 'manly' rigour of language and expression which women could emulate but never properly attain. Thus the *Vindication* is criticized because it is not written in the emotional style appropriate to a woman; it is amazonian, 'containing sentiments of a rather masculine description and, it must be confessed, occasional passages of a stern and rugged character, incompatible with the true stamina of the writer's character'. But it is clear that his gendered critical framework makes it impossible for a woman ever to show strength or to challenge prevailing ideas without violating codes of literary propriety. Strength of mind and statement are inextricably bound up with the masculine: merely showing that women possess these qualities makes them transgressive.

The difficulties involved in even speaking of women's sexuality or creative capacity serve to demonstrate the extent to which men's rights and privileges were claimed, not as a facet of a broad and potentially shared humanity but as masculine rights and capacities, defined by contrast with feminine subordination and incapacity. The Rights of Man could never simply be claimed by women, since much of their meaning came from the fact that men alone were entitled to them. On the one hand, as their opponents recognized, this meant that the very idea of the Rights of Woman raised fundamental questions about sexual difference and sexual hierarchy. At the same time, by keeping debate within the framework of natural rights, those concerned about the situation of women addressed only certain aspects of women's subordination—demanding recognition of their rationality, but failing to challenge the overall ways in which men claimed the areas of human sexuality, of creative capacity, and even of feeling, for their own sex.

Battersby, C., *Gender and Genius: Towards a Feminist Aesthetics*, London, 1989; Davidoff, L., & Hall, C., *Family Fortunes: Men and Women of the English Middle Class, 1780–1850*, London, 1987; Gatens, M., *Feminism and Philosophy: Perspectives on Difference and Equality*, Cambridge, 1991; Jordanova, L., *Sexual Visions: Images of Gender in Science and Medicine between the Eighteenth and Twentieth Centuries*, Hemel Hempstead, 1989; Kowalski-Wallace, E., *Their Fathers' Daughters: Hannah More, Maria Edgeworth and Patriarchal Complicity*, New York, 1991; Landes, J., *Women and the Public Sphere in the Age of the French Revolution*, New York, 1988; Laqueur, T., *Making Sex: Body and Gender from the Greeks to Freud*, Cambridge, Mass., 1990; Myers, M., 'Reform or Ruin: A Revolution in Female Manners', *Studies in Eighteenth-Century Culture*, 11 (1982), 119–26; Rendall, J., *The Origins of Modern Feminism: Women in Britain, France and the United States*, Basingstoke, 1985; Sapiro, V., *A Vindication of Political Virtue: The Political Theory of Mary Wollstonecraft*, Chicago, 1992; Taylor, B., 'Mary Wollstonecraft and the Wild Wish of Early Feminism', *History Workshop Journal*, 33 (1992), 197–219.

5 · EMPIRE   JOHN GASCOIGNE

The British empire was a mirror which both magnified and distorted the characteristics and idiosyncrasies of the home power. And in the period from the American Declaration of Independence to the Great *Reform Bill, Britain passed through a number of jolting experiences which were reflected in its dealings with the territories under its control. It had to absorb the shock of the *American Revolution, the humiliation of defeat, and, soon afterwards, the cataclysm of the *French Revolution, which coloured all aspects of political life. Even after the defeat of *Napoleon in 1815, the long shadow of the French Revolution gave a sinister hue to the moves for reform which were partially and belatedly implemented in the wake of the Reform Act of 1832.

Naturally, these upheavals at home left their mark on the empire and gave our period some measure of distinctiveness in the sphere of imperial relations. Fear of colonial revolt which had been prompted by the American Revolution was strengthened and given a much sharper ideological edge by the impact of the French Revolution. The forms of colonial rule were shaped by the distrust of popular participation which these experiences had instilled in the minds of the British governing classes. In this counter-revolutionary climate the traditional practice of allowing colonies representative institutions was weakened—particularly as such colonial replicas of Westminster had proved so inimical to British interests, not only in the Thirteen Colonies of America but also in Ireland where Protestant 'patriots' and parliament had been obstreperous and independently minded.

Moreover, British policy towards India had moved in the direction of maintaining firmer control—even, if necessary, at the expense of the traditional privileges of the *East India Company and the demands of British residents. As Lord Stormont remarked of the machinery established by the India Act of 1784, which vested supreme power over Indian affairs in a governmental Board of Control, the goal was 'a strong government in India, subject to the check and control of a still stronger government at home'. Policy towards India, then, reflected the prevailing view that in the imperial sphere the traditional checks on the power of the Crown should largely be pruned in the interests of effective government. After all, the American experience appeared to show that if the imperial government allowed its powers to be largely superseded by local authorities, the reassertion of centralized control was likely to prove a difficult and hazardous enterprise.

Fear of *revolution [1] was compounded by the exigencies of *war [2], so that colonies captured from the French or their allies during the revolutionary and Napoleonic wars were generally given the political forms of a Crown colony whereby a strong executive, largely unimpeded by representative institutions, could if necessary act resolutely to meet the needs of war. The British experience of dealing with the problems of Quebec did much to develop such an alternative to the traditional pattern of creating some form of representative body as a bridge between the British settlers and the royally appointed governor. In Quebec, Britain faced the novel problem of creating political forms to accommodate the needs of some 80,000 European but non-British settlers. Since the loyalty of such recent and involuntary subjects of the British Crown was inevitably uncertain, it was naturally feared that the erection of representative institutions might provide the forum for continuing frustration of British rule or even for revolt—revolt that might infect the increasingly tense relations between Britain and the nearby Thirteen Colonies. Moreover, the French settlers themselves, having been nurtured on the practices of the French absolutist state, found such representative institutions alien to their traditions.

The result was the Quebec Act of 1774, which placed power firmly in the hands of the Crown or, in practice, the royally appointed governor. An elected assembly was rejected in favour of a council drawn from both the French and British settlers and nominated by the Crown in consultation with the governor. It was, moreover, a council whose powers were closely circumscribed, especially in the critical area of taxation. At the local level the Act also left in place much of the traditional pattern of French seigneurial rule allied with a privileged position for the Roman Catholic Church. This ensured the long-term loyalty of the *Canadiens*—even if it further inflamed the suspicions of the American colonists about the sinister intentions of the British Crown. The Quebec Act of 1774 did achieve its most basic goal of securing the stability and loyalty of an area of strategic significance and uncertain intentions. Naturally, then, it was a model to which the British government turned when having to deal with the problems of administering newly acquired territories which had an alien European population or which were of strategic significance.

Such problems became ever more manifest as the fortunes of war brought under British control an increasing number of colonies once ruled by the French or their allies. Thus, in the former French colonies in the West Indies all executive powers were placed in the hands of the governor. The governor was advised by a nominated council, but he was free to disregard its advice. In adopting such autocratic forms the British were largely preserving the style of old-regime government already in place under their predecessors. This was also the case in the former Dutch colonies of the Cape and Ceylon, or in Spanish colonies such as Trinidad which passed to Britain during the revolutionary and Napoleonic wars.

However, the traditional practice of granting British colonists representative institutions was not extinguished by the counter-revolutionary tide. In Canada, the Quebec Act of 1774 was modified in 1791 in order better to quarantine the country from the political contagion of the newly formed United States and to meet the demands of the increasing number of British settlers who regarded representative forms of government as part of their birthright. The result was a constitutional amalgam which reflected both the counter-revolutionary tenor of the times and a more traditional attachment to representative forms. Colonists were granted an assembly, but it was hoped that any democratic excesses would be checked by yoking it to an upper house made up of members nominated by the Crown—an upper house which was intended to act in the manner of the House of Lords by providing a form of aristocratic stability. In order to avoid conflict between the French- and English-speaking colonists, Canada was divided into two provinces with names which reflected their position on the critical St Lawrence River: an English-speaking Upper Canada and the predominantly French-speaking Lower Canada, each with their own assembly kept in check by a nominated legislative council which, it was vainly hoped, might eventually give birth to a colonial aristocracy.

Since the threat of revolution was a challenge to the constitution of both the Church and the state, imperial policy sought, where possible, to promote religious as well as political institutions which might serve to contain revolutionary impulses. Just as colonial analogues of the House of Lords were seen as a bulwark against revolution, so too it was hoped that the promotion of another pillar of the traditional constitution, the Church of England, would serve a similar goal. For many in Britain regarded the American Revolution as being proof that religious Dissent led to political dissent. In Canada, moves to shore up the position of the Church of England could be justified as following the entrenched precedents created by the founders of New France in bestowing privileges on the Roman Catholic Church. Thus, under the terms of the 1791 Act, the Crown was authorized to devote a seventh of the lands not yet allocated to European settlers to the maintenance of clergy 'according to the establishment of the Church of England'. This association between British rule and the advancement of the Church of England gathered pace in the wake of the French Revolution, the de-Christianizing rhetoric of which appeared to confirm the view that the traditional political and social order needed the ideological mortar provided by the established Church. When the bishoprics of Jamaica and Barbados were created in 1824 the imperial government ensured that they were well endowed. In the following year the governor of New South Wales was instructed to set aside one-seventh of public land to support schools based on *Anglican principles, while in 1831 the governor of British Guiana was commanded to establish schools which would provide religious instruction 'according to the Doctrine of the United Church of England and Ireland'.

However, such counter-revolutionary-inspired attempts to make the Church of England a virtual established church throughout the empire were checked by countervailing forces. In the first place, imperial administrators were well aware that too obvious an alliance with the Church of England could inflame the suspicions both of non-Christian native peoples and of

European settlers outside the Anglican fold. The imperial government also had to reckon with the increasingly well-organized political voice of Protestant Dissent both at home and abroad—particularly after the Repeal of the Test Act in 1828 removed from Dissenters any restriction on their involvement in the political life of the nation [see *toleration]. Furthermore, the advancement of *religion [10] by state power was difficult to combine with *Whig traditions of promoting at least some measure of religious and political liberty—traditions which slowly began to reassert themselves in the 1820s and 1830s as the shock of the French Revolution began to abate. By 1835 the Whig Colonial Secretary, Lord Glenelg (1778–1866), could acknowledge the futility of choosing 'any one Church as the exclusive object of public Endowment' in Australia, and the Colonial Office discouraged plans for the further endowment of Anglican rectories in Upper Canada. It is a measure of the limits of the alliance between the imperial government and Anglicanism after 1776 that nowhere in the empire was the Church of England formally made the established church.

Though, as we have seen, imperial policy was deeply coloured by the counter-revolutionary attitudes of the British oligarchy, the actual form assumed by imperial rule was also influenced by the local traditions of the colonies, whether (as in India) of the indigenous inhabitants or (as in most of the territories annexed during the French wars) of the former colonial powers which the British had superseded by force of arms. Even the phrase 'the British Empire' exaggerates the uniformity and cohesion of the rag-bag collection of territories which had fallen into British hands as the result of the vagaries of military or commercial success. Since, for much of our period, those directing the British state were chiefly concerned with resisting the threat of foreign domination or, to a lesser degree, popular *insurrection at home, the affairs of distant colonies were generally given scant attention. Only towards the end of this period did greater stability at home and the development of more effective bureaucratic forms permit the luxury of a coherent examination of the direction of imperial policy and a consideration of the ways in which the scattered threads of empire could be gathered together.

The result, then, was that in the late eighteenth and early nineteenth centuries the British empire was a coat of many colours, as local traditions gave the forms of government in its different parts their own distinctive hues. The former French colonies in Africa or the Caribbean retained some of the forms of old-regime absolutism while former Dutch colonies such as the Cape Colony also remained largely autocratic in their patterns of government. In the traditional British West Indies, by contrast, longer British settlement had left a deeper British imprint in the form of representative institutions. These institutions to some degree mirrored those of the homeland, yet were at the same time distorted by the phenomenon of *slavery [6], which made the white planters a virtual aristocracy, free from many of the constraints in dealing with their social inferiors to which even members of the House of Lords had to submit. In New South Wales the cleavage between the mass of the unfree convict settlers and their rulers was more openly acknowledged by adopting the forms of military government. A great range of legal systems also continued to exist under the British imperial flag. Lower Canada and St Lucia were controlled by old-regime French law, Mauritius by an amalgam of pre- and post-revolutionary French codes; former Dutch colonies such as the Cape, British Guiana, and Ceylon retained Roman-Dutch law modified to some extent by the enactments of the Batavian republic; in Trinidad Spanish law prevailed, and in Heligoland Danish. In India, of course, there was no single legal code, as indigenous and British legal forms coexisted. And, despite the attempts to give the Church of England a privileged position, the empire had a heterogeneous religious composition. The Roman Catholic Church retained much of its traditional prominence in former French and Spanish colonies, and predominantly Protestant settler societies, such as the Cape and Australia, supported a range of denominations jealous of any signs of particular government favour to the Church of England.

Variegated though the empire of our period was, common threads of unity ran through the whole, and were also linked with the political and cultural structures of Britain. The empire naturally reflected the values of a governing landed class which had become convinced of the possibilities of increasing wealth by the application of improving techniques, whether in agriculture, manufacture, or in response to such social problems as the *poor law. The greatly increased yields made possible by the techniques associated with the *agricultural revolution reinforced the cultural values of the **Enlightenment [32]** with its confidence in the fruitfulness of experimental and scientific techniques and the possibilities of human progress [see *land, 16].

Both at the metropolitan level and through the local colonial élites, the techniques of improvement offered the possibility of meshing the diverse fruits of empire into a web of trade, with the mother country at its centre. Hence the endeavours promoted by prominent agricultural improvers such as Joseph *Banks and Lord Sheffield (1735–1821) to enhance British self-sufficiency by attempting to promote the growth of cotton in the British West Indies or tea in India, or to transplant cochineal by surreptitious means from South America to British colonies. The ideal of improvement not only offered the possibility of greater wealth and self-sufficiency for Britain but also provided some moral veneer to soften the crude realities of imperial expansion. Improvement, it could be argued, not only benefited the home country but also offered the indigenous people some hope of relief from the traditional scourges of disease and famine. At home, improvement was promoted by such institutions as the Board of Agriculture or the Society for the Encouragement of Arts, Manufactures and Commerce— institutions which were reflected in colonial miniature in societies such as the Jamaican

8. *Europe Supported by Asia and Africa*, an engraving by William Blake personifying the spreading British empire, and illustrating J. G. Stedman's *Narrative, of a Five Years' Expedition, against the Revolted Negroes of Surinam* (1796). Stedman expressed an accompanying wish regarding the peoples of all three continents that 'in the friendly manner as they are represented they may henceforth and to all Eternity be the prop of each other'.

Society for the Cultivation of Agriculture and other Arts and Sciences, or the Society of Arts of Barbados. Though such colonial replicas were often short-lived, they testified to the dissemination of cultural values which helped to bind the metropolitan power with the colonial élites of the scattered empire, just as the goals of improvement had done much after the *Act of Union to weld Scotland and England into a more effective greater Britain.

The need for such informal ties was the stronger because of the lack of a clear institutional mechanism for the conduct of empire. Though the scale of British government had ineluctably expanded in response to the needs of war, the bureaucratic apparatus for dealing with the greatly increased scale of empire occasioned by naval *exploration [37] of the Pacific and military success against the French lagged well behind. In the late eighteenth century imperial concerns were untidily divided among a number of governmental agencies as the machinery of government belatedly and inadequately began to catch up with changed imperial realities. Indian affairs largely fell to the Board of Control, commercial matters to the Committee of the Privy Council for Trade and Plantations, while other colonial problems came under the Home Office or, as imperial expansion and warfare became more closely intertwined, under the War Office. It was symptomatic that when a colonial secretaryship was eventually established in 1801 its full title was Secretary of State for War and the Colonies: the order in the title reflected the priorities of the office, and recognized that new colonies were an often unintended by-product of war. Nor did colonial affairs really emerge from under the shadow of the immediate and pressing needs of war until 1812, when Henry Goulburn (1784–1856) was appointed Parliamentary Under-Secretary of State for the Colonies under Henry Bathurst (1762–1834), the first Secretary for War and Colonies to take a close interest in colonial affairs. Further bureaucratic recognition of the importance of colonial affairs came with the establishment of a Permanent Under-Secretary in 1825. Between 1836 and 1847 this office was held by Sir James Stephen (1789–1859), under whom the Colonial Office was put on a firm organizational footing and rendered an effective instrument in advancing representative government and in opposing the slave trade.

The slow rise of the Colonial Office and the apparent bureaucratic confusion in dealing with colonial affairs has masked the fact that late-eighteenth-century imperial policy was actually given a large measure of direction and coherence. It was mainly shaped by a group of prominent landowners who shared a similar conception of the goals of empire—goals which, in their emphasis on a large degree of metropolitan control over the affairs of the empire, naturally meshed with the counter-revolutionary climate of the period. The most important of these were Charles Jenkinson (from 1786 Lord Hawkesbury and from 1796 Earl of Liverpool), Secretary at War, 1778, and from 1786 President of the Privy Council Committee on Trade; John Holroyd, Lord Sheffield, President of the Board of Agriculture, 1803, and a Lord of the Board of Trade, 1809; William Eden, Lord Auckland, First Lord of the Board of Trade and Plantations, 1776, and Joint Postmaster-General, 1798–1804; and Joseph Banks, President of the Royal Society, 1778–1820, and from 1797 a Privy Councillor and member of the Committee on Trade. These dominant voices in determining late-eighteenth-century imperial policy shared a common commitment to the goals of improvement and, with it, a largely *mercantilist conception of the place of the colonies. In their view, colonies should be improved to some extent for their own benefit but primarily for the contribution they might make to the economic well-being of the mother country.

At the Board of Trade, which in the late eighteenth century became the chief instrument for promoting imperial policy, Jenkinson, with Banks's assistance, promoted such improving schemes as attempting to establish tea or hemp in India or cotton in the West Indies—schemes which accorded well with the view of commerce put forward a century earlier by the arch-mercantilist Jean-Baptiste Colbert, who wrote that 'Commerce is the means to augment the power and grandeur of his Majesty and to lower that of his enemies and rivals'. Jenkinson's determination to maintain at least the basic machinery of mercantilism, despite the irritation it had caused to the American colonists, was most evident in his support for the last great Navigation Act of 1786. It was an Act that rejected the earlier view of Lord *Shelburne, expressed in 1782, that 'We prefer trade to dominion', for it attempted to prevent trade between the West Indies and the United States with the goal of protecting British trade and British maritime and naval supremacy. As Jenkinson told the Commons during the passage of the Act: 'If proper means could be devised to secure the navigation trade to Great Britain, though we had lost a dominion, we might almost be said to have gained an empire.'

Such attempts to maintain the traditional mercantilist forms of empire were strengthened by the fact that the representatives of the landed classes, who had such a strong voice in shaping imperial policy, were increasingly committed to protectionist policies at home, as the rise of imported foodstuffs—and especially corn—came more and more to pose a threat to their incomes and position. Both Lord Sheffield and Joseph Banks, for example, were active in forming the landed interest into an effective lobby group with the aim of countering what they considered was the undue power of the manufacturing classes. Agricultural protection at home and mercantilist policies were, then, naturally complementary in the minds of such landed gentlemen, who regarded the empire as an extension of the agricultural and commercial wealth of Britain. After all, had not the great Chatham (1708–78) considered 'the sugar islands as the landed interest of this kingdom'?

Such informal methods of formulating and directing imperial policy and, with it, the strong bias towards the views of the landed interest were, however, gradually supplanted as the machinery of the British state was belatedly compelled to expand and readjust to take account of the growing girth of empire. The ineluctable need for the British state to become involved in the affairs of India as the scale of imperial involvement surpassed the competence of the East India Company paved the way for greater state direction elsewhere in the empire. The India Act of 1784 and the establishment of the Board of Control proved to be the first large step on a path which led, first, in 1833 to the East India Company ceasing to trade, then to the elevation of the governor-generalship of Bengal to the governor-generalship of India as a whole, and in 1858 to the abolition of the Company. In 1821 the remnants of another of the chartered companies, the Royal African Company, were abolished and its forts were taken over by the Crown.

The demise of the Royal African Company was also testimony to the force of the *abolitionist movement which drew the British government more and more into the internal workings of its colonies in order to stamp out the slave trade. In combating the slave trade the British state's main agency was the Colonial Office. Under Lord Bathurst's supervision from 1812 to 1827, this established a reputation and routines which gradually enabled the British government to exercise a more direct role in directing the affairs of empire. Though the Colonial Office long remained too understaffed and too politically marginal to be fully equal to such a mission, its activities were an indication that the British state was beginning to turn its attention to the long and never fully completed task of drawing the diverse and scattered fragments of empire into a more coherent whole.

The activities of the Colonial Office in fostering representative government were also indicative of the waning of the counter-revolutionary climate which had dominated much of the period from 1776. In 1823 even the distant gaol of New South Wales received the forms of a Crown colony with a nominated council, a constitutional concession extended in 1825 to the Cape Colony—a colony where autocratic control had been well established because of its strategic significance and its volatile mixture of Dutch, British, and African inhabitants. Settlers in New South Wales and the Cape followed their English-speaking counterparts in Canada by showing that the forms of a Crown colony could be moulded to correspond more closely to representative institutions, as the memberships of councils were expanded to include non-officials and even elected members. Predictably, fully-fledged representative government followed in New South Wales (1843) and the Cape (1853), while Canada—the traditional pace-setter in imperial constitutional affairs—gained a form of de facto responsible government from 1848.

   Such moves down the path to an empire in which the traditional conception of the ultimate sovereignty of the British parliament became more and more attenuated was, of course, chiefly evident in areas where British or, at least, European settlers had settled in large numbers. By contrast, in places such as India, where the Europeans were vastly outnumbered by the indigenous peoples, more autocratic forms of government were retained. None the less, however partial, the gradual dismantling of these often autocratic forms of imperial control was an indication that the empire was acquiring a new form, as the fear of revolution began to abate. The growth of free trade also contributed to the dismantling of many of the mercantilist controls over empire with which Hawkesbury, Sheffield, and their allies had attempted to shore up British economic, strategic, and political power. In 1776 the shock of the American Revolution marked the beginnings of an imperial policy which was based on fear of revolution and which was wary of too great a measure of colonial autonomy. By 1832, in contrast, at least the general outlines of another conception of empire, which allowed for a considerable loosening of the reins of political and economic control, could be discerned.

Bayly, C. A., *Imperial Meridian: The British Empire and the World 1780–1830*, London, 1989; Cain, P. J., & Hopkins, A. G., *British Imperialism and Expansion 1688–1914*, London, 1993; Harlow, V. T., *The Founding of the Second British Empire, 1763–1793*, London, 1952; Holland Rose, J., Newton, A. P., & Benians, E. A., eds., *The New Cambridge History of the British Empire*, ii: *The Growth of the New Empire, 1783–1870*, Cambridge, 1940; Hyam, R., *Britain's Imperial Century, 1815–1914: A Study of Empire and Expansion*, London, 1993; Knaplund, P., *James Stephen and The British Colonial System 1813–1847*, Madison, Wis., 1953; Mackay, D., *In the Wake of Cook: Exploration, Science and Empire, 1780–1801*, London, 1985; Manning, H. T., *British Colonial Government After the American Revolution*, New Haven, Conn., 1933; Marshall, P. J., *Problems of Empire: Britain and India 1757–1813*, London, 1968; Morrell, W. P., *British Colonial Policy in the Age of Peel and Russell*, Oxford, 1930.

6 · SLAVERY   JAMES WALVIN

Black slavery lay at the heart of the late-eighteenth-century British Atlantic empire. It dictated the pace and direction of much of the flow of people and goods along those complex trading routes which were at once the lifeblood of *empire [5] and the sustenance of expanding metropolitan business, trade, and taste. It was also a system which crucially intersected with, and depended on, an even wider global commercial network which stretched from China to the interior of Africa. However, in these years the slave system was utterly transformed. On the eve of American independence, few could contemplate British life without the slave empires of anglophone America. By 1832, British slavery was doomed.

   The figures provide the framework. Whites outnumbered blacks by two to one in the British Americas by 1776, but African slaves constituted by far the higher proportion of migrants. Since the early seventeenth century some 815,000 whites had migrated to the British settlements, compared to 2,339,000 African slaves. Of course, the Africans and their local-born descendants (who inherited their mothers' bondage) were spread unevenly. They were concentrated overwhelmingly in that string of possessions across the Caribbean sugar islands (territories greatly augmented by the gains of the treaty that ended the Seven Years War) and in those mainland settlements which had flourished on the back of plantation-based staple production, notably tobacco in the Chesapeake and rice in South Carolina.

Africans were imported into the Americas to work for their (mainly white) owners. Whatever else they achieved (normally under the most testing of social and physical conditions) they were valued—and priced—for their labouring strengths and skills. In time, slaves came to fill a remarkable range of occupations in the Americas—from gunsmiths to cowboys—but initially the Europeans wanted merely their muscle-power. In the early days of settlement Africans worked alongside Europeans and local Indians, cutting back the wilderness and bringing the land into fruitful cultivation. From one colony to another, the first years were uncertain and survival unsure. Once the ideal local economic formula had been discovered, however, once the most suitable export crop had been planted, slavery developed as the backbone of the local plantation system. Nowhere were the slaves more visible, more spectacularly successful (for others, if not for themselves), than on the sugar plantations of the Caribbean.

The sugar islands struck visitors as an image of Africa, their large-scale plantations worked by huge gangs of slaves who laboured from childhood to old age at appropriate tasks. As the settlements matured, slaves acquired that range of skills necessary to all rural industries and to local society at large. The sugar industry of the late eighteenth century, for instance, required more than simple muscle-power for its economic success, and much the same was true of other slave-based economies. In tobacco, rice, and in a host of generally overlooked crops throughout the Americas (cotton, indigo, coffee, and chocolate), slave skills and experience were crucial ingredients in local economic success.

The whole edifice of British Atlantic slavery hinged on two main factors: regular supplies of new Africans delivered by the slave ships, and markets for slave-grown produce. It was, however, a remarkably complex commercial empire (so often misrepresented by the concept of a 'triangular trade'), for each point of the trading system was linked to a much broader system of global trade. Stated crudely, the Atlantic slave empire was but one element of a massive global trading system which stretched from the furthest points of Asian commerce to the unknown point of enslavement in Africa, and on to the insecure frontier of the Americas. Africans, for example, were bartered for and purchased at those myriad spots on the sub-Saharan coast, in return for a multitude of commodities culled from Britain's pervasive world trade: Indian textiles, French wines, English metalware, cowrie shells from the Maldives—all and more were handed over in return for cargoes of African slaves.

For all its inhuman cruelty and violation, the British trade on the African coast had, by our period, become a well-established and sophisticated branch of maritime business. From Sierra Leone to Angola slave-traders roamed the coast, dealing with communities of resident Africans and Europeans for coffles of slaves from the interior. The business was environmentally dangerous for Europeans and took a horrific toll of white sailors and traders. Such risks failed to deter the flotillas of European slave-traders arriving in growing numbers throughout the century. Moreover, European losses and sufferings were as naught compared to what happened to the African slaves consigned to the unsanitary, crammed, and disease-ridden slave ships.

The African survivors of the consequent horrors of the Atlantic crossing (some eleven million in total) were destined to produce crops to satisfy mounting Western *consumerism [19]. Of all the slaves landed in the Americas, some 70 per cent worked in sugar, a crop which, more than any other, utterly transformed the taste and social habits of the Western world. Sugar cane, in some ways similar to the black and white populations of the Americas, was an alien, transplanted commodity. By the early eighteenth century, however, slave-grown sugar had made the leap, so common to a host of tropical staples, from luxury to necessity. What had once graced the tables of only the rich and influential was now to be found in the lowliest of homes, and could be bought, for pennies, from humble local shops in the most inaccessible corners of the British Isles.

Sugar was an additive for ever more foodstuffs, but it was as an ingredient in drinks—most notably tea—that its pre-eminence was secured. The West India lobby, that nexus of planters, shippers, financiers, and agents which formed so powerful a group in mid-eighteenth-century London, was keen to promote tea-drinking, a habit which had taken root in the years from 1685 to 1700, thereafter remaining a characteristic feature of the British social landscape. The more tea the British consumed (secured from traders in Canton), the more sugar was required from the slave fields of the West Indies. And the same was true of other tropical drinks, such as coffee and chocolate, so recently adopted by the British. All were bitter drinks, made palatable to Western taste only by the addition of slave-produced sugar. Tea from Canton, coffee initially from the Yemen, chocolate from Aztec Mexico, sugar from the Caribbean; here in a specific form was an illustration of the complexity of international commerce which underpinned slavery itself.

The British consumption of slave-grown produce increased spectacularly in the eighteenth century. In 1700 the British imported 23,000 tons of sugar; a century later the figure stood at 245,000 tons. Much of that sugar was stirred with tea, some nine million pounds of which came to Britain in the 1720s. This figure rose to more than twenty million by the 1740s and stood at thirty-seven million pounds at mid-century. Despite high excise duties, a thriving tea-smuggling industry conspired to bring the British consumer enough tea to be able to consume more than two pounds per head annually. Drinking sweetened tea became a habit which brought more than mere pleasure; it transformed the routines of domestic life and shaped key areas of sociability. The pattern of the day came to be structured around a host of tea-drinking rituals, from the fashionable tea parties of ladies of *sensibility [11] (displaying the finest of imported 'china') through to labourers interrupting their toils to drink hot sweet tea.

Sugar, then, had brought about the most spectacular consequences in Britain. But other slave-grown staples also proved instrumental in redefining both taste and social style. Tobacco, for example, was as British as sweet tea by the mid-eighteenth century. Sold in *taverns, *coffeehouses, and apothecaries, it was also readily available from a proliferating number of specialist shops, markets, and pedlars. When people could not afford their own pipes, they could smoke from the communal pipe passed round in the drinking-place. And all

9. This advertisement, c.1815, from the slave-trading port of Bristol uses an exotic Amerindian as a sales device, glossing over the slave labour which supported the tobacco plantations in America.

of this was made possible by the slaves of Virginia and Maryland. The 65,000 pounds of Virginian tobacco exported to Britain in the 1620s had risen to 220 million pounds fifty years later, a massive expansion made possible by the switch from white indentured labour to enslaved African. To populate the rapid expansion of the Chesapeake tobacco plantations, some 100,000 slaves found themselves deposited in the region between 1690 and 1770. Their labour generated a massive export of tobacco, costs fell, and, despite hefty duties, the British consumer had by the early eighteenth century become addicted to smoking on a lavish scale.

The habit was sustained, as was the taste for sugar, by a national network of thousands of small shops whose main source of income was the sale of recently established exotic and tropical staples. As the habit spread across the social divide, tobacco lost its initial social cachet. By the late eighteenth century, tobacco consumption had also become progressively more masculine, aided in large measure by the influence of the military (notably the navy) and the fact that, during that century of ubiquitous warfare, so many men spent time in the services. Yet here was a simple Indian crop, once culled from the wild, now disciplined and cultivated by slaves throughout the Chesapeake, and which laid the foundation of a massive trans-Atlantic business, with repercussions which stretched from the most miserable of American slave huts to the emergent prosperity and physical grandeur of late-eighteenth-century Glasgow. Once again, a product of the slave empire and global commerce had so deeply embedded itself in British daily experience that its social and economic origins passed unnoticed. Behind these apparently innocent aspects of domestic consumption was the exercise of imperial power and commercial dominion which enabled the British to transplant peoples and commodities from one side of the world to the other in a complex commercial exchange shored up by maritime power.

With a few exceptions (Barbados most notably), slave populations in the islands failed to increase naturally. Problems of sex and age ratios, infertility, high mortality, and a host of ailments (all in a context of harsh work in an alien environment) served to prevent normal, healthy slave reproduction. Cruelty played a part, of course, though by mid-century all but the most callous of planters were coming to recognize that they needed to care for their slaves—if only to get the best economic return on their investments in human capital.

From first to last, West Indian planters and their British backers cried out for still more Africans. The ending of the original monopoly system of supply, and the opening of the slave trade to competition (though within the restrictions of contemporary *mercantilist ideals), led to a rush of slavers, investors, and associated British industries eager to satisfy the slave-owners's needs. In the first half of the eighteenth century, British slavers delivered some 20,000 Africans each year. For the rest of the century the figures rose to between 35,000 and 40,000 annually. Between the end of the Royal African Company's slave trading monopoly in 1698 and the abolition of the British trade in 1807, perhaps 11,000 ships were dispatched from Britain to trade in African slaves. Slavers transported about three million slaves in that century—almost half of all the Africans shipped into the Americas. London led the way, followed in the early eighteenth century by Bristol (with its ready-made advantages of maritime links to the west). But by about 1750, the growing city of Liverpool had become the nation's, and Europe's, pre-eminent slave port. In the last generation of the slave trade, something like three-quarters of all the British slave trade was fitted out in that city. Around £1,000,000 per year was invested in the slave trade in Liverpool alone by 1800. However, a multitude of smaller ports also dispatched a regular flow of ships in search of African slaves, from Preston and Poole, from Lyme Regis and Bideford, and in the hinterland of such ports, manufacturers and producers, shopkeepers, and farmers supplied the slave ships.

The Atlantic slave trade did more than profit its lucky, or persistent, investors. It served to recast the face of eighteenth-century Britain, often in ways which remain unrecognized. Its most obvious impact took the form of bands of ex-slaves cast adrift in British ports—the human genesis of the first British black communities. The slave trade also enhanced the material prosperity of British ports. Profits for the trade hovered at around 10 per cent by the late eighteenth century, and those who stuck with their investments saw their family or business fortunes mount. From the Atlantic trade they were able to acquire those trappings of eighteenth-century material well-being and *design [25] which were disgorged with ever greater abundance by consumer industries on both sides of the Atlantic. The most successful slavers constructed fashionable central city homes, brimming with the most stylish of fittings; they built business headquarters of the most elaborate kind; and they enjoyed regular trips to the most fashionable of watering-places. Indeed, the vulgarity of slave-based wealth became something of a caricature among observers of social life at English *spa towns (notably Bath).

There was, then, a widely diffused interest and investment in slave trading which manifested itself in a multitude of forms across the face of eighteenth-century Britain. From the craftsmen who built and equipped the ships through to distant suppliers of goods for the ships' holds, all found their interests intimately linked to the prosperity spawned by slavery. This coalition of interests formed an entrenched, and socially varied, lobby across Britain, ready to offer a fierce defence of slave trading when the early proponents of *abolitionism raised their initial objections in the 1780s. In 1787 a small band, mainly of *Quakers—men of sensibility who approached slavery from varied religious and humane positions—formed a committee in London to demand an end to the Atlantic slave trade. It must have seemed a forlorn hope. However, within a mere four years they were able to muster more than 500 *petitions from across Britain, with 400,000 names objecting to the slave trade. It was an extraordinary—and quite unexpected—salvo against a slave lobby which had assumed that its business was secure because it contributed so massively to Britain's well-being. Abolitionists achieved this rapid development because they were well connected; Quakers had friends in most corners of the nation, willing to provide help for speakers or to distribute publications. But they also caught that rising tide of literate political awareness, first noticed under John *Wilkes and destined to become still more pronounced with the *corresponding societies movement in the early 1790s.

The London committee, though spiritually devout, consisted of practical businessmen who quickly appreciated the need for a national, popular campaign. In Thomas *Clarkson they found the ideal peripatetic agent, ceaselessly spreading the abolitionist word throughout *106* Britain—often at risk to himself. Abolition was above all else a brilliant propaganda campaign which used the printed word and a host of graphic and material images to broadcast the horrors of the slave trade. In a society already marked by the drift to urban life, by the early shift in key areas to industrial change (notably in Manchester), and by ever more people able to purchase more and more goods, the British people were in a state of remarkable flux, and prone to change or adopt new ideas.

The abolitionist groups which flowered nationally were products of the aftermath of the *American Revolution. They spoke in a political tone, and to issues that were unmistakably shaped by the American war and by the loss of the colonies. That national humiliation proved to be a catalyst which prompted a reappraisal of a host of British ideals and systems. The conflict had hinged on questions of representation, but had also aroused wider debate about liberty—and the supposedly 'freeborn' British had been seen as constitutional transgressors and violators of human rights. Anti-slavery provided the opportunity of restoring the British belief that they, above all others, were a people wedded to liberty. After all, what institution seemed more violent and more thoroughly a denial of liberties than the Atlantic slave system?

To ever more people, slavery seemed both wrong and oddly old-fashioned; a throw-back to a mode of conducting business (through a system of strict protection) and a way of dealing with mankind which sat uncomfortably with a rising attachment to sensibility, progress, and modernity. The abolitionist committees enabled the emergent, provincial, urban middle classes to come together, and to speak out in favour of a reform which was itself congruent with their broader social and economic interests. Abolition was, then, construed as a blow for progress against an outdated, backward-looking, and cruel economic system. It struck a strong chord with the sentimental movement in literature, which emphasized suffering, pathos, and emotional expressiveness—well illuminated in the literary exchanges between ex-slave Ignatius *Sancho and novelist Laurence Sterne (1713–68). Perhaps the most remarkable aspect of the abolitionist campaign in the 1780s and 1790s was its ability to embrace more than the newly vitalized propertied orders. Artisans and working men, large numbers of women (traditionally beyond the political pale), and even children (courtesy of the proliferation of abolitionist *children's literature) were rallied to the abolitionist banner. On the eve of the *French Revolution, the social and political alliances forged by the anti-slave trade movement enabled the campaign to claim to be the most popular movement demanding major political change.

Demands for the abolition of the slave trade—the easiest, most practical entrée to the wider problem of colonial slavery itself—were firmly lodged in parliament and supported by a massive national base well before the upheavals of 1789. The Revolution changed everything of course. Initially, the simple weight and logic of the Revolution's basic ideology—the rights of man—gave abolition added impetus. But for many of the propertied, the issues began to blur. The links between black freedom and broader social rights—and the subsequent degeneration of the Revolution into factional violence—raised the serious spectre of levelling and social unrest. This was especially pressing when the British debate was played out in the context of revived plebeian radicalism and the related onset of distress in 1792. It now seemed dangerous to discuss major political change—including abolition—with the example of France to hand. The slave revolt in St Domingue in the early 1790s merely confirmed the point.

The Revolution, inevitably, had major repercussions in French colonial possessions, spreading thence to the British islands, where white élites were terrorized by fears of slave unrest. The early sectional and racial bickering in St Domingue deteriorated after 1791 into a major slave revolt. In the ensuing conflict the sugar economy was destroyed, along with the power and the very being of the local plantocracy. The British, keen to seize another lucrative sugar possession for themselves, dispatched an invasion force to St Domingue, but slave armies—and tropical disease—destroyed the British just as they had destroyed the French. The eventual rise of an independent black republic—Haiti—seemed to confirm the West India lobby's worst fears and predictions. After 1792, the abolitionists could never fully convince waverers (even those sympathetic to ending the slave trade) that abolition would not lead to slave insurrection.

The Revolution—and its seismic results on the far side of the Atlantic—thus entombed abolition for a decade. Concepts of liberty rapidly passed into disrepute, even among men and women who had been firmly on their side before 1789. When abolition came in 1806–7 it did so under a fresh administration and thanks to a switch in parliamentary tactics used by William *Wilberforce. Yet from 1792 onwards there was no doubting the mood of the British people about the slave trade. They had turned decisively against it, whatever its economic benefits, nudged in that direction by a powerful and subtle propaganda campaign able to harness the emergent forces of mass literacy and the power of new, mainly urban, nonconformist communities. This mood chimed with a growing material interest in social and economic freedoms among the middling orders. The restraints and restrictions of the old economic order seemed designed to hold them back. And slavery and the slave trade were perhaps the most blatant creations of 'Old Corruption': an economic system which, for all its material bounty, was rooted in an economic and political philosophy increasingly out of kilter with the changing mood of the last years of the eighteenth century. Though Adam *Smith may have been the apostle of the new philosophy of *political economy [33], it was shared, at a humbler, more self-interested level, by an alliance of middling ranks whose personal fortunes were best served by a greater liberality in the conduct of economic affairs. It was precisely these people who formed the bedrock of the abolitionist campaign up to 1792.

The abolition of the slave trade in 1806–7 cut the supply of African slaves and ultimately transformed slavery in the colonies. Planters had to treat their slaves differently, in order to make the most of their human capital. There were other changes, however, which few could have predicted at the time. The decline of the older African population and the rise of a local-born one compounded many local tensions, especially expectations among local-born and skilled slaves for preferential treatment and better prospects. The planters' need for field-hands served to frustrate those ambitions. Caribbean tensions were compounded by the development of a political debate in the islands which embraced black and white, and which was partly literary, enhanced by the rapid growth of newspapers throughout the islands. Most important of all, perhaps, was the dramatic rise of local (mainly Nonconformist) churches among the slaves and the swirl of abolitionist news from Britain.

After 1824 the British campaign for the full abolition of slavery fanned the embers of slave discontent (which had already erupted in Barbados in 1816 in a revolt—for that island—of unusual savagery). Barbados witnessed a miserable reprise of a familiar tale; black grievances, an initial slave outburst, suppression by plantocratic violence on a massive and, in British eyes, horrifying scale. The pattern was repeated, with even more horrible consequences, in Demerara in 1823 and, most savage of all, in Jamaica in 1831–2. Slave resistance, of course, had been as characteristic of colonial slavery as plantocratic violence. But the revolts of the early nineteenth century were different. Viewed from Britain, they seemed a throw-back to a world which had long gone; to massive social discontent, savage suppression, and legalized violence of a kind not seen since the Scottish and Irish troubles of the previous century. To a society progressively influenced by a new sensibility about matters of cruelty, the fate of the West Indian slaves seemed unjustifiable. And all for what? To maintain an economic system which was itself increasingly prone to expert criticism.

The churches formed the key element. Tens of thousands of slaves were now Christian, caught in a web of Nonconformist organizations and belief which had been spun by *missionaries throughout the islands and which had links to their mother churches in Britain. Slave congregations, slave preachers, biblical imagery to advance the cause of freedom—all served to integrate the progress and fate of West Indian slaves more closely into the considerations of domestic British congregations. When the British read about the slaves, or listened to preachers returning from the slave islands, they viewed them as persecuted co-religionists. There was then a rising sense of outrage among British congregations about the fate of West Indian slaves. Treatment which had once gone unchallenged—the everyday stuff of slavery—now seemed utterly at odds with a changed Britain. Here was a slave system which could only be kept in place by the most fearsome but worthless application of state and plantocratic violence.

The campaign launched against colonial slavery from the mid-1820s turned to well-tried abolitionist tactics. It was carried forward by a much deeper surge of reforming sensibility and organization evident in the campaigns for *parliamentary reform. The tactics, the personnel, even the vocabulary were similar. Grass-roots pressure persuaded MPs to adopt slave emancipation. The declining band of parliamentary defenders of the slave system found themselves harried inside and outside parliament. It was, however, the reform of parliament in 1832 which sealed the fate of British slavery. By changing the electorate, by curbing the power of 'Old Corruption', and by enfranchising newer sectors of the population, the numbers of emancipationist MPs increased and their pro-slavery opponents were reduced—in numbers, power, and persuasiveness. With parliament reformed, it was but a matter of time—and detail—before British slavery was given the parliamentary *coup de grâce*.

Why should the capitalist metropolitan power, growing in riches throughout much of the eighteenth century, turn so quickly and so vigorously against the institution which had yielded such profit? That slavery remained profitable up to its dying days (its most active participants were, after all, loudest in its defence) merely compounds the enigma. Slavery was, to repeat, only one of a host of congruent issues which focused on Britons' freedom of labour, of capital, and of management to conduct their economic lives untrammelled by restrictions and controls. This was the very essence of a new kind of British economic power. After 1776, thanks in part to the influence of Adam Smith, it was also the core of a new economic thinking. To attack slavery was to advance a new social and economic orthodoxy by asserting the primacy of freedom in all things.

In all this, the temptation is to see things narrowly: to view black freedom (conceded partially in 1834, completely four years later) as a metropolitan concern. Yet the slaves were clearly an agent in their own freedom, for it was the changes in Caribbean slave societies which persuaded more and more people in Britain that slavery was doomed. The slaves were, increasingly, Christian. The most impressive of slave forums was that proliferation of congregations across the islands in which slaves expressed themselves in a biblical vernacular (if not a style) familiar to any British observer. News from slave communities quickly filtered back to all corners of Britain. The ultra-radical mulatto Robert Wedderburn (c.1763–c.1835) in 1819 alleged that he received a continuous stream of slave news from the compounds of Kingston, Jamaica. Equally, news from Britain seeped into the slave quarters, bringing encouragement and the conviction that salvation was in sight; a sense that the local, white oppressors were out of kilter with the changing mood in Britain itself.

When slavery passed into oblivion (in the British empire at least—elsewhere it survived much longer), 750,000 freed slaves celebrated in and around their churches. Here was an institution conceived and maintained in conditions of extreme violence but which ended peacefully. Black freedom also heralded the precipitous economic decline of the former slave islands. Those planters still in need of malleable labour persuaded the Colonial Office to recruit indentured labour from India (creating a system which survived until the First World War). However, such changes failed to prevent the rapid decline of the economic power and influence which the Caribbean had once mustered in British imperial affairs. Soon, it was hard even to imagine how important the islands had once been. As the British looked elsewhere for trade and dominion, the Caribbean seemed little more than a troublesome backwater—a reminder of a former but now redundant empire. What had made the West Indies so important—so crucial an element in the eighteenth-century imperial scheme of things—was their centrality in a global economic system. Slavery belonged to that broadly based Atlantic empire which formed the heart of the old imperial system. The 'triangular trade' is a crude way of expressing a complex network on which had been created a major trading system linking Britain, Africa, and the Americas. It is clear beyond doubt that the old Atlantic empire, its foundations secured by enslaved humanity, was the rock upon which much else was constructed. The legacy of slavery lived on, of course, most notably in the form of the communities of free black peasants of the West Indies. But it survived much closer to home in the habits of the British people themselves. The fruits of slave labour had shaped key habits and addictions of the British people and of millions of counterparts round the world. But who among the former imperial masters so much as thought of the ex-slaves when they sweetened their tea, or lit the tobacco that gave pleasure to their daily lives?

Bailyn, B., & Morgan, P. D., eds., *Strangers within the Realm: Cultural Margins of the First British Empire*, Chapel Hill, NC, 1991; Blackburn, R., *The Overthrow of Colonial Slavery*, London, 1988; Coleman, D., 'Conspicuous Consumption: White Abolitionism and English Women's Protest Writing in the 1790s', *English Literary History*, 61 (1994), 341–62; Eldar, M., *The Slave Trade and the Economic Development of the 18th Century*, Lancaster, 1992; Geggus, D., *Slavery, War and Revolution*, Oxford, 1982; Kulikoff, A., *Tobacco and Slaves*, Chapel Hill, NC, 1986; Oldfield, J. R., *Popular Politics and British Anti-Slavery*, Manchester, 1995; Walvin, J., *English, Slaves and Freedom*, London, 1986; *Fruits of Empire: Exotic Produce and British Taste, 1660–1800*, London, 1996; Ward, J. R., *British West-Indian Slavery 1750–1834: The Process of Amelioration*, Oxford, 1988.

7 · POLICING DAVID PHILIPS

The age of Romanticism and *revolution [1] in Britain was also one of growing social discipline. The period from the 1770s to the 1830s saw a new industrial discipline devised and enforced in the burgeoning *factories, and a tightening-up of the *poor law, especially after 1834, so that it came to regulate rather than relieve the lives of growing numbers of urban and rural poor [see *poverty, 12]. It was also the key period for the transition from an 'unpoliced' to a modern 'policed' society. The first professional, full-time, uniformed *police force was appointed in 1819, known as the Metropolitan Force for Greater London. Over the next three decades, that idea of a professional, full-time police force was gradually extended piecemeal over the other cities, towns, and counties until 1856, when the County and Borough Police Act extended the 'new police' to every part of the country, and imposed greater centralized control over finances and a national inspectorate. Full-time, paid, uniformed police forces had become the norm, as they have remained ever since.

Eighteenth-century British society certainly had agencies of policing, but they were not the modern professional police forces with which we are familiar. The key institutions were the Justices of the Peace (JPs) and parish constables. JPs in the counties were magistrates appointed by the Lord Chancellor to keep the peace within the jurisdiction for which they were appointed. They were usually landowners, while constables were often farmers, artisans, or tradesmen. Both offices were part-time and unpaid (the constable's office was meant to be filled annually by local ratepayers, though a paid deputy often did the actual work). The theory was that the JP kept law and order in each small parish or township largely by his influence and paternalist control over 'his' people; the constables, well-known to the local inhabitants, did the day-to-day work of arresting offenders and serving warrants. The process of *law [8] enforcement was essentially one of collective self-help with some local state assistance: if an offence was committed against property or persons, the latter were responsible for setting the machinery of justice in action. If they could suggest likely suspects, the constable could arrest them and the JP issue a warrant for the constable to search their home or premises. The victim of the alleged crime was then expected (with some financial reimbursement, after the event, from the county or borough) to prosecute—summarily at petty sessions for less serious offences; on indictment at quarter sessions or assizes for more serious crimes. The system thus relied on a considerable communal input, such as offenders being caught red-handed by citizens, or the victim suggesting a probable suspect; where these were absent—unless the crime was seen as a serious one—it was highly unlikely that the constables or JPs would take steps on their own to try to find the criminal. This offered considerable scope for private initiative to supplement the official institutions. By the late eighteenth century, property-owners in most parts of the country had established many hundreds of associations for the prosecution of felons as a form of crime insurance. In return for a subscription to an association, members were given assistance in finding, apprehending, and prosecuting offenders against themselves. By the early nineteenth century some of these associations had set up their own small private police forces, paid for by subscription. The large towns and the parishes of the metropolis employed watch forces to patrol their streets at night. By 1805 London also had a horse and foot patrol, and small paid police forces attached to the Bow Street office and the offices of the salaried police magistrates established in 1792.

The most glaring area of weakness on the part of the local constables was in dealing with *riots or disturbances of any seriousness. The authorities used troops to quell disturbances—often regular troops, sometimes volunteer yeomanry—and could swear in as many special constables as they felt the occasion required. This remained the case throughout the period. Troops were used to suppress the *Gordon riots in 1780; troops tried to catch the *Luddites in Nottinghamshire, Yorkshire, and Lancashire in 1811–12; yeomanry and regulars charged into the crowd in St Peter's Fields in Manchester in 1819, occasioning the *Peterloo massacre; troops and special constables confronted the Captain Swing agricultural protesters in 1830–1; and troops and yeomanry—with military pensioners enrolled as more effective paramilitary special constables—still took the major role in trying to contain the uprisings of the *Chartist movement in the late 1830s and 1840s. By this last period, however, the new police forces were starting to take over from the troops this public-order role. An important part of the pressure for new police forces was the appeal of substituting, for the lethal infantry volley or cavalry charge, the baton charge of a trained police squad; riot control was a major part of the training of all the early police forces. This emphasis is scarcely surprising when we consider that the ruling class of England had lived through the *French Revolution and the reign of terror, and had seen the development in Britain of a new urban industrial proletariat and mass democratic movement which mounted significant challenges to the political system on a number of occasions [see *industrialization, 14 and *democracy, 3]. The development of modern police forces joined a number of other strategies designed by the ruling class to restore the social discipline and social order which were seriously challenged by the simultaneous impact in England of the French and industrial revolutions.

However, if police reform had been simply a concern about public order, then England would have had a strong national police force long before the piecemeal spread of discrete bodies which finally covered the country in the 1850s. The government's measures to repress the radical movements of the 1790s and the immediate postwar period did not include establishing a professional police, although we shall see that developments of this kind were a feature of early-nineteenth-century governance in Ireland. Many of the landed gentry feared such a paid force in government hands, and associated traditional English liberties with an absence of police. The 1689 Bill of Rights, the key piece of legislation arising from the *Glorious Revolution of 1688, had outlawed the ministry and Crown maintaining a standing army in times of peace without parliamentary consent. The clergyman William *Paley stated in his 1785 *Principles of Moral and Political Philosophy* that the 'liberties of a free people . . . permit not those precautions and restraints, that inspection, scrutiny, and control, which are exercised with success in arbitrary governments'. These ideas became the basis of a strongly articulated gentry resistance to government attempts, from 1785 onwards, to bring in a paid police force. The argument turned on the necessary trade-off between order and liberty. In return for the great blessing of the 'freeborn Englishman' being able to manage without a state-run police (unlike his oppressed French counterpart, both before and after the Revolution), society would have to tolerate a degree of crime and disorder. The *Daily Universal Register* (subsequently *The Times*) encapsulated this view in its opposition to the government's abortive Police Bill for London in 1785:

Although many inconveniences arise from an excess of liberty in this country, yet they are so greatly overbalanced by the advantages, that we cannot be too careful to preserve a blessing which distinguishes us from all the world . . . Our constitution can admit nothing like a French police . . . Mr. Reeve's bill intended to amend the *police*, if passed into a law would have tended to destroy the *liberty of the subject*.

The late-eighteenth-century landed class held to a paternalist theory of rule, which required them to maintain order in their own parts of the country without the formal institutional support of a regular police. The theory maintained that they should rule by personal example and conduct. But they supplemented this with a selective invocation of the 'bloody code'—the savage eighteenth-century criminal law with its more than 200 capital offences—to punish those who stepped badly out of line. The historian Douglas Hay has described this system as a 'calculated blend of terror and mercy under the strict rule of law'. Despite the absence of a professional police, the gentry made this system work successfully, and kept the lower orders under control in typical small parishes or towns. Such face-to-face intervention in the legal process by the landed classes has been seen as important source of British ruling-class stability during a period when many foreign governments were being rocked by revolutionary tremors. Where legal paternalism began to break down seriously and noticeably was in London by the mid-eighteenth century, and in the rapidly growing provincial industrial or commercial towns by the early nineteenth century. A supposed increase in property crime and social disturbance gave rise, from the 1750s onwards, to a series of 'moral panics' about a growing and un-stoppable crime wave and the perceived breakdown of the moral, social, and political order. These 'moral panics' were articulated and used by a number of influential figures to try to persuade the governing class of the need for a regular, organized police.

The novelist Henry Fielding (1707–54) also made his mark as the first salaried magistrate at London's Bow Street police office. Writing in the 1752 *Covent Garden Journal*, he expressed concern about the growth of 'that very large and powerful body which form the fourth estate in this community, and have long been dignified and distinguished by the name of *The Mob*', who, in London, were no longer subject to the traditional forms of control by their social superiors. This panic over 'the mob' is also voiced in Fielding's *An Enquiry into the Causes of the Late Increase of Robbers* (1751), designed to frighten people into supporting the need for a paid police force to deal with crime and to discipline the lower orders. He was succeeded as chief Bow Street magistrate, after his death, by his half-brother Sir John Fielding (d. 1780), who had worked with Henry as assisting magistrate and who turned Henry's few paid thief-takers into a permanent small force—the famous 'Bow Street Runners'. Sir John continued to agitate for a regular policing agency, not just for London, but with national scope, co-ordinating activities all over the country. Both brothers believed that crime was becoming markedly more professionalized, and that the police had to follow suit.

Patrick *Colquhoun, a wealthy Glasgow merchant turned London stipendiary magistrate, continued the pressure with his *A Treatise on the Police of the Metropolis*, which drew on his experience as a London magistrate and went through seven editions between 1795 and 1807. Colquhoun used large numbers of tables, based on often highly dubious if not simply fabricated *statistics, to provide 'scientific' backing for his claims that London faced a major crisis, comparable to that of Paris in the French Revolution. The crisis, he felt, arose from the conjunction of a number of factors: the large number of poor in London unable to support themselves honestly; the breakdown of traditional methods of control of the lower orders in the huge anonymous metropolis; and the vast growth in commercial wealth, *transportation, and movable property, especially stemming from London's docks, which was a perpetual temptation to plunder. The result of this crisis, claimed Colquhoun, was an urgent need for 'a *new Science*' of police, which would achieve 'the PREVENTION and DETECTION OF CRIMES, and . . . those other Functions which relate to INTERNAL REGULATIONS for the well ordering and comfort of Civil Society'. A professional police force would protect property by keeping the poor under constant surveillance; they would arrest and punish the criminals, but they could also use popular forms of recreation 'to give the minds of the People a right bias'. Drawing a metaphor from the industrialization occurring around him, Colquhoun stated: 'Police is an improved state of Society . . . like the Mechanical power applied to a useful Machine'; properly used, that new machine could 'gradually . . . lead the *criminal*, the *idle*, and the *dissolute* members of the community into the paths of innocence and industry.'

Colquhoun's friend and mentor Jeremy *Bentham applied the philosophy of *utilitarianism, based on a belief that humankind is ruled by responses to pleasure and pain, to the police debate. As a part of his larger arguments for the reform of England's criminal law and penal code, he advocated the need for a preventive police—a police force designed to stop crimes being committed, rather than to detect and punish the offenders after the event. The disciple who developed this aspect of the master's thought furthest was Edwin *Chadwick. In an article entitled 'Preventive Police' (1829), Chadwick set out the Benthamite argument for such a force. And as the leading member of the Royal Commission into a constabulary force for England and Wales in the years 1836–9, Chadwick drafted the Commission's report, which painted a terrifying picture of the vulnerability of the English countryside to a constant horde of itinerant criminals, vagrants, and beggars. That report, Chadwick claimed, 'proved' that crimes against property were not 'caused by blameless poverty or destitution' but by 'the temptations of the profit of a career of depredation, as compared with the profits of honest and even well paid industry'. Chadwick was also the author of the deterrent New Poor Law of 1834, with its central principle of 'less eligible' treatment for paupers in workhouses; the constabulary force Commission report was designed to complement the Poor Law, with a similar philosophy—a new national police force would deter criminals and vagrants from their careers of crime. Though not implemented in its entirety, the report formed the basis of the legislation establishing county police forces, and had a powerful influence on Victorian ideas about crime and criminals. Charles *Dickens detested Chadwick as the author of the New Poor Law, and yet he was much closer to him than he might have thought: the picture Dickens offers of crime in the London slums in *Oliver Twist* (1837) could have come straight out of Chadwick's report, or out of the writings of William Augustus Miles (1796–1851), chief researcher for the Royal Commission, who supplied Chadwick with much of its lurid evidence about crime and the habits of criminals.

However, the efforts of these 'moral entrepreneurs' to influence government and parliament met considerable political resistance to the idea of an organized police. Most government attempts from 1785 onwards to set up a state-run force for London were repeatedly defeated or blocked in parliament, before they finally succeeded in 1829. It is worth noting that what the parliament rejected for the 'freeborn Englishman' it readily accepted as necessary to control the rebellious Irish. The Bill rejected for London in 1785 was applied to Dublin the following year, and legislation in 1814 and 1822 gave Ireland a nationwide constabulary before one had even been established for London. And whereas the early English forces were deliberately unmilitary—dressed in top hats and blue tailcoats and armed only with truncheons—the Irish constabulary were paramilitary forces, in military uniform, stationed in barracks, and armed with carbines and pistols.

The extent and success of this parliamentary resistance to a police force in England was not the result of any strong civil libertarian impulse among MPs. The House of Commons before 1832 was elected on a very narrow *class [15] basis, and showed no great concern with ordinary people's civil liberties; it suspended habeas corpus to deal with the radical agitations of the 1790s and the immediate postwar period, it resisted initial moves to reduce the number of capital crimes, and it defended their narrow electoral base against calls for *parliamentary reform and *Catholic emancipation. The opposition to a paid police was mainly a fear of the consequences of a police in the hands of a potentially over-mighty central government. Backbench country squires, in particular, felt that the defence of their own liberties and privileges—especially their autonomous local powers as JPs—required them to resist a government-run police, and they continued to put forward the argument about the necessary trade-off between order and liberty. Widely shared, if diffuse, *constitutionalist assumptions and memories based on the legendary tyranny of the late Stuart monarchs bolstered such resistance.

The 'new police' idea only began to be translated into practical politics by Robert *Peel. As

Peel's Police,
RAW LOBSTERS,
Blue Devils,

Or by whatever other appropriate Name
they may be known.

────────────────

Notice is hereby given,

That a Subscription has been entered
into, to supply the **PEOPLE** with
STAVES of a superior Effect, either
for **Defence** or **Punishment**, which will be
in readiness to be gratuitously distributed
whenever a similar unprovoked, and therefore unmanly and blood-thirsty Attack,
be again made upon Englishmen, by a
Force unknown to the British Constitution, and called into existence by a
Parliament illegally constituted, legislat-
ing for their individual interests, consequently in opposition to the Public good.

——*000*——

" Put not your trust in Princes."—DAVID.
" Help yourself, and Heaven will help you."—FRENCH
MOTTO.

──────

10th Nov 1830   Eliz. Soulby, Printer, 91, Gracechurch Street.

10. Broadsheet of 1830 showing radical opposition to Home Secretary Robert Peel's founding of the Metropolitan Police force in 1829, sentiments also shared by many landowners who feared state centralism.

*Tory Home Secretary in the 1820s Peel had learned his policing ideas as Chief Secretary for Ireland, when he was responsible for the first Irish county forces in 1814. As Home Secretary, he began with criminal law reform, abolishing many of the capital offences of the old 'bloody code', and moved on to police reform, succeeding in establishing the Metropolitan Police in 1829. To the traditional landed idea of 'liberty' as consisting in the absence of central government control, Peel now counterposed the notion of 'true liberty' as being the freedom from criminal invasion of one's life and property—an idea which appealed strongly to the growing urban middle class. In support of this argument, Peel could cite official criminal statistics which had been published from 1805 onwards. These figures undoubtedly showed a steady increase in committals to trial for indictable offences, an increase much greater than the increase in *population. Whether these figures represented a *real* increase in crime—as opposed to an increase in arrests and prosecutions or a greater public awareness of crime through the growth of *newspaper reading—is highly debatable. Nevertheless Peel used them skilfully to inspire a climate of fear about crime and disorder and a commensurate support for his police. This alarm about growing crime, combined with anxieties about the maintenance of public order, continued to concern the authorities during the 1820s and became prominent with the crises of Catholic emancipation, Captain Swing, and the *Reform Act of 1832. It was because of the pervasiveness of this fear and the success of the widespread campaign of moral panic that Peel could argue, as he did in parliament in February 1828:

the time is come when, from the increase in its population, the enlargement of its resources, and the multiplied development of its energies, we may fairly pronounce that the country has outgrown her police institutions, and that the cheapest and safest course will be found to be the introduction of a new mode of protection.

Such arguments enabled Peel, with the support of his Tory Prime Minister, the Duke of *Wellington, to overcome the long resistance to systematic policing with surprising ease, and to establish his force for London. In 1832, Lord Melbourne (1779–1848), as Home Secretary in the *Whig government of Earl Grey (1764–1845), produced a Bill for a paid police to cover much of the country, under the control of stipendiary magistrates rather than unpaid JPs. The Bill was dropped without being presented to parliament, but it shows that, by 1832, the national leadership of the Whigs, as well as the Tories, had been converted to a belief in the need for a 'new police'. In 1835, as part of their municipal reforms, the Whig government extended the 'new police' to all corporate towns, requiring them to set up forces on the metropolitan model. But, while the national political leadership had adopted the new thinking, and the urban areas accepted their new police with relatively little protest, there remained strong local resistance to the idea of an organized national police force (or forces) to cover all the counties including rural areas. The county JPs could express their political resistance in parliament; but their real bulwark lay in quarter sessions, from which they governed their counties. Between 1839 and 1841 this power was mobilized to resist the permissive County Police Act 1839, which allowed (but did not compel) quarter sessions to establish county police forces. Many of the JPs came out strongly with the traditional doctrines: a police force would be an unconstitutional 'standing army'; it would be an armed *gendarmerie*, which threatened civil liberties; it represented the thin end of the wedge of centralization, government power, and the end of the unpaid magistracy. Stressing the marked differences between urban and rural policing needs, the JPs resurrected and defended the paternalist theory that they should rule without the support of formal institutions of repression such as a professional police. They put up a formidable opposition in many quarter sessions, and succeeded in ensuring that half of the English counties refused to set up a county force under the Act.

However, traditional paternalist ideas had come under increasing challenge since the end of Napoleonic *wars [2], particularly in the area of the Poor Law. The Captain Swing rising of agricultural labourers in 1830–1 had dramatically demonstrated the falsity of the benevolent image of JPs ruling paternally with the full trust of their tenants and labourers, and it had seriously dented conventional assumptions about the deference and quiescence of rural workers. The 1830s proved to be a watershed decade, in which landed gentlemen increasingly began to accommodate themselves to a new conception of relations between rulers and ruled in the counties. This was shown by their reaction to the New Poor Law of 1834, for although the Act violated paternalist notions of the mutual obligations of rulers and ruled, most landowners accepted it relatively easily, and co-operated in its implementation. In the area of policing, although most still opposed a full-blown, Benthamite, centralized police, they increasingly accepted the need for some form of paid, trained professionals to supplement or replace the old parish constables. For this purpose, many landowners were actively involved in the 1830s in setting up and running a range of police experiments under their own local control: the Cheshire Constabulary Act of 1829 (a private Act obtained by the Cheshire quarter sessions to enable them to appoint their own paid police); forces set up under local acts obtained by towns; forces established by adopting the Lighting and Watching Act of 1833, which enabled parishes to levy a rate to pay for a police; forces set up by poor law unions and paid for from the poor rates (until this was declared illegal in 1836); and, in growing numbers by the late 1830s, forces established and sustained by voluntary subscription, and run by local magnates. By the time of the quarter sessions debates over adopting the County Police Act, the landed resistance was diminishing, and the traditional constitutional arguments were starting to look old-fashioned. Leading figures in many of the quarter sessions argued that (in the words of Lord *Ellenborough in the Gloucestershire debate) 'the great change which had taken place in society of late' now made a police force an inevitable necessity.

The major area of concern in the debates shifted from the constitutional and civil libertarian arguments to disputes about the cost and control of the new police forces. The Act placed the entire financial burden of a force on any county choosing to establish one, which sparked a ratepayer revolt in many counties, pressuring their magistrates to oppose a force. Some JPs objected to their old local control of the parish constables giving way to a new force under a Chief Constable and the quarter sessions police committee, and resented the fact that the Home Secretary had control (in reality, very faint) over the force. A few reactionary or paternalist diehards clung to the old ideas, but, for most of them, the basic principle of the need for full-time professional police forces had been accepted. By the end of the 1830s a notable change in thinking about the state and its role in policing can be seen even among the landed gentry; they had essentially moved away from the paternalist idea that social discipline could and should be maintained by their personal influence, and had accepted the modern idea of the need for a formal, government-run, professional institution to enforce discipline on the lower orders. The middle and especially commercial sectors of the cities also became increasingly supportive of the new police as providers of crucial services such as the protection of property; the suppression of traditional sports, *fairs, and pastimes [see *popular culture, 23]; the removal of vagrants; and the enforcement of drinking hours. Even so, the architects of the new police had always to tread carefully for fear of arousing traditional ruling-class anxieties about continental-style state policing. Some care was taken to avoid recruiting ex-soldiers as constables, preference being given to agricultural workers willing to accept the relatively low pay of 17 shillings per week. Rigid moral codes were enforced in order to control the behaviour of the new force, especially in respect to drink, sexual propriety, and fraternization with known criminals. The new police officers were also issued with uniforms which avoided any resonance of the military, and they were armed with rattle and truncheon rather than the sabre formerly used by Bow Street Runners.

Even so, acceptance of the new police was more protracted and uneasy amongst the urban working classes, especially in the docklands and East End of London. Traditional suspicions of the police as enforcers of state tyranny persisted and may even have grown, given the increased role of the new police in the surveillance and arrest of political radicals. A dramatic instance of such popular resentment occurred at a Coldbath Fields reform meeting in 1833, when a crowd clashed violently with 200 armed constables, leading to the death of one policeman followed by a notorious verdict of 'justifiable homicide' issued by the coroner's court jury. It is likely that such popular dislike of 'Peel's bloody gang', or the 'blue locusts', as the police were variously nicknamed, acted as a constraint on the shaping and implementation of professionalizing police bills throughout the early nineteenth century. On the other hand there is also evidence of a growing, if gradual, acceptance amongst urban artisans and labourers of the usefulness of the police in protecting their own property and persons from the threats posed by roughs, criminals, and vagrants.

We end, then, with something of a paradox. The French historian Alexis Comte de Tocqueville (1805–59) noted in *Democracy in America* (1835) that it was precisely the democratic nature of American society which led to it pioneering the repressive new penitentiary *prison.

Just as he had argued that the French Revolution resulted in the institution of tyranny in the form of administrative government, de Tocqueville argued with reference to America that a society with so much freedom and so few traditional social bonds felt the need for strong new forms of discipline to maintain order. Britain in the Romantic age was certainly no democratic society, but it was a society dramatically changed by the two great revolutions of the period. Industrialization produced large urban populations, freed of most of the traditional restraints of parish life and official religion; it spawned ideas of economic individualism and free-market forces, of *liberalism and proto-*socialism. The French Revolution disseminated ideas of the Rights of Man, political freedoms, and democracy. Fear of the potential effect of these greater freedoms on the masses, no longer restrained by traditional forms of control, led the governing class to abandon its long-held opposition and introduce professional police forces, in a bid to re-establish control through these new institutional means. That new model of policing is still with us today.

Critchley, T. A., *A History of Police in England and Wales*, London, 1978; Emsley, C., *Policing and its Context 1750–1870*, London, 1983; *Crime and Society in England 1750–1900*, London, 1987; Hay, D., 'Property, Authority and the Criminal Law', in D. Hay, P. Linebaugh, & E. P. Thompson, eds., *Albion's Fatal Tree: Crime and Society in Eighteenth-Century England*, London, 1975; Hay, D., & Snyder, F., eds., *Policing and Prosecution in Britain 1750–1850*, Oxford, 1989; Palmer, S. H., *Police and Protest in England and Ireland 1780–1850*, Cambridge, 1988; Philips, D., 'A New Engine of Power and Authority': The Institutionalization of Law-Enforcement in England 1780–1830', in V. A. C. Gatrell, B. Lenman, & G. Parker, eds., *Crime and the Law: The Social History of Crime in Western Europe since 1500*, London, 1980; Philips, D., & Storch, R. D., 'Whigs and Coppers: the Grey Ministry's National Police Scheme, 1832', *Historical Research*, 67 (1994), 75–90; Radzinowicz, L., *A History of English Criminal Law and Its Administration from 1750*, iii, London, 1956; Silver, A., 'The Demand for Order in Civil Society: A Review of Some Themes in the History of Urban Crime, Police, and Riot', in D. Bordua, ed., *The Police: Six Sociological Essays*, New York, 1967; Wiener, M. J., *Reconstructing the Criminal: Culture, Law and Policy in England, 1830–1914*, Cambridge, 1994.

8 · LAW   DAVID LEMMINGS

In his *Commentaries on the Laws of England* (1765–9), the judge and legal writer Sir William *Blackstone offered the following reading of British law as the guarantor of individual rights:

In these several articles consist the rights, or as they are frequently termed, the liberties of Englishmen . . . to vindicate these rights, when actually violated or attacked, the subjects of England are entitled, in the first place, to the regular administration and free course of justice in the courts of law; next to the right of petitioning the king and parliament for redress of grievances; and last to the right of having and using arms for self-preservation and defence. And all these rights and liberties it is our birthright to enjoy entire; unless where the laws of our country have laid them under necessary restraints. Restraints in themselves so gentle and moderate, as will appear upon farther enquiry, that no man of sense or probity would wish to see them slackened.

This encomium had the status of a dominant creed in eighteenth-century England. It was certainly a commonplace for his fellow *judges and *lawyers to celebrate the surpassing virtues of English law and legal institutions in this way. And as the European perspective of Montesquieu's *De l'Esprit des Lois* (1748) implied, a variegated but widespread consciousness of the supposed advantages of 'the rule of law' was the clearest feature of that patriotic superiority complex which distinguished the English in their own eyes and among foreigners around mid-century, when Blackstone first conceived his *Commentaries*. The rule of law was a uniquely inclusive and participatory ideal in English society.

Indeed, the concept and practical administration of law had never before been invested with so much capital. After the seventeenth-century crisis of rebellions against Church and king culminating in the *Glorious Revolution of 1688, the increased currency of ideas about *natural rights and a likely decline in the power associated with both the *monarchy and the established Church seems to have elevated the importance of law at several levels. Among the élites, the twice-yearly visitations of the assize judges to the county towns of England and Wales remained an essential administrative point of contact between the centre and the localities; they were also perceived by Georgian governments as primary media for communicating the good news about equal rights under common law and for moral suasion of the lower orders. And in the absence of real **policing** [7], substantial property owners and the proliferating business community in London and other cities looked to the criminal law as the primary safeguard for their property against what they were inclined to believe was a growing love of luxury and idleness among their inferiors. On the other hand, the common lawyers and judges, and the legal instruments and rules they invented, were required to order and facilitate the normal course of micro-economic affairs, especially money matters, which were increasingly complicated and largely unrestrained by any consensus of moral ideas transcending individual interest.

At the popular level, participation in the legal punishment of criminals at the cart's tail, the pillory, or the scaffold was a riotous community activity among the common people [see **class, 15**]. Indeed, at times of stress, many of the labouring multitude confidently articulated crude notions of customary law and common justice to justify direct action for securing the social values of their own communities: such action might take various forms, ranging from loyal *petitioning or threatening those in authority to *riot and even local *insurrection. The continuance after 1688 of quasi-mystical and religious ideas about 'loyalty and honesty' centred in the person of the monarch, alongside modern claims of 'liberty and property', was therefore perfectly compatible with normal belief in law as a guarantee of individual rights.

In sum, practically every British citizen appears to have accepted a version of Blackstone's premise about the positive value and necessity of government by law. Admittedly, the notion of the 'Englishman's birthright' was not generally extended to Scotland, whose separate (semi-Roman) legal system actually conveyed some rights not enjoyed in England, but where patrician judges did not scruple to dismiss the common people as a 'rabble' whose part was merely to obey. And in Ireland, although English law was applied by the courts, the indigenous Catholics were not thought worthy of its full advantages until 1829, by which time English institutions had been thoroughly tainted. Moreover, the positive rights of English **women** [4] were severely limited under common law. But despite these serious qualifications, and although there was no general agreement about either the law's substance or its purposes, English citizens of all classes shared an awareness of the rights and liberties they had inherited from the struggles of the seventeenth century and which were guaranteed by the constitution and the common law in the eighteenth. Law therefore represented a broad consensus of high expectations in Georgian England, and Jeremy *Bentham was expressing a general view of its importance as a unifying ideal when he wrote (probably in the 1770s): 'The law is every man's best friend . . . To her the rich man owes his wealth; the poor man his subsistence; every man who is free, his freedom.'

There is a subtle but radical difference between this statement of Bentham's and Blackstone's panegyric, however, in that Bentham defined law in society as the positive origin and source of rights, rather than the consequence of natural rights and natural law which were somehow antecedent and independent of society, or at least were demonstrated to be fundamental by their supposed origins in ancient common law. Bentham therefore entirely rejected the common law tradition, by which law was supposed to have evolved historically out of popular custom and participation in the court system via the judges' declarations of shared community values. Rather than representing the accumulated wisdom of the whole community about the protection of individual rights to liberty and property, Bentham believed that the common law was a confused and obscure rag-bag of fictions and contradictions which amounted merely to the corporate self-interest of the legal profession. Even the potential for corrective parliamentary legislation was rendered useless by its particularism. In his ideal conception, law should be the instrument of government, and it could therefore be changed to suit government's purposes: it was legislation created by a sovereign will, and not limited by any metaphysical notions about natural rights. Indeed, Bentham's *Fragment on Government* (1776) was the opening salvo in a long personal campaign which was designed to expose the manifold inadequacies of the Blackstonian legal system. He advocated root-and-branch law reform and positive legislation according to a more pragmatic standard than rights: namely, the *Enlightenment [32] ideal of utility, or in Benthamite language 'the greatest happiness of the greatest number' [see *utilitarianism].

In 1776, although there were many practical criticisms of particular aspects of the law (especially penal policy), wholesale theoretical and practical condemnation of the common law tradition was exceptional. It was equivalent to shouting against a cherished national myth, maintained in political discourse by conservative propaganda, radical subscription, and popular belief. Even in 1832, when Bentham died, emphasis on the substance and administration of common law, and on historical continuity as proof of legitimacy, remained important in relation to British legal and constitutional theory. But the shocks of *revolution [1] in America and France had diminished British sympathies for natural rights in relation to law. And by the 1830s the administration of English law was a touchstone for scandal in many educated circles: public opinion had taken a decisive turn against the bloody and saturnalian rituals of Tyburn executions and the archaic process of Westminster Hall. Both criminal law and civil procedure were the subject of prolonged parliamentary scrutiny.

Rather than continuing to rely on the common law courts as devolved agencies of propaganda, deterrence, and administration, and tolerating the development of new law by their judges, early-nineteenth-century ministers found themselves more frequently resorting to law as an instrument of central government. This took the form of parliamentary legislation for purposes of social control, if not yet social engineering. So although we cannot discern a conscious change in mentalities relating to law along Benthamite lines during this period, there is evidence of a widespread decline in the amount of confidence which contemporaries were prepared to invest in the ideals and apparatus of the common law tradition. It does appear that a change of emphasis was under way, a shift which anticipated the modern British tradition of positivist law reform and legislative governance. The roots of changing attitudes to the law have to be located in the administrative challenges posed by rapid social and economic development and in the psychological impact of revolution. Notwithstanding Bentham's ultimate importance, these developments seem to have inspired many others to depart from the prescriptions of the common law tradition in the century after 1750. Their impact will be assessed in the areas of civil law, criminal law, and legislation. But above all it is necessary to place law in the perspective of the *constitution.

The legislative inheritance of the Reformation and the political legacy of the seventeenth century meant that after 1688 it was not possible at a theoretical level to dispute explicitly the supremacy of King-in-parliament as a source of law and government. The Act of Settlement (1701), the Act of Union with Scotland (1707), the Septennial Act (1717), and the Irish Dependency Act (1720) were dramatic affirmations of that supremacy (as were the *Act of Union with Ireland in 1800 and the Catholic Relief Act of 1829). Nevertheless, hidden tensions between the continuance of the common law tradition and the full exercise of parliamentary sovereignty became apparent during the reign of George III. In the first place, the legal establishment took it for granted that the common law courts should remain the foundational source of regular legal development. Hence the Westminster Hall jurisdictions of *King's Bench, *Common Pleas, and *Exchequer remained the centre of the legal universe in England until the Victorian period. Although parliament became more productive of legislation during the eighteenth century, especially in the area of criminal law, several writers deplored this growing positivist activism by parliament as introducing contradiction in the law, and as interference which corrupted the ancient common law and threatened the liberties of English citizens. Blackstone's belief in the centrality of common law principles was such that his *Commentaries* were conceived (*inter alia*) as a project for educating potential legislators in the common law. But for traditionalists this was a second-best option, measured against the proper development of the law in the courts. The construction of the commercial law by Lord Chief Justice *Mansfield between 1756 and 1788 was the clearest contemporary example of the continuing willingness of common law judges to create substantive law independently of the legislature, despite their modest claims to a merely declarative function.

Moreover, in the absence of legislation for devolved local government, the central courts and their judges maintained some administrative functions. These took the form of the regulation of the corporations and parish rating authorities by *prerogative writ in King's Bench, as well as the practical supervision of local affairs through presentation by the grand jury at the twice-yearly assizes. After the abolition of the provincial councils and prerogative courts in the seventeenth century, courts and judges had no rivals in these administrative roles, and their only serious judicial competitor was the Chancellor's court, which was fast developing settled rules along the lines of the common law. Furthermore, as long as the courts continued to be regarded as the primary institutions for protecting individual rights in society, they were able to articulate important public principles on the basis of common pleas. These included pronouncements on the limited legality and 'odious' condition of **slavery [6]** in England (1772), on the freedom of the subject from arrest and of his property from confiscation on a general warrant from the Crown (1776), and (more gradually) on the freedom of contract. Indeed, the centrality of individualistic rights to politics and the constitution in eighteenth-century England ensured that sensitive political and constitutional issues (for example the questions of personal, electoral, and press freedom raised by the *Wilkites in the 1760s and 1770s) were still frequently fought out in the courts rather than in parliament. So while formal constitutional principle meant that the courts were ultimately vulnerable to the assumption of positive sovereignty by parliament, along the lines of the theories articulated by Bentham, the persistence of traditional attitudes allowed them a significant place in the practice of government.

The obsessive individualism of mid-Georgian England also underlay the second and more serious tension between the common law tradition and parliamentary governance. At a time when the language of politics was largely built from a legal vocabulary centred on rights, it was inevitable that the courts should be regarded by radical minorities opposed to the government as an appropriate forum for negotiating with the power of the executive. They were frequently encouraged by the tendency of common law judges (who were often party politicians themselves) to make quasi-absolute statements about the fundamental status of common law as the protector of individual liberty and property under the Glorious Revolution settlement of the constitution.

Even at the level of sober theory, the individualist natural law ideology which Blackstone and most other eighteenth-century legal writers articulated as the legitimating basis of law and the constitution could easily be interpreted as an absolute limit to parliamentary sovereignty, if an admittedly vague one. Moreover, emphasis on the historical origins of common law could easily extend into the classical populist tradition of the 'ancient constitution' which had often been used to argue for fundamental and inalienable freedoms. Blackstone himself, the conservative constitutionalist of the *Commentaries* (book 1), was careful to downplay such radical implications by both insisting on formal parliamentary supremacy and precisely delimiting the extent of 'the absolute rights of man' under the law of nature. Though he rejected the idea of residual popular sovereignty contained in the contractual theory of government, it was difficult to prevent this dangerous notion from gaining popular currency.

The potential contradictions between the common law tradition and the real business of eighteenth-century parliamentary government were presented in their most concrete and fundamental form by the offshore revolutionary challenges of 1776 and 1789. The American revolutionaries clearly felt that, by attempting to enforce its will on the colonists through legislation and military coercion, the corrupt British government of King-in-parliament had acted in an arbitrary way which abridged their natural and legal rights as freeborn Englishmen. Their instinctive constitutional remedy, as good followers of *Locke and *Rousseau, as well as of Sir Edward Coke (1552–1634) and Blackstone, was to declare their contract with the tyrannical George III dissolved, to enact a written constitution accompanied by an independent Supreme Court, and to establish a Bill of Rights. In other words, they created a fundamental charter of natural rights and set up a supreme common law court which developed powers of legislative review to prevent a recurrence of repressive parliamentary government. Alexander Hamilton (1757–1804), George Washington's private secretary during the *American Revolution, justified these developments on the grounds that 'though individual oppression may now and then proceed from the courts of justice, the general liberty of the people can never be endangered from that quarter'.

A radical interpretation of common law ideology, which emphasized individual natural rights and looked to the judges as the guardians of those rights against executive power, was therefore the essence of the constitutional challenge which the Americans presented to Britain in their fundamentalist statements of 1776, 1788, and 1791. By contrast, the French revolutionaries of 1789 and after were not, of course, common lawyers. But their uncompromising and violent assertion of the absolute rights of man against tyrannical government, although external to the British constitution, represented an even more serious problem inherent to the natural law elements of the common law tradition. Indeed, the successive publications of Thomas *Paine revealed the extent to which crude ideas about inalienable natural rights might not only undermine government in America and France but also offer the threat of revolution in Britain.

In these circumstances it is hardly surprising that the common law tradition as expressed by Blackstone and his more rhetorical judicial colleagues in the middle of the eighteenth century seems to have been modified in constitutional discourse after 1789, and the individualist and consensual associations of law effectively downgraded. The resurgence of radicalism in the 1770s and 1780s, and the far more dangerous political theory and example of the *French Revolution, required a restatement of constitutional theory in the form of a high doctrine of sovereign authority, and this was appropriate to a parliamentarian rather than a jurist. Thus, Edmund *Burke, in his *Reflections on the Revolution in France* (1790), explicitly rejected radical interpretations of the rights of man tending to popular sovereignty. True, he wrote respectfully of Blackstone as one of 'the great men' of English law, and appealed at moments to the legal writings of the seventeenth-century jurists Edward Coke and Matthew Hale (1609–76). Yet Burke took pains to purge the common law tradition of the elements of Enlightenment rationalism which the *Commentaries* had deployed to explain and justify the constitution of civil society, and which ultimately implied accountability to individual reason and individual interests. Burke thus expressed the common law tradition in collectivist rather than individualist terms, and entailed it specifically upon the legislature as a body which represented the inherited interests of the whole community. In this way the logic of legislative assertiveness of the 1688 Glorious Revolution was fulfilled a century later by a fully consistent theory of practical legislative sovereignty which effectively superseded populist appeals to the common law and individual natural rights.

Burke's rhetorical rejection of the rights of man in the face of revolution had its practical corollary in the repressive anti-libertarian legislation passed by the government in the 1790s, known as the *gagging acts, which suspended habeas corpus, prohibited unauthorized public meetings, and brought criticism of the constitution within the scope of the treason laws. It may have been indicative of changing attitudes to law that the 'Two Acts' of 1795 were passed by parliament after the common law courts had failed to deal with the radical reformers Thomas *Hardy, John Horne *Tooke, and John *Thelwall [see *Treason Trials]. By contrast with the compliant Scottish courts, which sentenced several radicals to transportation on flimsy grounds, English juries would not stomach the crown's far-fetched arguments about constructive treason. The passage of these statutes with large majorities amounted to the abandonment by a frightened government of even lip-service to notions about the fundamental rights of Englishmen under the common law, as opposed to the stated necessity to protect 'the people's rights' by statute. Indeed, when defending these measures, the Prime Minister, William *Pitt, was ultimately forced into the absurd position of claiming that statutes themselves had rights:

We trust whatever attempts may be made to resist their operation, the power of the laws themselves will be found sufficient to defeat them and to vindicate their rights.

As historian E. P. Thompson has shown, many of the working men who had believed in the rule of law and the ancient constitution as the guarantors of their rights as freeborn Englishmen were educated about their true relation to the law in the cold light of Pittite Britain. For Percy *Shelley, writing after *Peterloo, the Englishman's birthright had proved to be 'Golden and sanguine laws which tempt and slay'.

Of course the legislative repression was temporary, and the common law tradition endured the 1790s. It survived most obviously as a theory of the constitution which combined conservative and progressive elements: in its persisting emphasis upon continuity with the past; in the promise of limited civil liberties to the subject and protection of private property; and most concretely in the requirement for 'due process' by the community before interference with those liberties—especially trial by jury in serious criminal cases. But the characteristically eighteenth-century concept of the law of the land as the guarantor of fundamental individual rights and the symbol of popular participation in government moved into decline. In addition to the corrosive effects of the American and French revolutions, it was further diminished by the gradual resort to increased statutory intervention in the affairs of the community after 1800, tending to regulation and ultimately to direct administration and the exercise of wide discretionary powers from the centre. The early stages of this process represented the growing influence of Bentham and his followers, who were openly contemptuous of the common law. Yet the resilience of common law attitudes inhibited the growth of central government until the second half of the nineteenth century. Ultimately, common law loyalties were only overturned by the imperatives of the new society, rather than by the criticisms of the Benthamites.

The clearest examples of early legislative assertiveness at the expense of common law tradition and practice—a process which was substantially under way by the 1830s—may be seen in the new administrative bodies created by the Poor Law Amendment Act and Factory Act [see *poor laws and *factory system]. But a gradual failure of the common law tradition can also be perceived in the areas of civil litigation and criminal law. In both these spheres, as in the connected areas of local government, labour conditions, and the management of the poor, the limited machinery of the common law proved inadequate in the face of social and economic growth, just as the popular ideal of common law had failed as a unifying principle in the face of revolutionary challenge.

Despite the claims of the lawyers and judges for equal access to justice under the common law, it is evident that the eighteenth-century central courts did not live up to their ideal as open 'law shops' for the adjudication of a wide range of private, interpersonal disputes. Although they remained accessible in theory via the *nisi prius* arrangement of hearing civil suits at the provincial assizes, all the common law tribunals and the court of Chancery suffered a massive loss of civil business which reduced them to a nadir around mid-century. While there were various possible reasons for the decline, it is clear that rising legal and clerical fees and the connected problem of labyrinthine process were major deterrents against going to law, not to mention the uncertainty inherent in doctrine which was buried in a mass of case reports. Long-standing criticisms along these lines were multiplied after 1800, as economic and *population growth began to increase demand. *Newspapers and periodicals like the *Edinburgh Review* and the Benthamite *Westminster Review* provided a platform for complaint, with the result that several parliamentary investigations were commissioned, beginning with inquiries about Chancery delays in 1811. Reform came slowly, and in piecemeal fashion, often against resistance and reaction from diehard conservatives among the bar and bench. However, during the second and third quarters of the nineteenth century, middle-class public opinion forced considerable legislative simplification of process and consolidation of jurisdictions, culminating in the formation of the unified Supreme Court of Judicature in 1873–5.

Late Georgian and early Victorian working people were most likely to connect with the common law world of courtrooms and scarlet-clad judges in its more draconian aspect as the administration of the criminal law. This area of law—defined by Blackstone as relating to the prohibition and punishment of 'public wrongs'—was naturally most liable to the intervention of the legislature. Indeed, penal sanctions had already undergone considerable 'reform' by parliament before the middle of the eighteenth century, first in the shape of successive statutes which either withdrew benefit of clergy from existing felonies or created new ones, thereby making capital punishment the formal sanction for a great range of offences against all kinds of private property; and secondly by the introduction of an effective form of secondary punishment in transportation to the American colonies. The latter, established by the Transportation Act of 1718, constituted an absolute break with common law ideals and traditions, in that it inaugurated a form of punishment which disallowed the more or less active participation of the public, customary at hangings and whippings and essential for standing in the pillory. Instead transportation isolated offenders from the community.

After 1750, the harsh customary and participatory sanctions which were typical of medieval and early modern criminal law were subjected to increasing public criticism under the influence of Enlightenment thinkers such as the Italian legal theorist Cesare Beccaria (1738–94), who rejected disproportionate and uncertain punishment and excessive use of capital punishment. His concerns chimed with the extensive growth of sentiment in polite society, which entailed a concern for rehabilitating the morally 'fallen' [see *sensibility, 11]. This public criticism also drew crucial support from more practical concerns about the doubtful effectiveness of existing penal sanctions in the face of rapid urban growth, exemplified by considerable fear of crime and disorder in London from the late seventeenth century and more generally in the new industrial towns a century later.

This widespread criticism resulted in more legislation—acts of parliament which extended the range and scope of secondary punishments to be applied in place of death, while reducing the uncertain role of the local community and the unsavoury or morally dubious influence of popular custom. Statutes of 1776, 1779, 1815, 1823, and 1835 paved the way for the greater use of imprisonment with hard labour; the removal of public executions in London from Tyburn to Newgate in 1783 restricted the opportunities for public carnival. And after 1808, when Samuel *Romilly began his parliamentary campaign for reform, there was a retreat from the death penalty for some of the less serious offences against property, and a more gradual

11. *The Newgate Drop*, illustration to A. Knapp and W. Baldwin, *New Newgate Calendar* (1810). Executions by hanging were removed from the infamous 'Tyburn Tree' gallows to the exterior of Newgate prison in 1783.

abandonment of public and corporal punishment generally, culminating in the abolition of public execution in 1868. Already by 1840, after the successive criminal law consolidating and reforming statutes of conservative and liberal ministries, public whipping was limited to adult males, the pillory had been abrogated entirely, and capital punishment was largely confined to crimes which involved violence against the person.

Although state *prisons were not built on a large scale until after 1850, the progressive shift to the isolationist penalties of transportation and incarceration clearly tended to enhance the role of the state in punishment as it diminished that of the community. Moreover, the increased legislative prescription of practical sanctions short of death meant a reduction in the amount of discretion available to trial judges in sentencing, and an end to the need for *pious perjury to moderate the rigours of the law themselves. Indeed, while the central principle of trial by one's peers was maintained for serious offences, and the uniformity of justice was certainly improved by limiting the discretionary role of the judge and allowing defence counsel to participate fully in trials, the development of legislative precision in penal policy was a significant departure from the common law tradition of devolved decision-making in the administration of English criminal law. A common law preference for judicial discretion over parliamentary prescription may explain why the campaign to limit the application of capital punishment was resisted to the last ditch in the early nineteenth century by Lord Chancellor *Eldon and Lord Chief Justice *Ellenborough. Ellenborough maintained this preference in 1810 when opposing the removal of capital punishment from conviction for shoplifting, saying that 'There were always circumstances which aggravated or mitigated the crime, but it would be impossible to make them the subject of an act of parliament.' The increasing exercise of summary criminal juris-diction by JPs—common in the eighteenth century and confirmed and regularized by statute in 1848—departed from common law in a slightly different way. In the nineteenth century the confirmation of summary jurisdiction meant that an increasing number of minor offenders were tried and sentenced (often to terms of imprisonment) by one or two magistrates, rather than by twelve of their peers. Such an authoritarian regime may have seemed appropriate because the urban poor were identified increasingly as a criminal class. This perception entailed support for laws which created a network of institutions for their management and disciplining: through the penitentiary, the police, and the new poor laws.

In conclusion, by the 1830s, when legislation which established the Poor Law Commission, the Factory Inspectorate, and the Registrar-General of births, deaths, and marriages was passing in parliament, the substance and theory of English law had travelled a long way from the Blackstonian ideal, when the law administered in the courts was both the essence and the practical limit of government. Under this earlier system, ordinary eighteenth-century people enjoyed a large measure of individual and community self-government, autonomy, and even occasional anarchy under what Blackstone referred to as the 'moderate restraints' of the common law. Moreover, the common people witnessed and occasionally might be involved in the administration of the law as jurors, constables, and spectators of punishment. And the egalitarian and participatory implications of common law were sometimes used to justify direct popular action.

By contrast, in 1832, just as Jeremy Bentham died, the first *Reform Act initiated a trajectory of *parliamentary reform by which the legislature ultimately took upon itself the entire mantle of popular legitimacy. The Act symbolized the lengthy and complex process by which law and government were becoming merely representative of the community rather than legitimating individual participation in the name of the rights of freeborn Englishmen under the common law. Such participation was rendered dangerous by the events of 1776 and 1789, and impracticable by late-eighteenth- and early-nineteenth-century social developments. The age of popular protest and populist litigation under the aegis of common law was passing. The act of popular consent was confined increasingly to the regular exercise of the vote, and the law was identified with the command of the sovereign legislature legitimized by that act. Victorian people would surely have recognized their relationship to law and government in the prescient statement of Blackstone's successor as Vinerian professor of English law at Oxford, Sir Robert Chambers (1737–1803), that parliament 'has a civil right to obedience from its subjects, whose execution of its laws is only ministerial and who are considered not as agents but as instruments'.

Atiyah, P. S., *The Rise and Fall of Freedom of Contract*, Oxford, 1979; Beattie, J. M., *Crime and the Courts in England 1660–1800*, Oxford, 1986; Brewer, J., & Styles, J., eds., *An Ungovernable People: The English and Their Law in the Seventeenth and Eighteenth Centuries*, London, 1980; Brooks, C. W., 'Interpersonal Conflict and Social Tension: Civil Litigation in England, 1640–1830', in A. L. Beier, D. Cannadine, & J. L. Rosenheim, eds., *The First Modern Society: Essays in English History in Honour of Lawrence Stone*, Cambridge, 1989; Gatrell, V. A. C., *The Hanging Tree: Execution and the English People 1770–1868*, Oxford, 1994; Holdsworth, W., *A History of English Law*, London, 1922–66; Ignatieff, M., *A Just Measure of Pain: The Penitentiary in the Industrial Revolution 1750–1850*, Harmondsworth, 1978; Lieberman, D., *The Province of Legislation Determined: Legal Theory in Eighteenth-Century Britain*, Cambridge, 1989; Postema, G. J., *Bentham and the Common Law Tradition*, Oxford, 1986; Thompson, E. P., *The Making of the English Working Class* (1963), Harmondsworth, 1968.

9 · UTOPIANISM GREGORY CLAEYS

'Utopianism' can be taken in several senses: as the aspiration to imagine, establish, or discover a more perfect society and, after Thomas More's *Utopia* (1516), as the literary genre commonly associated with such aims. The utopian desire can assume many forms, such as *millenarianism, scientific enthusiasm, speculation about distant worlds, the description of model constitutions, imagined futures and communities, and conceptions of the past or 'golden age' of any society or mankind in general. The literary genre, in addition, is usually taken to encompass a spectrum of speculative works including dystopias, or satires upon perfectionist aspirations.

Eighteenth-century Britain was by and large a profoundly practical society. There was no shortage of speculation, but this tended to be as much commercial as political, religious, or philosophical. Rapid commercialization, urbanization, and *industrialization [14] occasioned frequent reflections upon the loss of purity and simplicity of manners, and the dangers this entailed for patriotism and civic virtue. Central to the assumptions of both utopian and anti-utopian texts was the understanding that Britain had undergone a process of rapid and extensive social transformation in which the naturally virtuous mores of a closely knit, largely agricultural society were being supplanted by more selfish, impersonal, aggressive manners dominated by money-getting and the diffusion of luxury goods. *Satirists found much to sustain them in the rising social expectations of tradesmen. Concern was widespread that unabashed greed, accompanied by a sharp growth in the *national debt, spelt the irrevocable decline of civic as well as private virtue, and threatened Britain's economic pre-eminence. The discovery of new lands and previously unknown cultures inflated a sense of national superiority, but also fuelled the sense of lost innocence. Along with the satirical reflection that no return to a simpler age was possible, or necessarily even desirable, this nostalgia underpinned much of the utopian/anti-utopian debate throughout the period.

Most utopian speculation from 1660 to 1790 was a combination of three basic types: the scientific and technological, modelled on Francis Bacon's *New Atlantis* (1627); imaginary *travel literature, inspired by the voyages of *exploration [37], usually to more virtuous primitive societies; and models of ideal moderate constitutionalist societies, often in the tradition of James Harrington's *Oceana* (1656). Usually deeply critical of existing social and political arrangements in the tradition of Plato and More, the utopias frequently advocated the limitation of property accumulation as a means of restraining the inequality of wealth. Thus Thomas *Reid, for example, contrasted 'the system of private property' to the 'utopian' system.

The literary genre of eighteenth-century British utopianism was greatly influenced by two novels: Daniel Defoe's *Robinson Crusoe* (1719), an 'individualist' fantasy of discovery, self-mastery, and providential salvation; and Jonathan Swift's satirical *Gulliver's Travels* (1726), which lampoons excessive scientific enthusiasm as well as efforts to proclaim the superiority of primitive society, while maintaining 'Country party' ideals. This last belief encompassed a critique of political corruption whereby an ideal of independent country gentlemen monitored both the King's servants and parliament in the interests of cheap government, a citizen militia, and moderate property-owning. Each of these texts established a widely imitated sub-genre, known as the Robinsonade and the Gulliveriana, through which much of the utopian thought of the subsequent century was expressed. The latter, in particular, was routinely used to satirize the often overt primitivism of the utopian tradition (notably in Edmund *Burke's *Vindication of Natural Society*, 1756, and Samuel *Johnson's *Rasselas*, 1759).

Predictably enough, the revolutionary politics of the last quarter of the century witnessed an unprecedented surge of non-religious utopianism rarely sustained previously [see **revolution, 1**]. As the radical orator Henry Redhead Yorke (1772–1813) put it in 1800, 'Astraea, who had been gone up to heaven for so long a time, is now come down to earth again, and the reign of Innocence and Concord is going to be revived among mankind.' The initial impetus fuelling this burst of idealism was the *American Revolution, which soon joined more familar but persistently influential models drawn from Roman, Greek, Venetian, Anglo-Saxon, and Celtic antiquity as an ideal of European utopianism. Radical political thought in Britain was widely inspired by the notion that the more equitable conditions of society in the young United States could be emulated in Europe. Utopian conceptions of America also encouraged schemes for migration, such as S. T. *Coleridge and Robert *Southey's ill-fated plans to set up the model community of *Pantisocracy on the banks of the Susquehanna River in the New World.

The importation of the American model into British politics was particularly associated with the doctrines of Thomas *Paine's immensely popular *Rights of Man* (1791), but the utopian aspects of British radicalism in the 1790s had other important sources as well. The libertarian poetry of provincial poets such as Gray, Collins, and Thomson in the 1740s and 1750s, extolling bardic and indigenous model societies located in the remote British past, remained a continuing source of inspiration for oppositional intellectuals such as John *Thelwall and William *Blake. William *Godwin's *Enquiry Concerning Political Justice* (1793), however, drew more heavily on **Enlightenment** [32] and Dissenting intellectual traditions to envision the removal of external constraints on individual opinion as actually promoting personal morality. The state's influence was thus construed as merely negative; it had to be curtailed. Social equality in Godwin was to be promoted by a voluntary redistribution to the needy and meritorious. The powers of mind might eventually, thought Godwin, bring a great prolongation of life, while mechanical inventions would greatly reduce the burden of necessary labour. Such views were popularized by radicals like Joseph *Gerrald, whose *A Convention the Only Means of Saving Us from Ruin* (1793) imagined a day when the greater public virtue, resulting from *republicanism, would end the need for any system of punishment. As early as the 1780s a more collectivist strand in republicanism was being developed in the writings of Thomas *Spence, whose *agrarian utopia was founded on the nationalization of land and its management at the parish level.

Spence himself participated in the revival of utopia as a literary genre that went along with this kind of political speculation. In *A Supplement to the History of Robinson Crusoe* (1782), the European inhabitants of Crusoe's island, having intermarried with the natives, regret the burdens of the system of private property-holding, and, after abolishing landlords, enjoy a life of comfort and plenty. To this Spence and his followers often added an even older British strand of utopianism associated with the millenarian restoration of an ancient Jewish constitution and homeland. They also saw the 'Jubilee Day' expounded in Leviticus 25, when Moses dramatically freed the slaves and restored the alienated lands of the Hebrew tribes, as a loose revolutionary model for the re-establishment in Britain of a democratic, smallholder, agrarian republic. Many *Spenceans thus sought, in the manner of Blake, to bring about the advent of a new Jerusalem in England's 'green and pleasant land'. Spencean utopias were scarcely disguised manifestos for revolutionary political change; but at least half a dozen less programmatic literary utopias also emerged in response to the early stages of the *French Revolution. The satirical *A Voyage to the Moon* (1793) describes a kingdom of snakes called Barsilia, where the lower orders are afflicted by misery and wretchedness, political corruption, and the avarice of the privileged. *Modern Gulliver's Travels* (1796) attacks the anti-Jacobin *Association for Preserving Liberty and Property against Republicans and Levellers, as well as the corruptions

55

of courtly life, the effects of heavy taxation on the poor, the tendency of the monarchy to foreign conquests and adventurism, existing legal abuses, and the efforts of a loosely disguised Edmund Burke to secure a pension by writing a work entitled 'Beauties of Aristocracy', an allusion to his *Reflections on the Revolution in France* (1790).

The most prominent Paineite constitutionalist scheme cast in utopian form in the 1790s was that of the London physician and radical William Hodgson (1745–1851), *The Commonwealth of Reason* (1795). This takes 'corruption' to be 'the most dreadful evil that can possibly affect either public or private life', and offers a plan of social and constitutional reforms, including ensuring popular sovereignty, political rotation, freedom of religion, speech, and writing, the creation of a popular militia, and the provision of a minimum wage. Godwin's ideas were diffused in utopian form in a work by the liberal intellectual Thomas Northmore (1766–1851). Northmore's *Memoirs of Planetes, or A Sketch of the Laws and Manners of Makar* (1795) rediscovers a primitive society on a Pacific island (following *Cook's and *Bligh's voyages, the favourite venue for such accounts). Here, revolution has established a representative republic, pending the eventual perfectibility of humanity and cessation of the need for government. Private property is preserved, though the laws of primogeniture and entail are abolished. Marriage—a significant source of oppression for Godwin—has become a mere civil institution, with divorce granted after six months' separation. Freedom of religion prevails, and capital punishment has been eliminated. This constitution rests upon restraint, the Makarians being 'almost total strangers to luxury; they are plain and simple in their diet, living chiefly upon the various fruits of the earth, and eating very little animal food'. Their manners are dominated by sincerity and the love of truth. Their women are 'chaste, handsome, and well educated', and, unlike in England, fecundity is regarded as a blessing. As is evident, the rich vein of eighteenth-century scholarship on *mythology [36] and comparative religion was tapped for utopian detail. Fletcher *Christian's mutiny in the Pacific against Captain Bligh and the *Bounty* in 1789 also gave a fillip to imagined communities based around the supposedly natural and sexually free societies of Otaheite or the Tonga isles. *Byron's poem *The Island* (1823), for example, was both anticipated and then imitated by libertarian South Seas utopias published by radicals James Ridgway (*fl.* 1782–1817) and William *Hone.

Imaginary lands closer to home could be deployed in either utopian or dystopian modes. The radical doctor James *Parkinson, writing under the pseudonym of 'Old Hubert', produced scathing satires of 'Bull-land' in the 1790s; while at the end of the decade *Libellus: or, A Brief Sketch of the History of Gotham* (1798) depicted a virtuous and utopian monarchy where the nobility are devoted to public affairs. Here the clergy also embody piety and dispassionate service; and the House of Commons, undistracted by partisanship and disdaining all corruption, is elected by a fair and free franchise (the principles of whose exercise, as in many works of this period, are detailed at length). Manners once again underpin political virtue: 'In no country is every species of vice more rarely to be found than amongst the Gothamites.' Morality is derived from the Bible, and while lapses from virtue such as prostitution occur, they are subject to rational, rather than merely puritanical, regulation. A substantial degree of social equality is enforced by restricting the size of landed estates. Idleness has virtually been banished, and there is toleration for all religions (though not for infidels).

Utopian idealism suffered a severe setback with the defeat of radicalism in the mid-1790s: radical aims were satirized in at least one anti-Jacobin dystopia, John *Reeves's *Publicola: A Sketch of the Times* (1810). Equally important was the publication of the most important modern anti-utopian tract, Thomas *Malthus's *Essay on Population* (1798). Here Godwin was a special target, and vice, in the form of the seemingly inextinguishable desire to procreate, triumphed over virtually every proposal for assisting the poor. Some apocalyptic anti-utopias were constructed with Malthus's ideas partially in mind. *The Last Man, or Omegarus and Syderia* (1806) is one example of a narrative in which human greed, by consuming irreplaceable natural resources, also plays an important role in inciting divine retribution against mankind.

Malthus, however, is blithely disregarded in James *Lawrence's extraordinary *The Empire of the Nairs; or the Rights of Women. A Utopian Romance* (1811), arguably the most important feminist tract between Mary *Wollstonecraft's *Vindication of the Rights of Woman* (1792) and William *Thompson's *Appeal of One-Half the Human Race* (1825). Lawrence recounts, amidst endless adventures illustrating the evils of the existing European system of marriage, the sexual customs of a vibrant South Asian matriarchy on the Malabar coast. This tract in turn exercised a strong influence on Percy *Shelley's *Queen Mab* (1813), a fervently anti-Christian free-love utopia which was later to gain a considerable popular as well as élite readership. Although a more liberal attitude towards marriage, and the insistence that unions be bonded by affection rather than by financial mergers, are pervasive in eighteenth-century utopias, Lawrence and Shelley's pleas for complete sexual freedom, where motherhood of any type was highly rewarded and the concept of 'father' was unknown, went well beyond such modest proposals. Like most of the utopias of discovery, where primitivism is equated with virtue, it is for Lawrence and Shelley the path of 'nature' which forms the basis of a romantic ideal of love. But this equally entails a turning away from the hypocritical dual standard of courtly and chivalric romanticism, with its inflated conception of female virtue.

Both Lawrence and Shelley also drew inspiration from utopian models and genres associated with the East. *Hellenism had long been rivalled by traditions of antiquarian scholarship [see *antiquarianism, 35] and travel which located the source of ancient wisdom and knowledge in Egypt or India. Opprobrious images and accounts of Turkey and Islamic culture dating back from the Crusades were to some extent reversed early in the eighteenth century by the dazzlingly popular impact of English translations of the *Arabian Nights Entertainments*. Its sensational exoticism, in combination with learned studies of Eastern culture from poet-philologist Sir William *Jones and Sanskrit scholar Sir Charles Wilkins (c.1749–1836), helped to inspire the Eastern poetic utopias of Byron, Shelley, and Thomas *Moore. Egypt, Persia, China, and the Islamic dynasties of northern India become real or fabulous sources for alternative communities and polities. An equally powerful Eastern dystopian model, however, derived from translations of the work of Constantin *Volney. His *Travels in Syria* and his enormously influential freethinking tract depicting a magical voyage through the past and future, *The Ruins; or a Survey of the Revolutions of Empires* (1791), contrasted the residues of great classical and Eastern civilizations such as Palmyra in Syria, which he depicted as ruined by religious fanaticism and war, with a golden future in which a democratically organized people lived and ruled themselves according to the laws of nature.

The revival of the political reform movement in the postwar era aided a resuscitation of such political and constitutional utopianism. One of the most prominent *Whig radicals of the early 1790s, the lawyer Thomas *Erskine, wrote *Armata* (1817) to reinterpret the British response to the American and French revolutions. His aim was to further reform causes, constitutional and legal as well as moral and social, while avoiding Spencean extremism; the utopia thus became a relatively risk-free forum for political speculation. Here it is constitutional degeneration through the vicious selfishness of the ruling classes and failure of the old aristocracy to uphold its ancient duties which has weakened Britain and left the nation open, through heavy taxation and an oppressive national debt, to the same scenario which occasioned the fall of the *ancien régime* in France. Even so the liberal utopia of universal prosperity based on the free market is also present at times. Pauperism, writes Erskine, 'would soon entirely disappear', if the mites of the poor were taxed equally with land and moneyed wealth, if savings schemes were used by labourers, if only the deserving poor were given relief, and if the existing system of ranks were reformed rather than abolished, 'the multitude' being 'more governed by visible and permanent distinctions, than by reflections on what is wise or just'. 'Equality' is thus seen in Erskine's utopia as much less useful than fine gradations of rank, which have been the principal cause of Britain's stability but which are now threatened by increasing impoverishment—although, as a sop to republican egalitarianism, barbers and aristocrats dress alike to inhibit the passion for social envy.

Simplicity is also central to the considerably more radical republican colony set up at the centre of the United States in *New Britain* (1820). There only water is drunk with meals; each member of the population farms and has a trade; labour is confined to four hours daily, and is based upon a principle of 'moderation and equity'. None possesses more land than is 'requisite for comfortable subsistence'. Money and barter have been abolished; and labour and trade are governed by the principle that it is wrong 'for a man to acquire all he can'. Machinery is widely used, but only where it decreases labour. Elected officials are unpaid; there is universal free education; and the death penalty has been abolished. 'Patriotism' has been replaced by 'philanthropy', and *Deism is the dominant religion. *New Britain* is one of the last republican utopias (probably influenced by Godwin) in which an agrarian law and the abolition of commerce ensure considerable social equality, with the final aim being 'to bring mankind as near as we possibly can to that state, in which they would be, if they were sufficiently virtuous to live in a society without laws'.

Out of the decline of the American republican utopia, which seemed increasingly less ideal as the realities of inequality in the United States became more apparent, emerged *socialism, which, in the period before 1848, has been understood as 'utopian' in several senses. First, it inherited those ideas of economic regulation and the common ownership of substantial resources associated with the tradition of More's *Utopia*. Second, it aimed to transform society slowly and peacefully, by the example of superior experimental communities, appealing thereby to the higher ethical interests of all members of society, including the property-owning classes. Finally, it envisioned a dramatic improvement in human relations, including the abolition of war, of exploitative systems of trade, and of the domination of man over woman, white over non-white, and the powerful over the weak, resulting from the diffusion of its principles.

The term 'utopian socialism', developed later in the writings of Marx and Engels, was used to distinguish their 'scientific socialism' from, for instance, *Saint-Simonianism in France and Owenism in Britain. The distinction was primarily based on the faith such movements showed in public opinion as a means of changing society. The appeal to all classes, on the basis of reason and justice, appeared historically naïve to Marx and Engels who argued that only class struggle, derived from a 'scientific' theory of history, could bring about socialism in the late nineteenth century. From 1820 to 1850, Robert *Owen tirelessly pushed his vision of rural communities in which needs, rather than wants, would be satisfied, and in which machinery would be introduced only to lighten the burden of human labour. Antipathy to urban growth had been a constant in utopian thought. More had commended the rotation of population between country and city, and as recently as the 1790s the Godwinian *An Essay on Civil Government* had proposed a limitation of cities to a population of 20,000. Owen's communities were to have only a few thousand inhabitants, and thus, he hoped, the sense of immediacy and intimacy of a village could be preserved. His communitarianism was thus chiefly rooted, like the agrarian ideals of Spence, William *Cobbett, and the great *Chartist leader Feargus O'Connor (1794–1855), in a pre-industrial past in which most of the population thrived on the land rather than festered in the wen of demonic cities. The rural ideal in early socialism is typified in one of the better-known literary utopias of the Owenite movement, philanthropist John Minter Morgan's (1782–1854) *Hampden in the Nineteenth Century* (1834), which verges occasionally on nostalgic *pastoralism. Socialist communitarianism collapsed after the failure in 1845 of the Owenite colony at Queenwood, but even Marx and Engels continued to support (through the 1848 revolution and the *Communist Manifesto*) the notion of transplanting the unemployed to country 'palaces' which would combine the advantages of rural and urban life.

Retrospectively what seems chiefly 'utopian' in the early socialist vision was the notion that modern society could be bypassed, and urbanization and the accumulation of wealth regulated by purely voluntary principles of moral restraint, without a substantial degree of coercion. Owenism never acknowledged the need for the latter, but coercion was finally to usurp the humanitarian elements in the 'scientific' socialism of Marx, Engels, and their successors. The Owenite ideal of 'community' relied instead upon the vigilance of one's neighbour, rather than the secret police, to ensure conformity to prevailing mores.

The most impressive literary utopia produced by the Owenite movement was John Francis Bray's (1809–97) *A Voyage to Utopia* (1842). Here the contrast is between a 'semi-barbarous nation', Brydone, and the narrator's home country, Utopia. Londo is a mass of congested humanity at each other's throats in 'one continual scene of turmoil'. An enormous weight of taxation benefits the 'aristocs' and 'Kin-kin', but oppresses the majority of distressed 'commos' living a hand-to-mouth existence and suffering under long hours of labour and poor working conditions. Their sole source of amusement is dissipation in 'fire-water houses'. Religious superstition and obscurantism based on the worship of 'Fe-fo-fum' prevail. Utopian worship by contrast is unitarian and pantheistic. Women in Brydone are held in thrall by laws which restrict their property ownership and succession rights, and by customs which limit their freedom and education. Corrupt governments propelled by worthless leaders export aggression and slaughter with weapons unknown in Utopia. Blacks are enslaved, and the neighbouring island of Erino is held in subjection. No nation conquered by the Brydons is regarded as anything more than 'a field on which the aristocs may pasture, and its people are transformed into beasts of burden, to toil for task-masters who know no mercy', the benefits of civilization never being extended to subject peoples. Internal disputes benefit only 'sharkos' who prey on the ignorant and unwary, while the greatest villains escape punishment entirely. A rationalist, cosmopolitan, enlightened egalitarianism is thus the basis for the critique of British institutions. Moreover, this critique is extended to 'Amrico', a former colony of Brydone. Here the narrator expects to find a 'second Utopia', and is surprised to discover that 'the great and small aristocs, with the sharkos and pestos, although of a somewhat different breed to those in Brydone, were equally as rapacious and unscrupulous, and devoured among them almost as much as was in the other case consumed by the Kin-kin and his soldos and polos.'

The rejection of modernity in the first decades of the nineteenth century also assumed non-socialist forms. Conservative critics of both *democracy [3] and unlimited *laissez-faire* sought refuge in images of a more virtuous, stable past where Greek, Roman, and Anglo-Saxon models continued to have some appeal, though the era of Sparta and the ancient Jewish constitution seems finally to have passed. Many in fact took the past century as their principal focus. In his *Colloquies of Society* (1829) Robert Southey, notably, evoked a nostalgia for earlier ages, and a more sympathetic treatment of the poor. Reaching further back, Thomas *Carlyle helped inspire a medieval revival in his *Past and Present* (1843), which was carried forward in the Victorian period by John Ruskin (1819–1900) and William Morris (1834–96).

The advent of *Catholic emancipation in 1828 spawned an explicitly anti-Catholic dystopia centred on *The History of Bullanbee and Clinkataboo: Two Recently Discovered Islands in the Pacific* (1828). The inhabitants of these South Sea islands are industrious, brave in war, grave and reflective without becoming melancholy, generous and liberal, humble and disdaining of servility. Their needs are limited; they trade (solely with Japan) without desiring luxury or superfluity. They are still prey to warfare, to outbreaks of public violence, to crime, and to the pangs of romantic desire unfulfilled. But a sudden change of religion converts 'this Eden into a land of strife', for the new religion, clearly modelled on Catholicism, is superstitious and corrupt in the extreme. Its priests manufacture relics, and are distinguished by their greed and utter disbelief in their professed principles. Ironically, this conservative anti-Catholicism thus reconnects with the anticlericalism of earlier radical Enlightenment utopias like Volney's *Ruins* (1791).

A second occasion for conservative warnings of Britain's future was the Great *Reform Bill (1832). *Great Britain in 1841* (1831) prophesies that it would bring the confiscation of church livings and university places, the decline of commerce, the diffusion of religious scepticism, the advent of mob democracy, the destruction of agriculture following free trade in corn, and eventually the collapse of society into civil war. In *The Mummy: A Tale of the Twenty-Second Century* (1827), similarly, the passion for equality has brought democracy, but the desire for work has evaporated, anarchy results, and the ancient nobility are recalled to restore order to society.

The best Tory dystopia of the period is Benjamin Disraeli's (1804–81) *The Voyage of Captain Popanilla* (1827), whose main target is Benthamite *utilitarianism, the central axiom of which is described as being 'that everything can be made perfect at once, without time, without experience, without practice, and without preparation'. But Disraeli also examines the growing early-nineteenth-century predominance of the notions of material progress. Here, in a strikingly proto-ecological satire, the notion that primitive societies acquire meaning only through 'development', that only through cutting down forests can we 'discover the utility of timber', are brilliantly portrayed in the contrast between the primitive isle of Fantaisie and the 'developed' Vraibleusia. Whiggish political economy's portrayal of 'competition' as an end in itself is lampooned, as are the national debt and paper money, the aristocracy's greed in keeping up corn prices artificially, the manners of the *nouveaux riches*, and the dangers of overproduction. More often, however, conservative social impulses assumed dystopic forms, as in John Trotter's (1788–1852) *Travels to Phrenologasto* (1829), which satirizes the scientific pretensions of the age. The claims of *phrenology, and the attempt to guide behaviour solely by 'reason' rather than by feelings, are especially lampooned. Here all individuals are assigned jobs on the basis of a national phrenological evaluation of their talents, with chaotic results. Similar futurological themes are canvassed in several light, adventuresome romances interspersed with ripping yarns, such as *The Mummy* and *The Triumph of Woman* (1848). Though evincing little serious utopian intent, these foreshadow a long dystopian tradition in warning, like Mary *Shelley's *Frankenstein* (1818), of the dangers of a hubristic scientific tampering with the mysteries of nature.

*Liberalism, too, was capable of moving in a distinctly utopian direction, and of doubting the optimistic vision of an unlimited commercial or scientifically material society. John Stuart *Mill, for example, was by the time of the revolutions of 1848 the most popular classical political economist of his day. But he then broke from the Ricardian tradition [see David *Ricardo] in his *Principles of Political Economy* (1848), confessing that economic laws might be historically limited, and bravely giving greater credence to the possibility that some forms of socialism might foreshadow a superior, more cultured, and less narrowly selfish society. Mill also proposed limiting the right of private property in land, and even suggested that a 'stationary state' might some day be reached in which population would no longer expand, affluence would be more widely shared, and greater stress would be laid on mental, moral, and social progress.

Other, less well-known liberal and radical utopias of this period likewise stop short of socialism. In Henry Forest's *A Dream of Reform* (1848), the workday in 'Philotopia' has been reduced to eight hours, factories have been removed from dwelling-places, leisure and education for all classes are the norm, and cultural activities are subsidized by the government. Cities are built to accord with principles of order and cleanliness, and with efficient sewers and provision of clean water. The monarchy is elective, hereditary titles have been abolished, and political partisanship is unknown. Prostitution has not been abolished, but women can enter many trades and professions, and wealthier classes take 'the initiative in cultivating a healthier and higher tone of morality amongst the female portion of our community'. Lady Mary Fox's prescient *An Account of an Expedition to the Interior of New Holland* (1837) imagines eleven federated colonies of Europeans ranging from hereditary monarchies to republics. Similarly, the pickpocket George *Barrington and other ex-convict chroniclers were to testify, in a burgeoning genre of Botany Bay voyages and apocryphal settler accounts, that a penal society on the other side of the world could hold out the promise of utopian paradise.

Utopianism in the Romantic age thus remains a discourse on corruption and degeneration on the one hand and the virtues of simplicity on the other. An epoch which witnessed the greatest diffusion of luxuries to the lower orders was, however, bound to weigh very critically proposals for reversion to simpler societies. Very little socialist writing and very few utopias appear in Britain during the affluent and complacent decades between 1850 and 1880. Thereafter—as in the 1640s, the 1790s, and the period from 1820 to 1845—it was the issue of crushing poverty which induced a profound utopian and socialist revival.

Claeys, G., ed., *Utopias of the British Enlightenment*, Cambridge, 1994; ed., *Modern British Utopias 1700–1850*, London, 1997; ed., *Restoration and Augustan Utopias*, New York, 1998; Davis, J. C., *Utopia and the Ideal Society: A Study of English Utopian Writing, 1516–1700*, Cam-bridge, 1981; Goodwin, B., & Taylor, K., *The Politics of Utopia*, London, 1983; Morton, A. L., *The English Utopia*, London, 1952; Sargent, L. T., *British and American Utopian Literature, 1516–1975: A Bibliography*, New York, 1988.

· II ·

REORDERING SOCIAL
AND PRIVATE WORLDS

10 · RELIGION R. K. WEBB

The structural foundations of religion in the British Isles are sunk in a terminological swamp. In 1736 William Warburton (1698–1779), a future Bishop of Gloucester, published *The Alliance between Church and State*, in which he set out the essential terms of the relationship. As he saw it, the ruler would 'establish'—that is make official and supported by the civil power—the religion of the majority of his subjects; the two powers would then enter upon a compact defining the precise obligations of each.

The Church of England, which assuredly claimed the allegiance of most English men and women, was in theory the ecclesiastical parallel to civil society. Under the governance of the king, there were ecclesiastical and civil legislatures, ecclesiastical and civil laws and taxes, ecclesiastical and civil courts, and, accordingly, a subject who rejected the Church could rightly be deprived of some of his privileges as citizen: hence Warburton's defence of the Test Acts of 1673 and 1678, which kept Roman Catholics from holding office under the Crown or sitting in parliament. Protestants who refused to conform to the Church of England were similarly affected with respect to office-holding but were not barred from parliament, while the Corporation Act of 1661 excluded both Catholics and Nonconformists from municipal corporations, unless they qualified by taking communion in an *Anglican church.

In fact that alliance, which Warburton held to be mutually advantageous, was more than a little unbalanced. The twenty-six Anglican bishops sat of right in the House of Lords, where in the middle quarters of the eighteenth century they formed a generally dependable pro-government block; by the same token, the clergy were ineligible to vote for or to serve as members of the House of Commons. But the Church's own parliament, convocation (divided into separate convocations for the two provinces of Canterbury and York), lost its principal claim to existence when its right to tax the clergy was surrendered to parliament shortly after the Restoration. It was allowed to transact business only in the fractious years between 1701 and 1717; thereafter, with one futile exception, it did not meet again until 1855. By the mid-nineteenth century church courts had lost all their ancient jurisdiction over lay persons. The civil power continued, however, to enforce the Church's right to certain incomes, such as tithe for support of the clergy and church rates for the upkeep of church buildings and churchyards, a right much changed and eroded in the nineteenth century.

The intrinsically problematical character of Warburton's analysis—which he had insisted was rooted in the order of nature—is underscored by the ways in which establishment elsewhere in Britain and Ireland was realized. The Presbyterian Church of Scotland, descending from the sixteenth-century Reformation, was governed (again under the King, who adhered to different religions north and south of the border) through a hierarchy of mixed lay and clerical bodies culminating in the General Assembly, an arrangement confirmed following the *Glorious Revolution of 1688–9; Scottish Episcopalians, who to the distress of their Anglican counterparts in England had been firmly discriminated against, were given the right to use the English liturgy only in 1712, when an Act of Toleration was passed by the parliament of the new United Kingdom of Great Britain [see *toleration].

Across the Irish Sea, the Church of Ireland, too, was Protestant, although (contrary to Warburtonian theory) the overwhelming majority of the inhabitants were fiercely Roman

Catholic, while in the northern provinces a majority of Presbyterians, resulting from early-seventeenth-century Scottish plantations and later immigration, led a beleaguered existence that was to have profound effects in the distant future. The Church of Ireland ministered to a tiny minority of mostly English residents through a parochial system supported by taxes levied on the entire population and an overblown hierarchy readily available for political and ecclesiastical patronage. From 1801, when the Irish and British parliaments combined under the *Act of Union passed the previous year, the two churches were also merged. Meanwhile, the political and economic discrimination that weighed so heavily on Irish Catholics at least down to 1829 intensified their sense of religious identity and exacerbated political as well as religious relations with England.

In Wales, the Church had been incorporated into the Church of England when the principality became a part of the larger nation in 1536, but its ministers presided over a population increasingly alienated by culture and language. Although by the middle of the nineteenth century the Church of England began to act more responsibly towards such Welsh communicants as had not joined the highly successful Dissenting sects, the demand for disestablishment became a gauge of nationalism and a pressing political issue for decades until, in 1920, the four Welsh dioceses were separated into a voluntary Church in Wales.

The principal institutional structures of English religion in the mid-eighteenth century were the Church of England and the loose grouping of denominations outside the Church known collectively as Nonconformity or Dissent, destined to play a significant role in both the revolutionary and the Romantic insurgencies. Roman Catholics may have been an overwhelming majority in Ireland and a significant presence in the Highlands of Scotland, but in England they were a small minority, perhaps 80,000 in 1770, with disproportionate representation among old aristocratic and gentry families who had the standing to survive the pervasive anti-Catholic prejudice endemic in most of the population. Unobtrusive and deeply concerned to demonstrate loyalty, English Catholics were numerically insignificant until swelling Irish immigration and some dramatic conversions from the Church of England changed the character of their Church in the first half of the nineteenth century.

So, too, English *Jews, readmitted to the country only in the mid-seventeenth century, remained a tiny minority in the eighteenth, subject to obloquy and legal restriction, until growing prosperity and the immigration of many poor Jews from the Continent at the end of the century began to alter their community and its place in English society.

Principled rejection of one or another aspect of the liturgy and organization of the Church of England ran back at least to the period of the sixteenth-century Reformation. In the rigorous but protean guise of Puritanism, it was an important dynamic in the Civil Wars of the 1640s, and briefly triumphed when the Church of England was suppressed during the Commonwealth in the 1650s. When the Church was re-established in the Restoration of 1660, some gestures were made toward the possibility of accommodation or 'comprehension', but parliament eventually carried the Act of Uniformity of 1662, which required of ministers complete and unfeigned acceptance of the Book of Common Prayer as revised in that year, on pain of deprivation, and insisted on re-ordination of those clergymen who had entered the ministry during the suppression of the Church. Their inability to accept either or both of these stipulations forced more than 900 ministers from their livings, a number at least doubled by earlier deprivations and forced resignations from universities and schools.

In formally abandoning the old Christian ideal of unity, the Act of Uniformity brought Dissent into existence, but additional legislation penalizing both Dissenting ministers and laymen and sporadic, often severe, persecution over the next quarter-century made clear the determination of lay and ecclesiastical authorities that Dissent would be a short-lived phenomenon. But persecution did not work, and in 1689, following the revolution in the preceding year which brought William and Mary to the throne, the Act of Toleration gave legal recognition to Dissenting congregations which complied with certain restrictive standards.

In the early eighteenth century, Dissenters accounted for around 6 per cent of the population, unevenly scattered about the country; there was thought to be (and probably was) a falling-off down to mid-century. A brave show of Dissenting unity after 1688 had quickly collapsed, but clear denominational lines were long in being established. In actuality or in tendency, there were three principal groupings: roughly in order of wealth, education, and social standing, they were Presbyterians (differing significantly from their Scottish or Irish counterparts), Congregationalists (or Independents), and Baptists.

A fourth Dissenting group, the Society of Friends or *Quakers, had played a highly visible, sometimes violent, role after their emergence in the mid-seventeenth century, and demonstrated remarkable cohesion during the persecution of which they were the principal victims. After toleration, they quickly moved to secure certain special privileges, such as affirming instead of swearing oaths; but in the eighteenth century they retreated generally into quietism and isolation, enforced by distinctive speech and dress and by a rigid prohibition against 'marrying out'. As a result of these peculiarities and of their tendency to splinter, the Quakers declined in numbers though not necessarily in significance, and their rejection of a formal ministry and of liturgy in favour of silent meetings remained a steady challenge to other Protestant traditions in English religion, as did their emphasis on direct communication with the divine through the 'inner light'.

In the seventeenth century, the 'three denominations' which historians have come to call 'Old Dissent' were united by their adherence to Calvinist theology, with its emphasis on predestination and on a tiny spiritual élite whose salvation was secured by divine decree. Arminian views—tending to emphasize the availability of salvation to all and to stress the efficacy of good works—began to take hold among the Presbyterians, as they had somewhat earlier among Anglicans. The rapid spread of rationalistic views after the middle of the seventeenth century had led to considerable debate in the Church of England about the doctrine of the Trinity, but it was only in the early eighteenth century that the so-called Arian view that Jesus was created and that His divinity was subordinate to that of God the Father began to penetrate Dissent and after mid-century to grow among more progressive thinkers, again chiefly Presbyterians, into insistence on the fully human nature of Jesus (the doctrine of Socinianism).

These heterodox tendencies, nourished in a few of the *Dissenting academies that had grown up to educate young men excluded by their Dissent from the universities, led gradually to estrangement from those who continued to hold orthodox beliefs and to the clearer definition of denominational boundaries. Many Presbyterian congregations splintered, with their orthodox members moving usually to Congregationalism, while the remaining English Presbyterians underwent a gradual absorption into the new denomination of *Unitarianism, which also claimed a small remnant of the Baptists who had from their beginnings held to the possibility of universal redemption.

Unitarians retained the traditional leadership that had been exercised by Presbyterians over Dissent as a whole, notably in the Dissenting deputies, established in the early eighteenth century to protect the rights of Dissenters and, if possible, to advance them. The deputies did little more than hold ground already taken, until in 1813 they obtained an Act extending toleration to Unitarians, which had been denied under the Act of 1689. They also played an important part in the repeal of the Test and Corporation Acts in 1828, which removed the seventeenth-century impediments to participation of Dissenting laymen in national and local government. But by that time Unitarian Dissenting leadership was under challenge from the newly confident and burgeoning ranks of orthodox Dissent. Not only did Unitarians lose their traditional primacy, but they came close to losing the chapels and trust funds they had inherited from their Presbyterian forebears and were rescued only through the political clout—the small Dissenting representation in parliament was predominantly Unitarian—that secured passage of the Dissenting Chapels Act of 1844.

When William and Mary came to the throne in 1689, some Churchmen, among them the Archbishop of Canterbury, could not bring themselves to break their oaths to James II, King by divine right, and to swear fealty to monarchs ruling by a less clear and arguably parliamentary title. These so-called non-jurors survived in dwindling numbers as a schismatic church for most of the eighteenth century, but early on, in alliance with some High Churchmen within the establishment, they gave spirited battle against Dissenters and the increasingly entrenched *Whig bishops. Moreover, there was strong sentiment, particularly among the country clergy, in favour of a narrow construal of the Church and even in support of the exiled Stuart dynasty.

While the enmity between the *Tory and Whig parties, running back to the 1670s, was resolved politically in favour of the Whigs after 1714, Tory sentiment in the country remained powerful. The official line of Church leaders was that toleration of Dissent was a firmly established part of the constitution, though there was little wish to extend Dissenting privileges further, but among the parish clergy who had to cope directly with the sometimes unsettling effects of Dissent, a narrow exclusiveness held sway as a major ingredient in a submerged Toryism. Grateful for what privileges they had received, Dissenters after 1714 were generally loyal supporters of the House of Hanover and of successive Whig governments.

Conservatively minded Churchmen took aim not only at Dissent and Whig politicians on and off the episcopal bench but at doctrinal developments as well. The rationalism that eventually became domiciled in certain segments of Dissent had made much greater inroads in the Church much earlier. The potent alliance of rationalism and science clearly in evidence within a few years of the Restoration ran in several directions. To some convinced rationalists, adherents of what came to be known as *Deism, it seemed that the religion of nature taught everything people needed to know, not only about the physical universe but about moral questions as well; accordingly, Revelation could be dispensed with. In the first half of the eighteenth century Deism was the great bogey to the devout, liberal and conservative alike, a fear compounded by the tendency of many Deists to political opposition. But not all rationalists were Deists, and increasing numbers of Churchmen came to adopt a rationalistic approach to understanding both nature and the *Bible.

Firmly planted in a tradition of tolerance and adaptation that ran back to Erasmus and other Continental scholars, these soon came to be known as Latitudinarians—from the nickname 'Latitude-men'. Like all such portmanteau words, Latitudinarianism covers many complexities and differences and varies over time, but it did claim the allegiance of many of the best intellects of the age. Latitudinarians formed friendships and alliances with heterodox Dissenters, and in time some of them actually turned Unitarian. The first openly Unitarian chapel in the country was established in 1774 in Essex Street, London, by Theophilus Lindsey (1723–1808), who had been vicar of Catterick in Yorkshire and who, like many liberally inclined Anglicans, was discouraged by the failure of an effort in the Feathers Tavern petition of 1772 to persuade parliament to relax the requirement that the Anglican clergy subscribe to the Thirty-Nine Articles, the Church's basic doctrinal statement, and to substitute a simple declaration of belief in the Bible as the source of truth. Latitudinarians were particularly well represented in Cambridge, where they spearheaded the unsuccessful drive for university reform, and by the 1780s formed an impressive, though gradually diminishing, phalanx of advocates of political and parliamentary reform.

In the 1760s the efforts of the young George III to assert the prerogatives of the *monarchy he was convinced had been frittered away by his grandfather, George II, provoked much resentment, which soon developed into an oppositional cast of mind and created a myth of unchecked royal power. Among some advanced thinkers like the pioneering chemist and Unitarian minister Joseph *Priestley or his good friend the Arian minister and philosopher

Richard *Price, monarchical aggression seemed paralleled by ecclesiastical aggression aimed at limiting or even rolling back Dissenting gains. Secure in his new-found Unitarianism after 1768, Priestley advanced a comprehensive view of religious liberty, which insisted that large areas of human experience, notably religion and *education [17], were better left to the individual freed from any collective interference, and many liberal-minded Dissenters soon came to share this way of thinking.

Such confident argument put forward Dissent as a set of principles involving liberty, independence, openness, and rational progress, and tended to stigmatize even friends and allies within the Church as venal compromisers. It also fed and was fed by a 'Commonwealth tradition', long buried in Dissenting memory and revived with some forgetfulness of the narrow dogmatism it had displayed a century earlier. The onset of the *American Revolution shook the traditional loyalty of many Dissenters, who took heart from the creation of a new nation 'conceived in liberty', and from the seemingly bright promise of reform in Britain in the 1780s. There was, accordingly, widespread enthusiasm for the *French Revolution, at least in its early stages.

Once *war [2] began in 1793, however, and the French Revolution seemed to pose a threat to stability within Britain itself, this forward movement was halted and then reversed, a shift anticipated by Edmund *Burke in his *Reflections on the Revolution in France* (1790), a direct reply to a sermon by Richard Price glorifying the Revolution of 1688. A few hardy souls became more and more radicalized—Priestley, the eccentric Cambridge classicist Gilbert Wakefield (1756–1801), and a number of students in the more liberal of the Dissenting academies. But the Birmingham riots of 1791, in which the two Unitarian chapels, several houses belonging to Dissenters, and Priestley's house, library, and laboratory were burnt, showed the depth of the reaction, and Unitarians were long in recovering their nerve and optimism from the disasters of the 1790s. Priestley emigrated to America in 1794, and so did a number of other Unitarians, while still more thought seriously about it as an escape from an England beyond reforming.

While the Deist champions of the early part of the century had appeared vanquished, scepticism or frank unbelief made their way quietly in higher intellectual circles. The most eminent eighteenth-century instance was the highly influential—and much controverted—philosopher David *Hume, but such views survived the French Revolution to surface in the scepticism or outright atheism of philosophers like Jeremy *Bentham and James *Mill, or of poets like Lord *Byron and Percy *Shelley.

Anti-clerical views also made considerable headway in an awakening popular opinion, drawing on old resentments of clerical presumption and on a new awareness of abuses in the administration of the Church. Clergy with their eyes on promotion and emoluments; absentees who turned the spiritual care of their parishioners over to ill-paid curates; the widespread practice of holding more than one living: all these defects were looked on with genuine concern by church reformers, but little progress was to be made in remedying them until the 1830s. In the countryside, tithe was particularly vexing because it was assessed in kind and offered the occasion for bitter disputes between clergymen and farmers, while church rates, an obligation of all occupiers of premises whether Anglican or not, were an added grievance, along with other fees exacted by the clergy. Even one of the presumed advantages of the parochial system, that it secured the presence of a gentleman in every parish, could provoke egalitarian hostility, the more so as increasing numbers of clergymen began to act as magistrates and so became involved with the imposition of often harsh legal penalties such as those visited on the Swing agricultural rioters after 1831 [see *riots], and as most Anglican ministers rallied to the anti-radical cause, seeking to reinforce social stability through loyalist *sermons, pamphlets, and condescending parochial effort.

With the outbreak of the French Revolution and the stimulus it gave to working-class

12. Caricature by George Cruikshank, 1819, lashing the popular radical publisher Richard Carlile as a fomenter of satanism through his revival of the Deistic writings of Thomas Paine.

radicalism in England, vulgar Deism or 'infidelism' gained new appeal, extending even to deliberate blasphemy. Clergymen increasingly became targets for the scorn and ridicule of radical pamphleteers and *satirists. When the Church reformers set to work in earnest in the 1830s, they were acutely aware that the reputation of the Church had been brought to a low point and that, unless corrective action were taken, disestablishment might well follow. Indeed, in some respects, the Church's position had already been diminished by two important parliamentary acts. The repeal of the Test and Corporation Acts in 1828 essentially proclaimed Dissenting equality within the constitution—though many other discriminations remained—while so-called *Catholic emancipation in 1829, a response to an Irish agitation that came to a head in that year, allowed Roman Catholics to sit in parliament, thus breaking a Protestant monopoly on legislative power.

In the early 1830s, attempts were made to reform the bloated Church of Ireland by suppressing some bishoprics and diverting the savings to secular purposes such as education. Not entirely successful, and attended with profound political and religious consequences, this project nevertheless made plain the power that the secular state could exercise over what many Churchmen believed was the sole province of the Church.

Victorian Christians looked back on the worldly, unreformed churches of the eighteenth century with palpable disdain. They were even more scornful of the rationalism of that century, which struck them as cold and inimical to a properly aesthetic and emotional approach to religion. Denominational lines in Old Dissent had hardened, while a gradual resurgence of Anglican exclusiveness and a revival of patristic learning gave new life to the long-isolated High Church party. Preachers and writers who were heirs to these developments, and most historians since, have given less credit than is due to the eighteenth-century sources of later religious currents, to the compatibility of rationalism and devotion, and to the continuing influence of rationalism at the very centre of nineteenth-century life.

The last point need be touched on only briefly. The remarkable conquests of nineteenth-century science grew out of the assumptions and methods of preceding generations, and it is increasingly appreciated that the old reliance on natural theology survived well into the latter part of the nineteenth century. Many men of science took for granted that nature and Revelation could not ultimately conflict, given a proper understanding of both [see **natural philosophy, 34**]. But that implied a steady application of critical study to the Bible, an enterprise launched by the Deists and gradually developed among Latitudinarians and Unitarians.

German biblical criticism, with its careful attention to textual accuracy and historical context, was slow to penetrate English awareness, but on two occasions it did so explosively: the publication of a translation of D. F. Strauss's *Leben Jesu* by Mary Ann Evans, the future George Eliot, in 1846; and the appearance in 1860 of *Essays and Reviews*, in which seven Anglican academics and scholars assessed the recent critical trends. As an early response to this challenge, some religious people from the 1820s began to insist on a strictly literal interpretation of the entire Bible, but a sharp division of believers on this point did not become important until well into the twentieth century.

A decisive influence on religion in the eighteenth century was the reaction against the 'immorality' of the Restoration period which preceded the related but much later and better-known phenomenon of *Evangelicalism by almost a century. One manifestation of this moral revolution was the founding of a number of societies to forward specific goals: many societies for the *reformation of manners and, at the very turn of the century, the Society for Propagating the Gospel in Foreign Parts and the Society for Promoting Christian Knowledge. The last-named stood at the centre of the notable movement for the establishment of charity schools to bring learning to children at more humble social levels than those catered to by the long-established grammar schools. Although the impetus of this broad movement was not maintained at the initial level, these institutions survived and tied in with the extraordinary multiplication of agencies for social welfare and reform at the beginning of the nineteenth century [see *poverty, 12].

Equally important was the widespread practice of private devotions throughout the eighteenth century, which united households and groups of friends in worship. Important research has pointed to the intensity of religious feeling to be found in the Midlands town of Northampton and particularly in the Castle Hill congregation, where the great Evangelical figure Philip Doddridge (1702–51) ministered from 1729 to his death. But while Doddridge, like many others, wrote books to guide individual and family devotions, evidence suggests that the primary obligation ran the other way: that conditions in Doddridge's congregation allowed him to exercise a ministry notable for its sensitivity to the spiritual state of individual men and women, as the students in Doddridge's academy admiringly noted.

Near Doddridge's Northampton lived William Law (1686–1761), a non-juror whose *Serious Call to a Devout and Holy Life* (1743–4) was one of the great inspirational books of the century. At the centre of a small group of devout friends, Law became more and more deeply concerned with mystical experience akin to that evidenced among the Quakers, and he was often read in conjunction with the mystical writings of Jacob Boehme [see *Behmenism]. No doubt, Law's peculiar isolation as a non-juror contributed to the intensity of his religious feeling and experience, but it is to be found as well in High Church circles within the Church of England.

Such a background helped to form John *Wesley. Samuel Wesley, his father, was a High Church parson in remote Lincolnshire; Susanna Wesley, his mother, was the daughter of a prominent Dissenter. From this earnest and devout household, John and his brothers drew their determination to undertake the systematic practice of piety at Oxford, both in good works, such as *prison visiting, and in personal devotion pursued with such rigour and

precision that their contemporaries unkindly dubbed them 'methodists' [see *Methodism].
On his way to a brief career as a *missionary in the new colony of Georgia, John Wesley fell in
with a group of *Moravians, a German pietistic sect founded a decade earlier by Count
Nicholas Ludwig von Zinzendorf. When he returned to London in 1738, Wesley attended a
meeting at a Moravian chapel and there underwent the spiritual conversion that drove his
mission to convert the British Isles, and particularly those among its inhabitants whom the
regular forms of Christian worship were failing to reach. Much of his success has been interpreted as a response to the failure of the Church of England to adapt to the titanic new forces of
urban power and *industrialization [14] during this period.

Among Latitudinarians, and perhaps more among austere civic Anglicans concerned with
church discipline in country parishes, Wesley's brand of religion came to be dismissed or
reviled as *enthusiasm, the sense of direct communication with God without the need for
churchly mediation, especially because early Methodism often served as a slipway for
*millenarian prophets. Wesley remained an intensely loyal son of the Church, however, and it
was only when pulpits were closed to him on his gruelling travels about the country that he
took to preaching in the fields, a practice immediately anticipated by the revivalist George
*Whitefield and at longer range by Welsh revivalists early in the century [see *field preachers].
But Wesley's followers were often driven by their new-found sense of sin into extreme emotional manifestations which only increased the distrust of conventional Churchmen, and
which helped to fuel the violence that was often directed against Wesley himself.

The Methodist societies were closely organized into 'classes', which sought to discipline
the individual search for salvation and to prevent backsliding; they also provided training
grounds for a generation of lay preachers. In time, the inveterate hostility of the Church to this
new manifestation of spirituality within its ranks led Methodists to consider leaving the
Church behind, an idea intolerable to Wesley. But after his death in 1791 there was a fairly rapid
distancing of the Wesleyans from Anglicanism, and by early in the new century Methodism
had to all intents and purposes become a new denomination. It showed an early tendency to
division, in part a response to the dictatorial ways of Wesley's successor, Jabez Bunting
(1779–1858), but also a reflection of differing social status and ambitions. This variety of
Methodists makes up the historical category of 'New Dissent'.

The highly personal, conversionist nature of Wesley's movement, with its emphasis on the
death of Christ for the sins of men, had wide repercussions. The new style took hold in the
orthodox ranks of Old Dissent, leading to very rapid growth and to a new aggressiveness,
directed against the Unitarians on one hand and against the Church on the other: it was among
the Evangelical Dissenters that the agitation for disestablishment was launched with new
intensity in the 1840s. Yet another source of division appeared among the Quakers, where an
Evangelical movement dominated the connection for much of the nineteenth century.

But the Church itself did not remain unaffected. An Evangelical movement also grew up
within the Anglican communion and, giving a new meaning to the term 'Low Church', revivified a Church that had remained firmly within its inherited civic and establishmentarian
assumptions. In Scotland, where the moderate party in the Church had considerably light-
ened the stern Calvinist heritage and had served as the principal carrier of the brilliant *Scottish Enlightenment, an emerging Evangelical movement challenged the moderates' easygoing
civility, a challenge that would eventuate, through a quarrel over lay patronage, in the Great
Disruption in 1843 and the creation of a parallel Free Church.

Since the emotional experience of conversion was at the heart of Evangelicalism, it was easy
for those of that persuasion to believe that there was a greater unity between those who had
undergone conversion than between those linked by loyalty to a mere denomination: in the
time-honoured phraseology, the 'invisible church' took on greater importance than the 'visible
church', a view that underlay much interdenominational collaboration in good works, such as

the Bible Society, founded in 1804. Obligated in doctrine, organization, and devotion to early eighteenth-century religious characteristics, Evangelicalism by its very scale and by the novel emotionalism of its message became a transforming force bridging the divide between the eighteenth and the nineteenth centuries.

The same kind of bridging is to be found in the influence of *Romanticism. Here, as with Evangelicalism, one must point to ground prepared by the new primacy accorded to the individual as a spiritual and emotional being, to the widespread practice of private devotion, to the religious intensity conveyed in the hymns of Isaac Watts (1674–1748) and Charles *Wesley—a poetic form that departed sharply from the old Puritan practice of psalm-singing—to the rise of *sensibility [11] and to a new awareness of the thrilling sense of impotence and terror conveyed by the *sublime in nature and art [see *hymnody].

These effects are to be found not only among Evangelicals but among Churchmen and even Unitarians. Indeed, two figures of the first rank in religious and Romantic history, S. T. *Coleridge and Frederick Denison Maurice (1805–72), abandoned their youthful Unitarianism for Anglicanism, without entirely abandoning their critical stance toward either the organization or the doctrines of the Church. But even Unitarians, so widely condemned for their coldness, displayed romantic and emotional tendencies in their preaching and devotional literature. In part, they were responding to the example of the compelling American preacher William Ellery Channing (1780–1842), but they were also reflecting the wide appeal of the poetry of William *Wordsworth, which spoke with special force to two generations of English men and women.

In 1833 John Keble (1792–1866) preached a sermon in Oxford which he entitled 'National Apostasy', an occasion to which John Henry Newman (1801–90) later pointed as the beginning of what came to be known as the Oxford Movement. Its leading figures were of widely varying backgrounds, but they were united in a protest, initially galvanized by the proposed reforms of the Irish church, against what they saw as the disastrous incursion of the liberal state and liberal ideals on the proper province of the Church.

In redefining the Church for a new age, the men of Oxford sought an identity in the Catholic traditions that had survived in Anglicanism. Some among them, most importantly Newman, eventually turned Roman Catholic, further discrediting a movement already suspect in the Church and in the country. But the Victorian period saw the legacy of the Oxford Movement, in pastoral concern, historical argument, and liturgical revival, spread throughout the Church and even into the Dissenting denominations.

That legacy—anti-revolutionary, profoundly Romantic, and with us still—serves as a fit stopping-place in this chronicle, though it may be less of a break than it has usually seemed. Nineteenth-century religious developments, so dramatically novel to their participants, may best be understood within a continuum of English religion descending from the mid-seventeenth century, a paradigm that may have emerged into a genuinely new avenue only at the end of the Victorian era.

Bebbington, D. W., *Evangelicalism in Modern Britain: A History from the 1730s to the 1980s*, London, 1989; Brooke, J. H., *Science and Religion: Some Historical Perspectives*, Cambridge, 1991; Everitt, A., 'Springs of Sensibility: Philip Doddridge of Northampton and the Evangelical Tradition', in his *Landscape and Community in England*, London, 1985; Hole, R., *Pulpits, Politics and Public Order in England, 1760–1832*, Cambridge, 1989; McCalman, I., *Radical Underworld: Prophets, Revolutionaries and Pornographers in London, 1795–1840*, Cambridge, 1988; Rupp, G., *Religion in England, 1688–1791*, Oxford, 1986; Semmel, B., *The Methodist Revolution*, New York, 1973; Watts, M. R., *The Dissenters: From the Reformation to the French Revolution*, Oxford, 1978.

11 · SENSIBILITY G. J. BARKER-BENFIELD

Britain became a consumer society in the period 1650–1750, although there were great *class [15], regional, and chronological differences in the new consumption patterns. Decline in the long-standing forms of suffering, brought about by natural and human causes, was accompanied by a widespread expression of the more refined kind of suffering that preoccupied the primarily middle-class cultivators of sensibility. Indeed, sensibility was the means whereby the middle class defined itself against a lower class still vulnerable to severe hardship [see *poverty, 12]. So great was the divide that as early as 1710 the *Spectator* could recommend perceiving the miserable and hungry in London's streets as 'a different species', and aggrandize the pleasure of 'a secret comparison' between 'ourselves and the person who suffers'.

Journals such as the *Spectator* were an important part of a public culture which encouraged its new middle-class audience to pursue the cult and language of sensibility. This word and its cognates denoted the receptivity of the senses—the material basis of consciousness—in a psychoperceptual scheme combining John *Locke's psychology with Isaac *Newton's explanation of the operation of the nerves. According to Locke, sensation was received by the organs and conveyed by the nerves to the brain, generating ideas, which were connected to each other by reflection. Locke later added the 'Association of Ideas' to sensation and reflection as the sources of consciousness. Newton's enormous intellectual authority provided sensational *psychology [39] with its understanding of the specific operation of the nerves: his view was that the nerves transmitted sense impressions by the vibrations of the 'most subtle spirit', ether, inhering in all solid bodies. The speed of such neurological transmissions depended on nerve elasticity, supposed by some to be highly developed among the middle class. Popularized by sentimental fiction and some popular forms of *religion [10] with which it coincided, this psychoperceptual scheme became a paradigm for consciousness in general as well as a particular kind of consciousness, one that could be further sensitized in order to be more acutely responsive to signals from the outside environment and from inside the body. Auditors and readers initially relished and eventually took for granted the system betokened by the words 'nerve', 'fibre', 'sensation', 'impression', and, of course, 'sensibility'. The flexibility of the term 'sensibility', synonymous with consciousness, with feelings, and eventually identifiable with sexual characteristics, generated a continuous struggle over its meanings and values.

As the new scheme was popularized, it was also gendered. Newton had not distinguished women's nerves and brains from men's, but his popularizing successors, especially the new medical experts, frequently questioned the operation of the will in women's putatively more delicate nerves, compounding the potential for passivity implicit in the association of ideas. The view that women's nerves were more delicate than men's, making them naturally creatures of greater sensibility, became a prominent convention of the eighteenth century. A high value was placed on this greater sensibility as grounds for imaginative capacity, but the refinement of the nerves (in 'effeminate' men, too) was also often identified with greater suffering, delicacy, and a susceptibility to disorder. Of course, late-seventeenth-century sensational, or environmental, psychology had promised women and men the power to construct selves and circumstance. However, the theoretical value attributed to the development of women's consciousness was in tension with a paradigm that could also rationalize their subordination on the basis of their finer sensibility. Eighteenth-century men cultivated sensibility, too,

13. 'Who can contemplate
such a scene unmoved?',
illustration by Charles Rolls
after Richard Westall to the
1822 edition of Hester
Chapone's conduct book,
*Letters on the Improvement of
the Mind.*

but this did not jeopardize other qualities or their participation in larger and more public goals.

Long having claimed regular, even daily, leisure at the alehouse, men found their pleasures amplified by the alehouse's absorption of the recreations banned from the churchyard since the Reformation [see *taverns]. Benefiting from the resurgence of internal trade, the alehouse became a new kind of economic centre, outside the old regulated market, more modern in its range and flexibility. However, puritan respectables apprehended it as 'a centre for public irreligion' and scorned it for its 'obscene talk, noise, nonsense and ribaldry . . . fumes of tobacco, belchings and other foul breaking of wind' that 'the rude rabble' esteemed 'the brightest happiness and run themselves into the greatest straits . . . to attain'. The attainment of this masculine happiness was, in large part, dependent on a sense of 'liberation' from the presence of 'womenfolk' in the place where most men spent the bulk of their time when not working. It was the base from which 'rakes' launched their individual and group assaults on people in the street, above all on women, marking men's traditional domination of public space. Physical and verbal assaults in the streets, along with cultural stereotypes in print, demonstrate the prevalence of a popular strain of misogyny. 'Rakes' or 'libertines' in eighteenth-century sentimental drama and literature can be seen as the most egregious representatives of a male culture being defined by its incompatibility with a new sense of public decency, that is, a new order in the streets and the non-brutalization of women.

That order was in part implemented by the century-long campaign for the *reformation of manners. Provoked by the post-Restoration proliferation of public pleasure centres, playhouses, and *coffeehouses, as well as of those uppity alehouses—and the freer expressions of behaviour associated with them—societies for the reformation of manners united their efforts with those of the government throughout the century [see *popular culture, 23]. Adherents to this campaign ranged from monarchs to manufacturers, bishops to commonwealthmen, *Tories, *Whigs, and feminists. Their weapons included blank warrants, licensing laws, theatre, poetry, sentimental fiction, and sovereign edicts (for example, against night violence on the streets). By definition they campaigned for a different kind of manhood.

Campaigning Latitudinarian divines argued that human nature was instinctively sympathetic and that passions naturally inclined men to virtuous actions which were reinforced by associated pleasurable feelings. Derived from Cambridge Platonism, this was the germ of 'moral sense', which also entered the culture of sensibility. Latitudinarians, too, drew upon the paradigm of sensibility; their *sermons reflected the same relationship between the narrators' affecting stories and the audiences' tears and sighs that informed the sentimental novel. Wesleyanism softened Latitudinarian doctrine still further by appealing to 'reasons of the heart' associated with 'peasants' and 'women'. John *Wesley opposed the world of the tavern, its cock-fighting and bear-baiting, and the rough music and wife sales embedded in the same culture. He opposed the sexual double standard by calling for 'male chastity', and he urged the replacing of the gamut of 'coarse' public behaviour with the manners of reformed gentlemen.

Though eighteenth-century religion may have contributed to the modification of the public manners of men, the historian John Pocock believes that the new mobile forms of property entailed the 'construction of a new image of social personality', based 'upon the exchange of forms of mobile property and upon modes of consciousness suited to a world of moving objects'. In the view of contemporaries, this new image was brought about by the multiplying 'encounters with things and persons', evoking 'passions and refining them into manners', experienced in turn as male sensibility. Commercial capitalists changed their manners in fostering new modes of mass mannerliness among customers—both groups primed to change by appetite, by mobility, by religion, by successful rebellions and reactions, as well as by emulativeness and the other possibilities nurtured by alehouse culture.

Trumpeting of the reformation of manners marked anxieties over the triumph of moneyed interests and attempts to uphold an eighteenth-century classical ideal of the landed patriotic citizen. The 'degeneracy' linked to the rise of the moneyed interest and decline of the citizen soldier was expressed in the gender-specific term 'effeminacy'. Those who warned Englishmen that effeminacy was the inevitable effect of luxury had the most powerful of all precedents in mind: the history of the degeneracy of Rome, from virtuous republic to luxurious empire.

Tension between the high evaluation of refinement in men and the wish to square it with manliness permeated the eighteenth-century novel, whatever the gender of the writer. Samuel Richardson (1689–1761), the author of what is usually regarded as the founding British sentimental novel, *Clarissa* (1748), made softened manhood the central goal of his participation in the reformation of manners, saying in his own voice that 'the man is to be honor'd who can weep for the distresses of others'. He made Sir Charles Grandison, the eponymous hero of his 1753 novel, a mid-century emblem of the ideals upheld by Adam *Smith and David *Hume, whose writings illustrate the proper limits placed on sensibility in men.

Hume recorded the physiological distinctions of men congregating in the splendid new houses and public buildings of Georgian Edinburgh, withdrawing from 'the grimy vitality of old Edinburgh to the prim and properness of the New Town', just as the same men rejected 'Scoticisms' for English speech [see *language, 40]. The 'skin, pores, muscles and nerves of a day labourer are different from those of a man of quality, so are his sentiments, actions and manners'. Hume specified how the creation of cities, with consequent increase in human contact, organization, knowledge, and pleasure, produced 'an increase of humanity', that is, humanitarianism. He argued that the more men refined their pleasures, the less susceptible they were to indulge themselves in 'beastly gluttony' and 'drunkenness', though not necessarily in 'libertine love'. He attributed to women 'a more delicate taste in the ornaments of life' and 'the ordinary decencies of behaviour', and he suggested that it was the easier and 'sociable' intercourse men had with women in the context of a consumer society that reformed men's manners, civilizing them, making them more humane, and thereby contributing to the improvement of public life. The same developments which humanized men benefited middle-class women by drawing them into pleasurable, amplifying, public social spaces. At one level, Hume recognized that sensational psychology showed women to be 'distinguished' or differentiated by custom, that is, by men's sexual 'prejudice', yet he still demonstrated the tendency of even enlightened men to assume that women were by their natures essentially creatures of sensibility (perhaps because men were thought to depend on them for refinement).

Adam Smith's *Theory of Moral Sentiments* (1759) and *Wealth of Nations* (1776) argue that better material conditions at home improved child-rearing and thereby nourished 'sensibility'. Poverty, he said, was 'extremely unfavourable to the rearing of children . . . the common people cannot afford to tend them with the same care as those of the better station.' By contrast, Smith extolled the feelings generated in a middle-class family, able to afford such psychological luxuries as careful child-rearing. Smith saw history culminating in the 'man of perfect virtue . . . he who joins to the most perfect command of his own original and selfish feelings, the most exquisite sensibility to the original and sympathetic feelings of others'. The company of women contributed to the development of such a character, but Smith also registered the danger that 'the delicate sensibility required in civilized nations sometimes destroys the masculine firmness of character'. Women's exposure to 'luxury', while stimulating the passion for enjoyment, could also endanger fertility.

At mid-century, British businessmen had long recognized the personal value of cultivating refinement. Clubs and societies had been established to encourage values of consideration, sociability, and charity. The urban historian Peter Borsay notes that the charity of male associations was thought to improve 'the social environment, making it a better place in which to trade, sell, borrow, and lend'. Civic leaders combined subscription with the exercise of political will to make streets, squares, and promenades 'islands of ordered elegance'. From 1700, squares and circuses were made so orderly and civil they functioned as 'open-air rooms', designed for socializing and mutual display among both sexes. But the continued co-existence of old and new public spaces also meant the shocking juxtaposition of drunk and violence-prone young males with the newly fashionable assemblies of the polite of both sexes.

Moreover, change in the behaviour of men was not as thoroughgoing as some women and other reformers wished. John Wilkes's rakish masculinity was central to his appeal to *Wilkite followers, even though he also represented himself as a patriot citizen. As men elaborated their political and economic sphere, *women [4] were often excluded from it. Nothing would be more significant for political feminism than that democratic politics—manhood suffrage—was generated in tavern associations [see *democracy, 3].

What did these changes in masculine culture and changing constructions of masculinity mean to women? Roy Porter and Carole Shammas note some significant changes that had taken place in women's work with the beginnings of *consumerism [19]. Central to the purpose of the culture of sensibility was the aggrandizement of the affectionate family and, at its heart, mothering, because it could legitimate traits desired by the middle class, including consumer desire [see *domesticity, 13]. Recent scholarship suggests that the increasing comfort of domestic space afforded by consumer innovations coincided with the democratization and relocation of prayer and Bible-reading as domestic, family rituals—rituals that persisted when the religious impulse waned. Women's new ritualistic power in the expert serving of tea is implied by the contemporary naming of teatime as a 'shrine of female devotion'. Men who spent much time drinking tea with women ran the risk of being called effeminate. By and large, tea-drinking was a domestic activity, even a domesticating one: the eventually ubiquitous stimulants of tea, coffee, and chocolate may have replaced the daily alehouse draught, although men continued to patronize the alehouse as it evolved into the tavern and coffeehouse.

Traditional mealtimes were also transformed. More time was now devoted to the consumption of food (by the fork, and from cheaper, lighter crockery and glassware) as well as its preparation, nourishing greater familial exchange and increasingly literate conversation. From mid-century, middle- and lower-class women more frequently joined other members of the household at the table for meals, whereas formerly they had stood to serve. Participating in literally more stimulating meals, perhaps recognized as more expert in the use of the new eating and cooking equipment, women must have been seen—by children, say—not only as less unequal, less unskilled than before, but as more influential than men, even as powerful players in the dispensation of food, the most fundamental form of production and consumption.

Women of the lower and middle classes joined increasingly in denunciations of male recreations, particularly drink, making it clear that booze, betting, paying for sex, and other forms of prodigal spending (and rakes were representative on this score, too) could be a prime absorber of their own and their children's prospects. Women's decisive part in consumer spending in the interests of improved domesticity and, eventually, of more sympathetic child-rearing practices enhanced their roles. Conversely, men of this same social background began to find at home more of the comforts they had previously sought in the tavern.

If middle-class mothers, as well as fathers, felt better about themselves, such feelings could be transmitted to their children through *education [17], to whom they now devoted more time. A trend towards greater literacy on the part of the parents was echoed by their children's, as commercial booksellers published and priced reading materials to reach all but the very poorest families of unskilled labourers [see *publishing, 21]. Reformers of manners, such as Hannah *More in her *Cheap Repository Tracts, joined this publishing drive, struggling to control the shaping of selves. Such works as *Pity's Gift: A Collection of Interesting Tales, to Excite the Compassion of Youth for the Animal Creation: From the Writings of Mr. Pratt*, 'Selected by a Lady' in 1798, abounded with 'exquisite sensibility' and contributed to its deification. The assumptions of sensationalist psychology and the perceived ductility of young and tender nerves made *children's literature a logical route by which reform could be implemented.

By late in the century, however, child-rearing literature and other advice books joined sentimental fiction in expressing concern over the effects of mothers indulging their children. The counterpart of the 'excessive social mixing of the sexes' to which *Female Government* (1779) ascribed current social problems was the new degree of intimacy between husbands and wives at home. The tract recommended that a boy be sequestered from his mother after weaning, so as to avoid the 'contagion of effeminate manners'.

Shifting work and spatial patterns allowed more women to find more time for literacy. It seems likely that by 1750 60 per cent of men and 40 per cent of women could read. The decisive popularity of Richardson's three novels, published between 1740 and 1753, reflected his responsiveness to the new audience of female readers. Richardson's popularity continued well into the nineteenth century, as his work was identified as a paradigmatic example of the language and culture of sentiment and sensibility. His work expressed the moral power of literate women and the potential conversion of men to the values for which women stood. This was the central thrust of the emerging literature of sensibility. The major truth expressed by the correspondence between the rise of sentimental fiction and the laws of the marketplace was that the themes of the fiction answered the interests of female readers, and it was in the genre of the *novel [31] that women wrote and read most. It may well be that the majority of novels published between 1692 and the end of the eighteenth century were written by women.

The feminization of the popular novel reflects the relative openness and non-traditional nature of the form, 'hedged round by no learned traditions, based on no formal techniques'. Anna Laetitia *Barbauld suggested in 'On Romances' (1773) that sentimental fiction was popular because 'few can reason, but all can feel'. Here, she said, was illimitable potential:

'Sorrow is universally felt.' Debarred from the educational establishment and usually from a knowledge of the ancient languages, women turned their hand to a form and subject they could master by themselves. If the supposedly 'unexacting' requirements of the novel's language were thought to suit women's nervous systems and education, the form also encouraged them to express their preoccupations with the gender arrangements governing domestic lives.

Women's entering fictional worlds coincided with their entering public life for pleasure, a dramatic reversal of their exclusion from most recreational culture. The burgeoning attractions of shopping and commercialized entertainments such as balls, *masquerades, and *concerts drew women irresistibly out of the home into the newly ordered urban spaces, such as *pleasure gardens, *theatres [24], and museums [see *music, 26 and *viewing, 20].

Assemblies had begun to meet regularly in the earliest resort towns before 1700, and soon weekly assemblies—for cards, dancing, and conversation—were being held in London and throughout the network of provincial towns. Here were public nodal points for women, debating fashionable literature as well as displaying and discussing fashionable clothes [see *fashion], formulating new cultural items for themselves—in short, cultivating new personal skills required by the public heterosocial gatherings praised by Hume and Smith.

Richardson complained against female consumer spending and women entering public space, apprehensions echoed by some early feminists such as Mary Astell (1666–1731) as well as by other campaigners for the reformation of manners. Typically, both Astell and Richardson also benefited from the new commercial system they criticized. If women were peculiarly susceptible to such pleasures, they were supposedly peculiarly endangered by them. The woman addicted to 'out-door pleasures' became a monitory type in sentimental culture: 'woman of the world', a female equivalent of the 'man of the world', a figure who unhesitatingly enjoyed the possibilities of commerce and consumption. Critical representations of such women (both in fact and in fiction), from parvenues to the Duchess of *Devonshire, symbolized their increasing involvement in travel and outdoor leisure activities. Emblematically, the resulting adoption by women of male riding-clothes provoked sharp debate over the meanings of femininity and masculinity.

Historically, 'luxury' and 'idleness' had been characteristic of the rich, but by the late eighteenth century Mary *Wollstonecraft observed that middle-class urban women were 'in the same condition as the rich, for they are born—I now speak of a state of civilization, with certain sexual privileges'. One quality of ladyhood to which they aspired was sensibility. Like Astell, Wollstonecraft recognized the value of sensational psychology to women, attributing their apparently inferior mental accomplishments to their upbringing. But, also like Astell, Wollstonecraft spelled out the dangerous implications that uncritical sensibility could hold for women. Without the cultivation of reason, women become 'the prey of their senses, delicately termed sensibility, and are blown about by every momentary gust of feeling'. Sensibility made women 'the plaything of outward circumstances'. Therefore, they became the 'prey' of men, 'love alone' concentrating the 'ethereal beams' of sensibility.

Sexual dangers also inhered in sensibility itself because of the supposedly automatic physiological responsiveness associated with it. Waiting for her lover, the heroine of Elizabeth *Ryves's *The Hermit of Snowden* (1789) found her 'passions were warm, and her bosom tremblingly alive to every touch of joy or sorrow'. This responsiveness accords with Hannah More's definition in 'Sensibility' (1784), although, crucially, her passion is pain rather than pleasure:

> Where glow exalted sense, and taste refin'd,
> There keener anguish rankles in the mind:
> There feeling is diffus'd thro' ev'ry part,
> Thrills in each nerve, and lives in all the heart.

That Ryves's heroine's response was a sexual one is confirmed by the hastily following qualification: 'yet her reason was sufficiently strong to regulate not only her conduct, but her wishes; and though she felt the thrills of sensibility, she always preserved an absolute dominion over herself.' Here we have an implementation of the code, usually termed 'delicacy', that was required to offset sensibility's dangers. Delicacy implied that, somehow, inhibition inhered in the female nervous system, a gendered expression of the 'moral sense'. Elizabeth Griffith (1727–93) said in *The Delicate Distress* (1769) that 'there is everything to be expected from *sensibility and delicacy* joined; but indeed, I have scarce ever known them separated, in a female heart.' The code of delicacy mediated a complex power struggle, exacerbated by women's widespread participation in recreational life and fuller expression of wishes in the marriage market.

Novels were supposed to exert a decisive effect on those who gave in to their sensibility. Elizabeth *Carter, a prominent member of the informal sociable circle of women called the *bluestockings, blamed the example of Julie, in Jean Jacques *Rousseau's *Julie, ou la Nouvelle Héloïse* (1761) for the elopement of Kitty Hunter with the married Earl of Pembroke. Anna Laetitia Aikin's marriage to an 'unstable Frenchman'—whereby she became Mrs Barbauld, theologian of sensibility—was attributed to the same novel. Even with no particular prospects of elopement, women were thought to be sexually aroused by reading novels, thereby readied for seduction. Throughout the century writers warned of this, even blaming novels for an 'alarming increase of prostitutes' in 1790. By definition, sentimental fiction was intended to stimulate readers to feel. Moralists simply wished to turn this power to reformation rather than allow it to further the individual pursuit of pleasure. For many women, sexual relations entailed denigration and the threat of brutalization, pregnancy, and disease. By contrast, fictional heroes stayed in the reader's control; they were shown respecting women's feelings—indeed, respecting women's definition of masculinity—and responding to them in appropriate ways.

The strength of women's wish for sensitive lovers supposedly made women easy marks for men who pretended sensibility in order to seduce them. Jane *Austen's *Sense and Sensibility* (1811) demonstrated that the culture of sensibility involved a short-circuiting of reflective thought which could lead to self-deception of drastic proportions. The literature also sometimes implied that women's attraction to rakish men might have derived from a kind of addiction to suffering. Marianne Dashwood 'courted misery' and, at first, repudiated Elinor's appeal to a more individualized, tougher-minded consciousness, crying, 'No, no . . . they who suffer little may be proud and independent as they like, may resist insult or return mortification, but I cannot. I must feel—I must be wretched—and they are welcome to enjoy the consciousness of it that can.' Preoccupation with women's 'excessive sensibility' expressed the possibility of women being able to enjoy any consciousness, controlled neither by taste, morality, men, nor anything but themselves. This led to the co-existence of an opposite explanation, based on their search for pleasure, for women's attraction to rakes and libertines. Eighteenth-century writers suggested that such male figures represented the attractions of prodigality, playfulness, and sexual pleasures to women. Women's possibilities, however, existed in a world where men still monopolized most power—power they could invest in their sexuality.

The continuing attractiveness of this style of manhood to women was also explained by the apparent inadequacy of men of feeling or, rather, by the unfathomed question of their sexuality. To make men more sensitive, more delicate, was, in the eighteenth century's own terms, to bring them closer to women and to run the risk of making them too 'effeminate' or 'feminine'. Henry Fielding's (1707–54) eponymous hero Tom Jones carried 'the most apparent marks of sweetness and good nature' and included 'spirit and sensibility in his eyes, which might have given him an air rather too effeminate had it not been joined to most masculine person and mien'. Women novelists, too, combined their advocacy of more sensibility in a man with the reassurance that heroines regard him as 'manly'. Still, the reformation of men in order to bring them closer to women raised the difficult question of irreducible difference, that is, of sex.

Many writers and reformers wished to reconcile the pursuit of pleasure with morality—identifiable with sexual restraint—and the old sexual orthodoxy. The wilful pursuit of pleasure could create women and men deemed to be sexual deviants in eighteenth-century terms, daughters who became women of the world or solipsistic, childless invalids, and sons who became rakes or effeminate. The dynamics of British consumer capitalism continuously worked to produce such figures, drawing women toward self-expression and outdoor, heterosocial pleasures, making them vulnerable to rakes as well as to accusations of bad mothering, and bringing men closer to women, in more comfortable homes or those irresistibly fashionable public places. Both tendencies were perceived to make women and men more like the other—women 'masculine', men effeminate. Women could make it clear that they could do without the duplicity, violence, and cruelty in the male treatment of women, but how to make sexual a new relationship built on mutual sensibility remained a problem. Sexuality betokened difference and possible conflict, continually to be renewed and resolved, when sensibility's most basic fantasy had become harmony. Evidence of women's interest in consumer pleasures had always gone hand in hand with attempts to control it. This is why the culture of sensibility insisted on a tasteful relationship with the goods and services supplied by the consumer revolution. Consumption could provide women with a new kind of power, but it also pointed to the moralization of its other possibilities. Here, too, 'delicacy' worked to influence a woman's taste more completely than it did that of a man. Tasteful objects and delicate nerves were thought to be attuned in the same system. The heroine of Ann *Radcliffe's *The Mysteries of Udolpho* (1794) finds it impossible to contain her feelings in a domestic space stuffed brim-full; 'where, alas! could she turn, and not meet new objects to give acuteness to grief?' There, 'indulging' her feelings and making a virtue of necessity, the heroine unwittingly helped to foster what sociologist Colin Campbell has called 'the psychology of consumerism'.

Along with *conduct books, sentimental literature taught readers to have the same sensitized and tasteful relationship to fashionable objects, selected from the increasing range of consumer items women wore, carried with them, or used to characterize domestic space. Enterprising new industrial manufacturers seeking to reach a mass market had to note women's wishes, given the centrality of home. Josiah *Wedgwood boosted the sale of black basalt tea-ware during a downturn in demand because he observed the fashion for delicate white hands symbolic of gentility. Black provided a tasteful contrast during the tea ceremony's civilities. Matthew *Boulton linked the social transformation he and his fellow manufacturers wrought with the parallel campaign for the reformation of manners, which purged cruel, animal-baiting sports and 'abominable drunkenness'. He aspired to replace such rough male activities by the heterosocial 'scene' in which men and women could put manufactured objects to good use. This was the Smithian vision of 'liberal arts'—manufacturers' intentions interwoven with the civilizing process. The historian Paul Langford sees a similar relationship between philanthropy and entrepreneurship. *Evangelical reformers, too, linked moral with material improvement.

Much of the suffering addressed by the humanitarian reformers of the later eighteenth century could be laid at the door of that masculine world against which the culture defined itself and which moral reformers wished to enter and to change. The wide range of 'obvious and pointless physical suffering' they protested came to include the cruel treatment of animals; the mistreatment of children, of the sick, and the insane; the corporal punishments of public flogging and executions; imprisonment for debt; *duelling; the abuse and exploitation of the poor [see *poverty, 12]; *press-gangs; political corruption; and the slave trade and *slavery [6]. Sensibility's galvanizing of public opinion was fundamental to the remarkable legislative initiatives aimed at humanitarian reform and *abolitionism during the last third of the century.

The reforming impulse of sensibility encouraged both the liberation of women from their internalized and brutally enforced constraints and the reformation of men. The former included self-assertion of mind, feelings, and moral value, though some modern critics also claim that excesses of sensibility led to indulgence in the feelings aroused by slaves or to a pre-occupation with the moral authority of the reformers rather than the conditions of the victims. This proved a source of concern to sentimentalists themselves. Frances *Burney suggested that if 'wayward Sensibility' could impel 'to all that is most disinterested for others', it could also 'forget all mankind, to watch the pulsations of its own fancies'.

The immediate purpose of sentimental fiction was to persuade men to treat women with greater humanity. That the non-gendered term 'humane' was elevated during this period with this in mind is of considerable interest to the historian of gender. Richardson's Clarissa expressly wished to 'reduce' Lovelace's explicit hard masculinity to 'a standard of humanity'. As the critic Robert Brissenden pointed out, 'Virtue in distress' was a term that referred to the experience of women at the mercy of men depicted as liars, cheats, frauds, hypocrites, rogues, and sadists. Encountering the complexity of social forms through which people in the world expressed themselves at first challenged and bewildered that group which, by and large, men had always restricted to the household and to which they had denied participation in worldly business. While sentimental fiction publicized its private virtues, what good could these be in a public world unless women had the economic and political power advocated by Wollstonecraft? Yet to be experienced, a 'woman of the world', was grounds for moral condemnation.

Another source of tension within sentimental culture was the growing evidence of shifts in men's characters, where clearly 'modern' men appeared able to move easily between 'homo-social' commercial worlds on one hand and heterosocial worlds of assemblies (or home) on the other. Sentimental culture clung to simpler notions of sincerity, and celebrated a range of retreats from the corrupt and duplicitous 'world'—to the home, to the countryside, to child-hood, to the feudal past, and to the grave. Such simplicities and retreats were all presented as morally superior to worldliness.

Sentimental literature raised fundamental questions about the nature and relations of each gender. It asserted the right of women to marry for love, in accordance with their own wishes rather than for mercenary reasons. It warned of the dangers of simply following one's own heart, a major ground for urging that sensibility be tempered by reason: women therefore required a proper education. A daughter's having a marriage choice made 'the tension between love and filial obedience' a preoccupation of women's writing. Central to many of the novels is the struggle between daughters and tyrannous fathers, as well as fantasized harmony and obedience to sympathetic ones. The desire to soften and improve relations between parents and children and wives and husbands are related themes. Sentimental fiction elab-orated women's claim to enjoy public pleasures with men, without threat of violent assault. Above all, women's literacy and women's fiction declared that women had minds and wishes of their own.

Sentimental novelists made a point of cataloging sexually backward views, putting them in the mouths of squires, rakes, and men of the world, who opposed domestic and domesticating qualities, and represented male resistance to the rise, consciousness, and wishes of women. Sentimental heroes opposed *gambling, oaths, drinking, idleness, cruelty to animals, and other elements of popular male culture. Because the sentimental hero was benevolent, com-passionate, humane, literate, and tasteful, he would make a better husband by placing a high value on a harmonious marriage and on domesticity. Above all, this man of feeling was shown to respect women and make common ground with them. Not only had men to give up their physical harassment of women, they were also asked to take care not to give women psycho-logical pain.

Sentimental fiction showed insensitive men transformed into men of feeling through conversion, in which women were given a decisive role. Their power derived in large part from tearfulness, fainting, and physical weakness, a style of sensibility which was sexualized as a source of arousal to unreformed men. At the same time, the conversion of a man's behaviour did not necessarily challenge the male's powerful legal authority as husband and father.

The fact that sensibility suggested a distinct world-view, infused with religious values and claiming to reform a fallen population by conversion, raises the possibility that sensibility did constitute the 'cult' that so many literary critics and scholars have termed it. A 1776 piece in the *London Magazine*, signed 'Rosaline', described 'The Birth of Sensibility' as the birth of a goddess. This literary deification coincided with a rising tendency of women to act in more specifically religious fields. Women of all denominations wrote *hymns, emotional verse, religious tracts, pamphlets, and missionary letters, all promulgating values of sensibility. Modern scholars see the 'feminization of religion' as coinciding with the 'feminization' of the novel. *Methodism, with women salient among its preachers, seems to have had most in common with the cult of sensibility. Wesley himself encouraged the convergence of sensibility and piety by his publication of properly edited sentimental novels and poems. Methodist recreation was supposed to take place within the family and home, and to dovetail with piety and prayer, shifting the centre of worship from church to hearth. Such a vision squares with the economic world-view of women managing the family purse, agents for the family's respectable prospects. Arguably, Evangelicalism of all kinds and the cult of sensibility were two branches of the same culture, nourished by the same roots in the awakening minds of eighteenth-century women and those men with whom their wishes overlapped.

If at first Methodists had been potentially disruptive, particularly of traditional male hierarchies, they were by the 1790s increasingly dominated by an élite of respectable, professionalized, male ministers, tightly linked to solid householders. Methodist rank and file hankered for respectability, leading to purges of radical elements, including women preachers. Methodist women, eager to become ladies, joined respectable evangelical women in formal reform societies. This aligned with general tendencies in the broader culture of sensibility, following the convulsive struggle over its subversive potentials initiated by British reaction to the *French Revolution, and interpreted by opponents as the result of excessive, Rousseauistic sensibility.

Of course, sensibility had conservative as well as subversive aspects to it all along, including courtly elements, pietistic values, and adherence to a moralized taste in consumerism. Together, the culture's language of gesture and word became a system attempting to define 'the sex' as 'ladies'. Approving neatness, cleanliness, decency, and piety in the poor, sentimental literature was disgusted by those who did not thus mirror the ideals of middle-class observers. According to Mary *Hays, sensibility was demonstrable in the distribution of charity, when it was accompanied by 'kind accents, tender sympathy, and wholesome counsels' to the 'indigent but industrious' cottagers. That More devoted her efforts to the founding of charity schools, as well as writing unrelievedly didactic and sentimental stories to be used in them, illustrates the relationship that existed between the gendered ideology of sensibility and the class-consciousness of its charitable efforts. One detects in sentimental fiction the fantasy of class harmony—even 'a feast of love'—in which hierarchy is fixed and accepted by the lower classes with joy. Sentimental fiction continued, however, to be extremely popular. Radcliffe's *Mysteries* typically hinted at its apparent dangers but continued to convey its tenets. And no one could prevent readers from identifying with figures the author intended as warnings against sensibility's 'excesses'. None the less, the ambiguous values of sensibility became a critical problem for many writers during the last fifteen years of the century. From the late 1780s, a spate of criticism of excessive sensibility was reflected in novels whose titles and themes anticipated Austen's *Sense and Sensibility*: *Excessive Sensibility* (1787); *The Illusions of Sentiment* (1788); *Arubia: The Victim of Sensibility* (1790); *Errors of Sensibility* (1793). These

14. *The New Morality* by James Gillray, published in the *Anti-Jacobin Review* (1798), attacked a congeries of radical intellectuals as supporters of voguish libertine ideals. Sensibility (on the right) is satirized with Justice and Philanthropy as one of the idols of the followers of the French Revolution. She holds a book by Rousseau and weeps over a dying bird (a reference to Paine's *Rights of Man*) with her foot on the head of Louis XVI.

novels dramatized the tensions between a sensibility governed by reason and a sensibility dangerously given over to fantasy and the pursuit of pleasure. Many also focused explicitly on what was seen as a particularly perilous source of excessive and enthusiastic sensibility, the over-charged *Gothic novels disseminated through the *Minerva Press.

Because the definition of gender was seen to be fundamental both to the Jacobin prospects for reform and to the anti-Jacobin attempt to maintain the natural order, the debate over sensibility became a key issue in British politics during the 1790s, one crystallized by the uproar over the posthumous figure of Wollstonecraft. Women writers—novelists in particular—came under still more severe attack for subverting the natural ordering of the sexes. Charlotte *Smith recorded in *Desmond* (1792) that novels were being accused of inspiring a range of immoral behaviour. This was six years prior to William *Godwin's revelations that Wollstonecraft exemplified all of these, in his *Memoirs of the Author of A Vindication of the Rights of Woman* (1798).

To defend Wollstonecraft, Godwin declared she was 'endowed with the most exquisite and delicious sensibility'—a view which she had in the *Rights of Woman* (1792) taught women to resist. However, his defence backfired, and attribution of Wollstonecraft's sexual unconventionality to her excessive sensibility, published at a crucial counter-revolutionary moment, only goaded the sexually puritanical attacks of opponents such as Richard *Polwhele and other *anti-Jacobin writers. Though Wollstonecraft had argued against the gendering of sensibility, she now became the embodiment of those apprehensions over the subversive

possibilities in female 'sensibility' run rampant. After her relationship with Gilbert Imlay, according to the *British Critic*, Wollstonecraft's 'senses were so *completely awakened* that she could not exist without their gratification'.

More's *Strictures on the Modern System of Education* (1799), written to refute Wollstonecraft's *Rights of Woman*, represented the century's final orthodoxy on sensibility, even as the subversive potentials in sensibility entered *Romanticism. More declared that men had not only 'a superior strength of body' but 'a firmer texture of mind . . . a higher reach and wider range of powers'. By contrast, women

had a certain *tact* which often enables them to feel what is just more instantaneously than they can define it. They have an intuitive penetration into character, bestowed on them by Providence, like the sensibility and tender organs of some timid animals, as a kind of natural guard to warn off the approach of danger.

Women's minds were to be strengthened, however, albeit for defensive purpose, to prevent their 'natural softness' from degenerating into 'imbecility of understanding'. More said that women ran the risk of that imbecility because of their 'indulgence' and 'the general habits of fashionable life'. Here was some common ground with Wollstonecraft.

More could not entirely avoid the environmental explanation for gender differences, a particularly vibrant issue during the Jacobin/anti-Jacobin debate. However, she accepted the differences as given, however induced, and on that basis claimed the separate but equalizing power conferred by feminine religious sensibility. The gendering of sensibility, and even the apparent deficiencies in education, rather than crippling the female personality, More declared, fostered a special propensity in women for an empowering Christian mission.

Out of the final 1790s fusion of Evangelicalism with sensibility would emerge the flood of reform organizations centred on a middle-class, female constituency. These often manifested the degree of tough-mindedness with which so many late-eighteenth-century female writers, including Wollstonecraft, had wished to harness sensibility. The stereotypes of false, merely fashionable sensibility, and of sofa-lying, excessive sensibility also remained, characteristic of nineteenth-century fiction. Across this spectrum, the 'naturalizing' of women's finer sensibility—connoting nerves and morality—continued to bedevil and aggrandize women's self-conceptions into the next century.

Barker-Benfield, G. J., *The Culture of Sensibility: Sex and Society in Eighteenth-Century Britain*, Chicago, 1992; Borsay, P., *The English Urban Renaissance: Culture and Society in the Provincial Town, 1660–1770*, Oxford, 1989; Brissenden, R. F., *Virtue in Distress: Studies in the Novel of Sentiment from Richardson to Sade*, New York, 1974; Campbell, C., *The Romantic Ethic and the Spirit of Modern Consumerism*, Oxford, 1987; Langford, P., *A Polite and Commercial People: England, 1727–1783*, Oxford, 1989; Lawrence, C., 'The Nervous System and Society in the Scottish Enlightenment', in B. Barnes & S. Shapin, eds., *Natural Order: Historical Studies of Scientific Culture*, Beverly Hills, Calif., & London, 1979; Pocock, J. G. A., *Virtue, Commerce and History: Essays on Political Thought and History, Chiefly in the Eighteenth Century*, Cambridge, 1985; Poovey, M., *The Proper Lady and the Woman Writer*, Chicago, 1984; Porter, R., and Brewer, J., eds., *Consumption and the World of Goods*, London, 1993; Rousseau, G. S., 'Nerves, Spirits, and Fibres: Towards Defining the Origins of Sensibility', *Blue Guitar*, 2 (1976), 125–53; Shammas, C., *The Pre-Industrial Consumer in England and America*, Oxford, 1990; Sheriff, J. K., *The Good Natured Man: The Evolution of a Moral Ideal, 1660–1800*, Tuscaloosa, Ala., 1982; Todd, J., *Sensibility: An Introduction*, London, 1986.

12 · POVERTY   SARAH LLOYD

The history of poverty cannot be written simply by establishing a measure or threshold of deprivation and looking for all who fell beneath it, since it is also a history of shifting definitions and perspective. The terms 'poverty' and 'poor' were particularly dense and highly contested concepts in this period. They described a social and economic situation which sometimes required charity or statutory relief, but they were also terms of political analysis which conveyed specific values, attitudes, and explanations of how society in general was composed and governed. Questions of the origins of poverty, its inevitability, and whether and how it should be relieved were established in Christian belief, economic principle, and theories of *population. Between 1770 and 1830, the experience and meanings of poverty came under pressure from *war [2] and rapid economic, social, and demographic change. By the early nineteenth century, commentators were no longer as certain as their eighteenth-century predecessors had been that ties of sentiment and models of social order required poverty to be met with charity. The redefinition of indigence as a state of unnatural dependence was central to the emergence of new thinking on social and sexual relations. Consequently, understandings of poverty went beyond an immediate response to the material conditions of the lower classes to touch upon and shape dominant nineteenth-century characterizations of Britain.

Who were the poor? This question preoccupied parish officials and magistrates; it concerned a range of political economists, ratepayers, landowners, clerics, and *Evangelicals who shared much of their social thinking and held a common interest in categorizing and analysing the circumstances of the lower classes. Many of these men responded to parliamentary interest in *poor law reform, contributing to an extensive published literature on poverty, and many had face-to-face dealings with the poor, who in certain respects resembled the inhabitants of a foreign land as unfamiliar objects for scrutiny. Two definitions predominated.

First, the poor were the destitute whose needs for discipline and sustenance were to be addressed either by voluntary donation or through statutory provision. In England and Wales the poor laws made parishes responsible for relief and employment of the settled poor, financed by the levying of rates; in Scotland, parish relief was generally funded from voluntary collections. Second, the poor were a more general category of labourers toiling to create the nation's wealth. This double definition overlay a tenacious belief in inherited status which underpinned the concept of the genteel poor, those unable to live according to the expectations of their rank. And it tended to supersede a long-established Christian tradition, reasserted by John *Wesley, that the poor formed a spiritual category, closer to salvation than the rich and respectable.

During this period, individual almsgiving was extensive. Charitable foundations or funds, many long established, still provided doles, almshouses, rudimentary *education [17], and other forms of assistance for the needy. A network of eighteenth-century urban charities catered for various specific categories of poor—orphans, prostitutes, pregnant women, injured labourers, the blind—who gained access through patronage rather than settlement. Throughout the country, parish pension lists were dominated by women and men unable to work or subsist because of illness, age (advanced years or extreme youth), or personal calamity (widows). These were most secure in their claim to assistance and to the title of 'poor', but parish officials also had extensive dealings with a larger group which received occasional relief—medical assistance, clothing, food, or cash to tide them over immediate crises. Discrimination between the undeserving and the deserving had structured attitudes to the poor for many centuries, but parish officials, unlike some pamphleteers, recognized the claims of the able-bodied. Indeed, a substantial proportion of the poor rates was paid as occasional relief to the able-bodied. Periodically, parishes might establish or reform a local poorhouse or workhouse to cut the cost of poor relief, discipline the recalcitrant, or establish some form of manufacture. Important incorporation and workhouse initiatives were undertaken in East Anglia (from the 1750s) and in Shropshire (from the late 1780s). However, these institutions were unpopular with the poor, and often disappointed expectations, becoming instead a place of last resort for the very young or the sick and exhausted.

By the late eighteenth century, decades of local experiment, tradition, and enabling legislation had produced a heterogeneous system of indoor and outdoor relief, and an extensive administrative structure which enabled officials to respond to economic crisis and social unrest by intervening in food markets, employment practices, and wage rates. In the 1790s, many Scottish parishes subsidized food. English parishes supplemented wages according to the cost of bread and the number of dependants, a practice dubbed the 'Speenhamland system' after 1795. They sent the unemployed—'roundsmen'—out to local employers, subsidizing their earnings. Overseers also hired out and apprenticed children, sometimes sending them over long distances from southern towns to Lancashire cotton manufacturers.

Thus the poor relief system linked the destitute with a much broader constituency of the poor, the great mass of 'inferiors' at the bottom of the social pyramid. In this sense, poverty was usually taken for granted as a natural state requiring neither redress nor explanation beyond providential sanction, and the particular theory of economic value on which it rested often went unstated or was left vague. Agriculture was still a major source of income for the labouring classes, although it had not employed a majority of the population since the early eighteenth century [see *agricultural revolution]. Many earned something from manufacturing, notably spinning and weaving at home, while urban occupations supported growing numbers of women and men. The poor, whatever their employment, had no property other than their own physical strength, yet during most of the eighteenth century *philanthropists and projectors devised schemes in the belief that the poor literally created national wealth in the form of population and commerce, and were thus the benefactors of the rich.

The history of Samuel Price, an 'honest and industrious' Monmouth labourer, as narrated by Frederick *Eden in his *The State of the Poor* (1797), illustrates the different meanings of being poor. Price's household lived mostly on bread and potatoes, consuming neither meat nor beer; the eight children still at home went without shoes or stockings, and all their clothes came from charitable donations. By 1795 this family was no longer poor in the sense that it scraped a living, but poor in the sense that it failed to do so. Price, his wife, and one son earned £25 a year, but outgoings were calculated as £30 14s. and Mrs Price was pregnant again; Samuel was in dispute with the Monmouth Corporation over rent arrears; and the Price children, who were illiterate and had been 'bred up in idleness', were said to be so saucy that no one would employ them. Such combinations of material and moral criteria, shaped by debates on the poor law, crime, trade, employment, taxation, social change, luxury, and Christian duty, determined observers' understandings of poverty.

Although opinion varied on whether the corrupt outnumbered the virtuous poor, observers assessed character by behaviour, notably drunkenness, thieving, insubordination, blasphemy, sexual incontinence, and love of fripperies; moral shortcomings with different implications in the male and female poor. Idleness was the coagulant around which other vices clustered. Clerics and commentators on trade alike declared that labour was a duty owed to God, nation, employer, body, and conscience. They read political and moral lessons from the social inferiority of the poor. Such inferiority displayed the ideal, hierarchical order of family and society; it was a necessary condition which guaranteed stability, civility, and deference between sexes and ranks. Writers imagined a tight mesh of economic, moral, and political bonds holding rich and poor together; consequently, the poor had a moral or natural, although not necessarily a legal, right to charity. Fear of disorder suggested prudential arguments for benevolence, while the possession of property and operation of pity morally compelled the rich to philanthropy, a duty which they thought they performed more magnificently than their counterparts in any other nation. Poverty was a 'relative' state, a social condition defined by its relation to other ranks.

When Arthur *Young commented in 1770 that the term 'labouring poor' was meaningless, he indicated the very utility of the term he dismissed. A term that means nothing can mean anything, a phrase into which contemporaries poured specific understandings shaped in heterogeneous contexts. It was the conglomeration of religious, political, economic, and social meanings that made exact definition of the poor so difficult and the source of endless discussion. However, Young's statement also signals a realignment of thinking on the causes and remedies of poverty.

Two contrasting approaches to poverty emerged in the closing decades of the eighteenth century. Critics of economic change blamed socially ambitious farmers, who paid cash and employed intermittently, for cutting the poor adrift from paternalist influence. By so doing these farmers encouraged the poor to spend money on luxuries rather than wages, thereby contributing to rising prices which cut so severely into meagre incomes. This critique helped produce a new meaning of poverty: those unable to live, however frugally, on what they earnt. Concurrently, many writers opened a conceptual gulf—a categorical difference—which would separate the destitute from those who toiled. It became commonplace to argue that philanthropic excess was misguided, dangerous, and self-indulgent, and that national wealth was not simply fostered through population growth. It was also claimed that public schemes to employ the poor neither improved their moral condition nor generated profits. Both lines of argument contributed significantly to a fluid discourse about social structure which anatomized the emergent middle class and the bases of social power and economic prosperity. Both addressed pervasive fears about an increasingly problematic poor.

These apprehensions were based in experience of agricultural change, as well as new manufactures, war, food shortages, and fiscal crisis. From the mid-eighteenth century, apprenticeship and the practice of boarding and feeding farm servants declined, particularly in southern England. This exposed increasing numbers to rising prices and seasonal unemployment, and cut off one major route to gaining a legal settlement and access to poor relief. Prices rose particularly fast from the 1760s, accelerating in the 1790s and outstripping wage increases. Parish officers in Presteigne, Radnorshire, for example, reported in the summer of 1795 that the poor were literally starving. Subsistence crises were especially severe in the 1790s, when typhus reached epidemic proportions. Cottage industry offered an increasingly precarious and meagre income as capitalists sought more control over manufacturing processes and agriculture slumped after 1815. War brought financial and commercial disasters, since taxation and rising *national debt, as well as the gathering and disbanding of great armies and navies, contributed to existing social hardship and aggravated the pressures of population increase. Although war increased demand for male labour, women and children required poor relief when men volunteered or were impressed; postwar, men returned to economic dislocation, personal difficulties, and, in counties like Norfolk, to an overstocked rural labour market.

Detailed patterns of poverty varied between parishes and regions. Pressures were most acute in England. Distinctive social and economic conditions in Scotland created less demand for relief, though Scottish parishes closest to the border were sometimes forced to adopt more generous English practices in the late eighteenth century. While marked differences in wages according to occupation, gender, and region, as well as differences between the experience and the statistics of poverty, make generalizations difficult, the poor were probably less comfortable at the turn of the nineteenth century than they had been thirty years earlier. In southern, arable districts, those who had been relatively well paid in the mid-eighteenth century were particularly affected by declining standards of living. Unlike agricultural areas in northern England, there was no alternative source of employment in manufacture to keep wages buoyant or encourage migration, and throughout this period fluctuating demand for labour during the course of the year left many in great hardship during winter. The urban poor experienced a different cycle of poverty, facing extreme distress during trade slumps and vulnerability to high food prices [see *famine].

Instability was marked by rioting over food prices and military recruitment, by industrial disputes, political conflict, and, in the 1790s, by fears of *revolution [1] spreading from France. Commoners contested land enclosure and loss of their customary rights. The Captain Swing rioters of 1830–1, who broke the threshing machines which threatened winter employment, are credited with finally tipping opinion towards poor law reform [see *riots]. Manufacturing districts and areas of rapid population growth had their own distinctive ecology of disturbance and violence. Machine-breaking erupted periodically in the north and south-west of England as an attempt to protect the existing organization of the textile industry [see *Luddism]. Riots reflected complex political and economic relationships embedded in local contexts, while the patterns of female participation in such disturbances mapped women's status in the household and local community. To the propertied, riots were simply a threat to property and social order.

The expense of the poor generated cumulative panic: poor rates in England and Wales rose from £1,720,316 in 1776 to a peak of £8,411,893 in 1820–1. Between 1770 and 1830 the population of England more than doubled, from under six and a half million to over thirteen million, increasing the number of dependent children. But until the first official census in 1801, the size of the population was a matter of conjecture. Observers throughout the period juggled with calculations, budgets, and estimates in an attempt to comprehend the individual and collective lives of the poor. Was the number dependent on relief rising at a faster rate than the population as a whole, endangering national wealth? What was the geography of poverty and how were differences to be explained? Parliamentary interest generated volumes of alarming *statistics, and private charity further inflated the sums. In the 1790s the philanthropist and writer

Sir Frederick Eden investigated and charted poverty, finding greater economy and resource-fulness in Wales, Scotland, and the north of England than in the southern counties. In 1806 Patrick *Colquhoun, police magistrate and philanthropist, guessed that one seventh of the British population lived on poor rates, charity, crime, and vice. Although Colquhoun took this as a sign of prosperity, many others were troubled both by the statistics of the period and by the uncertainty which surrounded them.

In this context, political economists offered significant new approaches which emphasized that the social environment shaped poverty. Adam *Smith, Edmund *Burke, Thomas *Paine, Frederick Eden, Thomas *Malthus, Jeremy *Bentham, Patrick Colquhoun, and David *Ricardo claimed to apply scientific, general reasoning about human nature and economic growth to questions of poverty and philanthropy, although they reached very different conclu-sions. Were the poor laws subject to commercial or constitutional logic, for example? Was necessity or reward the best incentive to labour; how beneficial were high wages? Smith offered an influential prospect of commercial expansion and improving living conditions, whereas Malthus shed the earlier optimism of the political economists and argued in the late 1790s that the poor were condemned to misery, since unchecked population growth would always exceed the means of subsistence.

Many historians take Malthus's *Essay on the Principle of Population* (1798) as the most significant intervention into the debate on poverty. His argument that population was neither the source nor even an indicator of economic productivity combined elements of **political economy** [33] and Evangelical *religion [10] to redefine the relationship between the poor, human nature, and national wealth. It tapped contemporary *millennial and counter-revolutionary fears, attracting considerable attention—both favourable and hostile.

Social theorists blended versions of political economy and more traditional approaches in order to create a new moral science of poverty. They preserved a hierarchical model of society ('inferiors' were rephrased as the 'lower classes'), but weakened the moral glue of 'depend-ence'. For much of the eighteenth century, dependence was the fundamental social and polit-ical relationship which bound servants to masters, children to parents, wives to husbands, subjects to rulers. Towards the end of the century, however, a range of social commentators challenged the moral value of male dependence, suggesting that parish relief and charity inter-fered with human nature, worsening problems of poverty.

Dependence on poor relief, it was frequently stated, destroyed every incentive to work hard and left the poor surly and insubordinate. Commentators compared the English poor unfavourably with those in Scotland, where poor relief was much less expansive. By the turn of the century, independence had lost many of its earlier pejorative associations with political presumption and claims for social autonomy, and now signified a healthy self-sufficiency that kept the labourer submissive and off the parish accounts. In this way it merely refashioned employees' 'natural' dependence on their employers, as a pattern of fluid and contractual eco-nomic relationships based on individual self-interest in place of an older pattern of fixed social ranks and reciprocal duties.

By 1800, the characterization of dependence was well established. It undermined older dis-tinctions between the deserving and undeserving poor, those willing to work and those unwill-ing, and so discredited much contemporary poor law practice. Self-sufficiency was not just a matter of living within present earnings, but an exercise in foresight and prudence. Reformers advocated new forms of assistance, including savings banks and benefit societies, as instru-ments to enable the lower classes to provide for themselves against times of sickness or un-employment, and to absorb 'surplus gains' which might otherwise encourage profligacy, luxury, and ostentation. By 1803 there were more than 9,000 *friendly societies in England and Wales, associated particularly with towns and industrial areas, but also promoted by farm-ers and clergymen. Enthusiastic proponents claimed that these funds would support the poor adequately, but not over-generously, in every contingency, requiring the charitable to manage rather than donate funds. The poor would need neither public-works nor material relief to survive. Promotional literature promised economic benefit to rich and poor, parish pensioners and ratepayers, while enforcing social proprieties and an Evangelical program of moral reform. Nevertheless, many societies fostered conviviality and sometimes industrial and political activity.

By the first decade of the nineteenth century a new and problematic type of person, the pauper, had been introduced into the social account. Pauperism was judged an unnatural, immoral condition to be eradicated rather than relieved: both characteristics marked it off from existing understandings of the poor. Although the distinction between the pauper and the poor was continually contested, undermined, and asserted only to be contradicted, the 1834 Royal Commission declared it the first and 'essential' principle of poor law reform. The pauper was a specifically delineated moral and economic category. Building on earlier definitions of poverty as a condition both of labour and of destitution, social commentators cut away a newly identified ambiguity to describe as paupers all who relied on the poor rates or charity to supplement their income. Pauperism was seen as individual moral failure, and parish relief, particularly wage supplementation, was condemned for paralysing moral independence and dissolving social ties. Symptomatic of this economic and moral disorder, the pauper's house was typically represented as dirty, cheerless, indolent, and demoralized. Pauperism chained English labourers to the African negro and Arabian slave; once this link was broken, observers discerned the labourers' pride and contentment in their cottages, gardens, and families.

The contrast between the pauper's dwelling and the thriving cottage was a particularly rich imaginary scene. Although descriptions were framed as true accounts of the lives of the poor based on observation and experience, they were subject to tight conventions which attributed very specific meanings to those lives. Responses to George *Morland's paintings of rural life indicate that observers were disturbed by 'realistic' depictions of the miserable and defiant poor. The garden surplus, which the independent cottager was urged to sell, was not an Arcadian abundance. More conventional, therefore, were glowing contrasts between a wretched hut and the humble, happy return of a labourer to the moral space of the cottage, his evening fire, family, and 'wholesome, but frugal plenty'. Such apparently simple accounts had complex messages to convey. Radicals, populists, and conservatives also marshalled these images, for different ends, in literature addressed to the lower classes. Cottages and hovels conveyed political and aesthetic values which framed the concept of pauperism and gave new emphasis to the male poor.

Reference to a generic 'poor man' was not new. What, however, became distinctive in the late eighteenth and early nineteenth centuries was a clearer focus on the poor as men, and in particular on the characteristics that constituted manliness [cf. the contested virtue *sensibility, 11]. For what the pauper lacked was manly virtue; the pathetic plight of the distressed and worthy labourer forced to apply for relief was discerned, as one contemporary claimed, in the 'downcast look and broken accents [which] fully declare, that the manly feelings of the heart are at variance with the deed'. Manliness was more than independence from the poor rates on which more women relied than men. It connoted moral strength and prudence. Above all it was a domestic virtue which took its meaning from an association with hearth and family. Late-eighteenth-century Evangelicals rewrote old arguments for contentment in terms of mended clothes and fireside cheer, and found a new incentive to labour in men's responsibility for the economic support of dependent wives and children, and adult children's responsibility for decrepit parents. By implication, female reliance on the parish, with its complicated implications of expense, dependence, and unruliness, was of pervasive concern.

The unit of social independence, and of national moral regeneration, was now the male labourer and his family. In contrast with the pauper, he was a 'competent' member of society, a

15. George Morland, *The Squire's Door*, *c*.1790. Morland's popular genre paintings, though often sentimental, purveyed a realism which ruffled traditional ideas about rural quietism and labouring-class domesticity.

condition which lent him political status. Although his lack of property fundamentally disqualified him from the government of society, this competency was the basis of more radical claims for political representation. Both William *Cobbett and more conservative writers shared a view of cottage cosiness, whether to emphasize the dignity of labour, the economics of poor relief, or the *reformation of manners. Many working-class men involved in radical politics, and supported by female dependents, adapted elements of this approach to advance their own independent claims for political rights. Thus by the 1820s, understandings of poverty formulated by the non-poor, and co-opted in distinctive ways by the poor themselves, entailed specific and new understandings of sexual difference.

It is tempting to interpret these discussions as an unproblematic assertion of a new ideology of separate spheres, of public and private domains, in which women of all classes were confined to the household and men to the public, economic, visible, even proto-democratic realm. Elements of this ideology certainly existed. Public-spirited gentlemen who took an interest in poor law business were said to display 'manlier feeling', while women writers carved out their own sphere for philanthropy, recommending a distinctly female practice of visiting poor women in their homes to give advice on household economy and childbirth. Poor women were associated with the comforts of home, as opposed to the wasteful temptations of the masculine realm of the *tavern and alehouse. The virtue of cleanliness moved further up the list of

16. *Sunday Morning (Bible Reading at the Cottage Door)*, c.1812–20, by Scottish painter Alexander Carse, presented the more conventionally acceptable view of labourers' lives in the late eighteenth century.

desirable qualities in the poor, and marked the maintenance of social and moral order as the sphere of women. However, contemporary debate and philanthropic practice also suggest inadequacies in the separate spheres model, and considerable ambivalence about women's social duties. Commentators recognized the value of women's work and linked economic with sexual vulnerability, while female philanthropists contested male prejudice against women and laid claim to national reformation.

Throughout the period women were paid less than men, and though their earnings were crucial in maintaining the household, marriage was for most an economic necessity. Realignments and intensifications of the sexual division of labour, including the reduction of female employment in southern arable farming, heightened philanthropists' dilemmas about the female poor. Sarah *Trimmer, who gave moral justification to new employment practices, feared that where there was no employment in spinning or knitting, women would leave the quietness of home for the bad company of routine agricultural work. She could suggest no remedy. Hannah *More recognized poor women as independent economic operators, not as dependants. But it was difficult to draw them into the new regime of self-sufficiency when, as she found in Cheshire, the weekly subscription for benefit clubs (around 1½d. in 1791) was almost beyond their means: More had to give widows their subscription money secretly. Women's employment in workshops and factories roused fears of social disintegration. Uneasiness about the proper bounds of female labour was perhaps resolved in the idealism of cottage scenes, but it signified a more general difficulty in reconciling understandings of social difference (what did it mean to be poor?) with concepts of sexual difference (what did it mean to be a woman?). And such inconsistency generated new moral concerns, including anxiety that domestic overcrowding improperly mixed sexes and generations.

Issues of dependence and independence framed various philanthropic proposals and attempts to reform the poor laws. Schemes to make the poor independent by renting them decent cottages with gardens or allotments became increasingly common after 1815. Legislation supported allotment schemes which were most commonly implemented in southern English counties, where rural poverty was acute and poor rates high. At a time of postwar social dislocation, advocates depicted a self-sufficient and well-managed poor, and promoted a grander scheme of social harmony established in a particular view of marriage and of relations between landlord and labourer.

From the late eighteenth century, agricultural labourers supplanted metropolitan dwellers as a focus of social concern, even though the former were of declining economic and demographic significance. However, interest in their plight involved a broader discussion of new forms of capitalism, including the *enclosure of common land: complaints that farmers destroyed cottages as a strategy to reduce poor rates encapsulated more general fears of social tension and conflict. This vision was shared by many labouring men who associated access to land with economic survival, comfort, and dignity. In one Hampshire parish at least, cottagers were prepared to pay high rents to get land. As a remedy for the new social affliction of pauperism, allotments were distinctly old-fashioned (rules typically forbade ploughing in favour of 'spade husbandry'), and were criticized on the very modern grounds that they encouraged population. Cottages represented a society of sturdy yeomen existing in some recent but ill-defined era before *agrarian change. The theory of pauperism, for all its scientific status, tended to presuppose a past age in which the poor were less dependent and corrupt.

Many who borrowed Malthus's concept of population surplus wavered between his analysis of the vigorous, reproductive body and an older tradition concerning human corruption. Nor was population theory fully integrated with the powerful rhetoric of manly virtue and domestic order. Malthus himself gave qualified praise to pleasure in love; but how were the joys of familial affection to be reconciled with warnings against early and imprudent marriage? The most significant resolution, which pre-dated Malthus's *Essay* by at least a decade, reserved domestic comfort, and by implication sexual enjoyment, for the independent poor man as an incentive and reward for useful employment.

As new work practices, including mechanization, increased human productivity, the simple link between population and economic prosperity grew less credible, and it seemed more important to preserve families of a particular type. Emigration was now discussed extensively. Proponents and critics of specific methods were much more concerned with family ties than early-eighteenth-century writers had been, and this became important in assessing the merits of charitable schemes and workhouses. Philanthropists were not above exploiting parental affection as a tool to secure the ends they desired. Workhouse critics argued against the cruel and impolitic destruction of family feeling which was so essential an incentive to labour and protection against pauperism, while those who devised punitive schemes to eradicate pauperism aimed to cut the familial and social connections through which the pauper drained the lifeblood of the nation, and this was an important element of workhouse proposals from the 1820s.

What philanthropists and campaigners for poor law reform usually agreed (and these were not necessarily discrete groups of people) was that the poor laws had gone awry—because they were out of date, poorly or corruptly administered, or established on bad principles. Calls for the abolition of the poor laws were the most radical response to poverty, a remedy suggested in 1786, echoed by Malthus and affirmed in the 1817 Report of a House of Commons Select Committee. Since the definition of poverty had shrunk from its earlier latitude, it was claimed that voluntary charity, exercised with due discrimination, would protect those few who were truly helpless. For the rest, fear or hope would stimulate appropriate behaviour. In 1819 Thomas Chalmers (1780–1847) led an experiment in one Glasgow parish to abolish poor relief. Though striking, this strategy was not endorsed by a majority in the debate. Nor was Bentham's elaborate 1798 plan adopted: to establish a vast centralized system of Panoptican workhouses, directed by a National Charity Company, in which all in need of any relief would be sent to work. More influential in the 1790s was Archdeacon *Paley's *utilitarian argument that the poor should be cared for by *law [8], and that they had a right to sustenance and charity founded in the law of nature, the origins of property, and divine will. By the early nineteenth century, however, this position was redefined in line with thinking on dependence; rising poor rates were generally cited as a reason for minimal legal provision, framed to deter harmful behaviour, foster self-sufficiency, and effect moral reform.

Early-nineteenth-century commentators, many of them influenced by an Evangelical sense of human sinfulness, were much less optimistic than their predecessors both about the moral condition of the poor and about the potential for intervention. But philanthropic activity did not decline; rather it flourished—established, so its supporters claimed, on a new, rational, scientific footing. Indeed, dismay at the moral condition of the lower classes and doubts about the efficacy of a statutory system of poor relief made philanthropy seem all the more necessary, creating a distinction between charity and legal provision not always evident earlier. Working within a framework based on 'laws' of human nature and of the economic market, clerics in particular saw properly constituted and well-exercised charity as the key to re-establishing harmony between social classes.

By 1822 London alone had nearly 500 benevolent institutions. Here and in the provinces, charity expressed more than one social vision and was an important focus for middle-class male sociability, political aspiration, and influence; it offered women formal opportunities to exercise patronage and assert their capabilities, albeit usually under the direction of men. The number and variety of charities founded suggest the vigour and diversification of philanthropy in the period. Thomas Barnard's Society for Bettering the Condition and Improving the Comforts of the Poor (established in 1795) publicized various experiments in relief, particularly cottages, cheap recipes, and friendly societies. The urban middle class contributed large sums of money for emergency relief of the poor in towns and cities, and organized mendicant societies to clear the streets of beggars. Working children were targeted for assistance. Metropolitan charities provided therapeutic sea-bathing, electrical treatments, trusses, and *vaccination. Various religious denominations funded *missions in Britain and abroad, and translated the English prayer-book into other languages. Prison discipline, night shelters, relief of debtors, rational recreation, and the investigation of cancer all found supporters.

Most significant were societies for the improvement of morals, and visiting and educational charities. The Proclamation Society (1787) and the *Society for the Suppression of Vice (1802) had powerful supporters in opposing popular immorality and reforming the habits of the poor. The practice of visiting gave philanthropic form to the new realization that individual responsibility and domestic management were the antidote to pauperism. It reflected growing interest in the details of particular cases, in creating a body of knowledge about the poor. Visiting was part of a broader shift away from institutional care, from hospitals and dispensaries, to assisting the sick poor at home. Thinking on poverty and philanthropy also influenced various educational initiatives: all were harnessed as a preventative against dependence. *Sunday schools were prominent in Wales and the industrial north, but spread throughout Britain, in both rural and urban areas. Compared with the early-eighteenth-century charity schools, they offered a restricted education; like the friendly societies, however, many were promoted, managed, and modified by the poor themselves.

The history of poverty, and of responses to it, is located fundamentally in a material environment. However, the connections between contemporaries' assertions about the poor and that material environment are neither simple nor self-evident. Although debates about poverty were firmly fixed in authors' claims that they were telling the truth about the lives of the poor, eighteenth- and nineteenth-century accounts cannot be regarded as unmediated representations of these lives. The true state of the poor remains elusive, as does the precise relationship between perceptions and experiences of poverty, and between understandings of poverty and the broader social and economic conditions in which historians set them. *Conduct books reveal little of how men and women, divided by class, lived according to either moral prescription or a sexual division of labour, while social attitudes are not readily discernible from evidence of economic change.

Questions of how political and economic change influenced social attitudes have shaped many historians' accounts of poverty and philanthropy. From the 'standard of living' debate (how well did the poor live?) to arguments about poor relief measures, historians have tended to give primacy to a material definition and context of poverty which either seeks to make sense of past attitudes or reveals that contemporary observers imperfectly understood their social environment, particularly structural economic change. But it is also possible to ask how *perceptions* of change influenced remedies for pauperism; how the generation and organization of knowledge about the poor infused economic practice; how eighteenth- and nineteenth-century definitions of poverty (however flawed in terms of modern research) shaped broader economic and political agendas.

Discussions about poverty in our period did not lead inexorably and uniformly to the new Poor Law in 1834. Ambiguities fractured thinking about cottages and population; fears of an unruly and suffering mass co-existed with a sense of national self-congratulation; various expedients at the local parish level ran counter to pamphlet opinion; and gentlemen argued about the benefits or cruel oppressions of workhouses and poor law reform. Contradictory analyses of poverty as the result of insufficient wages and the consequence of dependence were only partially resolved in the idea of the cottage. Nor is there historical consensus about whether the new poor law was a radical break from the old system of relief, or part of a longer process of intellectual adaptation by the ruling class.

From the late eighteenth century, a new analysis of poverty was developed in discussions of statutory and charitable relief. Sexual difference emerged as a key to understanding what had gone wrong with the system of poor relief and what could be done to remedy it. Dependence, cottages, self-sufficiency, and friendly societies were complex amalgamations of moral description, pragmatic proposal, and social imagination which turned on notions of manliness. Older and more eccentric opinions persisted, but the concept of pauperism and a new attitude to population grew increasingly dominant from the 1790s. The French revolutionary wars, agricultural dislocation, new forms of economic organization, and problems with the poor relief system contributed to feelings of unease and a growing certainty that something had to be done. Evangelical religion disseminated a particular outlook to the problem. Male agricultural labourers came back into view to embody the crucial difference between the pauper and the independent labourer.

During this period, the meanings of poverty were volatile. But they were also the basis for thoughtful and far-reaching analyses of national wealth, social harmony, human sinfulness, laws of nature, and the forms of government.

Andrew, D. T., *Philanthropy and Police: London Charity in the Eighteenth Century*, Princeton, NJ, 1989; Barrell, J., *The Dark Side of the Landscape: the Rural Poor in English Painting 1730–1840*, Cambridge, 1980; Cunningham, H., *The Children of the Poor: Representations of Childhood since the Seventeenth Century*, Oxford, 1991; Dean, M., *The Constitution of Poverty: Towards a Genealogy of Liberal Governance*, London, 1991; Devine, T. M., & Mitchison, R., eds., *People and Society in Scotland*, i: *1760–1830*, Edinburgh, 1988; Hall, C., 'The Tale of Samuel and Jemima: Gender and Working-Class Culture in Early-Nineteenth-Century England', in her *White, Male and Middle Class: Explorations in Feminism and History*, Cambridge, 1995; Himmelfarb, G., *The Idea of Poverty: England in the Early Industrial Age*, London, 1984; Innes, J., 'The "Mixed Economy of Welfare" in Early Modern England: Assessments of the Options from Hale to Malthus (*c.*1683–1803)', in M. Daunton, ed., *Charity, Self-Interest and Welfare in the English Past*, New York, 1996, 139–80; Oxley, G. W., *Poor Relief in England and Wales 1601–1834*, Newton Abbot, 1974; Poynter, J. R., *Society and Pauperism: English Ideas on Poor Relief, 1795–1834*, London, 1969; Snell, K. D. M., *Annals of the Labouring Poor: Social Change and Agrarian England, 1660–1900*, Cambridge, 1985.

13 · DOMESTICITY   CLARA TUITE

In his *Reflections on the Revolution in France* (1790), the counter-revolutionary and Romantic conservative Edmund *Burke wrote:

In this choice of inheritance we have given to our frame of polity the image of a relation in blood; binding up the constitution of our country with our dearest domestic ties; adopting our fundamental laws into the bosom of our family affections; keeping inseparable, and cherishing with the warmth of all their combined and mutually reflected charities, our state, our hearths, our sepulchres, and our altars.

As Burke suggests, the family is a political institution. 'Domestic attachments' and 'family affections' are the stuff that 'bind' a nation. Throughout his *Reflections*, Burke imagines the British nation *as* a family, in opposition to the French nation, which he imagines as a cabal, as a destroyer of the family. Burke's text initiated a new language of nationalism based on domesticity: it demonstrates the way in which both the threat of revolutionary incursion from across the Channel and a form of conservative or organic *Romanticism combined to produce a particular representation or ideal of the family, a particular *politicization* of the idea of the family, in our period.

The word family today suggests the exclusion of those who are not part of the biological or

17. James Gillray, *The Blessings of Peace/The Curses of War*, 1795. Produced on commission for a loyalist association, this print depicts the French Revolution as a threat to hearth and home.

nuclear family, constituted by the heterosexual couple and their biological offspring. These late-twentieth-century understandings of the family may be said to be the specific product of ideological developments which date from the eighteenth century, which have naturalized the social construct of the nuclear family, and which have regulated the understanding of the word 'family' to refer to biologically related individuals. In his 1755 *Dictionary*, Samuel *Johnson offered two definitions of the family: '1. Those who live in the same house; household. 2. Those that descend from one common progenitor; a race; a tribe; a generation.' Each definition suggests a quite different, and to some extent class-specific, understanding of the family: the first, implying a contained unit, limited in size and space and revolving around the house, points towards the labouring-class and middle-class arrangement of the family; the second, which is transgenerational and exceeds space and time, suggests an aristocratic idea of family. In one sense, the material, ideological, and cultural history of the family in the Romantic period is marked by intersections, tensions, superimpositions, and attempts to integrate these different meanings across the boundaries of *class [15] and gender.

The ideology of domesticity—the vast investment in the *idea* of the family across a range of social, cultural, and political discourses and practices—is linked to the broad historical process known as the 'rise' of the middle classes which occurred between the seventeenth and nineteenth centuries. This involved an accession to power on the part of the middle classes based on the development of capitalist strategies of production and *industrialization [14], but also on the growth of *cultural* power, through the control of *language [40], rhetoric, representation, and writing. Associated with the cementing of cultural authority through increased literacy and the commercialization of culture as a whole were changes in class and gender relations resulting from the *agricultural revolution and its practices of *enclosure and agricultural improvement [see *land, 16].

These changing modes of production were arranged materially and ideologically according to a gendered division of labour—one of the main features of the ideology of domesticity, whereby the pursuit of capital or work in the market-place was marked as an exclusively masculine form of labour, while *women [4] were confined largely to reproductive labour, housekeeping, and child-rearing (see *childhood). Of course, women's lives had always been circumscribed by their identification with the function of reproducing and raising children, but from the middle of the eighteenth century this identification was consolidated and elaborated in a particular way so as to facilitate capitalist production. The new division of labour was important materially in maximizing the efficiency of specialized labour within the capitalist market-place and workplace. Ideologically, the gendered division of labour *naturalized* the equation between women and maternity, suggesting that a woman's role was entirely comprehended and fulfilled by her function within the home.

This demarcation of the public and private spheres was also implicated in an attempt to reconcile religious principles with the pursuit of wealth in the market-place [see *religion, 10]. If we define the main material and cultural difference between the aristocratic and middle classes in terms of the aristocratic identification with land as opposed to the middle-class identification with liquid assets, one of the interesting things about the period is the way in which the middle classes authorize and legitimate capitalism and the mobility of cash and property. If the aristocratic ethos of land sees money as unstable and corrupting (despite the fact that in *practice* the aristocracy deployed *agrarian forms of capitalism from the seventeenth century), then part of the ideological work of the middle classes involved making money clean, virtuous, and only relatively—and not excessively—mobile. And it was partially to this end that the ideology of domesticity was promulgated. The home was idealized as a kind of refuge of affection away from the market-place. In this way, the moral ambiguities and tensions of an exploitative and profit-seeking market-place were hygienically separated from a feminized and purified realm of the home. Defining the metropolis and the market-place as masculine spheres enabled the retention of the domestic sphere as a pure space free from the vagaries and excesses of capitalist competition. For example, historian Anna Clark has pointed out in *Women's Silence, Men's Violence* (1987) that the myth that women are raped only by strangers or deviants emerged precisely at this time, to warn women against the dangers of straying outside their proper place in the home, thereby consolidating this material and ideological demarcation between the streets and the home.

In *Family Fortunes: Men and Women of the English Middle Class* (1987) Leonore Davidoff and Catherine Hall argue that the middle-class ideal of domesticity was imbricated with a particular kind of capitalist ethos which stressed not individual profit but the provision of wealth for dependants—or at least justified profit in terms of this provision. This led to the development of particular strategies such as the partnership, the annuity, and the life assurance, which were designed to expand the business while providing for family members and future generations. In this way, specifically bourgeois capitalist enterprises were dependent upon ties of family, kin, and friendship. And it was by maximizing the returns on wide investment that the middle classes managed to create their own dynasties modelled upon aristocratic dynasties based on land.

Implicated in this elaboration of domesticity as a moral and social ideal, and a corollary of burgeoning capitalism, was a new emphasis in the period upon the site of the home. The aristocratic conception of domesticity was associated with the estate as the 'family seat', and offered its self-representation through the contemporary aristocratic genre of the *conversation piece. This usually used an outdoor setting for its celebration of the aristocratic family, so as to take in the estate as both home and grounds. The middle-class counterpart, on the other

18. *Maternal Recreation*, an
anonymous engraving reproduced
for the 1816 trade catalogue of
Broadwood's, leading piano
manufacturers to middle-class
Britain.

hand, identified the home as a single dwelling, along with its contents. Middle-class representations, typified by 'Maternal Recreation', featured in an 1816 trade catalogue of the piano manufacturer Broadwood, thus tended to focus on an interior as a site of domestic 'recreation'. In
this particular epiphany of middle-class domestic life, the experience of domestic relations is
mediated by commodities such as tasteful furnishings, fashionable clothing [see *fashion],
a musical instrument—either harpsichord or piano, which were primary instruments of
domestic *music. Here domesticity is linked to consumer desire, emphasizing the domestic
interior as a site of conspicuous cultural and material consumption [see **consumerism, 19**].

A growing fascination with all aspects of the home—including, for example, how many
rooms were appropriate for how many children, for their physical and mental well-being—
underpinned the idea of the family as a close-knit cell and self-contained unit. The family
became increasingly enclosed—physically and conceptually—within the four walls of the
nuclear household, implicitly defined in terms of middle-class domesticity. The home
became the focus of the writings of reformers such as Edwin *Chadwick and James Phillips
Kay-Shuttleworth (1804–77), who surveyed and monitored the lives of the urban labouring
class and pondered the extent to which they conformed to middle-class ideals.

Ideas of domesticity were also implicated within the category of the 'natural' as derived from
natural sciences, particularly *evolution and biology, in terms of which socially constructed
differences between men and women were categorized as part of the natural rather than social
order [see **natural philosophy, 34**]. If women were contained within the home, women's
bodies were also contained both materially and figuratively in accordance with the ideals of virtuous motherhood that involved an extension of the maternal role beyond that of child-bearer
to that of biological carer and nurturer. This emphasis on the prolonged *corporeal* investment
of the mother in the child, and of the child in the mother, can be seen in the increased adoption
of breastfeeding by the natural mother in Britain from the middle of the eighteenth century. A
further sign was the developing emphasis upon hygiene, cleanliness, physical exercise, and
other forms of regulating the body, as well as on the provision of a salubrious domestic atmosphere within the home in order to ensure optimum conditions for such physical health and
beauty. Medical tracts like William Buchan's (1729–1805) bestselling *Domestic Medicine* (1769)
promulgated the practice of breastfeeding as a moral virtue: 'she who abandons the fruit of her
love . . . to the care of her nurse, must forever forfeit the name of mother.' Breastfeeding also
became a pervasive trope within middle-class critiques of aristocratic maternal patterns, which
did not place such a premium on the practice. The idealization of this bodily relationship
between mother and child was part of a new pedagogical, moral, medical, sexual, and commercial investment in childhood as a particular state with its own distinctive requirements,

interests, and rituals. This elevation of childhood as special state is also apparent in the proliferation of *children's literature and toys, and in the rapid growth of institutional schooling for the middle classes [see *education, 17].

The well-being and improvement of the biological family offered a new middle-class form of corporeal 'capital', consolidated through the professionalization of science and of social sciences such as **political economy [33]** and *statistics. Corporeal health was used by the middle classes to define themselves against the effete and interbred aristocracy, on the one hand, and the biologically impoverished poorer classes, vitiated by disease and uncleanliness, on the other. Although the extended family was often an economic necessity for urban and rural labouring-class people, middle-class reformers used it to stigmatize urban labouring-class families. In James Phillips Kay's (later Kay-Shuttleworth) *Moral and Physical Condition of the Working Classes in Manchester* (1832), for example, moral and physical threats to 'the sanctity of the domestic circle' are both the cause and effect of the impoverished condition of the urban Irish poor in Manchester. In effect, Kay's medical, social, and statistical diagnosis racializes **poverty [12]** and disease as the inherent natural condition of the urban Irish poor.

This identification of the poor with moral laxity and sexual excess worked to justify the middle classes in their moves to curb the power of the poor to reproduce. A key text in the middle-class regulation and socialization of sexual and procreative behaviour was Thomas *Malthus's *Essay on Population* (1798), which recommended 'moral restraint' as the solution to supposed 'overpopulation'. 'Moral restraint' was a regime of a delay in marriage which eschewed the vice or misery of 'irregular gratifications' such as masturbation, and stressed a concomitant outlawing of birth control, prostitution, and 'cohabitation'—the term for unconventional forms of sexuality such as *homosexuality. Malthus's paradigm of the procreative couple, who waited until they reached a certain age before marrying and reproducing, was a construct that neatly met the corporeal demands and domestic arrangements of capitalist production. Malthusian policies of the state, such as the 1834 *poor laws, which separated married couples, and the 1836 Illegitimacy Act, which punished single mothers, can be seen to arrogate procreation as a privilege of the middle classes, and to deny this as a right to the labouring classes. Apparent within this consolidation of the middle-class nuclear family is a less visible process which involves the ideological consolidation of domesticity through opposition to its unwelcome alternatives or outcasts: national; racial; social; economic; sexual.

While it is simplistic, as some recent cultural historians have argued, to reduce many historical and cultural complexities of the period to a narrative of the 'rise' of the middle classes, there is nevertheless a pervasive and self-conscious sense of destiny voiced on the part of middle-class professionals, writers, reformers, and educators. Not only does Malthus claim that the middle classes are the best suited to corporeal, financial, and moral improvement, but the radical *republican and feminist Mary *Wollstonecraft also speaks polemically and triumphantly of the middle classes, when she says in the *Vindication of the Rights of Woman* (1792), 'I pay particular attention to those in the middle class, because they appear to be in the most natural state.' This naturalization of middle-class ideological prerogatives is what constitutes the ideal of domesticity.

The domestic ideal, or the ideal of the sentimental or affective family, was self-consciously opposed by the middle classes to what they perceived to be the mercenary or dynastic courtship and marriage practices of the aristocracy. The conventional understanding of the institutions of bourgeois society, including that of companionate marriage, is that they do away with the kind of absolutism which had marked the patriarchal conception of marriage. Historically, the doctrine of patriarchalism, first elaborated in Robert Filmer's *Patriarcha* (1680), holds that political authority may be comprehended in terms of the governance of a household. Certainly, theorists such as *Rousseau and *Locke argued against Filmer and this idea of absolute paternal right. However, the bourgeois, liberal development of the companionate

marriage often remained merely a modified or 'enlightened' version of earlier patriarchal patterns and so carried its own forms of sexual injustice. For a start, it was often a companionate
marriage in theory only. For all practical intents and purposes, the liberal middle-class household remained male-dominated. While it has been claimed that an emphasis upon increased
'choice' of a marriage partner necessarily involved an improvement in the prevalent conceptions towards women, there is no real corroborative evidence. On the contrary, there are
important ways in which the idealizing of the sentimental domestic family provided a fresh
rationale for the subordination of women.

Companionate marriage could work to subordinate women because it further legitimized
male supremacy by claiming that the interests of the family were totally united, and because it
underwrote the stricter separation of women's spheres from the outside world, thereby reinforcing characterizations of women as creatures of sentiment rather than as rational citizens.
This ideological belief is expressed in the common law doctrine of 'coverture', by which the
wife's legal identity was subsumed under that of her husband [see *law, 8]. As Carole Pateman
has argued, the difference between early patriarchal conceptions of the family and modern
ones was that the extended family was diminished to be replaced by husband and wife, so that
the marriage contract fashioned domestic relations. It was this liberal-capitalist ideal, best
expounded by Locke, that informs the modern idea of the 'housewife', someone who is related
to her husband as a kind of contracted but unpaid worker in the home.

The widely read writings of Rousseau elaborated this version of family life. For Rousseau,
the family was naturally and necessarily patriarchal. He justified male rule on the grounds of
the necessity for the man to be sure his children are his own; however, the ethical *justification*
for patriarchal rule within the family was based on sentiment—a father will naturally act from
his heart in the interests of wife and offspring [see *sensibility, 11]. This belief that women's
interests were identified with and encompassed by the family was also elaborated in the classic
*utilitarian liberalism of James *Mill. His *Essay on Government* (1820) argued that women
could be legitimately excluded from voting rights because their interests were 'included in
those of their husbands and fathers'.

Radical critiques of marriage, such as that in William *Godwin's *Enquiry Concerning
Political Justice* (1793), implied that the ideal of companionate marriage masked an elaborate
mechanism for facilitating the transmission of private property, and for turning women into
pieces of private property. As Wollstonecraft wrote in her *Vindication*, women's 'persons [are]
often legally prostituted' in marriage. None the less, Wollstonecraft can be seen to offer a
different form of idealization of domesticity in her elaboration of an ideal of republican motherhood for women. She emphasized a woman's role as mother over and above, and even to the
exclusion of, her role as wife. By separating the normally conflated roles of wife and mother,
Wollstonecraft thus crucially revised the conservative middle-class ideal of domesticity.

The division of the world into public and private, masculine and feminine, rational and
emotional, intellectual and moral, was bound up just as much with class—and with shared
class interests across gender lines—as with a simple division between masculine and feminine.
Lower-class men, like middle-class women, were the object of the attentions of middle-class
reformers promulgating a particular version of conjugal domesticity. Hannah *More, for
example, directed her *Cheap Repository Tracts at lower-class men, with the aim of reforming them as domestic subjects, making them into responsible husbands and fathers. Tracts
directed against drinking and potentially disruptive collective activity stressed the positive
alternative of domesticity. Circulating in the same cheap, popular forms as radical material,
these tracts sought to effect the identification of the lower-class subject with the family as an
antidote to radical political activism. Some labouring-class women also had a middle-class
ideal of domesticity to some extent forced upon them when the increasing specialization of the
capitalist market-place squeezed them out of the labour market. They were also subject to

ideological strictures in terms of which they were accused of idleness if they did *not* engage in the production of wealth for the family. The writer and feminist Mary *Robinson highlighted this contradiction between the ideal of passive femininity and the actual lives of the vast majority of British working women in her *Letter to the Women of England* (1799):

If woman be the weaker creature, why is she employed in laborious avocations? why compelled to endure the fatigue of household drudgery; to scrub, to scower, to labour, both late and early, while the powdered lacquet only waits at the chair, or behind the carriage of his employer? Why are women, in many parts of the kingdom, permitted to follow the plough; to perform the laborious business of the dairy . . . to wash, to brew, and to bake, while men are employed in measuring ribands; folding gauzes?

Robinson here exposes the class bias of this construction of femininity, which reserves the prerogative and privilege of passivity to middle-class women. Wollstonecraft mounted a similar vindication of working women when she attacked Burke for representing working women as 'furies of hell', to which she responded ironically, 'probably you mean women who gained a livelihood by selling vegetables or fish'—that is, as street-sellers. While Wollstonecraft's immediate object was to vindicate the Parisian street rioters, she was also attacking the particular image of domesticity which underlay Burke's image of the female rioters, and the way in which it worked to present working women as unnatural and unfeminine. She was attempting to break this association between public women and prostitutes, and doing so, partly, to reclaim their status as virtuous mothers.

While we have been identifying the ideology of domesticity as a middle-class phenomenon, it is perhaps more accurate to say that it was predicated on a number of material and cultural factors which involved interrelations across classes. *Embourgeoisement* made an emphatic mark on the aristocracy as well as the labouring class during this period. Practices and patterns of marriage and will-making thus reveal a great deal about the material manifestations of domesticity at the nexus of class and gender. A crucial part of the story of domesticity has to do with intermarriage between the middle classes and the aristocracy. Intermarriage provided a means of social mobility for the middle classes and lower gentry, as well as a strategy of aristocratic recuperation and consolidation at a time of great economic instability. Marriage was the central strategy of material and cultural transmission that helped to stabilize class arrangements and yet to loosen these in order to allow a sanctioned and relative degree of mobility (akin to the sanctioning of *relative* mobility of capital within the economic sphere).

The British aristocracy of this period is often seen as having adopted the middle-class ideal of the sentimental family, i.e. they abandoned the ideal of marriage as a dynastic strategy, and the family as a patriarchal conception, in favour of companionate marriage. And while it has become something of a commonplace to narrate the development in the eighteenth century of an 'affective' family away from a mercenary, calculating model of marriage and family, it is important to acknowledge that this move was also in part strategic. The aristocracy was forced—for material survival and the survival of their names and estates—to come to terms with middle-class cultural dominance, primarily by marrying into middle-class money. Jane *Austen's novels are particularly interesting on this subject because of the way in which their formulaic courtship plots and marriage endings can be seen to serve the political purpose of encouraging social assimilation by marriage with previously unaffiliated groups or classes. Romantic love justified these new arrangements: tensions governing class relations were transformed into individualized, gender-specific traits. Austen's novels represent intermarriage between the lower gentry/middle classes and aristocracy as mutually beneficial: allowing social mobility for the gentry, and moral and financial regeneration for the aristocracy.

In *Pride and Prejudice* (1813), for example, Elizabeth Bennett's consciousness of Darcy's 'pride' is represented as the 'prejudice' of intelligent lower-gentry female subjectivity, whilst Darcy personifies an unbecoming 'pride' in not wishing to marry down into the landless gentry.

With the cancelling out of these traits, class antagonism is neutralized. In *Persuasion* (1817) Sir Walter Elliot must be 'persuaded' of the virtues of marrying into the professions to regenerate the estate, while *Mansfield Park* (1814) proposes the selective patronage of individuals from the outer ring of kinship relations. All these novels demonstrate the *embourgeoisement* of the aristocratic family—the process by which the aristocratic family became more like a middle-class family—as it went through a process of retrenchment and consolidation during this period, notable in the cutting back of patronage and dependent kin that we see in *Mansfield Park*.

The ideology of domesticity has been identified with the middle classes because of the way in which it served their social interests and aspirations for upward mobility. At the same time part of this bourgeois enterprise involved the renovation of the aristocracy. In this sense, domesticity was complicit in a symbolic recuperation of the family on behalf of the aristocracy and the *monarchy, as in Burke's sacralization of the aristocratic extended family. Burke attempted to naturalize the connection between filial devotion and the willingness of a subject to obey. His strategic naturalization effectively reactivated the Puritan patriarchalist conception of the family, which had been attacked and replaced in the work of Locke by the contractual model of state and family relations. Burke's rhetoric sentimentalized paternal authority, and hence became a key component in the larger sentimentalizing of marriage and familial relations.

Burke's elaboration of a specifically aristocratic sense of the family within the framework of a mythical interconnection between 'those who are living, those who are dead, and those who are yet to be born' had a number of ideological effects. First, it presented an idealized, mystified, aristocratic family which could stand symbolically for a hierarchically ordered nation. This sentimentalization of the aristocracy, and the mystification of property as something to be passed on with family values, reinforced and protected the principle of *primogeniture. Identifying women with the family and the home was one way of stemming the tide of revolutionary ideas that were seen as spreading like a disease across the Channel from France. Burke's text is exemplary in its multiple use of 'domesticity' to signify the private as well as the domestic, and the national as opposed to the foreign. He was as opposed to certain foreign elements within British society as much as without—such potentially subversive foreign elements could encompass the urban and provincial poor, the unmarried mother, the Jewish moneylender, and the homosexual man or woman. His domestic ideology worked to identify a certain type of subject as *the* national subject.

Burke is important for forging this subtle connection between private sentiments and public politics, which later became the commonplace of state-sponsored nationalism. *The Day* in 1809, commenting typically on the Royal Jubilee celebrations, declared: 'The whole nation [was] like one great family in solemn prayer and thanksgiving, for . . . the Father of his People.' It was the royal *family* and not just the monarch which acquired increased currency during the period, and indeed which could be seen to underlie and underwrite a kind of renovation of the monarchy. The ideal of royal domesticity was even more honoured when it was subverted, as in the case of the protagonists of the *American Revolution, who referred to George III as an unnatural father, and were referred to by *loyalists as parricides, and who sought to replace him with a new, benevolent father figure in George Washington, known from 1778 as 'the Father of His Country'. Even when the family ideal was dramatically broken, as in the notorious example of George IV's infidelity, the result was an unprecedented popular—and female and feminist— eruption of support for the 'wronged Queen' during the *Queen Caroline affair of 1820.

By 1832, the ideology of the family and of domesticity was firmly rooted in a whole network of interrelated social, scientific, moral, religious, and economic discourses that could be used as weapons against particular social, sexual, and ethnic minorities, as it was in the burgeoning movements of social science and political economy. The *Reform Act of 1832 is significant not only as the first explicit extension of democratic suffrage, but also, *through* this, as the first explicit exclusion of women from participating in the political process, so that empowerment of the middle class was to some extent dependent upon subordination of women. Arguments against female suffrage assumed that the woman's interests would be represented by her husband, who had the interests of his family at heart.

But perhaps the most powerful indicator of the way in which the identification of women with the family in this period was inextricably linked with the loss of individual rights for women was the Dower Act of 1833, whereby wives lost the absolute right to inherit. The dower was originally based on the idea of 'provision' as part of aristocratic property arrangements. Within middle-class property arrangements, however, the idea of provision worked in such a way that male trustees had access to the woman's capital to use in the pursuit of their own economic interests. By being identified exclusively with the family, a woman thus lost rights as an individual—rights that were maintained by men. Interestingly, such inheritance strategies did not bear as heavily on women who fell outside the pale of the domestic ideal: the unmarried heiress, non-heterosexual, or actively lesbian woman—or *sapphist, to use one contemporary term. That unmarried heiresses were not necessarily circumscribed by such laws is indicated in a less celebrated historical event of 1832—the 'clandestine marriage' between the young Yorkshire gentry heiress Anne *Lister and her companion and sexual partner, Ann Walker. With the marriage, Lister entailed her property upon Walker (and many unmarried heiresses similarly bequeathed property to friends). However, this subversion of aristocratic patrilineal conventions was intentionally temporary. Ann Walker's property was entailed back to Lister's family after her death in order to preserve the family name. Thus in a period of intense pressure to conform to new ideals of domestic orthodoxy, a young, lower-gentry practising lesbian was able to affiliate her unorthodox sexual practice and lifestyle with a dynastic family identity.

Armstrong, N., *Desire and Domestic Fiction: A Political History of the Novel*, Oxford, 1987; Binhammer, K., 'The Sex Panic of the 1790s', *Journal of the History of Sexuality*, 6 (1996), 409–34; Clark, A., *Women's Silence, Men's Violence: Sexual Assault in England 1770–1840*, London, 1987; Colley, L., 'The Apotheosis of George III: Loyalty, Royalty and the British Nation 1760–1820', *Past and Present*, 102 (1984), 94–129; Davidoff, L., & Hall, C., *Family Fortunes: Men and Women of the English Middle Class 1780–1850*, London, 1987; Hill, B., *Women, Work and Sexual Politics in Eighteenth-Century England*, Oxford, 1989; Liddington, J., 'Beating the Inheritance Bounds: Anne Lister (1791–1840) and her Dynastic Identity', *Gender and History*, 7 (1995), 260–74; Lynch, D., 'Domesticating Fictions and Nationalizing Women: Edmund Burke, Property, and the Reproduction of Englishness', in A. Richardson & S. Hofkosh, eds., *Romanticism, Race, and Imperial Culture*, Bloomington, 1996; Pateman, C., *The Sexual Contract*, Cambridge, 1988; Poovey, M., 'Curing the Social Body in 1832: James Phillips Kay and the Irish in Manchester', in her *Making a Social Body: British Cultural Formation, 1830–1864*, Chicago, 1995.

14 · INDUSTRIALIZATION   JOHN STEVENSON

The Romantic age and the cultural and artistic movement of *Romanticism occupy no firm temporal boundaries. In large part, however, they overlapped and interacted with the complex of changes which are subsumed under the name of the industrial revolution. The publication of the first parts of Edward *Gibbon's *Decline and Fall* in 1776 coincided with that of Adam *Smith's *Wealth of Nations* and the flurry of patents with which James *Watt created the first efficient form of steam power. By the end of our period, writers had begun to depict much more directly the social repercussions of industrialization. For Charles *Dickens, writing in 1840, the Black Country represented a land and people ravaged by the brutality of the machine: it was a

cheerless region . . . where not a blade of grass was seen to grow . . . where nothing green could live but on

the surface of the stagnant pools; [a world in which] strange engines spun and writhed like tortured creatures, clanking their iron chains. [Dismantled houses] here and there appeared, tottering to the earth,
propped up by fragments of others that had fallen down, unroofed, windowless, blackened, desolate, but
yet inhabited [by men, women and children] wan in their looks and ragged in attire, [who] tended
the engines, fed the tributary fires, begged upon the road, or scowled halfnaked from the doorless
houses.

These words epitomize the received image of the social repercussions of the industrial revolution: the creation of a mass urban society, governed by the regime of the factory and the pace of
the machine, an environment polluted and despoiled, its inhabitants rendered anonymous
and dehumanized. Dickens was only one of a number of figures in the early Victorian period,
such as *Carlyle, Disraeli, Kingsley, Gaskell, Engels, and de Tocqueville, whose views have
often been adduced as evidence about the social dimension of economic change. Discussion of
the social repercussions of industrialization, the 'Condition of England' question, occurred
well into the classic phase of the first industrial revolution, conventionally dated as beginning
in the late eighteenth century. The social criticism of the period prior to the 1830s, in the work
of figures such as Frederick *Eden and David Davies (d. 1819), both of whom were early
contributors to the debate on the *poor laws, was certainly concerned about *poverty [12],
squalor, under- and unemployment, crime, *policing [7], and demoralization, but its focus
was primarily the agricultural labourer and the rural poor. Similarly, William *Cobbett in
Rural Rides (1830) examined the plight of the agricultural labourer in the south, rather than the
workers in the towns of the north and of the Midlands: when Cobbett's testimony is called
on, it is concerning the repercussions of economic and social change on the *land [16]. His
writing on the state of the common people is dominated by his conviction that in the space of
half a century the countryside had become depopulated, its remaining population pauperized,
demoralized, and deprived of the wholesome fruits of their own toil, and that a once organic
relationship between farmers and labourers had been replaced by the cash nexus. *Rural Rides*
remains one of the most potent critiques of the effects of economic and social change as a
whole, an extended lament for a rural world that had been lost.

　　Cobbett and Dickens provide the two sides of what might be called the conventional picture
of the social impact of industrialization: an older rural world of security and prosperity, now
lost, contrasted with the squalor and degradation of the new mass society of the factory towns.
It is a view that remains deeply rooted, but in recent years historians have sought to qualify the
stark contrasts offered by the first commentators on Britain's transition to an industrial society.
In particular, they have sought to refine the view of the industrial revolution as a discrete phase
of development occurring, approximately, in the century before 1850. Although we need not
go so far as some in regarding the industrial revolution as a 'myth', it is necessary to recognize
that historians tend to use the phrase in different ways. Sometimes it is applied to the rapid
growth in the later eighteenth century of specific sectors of the manufacturing industry, particularly cotton and iron, and the associated development of factories, steam power, and new
forms of *transport. It is also taken to stand for the structural shift in the economy over a longer
period which saw Britain's transition from a primarily agricultural society to one in which
manufacturing, mining, and *engineering played the larger role. Overlapping with these views
is that of the industrial revolution as a marker of decisive change, in which the economy as a
whole moved from a state of gradual or intermittent growth into a more rapid and continuous
advance in national income, or 'self-sustained growth'.

　　Where the social consequences of industrialization are concerned, the central difficulty lies
in evaluating the effects of a process which is now seen as both complex and protracted. As a
result, it is no longer possible to accept without major modification the view of an earlier
generation of historians that the century prior to 1850 witnessed an overwhelming transformation of social life in both industry and agriculture. For example, the view that the industrial

19. An example of the genre of 'industrial sublime', Philippe Jacques de Loutherbourg's *Coalbrookdale by Night* (1801) romanticizes a scene earlier treated by Joseph Wright of Derby in more classical style. This is industrialism as a source of wonder, not yet synonymous with exploitation and evil.

revolution was paralleled by an *agricultural revolution which brought about radical changes in techniques, organization, and social relations over a relatively brief period of time has been so heavily qualified that it can no longer be sustained. The gradual and long-term nature of change in agriculture and rural life is now well recognized. Moreover, many of the social changes traditionally associated with the industrial revolution have been seen increasingly as part of longer-term processes which have a complex relationship to economic growth. Accordingly, there has been a shift in emphasis in writing about the social aspects of industrialization from a concentration upon the impact of change in the most advanced sectors of the economy towards a broader and more balanced assessment of society as a whole. While many recent studies of British society follow a conventional chronology by beginning the modern era in the latter half of the eighteenth century, most now accept that the eighteenth century witnessed only the start of processes which were to take much of the next century to spread to the economy and to society at large.

Modern work on economic growth, however, would describe an economy growing only gradually until the 1820s, with little evidence of revolutionary change outside an advanced industrial sector which as late as the 1840s accounted for less than a fifth of the male labour force. Moreover, studies of the eighteenth century have increasingly suggested the importance of urbanization, commercial expansion, the extension of communication [see *postal service], and the development of a consumer-orientated society as part of a long lead-in to nineteenth-century industrialization [see *consumerism, 19].

But as well as differentiating and attenuating the pace of economic growth, recent work has permitted historians to assess major themes in British social development from the eighteenth century in a way which allows the effects of economic change to be put into perspective. Hence, if we examine some of the broader social aspects of the 'classic' century of the industrial revolution we can discern the extent to which earlier preoccupations with an overwhelming and cataclysmic sequence of events have been replaced by a more sophisticated awareness of the complexity of the social response.

The received version of the social consequences of the industrial revolution is inseparable from the idea of *population growth. Whatever emphasis is given to the long-term development of the economy, there was a major discontinuity in the form of population increase. Taking England and Wales alone, population rose from below 6.5 million in 1751 to almost 18 million in 1851. The trebling of Britain's population in just over a century, if we take the figure to 1861 (20.1 million), seems the most startling parallel to economic growth. However, as has long been recognized, England and Wales did not possess the only rapidly increasing populations in the eighteenth and early nineteenth centuries. Other European populations were also growing, including those in places such as Ireland, Scandinavia, and eastern Europe where industrialization was clearly not responsible for population increase. Until quite recently, explanations for this growth centred on a lowering of death rates, interpreted as the result of a complex interaction of factors. At present it is not clear to what extent the lowering of death rates through improved health was the result of an autonomous decline in the virulence of disease or of increased resistance of human hosts to infection as a result of better food supplies and improved environmental conditions. It may well have been a combination of the two. But these were not effects confined solely to England and Wales or even to continental Europe, and showed few signs of having been primarily associated with Britain's role as the first industrial nation. Indeed, in so far as a link might be posited with one of the most obvious symptoms of economic development, the growth of the towns, it might be argued that the tendencies pulled in the opposite direction. Death rates were customarily higher in the growing towns and cities than in the countryside. Indeed, urban populations were only able to grow through a net influx of population from the countryside. On this reading, it was the parts of the country *least* affected by economic change which were providing the surplus people to swell the urban populations. Left to its own natural rate of increase, eighteenth-century London, like most other expanding towns of the period, would have stagnated or even fallen in population. Only an influx of between 8,000 to 12,000 people a year permitted the capital, and in smaller order the other early industrial towns and cities, to increase in size.

But a new complexion has been given to the question of the relationship between the course of economic change and the rise of population for England and Wales. Research suggests that the birth rate accounted for about 70 per cent of net population increase in the late eighteenth and nineteenth centuries, and that the decline in death rate on its own would have achieved much lower rates of population increase than actually occurred. It was the increase in fertility which marked England and Wales out from the rest of Europe. During the eighteenth century the growth rate of population in England and Wales was not especially high by continental standards, as the mortality rate declined in common with much of the rest of Europe. Only at the end of the century, when fertility also rose, did the population of England and Wales begin to grow more rapidly than other European countries. The explanation for this increase in fertility lies almost entirely in a lowering in ages of marriage and levels of celibacy, what has been called the trend 'towards earlier and more universal marriage'. Economic opportunity in a growing economy may provide the key to resolving the 'conundrum' of increasing marriage, higher birth rates, and the rapid acceleration of population growth from the late eighteenth century.

But economic growth was by no means exclusively or even primarily *industrial* growth. Much of it was commercial expansion based in the capital, in the burgeoning ports, and in the prospering centres of consumption, leisure, and civic life in the provincial capitals and *spa towns.

If the population history of England and Wales only partly fits the conventional chronology of the industrial revolution, the same might be said for the history of urbanization. On the face of it, this might seem surprising, for the one feature that does appear to coincide with the conventional idea of an industrial revolution starting at some point in the late eighteenth century is the increasing percentage of the population living in urban areas. In the space of just over a century Britain was transformed from a predominantly rural and small-town society to an urban one. By 1851 there were sixty-three towns in England and Wales each with over 20,000 inhabitants: in 1801 there had been only fifteen such towns. Moreover, the balance had shifted decisively away from London, the most dynamic urban centre of the seventeenth and eighteenth centuries. The capital continued to grow, but after 1801 it took a declining share of a swelling urban population as the highest rates of urban growth were registered in the new centres of commerce and manufacturing. The fastest-growing cities of the early nineteenth century were Liverpool, Manchester, Birmingham, Leeds, and Sheffield, some of which recorded growth rates in excess of 40 per cent in the single decade of the 1820s. Of the second-rank towns, Bradford, Salford, Oldham, Preston, and Wolverhampton were amongst those showing the most rapid increase. The broad impact of economic growth can also be seen from evidence showing that the four most industrialized counties (the West Riding of Yorkshire, Staffordshire, Warwickshire, and Lancashire) increased their share of the total population from 17 per cent in 1781 to 26 per cent in 1861.

Until the first half of the nineteenth century, the problems of urban growth had been identified with London rather than with anywhere else. In eighteenth-century literature, London became the focus of national concern about crime, riots, and social disorder, on account both of its vast size and of its opportunities for illegality. Cobbett was only trading on a well-established image in his famous description of London as the 'Great Wen'; literally, a great cyst. Even with the huge increase in the size of the provincial manufacturing and commercial cities, London remained the giant metropolis, almost too vast to comprehend, and the setting still (as in so much of Dickens) of novels of social concern. Indeed, London's dominant role in the literature of anti-urbanism was never fully displaced.

But urbanization is not in itself the major preoccupation of those concerned with the social repercussions of industrialization. The argument has always revolved around the rise of disruptive new patterns of work, the *factory system, and machine-driven production. Probably fewer than 12 per cent of the British workforce was employed in factories by 1850, and as late as 1871 the average size of a manufacturing establishment was under twenty employees. Indeed, craft and unmechanized trades were still the most numerous; there were more shoemakers than coalminers in 1851, and coalmining was itself hardly exemplary in its use of powered machinery, relying primarily on muscle-power for the hewing and underground movement of coal. Similarly, trades such as the Sheffield cutlery industry was virtually unmechanized, apart from powered grinding wheels, and remained organized on a small workshop basis well into the twentieth century.

Although agriculture ceased to be the principal sector of the labour force between 1801 and 1851, in absolute terms the number of those employed on the land was actually higher by the early nineteenth century. The rural population growth which fuelled immigration to the towns and overseas also produced the pauperization and underemployment described, but not fully understood, by commentators of the time. Genuine depopulation, in the sense of a fall in the *absolute* numbers of the rural population was, in spite of Cobbett's claims, only to be found in a few specialized cases. *Enclosure, as we now know, did not necessarily lead to a reduction in the labour force required, whatever other effects it may have entailed. A decline of the rural population and of the agricultural labour force was certainly taking place but it was only relative, and still left a substantial body of over 2 million agricultural workers by the mid-nineteenth century, still by far Britain's largest single occupational group.

If the spread and scale of manufacturing operations by 1850 can be exaggerated, there remains a powerful line of argument that, where it occurred, industrialization disrupted an older and, implicitly, better way of life. This view was consolidated by the historian E. P. Thompson's highly influential *The Making of the English Working Class* (1963). While accepting the case that there might have been some overall improvement in material living standards in the half century before the 1840s, Thompson argued that it was bought at the price of intensified exploitation, greater insecurity, and increasing human misery. However, this account oversimplifies a process which is protracted, piecemeal, and subject to highly complex variations of environment and experience.

The industrial revolution was often experienced on the ground as a gradual quickening of economic activity during the course of the eighteenth century. Even with the acceleration which took place from the end of the century or, in some cases, rather later, the long-term character of the growth of manufacturing did permit some adjustment to change. To take one example, Sheffield rose from a population of approximately 9,000 in 1736 to over 40,000 by the 1790s. This rapid growth was accompanied by some refurbishment and development of civic amenities. Assembly rooms and a theatre were built in 1762, a new market in 1786, and a number of new, large chapels established by the early nineteenth century. It would be a profound error to suggest that older, even legally unincorporated, communities were completely swamped by the growth of population. Indeed, several showed some vigour in responding to new needs: the booming silk town of Macclesfield saw the building of an impressive *Sunday school institution serving over 2,000 pupils by 1812, the opening of a town dispensary in 1814, a private Act of Parliament 'for the better Lighting, Watching and Improvement' of the town in the same year, and in 1823 the reorganization of the market area and a rebuilt town hall. In 1825 a further Act appointed *police [7] commissioners to improve the town's paving and lighting.

Hence it is extremely misleading to use the language of 'the frontier town' or 'urban chaos' to describe the reality of the experience of urban growth in most parts of England and Wales in this period. The true frontier towns, communities built up almost from nothing on the basis of industrial development, were rarer than is often thought: most urban development took place on the framework of existing administrative structures, frequently inadequate no doubt, but often showing more resilience than they have been given credit for. Incorporation, especially after 1835, provided the mechanism by which a more rapid and systematic response became possible.

This impression of something less than wholesale catastrophe in the face of an urban population explosion is reinforced by research work on the structure of the urban communities in early-nineteenth-century Lancashire. The historian Michael Anderson shows that there was a remarkably strong development of close kinship relations in the cotton towns, partly as a defence against the major vicissitudes of life: sickness, unemployment, and bereavement. Migrants to the early industrial town were not necessarily thrown into an anarchic and 'soulless' environment, but instead often relied on kin or neighbours for early support and sought to live near people from the same area as themselves. Indeed, the early experiences of town life may have strengthened purely instrumental kinship relations before the development of the neighbourly solidarities and sense of 'community' later to be associated with working-class urban life. The birth of a working-class community, with its associated mores, communal self-help, and often vigorous informal economy, was as much the product of industrialization as the dreadful physical environment which many had to endure [see *class, 15].

But to what extent was industrialization purchased at the price of a fall in material living standards? To an extent, the steam has gone out of this debate. It is now partially agreed that there was scope for some rise in material living standards even in the first phase of industrial growth before 1850. The experience of particular families and groups of workers is still difficult to assess because of the nature of the evidence. There are very few records of actual hours and days worked by individuals, or detailed evidence of expenditures on food, housing, and other necessities. It is even more difficult to make an accurate assessment of household 'income' as a whole, taking into account non-mainstream earnings and non-money exchanges of goods and services. Those records that do exist provide us only with examples for specific households in particular localities. That being said, in so far as the broad movements of prices and wage rates can be taken into account, we can perhaps isolate some of the main points of agreement in the debate. There was an overall rise in real incomes per head in the country as a whole, and an avoidance of a large-scale subsistence catastrophe such as the famine which afflicted Ireland in the 1840s. Britain was able to sustain a trebling of population in the century before 1861, and to feed it largely from its own resources. Clear evidence of rising real incomes for the working classes is most apparent for the later nineteenth century, but evidence for the period before 1850 is more patchy. This is particularly true if we look at shorter periods and specific groups. To take only one example, the revolutionary and Napoleonic *wars [2] occupy a crucial twenty-three years in the middle of the era of the industrial revolution. Here there is substantial evidence that particular periods of harvest crisis and inflated food prices produced a fall in real wages of a substantial magnitude. Compared with the relatively 'normal' year of 1790, real wages were reduced by as much as 10 per cent in 1795 and by as much as 20 per cent in the even worse crisis of 1800–1. Although neither of these episodes produced famine, they created extensive hardship, and considerable contemporary comment about the need to relieve the unparalleled hardships of the labouring classes. Similarly, the postwar depression, with its high unemployment, and the early 1840s stand out as episodes of short-term deflections from long-term trends.

To these temporal fluctuations must be added the plight of those who failed to benefit from economic growth or were adversely affected by it. One group were the pauperized agricultural labourers, whose real wage rates seem barely to have improved before the mid-nineteenth century, and who were the victims of the effects of overpopulation and chronic underemployment in rural areas. They and other workers were rendered technologically obsolete by mechanization, and their skills, traditions, and values were placed under particular pressure by economic change. The struggle of other groups of workers, particularly skilled artisans, to defend their status and earnings was often a losing one in a period of rapid technological change and economic development. Whatever long-term series and aggregate statistics may tell us, the experience of particular trades and occupations, notably those of handloom weaving and wool-cropping, was of a deterioration in both status and earning power. It is apparent that the sheer complexity of occupational groups and their differing circumstances, at least in the period before 1850, will always provide ammunition for both optimists and pessimists. The situation becomes even more complex if we add to the male-centred concept of principal occupation that of family earnings. The ability of women and children to find work in changed technological and economic circumstances would have played a critical part in the standard of living of particular families.

As a result, the standard of living debate remains finely poised. The circumstances affecting individuals and households defy succinct generalization. Problems of evidence about wages and prices, and especially about regularity of employment and household income, bedevil the argument. The influence of changes over time, periods of price fluctuation, trade boom and slump, and the fortunes of discrete groups of workers, as well as the operation of the 'family cycle' of changing demands upon households, permit a wide range of interpretation. Long-term, however, a powerful argument remains that it was only through economic growth that Britain avoided the wholesale pauperization which population growth brought to Ireland and much of rural continental Europe during the nineteenth century.

Almost from the beginning of the study of industrialization, historians have sought access to the attitudes of artisans, labourers, and their families as revealed by the *riots and protest movements which appear to dominate so much of the story of early industrialization. No account of the social impact of economic change is complete without its reference to machine-breakers, food rioters, and agricultural unrest.

*Luddism was undoubtedly a major and protracted episode of unrest, but we now know that it occurred against a background of sporadic and varied responses to machinery and new work practices in which attacks upon machines formed part of a wider repertoire of bargaining and protest, dating from as early as the seventeenth century and continuing well into the nine-teenth. The Luddites were not blind opponents of machinery. Often such attacks were not resistance to machinery itself, but attempts to regulate its use or bring pressure to bear upon masters by threatening damage to an important capital asset. In Yorkshire, for example, the spread of machine-breaking amongst the croppers came after the frustration of attempts to regulate the trade by other means and during a particularly intense season of high prices and unemployment. The textile districts saw a series of strikes, combinations, and negotiations between workers and employers, including the first strikes by the cotton-spinners of Lancashire, in 1799, 1800, 1802, and 1803. In 1810 they maintained a four-month stoppage supported by subscriptions totalling £17,000 drawn from several parts of the north. Only a fraction of the ink devoted to Luddism has been expended on one of the most impressive examples of early *trade union organization: the strike by the Scottish and north of England cotton-weavers in late 1812, in which 40,000 looms remained idle for six weeks over an area from Cumbria to Aberdeen. Concentration on Luddism should not obscure the most obvious feature of these years: the ability of workers to organize themselves and to deploy a range of tactics, in which violence and machine-breaking could play a part, in order to accommodate change as best they could. If these actions were often defensive, they were not exclusively either backward-looking or unsuccessful. Records of individual disputes even under the restrictions of the Combination Laws of 1799 and 1800 reveal that it was possible for workers to behave other than as helpless victims.

Similarly, it remains too simple to see food riots as a symptom of new depths in mass depriv-ation during the last years of the eighteenth century. In spite of much use of the term 'famine', famine proper was a distant memory by the time Britain embarked on the beginnings of indus-trialization. Food riots, which more properly should be termed price riots, appear to have developed from the early modern period, only reaching epidemic proportions in the latter part of the eighteenth century. Primarily an urban phenomenon, they marked the response of con-sumers to an increasingly market-orientated trade in foodstuffs. That being said, it is notable that the major aspects of food rioting in England and Wales appear to have occurred some time after the food trade became largely deregulated, and when the experience of marketing of produce of all kinds was well established. The largest outbreaks of food rioting, at the end of the eighteenth century, came not when people were exposed to the market mechanism for the first time, but long afterwards. Indeed, in many parts of the country, such as the small textile towns of the south-west, price riots had become a fairly routine part of what has been called 'community politics', less a desperate reaction to deprivation than an ongoing process of nego-tiation with the local authorities. Moreover, these disturbances were very largely a small-town phenomenon, a feature of the small market town or the emergent 'industrial village'. Although it is the case that in later harvest crises, particularly that of 1800–1, price riots began to affect the larger industrializing communities more markedly, this was a relatively short-lived phenom-enon. Price riots on a nationwide scale became a thing of the past after the Napoleonic wars, increasingly replaced by strikes, machine-breaking, collective bargaining, and political agita-tion. The era of price riots was therefore largely over when the most rapid phase of industrial-ization began after 1815.

There is a difficulty, then, in representing the various forms of violent protest that occurred in the century or so after 1750 as part of a response to 'industrialization', if we mean by that the coming of the factory system and the development of large factory towns. Price riots and machine-breaking belonged to strategies of protest and negotiation which had a long history. They were to reach a peak between 1795 and 1816 as much because of the peculiar and difficult conditions of the Napoleonic wars as through any direct consequence of industrialization. Similarly, a tendency to invoke the unrest surrounding the agitation for *parliamentary reform, especially in the years between 1816 and 1821, as part of a reaction to industrialization is liable to confuse rather than clarify. The forcible dispersal of the reform meeting at St Peter's Fields, Manchester, in August 1819—*Peterloo—is often taken to symbolize a whole era. In fact, the violence inflicted was wholly the responsibility of the authorities, the result of a clumsy and inept attempt to control an otherwise peaceful mass meeting for reform.

Any review of the social consequences of the industrial revolution has to come to terms with both its image and its reality. The public recognition that Britain was becoming an industrial nation dates, as we have seen, from the early nineteenth century. In practice, however, even as late as 1850 much of what would be defined as industrialization had still to occur. But for something like another century, the debate upon the effects of industrialization was carried on in terms coloured by the ruralist lament of Cobbett and the urban concerns of the 'Condition of England' novelists. Glossed increasingly with nostalgia, the rural world was counterposed to the squalor and misery of urban life, as in the writings of Flora Thompson, published on the eve of the Second World War. The powerful image of a landscape despoiled by industrialization, intensified by the interwar depression, is epitomized by Richard Llewellyn's *How Green Was My Valley* (1939). Similarly, the posthumously published compendium of the great lyric poet of British documentary cinema, Humphrey Jennings, *Pandaemonium* (compiled 1937–50; published 1985), speaks volumes for the received cultural impact of industrialization. From 1937 Jennings, who described his political beliefs as those of William Cobbett, collected items for *Pandaemonium* which testified to the impact of the 'machine' from the late seventeenth century to the end of the nineteenth. Such views were not surprising for artists who lived in a world recognizably similar to that witnessed by the first generation of critics of industrial society. When J. B. Priestley toured the country on his *English Journey* in the autumn of 1933, he found several 'Englands', including 'the nineteenth-century England, the industrial England of coal, iron, steel, cotton, wool, railways; of thousands of rows of little houses all alike . . . a cynically devastated countryside'. It was the same 'England' that George Orwell found in Wigan and Sheffield in the later 1930s, and which could, of course, be found in industrial south Wales and central Scotland.

This was an industrial England in interwar depression, whose decay and dereliction were to inform planners and policy-makers during and after the Second World War. In the various plans for the urban New Jerusalem which emerged from the Depression and the Blitz, slum clearance, zoning, and rebuilt cities would replace the damage wrought not only by the Luftwaffe but also by the Industrial Revolution. There was little doubt that what was to be swept away was the legacy of Dickens's 'Coketown'; the image as much as the reality of the industrial revolution which had first exercised the minds of writers and artists more than a century earlier.

Anderson, M., *Family Structure in Nineteenth-Century Lancashire*, Cambridge, 1971; Berg, M., *The Age of Manufactures, 1700–1820: Industry, Innovation and Work in Britain*, London, 1994; Hammond, J. L. L. B., & Hammond, B., *The Bleak Age*, Harmondsworth, 1947; Hoppit, J., & Wrigley, E. A., eds., *The Industrial Revolution in Britain*, Oxford, 1994; Thompson, E. P., *The Making of the English Working Class* (1963), Harmondsworth, 1968; Wrigley, E. A., *Continuity, Chance and Change: The Character of the Industrial Revolution in England*, Cambridge, 1988.

15 · CLASS EILEEN JANES YEO

Any discussion of class must now take account of culture and language. The historian E. P. Thompson, who left giant footprints across the historiography of both eighteenth- and nineteenth-century English history, transformed a whole generation's view of class. He relinquished the crude Marxist model of base and superstructure which gave primacy to economic production as the determining factor in social relations and which saw culture (including value systems and symbolic modes of expression and action) as reflective of this more solid layer of reality. Instead Thompson insisted that class relations and class consciousness developed often through conflict over time, and took cultural and political as well as economic forms. Convinced that both working- and middle-class consciousness were fully present by the 1830s, he was, however, cautious about attributing class consciousness to a society like eighteenth-century England, which experienced sharp social conflict but where the contesting parties remained within a mental horizon dominated by the gentry and did not have a clear or sustained conception of conflicting class interests within their cognitive system.

More recently, the issue has resurfaced in the form of whether a language of class is indispensable for expressing a consciousness of class, especially when it is clear that radicals and oppositionists, even between 1789 and 1839, frequently structured their collective identities in terms of other keywords and concepts, such as the category of 'the People'. Under the influence of modern constitutive models of language, several historians have argued that the language of 'the People' precluded class consciousness because it was primarily a political language which did not necessarily reflect social and economic grievance nor extend into social and economic analysis. Further, it has been argued that populist conceptions such as 'the People' or 'the constitution' were so capacious and inclusive of various British social groups and aspirations that they could neither express nor shape conflict. Taking a different approach, this essay argues that such revisionist historiography, though fertile in having rescued neglected 'languages' and discourses of collective identity, is now in danger of throwing out the baby with the bathwater. The latent and emerging language of 'class' in this period is often eclipsed in favour of new, all-encompassing master narratives. Moreover, a useful recognition of inclusive impulses within popular discourse has become an excuse for overlooking equally pronounced counter-tendencies expressive of conflict and difference.

This essay will focus on several multivalent discourses which were viewed and contested as particularly glittering prizes. As the Marxist philosopher V. N. Volosinov wrote in 1929, 'different classes will use one and the same language. As a result, differently oriented accents intersect in every ideological sign. Sign becomes an arena of the class struggle.' A substantial proportion of the British population struggled to form new, or re-form old, collective identities at a time when the country was experiencing large changes in agrarian, industrial, and commercial structures and processes. This essay will spotlight such contests, especially between contestants from above and below at significant moments in the development of social relations, by focusing on a series of major languages, particularly those of custom, *constitutionalism, *religion [10], *political economy [33], and, of course, class itself.

One of the key arenas in which social difference was defined and articulated in the eighteenth century was that of custom and customary relations. E. P. Thompson constructed a model of social relations which involved a power equilibrium between the gentry, whom he sometimes called the patricians (their own self-characterization), and the common people in the crowd, whom he called the plebs or plebeians. These two basic groupings exerted their distinctly unequal power in highly theatrical ways to call each other to order within the bounds of a commonly understood set of duties and obligations, what Thompson called the 'moral economy of the poor'. The crowd (another node of collective identity) who tipped their caps by day also posted anonymous threatening letters by night, reminding the gentry that freeborn Englishmen had customary rights: to food in the land where they laboured, to a fair day's wage for a fair day's work, and to freedom from arbitrary incursions by the armed force of the state. Thompson argued that 'custom was the rhetoric of legitimation for almost any usage, practice, or demanded right', and therefore that 'custom was a field of change and of contest, an arena in which opposing interests made conflicting claims'. In this society, where economic innovation was coming from above, Thompson's 'plebs' mounted their resistance in the name of defending custom, that is, rights and practices perceived to have been in place 'from time immemorial'.

If not appeased, the crowd might stage a *riot by day, particularly in times of bad harvests and high food prices. This riotous action was striking for its ritualized forms and limited use of violence. Hardly ever attacking persons, the crowd often seized the grain or bread and sold it at what they considered a 'fair' price. The ruling classes had their own theatrical ways of displaying their authority. By and large the actual landowners only met the plebs face to face when cloaked in the majesty of the *law [8] or prepared to shower mercy and charity in order to cool plebeian discontent; otherwise they operated as employers and landlords through a range of less benevolent middlemen.

This picture has been criticized as leaving out of account an emerging middle class, both commercial and professional, which, together with politically moderate gentry and aristocratic friends was creating a public sphere of literary culture and political action. Certainly by the 1770s, in the political disputes surrounding the *American Revolution, such groups were breaking free of the clientage/patronage relationship which pulled them magnetically towards the patrician interest. Instead, in agitations like those of the Middlesex electors [see *Wilkites] and the Association Movement [see *Wyvillites], they asserted a right to speak in the name of 'the People' in order to call for *parliamentary reform and to denounce what William *Cobbett memorably dubbed 'Old Corruption', a nickname for the unrepresentative parliament, sinecurist bureaucracy, and self-serving ruling classes.

In the wake of the *French Revolution, the ideology of reciprocity that governed relations between patricians and plebs fractured, and with it some of the viability of the appeal to custom as a language of persuasion and an emollient of relations between these social groups. Many developments were already leading in this direction: agrarian capitalists were organizing their production of crops for free movement and profitable sale in the market-place, statute law was enshrining absolute powers of ownership rather than differential use rights to property, and employers were imposing new work disciplines and redefining as theft what artisans regarded as customary perquisites of their trade. But the French Revolution and the fear of an English replay led the gentry and middle classes to suspect any customary form of popular action as Jacobinical. They defended repression partly in aid of the established Church against revolutionary infidelism, or radical free thought, and partly in obedience to what they perceived to be the natural *laissez-faire laws of the economic market-place. The middleman—once, according to traditional ideas of 'moral economy', the symbol of the evil exploiter of the poor in times of dearth—now became the political economist's hero, the rational calculator of profitable advantage.

Similarly formative in the changing languages of politics and economics was the repression launched against the new urban radical associations like the *corresponding societies.

Founded in London and elsewhere from 1792 onward, these were the first political associations to try to recruit 'numbers unlimited'. The Seditious Meetings Act of 1795, the suspension of habeas corpus, and finally the Combination Acts (1799–1800) [see *gagging acts] pushed these associations increasingly into a twilight zone of secrecy and closed down every other form of labour combination as well, making *trade unions and self-governing *friendly societies illegal. Repression and *loyalist sentiment silenced most *Whig and middle-class radicals and, with the exception of the oppositionist activities cohering around Sir Francis *Burdett during the early *Regency years, impaired effective cross-class radicalism until the reform agitation of the early 1830s.

With *Malthusian ideas of political economy gaining ever greater purchase amongst Whig and *Tory politicians and administrators, parliament also set about dismantling the legislative defences of labour in the first two decades of the new century, repealing laws like the Elizabethan Statute of Artificers which had allowed for regulation of apprenticeship, wages, and working conditions. *Petitions from wool-combers or framework knitters objecting to such actions in the language of custom and moral economy were dismissed as Jacobinical, in spite of *Byron's eloquent speech in the House of Lords in their defence [see *Luddism]. The way was now open for the development of the characteristic features of commercial and early industrial capitalism: low wages, long working hours, a large pool of casual (intermittent) or unemployed labour, and expanding export markets [see **industrialization, 14**]. Workers often experienced new labour disciplines together with low wages not as progression but as oppression, both in the new mechanized factory sector and in the old artisan trades, where intensification of work, driven by constant competition from a 'dishonourable' sector of sweated outworkers, achieved mass production. The repeal of the Combination Acts in 1824 led not

20. Banner of the United Tin Plate Workers' Society, *c.*1821. Friendly associations of this kind had developed in Britain prior to the repeal of the Combination Acts in 1824 which lifted the legal ban on trade unions.

only to a resurgence of trade unionism but also to a counter-attack from employers and government, culminating in the defeat of the Grand National Consolidated Trade Union in 1834.

The period from 1776 to 1832 therefore witnessed the emergence of a socio-economic structure based on the assertion and defence of property rights and on relatively unrestricted market relations rather than on customary rights and paternal obligations. Such concerted assaults on the culture of labouring freeborn Englishmen created in many cases a bitter sense of injustice, articulated from below partly in terms of a language of slavery and bondage, inflected by the discourses of constitutionalism, class, and religion—three major linguistic battlefields throughout the first half of the nineteenth century. Especially from the 1770s onward, those opposing 'Old Corruption' had used a rhetoric of *patriotism and constitutionalism to legitimize themselves and to castigate a tyranny that turned free Britons into slaves. During the eighteenth century the image of **slavery [6]** had also figured in critical writing about relations between men and women. From the 1790s, the rhetoric of enslavement gained new dimensions of meaning in reference to colonial slavery made increasingly visible by the propaganda achievements of the *abolitionist movement and the successful slave revolt in St Domingue in 1791. The reference to slavery as economic exploitation was absorbed into postwar radical analysis, for example when the striking cotton-spinners in 1818 compared black colonial slaves with white factory slaves. It became the dominating image of the campaign for the ten-hour working day after Richard Oastler (1789–1830) wrote his famous letter on 'Yorkshire Slavery' to the *Leeds Mercury* (16 October 1830), which declaimed on how, in *Wilberforce's own constituency, mill-owners were less concerned with human life than were slave-owners in the West Indies:

Ye live in the boasted land of freedom, and feel and mourn that ye are slaves, and slaves without the only comfort which the negro has. He knows it is his sordid, mercenary master's interest that he should live, be strong and healthy. Not so with you. Ye are doomed to labour from morning to night for one who cares not how soon your weak and tender frames are stretched to breaking!

A huge procession to the Manchester reform meeting of 23 August 1832 was headed by a flag with the representation of a deformed man, inscribed with the *abolitionist slogan 'Am I not a man and a brother?' and underneath 'No White Slavery'.

The political rhetoric of patriotism also continued to be contested terrain. While the government and ruling classes used a language of patriotism both to smear reformers with the taint of French Jacobinism and to fortify national resolve against Napoleonic *invasion, plebeians also struggled to appropriate a similar rhetoric by referring to themselves as the 'true' patriots and to their political and economic rulers as unconstitutional tyrants. The threatened London Corresponding Society spoke of 'the holy blood of patriotism' in 1795 and, over the next two decades, the government replaced the more libertarian 'Rule Britannia' with 'God Save the King' as the national anthem. Thanks both to growing war-weariness and to a series of scandals involving corruption in the administration of the armed services, oppositionists such as Burdett and Cobbett began in the early Regency years to regain the moral salient of patriotism and constitutionalism that had been lost to loyalism at the height of the 1790s Gallophobia. Peace in 1815 and the demise of *Napoleon completed the process: a new generation of postwar radical leaders such as T. J. *Wooler, Henry *Hunt, William *Hone, and Richard *Carlile renewed their attacks on Old Corruption with a *mélange* of constitutionalist ideas tacked together from Saxon mythology, natural rights theory, Christian communitarianism, and **Enlightenment [32]** freethought. Part of the appeal of constitutionalist rhetoric derived less from its inclusivity than its ambiguity: the right to remove tyrants from the throne had after all been enshrined in the *Glorious Revolution of 1688 which had also given rise to a national convention. Renewed calls for the latter by popular radicals could be cast in legitimate constitutionalist rhetoric while at the same time carrying the implicit menace of French revolutionary models.

During the early decades of the nineteenth century it seemed, moreover, as if the appealing plasticity of constitutionalist rhetoric could extend even to claiming political rights for *women [4]. Female radical societies proliferated in the north in 1818–19: at *Peterloo the Females of Royston typically carried a banner urging their sisters, 'Let us die like men, and not be sold like slaves'. The extraordinary explosion of popular sentiment during the *Queen Caroline affair the following year generated a plethora of radical press attacks on the sexual double standard. Caroline briefly joined a pantheon of constitutionalist popular monarchs alongside Saxon Alfred and Good Queen Bess. Even the seemingly more conventional rhetoric generated during the affair, whereby Caroline was represented as the heroine of a romantic melodrama, a wronged wife and mother betrayed by a gross royal voluptuary, could carry feminist implications. Recent scholarship has argued that women radicals and *Chartists mobilized a similar domestic ideal in the 1840s to make strong political claims for their rights as wives, mothers, and Christians to take public action in support of a wage capable of feeding and educating their families. Although this domestic and constitutionalist claim may ultimately have backfired when working women helped to pass legislation that enshrined the ideal of the male breadwinner wage, they had participated forcefully, vocally, and enduringly in very many facets of public culture and political activity.

Across the seas in Ireland, Daniel *O'Connell also deployed an ostensibly constitutionalist and religious rhetoric. Ironically, this harked back to the very limited 'Protestant Constitution' and independent Irish parliament of 1782 in order to make powerful democratic claims for the oppressed Catholic majority and later to mount still more radical challenges to the *Act of Union of 1800. O'Connell's spectacular success in mobilizing mass peasant support to win *Catholic emancipation in 1829 was unfortunately matched by the equally dramatic failure of his repeal campaign when the *Peel Tory government called his bluff and forced him to cancel a 'monster' meeting at Clontarf in 1843. In so doing, Peel's English government exposed the limits of the language and practices of constitutionalist protest: for one strand of O'Connell's embittered followers the only future hope was to lie in a return to the ideals of republican violence and sacrifice espoused by earlier Jacobin martyrs like Wolfe *Tone and Robert Emmet (1778–1803). For this revolutionary minority the secular languages of nationalism and Romantic blood sacrifice supplanted that of religious constitutionalism.

Counter-revolution both in Britain and Ireland was, however, also able to mount a telling cultural offensive based on a variety of traditional languages. From the 1790s onward the *Evangelical clergy and female philanthropists made attempts in country villages and in towns to operate a new degree of surveillance over the lives of the poor. Hannah *More set a pioneering example. Reversing the *laissez-faire* attitude to plebeian culture, More and her sister Martha, known as 'Patty' (c.1759–1819), helped create a pattern of cultural intervention which demanded more strenuous involvement in reaching and teaching the poor. They, like other Evangelicals, aimed to inculcate habits of piety, industry, forethought, and especially subordination by means of a new cluster of institutions, including female friendly societies and *Sunday schools whose teachers would make regular visits to the dwellings of the poor [see *poverty, 12]. Yet doing so often entailed storming male bastions: recent scholarship has shown surprising parallels between the language of Evangelical women enthusiasts like Hannah More and that of radical feminists like Mary *Wollstonecraft. Evangelicals also mounted fierce critiques of a ruling class that had relinquished its traditional paternal obligations in favour of urban decadence and dissipation. This pattern of heightened Evangelical interventionism continued into the *philanthropy of the 1830s, where the district provident societies, often run by a coalition of local Dissenters and *Anglicans, visited working-class households in cities, gave advice on domestic economy, and provided savings schemes.

The Evangelicals offered an activist Christianity which promised salvation for all. The More sisters also quite happily used spiritual blackmail to bolster their recruitment: 'My dear women which of you could bear to see your darling child condemned to everlasting destruction?' However, undercutting their own rhetoric about spiritual equality, they evoked three powerful representations which endured afterwards in the depiction of social difference: first, a language of colonialism which likened the poor in English villages to savages in darkest Africa, in need of a civilizing mission; second, a view of the poor as morally and politically diseased, in a powerful evocation of healthy and disordered social bodies; and finally, an image of the poor as naughty children in need of mothering from women of another social class.

The response of the Somerset village women is revealing. Despite initial reluctance, they started to send their children to Sunday schools, possibly responding to a religion of spiritual equality which valued them for the first time. They were prepared to reform their behaviour and postpone sex until after marriage. But relations between rich and poor women were still riddled with tension. Rich women wanted to give club benefits for marriage, childbirth, and sickness. Poor women wanted funeral payments. In one of the Mores' Somerset villages, a member declared: 'What did a poor woman work hard for, but in hopes she should be put out of the world in a tidy way?' The Mores found that this notion of putting the dead before the living 'was a pitch of absurdity almost beyond bearing'. But they put up with it because without such funeral benefit poor women refused to join the clubs.

The Sunday schools also continued to be arenas of cultural contest between the dispensers and receivers of education. Both Evangelical Anglicans and Wesleyan *Methodists were split on whether writing as well as reading should be taught to the poor. Religion had been an age-old battleground for assertions of collective identity between plebeian and patrician folk, and complex inheritances of self-assertion and resistance came through from the seventeenth century together with *millenarian strains which were activated particularly by the French Revolution. But the Peterloo massacre and its aftermath gave a new spur to the creation of visions of 'true' and 'false' Christianity by different social groups that were now also inflected by other emergent political and economic languages of class and constitutionalism. The immediate cause of offence was the interlocking of civil and religious oppression: two Anglican ministers were prominent among the magistrates who ordered the cavalry charge on a peaceful demonstration and then used the courts to punish the victims. With equal zeal, Anglican and Wesleyan officials in south Lancashire joined in the Home Office Secretary Lord Sidmouth's postwar drive to silence popular unrest by hounding suspected radicals out of their worship and their Sunday schools.

While the multi-faceted drive by the postwar Tory government to stifle popular political expression and participation pushed a minority of working people into the camp of infidelism or the popular political freethought espoused by leaders like Richard Carlile, it also provoked radical Christians to spell out a counter-Christianity: a 'Christian reformer' in the *Manchester Observer*, 6 June 1819, defined this as the need 'to deliver the religion of Jesus Christ from the disgrace brought upon it'. Their formulations of belief, developing further as need arose, were carried by a range of Nonconformist working-class chapels, sects, and movements over the next twenty years. From then on each political crisis tended to generate a religious dimension that resonated with assertions of class pride and anger at political exclusion and social oppression. The reform agitations in 1831 took careful notice of the fact that the bishops in the House of Lords had blocked the passage of the parliamentary *Reform Bill, and this antagonism continued in a series of skirmishes over church rates in various localities during the 1830s. Fittingly, it was the Chartist movement, espousing a core political programme first laid down by Rational Dissenters in the 1780s, which most vigorously fought the religious class war in 1839. The Chartist demand for Six Points of parliamentary reform starting with universal (manhood) suffrage now also absorbed the perspectives and personnel of the Ten Hours movement and the agitation against the 1834 *Poor Law Amendment Act.

The Chartists held a cluster of Christian beliefs which emphasized the rights of labour and the poor, and which offered a powerful critique of social oppression. Like the anti-poor law campaigners of the 1830s, they attacked the new workhouses, often called bastilles, which punished poverty as a crime and denied the rights of the poor to subsistence, now seen as founded on religious not customary authority; 'dwell in the land and verily thou shalt be fed' was a popular banner text carried in large demonstrations. Segregated by sex and by age, the workhouses also dissolved the sacred bonds of marriage ('None but he who rules the thunder/shall put man and wife asunder') and violated God's anti-Malthusian injunction to 'be fruitful, and multiply, and replenish the earth, and subdue it, for all is yours', a passage from the book of Genesis which received cheers whenever quoted.

The dignity of labour was underlined not only by the fact that Christ had come to earth as a working man but also by a theology which posited a special relationship between God and the working classes. After Peterloo, a Halifax reformer had insisted in the *Manchester Observer* (20 November 1819) that 'the Voice of the People is the Voice of God' and that the 'common people constitute the bulk and strength of the Kingdom'. By 1839 a more precise idea had developed: while God had created the earth as potential abundance, it was labour which actually turned the potential into fruits, wealth, and property. As Chartist shoemaker and preacher Abraham Hanson (*c*.1770–1855) put it, 'their labour was the source of all property—they performed that labour by the physical power of their bodies, they derived that power from none but God.' Labour had the first claim to the fruits (usually to a fair share rather than to the whole produce).

The truly Christian society honoured the divine rights of labour and the poor and also embodied Christ's teaching about mutuality: 'do unto others as ye would they do unto you' was a favoured text for Chartist *sermons which invoked the still-cherished popular ideals of moral economy. Those in power who ignored these rights were oppressors who had repudiated God: 'He who oppresseth the poor', ran another popular banner text, 'reproacheth his maker.' Like the Old Testament prophets and Christ, Chartists pointed to princes and other political rulers—unjust employers and state priests—as oppressors against whom the people—the working classes and their friends—could legitimately prepare to use defensive force. Christ had instructed his disciples, when injustice was rampant in the land: 'He that hath no sword, let him sell his garment and buy one.' This text was often coupled on banners with a line from Lamentations: 'Better to die by the sword than to perish with hunger.'

In August 1839, just as the Chartists prepared for their most extreme action, three 'Sacred Days' of general strike, the battle of the Bible began in earnest. The Chartists staged demonstrations in more than thirty parish churches to display that they had the moral and Christian authority in this time of crisis. They submitted biblical texts for the vicar to preach, the favourite being from James which began 'Go to now, ye rich men, weep and howl for your miseries that shall come upon you.' The clergy were in no mood to be told their business by a Chartist 'mob', and their sermons played on themes like submission to the powers that be, quietness as godliness, and compensation in the afterlife for contentment in this. Insults were hurled, as when the Revd Francis Close of Cheltenham (1797–1882) told women demonstrators that they had not only unsexed but dehumanized themselves into fiends akin to their French sisters who 'glutted themselves with blood; and danced like maniacs amidst the most fearful scenes of the Reign of Terror'. So provocative were these demonstrations, especially when Chartists commandeered the pews which were privately owned or rented, that armed force was sometimes paraded in the 'poor man's' church to keep out the poor, an irony not lost on Chartists. After the Newport rising in Wales in November 1839, the vicar of Dowlais argued relentlessly to the conclusion that 'the Church of England and Chartism totally oppose each other'. Such confrontations served only to accelerate Chartist attempts to set up their own places of worship, especially in Scotland, where Chartist churches became widespread, some even rotating the ministry among all members. The Glasgow Chartists took religious authority into their own hands and operated a primitive Christian democracy.

Chartist public rhetoric was mainly constitutionalist and gave paramount authority to 'the People'. Thus at New Year festivities in Barnsley in 1839, Chartists raised the first toast to the 'People, the only source of all power', rather than to 'the Queen', as at a conventional public dinner. 'The People' had been central to the constitutional as well as to the religious vocabulary since at least the seventeenth century, and not surprisingly, disputes about who should be included in or excluded from this category had recurred constantly since that time. During the 1790s groups like the corresponding societies had extended the concept to male numbers unlimited, utilizing Thomas *Paine's idea that humanity was property, and they carried his words, 'his person is his title deed', on banners right through our period.

The issue of which social groups constituted 'the People', that is, who had the right to be included within this category, was intensified during the agitation for the 1832 Reform Act. Tories like the Duke of *Wellington clung to a doctrine of virtual representation which identified the owners of landed property as those to whom political powers belonged and those who would 'virtually' represent the rest. Compromisers like Lord Grey (1764–1845) thought it expedient to attach 'the middle classes who form the real and efficient mass of public opinion' to the gentry. Reformers in societies like the National Political Union and the Birmingham Political Union insisted that 'the People' were the middle and working classes who together constituted the industrious, useful, intelligent, and virtuous classes. In 1830, Abraham Hanson addressed the issue directly in a meeting to establish a Moderate Reform Union:

What constitutes a people or nation? According to my opinion, it is composed of that class of inhabitants who, by their moral and intellectual qualities, and active pursuits, form, as it were, the kernel of the population. It is this class that furnishes the standard of manners, intelligence, and all the useful arts that are necessary for man;—it is from this class that an opinion ought to be founded—it is in this that the national character centres—(cheers, and cries of hear).

None the less, some middle-class reformers in the alliance for reform pressed for yet another version of virtual representation, with the middle class representing labour. Indeed, it was during the reform agitation of 1831 that the idea of the working classes needing leaders from above in order to fulfil their role as 'the People' was most systematically propounded. The key figure in the Birmingham Political Union, banker Thomas Attwood (1765–1838), always called the working classes 'the masses' until the addition of the productive element of the middle class elevated them to 'the People'. Attwood kept insisting, in different ways, that self-governing popular movements could not succeed: 'there is no instance in history in which political movements have been successful without leaders and in almost every instance those leaders have been men of wealth and influence.'

By the Chartist years, Hanson had changed his mind about the necessity of alliance with middle-class reformers. Many radicals became disillusioned with the reformed parliament, which immediately passed an *Anatomy Act allowing for medical mutilation of the corpses of the poor, and which then enacted the repressive Irish Coercion Act (1833), the detested New Poor Law (1834), and a Municipal Corporations Act (1835) which deprived many working people of their local franchise and which colluded in the transportation to Australia of trade unionists like the Tolpuddle Martyrs (1834) and Glasgow Cotton-Spinners (1836). The Chartist National Petition of 1837 asserted that 'the Reform Act has effected a transfer of power from one domineering faction to another, and left the people as helpless as before. Our slavery has been exchanged for an apprenticeship to liberty, which has aggravated the painful feeling of our social degradation, by adding to it the sickening of still deferred hope.'

Some Chartists began to evict both the middle and upper class from the category of 'the People' unless members of these groups committed themselves to the Six Points, in which case they became the 'friends of the People'. At the large outdoor meeting on Peep Green in 1838, at which Chartists elected their delegates to the General Convention of the Industrious Classes or the People's Parliament (in contradistinction to the Imperial Parliament), Hanson now made clear that only the labouring classes constituted 'the People', adding, ''twas said that labourers could do nothing; and yet they were continually doing everything. (Cheers.)' This radical conflation of 'the People' with labour became even more firmly cemented over the remainder of the Chartist years, especially in 1842, when a general strike affected twenty-three counties in Britain, and Chartists clearly targeted powerholders in economic as well as in political and religious realms.

The passages quoted so far from the 1830s frequently used an actual language of 'class'. But beginning in the later eighteenth century there was a noticeable fluidity of the terminology of class, the result of a society which was undergoing significant social and economic change. From the 1750s, the conventional ways of expressing social hierarchy in static designations like rank, order, degree, and station were being supplemented by classifications based less on birth than on income and wealth, and often using the word 'class' derived from the Latin *classis*, meaning a group for taxation purposes. By the 1760s a tripartite division into higher, middling, and lower classes had appeared, with the middle seen as moving towards the apex at the top. In the 1770s, however, celebration began of the middle as the golden mean between two extremes, a configuration which was to become important in middle-class self-definition. The new political economy also complicated the picture by its emphasis on a tripartite division of society into economic groupings of landlords, capitalists, and labourers.

From the period of the French Revolution onward, this emerging language of class was not only directed towards labelling and defining social groups but was also used to express the contrasting social worth and even superiority of different classes. The middle class, particularly in its battle to extend the franchise, made good use of the upper, middle, and lower divisions to assert its superiority over the two extremes on grounds of its intelligence, its industry, its moral probity, its religious commitment, and its useful and productive contribution to social life. James *Mill, in his 'Essay on Government' (1820), characterized the 'middle rank' as 'both the most wise and the most virtuous part of the community'. By contrast, since 'intellectual powers are the offspring of labour', the greater part of the hereditary aristocracy 'will, therefore, be defective in those mental powers'. Without the model of the middle ranks to guide them, the vast majority beneath could become 'a mob, more than half composed . . . of boys and women'. Outside the political debate, the middle class also rested its authority on its responsible Christian family life built around a redemptive wife and mother who presided over the private sphere of the home, the abode of peace and love, and a protector-provider husband who navigated the more turbulent public spheres of business, politics, and voluntary associations. This behaviour was contrasted with the frivolity, vanity, and barbarism of the upper classes and with the ignorance, vice, and anarchy of lower-class life.

As the reform agitation reached its climax, Henry *Brougham announced in 1831, 'by the People, I mean the middle classes, the wealth and intelligence of the country, the glory of the British name'. But by Chartist times a key distinction was beginning to be made between the middle classes (sometimes designated 'millocrats') and the working class who had usurped the category of 'the People'. A government-sponsored paper, *Voice of the People*, just after the presentation of the 1848 Chartist Petition, complained that Chartism was 'based upon a systematic attempt to raise a portion of the industrious classes—the non-capitalist portion— into the belief that they are exclusively "The People"'.

During the 1820s, the early co-operative and *socialist movements were developing a different idea of class which disrupted this adulation of the golden mean and bestowed its moral gloss elsewhere. Even when class was being described in terms of function in economic life, it was the moral value of each class contribution that was being underlined. Middle-class activists were keen on binary oppositions which dignified their social contribution, as in the industrious versus the idle classes, the productive classes versus the parasites, the useful classes versus the useless, and they mobilized all these juxtapositions in the reform campaign. Classical political economists like David *Ricardo believed that labour created surplus value, but none the less felt that capital was the indispensable catalyst to set inert labour into productive motion. By contrast, the economists within the co-operative and socialist movement considered that labour was entitled to the value it had created. Indeed, maverick Irish landlord William *Thompson, author of *Labour Rewarded* (1827), debunked capital as a '*cabalistic word* like church or state, or any other of those general terms which are invented by those who fleece the rest of mankind to conceal the hand that shears them'.

John Gray (1799–1883), in *A Lecture on Human Happiness* (1825), made a robust evaluation of the utility of all existing groups in the population, which awarded top marks to the working classes, inverted the status pyramid of landed society, and challenged the rival middle-class vision of social value. 'They only are productive members of society', Gray insisted, 'who apply their own hands either to the cultivation of the earth itself, or to the preparing or appropriating the produce of the earth to the uses of life.' Everyone else was not only an 'UNPRODUCTIVE' member of society and a 'DIRECT TAX upon the productive classes' but also 'USELESS unless he gives an equivalent for that which he consumes'. This definition immediately excluded capitalists or indeed any fraction of the middle classes from being called productive, the most positive label of the period—connoting not only those who were active and energetic but also those who created useful and valuable things. Gray considered that manufacturers employing capital only played a useful role when directly engaged in management, and he dismissed three-quarters of eminent merchants and bankers as unnecessary. The landed classes, comprising 12,900 temporal peers and 402,915 gentry, together with the 720 bishops, were damned as being both non-productive and useless.

The arguments of Gray and Thompson resonated in writings by co-operators and socialists all over the country for at least the next ten years, and helped to energize co-operative and communitarian ventures which aimed partly to give labour the value it had created. To counter political economy—the science of wealth—the socialists also developed a more democratic 'social science', or science of happiness, and not only imagined a state of affairs where working people would take all areas of cultural life into their own control but also tried to experience it in their halls of science. The co-operative movement mounted three national delegate congresses in the early 1830s and helped form a Grand National Consolidated Trade Union in 1834. As labour strength became more formidable, the reaction of the classical political economists became more alarmist and shrill. Those industrious classes who had once been invited to ally with or be guided by the middle class were now in some instances depicted as subhuman—either as savages or as wild beasts. James Mill warned that the spread of radical economic ideas 'would be the subversion of civilised society, worse than the overwhelming deluge of Huns and Tartars'. Popular publisher Charles Knight (1791–1873) saw that 'the triumphant song of "Labour Defended against the Claims of Capital"' could only take place 'amid the shriek of the jackal and the howl of the wolf'.

Language, especially rhetoric or the language of persuasion, needs to be considered as social communication and situated within the historical context of the social relations where it played an active part. The shift from eighteenth- to nineteenth-century Britain, by way of political repression, economic revolution, and cultural offensive from above, involved a fundamental realignment of social forces and produced much more antagonistic class relations between the labouring classes and their political and economic masters. The actual tensions and conflicts were not necessarily expressed in separate languages but often in rival versions of the same legitimating discourses, as different social groups tried to seize the moral power conveyed by concepts like 'the People' or 'the useful and productive classes'. Looking for an immaculate and adequate revolutionary language new-minted by a revolutionary class is like searching for the holy grail. Peoples everywhere have usually struggled in the resonant languages culturally available to them and remade these in the process. Working people, when involved in economic, political, and religious class conflict before 1850, drew promiscuously from a range of vocabularies and used them to fortify each other in order to express a wide-ranging experience of oppression and utter a call to concerted action. It is no surprise to find a Chartist hymn which managed to combine radical patriotism, constitutionalism, and Christianity, together with the rights of man and socialist mutuality; 'All for each—each for all':

Ye nobles of nature, ye scions of fame,
Ye foremost in liberty's van,
Hoist your standard aloft, and loudly proclaim
The duties and rights of man.

When nature first stamped us with life and with form
It was at equality's shrine;
Truth, justice, and reason, united, conform,
to hallow the sacred design . . .

Our motto is equal rights and laws
Our call is freedom's call
Our cause, the cause, the common cause,
All for each—each for all

No one imperially should tower,
Nor govern with iron rod:
The people are the sovereign power,
Their voice is the voice of God.

Briggs, A., 'The Language of "Class" in Early Nineteenth-Century England', in A. Briggs & J. Saville, eds., *Essays in Labour History*, London, 1967, 43–73; Corfield, P., ed., *Language, History and Class*, Oxford, 1991; Cunningham, H., 'The Language of Patriotism, 1750–1914', *History Workshop*, 12 (1981), 8–33; Davidoff, L., & Hall, C., *Family Fortunes: Men and Women of the English Middle Class 1780–1850*, London, 1987; Epstein, J., *Radical Expression: Political Language, Ritual, and Symbol in England, 1790–1850*, Oxford, 1994; Jones, G. S., *Languages of Class: Studies in English Working-Class History, 1832–1982*, Cambridge, 1983; Joyce, P., *Visions of the People: Industrial England and the Question of Class, 1848–1914*, Cambridge, 1991; McCalman, I., 'Popular Constitutionalism and Revolution in England and Ireland', in I. Woloch, ed., *Revolution and the Meanings of Freedom in the Nineteenth Century*, Stanford, Calif., 1996, 138–72; Thompson, E. P., *The Making of the English Working Class* (1963), Harmondsworth, 1968; *Customs in Common* (1991), Harmondsworth, 1993; V. N. Volosinov, *Marxism and the Philosophy of Language* (1929), trans. L. Matejka & I. R. Titunik, Cambridge, Mass., 1973; Wahrman, D., *Imagining the Middle Class: The Political Representation of Class in Britain, c.1780–1840*, Cambridge, 1995; Yeo, E. J., *The Contest for Social Science: Relations and Representations of Gender and Class*, London, 1996.

16 · LAND   ANNE JANOWITZ

Between 1780 and 1830 the rural territory of England—fields, estates, commons, wastes, villages—was the arena and the object of a bitter set of rhetorical and practical contests. Present-day historical consensus is that the *agricultural revolution was a much longer process than earlier scholars had thought, though perhaps even more thoroughly revolutionary than has been acknowledged. Agrarian capitalism, which had developed through a centuries-long process of agricultural alteration, reached both maturity and crisis in the early decades of the nineteenth century. It provided the material foundation for a massive increase in *population as well as a consolidated national market from which to launch into colonial and international spheres, and within which to establish the wage as the fundamental mode of payment for labour. Between the fifteenth and nineteenth centuries, the creation of a class of agricultural workers who had only their labour power to sell to tenant farmers, who themselves needed to intensify production and compete for markets, provided the paradigm for relations of exploitation throughout capitalist production. The response of the labouring poor to the inequitable shift from customary to wage arrangements was a key element of domestic social conflict between 1770 and 1830. The conflicts which were played out within the cultural practices of the period as debates between individualism, which accorded centrality to individual property rights, and communitarianism, which advocated common ownership of land and property; between common law and communal custom; and between market-determined wage and customary wastage, all related to the practice and rhetoric of 'improvement'. Improvement as a practice referred to the management and cultivation of land to render it more profitable; as a discursive and rhetorical term improvement came to refer to moral or social cultivation. In the context of European and trans-Atlantic warfare as well as trade, improvement had a global dimension. In the context of the culture of *Romanticism, the meanings of improvement range from an external set of incentives for increasing profit to a set of internal pressures for developing the Self. In the long run, the moral associations of the discourse of improvement outstripped its originally economic meaning, but in the late eighteenth and early nineteenth centuries the meanings of improvement were often contradictory and obscure, as questions of profit and decorum were at times experienced as congruent, and at others as irreconcilable.

The tradition of agricultural improvement can be traced from seventeenth-century Commonwealth agriculturists like Samuel Hartlib, in tracts such as Walter Blith's 1649 *The English Improver*, through the eighteenth-century agricultural writings of William Marshall (1745–1818) and Arthur *Young. By the end of the eighteenth century, this rhetoric had become an element in an *Enlightenment [32] and *laissez-faire ideology of progress. Strategies for increasing the profitability of the land were bound up with notions of beauty. Elaborated within the context of ideas of the *picturesque, which presented beauty as an unmediated and idealized absolute, ornament often became an aesthetic pretext for the profit motive. In Romantic landscape *poetry [29], the acceleration of productivity informs the aesthetic of the picturesque. For example, in William *Wordsworth's 'Lines Composed a Few Miles Above Tintern Abbey' (1798), enclosure boundaries are naturalized as 'hedgerows, hardly hedgerows, little lines / Of sportive wood run wild'. But what counts as advancement for one section of society may be experienced as deterioration in the living conditions of another. In the face of the massive extension of parliamentary *enclosure acts and the long and devastating *war [2] with France, a counter-argument to agricultural capitalist growth resurfaced, an argument made through rhetoric and practical resistance, and which had begun in the seventeenth century with the interventions of the Diggers and Gerrard Winstanley (*fl.* 1648–52). An alternative version of improvement was espoused in the urban artisan movement of radical *agrarianism, gathered around Thomas *Spence's programme for the redistribution of the wealth derived from farming. Other, less far-reaching critiques of capitalist improvement encompassed Oliver Goldsmith's (?1730–74) sentimental regret and George *Crabbe's virtuous compassion, as well as the more radical Paineite ideas linking redistribution of wealth to social and *parliamentary reform. Practical responses were even more formidable, ranging from framebreaking, hedgerow destruction, and rick-burning to the politicization of traditional *friendly societies. The *famines of the 1790s and early 1800s, during the wars with France, precipitated multiple local uprisings, and linked the global politics of war and *empire [5] to the practices of agricultural capitalism.

What form did improvement of the land take? Major alterations in agricultural production transformed the configuration of the acreage used in farming. Principally this was done

through the enclosure of open-field farms, commons, and wastelands, the draining of bogs and fens, the conversion of arable to pasture land, the consolidation of land into larger holdings, and the use of better techniques to cultivate the newer nitrogen-rich animal-feeding crops such as turnips. Between 1762 and 1844 there were more than 2,500 enclosure acts, engrossing over 4 million acres of land fanning out from the centre of England: almost 43 per cent of all parliamentary enclosure acts took place during the period of the wars with France. A vast literature about farming reform was generated between 1770 and 1830: Arthur Young's *The Farmer's Calendar* (1771), for example, had gone through ten editions by 1820. A range of national and local organizations prospered as well, including the government-sponsored Board of Agriculture, established in 1793. The significance of these alterations to the land and physical environment can be measured not only by increases in productivity but also by the way in which modifications to the terrain altered ideas about geography as well as the patterns of everyday lives. For example, the agricultural organizations which fostered improvement became messengers for an increasingly national agricultural market, particularly during the French wars. This in turn gave ever greater urgency to the predominance of the national interest over the local interest in both agricultural and political spheres. These organizations were also used to defuse a growing sense of alienation felt by rural labourers dependent upon customary rights which were being eroded. Some groups gave prizes both for significant animal-breeding techniques and for labourers who could demonstrate a specialization in their skills and a capacity to live within their increasingly straitened means.

While the enclosure of open-field farming meant changes to capitalist agricultural production, the aspect of improvement between 1790 and 1815 that resounded most importantly in labourers' lives was the enclosure of wastelands. For farmers, the enclosure of the wastes appeared to foretell universal enrichment: with more land opened up to both arable and pastoral farming, greater productivity and more diverse forms of land utilization seemed possible. It was, however, from the wastes that most waged farm labourers supplemented their earnings. The rights of sheepwalk, estover (wood-gathering), piscary (fishing), turbary (peat-cutting), and gleaning (picking up stray stalks of wheat after the harvest had been gathered), maintained or eased the embattled life of the agrarian labouring family. The Speenhamland system of poor relief, which came into existence in 1795, offered outdoor poor relief to wage-earners only if the price of bread dropped below a minimum, or if the labourer's children exceeded a number maintainable on his wages [see *poverty, 12]. The interaction of the Speenhamland system with the practice of waste enclosure produced an immediate deterioration of labourer's living conditions. The attack on customary rights also caused numbers of workers to leave their homes and villages in search of employment; hence the great abundance of wanderers and vagrants in nostalgic rural poems, from Goldsmith's 'The Deserted Village' (1770) through Wordsworth's depictions of discharged soldiers, rural beggars, and the suffering Margaret of 'The Ruined Cottage' (1814). Indeed, even though the ruined village is a long-standing trope, such poetry is often an important documentary location of the social destructiveness wrought by improvement. One of the prevalent poetic themes of the end of the eighteenth century was lament over the dispersal of traditional communities into the large networks of local, national, and global movement. In 'The Deserted Village' Goldsmith presents the double-sidedness of improvement: 'The country blooms—a garden and a grave.' And though his central focus is on the process of becoming a poet, he voices the links between the expansion of a global empire, presented as a frightening terrain of silent bats and dark scorpions, and a transformed locality left behind, where 'even the bare-worn common is denied'. In this population movement from

21. *Ye Gen'rous Britons, Venerate the Plough* by Valentine Green, 1801, with an inscription from James Thomson's poem *The Seasons*. The print ambiguously invoked both the pastoral defiance of Thomson's 'Spring' (1728) and the improving values of the Board of Agriculture to which it was dedicated.

the country to the city, and from city to parts foreign, many of the sources for the nostalgic myth of rural England were generated. The intensity of capitalist production in the countryside in Britain precluded the absolute rejection of the country for the pleasures of urbanity that characterized other European nations, and gave rise to a peculiar ideological investment in the country and its mystification. This mystification of the rural landscape as idyll involved presenting the country as a retreat or alternative to the city, drawing on long-standing *pastoral and arcadian themes, thereby glossing over its status as a motor of economic activity.

Poetic themes were not confined to a rhetoric of regret and nostalgia, for the success of agrarian capitalism went beyond economic profit: it was also responsible for the improvement of farming technology and for a whole aesthetic of landscape improvement. The largest landlords and farmers reshaped chunks of the physical and human geography of south-east England into an ersatz unblemished countryside: whole villages were moved outside park grounds, while serpentine rivers were inserted. While enclosure of commons and wastes was proceeding outside the walls of the estate park, inside the legacy of the previous generation moved towards less formal estate design. This in turn led directly into the debates amongst
95–6   Richard Payne *Knight, Lancelot 'Capability' *Brown, and Humphry *Repton about how best to mimic unadorned nature. The landscaped park was often fitted out with bogus versions of historical remains, as the taste and sentiment for ruins of the eighteenth century persisted into the nineteenth. Even so, care was taken to divest such ruins of associations with a countryside crowded with historical event and engagement, making them appear instead as part of an apparently empty landscape, filled now with an immaculate and, paradoxically, unpopulated 'Nature'. Similarly, the location of ruins within the countryside naturalized an association between 'country' as rural terrain and 'country' as nation, which served to underwrite the nationalist myth of rural England.

The poetic and artistic rhetorics of the *sublime and the picturesque were direct beneficiaries of estate improvement. *Landscape gardening created a taste, based on the estate park, which was applied to the countryside in general. The struggle over whether or not to improve the extensive heaths became a matter of debate between agriculturists, who urged farmers to
90–1   enclose heaths, and prose writers of the picturesque, such as William *Gilpin, who were developing an aesthetic appreciation of unrecovered belts of land. The further into the nineteenth century and the closer to London, the greater became the argument against destruction of the wastes on aesthetic grounds: commons were increasingly seen as spots where one might elude the pressure of the teeming city. In semi-isolation, one might locate and refine the transcendent, all too often alienated 'Self', the model for the Romantic version of consciousness over the entire next century. As a landowner himself, however, Sir Uvedale *Price, author of *An Essay on the Picturesque* (1794–8), was very clear that 'wanton' labourers should be discouraged (by law) from gathering fuel.

The criminalization of customary right became an important subtext of contemporary discussion of the agriculturally and aesthetically improved landscape, at a time when the productive activity of rural commoners was being erased from the picturesque vista and from market-driven considerations of agrarian capitalism [see *law, 8]. On the other hand, both realistic and sentimental versions of agricultural labour were a popular theme in *landscape painting and illustration—in the work, for example, of John *Constable, Thomas *Gainsborough, George *Morland, and Thomas *Bewick. Farther afield, in rural areas outside central England, in the Lake District, and in Wales, lay the space where the sublime might supervene over the picturesque, offering to visitors or to readers of poetry the experience of the overwhelming differences between Self and Nature. So one might get a taste of the vertiginous and unencompassable depth of the visible world, as Wordsworth did upon Mount Snowdon, viewing the 'gloomy breathingplace' where 'Mounted the roar of waters, torrents, streams / Innumerable, roaring with one voice' (*The Prelude*, 1805).

Floating somewhere between the self-sustaining landscaped estate park on the one hand and the claims of individual consciousness and the sublimity of natural expanse on the other lay the world of the village. The enclosure of open-field farms resulted in a shift in the physical layout of villages. With farm buildings increasingly being built beyond the village, the network of social relations within it was fundamentally altered. Yet when village populations were dispersed and the farms where they might labour gathered into larger estates, these were brought into closer relation with the roads to cities and towns (the chief destination of produce), allowing a growing social connection between urban and rural residents. This, combined with improvements in *transport, made it increasingly possible for the radical languages of the city to reach the farm labourer, and so be incorporated into the struggles to produce an alternative, 'people's' version of improvement. For women labourers, used to the community practices of village life, improvement meant important changes in the character and value of labour. In addition to the tyranny of the wage, they faced the erosion of customary rights which had provided additional sustenance for their families and a significant role for themselves in the productive process. The increasingly gender-specified character of the division of labour meant that in some parts of Britain women were pushed further away from production itself. For example, the growing capital intensification of the dairy industry opened up new markets for cheese and milk in the city, but also diminished the value of the skills and expertise traditionally linked to women, whose domestic 'arts' were replaced by the mechanized manufacturing techniques of industrial production or by sweated piecework systems of commercial capitalism.

The expansion and intensification of agrarian production and its involvement in a network of physical and mental communications also meant that the landscape of a larger Britain was increasingly engrossed in the process of improvement. So, the rural labourers of Scotland had their lives dramatically changed by the introduction of large-scale sheep farming in both lowlands and highlands; while the intensification of cattle-ranching in Ireland contributed to widespread rural disturbances as well as to the substantial movement of population to England.

All in all, improvement was closely linked to a decrease in the real wages of the labouring poor. Of course, negative effects could be felt by farmers as well. While there were gains in the rate of productivity derived from agricultural workers, there were also losses, including increased labour unrest, the price of enclosure, and the effects of *poaching, which itself tended to become more large-scale and business-like. Agricultural improvement indexed to farming profitability also resulted in instances of severe ecological short-sightedness: for example, the rush to enclosure resulted in a reduction of woodland all over England: 'Ye banish'd trees, ye make me deeply sigh—/Inclosure came, and all your glories fell,' wrote John *Clare. These losses were linked not only to the consolidation of ever bigger farms, but also to the intensification of shipbuilding for extensive foreign ventures and war. Oaks were planted in Crown forests in an unsuccessful attempt to build up a store for shipbuilding, without regard for the necessary ecological balance of plants required. When enclosed, Crown forests became private property and, for the most part, new owners immediately cut the trees down. Moreover, landlords were known to destroy woodland and enclose it when they met with resistance to the enclosure of the open-field farms. The loss of woodlands was hardly compensated for, and, when it was, almost wholly within private estates and parks. In some cases estate planning was badly executed. In his *Rural Rides* (1830), William *Cobbett remarked upon estates in which faulty landscaping plans of 'enclosure and plantation have totally destroyed the beauty of this part of the estate'. While worldwide expansion of trade resulted in the importation of a vast number of plants, it is noteworthy that these new varieties had virtually no productive value: they were brought into gardens and parks as novelties and ornaments, and suggest how demands of *consumerism [19] further encroached upon popular access to productive land.

Most alarming to farmers and owners was the volatile response of the population to enclosing schemes. During the rapid enclosure of wastelands, numerous instances of local resistance culminated in physical struggle between farmer and labourer. When an 1801 Bill to enclose part of Oxmoor eventually passed through parliament, it was greeted by rural resistance, a pattern repeated in 1830, when Oxmoor villagers destroyed the fences and hedges that had been erected. This kind of history of local resistance and *insurrection was repeated throughout the country. Attempts to mitigate the anger of local agricultural labourers included the beginning of the allotment movement: by 1833, allotments had been organized in well over a third of English parishes.

Along with spontaneous resistance to improvement, there emerged a fully-fledged counter-vision of how the abundance of the land might be used. While discussion of improvement from the point of view of estate owners was both explicit and well publicized, oppositional arguments were less easily heard. The rhetoric of a 'people's' improvement, in counterpoise to that of agricultural capitalism, can be traced as both a language and a practice within and beyond farming areas. The democratic *republican rhetoric that arose in the metropolis, linking native traditions of middle-class Dissent with *Scottish Enlightenment and French thought, as well as with republican rhetoric from America, was also inflected by issues arising from agricultural change. Thomas *Paine's *Agrarian Justice* (1796), for instance, argued for an ameliorative agrarian capitalism. Although Paine did not advocate the expropriation of farm-owners, he none the less argued that they had responsibilities to their communities which derived from an original common ownership of the land. In legal title, the commons and wastes, like the open fields enclosed earlier, belonged to the lord of the manor. But Paine argued that an original commonality should be interpreted as the provenance of a land tax whose revenues would be used to better the lives of the rural poor: 'it is the value of the improvement only, and not the earth itself, that is individual property. Every proprietor, therefore, of cultivated land, owes to the community a groundrent.'

The *corresponding societies in London attempted, albeit unsuccessfully, through a set of marches and *petitions presented to parliament during the famine years of 1794–5 and again in 1801, to link their demands for political reform with a mass of agricultural labourers made volatile by the hunger in the countryside. This, too, was to be the enduring goal of republican and nationalist politics in Ireland. While elsewhere in Britain this pattern in the network of political relations between city and country developed under the auspices of the parliamentary reform movement, another pattern was grounded in the communitarian tradition. Forging links between Enlightenment rationalism and customary heritage, Thomas Spence recast the communitarian rhetoric of agrarianism. Outflanking Paine to the left by his call for the rights of *women [4] and infants as well as men, Spence's 'Land Plan', first advanced in 1775, advocated the community distribution of the bulk of wealth derived from agriculture. The theory of 'Spenceanism' travelled back and forth from city to country via radical journalism and community links amongst agricultural and urban workers, leaving a legacy for the *Chartist Land Plan and the *socialist movement at the end of the nineteenth century. Significant as well was the manner in which a 'people's farm' idealization of the land differed from that proposed by the poets of solitude and retreat. Instead of a landscape most noteworthy for its coalescence with pure consciousness, Spencean agrarianism presented a landscape meant to feed the body. The hairdresser E. J. Blandford (*fl.* 1818), a follower of Spence, wrote:

> When nature her pure artless reign began,
> She gave in entail all her stores to man;
> The earth, the waters, eke the air and light,
> And mines and springs, men held in equal right . . .

This sentiment formed an important strain within popular *ballads: 'In olden times the poor could on the common turn a cow / The commons are all taken in, the rich have claimed them now.'

Cobbett and Wordsworth each observed the gains and losses of improvement over many decades. Just as the agriculturist Arthur Young's experience led him to shift from advocating enclosure to fiercely arguing against it, so Cobbett moved closer and closer to identifying with the position of the labouring agricultural worker. Cobbett participated in the practices of improvement; but while other farmers strove to reduce the number of workers and raise the level of productivity, Cobbett aimed, in his 'radical husbandry', to make the agricultural worker a self-sufficient producer. In this context the description of Cobbett as a 'Radical Tory' is a misnomer, since he developed a *class [15] analysis of rural oppression, supporting the Captain Swing rural *riots and by the early 1830s taking seriously Spencean land proposals. In Wordsworth's landscape poetry, we find an ameliorative version of improvement. Wordsworth's attention to the migrations produced through the displacements of war, famine, and the enclosures of wastes brought into his poetic prospect a population of marginal wanderers; yet Wordsworth increasingly naturalizes such economically and socially engineered dissonance in the countryside. He introduces dislocated humans into a vocabulary of natural waste: 'as in nature so he lived, so let him die', he writes of the 'Old Cumberland Beggar' (1800). When he turns from the marginal lives of Dorset to the sublime landscapes of the Lake District, human elements are even further attenuated, until it appears that there is only the singular Self of Wordsworth in the sublime surrounding. What John *Keats called the 'egotistical sublime' supervenes upon the labour of the land.

Wordsworth's poetic vocation linked him to landowning elements of rural society. His literary defence of the Lake District from what he saw as an onslaught of the urbanism and rationalism of the *Edinburgh Review*, epitomized by the appearance of Henry *Brougham as a parliamentary candidate for Camelford in 1810, reflected deep anxieties about a potential alliance of middle-class Rationalist intellectuals with a dissatisfied rural population. Wordsworth may have explicitly responded to the claims of the Spenceans in his defence of *his* version of 'nature'—certainly Robert *Southey felt bound in 1817 to attack them at length in print.

William *Blake, as a poet of London, and with links to communitarian traditions and artisanal conceptions of human labour, was able to pierce through the increasingly mystified version of nature. He poetically recovered the natural world not as a vista to be surveyed, but as a dialectic between human labour and earth, in which a distinction between society and nature has no meaning: 'Where Man is Not, Nature is Barren'. When Blake does represent nature, he always introduces the practices of labour: even when his poetic language is at its most mythic and apocalyptic, he renders persons working the land and cultivating the soil. Blake satirically produces an anti-capitalist aesthetic: 'Improvement makes strait roads, but the crooked roads without Improvement are roads of Genius' (*The Marriage of Heaven and Hell*, 1790, 1793). Such roads are outside the estate parks. In John Clare's poetry and autobiography we find the most explicit presentation of the toll that enclosure had taken on the lives of rural workers; his poetic borrows from the generic stores of pastoral, but his sense of landscape feels the constant pressure of the local changes which have altered daily life. Poets with even fewer links to the metropolitan literary world than Clare also wrote interventionist verse against improvement and enclosers: 'So take care who comes out at night / For we will do all the mischief that we can' [see *peasant poets]. In the 1830s and 1840s Ebenezer Elliott (1781–1849), known as the 'Corn Law Rhymer', returns to the figure of the common, 'sown with curses loud and deep / [which] Proclaim a harvest, which the rich shall reap'.

Enclosure was not the only motive for resistance, and rural disturbances mark our period throughout England, Ireland, Wales, and Scotland. In Caernarvonshire, rents and bread prices caused many disturbances in the 1790s and early 1800s. The loss of customary right was significant here too. Rights to cut turf for fuel were eroded, leading in Cardiganshire to the assertion of a people's 'Turf Act', protected through the cultural practices of direct confrontation and effigy-burning. Such tactics of rural resistance perhaps passed backwards and forwards across the Irish Channel through contacts with Irish Whiteboys and Ribbonmen— implied in Thomas *Moore's tract *Captain Rock* (1824). In the south of England hunger was intermittent but widespread, and in the years 1794–5 and 1801 it reached famine proportions, provoking a series of rural riots and demands for cheaper bread. The riots associated with food shortages became linked in the 1810s with frame-breaking disturbances [see *Luddism]. Rural workers also agitated for changes in poor law relief and for implementation of a minimum wage, as the techniques and strategies of urban artisans and labourers made their way into the countryside.

The struggle over improvement also had a broader dimension. The subjugation of the rural community—or, as improvers might think, its liberation into free wage labour—was a project conceived on the model of imperial conquest. In 1803 Sir John Sinclair (1754–1835), President of the Board of Agriculture, urged his class: 'Let us not be satisfied with the liberation of Egypt, or the subjugation of Malta, but let us subdue Finchley Common; let us conquer Hounslow Heath, let us compel Epping Forest to submit to the yoke of improvement.' And beyond the borders of the islands of Britain, the colonial production of commodities significantly affected the lives of agricultural workers. The example of the consumption and production of sugar epitomizes an economy which constructs a global economic ecology. The sugar produced by slave and indentured labour in the British-controlled colonies of the West Indies became a part of the staple diet of the English labouring class, who were now attracted to the stimulants of tea and coffee with sugar, in part to compensate for nutritional deficits caused by the erosion of their customary rights and their changing role as wage labourers [see *slavery, 6]. Within Britain, the attack on the community's rights to its environment, backed up by the military, is linked to the perceived growth of crime in the city. In London, the punishment as legal crimes of what had recently been social customs (for example, the retention by shipwrights of 'chips' or waste timber), in order to increase productivity, reveals economic motives which often underlay various supposedly reformative and rational processes.

Interestingly, the period we have come to designate as 'Romanticism' coincides exactly with the years of the greatest number of parliamentary enclosure acts. And the best, or at least most canonical, of what we have come to call 'Romantic' nature poetry often lies on the borders, or acts out the contests, of improvement. That is to say, poetry by Wordsworth, Blake, and Clare, amongst others, tests and works against conceptions of Self as part of a rural community and as an isolated transcendent consciousness. In poems by Wordsworth and *Coleridge we are offered a poetic of transcendence, *lyric solitude, and private meditation which displaces the drives of improvement. However, poems by Blake and Clare, and lesser-known Spencean artisans such as Blandford and the shoemaker Allen *Davenport, offer a Romanticism of polemical militancy which invokes political activism. If we look at the double intention within Romanticism, as part of a literary-historical dialectic, we can see that the contest between individualism (grounded materially in the superseding of customary rights by the rights of private property and its legal apparatus) and communitarianism (grounded materially in the customary rights of the countryside) yields, in the course of the nineteenth century, to both the triumph and the crisis of liberal individualism, and to the rise of socialist and *utopian [9] communitarianism. Romanticism, then, in this context is a cultural theatre of contest between the rhetorics of traditional and capitalist society earlier in the eighteenth century, and between those of liberalism and socialism later in the eighteenth and early nineteenth centuries. The sublime of Romanticism presents an absolute distance between personal identity and nature; the communitarian strain in Romanticism demonstrates the inextricability of the human and the natural terrain. So it is, then, that romanticism offers itself to us as both an intervention against, and aesthetic authorization of, the material and ideological developments of capitalism.

Chase, M., *'The People's Farm': English Radical Agrarianism 1775–1840*, Oxford, 1988; Neeson, J. H., *Commoners: Common Right, Enclosure, and Social Change in England, 1700–1820*, Cambridge, 1993; Payne, C., *Toil and Plenty: Images of the Agricultural Landscape in England, 1780–1890*, New Haven, Conn., 1993; Snell, K. D. M., *Annals of the Labouring Poor: Social Change and Agrarian England, 1660–1900*, Cambridge, 1985; Turner, M., *Enclosures in Britain, 1750–1830*, London, 1984; Valenze, D., 'The Art of Women and the Business of Men: Women's Work and the Dairy Industry, c.1740–1840', *Past and Present*, 130 (1991), 142–69; Wells, R., *Wretched Faces: Famine in Wartime England, 1793–1801*, Gloucester, 1988; Williams, R., *The Country and the City*, Oxford, 1973; Wood, E. M., *The Pristine Culture of Capitalism*, London, 1991; Worrall, D., *Radical Culture: Discourse, Resistance and Surveillance, 1790–1820*, New York, 1992.

17 · EDUCATION   IAN BRITAIN

In Romantic-period parlance, the words 'education' and 'culture' had similar connotations and could be used interchangeably. The association of educative processes with the cultivation of human faculties suggests that much more was envisaged in the term 'education' than institutional instruction or learning. It was a term that could include the operation and application of much wider environmental influences, within nature as well as society, from earliest childhood onwards. This was certainly the general understanding—for all the differences in their ideas and schemes—of the three leading educational theorists, *Locke, Helvetius (1715–71), and *Rousseau; and it was an understanding shared—indeed, passionately articulated at times—by educational pundits or practitioners as varied as the liberal experimenters Thomas *Day, Richard *Edgeworth, and Maria *Edgeworth, rationalist radicals such as William *Godwin or Robert *Owen, the utilitarian philosopher James *Mill, and the Romantic poets *Coleridge and *Wordsworth.

Their need to articulate these wider senses of education testifies, however, to the extent that the term or concept was now 'commonly confined' to schooling, as Mill complained in 1815 when composing an entry on 'Education' for the *Encyclopaedia Britannica*. His own educational concerns were often with matters of formal instruction in schools or institutions of higher learning; and neither he nor the other writers listed above completely disdained the uses of such instruction, as some more radical voices were inclined to do. ('I hold it to be wrong,' William *Blake is reported as saying; 'despicable cant and nonsense,' chimed in William *Cobbett.) How much and what types of instruction should be conducted in institutions, as distinct from in the home or through individual self-instruction, remained a major issue of debate in British society.

There was at least as much debate about the levels of instruction appropriate to the various levels and sections of British society. Did the bulk of the lower ranks, engaged in manual or menial labour, need literacy or numeracy, let alone systematic access to more developed skills and areas of knowledge? Cobbett, for one, felt that what they needed more urgently was greater material sustenance to quell 'the gnawings and ragings of hunger', and that schools were only a distraction from these pains, a kind of anaesthetic that ended up compounding 'servility, pauperism and slavery'. On the other hand, many radically inclined representatives of the working class, or sympathizers with its plight from higher ranks, looked favourably on *popular education (of various kinds, and up to the most sophisticated levels) as a positive aid to independence or liberation. More conservative forces in British society generally came round to the view that the spread of basic literacy could have a stabilizing (if not anaesthetizing) effect on the mass of the population, by facilitating the inculcation of moral homilies based on orthodox Christian dogma, but this strategy entailed strict control over reading and teaching practices. Hannah *More and Sarah *Trimmer, as well as involving themselves in *Sunday school schemes and programmes, produced a plethora of exemplary tales and exhortatory *Cheap Repository Tracts to counteract the influence of more fanciful, ribald, or satirical brands of popular and *children's literature. Some deeper-dyed conservatives so feared the effects of undirected literacy in encouraging an appetite for seditious or salacious books that they urged that classroom reading, where it was to be countenanced at all, be restricted entirely to the *Bible.

The scope and content of *female education provided another major focus of debate. 'What have men to do with the education of girls?' the narrator of Rousseau's *Émile* (1762) asked at one point. Little in practice, he could plausibly plead, speaking of French society in the mid-eighteenth century; but this did not deter him from pontificating on the subject at great length; and (partly under his influence, or in reaction against him) it was a subject which increasingly engaged British authors of both sexes. Rousseau made clear his objection to any notion that women should be brought up in ignorance and assigned exclusively to housework; but in advocating that 'they cultivate their minds as well as their persons', his concern was not to enhance their own freedom or independence. Rather, it was to make them more effective and stimulating companions for their husbands. Within the general constraints of the domestic ideology and structures of the day, this necessarily involved limits on the intellectual freedom of women [see *domesticity, 13]. 'They should learn many things,' the narrator of *Émile* declared, 'but only such things as are suitable.'

The question of where the limits started, of what 'suitable' meant, was the basic one in the debate on female education, underpinning other issues such as whether this education should take place at home or at school. Among the most active supporters of increased educational opportunities for *women [4] (and they included some conservatives like More, as well as liberal reformers such as the Edgeworths and Erasmus *Darwin), only a tiny radical fringe came anywhere near to entertaining the prospects of parity with male education, and even its representatives had to bow to limits, endorse discriminations, necessitated by traditional divisions of occupational and family roles. Catharine *Macaulay and Mary *Wollstonecraft each advocated forms of co-education aimed at dissolving certain social as well as gender distinctions in the classroom, but these were selective and restricted forms. Wollstonecraft, who went further down the radical path, none the less clung to a belief that 'after the age of nine, girls and boys, intended for domestic employments, or mechanical trades, ought to be removed to other schools . . . the two sexes still being together in the morning; but in the afternoon the girls should attend a school, where plain work, mantua-making, millinery, etc., would be their employment.'

The variety of opinion expressed in the debates over modes, levels, and types of education in Britain in this period was in part a reflection of the profusion and variety of educational facilities already available, in all their transparent strengths and weaknesses. As early as 1678, Christopher Wase was sufficiently struck by the 'multitude of schools . . . in England' to produce a detailed excursus on one variety that he particularly valued: the so-called 'free schools'. The intensity of the debates on education in the next century and a half reflected a concurrence of various pressures, old and new: lingering tension between the religious establishment and Dissenters of various kinds, with their competing claims for children's souls [see *religion, 10]; the intellectual ferment of the *Enlightenment [32], with its predominant view of human

Frontispiece.

Blake inv. & sc.

Look what a fine morning it is. Insects, Birds, & Animals, are all enjoying existence.

Published by J. Johnson, Sep.ᵗ 1ˢᵗ 1791.

22. An engraving by William Blake for Mary Wollstonecraft's *Original Stories from Real Life* (2nd edn., 1791), a didactic fiction designed for the education of young girls. Wollstonecraft went further than most in attempting to tease from Rousseauist ideas a rationale for women's independent learning.

differences as environmentally determined, rather than hereditary, and therefore amenable to adjustment through changed material and educational circumstances; the visible advent of a mass society clustered in cities, stemming from the unprecedented demographic and economic changes associated with large-scale 'revolutions' in agriculture and industry; and the spectacle of democratic, or would-be democratic, *revolution [1] in political regimes across the Atlantic in America and across the Channel in France.

Across the border from England in Scotland existed the only comprehensive network of schools in the nation. These were under the aegis of the Church of Scotland, whose Calvinist allegiances committed it to the growth of literacy as a means of spreading the word of God through the Scriptures. Nearly every parish boasted at least one of these schools, which (from 1696) were subsidized regularly by ratepayers, and which educated children at least up to elementary level. The sprinkling of Catholics, Episcopalians, and other smaller sects to be found in Scotland added some variety to educational practices there but no great challenge to the establishment. There were also some small-town, or 'burgh', schools which offered more advanced education, along with city grammar schools which specialized in Latin and Greek and prepared pupils for entry to the universities.

In Scotland, universities or university colleges existed at St Andrews, Glasgow, Aberdeen, and Edinburgh, the earliest of them dating back to the fifteenth century. Collectively, these institutions almost trebled their enrolments over the course of the eighteenth century, though it has been calculated that only about one in a thousand Scots gained admission to them. Their clientele was increasingly drawn from England, Ireland, Wales (where there was no university until the foundation of a college at Lampeter in 1822), and the colonies. Part of the attraction of these institutions was that they did not enforce residence on students (and the fees this would have entailed), nor any exclusionary religious prerequisites. They also offered a wide range of courses, including relatively 'modern' ones in the physical sciences and in vocational disciplines such as *medicine [18] and *law [8].

In England, the *Anglican Church exercised direct or indirect control over many educational institutions at the higher levels: the two famous universities dating from the Middle Ages, Oxford and Cambridge, and the bulk of the schools which fed those universities their students. At more modest levels of schooling, however, the Church of England's field of influence was much patchier than that of the established church in Scotland, and its record of active involvement desultory.

Until 1828, Oxford and Cambridge were the only two universities in England. Each comprised a collection of autonomous colleges, all of which were Anglican institutions. As a general rule, official teaching positions at these places were confined to ordained clergymen. Long-established conventions, some enshrined in law, effectively excluded Dissenters, Catholics, and *Jews from the undergraduate body; at Cambridge—though not at Oxford—Nonconformists were occasionally permitted to study, but they were still barred from taking a degree.

The number of students attending Oxford in the eighteenth century was at a low ebb (no more than 250 freshmen in any one year, compared to the 450 or so matriculating around the time of the Restoration), and Cambridge's student intake declined even more over this century. The social range of the students narrowed markedly during the same period. Oxford matriculants registered as 'poor' fell from 27 per cent to 1 per cent, with students from professional families joining those of the older landed ranks to become the dominant element. Numbers at both universities were to return to their former heights by the end of the Napoleonic *wars [2]. The growing prosperity and ambition of the middle class during the Industrial Revolution may have been a factor in these increased enrolments, although the commercial sectors of this class were troubled, even as they were beguiled, by the air of aristocratic nonchalance which seemed to prevail at the old universities. This laxity permeated the teaching and examining practices of these institutions; and there was further cause for concern in the conservatism of the teaching curriculum.

In the first decade of the nineteenth century, some reformist pressure from within Oxford itself brought about a considerable tightening up of examination procedures at the two levels—pass and honours—at which undergraduates could pursue their degrees; the old routine of answering standard questions known in advance was now replaced by a much more searching succession of tests in the various branches of *Literae Humaniores* (classical studies) as well as in mathematics and science. Cambridge had never formally observed a distinction between an honours and an ordinary pass degree, but it introduced this system in 1828. There were still no major changes or extensions made to the curriculum at either institution. Most undergraduates at Oxford concentrated exclusively on the classics. There was greater scope at Cambridge to pursue mathematics, but at a fairly rarefied level that had little direct connection with the everyday needs of an age witnessing unprecedented technological change. Both universities appointed professors to give public lectures in a variety of other fields (such as natural philosophy, astronomy, chemistry, mineralogy, botany, anatomy, medicine, and modern history), but as these did not form the basis of undergraduate courses attendance at the lectures was often minimal, and the appointees often appear to have felt under no obligation to turn up themselves.

Oxford and Cambridge survived lean periods partly because a classical education was still regarded as a necessary basis for the careers of clergymen, schoolmasters, civil lawyers, and physicians; but, as professional training-grounds, the two universities faced considerable competition not just from their Scottish counterparts but also from the so-called *Dissenting academies set up by leading Nonconformists in England. In the century following the *Toleration Act of 1689 more than seventy of these institutions were in operation for varying periods of time and in various spots around London or in the provinces. There remained some insecurity in the legal position of Dissenters, with respect to education, but this was brought to an end in 1779 by an act of parliament formally ratifying their right to follow the teaching profession. The academies as a rule prescribed no exclusionary religious tests, and managed to attract a cross-section of pupils from other religious backgrounds, including Anglican and Catholic. They offered a broad curriculum which did not exclude the classics but which emphasized more modern, scientific, and commercial subjects; and the level of instruction at the best of these institutions was up to the equivalent of a university degree.

During the 1790s, at the height of the conservative reaction to the *French Revolution in Britain, some of the academies were suspected of being dens of political as well as religious dissent, and underwent a downturn in their fortunes, where they were not shut down completely. It was to be another three decades before the establishment of a university, at London, consolidated and extended the role of the academies in providing advanced education without religious tests and in a range of modern and traditional subjects.

In 1824–5 the poet and literary editor Thomas *Campbell first mooted the scheme for a University in the English capital. It was soon taken up by James Mill and other leading *utilitarians, such as George Grote (1794–1871) and Henry *Brougham, and it had the endorsement of their panjandrum, Jeremy *Bentham, to whom it appealed as a version of his own ideas for a broad and rational school curriculum concentrating on practical, largely scientific subjects (his 'Chrestomathia'). A prospectus for the 'University of London' was issued, an appeal launched, a joint-stock company founded to manage the funds, and some distinguished academic staff appointed (predominantly from Scotland or abroad). Around 300 men were admitted as students in 1828. Various forces within the English academic and ecclesiastical establishments strongly opposed the new institution, and it had to wait another eight years before it was granted a charter, which officially renamed it 'University College, London'. Meanwhile, the establishment forces had set up a counterpart in the metropolis, King's College, which retained Anglican affiliations and stressed the crucial importance of religious values while also offering a 'liberal and enlarged' curriculum. In 1836 the two rival colleges were each empowered to present students for the conferment of degrees by a newly constituted University of London. Three years earlier, at Durham, the first of the new provincial universities in England had been established through Anglican initiatives.

Students at the universities were drawn from homes throughout (and in some instances outside) the country, lending these institutions a geographical reach that far exceeded their immediate locality. Most schools remained much more localized in their constituency. Landed upper-class families might opt to send their children (particularly their male children) to some élite boarding school in another part of the country, but many such families employed a private tutor to instruct their children *in* the home. Household or 'domestic' education had been a common practice among the highest social ranks in the middle ages, and this old custom became a new fashion from the later years of the seventeenth century. Some advanced educational commentators, led by Locke, developed an aversion to institutional or 'public' education because of the risks it might involve of exposure to moral contamination, or because of the constraints of the collective classroom on the free growth of the mind. The pedagogic theories of Rousseau and his English disciples helped sustain and spread the fashion. It was attacked by various other commentators and never became the dominant practice; but throughout the eighteenth century, up to a quarter of the aristocracy and a third of the gentry had no public schooling.

Even some of the top-level boarding-schools attended by the rest of these classes had initially been set up to educate local boys. The original idea behind such establishments, some of which dated back to the Middle Ages, was to subsidize talent from the poorer ranks in their vicinity—those who could not afford private tuition—and to direct it by careful nurturing into the professions, especially ones connected with the church. These, then, were nominally 'free schools' (though much debate ensued over whether that meant free of all charges for every pupil); and they were also known as endowed grammar schools ('endowed' after their source of their funding, a charitable bequest from a monarch, church dignitary, or wealthy layman; 'grammar' after their curriculum, dominated by the classical languages) or public schools (to distinguish them from private tuition in the home or from various places of instruction set up as a business to make profits for their owners and administrators).

Nicholas Carlisle's (1771–1847) *A Concise Description of the Endowed Grammar Schools in England and Wales*, published in 1818, recorded the existence of nearly 500 of these institutions at the time; and according to the report of the first parliamentary select committee on education, set up in 1816 and headed by Brougham, there were another 212 endowed schools in Scotland, though it did not stipulate how many of these were the higher-level grammar schools. The names 'endowed', 'free', and 'public' still remained in common use during this period, and still occasionally overlapped. Over the centuries, however, they had taken on different shades of meaning, with 'public schools' coming to connote an élite subtype which still made gestures towards retaining a charitable function on behalf of poorer scholars but increasingly recruited its clientele from fee-paying boys of higher rank and from far and wide.

The endowment statutes of Winchester and Eton, the oldest schools in this choice band, had provided loopholes which from the start had encouraged the admission of a selection of non-local pupils. This practice became the routine policy of the school at Westminster which Elizabeth I founded in 1560, and an increasing trend over the next 300 years at a range of the more ambitious endowed schools in London or the provinces, including St Paul's, Charterhouse, Merchant Taylors', Rugby, and Harrow. It was these very establishments (with the exception of Harrow) which Sydney *Smith named when specifically attacking 'public schools', and their pretensions to eminence, in an *Edinburgh Review* article of 1810.

The fees that wealthier families could afford to pay, or the social lustre attaching to their name, were clearly a strong attraction for school governing bodies. By 1800 fee-paying students at Eton, the most illustrious of these establishments, had come to outnumber the subsidized scholars by as much as seven to one. Eton's enrolments, which stood at about 400 in that year and rose to 600 by 1830, exceeded those of all but one other school in the nation.

The largest school of all was Christ's Hospital in London, with enrolments exceeding 1,000 throughout this period. Established in the mid-sixteenth century through an endowment of Edward VI, it still had 'no rival' among 'charitable establishments', according to the text accompanying Rudolph *Ackermann's engravings of selected English schools, published in 1816; and it was expressly labelled a 'Free School' there. In the same year, Brougham's parliamentary committee on education noted the 'very many instances' at Christ's Hospital 'of children being admitted, whose parents are totally destitute'. But all the other establishments selected for inclusion in the Ackermann volume were identical to those in Smith's list of 'public schools' (with Harrow now added as well), and the text quoted a statement by Charles *Lamb, a former pupil of Christ's Hospital, recommending expansion in its recruitment of 'respectable clientele', and warning against degeneration into a 'mere charity school' of the kind which drew on 'none but the very lowest of the people'.

Technically speaking, all endowed schools (including Eton) were charity schools, but in the eighteenth century a distinction was drawn between those institutions which had been established by a single founder, in the form of a gift or bequest, and those established by a group of subscribers contributing to a fund. As part of its campaign against the possible resurgence of Roman Catholicism in England, the Society for Promoting Christian Knowledge had been particularly active in the early part of the century in encouraging the growth of charity schools offering elementary instruction to the poorer ranks. There was a spread of over 1,300 such schools by the 1720s. Collectively, they constituted the nearest Anglican equivalent to the network of parish schools in Scotland; but because their funding was by voluntary subscription and did not come out of parish rates, they had no real security. As the fears of Catholicism subsided among the higher social ranks over the course of the eighteenth century, subscriptions for charity schools began to dry up, and their expansion halted.

Anything approaching systematic organization of lower-class schooling in England and Wales, let alone an integrated national structure supervised or subsidized by the state, had to await the nineteenth century. Individual enterprise filled many gaps, however. A large array of institutions, embracing a large range of age groups, pedagogic methods, and social levels, were represented under the category of 'unendowed' or 'private venture' schools, as used by the Brougham parliamentary committee early on in the new century. It is no wonder that it was the largest category, swelling to over 14,000 by the time the committee's figures were being compiled. Here were included the surviving Dissenting academies, a gallimaufry of day and boarding-schools, from the genteel to the rough, and the so-called 'dame schools' to be found in nearly every parish (most of them little more than child-minding centres, though in some instances supplied with a reading and writing master). The only common feature of these institutions was their dependence on pupils' fees, rather than on any proceeds of an endowment or trust. This could give them something of a cachet, even in poorer areas. The Brougham committee noted how charity schools were unpopular where the instruction they provided was 'completely *gratis*', and that some establishments now charged a nominal fee to avoid the impression of a handout.

As a means of adjusting to the pressures of the new industrial age, members of the working classes often took the initiative in their own education. While much of their activity in this field was on a casual and individual basis, it sometimes took on more regular, collective forms, as in the Sunday schools which they organized from the 1780s on. Some of these enterprises not only taught the rudiments of literacy; they also attempted to replace the religious indoctrination of the Sunday schools run by the likes of Mrs Trimmer and Mrs More by a more rational education, involving the reading and discussion of political literature.

At all age levels, and in all classes, the formal schooling of women was not nearly as far advanced as men's, and female literacy, while increasing steadily between 1750 and 1850, still lagged behind male rates by as much as 25 per cent. But although restricted by the imperatives of domesticity, opportunities for female education were far from negligible, and struck a visiting Frenchman of the mid-1780s, cited in the *Gentleman's Magazine* for October 1795, as 'less regulated and subject to prejudices than in France'. Upper-class girls continued to be educated mainly at home; there was as yet no equivalent for them of the great public schools, although a few of the endowed grammar schools (including Christ's Hospital) did take a proportion of female pupils, and among the charity and dame schools for the poorest ranks there had always been many open to both sexes. For middle-class girls, private boarding-schools or academies started to spring up; in some of the bigger cities at least, these started to outnumber the boys' variety by the early decades of the nineteenth century.

The same decades witnessed the advent of the *monitorial system, based on competing schemes devised by the *Quaker Joseph Lancaster (1778–1838) and the Anglican clergyman Andrew Bell (1753–1832). This system found its main institutional form in a string of new elementary schools where the instruction was carried out almost entirely by a selection of the pupils, supervised by a single teacher. Not since the heyday of the charity schools a century earlier had the Anglican establishment become so exercised in the matter of popular educa-tion. It set up the 'National Society for Promoting the Education of the Poor in the Principles of the Established Church' as a direct counter to the Lancaster faction's promotional organ-ization, which became known as the 'British and Foreign School Society'. There are grounds for arguing, however, that the rivalry of these two bodies, and of the forces they represented, did as much to impede as to aid the spread of education through the British nation at large. It was a deadlock between these forces that frustrated the attempt by Brougham, following his parliamentary enquiry into schools, to legislate for a measure of direct state participation in the extension of educational provisions for the lower classes. Even the question of indirect state participation, through financial subsidies to the religious bodies concerned, remained a deli-cate one, and it was not until 1833 that parliament found its way to providing a small grant-in-aid for school-building programmes of the National Society and the British and Foreign School Society, to be divided almost evenly between them.

The new schools set up by the two societies were not the only ones with aspirations to being 'national' or 'British' institutions. Claims to national status were voiced by, or on behalf of, some of the oldest institutions, notably Oxford, Cambridge, and the public schools, even though their representativeness, as judged by the sex, social class, and religious affiliations of their main clientele, remained very limited. Writing in the 1780s, the historian Edward *Gib-bon, who had received part of his schooling at Westminster, supposed it was 'the common opinion, that our Public Schools, which have produced so many eminent characters, are the best adapted to the genius and the constitution of the English people'. It would be impossible to prove this was the common opinion across the whole of the nation, and a couple of decades later Sydney Smith, an old boy of Winchester, attempted to show that individual geniuses in a variety of fields were likelier to have received their formative education at more modest estab-lishments, several of which were located in Scotland. On the other hand, we find a classic speci-men of this breed, Sir James *Mackintosh, writing of the English public schools: 'though I am a stranger to their advantages, yet no British heart can be a stranger to their glory . . . I have often contemplated with mingled sensations of pleasure and awe, those magnificent monuments.'

For those Britons alarmed by the overthrow of the *ancien régime* in France, it became all the more urgent to sing the praises of their nation's long-standing institutions and landmarks. A history of the River Thames, published in 1794, offered this reverie on the spectacle of Oxford:

> The lofty spires and antique towers rise, in solemn arrangement . . . And as we view the numerous youth who range along the bank, . . . the animating hope springs up, that there may be superior characters among them, who will form the honour, the support, and the pride of their country.

Sydney Smith pronounced the Scottish universities 'far more pure and perfect' than Oxford or Cambridge, yet the very impurities and imperfections of the English universities made them the more newsworthy. Poets and novelists who had studied at one or other of these institutions often invoked them as symbols or included them as settings. (Wordsworth's detailed and ambivalent re-creation of his days at Cambridge in the earlier sections of *The Prelude* is only the most notable example.) And more than occasionally there were references to Oxford and

85

Cambridge in the works of writers who had no formal connections with these institutions—such as Jane *Austen or Benjamin Disraeli (1804–81). Few such prominent authors dealt with comparable institutions elsewhere in Britain. (Among these rare instances were Mrs *Barbauld's elegies for the Dissenting academy at Warrington, and Walter *Scott's less flattering vignettes of 'Glasgow College' in his novel *Guy Mannering*, 1815.)

In the mid-1770s, *Wedgwood potteries supplied a dinner service for Catherine the Great of Russia which displayed views, the catalogue explained, of 'the most remarkable buildings . . . and other national curiosities which distinguish Britain'. Only two educational institutions were selected for representation: Eton College and Christ Church, Oxford. Four decades later, just prior to his set of public-school engravings, Ackermann completed a lustrous four-volume series of interior and exterior views of various colleges at both Oxford and Cambridge. That Ackermann was a German émigré, and the Wedgwood family of *Unitarian faith and thereby effectively excluded from either of the English universities, may be a measure of the extraordinary enchantment of these places for outsiders.

In accordance with their wider range, the attention given to non-public schools in British literature was much more extensive than that given any of the alternatives to Oxford and Cambridge universities. However, it was usually just as emblematic types ('village', 'ladies', 'private') that such schools were represented in poems and novels. Representations of public schools, on the other hand, tended to identify them with actual institutions—to specify them, whether in praise or criticism, by name, as Eton was by *Shelley, Harrow by *Byron, or Westminster by *Cowper. Most other schools lacked this opportunity for precise registration in the public consciousness.

There were myriad visual representations of all varieties of British school in paintings, engravings, and book illustrations, but the evidence of contemporary sales, exhibition, and print-room catalogues suggests that the best-known or most sought-after of such images were those which concentrated on the public schools. Eton, in particular, had long provided subject-matter for visual artists, most of whom had never been educated there. In addition to

23. *Eton College Chapel from the South*, executed by Paul Sandby in the 1770s. One of the largest endowed schools, Eton was for many a symbol both of architectural excellence and educational privilege.

Wedgwood and Ackermann, the non-Etonian painters or engravers attracted to this subject in the late eighteenth or early nineteenth centuries included Sir Thomas *Lawrence, Sir William Beechey (1753–1839), Paul *Sandby, J. M. W. *Turner, and even (though under commission from an obscure patron) William Blake. The charms of Eton's rural setting and the antiquity of its buildings were evidence of its connections with the country's past traditions and a sufficient basis, perhaps, for its particular appeal to artists, regardless of any deficiencies or excesses they might have perceived in its curriculum or clientele.

Bantock, G. H., *Studies in the History of Educational Theory*, ii: *The Minds and the Masses, 1760–1980*, London, 1984; Camic, C., *Experience and Enlightenment: Socialization for Cultural Change in Eighteenth-Century Scotland*, Chicago, 1983; Kamm, J., *Hope Deferred: Girls' Education in English History*, London, 1965; Laqueur, T. W., *Religion and Respectability: Sunday Schools and Working-Class Culture, 1780–1850*, New Haven, Conn., 1976; Mack, E. C., *Public Schools and British Opinion 1780–1860*, London, 1938; McLachlan, H., *English Education under* the Test Acts: Being the History of Nonconformist Academies, Manchester, 1931; Richardson, A., *Literature, Education, and Romanticism: Reading as Social Practice, 1780–1832*, Cambridge, 1994; Simon, B., *The Two Nations and the Educational Structure 1780–1870*, London, 1974; Stone, L., ed., *The University in Society*, i: *Oxford and Cambridge from the 14th to the Early 19th Century*, Princeton, NJ, 1974; Tompson, R. S., *Classics or Charity? The Dilemma of the 18th Century Grammar School*, Manchester, 1971.

18 · MEDICINE ROY PORTER

The decades around 1800 brought unparalleled transformation in Britain as elsewhere: native radicalism, some of it responding to the *French Revolution; the Industrial Revolution; the making of a *class [15] society; to say nothing of the cultural upheaval that *Romanticism itself constituted. But did those years bring a revolution in medicine and in health?

In most respects the answer is no. The old political and ecclesiastical order might have been shaken, but the biological and epidemiological *ancien régime* continued through the nineteenth century. It seems plausible to argue that scientific medicine, whatever precisely that may mean, did not really begin until the creation of laboratory-based medicine in the mid-nineteenth century and the bacteriological revolution forged by Louis Pasteur and Robert Koch in the 1870s. Therapeutically, one can argue that medical interventions did not radically improve life chances until well into the twentieth century, with the development of sulfa drugs in the 1930s and above all antibiotics in the 1940s.

During the eighteenth-century biological *ancien régime*, humans died inexorably of all sorts of fevers and infections; from the most serious, like smallpox, down to what we would consider to be the trivial, such as stomach upsets and influenza. Nothing had changed in this respect by the close of the Romantic era. With the possible exception of smallpox (for which inoculation had gradually been introduced during the eighteenth century and a *vaccination developed by Edward Jenner from 1796), all the other endemic epidemic diseases continued to be lethal into the nineteenth century. Indeed, at the very close of the Romantic era terrible cholera pandemics moved from their traditional home in the Indian subcontinent and swept round the globe in six catastrophic episodes, beginning around 1830. There were, indeed, features of medicine that changed around 1800; but it would be unwarrantable to imply that the age constituted some revolutionary watershed that transformed clinical medicine and gave *physicians and surgeons far greater powers than before to heal and cure, or even to understand the hidden causes of disease. Such advances were made in the latter years of the nineteenth century and during the twentieth.

The late Georgian period brought unprecedented *population growth in Britain. But practically all historians now agree that this rise was due not to a diminution in the death rate but to a rising birth rate—possibly thanks to greater fertility, but more likely a demographic response to earlier marriage. Before the first national census of 1801 and the development around 1830 of epidemiology and of *statistics—associated with the work of William Farr (1807–83), who inaugurated the new science with a lecture on 'Vital Statistics' in 1837—it is very difficult to quantify exactly the incidence of particular diseases or even the chief causes of death. But there is ample evidence that deadly fevers—those we would now term typhus, typhoid, dysentery, scarlatina, influenza, measles, smallpox, and so forth, diseases both bacteriological and virological—were extremely common and very frequently lethal in late Georgian England. The very young were particularly vulnerable to such diseases. A shockingly high percentage of babies and infants died of various forms of summer diarrhoea, dysenteric disorders, and respiratory conditions. Mothers also suffered from puerperal fever, often as a result of inept obstetrics, and many died.

Maybe up to two out of every five infants died before they reached their fifth year. Children were particularly vulnerable to smallpox, which was still common. The rise of towns associated with *industrialization [14] resulted in slum conditions; physicians in Manchester, Birmingham, Sheffield, Leeds, and Glasgow noted a growing prevalence of the various forms of fevers we can call 'filth diseases'. The work of *prison reformers (notably John *Howard), pioneer sanitarians, medical reformers, and urban physicians like the London *Quaker John Coakley Lettsom (1744–1815) pointed to the dangers of poor ventilation, overcrowding, dirt, and malnutrition. Schools, gaols, camps, barracks, and workhouses were extremely vulnerable to fevers (typhus). Tuberculosis ('the white plague') was recognized to be worsening, particularly amongst the urban poor, and the links between tuberculosis and slum conditions were evident [see *poverty, 12].

Faced with such health risks, people had access to a widespread lay culture of advice and action regarding health and sickness. Medical self-help was universal and every family had its own preferred forms of treatment. 'Primary care' meant care by the head of the household, the cook, a trusted servant, neighbours, or the 'lady bountiful' perhaps—the clergyman's wife. Self-help came first and the recourse to professional medical treatment was secondary. There was a growing market for medical self-help books like William Buchan's *Domestic Medicine*, first published in 1769 and still in print seventy years later. John Wesley's *Primitive Physick* (1749) remained a bestseller, a book designed for the very poor, showing that practically all diseases could be treated (if not cured) with the aid of onions, lemon, cold water, brown paper, and prayer. This resort to medical self-help was a sign of a distrust of the doctors. It was not that people rejected the aid of medical attendants, regular or irregular—far from it. But a healthy scepticism about the powers of the physician meant that a 'belt and braces' approach prevailed, whereby sick people sought remedies of their own as well as using a variety of physicians. Alongside a shelf of self-help medical books, many kept medicine chests, bought proprietary nostrums from the local general store, and used the services of travelling nostrum-sellers.

This flourishing culture of medical self-help, which stretched from the heights of the aristocracy down to the labouring poor, did not, however, preclude the growing presence of medical practitioners. Indeed, medical historians have shown that this was a time of rapid expansion in the numbers of medical men (and in those days all were men: women were essentially excluded from professional ranks). There was not just an expansion in numbers, but also a rise in income and status which can be explained not so much in terms of the growing success of the medical profession in achieving cures and improving health but rather as a function of

growing disposable incomes amongst a swelling sector of the British population. A consumer
boom was in progress, and increased surplus income was going into all manner of goods and
services, pleasures and household goods. The purchase of medical services was one manifestation of the growing prosperity of what has been called an early consumer society. The distinctive cultural formation of *spa towns operated precisely at this nexus of **consumerism**
[19] and medicalization.

   Historians of eighteenth-century medicine used to present a picture of an ordered, hierarchical, pyramidal medical profession, one with an élite of physicians at the top, a larger number
of surgeons in the middle, and a heap of apothecaries at the foot. Medicine was regulated by
corporations. Physicians commanded greatest prestige because they had been trained at university, and 'physick'—the art of diagnosis and prescribing—was seen as a science of the mind
involving book learning. Surgery, by contrast, carried less prestige because it was a manual art
or craft, and involved the shedding of blood. The apothecary's trade was least dignified,
because it was seen as shopkeeping. This image of a hierarchical, closed profession has been
undermined by recent research. Medical historians now suggest that the practice of medicine
was far more widespread, fluid, and heterogeneous than traditionally assumed. On the whole,
medical regulation was breaking down in Georgian England. Strict distinctions between
physicians and surgeons and apothecaries were being challenged or circumvented. This
resulted partly from the enormous popularity of Edinburgh as a centre of medical education.
Unlike Oxford and Cambridge, Edinburgh trained its graduates both in the art of physic and
in surgical skills. Edinburgh medical graduates tended to become what we nowadays call general practitioners, uniting the functions of physician, surgeon, and apothecary. Many such

24. *Thinks I 'tis all over—my
sentence is past. / And now he is
counting how long I may last.*
Family doctors, or general
practitioners, were a relatively
new phenomenon in early
nineteenth-century provincial
towns: this print appeared in the
Bath Guide of 1807.

family doctors set up in the market towns and new industrial centres of England, the first medical graduates ever to venture deep into the provinces. Their professional skills were much in demand.

Not least, many of these surgeon-apothecaries or emergent general practitioners practised obstetrics. Traditionally, delivery of babies had been the work of village midwives who were often uneducated. The midwife was increasingly elbowed out by the aspirant man-midwife (*accoucheur* or obstetrician), who claimed to be superior because of his possession of better anatomical skills and of forceps, and also because of his deeper medical learning. The growing numbers of well-trained, rank-and-file medical practitioners threatened the physician and surgeon élites, and led to growing tensions. General practitioners demanded full entry into the profession, equality of rights alongside their senior brethren, perhaps even their own college. And they were driven to a radical critique of oligarchy and nepotism. Such a critique found expression in the *Lancet* magazine, set up in 1823 by Thomas *Wakley, a pugnacious medical practitioner who attacked the medical top brass and stood up for the little man. In 1832 the British Medical Association was founded as a pressure group for GPs.

Yet these general practitioners were themselves being attacked from below. This was partly through the rise of chemists and druggists, tradesmen with no medical training at all who set up shop and sold medicines, thereby threatening the livelihood of the doctors. And it was also partly because of the growing number of *quacks and empirics, such as the flamboyant *dentist, inventor, and healer of fistulae Martin Van Butchell (1735–?1812). Many of these medical entrepreneurs shared qualities with the new captains of industry. They were adept at consumer psychology, they pioneered medical *advertising, they manufactured and sold in bulk, and they made use of the new turnpike roads, canals, *newspapers, and other commercial outlets [see *transport]. As early as the 1760s Dr James, who patented 'Dr James's Fever Powders', was able to sell approximately two million doses of his powders. By the 1830s James Morison (1770–1840)—part quack, part alternative healer—was peddling millions of his 'Special Vegetable Pills'. Slightly later, Thomas Holloway (1800–83), another pill-monger, became one of the top entrepreneurs in the nation, eventually founding Royal Holloway College in London. Large amounts of money were to be made especially by exploiting anxieties and shame associated with venereal disease, increasingly rampant in urban centres containing concentrations of servicemen. Medical men were deeply perturbed by threats to the profession from trading outsiders. Some were worried that medicine itself was not an ethical profession with a high sense of vocation, but was operating too much as a mercenary trade. Radical physicians like Thomas *Beddoes, a supporter of the French Revolution, vitriolically attacked the British medical profession represented by prestigious figures such as the brothers William and John *Hunter as a mere 'sick trade', cashing in on the new opportunities for advancement that medicine offered, not least by whipping up health anxieties. Beddoes portrayed a conspiracy between fashionable patients and toadying practitioners who would endorse the cranky health ideas of their rich patients. This cry could be heard well into the Victorian era amongst doctors like the Guy's Hospital lecturer Thomas Hodgkin (1798–1866), who thought the 'sick trade' corrupted the medical profession's morals while doing the nation's health no good.

Yet it was not clear what could be done. In his pioneering *Medical Ethics* (1803) the Manchester physician Thomas Percival (1740–1804) admitted that in medicine the rule was 'he who pays the piper calls the tune'. It was inevitable, Percival admitted, that in the medical market-place private customers would secure the compliance of the medical profession. Only over poor and charity patients could the physician command due authority. In many ways a medical politics thus emerged in this period, mirroring the wider political struggles of the period. Was there going to be medical reform or medical revolution? Should the medical profession be the legislators of mankind, possessing a scientific expertise which would maybe, as with Benthamite *utilitarianism, dictate the laws of health to the people and ensure the greatest health of the greatest number? Or were medical practitioners to remain, in *ancien régime* fashion, the lackeys of the rich? These issues were not resolved in Britain in the Romantic age. Medical reform was achieved elsewhere, as in France, where the Revolution had led to the dissolution of the medical corporations. The Jacobins had grandiose plans for the total transformation of all medical institutions and the medical profession, which involved throwing the profession open to all. Partly as a consequence of this, radical medical change occurred in France, above all in Paris, where a new hospital system was established stressing anatomy, pathology, and statistics, and therefore accenting the scientific study of disease. No such transformations, however, occurred in Britain. In medical politics, as in politics in general, the *ancien régime* survived its buffetings to live into the Victorian era. The conservatism of British medicine was accurately sketched by George Eliot in *Middlemarch*, set in 1832, where the ambitious, idealistic, and abrasive young practitioner Tertius Lydgate, just returned from radical France with new medical ideas, is treated with suspicion and to some degree cold-shouldered by local provincial society.

In many respects, therefore, the decades spanning 1800 were years of continuity. And yet it would be foolish not to point to areas where change was taking place. Under the old *poor law, a growing number of surgeon-apothecaries were being employed to give medical assistance to the poor. There was the founding of and massive growth in the dispensary movement, providing outpatient services for multitudes of poor people in London and in other major urban centres. At the same time the hospital movement, growing in London from the 1720s and shortly after in the provinces, reached the new industrial towns. Places like Nottingham and Hull (both 1782) and Sheffield (1797) acquired their first infirmary.

One particular field of medicine saw striking growth: the treatment of mental disorders. Before the age of George III, very few institutions in Britain specialized in *madness. Apart from Bethlem Hospital (Bedlam) and St Luke's in London, there were hardly any *madhouses. From around 1760, charitable lunatic asylums were set up in Leicester, Newcastle, Manchester, and York. Private asylums were also being founded by enterprising medical men cultivating the new specialty. Many of these private madhouses, engaging in 'the trade in lunacy', were corrupt and brutal. But others pioneered innovations in psychotherapy. So also did the York Retreat, opened in 1796 on the initiative of a group of Yorkshire *Quakers, and beginning what was known as moral management and moral therapy. According to the moral therapists, madness was not primarily or solely a disease of the body and its organs, but a disordering of the mind, the emotions, and the imagination. Its champions argued that the insane must no longer be seen as wild animals, or as devoid of reason and human feelings, but might better be viewed as victims of circumstances. It was essential therefore that such unfortunates be treated with humanity, gentleness, and reason—a viewpoint which gained greater purchase due to George III's notorious bouts of insanity, now thought to be a symptom of porphyria. This programme of curing madness with kindness was particularly pursued at the York Retreat: its philosophy was outlined in Samuel Tuke's (1784–1857) book, *A Description of the Retreat at York* (1813). When in 1815 the House of Commons set up a committee to investigate madhouses, Bedlam was criticized for its benighted and brutal treatment, and the York Retreat praised as the beacon for the future.

In the field of mental health the Romantic era brought a break with the past. Indeed, if we are looking for 'Romantic medicine'—whatever that might be—it is in the treatment of the psyche that it can most easily be found. Mary *Wollstonecraft's *The Wrongs of Woman; or Maria a Fragment* (1798) invited the reader to identify with the mad woman as victim. The Romantic vision that 'the world is too much with us' saw people driven insane because of the crazy pressures of wealth, ambition, emulation, and self-deceit. New stress was laid upon the *Rousseauist healthiness of solitude. It was no accident that the York Retreat was sited, like so many other new asylums, outside the city: as with so much Romantic *poetry [29], the countryside was seen as a spring of solace and recovery.

And it is no surprise that the Romantic poets themselves became fascinated by the condition of madness. This might be seen by them as the consequence of social evils, as a form of higher health, or as a source of insight. The mad could be viewed as superior beings, in touch, through the imagination, with great transcendental creative powers. William *Blake revelled in the idea that he was himself mad. In his poem 'Julian and Maddalo' (1824), Percy *Shelley presented a sympathetic portrait of a madman as a tragic hero, driven to insanity by society. In his ode 'On Melancholy' (1820), John *Keats aspired to the condition of a melancholic, implying that depression was the wellspring of poetic creativity and the most inspirational human experience. Ironically, it took another Romantic, Charles *Lamb, to challenge as sentimental these attitudes towards mental disturbance. As the brother of Mary Anne *Lamb who, in a mad fit, had killed her mother with a carving-knife, Lamb could not afford to fantasize about madness. Faced with the conundrum of madness and creativity, Lamb wrote an essay entitled 'The Sanity of True Genius' (1833), rebutting the Romantic conceit that is was the mad who were the truly great poets [see *genius].

Were there specifically Romantic *attitudes* towards health and sickness? Was illness given any distinctive meaning by the Romantics? Recent studies have demonstrated beyond doubt that many Romantics were deeply versed in medical and scientific knowledge. In certain respects sickness was seen by Romantic writers and artists not simply as a physical effect—not merely a breakdown of the body machine—but as an expression of the soul or personality, a view which paralleled some Christian and folk beliefs. This is particularly apparent in the mythology of the tubercular personality. It was believed that the consumptive possessed a unique sensibility, an erotic intensity. The wasting of the flesh was the intensification of the spirit, with Keats offering a particularly clear embodiment of such views. Tuberculosis came to be seen by many later nineteenth-century commentators as the distinctive 'Romantic' disease, a view which glossed over its brutal, harrowing symptoms and almost plague-like incidence amongst the urban poor.

Another Romantic sufferer for whom illness meant more than mere bodily breakdown was S. T. *Coleridge. Throughout his life, Coleridge suffered desperate pains which defy retrospective diagnosis. In August 1808, he wrote to Robert *Southey:

Your Letter affected me very deeply: I did not feel it so much the two first Days, as I have since done. I have been very ill, & in serious dread of a paralytic Stroke in my whole left Side. Of my disease there now remains no Shade of Doubt: it is a compleat & almost heartless Case of Atonic Gout. If you would look into the Article Medicine, in the Encyc. Britt. Vol. XI. Part I.—No. 213.—p. 181.—& the first 5 paragraphs of the second Column you will read almost the very words, in which, before I had seen this Article, I had described my case to Wordsworth.—The only non-agreement is—'an imaginary aggravation of the slightest Feelings, & an apprehension of danger from them.'—The first sentence is unphilosophically expressed / there is a state of mind, wholly unnoticed, as far as I know, by any Physical or Metaphysical Writer hitherto, & which yet is necessary to the explanation of some of the most important phaenomena of Sleep & Disease / it is a transmutation of the *succession* of *Time* into the juxtaposition of space by which the smallest Impulses, if quickly & regularly recurrent, *aggregate* themselves—& attain a kind of visual magnitude with a correspondent Intensity of general Feeling.—The simplest Illustration would be the *circle* of Fire made by whirling round a live Coal—only here the mind is passive. Suppose the same effect produced ab intra—& you have a clue to the whole mystery of frightful Dreams, & Hypochondriacal Delusions.

With its witch's brew of fantasy, suffering, and erudition, the letter continues for several further pages. The medications Coleridge took to counter his ailments, in particular large doses of opium, intensified his pains, deprived him of sleep, reinforced his hypochondria, and rendered his melancholic imagination more nightmarish. Suffering turned Coleridge in upon himself and led him to explore his soul, through the medium of sickness. Thomas *De Quincey offers a parallel case.

The experience of illness involves an intense, often painful subjectivity. It enhanced the Romantic exploration of the self, its analysis of unconscious processes and the complicated interworkings of self, psyche, and soma. Certain developments in medical theory and in fringe *medicine supported the Romantic collapsing of traditional mind–body dualisms, of the traditional Cartesian distinction between object and subject, and furthered the emphasis on a unitary self. Developing in Scotland from the 1750s, medical theories associated with Robert Whytt (1714–66), William Cullen (1710–90), and their followers saw health and disease as a function of the nerves. The nervous system united the body, with its nerve-endings in the extremities, with the brain and mind. The doctrine of the nervous rooting of disorders related the physiological to the psychological. Neurological theories suggested that disease was sympathetic, and so provided sound physiological explanations of hypochondria and hysteria. On the medical fringe, the popularity of mesmerism, and later of *phrenology, both developed in Europe before being brought to England, where the former was known as *animal magnetism, also resulted in the breaking down of supposedly clear-cut distinctions between mind and body. Those practising hypnotism were able to obtain control over their patients' bodies through the use of mental methods, such as fixing eye to eye or the incantation of phrases. The power contained in hypnotism fanned fears of the destructive potential of medicine and science, of a kind voiced in Mary *Shelley's *Frankenstein* (1818), but it was also conversely

25. *Animal Magnetism—The Operator putting his Patient into a Crisis*, an illustration to Ebenezer Sibly's *A Key to Physic, and the Occult Sciences* (1794), showing the potent powers of the mesmerist.

attractive to poets like Shelley and Coleridge, eager to experiment with the vitalist forces of the imagination. Theories of the nerves and of hypnotism helped to undermine the entrenched idea that the body was essentially mechanical and that the mind, or soul, was a mere ghost in the machine. The dualism introduced by the scientific revolution, endorsed by the philosophy of Descartes and associated in the *Enlightenment [32] with the progress of science, was increasingly challenged by Romantic belief in the unitary, holistic nature of human experience, and in the complex intertwining of the physical, the mental, and the imaginative.

The Romantic era did not transform the practice of medicine in Britain, and certainly did not result in statistically documentable improved health and longevity. Nor, even, did the outlooks of Romanticism transform orthodox medical theories and philosophies. But the experience of the body and of suffering was an essential component in that journey into the self that constitutes the intense subjectivity of the Romantic interlude.

Bynum, W. F., & Porter, R., eds., *Medical Fringe and Medical Orthodoxy, 1750–1850*, London, 1987; Crook, N., & Guiton, D., *Shelley's Venomed Melody*, Cambridge, 1986; de Almeida, H., *Romantic Medicine and John Keats*, Oxford, 1991; Digby, A., *Making a Medical Living: Doctors and Patients in the English Market for Medicine, 1720–1911*, Cambridge, 1994; Durey, M., *The Return of the Plague: British Society and the Cholera, 1831–2*, Dublin, 1979; Lawrence, C., *Medicine in the Making of Modern Britain, 1700–1920*, London, 1994; Porter, D., & Porter, R., *Patient's Progress: Doctors and Doctoring in Eighteenth-Century England*, Cambridge, 1989; Porter, R., ed., *The Popularization of Medicine*, London, 1992; Porter, R. & Porter, D., *In Sickness and in Health: The British Experience, 1650–1850*, London, 1988; Waddington, I., *The Medical Profession in the Industrial Revolution*, Dublin, 1984.

· III ·

CULTURE, CONSUMPTION, AND THE ARTS

19 · CONSUMERISM ROY PORTER

Disputes rage as to the right term to describe the distinctiveness of the contemporary Western world. Labels like 'democracy', 'the first world', 'post-industrialism', and 'capitalist society' all circulate, but one favoured tag is 'the consumer society'. With that concept in mind, historians have, not surprisingly, peered back into the past in search of the roots of consumerism, and in particular in hope of unearthing the first consumer society. They have also undertaken historical analyses seeking to elucidate the essential core of 'consumerism'.

The seventeenth-century Dutch Republic has as good a claim as any to be called the first consumer society: a high percentage of the population was bourgeois, that is, lived in towns, and enjoyed sufficient economic surplus to be able to purchase large quantities and a wide range of luxuries, on top of necessities. Dutch culture found the very idea of a world of goods fascinating yet also morally perilous: the still-life paintings of the Golden Age made a great display of universal abundance, while encoding moral warnings against the seductiveness of things (*vanitas*) in a Providential order in which the godly knew it was easier for a camel to pass through the eye of a needle than for a rich man to enter into the kingdom of heaven.

Alongside the Dutch Republic, Hanoverian England was also a trail-blazing consumer society. Consumption rose amongst all manner of products, from potatoes to porcelain. The idea and the practice of consuming (the acquisition and enjoyment of goods) grew more central as an expression of lifestyles and aspirations, as numerous satires against snobs and *bon viveurs* suggest. Spreading, but by no means universal, prosperity permitted more people to have a taste of more of the good things of material life; *Enlightenment [32] outlooks set greater store by the value of the material world.

The face of England (and, to a lesser degree, the rest of the British Isles) was undergoing piecemeal yet substantial change throughout the eighteenth century, a process accelerating in the decades spanning 1800. While not ignoring the growing numbers of the poor and dispossessed—ubiquitous casualties of all-conquering capitalism—it would equally be mistaken to disregard the swelling throng of middling people—masters, craftsmen, clerks, and shopkeepers—who were enjoying rising incomes and higher standards of living, new comforts and pleasures. A child born at the accession of George I, who had then fallen asleep only to awake in extreme old age around 1800, would have been surprised to encounter myriad minor changes in the fabric of life which, while individually petty, were cumulatively transforming the quality of life and imparting to the nation a far more 'modern' feel. Our awakening octogenarian would have found in houses of ordinary people all kinds of domestic goods which had hitherto been the preserve of the rich: possessions like curtains and carpets; upholstered chairs; tablecloths; glass and china-ware; tea services; fancy pottery; looking-glasses; clocks; cases of books other than just the Bible, supplied by *circulating libraries such as William Lane's *Minerva Press; prints or ornaments to put on the wall or the mantelshelf; and all manner of bric-à-brac and decorations. Shop-bought toys, games, and jigsaw puzzles for children had become common. Not least, diet was more varied, with a greater range of fruit and vegetables. People owned more changes of clothes, particularly with the growing availability of cheaper calicoes and cottons. Efficient oil-lamps dispelled the age-old stygian gloom; gas lighting arrived with the new century, soon to be followed by railway travel and the electric telegraph.

Outside the home, urban space was being spruced up. In many towns, straight, well-demarcated streets replaced the labyrinthine old warrens of alleys and yards. House numbering, pavements, and kerbs appeared, making sauntering agreeable and encouraging window-shopping—a new delight. The much-admired new-style retail shop was, with its gorgeous and well-lit display behind huge glass windows, a far cry from the dingy workshops of old. Sophie von La Roche, a German visiting London in the 1780s, was impressed by the bow-windows and the attention to display:

Behind the great glass windows absolutely everything one can think of is neatly, attractively displayed, in such abundance of choice as almost to make one greedy. Now large slipper and shoe-shops for anything from adults down to dolls, can be seen; now fashion-articles or silver or brass shops, boots, guns, glasses, the confectioner's goodies, the pewterer's wares, fans, etc.

During our octogenarian's lifetime thriving cities and market towns acquired assembly rooms, *theatres [24], *coffeehouses, parades, and public *pleasure gardens—to say nothing of hospitals, *prisons, and workhouses. New turnpike roads and coaching services linked provincial centres like York, Norwich, and Exeter with the metropolis. Widespread *advertising in *newspapers diffused *fashion, fanning acquisitiveness. Foreigners were struck by the brilliant animation of English life: 'The road from Greenwich to London was actually busier than the most popular streets in Berlin,' judged the Prussian Pastor Moritz, 'so many people were to be encountered riding, driving or walking. Already we saw houses on all sides, and all along the road at suitable distances lamp-posts were provided.' And with activity went speed: 'no country is so well arranged for comfort and rapid travelling as this,' observed another traveller. Most admired this bustle, though critics complained the English had no time for anything but moneymaking. Ever pressed for time, they had even pioneered the fast-food take-away: 'I happened to go into a pastrycook's shop one morning,' observed Robert *Southey,

and inquired of the mistress why she kept her window open during this severe weather—which I observed most of the trade did. She told me, that were she to close it, her receipts would be lessened forty or fifty shillings a day so many were the persons who took up buns or biscuits as they passed by and threw their pence in, not allowing themselves time to enter. Was there ever so indefatigable a people!

Southey's pseudonymous *Letters from England* (1807) portrays a nation of shopkeepers and shoppers being seduced by a novel and pervasive commercial culture.

In short, independently of the transformations wrought by the industrial revolution [see *industrialization, 14], England was being transformed during the eighteenth century into a commercial and consumer society. Not everyone approved. 'Everything about this farm-house was formerly the scene of *plain manners* and *plentiful living*,' remarked William *Cobbett, that traditionalist man of the people who deplored the rise of the *nouveaux riches*. In *Rural Rides* (1830), an anatomy of the rural counties of southern England, he observed of the homes of rich and swanky farmers, 'there were the decanters, the glasses, the "dinner-set" of crockery ware, and all just in the true stock-jobber style'. Nevertheless the prosperity of the many, if not exactly the masses, made Britain the envy of Europe and created the self-satisfied feeling that it was good to be a John Bull whose spreading girth suggested enviable consumption levels.

Certain characteristics of the progress of consumption, a trend accelerating around 1760, are worth brief individual mention. For one thing, *population growth spurred general economic expansion. The population of England and Wales had been stagnant in the late Stuart era, even dipping somewhat during the 1720s and 1730s. But it rose with increasing momentum after mid-century, from some 6 million in 1750 to around 8.5 million in 1800 and an astonishing 14.7 million by 1840.

Due partly to better communications and partly to rural dispossession and migration, urban population shot up particularly dramatically [see *land, 16]. London, for example, expanded from around three-quarters of a million in mid-century to almost a million in 1800 and then to two million by 1830. Alongside the capital, centres of manufacturing—for example, Birmingham and the Black Country—grew with great rapidity, as did the cotton towns of Lancashire and the woollen centres of the West Riding of Yorkshire. Urbanization gave a special boost to consumption, in view of the concentration of trading, markets, shopping, processing, and distribution. Innovations in *transport and communications spurred commercial activity. The dissemination of newspapers throughout the country and in particular the growth of a provincial press—by around 1770 almost all sizeable centres in England had their own individual title—resulted in an information revolution, putting locals in the picture about fashion items, innovations, and imports, and generating demand for new goods and services.

The improvement and spread of turnpike roads made it possible to transport goods and materials more swiftly all through the year. From the 1760s the canal system reduced haulage costs for bulk materials and lessened breakage risks, a factor that had always hindered the national marketing of more fragile goods like ceramics. This transportation revolution was completed from the 1830s by the laying of the railways. Freight carriage loomed large in the business plans of the early railway entrepreneurs.

Merchandizing of goods was transformed by what several scholars have identified as an 'urban renaissance' in Georgian England. It has been argued that the Tudor and Stuart era had brought widespread 'urban crisis'. By contrast, many historians believe the Georgian period saw the transformation of towns from essentially functional centres to foci of taste in their own right, with a new accent on encouraging people to congregate (a crucial role being played by inns, coffeehouses, assembly-rooms, and other public buildings), on creating attractive entertainment centres (theatres, race-tracks, ballrooms, and the like), and on marketing the pleasures of shopping. Fashionable London in particular became a customer's paradise: it was mainly for the shops that Jane *Austen loved to come up to town. The late Georgian age saw the establishment of such famous West End shops as Lock's the hatters, Hawkes the gentleman's outfitters, Asprey, specializing in dressing-cases and silverware, Fortnum and Mason—and their nearby rivals, Jackson's—for food, Hatchard's the booksellers, and even Hamley's toyshop, to say nothing of Christie's the auctioneers.

Concrete proof of the growing availability of goods derives from evidence about the changing nature of household interiors [see *design, 25]. Analyses of inventories and legal deeds published by Lorna Weatherill, Peter Earle, and Carole Shammas have created a more precise account of the growth of belongings. Their meticulous studies have drawn particular attention to the large number of exotic goods in circulation, especially in London (for instance, Asian fabrics and furniture); to the crucial role played by transportation improvements (in areas off the beaten track the revolution in goods was considerably retarded); to the considerable reduction in item costs during the eighteenth century, notably of commodities like tea and sugar; and to the dynamism of the fashion industry and the growing habit of buying relatively ephemeral items. Josiah Tucker (1712–99) and numerous other economic commentators noted with approval the growing ability to lay out money on 'decencies', suggesting that the luxuries of former centuries—for instance, clocks—became necessities no self-respecting person could afford to be without.

Proof of this may be found in the howls of horror against so-called 'luxury'. Sanctimonious moralists viewed the mushrooming of goods—the growing preoccupation with the material world—as symptomatic of a degenerate society in which hedonistic pursuits were supposedly sapping virtue, undermining political morale, rendering the nation more effeminate and less self-reliant, and resulting in the general 'corruption' of national spirit. Crusty conservatives and dissenting radicals alike deplored the seductiveness of objects, the licensing of greed, and the subordination of personal, family, and religious values to a *utilitarian, mercenary temper.

In short, there was a major surge of consumption in Georgian England. The delicate question is: does that mean that the term 'consumerism' is applicable and valuable? The case for an eighteenth-century 'consumer revolution' has been made by various historians, notably Neil McKendrick. More is at stake than the elementary and readily substantiated claim that a greatly increased consumption of commodities took place at this time. For the argument further runs that such an increase in consumption must also possess authentic explanatory power for uncovering and comprehending the roots of *modern* consumerism; that is to say, the outlooks of and the techniques pioneered by the frontiersmen of eighteenth-century consumerism should be seen to lead directly to the characteristic business strategies and structures of modern consumer society (mass production, taste and marketing, consumer psychology, innovations in advertising, and so forth). And it is additionally contended that growing consumer power (that is, home demand) provides a convincing, though not total, explanation of the dynamic acceleration of the industrial revolution itself. Recent years have brought fierce debate as to whether it is useful to speak of an 'industrial revolution' at all, and, if so, whether it took the form that economic history textbooks have so long retailed. Some who find the term useful have stressed entrepreneurship as the cause of causes; others have emphasized technological transformation, others the significance of capital formation and investment, while others have underscored the crucial role of overseas exports. But over the last twenty years various economic historians, McKendrick in particular, have argued that one major cause, and possibly the key cause, of the industrial revolution was the articulation of effective home consumer demand. Even if by the early Victorian age—arguably the peak decades of industrial transformation—economic dynamism was primarily associated with steam-powered factories and also with the pumping out of heavy industrial products and capital goods (coal, iron, steel, chemicals, steam engines, railways, ships, machine tools, and factory plant), the initial industrial quickening from around 1760 is said to have involved first and foremost a growing capacity to meet rising demand by boosting output of fairly familiar and inexpensive goods (locks, belts, buttons, straps, saddles, buckets, files, planes, tools, guns, knives, swords, cutlery, and other ordinary domestic goods).

Attention has been drawn by champions of such an interpretation to the skill with which manufacturers great and small were able to stimulate and tap 'latent' demand for all manner of goods and services. McKendrick has studied the achievements of Josiah *Wedgwood in applying consumer psychology in the design of his ceramics, and in their naming, display, and advertising.

Wedgwood recognized that acquisition and consumption had to be transformed into a pleasurable, arousing, addictive experience. Based in Staffordshire, he took the plunge in 1765 and opened a London showroom in Grosvenor Square; it was a genuine innovation. He targeted his display at the Quality, convinced that 'fashion is infinitely superior to Merit in many respects'. He succeeded. Soon he needed bigger premises, 'an Elegant, Extensive and Convenient showroom'. Would Pall Mall do? Probably not, because it was too easy of access to *hoi polloi*: 'my present sett of Customers will not mix with the rest of the World'. Hence he moved to Portland House in Greek Street, where the accent was on lavish presentation and spectacle. He had the brilliant idea of setting out whole dinner services as if ready for a meal. Wedgwood understood the shopping secret:

I need not tell you the many good effects this must produce, when business and amusement can be made to go hand in hand. Every new show, Exhibition or rarity soon grows stale in London and is no longer regarded after the first sight, unless utility or some such variety as I have hinted at above continues to recommend it to their notice . . . I have done something of the sort since I came to Town, and find the immediate good effects of it. The first two days after the alterations, we sold three complete Setts of Vases at 2 & 3 Guineas a sett, besides many pairs of them, which Vases had been in my Rooms 6–8 and some 12 months & wanted nothing but arrangement to sell them . . . I need not tell you that it will be our interest to amuse and divert & please & astonish, nay, even to ravish, the Ladies.

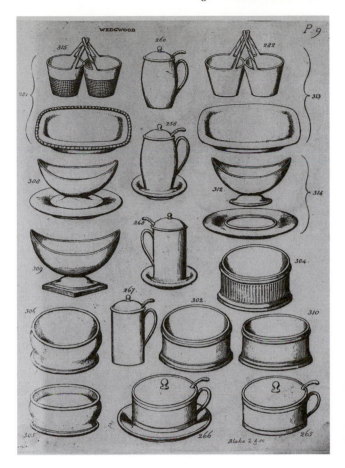

26. Creamware shapes engraved by William Blake for Josiah Wedgwood, 1817. The real dinner service would be set out in Wedgwood's showrooms to 'divert & please & astonish, nay, even to ravish, the Ladies'.

But it was not only great manufacturers who were able to exploit new market possibilities. George Packwood began as an inconspicuous manufacturer of razor strops, but by ingenious saturation advertising campaigns in the newspapers he built up a large business. Through exploiting health fears, *quack medicine vendors created vast markets for their wares. Dr Robert James (1705–76), whose powders were the eighteenth-century equivalent of aspirin, managed to sell over two million doses of his nostrum over two decades [see *medicine, 18].

It may thus be argued that the concept of 'consumerism' is useful, because pioneering manufacturers had a vision of a socio-economic system in which surging domestic consumption would turn the wheels. But the notion of 'consumerism' requires further elucidation. Traditional *political economy [33] took 'demand' itself for granted; it was an unexamined assumption that unlimited 'demand' was always present, checked only by want of money in consumers' pockets or by production bottlenecks. Once these hindrances had been removed, 'demand' would automatically take off like a rocket, since 'economic man' was assumed to be a rational hedonist, concerned to maximize his utilities via *Bentham's felicific calculus. *Homo economicus* has also been envisaged as emulative in his psychology: the self-evident urge to 'keep up with the Joneses' would mean that potential consumers would continue to spend, even once basic needs were satisfied. Such views were, of course, being set out in the eighteenth century, not least in Bernard Mandeville's *Fable of the Bees: or Private Vices Public Benefits* (1714), which stressed the value of envy in creating demand for goods and hence in fuelling economic growth in commercial society.

Sociologists, psychologists, and anthropologists have recently counter-argued that such acquisitive and emulative behaviour patterns are not an elemental expression of 'human nature'. Not all populations are acquisitive; in various societies, generosity and indifference to material goods have been prized and pursued. The 'consumer', in other words, is not a universal given; such a type needed to be 'fabricated'. Hence some have claimed that not the least invention of the industrial revolution was the invention of the 'consumer'.

The creation of the consumer may partly be understood in the light of the analysis offered by the Marxist political historian C. B. MacPherson of the rise of 'possessive individualism'. Addressing texts from Hobbes to the classical Smithian economists, utilitarians, and liberals, MacPherson showed how theories of politics and political economy, radical and authoritarian alike, increasingly grounded themselves upon the (presupposed) sovereign desires of the individual (possession, property, security, liberty). Giving plausible political priority to the autonomous individual (natural man) laid the foundations for a model of the want-filled consumer which thereafter proved highly serviceable for the apologists of market capitalism. Hobbesian man was fleeing from a state of nature in which there were 'no arts; no letters; no society, and which is worst of all, continual fear and danger of violent death; and the life of man, solitary, poor, nasty, brutish, and short': infinite fear bred infinite need for security. The more sunny days of the Enlightenment transmuted Hobbesian horror into an infinite aspiration for felicity, the boundless longings essential for mobilizing consumerism. Within this ideological framework it was the essence of human nature to desire to possess.

A more nuanced theory of the consuming individual has been outlined by the sociologist Colin Campbell. Campbell has drawn attention to Max Weber's problematization of the capitalist. Weber had contended that the capitalist ceaselessly ploughing his profits back into the business was not 'timeless' but had appeared as a type in time to facilitate the industrial revolution. Weber maintained that such an individual could be understood not in economic terms but only by reference to an 'ethos', and that 'ethos' could in turn be regarded essentially as an attempt to resolve dilemmas about self-worth and salvation posed by Protestant theology. The capitalist found fulfilment and assurance only in interminable justificatory labour.

In a manner owing much to Weber, Campbell contends that the postulation of an ethos is similarly necessary for understanding the counterpart of the capitalist; that is, the consumer. For Campbell, it was not Calvinist theology that was destined to induce a population to turn 'consumer', but rather the new epistemology of sensory experience and the aesthetics of subjectivity ('taste') developed by *Locke, amplified by Shaftesbury and Hutcheson, and finding fruition in *Romanticism. Consumption was a structure of feeling.

Locke's empiricist philosophy created a model of man not as 'given' but as the product of experience; that is, as a consumer of sensory inputs. Such a persona would thus need to absorb all possible 'goods' in order to become a whole and progressive individual. Thus Enlightenment empiricism and Romantic introspective individualism rationalized and legitimated the consumer in terms of the self-creation of mankind.

MacPherson's and Campbell's formulations are valuable, since the creation of a consumer mentality in the Georgian and Romantic eras involved massive ideological work in overcoming not only the traditional Christian suspicion of greed, envy, gluttony, and the other deadly sins but also the entrenched civic humanist or 'commonwealth' philosophy of virtuous poverty, community action, and hostility to personal indulgence.

There are, of course, risks in the casual application of the words 'consumer society' or 'consumerism' to describe Britain around 1800. After all, a growing proportion of the population was in the process of being proletarianized, indeed, pauperized [see *poverty, 12]. It would be offensive to give the impression that the populace at large was somehow in a position to indulge a taste for the new cornucopia of goods. It would also be anachronistic to suggest that mass production had arrived by 1800. Although, as Asa Briggs has emphasized, during the

Victorian period many consumer goods became standardized and cheap, it was not until the dawn of the twentieth century that, thanks to production-line techniques, manufacturers like Henry Ford were able to introduce the distinctive objects of mass society, epitomized by the Model T Ford.

Such caveats notwithstanding, the idea of consumerism is valuable as a partial explanation of the industrialization process beginning in the late eighteenth century and accelerating in the nineteenth. It also reflects the fact that late Georgian society increasingly indulged, and was proud to indulge, a taste for the decencies, comforts, and conveniences associated with the world of goods.

Adburgham, A., *Shopping in Style: London from the Restoration to Edwardian Elegance*, London, 1979; Alexander, D., *Retailing in England During the Industrial Revolution*, London, 1970; Brewer, J., & Porter, R., eds., *Consumption and the World of Goods*, London, 1993; Campbell, C., *The Romantic Ethic and the Spirit of Modern Consumerism*, Oxford, 1987; Earle, P., *The Making of the English Middle Class: Business, Society and Family Life in London, 1660–1730*, London, 1989; McKendrick, N., Brewer, J., & Plumb, J. H., *The Birth of a Consumer Society: The Commercialization of Eighteenth-Century England*, London, 1982; Mui, H., & Mui, L., *Shops and Shopkeeping in Eighteenth-Century England*, London, 1987; Plumb, J. H., *The Commercialization of Leisure in Eighteenth-Century England*, Reading, 1973; *Georgian Delights*, London, 1980; Shammas, C., *The Pre-Industrial Consumer in England and America*, Oxford, 1990; Weatherill, L., *Consumer Behaviour and Material Culture 1660–1760*, London, 1988.

20 · VIEWING C. SUZANNE MATHESON

The period from the foundation of the *Royal Academy in 1768 to the opening of the building of the National Gallery of Art in 1838 embraces many changes in the nature, scale, and composition of art and its audiences. The emergence of new paradigms of *patronage, new institutions to encourage the production and dissemination of work, and changes in the perception of private collections and galleries mark Britain's tentative steps towards a fresh formulation of the public sphere. This essay will address two broad aspects of the cultural politics of British art in the era: changing notions of the place and professionalism of art, and changing notions of the social and political constitution of the spectator.

The first professional body of exhibiting artists in England, the Society of Artists, grew from a charitable venture initiated in the 1740s by the painter and engraver William Hogarth (1697–1764), who formed a scheme of donating paintings to embellish a newly instituted hospital for abandoned and destitute children in London. The Foundling Hospital was a realization of the *philanthropy of a private individual, Thomas Coram (?1668–1751), a retired naval captain and city merchant. From its inception, his Hospital enjoyed the support of powerful patrons and subscribers, as well as a number of creative and mutually beneficial collaborations with the era's prominent artists and musicians. Hogarth's own gifts to the Foundling Hospital, which included *Moses Brought Before Pharaoh's Daughter*, his *March of the Guards to Finchley*, and a portrait of the founder, were matched by contributions from other artists alert to the fact that their benevolence could lead to greater professional visibility. Through Hogarth's example, the Foundling Hospital effectively became the country's first public picture gallery [see *painting, 27].

The Foundling Hospital venture convinced artists of the necessity of regularly bringing their work before a viewing public. In 1760 a very successful exhibition of the work of living British painters was held in the rooms belonging to the Society of Arts in the Strand. A Society of Artists was instituted the following year and it organized annual shows which were intended, as Samuel *Johnson explained in the preface of the 1762 exhibition catalogue, 'not to enrich the Artists, but to Advance the Art'. Johnson's cautious separation of an agenda for art from the commercial fortunes of its practitioners is indicative of the difficulties that faced the artists once they disengaged themselves from the respectable sphere of philanthropy. At the Foundling Hospital, art had been assigned the task of representing and rationalizing the social virtues; in turn virtue had provided the artists with a superlatively respectable showroom for their work, and with an audience morally guided to admire the conception and execution of their labour. The loss of this prefabricated exhibition space, with its clear social margins and sympathetic, sensible audience, was considerable, as suggested by the material and philosophical problems faced by the artists in the following years of independent exhibition.

Relations between members in the Society of Artists and between artists in similar bodies were frequently marred by dissension over the selection and arrangement of pictures in exhibition, the question of charging the public an admission fee, and the deployment of the receipts from its events—in short, by practical manifestations of the ongoing debate over the nature and function of art exhibition and the social composition of its viewing public. The boisterous early years of the Society of Artists exhibition are a case in point. In 1761 their exhibition was so popular and their estimated 20,000 viewers so rambunctious that thirteen pounds and six shillings were laid out afterwards to repair windows broken during the show. In an attempt to regulate not only behaviour but also the class of people attending its show, the Society instituted a one-shilling admission fee and called on Johnson to rationalize the measure in their 1762 catalogue: 'every one knows that all cannot be judges or purchasers of works of art.' Johnson's statement is a frank reading of connoisseurship's alignment with ready capital. These early exhibitions represent a moment in which the ritualistic or cultic value of art (its association with civic virtue) gave way to an apprehension and more overt acknowledgement of market value. The tension of art's passage from a rhetorically privileged position within a charitable enterprise to the arena of promotion and consumption was played out in the public sphere of the gallery [see *consumerism, 19]. The difficulties experienced by the first art societies in determining the tone and organization of their exhibitions, and regulating their enthusiastic viewers, were practical manifestations of their need to revise fundamental notions of the place and function of art in Britain.

The Society of Artists went through an administrative mitosis in 1768, with one faction staying on to become the Incorporated Society of Artists and a group of dissenting artists leaving to form the inner circle of the Royal Academy of Arts. The Royal Academy initially seemed to answer the vexed questions of how best to promote British art, fix the status of the artist, and locate the viewer. An Act of Institution, ratified by George III in December 1768, made provision for the appointment of 40 Academicians and 6 associates, for the conduct of the schools, and for the organization of an annual exhibition. In the words of its first President, Joshua *Reynolds, the Academy was 'to furnish able men to direct the Student' and to be 'a repository for the great examples of the Art'. The *Discourses* of Reynolds outline an agenda followed in modified form through the subsequent presidencies of Benjamin *West (1792–1805 and 1806–20), James *Wyatt (1805–6), and Thomas *Lawrence (1820–30). According to Reynolds, the artist's object was the expression of general and intellectual ideas that 'raise the thoughts, and extend the views of the spectator; and which, by a succession of art, may be so far diffused, that its effects may extend themselves imperceptibly into public benefits, and be among the means of bestowing on whole nations the refinement of taste.'

In the Academy's foundation document, the King is styled the 'patron, protector and

supporter' of his institution. The monarch served as a focal point for defining the social position of the Academy and its members—literally so in a well-known engraving of the 1787 exhibition executed by Pietro Martini and J. H. Ramberg, in which his *factotum*, the Prince   *38*
Regent, is guided round the gallery by Reynolds. In hard fiscal terms, however, the Academy's
most important patron was its viewing public, for a significant portion of the institution's
income was derived from the returns of the annual spring exhibition. In spite of this relationship, the Academy displayed a surprising ambivalence towards its public in the latter part of
the eighteenth century. Joshua Reynolds's caution to young artists in the *Discourses* against
indiscriminate attempts to please 'the mixed multitude that resorts to an exhibition' is an
expression of equivocation towards the general public played out on an institutional level in
the arrangement and regulation of the annual Royal Academy show.

The first Royal Academy exhibition was held in April 1769. It consisted of 136 works displayed in Pall Mall chambers that had formerly housed a print warehouse. In the advertisement
to the 1769 catalogue, the Academicians apologized for charging an admission fee to an event
supported by royal munificence, but confessed 'they have not been able to suggest any other
Means . . . to prevent the Room from being filled by improper Persons, to the entire Exclusion
of those for whom the Exhibition is apparently intended'. The qualifications within this brief
statement are striking. The traditionally privileged space of the collector and patron, a gallery
that stands as an embodiment of 'royal munificence', is placed under stress by a diverse and as
yet unidentified body of spectators. The spring exhibition evokes the conventions and mores
of noble patronage and private display but, unusually, does so in the creation of a public spectacle. The combination is clearly an unsettling one for the exhibition's organizers. The viewing public is obliquely situated between the monarch and a faceless multitude who threaten to
disrupt the gallery. This dilemma persisted when the Academy exhibitions were relocated
from Pall Mall to the grand salon of old Somerset House in the Strand.

The founding of a Royal Academy had an enormous impact upon notions of spectatorship
and publicity in the period, as well as on the practical administration of art in the capital. One
logical outcome of the entrenchment of an academy was the appearance of a number of smaller
art societies formed to redress artists' isolation within or exclusion from the institution.
Engravers were debarred from full membership in the Academy on the grounds that theirs was
an imitative and mechanical, rather than imaginative or intellectual, art. Partly in protest at this
exclusion, a Society of Engravers was formed in 1802 to promote the dignity and fortunes of the
work and its practitioners. Ironically, Francesco Bartolozzi (1727–1815), the first President of
the Society of Engravers, had been made a full Royal Academician some years previously
through the stratagem of exhibiting one painting at the annual exhibition. In 1804 a Society of
Painters in Water-Colours was formed in response to artists' concern over the treatment of
their work in the annual Academy exhibitions. The watercolourists claimed that their compositions were habitually hung in poor locations in the Academy gallery and that *watercolour
paintings were inevitably eclipsed if placed in proximity to oil paintings. The Society opened
a gallery in Lower Brook Street that was designed to give the work of its members due recognition. A related society, the Associated Artists in Water-Colours, was formed in 1808, and
exhibited at the same location.

The Royal Academy enjoyed a monopoly on annual institutional exhibitions until the
formation of the British Institution for Promoting the Fine Arts in 1805. The British Institution
was organized to encourage and disseminate the work of contemporary British artists and (that
most quotidian of objectives) to improve the public taste. According to its by-laws these goals
would be reached through establishing 'a PUBLIC EXHIBITION, for the sale of the productions of British artists'; by exciting 'the emulation and exertion of the younger artists by
PREMIUMS' and endeavouring to form 'a PUBLIC GALLERY of the works of British
artists'. Its structure and purposes were intended to complement rather than compete with the

Royal Academy; for instance, as a gesture of professional courtesy the Institution closed its exhibition during the period of the Academy's annual show. John *Britton enthused that the foundation of the British Institution opened a new era of publicity pleasing to 'connoisseur, patriot and artist', a statement of approbation that unconsciously evoked the administrative hierarchy of the organization. The Institution was guided by a group of prominent amateurs, connoisseurs, and collectors; the professional artists whose interests formed the basis of the enterprise were excluded from its administration. Regular spring exhibitions of contemporary work were held from 1806 in the Pall Mall chambers that had once housed John *Boydell's Shakespeare Gallery. In addition to its active promotion of contemporary British art, the British Institution organized annual summer exhibitions of the work of Old Masters. Paintings were loaned to the Institution from the private collections of its subscribers and benefactors and displayed against a vivid scarlet paper copied from the decorations of Windsor Castle. Six exhibitions of masterpieces of the Italian, Spanish, French, Flemish, and Dutch schools were held between 1813 and 1828. In 1813 a retrospective of the work of Joshua Reynolds was mounted (the first such exhibition in the country) and followed by similar events focusing on Hogarth, *Gainsborough, Richard *Wilson, and *Zoffany. Admission to the Institution's galleries was fixed at a shilling, a price which effectively excluded the lower orders.

The importance of these early institutions may only be understood if viewed in relation to the limited opportunities for exhibiting and viewing art in the period. A number of private galleries in London and the provinces could be viewed upon application to their proprietors, but access was not easily obtained by members of the general public. Joseph, Count Truchsess, founder of the 'Truchsessian Gallery' visited by William *Blake in 1804, noted in a subscription circular of his gallery the difficulties of viewing private holdings. 'Many', he claimed, 'have resided in London for years, without having seen a single picture belonging to a collection', a situation which obliges 'the Englishman desirous of instruction to travel abroad to see a Gallery of Paintings at Paris, Florence, Dresden, Dusseldorf &c.'

The first private collection in London to be opened regularly to the public was the gallery of the Marquis of Stafford at Cleveland House, where many of the principal pictures from the Orléans collection, sold by the Duc d'Orléans in 1792, were on display. The Stafford gallery was open on Wednesdays from May to July to visitors known to the Marquis or a member of his family, or to artists recommended by a member of the Royal Academy. Applications for tickets were inserted in a porter's book and vetted for the following day, a procedure that further limited the composition of the gallery crowd. Generally, visitors who gained permission to view a private house or gallery could expect to be accompanied on their tour by a housekeeper or servant who acted as a steward and animate catalogue to the works on display. Frequent complaints were made about the bribes and tips expected by servants guiding visitors around a property, especially at country houses. A correspondent to the *Monthly Magazine* in February 1760 claimed that he was fleeced of six shillings while touring the rooms and garden at Wilton, the Wiltshire residence of the Earl of Pembroke noted for its collection of pictures and antiquities. Even so, he fared better than William *Hazlitt early in the next century, who found his petition for admission to Wilton rejected altogether. 'Do these Noble Persons', Hazlitt angrily demanded in his *Sketches of the Principal Picture Galleries in England* (1824), 'wish to set bounds to and disappoint public curiosity? Do they think that the admiration bestowed on fine pictures or rare sculpture lessens their value, or divides the property as well as the pleasure with the possessor?'

Issues of connoisseurship and aesthetic property are also evoked in the history of the Dulwich Picture Gallery, founded in 1811 through a bequest from the Academician Peter Francis Bourgeois. A large portion of Bourgeois's collection of Dutch, Flemish, Italian, and German paintings was acquired from the picture dealer and prominent amateur Noel Desenfans. Desenfans had been actively employed as an art agent for Stanislaus, King of Poland, in the last decades of the eighteenth century. When Stanislaus lost his throne in the partition of Poland in 1795, Desenfans was left holding a large body of paintings he had acquired for a proposed national gallery in Warsaw. Initially Desenfans exhibited the works for sale by private contract at a gallery in Berners Street, writing an exhaustive and at times vituperative descriptive catalogue in which details of the paintings, aesthetic commentary, and political diatribe were dealt out in equal measure. At his death in 1807 Desenfans's collection was left to his friend Bourgeois and became part of the latter's bequest of more than 350 pictures to Dulwich College four years later. A structure designed by John *Soane to contain the collection and, more startlingly, a mausoleum for Bourgeois, his wife, and Desenfans, was completed in 1814 [see *architecture, 28]. The oldest public picture gallery in Britain thus bears the stamp of its patrons in an unusually corporeal manner. Admission to the Dulwich Gallery was carefully regulated to exclude the local (primarily artisan) population of the area. No entrance fee was charged, but the necessary admission tickets could only be had from a number of specific print and booksellers in London. School groups and children under 14 were debarred, and the catalogue formally requested that visitors refrain from tipping the servants.

The paucity of public venues for viewing art in London was a source of perpetual lamentation for travel and guidebook writers in the period. An attempt had been made in 1773 to encourage a fashion for pictures in English churches. A group of Academicians led by Joshua Reynolds approached the Revd Dr Thomas Newton, Dean of St Paul's, with a plan for decorating the cathedral with large paintings on biblical themes. Benjamin West, Angelica *Kauffman, and James *Barry were among the artists who offered their labour, but the scheme was rejected by the Bishop of London, who 'would never suffer the doors of the metropolitan church to be opened for the introduction of popery'. The King's Gallery at Kensington Palace was accessible but largely despoiled of significant works in this period. The State Apartments at Windsor Castle were open to properly vetted visitors by the end of the seventeenth century, although William Hazlitt opined in 1824 that the residence contained ten or twenty unforgettable paintings mixed with a surfeit of Verrocchio's and West's work, and 'too many rubbishly pictures of kings and queens'. Hampton Court was regarded as the proper repository of the Raphael Cartoons, a series of seven large watercolour sketches of biblical events that had been executed by the Italian painter for tapestry designs. The Cartoons, which had been acquired by Charles I, were an aesthetic and political reference-point in the period's art writing. When George III removed the works from Hampton Court to his new residence near St James's Park in 1763, there was a public outcry. They were returned to Hampton Court in 1809.

Some paintings, drawings, and engravings, and a good deal of antique *sculpture could be viewed at the *British Museum in Great Russell Street. The Museum was founded by an Act of Parliament in 1753 to house the Cottonian Library (begun by Robert Cotton in the era of Elizabeth I), the Harleian Library accumulated by Robert Harley, Earl of Oxford, and a cabinet of curiosities bequeathed to the nation by Hans Sloane. The Museum's holdings of fine arts and antiquities grew dramatically with the acquisition of the first of William *Hamilton's Greek vase collections in 1772, and with Charles Townley's (1737–1805) Greek and Roman marbles in 1805. The Phigaleian Marbles from the Temple of Apollo at Bassae were purchased in 1814 and the *Elgin Marbles from the Parthenon were installed in the Museum in 1816. In 1810 the famous 'Portland Vase' was deposited on permanent loan.

The British Museum was created as a public repository but the complicated entrance regulations instituted by the Trustees in its early period were a discouragement to many potential visitors. Small groups of individuals whose avidity survived the admission procedures (which not infrequently took several weeks) were taken around the rooms at a very brisk pace by a member of staff, a practice not discontinued until 1810. The bookseller William Hutton of Birmingham was enraged in 1785 when he was whisked past 'ten thousand rarities' in thirty minutes flat, and this after paying a scalper two shillings for a ticket. The Museum primarily served men of letters and artists in this period; in the words of a Parliamentary Act of 1808, 'gratifying the curiosity of the multitudes, who incessantly resort to it in quest of amusement' was regarded as 'a popular though far less useful application of the Institution'. The expenditure of public funds on creating and maintaining collections that were predominantly scientific and ethnographic in nature was not welcomed by connoisseurs and artists whose first desire was the establishment of a National Gallery of Art. The notion of a gallery that could educate artists, impress foreigners, and definitively answer the aspersions cast against the taste of the British public, had been advanced periodically through the century. However, development of a national gallery in England was hampered by political apathy, the expense of successive wars, and latterly by the whiff of *republicanism that accompanied the notion of a public art collection. The Musée du Louvre was famously enriched in the period by plunder from private and foreign institutions. British visitors to the Louvre during the Peace of *Amiens were routinely overwhelmed by the richness and scope of the art work gathered in the French capital, although most expressed decorous horror at the means by which it had been accumulated.

A national gallery in London was not brought about through any such energetic redistribution of property, but rather through the nation's orderly purchase of forty-three paintings from the estate of a banker, John Julius Angerstein. Angerstein's collection, admired for its Claudes, Titians, Rubenses, and Rembrandts, was purchased by parliament in 1824 for £60,000 and initially housed in inadequate quarters at 100 Pall Mall. The collection later shared space with the Royal Academy before construction of the gallery at the present Trafalgar Square site began. The building was designed by William *Wilkins and completed in 1838. The foundation of a gallery that was public in conception and practice culminated nearly a century of proposals, schemes, and genteel political lobbying. As John Landseer (1769–1852) put it in an 1834 catalogue of the National Gallery, the institution was designed to be 'permanent and perennial, so that the public mind may there luxuriate and dwell, and reflect upon, or at its pleasure, revisit, what is there reposited'.

At the same time as the project of the National Gallery was being pursued, London saw the emergence of a number of commercial, promotional art galleries—permanent collections of paintings originally commissioned for a specific publication and displayed in purpose-built galleries to publicize the venture. These galleries offer an important new paradigm for the association between audience, artist, and patron in the era, while the content of their exhibitions reveal a rapidly evolving awareness of the utility of visual art in constructing the nation's cultural history. The best-known example of this species of exhibition is the 'Shakespeare Gallery' assembled by the publisher and entrepreneur John Boydell. Alderman Boydell was a prominent printseller and patron of British art who made efforts to fortify the reputation of and market for British reproductive *prints [22] in the 1770s and 1780s. A number of his ventures blurred the lines between national and self-interest, art patronage and business, and even the generic divisions between the private pleasures of the illustrated book and the rhetoric of a public exhibition space.

According to the painter and diarist Joseph Farington (1747–1821), the idea of bringing forward a deluxe edition of *Shakespeare's plays was proposed late in 1786, during after-dinner conversation between Boydell, Benjamin West, George *Romney, William *Hayley, the bookseller George Nicol, and several others. A number of prominent contemporary artists were commissioned to produce paintings that would be engraved for illustrations, and a prospectus of the venture was published just one week after the party's sociable discussion. Boydell purchased 52 Pall Mall, premises formerly owned by the picture dealer Vandergucht. Its façade was reconstructed to a design by George *Dance the younger, and embellished with an allegorical sculpture of Shakespeare by Thomas Banks (1735–1805)—precariously balanced between poetry and painting. Interest in the project was intense: Edmund *Malone noted in a letter of 9 June 1787 that 'near 600 persons' and among them 'not above twenty

27. Henry Fuseli's *Titania and Bottom*, 1786–9, one of his celebrated paintings of scenes from the plays, executed for John Boydell's Shakespeare Gallery.

names . . . that anybody knew' had signed as subscribers before the proposals were entirely printed off. The first exhibition of paintings at the Shakespeare Gallery opened 4 May 1789. It featured thirty-four compositions by eighteen artists including Joshua Reynolds's *Death of Cardinal Beaufort*, James Barry's *King Lear*, and scenes by Henry *Fuseli from *A Midsummer Night's Dream* and *Macbeth*.

In the early weeks of the exhibition the rooms were crowded to capacity. Charles James *Fox, the Prince of Wales, and the Duke of York were reported to have attended, the prince 'enjoying the envied privilege of mingling undistinguished among the people it is possible he may one day govern, in a plain frock and slippers—with AFFABILITY the only *Star* about him'. His anonymity seems to have been short-lived, for he appears in full court dress in Francis *Wheatley's watercolour of the 1790 opening day, *Interior of the Shakespeare Gallery, Pall Mall*, along with Joshua Reynolds, the Duchess of *Devonshire, the Duke of Clarence, R. B. *Sheridan, the Countess of Jersey, and other similarly inconspicuous spectators.

The initial success of the Gallery must in some measure be attributed to the reputation of its central cultural icon. Boydell's venture responded to and benefited from the cultural and political rediscovery of Shakespeare at the end of the century. In a companion guide to the 1789 exhibition entitled *The Bee*, Humphry *Repton acknowledges the universality of the Gallery's subject-matter: the artists 'illustrate scenes with which we are all acquainted—events in which we all participate—and subjects that touch the heart, and come home to men's bosoms'. This appeal to the cultural authority of Shakespeare as a force transcending rank (if not gender) made Boydell's Gallery different from other exhibition venues. Unlike the display of a private collection, the representations of scenes from the plays did not form an exhibition constructed around the taste or inclination of an individual. Moreover, the works were not passed through the institutional filter of an Academy show or temporarily brought together in the saturnalia of the auction house. Rather, a direct address was made through the paintings to the sentiments, knowledge, and sociability of a viewing public, and the mediating presence of Shakespeare ensured both depth and a sense of historical continuity not entirely contingent upon the commodities themselves.

The Shakespeare Gallery was open from 1789 until 1805, by which time 167 paintings were on display. The appeal of the exhibition had lessened with its novelty, and the change is clearly discernible in the tone of its reviews. Adulation for the nature of the scheme gave way to colder evaluations of the performances themselves. Boydell's firm ran into financial difficulties over the protracted publication of the Shakespeare edition, coupled with the collapse of the lucrative foreign print market as a result of the *war [2]. An Act of Parliament was passed in 1804 to allow Boydell to dispose of the paintings by lottery, with the contents of the Gallery offered as first prize. About 22,000 tickets were sold for a draw on 28 January 1805. The winner was William Tassie, who later resold the paintings through Christie's auction house.

Boydell's venture sparked a number of imitations, such as the Historic Gallery instituted by Robert Bowyer at 87 Pall Mall. Drawing largely from Boydell's pool of artists, Bowyer commissioned sixty paintings to illustrate a new edition of David *Hume's History of Great Britain (1754–62). The publisher Thomas Macklin announced plans for a Gallery of the Poets shortly after the appearance of Boydell's prospectus and managed to open his exhibition in April 1788, a year in advance of the Shakespeare Gallery. The first exhibition was held in the Pall Mall buildings formerly occupied by the Royal Academy and featured nineteen compositions by as many artists—Reynolds, Fuseli, and Gainsborough among them. New paintings on poetical subjects were added to the exhibit each year, and in 1790 a whole new category was offered to viewers in the form of representations of biblical history. However, like Boydell's venture the Gallery of the Poets was a commercial failure, its contents being dispersed by lottery in 1797.

Henry Fuseli's attempts to rework the promotional gallery formula suggest the limited opportunities for artists to exhibit independently and promote their work. In 1790 he had been engaged by the publisher Joseph *Johnson to paint thirty pictures to illustrate a grand edition of *Milton's poetical works. The text was edited by William *Cowper, but the poet's mental indisposition prevented him completing the work and Johnson abandoned the project. Fuseli used the four pictures he had finished for Johnson, including Satan, Sin and Death, for his own enterprise. The Milton Gallery opened on 20 May 1799 with an exhibition of 40 works. Admission was fixed at one shilling and a catalogue providing the relevant portions of text priced at sixpence. In the first month the Gallery realized a disappointing sum of £117—the receipts from roughly 1,600 visitors if one conservatively estimates that each purchased a catalogue. The Milton Gallery closed after two seasons.

Another commercial venue in which a portion of the public could view works of art— especially the Dutch, Flemish, and Italian pictures prized by the collectors and connoisseurs— was the auction house. Theoretically the auction rooms of firms such as Christie's, Skinner and Dyke, Phillips, Bryan, and Langford offered an antidote to a dearth of accessible art galleries in London. Auctions of art and other goods were scheduled with an eye to the London season, with the most important sales taking place between March and May. Firms advertising in the period commonly stressed the gentility of spectators attending their sales. The social stratification of the auction room was nicely summarized in comments made on the sale of the late Lord Bishop of Bristol's paintings in 1788. One reviewer commended the fact that 'people not decently dressed, who have offered their money as others, to enter the Rooms, have been constantly refused admittance . . . that stricture is become necessary where people of rank and fashion are resorting'.

The private views preceding a sale at a firm like Christie's were often much more exclusive affairs, sometimes taking the form of a glittering evening reception. On one notable occasion in 1796 an official from the opera was stationed at the auctioneer's doorway to vet the clientele. The assumption that these distinct commercial and theatrical spectacles shared an audience was repeated in other accounts of high society life. A satirical 1813 ballad entitled 'A Day of Fashion' rehearses the sequential delights of the auction room, the opera, and the *pleasure garden to the accompaniment of illustrations by George *Cruikshank.

The activities of art purchasing and viewing were stoked by a dramatic increase in the number, size, and quality of art auctions as the century turned over. The strife that spread in concentric circles from France following the *French Revolution swept a vast amount of art to the 'auction block' in London. Britain was a uniquely stable art market amidst the political and economic upheaval on the Continent, and the 1790s were remarkable for the historically associative and aesthetically rich collections that passed through the sales rooms of London. One exhibition and sale that left its mark was the dispersal of the extensive Orléans collection from the Palais Royal in Paris. The 485 works that had constituted one of the finest galleries in Europe were sold in 1792 by 'Philip Egalité', Duc d'Orléans, to raise money for pro-revolutionary purposes. The Dutch and Flemish portion of the collection was brought from France and displayed for sale by private contract at the old Royal Academy rooms, Pall Mall, in 1793. The Italian pictures were exhibited and sold at the Lyceum in the Strand in 1798. The exhibition of the latter commenced on 26 December 1798 and generated great excitement during its six-month engagement. In the last week over £100 per day was taken at the door—with admission fixed at a shilling, the final view drew in over 2,000 daily visitors. The art dealer William Buchanan claimed that the 1798 exhibition of the Orléans cabinet in London effected a revolution in the taste of British collectors, turning the fashion away from the Dutch and Flemish works favoured by collectors such as the Prince of Wales towards specimens of the early Italian schools.

A much more egalitarian commercial venue for viewing images was the printshop window. Rudolph *Ackermann's 'Repository of Arts' in the Strand, the shops of Carington Bowles in St Paul's Churchyard, Colnaghi on Cockspur Street, Molteno on Pall Mall, and the windows of caricature specialists like Samuel William Fores and William Holland entertained passers-by with enticing displays of their wares. To judge from the comments of foreign visitors to London in the period, the informal, streetside exhibition created by the printsellers was regarded as a definitively British phenomenon. 'A prodigious number of little shops, particularly about Westminster-hall, are every day lined with prints,' reports a P. J. Grosley, while the German tourist Archenholtz tellingly regarded printshops as 'the real galleries' of the country. Naturally the audience for such open-ended displays of graphic reproductions and caricatures was more socially diverse than would be found inside a gallery, museum, or auction room. Charles *Lamb, for instance, recalled as a schoolboy 'shivering in front of printshop windows to extract a few hours' amusement'.

Visual representations of individuals gathered before printshop windows are numerous enough in the period to warrant their designation as a distinct type of *conversation piece. J. R. Smith's mezzotint *Spectators at a Print Shop in St. Paul's Churchyard* (republished 1774) shows two separate dramas unfolding in front of Carington Bowles's premises: a young lady directs her gallant's attention towards a portrait of a clergyman, while a man absorbed in contemplation of the prints is tapped on the shoulder to be arrested. Such works offered a means of engaging self-promotion for the printseller, as well as an opportunity to extend the spirit of satire from the prints displayed to the consumers themselves. J. Elwood's charming pen and watercolour drawing *A Crowd Outside a Print Shop* (1798) shows a large corner window of a generic map and print warehouse filled top to bottom with historical subjects, sporting scenes, and portraits. The orderly congestion along the pavement includes a barrow-woman, a sooty chimney-sweep, several delivery-men with their wares, including a Hogarthian butcher with a joint hoisted to his shoulder, fashionable ladies and *dandies, a cobbler, a connoisseur, and a squire in riding kit. The artist stresses the egalitarian nature of the spectacle as well as the comic potential of this mixing of disparate types, but he also seems concerned to indicate that the moment is simply part of the commercial pulse of the city. The danger of the indiscriminate attraction of the window is defused through the clear hierarchy of labour indicated in the composition of the print.

Between the creation of the Royal Academy of Art and the foundation of a National Gallery in London there are significant developments in the material conditions of art viewing that affect the direction of exhibition and the definition of the spectator. The period is fascinating for the scale and concentration of these changes as well as for the emergence of many aspects of institutional organization and art display that are now perceived as conventional. The Royal Academy occupied a unique position between the spheres of noble patronage and civic obligation; the annual exhibition that was the centrepiece of its promotional and public mandate exposed the stresses of the institution's relationship with its viewing public even as the relationship was celebrated and turned to spectacle. Innovative projects such as the entrepreneurial galleries of Boydell, Macklin, and Bowyer directly addressed the experience of the spectator by positing alternative intellectual frameworks for exhibition, a development linked to the publishers' attempts to restructure the economic basis of art patronage and exhibition. The decades between the late 1760s and early 1830s are also fascinating for the emergence of the notion that what a nation collects or accumulates is as much a part of its cultural capital as what it produces artistically. In this formula the cabinets of curiosities and art treasures formed by private individuals could be and were included in a contemporary definition of nationhood. Events such as the dispersal of the Walpole collection at Houghton Hall and

the various schemes proposed for the establishment of a National Gallery are part of a halting articulation of what might now be termed a sense of national 'cultural heritage'. The history of art in the Romantic era is the gradual revelation of the role of art and its publics within this construct.

Barrell, J., *The Political Theory of Painting from Reynolds to Hazlitt*, New Haven, Conn., 1986; Friedman, W., *Boydell's Shakespeare Gallery*, New York, 1976; Hazlitt, W., *Sketches of the Principal Picture Galleries in England*, London, 1824; Pye, J., *Patronage of British Art: An Historical Sketch*, London, 1845; Solkin, D., *Painting for Money:*

The Visual Arts and the Public Sphere in Eighteenth-Century England, New Haven, Conn., 1993; Vergo, P., ed., *The New Museology*, London, 1991; Waterford, G., *Palaces of Art: Art Galleries in Britain 1790–1990*, London, 1990.

21 · PUBLISHING   JOHN BREWER AND IAIN McCALMAN

In his *Life of Napoleon Buonaparte* (1828–39) William *Hazlitt claimed that the *French Revolution 'might be described as a remote but inevitable result of the invention of the art of printing'. By this he was acknowledging the specific historical conditions—the growth of literacy and the dissemination of knowledge through printed texts—which had led to the overthrow of Louis XVI, but he was also recognizing how books and the literary market-place had created a new kind of public, the mass of readers, conscious of their capacity to play a part in the evolving drama of national politics. By 1776 this reading public was well established and the cultural and especially political implications of its composition were vigorously debated. What were its boundaries? Should the reading public be monitored, or learn to discipline itself? For the bookseller James *Lackington, the expansion in the reading public was a development to be welcomed, especially insofar as it reflected on his own achievements. In his self-aggrandizing *Memoirs* (1791), Lackington commented 'that the sale of books in general has increased prodigiously within the last twenty years'. He went on:

The poorer sort of farmers, and even the poor country people in general, who before that period spent their winter evenings in relating stories of witches, ghosts, hobgoblins, &c. now shorten the winter nights by hearing their sons and daughters read tales, romances, &c. and on entering their houses, you may see *Tom Jones, Roderick Random*, other entertaining books, stuck up on their bacon racks &c. If *John* goes to town for a load of hay, he is charged to be sure not to forget to bring home 'Peregrine Pickle's Adventures'; and when *Dolly* is sent to market to sell her eggs, she is commissioned to purchase 'The History of Pamela Andrews'. In short, all ranks and degrees now READ.

Others regarded this expansion of the reading public with less equanimity: instead of the novels of Henry Fielding and Samuel Richardson, the poor were to be seen reading texts such as Thomas *Paine's *Rights of Man*, the phenomenal success of which led T. J. *Mathias to comment: 'We no longer look for learned authors in the usual places, in the retreats of

28. J. Elwood's *A Crowd Outside a Print Shop* (1798) exemplifies a form of the eighteenth-century conversation piece, portraying the mixed urban world of commerce, class divisions, and popular art.

academic erudition, and in the seats of religion. Our peasantry now read the *Rights of Man* on mountains, and on moors, and by the wayside.'

That Mathias should even contemplate a reading peasantry and the penetration of the printed word beyond the spheres of the universities and the church is a sign of the tentacular outreach of the late-eighteenth-century print trade. When Richardson's *Pamela* was published in 1740 there were about 400 outlets for books in nearly 200 towns. By the 1790s, there were nearly 1,000 firms in more than 300 places. Larger towns acquired an enviable range of printing and publishing services. By 1790 Newcastle upon Tyne had not only twenty printers, but twelve booksellers and stationers, thirteen bookbinders, and three engravers, including Thomas *Bewick.

By 1785 the publishing industry was so diverse, complex, and dispersed that the bookseller John Pendred (c.1742–93) brought out the first guide to English publishing, *The London and Country Printers, Booksellers and Stationers Vade Mecum* (1785). Pendred's world extends far beyond the traditional confines of St Paul's Churchyard and Paternoster Row. His account of the metropolitan trade lists nearly 650 businesses engaged in thirty-two different occupations. Disentangling the functional implications of these specific occupations is admittedly difficult. Both the terminologies and the structures of eighteenth-century publishing were in a state of transition. The term 'publisher', denoting those in the book trade who controlled the processes of production from commissioning to distributing books, was gradually supplanting earlier terms such as 'stationer', meaning a publisher/bookseller who belonged to the ancient chartered corporation of the Stationers' Company, or 'bookseller', signifying an earlier blending of retail and publishing functions. By the late eighteenth century, selling and publishing were increasingly being distinguished, and 'stationer' had come to mean a dealer in paper and writing materials. Pendred reveals how highly specialized the world of late-eighteenth-century publishing had now become: stationers and booksellers outnumber printers, who are enumerated alongside engravers; map, music, and print sellers; bookbinders; paper, card, and board makers; typefounders; and warehousemen. Fancy booksellers list their premises in Oxford Street, Piccadilly, Berkeley Square, and on Pall Mall, engravers work in the artists' quarter of Covent Garden as well as in the fashionable West End, and there are printers and publishers scattered all over the city. One clear implication of the guide is that the formerly blended operations of printer, bookseller, and publisher have definitely begun to separate into specialized commercial and technical functions.

But the most important part of the guide is concerned not with London but with the provinces. For one of Pendred's main purposes was to provide the London trade with valuable information about how to exploit provincial *advertising and distribution networks. When he lists the forty-nine country *newspapers printed in thirty-four towns, he gives two crucial pieces of information: the names of the owners and the addresses of their London agents. Booksellers could thus place advertisements in the provincial press through metropolitan agents, or they could contact newspaper proprietors directly in order to exploit the distribution network of newsagents and booksellers that the latter had established. What had begun as a metropolitan trade had become a national business.

A crucial date in the emergence of the modern publishing industry in the late eighteenth century was 1774, the year of the decision in the case of *Donaldson* v. *Beckett* which ended the English booksellers' right of perpetual *copyright. In the years following this decision, the landscape of the publishing industry was radically altered. The ending of perpetual copyright led to a rush of reprints in serial publications such as John Bell's *British Theatre* (1776–8), and a temporary fall in the price of books due to increased competition. Lacking the incentive jointly to protect copyrights in particular titles, publishers broke away to form individual enterprises such as the firms of Longmans, Rivington, and Murray [see *publishing companies]. London also faced competition from thriving alternative centres such as Scotland, where the houses of Constable, A. & C. Black, Blackie, and Collins were established by 1820. These firms introduced innovative publishing strategies that transformed the industry. Archibald Constable (1774–1827) inaugurated the modern bestseller with Walter *Scott's *Waverley* (1814), published in a 1,000-copy first edition and later cheap reprints, achieving total sales of 40,000 copies by 1829. Enterprises such as this were facilitated by technological changes after 1800 such as the mechanization of paper-making, lithography (introduced to Britain in 1801), and the steam-driven printing press, first used commercially on *The Times* in 1814 [see *prints, 22]. Only typesetting remained unmechanized until late in the nineteenth century. Just how crucial copyright protection could be by the early nineteenth century is well exemplified in the cases of Robert *Southey's *Wat Tyler* (1794) and *Byron's *Cain* (1821). Both were denied legal protection on the grounds of their blasphemous and seditious content, thereby enabling a host of predatory publishers to produce cheap pirate editions. Part of the reason for Byron's extraordinary circulation figures was precisely the inability of his legal publishers to prevent such piracy.

Piracy might have been a problem for law-abiding British publishers, particularly because of the difficulty of policing the activities of systematic operators like Patrick Byrne (*fl.* 1789–1802), who worked out of the lively provincial publishing centre of Dublin, but at least compared to other European nations, the British press was relatively free. Prior censorship of published works (though not of theatrical performances) ended with the lapse of the Licensing Act in 1695, and the government's use of special 'General Warrants' to incarcerate authors, printers, and publishers ended in 1765. Charles James *Fox's Libel Act of 1792 also meant that juries, not judges, determined what was a libel, a practice that on the whole helped the defendant. But the government still had at its disposal a number of means of harassing those whose views it did not like. Taxes on paper and print were imposed not just for revenue but to restrict readership, printing presses had to be registered with the government after 1799, and there

29. George Cruikshank's *Pursuits of Literature, No. 3, Law of Libel*, 1813, illustrates the dangerous life of the literary hack, always susceptible to the threat of charges of obscene, blasphemous, or seditious libel instigated by the government or private prosecuting societies.

were frequent attempts to suppress the lending or sale of cheap materials by street vendors. Government prosecution under the libel or blasphemy laws was not necessarily used in the hope of securing a conviction, but to jeopardize the financial affairs of booksellers and printers. In such ways the government frequently intervened in an attempt to define the content and scope of printed matter. Modern historians who assess the effectiveness of British state censorship purely by counting the numbers of successful government prosecutions seriously underestimate the operations of an informal system of harassment which as often as not silenced publishers through the debtors' courts. British governments were adept at avoiding the appearance of state censorship by encouraging the initiatives of private prosecuting societies, such as the *Society for the Suppression of Vice, or by using paid ministerial pressmen to bring forward civil libel suits and to press debt claims against perceived state enemies. One of the *Pitt government's most irritating political gadflies, Dr Sampson Perry (1747–1823), editor of the radical daily *Argus*, fled to exile in France in 1792 under the weight of just such a barrage of intimidatory libel threats and prospective debts. Nevertheless the history of this period is also studded with government attempts at political prosecution which backfired badly when truculent juries refused to convict, perhaps most notably in the case of William *Hone's three trials of 1817 for publishing a political parody on the *Anglican litany.

Providing they could avoid such hazards, what was the prognosis for would-be literati in our period? The number and variety of authors who embarked on the journey into print was remarkable. Aristocrats who wanted to publish their poems and obsessions, clerics bent on controversy and preferment, women poets, essayists, and novelists from every rank of society, and persons of 'low means' all succeeded in reaching the reading public. How did such a heterogeneous body of authors find their way into print? The crucial vehicle was the periodical press. Any aspiring author seeking fame, fortune, or just the pleasure of seeing their words in print could send their work to a magazine proprietor, and many a career began with such an unsolicited contribution. For some, like Thomas *Chatterton, the periodical press was a lifeline, feeding empty stomachs and fostering literary ambition.

Periodical editors were conscious of their importance in creating a republic of authors, a world of contemporary equality, in what was otherwise a highly stratified society. In an essay on what he called 'periodical performance', the proprietor of *The Bee*, an Edinburgh magazine that first appeared in the 1790s, emphasized the open character of the periodical: 'full liberty is given for every individual to become a writer when he feels a propensity to it, without any further limitation than good manners and becoming politeness requires.'

Periodicals also made possible a career dedicated solely to writing. Magazine proprietors were inundated with unsolicited material, some of which came gratis, and the growing competition between the magazines meant that the demand for material exceeded supply. Professional authors stepped into the breach with *essays, *reviews, poems, and criticism to enliven and enlighten the public; publication enabled them to earn a living. By the 1760s there were more than thirty London periodicals to which they could contribute; by the end of the century there were more than eighty. Still, while journalism may have been the first refuge of writers, it was a perilous and insecure career. More regular employment than was offered by writing periodic reviews, essays, and articles was best secured either by producing a magazine section—in effect, writing a regular column—or by acting for a bookseller as the literary editor of a periodical.

Contemporaries contrasted the genteel camp of 'liberal' writers, populated by men and women of large vision and good taste, with the squalid and impecunious quarters inhabited by authors of partial vision, venal aspiration, and grovelling subordination. Pastiche, the periodical, and compilation of every sort created publications whose parts were produced by writers but whose whole belonged to the publisher. Their design was formed not by the literary inspiration of the hacks who scribbled the copy but by the publisher's sense of the market. Without means and control, writers became manufacturers of components in the factory of literature. Such fragmentation undermined the integrity of writers, who came to bear only a marginal relation to the works they helped to produce. What they wrote was not properly theirs: it was designed by another and had value only as part of a larger whole. They had no vested interest in the completed work, for it was not a thing they could or might wish to acknowledge as their own. Writers were not *authors* but protean figures whose value lay in their ability to assume a number of authorial roles.

How could writers be paid but remain respectable? The answer, slow in coming, grew out of two seemingly unrelated debates, one about artistic value, the other about intellectual property. The former focused on the high-minded issue of creativity, the latter on the prosaic question of copyright; both helped to formulate and clarify the notion of the author as the creator of a unique property, owned by virtue of a singular, imaginative act. The liberal criterion of what made authorship legitimate was traditionally a social one. Financial independence produced good writing; the market-place produced trash. Against this claim, Samuel *Johnson and his allies now argued that the ability to produce valuable literature was not determined by economic conditions but was rather a matter of individual ingenuity and *originality. 'The highest praise of genius', wrote Johnson in his *Life of Milton* (1779–81) 'is original invention.' Originality distinguished the true author from the hack. Both might be paid, both embark on projects suggested and financed, like most of Johnson's major works, by booksellers, but an author had creative powers that the compiler and pastiche writer lacked. The emphasis on originality and novelty underscored the special relationship that the writer bore to his text. If a work was original it was also unique, the distinctive consequence of a writer's *imagination. Each text bore the distinctive impress of its author's mind. As represented in editions of his work such as Edmund *Malone's 1790 *Plays and Poems*, *Shakespeare was the presiding example of the Romantic concept of the autonomous author, the creative *genius whose work was the expression of complex subjectivity.

The professional author, the creator of the unique work of literature, had by the late eighteenth century become a recognizable type, distinguishable from both the liberal writer and the hack. But if the author fabricated and fashioned literary works, there was still the question of what right he had to own them. Establishing the legitimacy of the idea of professional authorship did not secure the careers and status of individual writers, which depended on more mundane matters: how effectively and skilfully they were able to understand and exploit the resources and opportunities of the literary system. The author's first task was to seek entry into the underworld of publishing. Without the resources of an aristocrat and despite the opportunities afforded by the periodical press, the writer almost certainly needed to procure the services of a bookseller/publisher. Only such a commercial middleman had the resources necessary to produce and distribute books.

If the author lived near London, this intimidating task was best accomplished in person. It required him to seek out a publisher in the numerous booksellers' shops and offices that huddled in the shadow of St Paul's Cathedral. Better still, he could hasten to the Chapter coffeehouse in Paternoster Row, where he would find many of London's most distinguished booksellers, stationers, and printers. If more desperate he might try to hire his pen to bookseller/publishers such as James Ridgway (c.1782–1838) or John Bew (*fl.* 1776–89), who specialized in producing blackmailing memoirs or *chroniques scandaleuses*. By the 1820s a distinct *pornography quarter had grown up in Holywell Street, London, presided over by ex-Quaker radical William Dugdale (c.1815–68), who operated several shops and writing-houses where smut was produced with factory-like efficiency by penny-a-line hacks. Confronting a bookseller directly—whatever his specialism—was not, of course, possible for many provincial writers, however desperate they might be. They had to use the *postal service, choosing a bookseller, often with local advice, whose imprint they had seen in newspaper advertisements or on title-pages.

Whether the writer approached a bookseller in person or solicited his support through importunate correspondence, his reception was rarely warm, occasionally tepid, and often cold. The arrogance and hauteur of the bookseller, brilliantly captured in Thomas *Rowlandson's pen and wash drawing *Bookseller and Author*, was an authorial cliché and long-standing grievance. Still, Rowlandson's sneering bookseller, whose corpulent prosperity contrasts with the cringing, emaciated figure of the imploring author, is a caricature. Though there were booksellers who abused both their position and the writers they employed, most members of the trade were prudent, honest, and conservative men of business who faced problems that most authors were eager to avoid. The bookseller bore the risk of publication and needed to make a profit. He was inundated with manuscripts, many of which were without merit and (more injuriously) were unlikely to make money. The sheer volume of material made it hard for the bookseller to discriminate, to pick out the work that would prove a success. It was much less risky to publish and trade in the copyrights of established figures. Only the most adventurous booksellers preferred an unknown living author to a dead literary legend.

How, then, was the hapless writer to overcome the bookseller's reluctance to help him into print? Improbable as it may seem, one of the best stratagems was to appeal to his personal interests and sympathies. Though Rowlandson, like many embittered authors, depicted booksellers as venal monsters and ruthless, profit-seeking entrepreneurs, most held certain subjects and certain causes close to their heart. Many booksellers were doubtless aware of the fragile status and insecure financial state of authors and made allowances accordingly. Some were more generous. They opened their houses, their tables, and their cellars, creating literary salons and circles at which authors could satisfy their hunger and slake their thirst with stout victuals, intoxicating drink, and hearty conversation. The brothers Edward (1732–79) and Charles Dilly (1739–1807), whose firm published James *Boswell's *Life of Johnson*, were famous for the literary dinners held at their shop in the Poultry and later at Charles's retirement home in Brunswick Row, Queen Square. Boswell and Johnson frequented the Dillys' shop; the dramatist Richard *Cumberland and the radical scientist Joseph *Priestley were among the guests at their table. John Newbery (1713–67), famous publisher of *children's literature, kept Oliver Goldsmith (?1730–74) off the street and out of debtors' prison by paying his rent. Numerous publishers advanced authors loans, tried to put their financial affairs in order, helped to organize subscription editions, and arranged reviewing work—as, for example, the radical Dissenting publisher Joseph *Johnson did for Mary *Wollstonecraft, John Horne *Tooke, and others. Lower down the social scale the radical bookseller/publisher William Sherwin (b. *c*.1799) helped to launch ambitious Devonshire ex-tinmaker Richard *Carlile on his own remarkable career as a freethinking publisher, bookseller, and journalist.

Both bookseller and author shared in the balancing act between pecuniary reward and intellectual interest that gave eighteenth-century publishing much of its energy. Yet the liberal tradition of writing, which was so concerned to deny the legitimacy of writing for money, died hard, even amongst those who became professional authors. The enthusiastic recommendations of a colleague might make an author's work more credible in the eyes of the bookseller, but it only marginally reduced the latter's financial risk. Such a reduction could be achieved in one of two ways: by getting someone else to bear—or help to bear—the costs of publication, and by guaranteeing a certain number of sales by organizing a subscription of purchasers prior to publication. Both methods required the support of patrons.

The question of *patronage was and remains a vexed one. The old relations between patron and client, in the eyes of many, had created a form of literary prostitution. In the politically charged climate of eighteenth-century Britain, dependence on a private individual, even dependence on the monarch, was deemed incompatible with the requirements of modern authorship. A professional writer, it was felt, should be servant of no one but the public. His work should not reflect the etiolated taste of a sybaritic aristocrat but rest on the firmer foundation of public approval. In the complex, often fraught relations between patron and authorial client, the balance of power slowly but irreversibly shifted in favour of the writer. Because authors increasingly had the alternative resources of a commercial literary world, they became less dependent on individual largesse. This did not make them any less eager to secure aristocratic support, but what they wanted was not, on the whole, the rather demeaning place of the household servant, but rather pecuniary aid—underwriting an edition, paying for its production costs—and, most important of all, someone to talk up their books in polite society. Welsh *Deist preacher and educator David *Williams become so concerned at the dependence and vulnerability of writers that he managed, after decades of lobbying, to launch a public subscription in 1790 for the purpose of founding a Literary Fund to support deserving authors fallen on hard times. Future beneficiaries were to included S. T. *Coleridge and hosts of lesser-known scribblers who found themselves patronless. Yet, ironically, even the fund itself remained shaky until Williams managed to persuade the Prince of Wales to provide it with generous patronage.

The shifting role of the patron from commissioner and controller of literary work to its consumer, publisher, and promoter was best epitomized by the practice of book subscription. The object of subscription was to secure down payments on—and promises to purchase—a book before its publication. This ensured that its production and distribution costs were covered before it went to press, an arrangement that was obviously congenial to the booksellers because it cut back their risks and could even promise large profits. Authors solicited some of the subscribers by getting jobbing printers to produce proposals and by hawking their wares in the drawing rooms and at the assemblies of the great. The booksellers and authors' friends handled many more.

Subscription publication brought together the interests of author, patron, and bookseller. For the author it helped to get expensive and scholarly tomes into print that might otherwise never have been published. It was the main means of publishing a collected volume or volumes of a single author's works in either prose or verse. A well-managed subscription could also prove popular and profitable enough to secure an author's financial independence. In the case of the subscriber it was an opportunity to be seen to be supporting an author without the difficulties that attended a more personal relationship between patron and client. For the publisher, not only was there a reduced risk but also the chance of additional sales through the network of retail booksellers, encouraged by the publicity obtained by a list of distinguished subscribers. Subscription publication increased as the nature of patronage changed. The number of subscription volumes rose rapidly between the late seventeenth century and the 1730s, levelled off until the 1760s, and spurted again during the last two decades of the century. Poems, *sermons, music [see *music publishing], histories, medical and advice manuals, biography, theology, mathematics, husbandry, and, by the end of the century, even *novels [31], plays, and *encyclopedias were published through subscription.

Up to this point our perspective on publishing has been largely internal; we have examined its inner workings with only an occasional glance to the public outside. But what of the reader, the all-important figure without whom the literary text remains an inert commodity? In the history of reading the issue of literacy has naturally had an important place. The long-term trend in Britain between the sixteenth and late eighteenth centuries was one of growing literacy, a trend stimulated by the increased provision of reading matter which in turn changed the nature of reading itself [see *popular education and *language, 40]. What sorts of book were available to the British reading public during our period? Perhaps surprisingly, the sermon proves to be the single most important literary form. On average about three new sermons were published every week—with still greater concentrations at the beginning and end of the century.

The latter may be explained largely by the revivals of *Methodism and *Evangelicalism, and their emphasis upon spreading the word of God through increased literacy. Moreover, in the wake of the French Revolution, as the radical and democratic literature, for example, of Thomas Paine underwent huge mass circulation amongst the artisan and labouring classes, religious conservatives had to win back their constituency by more sophisticated methods. Projects such as Hannah *More's *Cheap Repository Tracts offered moral as well as political advice in popular form.

As the number of books increased and the system for their distribution grew, it became easier to find them. Books could be bought, hired, or borrowed either from commercial establishments and institutions or from individuals. The humblest literature—*almanacs, *ballads, chap-books, and other forms of *street literature—could be purchased from the itinerant pedlars and chapmen who travelled the countryside selling trinkets, gifts, household goods, and toys. Even the most prosperous establishments stocked items other than books, for bookselling alone was rarely sufficient to make a decent living, and not all the commodities and services the bookseller offered were directly connected with the culture of print. The provincial bookseller—there are 988 listed in 316 towns in the *Universal British Directory* for the 1790s—carried a varied stock that typically included not only books but also stationery and patent medicines; the shop might even carry groceries such as tea, coffee, and sugar.

In regional cities, well-established bookshops carried a range of topical titles; elsewhere theology, bibles, legal manuals, and what the bookselling entrepreneur James Lackington dismissed as 'nothing but trash' was all that was to be found. The adverse effects of such poorly supplied premises were greatly ameliorated by the ease with which booksellers could order from the wholesale booksellers in London. The retail customer, who had probably seen an advertisement for a book in a newspaper, would place an order with the local bookseller. A conscientious reader, who kept abreast of new publications by scanning the advertisements and listings in newspapers, periodicals like the *Gentleman's Magazine*, and the reviews, could collect a currently available title from his or her local bookseller within a week of ordering it.

The parlous stock of most booksellers outside London and the use of 'mail order' to obtain books meant that a great many titles were requested by customers who had little knowledge of their contents. On the whole bookshops were not places to browse in. Retail booksellers tried to compensate for this absence by lending books to their customers at a nominal fee. This elision of borrowing into purchase makes it difficult to distinguish the growth of bookselling from the development of the first commercial libraries, the so-called *circulating libraries. Though in the long term bookshops and libraries emerged as separate institutions, for most of the eighteenth century their histories were intertwined.

The patrons of circulating libraries were not poor. Both Joseph Barber in Newcastle and Francis Noble in London charged their customers 3 shillings a quarter. This amount would not have stretched the budget of a gentleman, merchant, member of the professions, or prosperous trader—it was even within the means of a skilled artisan—but it would have given pause for thought to someone who earned between £40 and £80 a year. Nevertheless circulating libraries were good value. New books were not cheap; by the third quarter of the century a bound duodecimo novel usually cost 3 shillings a volume; a substantial history, piece of *travel literature, or biography was more expensive than an annual subscription to a library. In the last quarter of the eighteenth century book prices, stable for half a century, began to rise steadily. Novels that had once been 3 shillings a bound volume cost a minimum of 3 shillings in sewn papers; three-volume novels, a common length, cost 10 shillings and sixpence sewn. As prices increased, even affluent readers preferred to borrow rather than buy. The popularity of circulating libraries is evinced by their growing numbers: by the end of the century there were nearly 1,000 in the provinces and more than 100 in London.

The conventional wisdom about circulating libraries represents them as repositories of fictional pap, served up to women of leisure who had little to do but surfeit themselves with romantic nonsense. Actually women were not the main public of the circulating library, though they were more prominent there than in other book-lending institutions. Even at Marshall's circulating library in Bath, whose clientele notoriously comprised young ladies of leisure, women subscribers were in a minority: 35 per cent of readers in 1793 and only 22 per cent in 1798. And even at Marshall's, patrons could read a range of works that extended well beyond fiction. It may well have been, however, that the rise in the price of novels meant that more and more of them were borrowed from circulating libraries, so that their clients could concentrate their book-purchasing on what were regarded as more durable sorts of literature.

The concerns of the circulating library complemented those of two other institutions, the subscription library and the book club. The former focused on serious non-fiction and stocked relatively few novels, while the latter usually specialized in small pamphlets and printed ephemera in which current political and religious controversies were vehemently rehearsed. The holdings of these libraries mirrored the civic preoccupations and commercial interests of their members. Liverpool held an outstanding collection of works on the pros and cons of the slave trade; Manchester specialized in technical works; while Bristol housed a large collection of travel literature on the Levant, the Mediterranean, and North America—all areas important to the city's trade. Though the shape of collections in subscription libraries was fairly uniform, they all contained little fiction and large numbers of books of history, travel literature, belles-lettres, theology, natural history, philosophy, and jurisprudence. The books were not seen, on the whole, as of merely utilitarian value, but reflected the larger interests and preoccupations of the merchant and trading classes.

Subscription libraries were enduring institutions: they acquired their own premises, complete with padded armchairs; they printed catalogues to boast of their holdings; and they saw themselves as one more star in the galaxy of institutions—*literary and philosophical societies, assembly rooms, and *theatres [24]—from which emanated the bright glow of civic pride. Book clubs were altogether more evanescent: little associations (membership rarely exceeded twenty) set up by gentlemen, clerics, attorneys, and tradesmen who wanted access to new books but did not want to pay full prices.

The book club was a phenomenon of towns and large villages; it brought together the local élite of professional men, merchants, affluent farmers, and minor gentry in the clubbable atmosphere and convivial environment of the local inn or *tavern, where together they chose the club's acquisitions, debated the issues of the day, and last, but by no means least, ate and drank. Towards the end of our period mutual improvement societies extended the realm of such book clubs to artisans and skilled workers. The books bought were almost always controversial and topical, typically the pamphlets and duodecimos that contained current debates on politics and religion. The ephemeral nature of these books is indicated by the common practice of auctioning them or selling them by lottery to members at the end of each year. Lack of storage space may also account for these sales, but the value of many of the books was as short-lived as the controversies they contained.

Noting the emphasis on institutional resources and public places where books were bought, read, and borrowed should not obscure the importance of private collections of books, and of personal borrowing and lending. Any country-house visitor in the eighteenth century would expect to have the run of its library. Books themselves had become such numerous and frequent features that they were given their own rooms. In 1650 few country houses had libraries and even fewer had them incorporated into their design, but by the late eighteenth century a house without a library was almost unthinkable. In older houses the long galleries, once used for recreation and conversation, were now lined with shelves and stuffed with folios, octavos, quartos, and duodecimos. By the early nineteenth century the library had become the centre of indoor sociability for the country-house guest, as well as the envy of the domestic *tourist.

Its counterpart, William *Cobbett observed in *Rural Rides* (1830), was the proud display of a handful of volumes over the fireplace of the humblest cottages.

Books, print, and readers were everywhere. Not everyone was a reader, but even those who could not read lived to an unprecedented degree in a culture of print, for the impact of the publishing revolution extended beyond the literate public. People who could not read were encouraged to buy a few books so that their literate guests and friends could read to them. Reading aloud, both in public and in private, was a universal practice that enabled non-readers to share in the pleasures of the literate. In homes, taverns, *coffeehouses, in fields, and on the street, oral and literate cultures were married through the ministrations of the public reader.

Even those who often read alone and in silence enjoyed the pleasures of reading aloud. When Henry Austen wrote a biographical appreciation of his sister, Jane *Austen, for the 1818 edition of *Northanger Abbey* and *Persuasion*, he drew attention to her powers of reading: 'She read aloud', he wrote, 'with very great taste and effect. Her own works, probably, were never heard to such advantage as from her own mouth.' Public reading was not just a bridge between literate and illiterate but an attribute of a cultivated and genteel person, one of the most important ways in which values and ideas were shared in an age before electronic media.

On the one hand, changes in the organization of publishing after the lapse of the Licensing Act created a national, relatively unified, and quite coherent literary system. Thanks to a highly developed network of literary distribution, a rural shopkeeper like Thomas Turner (1729–93) had access to—and indeed read—much that was on the bookshelf of many a London gentleman. These same links between metropolis and province made it possible for a poet and critic like Anna *Seward to be one of London's most formidable literary figures while continuing to reside in the cathedral town of Lichfield. In the pages of periodicals, notably the *Gentleman's Magazine*, she published poems and reviews, castigated James Boswell's sycophancy to Dr Johnson, and argued the merits of the great English poets.

On the other hand, in unity there was diversity and division. Britain's literary system spawned a race of hacks who produced fragments of literature; as it grew, so its constituent parts became more and more specialized, with authors and booksellers working in distinctive and incommensurate sorts of literature. More seemed like less: the universal wisdom of the great ancient texts was in danger of being buried under an avalanche of modern dross. The unity and intelligibility of learning was under threat. While some commentators revelled in an explosion of particulars, savouring the myriad details that made up the fabric of modern learning, others looked back to a golden age whose order and manageability contrasted with the present indiscriminate growth of information and lack of control over its distribution. Out of the publication revolution emerged questions that have vexed authors and critics ever since: how could you affect the taste of the public, how could you discipline and control it in the world of a free press, and how were you to re-establish firm boundaries in a culture that was in flux?

Feather, J., *The Provincial Book Trade in Eighteenth-Century England*, Cambridge, 1985; 'British Publishing in the Eighteenth Century: A Preliminary Subject Analysis', *Library*, 8 (1986), 32–46; Houston, R. A., *Literacy in Early Modern Europe: Culture and Education, 1500–1800*, London, 1988; Kaufman, P., 'English Book Clubs and Their Role in Social History', *Libri*, 14 (1964), 1–31; *Libraries and Their Users*, London, 1969; Kernan, A., *Printing Technology, Letters and Samuel Johnson*, Princeton, NJ, 1987; Klancher, J., *The Making of English Reading Audiences, 1790–1832*, Madison, Wis., 1987; Korshin, P., 'Types of Eighteenth-Century Literary Patronage', *Eighteenth-Century Studies*, 7 (1974), 453–69; Lackington, J., *Memoirs of the First Forty-Five Years of the Life of James Lackington: the Present Bookseller in Chiswell Street, Moorfields, London, written by himself in a series of letters to a friend*, London, 1791; Neuburg, V., *Chap-books: A Guide to Reference Material*, London, 1972; Raven, J., Small, H., & Tadmor, N., eds., *The Practice and Representation of Reading in England*, Cambridge, 1996; Rose, M., *Authors and Owners: The Invention of Copyright*, Oxford, 1993.

22 · PRINTS DAVID BINDMAN

Before photography, almost the only method of producing multiple images was by making a design on a copper plate, stone, or woodblock, applying ink to it, and then pressing the inked design onto a sheet of paper to form a print. Hence from the end of the fifteenth to the mid-nineteenth century, prints in a certain sense controlled the ways in which the world was made visible to all but the few who had access to *paintings [27] and drawings, or to ceremonial forms of representation. Prints provided an almost limitless range of services, from the reproduction and multiplication of works of art to the commemoration of public hangings in broadsides sold at these events. All *advertising beyond a simple letterpress announcement required the services of a printmaker, and the religious life of ordinary people was reinforced by mass-produced, single-sheet, moralizing broadsides set around a relief-printed image. From its fifteenth-century beginnings, printmaking had become a multi-faceted profession which encompassed a wide range of skills and techniques, and offered many products in conjunction with letterpress or other forms of printing. Between 1776 and 1832 it was at its height, carried along by the growth of trade to which it made a notable contribution. Ironically, however, the very dynamism of printmaking contributed to its demise, for its technological innovation eventually led to its own replacement: photography was, after all, a mode of printmaking, which grew out of the perceived limitations of the processes then available.

100

While the products of the printmaking industry in the period are still part of common experience—available in museums and libraries, reproduced in books, and hanging in private homes—the culture which grew up around them has been lost. This culture, the milieu of the printmakers themselves, their rivalries, and their negotiations with each other and with purchasers, was essentially urban and overwhelmingly London-based, though there were independent centres of print production in the major provincial cities such as Edinburgh, Dublin, and Belfast. Like other industries in the period, printmaking was the locus of perpetual demarcation disputes and agitation, caused by the introduction and exploitation of new technologies and artificial attempts to confer value on new products.

The lives of printmakers were, therefore, dominated by unstable hierarchies. Printmaking had itself a place, though a low one, within the hierarchy of the visual arts [see *viewing, 20]. With the foundation of the *Royal Academy in 1768, line-engravers hoped that they would achieve recognition and be allowed full membership within this self-proclaimed professional élite. This was denied to them on the grounds that they were 'mechanics' and not practitioners of a liberal art—a rejection greeted by strong protest at the time and resulting in long-standing resentment. The line-engravers were the most conservative and status-conscious of all printmakers, jealously guarding methods going back to sixteenth-century Germany and Italy. Their practice involved the use of a burin, a short steel rod cut obliquely at the end to provide a point used to gouge lines out of the copper. The plate would be printed by inking and wiping it, and then squeezing the ink from the lines on to the paper by means of a special press. This technique had developed by the late eighteenth century into a highly formalized system of parallel lines and cross-hatching which could provide a kind of equivalence to a painting, but could never pass for a facsimile. In the hands of the best practitioners, like William *Sharp, engravings could produce remarkable effects of tone: they retained a strong aura of probity and

53

ancient craft, but they never claimed to capture the texture of the original. Painters, when making prints themselves, almost always preferred the less laborious and infinitely more spontaneous medium of etching, which required them not to wrestle with a burin but simply to scratch with a needle-pointed tool through a wax coating applied to the surface of the copper. The plate would then be placed in a bath of acid which would eat into the copper exposed by the needle, enabling the lines to hold ink and be printed by the same method as engravings.

Line-engraving and etching were instantly recognizable as printmaking techniques in their own right, but from the mid-eighteenth century onwards there was an increasing interest in imitative techniques which would provide a more precise equivalence of other media. Much effort, mainly in England and France, was expended in attempts to make facsimiles of the original painting or drawing from which the print was derived, so that its fugitive qualities could be captured and multiplied. A premium was increasingly placed on achieving a softness of effect, mitigating the hard linearity of traditional engraving. This was achieved by the use of tools which made fine dots on the surface, or by chemical means to create a delicate granular surface.

31 Mezzotint, a technique invented in the seventeenth century which involves scraping white highlights from a previously roughened copper plate, already provided a reasonable imitation of the tones and handling of oil paint on canvas. From the mid-eighteenth century onwards mezzotinters achieved a high standing in the profession, based on their skill but also on a careful control of the market. Since mezzotint involved working the surface of the copper plate, rather than cutting into it as with line-engraving, the plate wore very quickly. This meant that there was a visible difference between early impressions from the plate and those that had been taken further down the print run. Hence for collectors there was a high premium on proof impressions before the plate had been issued. In order to capitalize on this premium, mezzotinters often produced several impressions before the lettering was finished, no doubt with the collusion of the painter who had provided the design. These 'proofs before letters' became much sought after, but by definition could only cater to a very limited market, despite the fact that the production of such 'rarities' became notoriously open to abuse. In the nineteenth century the practice was even formalized into the publishing of 'proof editions'.

Mezzotint continued to provide the most persuasive rendering of oil painting, but by the end of the eighteenth century several other surrogate techniques were readily available. Stipple-engraving, which involved dotting the surface of the copper, imitated chalk drawing so that decorative prints in the French manner could be produced in large numbers to comple-
90–1 ment interiors in the style of Robert *Adam. Aquatint, in which fine resin was bonded to the plate before etching, could imitate wash drawing, thereby allowing the production of particularly elegant collections of views. In the face of these new imitative methods, traditional line-engraving was open to criticism as inexact, labour-intensive, and old-fashioned. However, partly through judicious compromise with new demands, it continued to hold its own well into the nineteenth century.

For the professional printmaker these new techniques raised the fundamental question of whether he (printmakers were almost always male) should be content to reproduce the characteristics of another medium, or should, on the contrary, make a virtue of the specific tech-
8, 22 niques of printmaking. The case for line-engraving was stated most eloquently by William *Blake, who had undergone a seven-year apprenticeship with James Basire (1730–1802), the most distinguished antiquarian engraver operating in London at the time. In his notebook drafts known as the 'Public Address' (*c.*1810) Blake condemned 'What is call'd the English Style of Engraving, such as proceeded from the Toilettes of Woolett & Strange'; these engravers, who were as it happens the most vociferous defenders of the profession in the face of the Royal Academy's rejection, had in Blake's eyes sacrificed the linear qualities of traditional engraving for softer and more imitative styles. This rejection of outline, he claimed, represented also the sacrifice of independence, in favour of work 'Suited to the Purposes of

Commerce . . . for Commerce Cannot endure Individual Merit'. The entrepreneurial efforts of 'Alderman' John *Boydell, who had sought, like Josiah *Wedgwood, to bring advanced business methods to the marketing of his product, were therefore inimical to the independence of the honourable traditions of engraving [see *design, 25].

It goes without saying that Blake's opinions were highly tendentious. A golden age of line-engraving had never existed in England, and Blake himself was as eclectic in method as any of those that he dismissed so fiercely. Furthermore, he gained more than he was prepared to admit from the increase in demand for prints and from the apparatus of speculative print publishing and selling. If old ways were under threat there were also new opportunities: the unique method of relief etching that Blake used for his visionary *prophecies was also the product of an age which sought to bring new technologies to bear on old problems. In his case this was the problem of reconciling on one plate text and design, which, if letterpress were used, would have to be printed separately.

Such debates were relevant to what was agreed to be the top end of the trade; there was perceived to be a huge gulf between line-engravings and broadsides as well as other forms of *street literature, decorated by woodcuts and relief prints, put out by the firms of James Catnach and John Pitts in Seven Dials, London, and sold by hawkers throughout the country. Such firms, which carried on through their successors right up to the last quarter of the nineteenth century, offered a diverse production but one which almost always contained text and design, taking advantage of the fact that while an engraved plate was incompatible with letterpress, a woodblock or relief plate (including the finer technique somewhat misleadingly known as wood-engraving) could be locked into a page of type. Their production ranged in size from the ballad slip to the full broadside intended for display in cottage parlours, pubs, or religious meeting-places. The production was enormous but it is poorly documented, for it was a dying trade by the time that Victorian social commentators like Henry Mayhew (1812–87) began to take an interest in it, and a very great deal has been lost because of poor paper, the disdain of collectors, and the practice of pasting the broadsides directly to walls. Even so it also contained its modernizing tendencies, for it is clear that by the 1820s stereotypes of woodblocks were already being used to prolong the life of the image. It is probably not coincidental that the period in which modern technology was introduced also saw the first signs of nostalgia for the lost world that they supposedly represented. Writing in the 1820s Thomas *Bewick could not

help lamenting that in all the vicissitudes which this art has undergone, some species of it, is lost & done away—I mean the large blocks, with the prints from them, so common to be seen, when I was a boy, in every Cottage & farm house throughout the whole country . . . these prints, which were sold at a very low price, were commonly illustrative of some memorable exploits . . . besides these, there were a great variety of other designs, often with songs added to them, of a moral, a patriotic or a rural tendency which served to enliven the circle in which they were admired.

Caricatures were often stigmatized at the time as belonging in the vulgar milieu of Seven Dials, but they also carried with them the aura of a gentlemanly hobby, for they were practised by aristocratic amateurs who had often learned to make them on their *Grand Tour, and they were collected avidly in fashionable circles. Graphic satire, or caricature as it is usually called (strictly speaking, caricature is a method of graphic satire which creates a humorous effect from the exaggeration of a single feature of the person caricatured), was perhaps the most successful of all branches of printmaking in the late eighteenth century, and was noted as a distinctive feature of London life by foreign visitors [see *satire]. Much of its reputation was due to the authority and fame of such artists as James *Gillray and Thomas *Rowlandson, both of whom gained reputations abroad, especially in Germany. Gillray and Rowlandson, despite the often lewd and scatological nature of their imagery, were in fact sophisticated purveyors of luxury goods aimed at the wealthy and politically powerful who might open their volumes of satires underneath their portraits by Thomas *Gainsborough or Joshua *Reynolds, or place them on shelves alongside the 1802 edition of prints of works housed in Boydell's Shakespeare Gallery. None the less, their work was also made available to a popular audience in print-shop windows, where they were displayed for free. Gillray and Rowlandson were both Royal Academy-trained, their work was undeniably 'artistic' and produced in relatively small numbers, and the imagery of their satires was consciously aimed at those conversant with literature and painting, and with the political debates of the time. Though their work has a raffish air, and Gillray's in particular cruelly mocked the royal family, it tended to be populist and volatile rather than conventionally radical or consistently conservative. Both produced some strongly *loyalist satires at the time of the *French Revolution debates in 1792–3, and Gillray was responsible for some of the crudest as well as the most elegant attacks on Charles James *Fox and other French sympathizers.

The success of Gillray and Rowlandson undoubtedly encouraged others to set up as satirists, and there were many who sought different and more radical paths. Unlike reproductive printmaking, which required the most meticulous craft skills and immense patience, caricaturists almost always used the free and rapid medium of etching, and so it was possible to achieve a certain success as a caricaturist without training. This left the door open to amateurs who might be gentlemen, like the Norfolk landowner Henry Bunbury (1750–1811), described by contemporaries as 'the second Hogarth', or evidently self-taught artists like William Dent (*fl.* 1783–93), who turned out hundreds of ribald political caricatures in the period. Somewhere in between amateur and professional was the extraordinary Richard Newton (1777–98), who produced a substantial œuvre despite his death at the age of 21. He drew brilliantly from the age of 15, and his social and political caricatures are marked by a scatological humour directed at the royal family or the *Pitt government. If Gillray, who had his own publisher in Hannah Humphry, tended to uphold the Pitt government, Newton's publisher, William Holland, was firmly on the radical side, publishing Thomas *Paine's *Letter Addressed to the Addressers* (1792) and spending time in Newgate prison.

The profusion of political caricature from the 1780s onwards raises the question of its efficacy as propaganda. It is hard to measure its impact because it was almost always part of a larger campaign involving pamphlets and *newspapers. There is certainly anecdotal evidence that Fox was damaged by James Sayers's (1748–1823) caricatures in the row over the India Bill of 1784, and it is hard to believe that the slow drip of Gillray's ceaseless portrayal of Fox as a sleazy, cowardly, and hypocritical opportunist did not undermine his credibility in some quarters at least. Certainly William Pitt and his colleagues felt more comfortable having Gillray on their side as a government pensioner in the later 1790s, though Gillray did not hesitate also to attack Pitt's new system of taxation. In the early nineteenth century, with the Napoleonic *wars [2], caricature tended to direct its energies abroad, and though many of George *Cruikshank's satires of *Napoleon are ribald and effective they lack Gillray's sharp edge. There is also a perceptible lessening of intensity among Cruikshank's contemporaries, like William Heath (1794–1840), and the end of the decade saw the virtual demise of the single etched and hand-coloured satirical print in the face of new technologies.

Overall, printmaking in late-eighteenth- and early-nineteenth-century Britain had the characteristics of a diverse and successful industry. The reproductive line-engravers had succeeded in replacing imports from France, the traditional producer, and had built up a Europe-wide dominance in the field of decorative engravings. Successful engravers like William Woollett (1735–85) had become celebrities, and the engraver-turned-entrepreneur John Boydell was briefly able in the 1780s to broach the possibility, abortive as it turned out, that serious *history painters might find a public through engravings after their work and thus be compensated for the neglect they suffered from the wealthy. If import replacement was a

30. *Caricature Exhibition, 1794*, by the young engraver Richard Newton, sardonically depicts an aristocratic clientele admiring lampoons of itself at the showroom of his publisher, William Holland. Graphic satire was the contested preserve of both loyalists and reformers during the revolutionary decades.

sign of printmaking's success, technological innovation and division of labour were signs of its modernity. A plethora of new or adapted techniques enabled paintings and drawings to be imitated as never before, making something of the experience of owning paintings or drawings available beyond the small circles of connoisseurs.

Though some printmakers capitalized specifically on the rarity value of their products by limiting editions and offering carefully contrived variants, for most, economic success was dependent on producing large numbers of prints from each copper plate. Copper had one serious disadvantage: as a soft metal it wore down imperceptibly each time it was printed, with the result that there was a limit on the number of satisfactory prints which could be taken from one plate. In the early nineteenth century copper was increasingly, though never completely, replaced by other means: lithography, steel plates, and Bewick's method—the use of the end-grain of hard wood. Lithography was the most adaptable printing method, for it was a chemical process, allowing an artist to work easily and freely with a greasy medium on the block of fine limestone it usually required. It also had great commercial potential; because the image was printed from the surface of the stone it could be made compatible with letterpress. Steel plates came into general production in the 1820s and they effectively replaced the use of copper, enabling increasingly large editions of line-engravings and book illustrations. Under

59 Bewick, working in Newcastle, the use of wood-engraving burgeoned to the point that it practically forestalled the success of lithography, becoming an important element in the mass-
production of images characteristic of Victorian serial publishing.

Though printmaking in the period was predominantly a means of reproduction, many of
the best artists were drawn to it as a means of expression, as well as a way of making their work
available to a wider public. The latter part of the eighteenth century saw much experimentation by artists seeking independence from publishers and the opportunity to develop their
techniques in other media. Gainsborough produced a series of prints using soft-ground etching and aquatint from the mid-1770s onwards which replicate the effect of his chalk and wash
drawings, while George *Stubbs, an inveterate experimenter who had worked briefly with
Wedgwood on porcelain supports for his paintings, produced prints of a fine-grained texture
based on the free use of stipple and engraving tools.

William Blake, though trained as a line-engraver, was perhaps the most far-reaching innovator of all. His main achievement was the combination of image and text on the same plate,
while at the same time controlling all the processes within his workroom. He developed a
process which he called, probably with reference to medieval manuscripts, 'Illuminated Printing'. This was, strictly speaking, a form of relief etching, which involved printing from the
surface of the copper plate, like traditional woodcut, but also incorporated etching away the
parts of the copper which did not print. Such a method allowed him to work freely between
text and image, moving from images which occupied the whole plate, to marginal decorations,
to the poetic text. He used this unique method almost exclusively to produce hand-made
editions of his prophecies, and though achieved by technological innovation, it contributed to
the other-worldliness of their appearance.

In the early nineteenth century, with the invention of lithography and the steel plate, the initiative in developing printmaking techniques effectively passed out of the hands of artists. J. M. W.

31. Frontispiece to J. M. W. Turner's *Liber Studiorum* (1807–19), etching and mezzotint.

*Turner and John *Constable both produced volumes of prints illustrative of their methods of *landscape painting. In his *Liber Studiorum* (1807–19), Turner combined outline etching by himself and mezzotint added by a professional engraver to provide a reasonable approximation of sepia drawings, while Constable, in his *Various Subjects of Landscape* (1830–3), also used mezzotint, but this time on steel and in a quite different spirit. Constable employed David Lucas (1802–81) as a printmaker to work mainly from paintings, but actively intervened in the production of the prints. Here Constable sought in miniature the dramatic effects of his bold handling of oil paint, aiming in the process to lose any sense of mechanical reproduction. John *Martin also used mezzotinting for his large biblical scenes dating from 1826. The tonal values of mezzotint suited the visionary qualities of his art; and with the use of steel plates he was able to produce them in large numbers. Lithography did not have much success with artists in Britain, except perhaps for the painter and caricaturist John *Doyle, though a great many produced experimental plates in the early part of the century. The one artist to take it seriously in Britain was the French painter Géricault (1791–1824)—not surprisingly, since Paris publishers were far advanced in lithography. On his brief visit to London in 1821, Géricault produced twelve prints entitled *Various Subjects Drawn from Life on Stone*. Here a brilliant grasp of the technique of lithography worked to produce a searching vision of the misery of a great industrial city in formation. *83*

The modernizing tendencies of printmaking were confirmed by the growing division of labour which characterized its development throughout the period. The characteristic type of mid-eighteenth-century printmaker was someone like George Bickham (d. 1758), who among other things made caricatures, music sheets, and drawing manuals, and sold prints to collectors. By the end of the century there were specialists of all kinds, the best of whom had established considerable public reputations. Print publishers and sellers were no longer necessarily engravers themselves, and the processes involved in production tended to become increasingly specialized. In the early part of the century a workshop would also be the point of sale; by its end there were rival publishers in the fashionable parts of town. Blake, writing in 1800, remarked; 'There are now, I believe, as many Booksellers as there are Butchers & as many Printshops as of any other trade. We remember when a Print shop was a rare bird in London.' The designer, the engraver, and the publisher of a large plate would all be clearly differentiated in the caption below the print, and by the early nineteenth century a plate printer like W. B. McQueen might also have his name on the plate.

There is a tragic irony in the fact that popular printmaking of the Seven Dials variety should outlive, though not by many years, the whole apparatus of the printmaking industry with its ceaseless quest for improved status and its ancient craft traditions. Yet, remarkably, one printmaker survived into modern times. This was Ross & Co., which was discovered to be still printing off some of its inheritance of copper plates in London's Hampstead Road until it moved in 1966. It had retained many of its records, and it proved also to have inherited many of the most important plates of the eighteenth century because, as other printmakers collapsed in the nineteenth century, Ross & Co. was able to acquire the stock, which included still printable plates by Gainsborough and Stubbs. Whatever future remains for this stock—and the company is no longer in the hands of its original owners—it remains the greatest monument to and source of knowledge of the lost milieu of printmaking.

Bain, I., 'Thomas Ross & Son: Copper- and Steel-Plate Printers since 1833', *Journal of the Printing Historical Society*, 2 (1966), 3–22; Bindman, D., *The Shadow of the Guillotine: Britain and the French Revolution*, London, 1989; Donald, D., *The Age of Caricature: Satirical Prints in the Reign of George III*, New Haven, Conn., 1996; Duffy, M., ed., *The English Satirical Print 1600–1832*, Cambridge, 1986; Essick, R. N., *William Blake, Printmaker*, Princeton, NJ, 1980; George, D. M., *English Political Caricature: a Study of Opinion and Propaganda*, vol. i, to 1793; vol. ii, 1793–1832, Oxford, 1959; *Hogarth to Cruikshank: Social Change in Graphic Satire*, Harmondsworth, 1967; Godfrey, R. T., *Printmaking in Britain*, Oxford, 1978; Gretton, T., *Murders and Moralities: English Catchpenny Prints, 1800–60*, London, 1980; Twyman, M., *Lithography 1800–50*, Oxford, 1970; Viscomi, J., *Blake and the Idea of the Book*, Princeton, NJ, 1993.

23 · POPULAR CULTURE

IAIN McCALMAN AND MAUREEN PERKINS

Modern studies tend to find popular culture an elusive concept, though there is rough agreement that it encompasses the common people's world of work, attitudes to the natural world, education, literacy and knowledge, health practices, gender and generational roles, religious beliefs, recreational and leisure pursuits, and community customs. Since the 1960s historians have also tended to advance two overarching theses about popular culture in the Romantic age: first, they have contended that a long-term process of polarization between élite and plebeian cultures widened into a yawning gulf; second, that over this same period the British middle and ruling classes subjected the culture of the common people to intensifying attack in order to eradicate or reform traditional customs and morality. Popular culture, they have argued, thus became increasingly oppositional and embattled, the domain of the labouring poor and outcast. This process of marginalization was compounded by the modernizing forces of commercialism and *consumerism [19].

Such unanimity of interpretation is strongly based: narratives of reform from above and of resistance from below are inscribed on many of the source materials through which modern historians must work. We depend heavily on the records of police informers, court prosecutors, local magistrates, and zealous *Evangelical morality campaigners, all anxious to discipline potential sources of social, political, and religious disorder. At every turn we encounter the social ripples created by pushy commercial and industrial entrepreneurs keen to control the space, time, and energy of the labouring masses. The accelerating urgency of *fin de siècle* campaigns to reform popular manners and morals can be clearly linked to the traumatic impact of *revolution [1], *war [2], sectarian struggle, *riots, and reform protest that studded our period from the 1770s to the 1830s. In the face of such multiple threats it is not surprising to find that Britain's ruling classes tended to subscribe to ideologies which aspired to a unified, consensual society. As Marilyn Butler shows in this volume, the flowering of cultural *antiquarianism [35], particularly in the popularly orientated folk collections of Francis *Douce, Joseph *Ritson, and William *Hone, displayed both a nostalgic yearning to capture vanishing organic folk-ways and a radical Romantic inclination to defend them as manifestations of a golden age of democratic *utopianism [9].

That so many late-twentieth-century analysts have sympathized with Marxist cultural materialist approaches has also reinforced a historiographical inclination to produce narratives of popular resistance and struggle, including one of the most inspirational and influential historical writings of our time, E. P. Thompson's *The Making of the English Working Class* (1963). In this vein of 'history from below', scholars like Robert Malcolmson have shown that the 'traditional' recreational pursuits of the broad mass of the lower orders evoked a marked desire for control and containment on the part of the Georgian ruling classes. Particularly amongst the urban middling sort, we find a growing moral disapproval of blood sports such as bull-baiting and cock-fighting. This fear of and desire to delimit popular festivity was related in part to processes of *class [15] formation. Campaigns for the *reformation of manners also intensified with the sentimental revolution of the 1760s and 1770s whereby a relatively broad-based code of feeling came to be asserted against the more exclusive and cynical aristocratic values associated with Lord Chesterfield's *Letters* (1774), as well as against the supposed brutishness of the plebeian. *Sensibility [11] of this sort, often enhanced by Evangelicalism's new emphasis on activist, work-based religious reform, generated sundry attempts to legislate against popular blood sports (excepting the impregnable aristocratic and gentry preserve of fox-hunting). It was also seen as imperative to control public spaces and rituals, including *fairs and football matches, where congregations of the common people could become unruly and dangerous. The gradual shift of public executions from the carnivalesque public festival of the Tyburn Tree to an almost covert private ritual within the interior of Newgate gaol is a notable example [see *prisons]. Legislative efforts were also made to head off potential disorder by silencing commercial *debating societies, by tightening restrictions on Sunday trading where groups of the common people might cluster, and by licensing popular chapels, *coffeehouses, *taverns, and alehouses as a means of controlling both proprietors and attendants [see *gagging acts].

11

Changes in popular custom have not, however, been ascribed only to the intervention of anxious ruling-class reformers. The dwindling of common land due to *enclosure limited the practice of public sports. The growth of towns and the attendant commercialization of leisure activities, as well as the regulation of work-rhythms through *industrialization [14], also played some part in restricting open-air activity, contributing to the importance of the pub, coffeehouse, dramshop, and other venues of primarily masculine social drinking. At the same time an element within the working class began in the early nineteenth century to campaign strenuously for the liberation of the populace from the effects of idleness, drunkenness, and superstition. Men like former breeches-maker Francis *Place argued that the pleasures and benefits of *self-improvement could be advanced by rational recreations such as visiting museums, enrolling in *friendly societies, joining reading circles and radical *corresponding societies, and attending public *lectures. While the eighteenth-century 'blackguard tradesmen' revelled in rough, masculine conviviality, consciously respectable artisans often encouraged their wives to participate in the new self-improving recreational culture and to undertake the education of their children [see *popular education]. A freethinker himself, Place illustrates, too, how criticism of popular manners and morals was further exacerbated by conflicts in religious outlook. His autobiography was scathing about the apathy and fatalism of the superstitious labourer. Attempts were also made by some Evangelically minded reformers to replace the boisterous celebration of maypoles and morris dancing—seen as remnants of paganism—with *Sunday school feasts and processions. Such reforming worthies strongly disliked those traditional festivals and saints' days that smacked of the persistence of popery. Lastly, reform could be seen as an expression of changing attitudes towards productivity, manifesting itself as a concern about the correct stewardship of time. The rational recreations which many reformers preferred the working classes to pursue, such as studying useful knowledge publications, attending Sunday schools, or listening to Mechanics' Institute lectures, were primarily intended to refresh and strengthen the mind and body in order to facilitate a diligent week's work.

Temporal responsibility was a fundamental part of Evangelicalism; John *Wesley's favourite verse of Scripture was said to be 'Redeem the Time'. The secular world, too, was during this period finding temporal precision both easier to achieve and more desirable. E. P. Thompson has famously argued for the growing influence of the clock, internalized within the time-consciousness of worker and employer alike. Contestation over this area of culture intensified as the pace of life increased with technological change and the imperatives of trade: Robert *Owen, for example, encountered persistent resistance to the use of a factory time-clock from workers at his New Lanark factory. The rise of a unified public sense of time also testified to the drive of middle-class reformers to make plebeian culture as standardized and controllable as possible. The many varied work rhythms which Thompson described as part of task-orientation were overridden by the demands of factory timetables. A public time schedule, fitting leisure around a predominantly regular working week, was becoming the norm, and its eventual dominance was to drive many heterodox and marginalized temporalities out of sight.

The triumph of the public calendar was clearly linked to factory schedules, to the standardization of timetables (of post coaches in the 1780s and then railways in the 1840s), and to the increasing precision of technological measurement. Less explored, however, has been the way in which desire for a new uniform temporality reached even into the private lives of the common people. It is difficult to see how economic production or social order could possibly be threatened by individuals applying herbal medicine within their own homes, or planning their journeys according to lunar-based weather predictions, or practising conception and contraception according to lunar phase. Yet a host of Evangelical moralists, eager *philanthropists, and vigilant local magistrates were clearly worried by the persistence of such behaviours, and the removal of popular 'superstitions' associated with temporality comprised a significant part of cultural reform.

*Fortune-telling, for example, was one surprisingly salient target. It was one of the social evils identified by the 1802 *Society for the Suppression of Vice, and in 1824 the Vagrancy Act made it punishable by a fine or three months imprisonment. Numbers of plebeian women and men were prosecuted, on the understanding that their claims to predict the future were a form of fraud or 'gammoning' of money from the gullible. Other methods of telling the future such as weather prediction, dream visions, and *prophecy attracted similar suspicion, indicative of the fact that the ruling classes were coming to see the conceptualization of the future as a matter of great significance. While vulgar *millenarian prophets such as Richard *Brothers were predicting an imminent time of suffering, leading to redemption, governments were eager to hold out the promise of progress. The future was to be conceived as new and better—fatalism and fecklessness needed to be eradicated. Like the similar conceptual shift in the meaning of the term 'revolution' from astronomical return to total transformation, the future was now cut free from the past, notwithstanding the irony that industrial capitalism demanded a considerable degree of forward planning. In suggesting that it was possible to see the future, popular predictive or 'superstitious' practices threw an unquantifiable factor into this planning. If indeed the flow of time was not as equable as *Newton's definition had claimed it to be, then the outcomes of scientific experiment, political policy, and technological advance were dangerously uncertain.

The multiplicity and intensity of such pressures to transform plebeian beliefs and morals has, however, led to some exaggeration both of the degree of cultural dominance achieved by the ruling classes during our period and of the extent to which plebeian culture took exclusively oppositional forms. Recent revisionist studies—exemplified by Tim Harris's collection of essays *Popular Culture in England*, c.1500–1850 (1995)—modify the prevailing model of cultural attack and resistance in several ways. First, these revisionists argue, it is misleading to see popular culture as fixed and homogeneous, whether in pre-industrial or modern forms. Rather, we should treat it as a fluid dialogical process, or at least as a field of study characterized by considerable pluralism arising from regional, sectional, and above all gender differences. Second, they argue, conventional bipolar divisions between élite and popular, polite and vulgar, or pre-industrial and modern tend to elide the considerable degree of cultural appropriation and exchange that took place among different social groupings. Finally, they contend, popular culture in our period was often more flexible, resilient, and adaptable to modernizing impulses than many historical accounts would have us believe.

In the remainder of this essay, then, we propose to explore the force of some of these revisionist criticisms by examining the experiences and cultural expressions of three of the period's most notable plebeians: the brilliant Northamptonshire *peasant poet John *Clare, the celebrated Devonshire servant-prophetess Joanna *Southcott, and London's bestselling writer-journalist Pierce *Egan.

At once we are confronted with the range of dissimilarities and particularities which the term 'popular culture' must encompass. The son of a thresher in Helpstone, John Clare worked for much of his life as a day-labourer as well as a poet; ploughing, shepherding, lime-burning, and scribbling 'rhymes'. With brief exceptions he lived in a world bounded by the village of his birth and the nearby rural town of Stamford; his poetry evoked with vivid specificity the landscape, idiom, songs, and folk-ways of the fen country. Pierce Egan, by contrast, was the son of an Irish roadmaker living in Holborn. His only education was as a printer's apprentice and hack of *street literature; the vivid social world of his writings was evoked from the sporting venues, alehouses, theatres, and bordellos located in the couple of square miles around Piccadilly. Joanna Southcott followed the typical trajectory of a poor tenant farmer's daughter by working as a domestic servant in Exeter. In 1792 she suddenly felt the call, at the age of 42, to declare herself a prophetess, the 'woman clothed in the sun' cited in Revelation. Her near-illegible, ungrammatical, and phonetically spelt spirit-writings drew on a syncretic blend of Devonshire pagan folk belief and Christian millenarianism. Local harvest failures and food *riots, as well as international war and revolution, provided the backdrop for her national mission from 1801 to announce the awful days leading to the Second Coming.

Despite this diversity of background, one is struck by how the cultural experiences and expressions of all three mark a confluence-point where orality and print, canonical literary works and street genres, combined and exchanged in complex ways. According to his *Autobiographical Fragments* (1821–8) John Clare regarded Helpstone as an 'unlettered' village, yet there he was able to nourish his imagination on a rich pabulum of both print and orality. As well as the standard village staples of the Bible, *hymns, weekly *newspapers, and *almanacs, he frequently listened to his father hum songs from penny songbooks like *Robin Hood's Garland*, and he both read and had told to him chap-book tales like *Tom Hickathrift* or jokes adapted from *Joe Miller's Jestbook*. If reading the classical lines of James Thomson's *Seasons* (1726–30) launched Clare's attempts at formal **poetry [29]**, equally influential were the obscure dream verses of John Pomfret's *Love Triumphant Over Reason* (1746), as well as several sonnets by Charlotte *Smith reprinted in the local Stamford newspaper. From vendors and pedlars at fairs in Deeping Market and Stamford he assembled the same *mélange* of second-hand works on topics such as gardening, mensuration, *astrology, herbals, perspective drawing, and domestic medicine that was available to urban artisan bricoleurs like Pierce Egan. While working in Soho, Egan imbibed an eclectic mix of fiction from Augustan worthies like Sterne, Fielding, and Smollett, alongside a plethora of underworld topographies, chap-book *romances, gallows speeches, and *Newgate Calendar* biographies [see *Newgate literature].

John Clare's zest for song, *satire, fiddle-playing, and dancing was nourished at a local gypsy camp and at convivial gatherings held in a 'ruinous thatched cottage' called Bachelor's Hall owned by his neighbours, the Billings brothers, who were part-time poachers with a cupboard full of sixpenny ghost stories. Egan's famous repertoire of stories, jokes, and burlesques was performed mainly at comparable free-and-easies held by the Daffy Club, a diverse group of drinkers and sportsmen who met at the Castle Tavern in Holborn, presided over by former world champion prizefighter Jem Belcher. Egan's influential history of pugilism, *Boxiana* (1812), and bestselling fictional social topography, *Life in London* (1821), inaugurated new serialized forms of cheap, mass-circulating literature, but these same texts were also peppered with cant and crambo (doggerel) whose origin was as much oral as literary. The richness and vitality of his language may also have owed something to his Irish cultural origins, shared by so many of the doyens of London popular journalism. Writing for proto-tabloid newspapers like *Bell's Weekly* in the early 1820s, Egan pioneered new modes of sporting, documentary, and

32. *Jem Belcher*, pen and water-colour by Thomas Rowlandson, *c.*1805–10, portrays the champion boxer who knew Pierce Egan and inspired his history of pugilism, *Boxiana* (1812). Prizefighters such as Belcher, and later Jack Randall, were revered by the 'Fancy', a wide social range of male gamblers, drinkers, and sports fanciers.

crime reporting which looked forward to the work of the young Charles *Dickens. William *Hazlitt's 'The Fight' and Thomas *De Quincey's 'On Murder Viewed as an Art Form', now regarded as classic examples of Romantic *essay-writing, were actually built on popular foundations laid by this now forgotten writer.

Egan's fiction could also provide cultural markers for a 'rhyming peasant' like Clare when he made four separate visits to the dislocating modern vortex of London between 1820 and 1824. Clare wanted to negotiate with bookseller-publishers, to promote his achievements as a peasant poet, and simply to experience the exhilaration of metropolitan intellectual life. Although he sensed his very identity shaken as the coach first rumbled past the strange new urban landscape, he felt partially prepared for negotiating the city's perils and pleasures through his prior familiarity with a sixpenny chap-book guide to London low-life. Egan's *Life in London* grew out of this same centuries-old genre of rogue guides and warnings, but he skilfully adapted it to encompass the brilliant engraving talents of Robert and George *Cruikshank and the bustling commercial spirit of the 1820s [see *prints, 22]. It is not known whether, on reaching the metropolis, Clare read one of the numerous cheap editions of *Life in London*, or encountered the torrent of merchandise, ranging from beer-mugs to firescreens, that displayed its leading characters, or, still more likely, attended one of the numerous adaptations of Egan's work being performed at the *theatre [24] (W. T. Moncrieff's version of it staged at the Adelphi Theatre ran continuously for more than 300 nights). However, there can be little doubt that Clare modelled his own metropolitan tourist programmes on the 'sprees and larks' of Egan's fictional heroes named Corinthian (a frequenter of a brothel) Tom, Jerry Hawthorn, and Bob Logic. When Clare first read *Don Juan* in September 1824, he recorded in his journal that Byron's 'Hero seems a fit partner for Tom and Jerry fond of getting into scrapes and always finding means to get out agen for ever in the company of ladys who seem to watch at night for oppertunitys for every thing but saying their prayers'. And like Egans's 'sporting coves', Clare and several friends went on pub-crawls; they admired the elegant Cyprian (harlot) 'ladies of the town' at Covent Garden; they took pride in joining the 'Fancy', the committed followers of the ring who avidly watched plebeian prizefighters like 'Sailor Boy Jones' fight at the Fives Court; they were dazzled by the fairy-tale splendour of the Vauxhall *pleasure gardens; they placed bets at Tattersalls; they tried to visit the Beggar's Bush, a famous rogues' tavern and vaudeville at Holborn; and they exercised sensibility by giving money to a poignant African beggar, who may even have been the actual Billy Waters, celebrated 'King of the Beggars', whom Egan had inserted in his mixed fictive and documentary account.

As a woman in humble circumstances, Southcott typically had far less exposure to literature than male counterparts like Clare and Egan—her early reading was virtually confined to the Bible and an aunt's hymn-book. Yet her famous prophecies were also deeply influenced by half a dozen chap-book romances which she later transformed into Christian allegories, as well as by ubiquitous popular almanacs in the vein of *Moore's* and, more surprisingly, by detailed daily news stories which disciples read out to her. Underpinning all these was a wealth of oral lore and legend about witches, remedies, astrology, dreams, visions, portents, riddles, signs, and signatures which she had imbibed while growing up in the small Devon village of Gittisham. Overall this informal education gave her access to a potent mix of old and new ideas. Even so, Southcott might well have remained merely a local wise woman in the mould of Elspeth 'Lucky' Buchan (c.1738–91) in Scotland had she not chosen to turn her prophecies into print. Beginning with a prophetic anthology, *The Strange Effects of Faith*, published by an Exeter bookseller in 1801, she went on in the next fourteen years to produce sixty-four further prophetic books and pamphlets, as well as scores of posters and newspaper columns. These, in conjunction with several provincial preaching tours, carried her words to tens of thousands of followers ranged over the West Country, the Midlands, and the industrial North.

This blend of traditional and modern belief was as evident in the content as in the form of many popular cultural products of the day. Clare cited numbers of his Helpstone friends, including a relatively well-educated farmer's son, John Turnill, who believed in the vivid real-ity of supernatural forces such as ghosts, spirits, and witches. Clare himself was always unper-suaded by the attempts of *Enlightenment [32] philosophers to explain away as natural phenomena the flickering lights of 'will-o'-the-wisps' and similar mysterious spirits; in this respect he echoed the anti-Newtonianism of his urban counterpart William *Blake. While walking Blake's 'charter'd streets' in the 1820s, Clare could not even bring himself to go down Chancery Lane at night for fear of 'thin death like shadows and goblings with sorcer eyes'. He recalled, too, how his father, Parker Clare, had been dazzled by the patter of an itinerant 'medical prophet' who attracted crowds of villagers using both scientific legerdemain and claims to supernatural powers based on being the seventh son of a seventh son. The shrewd villagers, however, decided the doctor was a *quack when, unlike the prophets of old, he charged payment prior to healing. Clare discerned the same blend of modern scientific theory and traditional fairground showmanship in the performances of the famous London *phrenologist Deville. Clare's own magpie mind conjoined the countryman's minute and ani-mistic knowledge of local flora and fauna with complex theories of botanical classification derived from works like John Ray's *Historia Planetarum* (1686–1704) and John Parkinson's *Theatrum Botanicum* (1640). Scientific and folk cosmologies could thus find themselves in unlikely couplings. Belief in the possibility of glimpsing the future was one of the attractions of the contemporary vogue of *animal magnetism. New wonders of science claiming to be able to galvanize a body into life with *electricity, or magnetize away blockages in the invisible and incorporeal ether, were conveyed throughout the provinces during the early nineteenth cen-tury by itinerant lecturers of humble origin. In the process they unleashed new possibilities of occult speculation on the part of a 'jack of all trades' intellectual like Clare.

True, Egan's works showed signs of the more secularizing influences of the city. Neverthe-less his criminal biographies of the 1820s are replete with ghastly portents and mysterious supernatural intimations. He also opens *Life in London* with the traditional folk invocation to the ghosts and shades of past writers. At one point, too, he has Corinthian Kate and her friend, Sue, hurry to a fortune-teller in order to discover their prospective successes or failures in love. Concern with identifying a future husband was one of the most common features of both fortune-telling and chap-book literature. The prominence of the topic of marriage no doubt reflects the importance of courtship in the lives of the readers, and of marriage as the one sure means to economic survival for many. The average age of marriage for the majority of the lower orders in most of Britain (excluding Ireland) was quite late, around the mid-20s, and the extensive period during which courtship loomed large was reason enough for young women to want to read or consult fortune-tellers about the subject of marriage, and to be reassured that they could have recourse to supernatural help in seeing, or even finding, their future partner.

Corinthian Kate and Joanna Southcott might seem to have had little in common. However, the Devonshire prophetess was also much preoccupied with love: she exercised a holy courtship with Christ, refracted her often erotic language through Scripture, and claimed her false pregnancy of 1814 to have been a consequence of spiritual impregnation. Significantly, she also attracted a majority of women followers, often domestic servants. Perhaps such unprotected and isolated women, many of whom were also single, found solace in Joanna's reassuring predictions, supportive community, and talismanic printed seals. Critics compared the last to the relic and icon worship of medieval piety cults. Southcott herself had no doubt that it was possible to glimpse the future through astrological influences, bewitchings, dream portents, and gypsy prognostications, but she warned her followers that most such powers were satanic and needed to be combated by her own spiritual revelations. As a millenarian prophetess she could turn her poverty and lack of education to unique advantage; she presented herself as an appropriately innocent and unencumbered medium for the automatic workings of the Holy Spirit. At the same time she was sophisticated enough to attract some highly educated disciples, to assemble a formidable national organization and publicity machine, to write tracts combating the *Deism of Thomas *Paine, to persuade some reputable doctors that she had achieved a virginal pregnancy, and to undertake large-scale financial transactions with London's most devious moneylender, Jonathan 'Jew' *King.

King, who initially presented himself as a sympathetic patron of the Southcottians only to sue them subsequently for failing to pay his exorbitant interest demands, typifies another troubling dimension of cultural interaction which plebeians like Southcott, Clare, and Egan had to endure if they were to succeed in a national arena. The support of patrons from the superior classes, though essential, was often obtained at a heavy cost. In a counter-revolutionary climate, this generally included having to exercise personal deference and to espouse politically conservative sentiments. True, there is reason to believe that Southcott, Clare, and Egan were all in their own ways natural conservatives, inclined, like so many of Britain's labouring and middling sort, to give support to the *monarchy, aristocracy, and the 1688 constitution. Clare claimed to have recoiled from radicalism after reading a pamphlet outlining Robespierre's bloody crimes, and Egan liked to extol the prizefighter as the embodiment of British (and Irish) patriotic virtue and toughness in contrast to the effeminate, freethinking continental. Clare seems genuinely to have admired the bluff, aristocratic paternalism of his patron Lord Radstock, a flesh-and-blood counterpart of Egan's rural sportsman Jerry Hawthorn. Like Egan, Clare seems also to have discovered a satisfying sense of urban pastoral in the sporting camaraderie of the 'Fancy' and the boisterous drinking rituals of alehouse free-and-easies. Here, in an atmosphere of mutual respect and intimacy, if not of equality, Corinthians like Jerry Hawthorn and scholars like Bob Logic could rub shoulders with dustmen like Nasty Bob and women of colour like African Sal. At one time Clare was even moved to wish himself a lord so that he might act as a patron to prizefighters. Yet Clare later found that this particular version of pastoral was emphatically not sanctioned by most of the patrons who wished to market him as an exemplary peasant poet and patriotic cottager. Ambitious bookseller-publishers like Edward Drury of Stamford and John Taylor (1781–1864) of London decried his 'preposterous ambitions', rough idiomatic writing, bawdy and drunken proclivities, and his dangerously radical views on the subjects of enclosure and agricultural 'improvement' [see *land, 16]. Other patrons like Mrs Emmerson and Lord Milton plied him with morally improving propaganda or sought to curtail his independence in exchange for subsidized accommodation.

By comparison, Joanna Southcott experienced relatively slight pressures from patrons, in part because her moral values were largely compatible with the strenuous Evangelicalism of prominent women campaigners like Hannah *More. Middle-class widow Jane Townley and her assistant Ann Underword placed their independent wealth and learning entirely at Southcott's disposal, and they affectionately shared a Cotswolds cottage with her. Yet Southcott was made acutely aware through newspapers of the day of the profound ruling-class suspicion of millenarian prophets and enthusiasts, widely viewed as potential assassins or auxiliaries of revolution. Consciously or otherwise, she strained every fibre to show that her prophecies and followers were quietistic and patriotic; it was not for nothing that she excoriated Napoleon as the latter-day Antichrist and heaped praise on the British monarchy.

Yet even Joanna, the victim of history's 'enormous condescension' from her own day to this, could not help but display a strain of feisty populism that seems to have informed much popular culture in our period. Though initially deferential to the leaders of both *Methodism and *Anglicanism, she began issuing pungently anticlerical prophecies during the *Regency years. She lashed the complacency, snobbery, and worldliness of the male clergy who so frequently attacked or mocked her mission. Though she espoused a democratic universalism akin to the early John *Wesley, she was also adamant that it was the poor as God's chosen people who stood closest to her heart. Her 'spirit' told her that she was born poor in order to humble the pride of the mighty. Clare and Egan similarly extolled the superior virtues of the common people. Egan's *Life of London* contrasted the artificiality of the 'Swell's' gambling club,

33. Entitled *Lowest 'Life in London'*, this illustration to Egan's *Life in London* (1821) by George and Robert Cruikshank sports Tom, Jerry, and Bob Logic at the East End tavern, All-Max, in implied contrast to the snobbish social life at Almack's club in the West End.

Almack's, with the exotic vitality and exuberance of the rogue's tavern, All-Max. Above all, he felt, 'it is the lower orders of Society who really enjoy themselves'. Upper-class *dandies who affected superiority and disdain for the lower orders found themselves on the receiving end of Bob Logic's knuckles. Such belligerent male populism anticipated both the sensationalist Victorian journalism of G. W. M. Reynolds (1814–79) and later Tory alliances between working-class roughs, publicans, and sporting aristocrats.

Though Clare longed while living in Helpstone to join the company of metropolitan literary lions like Hazlitt, *Lamb, and *Coleridge, he found the actual experience profoundly disillusioning. During his London visits of the 1820s he quickly became aware that most middle-class intellectuals viewed him as a vulgar curiosity, part of a dangerously ephemeral fashion inaugurated by the peasant poet Robert Bloomfield (1766–1823). Since boyhood, when his mother had bought him a fairground handkerchief carrying the tragic image and verses of *Chatterton, he had been sorely conscious of the fate of the failed poet. Of all the literary figures he encountered in London, Clare really warmed only to unpretentious John Hamilton Reynolds (1796–1832) whose appetite for drink, jest, and the 'Fancy' chimed with plebeian tastes. Clare also sensed that his own beloved rural culture was fast becoming a commercial item. The language, customary calendar, recreational rituals, and modes of work of his early life were being marketed as objects of nostalgic consumption. Influential antiquarian works like *Brand's *Popular Antiquities* (1777) and *Strutt's *Sports and Pastimes of the People of England* (1801) triggered a flourishing élite interest in popular festivities, folk legends, and ritual— British counterparts of the pioneering work on German folklore and national character conducted in the 1770s and 1780s by Johann Gottfried Herder (1744–1803). An article by Clare in William Hone's *Everyday Book* of 1826, aimed at a more popular market, expressed grave fears that the poet's song might soon be the only genuine refuge of traditional rural folkways.

In 1837 Clare was eventually admitted into Matthew Allen's private *madhouse at High Beach, Epping. Here he began mimicking the identities of notable contemporary figures, all of whom he imagined as rebels against the sorts of social deference that had contributed to his own neurosis and eventual *madness. One such figure was Robert *Burns, the only peasant poet of the era who, thanks to the long-established tradition of Scottish folk scholarship, had managed to become a literary celebrity without relinquishing his political independence or raffish ways. One imagines that Clare longed similarly to be able to get away with writing a pungent, anti-establishment satire like Burns's 'Holy Willy'. Another favourite hero and Clare persona was the plebeian prizefighter Jack Randall, whose brawn had defied all comers and whose pugilistic skills had been eagerly sought after by aristocrats like Lord *Byron. The latter Clare admired most of all: he saw Byron as an exile, outsider, and bold sexual libertine who had managed to produce bestselling poetry which spoke to all classes but deferred to no one. In a moving account of his third visit to London in 1824, Clare described the experience of standing in a crowd of labouring folk as they watched Byron's funeral cortège. While the rich sniggered and preened themselves, the common people stood in profound and reverent silence. Clare speculated that it was Byron's 'liberal principles in religion and politics' that had attracted such popular respect: labouring folk had no time for the 'mildewing censure' of the 'Reverend and Moral' who had hounded this aristocratic friend of the people. For a brief moment Clare's fractured identity was healed. He felt proud of and in harmony with the multi-stranded popular culture that had shaped him:

for the common people of a country are the best feelings of a prophesy of futurity—they are below or rather [above] the prejudices and flatterys the fancys and dislikes of fashion—they are the feelings of natures sympathies unadulterated with pretentions of art and pride they are the veins and arterys that feed and quiken the heart of living fame the breathings of eternity and the soul of time.

Burke, P., *Popular Culture in Early Modern Europe*, London, 1978, rev. edn. 1994; Cunningham, H., *Leisure in the Industrial Revolution, c.1780–1880*, London, 1980; Harris, T., ed., *Popular Culture in England, c.1500–1850*, Basingstoke, 1995; Hopkins, J. K., *A Woman to Deliver Her People: Joanna Southcott and English Millenarianism in an Era of Revolution*, Austin, 1982; Malcolmson, R. W., *Popular Recreations in English Society 1700–1850*, Cambridge, 1973; Perkins, M., *Visions of the Future: Almanacs, Time, and Cultural Change, 1775–1870*, Oxford, 1997; Reid, J. C., *Bucks and Bruisers: Pierce Egan and Regency* *England*, London, 1971; Robinson, E., ed., *John Clare's Autobiographical Writings*, Oxford, 1986; Shiach, M., *Discourse on Popular Culture: Class, Gender and History in Cultural Analysis, 1730 to the Present*, Cambridge, 1989; Storch, R. D., ed., *Popular Culture and Custom in Nineteenth-Century England*, London, 1982; Summerfield, Geoffrey, ed., *John Clare: Selected Poetry*, Harmondsworth, 1990; Thompson, E. P., 'Time, Work-Discipline and Industrial Capitalism', *Past and Present*, 38 (1967), 56–97.

24 · THEATRE   GILLIAN RUSSELL

Until comparatively recently, the predominance of Romantic literary studies in accounts of the culture of this period meant the marginalization of theatre and drama. Even theatre historians felt compelled to apologize for the fact that there was no Romantic equivalent of *Shakespeare, no drama of enduring literary merit to stand with the poetic achievements of *Wordsworth and *Coleridge. This is in spite of the fact that the age was preoccupied to the point of obsession with the theatre as an institution and with the theatricality of social, political, and personal behaviour. The discourse, practices, and images of the theatre pervaded all aspects of the culture. Politics, encompassing the ritual of protest and mass demonstration, the hurly-burly of the *election, parliamentary performers such as Charles James *Fox, and the textual strategies of ultra-radicals such as Daniel Isaac Eaton and Thomas *Spence as well as their arch-opponent, Edmund *Burke, was shaped by theatrical models. The macabre theatre of the public execution, and the pomp of the assize procession, indicate the importance of performance and display to the *law [8]: even warfare, in the rituals of military training, discipline, and the conduct of battle, as well as the costume-like uniforms of both the general and the sub-altern, was profoundly theatrical [see *war, 2]. Other art forms, such as *painting [27] and the *novel [31], intersected in significant ways with the theatrical. This is apparent in the momentous drama of *history painting, displayed in exhibitions which were themselves sites of communal performance, in the association between gendered subjectivity and performance in the work of novelists such as Frances *Burney and Jane *Austen, and, indeed, in the *conduct book tradition which their fiction both reflects and critiques. At the centre of this was a vital theatrical culture, dominated by London but extending throughout the kingdom and *empire [5]. This essay will explore various aspects of this culture, such as the composition of audiences, the role of theatre in provincial society, and the range of dramatic experimentation in the period. However, in order to appreciate fully the significance of theatre in late Georgian Britain, it is first necessary to understand how and why it was controlled.

Government regulation of the stage, in force until 1968, was a reflection of the dubious standing of theatre in public culture. Traditionally associated with other potentially disorderly and 'immoral' forms of recreation such as *gambling and prostitution, the theatre was a frequent target of criticism from both the pulpit and the magistrate's bench. Its political status made it doubly dangerous: for most of the eighteenth century the major London theatres of Covent Garden and Drury Lane were regarded as alternative representative assemblies, the other national 'houses' in which the polity could define its image. This role was reinforced by royal sanction of these theatres, and by their construction in ways which enhanced their significance as expressions of the body politic. With so much invested in the theatre as a political forum, it is not surprising that government, at both a local and national level, should keep a close eye on its proceedings.

Two earlier acts of regulation exerted a powerful influence on the theatre of our period— Charles II's granting in 1662 of exclusive rights or patents to perform drama to the courtiers Davenant and Killigrew, and the Stage Licensing Act of 1737. The patents subsequently became the property of successive owners of Covent Garden and Drury Lane playhouses, known as the major or patent theatres, who used them to justify a duopoly over spoken drama in the metropolis. Any challenge to the patent theatres was interpreted by their owners as a threat to the security of property rights in general and as an attack on the authority of the *monarch. The 1737 Licensing Act reinforced the power of Covent Garden and Drury Lane by restricting theatrical entertainment to Westminster and the royal residences; it also required the texts of plays to be submitted to the Office of the Lord Chamberlain for censorship prior to performance. However, the terms of the Act were complicated in 1752 when, in an attempt to curb 'disorderly houses' such as Sadler's Wells, a further measure of regulation was introduced. This empowered the Lord Chamberlain to license places of public entertainment other than theatres within Westminster and the city of London. A similar authority was granted to magistrates in respect of the area outside Westminster and the city within a twenty-miles radius. The full implications of this latter measure only became clear later in the century, when it was used to license playhouses in the new centres of population to the east of the city and south of the Thames. These theatres, known as the minors, were prohibited by the Licensing Act from performing the 'legitimate' drama—tragedies, comedies, interludes, operas, plays, or farces—but they evaded the law by devising protean entertainments such as the burletta, a combination of song and recitative, which became more dramatic in content until there was little to distinguish it from the legitimate forms. The ensuing contest between the patent theatres and the minors for rights to the spoken drama had significant ramifications: it indicated the declining political and cultural authority of the fashionable 'town', identified with Westminster and the West End of the city, and the rise of the more socially and politically heterogeneous metropolis. It also reflected the increasing tensions between the theatre's traditional ideological role as a representative assembly, a mirror of society, and the demands of the marketplace. Both sides in the conflict between the patent theatres and the minors justified their essentially commercial motives in terms of their duty to represent the 'public', the definition of which became a central issue in theatre politics. What kind of public could the theatre audience be said to represent? What, if any, acknowledgement was it owed by those who profited from it?

The regulation of theatre in the provinces had similar far-reaching effects. The Licensing Act was administered haphazardly outside London, and in practice dramatic activity came under the control of individual magistrates and notables. In the course of the century a number of prominent towns and cities sought to establish theatrical entertainment on a more secure footing by appealing to the monarch for permission to perform on the same basis as the patent theatres in London. In 1788 an attempt was made to systematize the regulation of the provincial theatre by giving magistrates the power to license performances, provided they did not take place within twenty miles of London, Westminster, and Edinburgh, or within eight miles of an already licensed theatre. The assurance of legal protection encouraged provincial entrepreneurs to construct permanent playhouses, and the ensuing boom in theatre-building was given further stimulus by the French wars of 1793–1815. Soldiers and sailors were inveterate playgoers, and throughout the south and east of England theatres sprang up to meet the demands of the leisure economy of wartime. In a survey made in 1803–4, the theatre manager

Delivering Play Bills in the Country.

My first Appearance, 'pon my honour,
Sir, in Hamlet the Great Prince of Denmark.

34. Detail from Richard Newton's *Progress of a Player* (1793), an actor's sequence of attempts to make good by moving from the country to the city. Here he woos his potential audience.

James Winston (1773–1843) noted the existence of 280 playhouses in places such as Abergavenny in Wales and Worksop in Derbyshire. These theatres ranged in quality from barns and wooden constructions that alternately served as stables or carpenter's shops to the grand theatres royal of Edinburgh, Bristol, Bath, and Norwich. Beyond this network of permanent theatres were the temporary stages of the strolling players who roamed the country in search of audiences. Even in comparatively isolated rural areas it was possible to see a play: in 1798, for example, Wordsworth's boyhood home of Hawkshead was visited by an itinerant company of actors who performed there with what the *Monthly Mirror* described as 'considerable success'. And further afield, satellites of the metropolis such as Kingston, Calcutta, Cape Town, and even the convict outpost of Sydney had their own theatres, and in some cases established companies of professional actors. Some of the latter were migrants, seeking their fortune in the colonies; others were itinerants who would return to Britain. They were augmented by a constant supply of enthusiastic amateurs—military officers mostly and, in some cases, their wives (though the involvement of the latter was usually confined to amateur productions). These imperial stages attempted to recreate the theatrical world with which the actors were familiar by means of the performance of plays that could be seen in Britain, the construction of buildings that even in the most primitive form could still be labelled a 'theatre royal', and the

reliance on conventions such as the prologue and epilogue and the playbill. Such performances affirmed British imperialism as a global strolling theatre, transportable and adaptable to
every contingency.

   Within Britain itself, the provincial theatre also had an important politico-cultural role. It
functioned as a place of assembly in which the collective experience of a town or city could be
registered. The acquisition of a royal patent for a playhouse was regarded as a considerable
coup, marking a community's coming of age. As those petitioning for a theatre royal in Edinburgh claimed in 1768: 'The state of arts and literature in any kingdom, and the taste of the
people, are best known by the amusements they follow: those of the theatre are the most rational in which the human mind can delight.' The construction of a playhouse was often associated with the development of other cultural activities such as *circulating libraries,
bookshops, *coffeehouses, and assembly rooms which not only proclaimed the civility of a
town but also stimulated the local economy. Playgoing was an integral part of cultural and political rituals such as elections, the assizes, and military mobilization, while the theatre was also
an important arena for the display of *philanthropy. Groups such as the *freemasons, the
*volunteers, and prominent women of the gentry class sponsored charity performances which
enhanced their own worth to society as well as benefiting the poor. During wartime the provincial theatre came into its own in a threefold way: as a site of conviviality and assembly for the
regular and auxiliary forces; as a forum in which British victories could be celebrated in the
form of spectacular re-enactments; and as a place in which the political issues of the war were
articulated and sometimes violently contested. In the 1790s and early 1800s there were numerous disputes in country theatres over the singing of 'God Save the King', often inspired by
military and naval officers who demanded the performance of the anthem as a test of the loyalty
of the audience. Such behaviour was a sign that, as in London, the identity of the provincial
theatre's true 'public' was in question. Who had a 'right' to attend the playhouse? What kind
of political or civic 'rights' did attendance confer?

   As far as the freemasons, the volunteers, and genteel women were concerned, their 'rights'
to the theatre were self-evident. For them, the playhouse was a powerful forum through which
they could express their entitlement to a say in local decisionmaking; likewise for the burghers
of Edinburgh the theatre functioned as a symbol of pride, not only in the city but also in Scottish identity as a whole. The politicization of the theatre in these terms, its appropriation in
the name of the middling orders, was encouraged by the leisure entrepreneurs who built the
theatres royal and who themselves belonged to this social grouping. However, as in London,
the politics of the provincial theatre was also influenced by the idea that the institution should
be representative of the community as a whole. This idea was most commonly expressed in the
definition of the audience in terms of 'box, pit, and gallery', a reference to the socially encoded
divisions within the auditorium. The boxes were the preserve of the upper classes and gentry,
the pit was the realm of the middling and professional orders, while the gallery belonged to the
artisans, the servant class, soldiers, and sailors. These areas of the auditorium were priced
accordingly. At the beginning of our period, seats in the boxes at Covent Garden and Drury
Lane were the most expensive at 5 shillings, the pit cost 3, while a gallery ticket could be bought
for between 2 shillings for the first gallery and 1 shilling for the upper. The affordability of the
gallery was enhanced by the custom of half-price which admitted patrons for sixpence after the
end of the third act of the principal item of the bill. This meant that playgoing could in fact be
less expensive than a evening spent in a *tavern, where a pint of ale cost threepence. Of equal
if not more importance than the monetary value of a half-price gallery ticket was its symbolic
value—the fact that it acknowledged the right of the servant or the artisan to a place within the
local or national theatre. Attempts by theatre managers to abolish the custom were stoutly
resisted by gallery audiences. In 1792 Covent Garden was the site of a serious disturbance
when gallery-goers discovered that they were no longer entitled to the privilege of half-price. In

35. The boxes and pit of Drury Lane Theatre, as adapted by the architect Henry Holland in 1794.

this case the managers capitulated, but the underlying tensions in both theatrical and 'real' politics were not so easily resolved. They broke out again in what were the most prolonged and violent of the theatre riots of this period—the Old Price disturbances of 1809.

The causes of these riots, which dominated Covent Garden and the national press for sixty-six nights, were the raising of the prices of admission after the reconstruction of the theatre following the fire of 1808, the inclusion of private boxes for hire by wealthy patrons (widely interpreted as places for the entertaining of prostitutes), and the fees paid to the Italian singer Angelica *Catalani. At a deeper level, however, the contest was also a struggle for the meaning of theatre in late Georgian politics and culture. By asserting his proprietorial rights the manager of Covent Garden, John Philip *Kemble had threatened the idea of theatre as a representative assembly. His opponents interpreted the raising of prices as suggesting that admission was a matter of capacity to pay rather than a recognition of a right to entertainment at a price one could afford. Implicitly this right was also a political right to a place within the national theatre of Britain, expressed by the slogan-like status of the phrase 'box, pit, and gallery'. The riots only served to confirm that the culture's confidence in this formulation was in crisis: the experience of the 1790s and the French wars had caused 'box, pit, and gallery' to split apart.

A sign of this crisis was the phenomenon of *private theatricals. Aristocratic women such as the Margravine of Anspach (1750–1828) and Albinia Hobart (1738–1816), later the Countess of Buckinghamshire, staged their own performances before carefully selected audiences of their peers. These widely reported occasions signalled that the fashionable world no longer felt the need to associate with the lower orders in the public theatres, a move that was greeted with dismay by managers and theatre owners, who sought to woo back this influential section of the audience by offering them the exclusivity of separate entrances and private boxes. Such measures were to no avail, however, as the *bon ton* continued to desert the increasingly unfashionable Covent Garden and Drury Lane. A similar development is observable in the provinces: by 1835 the *Colchester Gazette* could remark that 'few respectable people are ever found within the walls of country theatres. When any are there they avoid recognition—a fair criterion by which to estimate how much additional respectability they obtain within the walls of the playhouse.' By lamenting the fact that people of gentility no longer attended the theatre, such comments implicitly drew attention to those who did—the artisans and servants of the gallery who increasingly made up the bulk of audiences. Claims that the stage was in decline and that the beauties of Shakespeare were threatened by inferior forms of entertainment such as *pantomime were also implying that the tastes of the gallery now dominated. The extent and profundity of the anxiety at this development cannot be easily appreciated by twentieth-century observers. Why, for example, was *Byron drafted to 'save' Drury Lane in 1812? Why did Edward Bulwer, later *Bulwer-Lytton, set up a parliamentary committee to investigate the decline in dramatic standards at the height of the *Reform Bill crisis in 1832? Why was the theatre felt to be so important? The answer is to be found in the power of 'box, pit, and gallery' as an emblem of cultural and political order which late Georgian society would not easily relinquish.

The absence from the canon of English literature of plays from this period, with the exception of some of the productions of R. B. *Sheridan, can be traced back to the response of Romantic writers and critics to this prevailing sense of cultural crisis. Debating the extent to which the drama of this period qualifies as 'great' literature ignores the complexity of the theatre at this period, the fact that the patent theatres were multimedia enterprises employing visual artists, scene designers, mechanics, musicians, and dancers, as well as actors and dramatists. To focus on the playwright as the sole source of the play ignores the achievements of innovators such as Philippe Jacques de *Loutherbourg, whose work in stage design and lighting influenced a range of dramatic forms from pantomime to high tragedy, William Capon (1757–1827), whose medieval castles, banqueting-halls and bridges established the architectonics of *Gothic drama, and the *Dibdin family, whose songs and entertainments defined Britishness during the French wars and after. *Music [26] was an integral element of all forms of theatre in this period, many of the leading singers, including Braham, Incledon, *Billington, and *Crouch, having notable stage careers.

The multimedia experience of an evening at the patent theatres began normally with a main-piece drama followed by a musical interlude and an afterpiece—a farce, pantomime, pageant, or *ballet. The evening's show, which might last for up to seven hours, thus catered for a wide variety of tastes. The most prestigious item on the bill—the main-piece drama—was the preserve of Shakespeare and the Restoration and early-eighteenth-century playwrights Rowe, Otway, Southerne, Dryden, Congreve, Farquhar, and Addison, of works of mid-century figures such as Murphy, Goldsmith, and Colman the elder, and of contemporaries such as *Inchbald, *Cumberland, *Holcroft, Sheridan, and *Colman the younger. The most frequently performed plays by Shakespeare included *Macbeth, Hamlet, Henry V, King John,* and

Richard III, but his work did not meet with universal acceptance by managers and censors. *King Lear* was not performed for a period due to George III's illness, while *Julius Caesar* and *Coriolanus* were often avoided because Shakespeare's depiction of tensions between the governing classes and plebeians struck too close to home. Other notable stalwarts of the repertory were the pathetic tragedies *Venice Preserv'd*, by Thomas Otway, and Nicholas Rowe's *Jane Shore* and *The Fair Penitent*. All three plays offered meaty roles for actresses, but their themes, focusing on the fateful collision of private desires and public virtues, crossed the gender divide in appealing to both male and female adherents of the cult of *sensibility [11]. *Venice Preserv'd*, which involves a conspiracy against a corrupt ruling order, was interpreted anew by different audiences in changing political circumstances. It was withdrawn from the stage in 1795 because it was felt to be too politically sensitive, but in 1832 it was still being interpreted by audiences in the context of the Reform Bill crisis. The performance history of *Venice Preserv'd* illustrates the problem faced by the censors in monitoring the political atmosphere of the theatres. The 1737 Licensing Act obliged managers to submit new plays for censorship by the Examiner of Plays. However, the government could not legislate for the tendency of audiences to take apparently innocuous passages from old plays and apply them to topical contexts. Thus, in 1795, when the conspirator in *Venice Preserv'd* declared 'Curs'd be your Senate, curs'd your constitution', he was enthusiastically applauded by a section of the audience, including John *Thelwall, who had gone to see the play with the intention of transforming his attendance into a political demonstration. The Examiner of Plays ensured that censorship of new plays was thorough, excising any comment that could be interpreted out of context, or preventing the performance of a play altogether. But this does not mean that the drama of the period was apolitical. Playwrights went elsewhere to explore political concerns, in particular to historical drama, which allowed the displacement of contemporary issues to different eras and contexts. The England of the 1790s, 1800s, and 1820s found itself mirrored in the Englands of plays such as *The Surrender of Calais* by George Colman the younger, *England Preserved* by George Watson, William *Godwin's *Faulkener*, and Sheridan Knowles's *Virginius*. Like the history play, Gothic drama was also amenable to political interpretation: its representation of cliffside castles, disintegrating bridges, dungeons, and prisons, of divided families and marauding banditti, penetrated the extremities of a political and social order under stress. Moreover, the themes of incarceration and surveillance in Gothic plays such as *Lewis's *The Castle Spectre* and *Maturin's *Bertram* found added resonance in a theatre which was itself a site of surveillance by the monarch. This is not to imply that the genres of the Gothic or the history play were subversive: while indicting a corrupt aristocracy, many of these plays suggest a reformation of that order from within through the plot device of the disinherited son or brother who is restored to his rightful place, often after living in disguise and learning from the virtues of a poor family. Such plays suggested that those in power could absorb the impact of change by accommodating rather than resisting it. A similar message was conveyed by the sentimental comedies of Holcroft, Inchbald, O'Keeffe (1747–1833), Tobin (1770–1804), and Colman the younger which, in proclaiming the virtues of the farmer, the servant, the soldier, the maidservant, the Irishman, suggest that the unity of the nation can only be maintained by admitting other ranks, ethnicities, and voices.

The identification of the theatre with British values did not render it immune to foreign influences: the performers, technicians, and musicians who proclaimed that Britons ruled the waves represented the triumph of multiculturalism, not chauvinism. As it had been throughout the century, the London theatre continued to be dominated by the Irish—the actresses Dorothy *Jordan and Elizabeth *Farren, the child prodigy 'Master' William *Betty, the playwrights John O'Keeffe and Charles Macklin (?1699–1797), the musician and composer Michael *Kelly, and Sheridan himself all had Irish backgrounds. The stage offered opportunities for groups that were stigmatized for reasons of religion or gender—Catholics such as John

Philip Kemble and Elizabeth Inchbald, and women in general. Indeed, the theatre represented one of the few career paths for women, who used it as a springboard for social elevation—Elizabeth Farren becoming the Countess of Derby—or as a space for formidable artistic expression. According to one spellbound viewer of Sarah *Siddons, 'none knew the troubled grandeur of guilt till they saw her in *Lady Macbeth* . . . Shakspeare's self had learned something then from a sight of Siddons.'

The British theatre was also ready to look to foreigners such as de Loutherbourg for inspiration and innovation. Significant influences included the German dramatists Schiller and Kotzebue and the Frenchmen Beaumarchais and de Pixérécourt. The latter's *Coelina*, translated by Holcroft as *A Tale of Mystery* in 1802, was the first *melodrama to be staged in Britain. Plays such as Douglas Jerrold's (1803–57) nautical melodrama *Black Ey'd Susan* and John Walker's (*fl.* 1825–34) *The Factory Lad* brought hitherto marginalized figures—the sailor, the factory worker, and the artisan—to centre stage, as agents in their own destiny; in doing so, melodrama became identified with the shift in the locus of theatrical activity from the West End to the minor theatres south of the Thames. Equally if not more important was the pantomime, another foreign genre which had been appropriated earlier in the eighteenth century. By our period it had become thoroughly naturalized under the influence of the comic genius Joseph *Grimaldi. Pantomime combined knockabout comedy with sophisticated spectacle, topical satire with the archetypal struggle between youth and age, the oppressed and the oppressor.

Playgoers of the period were often avid play-readers. Books of the play could be bought at the theatre and read between the acts. Sheridan's eagerly awaited *Pizarro* sold a phenomenal 27,000 copies within a few weeks of the play's first performance in 1799. Managers would occasionally buy *copyright from a dramatist and prevent publication of a play in order to maintain audience interest; conversely, provincial managers colluded with publishers to pirate an edition of the latest London success in the hope of building audiences. Playwrights often used publication as a form of protest against changes made in the theatre or by the censor. In general the market for the playbook was huge, rivalling that for prose fiction: it ranged from the gentleman connoisseur such as Edmund *Malone competing at an auction for a Shakespeare folio to the lady's maid buying her sixpenny instalment of serial collections such as *Bell's* or Inchbald's *British Theatre*.

Such a readership was conducive to the production of dramas that were designed to be read rather than performed. These *'closet dramas' allowed for experimentation with form and subject matter. Horace *Walpole's *The Mysterious Mother* dealt with the taboo subject of incest, while Joanna *Baillie's influential *A Series of Plays* (otherwise known as *Plays on the Passions*) probed the recesses of monomania. Other closet dramas became a forum for those disaffected with the theatre, who felt that the home of Shakespeare and the repository of national virtues was in chronic decline. Subscribers to this view included the leading Romantic writers and critics, such as Charles *Lamb, who argued that the contemporary stage was unequal to the genius of Shakespeare, indeed that Shakespeare could not be adequately represented in any theatre.

Lamb's relationship with the theatre, like that of other Romantic writers, was a highly ambivalent one. Scathing in their condemnation of production standards and audience taste, they were at the same time profoundly attracted to the stage. At varied points in their careers many felt compelled to produce dramas, some of which achieved success in the theatre. Most of these works, such as Wordsworth's *The Borderers*, Lamb's *John Woodvil*, and *Keats's *Otho the Great* remained closet pieces. The attractions of playwriting were manifold. Becoming a dramatist was still a useful way of asserting one's place in the republic of letters, gaining attention, prestige, and income. No less significant was the fact that it enabled the aspiring writer to emulate the genius of Shakespeare. Writing for the stage, at least putatively, also touched on many of the central preoccupations of Romantic writers—the fraught relationship between thought and action, the complicated burden of personal and national histories, constructions of manliness and femininity, and ideas of community. Above all, it raised issues of representation, not only in terms of how, in becoming a playwright, an author could be said to represent or speak for 'the public', but also in terms of the theatre's use of other forms of representation, apart from the word. Hannah *More, herself an erstwhile dramatist, claimed that the theatre conveyed 'doctrines, not simply expressed, as those of Sunday are, in the naked form of axioms, principles and precepts, but realised, embodied, made alive, furnished with organs, clothed, decorated, brought into sprightly discourse, into interesting action'. In More's view the power of the word, in this case the biblical logos, was threatened by the many voices, bodies, and images of the theatre, what she described as 'a complicated temptation' to which 'frail and erring creatures' should not be exposed.

Romantic writers were both attracted and repelled by this power. The theatre was for them a site of adulteration in which the changes taking place in late Georgian culture—the impact of commercialization, competing definitions of the public, the emergence of new cultural forms such as melodrama to challenge established genres and hierarchies, the struggle for cultural authority through literary authorship, and the increasingly uncertain distinctions of gender and rank—were all too pressing. The response to the 'complicated temptation' of theatre of writers such as Coleridge and Byron is a sign of the theatre's centrality to the preoccupations of Romanticism, not its irrelevance, as has often been supposed.

If such a category as 'Romantic drama' exists, therefore, it should be extended to include not only the dramas of the canonical poets but also plays such as John Home's (1722–1808) *Douglas*. First performed in 1757 and frequently staged thereafter, this Scottish tragedy is profoundly Romantic in its enactment of the doomed desire for restoration, in both a familial and a national sense. *Douglas* would be joined in this revised canon of the Romantic drama with other plays such as Lewis's *The Castle Spectre*, Maturin's *Bertram*, and *Ireland's *Vortigern*, as well as with *Macbeth* and *Hamlet, Venice Preserv'd, Jane Shore*, and *The Fair Penitent*, the comedies of Inchbald and Holcroft, the harlequinades of Grimaldi, de Loutherbourg's experiments in light, colour, and space, and last but not least the theatre of embodiment—the glittering self-fashioning of actresses such as Elizabeth Farren, Dorothy Jordan, and Mary *Robinson, the muscular femininity of Sarah Siddons, the stare of Edmund *Kean that marked an epoch. This theatre of embodiment would also include those who pressed to see such figures—Coleridge, *Hazlitt, Byron, Lamb, and others—men and women who recognized in these actors the expression of their own theatricality and that of the culture as a whole.

Baer, M., *Theatre and Disorder in Late Georgian London*, Oxford, 1992; Bate, J., *Shakespearean Constitutions: Politics, Theatre, Criticism, 1730–1830*, Oxford, 1992; Carlson, J. A., *In the Theatre of Romanticism: Coleridge, Nationalism, Women*, Cambridge, 1994; Conolly, L. W., *The Censorship of English Drama, 1737–1824*, San Marino, Calif., 1976; Davis, T. C., *Actresses as Working Women: Their Social Identity in Victorian Culture*, London, 1991; Hays, M., & Nikolopoulou, A., *Melodrama: The Cultural Emergence of a Genre*, New York, 1996; Litvak, J., *Caught in the Act: Theatricality in the Nineteenth-Century English Novel*, Berkeley, Calif., 1992; Nicoll, A., *The Garrick Stage: Theatres and Audience in the Eighteenth Century*, Manchester, 1980; Russell, G., *The Theatres of War: Performance, Politics and Society, 1793–1815*, Oxford, 1995; Straub, K., *Sexual Suspects: Eighteenth-Century Players and Sexual Ideology*, Princeton, NJ, 1992; Thomas, D., ed., *Restoration and Georgian England, 1660–1768*, Cambridge, 1989.

25 · DESIGN CELINA FOX

Design had a range of meanings in the late eighteenth and early nineteenth centuries. In academic art circles it traditionally meant the expression of creative ideas, employing the principles of drawn composition which circumscribed all the arts. But increasingly design was used in contexts which suggested a distinction from the fine arts, particularly in connection with manufactured ornamental goods. Not that any opposition was necessarily denoted by this change of emphasis: it was universally accepted that if the more exalted branches of design—*painting [27], *architecture [28], *sculpture—flourished, then the humbler ends of industry would of course be answered. Their essential affinity is spelt out in the title of the Society for the Encouragement of Arts, Manufactures, and Commerce, founded in 1754 by the drawing master William Shipley. There was a widespread belief that artists could confer on goods something which manufacturers and artisans lacked. That something was called taste in design.

The principles of design were based on antique precedent, the classical orders of harmony and proportion reinterpreted in the Renaissance and purveyed through numerous illustrated academic treatises. But by the middle of the eighteenth century the study of ancient Greece and archaeological discoveries in Rome, Herculaneum, and Pompeii had led to a new understanding of the antique [see *Hellenism]. The influential writings of the German art historian Johann Joachim Winckelmann (1717–68) advocated a return to the noble simplicity and calm grandeur of Greek art. The classical tradition represented universal and timeless values of truth, purity, and honesty, freed from the intervention of the Renaissance and the artificial fripperies and degenerate deceits of the Rococo. The international movement which advanced its cause was later dubbed (pejoratively) *'neoclassicism', but at the time was understood as a return to the 'true style'.

This style was introduced to Britain by architects who had travelled to Greece and Rome to make a special study of classical remains and who came into contact with like-minded spirits from France, Italy, and Germany en route. James 'Athenian' Stuart (1713–88), the painter and architect and leading member of the Society of Dilettanti, was the first to design in the new manner, swiftly followed by Robert *Adam.

Their publications—Stuart and Nicholas Revett's (1720–1804) The Antiquities of Athens (4 vols., 1762, 1790, 1795, 1816), Adam's Ruins of the Palace of the Emperor Diocletian at Spalatro (1764), and The Works in Architecture of Robert and James Adam (published in numbers from 1773 and in volume form in 1778–9)—ensured a widespread influence. Inside Spencer House, Stuart created the first neoclassical decorative ensemble in England, while Adam created integrated interiors at Harewood, Kedleston (where he ruthlessly supplanted Stuart), Syon, and other great houses, utilizing a profusion of light and elegant ornamental motifs derived from antique Greek forms. Both involved the leading craftsmen and manufacturers of the day in their schemes.

Architects were in a position, as Josiah *Wedgwood expressed it, to act as 'godparents' to manufacturers' products. Adam made designs for the Carron Iron Works in Falkirk, where his brother John was a partner, ensuring the spread of anthemion motifs on everything from railings to fire-grates. Mrs Eleanor *Coade's famous artificial stone was employed by all the leading architects for outdoor ornament; she in turn based her designs on the Adams' work and on other reference books and imported antiquities, as well as employing the sculptor John Bacon (1740–99) to make designs in the neoclassical style. John Mayhew and William Ince's partnership in the second half of the eighteenth century produced high-quality furniture for aristocratic clients in association with the king's architects, Sir William *Chambers and Robert Adam.

Other London-based manufacturers catering for the luxury market used artists who were familiar with the new style. Benjamin Vulliamy (1780–1854), one of London's leading clock- and watchmakers, employed the young sculptors John Deare, Charles Peart, and John Rossi, as well as Bacon, to model figures for his clocks of neoclassical design, which were then produced in biscuit by William Duesbury's (1725–86) Derby porcelain works. The royal goldsmiths Rundell and Bridge (Rundell, Bridge, and Rundell after 1805) placed the Royal Academician William Theed (1804–91) in charge of their art department, and after his death in 1817 the sculptor John *Flaxman took over in an advisory capacity.

Large-scale manufacturers combined bespoke with off-the-peg production in businesses which encompassed a range of different skills. From their premises in Soho, Mayhew and Ince acted as cabinet-makers, carvers, upholders (upholsterers), plate glass manufacturers, and even auctioneers. The largest furniture-making firm in London in the last quarter of the eighteenth century, George Seddon, squeezed most of the trades involved onto one site in Aldersgate, employing some 400 men by 1786, ranging from carvers, joiners, and gilders to mirror-workers, upholsterers, girdlers, and locksmiths. A year later his insurance policies amounted to £17,500 (compared with £500 in 1756–7 and £7,700 in 1770). Rundells was involved in a number of subsidiary businesses including a diamond-cutting business in Spitalfields and a modern plate workshop, first in Greenwich and after 1807 in Soho, which supplied them with their stock and work on commission.

But the largest manufacturers to exploit the neoclassical taste lay outside London, where production could be undertaken on an industrial scale [see *consumerism, 19]. In the early 1760s Matthew *Boulton built his Soho factory at Handsworth, Birmingham, and with his partner John Fothergill redeemed the poor reputation of Birmingham goods by producing 'toys' in iron, brass, and silver plate—buckles, buttons, watch-chains, jewellery and other trinkets—of sound workmanship and in good taste. Through the division of his 800-strong labour force into workshops carrying out specialized tasks, he secured the firm's competitive edge. Water gave him the power to operate the rolling mills, lathes, and stamping and polishing machines essential for large-scale production. With these newly industrialized processes he exploited the invention of Sheffield plate—copper fused to a silver veneer—boosting the rate of production and lowering manufacturing costs.

His friend Josiah Wedgwood employed water and wind power in his new factory, built on a 350-acre estate lying between Burslem and Hanley in the Staffordshire potteries and opened in June 1769. He bought engine-turning lathes from Boulton for fashioning pots and decorating by incising designs on them before firing. He too divided his labour force into different specializations, to create the first pottery in Europe conducted on industrial assembly lines. At the core of his business lay his own skill as an experimental chemist, constantly researching new bodies and glazes.

Both Boulton and Wedgwood had pretensions to manufacture goods that were not merely 'useful' but also 'ornamental', displaying the highest principles of design according to classical precedent. Boulton saw his factory as a 'Temple of the Vulcanian Arts'. Besides manufacturing toys and Sheffield plate on a large scale, he started in the late 1760s to produce high-quality ormolu and silverware, the latter greatly stimulated by the establishment of an Assay Office in Birmingham in 1773, largely through his efforts. Wedgwood named his new factory 'Etruria', on the generally but mistakenly held belief that the Etruscans made the finest antique vases. By selling 'Vases, Urns and other ornaments after the Etruscan, Greek and Roman modells', he aimed to become 'Vase Maker General to the Universe'. He produced glazes which imitated

Roman stones—marble, granite, agate, lapis lazuli, porphyry—and transformed a traditional Staffordshire body known as 'Egyptian black' into the hard 'Black Basalt'. In 1769 he took out a patent for 'encaustic' or matt enamel painting to emulate classical Greek red-figured vases. By the mid-1770s he had perfected his own invention of 'Jasper', a pure white porcelain biscuit which, when used as a coloured ground with contrasting white applied relief, could imitate the effect of antique cameos.

The principles of design were diffused to these provincial centres of manufacturing through a number of channels. First was the medium of the engraved plate and printed book. Boulton and Wedgwood acquired the latest illustrated treatises on antiquity which both marked and stimulated the rising tide of the classical revival, notably Pierre François Hugues D'Hancarville's (1719–1805) *Collection of Etruscan, Greek, and Roman Antiquities*, issued in four volumes in Naples in 1766–7, illustrating Sir William *Hamilton's first collection of Greek vases, sold to the British Museum in 1772. According to the preface, one of the motives behind its publication was specifically to encourage manufacturers to use correct classical models.

Another channel was provided by personal contact with the most knowledgeable connoisseurs in the land. One of Wedgwood's early patrons, Lord Cathcart, was married to Hamilton's sister and lent him plates from the D'Hancarville volumes before he acquired his own edition. His partner and London manager, Thomas Bentley (1731–80), was a friend of Hamilton and had access not only to unpublished drawings from the catalogue but also to the original vases, and was able to seek advice directly from Hamilton himself. Bentley in turn advised Wedgwood on artistic trends and current fashionable taste. Both Boulton and Wedgwood visited—on at least one occasion together—the collections of their patrons.

They also had direct contact with painters, sculptors, and architects who were familiar with the new style. Sir William Chambers supplied Boulton with some 'valuable, usefull and acceptable modells' when they met in 1770. Robert Mylne (1734–1811) and James *Wyatt provided designs for his silverware in the 1770s, while James's cousin John Wyatt was Boulton's London agent for the toy business. In addition to the modellers based in Etruria, Wedgwood commissioned original work through Bentley from a number of the most talented artists in London. John Flaxman followed his father, a plaster-cast maker, in working for Wedgwood. He created designs and wax models in bas-relief for portrait medallions. His classical scenes were applied to Wedgwood's Jasper vases and tablets intended for chimney-pieces and larger decorative schemes. When Flaxman went to Rome in 1787, Wedgwood asked him to supervise on an informal basis the modellers whom he had employed there to supply casts and copies of antique sculpture.

Both Wedgwood and Boulton were constantly on the lookout for fresh ideas and motifs which could be copied or adapted to customers' wishes or to fit the requirements of production. The 'elegant simplicity' of objects decorated in the neoclassical style, rejecting complex illusion and elaborate contrasts of texture in favour of a uniform surface and mechanical precision of form, suited industrial needs. Relatively standardized models could be produced rapidly, while variations were created by mixing components of different designs. The mechanical imitation of antique effects, using a range of new materials, could be justified as being merely an extension of the hallowed practice of copying from the antique.

But both men recognized from the start that if they wanted their wares to sell and to keep their businesses afloat, the approval of royalty, the nobility, and the gentry counted as much as the intrinsic correctness, elegance, and beauty of the product. They welcomed a stream of distinguished visitors to their factories, which were showplaces of cleanliness and efficiency. Boulton had a retail warehouse at his Soho works, and in the early 1770s held exhibitions and sales of his finest pieces in ormolu at Christie's in London. Wedgwood went further and opened a permanent London saleroom sufficiently large to welcome the 'shoals' of ladies who came to inspect a changing display of dinner services laid out on tables and vases set against the walls. The urbane presence of his partner Bentley undoubtedly contributed to its success. In 1774 visitors flocked to see the 952-piece dinner and dessert service ordered by the Empress Catherine of Russia and decorated with hand-painted views of English architectural landmarks and beauty spots. In 1790 they came to marvel at the copy made in Jasper after the Roman cut-glass Barberini or Portland Vase. The original had been acquired by Sir William Hamilton, who sold it to the Duchess of Portland; on her death in 1785 it was bought by the third Duke of *Portland, from whom Wedgwood borrowed it to make a copy. Sir Joshua *Reynolds vouched that Wedgwood's version was a 'correct and faithfull imitation, both in regard to the general effect, and the most minute details of the parts'.

Admission for both events was restricted: in 1774 to those who had a ticket and in 1790 to those who were invited, thus conspiring to enhance the aura of privilege, exclusivity, and shared standards of taste. But there was always a danger in going further and being flattered into allowing distinguished clients to dictate demand, with the inevitable outcome of uneconomical short runs or over-large stocks of unsold goods. Boulton and Wedgwood were particularly vulnerable, as they had over-expanded and were under-capitalized for the huge investment they had made in plant and equipment. Their pricing policies were haphazard and took little account of fixed overheads. Costs needed to be assessed with greater accuracy; production runs needed to be lengthened, stocks reduced, and prices adjusted. Above all, new markets had to be exploited, especially those of the middle classes, whose level of consumption had been rising throughout the century. By the mid-1770s Boulton had largely abandoned his prestigious but loss-making production of ormolu, concentrating instead on large-scale Sheffield plate and toy manufacture. His energies were taken up with the development of the steam engine under patent with his new partner, James *Watt. Wedgwood also realized that he must drum up demand where he as a manufacturer most needed it. As he wrote to Bentley in 1772, it was at first necessary to charge the 'Great People' a great price so that they should esteem his vases 'Ornaments for Palaces'; but once their 'character' was established, the much vaster numbers of the 'Middling Class of People' would probably buy quantities of them at a reduced price.

Both Boulton and Wedgwood exploited the general emulative acquisitiveness of the middle classes, and in doing so ensured that the principles of design spread beyond the 'great people'. They manipulated this burgeoning market using a range of sophisticated promotion and sales techniques. Catalogues were a novel way of reaching retailers throughout the country and abroad, helping to acquaint them and their customers with the latest fashions. The illustrated trade catalogue emerged in the 1770s and was associated particularly with the West Midlands metal trades and the fused-plate manufacturers of Sheffield. As the largest single manufacturer of Sheffield plate, Boulton sent out illustrated catalogues of his wares directly to his extensive network of agents throughout Europe. In 1774 Wedgwood produced his first catalogue (and the first in the ceramics trade) of Queen's Ware. He also took to *advertising and offered free carriage to all parts of the country, replacement for breakages and satisfaction guaranteed. He employed travelling salesmen throughout Europe and sent out boxes of samples on continental tours. To reinforce brand loyalty as well as to guard against inferior imitations, every piece went out impressed with his name on the base.

Wedgwood was never competitive in price, despite his advanced methods of production which should have reduced costs. But these were inflated by his investment in land, buildings, and machinery, as well as in research, development, and training. His marketing expenses were exceptionally high. He continued to make unique pieces, which were usually sold at a loss. Above all, he would not compromise on quality. At the same time, these very features—inventiveness, marketing, and quality—underlay his success. In other words, he managed to create and maintain a 'limited edition' market, midway between the traditional reserves of exclusive patronage and a limitless flow of low-cost products.

Wedgwood had little reason to fear competitors, and would probably have maintained that imitation was the sincerest form of flattery. Indeed, the lack of *copyright law before 1842 encouraged the free flow of designs throughout specialized branches of manufacture. Their dissemination was aided by an extraordinary growth of pattern books, available increasingly at a reasonable cost. Those pertaining to cabinet-making are a case in point. George Hepplewhite's *The Cabinet Maker and Upholsterer's Guide*, published after his death by his wife in successive editions of 1788, 1789, and 1794, was the first major furniture pattern book to appear after the third edition of Thomas Chippendale's *Director* in 1762, and was heavily dependent on Adam. Thomas Sheraton's (1751–1806) *The Cabinet-Maker and Upholsterer's Drawing Book*, published in parts between 1791 and 1794 (with a second edition in 1794 and a third in 1802), attracted 700 subscribers, including cabinet-makers, joiners, carvers, gilders, musical-instrument makers, engravers, painters, and drawing masters, but significantly no wealthy patrons. Sheraton's role was that of interpreter to the trade rather than creator of exclusive designs. Similarly, *The Cabinet-maker's London Books of Prices* (1791–4) provided craftsmen with precisely costed and illustrated designs.

Many of the pattern books urged cabinet-makers to study basic principles of perspective and geometry, recognizing their dependence on a higher source, that of architectural design. Nevertheless, Wedgwood was the first to concede that in the eye of the consumer, fashion might count for more than merit; cosmetic appeal might prove more tempting than conformity to basic principles. He led the way in manipulating the market by feeding the engine of consumption with a constant stream of invention, boosted by a heavy dose of marketing. In the wake of this example, the ever-growing cycle of productive capacity, marketing drive, and appetite for consumption had by 1800 resulted in an unprecedented thirst for novelty, increasingly distanced from the chaste neoclassical 'true style'. The fascination with alternative sources of design can be traced back at least to the early eighteenth century, when rich, eccentric men of taste toyed with a variety of architectural styles from the *Gothic to the Chinese [see *chinoiserie]. But a century later, rather than resulting simply in one-off buildings stuffed with products commissioned *en suite*, the growth of industry and the market, as well as the diffusion of examples in catalogues and pattern books, encouraged the manufacture of goods in a plurality of styles on a hitherto unprecedented scale.

Fashionable taste in the first years of the nineteenth century tended to the exotic, a Euro-centred interpretation of the appearance of other civilizations, particularly those with which the country was acquiring increasing diplomatic, trade, and colonial ties [see *empire, 5]. Thus the European trading companies established at Canton in the eighteenth century provided a fragile foothold in China and encouraged the growth of interest in products of the Chinese empire. The creation in 1790 of a Chinese Room at the Prince of Wales's London residence of Carlton House, followed in 1802–4 by the decoration of the Regent's Pavilion at Brighton in a fanciful Chinese style by the firm of Crace, took place during a period of increasing diplomatic activity, culminating in Lord *Macartney's mission to the Emperor Ch'ien Lung in 1792–4. At the same time new stables were constructed for the Pavilion in an Indian style by William Porden (1755–1822), one of the first manifestations of the influence of *Views of Oriental Scenery* by Thomas and William Daniell, published in 1795–1808. These aquatints constituted a detailed record of many aspects of Indian architectural history compiled during the Daniells' tours from 1786 to 1793, starting from areas under British control.

Wedgwood had been producing wares using Egyptian styles and motifs since 1770, the main source for his designs being Bernard de Montfaucon's *L'Antiquité Expliquée* (1719–24), which reproduced antiquities from several ancient cultures, including specimens from Egypt of dubious authenticity [see *Egyptology]. Wedgwood's designers in turn adapted the images to suit neoclassical tastes. Popular interest in Egypt was rekindled by *Napoleon's expedition to Egypt in 1798 and *Nelson's victory over the French fleet at the battle of the Nile. Baron Denon's *Voyage dans la Basse et la Haute Égypte* (1802) provided the motifs for a style whose popularity was regarded as patriotic. Robert *Southey's *Letters from England* (1807) directly related the fashion to the military campaigns, contrasting the returning wounded soldiers with the elegant modes inspired by Egypt: 'the ladies wear crocodile ornaments, and you sit upon a sphinx in a room hung around with mummies.' Wedgwood produced a tea set decorated with Egyptian motifs and with crocodiles as handles; the same shapes were also available decorated in the Chinese manner with stylized blossom.

The famous Chinese-inspired blue-and-white 'Willow' pattern was first created by Thomas Turner (1749–1809) at the Caughley pottery in Staffordshire, being adapted and sold on to other manufacturers by an apprentice engraver, Thomas Minton, when he left the works in 1785. The new technique of transfer-printing designs engraved on copper plates onto biscuit earthenware enabled copies of Chinese blue-and-white landscapes to provide an alternative source to Canton, which was proving increasingly unreliable and expensive. The manufactory started in Stoke-on-Trent by Josiah Spode (1733–97) in 1770, and developed with his son Josiah II (1754–1827) and William Copeland, thrived on the production of blue printed earthenware. At their London warehouse, complete services were on sale, decorated with scenes culled from Wilhelm Tischbein's *Collection of Engravings from Ancient Vases* (1791–5), which recorded the second collection formed by Sir William Hamilton, J. Merigot's *Views and Ruins in Rome and its Vicinity* (1797, 1799), Luigi Mayer's *Views in Egypt, Palestine and other parts of the Ottoman Empire* (3 vols., 1801–3), and the illustrations to *Oriental Field Sports, and Wild Sports of the East* (1805–7) by Captain Thomas Williamson, with coloured aquatints after watercolours by Samuel Howett.

Furniture makers were also becoming increasingly eclectic in their use of sources. Sheraton's last work, *The Cabinet-Maker, Upholsterer, and General Artist's Encyclopaedia* (1804–6), contained designs in the Egyptian style and chairs and sofas adorned with swords, ropes, and anchors to commemorate Nelson's victories. But Southey was probably satirizing

36. 'The Egyptian Room', from Thomas Hope's *Household Furniture and Interior Decoration* (1807), reflected the contemporary vogue for exotic design.

above all Thomas *Hope's *Household Furniture and Interior Decoration* of 1807. The first work in English to use the term 'interior decoration', Hope's influential publication contained views of the principal rooms and measured drawings of individual pieces of furniture in his own London house in Duchess Street, off Portland Place. The most striking ensemble was the Egyptian Room, decorated in suitably Egyptian shades of blue-green and pale yellow relieved by black and gold and with a large frieze of figures drawn from Egyptian papyrus rolls. The sofa and armchair designs by Hope had an archaic splendour and were avowedly taken from Egyptian precedents. The materials used in the cups, canopic vases, and figures displayed— porphyry, granite, and basalt—reflected Hope's determination to recreate the monumental character of Egyptian antiquities. The Aurora Room, which centred on Flaxman's marble group, *Aurora Visiting Cephalus on Mount Ida*, was lined in yellowish-orange satin, with furniture and ornaments in the Greek style.

Hope's aim was to improve the standard of design by providing specific models in a range of antique styles founded on serious research, though he hoped they would not lead to 'servile copying'. He himself mixed Greek and Egyptian motifs, sometimes to bizarre rather than impressive effect. He knew the French designers Charles Percier and Pierre François Léonard Fontaine, whose sophisticated *grand luxe* neoclassical rooms for the new French Emperor, as catalogued in *Recueil de Décorations Intérieures* (issued in instalments from 1801 and in a single volume in 1812), were an important influence. Hope also owed an unacknowledged debt to the work of Henry *Holland's assistant, Charles Heathcote Tatham, whose *Etchings of Ancient Ornamental Architecture drawn from the Originals in Rome and other Parts of Italy during the Years 1794, 1795 and 1796*, went through three editions before 1810. But, unusually for a pattern book, all the objects illustrated in Hope's *Household Furniture* had actually been made by the finest craftsmen and existed for visitors to see, when furnished with a ticket issued after 'an application signed by some person of known character and taste'. Not surprisingly, within a year of Hope's publication George Smith had issued his *Collection of Designs for Household Furniture and Interior Decoration*, lifted largely from Hope as well as from Sheraton, Percier, and Fontaine, but providing designs for a complete range of domestic furniture aimed at a cheaper market.

At the same time, the first illustrated British magazine to be principally concerned with styles of domestic consumption made its appearance. Rudolph *Ackermann's *The Repository of Arts, Literature, Commerce, Manufactures, Fashions and Politics* was launched in January 1809 with a dedication by permission to that indefatigable consumer, the Prince of Wales. Until its closure in December 1828, it lived up to its title with an enormous variety of short articles and plates illustrating the latest fashions, textiles, manufactures and inventions, topographical views, and notable residences. Its devotion to the world of goods was demonstrated in its first year with the publication of six illustrations of leading retail showrooms in London. In 1810–11 it published a series of nineteen plates showing the innovatory furniture designs produced by the Strand firm of Morgan and Sanders—the Metamorphic Library Chair and Merlin's Mechanical Chair for instance—which pushed novelty and invention to the limits. From 1816, George Bullock's fashionable furniture and furnishing schemes were illustrated, and in 1825–7 the magazine promoted Augustus Charles *Pugin's designs for Gothic furniture, the twenty-seven plates being republished as a book in 1829 under the title *Pugin's Gothic Furniture*.

There had been 'revivals' of the Gothic style for a century or more. In *Ancient Architecture, Restored, and Improved* (1742), Batty Langley attempted to recover the principles which underlay Gothic architecture akin to those underlying classicism. The ensuing craze for Gothic ornament conspicuously failed to subscribe to any serious order, but at Sir Horace *Walpole's Strawberry Hill, ancient woodwork and stained glass were incorporated in rooms with Gothic fittings, copied from engravings in antiquarian books on medieval cathedrals and abbeys. From the 1750s until Walpole's death in 1797, Strawberry Hill was continuously extended to provide a suitable environment for its owner's collections of medieval and early Renaissance

56

37. 'Merlin's Mechanical Chair',
published in Rudolph
Ackermann's magazine *The
Repository of Arts* (1811),
appealed to consumer desire for
commercial innovation.

antiquities. Walpole's own *Description* (published in two editions of 1774 and 1784, the latter extensively illustrated) was used by streams of visitors to the house who ensured it became the most celebrated example of the Gothic Revival of its day.

James Wyatt was the leading architect of the Gothic Revival around 1800, notably at Fonthill, where his original design of 1796 for a ruined convent was endlessly enlarged at the behest of William *Beckford to house his *Wunderkammer* of a collection. From about 1806, a series of Gothic interiors were designed for the Prince of Wales's neoclassical Carlton House, with furniture and fittings which included oak chairs probably designed by James Wyatt for the library, and candelabra supplied by Mrs Coade for the conservatory. Such self-consciously theatrical sets and the treatment of architecture as scenery were characteristic features of the *picturesque, as discussed in the writings of William *Gilpin, Uvedale *Price, and Richard Payne *Knight. Overlying the antiquarian interest in medieval British history and archaeology was a Romantic fascination with the medieval age, with chivalry, heraldry and traditional festivities [see *medievalism], related in ancient British ballads and later in the novels of Walter *Scott. Indeed, George Bullock provided Scott's Abbotsford, reconstructed in Scottish Baronial style, with an eclectic mixture of armour, furniture, chimney-pieces, and ornament in a predominantly Gothic taste.

The state rooms at Windsor Castle, remodelled by Jeffry *Wyatville once George IV had ascended the throne, provided the opportunity for the young Augustus Welby Northcote *Pugin to begin in 1827 to design Gothic Revival furniture made up by Nicholas Morel and George Seddon. Some pieces were in plain oak following medieval precedent, but others in rosewood, with gilding and gilt bronze enrichments, were probably better suited to the taste of his patron. Around the same time Pugin was working for the royal goldsmiths, Rundell, Bridge, and Rundell, producing designs for medieval-style plate mounted with precious jewels, to be used at Windsor. His impassioned rejection of materialism for a society based on faith in *Contrasts* (1836) and his elucidation of *The True Principles of Pointed or Christian Architecture* (1841) lay ahead.

The extravagant patronage and opulent display favoured by rich connoisseurs like William Beckford and the Prince of Wales established their role as arbiters of taste. But the resetting of stones in newly commissioned historicist ornamental works of art was a habit few could afford to indulge. Likewise, acquisition of the finest pieces of eighteenth-century French furniture, bronzes, and Sèvres porcelain dispersed during and immediately after the Napoleonic Wars, which set the seeds for the so-called Louis XIV style (in fact a recreation of the Rococo), again led by the Prince and Beckford, was only pursued by the very rich. The *Regency period afforded many opportunities for conspicuous consumption. London was the wealthiest city in the world with a globally dominant economy, its commercial might expressed in the construction of new docks, its financial power accrued through sophisticated banking and insurance systems. In tune with this material confidence, Benjamin Dean Wyatt (1775–1850), son of James Wyatt, installed Rococo revival interiors in Belvoir Castle, Apsley House, Crockford's Gaming House, York—later Stafford (now Lancaster)—House, and Buckingham Palace. It was an expensive, showy style which George IV, for one, had difficulty paying for. When he died in 1830 he owed the firm of Morel and Seddon nearly £200,000, which was only grudgingly repaid by the Treasury after a Select Committee Report at the end of 1831, and then not *in toto*.

The 'Louis XIV' style was deemed degenerate even by the eclectic standards of the time. Though visitors were impressed by the gilded magnificence of such interiors, many like Thomas Hope who were used to the simple forms of a purer style attacked it for its tasteless excess of materials and overloaded profusion of ornament. But fears about national standards of taste were more far-reaching. *The Repository of Arts*, which probably contributed to the move away from a unitary style to plurality of choice, frequently urged artists and architects to descend from their lofty position and make it their business to select and improve designs for carpets, curtains, and furniture based on classical precedent. It pointed out that in France artists did not think it degrading to produce patterns for manufacturers, and workers had access to art in public galleries. In Britain, by comparison, artisans and manufacturers had few opportunities to see art and, under the then system of *education [17], could not be expected to ascend to higher sources of elegance.

The fear of competition from French manufacturers provided the spur for the Parliamentary Select Committee of 1835 appointed 'to inquire into the best means of extending a knowledge of the Arts, and of the Principles of Design, among the People (especially the Manufacturing Population) of the Country'. Its avowed purpose differed little from that of the Society for the Encouragement of Arts, Manufactures, and Commerce, launched some eighty years earlier. But whereas the Society's aim to encourage industrial art through prize competitions had foundered through lack of support, the Select Committee enjoyed the active participation of both members and witnesses with commercial or industrial interests. At the same time, its forty-nine members included 'men of taste' sympathetic to the views of the Royal Academy as to the primacy of the fine arts. And conspicuous among the witnesses called to give evidence were those who most rigidly adhered to conservative academic values.

They maintained that design was no longer controlled by men of taste but was being manipulated by men of commerce, and that, with a multiplicity of choice, objective standards in art were being abandoned under the force of economic pressures. The architect Charles Robert Cockerell (1788–1863) spoke bluntly: 'I believe that the attempt to supersede the work of the mind and the hand by mechanical process for the sake of economy, will always have the effect of degrading and ultimately ruining art.' According to the President of the Royal Academy, Sir Martin Archer Shee (1769–1850), the principles of commerce and the principles of art were in direct opposition to each another. Political economists who adapted to the arts a principle which belonged only to trade were entirely mistaken in their views: 'the moment you make art a trade you destroy it.'

Such an opinion seemingly ignored the successful efforts that had been made over the preceding half-century to apply the principles of design to manufactures, and of taste to consumption. Cockerell maintained that taste was more under the control of fashion than the direction of principle. Other witnesses acknowledged the efforts of Wedgwood, Boulton, Mrs Coade, and Rundells, but asserted that their influence was necessarily limited. The works of Flaxman and Hope, and the publications on Sir William Hamilton's vases, were shut up in private collections and produced little effect on public taste, compared with the free access the public had to libraries and museums in France. The superior designs from painters, sculptors, and architects were supplied at a cost in England, compared with France, which contributed to the expense of production and thereby restricted sales. As a result, manufacturers were no longer employing artists of eminence. It was pointed out that Wedgwood's prices had never been compatible with those of other potters and that he consciously manipulated the market to increase prestige. Edward Cowper (1790–1852), patentee of the Applegarth and Cowper steam printing presses and a manufacturer of terracotta vases in the antique style, maintained that Wedgwood retained a little of the prejudice of keeping art at a high price. After he had sold thirty copies of the Portland Vase at 25 guineas each Wedgwood had destroyed the mould in order to render them more rare. Cowper considered this 'a very erroneous feeling because it was so far preventing the diffusion of taste throughout the country'.

The Select Committee provoked the question as to whether it was possible to uphold the principles of design derived from high art when on the one hand there was increasing diversity of tastes and on the other the increasing productive capacity to service them. As the nineteenth century progressed it seemed as if the unique or limited-edition art object would be replaced by mass-produced commodities which satisfied the greatest number; in effect, quality was being ousted by quantity. This applied particularly to non-luxury trades, where machinery had largely superseded human labour, as was the case with cotton goods. The new power machinery and printing technology allowed for the cheap production of an increasingly diverse range of goods for particular markets, subject to frequent changes of style according to the latest fashions. In order to keep up with trends and keep down costs, manufacturers relied on copying high quality samples or designs. The Select Committee exposed a serious division of opinion between the protectionists, who wanted to introduce a copyright law on original designs, and the free trade manufacturers, who pushed the economics of scale to the limit. The former, who were mainly fine printers producing the most original, complicated, and expensive designs for the middle classes, asserted that the patrician character of the original was impaired when it became plebeian. The latter, the machine printers, asserted that there was no such thing as a unique design, that protection was tyrannical and injurious to trade and that the reduction in prices was beneficial to the lower classes.

Thus the architects, artists, and sculptors blamed the manufacturers for their failure to understand the basic principles of design and the artisans for their want of education in executing them. The manufacturers and artisans blamed in return the architects, artists, and sculptors for artificially restricting access to the best examples of design. And all blamed the general public, from the West End to Wapping, for their pursuit of meretricious finery rather than true design principles. The final Report of the Select Committee published in 1836 concluded 'that, from the highest branches of poetical design down to the lowest connexion between design and manufactures, the Arts have received little encouragement in this country'. Spurred into action by the example of other 'frequently more despotic' countries with a weaker manufacturing base, it turned to art education as a solution. It recommended that art schools should be established throughout the country, and that local schools should be specifically related to the needs of local manufacturers. In 1836 the government's vote of £1,500 for the establishment of a school of design in London marked the beginning of a new era which saw the development of design in relation to the fine arts on the one hand and industry on the other. It was no longer to be the concern of a privileged few, nor yet of enlightened manufacturers, but a state responsibility shouldered, albeit reluctantly, for the general good of all.

Brewer, J., & Porter, R., eds., *Consumption and the World of Goods*, London, 1993; Fox, C., *London: World City, 1800–1840*, New Haven, Conn., 1992; Morley, J., *Regency Design, 1790–1840: Gardens, Buildings, Interiors, Furniture*, London, 1993; *Report and Minutes of Evidence from the Select Committee on Arts and Manufacture*, (598) V, 1835, & (568) IX, 1836; Wainwright, C., *The Romantic Interior: The British Collector at Home, 1750–1850*, New Haven, Conn., 1989.

26 · MUSIC   CYRIL EHRLICH AND SIMON McVEIGH

Music was central to the age of *Romanticism and revolution. Irresistibly vigorous, the work of Bach and *Haydn, *Beethoven and *Mozart, *Weber, and *Mendelssohn, demanded to be listened to, not merely overheard. It was seized upon, first by musicians and amateurs, then by an ever-widening public, eager for its excitements and solace, both intellectual and sensory. Much of this classical repertoire has survived, its canon acknowledged as one of Western civilization's proudest achievements [see rise of the *classics]. The new music took command of European sensibilities with varying national emphasis. In France it was public and political, with the 'Marseillaise' the clarion call of revolution and Romantic fervour. In Italy it was the quintessential public art of opera, immediate, singable, and internationally exportable, with Rossini the most popular of all composers. In Germany it was expressive of the spirit of the age, the heroic status of Beethoven, firebrand and philosopher, epitomizing the emergence of the composer as national icon.

   Britain contributed to this efflorescence primarily through commercialism, craftsmanship, and consumption. One observer declared in 1792, 'there is positively no Nation in Europe, where Music is so generally patronized and so little professed, as in our own'. Though Britain could take credit for patronizing leading continental musicians from J. C. *Bach and Haydn to Weber and Mendelssohn, its own composers—the likes of Stephen *Storace, Cipriani *Potter, and Samuel *Wesley—have been typically described as a good 'second eleven'. In keeping with gentlemen-amateur traditions, these composers appeared to lack the visionary single-mindedness which activated their continental contemporaries. Though they were no feebler than their immediate predecessors, their limitations were now laid bare by contrast: creative impotence was openly mocked by fecundity throughout Europe. Only such craftsmen as Broadwood, Dodd, and Tubbs, and a few performers, particularly women, were truly fit to join the newly exalted company of musicians [see *women musicians and composers]. This embarrassing trough has never been adequately explained, still less successfully contradicted by occasional patriotic gestures of denial. Contemporaries were certainly in no doubt of the inferiority of British music-making, even when driven to mock foreign intrusions and idiosyncrasies. The lack of patronage structure no doubt played its part: though George III's support of William Boyce (1710–79) during the 1760s and 1770s seemed to augur well, neither royal nor aristocratic patronage was ever sufficiently generous and consistent to achieve anything lasting.

Critics clung to ideals of British qualities of purity, simplicity, and sublimity, while recognizing the energy and sensuality of foreign music-making. Thomas Arne (1710–78) and Boyce were modestly successful in the mid-eighteenth century, but thereafter every promising British composer somehow became sidetracked: Stephen Storace, William *Shield, Thomas Attwood (1765–1838), and Henry *Bishop moved into charming but inconsequential English *opera, Samuel Wesley into *church music. Thomas *Linley and G. F. Pinto (1785–1806) died young, John Field (1782–1837) left for St Petersburg, and William *Crotch's interests became narrowly academic. There was hope for a native genre, the *glee, its practitioners devising the impressive-sounding British Concerts of 1823, but these failed after only one season. Samuel *Webbe and William Horsley (1774–1858) undoubtedly produced fine examples of the genre, a serious link with the glorious cathedral and madrigal traditions; but this proved no basis for national revival. More promising initiatives were a summer English Opera House (1816), the Royal Academy of Music (1823), and the Philharmonic Society's 'trials' of new compositions: here Cipriani Potter could confidently challenge foreign symphonists such as Ferdinand *Ries and Louis Spohr (1784–1859). However, the only really enduring British contribution was made by a group of foreign-born *pianists—the important 'London Pianoforte School' of Muzio *Clementi, J. B. *Cramer, Jan Ladislav *Dussek, and later Ignaz *Moscheles. Their piano music was both imaginative and influential, as well as pioneering in its relationship with the emerging piano technology.

Reaction against foreign music concentrated upon a predominantly Italian opera house, nourishing *patriotism by an odd assortment of prejudices and misconceptions. Literary and philosophical intellectuals, wedded to an exclusively verbal discourse, required only 'legitimate' theatre, puritans no theatre at all. Patriots and radicals shared a distaste for patrician and fashionable indulgence in cultural traditions which smacked of the foreign or exotic: lingo, secco recitative, castrati, and displays of bravura and temperament all seemed alien to British sensibilities, especially during wartime when patriotic values were threatened [see *war, 2]. A hackneyed routine of insult, dating back to Swift, Defoe, and *Johnson, found no counterweight in widespread practical experience of opera. For outside the metropolis, in stark contrast to the Continent, there were few chances to catch a performance; and even a cheap seat at the King's Theatre, which boasted such star performers as Gertrud *Mara and Angelica *Catalani, cost more than most Londoners could earn in a day. Consequent neglect of what constituted the continental Romantic musician's essential training-ground cost the British nation's music dear.

On the Continent a popular music theatre (with spoken dialogue) developed alongside Italian opera, leading directly into German Romantic opera via Mozart's *Die Zauberflöte* (1791) and Weber's *Der Freischütz* (1821). By contrast, English ballad opera, originating with Gay's *The Beggar's Opera* (1728), never really transcended its origins. Though the British associates of Mozart (Storace and Attwood) could certainly craft ensembles in high classical style, even they were forced back into pasting together ballads with scraps of Continental operas: Storace's overture to *The Siege of Belgrade* (1791) unashamedly draws on Mozart's Turkish rondo. Bishop, master of the sentimental ballad, was similarly adept at stitching together an opera from other sources.

If many British composers simply lacked the technique to create large musical forms, there was clearly little demand anyway for serious and well-constructed musical drama. When foreign masterpieces did reach the playhouse stage, they were ferociously hacked about: in Mozart's *Figaro* at Covent Garden in 1827, Susanna even introduced the popular ballad

'I've been roaming'. London cannot have been entirely averse to the new German Romanticism, for Weber's *Der Freischütz* (in translation) was the great hit of the 1824 season. Yet the metropolitan stage tradition was so degraded that when Weber himself arrived in 1826 to write his commissioned *Oberon*, he was presented with nothing better than the dramatically unsatisfactory libretto by J. R. Planché (1796–1880).

However, while the British may have created little music of lasting distinction outside the piano repertoire, their activities as consumers were universally acclaimed as prodigious. Music in late-eighteenth-century Britain is commonly thought to have been in rapid transition from aristocratic patronage to bourgeois consumption, in line with general trends in *consumerism [19]. Yet such assumptions generally lack a necessary foundation of historical research; they rest upon supposition about repertoire (what was performed?), participation and reception (who played and listened, where and when?). Information about magnitude and representativeness (how many, how often, how typical?) is unavailable or unconsidered. Attempts to pin images of modernity to the economic and social context of music over this period probably anticipate events by at least half a century. Where relevant research has been undertaken, on the economic history of the piano industry, for example, it emerges that production, ownership, and use of the piano only became widespread in the late nineteenth century—more than a generation later than has generally been assumed—when mechanization, international competition, and economies of scale finally lowered costs. In similar fashion, the diversity of the working life of important figures such as Clementi will surely come to be better understood as a response of talent to the constraints and distortions imposed by an immature and uncoordinated domestic and public demand for his services.

Only in the second half of the nineteenth century (with the development of railways, steamships, and a burgeoning Atlantic economy) could large numbers of performers and their promoters break out from geographic and economic constraints to articulate and exploit ever wider markets. In 1776 Britain's *potential* market for music and musicians was undoubtedly rich—probably more so than anywhere else—in the essential ingredients of purchasing power and leisure. Musicians were already becoming aware of the new possibilities, and were sometimes enterprising by comparison with their predecessors. However, their activities were still circumscribed by limitations of space, cost, and education, which in turn restricted the demand for each of four interlinked 'products': performances, instruments, lessons, and sheet music.

Even in London, where demand was most concentrated, and seekers of pleasure least hindered by poor communications and social constraints, the market forces of nascent capitalism were readily stifled. The Concert of Ancient Music, for example, was launched in 1776, 'against luxury and fashion', or any taint of association with commerce and the middle class, and became a rigidly exclusive club under the dominance of such patrons as the Earl of Sandwich and the Archbishop of Canterbury. It promoted a dozen or so concerts, predominantly of *Handel and Corelli—Mozart was prohibited until 1826, Haydn until 1829—between February and May, when 'society' was in town. These intensely patrician gatherings, administered and publicly supervised by lofty non-musicians, could hardly have been better insulated from the consumer appetites of the rising middle classes and the spirit of the age—indeed deliberately so, for the veneration of older music was an unspoken metaphor for the continuation of traditional social values.

In complete contrast, the annual concert series at the Hanover Square Rooms, the Bach-Abel, the Professional, and Salomon's great ventures with Haydn in the 1790s, managed both to appeal to fashion and to carry a modern repertoire [see *concerts and music societies]. Yet even these were based upon exclusive subscriptions, without sale of single tickets. In this way the organizers hoped to gain sufficient guarantee of finance, and subscribers some protection against unwanted company: it was not a system devoted to the exploitation of market opportunities. By 1790 a London opera and concert diary might have looked busy, but on closer inspection limitations become apparent. Nothing happened for half the year outside the 'season' and, though the *pleasure gardens provided some employment during the summer, the most eminent performers left for the country estates of their aristocratic patrons. Musicians continued to focus their attention on high society, making little effort to nurture a broader audience, to the extent that Wilhelm Cramer's (1745–99) promotion of two city benefits during the 1780s was regarded as a surprising new initiative.

After Haydn's departure in 1795, despite the stimulus of war and refugees from the *French Revolution, public musical life in London became rather dull. Not until 1813 was there a new lease of life, with the launch of the Philharmonic Society. Though still essentially bounded by exclusiveness, it showed vigour and professionalism, being founded and managed by musicians themselves. The Philharmonic Society also encapsulated a new spirit, a genuine attempt to define and perpetuate artistic qualities in modern music (as the 'Ancients' had already done for earlier styles). Explicitly opposed to the tides of fashion, the Society's membership was vetted for devotion to music, while its programming eschewed triviality and emphasized instrumental masterworks. Music was to be protected against the ravages of public taste—an articulation of the nineteenth-century concept of aspiration rather than enjoyment. While virtuosity was soon readmitted, its practitioners were always reminded that an invitation brought prestige, and were therefore under-rewarded in financial terms. Symphonies and overtures remained the backbone of the Society's endeavours, whether already canonical or else newly commissioned, as with Mendelssohn and his compatriot Louis Spohr. At first the Philharmonic's stance of high art also paid off financially, but by the 1830s audiences were in retreat. Mendelssohn was amused by the quaint ritual of being 'led to the piano like a young lady', and Moscheles complained bitterly that every new initiative was stifled.

If the Ancients and Philharmonic remained exclusive in their different ways, there were nevertheless the beginnings of an appeal to wider audiences during the postwar period—a transitional phase in London's musical life. More public concerts were staged—nearly eighty in two months of 1829, including virtuoso benefits with less rarefied programmes and the popular Lenten 'oratorio concerts' with their staggered price-levels [see *oratorio]. Even the opera edged downmarket. In 1827 Lord Mount Edgcumbe commented sniffily on the mixed company and lack of full dress at the King's Theatre, as box subscriptions began to be shared and pit tickets sold off cheaply. Concerts also started invading new territory, especially in the City. Here clubs of amateur musicians had long been active; indeed, the Harmonic Society was largely responsible for popularizing Mozart's music during the 1800s, and City enthusiasts were developing a reputation for allegiance to high musical values and to the Viennese classics. But it was not until 1818 that a subscription series was tentatively established in the city, initiated by a group of merchants, bankers, and professionals: and even here exclusiveness remained, for those engaged in retail (however respectably) could not be admitted.

Meanwhile individual musicians were developing more commercial awareness and aptitude. A benefit concert could bring great profits, if one avoided competition and high expenses, but continuing restraints were noted by Mendelssohn in 1829: 'Here they pursue music like a business, calculating, paying, bargaining, and truly a great deal is lacking . . . but they still remain *gentlemen*, otherwise they would be expelled from polite society.' For polite society was still, of course, an essential source of patronage for the best (usually foreign) musicians. When Rossini appeared at Almack's in 1824, the old system of aristocratic patronesses was revived to ensure a select audience. City merchants and bankers promoted some of the most opulent private concerts (Moscheles was patronized by the Rothschilds), and while such patronage was still available there was little incentive for risky entrepreneurial venture in the market-place. Polite society still held the cultural reins, deciding which musicians were to be 'in' and which 'out'.

How did these celebrations of high art relate to everyday musical life 'downmarket'? Contemporary reports are hard to find, but music societies undoubtedly flourished at city *taverns during the late eighteenth century. In his *Reminiscences* Henry Angelo (1756–1835) describes one (*c.*1780) where tickets cost two shillings, and the performers were part professional, part amateur. The principal attraction was Daniel Arrowsmith, a tenor whose experience at public concerts enabled him to give lively impersonations of all the leading *singers of the day; he also 'excelled' on the violin, cello, and flute, and recited his own poetry. Supper followed in the tavern parlour. In 1785 John Marsh (1752–1828) visited a weekly amateur concert in Newman Street, where a dancing-master proved an unsteady leader, even accusing the horns of mistaking an entry (as they were hired professionals, they let it pass). At another tavern society, where the programme alternated glees, songs, and overtures, the gentlemen smoked throughout the concert, except during Mrs Goodban's song, when the president asked them to lay down their pipes ('it appeared as if we were all in a fog there').

The singer Henry Phillips (1801–76), who rose to sing for the Ancients, tells of 'very miscellaneous' semi-amateur concerts (*c.*1815) in a 'large, dark, dingy room in Lincoln's-Inn Square', with 'songs, duets, instrumental solos on flutes, horns, bassoons, and pianofortes', an amateur comic, and a separate pulpit for readings. And at a theatre in Berwick Street, Soho, near the instrument-makers' and musicians' lodgings, the amateur leader would start the overture beating three instead of four with 'a complacent smile', assisted by a trombone player who had 'unfortunately for us' survived *Waterloo. Even the celebrated violinist Niccolò *Paganini, who invented the idea and perfected the practice of demonic Romantic virtuosity, was also thought by some to be vulgar in repertoire and undiscriminating in choice of venue. He played, for example, at the London Tavern in the City, which Moscheles 'thought unworthy of a great artist; but it was all one to him, for he makes money there'.

Outside London, less music was made in public and it was still predominantly amateur, with occasional 'strengthening' by local professionals (or, on rare occasions such as *music festivals, from further afield). London stars with sufficient drawing power to encourage an impresario might be persuaded to visit out of season, though possibilities were limited by poor communications, lack of suitable accommodation, and generally high costs. Celebrities endured punishing schedules. During one week in 1820, Mrs Salmon (1787–1849) performed throughout southern England: Monday, rehearsal at the Ancient Music and concert at the Philharmonic; Tuesday in Oxford; Wednesday in London at the oratorio and Ancient Music; Thursday in Oxford; Friday in Bath; Saturday in Bristol. Tired voices and repertoire were already being attributed to such timetables.

Dublin and Bath were exceptions to the general amateur character of provincial musical life, achieving and finally losing prominence in response to social and political change. During the eighteenth century Dublin society took pride in cultivating musical activity appropriate to its status as the second city of the British Isles. Musicians of some reputation, including Geminiani and Giordani, took up residence in the city during their declining years. Later the boy John Field secured a platform there, before joining Clementi for tuition and wider horizons; and Dublin experienced auspicious visits, none so famous as Handel's extended stay in 1741–2 when *Messiah* was first performed. But for the most part standards of musicianship and audience expectations were mediocre, due largely to geographical isolation from centres of excellence. After the 1800 *Act of Union and abolition of parliament, rich patronage inevitably declined and amateur activity prevailed, with occasional visits by such celebrities as Catalani and Paganini. Sufficient pomp and circumstance remained for the conductor George Smart (1776–1867) to collect a rewarding, if challenged, Irish knighthood on his steady climb from trade to a niche in London society, and to his consequent authority among musicians as fixer and manager.

Bath's ascent and subsequent decline, in music as in all objects of fashion, was far more spectacular. Queen of *spas, its reputedly health-giving waters served as an excuse—not too far out of London—for conspicuous consumption, the exercise of the marriage market, diversion, and pleasure. By mid-century the town was entertaining at least 12,000 visitors in a high season extending from late October until Christmas. Here was an ideal concentration of audience and purchasing power, a community much given to tattle, which incidentally served to document more musical gossip for future historians than was common at the time. For its entertainment a local establishment of musicians was joined by visiting celebrities, aspirants, and protégés. George Bridgetower, 11-year-old 'son of an African prince', soon to be taken up by the Prince of Wales and to join Beethoven in the 'Kreutzer' Sonata's first performance, earned 200 guineas for a single appearance in December 1789 (some tickets selling at £5). The 13-year-old Hungarian pianist Johan Nepomuk Hummel (1778–1837) was less successful in October 1791, but soon returned to great acclaim with his own lessons and concertos. Celebrated London instrumentalists like Fischer the oboist were frequent overnight visitors.

An extraordinary group of musicians settled in Bath at various times. They engaged mainly in *music teaching, playing, and organizing for the visitors, but sometimes exerted longer and wider influence. There was William *Herschel, later astronomer royal; Venanzio Rauzzini (1746–1810), for whom Mozart wrote *Exultate Jubilate*, and whose pupils included a clutch of great singers and particularly *women musicians; and the famous Linley family. We do not know exactly what was played, but Bath society generally preferred novelty in music, as in all things, except for a few familiar oratorio excerpts, soprano arias, and Corelli's *Christmas Concerto*. In more sober mood it began to endorse Charles *Burney's 'revolution in taste', from ancient to modern, and by the 1780s there was some move towards stability in serious areas of modern repertoire: keyboard works by Clementi, much Haydn, and a little Mozart. Significantly, perhaps uniquely, Bath for a time provided a cultural environment capable of nurturing such local talents as the Linleys and Jane Mary Guest (c.1765–after 1814)—daughter of a lodging-house keeper, who probably picked up the rudiments from visiting musician lodgers to become a fashionable pianist, composer, and teacher. Even more remarkable was the rise of Lucy Philpot (1797–1878), daughter of an obscure double bass player, who as Mrs Anderson, most eminent of early Victorian pianists and formidable wife of the Master of the Queen's Music, became teacher of the highest ladies in the land, and a manipulator of wide patronage.

But as Haydn shrewdly observed in 1794, only a constant stream of visitors could guarantee prosperity; and when fashion turned, Bath became 'sedate and dull', no longer a place of musical interest. One of its stars who had good reason to look elsewhere was Felix Yaniewicz (1762–1848), a violinist from the Polish court, colleague of Haydn and Mozart, and later a founder member of the Philharmonic. Such was his popularity in Bath that, according to the *Bath Journal*, he could rouse an audience to sing along in accompaniment and barely desist from 'capering about the room'. Yet in a notorious incident he was thrown out of the Assembly Rooms on account of his inferior social status as a public performer. He settled in Liverpool in 1803 to sell music and instruments, compose a little, and still occasionally play at good venues, particularly Edinburgh. Such a career, diverse like Clementi's, shows a clear response to changing opportunities and constraints.

Meanwhile, provincial music necessarily developed its own roots. In the 1770s the important places for music outside London were still Dublin, Bath, Norwich, Edinburgh, York, and Bristol. Soon the locus would shift to the industrial Midlands and North. Deepest were the choral traditions of *Anglican church music and *hymnody, but northern *Methodist chapel singers also registered a new enthusiasm. Handel already formed the mainstay of northern musical taste: as early as 1788 Charles *Dibdin discovered that many Halifax chorus singers knew the whole of *Messiah* by heart. Instrumental societies also sprang up in every major town, and in many villages too, primarily for gentlemen amateurs to enjoy instrumental performance—initially of Baroque concerti grossi, later of the less demanding of the new symphonies. Edinburgh boasted the best-established music society, based on amateur players, but with some professional 'strength' hired from London. Merchants and manufacturers of northern industrial towns were not slow to emulate these sophisticated amusements. By 1823 a journalist for the burgeoning specialist genre of the *musical press noted approvingly that there were music societies in Manchester (one established as early as 1770), Liverpool, Bolton, Rochdale, Preston, Stockport, and Macclesfield. True, these new developments failed to inspire much in the way of lasting creativity, since no provincial composer emerged as a successor to Charles Avison (1709–70) at Newcastle, but the pace of provincial musical life was accelerating. So international stars found it worthwhile to tour the country extensively, often following up a successful London season. Catalani, Moscheles, and Paganini all toured to maximize profits while their reputations lasted, tapping local interests with such offerings as Moscheles's fantasia *Anticipations of Scotland*.

All these strands came together most spectacularly at provincial music festivals, the culminating events in the acquisition of metropolitan pleasures. The late-summer festival spread from the Three Choirs in the west through southern cathedral cities to Birmingham, the northern towns, and eventually Edinburgh, which in 1815 offered seven performances, including Haydn's *Creation* and a symphony, *Messiah* and other Handel excerpts, Beethoven's Second Symphony, and such other Philharmonic standards as the overtures to *Anacreon* by Cherubini and to Mozart's *Magic Flute*. Yaniewicz was there, with the double-bass virtuoso Domenico *Dragonetti, the cellist Robert Lindley (1776–1855), and other leading London players. Often at such festivals the orchestra and choir were of enormous size, following the tradition of the 1784 Handel Commemoration at Westminster Abbey. Originating as charitable fund-raisers and expressions of spiritual and moral uplift, the festivals continued to give a platform to local musicians. Chapel singers were especially dedicated to their cause, even walking from one festival to the next; and enthusiasm was maintained as these informal gatherings began to coalesce into dedicated choral societies. Notable manufacturers were leading patrons, since star performers and colossal orchestras brought trade and status to an emerging city. Distributing international music in response to market opportunities, the festivals also demonstrated social ambition and exclusiveness through highly visible 'insignias of leisure' such as pricing and dress regulation.

Metropolitan and provincial concerts were only one aspect of the market for late Georgian music-making; professional musicians were also compelled to piece together a living by dealing in instruments, sheet music, and lessons. Even the most distinguished virtuosi would take pupils, predominantly young women, and customarily those with status, time, and cash rather than particular talent. Lessons, like concerts, had to be crammed into the short season in London and Bath. Playing, music teaching, composition, *music publishing, instrument-making, selling and tuning (a new specialized skill for pianos) were all intimately linked, with opportunities for promotion and special 'terms'. Publications of Hummel's music were advertised in Bath to coincide with his visit. Conversely, singers eagerly promoted other people's music: violinist William Parke (1762–1847) noted that they would sing anything at all at the Lenten 'oratorios', if the composer or the publisher paid them to stimulate sales. By the 1840s this had developed into an organized system, based on the 'royalty ballad'. Some publishers even opened their own halls for thorough exploitation. Appealing to a wider market because paper travelled more easily than all other music products, successful public works could be immediately rushed into print for domestic consumption [see domestic *music]. Weber's quintessentially German Romantic opera *Der Freischütz* conquered England in 1824. Mary *Shelley wrote to Leigh *Hunt about its owls, toads, fiery serpents, and ghostly hunters. The journal *John Bull* fumed at its 'absurd' drama, the 'very name sickening . . . not a booth, not a barn but has gotten up *Der Freischütz*'; at the same time it carried advertisements from various publishers covering every kind of arrangement: for one or two players at the piano, with flute and cello *ad libitum*; for large or small orchestra; for flute and strings; for piano, flute, and violin.

Yet neither music nor instruments were cheap. A piano score of *Messiah* cost 21 shillings in the 1830s; fifty years later, at 1 shilling, it entered most musical households. Similarly the piano was already acting as 'household orchestra', but only for select families. One decisive shift before 1800, however, indicated an age firmly wedded to technological progress by rejecting the old and embracing the new. Pianofortes of various shapes and sizes decisively drove out harpsichords and spinets, which disappeared, along with knowledge of how to make and play them, for more than a century. We do not know how many pianos were being made during this period, but without economies of scale productivity was very low, distribution was primitive, and prices were therefore high. Despite some contemporary expressions of enthusiasm, 'piano mania' had scarcely begun to affect the mass of people, as it would a generation later [see London *keyboards].

Most aspects of musical life which we loosely associate with nineteenth-century Britain were similarly incipient or underdeveloped. Amateur choral societies, which began to flourish in most towns of 20,000 people or more by mid-century, were in 1830 thin on the ground and predominantly male: the Concert of Ancient Music, for example, still had a professional choir with boy trebles. Similarly the entirely male brass band 'movement' had scarcely begun [see *military bands]. Key elements in the development of modern popular music (expansion, diversification, and nationalization) can hardly yet be discerned. If the success of Romantic music was undoubted, it still awaited exponents of charisma and entrepreneurs capable of wide diffusion. Paganini came in 1831, defining virtuosity; Liszt toured the provinces in 1840–1, and his successors perfected large playing to large audiences. But it was only in the 1830s and 1840s that British musical life began to move towards modern patterns of organization. John Ella's Musical Union (founded in 1845) reunited aristocratic and upper-middle-class patronage in the support of a professionally run society—in this case dedicated to chamber music, part of a general trend towards specialist recitals. At the same time a populist movement began with the importation from Paris of the promenade concert, and Jullien's attempt to woo the 'one shilling public'.

Middle-class values were embodied in the founding of the Sacred Harmonic Society, initially born of religious dissent and social upheaval during the 1830s, but later redirected at the Crystal Palace Handel Festival of 1857. Meanwhile music tuition was becoming more widely available through Mechanics' Institutes and singing classes [see *popular education].

Britain's contribution to the early Romantic movement in music was reluctant and patchy: indeed in some ways the country remained a sceptical outsider, looking in on continental developments. An important indigenous Romantic tradition was, however, represented by the collections of folk-song (unbowdlerized) by Shield and Joseph *Ritson, the exotic or *Gothic settings of some English operas, even the revival of old music as a memory of a chivalric past. And everywhere there remained a sentimental attachment to Celtic folk culture, as concert pianists wrote their fantasies or 'recollections' on Irish melodies; Ries even incorporated six harps into a Bardic overture. But in George *Thomson's collections the folk-songs were decorously harmonized by mainstream composers like Haydn and Beethoven. Thomas *Moore's *Irish Melodies* were similarly domesticated by Henry Bishop for the drawing-room; and even the Welsh *eisteddfod movement became incorporated into the respectable mainstream by the 1820s. It was much the same with opera, whose supernatural or magical settings all too easily descended to routine balladry and superficial colour: Bishop's *Aladdin* was no match for Weber's fantastical *Oberon*. There was, also, a growth of popular and ethnographic interest in music outside Britain and Europe at this time, particularly in *Indian music, a fascination generated by the increased colonial development and settlement of India during this period.

Only in the 1830s did a recognizable early Romantic school emerge, with younger composers like Barnett, Sterndale Bennett, and Macfarren. 1834 saw both the opening of a dedicated English Opera House and the founding of a Society of British Musicians. Literature and music came together at Vincent *Novello's music parties, where Percy *Shelley and John *Keats were regular guests, and where Charles *Lamb listened to Bach and the Viennese masters in a state of bliss for hours on end [see English *Bach movement]. In 1834, again, John Barnett set *Byron, Shelley, and *Wordsworth in his *Lyric Illustrations of the Modern Poets*. This new determination and creative optimism were promising signs indeed, but they cannot disguise an underlying frailty in British musical life. Perhaps Mendelssohn, most revered of foreign visitors, came closest to an identification of national failing: 'The musicians are worse than ours, for there is more competition, and unlike the craftsmen this makes them not better, but more mistrustful and intriguing. In general they have everything that can be cultivated by external means, practice, money, formulas, and the like . . . but everything spiritual is lacking.' The British, he concluded, have 'no respect for the work of art'—this was the true touchstone of German Romanticism, and something that was only gradually to change as the nineteenth century progressed.

Beedell, A. V., *The Decline of the English Musician 1788–1888*, Oxford, 1992; Boydell, B., *Rotunda Music in Eighteenth-Century Dublin*, Dublin, 1992; Ehrlich, C., *The Piano: A History*, London, 1976; *The Music Profession in Britain since the Eighteenth Century: A Social History*, Oxford, 1985; *First Philharmonic: A History of the Royal Philharmonic Society*, Oxford, 1995; Fiske, R., *English Theatre Music in the Eighteenth Century*, 2nd edn., Oxford, 1986; Johnstone, H. D., & Fiske, R., eds., *Music in Britain:* *The Eighteenth Century*, Oxford, 1990; Leppert, R., *Music and Image: Domesticity, Ideology and Socio-Cultural Formation in Eighteenth-Century England*, Cambridge, 1988; McVeigh, S., *Concert Life in London from Mozart to Haydn*, Cambridge, 1993; Temperley, N., ed., *Music in Britain: The Romantic Age 1800–1914*, London, 1981; Weber, W., *The Rise of Musical Classics in Eighteenth-Century England: A Study in Canon, Ritual, and Ideology*, Oxford, 1992.

27 · PAINTING   MARK HALLETT

On 1 July 1787, a London printseller named A. C. de Poggi published an elegant engraving by Johann Heinrich Ramberg and Pietro Martini which depicted that year's *Royal Academy exhibition at Somerset House, crowded with people and paintings. By this date the Academy, set up in 1768, had already become Britain's most powerful institution of the visual arts [see *viewing, 20]. As well as providing its forty full and twenty associate members with a prestigious institutional base, it also functioned as a school for a new generation of British painters, offering a range of classes in drawing, *architecture [28], and anatomy to scores of enrolled students. Moreover, as Ramberg and Martini's print illustrates, the Academy provided a prime exhibition space for established and younger artists in the nation. Each year, during the spring and summer months, hundreds of modern British paintings, *sculptures, and drawings were put on display at Somerset House. Entrance to this exhibition cost a shilling, and attendance quickly became an annual ritual of polite urban society. *The Exhibition of the Royal Academy, 1787*, shows a typically fashionable throng of visitors picking their way through the Academy's main exhibition room. The paintings, large and small, that surround this cluster of connoisseurs and socialites make up a dense jigsaw of wood, canvas, and paint, reaching down to within inches of the floor and squeezing up underneath the rafters.

38. *The Exhibition of the Royal Academy*, 1787, by Pietro Martini and Johann Heinrich Ramberg.

This print, looked at a little more closely, offers us an eloquent introduction to the narratives of British painting in the later decades of the eighteenth century. Let us begin with the two men who are shown strolling through the centre of the exhibition-goers. The flamboyant figure of the Prince of Wales, the son of King George III, quickly catches the eye [see *Regency]. He stands holding a catalogue and a cane in his left hand. By his side Sir Joshua *Reynolds, the President of the Royal Academy, points towards the hanging pictures. This pair, and the dialogue that we are asked to imagine them enjoying, suggest an ideal partnership between British royalty and Academic artists in the period. The inclusion of the Prince of Wales indicates the prestigious origins and connections of the Academy, which had been set up by royal charter. Reynolds, meanwhile, exemplifies the figure of the Academic artist. He was not only the most highly regarded painter of the day, but was also someone who, in his published presidential addresses to students and patrons, provided the Academy with an elevated theoretical programme of taste and judgement.

In these *Discourses*, delivered between 1769 and 1790, artists were consistently directed towards executing works in what Reynolds called the 'grand style': that is, pictures which showed heroic figures from the highest branches of literature, from mythology, or from biblical or national history, and which were painted in an appropriately expansive scale and manner. As in the theoretical formulations of the older French Academy of Painting, this kind of work—known as *history painting—was placed at the head of a hierarchy of pictorial categories by Reynolds, where it was followed by picture types that were given a progressively diminishing aesthetic status: *portraiture, *landscape, genre, and still-life painting. This hierarchy's gradations unapologetically echoed the social and cultural divisions of eighteenth-century Britain itself: as we move from history painting and grand portraiture to (for instance) genre pieces showing humorous scenes from everyday life, we move from works that tended to depict the heroic figures of the great and the good to those that tended to picture non-aristocratic, and often plebeian, protagonists. Reynolds's *Discourses* thus mapped onto the territory of British art a class system for painting, one that conformed to the patrician and élitist pretensions of the Academy, and that reflected broader patterns of differentiation existing within society as a whole.

To execute the history paintings that Reynolds saw as the basis for a prestigious British school of art, individual artists would not only need to be technically proficient, but would also have to demonstrate intellectual sophistication in their choice and handling of subject. The *Discourses* encouraged the Academy's artists and students to concentrate on grand, universal ideas, and to focus on the central, ideal forms that underpinned the variety and particularity visible in the natural world. If 'the Art which we profess has beauty for its object,' Reynolds declares, 'the beauty of which we are in quest is general and intellectual; it is an idea that subsists only in the mind; the sight never beheld it, nor has the hand expressed it: it is an idea residing in the breast of the artist.' Through such high-flown language, the artist is thoroughly disassociated from the mechanical skills of craftsmanship, redefined as a liberal intellectual working within an enlightened Academic community, and mythologized as someone constantly seeking to 'raise the thoughts, and extend the views of the spectator'.

As well as offering a morally and culturally elevated position for the modern artist, the *Discourses* sought to define a proper public for painting in Britain. This public was imagined as a body of cultivated gentlemen whose education and leisure allowed them to interpret and appreciate successfully the exemplary subjects of grand history paintings. Through both intellectual and financial *patronage this constituency would guarantee the future growth of a specifically British school of history painting. And if we return to Ramberg and Martini's print, we can see that the figures of Reynolds and the Prince of Wales are shown to be acting out this gentlemanly alliance between British painters and élite patrons. We are encouraged to assume that they are discoursing learnedly on the exhibition display, and that they focus in particular 89 on the two large history paintings by John *Opie and James Northcote (1746–1831)—*The Assassination of David Rizzio* and *The Death of Wat Tyler*—that dominate the walls on either side of the room. If the two men's pictorial centrality and choreographed body language are indicative of a broader cultural partnership, even more telling is the way in which this partnership is symbolized within the exhibition itself. For, dominating the background and situated just above the two men's heads, we can see Reynolds's own highly ostentatious full-length portrait of the Prince. The utopian harmony between painter and patron that is symbolized by the two men's presence in the middle of the crowd is thus confirmed, at the level of oil and canvas, in the middle of the crowd of exhibited pictures.

On further inspection, however, *The Exhibition of the Royal Academy, 1787* also seems to undercut the rarefied agenda for British art that we have been describing. Our eyes, scanning the engraving, encounter paintings which refuse to fit into the ideal of a public art sketched out in the *Discourses*, and bump into people who dramatically fail to conform to Reynolds's notion of the proper public for that art. Swarming around the history paintings and the grand portrait of a Prince are pictures of beggars, flowers, waterfalls, witches, landscapes, birds, dogs, and horses. Modestly sized portraits of eminently unheroic people—women in fancy hats, humble prelates, and country gentry—jostle at the edges of Opie's and Northcote's history paintings, and hover beneath Reynolds's huge canvas. Furthermore, the crowd of visitors who attend the exhibition is made up not of a select group of élite males, but of a more motley crew of men and women (and children). Many seem wholly uninterested in the paintings on show, and more preoccupied with enjoying the event as an opportunity for entertainment and gossip. In this satirical context, the array of canvases becomes little more than a decorative background to a theatrical parade of high fashion, to a comic series of flirtations, and to laughable displays of misguided connoisseurship. Look, for instance, at the trio of figures on the right. We see a pretentious, somewhat misshapen aficionado of the arts showing off his knowledge to a fashionable woman, while failing to recognize that she is far more interested in the attentions of a handsome young beau.

Here, the exhibition is revealed as an event which encourages a very different set of relationships between the painter, the painting produced, and the audience than that envisaged by Reynolds's *Discourses*. Rather than flaunting education and high-mindedness, the artist is suggested as someone who needs to produce pictures that a mixed and easily distracted crowd will quickly understand and find novel and entertaining. Given these requirements, it is not surprising that the Academy walls filled up with portraits of contemporary celebrities, aristocratic beauties, and civic worthies, and with anecdotal genre-pieces, exotic landscapes, sentimental animal paintings, and gaudy still lifes. These are pictures designed to catch, and momentarily to hold, a succession of glances from a wide array of visitors, rather than be scoured by the eyes of a sophisticate. Paintings, whether executed for aristocrats, picture dealers, or print publishers, or produced as speculative ventures to be sold on the open market, thus increasingly depended for their success on the approbation of a broad urban audience, as much as that of an individual patron. So did painters, who anxiously watched their reputations rise and fall in the rooms of Somerset House.

While Reynolds's *Discourses* manifest a deep anxiety about these developments, contemporary press criticism offered a more positive, attentive, and subtle response to the new exhibition culture [see *prose, 30]. The period saw the rise of the journalistic art critic, a figure who mediated between the mass of paintings on show in the capital and the expanding metropolitan audience for art. The writings of such critics—often published anonymously, or under a humorous pseudonym—recognized that the viewers of painting in the capital appreciated the Academy shows not only as opportunities to exercise artistic refinement but also as commercialized forms of urban entertainment. Consequently, daily and weekly reviews of the exhibition in *newspapers and journals tended to take the form of snappy, gossipy, and frequently scathing responses to the painters and paintings on view. Rather than offering extended interrogations of individual paintings, journalistic art criticism normally mimicked the wandering path of the walker around the exhibition, and took in the ensemble of pictures as a whole. Paintings flit in and out of view, and are often discussed with a free-wheeling disregard for the decorous proprieties of Academic taste.

In this process, the published pronouncements of a painter-theorist like Reynolds became contested by an alternative form of discourse, generated from outside Somerset House. The irreverent language of pamphlets like *The Royal Academicians: a Farce, of 1786* by Anthony Pasquin [see John *Williams], or *Lyric Odes to the Royal Academicians* (1782–5) by Peter Pindar [see John *Wolcot], published regularly over the last two decades of the eighteenth century, offered a satirical and sophisticated rebuttal to the Academy's lofty claims to grandeur. And by the time William *Hazlitt was writing about contemporary art for publications like the *Champion* and the *Morning Review* in the second decade of the nineteenth century, art criticism was confidently assuming the same kind of critical and theoretical authority that had been assumed by Reynolds as President of the Academy, and fusing that authority with the demands of satisfying a broad urban audience. Hazlitt's criticism, parcelled out amongst a variety of newspapers and magazines, and combining the most stringent theoretical rhetoric with an entertaining, idiosyncratic, politicized, and highly personalized form of reportage, testifies to the art critic's growing role as a virtuoso and connoisseur catering to the private pleasures of thousands of individual readers.

How did artists respond to the new exhibition culture described by Pasquin, Pindar, and Hazlitt? While most painters sought to gain entrance into the annual shows at Somerset House, others began organizing independent exhibitions of their own work. Portraitists like Thomas *Gainsborough, for instance, transformed their showrooms into recognized exhibition spaces. These rooms, typically standing next door to the painter's studio, had traditionally functioned as sumptuous places of advertisement, allowing prospective clients to inspect an artist's output in comfort. After a much-publicized quarrel with the Royal Academy in 1784, Gainsborough put on regular exhibitions in his remodelled showrooms in Pall Mall. Visitors were confronted by a multiplicity of full-length portraits of idealized aristocratic and royal sitters, both male and female. Such an ensemble must have functioned like a painted hall of mirrors, reflecting back on the clutch of spectators their own sense of social refinement and worth. Meanwhile, newspaper journalists were invited into Gainsborough's house, both before and during his shows, to report on his sitters and their portraits. This publicity, which fused the vocabulary of artistic appreciation with that of high-class gossip, helped turn the traditional showroom into a fashionable site of sociability, spectacle, and patronage that, in Gainsborough's case at least, competed with the exhibitions at Somerset House.

In an even more novel development, the 1780s also witnessed the rise of one-man exhibitions of modern history painting. Painters and businessmen, having seen the success of the Academy exhibitions, quickly realized the profits that could be made by charging visitors to see large-scale, spectacular, and topical works by celebrated artists, and by reproducing these pictures as engravings [see *prints, 22]. Such ventures, however, were risky. They depended on the notoriously fluctuating state of the individual artist's appeal. The choice of subject painted was also vital, needing to be impressive and appealing enough to draw thousands of people away from the major public exhibitions. Finally, preparing for a one-man show was time-consuming and costly; failure might mean heavy debts and long-term damage to an artistic reputation. Even an artist as successful as Joseph *Wright of Derby lost out with his own one-man show of 1785, which centred on an enormous canvas of *A View of Gibraltar during the Destruction of the Spanish Floating Batteries*. Yet the rewards could be substantial. In one of the more successful of such events John Singleton Copley (1737–1815), an American artist who had settled in London and become an Academician in 1779, rented a large room in

4   the Haymarket to exhibit *The Death of Major Peirson* for two months in 1784. The painting had been commissioned by the print-publisher John *Boydell, for the large sum of £800, and Copley, charging a shilling a ticket and flagging his show in the London newspapers, also took the proceeds from this immensely popular exhibition.

Copley's picture depicted the recent triumph of British forces against the French in Jersey, and the tragic shooting of the young English temporary commander at the point of victory. As such, the painting could be appreciated as a contemporary, highly legible version of a theme—masculine heroism and loyalty in battle—that had been a staple of history painting for centuries. While dressing up this theme in modern uniform, and tying it to an explicitly nationalistic narrative, Copley also subdivided his painting into distinct pictorial sections. This compositional strategy allowed different parts of the canvas to be read simultaneously by different portions of its audience. Meanwhile, the individual spectator moving through this audience, and moving across the picture-space as he or she does so, is given an almost theatrical sense of different scenes following one from the other. Even as it offers its viewers an exemplum of heroic selflessness, painting is thus turned by the dynamics of exhibition into a form of modern drama.

This reconciliation of ambitious painting with the rituals of urban entertainment was further exploited by Copley's patron at the end of the decade. In 1789, John Boydell's Shakespeare Gallery opened in the print-publisher's specially converted premises in Pall Mall. As Francis *Wheatley's sketch of the following year's official opening indicates, this permanent Gallery was crowded with canvases depicting scenes from *Shakespeare, painted by Britain's leading artists and destined to be reproduced as engravings by Boydell. The choice of Shakespeare as a source of subjects allowed the entrepreneur to market his project as a patriotic attempt to 'establish an English School of History Painting'. At the same time, the variety of the playwright's output enabled Boydell to exhibit very different kinds of image—tragic, comic, sentimental, and erotic—alongside each other. The most ambitious and provocative canvases on show, pictures like Henry *Fuseli's *Titania and Bottom*, seem indeed to have internalized and exaggerated the Shakespeare project's eclecticism. Here, a grotesque protagonist, a miniaturized male nude, and an eroticized heroine intermingle promiscuously across the picture's centre, looked at by a circle of fairies whose fashionable, contemporary dress and elegant deportment provide a laconic echo of the female spectators who would have looked at the painting in the gallery itself. Such paintings offered an eerie, *Gothic alternative to the kinds of history painting produced by artists like Copley, one in which the masculine clamour of battle is replaced by an alternative, more fantastical form of patriotic symbolism, laden with the traces of a femininity both alluring and dangerous. 27

Even before the opening of the Shakespeare Gallery, the *Morning Herald* had declared that 'at no period do we remember so many exhibitions at one time as are now open. In every street, the word Exhibition, in great letters, admittance one shilling, strikes the eye—and at every exhibition we see company—a proof that we either have more money or more virtu than heretofore.' Yet this seeming success story—one that implied a parallel resurgence of British painting—was not without its failures, its victims, and its critics. Most importantly, the new exhibition culture only intermittently allowed women painters into its ambits, and then only on specific terms. While artists like Maria Cosway (1759–1838), Mary Moser (d. 1819), and Angelica *Kauffman did exhibit at the Royal Academy and elsewhere, and frequently showed history paintings as part of their contributions, their success in the genre largely depended on producing pictures that focused on allegorized female protagonists, and on the sentimental, 79 private virtues that contemporary culture defined as particularly feminine in nature. Women

39. *A Vase of Flowers* by Mary Moser, one of the few eighteenth-century women artists favoured with royal patronage. She was from the 1760s to the 1790s a prolific painter and exhibitor of flower pictures.

painters were more usually expected to paint pictures which focused on the domestic and the decorative, and their still lives, flower paintings, and portrait miniatures typically occupied the margins of exhibition space. Typically, women painters were expected to be amateur water-colourists rather than professional practitioners in oil, and thus to work in a medium that was still understood as an essentially private, intimate, and understated vehicle of expression [see *watercolour painting].

If women artists found it difficult to move into the centre of the fine arts because of their sex, other painters felt themselves being forced to cultivate countercultural identities on the fringes of the established exhibition circuit. Two of the most notable examples of this phenomenon are James *Barry and William *Blake. In 1777, Barry, an Irish-born painter who had regularly exhibited at the Academy, won a commission to paint a narrative of *The Progress of Human Culture* on the walls of the Great Room of the Royal Society of Arts in the Strand. He planned to turn this huge series, which he had agreed to execute for free, into a commercial loss-leader, which would be financially redeemed after its completion by a one-man exhibition of the finished paintings, and by the sale of engravings after them. The exhibition opened in April 1783, followed by a second a year later, and was accompanied by a catalogue dramatizing Barry's noble conception, grand style, and unusual self-sacrifice in pursuing the scheme. The relatively low attendance and meagre takings of these exhibitions—understandable in the light of the paintings' obscure iconography and esoteric narratives, but made even more galling by the work's extraordinary scale and long period of gestation—left the artist badly out of pocket. They also came to confirm Barry's increasing self-mythologization as a lone artist fighting heroically against a corrupted and unsympathetic artistic establishment.

The kind of self-mythologization, which offered an embittered mirror-image of more dominant narratives of artistic celebrity, was to be shared by William Blake. But while the Society of Artists paintings stood as monolithic testaments to Barry's genius, Blake exalted small-scale, handcrafted, and mixed-media productions as a means of defining his own artistic difference. Failing to find regular employment as a professional engraver, he sought to achieve a select form of patronage by producing small, densely worked 'experimental pictures' that filtered the nationalistic, heroic, and religious themes of history painting through a highly individualized matrix of medium, technique, and visionary symbolism. This experimentalism was also used as a platform for Blake's self-appointed and highly politicized role as a reformer of British painting, which he too saw as having been undermined by an oligarchical clique of painters and dealers. For Blake, even the oil paint used by Academic artists on their canvases was fatally tainted by the forces of commerce. In a one-man exhibition in 1809, held in the unpropitious environment of his family's hosiery shop, Blake displayed a series of 'portable frescos' of patriotic subjects, executed in the antiquated medium of tempera, which he hoped might provide the basis for a revitalized, purified form of ambitious artistic practice in the nation. The stridency of his accompanying *Descriptive Catalogue*, which bemoaned the state of the arts in a corrupt society, only served to suggest the cultural marginality of the works he had produced.

Blake's denunciation emanated from an embattled, radicalized sector of the art world. A similarly searching attack on contemporary taste came from within the centre of Academic culture itself. In one of his annual lectures as Professor of Painting at the Academy, Henry Fuseli, who served in the post from 1799 to 1804, declared: 'if we apply to our Exhibition, what does it represent, in the aggregate, but a gorgeous display of varied powers, condemned, if not to the beasts, at least to the dictates of fashion and vanity?' Fuseli's outburst indicates a newer, far gloomier prognosis for the fate of high art in a commercial society than that encouraged by the initial success of Boydell's Shakespeare Gallery. The Gallery's fortunes had subsequently been catastrophically affected by war with France, which cut off the crucial international markets for Boydell's engravings. More generally, the war years of the 1790s saw a dramatic slump in patronage for native painting, a depression accentuated by the wide interest in the Old Master pictures flooding into the country from war-torn Europe. These circumstances severely hampered Fuseli's own one-man exhibition project of the period, in which he single-handedly planned and painted a Milton Gallery. The ultimate failure of both Boydell's and Fuseli's schemes served to suggest that the alliance between British history painting and the narratives of commerce had been only a temporary truce, one that remained far too dependent on a fickle metropolitan audience and on an unstable international print trade to constitute a viable option for artists and entrepreneurs.

This crisis of history painting allowed other pictorial genres to claim a new status in the fine arts. In particular, the turn of the century saw landscape painting begin to acquire a growing importance as a bearer of public and patriotic narratives, and as a vehicle of high artistic ambition. Already, in the late eighteenth century, painters like Thomas Gainsborough had pro-   72 duced 'fancy-pictures' and landscape oils that offered a bucolic mythology of cheerful, pictorially cleansed peasants performing the unthreatening rituals of gathering wood, going to market, and raising multitudes of children. In the early decades of the nineteenth century, this pictorial remodelling of the British landscape was maintained by scores of professional artists, who travelled the nation with sketchbooks in hand and who returned to their studios to transform preliminary studies into finished exhibition canvases. Such works offered spectators a doubled representation of the rural as a space that was subtly infiltrated by modern narratives of commercial improvement and expansion, but one that was also an uncorrupted repository of morality, tradition, and hierarchical social values standing outside the clogged, mixed, and ever-expanding metropolis. Paintings such as John *Constable's *Flatford Mill* of 1817, exhibited at the Royal Academy and the British Institution, or the views of the Thames exhibited by J. M. W. *Turner in his London gallery during the first decade of the nineteenth century, exemplify this dualized representation of the landscape.

Constable's canvas invites our eye to travel along the pathways of a working mill and waterway on our left, and to potter around the picturesque foreground on our right. Contemporary writings on the arts tied such visual journeys to specific modes of reading. In the associationist theories of spectatorial response articulated by the Revd Archibald Alison (1757–1839) in his *Essays on the Nature and Principles of Taste* (1790), the viewer is encouraged to be stimulated by individual pictorial signs into a train of associations, both moral and intellectual. It is these associations—made more fluent and expansive by the degree of education and sensibility enjoyed by the spectator—that provide aesthetic pleasure and emotion, rather than the object that is being looked at. Here, in contrast to Reynolds, the informed viewer is excited not so much by the idealized forms and heroic narratives that were depicted most clearly in history painting as by the imaginative aftermath of the first encounter with any given image, when the spectator's own refined sensibility goes to work. Significantly, a section of Alison's treatise is devoted explicitly to landscape painting, which testifies to his belief that such pictures could legitimately enter the realms of high art. The depiction of a provincial pocket of landscape such as Constable's *Flatford* could now be seen as a rich starting-point for a meditation on broader, more general themes: the barge, the working boys, and the distant mill buildings might, for instance, be understood to resonate with the narratives of national improvement and agricultural prosperity, while the cultivated beauty of Constable's landscape could be reread as expressive of a Divine order: the 'union of devotional sentiment with sensibility to the beauties of natural scenery', Alison suggests, 'forms one of the most characteristic marks of human improvement, and may be traced to every art which professes to give delight to the imagination.'

While Alison's theories offered one avenue of interpretation and justification for pictures like *Flatford Mill*, the *picturesque theory of writers such as William *Gilpin and Uvedale *Price gave objects like Constable's gnarled tree, clump of plants, twisting brook, and battered

stump an independent aesthetic value as signs of an unspoilt, weathered, and 'natural' British
90–1 landscape endearingly resistant to the claims of modernity. Gilpin's *Three Essays: On Picturesque Beauty; On Picturesque Travel; and of Sketching Landscape* (1792), suggested that the
qualities of the British landscape were best appreciated if the traveller was able to map imaginatively the encountered scene onto those environments depicted in certain kinds of painting,
in particular the rugged landscapes executed by the seventeenth-century Italian artist Salvatore Rosa. This visual editing of the landscape celebrated the irregular, the wild, and the
rough, and turned the eye away from the modern signs of agricultural improvement and industry. This aestheticization of the irregular was refined by Price's *Essay on the Picturesque* of 1794,
in which the humble objects and quotidian narratives found in seventeenth-century Dutch
landscape painting—and reproduced in Constable's work—are imported into a mythical
vision of an untroubled, harmonious English countryside, quietly resplendent under the
paternal supervision of a landed élite. Gilpin's and Price's texts not only offered an aestheticization of rural Britain but were also explicitly intended as blueprints for landscape painters
to follow in their own work. *Flatford Mill* remains redolent of the picturesque aesthetic such
writers formulated, even as that aesthetic's components are shunted into a snug pictorial
corner.

Turner's Thames paintings offered a similarly comforting depiction of a river that had
became a powerful symbol of Britishness. Here, exquisite technique is fused to a loaded form
of pictorial organization that frames the river with the patriotic silhouette of the royal castle on
the one side and with the reassuring imagery of a deferential and productive rural populace on
the other. Other kinds of landscape painting, such as the dramatic depictions of Britain's
wildest outposts and newly emergent industrial landscapes executed by Philippe Jacques de
*Loutherbourg, offered a more unconventional iconography of Britishness. In Louther-
19 bourg's work, dramatically lit factories and vertiginously inaccessible crags articulate a
double-sided narrative in which the sights provided by a modern industrial heartland are complemented, in other paintings, by spectacular views of uncultivated and depopulated environments existing at the nation's edges.

The pictorial tourism offered by paintings like these sought to provide a version of that
*sublime experience theorized by Edmund *Burke in *A Philosophical Enquiry into the Origin
of our Ideas of the Sublime and Beautiful* (1757). Burke had declared that 'whatever is fitted in
any sort to excite the ideas of pain and danger, that is to say, whatever is in any sort terrible, or
is conversant about terrible objects, or operates in a manner analogous to terror, is a source of
the sublime.' Given a certain form of physical distancing, and a recognition that one was not in
actual danger, the encounter with a terrifying object or scene could be a highly pleasurable one.
It generated a keen thrill of the nerves, a 'tranquillity tinged with terror; which as it belongs to
self-preservation, is one of the strongest of all the passions'. Loutherbourg's landscapes, like
many other landscape paintings of the period, self-consciously introduced the vicarious experience of the sublime into aesthetic response, and in doing so they participated in a broader
theatricalization of terror in British visual culture, most vividly illustrated by the dramatic
shows put on in the *panoramas and dioramas of contemporary London. The vast apocalyp-
83 tic paintings of Francis *Danby and John *Martin even offered a glimpse of the most dramatic
theme of all—the sublime terror of the 'last days'.

A different, more sentimental kind of pictorial theatre was provided by the previously
humble category of genre painting, which was, in the first decades of the nineteenth century, to
undergo a similar re-evaluation to that enjoyed by landscape painting. Foreign genre pictures
had long been collected by aristocratic connoisseurs who appreciated their technical sophistication and humour, even though the typically vulgar subjects of such images meant that they
occupied a low place in the traditional hierarchies of the fine arts. At the same time, aestheti-
cized versions of low-life scenes produced by British artists had provided an enduring staple

40. David Wilkie's *Chelsea Pensioners Reading the Gazette of the Battle of Waterloo* (1822) attracted such jostling crowds that a guard-rail had to be erected for the first time in an Academy exhibition.

of the London exhibitions. In the most popular genre paintings of the first decade of the nineteenth century, those exhibited at the Royal Academy by the Scottish painter David *Wilkie, a thoroughly Dutch pictorial vocabulary appealing to wealthy collectors was fused with a comic and sentimentalized representation of rural society that was immensely attractive to a broad urban audience. In subsequent years Wilkie progressively raised the moral and social tone of his subjects, made his pictures larger in scale, and painted them in a more conventionally Academic technique. In doing so, he gradually gave them the status of anecdotal history paintings that offered an easily digested public theme. Typical of this development is his painting of the *Chelsea Pensioners Reading the Gazette of the Battle of Waterloo* of 1822. Here, genre painting situates itself as a quotidian, humorous, but similarly patriotic successor to the kind of work produced by Copley some forty years earlier, one which replaces the narratives of individual heroism in contemporary battle with a compensatory, collective heroism of the home front, pictured with a new concern for entertaining detail and everyday comedy. The commotion that Wilkie's painting caused on its exhibition at Somerset House—the crowds of people fighting to look at his work meant that, for the first time, a guard-rail had to be erected in front of an exhibited canvas—offers a powerful confirmation of the growing importance of genre painting in exhibition culture.

Nevertheless, it would be misleading to end our account with Wilkie's painting, for the portrait continued to remain the most ubiquitous element of the exhibition display. Writing in 1812 Benjamin Robert *Haydon, an artist who bemoaned this development, was forced to recognize that the privatized representations of portraiture had won out over the public narratives of his beloved history painting: 'nobody refuses portraits of themselves or their friends on canvases 8, 10, 12 feet long, but every one shuts his door against the illustrious deeds of our own and of other countries unless on the pettiest canvases.' While Haydon exhibited enormous paintings of traditional heroes for ever-diminishing returns, portrait painters like Thomas *Lawrence not only became wealthy and famous, but acquired increasing institutional authority at the Academy. Lawrence became President in 1820, replacing Benjamin *West, who had succeeded to the post on Reynolds's death. Under West and Lawrence's presidencies, the Academy's walls were often dominated by a genteel parade of pictured individuals, themselves painted by increasingly celebrated individual portraitists. Meanwhile, thanks to the fact that the fine arts were being promoted as a fashionable and affordable pursuit for an expanding sector of urban society, the exhibition audience who circulated in front of these paintings was becoming more recognizably middle-class in character. This is clearly evidenced in the representations of later Academy exhibitions, for example George Scharf's (1788–1860) watercolour of *The Royal Academy Exhibition, 1828*. Scharf's image, packed with portraits painted by the stars of the Academy, and with the top-hatted, besuited, and beribboned members of the urban bourgeoisie who have come to view them, usefully reveals that the Romantic cult of the individual exemplified by the boom in portraiture was being articulated along a collective, commercialized circuit of taste. Each sitter and viewer takes his or her place in a strikingly homogeneous, undifferentiated, and repetitive mass of paintings and people, offering a sardonic confirmation that painting, even as it dramatized a modern notion of individuality, simultaneously served as a crucial means of confirming a bourgeois community's cultural uniformity, both within and without the Academy's walls.

Barrell, J., 'The Body of the Public' in his *The Political Theory of Painting*, New Haven, Conn., 1986; ed., *Painting and the Politics of Culture: New Essays on British Art 1700–1850*, Oxford, 1992; Bermingham, A., *Landscape and Ideology: The English Rustic Tradition, 1740–1846*, London, 1987; Eaves, M., *The Counter-Arts Conspiracy: Art and Industry in the Age of Blake*, Ithaca, NY, 1992; Gage, J., *J. M. W. Turner, 'A Wonderful Range of Mind'*, New Haven, Conn., 1987; Hemingway, A., *Landscape Imagery and Urban Culture in Early Nineteenth-Century Britain*, Cambridge, 1992; Lukacher, B., 'History Painting: Blake and His Contemporaries' and 'Nature Historicized: Constable, Turner, and Romantic Landscape Painting', in S. F. Eisenman et al., eds., *Nineteenth Century Art: A Critical History*, London, 1994; Rosenthal, M., *Constable: The Painter and His Landscape*, New Haven, Conn., 1983; Solkin, D., *Painting for Money: The Visual Arts and the Public Sphere in Eighteenth-Century Britain*, New Haven, Conn., 1993; Waterhouse, E., *Painting in Britain, 1530–1790*, New Haven, Conn., 1994.

28 · ARCHITECTURE   DANIEL ABRAMSON

Between the mid-1770s and the mid-1830s, architecture in Britain flourished as hundreds of new buildings for government, industry, commerce, culture, religion, and leisure were constructed across the country. In design terms, architects stuck largely to conservative habits for large public buildings, but at the professional and theoretical levels they reacted with great innovation to economic, political, and social developments usually, however, beyond their full comprehension and control. Indeed, so destabilizing were the effects upon architecture of commercialization, war, and market culture that by the mid-1830s a consensus had formed that the work of the previous decades had failed. However, such condemnation obscured the complex struggles and real achievements of the period.

To gain an overview of architectural production between the mid-1770s and mid-1830s it is useful to divide the period roughly into three twenty-year segments. From the mid-1770s until the outbreak of *war [2] with France in 1793 a handful of major government projects dominated the scene. In London, there was Sir William *Chambers's Somerset House (1776–96),   97 a palatial administrative and cultural complex along the newly embanked Thames River; in Edinburgh, Robert *Adam's Register House (1774–92); and in Dublin, Thomas Cooley and James *Gandon's Four Courts judicial complex (1786–1802), new Customs House (1781–91), and Parliament House additions (1784–7). More typically, for a nation habitually suspicious of centralized bureaucracy, government building was focused on the county level, for example Thomas *Harrison's administrative complexes at Chester (1788–1822) and Lancaster (1788–99). There was also a burst of *prison-building beginning in the mid-1780s and spurred by parliament and the efforts of *prison reformers such as John *Howard. While fashionable architects like Adam, George *Dance, John *Nash, James *Wyatt, and John *Soane all tried their hands at penal design, the field was dominated by specialists like William Blackburn (1750–90), intimate friend and colleague of Howard, and the designer of no fewer than nineteen prisons between 1785 and 1790.

From 1793 to 1815, the nearly constant state of war with France put an end to prestigious government projects, especially in London. One exception was Soane's dramatic expansion of the Bank of England (1788–1833), which added new offices for the administration of the *national debt and paper money supply. For commercial and industrial architecture the war posed no impediment: new docks, warehouses, exchanges, markets, customs houses, mills, foundries, warehouses, and *factories were built throughout the country. Socially, the war years had two distinct consequences for architecture. On the one hand, the disruptions of war, *industrialization [14], and urbanization prompted government and charities to erect countless new prisons, workhouses, *madhouses, orphanages, and hospitals whose objective was essentially the maintenance of lower-class order: for example, Thomas Hardwick's (1752–1829) famous Millbank Penitentiary in London (1812–13) and William Stark's   54 (1770–1813) Lunatic Asylum in Glasgow (1809–11), thought to be the first British asylum built on a radiating plan. At another social level, the increasing prosperity of Britain's middle orders engendered a remarkable new architecture of leisure. Especially in the urban centres of the provinces there appeared numerous athenaeums, libraries, newsrooms, academies, museums, theatres, hotels, and art galleries, usually designed by prominent regional architects. In Liverpool there was John Foster I's (1758–1827) Athenaeum (completed 1799), Union Newsroom (1800), and Theatre Royal (1802–3), as well as Harrison's Lyceum (1800–3). William Stark's Hunterian Museum (1804–5) in Glasgow was one of the earliest of thirty-six museums founded in Britain between 1800 and 1837. And in Plymouth, John Foulston's (1772–1841) extraordinary Royal Hotel (1811–13) joined together an athenaeum, theatre, and hotel with meeting-rooms for business and pleasure.

After *Waterloo, architectural production in Britain soared to unprecedented heights. John Foster II's (c.1787–1846) iron St John's Market in Liverpool (1820–2) and Thomas *Telford's River Conway Suspension Bridge in Caernarvonshire (now Gwynedd) (1821–6) represented some of the most technologically advanced structures in the world. For society's troubled, scores of new prisons, hospitals, and asylums continued to be erected. For the prosperous there were also important new buildings: Nash's Royal Opera House (1816–18) and Haymarket Theatre (1820–1), William *Wilkins's University College, London (1827–8) and National Gallery (1834–8), Sir Robert *Smirke's *British Museum (1823–46), Decimus Burton's (1800–81) Athenaeum Club (1827–30), and Charles *Barry's Travellers' Club (1830–2). All these were London buildings, and indeed the war's end returned the capital to national preeminence in royal, public, and ecclesiastical architecture. Already between 1815 and 1822, the Prince Regent was employing his favourite architect, Nash, for the exotic Royal Pavilion at

41. The Royal Pavilion at Brighton was remodelled by John Nash (1815–22) according to the taste of the Prince of Wales. Known popularly as the Regent's Palace, this expensive oriental pleasure-dome in Brighton became synonymous with Regency extravagance and dissipation.

Brighton, and in 1824 Jeffry *Wyatville began his considerable renovation of Windsor Castle. Most of all, Buckingham Palace, begun by Nash in 1825, seemed to fulfil a long-standing dream for ambitious royal patronage on a continental scale. The government contributed to London's development by commissioning Soane's Westminster Law Courts (1822–5), Smirke's General Post Office (1824–9), and Burton's Hyde Park Screen (1824–5) and Arch on Constitution Hill (1827–8). Of national importance was parliament's decision in 1818 and 1824 to spend one and a half million pounds to help build over 500 new *Anglican churches for the promotion of religious, political, and social obedience in the turbulent urban areas of London, Lancashire, and Yorkshire. In London, Barry and James Savage (1779–1852) specialized in these so-called Commissioners Churches, as did Thomas Rickman (1776–1841) in the Midlands.

A survey of British architecture from the 1770s to the 1830s would hardly be complete without some mention of town planning. London continued to grow in all directions. Dance planned a number of new areas in and to the east of the city between 1768 and 1810. Intensive development to the north and west, from Bloomsbury to Paddington, ceased only during the war years. To the south and west, Belgravia and Pimlico were built up in the 1820s as fashionable districts adjacent to the new Buckingham Palace. Little of this work, however, was done by well-known architects; instead, developers like James Burton (1761–1837) and Thomas *Cubitt, as well as builders and tradesmen, assumed the role of designer. London's most famous urban project was Nash's Regent's Park scheme (1811–26), a spectacular series of palatial whitewashed terraces ringing a new park, itself sprinkled with luxury villas. Connecting the park to the Prince Regent's Carlton House (designed by Henry *Holland, 1783–96) was the new Regent Street with its splendid variety of commercial and residential buildings. In Scotland, developments were equally dramatic as both Edinburgh and Glasgow gained fashionable gridiron extensions designed, amongst others, by James Craig (1740–95), Robert Reid (1776–1856), William Playfair (1790–1857), George Smith (1793–1856), and William Stark.

Industrial communities like Robert *Owen's New Lanark (begun 1799) were also projected during this period.

To many the architectural picture looked very bright indeed. For the first time, the prospering middle orders joined Crown and state as patrons of important public building. The notion was widely held that Britain's military, political, and commercial ascendancy was naturally going to be accompanied by comparable architectural triumphs. And yet by the 1830s the tide of opinion had reversed. Observers perceived modern London as monotonous and possessed of too few magnificent public buildings. Parliamentary inquiries into Nash's Buckingham Palace deflated public confidence, as did the 1825 collapse of David Laing's (1774–1856) London Custom House (1813–17). It was felt that architecture was becoming a commercial trade, populated by unscrupulous architects and, even worse, unskilled builders and tradesmen. It seemed also to have abdicated its traditional ideological work of marking social character and hierarchy. 'There must be something radically wrong', one critic wrote, 'where the same sort of portico may be applied to the New Bedlam, Carlton House, Covent-garden Theatre, and Mary-Le-Bonne church.' The press itself contributed to architecture's sameness, many felt, by being overly critical of innovation. Talent was further inhibited by the supposed want of taste in the middle class, the absence of sustained royal patronage, and the lack of a proper teaching academy. What particularly stung was British architecture's obvious second-rank status behind continental production. When the leading Prussian architect Karl Friedrich Schinkel came to Britain in 1826, it was not to survey recent public building but to investigate the country's industrial base represented by the Stanley textile mill near Stroud (1812–13), the Tanfield gasworks in Edinburgh (1824), and Telford's Menai Straits Suspension Bridge in Caernarvonshire (1819–26).

The disillusion of the time was most completely expressed by the young architect Augustus Welby Northmore *Pugin in *Contrasts* (1836). Focusing his anger on the often cheaply built Commissioners Churches, Pugin broadly indicted contemporary architecture for its lack of feeling, contrasting its plain and supposedly morally insincere style with the richly decorated, and therefore deeply spiritual, work of medieval architects. Pugin's damning opinion lives on today in the mythography of modern architecture, but its fierce negativity obscures a more complicated reality. To understand the paradox of the period—how architecture was so productive, yet also felt to be in crisis—and how architects bravely and imaginatively responded to novel conditions (notwithstanding Pugin's damnations), it is necessary to chart how changes in British economics, politics, and society complexly affected architectural practice and thought.

Above all else, economic developments had a profound influence on British architecture from the 1770s to the 1830s. Industrialization engendered new building types, like factories, and new material possibilities, like iron. But the former never rose to the level of architecture. Whilst Nash used iron and glass to great effect at the Brighton Pavilion, in general British architects failed to exploit new materials except where they could be used to reproduce existing idioms cheaply. Eleanor *Coade's artificial stone statuary, capitals, plaques, friezes, and chimney-pieces could be found throughout London's new West End, in Holland's Carlton House, Nash's Buckingham Palace, and Soane's Bank of England, and were extensively used by every client, builder, or architect eager for economical ornament. By the 1830s, however, Coade Stone had become a symbol of architecture's spiritless commercialism.

Indeed, it was commercialization rather than industry that destabilized the profession. Without the steady government and royal patronage enjoyed by their continental counterparts, British architects were at the mercy of the building cycle, itself profoundly sensitive to the mercurial booms and busts of a newly expansive free-market economy. In these circumstances, architects' economic and thus also social status became extremely precarious, a situation only slightly ameliorated by Soane's charitable 'Fund for Distressed Architects'. Competing in the market-place also meant little time for intellectual work on a par with that

produced, for instance, by government-employed architects in France. Furthermore, Soane
and others believed that recent commercial real-estate speculation had seduced unscrupulous
architects into becoming developers and contractors, and had enticed tradesmen to usurp the
architect's design role. It seemed that cheap, flimsy, monotonous architecture was rapidly
replacing the nation's rich architectural patrimony. In certain respects, then, the feeling of
crisis in the 1830s was a reaction to the commercialization of architecture. A modern market
economy seemed to have sacrificed artistic and material quality, and debased architecture to
the level of an insecure, unintellectual, and rapacious trade.

After the economy, the long war with France from 1793 to 1815 must be considered the second
major factor contributing to changes in British architecture. Most evidently, high wartime taxes
curtailed opportunities for ambitious public and private patronage, but the war also affected
architecture by loosening the ties between the state and the profession. Traditionally, the government's Office of Works had been run and staffed by prominent practitioners like Chambers,
Wyatt, Soane, Nash, and Smirke, who used their official positions to secure prestigious projects
and train younger architects. But over time the architects lost control of the Office and its prerequisites, in part because of their own mismanagement. Laing's Custom House and Nash's
Buckingham Palace were public scandals, and Wyatt's surveyorship (1796–1813) was an unmitigated disaster. More importantly, the administrative and financial stresses of war impelled parliament to reform and shrink government departments and spending, as a result of which
architects lost the leadership of the Office to professional administrators in the 1810s. By 1832
the Office itself was humiliatingly subsumed into the Office of Woods and Forests, and parliament had declared that major public projects would be commissioned through politicized competitions distasteful to architects. Thus the institutional link between state and profession was
extinguished, and architecture for the first time in any country was effectively thrust into the
brave new world of the commercial market-place without support of Crown and state.

The war had one other, perhaps more profound, psychological and practical effect. While
it lasted it severed Britain from the Continent, where for generations architects had travelled
for training and inspiration. As soon as peace came Soane, Smirke, and Nash immediately set
out for Paris. In 1818, half the catalogue of the major London architectural bookseller I. and J.
Taylor was composed of works in French. But by then the damage had been done. British
architecture was seen, rightly or wrongly, to have fallen well behind continental standards.

Changes in British society between the mid-1770s and mid-1830s also had substantial
consequences. First, as we have seen, was the emergence of a whole new class of institutional
architecture—prisons, workhouses, orphanages, asylums, and hospitals—built as a calculated
response to the destabilizing social effects of war, industrialization, and urbanization. Of wider
significance was the enrichment and expansion of the nation's middle classes. By the end of the
period the middle classes were acknowledged, with some reservations, to be the leading hope
for architectural patronage.

The rise of the middle classes also transformed the space and nature of public discourse on
architecture. In the 1770s, this discourse was closely circumscribed within the sphere of
architect-authored and often self-published books, builders' manuals, the *Royal Academy,
and a small group of élite practitioners, patrons, and connoisseurs. During the following
decades a middle-class, commercial cultural market revolutionized architectural media.
New art periodicals like Elmes's *Annals of the Fine Arts* (1816–20) and the *Library of the Fine
Arts* (1831–2) published on architecture, as did more general magazines like the *Quarterly
Review*, the *Edinburgh Review*, the *Westminster Review*, the *Foreign Quarterly Review*,
Blackwood's Edinburgh Magazine, the *Athenaeum*, *Fraser's Magazine*, *Colburn's New Monthly
Magazine*, the *Spectator*, the *European Magazine*, and the *Literary Gazette* [see *prose,
30]. Ambitious topographical publications also, initially, reflected the isolation and pat-
riotism of the war years: John *Carter's *Ancient Architecture of England* (1795–1814);

Edward Brayley and John *Britton's monumental *The Beauties of England and Wales* (25 vols. 1801–14); A. C. *Pugin and Britton's *Illustrations of the Public Buildings of London* (1825–8); and James Elmes and T. H. Shepherd's steel-engraved *Metropolitan Improvements* (1827–30) and *London in the Nineteenth Century* (1829–31). This novel media reached well beyond architecture's traditional reading public. The topographical publications and periodicals like the *Penny Magazine* and *Gentleman's Magazine* appealed to lower and middle-class patriotic, antiquarian sensibilities [see *antiquarianism, 35]. Britton wrote for 'professional and private gentleman', and Elmes lectured in 1819–21 in Birmingham and London to 'honourable and respectable classes of amateurs or non-professors', as well as to the 'literary and scientific world' and the 'more opulent of the middle classes'. Besides the consumers, the producers of the new architectural discourse also departed from traditional norms. Taking on roles previously assumed by architects were generalist men of letters and professional writers like Britton and Elmes, and commercial publishers like John *Boydell, Rudolph *Ackermann, I. and J. Taylor, and John Weale (1791–1862).

This was not a comfortable situation for practising architects. They seem in the first place to have largely withdrawn themselves from the discourse. While eleven practising architects, including Soane, Nash, and Smirke, did contribute to Britton and Pugin's *Public Buildings of London*, none of the major figures of the early nineteenth century except Soane ever independently published works on either their buildings or their theories. Moreover, because the new writing usually focused on surface style—inasmuch as non-architects comprehended little else—and was commonly penned in a critical manner, practising architects were often in conflict with it. More than once, Soane considered legal action against his detractors. The co-option of architectural discourse into middle-class, commercial culture decisively loosened architects' control over the public presentation and reception of their work. An already heightened sense of economic, social, and professional insecurity was thus further aggravated.

The most frequently recurring remedial action against such insecurity took place at the level of professional education, organization, and ideology. In the first instance, repeated efforts were made to strengthen young architects' training. Traditionally this consisted of a three- to seven-year pupilage, private drawing lessons, occasional lectures at the Royal Academy, and, if one were lucky, foreign travel. The weak link, as everyone recognized, was the lacklustre education provided by the Royal Academy in Somerset House. The Academy offered a mere six lectures a year (and then only when an architect could be found to deliver them), opened its library only briefly twice a week, and from its founding in 1768 to 1828 managed to sponsor only twelve architectural students' brief sojourns in Italy. (By contrast, the government-sponsored architecture school in Paris held bi-weekly lectures, had two extensive libraries which were always open, owned an extensive collection of artefacts, models, and plaster casts, and annually sent its top student to Rome for five years.) From 1809 onwards there were regularly published criticisms of the Royal Academy's failings and numerous proposals for reform. For example, the young Thomas Leverton Donaldson (1795–1885), future President of the Royal Institute of British Architects, founded the Architectural Students' Society in 1817 and petitioned for extended library hours and a School of Architecture. Soane did permit Academy students to study from his own private collections, and on his death bequeathed them and his house to the state. However, it would not be until 1840 that a real course in architecture would be offered by the new King's College, London.

The struggle for educational reform was ultimately about strengthening architects' occupational and social status in the ongoing battle to wrest *design [25] work away from tradesmen, surveyors, *engineers, and builders. A second tactic in this same battle was the creation of a modern professional organization that could define, promote, and protect their collective interest. The first tentative step was taken in 1791 with the founding of the Architects' Club. This group met monthly at the Thatched House Tavern in London, mainly to socialize, and its membership was strictly limited. In 1806, the more open London Architectural Society was founded. Its purpose was self-improvement, and fortnightly meetings featured presentations of original designs and essays. In 1831 forty younger men, again in London, established the Architectural Society with the aim of forming an academy. Its membership was the most democratic, open to anyone who had studied in an office for at least five years. However, the breakthrough date was 1834 when architects reclaimed part of the public discourse with J. C. *Loudon's *Architectural Magazine*, written largely by and for professionals. At the same time, no fewer than eighty leading practitioners from around the country banded together to found the Institute of British Architects. Dedicated to upholding the reputation of the profession, the Institute held its present and future members to an unprecedented code of ethics. This dictated the architect's professional role to be that of a financially disinterested intermediary between client and builder, as Soane had been urging for years. The Institute aimed decisively and publicly to distinguish architects, along intellectual, occupational, ethical, and social lines, from their untrained, profit-minded, ungentlemanlike rivals. In effect, the Institute (soon to be the Royal Institute) represented British architecture's most innovative response to the commercialization of architecture. Admittedly, it had taken a long time to arrive at this point. But this was because there had been no precedent to follow. This invention of a new professional ideology and national institutional formation was one of the great achievements of British architecture in the first third of the nineteenth century.

Less coherently, but no less interestingly, British architects also fashioned aesthetic and theoretical responses to the exigencies of the times. Classicism in one form or another was the dominant style for major public buildings because of its capacity to represent conventionally the values of order, hierarchy, magnificence, and tradition. Chambers's progressive Franco-Italian classicism held sway during the first half of the period, with its Roman emphasis on richly articulated wall surfaces. After about 1810, British architects adopted a restrained Grecian vocabulary whose basic structural element was the free-standing column (with a particular bias for the elegant Ionic order) and whose ubiquitous representational image was the detached temple front, a conventionalization of the mythological first primitive hut. The Grecian or *neoclassical revival thus stood for a return to the very beginnings of classicism, and its purity represented a conservative antidote to what Britton called the 'mangled corpse' of modern, heterogeneous architecture. Moreover, Grecian classicism's learned foundation in a series of archaeological investigations implicitly secured the profession's intellectual status. Also worth noting is the fact that these expeditions to Ottoman-controlled Greece and the Near East represented the informal, cultural wing of British foreign policy. Grecian classicism was therefore, among other things, an imperial style [see *Hellenism].

The war with France, however, undercut the dominance of élite cosmopolitan classicism and fostered a more populist, cultural nationalism, oriented towards *medievalism. During the war years—which for the most part precluded overseas expeditions—a series of commercially produced books publicized the nation's own archaeological patrimony, for example Britton's *Architectural Antiquities of Great Britain* (1807–14). These works engaged middle-class interest in the preservation of old *Gothic buildings and the construction of new Gothic-style structures, primarily for domestic and religious uses. Professional architects were, in general, less interested. Gothic was not part of their training. It lacked classicism's established language of order, rationality, and magnificence. Gothic architecture did, however, possess certain advantages. Its lightness of structure had long been admired, and it was also believed to be more physically pleasurable to look at than classical architecture. It possessed a greater surface richness, a more striking skyline diversity, and in general a much more fanciful play of light and shade. In a word, it was more *picturesque.

Uvedale *Price's *An Essay on the Picturesque* (vol. i, 1794; vols. i–ii, 1796–8) and Richard Payne *Knight's *An Analytical Inquiry Into the Principles of Taste* (1805) laid out the theoretical foundations of picturesque architecture. Derived from the examples of Robert Adam and John Vanbrugh (1664–1726), the architect of Blenheim Palace, Oxfordshire (1705–16), the picturesque's formal criteria were bold contrasts of light and shade, prominent projections and recessions, a richly varied skyline, an overall appearance of irregularity and roughness, and an intricate interior plan featuring a succession of rooms varied in size and shape. Based on the compositional, aesthetic imitation of the *landscape painting of Salomon Van Ruysdael or Claude Lorrain and above all else on the actual English countryside, picturesque theory valued variety, irregularity, mutability, and contingency. The ruin was the archetypal picturesque structure. Picturesque architecture was supposed to strike the eye with a more vivid physical sensation and, for the knowledgeable, evoke pleasant sensations of remembered paintings and scenes. Indeed, what is so remarkable about the theory of the picturesque is the degree to which it was conceived in relation to its audience. In a revolutionary gesture, picturesque theorists from Adam onwards claimed that architectural quality should be judged by the novel entity of 'public opinion'—that is to say, by the market—not by tradition, precedent, or principle. In practice, the picturesque was primarily a domestic style, as in the work of the country house architect Anthony *Salvin. It was rarely adopted for large-scale public buildings. Its abstract, formal pleasures militated against legible representations of order, utility, hierarchy, and tradition. Soane's Bank of England is perhaps the one major example of a picturesque public building. However, its novel ornamentation, complexly varied elevations, and intricate planning more often than not perplexed critics, who wanted public architecture to make sense, not just please the public eye.

The picturesque's visual diversity could be made architecturally meaningful by applying its principles to a mixing of recognizable historical styles. A creative eclecticism could borrow the best from all periods, add new elements, instantiate a national style, and, as the designer Thomas *Hope wrote in the 1830s, compose 'an architecture which, born in our country, grown in our soil, and in harmony with our climate, institutions, and habits, at once elegant, appropriate, and original, should truly deserve the appellation of "Our Own"'. Eclecticism therefore combined the indigenous traditions of Gothic and picturesque with classical cosmopolitanism and a new concern for the expression of contemporaneity. It also occupied a comfortable middle ground between convention and novelty. It was nicely adapted to market conditions, since it would always be producing new, contemporaneous forms. Moreover, its historical erudition could articulate new meanings for public architecture, while augmenting the profession's intellectual status. Eclecticism did, however, have one weakness. It was usually understood to be a theory of surface style, therefore failing to engage the full, three-dimensional reality of architecture.

Few theorists of the period essayed a conceptualization of architecture in depth, perhaps because of the obsession with style of the dominant lay criticism and the incomplete education of architects themselves. Soane was an exception. In his Royal Academy lectures he argued that the total design of every building—from its plan and façade down to the smallest ornamental detail—should uniformly express the building's unique, specific purpose or character. The concept of character appealed at a number of levels. It bore the prestigious stamp of contemporary French theory, an important consideration for Soane. More importantly, it addressed the need for ideological representations of social hierarchy by creating distinctive architectural expressions for every type of institution and building, high and low, new and old, from 'the Cathedral and the Church' to 'the Hall of Justice' to 'the gloomy Prison; nay even the Warehouse and the Shop'. The theory of character also subtly strengthened the architect's professional position, another important consideration for Soane, by extending his authority over every part of every single building type.

Ironically, Soane's concept of character prefigured the theory of one of his fiercest critics;

42. Joseph Gandy's bird's-eye view (1830) of John Soane's renovations to the Bank of England.

A. W. N. Pugin also believed in the idea that the best architecture represented a total, symbolic expression of its 'destination'. Pugin, however, understood 'destination' to be more than mere function, but also to encompass religious beliefs and values. Pugin therefore identified the Gothic cathedral as a concrete symbol created not by its architect but by the faith of perfect Christian society. It is a further irony of Pugin's ideology that while it was the most anti-modern of its day, it was also in a sense the most market-orientated. Whereas the picturesque theorists had only proposed that architecture should *please* its public, Pugin was proposing that the best architecture was in fact *produced* by its public.

His famous work, *Contrasts*, also involved a deep attack on the modern asylum, including prisons and hospitals, which Pugin rightly perceived as having usurped the role of the Church in nineteenth-century Britain as the guarantor of social morality and stability. Beginning in the 1780s, asylum designers refined the gathering, controlling, categorizing, and rehabilitating of society's outcasts. For the first time, architecture was judged on its explicit social utility: how effectively could it modify behaviour through classification, isolation, and surveillance? Architecture no longer just *represented* social authority but was expected to *instrument* that authority. Where once, in Pugin's view, a good society had created its perfect architecture, now the perfect architecture would produce the good society. Ironically, then, the modern British asylum was the logical correlative to Pugin's social-moral theory of architecture. By calling on

buildings to engineer social improvement, the marginal field of asylum design represented one of the most advanced theoretical positions in contemporary British architecture.

No single image better illustrates the complexities of the period than the remarkable water-colour of the Bank of England rendered for Soane by Joseph *Gandy and exhibited publicly at the Royal Academy in 1830. In this sweeping picture, Soane and Gandy attempted to reconcile the contradictions of the time: to represent the Bank as both picturesquely in ruins and professionally under construction; to equate modern invention with the venerated ruins of antiquity; to be both British and classical; to gift London with the Roman grandeur it seemed so sadly to lack; and, finally, for the most written-about architect of his day, to attempt to seize back control of public presentation of his work from the critics of the new commercial discourse.

Adams, B., *London Illustrated, 1604–1851: A Survey and Index of Topographical Books and Their Plates*, Phoenix, Ariz., 1983; Archer, J., *The Literature of British Domestic Architecture, 1715–1842*, Cambridge, Mass., 1985; Britton, J., *The Union of Architecture, Sculpture, and Painting*, London, 1827; Colvin, H., *A Biographical Dictionary of British Architects, 1600–1840*, New Haven, Conn., 1995; Crook, J. M., & Port, M. H., eds., *The History of the King's Works*, vi: *1782–1851*, London, 1973; Elmes, J., *Lectures on Architecture (1821)*, New York, 1971; Kindler, R., 'Period-ical Criticism, 1815–40: Originality in Architecture', *Architectural History*, 17 (1974), 22–37; Markus, T. A., ed., *Order in Space and Society: Architectural Form and Its Context in the Scottish Enlightenment*, Edinburgh, 1982; Schinkel, K. F., '*The English Journey': Journal of a Visit to France and Britain in 1826*, ed. D. Bindman & G. Riemann, New Haven, Conn., 1993; Soane, J., *Lectures on Architecture*, ed. A. T. Bolton, London, 1929; Summerson, J., *Georgian London*, London, 1988.

29 · POETRY JEROME J. McGANN

'Romantic Poetry' is a philological term for a style or movement in verse-writing historically located in the late eighteenth and early nineteenth centuries. It is important to realize that the term works according to a fuzzy logic: that is to say, it is the very looseness of the term that can promote helpful critical discussion. For the phenomena associated with *Romanticism and Romantic poetry are volatile even to this day.

Among the many meanings of the meanings of Romantic poetry, one has clearly dominated. It is not really a 'meaning', however; it is a list or canon of writers: *Wordsworth, *Coleridge, *Byron, *Shelley, and *Keats, with *Blake—the youngest and earliest—added somewhat later. This is the Pleiades of English Romantic poetry, and, like that famous six-star constellation in Taurus, well-observed and known to all. When more specialized instruments are trained on these Romantic skies, however, other heavenly bodies always appear, and the shape of the constellation itself will change slightly. These (many) others—collectively, the lost 'seventh' Pleiad of the constellation—help to explain why the logic of the term 'Romantic poetry' must be fuzzy. Here is a partial list of the lost Pleiad's names: George *Crabbe, Anna *Seward, Erasmus *Darwin, Robert *Burns, Charlotte *Smith, Sir William *Jones, Hannah *Cowley, Robert *Merry, Ann Batten *Cristall, Walter *Scott, Helen Maria *Williams, Mary *Robinson, Robert *Southey, Dorothy *Wordsworth, Mary *Tighe, Leigh *Hunt, Felicia *Hemans, John *Clare, Laetitia Elizabeth *Landon, Thomas Lovell *Beddoes, Winthrop Mackworth *Praed, Thomas *Hood.

If our observations of the constellation were being carried out from a different stellar position, we would see it differently, and might not perceive one or another of the currently visible six. That is important to realize when we begin to think about Romantic poetry. On the other hand, Romantic poetry is fatally (or objectively) shaped by the history that produced the term.

All this is by way of preface to the following set of ideas, which govern this brief introduction to 'Romantic poetry'. Because the term designates, in my view, a vital body of writing, our study needs to cherish its volatile character. One way of doing that is to read the poetry in terms of the lost Pleiad, a procedure that has recently gained considerable acceptance. As T. S. Eliot argued in a famous essay, a tradition changes to our view when new elements are brought into its equations. Another way, however—it is the road taken here—focuses on the unstable structure of the traditional and dominant phenomenon itself: on the tensions and contradictions that define that deceptively stable thing we call 'Romantic poetry'.

Although Romanticism has been read as a revolt against *neoclassical models of cultural order, if we measure the movement by the norms set out in Wordsworth's Preface to *Lyrical Ballads* (1800)—the most traditional way of proceeding—we see that Wordsworth's critical object is not Pope or *Johnson but something much nearer to home:

The invaluable works of our elder writers, I had almost said the works of Shakespear and Milton, are driven into neglect by frantic novels, sickly and stupid German Tragedies, and deluges of idle and extravagant stories in verse. —When I think upon this degrading thirst after outrageous stimulation I am almost ashamed to have spoken of the feeble effort with which I have endeavoured to counteract it.

Wordsworth's reaction is not at all against neoclassical norms of order, but against what he regards as contemporary forms of cultural and poetic *disorder*. His famous discussion of

Epic Poets.	Philosophical & Metaphysical	Dramatic.	Historical.
Spencer, Milton, Davenant.	Sir J. Davis, Phin. Fletcher, Giles Fletcher, H. More.	G. Gascoyne, Shakspeare, Massinger, Jonson, Beaumont & Fletcher, Shirley.	Niccols, Sackville, Daniel, Drayton, May, J. Beaumont.

Satyrical.	Pastoral.	Amatory, & Miscellaneous.	Translators.
Hall, Marston, Rowlands, Donne.	Warner, Drayton, Browne, Fairfax.	Raleigh, Drummond, Marlowe, Cowley, Carew, Corbet, King, Habington, Cartwright, Randolph, Suckling.	Fairfax, Sandys, Crashawe.

Epic.	Dramatic.	Lyric.	Descriptive.
Ossian. Hole. Cumberland. Southey.	Hoadley. Moore. Mason. Walpole. Home. Murphy. Colman. Cumberland. Jephson. Sheridan. Chatterton.	Gray. Mason. Warton J. Warton T. Sayers. Hole. Richards. Coleridge. Sargent. Whitehouse.	Cowper. Hurdis. Gisborne. Bidlake. Sotheby. Burges. Bloomfield.

Didactic.	Satyric.	Miscellaneous.	Translators.
Mason. Hayley. Downman. Polwhele. Darwin.	Churchill. Anstey. Wolcot. Gifford. The Author of The Pursuits of Literature.	Goldsmith. Beattie. Hayley. Barbauld. Burns. Langhorne. Cawthorne. Penrose. Scott. Pratt. Williams Helen. Smith Charlotte. Bowles. Seward. Pye. Rogers. Radcliffe. Maurice. Polwhele. Campbell.	Warton J. Colman. Mickle. Potter. Hoole. Jones Sir W. Boyd. Polwhele. Cowper. Beresford. Brooke. Boscawen. Carlysle. Sotheby.

43 *above* and 44 *right*. In an age of taxonomic enthusiasm, critics competed over the nation's poetic achievements. The table in Henry Headley's *Select Beauties of English Poetry* (1787) sets the greatest of these in the Elizabethan to Restoration period (Fig. 43). In *Literary Hours* (1798) Nathan Drake countered with a rival tabulation, including only contemporary poets and supporting his argument that the last fifty years surpassed anything that had gone before (Fig. 44).

'poetic diction' assaults many of the reigning poetical practices of the 1790s. As a late florescence of the age of *sensibility [11], the period continued the rich experimental ventures so characteristic of imaginative writing in the aftermath of the age of Pope and Johnson. But to Wordsworth the contemporary state of poetry seemed far too volatile, too enamoured of what he called 'arbitrary innovation'.

Like the satirists *Gifford, *Polwhele, and *Mathias before him, Wordsworth wrote to oppose the spread of various kinds of poetic extravagance. Erasmus Darwin, Matthew 'Monk' *Lewis, and the *Della Cruscan movement typify a general and for the most part deplorable condition. Although Wordsworth did not know Blake's art and writing when he wrote his Preface, the 'arbitrary innovation' of *The Four Zoas* (1795–1804) is as much the object of his critique as the 'false refinement' of Darwin's *The Loves of the Plants* (1789) or Lewis's 'sickly and stupid' *The Castle Spectre* (1798) [see *Gothic drama]. It is no aberration that Blake would denounce Wordsworth's ideology of Nature throughout his life.

The issues at stake here are not simply literary or stylistic ones. Once again Wordsworth's 'Preface' is a useful point of departure.

The human mind is capable of being excited without the application of gross and violent stimulants . . . For a multitude of causes unknown to former times are now acting with a combined force to blunt the discriminating powers of the mind, and unfitting it for all voluntary exertion to reduce it to a state of almost savage torpor. The most effective of these causes are the great national events which are daily taking place, and the encreasing accumulation of men in cities, where the uniformity of their occupations produces a craving for extraordinary incident which the rapid communication of intelligence hourly gratifies.

In this passage Wordsworth sketches the historical geography of his Romanticism. Paris and the *French Revolution, London and the *war [2] with France: these scenes and events are Wordsworth's emblems of dislocation. To live in their midst is to experience the crisis of the age; to cultivate such influences—for example, to centre one's life in London, as Blake did, rather than at Grasmere—is to court psychic and cultural destruction. As the opening of *The Prelude* shows, Wordsworth's move to the Lake District positively defines the special character of his Romanticism. Indeed, his lifelong residence there was to become a social index of his commitment to his ideals. For Blake, however, retirement to Felpham precipitated an imaginative disaster from which he felt he had barely escaped—back to London.

In arguing for a radical revision of poetic style—a cultivation of 'simple and unelaborated expressions'—Wordsworth was promoting a broad social programme. His project in the *Lyrical Ballads* is to construct a rural mythos directed at the urban centres of culture. Purifying the language of the 'extravagances' it had been cultivating for more than fifty years would, he hoped, help individuals and society at large recover spiritual and emotional equilibrium. Wordsworth's conviction here stems partly from his views on habitual activities, and partly from his ideas about the relation of poetry and language to thought and feeling.

For our continued influxes of feeling are modified and directed by our thoughts, which are indeed the representatives of all our past feelings; and as by contemplating the relation of these general representatives to each other, we discover what is really important to men, so by the repetition and continuance of this act feelings connected with important subjects will be nourished, till at length, if we be originally possessed of much organic sensibility, such habits of mind will be produced that by obeying blindly and mechanically the impulses of those habits we shall describe objects and utter sentiments . . . that the understanding of the being to whom we address ourselves, if he be in a healthful state of association, must necessarily be in some degree enlightened, his taste exalted, and his affections ameliorated.

A widespread revolution in poetic style will help to restore people to 'habits of expression' that are proper to a 'healthful' state of society. Wordsworth's argument is extremely pragmatic, even (in no pejorative sense) behaviouristic. Feelings and sympathies are purified and improved, or corrupted and debased, according to the linguistic habits we have acquired and cultivated.

Another point about Wordsworth's argument should be mentioned. His critique assumes that the debasement of contemporary culture represents a falling away from a natural condition of healthfulness. Wordsworth's rural ideal is a *Rousseauist trope for an 'original' psychic simplicity. Read in social terms, the trope argues that England can reverse its process of historical corruption. Appeal is made to a population 'originally possessed of much organic sensibility'—as if the bad poetry of the day were an evil visitation upon an otherwise innocent social body. Indeed, by valorizing the term 'organic sensibility' Wordsworth is implicitly arguing that the eighteenth century's traditions of sentimentality and sensibility are in themselves 'healthful'. One recalls here that Wordsworth's critique of culture is directed against what he saw as '*false* refinement and *arbitrary* innovation'.

It is important to understand that traditions of 'sensibility' and poetic experiment fed virtually all the poets of the 1790s. To Wordsworth's mind, however, some were rightful inheritors, some were not. From his vantage in the late 1790s, therefore, although 'all good poetry is the spontaneous overflow of powerful feelings', no good poetry permits linguistic extravagance. Wordsworth could appreciate the songs of Burns and Blake because of their simplicity and directness of expression. But despite the continual coaxing of Henry Crabb *Robinson, he would go no further with Blake. Roads of excess do not lead to a wise passiveness. Even more deplorable were those popular styles of the day, Gothic and Della Cruscan verse [see *Gothic].

The latter's characteristic eroticism would have been especially odious to Wordsworth, since the Della Cruscan movement positively encouraged women to write highly charged erotic verse. When he argued that a poet was 'a man speaking to men', his words carry a subtle reference to the mob of scribbling women—Polwhele's 'Unsex'd Females'—who became prominent during the 1790s.

This division that Wordsworth marks within the contemporary cultural scene—Coleridge replicates his position in a slightly variant form—will develop further fault-lines as the Romantic movement plays itself out, as we shall see. The most spectacular of these gulfs opens later, when Byron appears—the very incarnation of all that Wordsworthian Romanticism was trying to exorcise. As the two dominant poets of their age, Byron and Wordsworth fairly define the contradictions of Romantic writing in the agon of their poetic relationship.

These contradictions take many forms. For instance, sharp differences emerge when different poets engage the crucial preoccupations of Romanticism: *'imagination', for example, or 'feeling', or 'nature'. Romantic 'keywords', their centrality to the writing of the period has always been recognized. Indeed, it is exactly their historical importance, their ideological volatility, that gives such terms their critical significance. They point us toward those moments when the spirit (or spirits) of Romanticism are most active.

Take, for instance, Romantic Nature. In its Wordsworthian form Nature is animated with a spirit of benevolence: 'nature never did betray / The heart that loved her'. Indeed, in 'Lines Written in Early Spring' (1798) he does not shrink from declaring: 'And 'tis my faith that every flower / Enjoys the air it breathes.' Later critics misunderstand Wordsworth when they see 'affective fallacy' in such verse. The style is more radical than that. Far from ascribing human attributes to non-human phenomena, Wordsworth turns human experience into a figure for exploring the transhuman. His purpose is to reveal what a human-centred world, economically and socially preoccupied ('getting and spending'), often cannot see: the presence of suprahuman spirit. Giving one's self up to the influence of Nature leads, in 'Tintern Abbey' (1798), to

> that serene and blessed mood,
> In which the affections gently lead us on,
> Until, the breath of this corporeal frame,
> And even the motion of our human blood
> Almost suspended, we are laid asleep
> In body, and become a living soul:
> While with an eye made quiet by the power
> Of harmony, and the deep power of joy
> We see into the life of things.

This is one of the triumphs of sentimental writing. The spiritual condition it celebrates comes through a regimen grounded in the senses. Harmony is (paradoxically?) a function of pleasure, whose increase transports one to a new sensual order—an order where one may at last experience 'the life of things'. We must read this great passage in the simplest and most literal way. 'Things' apparently dead or subhuman are filled with mysterious and harmonic life. The near-cliché of the phrase 'the life of things' is brilliant exactly because it registers the subjective genitive 'of things' so indirectly. The lines thereby partly enact the argument, or rather the experience, they are celebrating.

Blake and Byron develop variances from this way of rendering Nature which to Wordsworth must have seemed catastrophic. Their departures are useful because they help to clarify the subtler differentials of, say, Coleridge, Shelley, or Keats. The following is a Blakean presentation of 'Nature'. Notable is this historical fact: the passage comes from Blake's *Milton* (1804–8), which was written in part as a severe critical reflection on his rural sojourn at Felpham.

> Thou perceivest the Flowers put forth their precious Odours!
> And none can tell how from so small a center comes such sweets
> Forgetting that within that Center Eternity expands
> Its ever during doors, that Og & Anak fiercely guard
> First eer the morning breaks joy opens in the flowery bosoms
> Joy even to tears, which the Sun rising dries . . .
> The Honeysuckle sleeping on the Oak: the flaunting beauty
> Revels along upon the wind; the White-thorn lovely May
> Opens her many lovely eyes: listening the Rose still sleeps
> None dare to wake her, soon she bursts her crimsn curtaind bed
> And comes forth in the majesty of beauty; every Flower
> The Pink, the Jessamine, the Wall-flower, the Carnation
> The Jonquil, the mild Lilly opes her heavens! every Tree,
> And Flower & Herb soon fill the air with an innumerable Dance
> Yet all in order sweet & lovely, Men are sick with Love!
> Such is a Vision of the lamentation of Beulah over Ololon.

Of first importance here is the contradiction: that this scene of the 'majesty of beauty' is fundamentally, paradoxically, 'a Vision of . . . lamentation'. Beulah's lamentation repeats the experience—detailed immediately before this—of 'all the Living Creatures of the Four Elements' who at the coming of Ololon (which is also 'the Lord coming')

> wail'd
> With bitter wailing: these in the aggregate are named Satan
> And Rahab; they know not of Regeneration, only of Generation
> The Fairies, Nymphs, Gnomes & Genii of the Four Elements
> Unforgiving & unalterable: these cannot be Regenerated
> But must be Created, for they know only of Generation.

Though all in this system appears 'in order sweet & lovely', 'Yet' in it 'Men are sick with love'. The apparitions of (natural) beauty, seen in the truth of Blake's 'Vision', are *fully* revealed (revealed in their illusion, revealed in their truth).

So far as Blake is concerned, both the truth and the illusion of the system of nature can be known, which is to say, can be named. The truth of Nature, for Blake, is that it is fundamentally fallen—'sick with Love', as this text and the famous lyric 'The Sick Rose' both declare. Its illusion is that such Love is 'joy'. On the contrary, in his *Milton* the sick loves of the plants are 'The cruel joys of Luvahs Daughters lacerating with knives / And whips their Victims & the deadly sport of Luvahs Sons'. For Blake, Nature will always betray the heart that loves her. That is the (satanic) nature of Nature. So it is unsurprising that he repeatedly denounced Wordsworth's ideas of nature (even as he praised Wordsworth's poetry), or that he fled Felpham to return to London.

The opposition is stark and fundamental. 'God made the country, and man made the town': Wordsworth endorses and massively elaborates William *Cowper's famous apothegm from *The Task* (1785). Blake, on the other hand, reads it antithetically because in his imagination man is god. The god that made 'the country' of nature is at best blind and misguided, at worst cruel and sadistic. 'The human form divine', on the other hand, makes the town—Jerusalem.

The difference between these ethical views of nature produces some interesting stylistic variances in their poetry. For example, when Wordsworth details his 'forms of nature'—birds and flowers, rivers and mountains, the weather—they constitute part of an expressive and organic system. Even individual human lives are part of this vast system. These 'forms' are the local habitations and the names—literally, the apparitions—of a vital force that subsists everywhere and nowhere. Following a biblical precedent, Wordsworth typically refers to this subsistent spiritual reality with indeterminate words like 'Presence', 'Power', 'Spirit', 'Being'. The divine wholeness of the system cannot be expressed directly, its 'god' cannot be named.

But Blake treats all existence as both knowable and nameable. This attitude springs partly from his conviction that all gods reside in the human breast, and partly from the meaning he gives to the idea of 'Regeneration'. In Blake's reading of the *Bible, the Old Testament is the book of a sky god and mystery religion, a book in which all the most important realities have been darkly imagined, and can never be named. Through it the highest truths must be approached obliquely; and language is at worst a godless babel, at best a symbolic structure pointing elsewhere, in need of constant translation. With the New Testament—he reveals in *The Marriage of Heaven and Hell* (c.1790–3)—comes the story of 'Regeneration' and 'the return of Adam into Paradise'. At that point, when the human name of the unnameable G–d is finally revealed as Jesus, all of language is redeemed. Understood in the name of Jesus, language ceases to be symbolic and recovers its Adamic literality. Blake's view is expressed with great simplicity in the 'Auguries of Innocence':

> God apears and God is light
> To those poor souls who dwell in night
> But does a human form display
> To those who dwell in realms of day.

That Blakean mythos, antithetical to Wordsworth's, produces the startling extravagances of Blake's prophetic books. Wordsworth's is an art of innuendo and suggestion where 'invisible worlds' come and go in momentary flashes of revelation. (The argument is that those moments, those 'spots of time', will never lose their healing power, no matter how dark the time grows.) Blake's, by contrast, is an art of inflection and high rhetorical declaratives. Hence he insists on 'minute particulars' in the passage from *Milton*: not merely a catalogue of named flowers, but the names of all orders of being (Og and Anak, Ololon and Beulah) and the precise articulation of the dialectic of their acts at the different scalar levels of their appearances. Everything is exactly as it is perceived and the perceptions are always multiple: illusion is illusion, reality is reality, and the dialectical relation between the two—'the furious Wars of Eternity'—is the grammar of their expression. Blake's earliest complete revelation of this humanist vision comes in *The Marriage of Heaven and Hell*, where illusion and reality, Vala and Jerusalem, are named Heaven and Hell, Devourer and Prolific; and

These two classes of men are always upon earth, & they should be enemies; whoever tries to reconcile them seeks to destroy existence.

In contrast, Wordsworth's and Coleridge's ideas of 'harmony' and 'reconciliation' founded their new Romantic symbolism. In Coleridge's famous formula, poetry is 'the balance and reconciliation of opposite and discordant qualities'. An artist of the grotesque, Blake sees black where they see white. Neither is the Lake view Byron's view, who like Blake also refuses to spiritualize nature. One of his typical moves, for example, is to study natural phenomena for moral analogies: the remarkable *epic similes in *The Giaour* (1813) provide good examples of this procedure. On the other hand, the sharp accuracy of Byron's descriptions, so pleasing to Ruskin, indicate the fundamentally scientific spirit of his Romanticism. Under other circumstances, of course, Byron might confront nature in a mood of piety similar to Wordsworth's and Coleridge's—as happens momently, if not momentously, in Canto III of *Childe Harold's Pilgrimage* (1812–18). Unlike Blake, Byron does not regard nature as an unmitigated evil. But neither does he give his heart to nature as Wordsworth does, for nature's benevolence seems to him strictly occasional. His refusal is dramatized when Manfred declines both the dominion and the aid of the beautiful and benevolent Spirit of the Alps. Nature is not the symbolic form of 'the One Life within us and abroad' because in Byron's view nature, like 'Life', is to be respected exactly for its multiplicities and contradictions.

Byron's faithfulness to his Lucretian views is clearest, appropriately enough, when he treats natural horrors or disasters—for example, in Canto II of *Don Juan* (1819–24). The story of the shipwreck and its aftermath shows us that nature might at any moment betray the heart that loves her, shows us the inescapable power of what he elsewhere called 'Circumstance, that unspiritual god'.

> At half-past eight o'clock, booms, hencoops, spars,
> And all things, for a chance, had been cast loose,
> That still could keep afloat the struggling tars,
> For yet they strove, although of no great use:
> There was no light in heaven but a few stars,
> The boats put off o'ercrowded with their crews;
> She gave a heel, and then a lurch to port,
> And, going down head foremost—sunk, in short.

But his scrupulous attention to the smallest details of the shipwreck story shows something else. No jot or tittle in the triumph of evil is to be neglected; Byron keeps the most fastidious set of books. In the process he revives the picture of a mind—as in 'Prometheus'—that knows how to 'make of death a victory' exactly by the pitiless way it records all the victories of death. The serial of Juan's adventures builds not a divine but a demonic comedy.

If Byron and Blake stand together, and against Wordsworth, in their ethical judgment of nature and the non-human order of things, Wordsworth and Blake clearly share, over and against Byron, a belief that a redemptive scheme shapes both individual and collective existence. Byron and Wordsworth, on the other hand, stand against Blake in the authority they assign to objective and material conditions. For Wordsworth and Byron, everything is *not* as it is perceived; indeed, the primacy of a 'real' independent of perception or imagination characterizes their descriptive writing. Blake, in contrast, stands much closer to Keats, whose descriptions are driven by desire and structured as an order of pure language.

It is important to emphasize this further differential because so much Romantic description involves imaginative acts of projection. Keats is a particularly important figure in this kind of Romantic writing because his projections, as in 'The Eve of St Agnes' (1820), are carried to wonderful linguistic extremes:

> And still she slept an azure-lidded sleep,
> In blanched linen, smooth, and lavender'd,
> While he from forth the closet brought a heap
> Of candied apple, quince, and plum, and gourd;
> With jellies soother than the creamy curd,
> And lucent syops, tinct with cinnamon;
> Manna and dates, in argosy transferr'd
> From Fez; and spiced dainties, every one
> From silken Samarcand to cedar'd Lebanon.

Here we are very far from Wordsworth and Byron; such Keatsian things never were on sea or land. Moreover, that Keats is aware of the extravagance of this writing—that he makes that awareness part of his subject—is exactly the point. What he wants to display is not an objective order but the power of art to mount an independent world in the sphere of pure language. The same desire controls even a poem like 'To Autumn' (1820), so often cited for the power of its close objectivity.

> Season of mists and mellow fruitfulness,
> Close bosom-friend of the maturing sun;

Conspiring with him how to load and bless
  With fruit the vines that round the thatch-eaves run;
To bend with apples the mossed cottage-trees,
  And fill all fruit with ripeness to the core;
  To swell the gourd, and plump the hazel shells
  With a sweet kernel; to set budding more,
And still more, later flowers for the bees,
Until they think warm days will never cease,
  For Summer has oer-brimm'd their clammy cells.

Keats is here constructing an autumn of desire, an autumn where death is magically expelled through a series of intense and meticulous linguistic transformations.

Keats's descriptions can resemble Byron's because both men like to develop a wealth of carefully articulated physical detail. Wordsworth's descriptions are far more sketchy and select-ive. This is because Wordsworth is most interested in the salient or symbolically charged detail, the feature that goes to what Gerard Manley Hopkins (1844–89) would later call the 'inscape' of a scene or event. Neither Keats nor Byron are 'symbolist' writers in that respect; both typically seek rather an immediate, even a voluptuous, plenitude. Shelley cultivates a similarly lavish expenditure of poetic resources—in 'To a Skylark' (1820), for example, where the poet scours his imagination in a failed effort to capture an adequate expression for the idea he pursues.

Unlike Keats and Byron, however, Shelley's descriptions *are* idealized—like Wordsworth's. In *Prometheus Unbound* (1820) he wants to reveal something for which nature and language itself can only provide veils and suggestions.

Life of Life! thy lips enkindle
  With their love the breath between them;
And thy smiles before they dwindle
  Make the cold air fire; then screen them
In those looks, where whoso gazes
Faints, entangled in their mazes.

Synaesthesia dominates the great lyric which these lines initiate. A confusion of the senses sig-nals the presence of a spiritual voice 'IN THE AIR, singing', as the stage direction in the text indicates. The passage is only in the most superficial sense a 'natural description'. Rather, Shelley wants his language to enact the kind of sympathetic exchanges which he takes to be the enginery of the governing law of the physical and human world. In this lyric a poetic language of images aspires to the condition of music.

The intellectual effort of Shelley's verses must fail, as the text itself declares ('Till they fail, as I am failing, / Dizzy, lost, yet unbewailing!'). This result comes about for two reasons. First, a gap in expression opens when an effort is made to render an idea in positive language. Second and more importantly, the failure is itself part of the process that the poem addresses. The sympathetic idea that Shelley pursues is vital rather than conceptual—that it can only be realized through a process of enactment, a transformational process necessarily involving that ultimate state of transformation: death, loss, 'failure'. Writing in this way, Shelley comes very close to Wordsworth, and to the Coleridge of poems like 'The Eolian Harp', 'Dejection: An Ode', and 'Kubla Khan'.

The theme of poetic failure emerges strongly in the work of the second-generation Roman-tics—Byron, Shelley, and Keats—and it fairly defines the legacy they passed on through writers like Hemans, Landon, Clare, and Beddoes. The cultured imagination—say, Matthew Arnold's (1822–88)—will later deplore the emergence of this theme, which can appear to threaten society's faith that its literary heritage preserves the best of its cultural deposits. For their part, Wordsworth and Coleridge thought they could enlist their new ways of thinking about poetry in the service of culture, which is why Arnold turned to them, rather than to the younger Romantics, for his immediate touchstones.

From the point of view of Romantic poetry itself, however, the theme of failure is simply a radical style for displaying the dynamic character of imaginative (as opposed to cultured) writing. The distinction between the two—between poetry and culture—is fundamental to any Romantic art, as Blake argued in his annotations on Boyd's Dante:

the grandest Poetry is immoral . . . Cunning & Morality are not Poetry but Philosophy the Poet is Independent & Wicked the Philosopher is Dependent & Good

Indeed, it could (and should) be argued that the second generation Romantics pursued the theme of failure to elucidate the deceptive meaning of the Lake School's Romantic project in poetry. Wordsworth conceived the *Recluse* project as a mechanism for healing society and culture, as the completed part of it, *The Prelude*, explicitly declares:

> Prophets of Nature, we to them will speak
> A lasting inspiration, sanctified
> By reason, blest by faith: what we have loved,
> Others will love, and we will teach them how.

But the lesson drawn by the younger Romantics was not quite what Wordsworth had hoped or expected. Shelley and Byron veered sharply away from Lakist ideas of nature and love, and while Keats began in a close kinship with Wordsworth's programme, in the end he too fell off. As he says in 'Ode to a Nightingale' (1820): 'Forlorn! the very word is like a bell / To toll me back from thee to my sole self!'

According to the Wordsworthian redemptive (cultural) scheme, an 'abundant recompense' waits upon suffered loss, but Keats's poetry here triumphs exactly by sinking into its loss. Neither is it difficult to show that the Wordsworthian scheme is founded upon what he himself called 'the anxiety of hope', and that the fulfilment of hope necessarily brings, at best, an equivocal recompense. Once poetry gathers into itself a logic of failure, once it solicits entropy, or what Blake called Satan, as a source of life and energy, contradiction will define its system. Coleridge's 'balance and reconciliation of opposite and discordant qualities' signals an effort to bring the new poetry under conceptual control.

Moreover, a deeper antithetical truth appears in the poetical events themselves: in Coleridge's case, most if not all of his greatest poetry is either unstable or manifestly beyond the conceptual controls he himself explicitly pursued in his poetic work. The flaw appears as soon as Coleridge writes a serious and important poem, for instance, 'The Eolian Harp' (1796), whose contradictory elements, set into play in the earliest version of the work, only grow more chaotic as he adds to and revises the poem over the years. As with 'Christabel' and 'Kubla Khan', however, or the great and desperate *Notebook* poems (like 'Limbo'), the work triumphs in its own resolute irresolutions.

In such poetry, a kind of demon lover appears to take over the work, as if the act of writing under the authority of imagination guaranteed the presence of positive evil, positive error, positive failure. Byron's work lives and moves and has its being in the great world of positive evil. Among the canonical Romantics, Keats provides some of the most dramatic examples of positive error and failure. 'On First Looking into Chapman's Homer' (1816) is, like Coleridge's 'The Eolian Harp', one of Keats's earliest important works; it is also marked by a great lapse in its famous grandiose conclusion: 'Or like stout Cortez when with eagle eyes / He star'd at the Pacific . . .'. Critics tend to regard the mistake here of naming Cortez for Balboa as an insignificant error in Keats's cultural literacy. But the truth is that the error exposes an astonishing depth in this poem's self-revelation. It is crucially a ludicrous error, hence a perfect sign of what

Keats's detractors saw as his Cockney pretentiousness. Remember that the sonnet's explicit theme is the discovery of culture, and that the fanciful style signifies how the sonnet appears to execute its own entrance to the 'realms of gold' it so desires. In thus enacting its own desires, however, it simultaneously exposes the spectacular frailty and even triviality of the realms of gold. As in certain medieval paintings, a small leering monkey has found its way into the work—indeed, has arranged to appear at its rhetorical climax. The poem thus implodes, imperilling both its own desire and the object of its desire. Keats thereby deploys his poem's worst moment as part of a logic of revelation that is forbidden to the reified eyes of culture. That dark revelation is a forecast of modernity.

Abrams, M. H., *Natural Supernaturalism: Tradition and Revolution in Romantic Literature*, London, 1971; Bloom, H., *The Visionary Company: A Reading of English Romantic Poetry*, London, 1962; Bostetter, E. E., *The Romantic Ventriloquists: Wordsworth, Coleridge, Keats, Shelley, Byron*, Seattle, Wash., 1963; Jackson, J. R. de J., *Poetry of the Romantic Period*, London, 1980; Kroeber, K., & Ruoff, G., eds., *Romantic Poetry: Recent Revisionary Criticism*, New Brunswick, NJ, 1993; Levinson, M., *Keats's Life Style of Allegory: The Origins of a Style*, Oxford, 1988; McGann, J. J., *The Poetics of Sensibility: A Revolution in Literary Style*, Oxford, 1996; Manning, P. J., *Reading Romantics: Texts and Contexts*, New York, 1990; Rajan, T., *Dark Interpreter: The Discourse of Romanticism*, Ithaca, NY, 1980; Russo, G. A., & Watkins, D., eds., *Spirits of Fire: English Romantic Writers and Contemporary Historical Methods*, London, 1990.

30 · PROSE   JON KLANCHER

The Romantic era has long been associated with revolutionary new kinds of *poetry [29]—those like Thomas Love *Peacock who instead saw *prose* in the ascendant around 1800 have been minority voices at most. Yet the new prose media—from the proliferating rhetorics of journalism, reviews, and political pamphlets to the emergent disciplinary languages of modern knowledge—were becoming powerful stimulants of social visions and cultural classifications as well as apologies for poetry in the age of *Romanticism and revolution.

By the early nineteenth century, British writers began describing a historic transformation in the language and media of their public culture, a change they often dated to the *French Revolution controversy that had made the British 'an inquisitive, prying, doubting, and reading people'. What might be called a prose revolution, however, had been in the making for a century before 1789, following the early modern transformation in print technology and the gradual formation of 'print capitalism' in the seventeenth and eighteenth centuries. When they began writing in vernacular English, French, or German instead of Latin around 1700, the educated classes of Europe effectively made prose the essential medium of what has been called 'discursive literacy', the mastery of argument and conversation that became, by the mid-eighteenth century, the major focus of modern *education [17] and *publishing [21]. Written prose flourished within a remarkable network of periodical and book presses created during the hundred years following 1690 and it formed the 'polite' language that graduated from the aristocratic court to the urban readers and conversants of Addison's *Spectator* (1711), Cave's *Gentleman's Magazine* (1731), and *Johnson's *Rambler* (1759). The intellectual society of the *coffeehouse patrons who read Addison and other journalists in the first half of the eighteenth century formed a discussion-centred 'public sphere', in Jürgen Habermas's phrase. More explicit ideological conflicts appeared in the rough, vigorous 'pamphlet wars' of the early eighteenth century, as Jonathan Swift and other combatants deployed prose weapons to stake out variously traditionalist or modernizing intellectual and political territories. By the 1750s, Samuel Johnson's *Dictionary* and other contemporary authorities claimed that the English had come to speak and write a standardized prose *language [40], fictional as well as non-fictional. Novelistic prose did yet not count as 'literature', and the difference between non-fiction and fictive prose tended in the new 'republic of letters' to replicate the older division between a prestigious classical language and a common, modern, vernacular language. 'Men of letters' were skilled non-fiction prose writers who demonstrated broad expertise across several genres of prose, speaking 'generally' in a world of increasingly specialized knowledges. Polite or bellicose, the face-to-face contacts of early eighteenth-century print culture were gradually replaced by a more heterogeneous, dispersed array of writers and readers who were welded together as a public by the practices of criticism and the literary *reviewing journals at mid-century.

In this larger process, Ralph Griffiths's (1720–1803) *Monthly Review; or Literary Journal* (1749) and Tobias Smollett's (1721–71) *Critical Review; or Annals of Literature* (1758) carved out an audience of avid mid-century book readers and buyers. The new reviews promoted a fourfold increase in British book production and consumption between 1750 and 1800. Their impact was much greater than their paid circulations (3,000–4,000 copies per month) would indicate—universities, reading societies, private academies, and libraries subscribed while readerships multiplied. Such reviews were not simply devices for promoting the sales of British booksellers. Working within the *Enlightenment [32] category of 'literature' as generally educated discourse—a spacious universe of written genres ranging from *natural philosophy [34], *historiography, moral philosophy, political philosophy, and *political economy [33] to poetry, drama, and criticism—the *Monthly* and *Critical* reviews attempted to be encyclopedic in their display of recent or emerging knowledges. Hence they employed scholars in linguistics, mathematics, *chemistry, classics, moral philosophy, and other disciplines to inspect 'all' books in both established and emerging intellectual fields. Such reviewers typically quoted long patches of the books under review, offering their readers a generous sampling of the new knowledges, alongside work in already established prose fields such as *biography, *autobiography, and *novels [31]. Yet their summary judgements on these books encouraged the accusation that, instead of allowing readers to 'think for themselves', the new reviewing establishment was imperiously imposing its own opinions (whether *Whig or *Tory) on an unsuspecting public.

A turning-point in the history of British reviewing culture developed in the early 1780s. Writers for the Whiggish *Monthly* and Tory *Critical* reviews had expressed their respective political outlooks with increasing indifference to any larger intellectual function of the world of 'polite letters'. The new *English Review* (1783), however, mingled writers from both conservative and progressive political camps to introduce a new category—'Public Affairs'. The *English* and the *Analytical Review* (1788) were the first to circulate the notion of 'public opinion' as a newly autonomous force in British public culture, and before long the *Monthly* and the *Critical* likewise took up the mantle of 'public opinion' as the political articulation of what had formerly been a mainly 'literary' public sphere. Renewing the promise to enable readers to 'think for themselves', political and religious dissenters gathered to edit and write for the leading 'literary' reviews so that, by 1791, England's four most influential reviews were supporting the French Revolution while demanding political change at home.

This critical mass of reformist ambition helped produce the remarkable intellectual counter-culture of the 1790s, including Joseph *Priestley, Richard *Price, Mary *Wollstonecraft, William *Godwin, Erasmus *Darwin, John Horne *Tooke, a young S. T. *Coleridge, Thomas *Paine, and Thomas *Beddoes. What Godwin's *Political Justice* in 1793 called 'freedom of social communication' became the credo of these progressive intellectuals who socialized together in clubs and at suppers, wrote for the same periodical media, and exchanged critical viewpoints with an intensity which could produce rapid changes in even the most unqualified intellectual positions.

Alone among the reformers, Paine's 'democratical' rhetoric reached beyond the intellectual journals to galvanize an audience of hundreds of thousands of literate artisans and labourers unaccustomed to philosophical prose, crossing well-established lines between the public sphere of the intelligentsia and what Arthur *Young anxiously described as plebeian 'assemblies in ale-house kitchens, clubbing their pence to have *Rights of Man* [1791] read to them'. Yet Paine's popularity can obscure the fact that he shared with Godwin, Wollstonecraft, Priestley, and others the ambition of modelling a political republic upon the literary republic. A meritocratic literary canon which 'brings forward the best literary productions, by giving to genius a fair and universal chance' offered Paine the ideal model for anti-aristocratic government. His idealization of the literary public sphere as a model for political representation would also be one of the last such visions to be entertained seriously by Britain's progressive intellectuals. One of the most successful of what Edmund *Burke called these 'political Men of Letters', Godwin would argue, in his 1797 *Enquirer*, that the medium of British prose had now historically developed to its full maturity: 'the spirit of philosophy has infused itself into the structure of our sentences.'

But at no time since the formation of the Enlightenment category of 'literature' had this modern vernacular canon of discourse and knowledge come under such pressure as in the intense culture wars of the 1790s. In the 1793 edition of *Political Justice* Godwin had triumphantly opposed 'literature' to pre-modern *romance and superstition. However, by the second and third editions of *Political Justice* in 1796 and 1798 he was omitting such confident claims for its progressive powers and investing new hopes in the minor and maligned genre of prose fiction. Meanwhile, anti-Jacobin writers like T. J. *Mathias had begun to put pressure upon the hitherto unproblematic category of 'literature' by issuing widely read and reprinted demands that it expose its political and national allegiances. His polemic in the voluminous footnotes to the satiric poem *The Pursuits of Literature* (1794–8) campaigned to discredit the progressive political and intellectual culture sustained by the later Enlightenment reviewers and the circles of Godwin and Joseph *Johnson. Though these anti-Jacobin intellectuals could often sound like old-fashioned reactionaries in the mould of a Swift, they were in fact a new breed of conservative writers who embraced the economic forces of modernity and forged strategies to reassert control over the 'engine' of Enlightenment by every possible means. The collapse of the *Analytical* and *English* reviews in 1796–8 signalled the success of this inventive counter-revolution, which was part of a portentous restructuring of cultural and economic capital that opened onto the new century.

The conservative reshaping of British public culture around 1800 took two especially far-reaching and innovative material forms. One was the emergence of the new scientific, philosophical, and literary *lecturing institutions, established when a group of 'improving' aristocrats founded the Royal Institution to carry out a programme of wedding science to commerce, philosophy to technology, and literary traditions to the newest conditions of modernity. For fashionable audiences, the Royal Institution and its successors converted the eighteenth century's discourse of 'natural philosophy' into a spectacular urban display of scientific know-how. Its leading light, Humphry *Davy, translated dry technicalities into star performances while instructing his audience that the inequality of property, rank, and taste was a founding precondition for scientific 'advance'. Davy's rapturous lectures on chemistry and *geology tended to infuse scientific discourse with British aesthetic vocabularies of *sublimity and *sensibility [11]. While his brilliant rhetorical flights dazzled the audiences of the Royal Institution and similar bodies, they also helped conceal the fact that original scientific enquiry was beginning to disappear from public view. Laboratories were being separated from lecturing platforms, and sure-fire displays replaced the uncertain outcomes of true experiments. Unlike the older scientific lectures conducted by Priestley and his contemporaries, viewers of these new lecturing exhibitions were not meant to learn how to replicate experiments themselves. Instead, by pioneering methods of modern scientific popularization, Davy built a techno-scientific constituency for whom he could synthesize the various arcana of the new sciences as a visible testimony to one evolving culture rooted in property and national feeling. By the 1820s, fully professionalized scientists like Michael *Faraday would replace the half-publicist, half-scientist figure of Davy. Faraday and his successors would henceforth speak publicly only on matters of secured scientific expertise and institutional qualifications. But it was thanks to Davy's tenure at the Royal Institution that a 'popularized' science inscribed in popular prose effectively displaced the older dialogue of natural philosophy by wider moral, historical, and political languages.

The lecturing institutions achieved even greater impact by sponsoring new voices in moral philosophy and 'literary' criticism as well as in science. Davy recruited Coleridge to lecture on poetry at the Royal in 1808, and thereby crafted a public partnership between the new, conservatively inflected science and British cultural traditions that reached back into the very resources of the national language. Over the next twelve years, Coleridge interpreted and transmitted to contemporary audiences a *Shakespeare whom he called a 'philosophical aristocrat', unexpectedly compatible with the social ethos of the London lecturing institutions. But the lecturing scene also diversified after 1808; the Surrey and Russell institutions sponsored William *Hazlitt's lectures on the English poets and novelists for audiences of *Quakers and Dissenters, and by the year 1818 middle-class Londoners could choose between duelling Shakespeare interpreters, as Coleridge, Hazlitt, and John *Thelwall offered competitive readings of a figure who had come by this time to represent 'literature' in a more psychological and internalized way than Shakespeare could have done within the wider spectrum of discourses that counted as literature in the late eighteenth century. Like the new quarterly reviews of the early nineteenth century, the scenario of institutional lecturing had the long-term effect of dividing the externalized showcase of scientific innovation from the increasingly internalized conceptions of poetry and thereby 'literature' which Coleridge, Hazlitt, and others were interpretively promoting through lectures on Shakespeare and *Milton. These lectures were, of course, 'oral' performances in a predominantly 'print' culture, but their quasi-academic format, as well as wide publicity among the *newspapers and periodicals, made them a key form of contemporary prose media.

The other great innovation in media during this period was the new-style literary 'review', inaugurated in 1802 by the lawyer-journalists of the *Edinburgh Review*. By professionalizing the practices of periodical print culture, the Scottish reviewers changed the scope and relation of knowledges open to discussion in the British public sphere. Behind Francis Horner (1778–1817), Francis *Jeffrey, Henry *Brougham, and other intellectual inheritors of the Edinburgh-based *Scottish Enlightenment stood a tendentious body of philosophical and historical arguments [see *history, 38]. Most readers would have encountered this, if at all, only in the writings of David *Hume, William *Robertson, or Adam *Smith; that is, in Scottish philosophical history, with its 'inevitable stages' theory of the development of British modernity, and in the new 'science' of political economy with its rationalizing of commercial society. The *Edinburgh* reviewers' aim was as much to roll back the political and intellectual influence of the 1790s London reviewing journals as to counteract the conservative impact of the *Anti-Jacobin* and *Quarterly* reviews. Jeffrey and his colleagues absorbed the controversy over the French Revolution by interpreting the Revolution as a calamitous yet historically necessary stage in the unfettering of the commercial classes of France. They celebrated the defeat of *Napoleon in 1815 as a removal of the last barrier against commercialized civil society posed by the old *republican ideal of an armed citizenry.

Thus fitted with a rationale for commercial modernization, the *Edinburgh Review* forged a set of media practices which would persist throughout the nineteenth century and into the twentieth. Reviewers no longer quoted books at length. Instead, the new reviewer's own critical performance largely displaced the language and the summarizing of the book under review, thereby setting aside the question of whether the readers of the *Edinburgh* or *Quarterly* reviews were truly being invited to 'think for themselves'. 'Selectivity' became the new byword: where in three monthly issues the *Monthly Review* might assess an average of 150 books, the *Edinburgh* and later the *Quarterly* reviewed an average of fifteen books each in the same quarter. Shrinking the number of authors and raising the profile of reviewers, the *Edinburgh* and *Quarterly* reviews thus created a cadre system of public criticism, leaving the impression that to be ignored by the new quarterly reviews was a telling sign of exclusion from the higher reaches of the literary market-place.

The curious division of ideological labour between these leading quarterlies prompted the later *Westminster Review* (1824) to call their professed Whig and Tory alignments a mask for a joint advocacy of aristocratic interests. But the class content of the quarterly reviews was ambiguous. They contested with each other and with the *Westminster*'s *utilitarian intellectuals for leadership of the emerging professional class who had one foot in commercial institutions and one foot in the institutions of state and church. While reviewing Maria *Edgeworth's *Tales of Fashionable Life* (1809), the *Quarterly* defined its own role as 'a strict literary police', claiming to inspect the 'weights and measures' of the commercial cultural economy with its *circulating libraries and (in the common conservative epithet of the time) its 'manufactured' *novels [31]. In this indirect way, the *Quarterly* identified itself with the older principle of absolutism or *Polizeiwissenschaft*—the philosophy of rule by state—as if to declare its opposition to the more liberal philosophy of commercial civil society promoted by Jeffrey in the *Edinburgh*. The common result was jointly to represent the uniquely British and uniquely productive tension between state and civil society, *polizei* and commerce, inscribing it in Britain's intellectual public culture as perhaps nowhere else in Europe.

The *Edinburgh Review* claimed to draw its readers from the 200,000 lower clergy, shopkeepers, teachers, and lesser professionals who composed the middling classes often regarded as the moral backbone of Britain—as though to suggest that the new quarterlies would speak to a wider social base than their eighteenth-century precursors. Still, Jeffrey's aggressive critical style soon made clear that it was his or the *Review*'s opinion which counted more than the 'public opinion' to which it often appealed. One way to speak on behalf of a presumed consensus of public belief was to partition the literary public sphere into 'sects' and 'schools', which the *Edinburgh* and *Quarterly* reviews often identified with a named writer. Reviewing Hazlitt's *Table Talk* (1821–2) became a means of classifying and excoriating 'the Radical School'; Robert *Southey's *Thalaba* (1801) became the sign of a 'sect of poets', the Lake School; while *Keats and *Byron became prime exhibits of a 'Cockney school' or a 'Satanic school'. Ironically, the reviews' practice of calling out the representative writer of this or that 'sect' also produced a long-run, unintended canonizing effect. Elevated from the wider group of mere verse-producers, such poets as Keats, *Wordsworth, Byron, *Shelley, and Coleridge entered a sphere of publicity that would help to accredit them as distinctively representative poets of an age. By imposing such divisions upon the early-nineteenth-century literary world, the quarterlies expanded the 'judging' power far beyond the scope known to eighteenth-century critics. Not content merely to prosecute this or that individual author, the new reviewers became masters of cultural classification, dominating the literary sphere as institutions having the power to institute other categories and groups.

The most unexpected prose genre that emerged in the early nineteenth century was the *essay in 'Romantic prose'—the phrase that literary history has conferred upon the writings of Hazlitt, Thomas *De Quincey, Charles *Lamb, John *Wilson, and Leigh *Hunt. *Blackwood's*

Edinburgh Magazine (1817) probably published more of this reflexive, self-consciously literary genre of the period than any other journal; it also translated the German Romantic and idealist philosophers and poets into English for wide circulation and influence in the 1820s, doing much to make the taste for what was only later to be called 'Romanticism'. John Wilson's essays and reviews for *Blackwood's* established that magazine's early predisposition to shape an audience of middle-class culture consumers. Indeed, the new figure of the intellectual consumer was made plausible by the impressive leap in circulation figures for the major reviews and magazines by 1820: while early issues of the *Edinburgh* and *Quarterly* reviews still had circulations of 3,000–4,000, like their precursors, the numbers jumped by 1817 to an average of 12,000–14,000 for the quarterlies and *Blackwood's*.

If the *Edinburgh Review* systematically translated commerce into 'political economy', *Blackwood's*, the *New Monthly Magazine* (1814), and the *London Magazine* (1820) cast their lot with a more concretely *arriviste* cultural economy to which they were giving tangible form. Writers for the *New Monthly* were especially fascinated by the 'mercantile phraseology' of *advertisements and other historic signposts of a fashion-driven *consumerism [19] which they alternately criticized and publicized. No journal of the period better carried out the magazines' promise to make their readers skilful interpreters of the social semiotics and pretensions of public fashion, helping such readers to escape being categorized themselves as belonging to the much-noticed and maligned 'fashionables' or the strenuously climbing and socially anxious middle class.

A baroque public prose emerged from many of the quarterlies, magazines, and lecture halls formed after 1800. Perhaps its most trenchant critic was William Hazlitt, whose intellectual roots lay in the Dissenting culture of the 1780s and 1790s, and whom the *Quarterly Review*

45. Self-portrait of the young William Hazlitt (1802), produced during his short-lived career as a painter and before his transformation into a trenchant cultural critic.

defamed as a 'Slang-Whanger', gabbling vulgarisms to the multitude. In his reply to the *Quarterly*, Hazlitt sketched out the identifying marks of the newly normative prose language of the reviews and magazines—its 'rich and rare phraseology', its 'substitution of foreign circumlocutions for the mother-tongue', its 'technical or professional allusions', a language 'besotted with words' written by 'hieroglyphical writers' in which 'objects are not linked to feelings, words to things, but images revolve in splendid mockery, words represent themselves in their strange rhapsodies'.

Yet his shrewd assessment of inflated verbal currencies in the public journals was itself couched in a kind of linguistic economics. Hazlitt's essay idealized the writer who used plain words and popular modes of construction. Against the new journalistic sophistication, this was an appeal to an old tradesman's ideal, the one Daniel Defoe had commemorated in 1720 as the capacity to speak to 500 people of different occupations and ranks and have them understand one's meaning all in the same way. Re-employed in 1821, the effect of this trade-language principle was to desituate and unsocialize the language of social and cultural criticism. Hazlitt opposed the natural syntax of the King's English to provincial or local usages appearing in the coteries of cultural conservatives like William *Gifford or John Wilson. Today, any knowledgeable reader of Hazlitt's prose must be struck by how attuned it was to the local idioms of his own publishing venues—journals like the *London Magazine*, *New Monthly Magazine*, the *Examiner*, or the *Edinburgh Review*—the very idioms of the professionalizing liberal middle class to which he owed his audience and ethos. This group and its language escaped scrutiny in Hazlitt's opposition between the prose that is misshapen by social and material circumstance, on the one hand, and the prose he wished to hear speaking from the inner logic of language and the transhistorical place of critical thought.

It was not casually that Hazlitt voiced his deep reservations about the positive tendencies of 'public opinion' in the literary magazine begun by John Scott (1783–1821) in 1820. The liberal *London Magazine* contributed as much as the conservative *Blackwood's* to sketching in the Romantic world picture by erasing the journalistic world from which it arose. The *London's* anthology of current discourses was anchored by the 'Living Authors' section, a cultural category which seemed to replace the older magazines' rhetorical claims upon living readers. A new intimacy between writer and reader was claimed for liberal political ends, either as Hazlitt's 'familiar' style, or as what Charles Lamb redefined as the authentically 'genteel' style, modelled on the relaxed language of the late-seventeenth-century model Sir William Temple as opposed to the strained, ornate, and status-conscious prose gentility of Temple's contemporary, the third Earl of Shaftesbury. Hence, a third level of public prose could be identified in addition to the older division that opposed the 'lofty' or 'refined' writers of the conservative reviews to the 'vulgar' or 'lowly' rhetorics of the plebeian radical journalists: the 'common', 'familiar', or, in Lamb's sense, the 'plain natural chit-chat' of the unostentatiously learned man.

Equally decisive was the *London's* fourfold classification system, representing 'all that is going forward in Literature, Art, Science & Politics'—a division of intellectual labour well advanced beyond the older, less differentiated category of 'literature' operating in the *Monthly*, the *Analytical*, or the early *Edinburgh* reviews. The new space between 'politics' and 'literature' was evident even among the middle-class radical writers who, like Leigh Hunt in the *Examiner* (1809), had once strenuously referred cultural matters to political contexts. Writing in 1822 to open his new review, the *Liberal*, Hunt now modulated the relationship. In what was effectively a new definition of liberalism, he claimed that the review was not political, but was rather an arena for contributing 'liberalities in the shape of Poetry, Essays, Tales, Translations'. To separate literature from science and politics was also protectively to distinguish critical writing from the intensely personalized culture battles being waged in reviews and magazines since 1798. Even authorship itself was no longer to be pictured in a war of manœuvre between cultural positions. From 1820 to 1825, in works ranging from Lamb's 'essays of

Elia' and Hazlitt's 'table talks' to De Quincey's *Confessions of an English Opium Eater* (1822), the *London Magazine* writers tried to distance authorship from its social location by practising Hazlitt's 'familiar style' or De Quincey's confessional prose as the discourse of a newly defined literary subject. This subject was an 'author', held to be irreducible to the position of the 'writer', who was both politically marked and striving to be marketed.

In 1780 the terms 'public' and 'literary' still enjoyed a close association: by the 1820s, these terms displayed an open contradiction. Thomas *Carlyle's remark in the *Edinburgh Review* that 'all Literature has become one boundless self-devouring Review' rendered in shorthand what others, including Coleridge, John Stuart *Mill, and Arnold, would elaborate as an inevitable antagonism between 'society' and 'culture', those greater abstract totalities drawn from the intense local, civil, and cultural wars of the turn of the nineteenth century.

Guillory, J., *Cultural Capital: The Problem of Literary Canon Formation*, Chicago, 1993; Habermas, J., *The Structural Transformation of the Public Sphere: An Inquiry into a Category of Bourgeois Society*, trans. T. Burger, Cambridge, Mass., 1989; Jacobus, M., 'The Art of Managing Books: Romantic Prose and the Writing of the Past', in A. Reed, ed., *Romanticism and Language*, Ithaca, NY, 1984; Klancher, J. P., *The Making of English Reading Audiences*, 1790–1830, Madison, Wis., 1987; Mann, M., *The Sources of Social Power*, Cambridge, 1986; Raven, J., *Judging New Wealth: Popular Publishing and Responses to Commerce in England, 1750–1800*, Oxford, 1992; Roper, D., *Reviewing Before the 'Edinburgh' 1788–1802*, Newark, NJ, 1978; Schaffer, S., 'Natural Philosophy and Public Spectacle in the Eighteenth Century', *History of Science*, 21 (1983), 1–43.

31 · NOVELS   FIONA ROBERTSON

During our period the novel achieved a heightened aesthetic status, a salient social role, and a literary history or tradition of its own. Reassessing but not rejecting the history of their genre—which was felt, not entirely accurately, to be a recent one—novelists created a tradition by which readers and critics could estimate their place in the much-debated eighteenth-century 'progress of romance', the title of a polemical dialogue by Clara *Reeve. Developing from other genres—*epic, *romance, the journalistic report, drama, spiritual autobiography, and criminal confession or 'rogue biography'—the novel had always been marked both by the traces of its origins and by an ongoing dialogue with them. The Romantic novel continued this dialogue, a process of self-definition reflected in the proliferation of categorizing subtitles: 'A Tale of Other Times' (Sophia *Lee's *The Recess*, 1783–5), 'A Domestic Story' (Mary *Robinson's *The False Friend*, 1799), 'A German Story, Founded on Incidents in Real Life' (Francis Lathom's (1777–1832) *The Midnight Bell*, 1798), 'A Romance, Interspersed with Some Pieces of Poetry' (Ann *Radcliffe's *The Mysteries of Udolpho*, 1794).

However, the novel was most closely and self-definingly concerned with the previously dominant form of long prose fiction, romance. Many works of this period described themselves not as novels but as romances: writers thought the distinction meaningful, if slippery. Romance—diverse and diffuse, but traditionally dealing with the other-worldly and the marvellous, with ideals of chivalry, knight-errantry, and feminine perfection—was conventionally regarded as an oppositional form by novelists seeking to represent the manners and speech of their own day. The origins of romance thus inspired heated debate, often conducted (as was the scholarly conflict between the editors *Percy and *Ritson) along ideological lines. Most importantly of all, romance was regarded as a mode of writing free from formal constraint, its irregularities reassessed in works such as Richard Hurd's (1720–1808) *Letters on Chivalry and Romance* (1762) and Reeve's *The Progress of Romance* (1785). Sir Walter *Scott's 'Essay on Romance' (1824) questioned the adequacy of Samuel *Johnson's definition of the novel as 'a smooth tale, generally of love'; instead he defined the novel as 'a fictitious narrative, differing from the Romance, because the events are accommodated to the ordinary train of human events, and the modern state of society'. To reflect on what Scott means by the events of a narrative being 'accommodated' to contemporary society is to raise some of the key aesthetic and formal questions facing novelists in this period.

The novel was not an automatically propitious genre for authors during our time. At the start of the period, the Preface to Frances *Burney's widely popular *Evelina* (1778) records and contests the lowly rank of the novel in the republic of letters; and many novelists might have recognized themselves as the 'injured body' vehemently defended by Jane *Austen in chapter 5 of *Northanger Abbey* (1818). It was common to place the novel as the lowest of literary forms: loose in structure, quotidian in its settings and references, epistolary and journalistic in its origins and compositional impetus, female in its readership and (often) authorship. Writing novels was simply supposed to be easier than other types of literary endeavour, while reading them was not thought conducive to moral welfare, particularly if the reader was fanciful and female. Novelists could and did break through such suspicion, as the careers of Burney and Maria *Edgeworth demonstrate; they could also make knowing and mischievous use of it, as scandalous publications from Matthew *Lewis's *The Monk* (1796) to Lady Caroline *Lamb's *Glenarvon* (1816) testify. More generally, they developed systems of defence, repeatedly proclaiming their fidelity to accepted aesthetic and moral standards. Most commonly of all, they proclaimed their desire to examine psychological truth. William *Godwin described this (in his preface to the 1832 'Bentley's Standard Novels' edition of *Caleb Williams*) as the use of his 'metaphysical dissecting knife', which claimed for novel-writing a precision akin to that of experimental science. The striving after psychological truth is apparent across the genres, linking William *Wordsworth's *Lyrical Ballads*, Joanna *Baillie's *Plays on the Passions*, and the novels of writers as diverse as Charlotte *Dacre, Mary *Shelley, and Edgeworth. All three novelists append to their fiction prefaces which emphasize the importance of tracing causality, of excavating social manners and behavioural idiosyncrasies in order to reveal what Dacre calls (in *Zofloya*, 1806) the 'actuating principle' beneath.

Burney's Preface to *Evelina* also records, but here does not contest, the perceived status of novel-readers: 'more numerous, but less respectable' than the readers of any other literary form. The division between critical reputation and readerly demand was to change dramatically in the course of the period, due largely to the impact of the highly regarded and spectacularly popular novels of Scott. The years 1780 to 1830 saw a rapidly expanding *publishing [21] industry, an important factor in changes in the production, distribution, and reception of novels. The expansion was underpinned by innovations in the mechanics and conditions of book production: most notably the building of the first hand-operated iron-frame printing press (invented by Stanhope) in 1800; the introduction of machine-made paper; and the development of the plaster-mould stereotype. These innovations created the circumstances in which new moves to capture a mass market for fiction could begin, in the 1820s, with projects such as Archibald Constable's (1774–1827) and Robert Cadell's (1788–1849) remarketings of Scott's Waverley novels. Meanwhile, the physical form of the novel moved towards a greater standardization, the dominance of the three-volume octavo work (commonly known as a 'three-decker' in the 1830s) becoming more absolute from the early 1820s. The demand for the novel was also affected by the expansion of that new concept, the 'reading public', estimated at 1,500,000 in 1780 and 7,000,000 in 1830. The ways in which this public had access to novels affected their reception and construction. Books were expensive commodities, and novels, as

46. Caricature by George Cruikshank after A. Crowquill, 1826, satirizing readers of four flourishing contemporary genres: the feminine romance; the scandalous erotic memoir; the radical political tract; and the bestselling regional-historical novels of Walter Scott.

long works in several volumes, were especially beyond the reach of most potential purchasers. As a result they were commonly borrowed from *circulating libraries rather than purchased, reinforcing their perceived critical status as light works for idle entertainment. *Literary and philosophical societies established in the second half of the eighteenth century commonly restricted their stock of light works such as novels, as did the Mechanics' Institutes set up to provide informative reading for the labouring classes [see *popular education]. (The revolution by which novels encroached upon the status of 'informative reading' is one of the important shifts effected by Romantic period novelists.) In contrast, circulating libraries were well stocked with novels; some, notably William Lane's *Minerva Press and Library, promoted and commissioned particular kinds of fiction. Through their in-house literary reviews, moreover, *publishing houses such as Blackwood's fostered communities of readers. Public taste was shaped by the reviews, while novelists entered into complex interaction with this parallel world of fiction and intellectual debate: James *Hogg planted the idea for his 1824 novel *The Private Memoirs and Confessions of a Justified Sinner* in a *faux-naïf* letter to *Blackwood's Edinburgh Magazine* the year before; while Scott cultivated curiosity about his anonymous authorship of the Waverley novels by appearing as a reviewer of his own *Tales of My Landlord* in 1817 [see *reviewing].

The reading public was increasingly presented not just with novels but with histories and classifying analyses of novels. One significant work of canon-creation is William *Hazlitt's article 'Standard Novels and Romances' (a review of Burney's *The Wanderer* for the *Edinburgh Review* in 1815), which considers the supposed decline of British novelistic achievement since the reign of George II. Hazlitt endorses the novelistic canon most generally accepted in his day:

Fielding (above all), Smollett, Richardson, Sterne. Of the full-length scholarly treatises, the most important is John Dunlop's (?1785–1842) *The History of Fiction* (1814), which begins with early Greek romance and ends with the novels of the past 100 years in Britain and France. The chapters of the book ('Origins of Spiritual Romance', 'Comic Romance', 'Pastoral Romance', 'Fairy Tales', 'Voyages Imaginaires', and others) reminded readers of the form's genealogy and variety, implicitly setting modern fiction in a complex and earnest formal context. Dunlop's work is a key indicator of the shifting status of the novel in the Romantic period, and of its search for a distinct genealogy which would define the genre's particularity against the more reputable forms of *poetry [29] and drama [see *theatre, 24].

The evolution of a literary history for the novel was structured in critical works such as Dunlop's, but facilitated by the popularity of collections of novels—among the most important John Cooke's (1731–1810) series in the 1790s, Anna Laetitia *Barbauld's *The British Novelists* (1810), and Charles Whittingham's (1795–1876) *Pocket Novelists* in the 1820s. These collections took advantage of the ending of perpetual *copyright in 1774, and they both indicated and consolidated readerly interest in the novel as a distinct literary form. The novels in such series gained support from each other and a discernible critical gravitas. This was heightened by the publication, between 1821 and 1824, of the ten-volume series Ballantyne's Novelist's Library, which prefaced a selection of out-of-copyright novels (by Fielding, Smollett, Le Sage, Johnstone, Sterne, Goldsmith, Johnson, Mackenzie, Walpole, Reeve, Richardson, Swift, Bage, Cumberland, and Radcliffe) with critical and biographical introductions by Scott. Modelled on Samuel Johnson's *Lives of the Poets* (1779–81), these introductions implicitly claim for the novel and its practitioners an artistic seriousness conventionally reserved for poetry. Ballantyne's Novelist's Library also reveals the nationalist element in the formation of a tradition for the novel. Previously, novelists had anchored themselves by reference to Cervantes or Le Sage. This continued, but it was overshadowed by references to the internal traditions of British writing. Some of this national isolationism has an obvious political context: the close interconnections between British and French epistolary and sentimental fiction in the 1770s and 1780s, for example, are less marked in the decades of revolutionary *war [2].

It is common for literary historians to pivot the Romantic period on the first *French Revolution, and—following through the line of inquiry established by contemporary reflections such as the periodical article 'The Terrorist System of Novel Writing' (published in the *Monthly Magazine* in 1797), de Sade's essay 'Idée sur les romans' (1800), and Hazlitt's lecture 'On the Living Poets' (1818)—to seek parallels between social and literary revolution. In the 1790s, the most fervent decade of British response to events in France, one group of novels seemed to offer the perfect illustration of the ways in which literature could enter, and influence, political debate. The works of the so-called *Jacobin novelists—Robert *Bage, Thomas *Holcroft, Mary *Wollstonecraft, Charlotte *Smith, Mary *Hays, and Mary Robinson—deployed existing novelistic conventions as a means of advancing a radical critique of society. The political theorist William Godwin published one of the most celebrated and influential novels of the period, *Things as they are: or The Adventures of Caleb Williams*, in 1794, the year after his controversial *Enquiry Concerning Political Justice*. The tale of Falkland and his servant Williams exposes the flaws in Burkean chivalry and the inequity of the judicial system while developing, through Caleb's internalization of the systems which oppress him, a powerful critique of institutionalized authority. The impact of *Caleb Williams* can be felt everywhere in the literature of our period, and not only among those writers sympathetic to Godwin's radical views. Godwin's later novels develop a range of social, historical, and psychological concerns, including gambling and the occult in sixteenth-century France (*St Leon*, 1799), marriage and obsessive jealousy (*Fleetwood*, 1805), and political and religious turmoil in Cromwellian England (*Mandeville*, 1817).

That the novel could claim to be a suitable medium for serious ideas was significant in itself. A few months before being imprisoned for high treason (and acquitted) in 1794 [see *Treason Trials], Thomas Holcroft asks in the preface to *The Adventures of Hugh Trevor* (1794, 1797): 'Is a novel a proper vehicle for moral truth?' He then takes a young man's choice of profession as an opportunity to expose abuses in the systems of law, church, parliament, and the universities. Like Holcroft's earlier *Anna St Ives* (1792), *Hugh Trevor* puts its faith in the operation of human reason and in the growth of moral intellect, setting these against ungoverned passions and the corruptions which all the Jacobin novelists present as the current state of society. The Derbyshire paper-manufacturer Robert Bage had examined such corruptions in novels written several years before 1789: all comment on contemporary issues in a spirit of a scepticism towards received thinking. *Man As He Is* (1792), spurred by the ***revolution** [1] debate, is more explicitly political; while Bage's last and best novel, *Hermsprong; or, Man As He Is Not* (1796), wittily sets an American-born freethinker amid English country society and is notable for including one of the period's most engaging portraits of an independent-minded young woman, Maria Fluart. The first novel of actor and playwright Elizabeth *Inchbald, *A Simple Story* (1791), develops the mother-and-daughter plot of *Shakespeare's *Winter's Tale* into a contrast between the spoilt and the forbearing in womanhood. Inchbald's second and more politically orientated novel, *Nature and Art* (1796), exposes society's arbitrary injustice and sexual hypocrisy, using the perspective of a child brought up naturally to counter the corrosive vanity of another child brought up to ape his elders. The theme of ***education** [17] is the major link between the two works. The social mores which replace moral thinking in the education of ***women** [4] are also a key underlying concern of Mary Wollstonecraft's two novels, *Mary* (1788) and *The Wrongs of Woman; or, Maria* (unfinished; posthumously published in 1798). More explicitly writing in order to make money, Charlotte Smith nevertheless decisively engages with sensitive contemporary issues. The titles of her early novels proclaim a somewhat mannered sentimentalism (*Emmeline*, 1788; *Ethelinde*, 1789; *Celestina*, 1791); but a strong political consciousness is at work and becomes increasingly obvious. The 'Preface' to *Desmond* (1792) comments on the money motive in writing fiction and on the rights of women authors; this novel, with *Marchmont* (1796) and *The Young Philosopher* (1798), develops political themes, although the popular *The Old Manor House* (1793) more artfully blends a sentimental tale with pointed questions about the nature of society and its treatment of women.

Novelists also took part in the backlash of anti-Jacobin writing in the increasingly repressive public culture of the late 1790s. As part of the move to enshrine values of 'hearth and home' in the face of *invasion and ideological threat from France, novels such as Jane *West's *A Gossip's Story* (1797)—with its narrator Prudentia Homespun—and *A Tale of the Times* (1799) counter freethinking and social experiment with the virtues of moderation and Christian acquiescence. The Jacobin thinkers and novelists are directly pilloried by George Walker (1772–1847) in *The Vagabond* (1799) and by Elizabeth *Hamilton in *Memoirs of Modern Philosophers* (1800). Other novels, such as Amelia *Opie's *Adeline Mowbray, or Mother and Daughter* (1804), caution against idealistic attempts to live independently of the rules enforced by society. Interpreted thus broadly, the anti-Jacobin tendency in novel-writing coincides with other conservative forces shaping the tone and subject-matter of the novel. The cult of sentiment and ***sensibility** [11] continued to permeate and complicate explorations of romantic love, especially by women novelists, among them Elizabeth Hamilton, Mary Hays, Eliza *Fenwick, and Helen Maria *Williams. Mary Wollstonecraft's *Vindication of the Rights of Woman* (1792) placed special emphasis on the dangers of this kind of fiction, taking *Rousseau as its main target, while Helen Maria Williams's *Julia: A Novel* (1790) is characteristic of fiction which challenges Rousseau's depictions of the feminine character. The sentimental novel does not die out, but enters a particularly self-conscious phase, and its conventions are self-critically employed in a wide variety of fiction. Jane Austen's *Sense and Sensibility* (1811) criticizes excess but retains key elements of the form, which for many readers has always seemed more like a cautious reinstatement of sentimentalism than a rejection of it. Typically, as Austen's novel demonstrates, sentimentalism destabilizes and disrupts, and it has had just such an effect on the modern attempt to reach critical consensus about its impact during this period. Much of the implicit problem of sentimentalism can be seen in Wollstonecraft's writing career: inveighing against sentimental conventions in so far as they work to undermine female rationality, her own two novels reinforce the counter-convention by which the appeal to feeling itself criticizes the legal and political subjection of women. This form of criticism is seen most clearly in Hays's two novels of the 1790s, *Memoirs of Emma Courtney* (1796) and *The Victim of Prejudice* (1799). The male counterpart to the heroines of Hays and Wollstonecraft, the 'man of feeling', exemplified in the work of Henry *Mackenzie, has almost as complex, and much more under-recognized, a pattern of development and redeployment: Godwin's *Fleetwood: or the New Man of Feeling* (1805) is the most elaborate example.

Like the novel of sensibility, what are now called *Gothic novels (after the sub-titles of Horace *Walpole's *The Castle of Otranto* (1765) and Clara Reeve's *The Old English Baron* (1778), but known more variously at the time as romances, German tales, and tales of terror) were dubiously regarded by contemporaries. The widespread critical opposition to such fiction was typically grounded on a combination of moral and stylistic factors. But other critics and many more readers praised the works of Radcliffe, Lewis, and their imitators for liberating novels from the dreariness of recognizable surroundings and all too probable events. The introduction of mystery to the novel was to be a significant technical development, involving readers in newly complex relationships with manipulative narrators who could tell but don't, and foregrounding story at the expense of much else. This second effect was highlighted by S. T. *Coleridge in his review of Radcliffe's *The Mysteries of Udolpho*: how is the novel to set a value on itself if it leaves nothing to be savoured on rereading? In her essay 'On the Supernatural in Poetry' (published posthumously in the *New Monthly Magazine*, 1826), Radcliffe proposes that there are two distinct categories of the works now grouped together as 'Gothic': works of terror (in which acts of violence and supernatural appearances are continually evoked) and works of horror (in which they actually occur). Radcliffe's own novels, based on Edmund *Burke's theories of the *sublime, deal in terror rather than horror; her consequent reliance on the 'explained supernatural' was regarded by some critics, notably Scott, as an unnecessary restriction on the reader's credulity. No such limitations are imposed in Lewis's concoction of priestly hypocrisy, incest, murder, and Satanic intervention. His most interesting successor was Charlotte Dacre, who in *Confessions of the Nun of St Omer* (1805), *Zofloya* (1806), and *The Passions* (1811) daringly extended Gothic's treatment of erotic obsession as experienced by women.

Both terror and horror fiction, however, are steeped in political significance. Both forms question the nature of power, the source of its authority in the oppressive past, and the ways in which it is reinforced by the family and by gender roles. Contemporary critics recognized what has become a favourite focus of modern interpretation of Gothic. De Sade's essay 'Idée sur les romans' explains the cult of horror in terms of revolutionary upheaval. The same source is identified in an English essay purporting to be written by 'a Jacobin Novelist', 'The Terrorist System of Novel Writing' (*Monthly Magazine*, 1797). In contrast, some saw sensationalist fiction as a reaction against the tameness of everyday life. This case is put most cogently in an article 'On the Cause of the Popularity of Novels' published in *The Universal Magazine of Knowledge and Pleasure* in 1798. The connection between politics and terror is especially inescapable in novels dealing with human helplessness in the face of mysterious and powerful institutions such as monasticism and the Inquisition. The secret societies (particularly the Illuminati) which, according to conspiracy theories such as those of the Abbé de Barruel, had provided the intellectual and organizational foundations for European revolution, were a particular favourite of terror-novelists; while the mystique of secret organizations led to the fictional popularity of the Vehme Gericht or Germanic Secret Tribunal, the fanatic cult, and the rites of Rosicrucianism and the alchemical occult [see *freemasonry].

The formulaic tendencies of Gothic, which were mocked in a series of satirical 'recipes' for would-be novelists, offered an opportunity for commercially appealing imitation (seized by the Minerva Press) and a considerable challenge for the wide range of writers on whom Gothic made an early and unforgettable impression. Among those acknowledging a debt to 'Radcliffe-Romance' was the Protestant Dublin cleric Charles Robert *Maturin, whose first novel, *Fatal Revenge* (1807), was singled out for its intensity by Scott. Maturin also wrote novels romanticizing Ireland (*The Wild Irish Boy*, 1808, and *The Milesian Chief*, 1812) and historical works (*The Albigenses*, 1824), but is best known for the dizzyingly varied Faustian tale *Melmoth the Wanderer* (1820), which in its anatomy of morbid psychology, religious persecution, and the corruption of a 'child of nature' restlessly excoriates the spiritual and emotional securities it seeks. Godwin's 'metaphysical dissecting knife' is clearly in evidence. Although Gothic novelists were often ridiculed for their historical inaccuracies, the form relied fundamentally on the revaluation of the modes of history which was such a strong impetus throughout the Romantic period. Whether it be traced in Catherine Morland's complaint in Austen's *Northanger Abbey* that history is all about men or in Jane *Porter's innovative approach to fictional treatments of historical figures (such as William Wallace in *The Scottish Chiefs*, 1810), the revaluation had lasting consequences for the development of the novel. Interest in the relationship between the individual and the social group had been underpinned by the *Scottish Enlightenment emphasis on the study of social man which encouraged the fictional representation of man in different societies and at different stages of development [see *history, 38]. This 'philosophical history' was thus an important factor in the development of historical and regional novels. It also influenced another growing force in the fiction of the period, novels which send their characters out to other lands for all or part of the action, often using letters home as the opportunity for commentary on the organization of emigrant and ethnic groups: Mary Shelley's *Lodore* (1835) is set partly in Illinois, John *Galt's *Lawrie Todd* (1830) in Canada, while Scott's *The Surgeon's Daughter* (1827) follows its lovers from Scotland to India.

More widespread even than the influence of philosophical history however, was the notion, partly indebted to Rousseau and partly to sentimentalism, that private and domestic history is as important as public history. Many novelists echo Burney's declaration at the start of *Camilla* (1796) that the history of external events is easier to tell than the history of the heart. One of the most influential and explicit statements on the subject is Maria Edgeworth's 'Editor's Preface' to *Castle Rackrent* (1800). Edgeworth questions how many readers benefit from reading history, with its exaggerated heroes and villains, and instead promotes the human interest to be found in documents of private life. The ideal historian, she suggests, does not mask partiality with authority but might be an uneducated and even naïve observer, such as the narrator of *Castle Rackrent* itself, the Irish steward Thady. *Castle Rackrent* initiated the form of the novel of regional and national manners, in which the novel becomes a sociological and linguistic record of vanishing ways of life. Earlier, Edgeworth had experimented in the epistolary style with *Letters for Literary Ladies* (1795), and had written an educational treatise with her father, Richard Lovell *Edgeworth (*Practical Education*, 1798). Afterwards she wrote further series of improving stories for the young (including *Moral Tales*, 1801) a Burneyesque novel of female character formation in *Belinda* (1801), and another epistolary novel, *Leonora* (1806), before turning to develop further the potential she had unlocked in *Castle Rackrent*. Her two series of *Tales of Fashionable Life* (1809, 1812) include the highly regarded Irish novels *Ennui* and *The Absentee*. *Patronage* (1814), which addresses issues of political life, *Harrington* and *Ormond* (both 1817), and later *Helen* (1834) maintained her high literary profile as the most intellectually respected novelist of the period before Scott.

A major influence on the Scottish novels of Walter Scott and John Galt, the regional novel could also manifest a sentimental and didactic parochialism, as in Elizabeth Hamilton's *The Cottagers of Glenburnie* (1808). Another brand of regional fiction, until recently not regarded seriously by most critics, was the flamboyant blend of high rhetoric, sensational events, and the bardic antique epitomized by Sydney *Owenson's *The Wild Irish Girl: A National Tale* (1806) and *O'Donnel: A National Tale* (1814). Much imitated, most directly by Maturin, these highly-wrought outpourings of national identity developed the brand of Romantic nationalism ignited by the *Ossian phenomenon of the 1760s and after, and took advantage of the fashion for setting works in Scottish and Irish wilds. National tales written by Owenson and by Jane and Anna Porter elaborated enduring fables of a people's past, and proffered reconciliation tinged with Romantic regret which served distinct political purposes in an attempt to integrate these lands into a new British identity. Gerald *Griffin and William *Carleton offered much grittier, more realistic and socially engaged evocations of Catholic peasant life in Ireland.

One of the greatest achievements of regional fiction in the period was the series of novels (or 'theoretical histories' as he preferred to think of them) set in the western lowlands of Scotland, published by John Galt between 1820 and 1826. Galt's uncertainties over the term 'novel' are another reminder of the degree to which the most experimental work of the period challenged traditional boundaries. Beginning with *The Ayrshire Legatees* (1820) and *Annals of the Parish* (1821), Galt's works specialize in humorous and often sharply ironic depictions of parochial life and local character. Galt studies political life in *The Provost* (1822) and *The Member* (1832), and demonstrates the influence of Godwin, and of Gothic studies in obsession, in *The Entail* (1822) and *The Omen* (1826). He turns a revisionist eye on the romance of Scottish history in *Ringan Gilhaize* (1823). Another revisionist force in historical and regional fiction is James Hogg. His novels of superstitious Scottish peasant life, *The Three Perils of Man* (1822) and *The Three Perils of Woman* (1823), are innovative in their use of dialect. They are increasingly regarded by critics as significant experiments in their own right, and not just as preparations for the novel which has always dominated considerations of Hogg—*The Private Memoirs and Confessions of a Justified Sinner* (1824), one of the most brilliantly inventive productions of the period and a sophisticated reflection on narratorial and historiographic method, the limits of explanation and self-knowledge, and the nature of evidence.

None of these newer developments displaced the most traditional of all the novel's subjects: courtship. Heroines face conflicts between parental ambition or despotism and romantic inclination, and between their own social delusions and their true (and sometimes misguided) affections. The success of Susan *Ferrier's first novel, entitled simply *Marriage* (1818), is representative of the growing appeal of novels which trace not just courtship but also consequences; the two-generational plot of *Marriage*, indebted most immediately to Inchbald's *A Simple Story*, uses highly conventional contrasts between mother and daughter, daughter and twin, to convey the desired elements of *female education and upbringing. The contrast between the twin daughters of the corrupted and corrupting Lady Juliana Douglas is a particularly clear example of the importation into novelistic fiction of the most ancient plot structures of myth, epic, and romance. Some of these elements also infiltrate the later works of Burney. A model of the self-effacing female author during the publication of *Evelina*, Burney learnt to capitalize on her fame with the novels written after her marriage (*Camilla*, 1796, and *The Wanderer*, 1814). She also revised her earlier hostilities to fanciful romance expressed in *Evelina* and *Cecilia* (1782), incorporating elements from the newly fashionable Gothic fiction in order to increase her novels' appeal to readers.

Meanwhile, the novel of moral etiquette exemplified by *Evelina* continued to attract new practitioners: its outlines are clear in Mary *Brunton's novel of sustained emotional pressure and heroinely resistance, *Self-Control* (1810). The novel of moral etiquette imports material from Gothic fiction, with which, particularly in the variety developed by Radcliffe, it has much in common. Social convention, male power, female helplessness and uncertainty: the mazes of social propriety in the novel of moral etiquette and the physical peril adumbrated in the Gothic often stand in for each other. The two forms also share a tendency, as marked in *Self-Control* as it is in *The Romance of the Forest*, to endorse in their endings a type of the *pastoral, a retreat from sophisticated social life and a trust in rural retirements of a refined but unpretentious simplicity. Jane Austen seems exceptional among novelists of the period for so unequivocally accepting the conventions and constraints of the novel of a young woman's education. Austen's assured ironic style exposes the pretensions and the follies of polite society, producing the early social comedies, *Northanger Abbey, Sense and Sensibility*, and *Pride and Prejudice* (1813); the later novels, *Mansfield Park* (1814), *Emma* (1816), and *Persuasion* (1818), are distinctly more reflective and more broadly questioning, though equally sharp. Austen's adroit handling of so many central, even stereotypical qualities of the novel can make her elusive, and modern criticism characteristically desires to decode her language, to uncover the political resonances which refuse to rise to the level of explicit debate. These are overwhelmingly questions of social order and of the moral and emotional lives of women. Technically, Austen develops the novel subtly but significantly. Her use of free indirect discourse (the source of the closeness readers feel to the emotional responses of her heroines) and her powers of characterization through speech create a psychological verisimilitude which has distracted attention from other ingredients of her fiction: fairy-tale elements in the plots, for example, make Fanny Price a Cinderella as well as a study in regulated jealousy. The fictionality of her fictions, clearly signalled by references to the reader's expectations, the author's arbitrary will, and the stock phrases with which characters are released into their future lives, acknowledges the fragility of the happy endings to which her novels, as social comedies, conform.

The traditions of the philosophical novel also continued. Mary Shelley's first novel, *Frankenstein* (1818), finds in the language and the intellectual debates of science a powerful analogue for the moral judgement of the ambitious individual. *Frankenstein* expands the subject-matter of the novel, but its interweaving of letters, reported oral confession, and interpolated tales also conducts a recognizable debate with the mechanics of authenticity, personal reflection, social delineation, and the narrative of a young man's (or Creature's) education. Mary Shelley's later novels, only recently coming into critical focus, continue these developments of the philosophical and psychological novel. *The Last Man* (1826) envisages the world of the late twenty-first century consumed by plague, and offers a pessimistic but impassioned portrayal of the ideals of poet-philosophers such as Percy *Shelley. Mary Shelley also develops, in her novels *Valperga* (1823) and *Perkin Warbeck* (1830), the historicism which was part of the legacy of a revolutionary age and so significant a part of Godwin's literary imagination. *Lodore* (1835) and *Falkner* (1837) examine family bonds and contemporary society.

The boundaries of the conventional novel were also challenged by the *satires and historical romances of Thomas Love *Peacock. Peacock draws significantly on elements of classical literary tradition: on the prose satires of Lucian and Menippus, on Aristophanic chorus, on Socratic dialogue. Strikingly alert to the technicalities and the expressive possibilities of a wide range of literary modes, he is best known for the satirical-conversation novels *Headlong Hall* (1816), *Nightmare Abbey* (1818), and *Crotchet Castle* (1831), in which enthusiasts in craniology, ichthyology, toxicology, and other 'ologies' display their quirks and their prognoses for the world in a series of (usually inconclusive) debates. Breaking with notions of psychological realism but advancing the novel's engagement with particular intellectual milieux, Peacock retains certain novelistic conventions (notably the courtship plot and the revelation of identity) while implicitly criticizing the tendency of novels to look inward to character and motive rather than outward to the changing world of ideas—scientific, economic, religious, and political. In *Melincourt* (1817) Peacock turns to the romance, creating a heroine in search of a knight errant in a modern society stained with mercenary marriages, electoral corruption, and paper money. *Maid Marian* (1822) further extends the use of romance and folk-tale in a mock-medieval satire on modern politics; while in *The Misfortunes of Elphin* (1829) Peacock blends Arthurian and ancient Welsh legend, a contest of the bards, and an allegory of *Tory ideology.

The works of Scott, however, provided historians of the form with the glorious revolution they sought. The novels which dominated the age were hailed as productions of natural genius and a taste uncontaminated by false models. In fact the series of works, beginning with subjects from Scottish history and later ranging across a dazzling array of times and countries, opened with a first novel, *Waverley* (1814), which in its introductory chapter carefully marked out its difference from the typical productions of the modern novel, describing itself as a maiden knight entering the lists of fiction. The romance motif, denied in this opening chapter and in the novel as a whole (which sets Edward Waverley as a variant of Quixote, encountering the reality behind the Romantic illusion of Jacobite Scotland), was in practice a key factor in Scott's appeal. The Waverley novels most easily rescued from the trough of Scott's twentieth-century reputation were those grounded in Scottish history and featuring a range of Scottish peasant characters generally agreed to steal the show from their nominal heroes: these novels include *Old Mortality* (1816), *The Heart of Midlothian* (1818), and *The Bride of Lammermoor* (1819). Recently, however, critics have returned to novels such as *Ivanhoe: A Romance* (1819)—probably the single most dominant cultural product of the nineteenth century—*Kenilworth* (1821), and *Quentin Durward* (1823) as novels which reclaim the historical imagination as a form of pageant. Scott's novels, notably *Redgauntlet* (1824), combine and rework conventions from a wide range of literary modes, including romance and anti-romance, epistolary fiction, and the journal. Scott confidently reclaims for the novel the wonders and far-flung adventures of romance, the traditions of folklore and *ballad, and the superstitions of past ages. He invites reflection on history, romance, and the novel as conflicting and contiguous modes of writing. Like his 'Disinherited Knight' Ivanhoe, Scott chose to conceal his identity from an avid public. This turned the convention of genteel anonymity into a guessing game, generating curiosity, speculation, and sales, and setting up complex framing devices around his fictions which together formed the most sophisticated reflections to date on the techniques, readership, and intellectual and social responsibilities of the novel. Scott's eclectic novels despise nothing in the traditions they inherit, and they offered to later writers a mode of fiction which suddenly seemed integrated, weighty, and achieved.

The marginalization of novelists as formative intellects of their age can be seen early in the Romantic period's construction of itself: Godwin and Scott are the only novelists admitted to the select company of representative men analysed in Hazlitt's *Spirit of the Age* (1825). Yet by 1830 the novel had structured its literary past and laid claim to a present in which it could rival the creativity of all other literary genres. A narrative of a tradition had been created, comparable in many ways to the narrative of national integration and progress that was rehearsed, more or less confidently, in the period's historical romances and national tales. Like these tales, the narrative of novelistic tradition tells of the defeat of an older, wilder, superstitious culture, the culture of romance; and in the telling makes sure of its return.

Butler, M., *Jane Austen and the War of Ideas* (1975), with a new introduction, Oxford, 1987; Cottom, D., *The Civilized Imagination: A Study of Ann Radcliffe, Jane Austen, and Sir Walter Scott*, Cambridge, 1985; Duncan, I., *Modern Romance and Transformations of the Novel: The Gothic, Scott, Dickens*, Cambridge, 1992; Ferris, I., *The Achievement of Literary Authority: Gender, History, and the Waverley Novels*, Ithaca, 1991; Kelly, G., *English Fiction of the Romantic Period 1789–1830*, London, 1989; Women, *Writing, and Revolution 1790–1827*, Oxford, 1993; Kiely, R., *The Romantic Novel in England*, Cambridge, Mass., 1972; Poovey, M., *The Proper Lady and the Woman Writer*, Chicago, 1984; Trumpener, K., 'National Character, Nationalist Plots: National Tale and Historical Novel in the Age of *Waverley*, 1806–1830', *English Literary History*, 60 (1993), 685–731; Watson, N. J., *Revolution and the Form of the British Novel, 1790–1825: Intercepted Letters, Interrupted Seductions*, Oxford, 1994.

· IV ·

EMERGING KNOWLEDGES

32 · ENLIGHTENMENT MARTIN FITZPATRICK

In the eighteenth century there was not one unified movement, 'the Enlightenment', but several 'Enlightenments'. These differed a great deal according to national context, and within national contexts exhibited their own variations and complexities. Nevertheless there were essential elements of similarity which make the larger concept of 'the Enlightenment' possible. Though the Enlightenment produced no single programme of reform, its guiding preoccupation can be seen as the application of critical reasoning to human problems in order to ameliorate the human condition and create a more harmonious, tolerant, and virtuous society and government. An underlying unity can be found in the shared assumptions upon which these general aspirations rested. Referring mainly to the French Enlightenment, Norman Hampson has described these assumptions as: first, that nature was a self-regulating system of laws; secondly, that man could study himself only as a part of nature; and thirdly, that man and nature were the creation of a beneficent providence. To these bulwarks of Enlightenment thinking may be added, as Henry May has done in his study of the American Enlightenment, the premises that the present age is more enlightened than the past and that we understand nature and humankind best through our natural faculties.

May suggests that although the Enlightenment thinkers rejected traditional religion, their attitude to life remained religious, for they 'seldom thought about any branch of human affairs without referring consciously to some general beliefs about the nature of the universe and man's place in it, and about human nature itself'. Such an approach acknowledges the diversity of the Enlightenment and provides us with a flexible way of looking at it in Britain—thus it could be more or less political, more or less religious, more or less class-based, more or less shaped by national aspirations. However, this approach does set boundaries to the Enlightenment beyond which lie either more extreme forms of modernity or more retrenched forces of tradition. In this view one could be a sceptic but not a total sceptic, a Christian but not an intolerant or rigidly orthodox one, an admirer of the status quo but not utterly uncritical.

With the unions between England and Scotland in 1707, and Ireland in 1800 [see *Act of Union], the dominant political tendency was towards unification, but the Enlightenment in Britain was never unified in this way. The *Scottish Enlightenment was in part an assertion of national identity by a country which had lost its statehood, and Enlightenment movements in Ireland and Wales later in the eighteenth century similarly contained particularist national elements. Yet none abandoned enlightened cosmopolitan values; Enlightenment thinkers both thought of themselves as citizens of the world and sought the cachet that went with it. For example, Sir William *Jones's mentality led him to seek common elements in distinctive cultures, to contribute significantly to the development of the comparative study of religion and linguistics, and to make the original and imaginative suggestion of a common linguistic structure for Indian and European languages [see *mythology, 36]. Yet Jones was no simple-minded universalist. He loved the specificity of the languages he studied, and showed many dimensions to his sense of identity: he was a Welshman, a Briton, a Brahmin, and a Citizen of the World.

However, such untroubled multiple identities sustained within a broad enlightened framework could not easily survive the crisis engendered in Britain by the *French Revolution.

Perhaps significantly, this first public fracture in progressive rational ideology began with a bitter controversy between a liberal Protestant Welshman, Richard *Price, and an orthodox Protestant Irishman of strong Catholic sympathies and affiliations, Edmund *Burke, both of whom lived in London—a natural centre for enlightened culture in Britain. Only Scotland possessed an Enlightenment movement strong enough to maintain a consistently distinctive culture over the course of the century, and even that claim requires some qualification. For example, the development of Edinburgh New Town which turned the city into the 'Athens of the North' also embodied a rejection of the distinctive Scottish history symbolized by the medieval old city perched on its formidable rock and embracing within its walls a Calvinistic cathedral. James Craig (1744–95), the gold-medal-winning designer of the New Town was inspired by the ideals of his uncle, poet and dramatist James Thomson (1700–48), a proud Scot who also wrote the words of 'Rule Britannia'. Yet if the Scots aspired to be British, and especially to purge their **language [40]** of the stigma of provinciality by eliminating 'Scoticisms', they were also proud to be Scottish. Enlightened accounts of cosmopolitanism drew on the classical notion of spreading circles of affections so that true citizens of the world would necessarily retain strong affections for their own community. Scottish Enlightenment thought was similarly both distinctive and yet recognizable as part of the wider enlightened quest to provide a general understanding of humanity. That quest thrived upon the exchange of ideas. David *Hume believed that philosophy should be conducted as 'a conversation', an apt model for an age when travel was becoming easier, when *newspapers, journals, and *reviews proliferated, when the post was generally reliable, and when intellectuals could meet each other in clubs and societies, if not quite regardless of station, at least in a relatively democratic atmosphere. Universities also provided a natural forum for debate [see **education, 17**]. Cambridge fostered *Whiggish Latitudinarian Enlightenment thought, while the Scottish universities distinguished themselves variously in moral philosophy, jurisprudence, **political economy [33]**, *chemistry, and metaphysics. There were particularly strong links also between Ireland and the University of Glasgow, in part because Protestant Dissenters could avoid the Test Acts by pursuing their university education in Scotland. An Irishman, Francis Hutcheson, (1694–1746), for example, played a major role in the development of Scottish moral philosophy. In England the *Dissenting academy at Warrington similarly set new educational standards by incorporating science and history into its curriculum; some of its pupils then completed their education in Scotland, particularly at the Edinburgh medical faculty. London, too, played its part in disseminating Enlightenment: Scottish, Welsh, and Irish thinkers moved there to pursue careers, to find publishers and outlets for their writings, or to talk with philosophers who gathered in the capital city.

All this helps to explain why, in comparison with the Continent, the Enlightenment in Britain began so early and moderately, providing the Continent with its subsequent heroes, Francis Bacon (1561–1626), John *Locke, and Isaac *Newton. While these figures had epitomized a changing attitude to knowledge by valuing the application of new ideas to the improvement of the lot of the ordinary man, and by extolling the experimental method, they had pitched their claims modestly, with a clear, confident understanding of the limitations of knowledge. They had also been convinced that their investigations were helping to gain insight into God's world. This was hardly a unique idea; a pervasive feature of the scientific revolution was that man was gaining a God-like understanding. More importantly, they had believed that revelation and reason could be harmonized. Enlightenment in Britain was thus profoundly religious; even those who questioned the value of revelation did so in order to create a rational, 'natural' **religion [10]**. Moreover, by emphasizing God's benevolent nature they made less dramatic the undermining of traditional beliefs in humanity's essentially sinful nature, the Augustinian doctrine of original sin. Criticism rarely spilled over into scepticism, and Enlightenment was associated with progress and improvement.

Many of the features of this moderate Enlightenment were carried over into the second half of the eighteenth century, but in this area, as in many others, the 1790s served as a watershed. The publication of Thomas *Paine's *Age of Reason* (1795) produced a flurry of replies in which *Tory High Churchmen, Whig Latitudinarians, and orthodox and heterodox Dissenters joined to refute him. But by then such co-operation was becoming unusual. The middle ground of gentle amelioration, measured toleration, and mild-mannered reform was crumbling rapidly. The various strands in the English Enlightenment began to fray, and eventually parted completely. Just before this happened, however, it developed a last burst of vigour unseen since early in the century. Added to intellectual brilliance came a new commitment to political and social reform. This paralleled developments in France, where French *philosophes* in the 1740s had out of a mixture of defensiveness and aggression formed a type of party. Under Voltaire's leadership they joined to their existing criticisms of irrational and outdated customs and practices a campaigning zeal to bring government and society up to date, primarily through law reform and the introduction of religious *toleration, but also through political and economic reform. In short, they became what modern historian Peter Gay has called the 'party of humanity'. One can see similar, if distinctively local, tendencies in Scotland and England, and rather later in Ireland and Wales. This essay will focus mainly upon Rational Dissent, a label which contemporaries took to mean the liberal wing of religious Dissent from the established Anglican Church. As the most vigorous 'party of humanity' in Britain, Rational Dissent was viewed as the standard bearer of Enlightenment philosophy in general. Consequently, the rejection of Enlightenment ideas and the development of Romantic sensibilities are best understood in relation to the sharp criticism which it endured in the late eighteenth century. But first a brief outline of Enlightenment trends in Ireland, Wales, and Scotland is necessary.

Some historians doubt whether it is appropriate to talk of an Irish Enlightenment at all because of the deep fissures within Irish government and society. Yet there is no disputing the reality of the *Irish cultural revival. Moreover, Ireland displayed marked Enlightenment trends, most discernible in the careers of outstanding individuals such as Edmund Burke. Before he finally embarked on a political career, Burke wrote a profoundly influential work of aesthetic theory, *A Philosophical Enquiry into the Origin of our Ideas of the Sublime and Beautiful* (1757), a work potentially subversive of Enlightenment ideas, yet also indicative of growing Enlightenment interest in innate ideas and internal feelings [see *literary theory, 41]. Though he began the treatise as a student in Dublin, he had left for the greater opportunities available in London by the time it was published. Dublin, however, remained an important centre for *publishing [21], especially because of the relative ease of evading *copyright there. In this it was rivalled by Belfast, a city also very conscious of its role in enlightened culture. The *Northern Star*, a Belfast newspaper launched in 1792, carried in the form of extracts a virtual synopsis of late-eighteenth-century British and European enlightened thought. The foundations for enlightened radicalism in Ulster had, however, been laid nearly a century earlier, when Lockean ideas of social contract and popular sovereignty were related to the Irish situation by thinkers such as William Molyneux (1656–98) and Robert, Lord Molesworth (1656–1725), who also contrasted libertarian Whig principles based on the *Glorious Revolution with those of ecclesiastical and political tyranny. Another Lockean, John Toland (1670–1722), a more vehemently anti-religious pantheist, also laid the foundations for a theory of toleration which could accommodate religious (and potentially cultural) differences. Such ideas exemplified the attachment of Irish Protestant Dissent to the belief that both Church and state were voluntary and mutually protective societies, which in turn explains the powerful appeal of Rational Dissent later in the century. The French and *American revolutions undoubtedly encouraged the Irish into action, but, as historian Marianne Elliott has observed, the seeds which produced 'that contradictory tradition of rebellious loyalism' were 'already germinating'. Irish 'rebellious loyalism' contained the potential for a reconciling enlightened nationalism, but repression by the British government in the 1790s stunted the growth of that particular plant.

Foreign revolutions also had a catalytic effect in Wales, yet, as in Ireland, the foundations for a *Welsh cultural revival or renaissance had been laid earlier, following the introduction of the first printing press in 1718. Originally this Welsh print culture purveyed rather dour puritanical sentiments, but by the end of the century many small towns had spawned book and *debating clubs which brought Enlightenment works to the people. Interest in the printed word led to a major shift in Welsh culture, which had until the mid-seventeenth century been predominantly oral; now books provided a new and broader sort of stimulation for Welsh cultural life. Not only were they produced in the Welsh language, but they also provided a means of preserving and meditating upon earlier cultural traditions. A number of societies worked to further the latter end, notably the Society of Ancient Britons, founded in London in 1715, and the more important Honourable Society of Cymmrodorion, founded in 1751. The Cymmrodorion, which attracted many members of humble origins, was a rather typical gathering of the moderate Enlightenment, socially conformist and self-consciously proud of hobnobbing with grandees. A group of London Welsh, finding it too stuffy and limited in its Welshness, separated off to form the Gwyneddigion Society in 1770. This group combined a radical political outlook with a strong desire to recover tradition, a not unusual association in late-eighteenth-century Enlightenments. Its success can be measured in scholarly book production, in the revival of the *eisteddfod, and in the emergence of similar, though often more specialized, societies in Wales and London.

London naturally attracted Welshmen of distinction, including three of the most important thinkers of the British Enlightenment as a whole: Richard Price, David *Williams, and Sir William Jones. The two former men were very much cosmopolitan figures, whereas William Jones, a supreme linguist, was more conscious of Welshness. Besides them a host of figures contributed in different ways to the Welsh cultural and intellectual revival. These included Thomas *Pennant, traveller, antiquarian, aesthetic theorist, and botanist; David *Samwell (Dafydd Ddu Feddyg), poet, surgeon, and traveller; Edward *Williams (Iolo Morganwg), Rational Dissenter, poet, and forger; and John *Jones (Jac Glan-y-Gors), satirical poet and democratic republican. The links between such figures and the Enlightenment in general can be seen in the lives of Pennant and Samwell. Pennant was a natural historian and proponent of the *picturesque, as well as author of the four-volume *British Zoology* (1768–70), published by the Cymmrodorion. His high ambition was to synthesize the work of the two greatest natural historians of the century, the French Comte de Buffon and the Swede Carl von Liné, known as Linnaeus. He was also friend and adviser of Sir Joseph *Banks, who was a promoter of the career of Johann Rheinhold *Forster, the German naturalist on Captain *Cook's second voyage of discovery. David Samwell was not a botanist but he was, like Pennant, a fine observer who travelled as a surgeon with Cook on his third expedition and kept a superb journal of the voyage. In his *A Narrative of the Death of Captain James Cook to which are added some Particulars concerning his Life* (1786) he wrote what many regard as the best contemporary account of Cook's death, portraying Cook as the very archetype of the enlightened explorer. It was another Rational Dissenter, Andrew Kippis (1725–95), who persuaded Samwell to publish his account, and who further perpetuated notions of Cook the enlightener in an influential biography, *The Life of Captain James Cook* (1788).

Dissent and especially *Unitarianism played a major role in the Welsh renaissance. Rational Dissenting hostility to church establishments found strongly sympathetic resonances in Wales where between 1727 and 1870 not a single Welsh-speaking cleric was appointed to the episcopate. Welsh Enlightenment also had cultural and especially linguistic dimensions which found no counterpart in Rational Dissent across the English border. Samwell regarded his written ability in Welsh as inferior to that of some of his friends, but he was secretary to the

Gwyneddigion Society for a while and, with Iolo Morganwg's help, organized one of the key precursors to the modern Welsh eisteddfod, held at Primrose Hill, London, on Midsummer Day, 21 June 1792. The likely attendance of William *Blake is one indication of the range of appeal of Druidic revivalism, reminding us that enlightened rationalism existed alongside appeals to a mythic past, which writers such as Iolo, the Scot James Macpherson [see *Ossianism], and the Englishmen Thomas *Chatterton and William *Ireland imaginatively recreated. Though these writings were technically forgeries, their knowledge of the past usually ensured initial scholarly acceptance: Iolo's imitations of the medieval Welsh poet Dafydd ap Gwilym were only exposed this century. Historians have struggled to understand the peculiar combinations of rationality and emotionalism which characterized such writers. Were theirs the dissociated sensibilities of intellectuals at the cusp of Enlightenment and Romantic culture? Or were they manifesting pre-existing creative tensions within the late Enlightenment, which might have been resolved differently had not the French Revolution provoked a destructive counter-Enlightenment?

The Enlightenment in Britain was predominantly an urban phenomenon. In Ireland, Scotland, and England great cities and thriving towns served as a focus for enlightened sociability. While possessing no natural capital city, Wales experienced considerable social and economic change, signalling both the onset of *industrialization [14] in many areas and the transformation of the gentry. This created an audience for enlightened ideas among growing populations of artisans, and also patronage of the Enlightenment by a gentry in the throes of modernization [see *Welsh artisan painters]. The works of Richard Price were read by the gentry of his native Glamorgan. In mid-Wales, Thomas Johnes spent a fortune creating a picturesque paradise at Hafod, near Aberystwyth, and so made a watering-place for the enlightened traveller. The Welsh Enlightenment was in part a mobile phenomenon, with London providing a centre for new societies and ideas, but, as historian Gwyn Williams has noted, 'the modernization of Wales generated a loose-textured but potent organic intelligentsia'. The French Revolution placed exceptional strains upon this intelligentsia when gentry support waned under the attractions and fears generated by *loyalism and repression. But though Enlightenment was fractured here, as elsewhere, it did not collapse completely. Stalwart support emerged in a distinctive pocket of enlightened radicalism in south Cardiganshire. Dubbed the Black Spot (Y Smotyn Du) by *Methodists, a cluster of Unitarian chapels emerged, supported by the local farming folk. They declared war on an alien religious establishment and on Methodistical enthusiasm alike, and formed an almost unique example of an enduring rural Enlightenment.

It was perhaps inevitable that in the overcharged atmosphere of the 1790s *millenarian ideas proved especially attractive. Mythic notions of the Welsh being the first to colonize America found expression in the search for the Welsh Indians. Welshmen such as Morgan John *Rhys sought salvation in America, where he hoped to create a new homeland in Beulah, Pennsylvania. Yet such schemes were less the expression of wild Celtic imaginative aspirations than of the flights of fancy and *utopian [9] hopes generally in the air at that time; Rhys had republished *Volney's *Ruins* in 1793. Moreover, these visionaries retained odd yet rather sympathetic rational universalist aspirations, epitomized by Iolo Morganwg's belief that the Druids were Unitarian. In a curious way they sustained enlightened values through the worst of times.

Whereas the Enlightenments in Ireland and Wales were in the main later eighteenth-century 'movements', with strong radical components, this is less true of Scotland, where the Enlightenment was a more robust and longer-lived phenomenon, exhibiting considerable social cohesion. Its most powerful and creative period, from about 1740 to 1780, saw the publication of an extraordinary range of works, almost all of European significance. Key figures included David Hume, Francis Hutcheson, Thomas *Reid, Adam *Smith, and Dugald *Stewart in philosophy; Colin Maclaurin (1698–1746) in *natural philosophy [34]; Joseph Black (1728–99) and

James *Hutton in the emerging sciences of chemistry and *geology respectively; the three Alexander Monros (grandfather, 1697–1767, father, 1733–1817, and son, 1773–1854), William Cullen (1710–90), and two products of the brilliant Gregory dynasty, John (1724–73) and James (1753–1821), in *medicine [18]; James Dalrymple (Viscount Stair, 1619–95), Henry Home (Lord Kames, 1696–1782), Thomas Erskine, John *Millar, and Hume again in *law [8]; Hume, Millar, Adam *Ferguson, and William *Robertson in *history [38]; and in the related fields of sociological, economic, and linguistic study, Ferguson, Millar, Reid, Smith, Stewart, Kames, Sir James Steuart (1712–80), James *Burnett, and Sir James *Mackintosh.

Many of the more specialist activities in the Scottish Enlightenment were informed by a general interest in the science of humanity, which was in large measure a result of the empirical trend of Scottish moral philosophy. Developing Locke's ideas, Hutcheson and Hume had emphasized the role of sense experience in the formation of moral knowledge. They had also persuasively attacked the belief that moral judgement rested upon rational deduction, so emphasizing the need to observe humans in their social setting in order to understand behaviour. This gave a 'historical' and 'psychological' dimension to many aspects of Scottish enlightened endeavours which would leave crucial legacies in the era of Romanticism, perhaps most notably in the historical novels of Sir Walter *Scott. However, Hume's claim that 'the science of man is the only sound foundation for the other sciences' gave Scottish Enlightenment history a rather different character. It became concerned to understand the stages of human development from primitive times, as well as the interaction of governmental, social, economic, cultural, and religious practices. Most accounts divided the stages into four: Adam Smith denoted them as 'hunting, pasturage, farming and commerce', and Adam Ferguson argued influentially that such stages effected a transition from savagery through barbarism to 'polished life'. As this historicism suggests, enlightened thinkers did not think previous ages superior to their own, yet the nascent anthropology which was embodied in their attempt to understand social forms in their own terms helped check simplistic ideas of progress, and influenced some enlightened explorers to be more sensitive to the structure and survival of native societies [see *exploration, 37].

Fears of political instability and religious sectarianism undoubtedly contributed to the cohesion of the Scottish philosophers, as well as their political caution, their dislike of enthusiasm, and their underlying sense of the fragility of civilization. Their philosophy both reflected and depended upon the maintenance of a polite stable society in which differences of opinion could be the source of civilized debate rather than of conflict. In such a society it was possible to believe that morality might rest upon the use of the faculty of sympathy (Adam Smith) or upon common sense (Thomas Reid). In Scotland, as elsewhere, the Enlightenment was fostered by new or reformed institutions: universities, academies, literary and reforming clubs and societies, and publishing ventures such as the first and second *Edinburgh Review* and the *Encyclopaedia Britannica*, whose title is indicative of the British dimensions of the Scottish enterprise. A further specifically Scottish aspect of enlightened sociability was the established Presbyterian Church. The Church was Calvinistic in its creed and organization, but in the eighteenth century it came to be dominated by a group of well-connected and able clergy whose aim was to foreclose divisive theological disputes, and to restrain *Evangelicalism by means of a moderate tolerant religion. The moderate 'credo' was also opposed to political fanaticism. Indeed, when the moderates came to form a party in the early 1750s, it was led by men like Alexander Carlyle (1722–1805), John Home (1722–1808), and William Robertson—a group of clergyman educated at Edinburgh University, who had served in the College Company of Edinburgh Volunteers in opposition to the Jacobite army. These clergy gained control of the general assembly of the Church of Scotland and used their powers to discipline evangelical and democratic tendencies at a local level. Their moderatism upheld the virtue of civility and politeness as characteristics of the Christian and good citizen, and drew strong support from a gentry and aristocracy educated in enlightened values. In civil affairs the moderate literati also emphasized the value of subordination and good order, though they drew on classical republican thought to advocate the need for a Scottish citizen militia. The Scottish Enlightenment thus seemed to have exemplified the pragmatic belief associated with Montesquieu that politics should be adjusted to circumstance, whereas elsewhere among enlightened forces in Britain, especially in England, there emerged much greater support for the view associated with *Rousseau that politics should be shaped by the will of the people in conformity to universal precepts.

While Scottish moderatism was flowering in the 1750s, the Enlightenment in England at this period appeared near-moribund. Attempts to synthesize science and religion had become tired and derivative, moderate religion had become genteel and boring, and liberal politics was threatened by the appropriation of its universal concerns and symbolism (predominantly neo-classical) for self-congratulatory patriotic ends. This mould of complacency was broken, how-ever, early in George III's reign with the revival of the cause of *parliamentary reform, the growing tension with the colonies which stimulated new political ideas [see *empire, 5], and the development of new religious and scientific ideas associated especially with Rational Dis-sent. Crucial to this liberal religious revival was the emergence of a new generation of leaders from outside the Presbyterian heartland, including Richard Price and Joseph *Priestley from Calvinistic Independent backgrounds and Theophilus Lindsey (1723–1808) from the Church of England. Rational Dissent was sustained by excellent educational institutions, most notably the second Warrington Academy (1757–83). It was also well served by printers and publishers drawn from their ranks or sympathetic to them. Joseph *Johnson began his career as a pub-lisher at Warrington, serving unofficially as the press for the Academy. Circles of printers formed important talking-shops for enlightened ideas, as did the numerous clubs and soci-eties. Of the latter, the Club of Honest Whigs in London, the Lunar Society in Birmingham, and the Literary and Philosophical Society of Manchester were especially important in the for-mulation of new ideas and in giving coherence and purpose to this phase of the Enlightenment [see *literary and philosophical societies].

There was also an important feminine dimension to this Rational Dissenting sociability, manifested particularly in both mixed and female debating clubs and writers' circles. Rational Dissenting women were often capable and independent-minded, such as Ann Jebb (1735–1812), Hannah Lindsey (1740–1812), and Mary Priestley (1742–96), and their company and advice were highly valued. Indeed, it is notable that many of the women writers of the late eighteenth century were Rational Dissenters or were influenced by them, including Anna Letitia *Barbauld, Lucy *Aikin, Catharine *Macaulay, Mary *Hays, Amelia *Opie, Mary *Robinson, Helen Maria *Williams, and Mary *Wollstonecraft. In the first half of the nine-teenth century their Unitarian successors would be at the forefront of the early feminist move-ment. They were to struggle with one of the most pervasive contradictions of enlightened thinking—an emancipatory tendency to extol *women [4] as rational in tension with anti-egalitarian social and cultural assumptions.

The attitude of Rational Dissent towards women is a reminder that the assumptions of the Enlightenment which they all shared could have very different practical manifestations. In the French Enlightenment of the late eighteenth century those assumptions began to lose some of their Christian dimensions. Nature alone, rather than God and Nature, came to dominate its thinking. Rational Dissenters did not reflect French Enlightenment trends towards secularity of thought, but they did share the radical tendencies of the French and American Enlighten-ments, particularly their expectations that the existing world could be reformed and trans-formed. Like many in the Enlightenment generally, they were primitivists *and* progressives. They hoped to purify Christianity of the corruption of the ages *and* to restore English people to their natural and Anglo-Saxon political rights. Typically, and somewhat inconsistently, in combining natural and historic rights they believed that the lost rights which they wished to recover were also appropriate for all humankind. Contractual and historical thinking of this sort inspired the *Society for Constitutional Information in which Rational Dissenters played a leading role. Such thought was often further infused with millenarian expectations for the renewal of the world, evidence for which could be found in Revelation, thereby adding an extra dimension to belief in the progress of truth and the extension of knowledge.

The development of sensationalist *psychology [39] by David Hartley (1705–57) in his *Observations on Man, his Frame, his Duty, and his Expectations* (1749) provides the best example of how these various currents could come together. Hartley suggested that our ideas are shaped by experience and association. Following suggestions made by Isaac Newton, he argued that sensations cause vibrations in the nerves. These were transmitted to the brain, where they triggered other ideas through association. Developing Locke's ideas that experiences of pleasure and pain shape understanding of good and bad, he suggested that painful experiences caused excessive vibrations. Man would become progressively more virtuous both by seeking the good and by rooting out bad associations. Such gradual improvement was linked with the inauguration of the millennium, evidence for which Hartley found in Revelation. Progress thus occurred by a dual process of purification and improved conduct. The spread of reason and knowledge would eventually defeat evil in the world and all would share in the benefits.

Hartley's ideas were not always accepted in detail, but they are indicative of the mood of late-eighteenth-century English Enlightenment thinking. He also contributed to the Rational Dissenting conviction of the importance of unfettered free enquiry and the candid exchange of ideas. These notions gave Rational Dissenters a radical edge. A constant willingness to challenge orthodoxy led them to advocate Unitarian religious ideas, to challenge the Church establishment, and to campaign for universal toleration, parliamentary reform, and the *abolition of the slave trade. Their main emphasis was on change effected through individual truth-seeking and honest persuasion, and hence they advocated greater political liberty primarily as a guarantee for civil rights and civil liberty. To criticize Rational Dissenters as radical *individualists* is to miss the point; their concern was to improve society and to curb the state, which was viewed with great suspicion. This both enhanced and limited their radicalism.

Tensions within Rational Dissent were held in balance by the belief in a culture of enquiry, despite differences over the meaning of such a culture. Some, like Priestley, favoured a restless experimental approach in all things and a rather strident notion of candour, others, like William *Enfield, were more cautious. Fittingly, the Enlightenment in England in this closing phase drew strength from debate and divisions rather than from a uniformity of views. This is even more true when one looks beyond Rational Dissent itself. David Williams, 'the Priest of Nature', developed *Deist ideas and worship and propounded a sophisticated view of political liberty; Thomas Paine exploded ideas of British *constitutionalism and advocated democratic *republicanism; William *Godwin envisaged the gradual but irresistible spread of enlightened ideas through small coteries of candid enquirers which would grow into utopian communities where law was maintained without coercion; Jeremy *Bentham secularized and developed *utilitarian dimensions of Joseph Priestley's thought based on formulation of the principle of the greatest happiness of the greatest number. All these thinkers could regard themselves as members of a common intellectual community; they attended the same or similar clubs, and shared friends, many on the Continent and in America. In one way or another their ideas continued to be influential into the nineteenth century.

Yet in spite of this intellectual vigour the Enlightenment as a movement in England was dispersed in the early 1790s. Paradoxically, its strength was also a source of vulnerability. Its intellectual diversity and lack of programmatic unity made it ill-equipped to cope with the dramatic backlash of the late 1790s. The drawing together of various wings of the conservative

Enlightenment and the focusing of hostility on Rational Dissent played a decisive part in the fissiparous process of decline. Tories like Edward *Gibbon were increasingly frustrated by the outspoken attacks of Rational Dissenters like Priestley upon the Church establishment, believing increasingly that the power of the state should be used against them. Gibbon was concerned mainly about social stability and public order, but he was joined by others who feared Priestley's attacks upon Trinitarian theology. Led by Samuel *Horsley and George Horne (1730–92), these Tories formed a counter-Enlightenment which defended the Church of England from its Unitarian critics. The French Revolution as mediated through the powerful voice of Edmund Burke brought these currents of criticism together. Burke's *Reflections on the Revolution in France* (1790) can only be fully understood in the light of this growing hostility to Rational Dissent, the dominant force in the late-eighteenth-century Enlightenment. Above all, it represents an unmannerly attempt to blacken the character of Richard Price, one of Dissent's patriarchs. Burke was ultimately decisive in turning more conservative voices within the Enlightenment both at home and abroad against Enlightenment as such. Enlightened universalism and cosmopolitanism were rejected in favour of uniqueness and particularity. In the process Burke shifted his ground away from the tradition of conservative enlightened thinkers, like Montesquieu and Hume, who favoured gradual reform appropriate to individual circumstances but along lines advocated by what they regarded as all right-thinking individuals. Burke's attack on enlightened abstract generalizations about human nature and human rights opened the way for thinking of nations and societies in more organic terms, an approach which would be favoured by Romantic thinkers. Burke's portrayal of the state as a 'sacred temple' invested it with a poetic quality which also foreshadowed Romantic thought such as that of S. T. *Coleridge, and his belief in its necessary 'consecration' by a 'state religious establishment' was welcomed in High Church quarters. From such perspectives on the state, Rational Dissenters who believed in universal toleration and the separation of Church and state were seen as subversives, lacking all reverence for Church and king. Burke both played on and added to fears of sectarianism by representing Rational Dissenters as purveyors of the abstract calculating spirit of the Enlightenment which would corrode government and society wherever it was manifested, and which was already doing so in France. As the French Revolution grew into war and internal bloodshed, the alarm he evoked spread among those who did not share his politics. The destruction of Priestley's home, laboratory, and library in the Birmingham *riots of July 1791 was the first sign that hostile words would spill over into deeds. The government, which hardly disapproved of such direct local action, added its own legislative fiats to repression [see *gagging acts].

Deliberate intimidation of the leadership of Rational Dissent was one reason for the loss of momentum of the English Enlightenment. In 1794 Joseph Priestley emigrated to America. But it is doubtful whether, despite his enormous prestige as a scientist and philosopher, he could have held the movement together. The English Enlightenment had never had the social, intellectual, and institutional coherence of the Enlightenment in Scotland, centred as the latter was in the universities and among the moderate Presbyterian clergy. Though Walter Scott could dismiss the remaining Scottish Enlightenment leaders as an 'antediluvian' company by the early nineteenth century, he overlooked the fact that Scottish Whiggism, exemplified in the work of men like Henry *Brougham, Sir James Mackintosh, and Francis *Jeffrey (founder of the second *Edinburgh Review*), developed many of the traditions of the Scottish Enlightenment, while Dugald Stewart ensured its philosophical influence in the nineteenth century by adapting Common Sense philosophy to the age of revolutions. Thus despite the loss of its old leaders, the very moderate nature of the Scottish Enlightenment had indeed enabled its perpetuation and metamorphosis. Even the most devastating Victorian attack upon Enlightenment assumptions, from a Scot educated at the University of Edinburgh, Thomas *Carlyle, was testimony to the continuing vitality of the Scottish Enlightenment.

In England the loss of leadership was more critical. During the 1790s the leaders of Rational Dissent were aged if not already dead. The loss of people of such energy, talent, and eminence critically weakened the culture of enquiry whose earlier vibrancy gave their Enlightenment its character: henceforth what had been creative intellectual tensions in the decades before the French Revolution became impossible strains. In retrospect, Rational Dissent had balanced irreconcilables. Although never a unitary movement, its dominant trend had been represented by Price and Priestley. The explosion of loyalist rage against these two after 1790 demonstrated the naïvety of their faith in providential optimism and unfettered enquiry. Some of the radical, secular, and religious dimensions of Rational Dissent now began to part company. Under Paine in the 1790s, a simpler, more strident, democratic republicanism emerged, while Godwin developed the relentless rationalism of the Dissenters into a creed of philosophical anarchism. Both exemplify in different ways the continuing belief in a world transformed by knowledge, but they saw such a transformation in secular terms. Moreover, in the 1790s the millennial dimension of such expectations was somewhat tarnished by the revival of radical millenarianism which relied on direct revelation. Although Priestley's millennial pulse quickened with the dramatic events of the 1790s, his religion remained balanced and urbane compared with that of the various millenarian enthusiasts like Richard *Brothers and William *Sharp, who emerged from the radical 'underworld' or from the enthusiastic strands of Methodism.

Priestley's philosophy was also challenged from quite another quarter. Philosophically and politically Priestley had come close to outright utilitarianism, but this was held in check by his typical early Enlightenment belief that what was useful constituted part of God's plan. Under Jeremy Bentham utilitarianism developed its own momentum and an entirely secular rationale. It would prove to be the longest surviving thread of the Enlightenment and would eventually give a new impetus to reform. Meantime in the 1790s utilitarian-style arguments had been used by a whole phalanx of conservative thinkers from Burke to William *Paley in order to expose some of the limitations of blending belief in historic contract, enlightened natural man, and natural rights. The English Enlightenment was thus not simply repressed, it was also seriously damaged by the intellectual attacks of both radical and conservative writers.

Yet in diverse ways the English Enlightenment lived on through the age of revolutions and *Romanticism. The calculating spirit was represented by Benthamite utilitarians, who did so much to develop the science of legislation and who were able to endow radical reform with a new theoretical cogency. They undoubtedly contributed to the preservation and development of 'constitutionalism and radicalism', identified by the modern political historian Franco Venturi as 'the two great products of the Enlightenment in Britain'. Partly because utilitarianism was more measured, intellectual, respectable, and apparently safer than universalistic natural rights notions, it did not entirely sweep these two great ideas away. The aspiration to create a world in which all human beings had access to certain basic and inalienable rights remained part both of the narrow programme and of the overall outlook of English radicals. It was also appealing to young Romantic spirits. The late-twentieth-century concern to defend and extend human rights to all people can be regarded as a legacy of late Enlightenment thought transmitted to posterity through the passionate attachment of Romantics like Percy *Shelley to the worth of all living creatures. Another important aspect of the Enlightenment lived on in the Unitarianism which developed out of Rational Dissent. Under the leadership of Thomas *Belsham, this tradition of rational religion perpetuated Priestley's *Necessitarian philosophy, developed critical biblical scholarship, and remained the firmest proponent of universal toleration. It was through his advocacy of toleration for Roman Catholics that Priestley had got to know the leading Catholic Enlightenment figure in England, Father Joseph *Berington, sharing with him scientific and philosophical interests as well as an outlook which was both tolerant and anticlerical. Like Priestley, Berington suffered from the reaction to the

47. The Auto-Icon of Jeremy Bentham at University College London. In accordance with Bentham's own instructions, his body was dissected before friends and then displayed at the college he had helped to found. His head, modelled in wax, and his clothing can still be seen today.

French Revolution, but the English Catholic community did recover its nerve. It was revitalized by the activities of men like Charles Butler (1750–1832), secretary to the Catholic Committee from 1782, John Milner (1752–1826), Vicar Apostolic of the Midland District, and William Eusebius Andrews (1773–1837), a fiery journalist and publisher who linked the cause of *Catholic emancipation with the wider campaign for civil and religious liberty.

Other elements of the Enlightenment were rather more fragmented. With the French Revolution, the scientific community was alarmed by the association of science with Dissent and reform politics. The English Enlightenment had always had an important gentlemanly element; at its most high-minded this involved a keen amateur dimension of science committed to a Baconian belief in the value of experimentation and observation. This naturally conservative dimension was strengthened under the long tenure of Sir Joseph Banks as president of the Royal Society. Banks was anxious to uphold the constitution in Church and state: he opposed the repeal of the Test and Corporation acts and probably exercised his influence against the advancement of Rational Dissenting scientists like Thomas Cooper (1759–1839). Despite this unpropitious climate Dissenters helped to take science into a new phase. It was John *Dalton, a teacher in the new Dissenting academy in Manchester, who took a decisive step in bringing about the rather long-delayed chemical revolution by which chemistry adopted predominantly quantitative, mechanistic models in the Newtonian tradition. Dalton's work was also encouraged by the Manchester Literary and Philosophical Society, which was dominated by Dissenters, many having close links with medicine and industry, a reminder that some of the Enlightenment societies lived on into Victorian times. Thus, safely removed from the domain of politics and theology, science continued to live by essentially Enlightenment ideals.

Although Romanticism is often associated with the rejection of Enlightenment science, the situation was actually more complex. Some Romantics like Coleridge were far from hostile to science, and significant figures like Humphry *Davy infused the enlightened scientific quest with Romantic enthusiasm. Goethe's *Zur Farbenlehre* (1810), a rather naïve attempt to overthrow Newton's theory that white light was made up of the colours of the spectrum, exerted a considerable influence on the painter J. M. W. *Turner. Its English translation of 1840 stressed the work's artistic significance rather than its anti-Newtonianism, though Blake had already inspired the latter tradition in England with his rejection of enlightened rationalism—'the tree of death'—and his assertion of the intuitive spirit of art, 'the tree of life'. John *Keats's *Lamia* (1820) was perhaps more typical of British Romanticism in its less extreme criticism of Enlightenment science as deadening to the imagination:

> Philosophy will clip an Angel's wings,
> Conquer all mysteries by rule and line,
> Empty the haunted air, and gnomed mine—
> Unweave a rainbow.

There was undoubtedly some shift in sensibility here, for it was Newton's *Optiks* (1704) which had, of all his works, fired the imagination of poets. Yet there were also elements of continuity between Romantic and Enlightenment sensibilities. The relationship between philosophy and art in the Enlightenment was close, not least in the Enlightenment's development of aesthetics as a separate philosophical discipline. Its legacies included picturesque ideas—in many ways an attempt to harmonize Burke's polarities of the *sublime and the beautiful—and the untameable terrors of the sublime which led to feats of the *Gothic imagination. Different aspects of Enlightenment aesthetics could therefore be seen as operating on the Romantic imagination. From the outset of the Enlightenment, the sensationalist psychology of Locke had possessed the potential for developing into a radical subjectivism. Bishop George Berkeley (1685–1753) had suggested in his *New Theory of Vision* (1709) that the eye sees 'only diversity of colours', a view foreshadowing Goethe's notion that through 'light, shade and colour' the artist could create 'a much more perfect world than the actual one can be'. Such ideas would appear to be infinitely more suggestive than Hartley's associationist psychology, which hardly allowed the individual to reconstruct his world. Yet two important features of Hartley's thought strongly influenced the Romantics: a transcendental dimension, which allowed for the possibility for the individual mind to participate in the divine mind; and a unified, or monistic, view of the world, permitting a spiritual as an alternative to a material interpretation. Priestley's science similarly saw the world as infused with God's presence, an idea which came to be associated strongly with William *Wordsworth.

Thus, although the first Romantics reacted against the Enlightenment and turned their back on its political liberalism, they were also, in part, creatures of the phenomenon. Coleridge even for a brief moment contemplated becoming a Unitarian minister, and William *Hazlitt was the son of one. Hazlitt provides a link to the second generation of Romantics, notably Percy Shelley (Godwin's son-in-law) and *Byron, who sympathized with democratic nationalist movements on the Continent. The Enlightenment in Britain had indeed been diverse enough to provide the early nineteenth century with a variety of ideas and programmes: the case for self-government from Richard Price; for anarchism through Enlightenment from

William Godwin; for utopian renewal from the enlightened millennial tradition; and for parliamentary reform, including the precise programme of *Chartism, from a whole range of Dissenting reformers of the late eighteenth century. Indeed, the Victorians themselves did not actually absorb many of the Romantics' objections to Enlightenment philosophy, even if they were willing to accept a Burkean rejection of the idea of 'the Enlightenment'. The English Enlightenment was more a casualty of the assault mounted on it by Burke and the early Romantics, and of a general Victorian distaste for the eighteenth century, represented as an age of 'Old Corruption' and immorality. For Victorians, the Enlightenment was an alien movement which they associated with French tradition. This view was reflected in the *Oxford English Dictionary*'s late Victorian definition of the Enlightenment, which associates it with the French *philosophes* as 'shallow and pretentious intellectualism, unreasonable contempt for tradition and authority'. This was Burke's last revenge. Yet behind such Victorian rectitude lay a sense of superiority founded upon a range of ideals and reforms actually originating in the Enlightenment. Excepting Scotland, not until the late twentieth century have the varied British components of the Enlightenment been recognized as crucial aspects of the European movement, as well as interrelated movements in their own right. In its late-eighteenth-century phase the Enlightenment in Britain was extraordinarily vigorous. An unfortunate conjunction of hostile circumstances critically fractured its various components (again excepting Scotland), but their vitality was reflected in the many elements of continuity and deliberate discontinuity which were present in the early-nineteenth-century world.

Elliott, M., 'Ireland', in O. Dann & J. Dinwiddy, eds., *Nationalism in the Age of the French Revolution*, London & Ronceverte, 1988; Gay, P., *The Party of Humanity: Essays in the French Enlightenment*, London, 1964; Hampson, N., 'The Enlightenment in France', in R. Porter & M. Teich, eds., *The Enlightenment in National Context*, Cambridge, 1981; May, H. F., *The Enlightenment in America*, New York, 1976; Outram, D., *The Enlightenment*, Cambridge & New York, 1995; Porter, R., *The Enlightenment*, New Jersey, 1990; Venturi, F., 'The European Enlightenment' in his *Italy and the Enlightenment: Studies in a Cosmopolitan Century*, trans. S. Corci, London, 1972; Williams, G., 'Beginnings of Radicalism', in T. Herbert & G. Elwyn Jones, eds., *The Remaking of Wales in the Eighteenth Century*, Cardiff, 1988.

33 · POLITICAL ECONOMY DONALD WINCH

There is a well-rehearsed version of the history—or rather, perhaps, metahistory—of something usually called 'classical political economy' that firmly associates the science that emerged after the publication of Adam *Smith's *Wealth of Nations* in 1776 with the heroic or rampant phase of capitalism in its modern industrial form. Robert *Southey may have been the first to make the connection between Smith and the 'manufacturing system', but Karl Marx was primarily responsible for creating 'classical political economy', by encapsulating the ideas of his 'bourgeois' predecessors and by distinguishing between the 'vulgar' or apologetic versions of the science and his own 'critical' enquiry into the iron laws governing capitalist development. Later economists of more orthodox persuasion reappropriated the term merely to describe an early phase in the development of the modern discipline that was followed later in the nineteenth century by something called 'neoclassical economics'. The twentieth-century economist John Maynard Keynes added his own twist to this story by extending the connotations of 'classical' to embrace all those classicals and neoclassicals who accepted the non-Keynesian assumption that full employment was the normal condition of capitalist economies. Unfortunately, all these approaches have imposed something of a teleological straitjacket on the history of political economy that obscures its broader cultural significance, particularly during the late eighteenth and early nineteenth centuries.

That other retrospective coinage, the 'industrial revolution', has increasingly come to operate more as a piece of excess baggage than as vital explanatory background when interpreting the eighteenth-century emergence of political economy as a new branch of knowledge, capable of guiding legislators through the puzzling combination of short- and long-term problems experienced during this formative period in British economic history [see *industrialization, 14]. Applying a twentieth-century economic definition of the industrial revolution as a process that inaugurated continuous improvement in per capita real incomes is to suppose an ahistorical understanding on the part of those legislators: there are good reasons why such an improvement did not and could not inform the expectations of a whole generation of people still strongly conditioned by pre-industrial circumstances. Recognition that British prosperity was increasingly dependent on urban manufacturing pursuits that made use of newly recruited work forces and innovative forms of machinery was entirely compatible with scepticism as to whether these expanding employments would be capable of surmounting various limitations posed by the predominantly land-using activities underlying the supply of both food and energy. Far from being the solution, the manufacturing system might simply be an expression of a deeper problem, particularly when broader questions of moral health and political stability were brought into the reckoning. Conventional modern historiography associates such concerns exclusively with the literature of protest, with proto-socialist diagnoses, with 'Romantic' attacks on mechanistic forms of materialism, and with *Tory humanitarianism rather than the *Whiggish or *Benthamite conclusions of orthodox political economy in this period. But no account of political economy would be complete if it did not show how profoundly the new science was involved in attempts to articulate the underlying dilemmas, political and moral, of British commercial and industrial development.

Why this should be so can be illustrated by returning to Adam Smith's priorities in the work that established the broad parameters within which his successors operated. The 'revolution of the greatest importance to the publick happiness' to which Smith referred in his historical account of the progress of opulence was the 'silent and insensible' one associated with the slow growth of commerce and manufacturing against a predominantly *agrarian background [see *agricultural revolution]. Acting singly, this development would have been vulnerable to the 'ordinary revolutions of war and government'. The outcome had been made more durable as a result of the unintended by-products of the shift in consumption patterns by feudal landowners—those with legal entitlement to the agrarian social surplus. As their expenditure shifted towards the manufactured luxuries produced or imported by merchants living in towns, and away from those military dependants and menial servants that had given them status and power, so their capacity to challenge monarchs had been undermined. They became less able to disrupt those civil liberties that could best be achieved through the centralized and impartial administration of the rule of *law [8].

Chief among these liberties was that basic security of property essential to the productive investment of savings: the frugality that came from the restless desire to improve our condition which Smith believed to be a universal aspect of the human condition when given scope for expression. By opting for luxuries, and hence for the ready means by which they could be purchased, feudal landowners had permitted land to fall into the hands of a rent-paying tenantry that was more likely to introduce agricultural improvements. Independent labour organized to exploit market opportunities had replaced 'servile dependency'. As a result, modern commercial society was increasingly characterized by a 'gradual descent of fortunes'. In this respect it differed from both its feudal predecessor and the ancient slave economies by gradually reducing absolute, if not relative, inequalities of wealth and income. For reasons partly con-nected with the constitutional arrangements that resulted from the *Glorious Revolution of 1688, England had so far been able to benefit most from these Europe-wide developments. On this more secure agrarian foundation rested the 200 years of slowly rising living standards that had elapsed since the beginning of the reign of Elizabeth, 'a period', according to Smith, 'as long as the course of human prosperity usually endures'. Smith's optimism is chiefly con-fined to what had been achieved in retrospect rather than what lies in prospect. He had no great confidence that wisdom would always prevent the 'ordinary revolutions of war and govern-ment' from putting an end to the growth of national opulence, and he believed that there was 'a great deal of ruin' in nations.

If any single discovery was crucial to the accidental and largely unwilled results of the previ-ous 200 years, it was the discovery and European colonization of the Americas rather than any-thing connected with technology or pioneering forms of entrepreneurship. Although merchants and manufacturers who reinvested their profits in farming brought valuable com-mercial skills to enterprises that were increasingly organized on a non-subsistence basis, their talents were more often and far less advantageously revealed in attempts to raise prices, lower wages, and increase profits by means of tacit combination and special legislative privileges achieved at the expense of consumers, wage-earners, and taxpayers. Indeed, for Smith, it was the 'policy of Europe' in giving artificial encouragement to commerce and manufacturing at the expense of agriculture that had now become the chief obstacle to the expansion and diffusion of those forms of 'publick happiness' that derived from economic growth. Hence what he described as one of the main purposes of the *Wealth of Nations* was to sustain a 'very violent attack' on all manifestations of *mercantilism—that mode of thinking closely associated with merchants and manufacturers which had captured the imagination of European legislators.

The revolt of Britain's North American colonies was coming to a climax as Smith was finishing the *Wealth of Nations*, and it provided him with an ideal opportunity to press home this attack. Indeed, since he delayed publication in order to complete his analysis of the under-lying causes of the deteriorating political situation, together with his remedies for dealing with it, it might be said that the *American Revolution was one for which Smith's political economy was almost literally tailor-made. Indeed, the two issues around which much of Smith's analy-sis turned—the *income tax and *national debt burdens of *war [2] and *empire [5], and the future of Britain's mercantile system—continued to preoccupy his followers during the first decades of the nineteenth century. Far from being a remote episode of no further significance, therefore, completion of the commercial revolution, by removing the inexpedient and unjust results of mercantile thinking, retained its role in British political economy during the early decades of the nineteenth century.

What had largely been a slow and silent achievement in Britain was being completed more rapidly and noisily by political means in France after 1789. Two of the most prominent early British detractors and defenders of the *French Revolution, Edmund *Burke and Thomas *Paine, laid claim to the basic insights of Smith's political economy of modernity. To Burke, French events proved that the advantages to be derived from commercial civilization were dependent on the maintenance of social and political stability within established institutions and forms of government. To Paine, on the other hand, France was taking the next step in a sequence begun by the North Americans, proving that only *republican forms of government were capable of realizing the pacific yet revolutionizing potential of commerce in uniting and transforming civil society. An over-neat characterization of this divided inheritance would run as follows: whereas Burke took a strategic look backwards to feudalism to provide reminders of the intricacy and potential fragility of existing arrangements, Paine projected Smith's vision for-wards, seeing commerce as a progressive impulse that had the power of 'rendering modes of government obsolete'. The characterization is over-neat, because Burke's political economy was equally forward-looking in its appreciation of the hard fiscal and commercial realities that underlay Britain's capacity to wage successful war against the French Revolution; and Paine's vision, an inspiration for many later radicals, went beyond Smith's in comprehending explicit measures of redistribution, using social insurance as a method of complementing the equalizing and democratizing potential contained in Smith's system of natural liberty [see *natural rights].

Although radicals and other opponents of the war with France continued to call on Smith's terminology to condemn 'unproductive' classes and the high taxes that supported 'Old Corruption', as well as the diversion of productive labour from constructive pursuits, it was Burke's realistic agenda rather than Paine's more pacific, anti-monarchical, and cosmopolitan one that prevailed during the Napoleonic wars. *Napoleon's attempted economic blockade and the Orders in Council that were Britain's response also raised acute questions about the basis of British prosperity. Had the French *Économistes*, rather than Smith, been more accurate in ascribing prosperity to the exclusive capacity of agriculture to produce a net social surplus? How vulnerable was Britain to threats to its foreign commerce? Would her prosperity survive if she was surrounded by what Bishop Berkeley (1685–1753) called 'a wall of brass'? Smith could be cited as believing that defence was more important than opulence, but one result of wartime anxieties was to reinforce the mercantile logic of the navigation laws and imperial self-sufficiency. When it became clear that war, instead of harming British trade, had actually acted as a stimulus to manufacturing and given her a virtual monopoly of international commerce, these short-term anxieties gave way to concerns that were more fundamental to the way in which post-Smithian political economy developed. Two other structural changes played their part in altering basic perceptions: the recognition after the first census of 1801 that the British *population was rising faster than earlier estimates had suggested (many had maintained that it was actually stationary or falling); and the signs that by the end of the eighteenth century Britain had become a net importer rather than a net exporter of grain products. War focused attention on the security aspects of these developments, and rising expenditure on outdoor relief for able-bodied paupers under the *poor laws during periods of food scarcity and *famine in 1795, 1800, and in the postwar period drew attention to longer-term dilemmas centring on Britain's capacity to support its growing population from domestic sources.

Thomas *Malthus's *Essay on the Principle of Population* was first published in 1798 as a polemical response to William *Godwin and the Marquis de Condorcet's post-revolutionary optimism about individual and social perfectibility. Revised in 1803, and over the whole war and postwar period, Malthus's *Essay* became the first major work since the *Wealth of Nations* to express and address these social and economic problems. Conventional contrasts between Smithian optimism and Malthusian pessimism fail, however, to capture the shift of focus, though Malthus did succeed in overturning an eighteenth-century assumption that Smith himself left largely unquestioned, namely the equation between increasing population and national greatness. By making the pressure of population on the living standards of the mass of society an 'imminent and immediate' problem rather than one that lay in some distant future, Malthus undermined some of the more extravagant hopes of achieving mastery over nature, including human nature, that were characteristic of rationalistic forms of the *Enlightenment [32], whether based on technocratic promise or universal benevolence and social transparency. Malthus also queried what he took to be an unwarranted implication of Smith's model of economic growth, the assumption that capital accumulation, when concentrated on manufactured luxuries rather than agrarian necessities, would invariably benefit the mass of society [see *consumerism, 19]. Although the term is usually associated with later and more radical *utopian [9] visions, Malthus could envisage growth as an 'immiserizing' process.

Smith had emphasized the priority of agriculture in any 'natural' scheme of progress, and had been too cautious to make any long-term predictions implying final deliverance from ancient evils of scarcity and oppression, whether by economic or political means.

Nevertheless, by providing a longer perspective on what constituted economic progress he had cast doubt on the relevance of the eighteenth-century literature of jeremiad—those insistent warnings about the enfeebling consequences of luxury that predicted depopulation and national ruin. Malthus entertained his own visions of gradual economic and moral improvement, if the rate of population increase could be controlled by 'moral restraint' (deferred marriage accompanied by sexual continence) and thereby kept in step with (or just behind) the growth in the means of subsistence. But his efforts to change public perceptions on the subject also brought the signs of population pressure to the surface—low wages, incessant toil, indigence, and high pre-adolescent mortality rates—with the arithmetic series he posited for the likely maximum rate of increase in subsistence later emerging as a law of diminishing returns that was to dominate post-Smithian political economy [see *poverty, 12].

As interpreted by Malthus, by his friend David *Ricardo, and by their respective followers, the law of diminishing returns entailed a defensible but (in hindsight) inaccurate assumption that improvements in technology when applied to land-using activities were only capable of postponing an inevitable trend towards higher food and energy costs and prices. In this highly qualified respect, at least, Thomas *Carlyle was justified in describing political economy as the 'dismal science'. However, since the point of expressing the underlying problem in this fashion was to focus on practical solutions that would raise living standards generally, the law of diminishing returns should not be confused, as it often has been, with 'blind materialism' and heartless fatalism.

In addition to Malthus's own ideal solution of deferred marriage, some of his more radical and secular *confrères* within the political economy community that formed during the first

48. *The Revd T. R. Malthus*, portrait by the devout Dissenter John Linnell in 1834.

decades of the nineteenth century advocated birth control within marriage. Neither Malthus nor any of the other *Anglican clerics who increasingly sought to combine their interest in political economy with natural theology could accept this neo-Malthusian remedy. Increase and multiply regardless of individual and social consequences was clearly a misreading of God's message, but the idea that God had designed a universe in which the struggle to overcome necessity was essential to optimal cultivation of the earth and man's moral enlightenment could not be abandoned. Political economy with natural-theological underpinnings reinforced the general presumption in favour of *laissez-faire* and individual responsibility that Smith had imparted to the original enterprise. 'Unnatural' expedients such as birth control constituted an evasion of responsibility in the light of such theological doctrines. This also explains the opposition to any levelling or communitarian solutions that blurred the distinction between the prudent and the improvident, removing the incentive to rise and the 'goad of necessity' built into penalties for falling in the social scale.

While natural theology was needed to provide such explicit justifications for those forms of social inequality that did not derive from unfair legislative advantages, many secular-minded political economists joined Malthus in accepting his population diagnosis and hence in condemning the poor laws as having a depressing influence on wages. Abolition or fundamental reform of the principles on which relief was granted was one of those major institutional reforms needed to prevent a return, in new form, to a system of degrading dependency on the part of those who were otherwise able-bodied. Assistance should be concentrated on those whose poverty was attributable to circumstances that no prudence could foresee. Negative reform on this front was associated with more positive methods of encouraging prudence through savings banks, public provision of *education [17], and the extension of all those civil and political liberties connected with the general aim of *embourgeoisement*.

On the other main solution to the population–subsistence equation—repeal of the *corn laws—the analytical and political running was made by Ricardo and his followers, John Ramsay McCulloch (1789–1864), James *Mill, and his precocious son John Stuart *Mill; though outside this tight circle others had reached similar conclusions on the basis of Smith's more straightforward case for free trade. Ricardo's *Principles of Political Economy*, first published in 1817, was an elaboration of a deductive model of growth and the distribution of its results between rent, profits, and wages that Ricardo had originally formulated as part of his case for the gradual withdrawal of agricultural protection in the corn law debates of 1814–15. It embodied a theory of rent derived from the law of diminishing returns, but in contrast with Malthus's more harmonistic formulation of this theory it underlined the conclusion that land-rent was a form of monopoly return or transfer payment by the community at large to the owners of a scarce resource, with rents rising when the price of food rose, and with the rate of payment for any given piece of land being dependent on inherent natural differences in fertility. The passivity of rent as a form of income, if not its illegitimacy, was underlined.

This allowed Ricardo to achieve a startling reversal of what had been one of Smith's most confident assertions: that since landowners received a form of income that rose in the course of economic growth, their interest as an economic class was identical with that of the community at large. Smith had based this assertion on the opinion that landowners, unlike merchants and manufacturers, possessed neither the inclination nor capacity to combine in furtherance of their collective interests—an opinion that was revealed to be overly complacent when the corn law debate resumed against the background of the threat of falling corn prices and the collapse of high rents negotiated under war conditions. Ricardo's motives in maintaining that 'the interest of the landlord is always opposed to the interest of every other class of society' were coolly scientific, but he had placed a potent weapon in the hands of those, such as James Mill and his son, who wished to fortify the Benthamite or philosophical radical attack on the aristocratic nature of society and the British constitution.

For Ricardians, free trade in corn, the main good on which wages were spent, was the most obvious way of escaping the restriction on growth, and hence on rising living standards, posed by diminishing returns and the agrarian bottleneck. It was also the last major step towards fulfilling the cosmopolitan promise contained within Smith's system of natural liberty. It was presented as an exemplary step towards reciprocity and multilateralism in matters of trade, by the nation that could both afford and expect to gain most from the opening of markets and the extension to the world at large of the gains from the division of labour. For this very reason, the proposition was later to be subjected to a different interpretation by latecomers to the business of applying machinery to manufacture. It was to become the mark of 'perfidious Albion', a conclusion of the despised English 'cosmopolitical economy', as the German liberal Friedrich List (1789–1846) called it, that had laid the foundation for what was later to be known as 'free trade imperialism'. Domestically, however, Ricardian logic pointed to the benefits which a heavily populated island could derive from embracing a policy of exchanging the products of its new workshops and factories for food and raw materials, rather than having recourse to increasingly inferior land at home.

Although Malthus appreciated all the steps in this argument and was in many respects to remain more faithful to Smith's enterprise than Ricardo, he became a reluctant apostate on the corn laws, lending cautious support to their renewal in 1815 and only accepting their abolition when it seemed that they might become a major source of political unrest. The agrarian bias imparted by his original point of entry into political economy via the population question led him to question the wisdom of relying on other nations to supply the necessities of life. It was only with difficulty that he persuaded himself that urban manufacturing occupations might be made a healthy substitute for rural employments, and he always regarded them as less stable because they were more open to the caprices of taste and the chances of emulation by other nations. Moreover, since his own interpretation of the scope of political economy made it part of a wider system of Christian morals, Malthus was willing to sacrifice the pursuit of wealth whenever his calculation of costs and benefits suggested that the moral cost to the bulk of the population became too high. This infringed one of the self-denying ordinances of Ricardo's narrower conception of the science, which taught nations how to become rich, but not whether it was a good thing for them to do so. Malthus was more wary of 'premature generalizations' and attempts to press the conclusions of any single theory or principle into practice regardless of changing circumstances and opinions. He was also more impressed than Ricardo by the irregular and cyclical nature of economic phenomena, and by the pains of adjustment from one state of equilibrium to another.

This underlies Malthus's most important act of apostasy: his refusal to accept the Say–Mill law of markets. This law held that aggregate demand for goods and services could always be guaranteed as long as the conditions of aggregate supply had been achieved. General gluts, defined as the simultaneous existence of excess capital and unemployment, could not occur: what could be observed as unemployment was the result of partial gluts and incomplete adjustment to shifts of demand and technological change. Malthus, on the other hand, held that there was symmetry between population growth and capital accumulation: just as that population could increase too fast for living standards to be maintained, so the same could hold for capital accumulation and the output of manufactured goods, with the results being revealed in prices that were too low to sustain production and full employment. This was part of Malthus's explanation for postwar depression, and it also underlay his belief that stable, long-term growth depended as much on counterbalancing increases in 'effectual demand' as on favourable conditions for the increase in production or aggregate supply. This was Keynes's reason for regarding Malthus as a worthy predecessor in his own battle with 'classical' economics. In the circumstances of his own day, however, Malthus's support for public works and unproductive expenditure on personal services by those in receipt of rental and other forms of income that were large enough to permit expenditure on luxuries merely compounded his reputation for being, in polite language, overly sympathetic to landowners' interests—a charge that was vigorously denied by Malthus himself, with the support of Ricardo, despite disagreement between the two thinkers on the theoretical and policy issues involved.

In terms of many of the pressing theoretical and practical problems of the first third of the nineteenth century, the *Wealth of Nations* frequently offered general inspiration to Smith's followers rather than detailed guidance. Even among those who explicitly acknowledged Smith's status as an authority, there was room for disagreement on fundamentals as well as healthy development in new directions. Some theoretical questions were 'technical', even 'metaphysical', notably the dispute over the causes and ideal measure of exchange value. But policy issues could be equally 'technical', involving specialized knowledge and terminology. This was true, for example, of currency questions arising out of the suspension of cash payments during the war, of the management and redemption of the public debt, and of the incidence of taxation. Political economists were increasingly called upon as expert witnesses before select committees and royal commissions that dealt with agriculture, emigration, bullion, the consequences of machinery, and the poor laws. Parliamentary debate on some subjects was dominated by them, with Ricardo and Francis Horner (1778–1817), who chaired the 1810 parliamentary committee into bullion, being only the earliest and most prominent examples.

There were no specialized journals exclusively devoted to the subject of political economy, but the *Edinburgh Review*, reflecting the Scottish paternity of political economy and the early public teachings of Dugald *Stewart as professor of moral philosophy at Edinburgh, came close to serving this purpose, forcing its Tory rival, the *Quarterly Review*, to follow suit [see *prose, 30]. The fact that *liberal Tories, many of them clerics, became experts on political economy also reflects the fact that its role as one of the most practical of modern moral sciences was thought to be too important to be left to Whigs and atheists. As a potent new public language, political economy achieved a status comparable to the older political languages forged over a longer period by *constitutional debate. It had acquired a role that befitted Smith's description of it as 'a branch of the science of a statesman or legislator'. It had also become an appropriate subject for Malthus to teach at the East India College to budding civil servants before they left to govern the affairs of the Indian subcontinent.

What also needs to be mentioned in conclusion, however, is that during the same period, largely as a reaction to its growing public prominence, political economy acquired some of its most persistent, even virulent, critics. Some radicals and *philanthropists, whether on the right or left of the spectrum, were outraged by the harsh logic of Malthus's population principle and his abolitionist position on the poor laws, though many of them also came to accept the need for a fundamental reform of the principles on which assistance to the able-bodied was granted. Nevertheless, Malthus's principle appeared either to dissolve the paternal relationship between rich and poor or to place the blame for the condition of the poor on the victim rather than on the moral and political defects of the system that generated pauperism. This explains why S. T. *Coleridge, William *Hazlitt, William *Cobbett, and Robert *Southey made Malthus the focus of their early attacks, and why 'Malthusian' became a permanent term of abuse in their vocabulary that could be used to condemn every manifestation of 'modern' political economy. Having decided that the science was the emblem or source of so much that all the Lake poets, including William *Wordsworth, deplored about modern society, Southey became the first, though by no means the last, to describe the *Wealth of Nations* as 'the code, or confession of faith' of the economic system that had developed further in Britain than elsewhere—a system that denied man's higher spiritual qualities by treating him purely as a 'manufacturing animal'. Again without being first or last to make such statements, Southey also counterposed 'moral' to 'political' economy. In view of Malthus's belief, in opposition to Ricardo, that political economy could not be divorced from morals, there is some irony in this which can only be appreciated by those prepared to believe that the identity of ideas is not fully described by their sociological allegiances or ideological appearances.

Neither Coleridge nor Southey would have been impressed by the *utilitarian character of Malthus's Christian theology. However, if they had continued to read the work Malthus published after 1803 they might have found some remarkable parallels between their own concerns and his. One of Coleridge's more interesting accusations was that political economy was guilty of 'denationalizing' public debate by undermining 'love of our own country'. This attacks some of the cosmopolitan features imparted to the science by Smith, but it more readily reflects the patriotism that became part of the Lake poets' 'conservatism'—a potent term of political art which, like its partner, 'liberalism', existed at the end but not at the beginning of our period. There were liberal Tory, even ultra-Tory devotees of political economy, though Thomas *De Quincey, in his exaggerated admiration for Ricardo and in related charges that the Lake poets were arrogant dabblers in such matters, seems to be alone in representing and defining the latter category.

Burke, one of the figures with whom the Lake poets came to feel most sympathy, was invested with those qualities which made up their own brand of patriotic and pious conservatism, though they were clearly ambivalent about his belief that political economy was an essential qualification for the statesman called upon to direct the affairs of opulent commercial nations. In this way the ground was prepared for what became known as the conservative revolt against the eighteenth century, and perhaps even the entire project of Enlightenment with which political economy retained firm links. That is certainly how John Stuart Mill, the one person to attempt a bridge-building exercise based on his knowledge of both sides, came to see the situation after his encounter with Wordsworth and Coleridge in the late 1820s. Mill's diagnosis of what divided the two camps did not, however, result in any bridge being built that was capable of bearing traffic across the divide. One of the enduring fault-lines in British cultural debate had now been created: where Coleridge and Southey had led, Carlyle, Ruskin, Marx, and their nineteenth- and twentieth-century supporters were to follow.

Blaug, M., *Ricardian Economics*, New Haven, Conn., 1958; Claeys, G., *Thomas Paine: Social and Political Thought*, Boston, 1989; Cookson, J. E., *The Friends of Peace: Anti-War Liberalism in England, 1793–1815*, Cambridge, 1982; Fetter, F. W., *The Economist in Parliament, 1760–1870*, Durham, 1980; Hilton, B., *The Age of Atonement: The Influence of Evangelicalism on Social and Economic Thought, 1795–1865*, Oxford, 1988; Pocock, J. G. A., 'The Political Economy of Burke's Analysis of the French Revolution', in his *Virtue, Commerce and History*, Cambridge, 1987; Poynter, J. R., *Society and Pauperism: English Ideas on Poor Relief, 1795–1834*, London, 1989; Winch, D., *Malthus*, Oxford, 1987; *The Secret Concatenation: Studies in the Intellectual History of Political Economy, 1750–1834*, Cambridge, 1996; Wrigley, E. A., 'The Classical Economists and the Industrial Revolution', in his *People, Cities and Wealth: The Transformation of Traditional Society*, Oxford, 1987.

34 · NATURAL PHILOSOPHY (SCIENCE)

RICHARD YEO

Any discussion of the term 'natural philosophy' has to begin with the recognition that it now stands for a set of belief systems and practices that are no longer current, being associated with an earlier historical epoch and social structure. Instead the word 'science' has become the generic term for the systematic pursuit of natural knowledge. This shift began to occur in our period. Before about 1760 the scope and method of natural philosophy seemed secure; it was defined broadly as an enquiry into the phenomena and powers of nature, and as such it had enjoyed a reputation as the 'handmaiden' of theology, the 'queen' of the sciences, from the high middle ages. By the 1830s, however, the subject was being radically transformed and superseded: the term 'scientist' had been coined, by William *Whewell, and the demise of the earlier natural philosophy was well underway.

Looking back in 1817 on events since the *French Revolution, S. T. *Coleridge commented that the political turmoil had been matched by upheavals in the intellectual world, a widely shared perception. In 1790 James *Watt wrote to Erasmus *Darwin, 'I feel myself becoming all french both in chemistry and politics'. Joseph *Priestley explicitly linked natural philosophy and politics: his *Experiments and Observations on Air* of 1790, announced that 'the English hierarchy (if there be anything unsound in its constitution) has equal reason to tremble even at an air pump, or an electrical machine'. In reaction, Edmund *Burke alleged that the hand of 'geometricians and chemists' was apparent in the disastrous interventions of the French 'analytical legislators'.

Scholarship in the history of science has begun to recognize the complex associations suggested by these contemporary remarks. At one level, such comments signal the end of the comfortable alliance between natural philosophy and the *Anglican Church—an arrangement already in place by the time of Isaac *Newton's death in 1727. Under this partnership, Newtonian natural philosophy bolstered the design argument of natural theology, delineating the order and laws of nature, God's 'second book'. But in spite of its influence, this official Newtonianism had to control a variety of theories about the matter and forces of nature, including those found in Newton's own published writings—not to mention his secret alchemical investigations. The natural philosophy sanctioned by the Church envisaged a world composed of inert corpuscles of matter; so that both initial and sustained movement required forces deriving from the power of God as creator. By the 1770s, this relationship between natural philosophy, orthodox *religion [10], and maintenance of the social order was more frequently challenged by those who linked the former with materialism and radical causes. Natural philosophy became a contested intellectual space in which opposing political and theological notions were associated with rival theories of the natural world.

Yet these developments are only part of the story of natural philosophy in the period of revolution and *Romanticism. When the alliance with Anglican theology was challenged in the late eighteenth century, more was involved than the attachment of natural philosophy to different theological and political positions. Historians have spoken of a second scientific revolution during our period, marked by major advances in the fields of mathematical physics, *chemistry, optics, electromagnetism, and biology. The names linked to these advances—Pierre-Simon Laplace, Antoine Lavoisier, John *Dalton, Thomas *Young, Humphry *Davy, Michael *Faraday, Georges Cuvier, Priestley—rival those of the scientific ferment of the seventeenth century, the period of the scientific revolution. The emergence of new disciplines in the organic sciences and the increasing specialization of all scientific activity strained the capacity of Newtonianism as a unitary category. As separate disciplines claimed intellectual autonomy, the earlier notion of natural philosophy could no longer stand for a unified range of beliefs and practices. During this period, scientific developments were thus accompanied by significant shifts in attitudes to the study of nature, and indeed to the concept of 'science' itself. This essay aims to consider some of the issues in the transition from 'natural philosophy' to modern 'science' as it occurred in Britain between 1770 and the 1830s.

In attempting to grasp contemporary understandings of natural philosophy we may begin with the *encyclopedias of the eighteenth century, just as readers of this *Companion* may treat it as a reference work of first call for information about British culture from 1770 to 1830. There are sound grounds for such an approach because encyclopedias were one of the great *publishing [21] enterprises of the period, and those described as dictionaries of arts and sciences were major carriers and disseminators of information on natural knowledge. How did these works define natural philosophy? At first glance their editors seemed to have little difficulty in producing short answers. In 1765 *A General Dictionary of the Arts and Sciences* said that natural philosophy 'considers the powers and properties of natural bodies, and their mutual actions on one another'. This was repeated in a four-line entry in the first edition of the *Encyclopaedia Britannica*, published in three volumes between 1768 and 1771. Another one-line entry on 'Physics' listed it as 'a denomination sometimes given to natural philosophy'. The editors also made the provinces of both 'Philosophy' and 'Moral Philosophy' intersect with the domain of natural philosophy: the former was the rational study of nature and morality; but moral philosophy was also said to depend on observations and reasoning from experiments.

Short, and circular, responses such as these immediately create unease, especially when the work, in the case of the *Britannica*, contained long articles (20–110 pages) on subjects such as astronomy, *botany, chemistry, mechanics, and optics. Indeed, the entries on 'natural philosophy' refer the reader to these articles on the various sciences. Hence the contemporary encyclopedias do not offer a simple account of the meaning of 'natural philosophy', but they do provide a clue—though a standard term for the study of nature, it was one already under stress by 1765. This reading is supported by the short description of 'Newtonian philosophy' as 'the doctrine of the universe, and particularly of the heavenly bodies'—again with a cross reference to more detailed articles on the relevant sciences. Earlier in the century, similar dictionaries gave this phrase a far wider licence, accepting Newton's work as a comprehensive programme for the proper pursuit of natural knowledge. In order to appreciate what was happening to the concept of natural philosophy from the mid-eighteenth century, we need to note its earlier, and still active, association with Newtonianism.

As in the title of Newton's *Philosophiae naturalis principia mathematica* (1687)—that is, mathematical principles of natural philosophy—the most commonly used eighteenth-century term for the study of natural phenomena was 'natural philosophy'. Yet the wording indicates that Newton was claiming to give his subject a mathematical foundation, thereby implying that this had not yet been adequately achieved. Indeed, John *Locke, one of Newton's ardent admirers, said that natural philosophy was a subject a gentleman should look into, but its reliance on 'experience and history' made him suspect that 'natural philosophy is not capable of being made a science'. Here Locke distinguished the ancient concept of *scientia*—a system of axiomatic knowledge—from the kind of natural knowledge produced by members of the Royal Society of London, such as the chemist Robert Boyle (1627–91). This so-called 'new philosophy' could not be considered as *scientia*, precisely because it depended on observation and experiment. However, with the success of Newton's mathematical approach to phenomena in astronomy and mechanics, natural philosophy appeared to have achieved the status of rigorously demonstrative knowledge. In building on the dynamics of Galileo, the descriptive astronomy of Kepler, and the cosmology of Descartes, Newton established a style of enquiry applicable to a range of astronomical and terrestrial phenomena. In his other major work, the *Opticks* of 1704, Newton presented a more experimental method. Although most of the *Principia* was strictly mathematical and deductive, its pairing with the work on optics allowed Newton's approach to stand as the exemplar of an experimental and quantitative natural philosophy concerned with the components of matter and the forces that act upon it.

Throughout the eighteenth century the 'Newtonian philosophy' had advocates in both scholarly and more public circles. Disciples defended it against the increasingly shaky Cartesian alternative in expositions suited to educated audiences beyond the small élite who could grasp the mathematics. It was also disseminated in a range of *lectures, demonstrations, textbooks, and encyclopedias. In John Harris's *Lexicon Technicum* (1704 and 1710) and Ephraim Chambers's *Cyclopaedia* (1728), Newtonianism was virtually synonymous with experimental natural philosophy. By 1761 a popular text, *The Newtonian System of Philosophy*, was able to use the figure of a precocious young 'Tom Telescope' as the model for the instruction of 'young gentlemen and ladies'. The book went through many editions and sold at least 25,000 copies in Britain.

However, despite its power and the efforts of its advocates (especially in Britain), Newton's work should not be seen as coterminous with natural philosophy, certainly not after about 1760. The various opponents of Newtonianism—from the Anglican High Church theologian and mathematician Bishop George Berkeley (1685–1753) to the radical printer and poet William *Blake—suggest that it was a complex and moving target. In our period, both Priestley and Coleridge were critical, in different ways, of the Newtonian legacy, while still maintaining that a sound natural philosophy was fundamental to a proper understanding of human nature and society. Their views allow a glimpse of the debates about natural philosophy in the context of revolution, as well as the way in which the former was giving way to separate scientific disciplines.

The scope of Priestley's activities—*Unitarian theologian, *language [40] teacher, author of political, educational, and historical works, experimenter in *electricity and chemistry—indicates the array of interests in which natural philosophy could be found. But while orthodox Newtonianism affirmed the established order, Priestley's natural philosophy was linked with his support of revolutionary causes. Inspired in 1758 by the electrical performances of the American patriot Benjamin Franklin, he began to connect the pursuit of electrical and chemical knowledge to the ideas of social reform shared by other members of Dissenting and radical circles, such as James Watt, Erasmus Darwin, Richard *Price, and Thomas *Beddoes. Priestley regarded the phenomena of nature not as something to be gazed at in a passive state of wonder before the power of God, but as something to be understood as part of a process of active *Enlightenment [32]. Once carefully gathered, scientific knowledge would thus extend itself 'in all directions . . . [and] be the means under God of extirpating all error and prejudice, and of putting an end to all undue and usurped authority in the business of religion, as well as of science'. Priestley did not reject the practice of linking science and theology—as sanctioned by Newton—but in his *Disquisitions Relating to Matter and Spirit* of 1777, he advocated an ontology in which matter was not an inert substance requiring the impress of an external force, but one in which force was inherent. In other words, his natural philosophy was a materialist one in which matter and force were identified and divine activity permeated the world, from the physical to the mental and spiritual spheres. This was precisely the outcome against which Newton's Anglican followers had always guarded, since it either removed God from the universe or equated Him with nature.

49. This portrait of Erasmus Darwin (1792–3) was among many that Joseph Wright of Derby painted of contemporary scientific luminaries. Wright met Darwin through mutual acquaintances in the Lunar Society of Birmingham.

In addition, Priestley explicitly linked the terminology of chemistry—gases, gunpowder, explosions—to talk about political upheavals. In a *sermon of 1787 he declared: 'We are, as it were, laying gunpowder, grain by grain, under the old building of error and superstition, which a single spark may hereafter inflame so as to produce an instantaneous explosion.' This presented Edmund Burke with a ready-made equation between chemistry and sedition, making Priestley an accomplice of the French chemists and *philosophes*: 'Churches, play houses, coffee houses, all alike, are destined to be mingled, and equalized, and blended into one common rubbish; and, well sifted, and lixiviated, to crystallize into true, democratic, explosive, insurrectionary nitre.' Although Burke appealed to the 'pattern of nature' and the 'order of the world'—presumably discerned by natural philosophy—he ridiculed the transfer of experimental methods from chemistry to the social world, charging that those affected by such a delusion treated men as if they were mice in an air-pump. Judged against this background, Humphry Davy's success in making chemistry attractive to the wealthy audiences at the Royal Institution in London after 1802 was considerable.

Priestley's departure from the Newtonian legacy was not confined to metaphysics and politics; it involved claims about the organization of scientific enquiry. His *History and Present State of Electricity* (1767) aimed to 'give pleasure' to those who have 'a taste for Natural Philosophy in general, as [well as] to electricians in particular'. The distinction here is significant when juxtaposed with his judgement that 'the business of philosophy is so multiplied' that it was 'high times to *subdivide* the business, that every man may have an opportunity of seeing everything that relates to his own favourite pursuit'.

This can be read as criticism of those who sought to embrace all natural philosophy under the rubric of Newtonianism. Priestley had two objections. First, the Newtonian philosophy, as promoted by its followers, no longer adequately represented the range of subjects or the variety of approaches pursued by cultivators of natural knowledge. He believed that the mature mathematical sciences of astronomy, mechanics, and optics unjustifiably overshadowed the recent work of experimenters in electricity and chemistry. Comparing the various sciences to branches of a 'large overgrown family', he celebrated electricity as the 'youngest daughter', setting the example and showing that 'she thinks herself considerable enough to make her appearance in the world without the company of her sisters'. Recent discoveries in this subject would extend the boundaries of science: 'New worlds may open to our view, and the glory of the great Sir Isaac Newton himself, and all his contemporaries, be eclipsed, by a new set of philosophers, in quite a new field of speculation.'

Second, Priestley argued for a more accessible natural philosophy open to the contributions and judgement of the public. As part of his campaign against Antoine Lavoisier's chemical theories he protested against the expensive equipment that the French savant employed, claiming that it rendered experiments immune from adequate testing by others who lacked such financial support. Priestley regarded natural philosophy as a means of cultivating the rational capacities that would allow the public—for example, the Dissenters excluded from Oxford and Cambridge universities—to resist 'the empire of superstition' [see *Dissenting academies]. His egalitarian theory of knowledge stressed the role of accident in the discovery of recent electrical phenomena and lessened the importance of genius. In Priestley's opinion, the adulation of Newton's genius had been excessive and owed much to the fact that his discoveries had been presented as a logical series of deductive steps. In contrast, discoveries in electricity were more usually made by a process involving guesswork and good fortune. 'Were it possible', Priestley suggested, 'to trace the succession of ideas in the mind of Sir Isaac Newton, during the time that he made his greatest discoveries, I make no doubt but our amazement at the extent of his genius would a little subside.' It is possible to see this as a celebration of what the modern theorist T. S. Kuhn described as the rise of Baconian experimental sciences, such as chemistry and electricity—a tradition of enquiry that had not been fully integrated within the mathematical work of Newton.

Though Coleridge, like Priestley, eventually became a sharp critic of Newtonianism, his earliest interest in natural philosophy was still essentially orthodox. The harmony of the mathematical laws of nature attracted him, and he was also enthusiastic about the efforts of Priestley and David Hartley (1705–57) to carry Newton's philosophical method into the study of the moral world [see *psychology, 39]. Indeed, his exposure to science was through contact with members of Dissenting, Unitarian and liberal circles, such as Erasmus Darwin, Thomas Wedgwood (1771–1805), Thomas Beddoes, and Priestley, to whom he dedicated a sonnet in 1795. However, Coleridge began to think that Newton's followers encouraged a mechanical philosophy that explained too much by secondary causes, leaving God as an indolent First Cause. He concluded that the concept of lifeless matter separated from God was a large step towards atheism; and secondly, that Priestley's alternative of active matter was a form of pantheism. Thus after about 1800 Coleridge sought a natural philosophy that escaped the atomistic and mechanical conceptions of the natural world. This search took him into German *Naturphilosophie* and its conception of nature as organic and dynamic, with the laws of nature being expressions of Divine ideas.

It is important to note the sciences to which Coleridge turned in his search for a new philosophy of nature. In 1818, in his journal *The Friend*, he remarked that no one could attend a lecture course on, or read about, modern chemistry 'without experiencing, even as a *sensation*, a sudden *enlargement and emancipation* of his Intellect'. This science promised to lead the way out of the dead world of Newtonian matter—as both Blake and *Wordsworth saw it—by evincing the dynamic and opposing powers and qualities of nature. Here the chemistry of Humphry Davy—who discussed poetry with Coleridge—was the great hope because, in contrast with the atomism of John Dalton, it stressed analogies between the forces of electricity, galvanism, and chemical affinity. Combining this with his German reading, Coleridge elaborated a transcendental philosophy in which nature was a system of polar forces interacting in a historical sequence culminating in the human mind, which in turn comprehended the Divine ideas governing this process.

The details of these reflections cannot be examined here, but the fascination with scientific fields beyond the core of the Newtonian system resonates with some of Priestley's remarks about a new direction for natural philosophy. For Coleridge, the departure was more extreme: he saw the sciences of chemistry, *geology, electricity, biology, and comparative anatomy as the foundations of a less mechanistic and atomistic, more organic and dynamic, natural philosophy. More so than Priestley, Coleridge stressed the qualitative differences between the various sciences, especially between the inorganic and the organic domains. He reinforced this point by claiming that major discoveries, rather than deriving from accident (as Priestley suggested), involved the grasp of 'some master IDEA' that bound together the phenomena of a particular subject. From this it followed that a thorough philosophy of nature must recognize the differences between the various sciences: concepts applicable to the organic realm could not be translated into those of the physical; biology could not be reduced to mechanics.

Coleridge's views on science, and his Kantian terminology, were not widely accepted in Britain. However, he highlighted a new feature of the intellectual landscape: the emergence of a group of scientific disciplines from the general field of 'natural history', the poor relative of natural philosophy. Whereas the latter studied what were purportedly the prime movers of nature—motion and forces—natural history was thought to be limited to the observation and recording of specific characteristics of minerals, plants, animals, and other organic phenomena. Following the work of Carolus Linnaeus it aimed also to achieve some classification, but never with the hope of attaining the mathematical precision of the sciences denoted by natural philosophy. By about 1800 it became obvious, though, that this field could no longer be seen as merely descriptive. Following the work of French researchers such as Lamarck, Cuvier, Bichat, and Saint-Hilaire, the new disciplines of biology, physiology, and comparative anatomy asserted themselves as scientific studies of living beings. These sciences speculated about the mechanisms and processes underlying the structure and diversity of organic life. There was a shift from a static natural history to a history of nature, one that sought a genetic account of the development of the present order from the past. The Scottish natural philosopher James *Hutton played a major role in the establishment of another new science, geology, arguing in his *Theory of the Earth* (1795) that earth history showed 'no vestige of a beginning—no prospect of an end'. This concept of 'deep time' (as it is now called) provided an explanatory framework for the study of the processes by which the strata of rocks were formed and eroded, and for the laws and causes governing the movements of glaciers, volcanoes, and earthquakes. Geology also linked with the organic sciences via palaeontology, the study of fossil remains. All these sciences relied on classification of diverse phenomena and historical causation; they attempted to comprehend the pattern of non-repeatable events. As such, their mode of explanation contrasted with the mathematical quantification and predictive power of the sciences included in natural philosophy.

Thus by the early nineteenth century natural philosophy was no longer a generic term for scientific knowledge of nature; instead, it more usually referred to the core Newtonian sciences—mechanics, optics, electricity, and magnetism—later known collectively as 'physics'. Together with astronomy and chemistry these disciplines constituted the physical sciences. Natural history was still a general label for the practice of collecting and describing plants and animals, but the intellectual direction now came from the new organic sciences mentioned earlier, each with its own increasingly specialized data and concepts. Just as encyclopedias by the 1770s were pointing readers from a short entry on 'natural philosophy' to detailed articles on the various physical sciences, so by 1800 they were breaking 'natural history' into biology, *zoology, physiology, geology, and comparative anatomy. It was still possible for individuals to cultivate more than one of these sciences, but there was no longer any meaningful framework, such as Newtonianism, in which to integrate all their specialized knowledge.

In 1817 Coleridge tried to retain such a philosophical unity in his plan for the *Encyclopaedia Metropolitana*. His map of knowledge displayed the relations between sciences and prescribed the order in which the treatises on each should be read, starting with the 'formal' sciences such as logic, geometry, and grammar, moving to the physical, experimental sciences such as mechanics, optics, and chemistry, and then to those within natural history, such as geology, botany, and zoology. In this way he aimed to convey scientific instruction and information 'not in a confused mass, but in the natural sequence of the sciences'. But this was one of the last attempts at a systematic, rather than alphabetical, organization of an encyclopedia: much modified, it appeared in 1845 and was not a commercial success. The *Encyclopaedia Britannica* (which was successful) had never sought a systematic arrangement of the various sciences, and in a preliminary dissertation to the six-volume *Supplement*, begun in 1815, the Scottish philosopher Dugald *Stewart defended its refusal to draw a map of knowledge. Stewart argued that such schemes of classification were purely arbitrary and could not do justice to the complexities of modern science. Whereas Coleridge believed an encyclopedia should rest on an analysis of the conceptual relations between the various sciences, Stewart advised that this could only occur after a consideration by specialists of the detailed accounts of the particular sciences. This implied the absence of sure ground for an intellectual synthesis; authority rested with the experts.

In the 1770s, when Coleridge read Priestley's book on theology and chemistry, they were shelved next to each other in the Bristol library. Priestley wrote at a time when natural philosophy was expected to embrace the theological considerations raised by particular views of the natural order. The radical direction of his thought was censured by thinkers like Burke, but not the fact that he mixed science and religion. Coleridge also sought to build moral and social commitments on a different natural philosophy informed by new chemical theories and the emerging organic sciences. But the exciting array of sciences that attracted him was itself a portent of the disintegration of his intellectual world, and the style of natural philosophy it supported.

What were some of the signs of this shift from natural philosophy to the modern constellation of sciences? Perhaps the most crucial has already been mentioned: the crystallization into disciplines with separate research agendas, technical apparatuses, methods, and concepts. These were recognized by large articles or treatises in the *Encyclopaedia Britannica* and some of its rivals, especially from the third edition begun in 1788, which recruited contributions from specialists who synthesized the latest discoveries and theories. The allocation of these articles to various letters of the alphabet encouraged a demarcation between the subjects, in spite of the efforts at cross-referencing. Each new edition advertised the inclusion of the latest scientific information, thereby implying that previous editions were partly obsolete.

Division of intellectual labour was also manifested in the appearance of scientific societies devoted to a single subject. The Linnean (1788), the Geological (1807), the Astronomical (1820), and the Zoological (1826) societies were founded against the protests of Sir Joseph *Banks, the president of the Royal Society, the body which had formerly spoken for all sciences. It is also significant that many of these new institutions supported the natural-history sciences—in other words, the increase in scientific activity did not reinforce the status of natural philosophy. In 1831 the British Association for the Advancement of Science (BAAS) was formed, partly in an attempt to co-ordinate the diverse research interests represented by the various single-science societies. The first secretary, the Revd William Vernon Harcourt (1789–1871), aimed to prevent the fragmentation of the 'commonwealth of science' under the pressure of specialization. But natural philosophy—a term significantly absent from the title of the BAAS—was no longer the banner under which this co-ordination of the sciences could be achieved. The annual meetings of the BAAS divided into separate sections, thus acknowledging the different scientific disciplines, but sought to keep them in contact by issuing summary reports of the recent advances in all the sciences. Specialization was seen as necessary for scientific progress, but it had to be balanced by effective communication among specialists, and between them and the public. In 1829 Thomas *Carlyle expressed disenchantment with this situation and mourned the loss of the solitary natural philosopher of independent genius:

No Newton, by silent meditation, now discovers the system of the world from the falling of an apple; but some quite other than Newton stands in his Museum, his Scientific Institution, and behind whole batteries of retorts, digesters and galvanic piles imperatively 'interrogates Nature',—who, however, shows no haste to answer.

Secondly, scientific institutions and societies, in their public platforms, eschewed the political, religious, and metaphysical debates that had been so closely associated with natural philosophy from Newton to Priestley. In 1821 the radical printer-publisher Richard *Carlile wrote a pamphlet entreating 'men of science' to vindicate truth against 'the foul grasp and persecution of superstition', as Priestley had done in the 1790s. The immediate context for his plea was to publicize the materialist anatomical lectures of William *Lawrence, which were under attack from more religiously orthodox medical men such as John *Abernethy. Carlile had no audience among the respectable gentlemen who founded the BAAS. Indeed, the unease provoked by a mention of Priestley's political and religious opinions at the first meeting at York convinced its leaders that the promotion of science would be undermined if such divisive topics were countenanced. Scientific enquiry was presented as an arena free from denominational and political disputes; by default, though, this position reinforced the so called Broad Church outlook of its predominantly Anglican leadership. At least in these circles, science, via natural theology, was again the ally of rational and liberal religious views.

This suggests that the separation of science from other issues should not be exaggerated. Supporters of science within the two ancient English universities recognized that these were clerical institutions governed by Anglican-influenced religious tests. Though some of these tests were repealed in the 1850s and the remainder in 1871, they had already markedly conditioned the way in which science was promoted, including the imperative to demonstrate its moral significance. Geologists, for example, defended their subject against attacks deriving from a literal interpretation of Scripture by asserting that their science revealed an awesome prehistoric drama leading to the appearance of man as God's special creation. Indeed, the new organic sciences were favoured as resources for the arguments of natural theology because they were thought to offer more immediate illustrations of Divine design than celestial mechanics. William *Paley's influential *Natural Theology* of 1802 began with the famous case of a watch as an indubitable example of mechanical design, but all the illustrations in the book showed design as the benevolent adaptation of anatomical structures to bodily functions, and the way this ensured the happiness of animals and humans. Here again, natural philosophy seemed to lose ground to natural history. Since men of science in early-nineteenth-century Britain did not enjoy the possibility of definite scientific careers (such as those in France), these moral and religious lessons allowed them to affirm the value of science in public forums.

In 1833 Coleridge forbade the use of the word 'philosopher' as a description of members of the BAAS. In response, in the following year Whewell coined 'scientist' as a collective term for students of the natural world. This was an indication that 'natural philosophy' no longer effectively captured the range of separate scientific disciplines from astronomy to palaeontology; but nevertheless many leading men of science, like Michael Faraday, refused to adopt Whewell's neologism and continued to call themselves 'natural philosophers'. Such expressions of self-identity, however, could not restore natural philosophy as a unifying framework: by the mid-nineteenth century the direction of modern science was firmly set by specialized disciplines. Increasingly, as each of these claimed autonomy from other scientific fields, they also rejected any dependence on non-scientific grounds of legitimation. In the eighteenth century, natural philosophy had successfully supplied an embracing rationale; by the 1830s, the various sciences were beginning to speak for themselves.

Crosland, M., 'The Image of Science as a Threat: Burke versus Priestley and the "Philosophic Revolution" ', *British Journal for the History of Science*, 20 (1987), 287–318; Cunningham, A., & Jardine, N., eds., *Romanticism and the Sciences*, Cambridge, 1990; Gascoigne, J., *Cambridge in the Age of the Enlightenment: Science, Religion and Politics from the Restoration to the French Revolution*, Cambridge, 1989; Golinski, J., *Science as Public Culture: Chemistry and Enlightenment in Britain, 1760–1820*, Cambridge, 1992; Levere, T., *Poetry Realized in Nature: Samuel Taylor Coleridge and Early-Nineteenth Century Science*, New York, 1981; Porter, R., & Teich, M., eds., *The Scientific Revolution in National Context*, Cambridge, 1991; Rousseau, G. S., & Porter, R., eds., *The Ferment of Knowledge: Studies in Eighteenth-Century Science*, Cambridge, 1980; Schaffer, S., 'Priestley and the Politics of Spirit', in R. Anderson & C. Lawrence, eds., *Science, Medicine and Dissent: Joseph Priestley (1733–1804)*, London, 1987; Yeo, R., 'Reading Encyclopaedias: Science and the Organisation of Knowledge in British Dictionaries of Arts and Sciences, 1730–1850', *Isis*, 82 (1991), 24–49; *Defining Science: William Whewell, Natural Knowledge and Public Debate in Early Victorian Britain*, Cambridge, 1993.

35 · ANTIQUARIANISM (POPULAR)

MARILYN BUTLER

Popular antiquarianism is the study of British national culture: of English, Welsh, Gaelic, and Irish as vernacular languages, and of their oral as well as their written traditions—not merely literary forms and art, but beliefs, customs, and festivities. It existed as a scholarly practice in England and Wales for at least two centuries before the eighteenth century, the use of the word 'popular' firmly distinguishing its content from that of classical, religious, and *orientalist learning. Notable early modern works in the field include Camden's *Britannia* (1586 in Latin, translated by E. Gibson, 1695) and *Remaines of a Greater Worke, Concerning Britain* (1607), John Stow's *Survey of London* (1598), and above all the rich *œuvre* of John Aubrey (1626–97).

Antiquarianism generally is a form of knowledge prompted and sustained by the early-seventeenth-century Baconian intellectual revolution. Francis Bacon (1561–1626) not only established but also popularized the notion that knowledge was to be actively sought for, in nature and in society, present and past. By the end of the seventeenth century the empirical scientists gathered in the Royal Society were matched by more informal networks of 'social Baconians'—political economists, educated travellers to other lands, and their similarly ethnographical reporters on regions of the British Isles, all of whom were pioneering social scientists and social historians. In this sense antiquarians have good claims to be the initiators of modern anthropology and sociology, but the purpose of this essay is to establish their contribution to cultural history and the professional modern study of both *language [40] and literature. The first part outlines the work of four exemplary figures, all active in diverse aspects of *popular culture [23] by the last quarter of the eighteenth century—John *Brand, Francis *Grose, Joseph *Ritson, and Francis *Douce, and one in the early nineteenth century, William *Hone. The second part explores the role of popular antiquarianism in the literary movement known as British *Romanticism.

In 1725 a Newcastle clergyman, Henry Bourne (1694–1733), published a diffident, probing volume of popular 'ceremonies and opinions', *Antiquitates Vulgares, or the Antiquities of the Common People*. Bourne was a tailor's son and a glazier's apprentice before a patron sent him to Cambridge. Just over fifty years later, in 1777 another Newcastle clergyman, John Brand, nephew and former apprentice of a cordwainer, subsequently a student at Oxford, appropriated Bourne's famous piece of local sociology and turned it into a dialogue. Each of Bourne's original chapters was followed by Brand's Addenda, or critical commentary, and the whole renamed, in English, *Observations on Popular Antiquities*. In this composite volume, the first seven of the thirty-one chapters, just under a third of the volume, are concerned with the ceremonies, practices, ornaments, beliefs, and terrors accompanying death and burial; the sixth and seventh chapters address churchyards and their customary inhabitants, dead bodies, mourners, and apparitions.

In the 1720s Bourne had expressed anxiety regarding the reception of his remarkable book. He was a strong Protestant, the avowed critic of the superstition and popery he detected in the beliefs and practices of the common people. As his lengthy subtitle states, one of his purposes is to analyse these 'Opinions and Ceremonies . . . [to shew] which may be retained, and which ought to be laid aside'. Yet in a sense he preserved the dubious practices by publishing them; he moreover dignified his region by giving Northumbrians an antiquity back to the Anglo-Saxons, Britons, and Romans. In turn Brand, who liked to ridicule Bourne for piety and fustiness ('wholesome meat . . . brought on upon wooden platters') elevated his predecessor into the co-author of a remarkably influential book.

In 1777, and even more in the expanded posthumous edition brought out by Henry Ellis (1777–1869) in 1813, Brand was able to draw on a variety of vocabularies to justify the serious study of popular mentalities as an end in itself. From 1784, based in London and Secretary of the Society of Antiquaries, Brand must have sounded at times a *Tory populist, at other times a provincial patriot, and at still others—as in the new Preface to *Popular Antiquities* published by Ellis—something of a Jacobin. In conveying a resentment of metropolitan ascendancy, he epitomizes British fringe subcultures from mid-century to the 1780s. Since the 1740s the public had been able to read works by Thomson, Macpherson, Gray, Smart, *Percy, *Walpole, and *Chatterton, all redactors or creative translators of folk or *faux naïf* materials of earlier times. In his more scholarly mode Brand, too, constructs national identity in opposition to French (or metropolitan) classicism and sophistication—though his concept of an insular specialness is not the chauvinistic, Protestant, or narrowly English identity that modern historians Gerald Newman and Linda Colley have concentrated on in recent studies of the rise of British nationalism in the eighteenth century. Instead, Brand adopts the universalist perspective of the *Enlightenment [32], and traces existing popular practices back to medieval Catholicism, or discerns in Catholic 'superstitions' hints of the paganism of 'ancient and heathen Rome'. The Irish historian Sylvester O'Halloran (1728–1807) in 1772 made nationalist claims that the Gaels might have come from Troy or 'the hidden sources of the Nile' [see

*Irish cultural revival]; drawing on such notions, Brand writes of British cultural streams that rose in Asia or Africa and 'have been running and increasing from the beginning of time'. Within the next generation readers were adjusting to even longer historical perspectives, the 'deep time' of the geologist James *Hutton or of the evolutionary natural scientist Charles Darwin. Brand's continuous yet miscegenated and complex notion of culture showed that it was possible to explore national identity without being driven by a nationalist imperative and without identifying the nation with the present nation-state. It was in his emphasis on oral, popular experience, and minority or conquered experience, that he was most at odds with contemporary *Anglican and Tory apologists such as Samuel *Johnson, Thomas *Warton, and *Edmund Burke, who all emphatically linked long tradition and hence cultural legitimacy with the nation-state and its sanctioned cultural expression in Scripture, law, history, and a canon of published great works by known authors.

The second exemplary figure, Francis Grose, ex-army captain, draughtsman, historian, lexicographer, satirist, jester, and collector of ephemera, had already begun his remarkable career as a commentator on culture before the appearance of Brand's *Popular Antiquities*. Grose's most massive if not his most original achievement is the *Antiquities of England and Wales*, (6 vols, 1773–87), a county-by-county record of surviving medieval buildings and ruins of note, partly illustrated by Grose himself. This was followed by the *Antiquities of Scotland* (1789–91), of which the second volume was posthumous. The first of these large folio volumes, 1773, opens with an eighty-three-page 'Preface' on the history and political role of medieval monasticism, down to the dissolution of the monasteries in 1536. This is also Enlightenment historicism [see *history, 38] in the manner of Voltaire and the *philosophes*. Grose detaches himself ironically from the errors of the past, conveying no nostalgia in his brisk account of four centuries of political engagement between the monastic system and the feudal monarchy. With the help of long footnotes he tells a story largely discreditable to the monasteries with their recurring scandals of gluttony, luxury, and sexual licence.

But Grose, who describes himself in his collected essays, *The Grumbler* (1791), as 'an Opposition-man and Grumble-man', was no better disposed to the monarchs and their wealthier subjects. His critique of feudalism and monasticism, and his use of this as a context to his account of the arts and learning, covered much the same ground as Thomas Warton's more sympathetic portrayal, in the latter's *History of English Literature, 1100–1603* (3 vols, 1774–81), of an ultimately ordered Christendom. But, because Grose's survey of *medievalism slightly pre-dated Warton's, he was never drawn into the truculent disputes over the interpretation of English literary culture in its relations with the state in the formative early period. Instead Grose came into his own as a distinctive voice in the mid-1780s, with a group of clever, original books on the spoken language (slang and dialect) and other forms of modern communication. His short, confident study *Caricaturas* (1788) represents the caricaturist as a dangerous figure, to be feared rather than esteemed; but 'satirical painting . . . may be most efficaciously employed in the cause of virtue and decorum, by holding up to public notice many offenders against both'. Just as he was drawn to the popular, almost universally readable art of caricature, which in the next decade was to rise to new heights with the work of *Gillray and *Rowlandson [see *prints, 22], Grose liked another uncensored form of publication, the personal newspaper *advertisement. In *A Guide to Health, Beauty, Riches and Honour* (1785) he assembles an entertaining collection of these notices from London *newspapers and journals, to disclose to 'those living remote from the capital . . . the vast improvement made within this century, not only in the more abstruse sciences, but in the arts and conveniences of life'. Grose's selection includes Mr Martin Vanbutchell, *dentist, of Upper Mount Street, Grosvenor Square, who exhibits his embalmed wife to anyone armed with an introduction, any day between 9 a.m. and 1 p.m. except Sunday [see *quackery]. In the *Guide* Grose anticipates *Southey and *Dickens in his curiosity about human wants and his eye for the grotesque.

Also in 1785, the year after the death of Johnson, whose great *Dictionary* (1755) enshrined the resources of the written language and of educated speech, Grose issued his account of informal English, the *Classical Dictionary of the Vulgar Tongue*. The first edition contained 3,000 words, the third (1796) 4,000. Like its French model, Le Roux's *Satirical and Burlesque Dictionary* (1718), the book contains offensive words and insults directed at unpopular groups, such as the higher clergy, apothecaries, soldiers, and tailors. Longer entries include woman (*toad-eater, rib*, or *crooked rib*), loose woman (*abbess, lightheeled, squirrel, stammel*), the sexual act (*plaister of warm guts, riding St George*), and the penis (*arbor vitae, lobcock, plugtail*). Grose implicitly connects his interest in the language of 'seamen at the cap-stern, ladies disposing of their fish, criminals en route for Tyburn' with the vast illicit production in French at this time of offensive print materials, including *pornography and personal scandal, though he contrasts in political terms the vulgar argot of Britain with that of France: 'the freedom of thought and speech privileged by our constitution gives a force and poignancy to the expressions of our common people not to be found under arbitrary governments'. In the next generation the journalist Pierce *Egan was one of many to reissue the *Classical Dictionary* (1823). Egan's own informal survey of metropolitan entertainments and slang, *Life in London* (1821–3), was surely in part based on Grose's midnight rambles with his servant Batch, and his socializing in the *taverns of more notorious districts from St Giles to Wapping.

Finally, Grose's *Provincial Dictionary* (1787) provides a shorter listing of dialect words from different parts of England, with the regions or counties specified, and some etymologies provided; a section given over to proverbs, again localized by county, but including London; and another section on popular superstitions. Grose evidently did linguistic fieldwork as well as history and archaeology as he travelled, and was still doing this when, on his trip to Scotland in 1790, he made a detour to visit Robert *Burns as not only a dialect poet but also a collector of folk-song. Burns gave him the superstitions attached to a nearby abandoned church, Kirk Alloway, first in prose and afterwards in verse as his comic *Gothic masterpiece, 'Tam o' Shanter', which accordingly first appeared in the *Appendices of the Antiquities of Scotland* (vol. ii, 1791).

Grose's striking arrival as a lexicographer of the spoken language and of popular belief and story, along with his exploration of journalistic forms, could be seen as a challenge to the values of Samuel Johnson, great lexicographer of the written language. Grose's work comes out of the remarkable dispute which began with a quarrel over the status of the supposed work of a fifteenth-century monk, Rowley, offered for sale by Thomas Chatterton, and ended with a schism between the leading literary scholars. The main anti-Rowleians, the party bent on proving Chatterton a forger, were the circle of Thomas Gray, who still mustered the most respected literary scholars and cognoscenti of the day. In addition to Thomas Warton they included the historian of painting and historical novelist Horace *Walpole, to whom Chatterton had attempted to sell a manuscript, the song-collector Thomas Percy, and the future editor of *Shakespeare, Edmund *Malone.

While some of Chatterton's 'friends', for example some Bristol antiquarians, did claim that the manuscripts Chatterton produced were genuine, others did not see the issue as one of authenticity or forgery at all. Much contemporary writing about the past took the form of 'modern romance', or pastiche; Horace Walpole had himself written, in *The Castle of Otranto* (1764), a novel purporting to be an old manuscript recently discovered. Pretence had come to seem allowable; success in it might require real learning, as in the cases of both Macpherson [see *Ossianism] and Chatterton. Fairly or not, Walpole and his friends provoked opposition by laying down the law at a time when provincial commercial-class opinion resented the privileges enjoyed by their competitors in the metropolis, in for example the print trades, and when local antiquarians resented the way wealthy collectors circulated their rare books and manuscripts among themselves. So the Chatterton row had already polarized Bristol, the booming second city, against London and against the literati. With the intervention of Joseph Ritson, a London conveyancer formerly from Newcastle, the quarrel entered a phase in which the issues of *class [15] hostility and intellectual property rights became for the first time fully explicit.

Ritson's emergence in Newcastle in the later 1770s coincided with the *American Revolution, the first speeches and pamphlets of the *agrarian communist Thomas *Spence, and Brand's *Popular Antiquities*. The provocation that brought Ritson onto the national stage was probably the contribution to the *Gentleman's Magazine* of a young scholar from Ireland, Edmund Malone, gifted enough to have won instant acceptance from the Walpole circle. In two articles, Malone laid down the qualifications needed to pronounce on the Rowley dispute:

I beg leave to lay it down as a fixed principle, that the authenticity or spuriousness of the poems attributed to Rowley cannot be decided by any person who has not a taste for English poetry, and . . . knowledge of . . . most of our poets from the time of Chaucer to that of Pope. Such a one alone is, in my opinion, a competent judge of this matter.

And Malone proceeded to assert that the Rowleians were not 'furnished with any portion of this critical taste'.

Ritson riposted with an ambitious fifty-page pamphlet, *Observations on the first three volumes of [Warton's] 'History of English Poetry'* (1782), in which he berated Warton for many negligent mistakes, accused him of 'fulsome and disgusting Egotism', and resorted at key points to the ungentlemanly words of lying and cheating. One 'lie' was Warton's omission of Saxon (pre-1100) language and poetry, on the grounds that it was 'unconnected' with the later English tradition; a second, his discussion of Christopher Marlowe as a poet, without a hint of Marlowe's religious unorthodoxy.

In an only slightly less ferocious pamphlet of 1783, Ritson lambasted the recent edition of Shakespeare (10 vols, 1778) by Johnson and George Steevens (1736–1800), again for scholarly negligence. A yet more important piece, the learned 'Historical Introduction' to his *Select Collection of English Song* (1783), was probably most notable at the time for its ridicule of Thomas Percy's 'Introduction' to his *Reliques of English Poetry* (1765). Percy had idealized the medieval minstrels, treated them as the initiators of English poetry, and placed them at court; Ritson replied that courtiers of the day spoke French and that the anglophone minstrels would have been considered rogues and vagabonds. Again, it was a cheat, or a form of theft, to suppose that culture belonged to the upper orders and merely trickled down to the people, if it reached them at all. While Ritson in at least one passage doubts the credentials of Macpherson's Ossian, he tends to brush off, as a diversion, the charges of forgery levelled against Macpherson and Chatterton: they had merely performed 'experiments on the public taste'. If anyone was a thief, said Ritson (in a private letter, leaked by his opponents), it was this 'lying cleric', Percy, who edited and altered oral culture for consumption by the polite classes.

The press weighed in on either side, and the debate in the letter columns of journals is of great interest for its class consciousness and class hostility, as well as its implications for the notion of culture. Francis *Douce privately bound up Ritson's *Observations* not with Warton's *History* but with the ferocious debate it spawned; he identifies the different combatants in the Bodleian copy, including Ritson himself, who intervened on his own side under two pseudonyms. Two decades on, Douce added as a frontispiece Gillray's brilliant caricature of Ritson in 1803. The occasion for this was the publication of Ritson's *Essay on a Vegetable Diet*, but the works referred to in the picture, by title or quotation, are Ritson's diatribes against the gentlemen-scholars in 1782–3 [see *vegetarianism]. Another twenty years on, the philologist and antiquarian Richard Price (1790–1833) reissued Warton's *History of English Literature* in a remarkable four-volume edition (1824), annotated, corrected, and criticized by four different

50. James Gillray's print of
Joseph Ritson (1803) caricatures
the scholar as an eccentric,
misanthropic vegetarian. With his
pen dipped in 'Gall', Ritson is
surrounded by various verbal
and iconic indications of his
supposedly inveterate bitterness.

scholars, including Ritson and Douce. Forty years after it had begun, Ritson's debate with
Warton was still considered worthy of extended treatment. Only after the virulence of this
quarrel had been confronted and its main issue (the nature of world medieval culture) neutrally
resolved, could the 'history of English literature' assume a professional academic form, and
begin to meet the needs of the modern university.

Last of the major anti-establishment scholars was Francis Douce himself. The great collection of illustrated books, manuscripts, and ephemera he left to the Bodleian Library, Oxford,
helps define his notion of culture as an endlessly fascinating treasure-cabinet of discrete,
expressive, but anonymous objects out of the dark ages of East and West. But Douce is also,
like Grose, a polished writer and at times an analyst. His more influential writings engage the
issues Warton launched, the nature of medieval culture and its interpretation in modern times.

While never offensively personal in his attacks on fellow scholars, Douce in the first half of
his career plainly sought to revise Warton's accepting notion of the medieval heritage. His first
major publication was his edition of the *Dance of Death* (1794), based on an edition of
sixteenth-century illustrations wrongly attributed to Holbein and engraved in the seventeenth
century by Hollar. In this version of the popular late medieval theme, thirty characters, most of
them wealthy, many titled, are snatched away by Death; the message is levelling, to humble the
proud. In 1794 Douce's prefatory essay, modified in the much-altered book with the same title
of 1833, has a political bite:

In the dark ages of monkish bigotry and superstition, the deluded people . . . had placed one of their
principal gratifications in contemplating . . . ideas the most horrid and disgusting . . . They had
altogether lost sight of the consolatory doctrines of the Gospel, which regard death in no terrific point
of view whatever . . . we may yet trace the imbecility of former ages in the decorations of many of our
monuments.

This politically suggestive, indeed tendentious passage helped fuel the 'German-mania' or peculiarly dark, negative medievalism of the mid-1790s. Using old *ballad and prose narrative forms in an archaic self-conscious manner, most English and Scots Gothicists of the late 1790s conveyed an anti-clerical undercurrent that was fully modern in its application: for 'Gothic' read 'old-regime'.

In the journal of the Society of Antiquaries, *Archaeologia*, Douce went on to publish a series of papers (gathered as a volume in 1825) which before 1810 typically carried political critique. The first, read to the Society on 27 November 1800, included a proclamation by Queen Elizabeth on the scarcity of grain, which orders the committal of anyone found 'engrossing' or buying up grain in order to drive up the price. The topic relates to a similar ruling against 'forestalling' in 1800 by the Lord Chief Justice, Lord Kenyon (1732–1802). But the most developed and scholarly of the pieces in *Archaeologia* is 'Some Remarks on the ancient Ceremony of the Feast of Fools', read on 10 May 1804. Douce acknowledges that the 'Ceremony' in question has recently been described by Joseph *Strutt, in his *Glig-Gamena Angel-Deod, Sports and Pastimes of the People of England* (1801), but he suggests that Strutt was not aware of its 'precise significance' as a symptom of a degenerate religion rather than 'part of the general mass of ancient mummeries'.

After medievalism, Douce's second target was the exclusive Shakespeare—both the canonical writer, only begetter of great plays, and the newly purified texts emerging from the coterie of scholar-collectors who liked to keep their manuscripts and their rare, expensive Folios and Quartos among themselves. In his best book, *Illustrations of Shakespeare's Characters* (2 vols, 1807), Douce concentrates on the comedies and low-life scenes in the English history plays, meticulously investigating their sources from his unrivalled knowledge of medieval *romance and narrative. Where Percy and his generation had sentimentalized and gentrified the figure of the minstrel, Douce promotes the figure of the fool as the literal embodiment and symbolic representation of the unruly populace. For Douce, the paradoxical proof of the greatness of the plays is that they allowed the parts of the clowns to be ad-libbed by leading jesters of the day, some of whom (like Ned Tarleton) can be named, while others are anonymous. Douce's *Illustrations* is in effect a commentary to accompany the already discursive *Variorum Shakespeare* (1794) of his friend George Steevens—a variety of edition greatly extended by its use of 300 scholarly annotations provided by Joseph Ritson. But it is also a sardonic echo of Warton's *History*, for example, in also including three appendices, one of them a dissertation on the 'Gesta Romanorum', an often scurrilous fifteenth-century collection of about 200 anecdotes or fabliaux thought to have been used as materials for sermons. Warton too dealt with the 'Gesta' in an appendix, though more decorously.

A democratic 'Citizen Shakespeare' indeed made real headway in the 1790s, the decade of the *Boydell Shakespeare Gallery, a generous commercial *viewing [20] venture to give the public a worthy illustrated version of the national poet. With Steevens once more in charge of the text, the overall impact of the unfinished but widely dispersed project, abandoned in 1802, was already Doucean, just as Douce's disaggregated Shakespeare somewhat resembled Boydell's final product. The popular antiquarians read fifteenth- and sixteenth-century literature, oral and written, as a historical resource; Shakespeare's plays likewise. In so doing, they were constructing a cultural history and a history of mentalities. By diagnosing late medieval culture as anarchic, disorderly, semi-pagan, and Rabelaisian, they were reading similar characteristics even into individual works. This should have massive implications for our understanding of Romantic form.

An appendix to the work of the late-eighteenth-century antiquarians came from the publisher and satirist William Hone, who was tried for blasphemy at London's Mansion House on three successive days in December 1817 for publishing three political satires, of which the best-known was 'The Political Litany'. Each of the offending texts parodied the prayer-book or the Old Testament, and in doing so threatened the constitution, according to the Attorney-General, who led for the prosecution: his argument, based on the seventeenth-century jurist Edward Coke, was that these sacred texts were 'parcel' of the *law [8] of England. Hone defended himself from the dock, on the second and third days before Lord Chief Justice *Ellenborough.

In outline Hone's case was drawn from the carnivalesque portrayal of culture found in Douce's work on the *Dance of Death*, the Feast of Fools, and the comic Shakespeare. But Hone was able on his own account to deliver a non-stop recital of amusing and embarrassing examples of parody by the populace from the middle ages, and more recently from all sections of the population, including the present government. Moreover the role of the accused as clown or fool, seizing the opportunity to make justice a mockery, went back to the memorable trial of the Leveller John Lilburne in 1649, an example already used to good effect in the earlier 1800s by the radical writer-publishers Thomas Spence and Daniel Isaac *Eaton.

Hone had an unusually theoretical case to make; he argued that Scripture had been common cultural property from the middle ages, when the miracle plays and profane festivals had freely rewritten and inverted sacred texts and ceremonies. Acquitted on successive days amid scenes of jubilation, Hone published *The Three Trials of William Hone* (1818), further satires such as *The Political House that Jack Built* (1819, illustrated by George *Cruikshank), and a number of antiquarian works: *The Apocryphal New Testament* (1820), *Ancient Mysteries Described* (1823, on the peepshows, processions, and dramas of medieval London), *The Everyday Book* (1826–7, dedicated to *Lamb, with contributions by *Clare), and *The Table Book* (1827–8, a second massive compilation). Appropriately enough, it was this down-market publisher who gave the urban crowd the concept of a popular cultural history.

When first-generation Romantic poets are picked off for individual study, they are removed from their exceptional environment—a new literary culture which was both old and self-consciously fashioned by figures such as Hone, Douce, Ritson, and Brand. Popular antiquarianism was part of a broader historical revival occurring in the third quarter of the eighteenth century within France's largest neighbours, in the German princely states as well as in Britain. Pre-modern nativist cultural forms threatened the modern cultural dominance of France and of francophile governing élites. The ground was laid for a major shift not just in literary fashion but in social attitudes and group identities.

Three basic narrative forms emerged in this revival and remained dominant through the Romantic period. First to become fashionable was the (medieval) popular ballad, a short narrative poem enacting universal, extreme experiences—passion, heroism, terror, and death. Second came the long verse romance, fashionable from 1800 and often made up of ballad-like elements. Coinciding with both, the 'prose romance' or historical novel began to deploy supernatural incidents and characters, or to introduce ballads, scholarly materials, and elaborate framing narratives, all hinting at a process of transmission over time or across cultures. The actual ascendancy of the historical manner in the half-century 1780–1830 sits oddly with some later critical suppositions—that the personal *lyric is the dominant Romantic form, or that the period belongs to the writer of *genius, supremely individualistic and self-generating.

The 1780s and 1790s saw the familiar personal lyric poem overwhelmed in the rush to publish the national archive of ballad and song. It is the age of Ritson, of Charlotte *Brooke's edited and translated *Reliques of Irish Poetry* (1789), and in the 1790s of two multi-volume collections of Scottish song, to which Burns contributed. The largest body of archaic writings of the British Isles, the Welsh, was issued, thanks to backing from the London Welsh community, by William Owen *Pughe and Edward *Williams (Iolo Morganwg) in 1789, 1792, 1794, and 1801–7 [see *Welsh cultural revival]. The English contribution here was to discover the historical roots of the Angles and Saxons in old German or Norse materials. 'German-mania' hit London, Edinburgh, Norwich, and Bristol circles around 1795, and reached the public as the period's first runaway commercial success, in verse, prose, and dramatic forms sensationally preoccupied with sex and violence. A core of German folk materials was revamped with huge brio by young, unknown authors; William *Taylor, Matthew 'Monk' *Lewis, *Scott, *Coleridge, and *Southey. The publisher William Lane was ready from 1790 with the *Minerva Press, a skilfully marketed series of translated and new novels aimed specially at women readers.

The longer Middle English romances, though much discussed since the 1760s, were more formidable fare for modern readers than ballads or prose fiction, and achieved publication only after 1800. Then Joseph Ritson published twelve important Middle English romances in 1802; Scott, following his Border ballads (1802), published 'Sir Tristram' in 1804, George Ellis (1783–1815) a further twenty romances in 1805, Henry Weber (1783–1818) ten more complete ones in 1810. In his chapter on 'Romance' in *Poetic Form and British Romanticism* (1986), the modern critic Stuart Curran describes these eight years as 'without peer in the history of British literary scholarship . . . the publication [of the romances] wholly altered the conception of British literature.' They came explained and contextualized by discursive introductions, and met with sympathetic, knowledgeable reviews. They coincided, moreover, with other important historical editions of Chaucer and Dryden, both brilliant narrative poets, and with a further shelf-ful of translations from, for example, Italian (William Rose, 1775–1843) and Portuguese (Robert Southey).

In order to present themselves as naïves or primitives, most writers became *de facto* intellectuals who had researched their manner and matter. Burns, for example, was not only bilingual in two dialects, standard English and Scottish English or Lallans, but also knew the verse forms appropriate to both: hence the assurance of his great volume, *Poems in the Scottish Dialect* (1786). The following year he signed up as a contributor to the first of the two large compilations of traditional Scottish song on which he spent much of his literary energy until his death in 1796. William *Blake, emerging as a poet with the childlike *Songs of Innocence*, was steeped in folklore, *hymns, *Spenser, Shakespeare, Ossian, Darwin's *Botanic Garden*, the Old Testament, and Norse mythology. A cultural omnivore, he achieved at last a poetic history of Britain with his last and longest prophetic book, *Jerusalem* (1820). Blake's work on this and on *Milton* began in 1804, and so coincided with the most massive of the anthologies of the Welsh scholars, the *Myvyrian Archaiology of Wales before 1200* (1801–7). Albion, hero of Blake's poem *Jerusalem*, was the ancient name for Britain. Blake's illustrations dwell on the character's tortured body, but also on the fibrous, tunnelled soil. Place-names map the island, stressing its disconnections—Mam Tor and Penmaenmawr, in the Celtic west, as well as the poorer suburbs of London. Like Arthur, Albion is asleep, but he awakens to fulfil the *prophecy of redemption. Meanwhile the woman named Jerusalem, the second protagonist, wanders mournfully in exile—an allusion to the series of women in the Old Testament who, Robert Lowth (1710–87) explains in his *Sacred Poetry of the Hebrews* (1753), symbolize a defeated people. Two national histories, those of the British and those of the *Jews, are thus interwoven and made exemplary.

The more prosaic Southey also represents the generation. As a lonely schoolboy he discovered Spenser and Warton. By 1789 he had formed his project to write a long poem on the world's major religions, or in effect on different medievalisms; he began to learn Welsh. In 1792 he found Frank Sayers's (1763–1817) *Dramatic Sketches of Norse Mythology* (1790), a series of imitations of the 'voices' of the different Dark Age inhabitants of Britain, written in an archaic verse form borrowed from the Greek chorus. As a radical Oxford student, Southey from 1793 began his own experiments with traditional forms—eclogues, ballads, laments, songs, inscriptions. He liked the dramatic mode; characters rather than the first person, poor rather than rich and famous, people who take charge of their lives. In 1794 he based a play on a rebel, Wat Tyler, in 1795–6 a long poem on Joan of Arc. In its turn, the anonymous *Lyrical Ballads* of Coleridge and *Wordsworth (1798) should be seen as an imitation—partly of the voices and mentalities of poor people, past and present, partly of Southey's almost Chattertonian reinvention of past communities. In a minority of the *Ballads* of 1798, true, and in most of the second volume added by Wordsworth in 1800, greater use is made of the reflective Wordsworthian narrator, who gives a proprietorial signature to this poet's later work.

Yet the main impact on literary production of the post-Warton debate reveals itself after 1800. Led by Southey's syncretic impression of the middle ages of Mohammedanism, *Thalaba the Destroyer* (1801), Welsh, Spanish, Teutonic, oriental, and Mexican romances, pastiche, burlesque, or allegedly genuine, vied with one another for the market, and recruited readers to narrative poems, preferably located in exotic places and times. Scott's *Lay of the Last Minstrel* (1805), *Marmion* (1808), and *Lady of the Lake* (1810) capitalized on tastes he was as a scholar helping to create, and told a version of Scottish history. Resuming Southey's topic, the compulsively saleable Middle East, *Byron broke records for poetry with the Spenserean *Childe Harold's Pilgrimage* (1812), and did yet better with *The Giaour* (1813), first in his series of 'Turkish Tales'. *The Giaour* has greater ethnic particularity than its successors: its plot centres on a Muslim practice (the execution of a faithless wife by drowning), and the story was allegedly heard as a ballad sung by a fisherman in a Turkish tavern. *The Hebrew Melodies* (1815) are lyrics on Old Testament stories that Byron wrote to accompany authentic synagogue music; in late 1816, on arrival in exile in Venice, he began to study the Armenian language and its early church history. By this time Byron's friend Thomas *Moore, who had achieved fame with his *Irish Melodies* (1807), was creating Eastern analogues for Ireland's colonial experience in the well-received story within a story, *Lalla Rookh* (1817).

The period's **novels [31]** too, combine to show how society is constructed through time by its culture; it is a localized society, small communities documented, analysed, and interpreted as though clearly seen for the first time. 'Social Baconianism' finds itself in the regional novel's minute accounts of clothing or the hospitality offered to strangers and (particularly exact in the Irish tales of Maria *Edgeworth, from 1800, and the Scottish fiction of James *Hogg and John *Galt) the nuances of regional dialect.

Thanks largely to Hone's trials and their aftermath, the landmark texts and multiple strands of cultural populism flourished. The lived-in past—carnivalesque, heteroglossic, violent, vastly and numinously archaic—became newly fashionable from 1818, to bear strange fruit in John *Martin's Old Testament paintings or Thomas Lovell *Beddoes's *Bride's Tragedy* (1822) 83 and *Death's Jest Book* (begun 1825). Scott portrayed a schismatic, ungovernable middle ages in three novels of 1820, *Ivanhoe*, *The Monastery*, and *The Abbot*; Mary *Shelley, a brilliantly complex and sophisticated sketch of a fourteenth-century city-state in *Valperga* (1823).

In their target (religious and political orthodoxy) and their technique of textual appropriation, Byron's later 'biblical' dramas, *Sardanapalus* (1821), *Cain: A Mystery* (1822), and its sequel, *Heaven and Earth* (1823), also draw on the issues brought up at Hone's trials. Indeed they are reminders of the trials, as proto-Shavian intellectual comedies which replay and substantially invert biblical episodes in order to convey a secular and satirical message. Douce also contributed to Byron's comic presentation of the Devil and Cain as heroes, and to the remarkable concept of the Assyrian King Sardanapalus as a jester and holy fool.

When in 1824 Richard Price came to review Warton's great *History of English Literature* in the light of what forty years' criticism had made of it, he concluded that Warton's main error was to confine himself to the history of one nation. International scholarship since had established that national boundaries are not fenced but permeable. Religious beliefs and myths, arts, sciences, and stories recur in different parts of the world, probably not by importation but in response to the same stimuli, a fact which leads Price to turn away from 'sources' and linear history in favour of general psychological explanations for culture. Price was not signalling a victory for Warton's critics, who were source-hunters too. Indeed, Warton's capaciousness, unprecedented in its day, prepared the way; no one scholar coming after him achieved so much. The judgement of posterity on the debate, as delivered by the jury of post-Wartonians, was rather that culture is infinitely complex and contradictory, even while its patterns recur. In this case the local, particular data provided by the many would always be needed. There were no winners, except the group.

Bodleian Library, *The Douce Legacy*, Oxford, 1984; Bronson, B. H., *Joseph Ritson, Scholar at Arms*, Chicago, 1938; Burke, P., *Popular Culture in Early Modern Europe*, London, 1978; Butler, M., 'Repossessing the Past', in M. Levinson et al., eds., *Rethinking Historicism*, Oxford, 1989; 'Sardanapalus: John Bull's Other Empire', *Studies in Romanticism*, 31 (1992), 281–94; Dorson, R. M., *The British Folklorists: A History*, Chicago, 1968; Hobsbawm, E., & T. Ranger, eds., *The Invention of Tradition*, Cambridge, 1983; Porter, R., & Teich, M., eds., *Enlightenment in National Context*, Cambridge, 1981; *Romanticism in National Context*, Cambridge, 1988.

36 · MYTHOLOGY NIGEL LEASK

Ideas about mythology and comparative *religion [10] were debated in this period with a ferocity and urgency that belies the association of the subject with Mr Casaubon in George Eliot's *Middlemarch*. What to a late Victorian mind had seemed to represent a hopelessly blinkered and outdated academicism was in the late eighteenth century a field which put in doubt the basic legitimacy of the Christian state and cut to the heart of anxieties about European power and identity. The new awareness of other cultures which the colonial enterprise brought with it was potentially challenging to Britain and Europe's sense of cultural pre-eminence [see *empire, 5]. A plethora of new information—presented in such diverse forms as writings on *natural philosophy [34], *travel literature, *missionary tracts, and military memoirs—had to be incorporated within the available systems of classification, the methodological tools of which were little more sophisticated than those inherited from the old universal histories of the seventeenth century.

*Orientalism produced a body of knowledge on comparative religion which worked to affirm the primacy of European religious and cultural traditions and so confirmed the legitimacy of colonialism, but this effort was not without its perils. Knowledge of other religions was always potentially a challenge to the classical and *biblical traditions, and even those scholars who ultimately sought to reinforce European superiority often found themselves accused of providing materials for the sceptics and freethinkers who used mythography in order to criticize the Christian hegemony. For the British public, India proved an especially important source of information, opportunity, and danger. Anquetel Duperron's translation of the Zoroastrian *Zend-Avesta* in 1759 and the *Upanishads* in 1786, together with the pioneering Sanskrit translations of Charles Wilkins (1749–1836), Sir William *Jones, and Nathaniel Halhed (1751–1830) from the 1770s, added Persian and Hindu deities to the more familiar Latin and Greek pantheons, and the Middle Eastern gods of the Old Testament. A renewal of interest in accounts of indigenous Americans, as well as the *exploration [37] of the Pacific by *Cook and others further extended the global pantheon of myths and deities. This mythographic revolution had a parallel in studies in European *antiquarianism [35]. Bishop *Percy's translation of Mallet's *Northern Antiquities* (1770) gave great currency to the Norse myths, the second volume presenting a translation of the ancient Icelandic saga *Edda*, and

James Macpherson's (1736–96) *Ossian collections kindled interest in the old Celtic myths of Scotland and Ireland.

Amid the welter of contributions to the literature of myth, two basic responses can be discerned which will serve to organize this essay: a sceptical, allegorical tradition which reduced all myth—including Christianity—to natural, erotic, and astronomical meanings, and a conservative response which saw all mythology as emanating from the primal catastrophe of the Flood. Both tendencies developed a comparative method which abolished the differences between heterogeneous cultures in order to create a single system so as to explain the nature of religion and myth. Another aspect of this homogenizing project was the *diffusionist* representation of diverse mythologies, the theory of the dispersal of all cultures from a common source. Diffusionism, with its monogenetic account of origins, was a feature of most Christian apologetics which sought to defend the authority of the Bible against mythographic attacks, but some scholars, most notably in the French *Enlightenment [32] tradition, denied the chronological and spiritual priority of the Pentateuch and asserted that the biblical narrative had derived from Hindu or Egyptian sources. Diffusionism was contested by the innovative and sceptical theories of writers such as Richard Payne *Knight, who preferred a polygenetic, and often a polytheistic, account of cultural origins. Both diffusionism and anti-diffusionism reveal a common taxonomic agenda of reducing the heterogeneity of cultures to a common standard, whether based upon revelation or reason.

New knowledge of non-Christian religious traditions served to deepen the sceptical currents established by Renaissance scholars, revitalizing the Greek and Roman pantheons and introducing a plethora of new, now mainly oriental deities into the European image-repertoire. The pagan myths of European antiquity assumed a new immediacy and universality as they were identified with the cults of the contemporary 'primitive' or oriental world, a factor contributing to the *Hellenism of poets such as John *Keats, Percy *Shelley, Thomas Love *Peacock, and Barry *Cornwall. The renewed interest in Hellenistic culture after the middle of the eighteenth century was closely linked to the 'oriental renaissance' instigated by Sir William Jones and his fellow scholars of the Asiatic Society of Bengal. The pioneering exercise in this kind of syncretism was Jones's essay 'On the Gods of Greece, Italy and India' (1784). Shelley's admiration for classical Greece in *Hellas* was closely linked to the search for the Asiatic roots of Greek myth, which he explored in *Prometheus Unbound* (1820). His poeticization of primitive and oriental 'Bacchic' elements in Hellenistic myth contested the norms of the polite classicism which was so fundamental to British élite culture, but it also levelled the charge of primitivism at Christianity. Shelley drew here on a sceptical tradition which exposed the irrationalism and psychopathology of the religious impulse throughout history.

Two different branches can be discerned in the sceptical tradition. One was dominated by the figures of Pierre François Hugues D'Hancarville (1719–1805), Sir William *Hamilton, Richard Payne Knight, Erasmus *Darwin, and Sir William *Drummond. These men were gentlemanly virtuosi, usually *Whigs in politics, although their libertine interpretation of religion appealed to plebeian infidels, such as Shelley's early publisher George Cannon (1789–1854), as well as to poets such as W. S. *Landor, Peacock, and Shelley. The other branch could be described as a Jacobin school as it had its roots in French infidelism and the Enlightenment tradition of Pierre Bayle (1647–1706) and Voltaire (1694–1778). Its characteristic voices were those of Charles Dupuis (1742–1809) and Constantin *Volney. Volney's *Les Ruines* (1791, published in English 1792) and, to a lesser extent, Dupuis's *L'Origine de tous les cultes* (1795) were popular in plebeian radical circles in Britain. They complemented the infidelism of Thomas *Paine's *Age of Reason* (1794–5), and exerted a considerable influence on works like Drummond's *Oedipus Judaicus* (1811) and Shelley's *Queen Mab* (1813) and *Revolt of Islam* (1817). Not unlike Darwin, Volney argued in *Les Ruines* that the 'Gods, who act such singular parts in every system, are no other than the physical powers of nature, the elements, the winds, the meteors, the stars, all of which have been personified by the necessary mechanism of language, and the manner in which objects are conceived by the understanding'. What differentiates Darwin from Volney is the latter's explicit attempt to expose Christianity as an astronomical allegory dressed up by conniving priests to oppress the people. Although Volney's book lacked the scholarly depth of Dupuis's *L'Origine*, it was short, accessible, politically charged, and rhetorically persuasive.

If Volney somewhat downplayed the sexual symbolism of D'Hancarville and Knight, Dupuis, one of the leading minds of the French Directorate, exuberantly restated it. In contrast to the rationalist Volney, who disparaged the myths he surveyed, Dupuis celebrated mythology as 'a physiology of nature written in a poetic-allegoric style'. Drawing on a long tradition of biblical scholarship, *L'Origine* pursued through six dense volumes the theory that all religions are based on a solar cult refined into a phallic and vaginal dualism. The publication of a one-volume abridgement in 1798 made Dupuis's theories much more accessible to general readers. Citing with approval the pantheism of the Brahmins alongside that of Pliny, Dupuis claimed that 'Christians are but sun-worshippers, and their priests follow the very same religion as those of Peru'. Christ he identified with solar symbolism from his birth at the winter solstice and resurrection at the spring equinox. It was an exegetical project which, as we will see below, would elicit the weighty apologetics of G. S. Faber's (1773–1854) theory of the mystery cults. Dupuis's work represented perhaps the most formidable sceptical challenge of the whole period, and it was further popularized by radical infidels such as the Revd Robert Taylor (1784–1844), the 'Devil's Chaplain', who lectured at the Blackfriars Rotunda in the early 1830s.

German biblical scholarship, typified by the work of Johann Gottfried Eichhorn (1752–1827), turned aside the sceptical charge by asserting the value of primitive mythic experience. Eichhorn and his followers accepted the full mythologization of Christian tradition, but claimed that myth and symbol were not simply primitivist but rather a paradigm for all thought. Influential though this counter-current was to be later in the century, its partisans in early-nineteenth-century Britain, who included S. T. *Coleridge and William *Taylor of Norwich, were few and far between. The task of assimilating the new mythological materials to a narrative of Christian pre-eminence was performed mainly by *Anglican clergymen or scholarly employees of the *East India Company—though the latter were sometimes suspected of undermining the primacy of the biblical tradition by treating their Indian materials with too much seriousness. In his seminal attacks on the sceptical tradition, *A New System; or Analysis of Antient Mythology* (1774–6), Jacob Bryant (1715–1804) argued that 'it is mere ignorance, that makes infidels . . . some may be won over by historical evidence, whom a refined theological argument cannot reach.' Bryant and his followers sought to find distorted linguistic and symbolic traces of Scripture in the mythology of the pagans, which they argued provided convincing external evidence for the prior authority of the Bible. Bryant asserted that 'there are in every climate some shattered fragments of original history; some traces of a primitive and universal language'. Following the Christian diffusionist tradition, he asserted the descent of all the peoples of the world from the survivors of the Flood. His system gave particular prominence to Ham, accursed for spying on his father's nakedness. Allegedly Ham's Cushite progeny, via his wicked grandson Nimrod, builder of the tower of Babel, colonized the world far and near after the dispersal, preserving and disseminating the original language of the world. Bryant argued with wearying predictability that the whole range of ancient civilizations were all of Cushite descent, a fact attested to by the Cushite roots of their languages. By means of an etymological recovery of these roots, he set about reconstructing the fragments of a universal mythology. He argued that all the myths and rituals of the pagan world were distorted narratives of the Flood after the original patriarchal monotheism preserved by Noah had become corrupted into idolatrous worship of the heavenly bodies. Ancient solar myths were distorted memorials of

Noah and his family. By means of his etymological method, uninformed by any knowledge of oriental languages, Bryant argued that Noah was the original of a range of ancient mythological figures from Prometheus to Osiris.

When in 1796 Bryant sought to disprove the historicity of the Trojan wars (an example of his disdain for Greek records, which he read as distortions of Cushite myths), his scholarly reputation, already damaged by his support for the authenticity of Thomas *Chatterton's Rowley poems, took a further plunge. Undoubtedly the most authoritative criticisms of Bryant came from Sir William Jones, whose work was informed by a scholarly and ethnographic rigour missing from his predecessor's. Jones's knowledge of several oriental languages, including Sanskrit, convinced him of the untenability of Bryant's methods; instead he advanced more cautious grounds for accepting the biblical account. In his 'Ninth Discourse', Jones argued that 'the Deluge is a historical fact admitted as true by every nation'. He believed that the children of Ham, Shem, and Japhet had settled in Iran but gradually lost their common original language, a process commemorated in the tower of Babel episode in Genesis. Only the children of Shem—the *Jews—maintained the record of universal history in an undistorted form. Jones concurred with Bryant in his account of the diffusion of the Cushite children of Ham—'the most ingenious and enterprising of the three, but the most arrogant, cruel and idolatrous'. Spreading out into India, China, America, Egypt, the Mediterranean, and Scandinavia, they preserved the common linguistic and mythological heritage explored in 'The Gods of Greece, Italy and India'.

Whatever his own motivations, this kind of speculation risked fuelling the fires of sceptics, particularly since Jones discarded Bryant's notion that pagan solar myths were actually distorted memorials of Noah and his family. At one point Jones even came close to the allegorism of Darwin, Volney, and Dupuis by asserting that 'the whole crowd of gods and goddesses in ancient *Rome* and modern *Varanes* mean only the powers of nature, and principally those of the SUN'. This was sailing very close to the wind, for on the strength of Jean-Sylvain Bailly's (1736–93) claim for the superiority of the Hindu to the Mosaic chronology in his *History of Ancient Astronomy*, fellow sceptic Louis Langlès (1763–1824), keeper of oriental manuscripts at the Bibliothèque Nationale, maintained that the Pentateuch and the five Chinese books of kings were derivations of the five Vedas. A host of other sceptics, including Volney and Dupuis, accordingly sought to recast the Christian story as an *astrological myth of Indian or Egyptian provenance. Jones energetically combated the sceptics by dismissing the Hindu chronology as a puerile 'astronomical riddle', denying that the Vedas were written before the Flood, and boldly asserting 'either the first eleven chapters of Genesis, all due allowances being made for a figurative Eastern style, are true, or the whole fabrick of our national religion is false'.

The work of Captain Francis Wilford (1761–1822), a fellow member of the Asiatic Society of Bengal, represents the most extravagant development of Jones's careful linguistic research. The ten articles which Wilford contributed to *Asiatic Researches* between 1799 and 1810 provided a rich source for poets such as Robert *Southey and Shelley, but in the end did much to damage the prestige of Indology in early-nineteenth-century Britain, explaining, for example, the anti-orientalism of James *Mill's *History of British India* (1817). Along with other articles in *Asiatic Researches*, Wilford's essays were pirated and translated into French by Langlès, with annotations by other sceptically minded scholars who often extrapolated a dangerously infidel meaning from the investigations of the Asiatic Society. Unlike the cautious Jones, who paralleled only Hindu and Graeco-Roman traditions, Wilford was more interested in tracing parallels between Hindu and Jewish traditions. He sensationally claimed to have discovered a Sanskrit version of the story of Noah which corroborated Bryant's 'Cushite' diffusion. In 'Mount Caucasus' (1801), Wilford argued for a Himalayan location of Mt Ararat, claiming that 'Ararat' was etymologically linked with 'Aryavarta', a Sanskrit name for India. Shelley embraced Wilford's thesis with enthusiasm: he set both his 'Alastor' (1816) and *Prometheus Unbound* in Wilford's Hindu Kush and Cashmere. The Greek Prometheus was redefined as a syncretic figure analogous to Dionysus, the Persian Zoroaster, the Jewish Noah, and the Hindu Rama. To the anonymous editor of the (unauthorized) fifth volume of *Asiatic Researches* Wilford's essays posed the subversive question of 'whether the Hindu Brahmins borrowed from Moses or Moses from the Hindu Brahmins'.

Worse was to come. In the eighth volume of *Asiatic Researches* (1805), Wilford, who had been extremely cavalier in naming the sources of his discoveries, announced that he had detected his Brahmin pundit in the act of forging various texts from the Puranas; but seemingly undeterred, he promptly launched into his most extravagant speculation to date. Wilford argued that Britain was none other than the Sacred Isle of the Hindus, that all European myths were of Hindu origin, and that 'the fundamental and mysterious transactions of the history of their religion, in its rise and progress, took place' in ancient Britain. In an elaborate account of the sacred geography of the ancient Hindus, Wilford even suggested that India had produced a second—or first?—Christ whose life and works closely resembled the protagonist of the Gospels. Wilford at least initially convinced many Anglican mythographers, but these were soon to regret their endorsement of his 'discoveries' given the opportunities they presented to sceptics and French allegorists.

The most important attempts to modernize Bryant's theories in the light of the researches of Sir William Jones and other Indologists were made by G. S. Faber and Thomas Maurice (1754–1824). Both were Anglican clergymen, and Maurice, despite his ignorance of oriental languages, also became keeper of oriental manuscripts at the *British Museum. In his *Memoirs* Maurice explained the ideological urgency of defensive mythography in the revolutionary decade of the 1790s: 'India, and the imagined antiquity of that vast Empire and the arts and sciences there calculated . . . were the *debatable ground* on which [the] atheistical rulers [of post-revolutionary France] had taken their determined stand, during their efforts to root out Christianity and demoralise the world.' Maurice viewed the Trinity as a primordial revealed truth 'coeval with Revelation; and the . . . incarnation coeval with the Fall'. Dedicating the whole of the fourth and fifth volumes of his *Indian Antiquities* (7 vols, 1793–1800) to the oriental Triads and their relationship to the Christian Trinity, Maurice argued that, although any direct comparison between the Hindu and Christian Trinities was 'an insult to the latter', the Hindu nevertheless represented a common descent from 'the venerable patriarchs'. This accommodation cautiously distinguished the revealed trinitarianism at the heart of Hinduism from the extravagant myths and polytheistic pantheon which represented its corruption by Brahmin priestcraft, the latter (following Bryant) traceable to allegories commemorating the universal deluge.

Given his apologetic task in the heated ideological climate of the 1790s, Maurice struggled hard to distinguish the universalist element in his theology from that of the French infidels who simply derived Christianity from Hindu and Egyptian mythology. Maurice counter-attacked on all the familiar fronts. He refuted Bailly on the superior antiquity of the Hindu chronology. He poured scorn on Volney's identification of Krishna and Christ, as well as his claim that the latter was 'only the solar orb rising in the sign Virgo, the twelve apostles are the twelve zodiacal asterisms, while the very name Jesus is as impiously traced to YES, the ancient cabalistical name of the young Bacchus'. Dedicating a third of the second volume of the *History of Hindostan* (2 vols, 1795–8) to an account of the life of Krishna, Maurice derived the *Bhagavadgita* story from the Apocryphal Gospels which he claimed had also inspired Brahminical ideas of incarnation and of the avatars, denying that Krishna was the mythological prototype of Christ. The influences of these ideas are strongly felt in Southey's epic poetry, which, like Maurice's own work, was to come under attack from *Evangelical critics for being insufficiently explicit in its missionary impulses.

Maurice's apologies failed, however, to safeguard his respectability in the eyes of an increasingly Evangelical reaction to the orientalists, particularly after the scandal of Wilford's forged *Satyavrayta* was first revealed in 1804. In an embarrassed self-defence published in 1812 entitled *Brahminical Fraud Detected*, Maurice sought to refute the charge that 'he had endeavoured to prop up the adamantine fabric of the Christian religion with pillars constructed of perishable Indian materials'; and he attempted to exonerate both Wilford and himself by turning his fire on 'the fraudful baseness of the sacerdotal tribe of India' who were leagued with French infidels to bring down the national religion of Britain and its Empire. Badly burnt by the controversy he had raised, Maurice spent his last years attempting to disprove the Hindu astronomical tables on which Bailly had based his infidel *History of Ancient Astronomy*.

Described by the young Shelley as 'chief of a band of Armageddon-Heroes [who] maintain their posts with all the obstinacy of cabalistical dogmatism', G. S. Faber epitomizes the growing Anglican revulsion from mythography in the 1800s and 1810s. In his Bampton Lectures at Oxford in 1801, Faber had originally endorsed Bryant's system with only a few qualifications, unambiguously following Maurice in allowing the gentile myths a glimmer of the reflected glory of Christianity. But his two major works, the influential *Dissertation on the Mysteries of the Cabiri* (1803) and *The Origin of Pagan Idolatry* (1816), represented at once a refinement and a rethinking of the doctrinal basis of his Bampton Lectures. Faber now recanted his earlier view that the trinities of the pagans were corrupt representations of the Trinity, arguing that the proof of the Christian theology 'rests solely on the declarations of the inspired volume; nor does it either admit or require any extraneous assistance from the demon-theology of paganism.' Faber's rejection of his earlier latitudinarian view of other traditions seems to have been influenced by the Evangelical mood evident in the reaction to the Wilford affair. In the *Dissertation* Faber turned on one of his former allies, the Revd Edward Davies, who had argued that the Druids preserved the pure religion of the Patriarchs, and that a trinitarianism revealed before the Flood had been preserved in the rituals of Stonehenge. Faber denied Davies's thesis completely, identifying the gods of Britain with pagan mysteries unconnected with revelation. If Faber's arguments provided Evangelicals with ammunition against orientalists of the kind tolerant of Hinduism, his attack on Davies partook of a similar animus against Celtic antiquarians and apologists for Irish Catholicism. Faber insisted that the saints and legends of Catholic Ireland were analogous to the heathen idols of Hinduism, and that St Patrick was in reality 'a mere adaptation of the worship of Taurus to the corrupt Christianity of popery' [see *Irish cultural revival]. Faber also mobilized Bryant's ideas in order to refute the astrological allegorism of Dupuis and Volney, subordinating it to sacred history; 'Noah and the sun were . . . regarded as one divine object; and the Ark, in which he was preserved, was profanely reverenced in conjunction with the moon'.

In both the *Dissertation* and *Pagan Idolatry* Faber took on the infidel argument that the symbols and rituals of all religions without exception were derived from the worship of the human genitalia as symbols of the generative principle of nature. Faber took the bold but rather perilous counter-step of translating the genital hypothesis into biblical terms; the Hindus had represented the Ark as the universal mother, 'under the disgraceful symbol of the Yoni', while Noah 'was typified by the *Linga* or Phallus'. In *Pagan Idolatry* he explored various mythic representations of the relationship between these 'two primaeval personages', including the incestuous coupling of the great father with his own mother, sister, or daughter, and (with specific reference to Dupuis) the idea of the 'blended hermaphroditic deity . . . at once the great father and the great mother'. Faber saw hermaphroditism as the symbolic origin of pantheism and materialism, 'the primitive double god . . . from [whose] productive womb was born the universe'. It is perhaps ironic that the discussions of solar symbolism with which Faber's work was littered, together with the explicit sexual themes which he sought to translate into the terms of the Mosaic account, made his books a digest of the most advanced mythographic ideas of the previous half-century, and therefore a readily available source-book for infidel poets and polemicists.

Faber's disdain for the pagan records is indicative of the decline of mythography in the 1810s, defeated not so much by its allegorist enemies as by its Evangelical allies. In 1801 Faber had censured *geology, regretting that 'the bowels of the earth are ransacked, to convince the literary world of the erroneousness of the Mosaical Chronology', but with the publication of William Buckland's (1784–1856) *Vindiciae Geologicae* (1820) and the more celebrated *Reliquiae Diluvianiae* (1823) a strong argument in favour of a universal deluge appeared from the unexpected quarter of science. Buckland's proofs obviated the need to rake around in the treacherous records of paganism for confirmation of the historicity of Genesis. At least for the time being, geology could serve as a more solid support for the Pentateuch than mythology; Faber, along with many other High Churchmen, was convinced to the extent of becoming one of Buckland's ecclesiastical patrons in the 1820s. In May 1820 the *Edinburgh Review* observed, in one of the only reviews of an Indological work to be covered in the postwar period: 'The fields of Indian Antiquities have been of late less diligently cultivated.' A similar lack of interest in mythography and Indology is evident in the Tory *Quarterly*, although the palaeontological works of Georges Cuvier (1769–1832) and Buckland *are* reviewed at length in the same period.

Only among working-class infidels can any exception to this process be found, since many of the popular *Deist preachers of the 1820s—pre-eminently Robert Taylor—popularized versions of radical Deism based on astrological critiques of Christianity. Richard *Carlile— the best-known working-class sceptic of the early nineteenth century—also shifted from Holbachian materialism to belief in astronomical theism during the early 1830s. Leaving this continuing plebeian interest in mythography aside, the polemical shift from mythography to scriptural geology is evident in the marked differences between Shelley's *Prometheus Unbound* and *Byron's biblical dramas *Cain* (1821) and *Heaven and Earth* (1823). Shelley's mytho- graphical drama is in a sense the last of the Romantic mythological poems in the tradition of *Blake, Southey, and Peacock. In contrast, Byron's works reacted directly to the new Evangel- icalism and to its intellectual buttresses, Cuvier and Buckland. Unlike Shelley, Byron showed no interest in allegorizing or syncretizing Genesis, but was drawn rather to reinterpret the moral emphasis of the Bible story. The decline of poetic interest in comparative mythology in Britain in the 1820s was accompanied by a predilection for the apocalyptical *sublime, the predominant mood of Byron's dramas and Mary *Shelley's novel *The Last Man* (1826). Metaphors and images of natural catastrophe and deluge were all the rage in the *paintings [27] of John *Martin and J. M. W. *Turner, as well as in *epic poetry such as Barry Cornwall's *The Flood of Thessaly* (1823). The emergent new attitude to myth is aptly expressed in Hartley *Coleridge's essay of 1822, 'On the Poetical Use of the Heathen Mythology'. Thwarted in his attempt to write a pious drama on Prometheus by Shelley's successful treatment of the same subject, Hartley took revenge upon the school of Keats, Shelley, and Cornwall by depoliticiz- ing mythographical poetry. He described pagan (and particularly Greek) myths as 'so many beautiful forms . . . if they were ever pernicious, they have now lost their venom, and may serve to show how much, and how little, the unaided intellect can effect for itself.' Pagan mythology was safely circumscribed within the aesthetic realm, its fragility and effeminate beauty provid- ing a marked contrast with the sinews of revealed Christianity. As Hartley declared, 'the moral being has gained a religion, and the imagination has lost one'. The poetical use of heathen mythology was represented as an ideologically (if not artistically) spent force. Although Hartley's father, S. T. Coleridge, persisted in a quixotic attempt to reconcile the arid discourse of Anglican apologetic with German mythography, his May 1825 lecture to a somnolent Royal Society of Literature on the *Prometheus* of Aeschylus was by his own admission a resounding failure. Hartley had rescued pagan myth from Evangelical philistinism to the extent that it was still usable from an aesthetic point of view, provided that poetry kept within its proper bounds;

but even with the most sophisticated German tools, there was clearly no longer any future for the mythological project of either sustaining or tearing down 'the adamantine fabric of the Christian religion'.

Butler, M., 'Myth and Mythmaking in the Shelley Circle', in K. Everest, ed., *Shelley Revalued: Essays from the Gregynor Conference*, Leicester, 1983; 'Romantic Manichaeism: Shelley's On the Devil and Devils and Byron's Mythological Dramas', in J. B. Bullen, ed., *The Sun Is God: Painting Literature and Mythology in the 19th Century*, Oxford, 1989; Curran, S., *Shelley's Annus Mirabilis*, San Marino, Calif., 1975; Hungerford, E., *The Shores of Darkness*, New York, 1941; Kuhn, A. J., 'English Deism and the Development of Romantic Mythological Syncretism', *Publications* of the Modern Language Association, 71, 1956, 1094–1116; Manuel, F., *The Eighteenth Century Confronts the Gods*, Boston, 1959; Marshall, P., *The British Discovery of Hinduism in the 18th Century*, Cambridge, 1970; Pratt, M. L., *Imperial Eyes: Travel Writing and Transculturation*, London, 1992; Schwab, R., *The Oriental Renaissance: Europe's Rediscovery of India and the East, 1680–1880*, New York, 1984; Shaffer, E., *Kubla Khan and the Fall of Jerusalem: The Mythological School in Biblical Criticism and Secular Literature, 1770–1880*, Cambridge, 1975.

37 · EXPLORATION   NICHOLAS THOMAS

Anthropological ideas in the second half of the eighteenth century have been most frequently discussed under the rubric of a 'four-stage' theory of social development, according to which the initial condition of humanity was one of hunting or foraging, succeeded by pastoralism, agriculture, and finally commercial society. *Scottish Enlightenment writers systematically elaborated this scheme in works such as Adam *Ferguson's *Essay on the History of Civil Society* (1767) and John *Millar's *Origin of the Distinction of Ranks in Society* (1771). Early forms of society were hypothetically reconstructed on the basis of what were taken to be elementary needs and impulses, and were often offered explicitly as rhetorical models rather than as characterizations of societies in actual existence. In the case of societies that had developed beyond the 'original' condition, however, the reports of eighteenth-century travellers to America such as Charlevoix and Lafitau, and classical accounts of Gauls, Britons, and Germans by Caesar and Tacitus, provided more particular information concerning pastoralists and agriculturalists [see *evolutionary theories].

Although the four stages were defined on the basis of modes of production, writers such as Ferguson and Millar were not primarily interested in technology nor in the social relations engendered by particular forms of labour, but rather in the degree to which property was institutionalized and in the moral conditions that emerged from various nomadic and settled ways of life. The 'rudeness' of hunters was regarded as the effect of their rootless existence. The use of the plough in agriculture, and the consequent emergence of property rights in land and soil, were taken to be fundamental to the emergence of co-operative endeavour that led, in turn, to various forms of political union, civil regulation, and institutionalized government. The harsh treatment of women was taken to be a sign of savagery, and its gradual amelioration to characterize the growth of civility.

While such a model indeed structured the comparative vision of many late-eighteenth-century ethnological writers, the idea that a 'four-stage theory' was their central concern tends to reduce their arguments to the elements that prefigure Victorian evolutionism. The concept of stages and the occasional use of grand analogies between the life-cycles of individuals and those of the human species as a whole did anticipate social Darwinism, but the evolutionary discrimination of peoples and the characterization of races was never an end in itself, as it later came to be. Scottish Enlightenment comparative studies of property, kinship, language, and political institutions should be seen not as part of a unified progressive scheme, but rather as a self-reflective analysis of problems of government, commerce, and refinement. Their interest was not in bolstering a sense of the superiority of the civilized world by displacing non-Europeans into antecedent epochs, but rather in diagnosing flaws and contradictions in European societies, through the evocation of their simpler or original forms. In Millar's work, for example, the detailed narrative in the *Historical View of the English Government* (1787) employed the same vocabulary and was motivated by the same underlying moral preoccupations as his *Origin of the Distinction of Ranks*.

The analysis of progress was never unambiguously celebratory, but always profoundly ambivalent. The conditions seen as conducive to 'politeness' also stimulated various forms of licentiousness and corruption; conversely, virtues present in the barbaric state were vitiated by settlement, political union, and the growth of civility. For some writers, such as Lord Kames (1696–1782), a conviction that the factors giving rise to the growth of civilization also produced its lapse from *patriotism into private vice, opulence, and effeminacy took on a particularly poignant cast. A key category in this analysis was that of luxury. While property was understood to be the primary source of civility, its excessive accumulation was thought to feminize the aristocracy and encourage political despotism, corrupting both rulers and ruled. While this might result from the sheer accumulation of wealth in any context, corruption was all the more likely to occur in a commercial society in which a proliferation of new goods continually stimulated an acquisitive appetite [see *consumerism, 19]. Though trade might rouse men to pursue wealth vigorously, it also caused them to be preoccupied with personal gain rather than public good. The ideal of active citizenship was further eroded by the specialization of labour and the emergence of professions, referred to as 'mercenary pursuits'. Some writers, such as Ferguson, were less negative about opulence than Kames, and there was a trend to reconcile virtue and commerce in the first half of the nineteenth century, particularly among *Evangelicals. Until that point, however, history was understood in cyclical as much as in progressive terms, and as a process in which virtue and corruption might co-exist almost indefinitely [see *history, 38].

Anthropological thought in the period was thus not a discrete body of theory, confined to general treatises, but a set of ideas that extended to other kinds of writing such as *travel literature. In such texts the four-stage categories were adapted, distorted, or abandoned to accommodate local, observed social differences that were frequently explained, broadly following Montesquieu (1689–1755), by recourse to an elastic notion of climatic determination. Features of particular peoples and societies were derived not from their mode of subsistence, but from their residence in torrid, temperate, or frigid zones; or from the action of more particular environmental effects, such as wind and sea air, or from combinations of the climate and mode of life. These considerations might in turn be overshadowed by innate propensities that were taken to characterize particular races, such as the 'treacherous Javanese' or the 'effeminate Hindoos'. Religious differences were particularly important for the categorization of European peoples, whom Protestant British travellers generally took to be degenerate according to the degree to which 'Popery' and superstition reigned. However, observations on southern European peoples frequently incorporated the same kind of discussion of the effects of climate that figured in accounts of non-Europeans.

Tensions between systematic ethnological or political argument and the particular circumstances and events of a journey are reflected in the divisions within most travel literature between a narrative of the journey, in a chronological and often diary form, and the inclusion of interspersed passages or chapters offering systematic and impersonal description. On one level the narrative voice of the writer might be highly personal, purporting to convey feelings of doubt and despair, fear, and embarrassment, while on another level it impersonally records responses to scenery, the explorers' diet, the weather, collecting, and encounters with individual natives. In journeys over land, such as the Scottish surgeon Mungo *Park's first investigation of the upper Niger, where the explorer is typically accompanied only by local guides or servants, sentimental narrative accentuates the person of the traveller. This sentimental mode was, however, eclipsed in the early nineteenth century by a more formal and less overtly reflective style, at least in accounts from official missions such as those by Sir John Barrow (1764–1848), John Crawfurd (1783–1868), and Sir Thomas *Raffles. Voyages by sea also tend to be described in a less personal fashion, structured as they were by the communal nature of shipboard life.

When these writers turn from descriptions of the particular circumstances and events of a journey, their expository ethnological reflections are marked by a universal present tense and by essentialized typifications of the characters of particular peoples encountered (for example, 'the Hindoos are an effeminate people'). 'Manners' and 'customs' are abstracted from particular events and catalogued with observations on the range of wildlife, the character of the terrain, and the availability of water. Descriptions that appear to deny the particularity of the situation and the writer's personal response may nevertheless founder around customs or events that resisted representation and interpretation. Indigenous gender relations, familial forms, and visually disorientating forms of indigenous art and bodily decoration such as tattooing, were in some cases simply beyond the reach of ethnographic languages available to exploratory writers. What the reader encounters, then, are expressions of puzzlement that place more emphasis on obscurity than the incident in question would seem to warrant. This obscurity conveys a sense of the *sublime which is initially threatening but subsequently empowering for its observer: the traveller perplexed or threatened by disorder is strengthened for having witnessed and withstood it.

Late-eighteenth-century British compilations of voyages frequently emphasized that earlier voyages (such as those of the Spanish) had been motivated by avarice and the lust for conquest, while in contrast those initiated under George III after the Seven Years War were distinctive for the purity of their interest in discovery. At a very literal level, this was arguable: Captain James *Cook, to take the most famous example, was not actually seeking plunder, nor had he plans to establish settlements. Nevertheless his voyages were implicated in larger strategic and commercial aspirations. The great southern land, which Cook was able to expose as an illusion on the second voyage, was important because it was imagined to be a bountiful country of prospective settlement, while the north-west passage, the goal of his third voyage, would have enabled more direct access to Asian trade. The importance of these commercial aims was obscured to some degree by the fact that Cook's findings in both cases were negative, though the settlement of Australia followed from the charting of the east coast on the first voyage, and exploration in other regions, such as West Africa, was more obviously directed toward the opening up of trade routes [see *empire, 5].

The Earl of Sandwich, first Lord of the Admiralty, in a meeting with the French Ambassador in London, allegedly repeated at least twenty times that Cook's second voyage was motivated purely by curiosity. The dissociation from commercial and acquisitive aims was so much stressed that what the voyages were *not* seemed to overshadow any positive idea of what, in fact, they *were*. Mungo Park was similarly unable to convince local authorities that he was travelling merely for curiosity's sake and not for trade. Given his declared hopes that the journey would open 'new channels of commerce', however, it is not clear that the confusion was entirely in the minds of the Africans.

The project of curious enquiry was in fact always understood to be implicated in commercial speculation. Both were regarded as the pursuit of a succession of novel and particularly foreign objects, governed more by a thirst or passion for new things or findings than by reason. Specimens—accumulated in all possible variety and abundance—seem to have been fetishized in much the same way as the commodity. Just as commerce had earlier been associated with

51. *Mr Banks shews the Indians
the Planet Venus on the Sun*,
frontispiece to the anonymous
*Voyage to the Southern Hemi-
sphere; or Nature Explored* (1775).

luxury and effeminacy, natural history was tainted with commerce because collectors traf-
ficked in specimens and antiquities. It was also linked with promiscuity, most obviously
because natural historians such as Joseph *Banks had notoriously entered into sexual relations
with local women. Natural history imagined a sexualized system, a world overwhelmed by the
desire to reproduce and multiply. Lack of discrimination was the virtue of its inclusive vision,
seeking out detail, particularity, and oddity rather than ideal forms and wholes. At a more
vulgar level, instruments such as the telescope had licentious and voyeuristic associations, not
lost on the viewers of a cheap engraving depicting Banks inviting the Tahitians to look through
his phallic telescope. Although Cook himself was above any explicit reproach, it is notable that
illustrations in the reprints of the voyages implied precisely these moral ambiguities, not
specifically for natural history, but for the voyage as a whole. One such illustration has two
striking features: a huge Union Jack that forms a backdrop to an encounter, in which a Tahitian
chief is said in the caption to 'present' his sister to Captain Cook. The courtly sense of 'present'
here also has distinct suggestions of sexual exchange, apparent in the way in which the chief
proffers the woman's wrist to Cook.

Interpreted as polite intercourse, this encounter typifies what is supposed to take place on the voyages. Establishing good relations with other populations and opening the way to mutual improvement and trade were part of Cook's charter. But it was only too well understood that this intercourse was frequently corrupting. Given the familiarity of British readers with the controversies over sexual relations with Tahitians that followed publications such as John *Hawkesworth's *An Account of the Voyages Undertaken by the Order of his Present Majesty for Making Discoveries in the Southern Hemisphere* (1773), the engraving could only have been read as a juxtaposition of a patriotic mission with the prospect, if not the actuality, of sexual and commercial corruption. So far from inaugurating the improvement of savages, the voyagers' introduction of prostitution, and eager traffic in supplies, specimens, and baubles, exacerbated the supposed voluptuousness that might already be present in native character. The corruption of the indigenous body politic by this commerce also occurred quite literally, as the sailors introduced and spread venereal disease, a subject discussed in print by one of Cook's most sexually predatory memorialists, surgeon David *Samwell.

Cook's voyages, together with that of Louis-Antoine de Bougainville (1729–1811), are especially famous for the identification of the Tahitian with the ideal of the noble savage, the most

52. *O-Tai (a Chief of Otaheite) accompanied with his Wife, &c. presenting one of his Sisters to Captn. Cook, on board the Resolution Sloop*, illustration to George William Anderson, *A Collection of Voyages Round the World Performed by Royal Authority* (1790).

famous exposition of this notion being Diderot's *Supplément au voyage de Bougainville* (written 1772, published 1796). An idealized Pacific was also highly visible in *pantomimes such as playwright John O'Keeffe's (1747–1833) *Omai: or a Trip around the World* (1785), with stage designs by Philippe Jacques de *Loutherbourg. However, the degree to which the noble savage informed perceptions of Pacific peoples in general, and even the Tahitians specifically, has been overemphasized. Most writers did not presume that the actual, historical Tahitians really inhabited the exemplary space that had been defined for them. There was abundant evidence in the voyage publications of political complexities and elements of corruption (as opposed to mere sensuality) in Tahitian life, that paralleled the flaws of European society. More importantly, the writer of one compilation of Cook's voyages noted that the 'ferocious New-Zeelander' and 'the gentle and voluptuous O-Taheitian' both exhibited 'accumulated proofs of frankness, disinterested generosity, and innate goodness'. In other words, what was instructive from the South Seas was not limited to the Tahitian condition, but could be extended to include a different, more martial society such as that of the Maori of New Zealand, whose ferocity did not preclude more positive qualities. The issue was explored at much greater length and more systematically by Johann Reinhold *Forster, who in 1778 published a natural history treatise, *Observations Made During a Voyage Round the World*, deriving from his participation in Cook's second voyage.

Forster's anthropologically sophisticated exposition is of particular interest for its reading of Pacific societies in terms of European political debates, and for an uneasy synthesis of two grand, temporal narratives. On the one hand, there is something like the evolutionary time usually taken to be characteristic of nineteenth-century Darwinism. Not only does Forster imagine savage and barbaric societies in terms of stages, but he likens their progression from animality through barbarism and civility to the life-cycle of the human individual, from infancy through the excesses of adolescence to maturity. From this perspective, certain populations such as those of New Zealand are antecedent to the happier peoples of tropical Polynesia, who have virtually emerged from barbarism into a kind of rudimentary civility. (Though Forster was unusual in crediting the Tahitians with such a degree of advancement, virtually all explorers, lettered or unlettered, shared the view that they were at a higher stage than other peoples, such as the Melanesians of the western Pacific.)

Simultaneously, Forster speculated correctly that the inhabitants of the Pacific islands had migrated from Asia, acquiring new manners at successive locations. As they moved south into more temperate climates, they lost the intricate knowledge, particularly of agriculture, that enabled their refinement in the tropics and became degenerate and cruel. In this scheme, then, Tahitians represented the 'before' of the Maori in New Zealand; the latter were seen not so much as having regressed in evolutionary time as having become uncivil in historical time. This propensity to degenerate was not thought to be peculiar to savages, but directly paralleled the loss of *sensibility [11], and even shifts in temperament and physique, that could be detected among Europeans who moved from their original homeland to the tropics: the lassitude and cruelty of the Boers in southern Africa, as well as the Portuguese in Asia and the British in the West Indies, was attributed to this process of climatic determination. Criticisms of this kind were particularly conspicuous in the literature of *abolitionism [see *slavery, 6].

Forster found that Tahitian civility was already partially corrupted by luxury as a result of a pre-contact traffic in ornaments with other Polynesians. Recognition of such nuanced evaluations complicates both the noble savage theme and the notion that exploratory discourse was obsessed with the mapping and ranking of racial types. It is clear that an idealized savage was sometimes evoked to rhetorical effect, but also that this dehistoricized figure was complemented both by the realistically ignoble savage and by a variety of historicized native peoples, whose societies were variously appealing and imperfect, in much the same way as European nations varied inconsistently in refinement, mode of government, and temper.

While writers often presented arrays of typified natives, contrasting Tahitian and New Hebridean, Hottentot and Kaffir, Negro and Arab 'types', this process of typification was rendered unstable both by a plurality of larger narratives and by the grounding of exploration in personal experience. It was widely noted that travellers within Europe were prone to generalize on the basis of fleeting encounters, often in a fashion that reflected their own prejudices or tempers rather than the authentic manners of the people notionally represented. The particularity needed to authenticate accounts of journeys often undermined systems of typification. Given the peculiar circumstances in which travellers encountered particular people, apparent disquisitions upon their essential natures were often no more than generalizations from circumstances that were plainly contingent and inessential. Where Park defined the Moors as 'a nation of lunatics . . . combining in their character, the blind superstition of the Negro with the savage cruelty and treachery of the Arab', he elsewhere made much of underlying human sameness. The response of the aged mother of one of his guides, on being reunited with her son after the latter's protracted absence, impressed upon Park that 'whatever difference there is between the Negro and European in the conformation of the nose and the colour of the skin, there is none in the genuine sympathies and characteristic feelings of our common nature'. This narrative thus incorporated both assertions concerning the peculiar natures of the races encountered and observations that denied those natures, as it ranged between affirmations of superiority and perceptions of affinity, and between topographic systematization and sentimentality.

In other texts, such as Barrow's important *Travels into the Interior of Southern Africa* (1801–4), essential characterization of the natives is rejected for political rather than sentimental reasons: the so-called Kaffirs and Hottentots were not in fact savage or beast-like, as they appeared in Boer propaganda, but rather were products of settler inhumanity. Barrow did not, however, take human nature to be subject to the same historical mutability in south-east Asia. In his *Voyage to Cochinchina* (1806, drawing upon a journey of 1792) he described Malay and Chinese races in the same essentializing language that he found inappropriate for southern Africans; the difference, pretty transparently, arose from the need to legitimize the British acquisition of the Cape in 1802.

The authoritative character of exploratory writing was undermined not only by these forms of incoherence but also by the association of the genre with fantasy and misrepresentation. While a few notable explorers, such as Cook and Park, were widely presented as exemplary heroes, others, including James *Bruce, were sometimes regarded as charlatans. Because the value of a particular journey was so closely identified with new discoveries and with the extirpation of previous errors, explorers always sought to discredit previous travellers and were led to exaggerate the significance of their own findings. Hence the shortcomings of explorer Thomas Shaw's (1694–1751) *Travels . . . Relating to Several Parts of the Levant* (1738) are rehearsed extensively, with much other ungenerous commentary, in Bruce's *Travels to discover the source of the Nile* (1790). Bruce is in turn frequently taken to task in later publications such as traveller Henry Salt's (1780–1827) *Voyage to Abyssinia* (1814). Explorers' treatment of native people, their estimates of the fertility and resources of places visited, their plans of antiquities and charts of islands, and the accuracy of published architectural, topographical, and ethnographic engravings were all frequently interrogated. Travel writers arguably insisted upon the faithful and authentic character of their narratives precisely because their books were widely presumed to be tendentious and inaccurate.

From the beginning of the nineteenth century, the character of travel and voyage writing seems to change, in a fashion consistent both with intellectual shifts and with the practical organization of exploration. While voyages by sea were obviously always elaborately planned ventures, depending on the patronage of the Crown, Admiralty, and Royal Society, exploration by land in regions such as West Africa became similarly highly organized, and therefore also directed toward more specific strategic objectives. Park's second mission, though concluding in the loss of the entire party, was on a considerably grander scale than the first, and was sponsored by the Colonial Office rather than the African Association. Salt's travels in the Horn of Africa in 1809–10 were also officially directed, in that case particularly toward establishing relations with the Abyssinian rulers, while Crawfurd's 1820s accounts of Java, Thailand, and China emerged from commercial investigations and diplomacy for the *East India Company.

A slightly earlier work might, however, be seen as the consummation of these developments—Thomas Raffles's *History of Java* (1817), written not from an exploratory voyage but from the author's administration during the brief period of British rule (1811–16). Like Forster's *Observations* of fifty years earlier, it consisted not in a journal but a systematic description of agriculture, religion, languages, manners, and manufactures, which was accompanied by a chronological history up to the time of the British conquest. While Forster's exposition of a similar range of topics served what he aptly called 'ethnic philosophy', or a combination of comparative anthropology and political reflection, Raffles had little interest in speculative discussion on the causes of variety in the manners and temperaments of indigenous people. Though he provided much general and antiquarian information, his description aimed to inform commerce, and more particularly to draw attention to the inefficient and unjust character of the Dutch regime, thereby vindicating his own administration. A 'Comparative Table of Languages' in Forster's book, though a remarkable instance of Linnaean systematization for its time, was intended primarily to demonstrate the close relationships between the Polynesian peoples. Their common descent from an ancestral Polynesian population informed Forster's arguments about the particular causes of advancement in some cases and degeneration in others. In contrast, a similar linguistic appendix in Raffles's volume was far more extensive. Though Raffles sought to contribute to knowledge, and included terms for body parts, religious concepts, and even for supposed equivalents of the signs of the Zodiac in Malay, Javanese, and other languages, his volume was directed more toward practical language use, and incorporated many terms and much usage relating to commodities and the conduct of trade.

It would be wrong, however, to imagine an even progression in exploratory writing which ranged from eighteenth-century texts of a sentimental, picaresque, and occasionally philosophical type to nineteenth-century descriptions with concrete objectives in the shadow of the Colonial Office or the Admiralty, rather than of Montesquieu. Publications that reproduced or purported to reproduce voyage narratives encompassing non-European peoples and places remained extraordinarily diverse. While renowned quasi-official works such as those of Raffles and Crawfurd were obviously influential, especially via bodies such as the Royal Geographical Society, non-élite accounts, such as the sensational narratives of shipwrecked sailors and the very different works of missionaries, were also widely read. For example, *Byron's poem *The Island, or Christian and his Comrades* (1823) drew heavily on William *Bligh's *Narrative of the Mutiny and Seizure of the Bounty* (1789) and on the popular *Account of the Tonga Isles* (1817), edited by meterologist John Martin from the experiences of shipwrecked sailor William Mariner.

Shipwrecked narratives, often described as 'colourful' in bibliographies and booksellers' catalogues, are frequently marked by wild inaccuracies and an almost refreshing indifference to the spurious precision that typifies much colonial science. Lurid accounts of cannibal feasts, unscrupulous traders, marriage to indigenous women, escapes, and adventures were of course contrived to appeal, but also provided an unsanitized view of the colonial periphery. While official accounts, and those of more refined travellers, tended to reaffirm the distance of Europeans and their superiority, the memoirs of those who had survived wrecks or mutinies revealed an emerging space of interaction between indigenous peoples and Europeans, marked by what could be seen as degeneration on the part of the latter. The view that colonists might lapse from European civility into something much closer to the savagery of the tropical populations they were attempting to dominate had been advanced much earlier, notably by

Diderot; but these accounts effectively provided much first-hand information to suggest that colonization was disorderly and morally ambiguous.

*Missionary literature was also very widely consumed, and provided a view of indigenous peoples distinct from that of natural historians such as Forster and Alexander von Humboldt (1769–1859) and of strategic or commercial assessors such as Barrow, Raffles, and Crawfurd. Although missionaries were frequently critical of exploitative traders, they found commerce problematic when linked with slavery or prostitution, rather than in its general political ramifications. Craft specialization and the manufacture of ornaments were typically connected not with luxury and corruption, but with industriousness. This in turn could prefigure higher forms of Christian productivity and discipline.

Evangelical exploratory writing tended to stress contests between natives and heroic, some-times martyred, missionaries contending with all the evils of heathen superstition—John Williams (1769–1839), killed and eaten in the New Hebrides, was one of the most famous. Such works were complemented by a genre of descriptive ethnography, typified in William Ellis's (1794–1872) *Polynesian Researches* (1832), which offered rounded manners-and-customs descriptions, but also predictably emphasized dark practices such as polygyny, war-fare, and infanticide. Many of these accounts could not, however, be absolutely negative; missionary endeavour could only be sustained if it were supposed that indigenous peoples could be saved, and were worth saving. Missionaries had to show that natives were contin-gently rather than essentially evil. One could much more easily anticipate conversion if heathen natures already possessed certain commendable features, that might range from child-like generosity to manual dexterity. The resulting mix of ambiguity and promise gave mission-ary writing a certain incoherence, comparable to Park's narrative but differently motivated, where a description might lurch between the denigration of savage practices or religious obser-vances and sentimental observations of shared humanity.

At the same time racial categories were undoubtedly becoming more rigid, as the conflation of space and time that had provided anthropological thought with a comparative framework since the work of Lafitau was given a new inflection. While eighteenth-century writers gener-ally equated non-Europeans with the peoples of classical antiquity, who were seen as relatively proximate in historical time, the nineteenth-century tendency was increasingly to identify them with primeval phases in prehistory, suggesting virtual animality and absolute distance. If this racist evolutionism is typically associated with Darwinism, and indeed acquired more systematic theoretical form in the late nineteenth century, most of its familiar elements were nevertheless in place by the beginning of the century, though they jostled with other ways of perceiving human variety.

Voyage and exploratory writing should not be understood as limited to the corpus of well-known voyages and descriptive works, but to include less renowned accounts, and even the cheap versions of famous works, which frequently introduced additional comment in pictorial form. This literature does not unambiguously endorse imperial expansion. Neither are its workings upon exotic societies limited to the celebration of types such as the noble savage. Travellers were not only exploring new lands, but also new ways of writing. Writers of voyages seem frequently to have been misconstrued in a generic as well as a geographical sense: the diverse popular, scientific, and official audiences for their works could not all be pleased at once. While scholars need to read travellers' accounts critically, uncovering the racism buried in objectivist description and sentimental rhapsody, we should also be conscious of the epi-stemological and moral uncertainties that are often displayed rather disguised in exploration.

Curtin, P. D., *The Image of Africa*, London, 1965; Forster, J. R., *Observations Made During a Voyage Round the World*, ed. N. Thomas, H. Guest, & M. Dettelbach, Honolulu, 1997; Pratt, M. L., *Imperial Eyes: Travel Writing and Transculturation*, London, 1992; Smith, B., *European Vision and the South Pacific*, New Haven, Conn., 1985.

38 · HISTORY   JAMES CHANDLER

Among historians of 'history' the Romantic period is recognized as a kind of watershed. Such dates as 1830, 1790–1830, 'the late eighteenth century', or 'the early nineteenth century' have commonly been used to mark the emergence in Western Europe of what is termed 'historicism'. What is actually understood by this term probably varies more than the period to which its emergence is normally assigned, though in most accounts it is understood to involve one or more of the following: a practice of reducing other forms of explanation to the genetic form; a tendency to pinpoint particular events and human characteristics in reference to a highly specified articulation of cultural times and places; a challenge to certain ways of taking historical bearings from the concepts of a transcendent providence or a universal human nature; a commitment to the view that, as Marx would later put it, 'men make their own history, but under conditions given them from the past'.

Even allowing that historicism, so understood, dates from our period, it might none the less seem strange to offer a substantial consideration of the subject here. For the literary culture of this period in Britain managed to produce not a single work of *historiography in English to equal the greatest works of David *Hume, William *Robertson, and Edward *Gibbon—all published before the end of the *American Revolution in 1783—or those of *Macaulay, Buckle, Acton, or Engels—all published well after the *Reform Act of 1832. There are certainly a few histories from the period that might deserve mention in an overview of British historiography. In the early 1780s Catharine *Macaulay, writing from a radical *Whig position, completed a history that revised Hume's magisterial account of the English past and, in the process, boldly defied gender codes about who is permitted to assume the responsibilities of political historiography; the misogynistic reception of her *History of England* (1763–83) indicates how deeply those codes could cut. A new Catholic perspective on the subject was opened up by John Lingard's (1771–1851) *History of England* (1819–30). Henry Hallam's (1777–1859) *View of the State of Europe during the Middle Ages* (1818) became an important touchstone for Victorian medievalism, as James *Mill's *History of British India* (1817) was to be for later writings on the colonization of South Asia. Histories were also produced by writers better known for work in other fields: William *Cobbett's *History of the Protestant Reformation in England and Ireland* (1824–7), for example, or Robert *Southey's historiographical rebuttals to Cobbett's radical account. Yet it remains one of the less appreciated paradoxes of this period that the writings to which we must look for the most convincing evidence of a new historical outlook turn out to be not works of historiography in the customary sense but rather historically self-conscious works of journalism, criticism, poetry, drama, and, above all, fiction.

The question of a Romantic historicism in Britain can be profitably approached by considering a distinctive coinage of the period. In 1831 the young John Stuart *Mill published a series of articles in four parts for the *Examiner* under the title 'The Spirit of the Age' which, he claimed, was 'a novel expression. I do not believe that it is to be met with in any work exceeding fifty years in antiquity.' Although the *Oxford English Dictionary* gives an 1820 letter by Percy *Shelley as its first recorded instance, the term has an earlier history in British writing, a history related to but distinct from the equally celebrated use of *Geist der Zeit* by Arndt and *Zeitgeist* by Hegel, in German writings dating from the first decade of the century. Already in

Hume's *History of Great Britain* (1754–62), for example, one finds anticipations of the later vogue for such references. There is wisdom in the *OED*'s chronology, none the less, in that events in Britain from the time of the *Peterloo massacre in 1819 to the coronation of Victoria seem to have occasioned a particularly intense reflection on the 'spirit of the age'—even as the 'age' in question is often understood to range back to the closing decades of the eighteenth century.

This interest becomes a kind of journalistic obsession in a particularly influential sequence of publications from the decade 1824–33. Best known, perhaps, along with Mill's series of 1831, are the literary portraits in William *Hazlitt's *The Spirit of the Age*, which appeared in 1825 and which included some magazine articles he had published under the heading 'Spirits of the Age' the previous year in the *New Monthly Magazine*. Thomas *Carlyle, who singled out Mill's essay for praise when it appeared, had himself in 1829 published a similar meditation entitled 'Signs of the Times'. Edward *Bulwer-Lytton included a chapter on 'The Intellectual Spirit of the Time' in his *England and the English* (1833). As the author of 'Letter on the Spirit of the Age' in *Blackwood's Edinburgh Magazine* (1830) put it: 'That which in the slang of faction, is called the Spirit of the Age, absorbs, at present, the attention of the world.'

We find in these works, and in Macaulay's related article on historiography in the *Edinburgh Review* (1830), a complex mix, impossible to sort out in this brief space, of *utilitarianism, *Saint-Simonianism, industrialism, 'mechanism', German idealism, and what we might now call the theory of everyday life. We find a simultaneous commitment to and suspicion of the public sphere of bourgeois opinion; a paradoxical characterization of the period in question as quintessentially transitional. Each of these works tries to explore, in its own way, the peculiar form of historical self-consciousness that characterizes contemporary public culture. Each addresses the point Mill emphasizes as novel about the age (an age that, in his account, distinguishes itself by the use of the phrase 'the spirit of the age'): 'The idea of comparing one's own age with former ages, or with our notion of those which are yet to come, had occurred to philosophers; but it never before was itself the dominant idea of any age.' In order to comprehend what it means for this 'idea' to dominate, one must understand what was seen to be at stake in comparing one age with another. History had traditionally been understood to teach by example, to supply a host of concrete instances of how or how not to conduct oneself. This is apparent in such Renaissance texts as Machiavelli's *The Prince*, and it is spelt out explicitly in England in Sir Philip Sidney's *Apology for Poetry*, where philosophy teaches by precept, history by example, and poetry by combining the two in a single form. When, as in the Britain of the 1790s, unprecedented acceleration of social change, technological development, and new broad-based political movements come to be recognized as radically restructuring human relations over time, it is no longer viable to assume the possibility of moral exemplification across period boundaries. The warm reception accorded William *Godwin's arguments about the effects of political institutions on the shaping of character and action, for example, suggests a growing public appreciation—no doubt abetted by events and debates in America and France—of the power of historically specific circumstances to shape human subjectivity. With the strong sense of the epochal constitution of human personality in place, history can no longer be said to teach by providing examples to moral philosophy. Instead, it teaches by indicating changing directions of change and presaging possible futurities. For similar reasons, the exemplifying function of history is no longer that of supplying timelessly apposite examples (positive and negative) for moral edification, but rather that of identifying persons in whom a given period, or period trait, is understood to be especially well realized: hence the new Romantic typology of what Hazlitt in England called 'spirits [plural] of the age', Hegel in Germany 'world-historical individuals', or Emerson in America 'representative men'.

In the English context, a number of Shelley's writings are particulary helpful for their precocious explorations of the new conceptualization of history in such terms. One especially important passage, which was probably composed a few months prior to the 1820 letter cited by the *OED*, was eventually published as the now famous final paragraph of *A Defence of Poetry* (1821). Indeed, one of the reasons that this passage has gained such prominence is that it has generally been read, understandably, as one of the earliest self-representations *of* that period as an entity unto itself, that is of the period as a historical movement or normative system of a certain kind. What lends further interest to the passage is that it is one of the first meditations in English on the problem of the period as defined by a political or aesthetic movement or as constituting a normative system. The issue Shelley addresses stems from his sense that his, indeed, 'will be a memorable age in intellectual achievements', and that he and his contemporaries 'live among such philosophers and poets as surpass beyond comparison any who have appeared since the last national struggle for civil and religious liberty'. In certain 'periods', he writes, 'there is an accumulation of the power of commemorating and receiving intense and impassioned conceptions respecting men and nature'. Great writers are 'compelled to serve' this power even while they 'deny and abjure' it: 'They measure the circumference and sound the depths of human nature with a comprehensive and all-penetrating spirit and are themselves perhaps the most sincerely astonished at its manifestations, for it is less their spirit than the spirit of the age.' At least part of Shelley's claim here seems to be that, given a certain understanding of the relation between historical movements and literary production, writers themselves cannot be expected to know the most important moral and political implications of what it is that they are writing—not even great writers, *especially* not great writers. The greatest writers of an age are going to be to some extent unconscious of the tendencies of their inspiration, and the reason given for this is that this inspiration itself exists on a higher level of historical generality than they can, in any final sense, comprehend.

Shelley did not originally compose this passage for the place it came to occupy in *A Defence of Poetry*, but rather for a quasi-Benthamite pamphlet that he began in late 1819: *A Philosophical View of Reform*. This pamphlet, in which Shelley argues for reform not only as a moral but also as a historical necessity, was written in the wake of the Peterloo massacre. Much of Shelley's language in this pamphlet, including the paragraph later cannibalized for the *Defence*, derives demonstrably from the idiom of the radical reform movement. On 19 September, after Henry *Hunt was received in triumph through the streets of London to stand trial for his role in the Peterloo Manchester affair, he stopped in the Strand to address a crowd that contemporary estimates put at 300,000 people. Hunt is recorded as having included in his address the following remark, which interestingly anticipates Shelley's comment on the spirit of the age: 'Gentlemen, the conduct and patriotism you have evinced this day is not altogether your own. It is but a part of that glorious feeling which runs through every breast, and animates the mind of the population of those districts from which I came.' This idiom appears in many different kinds of writing by Shelley in this period. In October he would compose perhaps his greatest lyric addressed to just this theme, 'Ode to the West Wind', in which the poet-speaker describes the historical movement that animates his own poetic lyre and spreads his words like so many ashes and sparks among mankind. In December, in the sonnet tellingly titled 'England in 1819', he would write about the 'glorious phantom' that would burst forth to 'illumine our tempestuous day'.

One of the conditions that makes it plausible for either Shelley or Hunt to refer to a glorious feeling or phantom of the moment, a spirit of the time in the nation at large, is the increasing regularity and pervasiveness of the public press. Peterloo could become so massive a *cause célèbre* in 1819 partly because it was 'covered' by reporters from three daily *newspapers, including *The Times*, which published accounts of the atrocities that were mutually corroborating and widely circulated. Like other protests in the months and years preceding it— Spa Fields in 1816 or Stockton in 1819—Peterloo thus amplified the experience of historical simultaneity: the simultaneous experiences of people assembled in mass demonstration were augmented by the simultaneous experiences of readers reading accounts of such demonstrations in their morning newspapers. When the British parliament passed its draconian legislation, the Six Acts, in response to Peterloo and its aftermath, it addressed both kinds of representational practices—the assembly and the account of the assembly—with equally vindictive measures [see *gagging acts].

The discussion of the 'spirit of the age' in the new historicism of our period, then, is to be understood as a function of the way time and spirit are increasingly, through the developing public sphere of eighteenth-century letters, periodized by periodical publication. In eighteenth-century Britain the history of the periodical forms an important part in any account of the periodization of history. Founded in 1731 as a monthly digest of materials from the weeklies, the *Gentleman's Magazine* added an index of the entire year for the assembled issues that made up the 1732 volume. Then, in 1735, it added its annual Supplement, which offered an 'Account of the Proceedings and Debates in the last Session of Parliament concluded'. The content of such reportage was extended dramatically in a new project begun in 1758 by Edmund *Burke, in collaboration with Robert Dodsley (1703–64). The first publication in this series is called *The Annual Register: Or a View of the History, Politics, and Literature of the Year 1758*. Here the publication of all the numbers of a given year gathered into a single volume appears as a new edition, and each passing new year produces a new volume in the series with a new dated title. The distinction is a rich one when we apply it to the ensuing debate on the reform of the British *constitution. It might not be wildly amiss to allegorize the debate between Burke and *Paine, on the question of annual parliaments and the concept of generations, in terms of the difference between a newly titled annual representation of the nation (Paine) and a new annual edition of a national representation bearing the same exact title as the year before (Burke).

Another important institutional use of the word 'spirit', not in the phrase 'spirit of the age', but still, as it were, in an epoch-making context, occurred in a series very much in keeping with the form of the *Annual Register*. This one was begun in the year 1798, and was entitled *Spirit of the Public Journals for 1797* and so on into the 1820s. Here the notion of a spirit of an age and a 'state of the nation' converge in the regularized time of the periodical press. When Shelley composed 'England in 1819' in the closing days of that tumultuous year, he sent it off to Leigh *Hunt, editor of the *Examiner*, with an exhortation to Hunt to write 'a paper on the actual state of the country, and what, under all the circumstances of the conflicting passions and interests of men, we are to expect'. In urging this exercise on Hunt, Shelley seems in fact to be invoking, though he does not explicitly mention it, a bold prediction that was made in the first week of 1819, when, in the initial *Examiner* for the year, writing under the editorial rubric 'The State of the World', Hunt had announced: 'This is the commencement, if we are not much mistaken, of one of the most important years that have been seen for a long while . . . [for] a spirit is abroad.'

Literary representations of the state of the nation become a way of making history in two senses: the construction in letters of a historically determined picture of things, on the one hand, and the influence on the course of events by the very act of making such a construction. Precisely because this kind of activity was regarded as so potent, it was jealously defended as a male prerogative. The case of Anna Laetitia *Barbauld illustrates this point. In 1812 she published a quarto volume comprising a single poem, 'Eighteen Hundred and Eleven', representing the state of England in the present year and criticizing some of its military policies in respect to France and America. Among its satirical strategies we find one, anticipating Shelley's *Peter Bell the Third* (1819) by several years, in which the narrator imagines London as an ancient city, already in ruin, and now become a tourist site for visitors from North America to survey and evaluate. This volume was so aggressively attacked by John Wilson Croker (1780–1857) in the Tory *Quarterly Review* that Barbauld never published again. Croker's attack commenced with the very idea of giving the poem a date for a title: 'We do not, we confess, very satisfactorily comprehend the meaning of all the verses which this fatidical spinster has drawn from her poetical distaff; but of what we do understand we very confidently assert that there is not a topic in "Eighteen Hundred and Eleven" which is not quite as applicable to 1810 or 1812.' For Croker, Barbauld's failure to understand dates—their uses and their specificity—is a symptom of the larger error implicit in her ambition to write, even to make, history. Her taking up public satire, with its interest in historical topicalities and practical aims, created a mismatch of gender and genre: 'We had hoped', Croker writes, 'that the empire might have been saved without the intervention of a lady-author.'

There is, however, an important coda to this unseemly episode. Though Barbauld did not publish after the event, she did continue to write in those years, and some of these writings were collected in a posthumous volume entitled *A Legacy for Young Ladies* (1826). The most substantial piece in the volume is a protracted four-part essay in epistolary form entitled 'The Uses of History'. Though the evidence is inconclusive, the essay can plausibly be read as Barbauld's reply to Croker's charge that women had no place in writing about historical affairs. Her explicit aim is to explain to her fictional correspondent, young Lydia, just what kind of knowledge is required to turn the study of history from an affair of mere 'adventure', as it must first appear to a young girl in her innocence, into something more serious and substantial. By spelling out the legacy of historiography for a young woman, Barbauld makes explicit some of the tacit assumptions that underlie this predominantly male enterprise.

Barbauld identifies 'geography and chronology' as the 'two eyes of history', and insists that by their means one should be able to envision what she calls 'the state of the world at different periods of society and improvement' and eventually to 'grasp the measured distances of time and space which are set between them'. Because of Barbauld's particular conception of social development in relation to general history—one which has to do with what she earlier calls relation between 'different periods of society and improvement', on the one hand, and 'the state of the world', on the other—she is committed to the view that general chronology is crucial to the understanding of any given national development. It is not just, as she says, that it 'may be desirable to keep one kingdom as a meter for the rest'; it is rather a matter of mutual illumination. As she puts it in her most forceful and revealing formulation: 'You do not see truly what the Greeks were, except you know that the British Isles were then barbarous.' 'The Uses of History' is Barbauld's attempt to explain to the Crokers of the world all that they failed to comprehend in her performance of 1811. Thus, the survey of Britain in 1811 retains a sense of the meaning of the date for other cultures as well. The poem makes Britain a 'meter for the rest', and at the same time measures the British achievement in the context of the state of development or decay among other nations of the world—as if to say that you cannot see what the British were in 1811 except you know that Greece was then in slavery to the Turks, the United States on a steep economic ascendancy, and the unliberated nations of the Americas on the verge (some of them) of rising up to assert their independence.

Barbauld's exposition of the uses of history in her time suggests a view of the relationship between ethnography and historiography which is, even on her own subsequent account, a relatively new development. It is a view that was systematized in the writings of the *Scottish Enlightenment, which were being circulated more widely than ever by proselytizing efforts such as those of Barbauld's friend Dugald *Stewart. Crucial to this new methodology is a dialectical sense of periodization in which particular 'societies' or 'nations', newly theorized as such by just these writers, are recognized as existing in 'states' that belong at once to two different and to some extent competing orders of temporality [see *exploration, 37]. On the one hand, each society is theorized as moving through a series of stages sequenced in an order that is more or less autonomous and stable. Insofar as the stages are also 'ages', these sequencings can be said to constitute temporal orders. On the other hand, this same historiographical discourse always implies as well a second temporality, which is the temporality in which these different national times can be correlated and calendrically dated in respect to each other.

53. *Boadicea, the British Queen* engraved by William Sharp after Thomas Stothard, 1812. The Romantic age turned increasingly to ancient British and pre-classical figures such as Queen Boadicea or King Alfred as the subject-matter for national histories.

Depending on the writer, this larger order might or might not be taken as having its own development sequence. Rates of historical change are measurable by comparing the progress of different societies with one another, and are to some degree explicable by relating the state of a society to the 'state of the world' at that same moment. To locate a given state of society within a given state of the world is to establish its age or epoch in the most complete sense, and thus to establish the most thorough understanding of it as a culture or a historical situation for the actions of those who inhabit it.

The relational paradigm I am describing abstractly here can be briefly illustrated by John *Millar's early study of class and gender, *The Origin of the Distinction of Ranks* (1771). When Millar discusses the 'state' of some society, he normally locates that state, explicitly or implicitly, in a sequence of the sort: barbaric, pastoral, agricultural, commercial. Each state has its attendant 'systems of manners', in a way that Hume had already begun to elaborate in his *History of Great Britain*. Millar is also concerned, however, with the larger state of things in which the society's successive cultural states are related. The relationship proves a crucial one in Millar, though it is not always explicit. Consider how it works, for example, in the following sentence from Millar's introduction: 'When we survey the present state of the globe, we find that, in many parts of it, the inhabitants are so destitute of culture, as to appear little above the condition of brute animals; and even when we peruse the remote history of polished nations, we have seldom any difficulty in tracing them to a state of the same rudeness and barbarism.' In such a framework one can describe peoples of two different historical moments as belonging to the same state of civilization: in this case the same state of 'rudeness and barbarism'.

It none the less remains true that being in the state of barbarism in the present 'state of the globe' and being in the state of barbarism in some past 'state of the globe' will not be quite 'the same', in Millar's analysis, because of the different global circumstances of such states of a nation. In social theory such as Millar's we have the basis for what Marx will come to call the principle of 'uneven development'. It is the same principle that Leon Trotsky famously used in *The History of the Russian Revolution* to explain how it was that the most 'backward' country in Europe managed successfully to stage the world's first proletarian revolution in 1917. Long before Trotsky or even Marx himself took it up, however, the Scottish Enlightenment principle of uneven development became the basis not only of the practice of writers such as Barbauld and Shelley but also of the most popular and widely imitated new form of historiographical practice in post-Waterloo literary culture, Walter *Scott's Waverley novels.

In these works, one can see how the dialectics of uneven development and the notion of a homogeneous empty time may be said to go hand in hand. That the logic of uneven development had indeed structured Scott's fiction from his first great experiment had been acknowledged in the final chapter of *Waverley* (1814), 'A Postscript, Which Should Have Been a Preface', where Scott attempts to situate his project in Scottish intellectual and material history:

There is no European nation which, within the course of half a century, or little more, has undergone so complete a change as this kingdom of Scotland. The effects of the insurrection of 1745—the destruction of the patriarchal power of the Highland chiefs—the abolition of the heritable jurisdictions of the Lowland nobility and barons—the total eradication of the Jacobite party, which, averse to intermingle with the English, or adopt their customs, long continued to pride themselves upon maintaining ancient Scottish manners and customs—commenced this innovation. The gradual influx of wealth, and extension of commerce, have since united to render the present people of Scotland a class of beings as different from their grandfathers as the existing English are from those of Queen Elizabeth's time.

'Queen Elizabeth's time' is comprehended within the time of England, whose headlong progress through the stages or states of society had until the eighteenth century been unrivalled in Europe, but which has now been outstripped by the acceleration of Scottish time in the century since the Union. In Scott's reckoning the time of Scotland, at least in the period we date to the eighteenth century, moves faster than the time of England by a ratio of more than a century to a generation—Elizabeth reigned from 1558 to 1603, and Scott follows the recently standardized sense of a generation as thirty years: the generation of the grandfathers is that of 1745, as Scott stresses in the subtitle of *Waverley*: '''Tis Sixty Years of Since'. The calendrical chronology—'1745', 'the last twenty or twenty-five years of the eighteenth century', '1805' (the date, as Scott later stipulates, on which he began the novel)—functions as the medium in which these different times-in-temporalities can been merged in a yet higher-order calculus.

To complete this survey of Romantic historicism in Britain, it remains only to say something about the attendant anxiety about cultural anachronism. When Scott takes up *Ivanhoe* (1819), his first historical novel not on a Scottish subject, he again addresses himself to the chronological coding of uneven development, declaring that in order to find a state of society in English history equivalent to the earliest he had described in Scotland, he found himself having to go back to the twelfth century. He also, however, expresses his concern over cultural projection from the norms of his own present culture onto the past on which he was writing. Shelley, writing independently of *Ivanhoe*, but not of Scott's influence more generally, expressed a similar anxiety in the Preface to his play *The Cenci* (1819). 'I have endeavoured as nearly as possible', he says, 'to represent the characters as they probably were, and have sought to avoid the error of making them actuated by my own conceptions of right and wrong, false or true, thus under a thin veil converting the names and actions of the sixteenth century into cold impersonations of my own mind.' Shelley's phrase 'the sixteenth century' identifies a historical culture in which norms are understood to be, at least to some degree, sufficiently different from those of his own time as to block any simple 'conversion' of the one into the other.

We must not fail to recognize that, along with their concern for cultural anachronism, both Shelley's play and Scott's fiction show a particular fascination with the history of casuistry and the concept of the moral case. In this conjunction lies a further line of enquiry into the question of how it is that Mill could insist on his age's general contemporary preoccupation with the comparison of itself with other ages. To accept the view that human character is profoundly conditioned by the state of society in which it matures is to understand that moral cases need to be framed not only in relation to situations understood by kind ('a case of self-defense') but also in relation to situations understood by state, or date, or epoch: Roman Catholics of the late sixteenth century such as the Cenci family in Shelley's historical drama, or Scottish Cameronians of the 1730s such as the Deans family in Scott's *The Heart of Midlothian* (1818). The question of cultural anachronism belongs, in short, to the larger problem of historically relativizing pressures in moral discourse, and to the Romantic invention of what we now commonly refer to as 'the historical situation'.

Arendt, H., *On Revolution*, New York, 1963; Chandler, J., *England in 1819: The Politics of Literary Culture and the Case of Romantic Historicism*, Chicago, 1996; Collingwood, R. G., *The Idea of History*, Oxford, 1946; Culler, A. D., *The Victorian Mirror of History*, New Haven, Conn., 1985; Foucault, M., *The Order of Things: An Archaeology of the Human Sciences*, New York, 1970; Gearhart, S., *The Open Boundary Between History and Fiction: A Critical Approach to the French Enlightenment*, Princeton, NJ, 1984; Koselleck, R., *Futures Past: On the Semantics of Historical Time*, Cambridge, 1985; Meinecke, F., *Historicism: The Rise of a New Historical Outlook*, trans. J. E. Anderson, London, 1972; Siskin, C., *The Historicity of Romantic Discourse*, New York, 1988.

39 · PSYCHOLOGY   ROBERT BROWN

In our period 'psychology' did not refer to an established science and its practitioners, but to a wide variety of topics concerning mental life that engaged the attention of educated people. Referring to the study of the soul, the term was known on the Continent in the mid-seventeenth century, and was used by David Hartley (1705–57) in his *Observations on Man* (1749). Hartley was one of the earliest proponents in England of a physiological psychology that was based on the twin doctrines of particle vibrations within the nerves and the resultant mental association of ideas [see *sensibility, 11]. But although the word 'psychology' was in use in Britain by the end of the century, it did not refer to a specific professional discipline. What then came to occupy the attention of various groups of professional people was the struggle to describe the form such a discipline might take. Would a science of mind consist, for the most part, in conceptual analysis, or would it be empirical? Would it be purely observational, based on the study of people's behaviour, or would it rely on self-observation and introspection alone? Could it be truly experimental as physiology seemed likely to become, and as physics and *chemistry already were? Above all, could a science of psychology develop the power to direct and change people's mental abilities, their attitudes, thoughts, and emotions—and so heal the mentally ill and cure the mentally defective? Was human nature sufficiently malleable for *education [17] to improve it greatly? These were the sorts of issues that were entwined in contemporary attempts to characterize a future discipline of psychology—if there was to be one.

Four groups of people were interested in discussing the topic in public: *physicians and scientists, who did physiological research; religious spokesmen, who were charged with the care of the souls of their congregations; philosophers, concerned with the description, analysis, and explanation of mental concepts, especially those bearing on free will and responsibility; and the mind-doctors who in considerable numbers treated the mentally disturbed [see *medicine, 18]. The first group contributed a diverse body of physico-mental speculation, notably physiognomical ideas through the widely read essays of Johann Kaspar Lavater (1741–1801), neurological theory through the treatises of Edinburgh physician Robert Whytt (1714–66), mesmerism through the British disciples of Frantz Anton Mesmer (1734–1815) [see *animal magnetism], and a lively cult of craniology or *phrenology through the lectures and demonstrations of Johann Caspar Spurzheim (1776–1832) and Franz Joseph Gall (1758–1828). Religious spokesmen and philosophers overlapped both in the offices that they held and in the problems that engaged their attention: the latter encompassed the epistemological grapplings of associationists inspired by *Locke and Hartley, by educational debates over the legitimacy of the environmentalist claims of *Rousseau, by a rich vein of early anthropological thought stimulated by the supposed social and mental interactions of primitive peoples abroad [see *exploration, 37], and by theories on the links between *language [40] and mind advanced through influential writings by James *Burnett, John Horne *Tooke, and others.

The position of the last group, the mind-doctors, was somewhat different. They were committed to influencing their patients' minds both by treating their bodies with physical procedures and by other means. Psychological speculation might contribute to the explanation of mental illnesses but it was not a substitute for medical, or any other, therapy [see *madness]. However, psychological techniques, as distinct from mere speculation, were often used to dominate the patients and sometimes to comfort them. Yet, in the extensive modern literature that deals with the history of mental illness, its *madhouses, its therapies, and the absence of medical education in universities and hospitals for mind-doctors until the latter half of the nineteenth century, there is little evidence that the medical practitioners of the period, despite their best efforts, actually contributed much to genuine psychological investigation. Some of them learnt how to manage patients non-punitively so as not to harm their prospects for spontaneous recovery. Some of the doctors were shrewd observers of psychiatric symptoms without being able to arrive at a helpful nosology—a classification of diseases that would distinguish different kinds of mental illness. But the powerful sense of the importance of the non-rationality of the depths and privacy of the human self, a sense that was so distinctive a contribution of the Romantic period, was neither successfully examined nor plausibly explained by the mind-doctors. It was left to writers of fiction and poetry in the period to describe and exhibit these aspects, and to much later psychiatrists and psychologists to try to give plausible explanations.

Beliefs that are both socially important and extensively ramified within a society do not often give way immediately to their successors. The process of replacement is usually prolonged, and the old and new beliefs commonly compete with each other for some lengthy period. We see, for example, the growth of interest by such writers as William *Blake, William *Hazlitt, Thomas *De Quincey, and earlier by Edward Young (1683–1765), in the strange, bizarre, mysterious, or unconscious aspects of mental life, and also in the emphasis that should be given to the unique character of each person. For the attention paid to these features was in competition with that previously enjoyed in the seventeenth and eighteenth centuries by the belief in the constancy of human nature—the view that human nature, and especially human reason, is

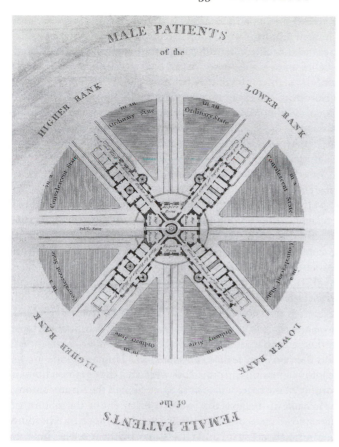

54. Plan of the Glasgow Lunatic Asylum by William Stark, from his *Remarks on Public Hospitals for the Cure of Mental Derangement* (1807). Considered the first madhouse in Britain to be built on a radiating axis, Stark's asylum made provisions for segregation and surveillance that reflected a new belief in the potential reform of patients, drawing on Jeremy Bentham's Panoptic theories about the malleability of human behaviour.

everywhere the same. David *Hume subscribed to this opinion in *An Enquiry Concerning Human Understanding* (1748), claiming in a well-known passage in section VIII: 'It is universally acknowledged that there is a great uniformity among the actions of men, in all nations and ages, and that human nature remains still the same, in its principles and operations.' William *Wordsworth agreed, giving to the poet an enhanced status as interpreter of this uniformity. In the Preface to *Lyrical Ballads* (1800) he wrote: 'In spite of difference of soil and climate, of language and manners, of laws and customs . . . the Poet binds together by passion and knowledge the vast empire of human society, as it is spread over the whole earth, and over all time.' In France similar views were expressed by Fontenelle, Rousseau, and Voltaire. All these opinions had two dimensions. The first was the claim that human nature is uniform and has been so throughout history. The second was that the uniformity of human nature is universally admitted. Still, neither view went wholly unchallenged or unqualified. The uniformity of human nature was said by Scottish political economist Sir James Steuart Denham (1712–80), in the opening sentence of *An Enquiry into the Principles of Political Economy* (1767), to be nothing more than people at all times and places acting from expediency, self-interest, passion, or duty. In that respect humans were similar, but in 'nothing else'. In his *Supplement to Bougainville's Voyage* (written 1772, published 1796) Diderot expressed his opinion that human beings had in common only a similar physical structure, their needs, their pleasures, and their pains. In brief, the various accounts of the qualities which were said to identify basic human nature were not themselves uniform. Large portions of that nature seemed to be highly malleable.

The supposed universal acknowledgement of the constancy of human nature was similarly restricted in practice, although human uniformity had long been an article of Christian faith. The European expansion overseas in the sixteenth and seventeenth centuries had revealed great diversity of custom and belief among the newly discovered peoples, a diversity so disturbing that the intellectuals of the eighteenth century felt called upon to defend remote foreigners against the common European belief that they were not fully human. So Hume's claim that it was universally recognized that 'there is great uniformity among the actions of men' has to be qualified; for it was not universally acknowledged, even by Hume, that all foreigners were complete human beings. In 'Of National Characters' (1798), he wrote: 'I am apt to suspect the negroes to be naturally inferior to the whites. There scarcely ever was a civilized nation of that complexion, nor even any individual eminent either in action or speculation. No ingenious manufactures amongst them, no arts, no sciences.' Thus the belief in human uniformity was inherited by thinkers at the end of the eighteenth century in the form of a problem: how was uniformity related to the exploration of private sensibility, and to the cultivation of personal feelings and attitudes whose pattern was unique to each agent? That is, which psychological properties contributed the private person and which the public—and how were these properties to be identified? The principle of uniformity standardized mental life, but the cultivation of personal sensibility and imagination diversified it. Was agreement possible between two such different attitudes?

In his *Discourses* on art, delivered at the *Royal Academy in London between 1769 and 1790, Sir Joshua *Reynolds gave an answer to this question. Reason and imagination have equal authority, he said. Both are 'known and reasoned upon in the same manner, by an appeal to common sense deciding upon the common feelings of mankind'. Human minds are as uniform as human bodies. Since the imagination can only work with what the common human senses provide, the known uniformity of the latter will ensure agreement of the former among different people. Hence it is a mistake to believe that we can learn about the nature of imagination merely by examining our own 'sensations'. True, we can learn much by attending to our own motives and sentiments, for their causes and effects may be the same as those in other people. However, we can be certain of this only through observation and experience of the passions of many other minds. Without this, we know ourselves 'very imperfectly'. We must submit our own opinion to the 'public voice'. In addition, says Reynolds, we have a 'sagacity' which does not rely on slow deduction but arrives immediately at the conclusion. Often we cannot give a supporting reason for it because we cannot organize and remember all our considerations, for they may be the result of a lifetime of experience. Nevertheless, we ought to be governed by this ability, since, if we always waited upon theoretical deliberation before acting, life would be at a standstill. We ought not, therefore, distrust feeling and imagination 'in favour of narrow, partially confined, argumentative theories'. It is true that in the end we must rely on reason; but on any given occasion we need it to tell us when 'reason is to give way to feeling'.

In *Table Talk, or Original Essays* (1821–2) the radical William Hazlitt, though ordinarily a sharp critic of Reynolds's cultural edicts, suggested similarly that as a result of their accumulated experience, people possess 'a series of unpremeditated conclusions on almost all subjects', and that these conclusions are called 'common sense'. They are the outcome of the association of our ideas; our experience of one member of a series can make us recall any one of the others without our needing to repeat the entire chain. Thus a feeling of pain or pleasure, or a judgement concerning morality, can be instantly revived by some brief impression before we are able to recall the circumstances that produced the original feeling or judgement. Since these sudden revivals of ideas precede our ability to account for them, they appear fanciful, irrational, and mysterious. Nevertheless, says Hazlitt, unpremeditated conclusions are both explicable later and worthy of trust at the time. In practical affairs we must rely on them;

reasoned scrutiny can only follow where they lead. This is one illustration of the fact, as Hazlitt remarked in a later essay in *Table Talk*, that

Man is not a merely talking nor a merely reasoning animal. There are geniuses of action and not only geniuses of thought. We cannot always judge an action merely by the amount of thought that it displays. Fighting battles and leading campaigns, making tools, painting pictures, playing music—all these require judgement and competence, and in addition, qualities such as perseverance, courage, self-control, secrecy, observation of character, and strength of will. Legislators, explorers, inventors, heroes, and founders of religion are not less worthy than abstract thinkers simply because people of action use different 'faculties of the mind'.

In *Essays on the Intellectual Powers of Man* (1785) Thomas *Reid, professor of philosophy at the University of Glasgow, published some of the material on which he had been lecturing for many years. In essay 1, chapter VII, when discussing the common distinction between the exertion of will and the operation of the understanding, Reid maintained that the use of one always required the use of the other: 'The understanding is always more or less directed by the will.' So all intellectual operations—for example, reasoning and judging, hearing, and seeing—display some form of activity, for we can have control of our thoughts and direct our attention as we wish. Conversely, an act of will must incorporate an intellectual operation, since the object of the will 'must be apprehended or conceived in the understanding'. Reid concludes that 'in most, if not all operations of the mind, both faculties concur'. To suppose that there can be direct warfare between the two faculties, or that we can describe one independently of the other, is seriously to misconceive their relationship. Just as for Reynolds human reason and human imagination could only operate in tandem and thus constrain each other, so for Reid the human will and human 'contemplative powers' could not operate separately.

Reid went on in chapter VIII to draw attention to 'another division of the powers of the mind', one that by contrast he thought not only was genuine and important but presupposed the activity of both will and understanding. This was the distinction between the social and the solitary operations of the mind. A man can judge and reason, says Reid, 'though he should know of no intelligent being in the universe beside himself'. Yet when he gives testimony, receives information, asks a favour, gives a command, or makes a promise, he is engaging in an act of 'social intercourse' with other intelligent creatures in society. Without such intercourse a person would have no language, for the expression of 'social intellectual operations' appears in children before they can reason. Such expression is 'the primary and direct intention of language'. What follows, then, from Reid's view is that the cultivation of private feelings and attitudes by a person—the cultivation of solitary mental activity—can only take place because the person has already participated in, and learnt to conduct, social mental activity. Without the sociability of human nature, and the underlying constancy of social instinct, there could be no private exploration by people of their concealed or mysterious or strange inner life. Far from human sociability and privacy arising in opposition to each other, the latter could only develop after the former was successful. Self-questioning and interior monologue can only be learned by our first engaging in social conversation and social activity. The later Romantic belief that only in solitude are people fully themselves needs the qualification that only in society can people be educated for a solitary life.

Yet how then should the inner and private mental life be studied? Thomas Brown (1778–1820), professor of moral philosophy at the University of Edinburgh, gave a philosopher's answer in his *Lectures on the Philosophy of the Human Mind* (1820). The science of mind, he said, was intellectual analysis—the distinguishing by careful reflection of the constituent elements that make up the exceedingly complex thoughts, sensations, and emotions of our mental life. The peculiarity of reflective analysis, as compared to chemical analysis, is that the same mind is 'the subject of analysis, the instrument of analysis, and the analyzing inquirer'. An emotion, for example, can grow with time and assume a complex character that appears to bear no relation to the simple feelings in which it began. To trace that development accurately is to make a discovery about the mind. That would not be possible if everyone had 'equal knowledge' of the ways in which his or her mind worked. If we could discriminate at a glance all the different relations of our feelings and thoughts we should not be able, nor have any need, to make discoveries about our mental life. However, the question left unsettled by this claim of discovery was whether the method of investigation was in any respect like that of an empirical science. The procedure appeared to be conceptual analysis of the ordinary philosophical kind. Nevertheless, Brown treated the 'science of mental analysis' as strictly analogous to the science of chemistry—for each tries to reduce compound substances and processes to elementary ones—and Brown thus thought that conceptual analysis and empirical scientific analysis were simply the same method applied to two different materials. Hence philosophical and scientific procedure are much the same. On this view, the philosophy of mind and the psychology of mind would be identical. The phrase 'science of mind' would not distinguish between them. Yet because he did not distinguish between the aims and methods of natural science and those of philosophy, the supposed science that he actually practised and advocated was simply the epistemological branch of philosophy under another name.

The widespread confusion as to the possible character of a science of mind was both the cause and the effect of a similar confusion about the character of the laws of nature. In the eighteenth century, the phrase 'laws of nature' was often used by practitioners of philosophy, economics, and history in a double sense: both to refer to what they took to be the actual constraining principles of human behaviour and to evoke the universal principles of morality that were supposed, but often failed, to constrain the vagaries of that behaviour. Both sorts of principle were thought to be 'scientific' regulations, or laws, and so it was difficult to explain the conflict that constantly arose between them. For if the social behaviour of people is controlled by empirical laws that are strictly analogous to the empirical laws of chemistry or astronomy, then these behavioural laws may often prevent people from obeying the universal principles of morality—the principles by which we judge the behaviour of all societies and their members. On the other hand, should not our moral principles take notice of what has been learnt about the regularities of actual human behaviour? How were these two kinds of principle to be reconciled in one and the same science of mind? Until this question was answered satisfactorily, the field of psychology could not lay claim to its own subject-matter and methods.

Practitioners of *political economy [33] in the early nineteenth century wished to use economic knowledge for social ends. Jeremy *Bentham, James *Mill, Thomas *Malthus, David *Ricardo, John Ramsay McCulloch (1789–1864), and Nassau Senior (1790–1864), for example, all believed that the science of economics could be used to improve the management of considerable portions of social life and to eliminate its mismanagement. All made psychological assumptions about human behaviour and relied on them to support the arguments by which they developed their economic and social views. For example, in his Oxford lectures of 1826–7, Nassau Senior claimed that one of the general propositions on which political economy rests is that 'every person has some unsatisfied desires which he believes . . . additional wealth would gratify'. Wealth included not only things that are valuable, exchangeable, and in limited supply, but personal qualities such as good health and knowledge. Disturbing causes, of course, might prevent people from acting upon their desires. Other psychological assumptions commonly asserted included the universality of self-interest in social transactions, the malign effects on people of their being economically dependent on others, and the beneficial results of work being made a duty. Such assumptions were not critically examined by the political economists, but the more general question raised by David Hume earlier in the century— are general psychological propositions open to scientific scrutiny?—did re-emerge in 1804 in the *Edinburgh Review*. Francis *Jeffrey, the founding editor, reviewed Dugald *Stewart's book *Account and Writings of Thomas Reid* (1803) and criticized Stewart, the professor of moral philosophy at Edinburgh, for joining his teacher Reid in agreeing with the analysis of scientific induction given by Francis Bacon.

Stewart mistakenly believed, Jeffrey wrote, that there would be great benefit in 'applying to the science of mind those sound rules of experimental philosophy that have undoubtedly guided us to all the splendid improvements in modern physics'. This attempt, Jeffrey thought, would not succeed. Its supporters were misled by drawing a 'false analogy' between the science of mind and the sciences of physics and chemistry. Not much improvement could be expected in the science of mind from trying to adopt the 'plan of investigation' used in the physical sciences. For we have to distinguish between those fields in which we can conduct experiments and those in which we can only make observations. In physics, for example, we deal with substances that are under our control; the enquirer can arrange them so as 'to disclose their most hidden properties and relations'. On the other hand, in observational fields, such as in the science of mind, the substances that we study are beyond our control. We can only subject them to observation and 'collect and record the laws by which they appear to be governed'. The most intense observation will not allow us to manipulate mental events or processes nor thus to experiment on them. Yet it is only by experiment that we have obtained both scientific knowledge of the 'material universe' and the ability to exert power over it. Without the capacity to experiment, says Jeffrey, our causal knowledge must remain limited. The 'sound rules of experimental philosophy' that Bacon recommended are largely inapplicable to the purely observational sciences such as astronomy, *geology, and the moral sciences—of which psychology is one. Moreover, increasing the accuracy of our observation does not by itself add to our power to control what is observed. Even arranging our observational results more methodically will not increase our knowledge of those facts that we cannot modify artificially for experimental purposes.

In Jeffrey's view, the most important benefit conferred by the method of experiment is that in it our knowledge comes from the fact that the enquirers themselves distribute and arrange the conditions that produce the phenomena. This gives us sound knowledge of the causal conditions; but in mere observation we must usually conjecture about the causal role of events that it is beyond our power to influence. So when we remember or feel or perceive something, our mental operations take place by means outside our control. We can observe but not change them. Since all people are familiar with the mental operations common to human beings—such as believing, imagining, and sensing—and with 'almost all the laws by which they appear to be governed', it is not possible to discover new mental functions and laws. Although they may be described satisfactorily for the first time by some educated observer such as a philosopher, they themselves must already be familiar to every human being. Otherwise, their existence will not be admitted by the general public, and the observer will not be able to rely for descriptive purposes on prior acquaintance with his own feelings, memories, perceptions, and thoughts. It is only because his mental capacities are similar to those of people in general that they will be willing to accept his account of mental functions and laws.

To Jeffrey philosophers should be cartographers or grammarians, not chemists, of mental life:

We acquire a perfect knowledge of our own minds without study or exertion, just as we acquire a perfect knowledge of our native language or our native parish; yet we cannot, without much study and reflection, compose a grammar of the one, or a map of the other.

Philosophers who become satisfactory cartographers of mental operations simply reorganize the information that we already possess. In that respect they resemble grammarians of our native language and the makers of our parish maps. What all three provide us with are the means for us to rearrange our ideas in a more methodical fashion. Still, in doing this we only come to think more adequately about what we knew earlier. No amount of scientific experimentation can change this fact.

In 1810, six years after these criticisms appeared, Stewart replied to them in his new volume, *Philosophical Essays*. Once again Jeffrey reviewed it critically, and took the basic question under discussion still to be whether the experimental procedures of the natural sciences could be applied profitably to the moral sciences—to political economy, politics, ethics, and psychology. Stewart began his reply to Jeffrey by agreeing with him that an observational science such as astronomy gave us no direct—that is mechanical—control over its phenomena. Indirectly, however, astronomy had given us control over some phenomena on earth, and had done so by the use of physical theories that explained events both on earth and in the heavens. Moreover, even if all our information about mental processes came from observation alone, it would not follow that the information would be less useful than if it were derived from experiment. In any case, Stewart says, it is not true that the science of mind cannot employ experiments. Bishop George Berkeley's (1685–1753) theory of vision, for example, describes the way in which experience teaches us to judge the size and distance of objects. The theory tries, experimentally, to decompose our perceptions; and there are many other attempts of the same kind by different thinkers. In addition there are experimental investigations of the use of language, habit, imagination, and attention. 'The whole of a philosopher's life, indeed, if he spends it to any purpose, is one continued *series of experiments* on his own faculties and powers', Stewart argues. Similarly, our methods of education, the arrangements of different societies, the many distinct types of personality, the varied character of human religion, art, laws, and commerce—all these are experiments by the 'hand of Nature' for our instruction. We can use them to learn almost everything that we could discover by deliberate experiments of our own. So observation and experiment differ only nominally as 'sources of knowledge'.

Stewart goes on to reply to Jeffrey's claim that, because all people are familiar with the mental functions and abilities common to everyone, it is impossible for us to discover new functions as we can discover new chemical reactions. This conclusion, says Stewart, would apply with equal force to the sciences of matter. A person unfamiliar with *Newton's third law of motion applies it when he pushes his canoe away from the shore with a pole, or when using a slingshot he makes use of the notion of centrifugal forces. Even a horse circling the ring under the direction of a lunging-rein adapts the obliquity of its body with 'mathematical accuracy' to the rate of its speed. Despite all our familiarity with the practical applications of physical and chemical laws, it is still a valuable discovery when we learn to state them explicitly. Who would deny the power and utility of Newton's laws simply because illustrations of their theoretical applicability were long known in daily life? Stewart claimed that the same holds true of the science of mind and our daily application of its unstated laws.

At the centre of the exchange between Jeffrey and Stewart were different conceptions of scientific experiment and observation. As a consequence, they give differing answers to the two questions 'Can the science of introspection yield testable generalizations? Can the method of introspection be made into a discipline with the essential features of the physical sciences?' Stewart answers 'yes' because he takes scientific experiments to include both deliberate actions and mere examples of natural powers, including psychological ones. Jeffrey answers 'no' because he restricts experiment to deliberate arrangements that are not only impossible to use when introspection is employed, but unnecessary for discovering what is already known. Jeffrey also detaches the activity of observation from both experiment and theory, forgetting that one observation of an item often leads to another observation, that the agent may apply a theory to explain them, and that it in turn can be tested by new observations and experiments. Thus reflection on our mental operations can set this process of discovery in train, and Jeffrey was mistaken in denying it. However, neither he nor Stewart considered the problem of how the observations produced by introspecting were to become parts of theories that could themselves be tested by introspection—or by any other means. New theories create new subjects of consciousness for introspection and hence new ways of characterizing them. So for both men there remains the basic and difficult question of the nature of introspection: that is, whether it is intuitive and non-inferential knowledge of our minds, or of certain kinds of mental states, or of both, and what sorts of mental states and minds are introspectable.

Both Jeffrey and Stewart subscribed to an introspectionism that was embedded in much philosophical procedure during the seventeenth and eighteenth centuries. Thus in the *Leviathan* (1651) Thomas Hobbes writes of the counsel 'read thyself' that it tells us this: 'whosoever looketh into himself, and considereth what he doth, when he does *think, opine, reason, hope, fear &c.* and upon what grounds; he shall thereby read and know, what are the thoughts and passions of all other men upon the like occasions.' Hobbes concludes by writing that each man will have 'only to consider, if he also find not the same in himself. For this kind of doctrine admitteth no other demonstration.' Anyone who took this view to be a statement of fact, as Stewart, Jeffrey, and many others of their contemporaries did, was then faced with the apparent conclusion that belief in the introspective method would actually prevent the application to the 'science of mind' of those experimental procedures of the natural sciences that Stewart wished to adopt. The doctrine of introspectionism, as it then stood, seemed to be both a formidable barrier to the development of scientific psychology and its indispensable starting-point.

Figlio, K., 'Theories of Perception and the Physiology of the Mind in the Late 18th Century', *History of Science*, 8 (1975), 177–212; Porter, R., *Mind-Forg'd Manacles*, London, 1987; Reed, E. F., 'The Separation of Psychology from Philosophy', in C. L. Ten, ed., *The Nineteenth Century*, London, 1994; Richards, G., *Mental Machinery: The Origins and Consequence of Psychological Ideas*, i: 1600– *1850*, London, 1992; Rousseau, G. S., 'Psychology', in G. S. Rousseau & R. Porter, eds., *The Ferment of Knowledge: Studies in Eighteenth-Century Science*, Cambridge, 1980; Vidal, F., 'Psychology in the 18th Century: A View from Encyclopedias', *History of the Human Sciences*, 6 (1993), 89–119.

40 · LANGUAGE   JON MEE

As perhaps it always is, language in our period was taken to be a crucial index of individual, social, and national identity. Challenges to that identity were perceived as coming from many different sources in a rapidly changing society. English was increasingly being valued over the classical languages as a national treasure, though the possession of Latin and Greek remained important markers of gentility, but this development brought with it a desire to stabilize English itself into a standard or 'classical' form. Texts concerned with such issues became an important growth area in the eighteenth century's expanding *publishing [21] industry. Fewer than fifty writings on grammar, rhetoric, criticism, and linguistic theory seem to have been published between 1700 and 1750, but over 200 in the second half of the century. Many of these improving texts were directed at a genteel readership, especially gentlewomen, warning of the dangers of vulgarity. A smaller number were intended for the improvement of the middling sort, but most grammarians who were prepared to address this new readership insisted that it conform to the usage of the metropolitan élite. Not to use language in certain ways was to threaten the imagined community of the nation and to court exclusion from the public sphere of polite society.

In the eighteenth century, it was commonly believed that a nation's 'genius' could be discovered in the characteristics of its language and, conversely, that remedying defects or halting decay in the language could play its part in preserving or improving the condition of the nation. Anxieties about the proper performance of the language can be found in the new concern with sound, style, and elocution. A plethora of pronouncing dictionaries flooded the market after 1750. Thomas Sheridan (1719–88), perhaps the pre-eminent figure in the so-called 'elocution movement', was convinced that the standardization of English pronunciation was necessary to a nation that believed itself united as the 'subjects of the same king'. When Sheridan, himself an Irishman, expressed his concern over the linguistic unity of the King's subjects in 1762, English was not the only language of the kingdom. The last native speaker of Cornish is believed to have died in 1777, but Welsh remained the predominant language in Wales until the late nineteenth century. The *Act of Union with Ireland only added further complications to the language map of the British Isles, but throughout the eighteenth century it was Scotland which caused most anxiety. As they had for several centuries, Lowlanders for the most part spoke Scots, a cognate language with English, which allowed them to communicate easily with their neighbours in England's northern counties. Highlanders, who more often spoke Gaelic, were unlikely to make a distinction between Scots and English speakers, and for most of the eighteenth century the Gaelic term 'Sassenach' was applied equally to both.

Notwithstanding the efforts of antiquarians, who in their different ways celebrated the ancient authority of the Gaelic, Irish, and Welsh tongues, in Ireland and Scotland at least strong cultural and economic pressures drove the populations towards the acquisition of English. Even Daniel *O'Connell, an Irish-speaking Catholic, believed that 'the superior utility of the English tongue, as the medium of all modern communication, is so great, that I can witness without a sigh the gradual disuse of the Irish' [see *Irish cultural revival]. In Scotland similar pressures had been leading not only to the devaluation of Gaelic but also to a desire to make Scots indistinguishable from the polite forms of metropolitan English. After the Union of 1707 those Scots eager to redefine themselves as Britons sought to excise so-called 'scotticisms' from their speech and, especially, their writing. Henry Home (1696–1782), Lord Kames, spoke Scots but encouraged the Scottish to use English in his *Elements of Criticism* (1762). Along with many other luminaries of the *Scottish Enlightenment, Kames subscribed to Thomas Sheridan's *Course of Lectures on Elocution*, delivered in 1761 to an Edinburgh audience anxious 'to cure themselves of a provincial or vicious pronunciation'.

Sheridan believed that 'even in England itself for want of such a method, there were such various dialects spoken, that persons born and bred in different shires, could scarcely any more understand each others speech, than they could that of a foreigner'. Quite apart from the issue of regional dialects, literacy was one of the important ways in which the language community within England itself was divided. The best available evidence suggests that while around 70 per cent of English men and 90 per cent of English women could not write their own names in the mid-seventeenth century, by the middle of the next century the figures had changed to 40 per cent and just over 60 per cent. On the basis of material drawn from the signatures required by Hardwick's Marriage Act (1753), literacy seems to have stagnated at around these levels for the next century or so.

However, the figures must be treated warily. First, there is the question of what 'literate' means. In the eighteenth century the term 'literacy' was continuing a process of evolution which was taking it away from the medieval association with the possession of Latin towards a broader definition based on the ability to read and write. Even so, there was no consensus as to what level of ability qualified as literacy. The evidence of the marriage registers as to who could sign their name does not tell us who had a practical proficiency in writing. Moreover, the writing skills of the tradesman might stop well short, for instance, of the expressive usage of the gentleman. Nor does the evidence take account of the potential gap between reading and writing, skills that were not always taught together, especially not to girls, who might only encounter writing as an optional extra [see *female education]. Only in the nineteenth century, when the two skills were more often taught together, does the gap between male and female statistics close. Second, the statistics mask social and geographical variations. The urban population became increasingly literate, for instance, while the rural population seems to have fallen back, although it should not be assumed that the inability to read and write was necessarily experienced as a handicap in communities where scriveners could often be found to provide for the needs of their illiterate peers. William *Cobbett pointed out as late as 1831, in *A Spelling Book with Appropriate Lessons in Reading*, that 'great numbers of people are very clever at their different trades, and earn a great deal of money, and bring up their families very well, without even knowing how to read'. Yet oral and literary cultures were in no way definitively cut off from each other. Books could be read aloud to groups, as proclamations often were in public places, while *ballads from the oral tradition could draw on printed sources, themselves often collected from itinerant singers. *Popular culture [23] took both oral and printed forms throughout the period. Attitudes to whether mass literacy was desirable or not varied greatly, especially in the wake of the *French Revolution. For some commentators a literate population produced the threat of a revolutionary mass political moment. Some anti-Jacobin writers such as T. J. *Mathias believed that Thomas *Paine's *Rights of Man* (1791) had not just spread subversion but also a dangerous literacy, whereas Hannah *More believed that reading, properly monitored, would provide a channel through which the antidotes of *religion [10] and morals could be administered.

The spectre of an increasingly literate population, whether real or imagined, desirable or undesirable, helps explain the urgency of debates from the middle of the eighteenth century about what constituted 'correct' English. While much of this writing was unapologetically prescriptive, it usually deferred to Horace's maxim 'use is the sole arbiter and norm of speech'. 'Usage' itself, however, was not an uncontested term, and frequent parallels were drawn with arguments over the definition of 'the people' in constitutional debates [see *class, 15]. The *locus classicus* for the analogy drawn between the state of the language and the state of the constitution was the third book of *Locke's *Essay concerning Human Understanding* (1690). The theory of language set out in this work, no less than Locke's constitutional theory, had the notion of 'consent' at its basis. Locke argued that words were not the signs of things but of ideas. These signs were not naturally tied to their meanings. Language, according to Locke, is a social compact—the product of an agreement that words should denote certain ideas. Consequently, grammar was the product not of what ought to apply rationally, so-called 'analogy', but of customary practice. However, this emphasis begged the question of exactly whose practice was designated as customary, just as Locke's theory of government raised the issue of exactly whose consent was necessary for constitutional rule. Locke's discussion of 'common usage' made it possible to argue that the usage of the vulgar could have no part in determining common standards.

The importance of 'common usage', based on the authority of Locke, frequently coalesced with the idea that the language was a reflection of the national genius of the English people. The freeborn Englishman was widely held to have a peculiar predisposition to liberty. A similar notion of the national genius was said to underpin the perceived irregularity of the English tongue, though by no means all writers viewed the perception positively. Robert Lowth (1710–87), in his *Short Introduction to English Grammar* (1762), made a distinction between 'practice', which 'oftentimes offends against every part of Grammar', and the true 'nature' of the language. 'Practice' here comprised even 'the English Language as it is spoken by the politest part of the nation, and as it stands in the writing of our most approved authors'. Appearing in twenty-two editions before 1795 alone, the book's grammar was perhaps the most influential of the eighteenth century (its impact endured well into the nineteenth century through the in-corporation of much of its detail and approach into Lindley Murray's (1745–1826) grammar discussed below). Yet despite its popularity as a practical grammar, Lowth's theoretical distinction between 'practice' and the true 'nature' of the language was already sounding rather old-fashioned. Lowth's philosophy of language was derived from James Harris (1709–80), who regarded languages as manifestations of a universal grammar. This universal grammar was taken to have its basis in pure acts of mind, although in practice the classical languages were taken to offer the best available model for it. However, by 1776 grammarians such as George Campbell (1719–96) could bluntly say: 'there cannot be such a thing as an universal grammar, unless there were such a thing as an universal language.' Correctness was increasingly seen as a matter of faithfulness to the peculiar idioms of English, rather than to the authority of a uni-versal grammar. Nevertheless, most writers on language agreed that the usage of only the most polite sections of society could serve as a model, and appeals to common usage usually took a very restricted definition of what 'customary' meant: as Campbell claimed, the

tattle of children hath a currency, but, however universal their manner of corrupting words may be among themselves, it can never establish what is accounted use in language. Now, what children are to men, that precisely the ignorant are to the knowing.

Hundreds of dictionaries and grammars insisted that the 'customary' language of the metrop-olis, usually manifested in the best authors, was the true standard of common usage. Usually 'customary language' did not refer to contemporary writing or speech, nor was it too archaic. Campbell identified 'reputable custom' with the writing of the period after the *Glorious Revolution of 1688 and prior to any living author; Queen Anne's reign was a more general favourite, but the underlying principle was common to most late-eighteenth-century writers on language.

It was a principle given a particularly powerful and influential form in the middle of the century by Samuel *Johnson's *Dictionary of the English Language* (1755). Johnson's use of literary illustrations implied that a native English tradition should determine correct usage. In practice these authorities were mainly drawn from the literature of the previous century, a third of them from the works of *Shakespeare, *Milton, and Dryden alone, which Johnson regarded as 'the wells of English undefiled'. Where the French academies attempted to regulate lan-guage by means of rational principles, Johnson conformed to 'the spirit of English liberty' by offering the models of great minds expressing the nation's genius. Nevertheless, Johnson's appeal to custom invoked a specific understanding of usage in which the need to escape foreign imports and local peculiarities of speech was emphatically linked to the need to avoid the 'fugi-tive cant, which is always in a state of increase or decay'. The model speaker was a gentleman, a man with a classical education, whose reading was informed by a knowledge of the 'best' English writers and whose private income and stake in the land could guarantee that his lan-guage was not infected by idiosyncrasies related to fashionable taste, the pursuit of a particular trade, or confinement to a particular locality. Originally, in the *Plan of a Dictionary* (1747), Johnson had seemed confident of his ability 'to fix the English language'. The completed pro-ject is presented with a more melancholy air which mourns the inevitability of change in a living language. Nevertheless, Johnson tried to slow the decay. Language was to be defended against both the unnatural changes of rationalizing reformers and the debasing corruptions of the lower classes. The *Dictionary* was to fix what was known so that common usage would become a matter of authoritative record rather than a matter of what people wrote or said. Just as Johnson's political pamphlets sought to safeguard English liberties by preserving existing constitutional arrangements, so too his *Dictionary* sought to oppose the permanent record of the English classics to 'the boundless chaos of a living speech'. Indeed, the parallel was made clear when he wrote that 'tongues, like governments, have a natural tendency to degeneration; we have long preserved our constitution; let us make some struggles for our language.'

Johnson's view that the language was permanently under threat from decay was widely shared. Corruption was identified, for instance, with servants who might introduce their fallen speech into the security of the nursery. For not dissimilar reasons, writings on correctness had long been directed at gentlewomen, who were seen as particularly liable to introduce imperfections. R. B. *Sheridan's comic character Mrs Malaprop, with her tendency to confuse similar-sounding words, is one of many literary examples from the eighteenth century of this kind of perception. The very first English dictionaries, published at the beginning of the previous century, had frequently been directed at young ladies in an attempt to regulate such errors. The attempt was to continue in the eighteenth century through books such as G. N. Ussher's *Elements of English Grammar* (1785), designed specifically for 'Ladies' Boarding Schools', although the task was not made too difficult: 'to render that study as easy and as useful to them as possible . . . all abstract terms that could be dispensed with, should be rejected; and all references to the learned languages omitted.' Writing in this vein frequently took Johnson's *Dictionary* as the definitive statement of customary usage which had to be defended against the encroachments of innovation and vulgarity. John Walker (1732–1807) wanted the language to 'remain as it stands at present [in 1775] in the monument of English philology erected by Johnson'. Walker was one of many in the elocution movement who presented himself as extending to pronunciation Johnson's success in providing a stabilizing authority for the language. His *Critical Pronouncing Dictionary* (1791) acknowledged the authority of custom, but followed Johnson and others in denying that custom was the same thing as 'the usage of the greater part of speakers'. No usage which 'is reprobated by the polite' was likely to be entertained at the beginning of the 1790s, a decade in which the relationship between language and politics became more explicit than ever before.

The vogue for 'unnecessary innovation' against which Walker was writing was associated with men like Joseph *Priestley, innovators in language as well as in politics. Priestley's approach to questions of correctness was a flexible one. He was prepared to appeal to rational analogy which would make the language consistent with itself in questions of disputed usage, although analogies with the classical languages were explicitly ruled out in his *Rudiments of English Grammar* (1768). But the final decision had to wait until 'all-governing custom shall declare in favour of the one or other'. Priestley's confidence in the rational evolution of human history meant that he assumed common usage would eventually come to disown irrational imperfections. As part of the collective effort towards creating this enlightened state, it was open to anyone to suggest improvements or alterations: 'it is vain to pretend that any person may not attempt to introduce whatever he thinks to be an improvement.' Priestley's desire for rational reform was always hedged about with a democratic spirit which insisted that the 'general prevailing custom, wherever it happens to be, can be the only standard for the time it prevails'. Its claim that the authority of 'custom' cannot reach beyond the grave offers an antidote to Johnson's conservatism, and anticipates Paine's rejection of *Burke's appeal to immemorial custom in defence of the constitution. Nevertheless even Priestley was willing to characterize certain kinds of usage as 'too low and vulgar'.

Collectors of popular antiquities, such as Francis *Grose, frequently offered a more spirited defence of class and regional dialects. Grose's *Classical Dictionary of the Vulgar Tongue* (1785) stands in direct, perhaps parodying, relationship to Johnson's *Dictionary*. Where Johnson saw the speech of the common people as 'fugitive' and not worthy of record, Grose celebrated that mutability as the product of English liberty, claiming that 'the freedom of thought and speech arising from, and privileged by our constitution, gives a force and poignancy to the expressions of our common people, not to be found under arbitrary governments'. Grose's use of the word 'classical' seems a deliberate challenge to Johnson's desire to find precedence only in high literary forms. Grose boasts that his examples 'have been drawn from the most classical authorities; such as soldiers on the long march, seamen at the cap-stern, ladies disposing of their fish . . . and the colloquies of the Gravesend-boat'. As a friend and patron of Robert *Burns, he was also active in encouraging kinds of cultural practice which refused to accept a narrow notion of correct usage. Grose's *antiquarianism [35] was part of a tradition which was to include figures like Francis *Douce, Joseph *Ritson, and William *Hone, and which sought to use its researches in offering a broader definition of the national language and culture. Others, such as Thomas *Spence, wished to reform the language in ways that would make it easier for the uneducated to participate in public affairs. Like Ritson, Spence wanted to reform spelling so that it was less mystifying to the unlearned. He believed that traditional orthography concealed 'the true pronunciation from all, except a few well-educated natives'. Spence played a committed part in the radical politics of the 1790s, publishing some of his pamphlets in his phonetic spelling system, and he was not alone in making language a political issue in that revolutionary decade and its aftermath. John *Thelwall's involvement in the elocution movement after 1800 and William Cobbett's interest in grammar had similar origins.

Perhaps the most influential of the radical critiques of linguistic ideas published at the end of the eighteenth century was John Horne *Tooke's Ἔπεα πτερόεντα, Or Diversions of Purley (1786–1805). Tooke's interest in language was explicitly bound up with his politics, reflecting an awareness of the way that language could be used to exert political control. His concern with theories of language had its immediate origin in his trial for seditious libel in 1777. His experience in the law courts convinced him that language was an important instrument through which the authority of the élite was maintained. Diversions sets itself up as an attack on what it refers to throughout as 'metaphysics', an attitude to language which Tooke identified with James Harris and James *Burnett, Lord Monboddo. The fundamental premise of the book was that parts of speech represented neither categories of things nor acts of minds. Ultimately Tooke traced all parts of speech to the noun and the verb. Nouns and verbs, the originals of all the parts of speech, did reflect mental acts in so far as they were the result of sense impressions, but with this change in perspective, language could be seen as the product of a material context. Where Burnett had claimed that language was the artificial construction of extraordinarily gifted individuals, versions of himself cast in primitive times, Tooke believed that 'artless men' had developed language. The Diversions abolished the distinction between a language of mind—associated with the classical educated élite—and the 'cant' which Johnson had argued was mired in the peculiarities of trade and region. Reinforcing Tooke's philosophical account of language was a historical insistence that Anglo-Saxon was the foundation of modern English. Where philosophers like Harris and Burnett wanted an English which reflected what they took to be the rational purity of a universal grammar derived by analogy from the classical languages, Tooke celebrated the Anglo-Saxon origins of English. The occlusion of these origins was for Tooke the linguistic equivalent of the Norman usurpation of ancient English liberties that was central to the radical political histories produced by Paine and other radicals [see *constitutionalism]. English as a language was effectively under the Norman yoke, and Tooke set out to free it by revealing its bases in the common language of the Anglo-Saxons.

Perhaps because of its often whimsical manner—its Greek title belying the English focus of much of its content—most reviewers chose to see the politics of Diversions as an unfortunate excrescence rather than as an essential part of the book's theory of language. By representing Tooke's dialogues as contributions to ideas about the philosophy of mind, the socio-political implications of their materialism could be played down by reviewers. From this perspective, even conservative reviews like the British Critic could paint Diversions in a positive light. An important exception to this response was Dugald *Stewart. For Stewart, etymology was a dangerous science when it insisted on the material basis of language. Where Tooke believed he could trace the development of words back to their Anglo-Saxon origins, Stewart insisted on

A S'UPL'IM'INT

Too thǐ Hǐſtǐre ǒv Rǒbǐnsǐn Kruzo, beǐng

TH'I H'IST'IRE 'OV KRUZONEA
ð.

R'OB'INS'IN KRUZO'z IL'IND,

Doun too thǐ prězǐnt Tim.

Kǒpeǐd frǒm' a Lětǐr ſěnt bǐ Mr Tǒmǐs Wǐſh-
ǐt, Kǎptǐn ǒv thǐ Good-'Intěnt, too ǎn' ǐǎtělǐ-
jǐnt Frěnd ǐn 'Inglǐnd, ǎftǐr beǐng ǐn a Stǒrm ǐn
Ma, 1781, drǐvǐn out ǒv hǐz Kǫrs too thǐ ſaḍ
Ilǐnd

Pǔblǐſhǐd bǐ thǐ ſaḍ Jěntǐlmǎn, fǒr thǐ agreǐ-
bǐl Pǐruzǐl ǒv Rǒbǐnsǐn Kruzo'z Frěndz ǒv aul
Sizǐz, ǎnd prǐntǐd ǐn thǐ

KRUZONE'IN M'AN'IR,

Thǐ 'Invěnſhǐn aul ǎdmir'd, ǎnd, ech, hǫu be
Too be thǐ 'Invěntǐr mǐs'd; ſo eze ǐt ſem'ḍ, ·
Wǒns found, whǐch yět ǔnfound moſt wǔd hǎv
'thaut 'Impǒſǐbǐl.
                              M'IL T'I N.

N U KAS'IL.
Prǐntǐd ǎnd ſold bǐ T. ṢANT, 1781,
Pris 6d.

55. Title-page to Thomas Spence's *A Supplement to the History of Robinson Crusoe* (1782). Spence's version of the island utopia has Europeans intermixing with natives and jointly abandoning private land ownership: he published some editions in his own idiosyncratic phonetic format designed to abolish the social barriers of contemporary English.

'the obscurity of their history'. Using a phrase resonant of the conservatism of both Johnson and Burke, Stewart argued that the authority of language consisted in 'the sanction of immemorial use'. Custom for Stewart was impervious to historical change.

Stewart was right to be nervous of *Diversions* in so far as it influenced a generation of radical writers about language. Perhaps the most lasting result of this influence is to be found in the writings of Noah Webster (1758–1843), which had a direct practical effect on the development of American English. Webster argued for the development of an American English that would be distinct from what he saw as the corrupted state of British English. Webster was one among many spelling reformers in the late eighteenth century who believed that orthography should have a clearer relation to pronunciation. He argued that the gap between written and spoken English was perpetuated and extended by writers like Johnson, who sought to keep knowledge in the hands of the élite. Compared to many of the other spelling reformers active in this period, Webster's changes were relatively modest—which may well account for his success in establishing 'honor', 'center', and 'defense' as standard spellings in American English. Webster justified such innovations as a return to a purer English, the language of the American yeoman farmer, which pre-dated what he characterized as the aristocratic corruption of eighteenth-century Britain. At times he even went so far as to suggest that the contemporary dialects of the unlearned were closer to the purest forms; more often he was intolerant about variation within American English, since he was concerned with developing a national standard in opposition to British English. Historically, Webster followed Tooke in tracing this purer language to the Anglo-Saxon: 'the common people, descendants of the Saxons, use principally words derived from the native language of their ancestors, with few derivatives of the foreign tongues, for which they have no occasion.'

A similar set of ideas about language was evident in a number of texts published in Britain in the 1790s. Paine's *Rights of Man*, for instance, provides a virtual compendium of what Tooke had called 'Metaphysical [that is, verbal] Imposture': the process by which the language operated in the interests of the powerful to exclude the unlearned from the public sphere. Perhaps the most innovative dimension of Paine's book is its attempt to provide a political thesis in a popular style. If *Rights of Man* repeatedly returns to the idea of the usurpation of Anglo-Saxon liberty by Norman oligarchy, so too its style implicitly signals that the language of the common people could be a valid medium and instrument of political change. Paine's is perhaps the most important application of Tooke's thesis that there was no special language of mind enabling the discussion of issues of national importance, but it had many imitators. In its very form, for instance, Charles *Pigott's much-reprinted *Political Dictionary* (1795) implied the importance of language in determining the political nation. Its contents sought to redefine a political vocabulary, in ironic terms, from a perspective which implied that there existed an entirely different and equally valid language of politics in which, for instance, 'Church' could be glossed as 'a patent for hypocrisy; the refuge of sloth, ignorance and superstition, the corner-stone of tyranny'.

Where writers like Johnson had seen the vernacular as corrupt and mutable, Paine and Tooke presented it as the repository of the true English spirit of liberty. As such, they were the representatives of a broad movement which sought to widen definitions of British cultural identity in the last decades of the eighteenth century. It was a movement which received its most famous, if rather attenuated, literary expression in the Preface to the second edition of *Wordsworth and *Coleridge's *Lyrical Ballads* (1800). The Preface calls for poetic language to remodel itself not on the 'reputable custom' which writers like Johnson and Campbell believed to be the highest form of language, but on the basis of 'a more permanent and a far more philosophical language' used by 'rustics'. According to Wordsworth, these rustics, rather like Webster's yeomanry, were 'less under the action of social vanity' than their urban counterparts. Their language was more philosophical and permanent because they 'hourly communicate with the best objects from which the best part of language is originally derived'. Tooke had argued that language had its origins in sense impressions, which gave rise to the nouns and verbs which were the bases of all the other parts of speech. Much of Wordsworth's early poetry seemed to seek to recreate this conversation with the source of language. The radical origins of this poetic theory are clear enough, but its enunciation in the *Lyrical Ballads* seems less directly political than Paine's or Tooke's use of such ideas. Certainly Coleridge was unhappy about its democratic implications from as early as 1802, when he dissented from Wordsworth's 'daring Humbleness of Language'. In the *Biographia Literaria* (1817) Coleridge was suggesting that the language of rustics was not one which could seriously qualify as philosophical and permanent:

A rustic's language, purified from all provincialism and grossness, and so far reconstructed as to be made consistent with the rules of grammar (which are in essence no other than the laws of universal logic, applied to Psychological materials), will not differ from the language of any other man of common-sense, however learned or refined he may be, except as far as the notions, which the rustic has to convey, are fewer and more indiscriminate.

Although elsewhere the *Biographia* castigates the overly elaborate speech of the refined, it is clear that Coleridge regarded the speech of rustics as inferior to the educated and sensitive man of common sense whose usage reflected the universal rules of grammar. Contrary to the challenge to the Johnsonian hegemony put forward in the Preface's redefinition of *Lyrical Ballads*, Coleridge now found that 'the best part of human language, properly so called, is derived from reflections on the acts of mind itself'. Indeed, these sentiments sound more like Lowth and Harris than many of the other writings on language theory published in the intervening fifty or so years.

Nevertheless, even while Coleridge was writing his *Biographia*, voices continued to be heard for whom language and culture were not solely to be defined in terms of the usage of the élite. William Cobbett, for instance, continued to write about language in the radical tradition. The influence of Webster and Tooke is apparent in the articles he wrote from America discussing the relationship between grammar and class for the *Political Register*. These articles culminated in *A Grammar of the English Language* (1818), which represented the issue of language as central to any attempt to redefine the political nation. At every turn, even in the illustrations he supplied to particular points of grammar, Cobbett made it clear that language was a political issue:

We are sometimes embarrassed to fix precisely on the nominative, when a sort of *addition* is made to it by words expressing persons or things that accompany it: as, "Sidmouth, with Oliver the spy, *have* brought Brandreth to the block". We hesitate to determine, whether *Sidmouth* alone is the nominative, or whether the nominative includes *Oliver*.

Cobbett's grammar was written specifically to enable labourers to participate in politics. For Cobbett, language was not debased by the usage of the lower orders, as it had been for Johnson and Coleridge, rather it was the use of language to sustain an unjust political system and to exclude the people from participation, which was genuinely corrupt and corrupting.

Cobbett's grammar was extremely successful. It sold 5,000 copies in two weeks, 50,000 by 1822, 100,000 by 1834. The contrast with its main competitor, Lindley Murray's (1745–1826) *English Grammar* (1795), is instructive. Both were popular texts in the sense that they were oriented towards readers outside the educated élite. Murray presented his readers with the task of conforming to stable grammatical truths. Carefully emphasizing the unoriginality of his approach, he commented: 'little can be expected from a new compilation, besides a careful selection of the most useful matter, and some degree of improvement in the mode of adapting it to the understanding, and the gradual progress of learners.' For Cobbett, this approach encouraged an uncritical acceptance of the authority of the élite in both language and politics; it 'inculcates passive obedience and softly promotes the cause of corruption'. Cobbett's presentation of his own material was very different. Not only did his grammar refer constantly to the role of language in politics, it also implied the validity of the existing knowledge of his popular readership. 'I need not tell you', he wrote, 'that I *was working* means the same as *I worked*, only that the former supposes that something else was going on at the same time.'

Nevertheless it was Murray who ultimately had the more enduring influence. The 1818 abridgement of his grammar went into 120 editions of 100,000 copies each. Over 300 different editions have been recorded in total. Its lasting status is illustrated by passing allusions to Murray in any number of Victorian literary works, including Charles *Dickens's *Nicholas Nickleby* (1838–9) and George Eliot's *Middlemarch* (1871–2). Murray's declared aim was to encourage learning and virtue together, and to this end he was careful 'not only to avoid every example and illustration which might have an improper effect on the minds of youth; but also to introduce, on many occasions, such as have a moral and religious tendency'. Murray no less than Cobbett was aware of the social and political significance of language—its importance as an indicator of moral and cultural value. Despite all the challenges mounted against the authority of the élite, a process of standardization continued powerfully to enforce the ideas of propriety promoted by Johnson and Lowth and transmitted through popular texts like Murray's grammar. If modern historians of nationalism are right to suggest that the period ended with an expanded notion of who constituted the nation, one of the prices of entry was conformity to an image of the language which depended on a very restricted definition of 'usage'.

Barrell, J., 'The Language Properly So-Called: The Authority of Common Usage', in his *English Literature in History 1730–80: An Equal Wide Survey*, 1983; Barry, J., 'Literacy and Literature in Popular Culture: Reading and Writing in Historical Perspective', in T. Harris, ed., *Popular Culture in England, c. 1500–1850*, London, 1995; Cohen, M., *Sensible Words: Linguistic Practice in England, 1640–1785*, Baltimore & London, 1977; Colley, L., *Britons: Forging the Nation 1707–1837*, New Haven, Conn., 1992; Cressy, D., 'Literacy in Context: Meaning and Measurement in Early Modern England', in J. Brewer & R. Porter, eds., *Consumption and the World of Goods*, London, 1993; Crowley, T., *Language in History: Theories and Texts*, London, 1996; Leonard, S. A., *The Doctrine of Correctness in English Usage, 1700–1800*, New York, 1962; Simpson, D., *The Politics of American English, 1776–1850*, New York & Oxford, 1986; Smith, O., *The Politics of Language 1791–1819*, Oxford, 1984; Vincent, D., *Literacy and Popular Culture: England 1750–1914*, Cambridge, 1989.

41 · LITERARY THEORY   PETER OTTO

Writing in *Tait's Magazine* for June 1836, Thomas *De Quincey looks back to his first acquaintance with the 'vast, billowy ocean of the German literature' as being akin to the sudden revelation, 'to an ardent and sympathising spirit, of the stupendous world of America, rising, at once, like an exhalation, with all its shadowy forests, its endless savannas, and its pomp of solitary waters'. As De Quincey's description proceeds one can find, in inflated form, many of the ideas often associated with Romantic aesthetics. First, there is the significance for British *Romanticism of German literature as a literature of expression in which the internal is made external. What William *Wordsworth describes as a 'spontaneous overflow of powerful feelings' has, in Germany, become an unpremeditated flood, from which each year pours 'a *literal myriad*' of books. Second, as a literature of *expression* (rather than *instruction*), it orients itself in relation to the national genius that casts it forth rather than to its audience. Third, instead of offering a mirror to the world, this 'spawn infinite . . . teeming and heaving with life' suggests a second nature or heterocosm that vies with the real. Fourth, as an exhalation that emerges without reference to the past, German literature divides itself from a 'lifetime of inheritance and tradition'. It is this which underwrites an association of German literature with America and, in turn, with the age of revolution. De Quincey's deft, if rather cavalier, juxtaposition of aesthetics with questions of subjectivity and politics is characteristic of literary theory in our period. Before we can turn to these matters, however, his account of the new German literature brings us to 'the transcendental philosophy of Immanuel Kant', identified by De Quincey as the 'central object' in the new world, 'the very tree of knowledge in the midst of this Eden'.

In the 'Preface' to the second edition of the *Critique of Pure Reason* (1781), Kant describes his transcendental philosophy as attempting a Copernican revolution in metaphysics. It is this revolution that, for De Quincey, gives Kant 'the keys to a new and creative philosophy'. The original Copernican revolution turned on the conviction, against both inherited belief and the evidence of the senses, that the earth revolved around the sun. The arguments for and against

Copernicus depended, at least in part, on the status ascribed to everyday perceptions (that the sun rises in the east, for example). Does perception simply register events in the external world, or does the observer in some way contribute to what is seen? Kant's revolution sets out to achieve an analogous turn to the subject and a revision of the evidence offered by the senses.

Against an empiricist philosophical tradition associated with John *Locke, which assumed that perception must conform to the object of perception, Kant proposed that objects (if they are to be perceived) must conform to conditions imposed on them by the human faculties through which they are known. Where Locke pictures the understanding working with simple ideas inscribed on the *tabula rasa* of the mind, Kant begins with the proposition that the understanding imposes conditions which must be met if objects are to be thought. The results of this turn to the subjective conditions of perception and cognition are extremely significant for the history of philosophy. Both space and time turn out to be necessary conditions for all experience, with their origin in the structure of our sensibility rather than in the external world. Similarly, the understanding is found to contain conceptions or 'categories' which, rather than being learnt from experience, are applied a priori to objects of perception in general. Objects which appear in experience must conform to conceptions. Some of the most remarkable effects of this epistemological revolution were in the field of aesthetics.

Eighteenth-century aesthetic theory often focused on the spectator's response to objects, incorporating affect and reception by default into the terms of classification of aesthetic categories, such as the *sublime or the beautiful. Edmund *Burke, for example, in his *A Philosophical Enquiry into the Origin of our Ideas of the Sublime and Beautiful* (1757) proposes, first, an 'examination of our passions'; next, a survey of 'the properties of things which . . . influence those passions'; and then the application of the rules deduced from this enquiry to 'the imitative arts'. Kant, in contrast, writes that the 'determining ground' of the beautiful is 'the feeling of the Subject, and not any concept of an Object'. His point was not that an experience of beauty arises without reference to objects; rather, a thing is judged to be beautiful 'solely in respect of that quality in which it adapts itself to our mode of taking it in'. The case of the sublime is even more striking, for while we may 'with perfect propriety' call many objects in nature beautiful, all we can say with regard to the sublime is 'that the object lends itself to the presentation of a sublimity discoverable in the mind'. Sublimity has its ground in 'the attitude of mind that introduces sublimity into the representation of nature'. In this way, then, Kant works against the conflation of reception and object that characterizes Burke's empiricism by explicitly restricting the sublime to the operations of the subject.

Kant's transcendental philosophy provided a point of departure for the extraordinary flowering of German idealism from the last decade of the eighteenth century to the death of Hegel in 1831. Mediated by this tradition, Kant's emphasis on the active role played by the subject in perception and cognition exerted a strong influence on German Romanticism. Kant's influence on British aesthetic and literary theory is a little more oblique, although more substantial than in other European countries outside Germany. At least four book-length studies of Kant were published in London between 1795 and 1798, an early high point in his reception, supported by frequent mentions in journals such as the *Analytical Review* and the *Monthly Magazine*. This early interest was contemporaneous with a rapid growth in popular curiosity about German literature and philosophy in general after 1790, witnessed by the appearance of the *German Museum* (1800–1), a journal devoted entirely to discussions of German culture, and by the work of William *Taylor, who between 1793 and 1799 published over 200 articles in the *Monthly Review*, many of them on German literature. Although most of the notices of Kant's work were not particularly sophisticated, they nevertheless created the impression of a philosophy that claimed to transform metaphysics.

Given this history of reception, it is hardly startling to find Kant firmly ensconced at the centre of De Quincey's version of the new German literature. What *is* surprising, however, is that De Quincey places him at the tree of knowledge, not at the tree of life. In a Romantic reworking of the story of the Garden of Eden, one would expect the latter to be identified as the productive *imagination, source of the organic life and literature, and the former to be the rational understanding. In Romantic psychologies, eating the fruit of the tree of life precipitates a fall into alienated, self-conscious identity. Indeed, De Quincey tells his readers that he has painted the 'glad aurora' of his first acquaintance with German literature 'in order adequately to shadow out the gloom and blight which soon afterwards settled upon the hopes of that golden dawn'. His disenchantment is as sudden as it is complete: 'Alas! all was a dream. Six weeks' study was sufficient to close my hopes in that quarter for ever. The philosophy of Kant... already, in 1805, I had found to be a philosophy of destruction... It destroys by wholesale, and it substitutes nothing.' If Kant's transcendental philosophy does emphasize the active role played by the subject in perception and cognition, how can it be a philosophy of destruction? Why should his power turn out to be that 'of a disenchanter—and a disenchanter the most profound'?

In the third of his *Letters to a Young Man*, De Quincey develops a comparison between a literature of knowledge and a literature of power, which is in broad terms analogous to the opposition he implied between the tree of knowledge and the tree of life. The literature of knowledge includes works that attempt to communicate information about an external, objective world (economics, politics, and so on). The literature of power draws our attention inwards, to the subjective world, by inducing us to 'feel vividly, and with a vital consciousness, emotions which... had previously lain unwakened'. By organizing and actualizing 'these inert and sleeping forms', this second kind of writing communicates a sense of our own power by revealing hitherto unrecognized dimensions of the self. Where a literature of knowledge tells us that we are dwarfed by the infinity of the external world, a literature of power startles us into a 'feeling of the infinity of the world within'. As De Quincey acknowledges, this distinction is derived from Wordsworth. One thinks in particular of the 'Essay, Supplementary' (1815), where the poet is described as creating taste and providing the foundation for knowledge by calling forth and bestowing power. It is also closely related to the distinction between the poet and the man of science found in the Preface to *Lyrical Ballads* (1800). Although it will postpone our return to Kant, we must consider the Preface at some length: first, because it illustrates some of the central issues of Romantic aesthetics; second, because it will enable us to show why Kant should engender such profound disappointment.

In the Preface to the *Lyrical Ballads*, whereas the Scientist is a solitary figure seeking 'truth as a remote and unknown benefactor', the Poet sings 'a song in which all human beings join with him'. 'He rejoices in the presence of truth as our visible friend and hourly companion.' The poet is

the rock of defence of human nature; an upholder and preserver, carrying every where with him relationship and love. In spite of difference of soil and climate, of language and manners, of laws and customs, in spite of things silently gone out of mind and things violently destroyed, the Poet binds together by passion and knowledge the vast empire of human society, as it is spread over the whole earth, and over all time.

The confidence manifest here is to some extent offset by the sense of crisis that pervades the Preface. Politics, modernity, and the emergence of a consumer society [see *consumerism, 19] all conspire to 'blunt the discriminating powers of the mind' and produce a 'degrading thirst after outrageous stimulation'. With these forces arrayed against him, Wordsworth is saved from melancholy only because he has a 'deep impression of certain inherent and indestructible qualities of the human mind, and likewise of certain powers in the great and permanent objects that act upon it'. These natural qualities and powers are most evident in the low and rural classes, who preserve language and manners which, quarantined from the modern world, arise in the interplay between the 'essential passions of the heart' and 'the beautiful and permanent forms of nature'. The speech of such classes is, Wordsworth implies, evidence of a 'primitive' or 'natural' language, in which words are not arbitrary signs of an idea (as they are in Locke) but preserve a direct link with both things *and* the powers of the mind. Confronted with a culture where words have separated themselves from both subjects and things, Wordsworth sets out a poetic programme aimed at stripping artifice from *poetry [29] to make it expressive of the elementary laws of our nature. This co-ordination of aesthetics and subjectivity introduces a political programme: the poet emerges as a prophet who speaks for human nature, creates a community of taste, and so binds together what modern life divides. In De Quincey's language, the poet's literature of power awakens individuals to a nature which, because it is shared with others, can form the basis of community.

The Preface to *Lyrical Ballads* is one of the most influential documents in the tradition of liberal humanism. Mediated by the work of J. S. *Mill and Matthew Arnold (1822–88), its account of poetry as an expressive, humanizing, and unifying medium, able to heal the divisions of modern life, has proved remarkably influential. It is, nevertheless, a project beset with difficulties. This is in part because it relies on a direct relation between nature and subjectivity (between nature, sense impressions, and thought) which, as it is propounded in the Preface, relies on the associationist *psychology [39] of David Hartley (1705–57). Outside this context, the belief that 'nature and the language of the sense' are 'The anchor of my purest thoughts, the nurse, / The guide, the guardian of my heart, and soul / Of all my moral being' can appear more tenuous. The year in which *Lyrical Ballads* was first published, 1798, saw a Britain engaged in *war [2] with France, and attempting to suppress Irish *rebellion and unrest over soaring bread prices and *famine. Measured against this background, the poet's work can seem merely defensive, a retreat from the disorder of politics and history. If this is so, then the poet is an enchanter rather than a prophet—and an enchanter the most profound—because he uses aesthetic order to disguise political disorder.

Such is roughly the opinion, making allowance for his heavily ironical tone, expressed by Thomas Love *Peacock in 'The Four Ages of Poetry' (1820). Peacock describes the Lake Poets (*Coleridge, *Southey, and Wordsworth) as an 'egregious confraternity of rhymesters' who 'wrote verses on a new principle; saw rocks and rivers in a new light; and remaining studiously ignorant of history, society, and human nature, cultivated the phantasy only at the expence of the memory and the reason'. A poet in the modern world is, according to Peacock, 'a semi-barbarian in a civilized community' because his craft belongs in a society where imagination and feeling are the only index to reality. Where Wordsworth turns to the poet to heal wounds inflicted by civilization, Peacock turns to the scientist and historian to dispel the merely subjective pronouncements of the poet. For Peacock, the literature of knowledge acts on the literature of power as an agent of disenchantment, a position which *Byron sketched in his suppressed Preface to *Don Juan* (1819–24) and put into practice in the rest of the poem.

This lengthy digression brings us back to De Quincey, who identifies Kant's philosophy as an agent of disenchantment all the more profound because it deflates the pretensions of the literatures of knowledge *and* of power, of the scientist *and* the poet. Against Peacock, De Quincey sides with Kant's (and Wordsworth's) account of the active participation of the mind in perception and cognition. One might even say that in bringing the mind's productive powers to light Kant has, for De Quincey, revealed the tree of life in the Garden of Eden. The problem is that in so doing he has also uncovered the limits of those powers. As Kant writes in the *Prolegomena to any Future Metaphysics* (1783), because our 'senses never and in no manner enable us to know things in themselves, but only their appearances, which are mere representations of the sensibility, we conclude that "all bodies, together with the space in which they are, must be considered nothing but mere representations in us, and exist nowhere but in our thoughts" '. Kant goes on to argue that this does not imply that his philosophy is an idealism, because he does not doubt that things in themselves really do exist. Nevertheless, it is Kant's circumscription of human knowledge that is the proximate cause of De Quincey's disenchantment. The impasse this produces for De Quincey can, in my view, be summarized as follows: no link can be established between the creative activity of the mind and the nature of things in themselves. At the same time, we cannot retreat from the subjective to the objective because we know nothing of the real world; our knowledge extends no further than appearance. The scientist simply does not recognize that, as De Quincey writes, 'In reality, the depths and the heights which are in man, the depths by which he searches, the heights by which he aspires, are but projected and made objective externally in the three dimensions of space which are outside of him.' There is, in short, no sure path from nature to sense impressions to thought. As De Quincey remarks, 'I belonged to a reptile race, if the wings by which we had sometimes *seemed* to mount, and the buoyancy which had *seemed* to support our flight, were indeed the fantastic delusions which he represented them.' Although Kant's philosophy reveals the tree of life in the Garden of Eden, this recognition is garnered from the tree of knowledge. Because it is formed under the guiding star of Kant, 'the new German literature' (although suggestive of a literature of power) is a literature of knowledge. Once one has eaten of the tree of Kantian knowledge, there can be no return to the Wordsworthian tree of life.

De Quincey locates his disenchantment with Kant in a historical moment (1804–5) which makes it roughly contemporaneous with the end of the first period of British interest in both Kant and German literature as a whole. In the twenty years after 1806 Kant was barely mentioned in British periodicals. This decline was in part owing to the conservative belief, propagated in journals such as the *Anti-Jacobin, that 'German culture *en bloc*' was a vehicle for the dissemination of 'Jacobin, republican and radical ideas'. This neglect was, of course, not universal. Madame de *Staël's *De l'Allemagne*, published in London in 1813, offered an account of German manners, literature, and philosophy which included a description of the transcendental philosophy. During these years, William Taylor continued to write on German literature. The most dramatic exception, however, is Coleridge, who, in his published and unpublished writings of the first decades of the nineteenth century, comes close to plagiarism in his reliance on Kant and the German idealist tradition.

The convergence between Kant's epistemological dilemmas and Coleridge's Romantic aesthetics can be glimpsed in the latter's discussions of the Brocken Spectre. This optical illusion, named after a peak in the Hartz mountains in Germany, is used by both Coleridge and De Quincey as a vehicle for speculation on the relation between the mind's productive powers and things in themselves, partly because its genesis depends on both subjective and objective conditions. If a Brocken Spectre is to materialize, the air must be filled with a diffuse mist, the sun must be near the horizon, and the initiate must stand with back turned to the sun. Under these conditions a 'natural magic' comes into play and a figure, sometimes of great size, is projected onto the mist. Coleridge uses this apparition in a variety of contexts. In *Aids to Reflection* (1825), for example, he writes that the work of *genius is 'a projected form of [the Beholder's] own Being, that moves before him with a Glory round its head'. In 'Dejection: An Ode' (1802) the same figure is used to characterize the creative component of perception. And in 'Constancy to an Ideal Object' (1825–6) Coleridge uses the Spectre to question the status of the ideal world glimpsed in art. The question that this third text directs to the Spectre and the Ideal Object—'And art thou nothing?'—seems apt in each of these contexts. At least at first glance, the obvious answer to this question is that the Brocken Spectre is indeed nothing; it is nothing more than an optical illusion. Moreover, the Spectre suggests a range of associations which, one assumes, an idealist poetics would want to forget. In 'Constancy to an Ideal Object' for example, Coleridge's description of the 'enamoured rustic' worshipping the 'fair hues' of the Spectre recalls Wordsworth's account of the rustic's ennobling exchange with

Nature; unfortunately, it also evokes Peacock's judgement that poets are 'semi-barbarians in a civilized age'.

Coleridge's use of the Spectre, however, implies that both naïve (the phantom is real) and sceptical (it is a mere projection from the spectator) explanations of the Spectre are misleading. Instead, it is both subjective and objective: it is a figure cast by the spectator, but this image is itself projected onto the mist by the sun. In other words, the mind's productive power (the imagination) is congruent with and enabled by a creative power residing in Nature. The mind's creations—whether the universe of perception or the world of art—carry a trace ('a glory') of this transcendent creative power, which is the absolute ground of both nature and the self. In *Aids to Reflection*, for example, the creative productions of genius are a projected form of the artist's own being; yet at the same time they are a sign of the creative power of Nature or God. Similarly, in 'Constancy to an Ideal Object' it is the 'glory' around the phantom's head that allows the possibility that the ideal world of art might be more than a mirage. De Quincey, as I have argued, doubts the validity of these claims. In his own meditation on the Brocken in *Suspiria de Profundis* (1845), he concludes that 'the apparition is but a reflex of yourself; and, in uttering your secret feelings to *him*, you make this phantom the dark symbolic mirror for reflecting to the daylight what else must be hidden for ever'. The apparatus which projects the Brocken is entirely within the self. For De Quincey, the relation between subject and object are therefore, at best, unknowable; this is why the hopes aroused by the 'glad aurora' of the new German literature prove to be illusory. For Coleridge, the glory seen illuminating the Spectre suggests both a correspondence and collaboration between the creative powers of the mind and those ultimately divine creative powers in nature. By identifying in imagination the absolute ground of both human and natural worlds, in a way which avoids the charge of solipsism, Coleridge hopes to close the gap between subject and object, mind and nature, thought and thing.

The privileged agent of this reconciliation is art, which Coleridge, under the influence of Friedrich William Schelling (1775–1854), defines in 'On Poesy or Art' (1818–19) 'as of a middle quality between a thought and a thing, or . . . the union and reconciliation of that which is nature with that which is exclusively human'. Yet how is this to be substantiated? How could one confirm the view of imagination on which it relies? The Brocken Spectre provides a remarkable analogy, but no proof. Without proof, there is little more than rhetoric to stop the slide to scepticism. Coleridge often approaches these questions obliquely, by providing fresh analogies or new discriminations which illustrate the role of imagination. In the thirteenth chapter of the *Biographia Literaria* (1817), however, he promises a 'deduction of the Imagination, and with it the principles of production and of genial criticism in the fine arts'. This is clearly a critical moment in the *Biographia* and in Coleridge's thought as a whole. Readers are, therefore, often surprised when they learn, after no more than three pages, that transcription of this important argument was interrupted by the arrival of a letter from a friend who, having read the chapter in question, advised him not to publish it; not because he had found a flaw in the argument, but because the chapter was too long, too difficult, and was likely to depress sales. Convinced by these arguments, Coleridge claims to have withheld the rest of the deduction and contented himself with 'the main result', the definition of the imagination. The paragraphs that conclude this chapter do align perception and artistic creation with an absolute creative force. The creative power evident in art (the secondary imagination) is an echo of the creative work manifest in perception (the primary imagination), which in turn is nothing less than 'a repetition in the finite mind of the eternal act of creation in the infinite I AM'. The work of art does indeed have a 'glory' around its head; but this is again a matter of assertion rather than demonstration.

In the absence of a deduction of the imagination, Coleridge's literary and aesthetic theory returns again and again to distinctions which differentiate the creative imagination and its works from the products and procedures of inferior faculties in such a way that the former are found to be coincident with the deepest impulses of life. Coleridge defines 'mechanic form', for instance, as the product of rules and conventions operating on inert matter. 'Organic form', in contrast, is the sign of a life which is able to shape and develop itself from within: the form corresponds to the life rather than to an external model. This distinction has the effect of aligning organic form with nature and life, mechanical form with artifice and death, which in turn implies two other interdependent propositions. If organic form is the type of all creative art, then Nature turns out to be 'the prime Genial Artist': 'Each exterior is the physiognomy of the being within.' If Nature is 'the prime Genial Artist', then the human genius repeats in his labours the creative work of Nature. *Shakespeare is 'himself a Nature humanized'. De Quincey's critical vocabulary offers a strong contrast to the terms used by Coleridge. Where Coleridge is drawn towards binary opposites which distinguish life from death, nature from artifice, the interior from the exterior, De Quincey's prose gravitates around terms and phrases which imply a promiscuous confusion of categories. In *Confessions of an English Opium Eater* (1822), for example, a scandalous correspondence is developed between opium and the imagination. How is one to keep mechanic and organic form apart when an inert substance is able to counterfeit the most profound affects of life?

The literary and aesthetic theories of Coleridge and De Quincey elaborate different but interrelated responses to the late-eighteenth-century 'turn' to the subject exemplified by Kant. It would not be an exaggeration to suggest that De Quincey's epistemological scepticism is for Coleridge the unwanted double that his aesthetic and literary speculations attempt again and again to expel. This double is at its most insistent whenever the question of the legitimacy of Coleridge's aesthetic and literary theories arises. For example, if, as I have argued, Coleridge's alignment of subjectivity, aesthetics, and nature is established on the level of rhetoric rather than actuality, then it would seem itself to depend upon the mechanical world it disavows. More importantly, if the correspondence between nature and art is to be more than a subjective intuition, if it is to be the touchstone of a politics, it must be formulated in the language of the world it wants to occlude. Similarly, one might say that Coleridge's dream of a correspondence between subjectivity, aesthetics, and nature haunts De Quincey's work.

It would be convenient if I were able to conclude this brief overview by proposing that Wordsworth, Peacock, Coleridge, and De Quincey, with Kant fortuitously providing a centre, represent the cardinal points of aesthetic and literary theory in Britain during our period. Unfortunately, literary and aesthetic theory between 1765 and 1832 has many more 'centres' than this scheme allows and more cardinal points than are possible in a compass. For example, although William *Blake would certainly subscribe to Coleridge's belief in the active role played by the human imagination, the influence of radical Protestant and *millenarian ideas on his thought gives this a very different inflection. At the risk of unnecessary simplification, one might say that, rather than grounding our imagination in Nature, Blake attempts to open Kant's categories (the fixed forms of Urizen) and the forms of time and space (Los and Enitharmon) to the ungrounded energies of Eternity. When Blake writes that the Man or Woman who is not a Poet, a Painter, a Musician, or an Architect, is not a Christian, and when he calls on the 'Young Men of the new Age!' to struggle against those who want to 'depress mental & prolong Corporeal War', he is therefore aligning subjectivity, aesthetics, and politics in a way that, one imagines, would be dismissed by Wordsworth, Coleridge, De Quincey, or Peacock.

What draws these diverse figures together is that their literary and aesthetic theories register, albeit in radically different ways, modernity's attempt to break with the models for thought and action offered by the past. It could be claimed that the field of aesthetics is the first to register the problems associated with this endeavour, because it is in aesthetic experience, particularly as constructed by a certain kind of Romantic, that subjectivity is divorced from temporal and everyday experience. It is because we still belong to the era opened by Romanticism that our modernity continues to reinvent and reshape itself in Romanticism's forms.

Abrams, M. H., *The Mirror and the Lamp: Romantic Theory and the Critical Tradition*, Oxford, 1953; Bowie, A., *Aesthetics and Subjectivity: From Kant to Nietzsche*, Manchester, 1990; De Man, P., *The Rhetoric of Romanticism*, New York, 1984; Eagleton, T., *The Ideology of the Aesthetic*, Oxford, 1990; Engell, J., *The Creative Imagination*, Cambridge, Mass., 1981; McGann, J. J., *The Romantic Ideology: A Critical Investigation*, Chicago, 1983; Michelli, G., 'The Early Reception of Kant's Thought in England 1785–1805', in G. M. Ross & T. McWalter, eds., *Kant and His Influence*, Bristol, 1990; Stokoe, F. W., *German Influence in the English Romantic Period, 1788–1818*, Cambridge, 1926; Wellek, R., *Immanuel Kant in England, 1793–1838*, Princeton, NJ, 1931; *A History of Modern Criticism: 1750–1950*, London, 1955.

INDEX TO PART ONE

This index covers Part One only; for comprehensive coverage of the Companion it should be used in conjunction with the alphabetical entries in Part Two. **Bold numbers** denote an entire essay on a topic. With the exception of *Lyrical Ballads*, titles are to be found under their authors. Similarly, individual periodicals will be found under the entries for journals or newspapers, except for the frequently mentioned *Blackwood's Edinburgh Magazine*, *Edinburgh Review*, *Monthly Magazine*, and *The Times*. Illustrations, captions, and bibliographies have not been indexed.

· PART TWO ·

A

ABERNETHY, John (1764–1831), as president of the Royal College of Surgeons, one of the most influential men in the medical profession in this period, who played a part in the advancement of William *Lawrence and Richard *Owen.

Educated in the theologically conservative atmosphere of Edinburgh, Abernethy unwittingly opened up a schism in the life sciences in his Hunterian lectures of 1814. His topic was the origin and nature of the so-called 'life-principle'. His intention was to reconcile recent discoveries in medical science with orthodox religious thinking by claiming that some 'subtle, mobile, invisible substance', beyond mere matter, was the vital principle of life. This attempt to conserve a place for the traditional idea of the immortal soul was contested by Lawrence, at first indirectly in 1816 and then with an outright attack on Abernethy in the Hunterian lectures of 1817. The controversy soon spilled beyond medical circles and became politicized with conservative opinion supporting Abernethy and radicals using Lawrence's ideas to attack orthodox Christianity. S. T. *Coleridge supported Abernethy in the controversy, while Lawrence gained an enthusiastic public amongst freethinking artisan intellectuals such as Richard *Carlile.   JM

abolitionism, a slippery term covering both the movement for the abolition of the slave trade, achieved by an Act of Parliament in 1807, and the subsequent agitation against *slavery [6] itself which culminated in the emancipation of slaves in 1833–8. The reasons for the unprecedented popularity of this campaign have been much debated, with historians arguing across a range of religious, moral, humanitarian, and economic motives. In the 1780s abolitionism also spawned a number of proponents of the colonization of Africa, who reasoned that it would be far more moral and profitable for Britain to trade in Africa than to trade in Africans. To this end Britain's black poor, their numbers swelled by ex-loyalist slaves, were rounded up and repatriated, but the experimental 'free' settlements on the west coast of Africa, in Sierra Leone and Bulama, were disastrous.

Thomas *Clarkson and William *Wilberforce are the names most closely associated with abolitionism in Britain, but there were a number of other major players, including two black writers who had themselves been slaves, Ottobah Cugoano (b. 1757) and Olaudah *Equiano. So fashionable was the movement in the late 1780s that almost everyone with literary pretensions penned anti-slavery verse, from *Cowper to *Coleridge to *Southey, not to mention innumerable contributions by women, such as Hannah *More, Helen Maria *Williams, and Anna Laetitia *Barbauld. That feminism has its antecedents in

abolitionism is clear enough in the work of the many Ladies' Anti-Slavery Associations which sprang up in Britain in the 1820s and 1830s, with radicals like Elizabeth Heyrick (1769–1831) propelling the movement in the direction of immediate rather than gradual emancipation of the slaves. But the centrality of women's role in the movement is there from the start: most evident, perhaps, in the early boycott campaigns, with their special appeal to the consciences of women as consumers and household organizers. The idea of the white woman's mission to the slave was also enforced by the link between abolitionism and the powerful *Evangelical *missionary movement to which so many women abolitionists belonged.   DC

ACKERMANN, Rudolph (1764–1834), publisher and bookseller. Born in Saxony, Ackermann moved to London in the 1780s, where, after a career as a coach designer, he established a *print [22] shop and drawing school in the Strand in 1795. His business, 'The Repository of Arts', combined the functions of shop, gallery, *circulating library, and social centre. As publisher of the magazine *The Repository of Arts, Literature, Commerce, Manufactures, Fashions and Politics* initiated in 1809 under A. C. *Pugin, and of topographical guides that exploited interest in the *picturesque and the exotic, Ackermann disseminated and influenced changing tastes in *fashion, **design [25]**, and *architecture [28]. His significant publications include the *Microcosm of London* (1808–11), an illustrated guide to the buildings of the metropolis with drawings by Thomas *Rowlandson and A. C. Pugin and text by W. H. *Pyne and William *Combe, and *The Tours of Dr. Syntax* (1809–11), also by Rowlandson and Combe. An innovator in technology as well as an entrepreneur, Ackermann experimented with paints, the waterproofing of paper and cloth, and axle design for coaches. He pioneered the application of lithography in Britain, and was among the first to introduce gas lighting to his place of business.   GR

37, 56

Act of Union, the Act of Parliament of 1800 which dissolved the old independent Irish parliament of 1782 and integrated Ireland constitutionally with England by returning 100 Irish members to the House of Commons. This Act became the hinge of modern Irish history, dominating Irish social, economic, and political affairs until 1922, and exercising almost equally profound effects on English politics.

The Act, which also united the Churches of England and Ireland, established free trade between the countries, and exacted a contribution towards imperial revenue, was prompted by English wartime

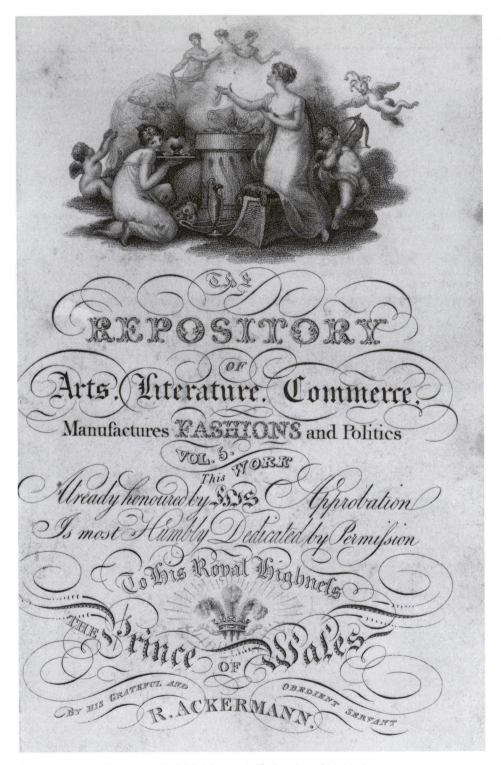

THE
REPOSITORY
OF
Arts, Literature, Commerce,
Manufactures FASHIONS and Politics
VOL. 5.
THIS WORK
Already honoured by HIS Approbation
Is most Humbly Dedicated by Permission
To His Royal Highness
THE Prince OF Wales
BY HIS GRATEFUL AND OBEDIENT SERVANT
R. ACKERMANN.

56. Title-page of the fifth volume of Rudolph Ackermann's *The Repository of Arts* (1823).

fears of buoyant Protestant Irish nationalism coupled with the dangers of a French *invasion following several unsuccessful attempts in the 1790s. William *Pitt referred to Ireland as a 'a ship on fire, it must be extinguished or cut adrift'. The English executive managed to push through the legislation by skilfully exploiting divisions of opinion in Ireland. Conservative Irish landlords supported the proposed union as a bastion against rising Catholic power, while conservative Catholics preferred English rule to that of Irish Protestants, and were further wooed with vague promises of religious emancipation [see *Catholic emancipation]. Some, mainly Northern business interests, also believed that economic benefits would flow from free trade. Even so, the English executive under Lord *Castlereagh had to institute an unprecedented campaign of bribery to secure parliamentary support.

Reaction against the union followed swiftly. Liberal and radical Protestants railed against their loss of independence, making the 'constitution of 1782' a rallying-point of future Irish nationalism. Catholic clergy and professionals were outraged at the betrayal of emancipation promises, which led to the rise of a more militant era of Catholic politics under the leadership of Daniel *O'Connell. Dublin suffered serious eclipse, as economic and social power drifted to London, and later Belfast. Above all, responsibility for the problems of Ireland now shifted centrally to Britain, which, by importing a bloc of Irish parliamentarians, paved the way for O'Connell's use in the 1830s of pledged voting, threats to the balance of power, and tactics of legislative wrecking. Repealing the union became the panacea of most shades of nationalist Irish politics throughout the remainder of the nineteenth century.
IMcC

ADAM, Robert (1728–92), architect and designer. Pre-eminent designer of town and country residences for the nation's élite, Adam developed a style that was a sophisticated synthesis of classical sources and influenced all levels of domestic *architecture [28].

Adam's father, William (1689–1748), had been the leading Scottish architect of his generation, and all four of his sons, John, Robert, James, and William, entered the family firm. This impressive architectural inheritance was not the brothers' only advantage. They also grew up in the midst of the *Scottish Enlightenment and cultivated friendships with the likes of William *Robertson, Adam *Smith, and David *Hume. Profits from the firm's responsibilities as architects to the Board of Ordnance in the aftermath of the Jacobite Rebellion of 1745 enabled the more ambitious Robert to embark on three years of continental travel and study in 1754. Based in Rome, he studied the full range of classical architecture and decoration, from the antique to the contemporary work of neoclassical designers such as Giovanni Battista Piranesi, with whom he developed a close friendship. Adam's affluence also afforded him the opportunity to support the French architect Charles Louis Clérisseau as his drawing instructor,

and to participate in the social scene enjoyed by aristocratic British travellers.

On returning to Britain, with James as his partner, Robert Adam quickly established a successful London firm concentrating on the interior decoration and renovation of aristocratic residences. Their most renowned works included Kedleston Hall, Derbyshire (c.1760–70), Syon House, Middlesex (1762–9), Kenwood House, Middlesex (1767–9), and Derby House, London (1773–4). Politically and economically uncertain times jeopardized large-scale building projects. Indeed, the credit crisis of 1772 halted the brothers' ambitious development on the north bank of the Thames, the Adelphi (1768–72), and nearly bankrupted them.

Rescuing themselves from the Adelphi disaster by organizing a lottery, the Adam brothers characteristically went on the offensive by publishing *The Works in Architecture of Robert and James Adam* (vol. i, 1773; vol. ii, 1779). In it they claimed to have revolutionized *design [25] through skill in planning and a concern for movement and variety in architecture. These terms were the bywords of the *picturesque movement, and the Adam brothers demonstrated in their residential designs an enthusiasm for spatial experience and perception akin to that formulated by the Revd William *Gilpin. In commissions such as Syon House or Home House, London (1773–6), they created sequences of spaces that exhibited a felicitous variety of plan shapes and decorative schemes corresponding to contemporary social patterns and tastes. Their three decades of fashionable dominance resulted from a constant refinement of style and an insistence on the highest quality of workmanship.

Adam explored the architectural ramifications of the picturesque by cultivating a so-called 'Castle Style'. Structures such as Culzean Castle, Ayrshire (1777–92), and Seton Castle, East Lothian (1790–1), resemble medieval fortifications but do not depart from the planning and compositional principles underlying his neoclassical designs. Adam's approach to the picturesque is that of Richard Payne *Knight, who advocated a mixed style as appropriate to modern life, rather than the revivalist attitudes of either James *Wyatt or John *Nash.

Adam practised mainly in Scotland during the last decade of his life. In Edinburgh he initiated a monumental urban development, Charlotte Square (1791–1807), and finally completed a major civic commission, the Register Office (1774–92).   SS

advertising. The commercialization of British society was manifested in and sustained by an expanding advertising industry which assumed its modern shape during this period. Agencies specializing in advertising were established as early as 1812, and despite the restrictions of stamp and advertisement taxes, press advertising thrived. The leading daily *newspapers became increasingly dependent upon advertising revenue for their profits. In the early nineteenth century the famous 'black' front page of *The Times* consisted entirely of minutely printed advertisements. Government influence via direct subsidy and official advertisements was rendered less effective because of the financial independence provided by commercial advertising. In this respect advertising made it more difficult for the government to control newspapers by direct means as the nineteenth century went on.

The quarterly and half-yearly journals developed their own advertising methods, John Bell (1745–1831) pioneering the co-ordination of advertising and main text in his ladies' fashion journal, *La Belle Assemblée*. The children's book industry was particularly significant for its innovative advertising techniques: the publisher John Newbery (1713–67) developed sales gimmicks such as free gifts [see *children's literature].

During the 1810s the distinctive display typefaces known as 'fat faces' or 'Egyptians' were widely introduced in the printing industry and were used in areas of advertising outside the press, giving rise to *prints [22] specializing in packaging and placards. Bill-posting became a large and well-organized trade with a considerable impact on the urban landscape. Robert *Southey claimed that in London 'whenever there was a dead wall, a vacant house, or a temporary scaffolding erected for repairs, the space was covered with printed bills', but these bill posters were rarely illustrated until the mid-1830s.

The volume of advertising and the parodic tendencies of many forms of advertisement permeated most literary media. As early as 1785 Francis *Grose published *A Guide to Health, Beauty, Riches, and Honour* composed entirely of preposterous advertisements. Mock newspapers mainly composed of *satiric advertisements had appeared by 1820. In the political sphere, advertising forms were adopted on a mass scale in the government-backed propaganda against France during the Napoleonic wars. Radical publicists, printers, and printmakers such as William *Hone, William *Benbow, and George *Cruikshank picked up on this material and developed their own anti-state satire based on a variety of advertising models in the years of political turmoil which succeeded *Waterloo.   MW

agrarianism, loosely termed 'back to the land', was a defining characteristic of popular radicalism. Some agrarians, like Thomas *Spence, called for the abolition of private property, while others desired a restored peasantry. Common to all was a belief in the viability of small-scale agricultural enterprise, and in the right of universal equal access to the *land [16].

Agrarianism derived from an awareness of how inequalities in landholding, which *enclosure was extending, reinforced all other inequalities. In this sense virtually all British radical reformers were agrarians. However, the term is more appositely applied to those who saw a return to the land as the essential prescription for social and economic ills generally. The agrarian vision was neither a nostalgic *pastoral nor an economically inert arcadia. It emphasized the partnership between labour and the soil. Its view of the landscape was starkly *utilitarian, rejecting an aesthetic based upon wild, unsubdued nature in favour of one emphasizing cultivation and

productiveness. This reflected both the uncertainties of labouring lives acquainted with scarcity and *famine and antagonism to *Malthusian views on the limits to growth.

Agrarianism might be summed up not as 'back to the land', but as 'forward to the land as it would be' in a polity which guaranteed access to the soil, a small-producer economy, and that control over daily life and labour which was widely held to be a casualty of both agricultural and industrial growth in this period.   MC

agricultural revolution is a contested historical term designed to denote a transformation in agricultural output and *agrarian practice, chiefly in England, between 1750 and 1850.

The term emerged in the historical literature of the late nineteenth century, usually in conjunction with the similarly contested notion of 'industrial revolution'. It focused on the 'heroic' achievements of eighteenth-century English farmers, such as Jethro Tull (1674–1741), in implementing revolutionary new farming techniques. These were linked with institutional innovations such as parliamentary *enclosure, which allowed for the replacement of small-scale peasant production with more economically viable single cash crops [see *land, 16]. This 'heroic' interpretation has long since been discredited, as historical research has drawn attention to the distinction between an 'economic' focus on agricultural output and an 'institutional' focus on enclosure and changes to property rights.

The 'economic' school of thought embraces three related criteria: changes to farming techniques, improvements to productivity—assessed as output per unit of input—and the ability of the agricultural sector to sustain an increasing population. The 'institutional' approach focuses on the transformation of feudal tenures into modern 'rational' tenures conducive to efficient agricultural production and the related issue of farm size, together with the structural changes to agricultural employment.

The question of culture in relation to the transformation of the countryside has been somewhat neglected in the literature on the agricultural revolution. But it is best represented by the work of the historian E. P. Thompson, who has focused on the transformation of agrarian practice, whereby changing definitions of property occasioned by the enclosure movement and technological innovations to farming influenced the declining role of custom in the texture of rural life: a 'revolution' witnessed in George Eliot's *Middlemarch*.   ARB

AIKIN family. John (1747–1822), Arthur (1773–1854), and Lucy (1781–1864), together with John's sister, Anna Laetitia *Barbauld, were a prominent Dissenting family whose literary and scientific accomplishments belie the faintly dismissive implications that a more specialized age reads into the aptly descriptive term 'miscellaneous writer'.

John Aikin was one of two children of an older John Aikin (1713–80), a tutor, first in classics and subsequently in divinity, at the *Dissenting Academy at Warrington. Aikin senior never moved beyond *Arianism, but his sister and his children adopted *Unitarianism. Deflected by weakness of voice from a ministerial to a medical career, the younger John Aikin escaped from an unprofitable apprenticeship in Rutlandshire to medical studies at the University of Edinburgh and a further apprenticeship in Manchester. He practised in Chester, Warrington, and Yarmouth, where he suffered severe prejudice owing to his religious views, and finally settled in London, near the thriving Dissenting intellectual community in Hackney. In 1798, when chronic illness forced him to hand over his practice to his younger son, Charles Rochemont Aikin (1775–1847), he moved to Stoke Newington, the centre of another impressive Dissenting circle.

Aikin's earlier literary avocation now became his vocation. The early biographical history of British *medicine [18] to the time of Harvey was followed by a ten-volume *General Biography* (1799–1815). To extensive publications on medicine he added books on *botany, geography, and topography, notably in his extended description of the country around Manchester (1795). He also wrote poetry, essays, literary criticism, and entertaining and improving books for children; and, as the friend, biographer, and literary executor of the prison reformer John *Howard, he did much to bring Howard's work to public attention. Aikin was literary editor of the *Monthly Magazine* from 1796 to 1806 and of the *Athenaeum* in 1806–8. His successful *Annals of the Reign of King George III* (1816), narrowly focused on political and diplomatic developments, does not reveal his own politics, which had taken a turn from *loyalty to disenchantment (common to many Dissenters) during the *American Revolution, and thence to warm support of the Foxite *Whigs.

Trained to be a Unitarian minister but never occupying a pulpit, Arthur Aikin won a distinguished reputation as a *chemist and mineralogist, publishing extensively in both areas; he was one of the founders of the Geological Society. Though he wrote mostly on scientific subjects, from 1802 to 1808 he edited and contributed to the *Annual Review*, a valuable survey of recent publications organized by field.

Arthur and Charles were educated in the school run by Mrs Barbauld and her husband in Suffolk. Lucy Aikin was taught at home by her father, a strong advocate of *female education and companionate marriage, positions which she too championed in verse and prose, usefully collected in *Epistles on Women, with Miscellaneous Poems* (1810). Like her aunt, Lucy Aikin was a poet and essayist—her first published work was a collection of poems for children (1801)—but she was best known by contemporaries as a historian of the reigns of Elizabeth, James I, and Charles I. Today's readers, however, will find much greater rewards in a correspondence with the famous American Unitarian minister William Ellery Channing (1780–1842), an invaluable commentary on British developments over sixteen years that inaugurated the age of reform. The Whig enthusiasm Lucy Aikin shared with her family did not extend to the new varieties of radicalism that surfaced in the 1830s. Nor is there any indication that the discontent she came to feel, under both Channing's tutelage and the subtle influences of Romanticism, with *Necessarianism was satisfied in any of the new religious movements in the Church or in Dissent in the latter part of her life   RKW

ALDERSON, Amelia, see Amelia *Opie.

alehouses, see *taverns and alehouses.

allegory. S. T. *Coleridge provides the paradigmatic instance of the Romantic rejection, at the level of *literary theory [41], of allegory in favour of symbol. Allegory is, he writes in *The Statesman's Manual*, 'a translation of abstract notions into a picture-language which is itself nothing but an abstraction from objects of the senses'. In the broadest understanding of the term, allegory speaks of one thing in the guise of another: it co-ordinates a 'literal' or 'visible' order of meaning with a second order of persons, ideas, and events. For Coleridge, allegory therefore has the dubious distinction of bringing together a first-order signifier and a second-order signification which have both been disassociated from their proper objects. The product of this 'unnatural' conjunction is like a ghost, present in yet divided from the world of the living: but 'the principal' and 'its phantom proxy' are 'unsubstantial, and the former shapeless to boot.' By contrast, a symbol, according to Coleridge, establishes a living, natural, and organic relation between form and content, thought and thing: it 'always partakes of the Reality which it renders intelligible; and while it enunciates the whole, abides itself as a living part in that Unity, of which it is the representative.'

Although a similar estimation of the respective merits of these terms can be found in Goethe and Schelling, amongst others, in practice Romantic writers were more ambivalent about this genre. In a letter to Butts dated 6 July 1803, William *Blake defines the 'Most Sublime Poetry' as 'Allegory address'd to the Intellectual powers'; yet in *A Vision of the Last Judgment* he maintains that 'Fable or Allegory are a totally distinct & inferior kind of Poetry' not to be confused with 'Vision or Imagination.' His own poetry establishes a remarkable pantheon of allegorical figures. Poems such as Percy *Shelley's *Prometheus Unbound* and *Keats's *Endymion* are allegories in a fairly straightforward sense; while recent accounts of the period note a tendency toward allegory in Romantic figuration. In Romantic allegory, the literal meaning is often co-ordinated with the elements of a *psychology [39], rather than with a fixed system of meaning such as that provided by Christian theology. For readers of these works, there is frequently no access to an autonomous, second-level order of meaning which decodes the literal meaning of the text; instead, we understand the former through attention to the features of the latter.

There is no consensus on the precise significance of Romanticism's ambivalent appreciation of allegory. The modern critic M. H. Abrams endorses the claims for the symbol made by Coleridge. He puts the reconciliation of subject and object, thought and thing, of which the symbol is an exemplar, at the centre of his account of Romanticism. For theorist Paul de Man, the symbol is always shadowed by allegory because the former is a defensive strategy designed to conceal the non-coincidence of subject and object which the latter proclaims. More recently, it has been argued that allegory and symbol compete and co-operate within Romanticism.

The roles of allegory are not exhausted by these debates. Its most protean manifestation is in political *satire, where it is used by writers of all persuasions, often to escape the attention of the law. As a mode of interpretation, it can be found in the procedures of comparative mythographers such as Richard Payne *Knight, Sir William *Drummond, and Sir William *Hamilton, who read religious myths as arcane, in effect allegorical representations of natural philosophy. If, as the critic Northrop Frye argues, 'all commentary is allegorical interpretation, an attaching of ideas to the structure of poetic imagery', then Romantic literary criticism must also be counted as one of the most remarkable of the flowers of allegory in this period.   POT

ALLEN, William (1770–1843), scientist and *philanthropist. Born into a *Quaker family of manufacturers, Allen trained as a *chemist, ran a laboratory, and *lectured at Guy's Hospital from 1808, when he became increasingly involved in philanthropic projects.

Long interested in the agitation against *slavery [6], friend of *Clarkson and *Wilberforce, he was also a founder member of the Society for the Diffusion of Knowledge upon the Punishment of Death (1809) which campaigned for a reform of the criminal code [see *prison reformers]. In 1813 he became involved with plans for a new London lunatic asylum with William *Hone, and Sir Richard Phillips (1767–1840).

Allen's other main interest was *popular education. He was a supporter of the Lancastrian *monitorial system, and after 1814 a member of the British and Foreign School Society, on which he worked closely with Francis *Place. Allen worked within the strong religious wing of the Lancastrian movement, which resisted the attempts by Francis Place and others like James *Mill to reduce its Christian emphasis. The controversy between the Bell and Lancaster schemes, together with his other reforming interests, was covered by Allen in his partisan journal, the *Philanthropist*, from 1811 to 1817. Many other schemes for social improvement were floated in the *Philanthropist*, including Robert *Owen's scheme at New Lanark which Allen joined, with Jeremy *Bentham, as a partner in 1814. Religious and other differences led to tensions between Allen and Owen, who withdrew from the partnership in 1829. Allen was no radical, and when the allied sovereigns visited London in 1814 he was introduced to them as a model Quaker. Owen believed that Allen's increasing contact with the ruling classes was turning his head. Allen devoted the rest of his life to various philan-

thropic schemes. Such campaigns often drew him into radical circles, but he remained a 'man of benevolence' rather than a political figure, a distinction which, as his experience with Owen suggests, often created tensions within the campaigns in which he was involved.   SR

almanacs (or almanacks) were calendars, either book or broadsheet, many of which included *astrological predictions as part of their overview of the year to come. They usually contained a calendar section, a chronology of significant dates, and articles on popular topics such as health or husbandry. Their format and function changed little throughout the eighteenth century, due to the virtual monopoly of the Company of Stationers, but at the end of the century they became the target for various attempts at reform [see *publishing, 21].

In 1776 the Company of Stationers was publishing about twenty-five different almanac titles. The bestsellers were those which dealt either with astrological prediction or with ancient *prophecy. *Vox Stellarum*, more widely known as *Moore's*, was by far the most popular, selling almost 400,000 copies in 1801, with a profit of over £2,500 [see *popular culture, 23]. Contemporaries claimed that it was enormously influential. This may have been because its authority derived from the ancient prophecies which it disseminated, interspersed with the comments of its pseudonymous author, 'Francis Moore' (the real Francis Moore had died in 1714).

For some, *Moore's* represented a superstitious world-view which tied the newly literate to a fatalistic lack of effort. Moreover, its visions of the future involved political comment, anathema to a *utilitarian understanding of the role of the printed word. Despite critics' fears, however, the overall message, at least of the Stationers' version, was of a reformist *Whig politics, in which peaceful campaigns for moderate change were extolled. In 1827 the liberal commercial publisher Charles Knight (1791–1873) persuaded the Society for the Diffusion of Useful Knowledge to finance the publication of the *British Almanac*, the first 'rational and popular' almanac ever produced [see *popular education]. Appearing in 1828, it was the first statistical almanac in England, its lists of 'legislation, public improvements and offices of state' forming a mounting litany of progress.

The 1830s brought two further developments. The first was the use of the genre by radicals who were campaigning for the removal of press restrictions [see *unstamped press]. Richard *Carlile was among a number of publishers who issued almanacs which left out royal birthdays and dates of accession, and included instead the birthday of Thomas *Paine. Most also expressed a disapproval of astrological almanacs, urging their readers to break away from the restrictions of superstition.

The other development was the repeal of the almanac duty in 1834. A Stationers' Company almanac, attracting a duty of 1s. 3d. a copy, could cost as much as 2s. 3d.; unstamped almanacs, including a substantial number imported from the Isle of Man, sold at between 2d. and 6d. The repeal of the duty opened the floodgates to every sort of campaigner. Christian denominations, temperance societies, patent medicine producers, *Chartist radicals, all resorted to almanacs to spread their messages. In the long run the Company of Stationers was unable to compete with the proliferation of cheap and simple alternatives.

When most people had neither watch nor clock, almanacs provided one of the few means of recording the passage of time. Through their chronologies they had considerable influence in forming communal memory and a sense of history; and through their use of prediction and prophecy they helped to shape expectations of the future. Whigs and radicals alike assisted in their transformation from a popular literary form to disseminators of a rational and utilitarian world-view.　　MP

American Revolution. From the British perspective, the American Revolution (1775–83) began as a rebellion, continued as a civil war, and concluded as yet another episode in the perennial eighteenth-century saga of conflict between the imperial European powers.

The war of independence which accompanied the revolution demonstrated the limits of Britain's fiscal-military state when it had no continental allies, depended on extended and vulnerable lines of communication, and was faced for the first time since the seventeenth century by Protestant as well as Catholic foes.

Military defeat inevitably accentuated dissension within Britain, building on existing political antagonism to the King's ministers. Within parliament, attention switched from fears of an over-mighty monarch to the issues of representation, *parliamentary reform, and government retrenchment, with the aim of destroying what was perceived to be widespread institutional corruption. The result was a powerful but short-lived crisis, beginning in the early *war [2] years and culminating in the ministerial dislocations of 1782–3, which briefly threatened the aristocratic élite's hold on the levers of state power and, in Ireland, led to the granting of legislative independence in 1782. The crisis abated after 1784, due to the shrewdness of George III and the renewed confidence in the political system engendered by the resilience of his new Prime Minister, William *Pitt. Fuelled by a complex mix of pro-American sentiment, uncertainty about legitimate war aims, temporary loss of confidence in the political capacity of the ruling élites, an upsurge in anti-popery, and, eventually, war-weariness, the crisis of the American war was not only parliamentary. It also marked the emergence of new extra-parliamentary pressure groups, feeding off a burgeoning press.

The American crisis, however, created as many problems for opposition groups as for the government. Opposition unity was to prove illusory, and for more radical groups, such as the *Society for Constitutional Information, the imperial nature of the crisis undercut the traditional oppositionist ideology combining *patriotism at home and jingoistic imperial-

ism overseas. With radicals unable thereafter to use it as a unifying device, patriotism—greatly enhanced by the growing cult of George III—gradually shed its radical past to become, by the time of a greater crisis in the 1790s, a bulwark of *loyalism.

Yet the American crisis was surprisingly short-lived. By the late 1780s Pitt's moderate reforms and sound administration had quelled fears that Britain's institutions were corrupt, and had renewed public confidence in the system of government. With hindsight, the American colonies' declaration of independence in 1776 enabled Britain to face *revolution [1] in France more united and better organized than would otherwise have been the case.　　MDU

Amiens, Peace of, between Britain and France, was signed on 25 March 1802 and lasted until hostilities were renewed in May 1803. During this fourteen-month period of peace, thousands of British tourists crossed the Channel to examine post-revolutionary France, to assess the new architecture and fashions of Paris, and, like the painters John *Opie and Benjamin *West, to see the art works looted during *Napoleon's Italian campaigns collected at the Louvre.

Many of the British visitors to Paris witnessed Napoleon's inauguration as Consul for Life on 15 August 1802, including W. S. *Landor, who felt it revealed Napoleon's new position as a dictator. Napoleon himself received a number of the visitors, including Charles James *Fox, whose meeting with the Consul was satirically depicted by James *Gillray in his caricature 'Introduction of Citizen Volpone & His Suite, At Paris' (1802), and criticized by William *Cobbett in the *Political Register* and Coleridge in the *Morning Post*.

William *Wordsworth, who was in France in August 1802 to meet Annette Vallon, was similarly contemptuous of those who crowded 'to bend the knee / In France, before the new-born Majesty'. Throughout his political sonnets of 1802, Wordsworth scornfully contrasted his experience of Consular France with that of Revolutionary France gained during his walking tour of 1790.

For William *Hazlitt, however, the visit to France was a revelation. For him the Louvre represented the ideal of art open to the people, symbolizing what he saw as the central democratic principle of the Revolution. Numbers of British visitors found themselves trapped in Paris when Napoleon suddenly resumed war in 1803. Their subsequent memoirs and accounts of internment contributed to the growth of the 'black legend' of Napoleonic atrocities which gained widespread currency in the British and *émigré press.　　SB

Anatomy Act of 1832, enabling the unclaimed bodies of institutionalized paupers to be sold to anatomy schools for dissection. Traditionally, the law had provided surgeons with the remains of executed murderers and suicides. With the expansion of medical schools the demand outstripped supply, and anatomists employed grave-robbers to exhume recently interred bodies [see *medicine, 18].

Popularly known as 'resurrectionists' or 'sack-em-up men', the robbers did not always restrict their activities to the newly deceased. Some, like the notorious Scots duo Burke and Hare, were murderers who smothered their victims. By the 1820s the complicity of medical men and the public disturbance created by body-snatching had become a matter of urgent public concern. The Anatomy Act and, in its wake, the Anatomy Inspectorate were created to secure the orderly supply of corpses to medical schools.

Dissection was viewed by all but a small group of reformers as abhorrent. Public sentiment ran strongly against the desecration of the corpse, and Christian orthodoxy decreed that the remains of the dead should be undisturbed until the Day of Judgement. The government's decision to execute and publicly dissect two London 'burkers' in 1831 did little to comfort those who viewed the Anatomy Act as post-mortem punishment for the crime of being poor. The Act's most vocal radical opponent, Henry *Hunt, countered the official argument that paupers maintained at public expense should repay society by allowing their bodies to be used for scientific research by claiming that government pensioners and sinecurists, as well as dissecting surgeons, should also make their bodies available. With the extension of franchise through the *Reform Act of 1832, the Anatomy Act became an emotive election issue in many industrial cities. In many ways a precursor of the 1834 *poor laws, the Anatomy Act met with even greater popular resistance after 1834.   LH

Anglicanism. The term strictly applies to the system of belief and worship embraced by those in religious communion with the see of Canterbury [see *religion, 10]. Anglican theological identity was only gradually formulated during the late sixteenth and seventeenth centuries in response to the political necessity of distinguishing the Church of England, as both 'Catholic' and 'Reformed', from Roman Catholicism on the one hand and Protestant Nonconformist churches on the other. The adjective 'Anglican' had gained limited currency by the end of the eighteenth century, but the term 'Anglicanism' has been aptly described by modern critic Stephen Sykes as 'a neologism of the 1830s', one of its earliest uses being attributed to John Henry Newman (1801–90) in his *Lectures on the Prophetical Office of the Church* (1837). In the seventeenth century, 'Anglicanism' had not been a term descriptive of a theological system in the way that Calvinism, Lutheranism, or Roman Catholicism has been. At that date, usage of the term 'Anglican', usually in its Latin form, denoted individual membership of the Church of England; it was primarily descriptive of a national church, linking civil government underpinned by the Royal Supremacy with traditional Catholic order, which set it apart from most continental Protestant churches. While neither 'Anglican' nor 'Anglicanism' were generally employed prior to the nineteenth century, they can be applied to describe the distinctive characteristics which contemporaries saw as defining the Church of England.

It is preferable to speak of 'the Anglican tradition' or 'the faith and practice of Anglicans' rather than 'Anglicanism' in the sense of a tight system or confessional creed. Anglicanism cannot be identified with any uniform understanding of church order, ministry, and sacraments, but it can be distinguished by a broad adherence to a particular theological method—a tripartite appeal to Scripture, tradition, and reason. Anglicanism has never had a dominant theologian such as Aquinas, Luther, or Calvin; the nearest approach to one has been Richard Hooker (1554–1600), whose apologetic *Of the Laws of Ecclesiastical Polity* is sometimes regarded as the true beginning of Anglicanism, and can be taken as the characteristic and enduring expression of an Anglican theological temper.

The doctrinal basis of Anglicanism is classically grounded in an appeal to Holy Scripture as containing all things necessary to eternal salvation, and corroborated by the testimony of the Fathers and councils of the early Church. 'Fundamental' doctrines were confined to the articles of the creed or deductions therefrom, and distinguished from 'nonfundamentals', which could be matters for discretion. Anglican identity, however, has traditionally been perceived in terms of episcopal order and a prescribed liturgical uniformity rather than of precise theological definition. The *Thirty-Nine Articles* (1571) are the only confessional statement of Anglicanism, but do not represent a complete system of doctrine; on the contrary, they have been sources of doctrinal dispute and susceptible of both 'Arminian' and 'Calvinist' interpretation among Anglican churchmen. While invested with unique authority by Calvinist and *Evangelical churchmen, the *Articles* have usually been regarded by High Churchmen as 'articles of peace' rather than as a rigid doctrinal standard. The *Ordinal* (1550), with its preface stressing the threefold ministry and episcopal ordination, is on a level with the *Articles* as a source of Anglican doctrine. The prayer-book formularies (contained in various versions of the *Book of Common Prayer*, notably those of 1559 and 1662), many of them derived from the ancient Church, have been the principal source of doctrine, notably over the sacrament of baptism, and a primary basis of the spirituality of both clergy and laity. Anglicanism should be viewed as much in terms of lay practice as of clerical theory. Parish Anglicanism revolved around the Prayer-Book liturgy with its set forms of prayer and worship in the vernacular, administration of approved sacraments, and provision of the 'rites of passage': baptism, marriage, and burial. The formal worship of the 1662 Prayer-Book carried on unaltered for over two centuries.

Anglican theological identity has been often obscured by the contradictions implicit in the English Reformation settlement. The resulting tensions were displayed in the Laudian experiment, which partly contributed to the overthrow of episcopacy (with the Anglican martyr Charles I) in the 1640s. Re-established in 1660, the Church of England was ultimately unable to contain the rise of Protestant Nonconformity. The secession of the non-jurors after 1690 weakened the Church, but recent scholarship has shown that Latitudinarian dominance of the eighteenth-century Church of England was less pervasive than historians once assumed. Theological conflict between 'High Church' and 'Low Church' parties in the reign of Queen Anne, which had overtly political overtones and mirrored battles between *Tory and *Whig, was only slowly defused. High Churchmanship, in a spiritual as well as political sense, revived after 1760, and more especially in the 1790s in reaction against the *French Revolution.

Prior to the Oxford Movement of the 1830s and 1840s, both liturgical uniformity and a common commitment to the English constitutional settlement in church and state maintained cohesion in the Church of England. The principle of religious comprehensiveness or 'moderation', itself a reaction to earlier clerical controversies, was widely regarded as a defining note of Georgian Anglicanism, and helped bind the clergy to the polity, articles, and liturgy of their Church. The *Methodist movement and Evangelical revival did much to renew the spiritual life of the Church of England and also provoked fresh controversy, but Methodism only separated completely from the mother church after John *Wesley's death in 1791. Anglican influence on the nation, however, remained as much social and cultural as doctrinal. Gentry and clergy were closely allied; the local parson was often the local landowner, so that the Church's ministry could be both defined and limited by its social character. At a parochial level, Anglicanism was a force for hierarchical social order and stability, but could also be a focus for plebeian loyalty, as attested by pro-Church mobbings of Methodist preachers and 'Church and King' *riots. Anglicanism was able to link rich and poor through a common 'Englishness', a major source of its appeal being an apparent harmony with the English character and temperament. Popular Anglicanism could often be a cultural focus for communal and local loyalties rather than a theological standard.

The social and cultural cement underpinning Anglicanism was weakened by the nineteenth-century forces of *industrialization [14] and urbanization, though recent scholarship stresses a greater degree of Anglican pastoral adaptation to the challenges of an industrial society than was once supposed. In the wake of the Oxford Movement, however, the erosion of the legal order of the Anglican establishment, and church reforms of the 1830s, the Church of England became more vulnerable to conflicts of theological interpretation of its ambiguous formularies and divergent readings of the past among different parties (High Church, Evangelical, liberal) battling for dominance. The Anglo-Catholic reinterpretation of the Catholic heritage of Anglicanism only provoked Anglican Evangelical opponents to emphasize the Church of England's Protestant past, while the emergence of modern biblical criticism among the liberal or broad church wing united the two former warring parties against the latter. *Missionary societies, *publishing companies, theological colleges, and even versions of Holy Scripture each tended to adhere to a particular party. The Church of England increasingly became an ecclesiastical patchwork. A particular parish became a stronghold of one party or another, on the basis of the views of the incumbent clergyman and sometimes of the patron of the living.

While the eighteenth-century Evangelical fathers sought to recover what they regarded as the Augustinian Protestantism of the Anglican reformers, the Tractarians sought to recover the supposedly neglected Catholic inheritance of Anglicanism; for the one, Anglicanism was a product of the Reformation, for the other, it was a product of the church of antiquity. Newman was responsible for trying to create the 'myth of a unique Anglicanism', embodying complete doctrinal coherence. The collapse of the myth was a factor in the conversion of Newman and other Tractarians to Roman Catholicism, but Anglo-Catholics remained loyal to the Tractarian ideal of a congruity between the Church of England and the ancient and even medieval church. In fact, the Anglican tradition has always been marked by an underlying religious diversity. The seventeenth-century divines from Lancelot Andrewes to the nonjurors might be regarded by High Churchmen as embodiments of 'classical Anglicanism' but they only represented a school within Anglicanism, not its definitive mouthpiece. Later Anglican Evangelical claims to be the true heirs of a dominant pre-Laudian orthodoxy characterized as episcopalian Calvinism had plausibility. While the Catholic revival enriched the sacramental life of the Church of England as a whole, later-nineteenth-century Anglo-Catholicism was even less uniquely representative of Anglicanism; it embodied a phase of mind in the Church of England, a merely tolerated school of opinion.   PBN

animal magnetism. Often known in Europe as mesmerism, animal magnetism comprised a body of quasi-scientific—especially medical—doctrines and practices associated with the teachings of Austrian physician Franz Anton Mesmer (1734–1815). By appealing to discontented literati in the 1780s and 1790s, it hastened the spread of unorthodox, occult scientific, radical, and Romantic ideas, particularly in France but to some degree in Britain as well.

Mesmer posited the existence of a universal invisible fluid, the blocking of which induced ill health in the individual or disorder in the social polity. Treatment initially consisted of making contact with magnetic rods in specially designed tubs of fluid, but this was later supplanted by mesmeric touch, gesture, or intense eye contact. Such treatment induced apparent crises and cures amongst a range of patients, beginning with the bored and fashionable classes on both sides of the Channel and later spreading to alienated Parisian literati and self-taught artisan intellectuals in London. Though Mesmer maintained that this fluid exerted a material and physical influence on the nervous system, expert scientific testimony in France and England attributed its effects solely to imaginative suggestion. In both countries animal magnetism also became entangled with a range of mystical, prophetic, and spiritualist ideas.

After being condemned in a French enquiry of 1784, it flourished briefly in London from around 1785 to 1790, and as a result a new term entered the language. Despite its proclaimed benefits, rival physicians and establishment figures denounced the practice as *quackery, thus illustrating the cultural processes of marginalization entailed in constructing legitimated scientific disciplines around the turn of the century.

The two earliest animal magnetizers were both trained in Paris. John Bell (1763–1820) recreated a mesmeric salon in Covent Garden, where patients could soak up magnetic fluid from a large oaken *baquet* through iron bars. However, the far more successful John de Mainauduc (*c*.1750–97), who allegedly earnt a fortune from his lectures and treatments, distanced himself from the discredited Mesmer, and used no magnetic equipment. This trained surgeon and man-midwife attracted several hundred people to his fashionable salon in Bloomsbury Square, including leisured members of the aristocracy, the newly wealthy wives of *Quaker industrialists, rival medical men, and occult enthusiasts such as the theatrical artist Philippe Jacques de *Loutherbourg.

De Mainauduc's basic technique resembled what we now call hypnotism. Placing himself opposite his patient—usually a woman—he stared intently into her eyes, and moved his hands round her body without touching her. Many women experienced a 'crisis'—manifested as convulsions, hysteria, or sleep—followed by a calm warmth; some of them also claimed that chronic physical ailments were alleviated. Like many physicians, de Mainauduc stressed the importance of maintaining the body's equilibrium. With a vitalist insistence that life depends on an immaterial principle, he taught that a magnetic therapist used his own 'volition' to divert diseased atoms emanating from a sick person's body and restore natural harmony.

Recognizing the profitability of this therapy, a few other animal magnetizers developed their own marketing tactics. Their theories and practices resembled those of other natural philosophers and medical men, and resonated with contemporary preoccupations such as the power of the gaze, the creative capacity of the *imagination, and the variety of states of consciousness. However, particularly after the *French Revolution, critics such as Robert *Southey marginalized animal magnetism by equating it with *enthusiasm and deploying it as a satirical weapon in a variety of debates. Erotic pamphlets and cartoons portraying scenes of sexual licentiousness explored women's sensitivity to this male-dominated practice and ridiculed its adherents [see *pornography]. 'Animal magnetism', the title of a popular farce by Elizabeth *Inchbald, became a versatile term of abuse for mocking physicians and natural philosophers, as well as religious and political factions.

Animal magnetism had virtually disappeared in Britain by the end of the century, but was re-imported from Germany by S. T. *Coleridge. Such new mesmeric practices influenced the work of other Romantic writers, notably Percy *Shelley, and became increasingly popular during the nineteenth century.   PF

Anti-Jacobin review and newspaper. The *Anti-Jacobin Review* was founded in 1798 to take the place of the short-lived *Anti-Jacobin* weekly *newspaper. The latter was the brainchild of George *Canning, though the chosen editor was William *Gifford. The newspaper was the focus for the talents of a group of *Tory wits which comprised John Hookham Frere (1769–1846), George Ellis (1753–1815), and Robert Jenkinson (later Lord *Liverpool), as well as Canning himself. The group also managed to procure the services of James *Gillray who provided caricature illustrations when some of the works were issued as broadsides [see *prints, 22]. The aim of the anti-Jacobins was not simply to attack the Foxite opposition but also 'to set the mind of the people right on every subject'. Unlike Hannah *More's *Cheap Repository Tracts, which had a more popular audience in mind, the fire of the anti-Jacobins was directed at politicians and intellectuals who were seen as bestowing a respectability on the so-called 'New Morality' associated with infidelity and *republicanism. *Fashion in general, from the taste for *sensibility [11] and the *Gothic novel to styles of dress copied from French models, was an object of their derision and suspicion. The *Anti-Jacobin* newspaper was succeeded by the more stolid *Anti-Jacobin Review*, and the Canning circle was largely replaced by *Anglican clergymen. The new brand of anti-Jacobinism was every bit as ferociously conservative, but rather humourless in style. Its periodical format moved the focus of the publication away from the daily business of parliament and towards a general critical survey of dangerous ideas.   JM

Arianism. Heresy of the third-century Alexandrian Arius, holding that Jesus and God were not of the same essence and, in extreme cases, that Jesus was not divine.

ARNOLD, Samuel (1740–1802), musician, composer, and editor who made important contributions to *music [26] in the *theatre [24], concert hall, and church. Educated at the Chapel Royal, and gaining his doctorate of music from Oxford in 1773, he began his career as a harpsichordist at Covent Garden in 1764, where his pastiche *opera *The Maid of The Mill* (1765) achieved great popularity. From 1769 to 1776 Arnold owned the *pleasure gardens at Marylebone, where burlettas (short, all-sung comic operas) were performed during the summer. In 1777 he moved to George Colman's Little Theatre in the Haymarket, where he composed for the summer seasons for twenty-five years. He held the post of organist of the Chapel Royal, then of Westminster Abbey, and in 1789 he became the official conductor of the Academy of Ancient Music. He composed and arranged nine *oratorios, and for several years he shared the direction of the oratorios at Drury Lane, but the main part of his career was devoted to opera, of which he composed or contributed to more than seventy works. Arnold was also a respected editor, who made the first collected edition of *Handel's works.　JG

ASHLEY family, English musicians and impresarios active in London and in the provinces 1780–1830. John Ashley (1734–1805), a bassoonist, was assistant conductor to Joah Bates (1741–99) at the 1784 *Handel Commemoration. From 1788 to 1793 and from 1801 to 1804 he promoted and played in large-scale *music festivals in the provinces, aided by his four sons: the violinist Charles ('General', 1770–1818), the organist John James (1772–1815), the cellist Charles Jane (1773–1843), and the viola player Richard (1775–1836). He was director of the Lenten *oratorio concerts at Covent Garden from 1795 until his death, and in this capacity was responsible for the first performances in England of *Haydn's *The Creation* (28 March 1800) and of *Mozart's Requiem (27 February 1801).

After John Ashley's death the management of the Covent Garden oratorios was taken over by General and Charles Jane Ashley. The two brothers also continued the family involvement with provincial festivals, as players, orchestral contractors, and on occasion as promoters, between 1807 and 1815.

The activities of the various members of the Ashley family illustrate the growing professionalization of *concert organization and promotion, and the ways in which orchestral musicians were able to diversify into these areas. The family is also significant for the role it played in the development of the provincial music festival.　PO

Association for the Preservation of Liberty and Property against Republicans and Levellers, founded in London by John *Reeves on 20 November 1792, sought to stimulate demonstrations of *loyalism throughout the country as an antidote to the escalation of popular radicalism.

The first nine months of 1792 had seen reformers assiduously circulating radical literature throughout the country, as well as the spread of reform societies among the populace. A Royal Proclamation against seditious writings in May 1792 and the prosecution of Thomas *Paine's *Rights of Man: Part the Second* for a libel on the British constitution proved equally ineffective in stemming these developments. By December 1792 a real fear of insurgence in London led the government to issue a further Royal Proclamation against sedition on 1 December, twelve days after the founding meeting of Reeves's Association. It is a matter of dispute how far Reeves was simply a government lackey, acting wholly on instructions from the ministry; but even if he acted independently there is no doubt that his initiative was warmly welcomed in government circles.

The Association printed resolutions in several London papers supporting the existing constitution, decrying the activities of French and domestic radicals, and urging loyal supporters to correspond with the London Association. The main aims were to generate further loyal associations throughout the country and to stimulate the detection and prosecution of subversives and radical activists. On both counts the

Association was successful. Several hundred provincial associations, with committees made up of men of property, local magistrates, and churchmen, sent in resolutions, and there is no doubt that many radicals found it more difficult to meet, speak, and publish freely. However, the activities of these local committees subsequently took second place in many areas to the spreading of anti-radical propaganda. The loyalist associations, but more particularly the correspondents of Reeves, played a major and innovative role in generating and circulating throughout the country propaganda and political pamphlets which sought to rouse members of the élite to the defence of the established order, to warn of the potentially horrific consequences of adopting 'French principles', to portray reformers as committed to a thoroughgoing egalitarianism and atheism, and to caution the lower orders as to the dangers of associating with men of seditious intent. Some of the publications were written by John Bowles (1751–1819), a barrister, magistrate, place-holder, and paid Treasury writer; others by the Revd William *Jones. Numbers of pamphlets and broadsides stemmed from unsolicited contributions from correspondents, many of whom were effectively bidding for inclusion within the political domain. By insisting on the urgency of the problem of vulgar radicalism and offering their services as educators of this class, their inclusion within a hitherto élite political culture became automatic.　MPH

astrology may be defined as the belief that celestial and terrestrial phenomena are connected in a way that can be interpreted and used to human advantage, usually to predict the future. Although widely ridiculed and dismissed by educated comment from the late eighteenth century, astrology remained an active component in the creation of middle-class and plebeian *popular culture [23].

Among the best-known astrologers were Henry Andrews (1743–1820), compiler of the popular *almanac *Vox Stellarum*, and John Worsdale (1766–c.1828), a friend of Andrews and a consulting astrologer based at Lincoln. Both men shared a deep commitment to a mathematically precise and Christian astrology. Andrews accepted requests from his readers to calculate their birth charts, and much of his spare time was taken up with a private astrological practice and the writing of unpublished astrological texts. Worsdale published many astrological works and was also widely known as a wise or cunning man.

Ebenezer Sibley (1751–99) was a successful astrological writer based in the south of England, whose blend of experimental *natural philosophy [34] and interest in the occult produced a new form of judicial astrology, one which would appeal to the emerging middle classes as a semi-erudite magical science. It was this more magical practice of astrology that appealed to John Varley (1778–1842), the astrologer and painter who worked with William *Blake on calling up the spirits of various dead celebrities. Varley calculated charts to show correspondences between the moment of the spirit's appearance and its physiognomy as sketched by Blake.

THE ANATOMY.

You nasty little ugly wretch, begone,
Get out, make haste and put your breeches on.

57. 'The Anatomy' from the popular almanac *Poor Robin* (1828). Astrological almanacs frequently came under attack in the nineteenth century from evangelical reform groups such as the Society for the Suppression of Vice who saw them as nourishing superstition and traditional unruliness.

The most widespread astrology, however, did not involve the casting of a chart. Natural astrology, found at all levels of society, linked visible celestial signs such as the phases of the moon or eclipses with terrestrial events, especially with the weather and with the fertility and health of plants and animals. Under the rubric of 'moonlore' it became a major topic of exploration by antiquarians later in the nineteenth century.

Two new astrological almanacs, Raphael's *Prophetic Messenger* (1826) and Zadkiel's *Herald of Astrology* (1832), signalled the emergence of a flourishing new version of judicial astrology which used personalized forecasts related to individual prosperity and fulfilment, far removed from the political or meteorological predictions of the seventeenth century. Some of the practitioners of this new astrology were prosecuted under the 1824 Vagrancy Act, designed to reduce *fortune-telling.   MP

AUSTEN, Jane (1775–1817), arguably the most important English novelist of this period, whose modest contemporary popular success developed into widespread critical, institutional, and popular acclaim in the late nineteenth century.

Born in Steventon, the daughter of the clergyman George Austen, Austen had access to a large library. As a teenager, she wrote numerous skits and mock-novels, mainly parodies of *sensibility [11] fiction (collected as *Minor Works* (1954)), which already show her invention and satiric bent. Her six main *novels [31] are usually divided into two periods, the first comprising *Sense and Sensibility* (1811), *Pride and Prejudice* (1813), and *Northanger Abbey*, the second comprising *Mansfield Park* (1814), *Emma*

(1816), and *Persuasion* (published posthumously with *Northanger Abbey* in 1818), though work on the novels proceeded continuously. The first group of novels draws together the concern with 'female difficulties' of the earlier novelists of sensibility, and the plot motif, used by Frances *Burney and others, of 'a young lady's entrance into the world'. The later novels retain this focus on the comic and ethical implications of courtship behaviour, but communal, family, and physical settings now have greater depth and resonance.

Austen was committed to novel-writing as a profession, and to making money through her work. There is clear evidence—contrary to myth—that her family respected this, providing her with time and facilities for writing, and promoting the publication of her books. Her sister Cassandra, with whom she shared a room, was probably the most important figure in her life. Austen addressed a large body of correspondence to Cassandra, written when staying with relatives. Unfortunately, however, much about their relationship must remain unknown, since Cassandra destroyed many of the letters after Jane's death.

All Austen's novels concern the life of the contemporary gentry, a broad social class which comprised both landed and landless gentry. Austen belonged to the landless gentry, though she enjoyed connections to the landed gentry and aristocracy through her mother, Cassandra Leigh, and her novels ceaselessly disclose the tenuousness and ambiguity of class boundaries. The tensions between money and status and the shifting correlations between manners, social position, and moral sensibility play an important role in her novels. Politics in the formal, and 'adventures' in the picaresque, sense are absent from her novels, but political issues, when redefined as personal, domestic, and gender concerns, penetrate them. Though apparently formal and decorous, Austen's novels offer at once sharp and amusing fictions of personal fulfilment, and searching commentary on social relations.

Though soon recognized by many critics, including Sir Walter *Scott and Richard Whately (1787–1863), as a compelling novelist who brought a new refinement, verisimilitude, and psychological complexity to the novel genre, Austen's later reputation during the mid-nineteenth century was hindered by the naïve assumption that her art was contaminated by the provinciality of the worlds she depicts.

Austen has often been claimed to offer a conservative depiction of human behaviour. Certainly, the irony of her novels depends upon a traditional assessment of the limitations, rather than the possibilities, of human nature. Read against the background of the *French Revolution and current English antagonism to progressive thought, the novels are, broadly speaking, counter-revolutionary, patriotic, morally and politically conservative.

On the other hand, read against the background of contemporary feminists like Mary *Wollstonecraft, the novels offer an often astringent focus on the position of *women [4] in contemporary society and radical scrutiny of masculine prerogatives and the self-deceptions, both male and female, that support them. Women's independence and autonomy are certainly important values in the books, particularly in their incarnations in the characters of Elizabeth Bennett and Emma Woodhouse. These figures in particular, and the novels in general, are shadowed by a pervasive sense of the tedium and unfulfilment threatening the life of a gentlewoman, whether married or not. However, these issues are complicated by the subtle and, in one case (*Mansfield Park*), not entirely coherent ironies of her texts.

Jane Austen's novels, following the early, unpublished, and melodramatic 'Lady Susan', break with the epistolary convention, and instead handle the form of omniscient narrative with a new flexibility, ironic inflection, and range. Increasingly in the earlier novels the narrative incorporates passages illustrative of the thought-sequences of characters. Beginning with *Mansfield Park*, individuals are represented both dramatically and in the new novelistic technique of 'free indirect speech'. This technique is marked by an absence of grammatical markers which indicate a character's speech, and therefore allows a subtlety of movement between the narrator and the supposed 'consciousness' of a range of figures, opening possibilities of irony that are exploited most successfully in *Emma*. Austen is able to utilize the representation of an inner monologue to suggest complex psychological processes, disclose self-deceptions to the reader, and to hint, through rhythmic and other means, at the dynamics of desire.

Within the conventional outline of the courtship plot and marriage-ending and retaining a surface politeness, the novels offer penetrating representations of the intricacies of family and sexual relations. *Mansfield Park*, in particular, contains a study of dependency and personal development that, despite its outward decorum, introduces a new depth of psychology to the English novel. Austen's interest in forms of repressed sexuality is also manifest in such figures as Mr Woodhouse and Mrs Norris.

After the death of her father in 1805, Austen settled with her mother, sister, and a friend at Chawton Cottage in 1809. It was here that she worked on her novels, including the unfinished and posthumously published *Sanditon* (1925), a satire on (among other things) the commercialization of leisure and medical faddism.   JW

autobiography. Writing in the *Annual Register* in 1807, Robert *Southey described his time as one in which 'booksellers, public lecturers, pickpockets, and poets become autobiographers'. The ubiquity of the genre can be gauged by the fact that the word 'autobiography' was actually coined in 1797 by William *Taylor in the *Monthly Review* (although Southey's use of the word in the *Quarterly* over a decade later is more often given precedence). Reviewing Isaac *D'Israeli's 'Diaries and Self-Biographies', Taylor suggested his word was a 'pedantic coinage', but it proved to be one which he and others used repeatedly in *reviews over the next few decades.

The eighteenth century had seen a growing interest in the techniques of life-writing in autobiography; in biography, such as *Boswell's *Life of Johnson*; and in *novels [31] such as Sterne's *Tristram Shandy*. Increasingly the formal public 'Character' was replaced in such productions by more impressionistic accounts of complex individuals. The most influential example at the end of the eighteenth century was *Rousseau's *Confessions*, published in English translation between 1783 and 1790. The last section of Rousseau's autobiography sanctioned a view of the social world as a prison, which may have passed from *Gothic literature on to the melancholy of *Byron's poetry. Rousseau also gave credence to reveries and solitude as a path to self-knowledge and may have influenced the technique of what is often regarded as the greatest creative autobiography of the period, *Wordsworth's *The Prelude*, although that poem is carefully distanced from Rousseau's emotionalism.

Something of the importance of the genre for the period can be gauged by the fact that *Coleridge cast *Biographia Literaria* (1817), his major statement of theory, in an autobiographical form; but the genre's popularity was to be found in every corner of the ever-expanding *publishing [21] market. *Evangelicals and *Methodists recounted their spiritual conversion and growth, and numerous autodidacts gave accounts of their journeys from ignorance to knowledge. Print itself was often the hero in these stories of *self-improvement. The wider literary public may have valued such productions as affirmations of the march of progress, but they frequently contained statements of intellectual independence which linked personal development to political activities. Published autobiographies by women remained relatively rare, but life-writing was a key part of the female literary experience in private diaries and journals such as those kept by Dorothy *Wordsworth.
                                                                                                JM

B

BABBAGE, Charles (1791–1871), *utilitarian political radical and mathematician who attempted to develop the mental process of calculation, and ultimately his notion of 'intelligence', into a machine and as a model for society.

His father, Benjamin Babbage, was a wealthy banker who sent Charles to Cambridge in October 1810, where the son was instrumental in forming the Analytical Society. In collaboration with John *Herschel, Charles sought to propagate a form of mathematics based on the French analytical method in opposition to the traditional form of British geometry. During this period he also came to admire, and regularly visited, the exiled younger brother of *Napoleon, Lucien Bonaparte, in Worcestershire. Bonapartism subsequently informed Babbage's politics and view of science.

In 1820 he was an important figure in establishing the Astronomical Society of London in collaboration with Herschel, the stockbroker Francis Baily, and a number of other commercially oriented men. He also considered a career in assurance, being appointed actuary to the short-lived Protector Society in 1824. During the early 1820s he began to design and build the Difference Engine—a machine designed to calculate and print basic mathematical tables for use in navigation, astronomy, industry, and commerce.

Throughout the 1820s Babbage sought to reform the intellectual and institutional structure of British science, his efforts culminating in *The Decline of Science* in 1830. He regarded science as a factory, in which the intellectual division of labour was carefully divided, with each operation a connected part of an overall system managed by élite engineers with a firm grounding in both theory and practice. His notion of intelligence was functional, standardized, and mechanical, inspired in part by the array of *factories visited throughout his career, coupled with a keen interest in railways. He codified his observations and suggestions in *On the Economy of Machinery and Manufactures* (1832), which later informed the work of both Karl Marx and John Stuart *Mill.

Babbage viewed the world as an analytical system which conformed to a prescribed programme designed by the ultimate engineer (God). He could thus argue, in response to the Bridgewater Treatises of the 1830s (a series of eight essays on natural theology written by leading figures of the Royal Society, including William *Whewell, founded at the behest of Frances Egerton, eighth Earl of Bridgewater (1756–1829)), that revelation and miracles were congruent with an original calculated programme. This was objectified into his plans for an Analytical Engine.   WJA

Bach movement, English, the introduction from around 1800 of the music of J. S. Bach into England, where it had previously been almost entirely unknown. It was marked by the first English performances and publications of Bach's music, and was led by a group of enthusiasts which included Benjamin Jacob (1778–1829), C. F. Horn (1762–1830), A. F. C. Kollmann (1756–1829), and Samuel *Wesley.   PO

BACH, Johann Christian (1735–82), London's principal resident composer and *pianist during the 1760s and 1770s. The youngest son of J. S. Bach, he began his professional career in Italy, moving to London in 1762 with an invitation to write for the opera-house. However, it was his instrumental *music [26] that secured his reputation: an important early symphonist, he cultivated an elegant, almost *Mozartian style. The symphonies were written for a long-running subscription series, the Bach-Abel concerts, which laid the foundations for modern *concert life. He also pioneered the newly emerging piano as a concert instrument.   SMcV

BAGE, Robert (1728–1801), industrialist and novelist. The generally positive reception of Bage's early *novels [31] soured in the 1790s, when he was stigmatized as a *Jacobin novelist.

Deeply involved with the English *Enlightenment [32], Bage participated fully in the flourishing provincial culture of Dissent. He was a member of the Derby Philosophical Society, close to men like Erasmus *Darwin, Josiah *Wedgwood, and the historian-topographer William Hutton (1723–1815), and in touch with the better-known Lunar Society in Birmingham [see *literary and philosophical societies]. The broad cultural and scientific interests of these circles are reflected in his six novels: *Mount Henneth* (1782); *Barham Downs* (1784); *The Fair Syrian* (1787); *James Wallace* (1788); *Man as He Is* (1792); and *Hermsprong, or Man as He Is Not* (1796).

The novels take the form of gently comic *satires whose digressive plot structures reminded contemporary reviewers of Smollett's fiction. At the centre of each novel is a villainous aristocrat who is a figure of political and domestic tyranny. Aristocratic manners and fashion are usually rejected by the sensible heroine in favour of middle-class morality. It is Bage's secondary female characters, culminating in Miss Fluart of *Hermsprong*, who are given leeway to be more original and independent, although their vivacity is significantly not rewarded with marriage to the hero.

There is no obvious break in method or style between the novels of the 1780s and 1790s, but the latter clearly position themselves as contributions to the reformist side of the revolution controversy. Although himself no advocate of popular insurrections, Bage was regarded as a Jacobin novelist, the *Anti-Jacobin* newspaper comparing his work to 'the trash' of Mary *Robinson. Walter *Scott chose the less-provocative novels of the 1780s for his Ballantyne's Library series in 1824, but still attracted the censure of the Tory *Quarterly Review* for doing so.   JM

BAILLIE, Joanna (1762–1851), dramatist, poet, lyricist. The most highly regarded female dramatist of her time, Baillie was the author of innovative forms of tragedy and historical drama whose imaginative power, *lyrical intensity, and complex psychological realism had far-reaching theoretical and practical effects on Romantic drama and *theatre [24].

Baillie spent most of her youth in Hamilton, with a brief period in Glasgow from 1776, when her father was appointed professor of divinity at the University of Glasgow. After her father's death in 1778, Joanna moved with her mother and twin sister to Long Calderwood, then to London, and finally to Hampstead in 1791. She remained here for the rest of her life, her home becoming a meeting-place for writers such as Lucy *Aikin, Samuel *Rogers, Anna Laetitia *Barbauld, and Maria *Edgeworth. In 1798 Baillie published anonymously the first volume of *A Series of Plays: In Which It is Attempted to Delineate the Stronger Passions of the Mind. Each Passion being the Subject of a Tragedy and a Comedy*, which caused a sensation. Subsequent volumes appeared in 1802 and 1812. Outlining a programme of theatrical reform, the 'Introductory Discourse' provided an important theoretical framework for the reception of the *Plays*, and criticized the superficiality of the sentimental drama and prevalent comic genres. Its powerful renovation of the sentimental ideal of sympathy as a Romantic dramatic principle underpinned a theory of a cross-generic, common, and natural *language [40] which anticipated *Wordsworth's celebrated 'Preface' to the *Lyrical Ballads* (1800). Of these plays (also known as *Plays on the Passions*), De Monfort, a tragedy on hatred, was Baillie's best-known and most successful play. It offered a new conception of tragic character independent of the action and causality of plot, and a *sublime conception of scenics in which landscape and external surroundings were emphasized to elaborate an alienated and contingent subjectivity. *De Monfort* was first performed in 1800 at Drury Lane, with a cast that included John Philip *Kemble and Sarah *Siddons. Although Jane De Monfort was a popular, widely celebrated showcase role, and a favourite of Siddons, the performed *De Monfort* did not match the excitement generated by the printed version.

Baillie's plays were always more popular with the reading rather than the theatre-going public, earning her a distinguished if problematic reputation as a writer of *closet drama. Lord *Byron, whose own poetic dramas were written in opposition to a contemporary stage generally perceived to be in decline, was a great admirer of Baillie, whom he saw as revitalizing British drama with the tragic genius of the

Restoration dramatist Thomas Otway (1652–85). He assisted a short-lived but warmly received revival of *De Monfort* in 1821. Baillie was also highly praised by Wordsworth, and habitually compared to *Shakespeare by Sir Walter *Scott. Scott befriended Baillie in 1807, and became an active supporter of her work. Her first negative review came from Francis *Jeffrey in his 1803 review of the second volume of the *Plays on the Passions* (1802) in the *Edinburgh Review*. Jeffrey found fault with Baillie's principle of the dramatization of a character through a ruling passion on the grounds that it was irrelevant to the whole, and attacked the moral pretensions of her dramas by claiming that drama could have no moral effect.

The Family Legend (1810), together with *Constantine Paleologus* (1808), enjoyed the longest stage run of Baillie's plays. It was based on the legend of the fifteenth-century clan feud told to Baillie by her friend Anne *Damer as the legend of her maternal ancestors. Like *De Monfort*, *The Family Legend* responds to contemporary pseudo-historicism with a historical drama of intense psychological and historical realism. Centring on the story of Helen of Argyll, the object of a tussle between two clans, the play explores the issues of legitimacy and inheritance with particular reference to their effects upon women. As in *De Monfort*, Baillie dispenses with the established heroic rules which dictated an unmitigated heroism in the good and unmitigated evil in the bad. She presents mixed characters in relation to shifting social and material circumstances.

Another of Baillie's contributions to the mixed historical genres that proliferated in women's writings during the Napoleonic period is represented by the non-dramatic poems *Metrical Legends of Exalted Characters* (1821), tributes to male and female heroes of Scottish history. In prefacing the legend of William Wallace, Baillie calls attention to the differences that frame the respective unions of Scotland and Ireland with England, and laments Ireland's *Act of Union as an effect of oppressive historical circumstances. In this way, Baillie develops historical setting as a mechanism for allegorizing current events. She thus resists the homogenizing impulses of much Romantic *antiquarianism [35] during our period, which celebrate local and regional identities as part of and subsumed within a larger national British identity and interest.   CT

ballads, narrative poems of oral origin usually thought to have arisen in the late Middle Ages. They were first printed in the sixteenth century in broadsheet form. Their subject-matter varied from traditional and semi-historical material to tales of love, the marvellous, and topical events.

In the eighteenth century the ballad, although still popular orally, was unfashionable in literary circles. Samuel *Johnson mocked its repetitive stanza and banal style:

> I put my hat upon my head
> And walk'd into the Strand,
> And there I met another man
> With his hat in his hand.

The rediscovery of ballads was initiated by Thomas *Percy in his *Reliques of Ancient English Poetry* (1765), which contains ballads from several sources, including authoritative versions of one of the most famous, 'The Hunting of the Cheviot', popularly known as 'Chevy Chase' [see *antiquarianism, 35]. The appeal of ballads to late-eighteenth-century readers was that, in contrast to the classical aspirations of Augustan culture, they represented a native tradition of *poetry [29] and gave voice to the common people. Percy was succeeded by other ballad editors, of whom the most notable was Joseph *Ritson, who produced the first collection of ballads associated with Robin Hood (1795).

Percy had commented that the north of England and south of Scotland were rich sources of ballads. That was confirmed in the work of Walter *Scott, whose *Minstrelsy of the Scottish Border* (1802–3) established the concept of the Border ballad, giving pride of place to the 'riding ballads' describing Border raids.

Later-eighteenth-century ballad editors supplemented printed sources by attempts to collect versions from contemporary ballad-singers. They were usually unable to collect the music, but Anna Brown (1747–1810) proved an exception. Her ballads, dealing particularly with love, magic, and witchcraft, were recorded in Aberdeenshire along with, in some cases, simple notation of her tunes.

The ballad in the eighteenth century was of more than antiquarian interest. It inspired imitation, and also influenced published poetry in more elusive ways. 'The Diverting History of John Gilpin' by William *Cowper is a humorous imitation of the urban broadsheet ballad. Thomas *Chatterton's ballad imitations were an attempt to re-enter the medieval world. Scott and Matthew 'Monk' *Lewis imitated the German horror ballad. John *Keats, though not particularly associated with the folk tradition, made use of the ballad motif of the human in thrall to a faery in 'La Belle Dame sans Merci' (1820). An eclectic use of the ballad tradition may be seen in *Wordsworth and *Coleridge's *Lyrical Ballads* (1798). Its title revealed a revision of the concept of the ballad: traditionally ballads were narrative and only incidentally *lyrical. Many of the poems in the collection were too autobiographical and reflective to be considered ballads, but two at least reached back to the narrative subject-matter of the traditional ballad. Wordsworth's 'The Idiot Boy' showed the ballad's concern with ordinary human experience; and Coleridge's 'The Ancient Mariner', which uses the ballad stanza, showed the tradition's concern with the human being caught up in the supernatural.

CL

ballet had been presented to the public in London's royal *theatres [24] throughout the eighteenth century, and vied with *opera in popularity. Patrons accustomed to its performances were inclined to regard opera-ballet as a charming entertainment or *divertissement* rather than a serious art form; but, while remaining intrinsic to many operas, ballet had gradually developed into a disciplined form of theatrical dancing, and was presented by impresarios as independent entertainment.

Most eighteenth-century English dancers were taught by dance-masters brought to London from Italy and the Paris Opera, although English choreographers were not unknown. Shrewsbury-born John Weaver (1673–1760) had endeavoured to introduce innovative and free movements to theatrical ballet in the early eighteenth century. His aim was to carry dramatic tales forward by movement rather than by words, but his dance dramas inspired scant popular support. *Ballet d'action* was successfully brought to the London stage by the celebrated actor-manager David Garrick, who introduced the dramatic ballets of French choreographer Jean-Georges Noverre to the London public in 1745.

In London, full-length ballets were customarily arranged by foreign choreographers and performed by imported dancers to *music [26] written by European composers. Lully had composed rhythmic pieces for court ballet, Rameau devised melodies to fit specific characters in opera-ballet, and Gluck created orchestral music for ballet drama. The young *Beethoven wrote pieces especially for the Italian choreographer Salvatore Vigano (1769–1821), who often worked in London, and in 1801 he composed the overture and score for the ballet *The Creatures of Prometheus*.

The fall of the *ancien régime* and the terrors of the *French Revolution caused many established dancers and choreographers to flee France. Ballet-master Louis Boisgirard and choreographer Jean Dauberval were exiled in London, which became a centre of ballet activity in the 1790s. Ironically, Dauberval had already broken with classical traditions to focus upon prosaic rural characters and country customs in his ballet *La Fille Mal Gardée* in 1789. He staged this influential ballet at London's Pantheon Theatre in 1791, where it received immediate public acclaim.

By the late eighteenth and early nineteenth century, ballet had developed into a dance form which required complete mastery of dramatic gesture, attitude, technique, elevation, and lyrical movement from professional dancers. Male dancers retained their presence, but ballerinas became more prominent on stage. New dramatic roles were created, as were new costumes, and in the process the ballerina helped to redefine feminine ideals of form and grace. By a series of design progressions, lighter, shorter costumes and flexible shoes revealed dancers' virtuosity of footwork that allowed imaginative choreographers to extend dancers' skills. Exposure of graceful arms, *décolletage*, shapely legs, and ankles allowed audiences to judge a female dancer's shape as well as her technical and dramatic performance. Agility, grace, and elevation were paramount, and the *pas de deux* featuring the male dancer supporting the prima ballerina became a focal point of Romantic ballets.

Choreographers' desire for artistic dance forms prefiguring the metaphysical, emotional, and transcendent aspirations of Romanticism hastened the creation of ballets which demanded even more physical and lyrical expression from dancers. Popular *folk legends provided inspiration, and themes drawn from neo-*Gothic, *oriental, mythical, *allegorical, and *romantic fictional genres formed the basis of many new ballets. Contemporary fascination with the Orient and the popular poem *Lallah Rookh* (1817), by Thomas *Moore, inspired choreographers with sensuous images of Arabian nights and slave harems. The pre-Romantic ballets, *Paradise and the Peri*, *Lallah Rookh, or, the Rose of Lahore*, and *Mokanna*, choreographed by Carlo Blasis (1797–1878), were based upon Moore's work.

Despite the Napoleonic wars London remained a centre for choreography and ballet performances, although the standard of the *corps de ballet* and teaching declined. After *Napoleon's defeat French dancers and choreographers were able to travel and work freely abroad, and Auguste and Armand Vestris, both talented French choreographers, arrived in London in 1815 to work at the King's Theatre. The Royal Opera House, Covent Garden, the Pantheon, the Theatre Royal, Drury Lane, Haymarket, Princess's, and Lyceum theatres also all provided ballet stages. Stage dioramas and elaborate stages were often flooded in artificial limelight. Stage machinery was used to create special effects such as mists, and orchestral music completed the atmosphere of fantasy. Dancers appeared in castle ruins, slave harems, and moonlit forests. Through the efforts of the entrepreneurial subscription librarian John Ebers, some of Europe's leading dancers were engaged to dance at the King's Theatre, where they were permitted to wear silk tights. *Newspapers began to review performances seriously and to describe dancers' techniques in poetic detail. French choreographical terminology, such as *arabesque*, *pirouette*, *jetté*, *en pointe*, became familiar terms.

England's first notable dancer was Louisa Court (*fl.* 1820–50), who appeared initially as Cupid in 1819 and later captured audiences with her audacious leaps and vivacious style. *The Times* and the *Morning Post* loyally praised her flight, grace, and stunning technique, but she could not compare with foreign dancers such Fanny Bias, who first danced on points in 1821, or Marie Taglioni, Fanny Elssler, and Carlotta Grisi cast as sylphs, fairies, gypsies, and harem slaves. By 1832 *The Times* could observe that ballet was 'an art worthy to rank with poetry and painting'.

Romantic ballet probably reached its peak in England in the 1830s with the first performances of *La Sylphide* (later *Les Sylphides*) and *Giselle*. Romanticism's influence, though not immediate, translated strongly into ballets which emphasized the dichotomy of the flesh and the spirit—ethereal female spirits and mortal men united only in death. By the 1840s, however, the popularity of such ballets was declining. Many choreographers and dancers of distinction had retired, and England, without national companies and schools, had little to offer. British ballet thus moved for a long period into the realms of musical theatre. SR

93 **BANKS**, Sir Joseph (1742–1820), scientific organizer, collector, and administrator. Banks's historical importance rests on his ability to place science firmly in the public domain. Though his own scientific achievements were slight, he could recognize talent in others and use his considerable abilities as a patron and an organizer to obtain support for their endeavours. As president of the Royal Society from 1778 to 1820, he guided the nation's oldest and most prestigious *scientific society in an age when Britain's stature in the world was growing as a consequence of its economic growth and increasing military and naval supremacy. Banks, then, became the de facto minister for science to the British government in an age when the needs of the economy, the *empire [5], and the armed forces called more and more for expert scientific advice. This Banks provided both directly and by acting as a conduit for the opinions of his many scientific clients.

Banks was educated in the bastions of the established order—Harrow (1752–6), Eton (1756–60), and Christ Church, Oxford (1760–3). He received little formal scientific education, though his interest in *botany began at Eton and was continued at Oxford, where, to compensate for the inertia of the university's professor of botany, Humphrey Sibthorp, he imported at his own expense the botanist Israel Lyons to give a short course of lectures in July 1764. These establishment institutions did, however, provide Banks with many of the connections which later enabled him to link science with the workings of government; and, at Oxford particularly, there was considerable opportunity to pursue his natural history interests in informal ways [see *natural philosophy, 34].

Banks's early apprenticeship as a practising naturalist was provided by his joining a naval expedition to Newfoundland and Labrador in 1766—an opportunity which was made possible by his long-standing association with his old Eton friend, the naval officer Constantine John Phipps (1744–92). The experience thus gained was to stand him in good stead when he set out on his great journey of *exploration [37] in the *Endeavour* in 1768. By linking the study of science and the naval exploration of largely uncharted territories, Banks helped to create the tradition of scientific-cum-naval expeditions which were, in the nineteenth century, to produce such glories of British science as Darwin's *Beagle* voyage and Huxley's *Rattlesnake* expedition. As president of the Royal Society Banks was himself to foster such expeditions, being particularly active in promoting Flinders's *Investigator* expedition of 1801, which had as its object the circumnavigation of Australia.

The return of the *Endeavour* in 1771 brought Banks public adulation and the admiration of George III; it was the beginning of a long association with the King which enabled Banks to utilize royal patronage for the benefit of science. One immediate outcome of this fruitful partnership was Banks's appointment in 1773 as the virtual director of the Royal Gardens at Kew, which he helped to develop into a major centre for imperial botany. The acclaim that Banks received on the return of the *Endeavour* did, however, lead him to overestimate his own significance. His subsequent attempt to pressure the navy into remodelling

51

*Cook's second great voyage—that of the *Resolution* (1772–5)—better to suit his scientific needs led to his stormy departure from the expedition. Having assembled a scientific party Banks organized a voyage to Iceland in 1772 as a partial and very inadequate substitute for a second circumnavigation of the globe. Thereafter, Banks's chief theatre of operations was London—apart from the annual summer pilgrimage to the family estates in Lincolnshire, where he kept in close touch with local activities and promoted the application of science to agriculture through the techniques of agricultural improvement [see *land, 16]. Banks's election to president of the Royal Society in 1778, followed by his marriage to Dorothea Hugesson the following year, marked a watershed in his life as the youthful adventurer gave way to the public man of science.

Banks's position as president of the Royal Society and his wide acquaintance led to his being called on more and more by government for expert advice. In 1779 his testimony before the Beauchamp Committee of the House of Commons, enquiring into possible sites for the transportation of convicts, did much to persuade the government seriously to consider settlement at Botany Bay, which finally came to pass in 1788. Thereafter Banks remained the early colony's chief advocate in London at a time when the government was almost entirely preoccupied with the conduct of *war [2]. It was Banks who determined the choice of many of the early governors and who helped to overcome the trading restrictions imposed on the infant colony of New South Wales by the *East India Company's monopoly. In return, he expected to be advised of any possible scientific or economic advantage which the colony might offer.

Banks provided the British government with scientific advice by means of several different channels, though his varied connections within the governing élite helped to give his activities coherence and direction. His close working relationship with Henry *Dundas, president of the Board of Control (for India) from 1793 to 1801, gave him some influence in shaping policy towards India in such a manner as to encourage crops and products which would serve Britain's economy. Banks's active involvement in the affairs of the Privy Council's Committee on Trade—an involvement officially recognized by his appointment as Privy Councillor in 1797—provided him with an even more important forum for linking science with imperial policy. And, in lesser ways, Banks could also bring his influence to bear on other governmental instrumentalities such as the Home Office, the Board of Longitude, the Board of Agriculture, and the Mint. Whatever the agency, his fundamental aspirations remained constant: that science and the techniques of improvement should be used, in the Baconian phrase, 'for the relief of man's estate' and, more particularly, to increase the wealth and prestige of the nation.   JGA

71 **BARBAULD,** Anna Laetitia (1743–1825). Precociously gifted as a child, Barbauld received a classical education from her father, a schoolmaster, later clas-

sical tutor at Warrington in the prominent *Dissenting Academy. In 1773, encouraged by her brother John *Aikin and Joseph *Priestley, she published her *Poems* and, together with Aikin, *Miscellaneous Pieces in Prose*. The *Poems* won general acclaim and in 1774 she was installed as the most up-to-date addition to Mary Scott's (1751–93) poem in praise of female worthies, *The Female Advocate*, and invited by an admiring Elizabeth Montagu (1720–1800) to help her set up a Literary Academy for Ladies. Having received a man-made education and grown up solely amongst boys, Barbauld declined the offer, arguing that the best way for a woman to acquire knowledge was 'from conversation with a father, a brother or friend, in the way of family intercourse and easy conversation, and by such a course of reading as they may recommend'. Shortly after this refusal, she married and opened a boarding-school for boys at Palgrave, Suffolk, with her husband, the Revd Rochemont Barbauld, a French Protestant whose later bouts of insanity threatened her life until 1808, when he committed suicide.

During the period that she taught English composition and geography at Palgrave (1774–85) Barbauld established herself as an educator of children, with publications such as *Lessons for Children* (1778) and her highly popular *Hymns in Prose for Children* (1781). From the late 1780s onwards she turned increasingly to political subjects, writing pamphlets and poems on *slavery [6], the repeal of the Test and Corporation Acts, the *war [2] with France, *democracy [3], popular *education [17], and the rights of *women [4]. Her poem 'The Rights of Woman' (c.1795), commonly misread today as a parody of Mary *Wollstonecraft's *Vindication of the Rights of Woman*, humorously rehearses the earlier text's desire that women, instead of being 'short-lived queens', obtain the 'sober pleasures that arise from equality'. She befriended a wide circle of eminent literary women, and was assiduously cultivated by up-and-coming young poets and polemicists like S. T. *Coleridge. Her last published poem was *Eighteen Hundred and Eleven* (1812), a prophetic work and important example of Romantic historicism [see *history, 38], which appears to look back to Coleridge's *Ode to the Departing Year* (1796) and forward to a time when the future belongs to America, leaving Britain and Europe enveloped by 'Gothic night', ruin, and devastation. The poem's pessimism and powerful anti-war sentiments aroused the ire of the *Quarterly Review*. Dismissed as 'the fair pedagogue of our former life', Barbauld was rebuked for 'exchanging the birchen for the satiric rod'.

Later years were spent as a professional editor. In 1810 she edited in fifty volumes *The British Novelists; with an Essay, and Prefaces Biographical and Critical*, a project in which she vigorously defended the novel and made acute critical observations on women as writers and consumers of novels. She also edited Akenside's *Pleasures of Imagination*, Collins's *Odes*, and Rogers's *Pleasures of Memory*. Her selection and publication of Samuel Richardson's *Correspondence* (1804) in six volumes was something of a flop, with Barbauld's long prefatory essay considered by many its only redeeming feature. A lifelong admirer of Addison and other Augustan writers, she also edited selections from the *Spectator*.

DC

BARRINGTON, George (1755–1804). London's most celebrated gentleman thief, Barrington (born George Waldron) was the son of skilled Irish artisans and attended Dublin's Blue Coat Grammar School. Following a violent altercation at school, he joined a travelling group of actors in 1771, making his theatrical debut in Drogheda as Jaffier in Thomas Otway's drama *Venice Preserv'd* (1682).

Barrington acquired pickpocketing skills from John Price, his theatrical and criminal mentor. After avoiding arrest in 1773 he escaped to England, where he worked for almost fourteen years disguised, alone, and largely undetected in London's *theatre [24] foyers and *pleasure gardens. Most notorious of his numerous celebrated thefts was pickpocketing Prince Orloff's diamond snuffbox at Covent Garden in 1775. The press dubbed him 'Prince of Pickpockets'.

Arrested fourteen times, Barrington managed to serve only three short prison terms, mainly because the courts were impressed by his gentlemanly demeanour and eloquence. Verbatim court reports, newspaper copy, and accurate engravings also ensured, however, that his face became too familiar. Sir William Beechey (1753–1839) painted his portrait and his caricature appeared on a Staffordshire mug, one of many depictions of him as the archetypal gentleman thief which also appeared in popular fiction, *ballads, and *melodrama.

His criminal career was eventually halted in 1790, when he was transported to Port Jackson for stealing. Unscrupulous London publishers exploited his absence and reputation, attributing to him a number of illustrated works on the colony of New South Wales. He served for eight years there as Superintendent of Convicts and died, allegedly insane, in Parramatta in 1804.

SR

58. An earthenware mug of the early 1790s, one of the popular souvenirs which circulated during Barrington's career and which somewhat hampered the notorious pickpocket's efforts at anonymity.

BARRY, Sir Charles (1795–1860), architect. The son of a successful stationer, Barry travelled extensively in Egypt and the near East (1818–20), gaining notice for his drawings of the region. He established himself with designs for Commissioners Churches in London in the early 1820s [see *architecture, 28]. His most notable buildings included the Travellers' Club House, Pall Mall (1830–2), the Manchester Athenaeum (1837–9), the Reform Club House, Pall Mall (1838–41), and Bridgewater House, Green Park (1846–51). His successful collaboration with A. W. N. *Pugin began with King Edward VI's Grammar School at Birmingham (1833–7) and culminated in the *Gothic Palace of Westminster (1840–60).   GR

60 **BARRY,** James (1741–1806), Irish-born history painter and polemicist whose art and writings were critical of contemporary *patronage. Barry's patchy early training in Ireland did not prevent him pursuing his aim to be a history painter, and his first important works were of this genre. His aspirations were fuelled by contact with Edmund *Burke, who helped finance Barry's move to London in 1764 and a visit to Italy from 1766 to 1771. In Italy he continued to paint serious historical subjects, and the influence of Renaissance and classical art blended with his adoption of Burke's notion of the *sublime and Johann Joachim Winckelmann's (1717–68) idea of the 'noble simplicity' of ancient sculpture.

On his return to England his career flourished: he became a member of the Royal Academy in 1773 and professor of painting in 1782. In published writings, especially his *Inquiry into Real or Imaginary Obstructions to the Acquisition of the Arts in England* (1775), he pointed out the deficiencies of contemporary English patronage, which he attributed to iconoclastic Protestant taste and the popularity of *portraiture. Barry felt that conditions for artists would improve if major public commissions were forthcoming, but a plan to decorate St Paul's Cathedral in 1771 was halted by the intervention of the Bishop of London. When Royal Academicians withdrew from another project to decorate the Great Room of the Society of Arts in London, Barry offered to take on the commission alone, without pay.

Between 1777 and 1783 he worked frantically for the Society of Arts to produce a series of six paintings, generally entitled 'The Progress of Human Culture'. These works traced the growth of culture from its early origins in agricultural production to its zenith in classical Athens. Another theme of the series stressed England's importance as a manufacturing and trading nation and paid tribute to potential patrons of the arts in this flourishing economy. In artistic terms the project was a success, but it did not inspire followers or patronage, and it led to poverty and mental distress for Barry. His outspoken attacks on Royal Academy procedure led to his expulsion from that institution in 1799, and he died in poverty. Ironically, his advocacy of *history painting echoed Royal Academy rhetoric, but his refusal to accept the social hierarchies of the art world branded him an outsider.   SW

BEATTIE, James (1735–1803), professor of moral philosophy and logic at Marischal College, Aberdeen, from 1760 to 1793. As a poet and public moralist, Beattie illustrates the *Enlightenment [32] combination of Christian stoicism, moral science, and sentimental expressivism that is best seen as a prolonged reaction against the scientific revolution.

In so far as he had any philosophical backbone, it derived from Thomas *Reid's 'Common Sense' realism, with which Beattie attacked David *Hume's scepticism in the grandly intended but somewhat distasteful *Essay on the Nature and Immutability of Truth* (1770). The performance was simplistic, comforting, and well timed; it gave the author instant national—and some international—fame, clerical favour, and a royal pension. It was closely followed by a more solid effort, *The Minstrel* (1771–4), a large poem, shaped in *Spenserian stanzas, on the edifying theme of the rise and progress of poetical *genius. In addition to poetical works, Beattie published *essays on moral, aesthetic, and religious topics, and an underrated condensation of his academic lectures, *Elements of Moral Science* (1790–3).

In much of his writing, Beattie explicitly promoted an Addisonian style of public moralizing, which he combined with a fervent Baconian ideal of useful knowledge. Hume's and Kant's justified scorn for the *Essay on Truth* has all but obliterated Beattie from the annals of philosophy, but he was in fact a moralist and literary figure of some substance who sustained a coherent argument against *slavery [6] and undermined the Enlightenment racism represented by his two great critics.   KH

BECKFORD, William (1760–1844), *Gothic novelist, *orientalist. The only son of a Jamaican planter, slaveholder, and city radical, from the age of 9 he was raised exclusively by his mother, a strenuously *Evangelical matron known as 'the Begum' to her precocious offspring. As well as the Fonthill estate in Wiltshire, the young Beckford's portfolio included a rotten borough, a county magistracy, a network of political patrons and placemen, and, when he came of age, marriage into a titled family.

In 1777 Alexander Cozens (1717–86), a cosmopolitan homosexual artist, became the adolescent Beckford's drawing-master. His obvious ascendancy displeased the Begum, so she promoted a close connection between Beckford and a flighty young married woman, Louisa Beckford, wife of his cousin. In 1779 Beckford also began a secretive love affair with a younger boy, William Courtenay, son of the Viscount Powderham. 'Kitty' to his friends, Courtenay was the model for the character Gulchenrouz in Beckford's fictional masterpiece, *The History of the Caliph Vathek* (1786).

Beckford was sent on successive European tours, beginning with Switzerland in 1777, the Netherlands in 1780, and Italy in 1782, where *Vathek* was written. By his 21st birthday in 1781 he had already acquired a reputation as patron, engineer, architect, choreographer, connoisseur, collector, and host to the rich and famous. Kept away from school and university by his meddlesome mother, he fantasticated Font-hill, its paintings, the banquet, the clan gathering, the hunting excursion, and the hallooing return with the spoils. His Gothic imagination and aesthetic was dominated by urban carceral *architecture [28], like the ziggurats of Hawksmoor (c.1661–1736) and the catacombs of Giovanni Battista Piranesi (1720–78).

Beckford's early writings showed brilliant and versatile gifts, transposing social interaction into sharp critique, and using the informal *autobiographic genres of the journal, travel sketch, and familiar letter. *Biographical Memoirs of Extraordinary Painters*, written about 1777, was a spoof catalogue of ancestral portraits by spurious canonical painters. *Dreams, Waking Thoughts, and Incidents*, begun in Italy in 1780 and published anonymously by Joseph *Johnson in 1783, linked *travel literature to the exploration of erotic and political difference, a mode which Lady Mary Wortley Montagu (1689–1762) had earlier exploited. Beckford started to translate Edward Wortley Montagu's (1713–76) manuscript collection of Arabian Nights tales into French, and went on to write original 'Arabian' and 'Persian' stories, imitating the *immoraliste* fiction of his literary forebear, Antoine Hamilton, Comte de Gramont (1646–1720).

The Caliph Vathek and the confessional *Episodes of Vathek* were written in French from about 1782, reviving the sodomitical wit of Voltaire embedded in infernal landscapes of hallucinatory intensity. *Vathek* is a masterpiece of camp, the plot a variation on Dr Faust's diabolical bargain. The Caliph Vathek is a precocious genius dominated by his voodoo-working mother and internally driven by a spectral father who is incontinent, incompetent, and maniacally legitimist.

In 1783 Beckford was shepherded into marriage with a suitable bride, Lady Margaret Gordon, a step towards securing a peerage and a career in politics. As an extra precaution, his first publication, *Dreams, Waking Thoughts, and Incidents*, was hastily withdrawn from sale by the tutor of Beckford's Hamilton cousins, Revd Samuel Henley, acting on the Begum's orders. In 1784 Beckford took his seat as MP for Wells, and his wife bore the first of their two daughters. However, a rumour that Beckford and the 16-year-old 'Kitty' had been caught *in flagrante* by a servant of Lord Powderham led Beckford to embark on a prolonged and politic tour of the Continent.

The Courtenay scandal of 1784, followed by the death of his wife in 1786, drove Beckford into temporary exile and permanent estrangement from British reviewers and readers. Eponymous authorship as 'the Caliph Vathek' ceased to be an enjoyable hoax, once Beckford did not dare to publish under his own name. On his tour of penance he delegated *Vathek* to the clergyman Samuel Henley to be bowdlerized and made saleable in English. Henley lost or destroyed the original, suppressed the nakedly autobiographical *Episodes*, and publicized *Vathek* as an Arabic original translated by himself. In 1787 Beckford brought out a doggerel French version from memory to contest Henley's false claim, but the English

version in Henley's fustian prose is indisputably the canonical text.

The outbreak of war in 1793 foreclosed on Beckford's European travels, though in 1794 he managed to visit the Portuguese monasteries of Alcobaça and Batalha, the subject of his latest and finest travel book, *Recollections of an Excursion to the Monasteries of Alcobaça and Batalha* (1835). He immured himself at Fonthill and turned his attention to book-collecting and *antiquarianism [35]. In the winter of 1796–7, during one of his frequent absences, his father's mansion collapsed, and Beckford seized the opportunity to rebuild on a titanic scale with the Gothic Revivalist architect James *Wyatt. In 1800 the rebuilt Fonthill Abbey hosted a fabulous evening reception for Sir William *Hamilton (another Beckford cousin), his second wife, Emma, Lady *Hamilton, and the hero of the Nile, Admiral *Nelson.

Ten years after *Vathek*, Beckford published two novels, *Modern Novel Writing; or the Elegant Enthusiast* (1796) and *Azemia* (1798), both under feminine pseudonyms. Like the early novels of de Sade, these cashed in on the entertainment value of Samuel Richardson's naïve feminine signatures and impressionable female readership, but they lack de Sade's relish for the female role. The reviews attributed them to Robert *Merry, ringleader of the *Della Cruscan women poets, or else to Charlotte *Smith, and Beckford preened himself as their 'divine authoress', but only for private circulation. In 1793 Beckford had stood out against fellow Jamaican landlords and publicly opposed the *war [2] against France. To his intimate circle, Beckford lampooned the *gagging acts of 1795 as 'the Act for General Silence', and England 'the Island of Mum', pointing to the link between political, verbal, and nursery regimes of repression.

Self-protective seclusion, and building mania, virtually ended Beckford's career, though Lord *Byron was to hail him as a closeted master in exile, with *Childe Harold*'s Satanic tribute, 'There thou too, Vathek! England's wealthiest son, / Once formed thy Paradise'. In 1822 Beckford's finances failed and his library had to be auctioned. Three years later Wyatt's Gothic great tower collapsed, and Beckford made his last home in Bath, where he died among the superannuated in 1844. JB

BEDDOES, Thomas (1760–1808), physician, *chemist, and democrat, and a prominent figure in the provincial scientific and medical world of the revolutionary period. He studied *medicine [18] in London and Edinburgh, where he became a pupil of Joseph Black (1728–99) and an admirer of French chemist Antoine Lavoisier. In 1788 he returned to Oxford, where he graduated MD and began a series of chemical lectures. His open avowal of radical political causes is likely to have cost him an endowed chair in chemistry.

Branded a dangerous and violent democrat by the government, he resigned under pressure in 1792 and moved to Bristol, where in 1798 he established the Bristol Pneumatic Institute at the *spa town of

Hotwells. Here he conducted the first systematic practice of medicine based on the chemistry of gases. While his promising experiments with nitrous oxide (laughing-gas) attracted the support of such fashionable radicals as *Coleridge, *Southey, Maria *Edgeworth, and Thomas Wedgwood (1771–1805), reports of these events were seized upon by his political enemies. Beddoes, his assistant Humphry *Davy, and his friends were denounced as dangerous enthusiasts, as intoxicated by their own imaginations as they were by the effects of the nitrous oxide. Beddoes's experiments became known as the 'nitrous oxide capers' and his career was all but destroyed. Research into the medicinal uses of the gas was subsequently abandoned by the scientific community and its anaesthetic properties, noted by Davy in 1800, lost to the world for another forty years.   JM

BEDDOES, Thomas Lovell (1803–49), poet. Beddoes's macabre obsessions with failure and death typify later Romantic preoccupations both with *Gothic themes in general and more particularly with the world of Jacobean tragedy.

Son of the radical physician Thomas *Beddoes, he immersed himself in Elizabethan and Jacobean literature while at Oxford. *The Improvisatore* (1821) was a collection of verse and stories with a strong Gothic flavour, a taste which he maintained in his pseudo-Jacobean drama, *The Brides' Tragedy*, published in the following year. The *poetry [29] he went on to write between 1822 and 1825, including 'Lines Written in a Blank Leaf of the Prometheus Bound' and 'Pygmalion', shows the influence of *Keats and *Shelley. He also attempted to write four more plays in the Jacobean vein which he never completed: *The Last Man* (1823), *Love's Arrow Poisoned* (1823), *The Second Brother* (1824), and *Torrismond* (1824).

In 1825 Beddoes went to study medicine in Germany, and never published again in his lifetime. Involved in radical politics, he was deported and finally settled in Switzerland, only infrequently revisiting England before his suicide in 1849. During his time on the Continent he had been working on his sprawling, macabre play, *Death's Jest-Book*, which was published posthumously in 1850.   JM

BEETHOVEN, Ludwig van (1770–1827), German composer. Whilst he never visited Britain, Beethoven had important connections with this country, partly cultivated through his pupil Ferdinand *Ries.

His symphonies quickly became standard repertoire of the Philharmonic Society, which in turn commissioned music from the composer, who in 1815 sent three overtures. More significantly, the Society inspired the composition of the Ninth Symphony. Whilst it was first performed in Vienna—the London premiere took place in 1825, to an uncomprehending audience—the Philharmonic nevertheless sent the composer £100 in response to a plea of poverty.

Beethoven's *piano music was undoubtedly influenced by the London Pianoforte School, and he himself owned a Broadwood piano. In turn, his heroic middle-period style was reflected by London composers such as Ries and *Potter; and through *Clementi's initiative several major works of Beethoven were first published in London.   SMcV

Behmenism, the mystical ideas of the German shoemaker Jacob Boehme (1575–1624), circulated widely in the eighteenth century among those seeking a *religion [10] of the inner light. First translated into English in the 1640s and 1650s, Boehme's writings were best known in the four-volume edition (1764–81) for which the *Anglican clergyman William Law (1686–1761) wrote an introduction, although they were frequently issued in cheap collections of prophetic and mystical material. Boehme's antagonism towards institutional religion and celebration of inspiration over learning help explain his readership among lower-class seekers after the inner light. Although his language seems obscure in the extreme, it found a ready readership among those familiar with popular traditions of alchemy and *astrology. Many of those attracted to *Swedenborgianism, including William *Blake, found Boehme's stress on the Christ within similarly appealing. Boehme's readership was not confined to lower-class enthusiasts, however; counter-*Enlightenment [32] thought of all kinds was often drawn to his mysticism. S. T. *Coleridge claimed that his philosophy was influenced by direct reading in sources like Boehme before he encountered German idealism, but sought to distinguish this 'meek and shy quietist' from the 'fev'rous energy' of the tradition of popular *enthusiasm.   JM

BELSHAM, Thomas (1750–1829), the principal *Unitarian theologian in the generation after Joseph *Priestley. The son of an independent (Congregationalist) minister, he was educated in the *Dissenting academy at Daventry between 1766 and 1770. He became a tutor there and, after a short ministry at Worcester, returned in 1781 to teach divinity. His gradual move from outward orthodoxy to *Arianism and Unitarianism ended with a dramatic resignation in 1789. He then became professor of divinity at New College, Hackney, until its closure in 1796 for financial insufficiency and radical excess. He had succeeded Priestley at the Gravel-pit Chapel, Hackney, in 1794, and in 1805 moved to the premier London Unitarian congregation in Essex Street, where he remained until his death.

His *Elements of the Philosophy of the Human Mind* (1801) was the leading textbook on *Necessarianism. An advanced biblical critic, who appreciated German textual and historical scholarship while resisting German theology and Kantian philosophy, he was the main force behind publication of an improved version of the New Testament in 1808 [see *Bible]. His many published *sermons and a brilliant controversial style in religious journalism established him as the foremost Unitarian apologist of his time and a bogeyman to the orthodox. Although he was a steadfast advocate of civil liberties for Dissenters, his political and social views came latterly to seem old-fashioned to some younger, more radical Unitarians. Then, within a few years of his death, the rise of a 'new school' of Unitarian thought, drawing on introspective rather than external religious proof, made him a symbol of what a Romantic age had come to regard, in both substance and method, as an outdated dispensation.   RKW

BENBOW, William (1784–1841). Best known as the author of *Grand National Holiday, and Congress of the Productive Classes* (1832), a work outlining the concept of a general strike, Benbow was an energetic activist and publisher through most of the 1820s and 1830s [see *publishing, 21].

Originally a Manchester shoemaker, he addressed huge crowds in Lancashire immediately before the 1817 suspension of habeas corpus ('Arms I say it is your right to have') and was imprisoned under its terms, whence he came to the attention of William *Cobbett who dedicated his *Grammar of the English Language* (1819) to him. In London he worked for Cobbett for a time and fell in with *Spenceans, occupying Cobbett's old premises and publishing enormous quantities of pro-*Queen Caroline material, including in 1822 a re-engraved William *Blake image of Harriet Quintin—a long-running target of Benbow under the pseudonym 'Edward Eglantine'. His wife, Jane, died in 1821 while he was producing the *Radical Magazine* which included freethinking and libertinist contributions by George Cannon (1789–1854), a Spencean intellectual and future *pornographer.

Benbow's semi-pornographic *Rambler's Magazine, or Man of Fashion's Companion* (1822) was advertised alongside his incessant pirating of *Byron (Benbow's attitude to whom was summarized by his shop, 'Byron's Head'). *Rambler's* carried material of R. C. Fair, a Spencean schoolteacher involved in the early radical publication of *Shelley's *Queen Mab* in 1813. It also noticed Helen Maria *Williams and the death of Shelley. In *The Grand National Holiday*, Benbow ('the prophet of your salvation') drew on Spenceanism's belief in using the 'spontaneous produce' of the *land [16] to sustain the idea of a month-long strike.

Benbow stayed true to the rougher, more violent side of Spencean–radical activism, in the 1830s opening a *debating club in Theobald's Road, joining the National Union of Working Classes, and continuing to discuss assassination plans. Though he supported *Chartist demands for universal suffrage, he thought this should be accompanied by the Spencean demand for an equal share in economic production, particularly the resources of the land.   DW

47 **BENTHAM,** Jeremy (1748–1832), philosopher, jurist, and reformer. Creator of what has become known as 'classical' *utilitarianism, Bentham left an indelible mark on the thought and politics of his day, and his influence has persisted in numerous spheres to the present time.

Bentham was educated at Westminster School and Oxford, where he was admitted aged only 12; he was called to the bar, but decided not to carry on his practice. He devoted his life instead to reforming the *law [8] and other institutions on the basis of his principle of utility, which he called in later years the 'greatest happiness principle'. Although he was not the first person to use the term, he transformed its use in the eighteenth century by combining a consistent critical use of the idea as the central principle of morals and politics with a rigorous empiricism which gave careful attention to the uses of *language [40] in political and philosophical understanding. In his early and perhaps best-known works, such as *A Fragment on Government* (1776) and *An Introduction to the Principles of Morals and Legislation* (1789), these characteristics are clearly evident in the critique of such ideas as natural law, *natural rights, sovereignty, the social contract, and in his attempts to identify a neutral moral language to clarify the concepts employed in the theory of punishment.

Fragment on Government attracted the notice of Lord *Shelburne (later Lord Lansdowne), and Bentham subsequently joined the circle of intellectuals associated with Shelburne's house at Bowood. Much of his early writing, including the *Introduction to the Principles of Morals and Legislation* and the material eventually published as the *Rationale of Punishment* (1830), were attempts to state the underlying principles and detailed provisions of a penal code. His writings on civil law evolved from a lifelong critique of William *Blackstone's *Commentaries on the Laws of England* (1765–9). He also wrote extensively on judicial organization, procedure, and evidence. The most important of numerous works, the massive *Rationale of Judicial Evidence* (1827), was edited by the young John Stuart *Mill.

His earliest contribution to *political economy [33], *Defense of Usury* (1787), was a critique of Adam *Smith's analysis of this subject in the *Wealth of Nations* (1776). If Bentham is not ranked among the major classical political economists, it is partly due to the fact that his economic ideas permeate a wide range of writings from those on public finance and government economy, judicial organization, civil and penal law, the panopticon *prison, and the *poor laws, to such topics as trade, taxation, money, and the other more commonplace themes of political economy. Though he could count such classical economists as James *Mill, David *Ricardo, and J. S. Mill among his followers, his economic ideas had greater influence later in the nineteenth century in the writings of neoclassical economists like W. S. Jevons and F. Y. Edgeworth.

54

Bentham's reforming proposals touched every aspect of the law as exemplified by his assaults on the unintelligibility of the common law, on the system of imprisonment and transportation, on the widespread corruption of *judges, *lawyers, and court officials, and on the exclusion of the poor from access to the legal system [see *poverty, 12]. As a follower of Montesquieu Bentham accepted the British constitution as embodying political liberty, but he was never, like Blackstone, an enthusiastic defender of its confusions and anomalies. At the time of the *French Revolution he wrote enthusiastically about the development of representative democracy in France and favoured the extension of universal suffrage, frequent parliaments, the secret ballot, and democratic institutions to Britain. He soon turned against the Revolution, but due to earlier contacts developed through Shelburne and to essays and proposals sent to France, he was made an Honorary Citizen in 1792. One important consequence of his involvement in France was his friendship with Étienne Dumont (1759–1829), the Swiss writer and reformer whom he met at Bowood. Dumont's recensions of his works, especially the *Traités de Législation, Civile et Pénale* (1802), made Bentham famous throughout the world.

His disappointment with the French Revolution did not mean he was lost to radical reform. With the publication of *A Plan of Parliamentary Reform* (1817), he became a well-known figure in the postwar movement, drafting motions with the help of Mill, *Cartwright, and *Burdett which were put before the House of Commons in 1818. The spread of his ideas also coincided with the early development of liberalism in Spain and Portugal in the 1820s and movements for national independence in Greece and Latin America. In his later writings he became an enthusiastic admirer of the constitution of the United States of America, which he regarded as the crucial empirical evidence that radical reform and democratic institutions could be created in various countries throughout the world. His own ideas about representative *democracy [3] were embodied in the massive and unfinished *Constitutional Code* (1822–), as well as related works on constitutional law written in the 1820s.

Many of Bentham's writings were never published during his lifetime. Besides the versions produced by Dumont, an inadequate and virtually unreadable edition was edited by his friend and literary executor, John Bowring, and published in eleven volumes (1838–43). This edition is now being replaced by the new *Collected Works of Jeremy Bentham* (1968–) in approximately sixty-five volumes. With the publication of volumes in the new edition, Bentham's reputation as a legal philosopher, theorist of democracy, utilitarian, and radical reformer has already undergone substantial revision, and this re-estimation of his work is bound to continue.   FR

BERINGTON, Joseph (1746–1827), Catholic writer, historian, and theologian. Born of a well-to-do Catholic family in Shropshire, Berington was educated and ordained at Saint Omer. Returning to England, he settled at Oscott in Staffordshire, and quickly emerged as a major apologist for the English Catholic community. His Catholicism was of an independent sort. He was a leader of a group who styled themselves as Cisalpines, and represented an English variant of Gallicanism, which was anticlerical as well as antipapal in its outlook and located its leadership amongst the aristocracy and gentry. Berington was also a historian, theologian, and metaphysician of advanced views. At home in the company of leaders of science and industry in the Midlands, including the heterodox theologian and

political radical Joseph *Priestley, he was regarded with suspicion by the English Vicars-Apostolic and was suspended twice for his liberal theological views. By the time of his death the leadership of the English Catholic community had passed from the landed laity to the clergy, and the complexion of the community had begun to change under the influence of Irish immigration. Berington had, however, played a useful part in gaining greater *toleration for the Catholic community by demonstrating both its loyalty and numerical inferiority (so limiting its potential as a threat) and the existence within it of varieties of *Enlightenment [32] thought. His personal willingness to proclaim his Catholicism and his acceptance of Catholicism as part of a wider Dissenting community caused anxiety amongst the Catholic hierarchy but eased the way for Catholics to play a future role in civic life.   MF

BETTY, William Henry West ('Master' Betty) (1791–1874), child actor. Born in Shropshire, Betty spent his youth in the north of Ireland. He made his first appearance on stage in Belfast in 1803 at the age of 11. Subsequent performances in Ireland and Scotland made him a phenomenon, trumpeted by the press, and culminated in his debut at Covent Garden in December 1804, as Selim in the tragedy *Barbarossa*. The latest fashionable sensation, he dominated the *theatre [24], the London press, and public opinion in general, eclipsing mature actors such as *Kemble and *Siddons, the latter making a tactical withdrawal from the stage while the craze for Betty raged. His notable roles included Frederick in *Inchbald's *Lovers' Vows*, Young Norval in Home's *Douglas* (depicted by *Opie), Romeo, and Hamlet, for which *Pitt was reputed to have adjourned a sitting of the House of Commons.

'Bettymania' effectively lasted for two years, between 1804 and 1805, and was curtailed by the onset of puberty as well as by the inevitably limited lifespan of such pyrotechnic celebrity. The reasons for Betty's appeal are complex: there had been nothing to galvanize the London theatre world since Siddons's debut in 1782 and audiences were looking for a new 'star' actor. As an adolescent boy whose sexuality was indeterminate and gender blurred—Siddons described him cuttingly as '*the Baby with a Woman's name*'—Betty had an erotic appeal for both men and women. He was also a focus for the Romantic preoccupation with childhood and youth as lost innocence and idealism (often, as in the dramatic criticism of *Lamb, *Hazlitt, and Leigh *Hunt, figured in terms of the writers' experiences as playgoers). As the apparently 'artless' actor, whose skills came naturally, he was thought to be the perfect mediator of the supreme 'poet of nature', *Shakespeare. It is ironic that a phenomenon which was the result of creative marketing and promotion—at least seven commemorative Betty medals were struck—should have been based on Betty's 'natural', childlike talents, his very lack of professionalism—indicating the complex response to the *consumerism [19] of culture. After his retirement in 1808 Betty returned to the stage as an adult actor, but never equalled the success of the heady days of 1804–5 when, according to one commentator, 'he and Buonaparte divided the world'. However, he was never faced with poverty, the financial success of his childhood sustaining him after the crowds had long gone.   GR

BEWICK, Thomas (1755–1828), *watercolour painter, engraver, and illustrator, who introduced to the art of wood-engraving a unique technical perfection, descriptive variety, and sensitivity to nature [see *prints, 22]. Bewick's major publications revolutionized the commercial application of wood-engraving to the book trade, and had an immediate and lasting impact on the British artistic and literary imagination.

Having throughout his childhood demonstrated a compulsive desire to draw his surroundings, Bewick was apprenticed in 1767 to the engraver Ralph Beilby, who ran the only general engraving business at that time in Newcastle. Like William Hogarth (1697–1764), Bewick was trained in the basic techniques of decorative and reproductive metal-engraving, working on copperplate illustration and on the ornamentation of precious metals. Although there was little room for imaginative expression in this work, the great formal variety gave Bewick a chance to judge the relative strengths and weaknesses of commercial metal-engraving. His diagrammatic line engravings for Dr Charles Hutton's (1737–1823) *Treatise on Mensuration* (1768–70) saw his first extended use of wood-engraving.

After an abortive and unhappy stay in London for nine months in 1796–7, Bewick returned to Newcastle and went into partnership with his former master. Like William *Blake, Bewick had to carry out his masterpiece engravings in time set aside from daily labours. Yet, unlike Blake, he was to score commercial and artistic hits with his *General History of Quadrupeds* (1790) and then the two volumes of the *History of British Birds* (*Land Birds*, 1797, *Water Birds*, 1804). Bewick planned his *Quadrupeds* as a book for 'the pleasure and amusement of youth'. He saw himself as rebelling against the crudeness of children's book illustration typified by Thomas Boreman's *Three Hundred Animals* (1773). Boreman's lifeless, and wildly inaccurate, relief copper-engravings stand in absolute contrast to Bewick's supremely delicate and wonderfully observed little masterpieces. Boreman's prints were cut in one width of crude line and are haphazardly pitted with black dots and white circles. Bewick's engravings mark the rivets attaching the plate to a woodblock, in order to raise the illustration up to the level of the printing type. Bewick engraved on end-grain blocks, which were cut at the exact height of printing type so that they could be set straight into the forme. Whilst printers were surprisingly slow to take up Bewick's practices, this had become the standard method for printing cheap illustrated material by the 1830s.

Bewick shared with Blake an ability to create monumental images in miniature, and to evoke a whole landscape within a couple of square inches. Bewick's engravings describe English northern landscape and seascape with an economy and sensitivity to detail unprecedented in graphic work on wood. They also give glimpses into the work and pastimes of the agricultural poor which are uncannily Wordsworthian. William *Wordsworth in fact celebrated Bewick's descriptive powers in *The Two Thieves* (1800), 'O now that the genius of Bewick were mine'.

Bewick's vignettes exhibit a tender and homely sense of humour that is never sentimental, but there is also an ability to confront the harsh, the brutal, and the uncanny in nature. To his contemporaries his vignettes contained not only charm but horror. The eponymous narrator of *Jane Eyre* (1847) presents Bewick as a master not only of Romantic landscape but also of the Burkean *sublime.   MW

Bible. Though our period saw perhaps the lowest ever ebb of formal religious observance, with the increase in literacy in the later part of the eighteenth century, probably at no time has the Bible been more widely read or discussed [see *religion, 10 and *language, 40]. Successive crises in traditional modes of interpretation ensured that textual and devotional exegesis was increasingly pluralistic: while typological readings were still common, higher critical and historical approaches were also gaining ground. After 1790, in the wake of the *French Revolution, conservatives, radicals, and *millenarians alike made use of apocalyptic texts (especially Revelation) to promulgate their beliefs within a cosmic context. Meanwhile, the relatively new concept of the Bible as aesthetic creation meant that it was also taken up—

59. From Bewick's *Vignettes*, 1827. Bewick's method of engraving on the end-grain of hard wood overtook metal-engraving processes in the late eighteenth century, and subsequently became the dominant form of Victorian serial illustration.

especially in the Authorized Version—as an example of the literary *sublime that rapidly displaced earlier Greek and Latin models of neoclassicism [see *literary theory, 41].

In 1678 a French Oratorian, Richard Simon, had published his *Histoire critique du Vieux Testament*. Its aim was to counter the Protestant principle that Scripture alone was necessary for salvation. Using scholarly techniques developed for classical texts, Simon claimed that so far from being the direct dictation of the Holy Spirit, the Bible had origins no less human, complex, and varied than other histories. Challenging the traditional belief that Moses was the author of the Pentateuch, he argued that these books were more likely to be a composite creation of scribes and compilers. Though his book was banned in France, and Simon expelled from his Order, the subsequent English translation was a major influence on the Oxford scholar Robert Lowth (1710–87), whose *Lectures on the Sacred Poetry of the Hebrews* (1753) is generally credited with beginning the critical revolution in biblical studies. For Lowth it was axiomatic that anyone seeking to interpret the Bible must begin not with any system of typological presuppositions but by trying to understand the text within its historical setting—i.e. as an ancient Hebrew.

In Britain biblical interpretation was as politically sensitive as in France. *Whig ideologists, by denying its status as the source of revelation and pointing out the human elements in its composition, had already tried to undercut the biblicism of their High Church *Tory opponents. Lowth, successively Bishop of Llandaff, Oxford, and London, was a relatively conservative establishment figure. His *Lectures* were first printed, as they were delivered, in Latin, and it was not until they finally appeared in English in the 1780s that their radical potential became apparent. Among many others, Thomas *Paine and Percy *Shelley cite them as evidence both for human origins to the Scriptures and for their popular and often anti-monarchist bias.

Abroad, Lowth's ideas were taken up by a new wave of German scholars, including Eichhorn, Michaelis, Lessing, Reimarus, and even Herder, and by the 1790s their historical and mythological interpretations, generally known as the 'higher criticism', were circulating in advanced *Unitarian and Nonconformist circles—especially among the radical intellectual group centred around the radical publisher Joseph *Johnson. *Anglican reaction was hampered by a lower level of education among the clergy—especially by ignorance of German—and initial suspicion was quickly reinforced by a general conservative backlash following the French Revolution. Nevertheless, S. T. *Coleridge, among the poets, and later Herbert Marsh (1757–1839, professor of divinity at Cambridge) and Julius Hare (1795–1855, Cambridge tutor and subsequently Archdeacon of Chichester) were exceptional in their knowledge and use of the new critical ideas.

Radical and anti-religious uses of Scripture were given new impetus by another of Johnson's publications: a translation of *The Ruins* (1792) by Constantin *Volney which traced all religion, and in particular

Christianity, to a common *mythological [36] origin in ancient Egypt at least 17,000 years earlier.

A widespread popular millenarianism associated with the French Revolution was also reflected in apocalyptic writings not merely by enthusiasts like Richard *Brothers and Joanna *Southcott but by radicals like Joseph *Priestley, and even Anglican bishops, applying biblical *prophecy to current events—often deducing from them signs of the end of the world.

Though there had been a number of translations of the Bible earlier in the eighteenth century, their lack of popular success only underscores the rising popularity and esteem of the Authorized Version. By far the most significant in the later century was Lowth's own *New Translation of Isaiah* (1778), important more for the accompanying dissertation and notes than for the text itself. These show that Lowth himself saw no essential conflict between typological and historical criticism, and constitute the best analyses of the period on the principles of translation in general.

The trend towards seeing the Bible as a cultural and aesthetic document in its own right coincides with the appearance of the modern idea of 'literature' in general as a culturally valorized form of writing [see *prose, 30 and *novels, 31]. Lowth writes of the 'ineffable sublimity' of the Hebrew poets, and favourably contrasts the simplicity and homeliness of their imagery with the elaborate formal diction of neoclassical poetry. In spite of Lowth's own translation, the cult of the Bible as a source of the sublime was increasingly attached to the specific language of the Authorized Version. Poets as different as James Macpherson [see *Ossianism], Christopher Smart (1722–71), and Blake were influenced by the sound and rhythms of this version, which, for many people, had ceased to be a translation and had become 'the Bible' in an absolute sense—and by the early nineteenth century 'bibliolatry' was a continual presence in English culture. Lowth's aesthetic views, especially his identification of the poet as prophet, are amplified by Hugh *Blair in his *Lectures on Rhetoric and Belles Lettres* (1784) and in this form were taken up again by *Wordsworth in his 'Preface' to the *Lyrical Ballads*. For Coleridge, in his 1796 *Lectures* and *First Lay Sermon*, the Bible is a source not merely of aesthetic principles but also of political ones. Shelley advances similar arguments, in a more secularized form, in his *Defence of Poetry*. At the same time biblical and associated legends, such as that of the Wandering Jew, provided increasingly popular sources for secular works, including Coleridge's *Ancient Mariner* and *Byron's *Cain*.   SP

BILLINGTON, Elizabeth (1765–1818), soprano singer, actress, composer. Billington was born into a musical family, the daughter of the oboist Carl Weichsel and singer Fredericka Weichsel, née Weirman. An intimate of the London *theatre [24] world from an early age, making her first appearance at Covent Garden at the age of 11, she received instruction in singing from J. C. *Bach and studied the pianoforte and composition.

In 1783 she married the double-bass player James Billington against her family's wishes. The couple travelled to Dublin, where Elizabeth began her professional career in earnest and conducted an adulterous affair with the theatre manager, and notorious womanizer, Richard Daly. Returning to England, Billington worked hard at improving her *singing and was soon in great demand across the country, appearing at *music festivals, *Handel Commemorations, and Concerts of Ancient Music, as well as the London *pleasure gardens and theatres.

She was notorious for her many romantic liaisons with, among others, the Prince of Wales. In 1792, in an attempt to blackmail the Prince, the radical hack and publisher James Ridgway (c.1782–1838) produced scandalous memoirs of Billington, alluding to incest with her father and brother. After the resulting scandal, she left Britain in 1794 for the Continent, where she was fêted by Sir William *Hamilton and his circle at Naples, and sang for Josephine Bonaparte. Her European stardom increased her celebrity in Britain on her return in 1801. Among her many successes in this period were appearances in Nasolini's *Merope* (1802) and *Mozart's *La Clemenza di Tito* (1806). She retired in 1811, dying seven years later in dubious circumstances in Italy, probably at the hands of her second husband, M. Filissent.   GR

biography. 'We talked of biography', James *Boswell noted of a meeting between Samuel *Johnson, Thomas Warton (1718–1790) and himself in 1776. Johnson considered that biography should instruct, delight, and impart 'real character'. Writing that conversation would reveal more of a man's character than 'formal and studied narrative, begun with his pedigree, and ended with his funeral', Johnson questioned the polite eighteenth-century art of the *Biographia Britannica: or, the Lives of the Most Eminent Persons.*

When Boswell published his *Life of Johnson* (1791), he modified eighteenth-century panegyric traditions of biography because 'in every picture there should be shade as well as light'. Observing that 'indolence and procrastination were inherent' in Johnson, and that 'the boy is the man in miniature', Boswell suggested the significance of *childhood and inner life for biography as well as adult activities and achievements.

William *Godwin went further in *Memoirs of the Author of A Vindication of the Rights of Woman* (1798), framing a tribute to 'a person of eminent merit' and 'what Dr Johnson would have called, "a very good hater"'. The *Memoirs* portrayed Mary *Wollstonecraft's experience of her father's despotism as formative; more controversially, Godwin gave a candid account of Wollstonecraft's 'personal and ardent affection' for the married Henry *Fuseli; her 'unhappy passion' for the American Gilbert Imlay (*fl.* 1793) and 'cool and deliberate' plans to commit suicide. The exposure scandalized readers like Robert *Southey, who later characterized the biographers of his age as 'a race of Resurrection-men . . . First come the new-writers, then the magazines . . . The sharking booksellers, ever on the watch to tempt and delude the curiosity of the lower public, then set their Ghouls at work . . . and lastly comes the over-zealous admirer.'

Southey's own works of biography celebrated distinguished national characters rather than anatomizing them: *The Life of Nelson* (1813) was republished as a portable 'eulogy of our great Naval hero', while *The Life of Wesley and the Rise and Progress of Methodism* (1820) concluded with the hope that *Methodism 'may again draw towards the establishment from which it has seceded'. Southey's extensive prefatory bibliography reveals the burgeoning production of individual histories since the 1790s. Actor and abolitionist James Field Stanfield's (d. 1824) *An Essay on the Study and Composition of Biography* (1813) signalled a developing theoretical interest in the subject.

Apart from dutiful celebrations of establishment figures such as John Gibson *Lockhart's *Memoirs of the Life of Sir Walter Scott* (1837–38), biography became a way of reintroducing the nineteenth-century reading public to its exiled poets. Recollections of Percy *Shelley by Mary *Shelley, Leigh *Hunt, and Edward Trelawny (1792–1881) justified Shelley's poetry and his character. Thomas *Moore's *Life* of *Byron (1830) fixed the character of Byron's genius for generations. The burning of Byron's own *Memoirs* (to which Moore was a party) points to a growing competition between Romantic biography and autobiography. Thomas *De Quincey's *Recollections of the Lakes and the Lake Poets* (1834–40) shows how, under the influence of the Romantic lyric self, memoirs, conversations, and table talk gave way to psychological exploration.

JS

BIRKBECK, George (1776–1841), medical doctor and educational reformer. Birkbeck trained in ***medicine [18]** at Edinburgh where he was a student of Joseph Black (1728–99) and Dugald *Stewart. After graduating, he took up the chair of natural philosophy at the Andersonian University in Glasgow. In 1800 he established a series of *lectures for local artisans designed to promote the application of science to practical purposes. The 'mechanics' class' which evolved from these lectures became the Glasgow Mechanics' Institute (1823) [see *popular education].

In 1804 Birkbeck moved to London and set up a successful medical practice. Throughout his career he was a friend, colleague, and collaborator of such prominent Edinburgh-trained medical and political reformers as Henry *Brougham, Francis *Jeffrey, Dugald Stewart, Leonard Horner (1785–1864), Peter Mark Roget (1779–1869), and John Playfair (1748–1819). He believed that the ***Enlightenment [32]** dream of the unceasing march of progress through knowledge was a valid goal and that working men, and even women, could share in this process.

Inspired by the success of the Glasgow Mechanics' Institute, Birkbeck founded a similar institution in London in 1823, and he was a leading spirit in the creation of many similar schemes throughout Britain. In 1827 he was one of the founders of

University College London, which like the mechanics' institutes adopted the central features and pedagogic ideals of the Scottish university system.   LH

BISHOP, Sir Henry Rowley (1786–1855), conductor; the leading composer of English song and theatrical *music [26] during the first two decades of the nineteenth century. Most of his works were premiered at Covent Garden or Drury Lane, where he was music director at both *theatres [24]. Typically Bishop's music consisted of an overture plus a dozen or so short vocal items, particularly songs, with plots adapted from *Shakespeare, *Scott, or *melodramas. They were also characteristic of English *opera in their incorporation of speech and restricted use of music as a dramatic medium. He turned the paucity of outstanding professional singers to advantage, tailoring many songs for *domestic music consumption. Written in an accessible style, the picturesque morality of songs such as 'Home sweet home', from *Clari, or The Maid of Milan* (1823), his best-known example, expressed prevalent contemporary values. Also aimed at the commercial market were his *glees.

Bishop followed custom in freely using existing music, producing often drastically inferior adaptations of operas by *Mozart. When in the mid-1820s audiences reacted enthusiastically to the more substantial German style of *Weber, Bishop's essentially undramatic idiom was found wanting. By the early 1830s he had largely ceased original composition. The 1840s saw him gain a knighthood and professorships at Edinburgh and Oxford (effectively sinecures), and though many of his songs retained popularity, he was eclipsed by Michael Balfe (1808–1870) and other rising British operatic composers.   GB

BLACKBURNE, Francis (1705–87), divine. He is chiefly remembered for his work, *The Confessional* (1766), which stimulated controversy about the thirty-nine articles of the Church of England, and for leading a campaign to abolish clerical subscription to them. His main concern was to create a church based on simple scriptural principles. He failed, and while he furthered the cause of religious reform outside the *Anglican Church he weakened the reformist wing within it at a critical time for liberal Christianity [see *religion, 10].

Educated at Catherine Hall, Cambridge, Blackburne was ordained as priest in 1739. He lived at Richmond for the rest of his long life. He was collated to the archdeaconry of Cleveland in 1750, and in the same year to the prebend of Bilton. He thereafter refused preferment because of scruples about re-subscribing to the thirty-nine articles. Although he shared the Latitudinarian desire for a comprehensive Protestant Church, he attacked the associated beliefs that the articles could be interpreted in different ways and that many religious truths were 'merely speculative'. Together with Theophilus Lindsey (1723–1808), who married his stepdaughter, he played a prominent role in organizing the Feathers Tavern Petition for the abolition of clerical subscrip-

tion and its replacement by a simple acknowledgement of the authority of Scripture. The petition was twice defeated in the House of Commons (1772 and 1774). Lindsey, believing success impossible, left the Church in 1773 and became a professed *Unitarian. Blackburne remained a staunch, if somewhat unorthodox, Churchman. Like many radicals and Latitudinarians of his generation, he believed that Roman Catholicism posed a major threat to Protestantism.

Ultimately, Blackburne's significance lies less in what he achieved than in what he helped to provoke: the emergence of a self-conscious movement of Rational Dissent, the revival of Dissenting claims for greater *toleration, and the questioning of the existing constitution in church and state. Even Roman Catholics would benefit from these developments. It is fitting that at the close of his life Blackburne abandoned many aspects of his anti-Catholicism and agreed that a 'perfect toleration' could be granted to those Catholics who were prepared to swear allegiance to the state in all civil matters.   MF

BLACKSTONE, Sir William (1723–80), judge and legal writer. A somewhat retiring and unsuccessful barrister who became Vinerian professor of English law at Oxford, the publication of Blackstone's lectures as *Commentaries on the Laws of England* (1765–9) brought him contemporary fame and ensured his subsequent reputation as conservative apologist for the British constitution and the common law, despite his criticism of the penal code and support for its reform.   DL

BLAIR, Hugh (1718–1800), clergyman and first professor of rhetoric and belles-lettres at the University of Edinburgh, who played a leading role in the *Scottish Enlightenment and in the *Ossian affair.

Blair's writings, particularly his widely read *Sermons* (1777–1801), exemplify the dominant Scottish moral and aesthetic theory based on Christian stoic virtue, sympathy, and sentiment. Like the other moderates in the Scottish clergy, he rejected a narrow, doctrinaire Calvinism and worked for a more tolerant Presbyterian Kirk that actively promoted the *Enlightenment [32] values of free expression, humanitarianism, and polite learning.

It was at Blair's urging that James Macpherson (1736–96), somewhat reluctantly, went ahead with the publication of the first volume of his translations from the Gaelic, *Fragments of Ancient Poetry* (1760). Blair provided a preface which argued that the *ballads still current in the Highlands were corrupted versions of ancient *epics. Both he and Macpherson assumed that the earliest periods of society produced the proper conditions for epic. Soon after the publication of the first volume of Ossianic poetry, Blair encouraged Macpherson to set off on a tour of the Highlands to discover the lost epic of Fingal which he imagined lay behind the fragments. The translation which took place on Macpherson's return was carried out under Blair's supervision. His *Critical Dissertation on the Poems of Ossian* (1763) celebrated the *sublime qualities of the epics

Macpherson produced as the authentically passionate effusions of an early society.

There is no doubt that Blair played such an active part as patron for the Ossian poems because they provided proof for his own theories of literature. These formed the basis of his Edinburgh lectures and were eventually published as *Lectures on Rhetoric and Belles Lettres* (1783). The *Lectures* played an important role in the development of taste for the sublimity and imaginative freedom of early literature. They were often reprinted and frequently deferred to as the pre-eminent work of *literary theory [41] for more than a generation.   JM

BLAKE, William (1757–1827), poet, prophet, painter, and engraver. Although he was either ignored or scorned as a madman for much of his life, Blake's *poetry [29] and *painting [27] were inspired by the notion of a prophetic tradition of liberty which looked to the models provided by *Milton and the *Bible but more fundamentally drew deeply on a popular tradition of Dissent.

Blake's family evidently provided him with a background of religious nonconformity, although its specific nature is unclear. His father was a hosier who provided Blake with no formal schooling, but apprenticed him to the antiquarian engraver James Basire in 1772 [see *prints, 22]. Basire's shop practices influenced the bold linear style of most of Blake's graphic work. On completion of his apprenticeship Blake studied at the *Royal Academy, where he was evidently at odds with the orthodoxy established by Sir Joshua *Reynolds and his followers. Subsequently Blake struggled constantly for independence. He earnt his living as an engraver from 1779, which established his social position for most of his contemporaries in the class of urban artisans. In the 1780s he briefly entered a partnership running a print-shop, but the enterprise was a commercial failure.

He enjoyed initial success, often working closely with the artist Thomas *Stothard. By 1790 he was doing most of his work for the publisher Joseph *Johnson. Over the next decade he engraved a dozen book illustrations after Henry *Fuseli (who may have introduced Blake to Johnson), and was probably known to other members of the Johnson circle including Thomas *Paine and Mary *Wollstonecraft. Certainly most of Blake's own work reflects a commitment to radical politics and an enthusiasm for the *French Revolution. A copy of a poem called *The French Revolution* is extant in proof form (it appears never to have been published) which names Johnson as publisher, though Blake's *millenarianism has more in common with the metropolitan culture of popular religion than the rationalism of most of Johnson's authors. Blake's prophetic inclinations had attracted him to *Swedenborgianism in the 1780s, but his interest seems to have waned by the early 1790s as the movement developed into a church in its own right.

The need to earn a living as an engraver dictated the amount of time Blake could spend on his own imaginative work, but he continually sought recognition as an artist in his own right. In the early 1780s he had been introduced to the circle of Revd A. S. Mathew (1733–1824) and his wife, Harriet, by John *Flaxman. Flaxman and the Mathews helped with the publication of Blake's first volume of verse, *Poetical Sketches*, in 1783. Thereafter Blake's poetry appeared in the form of the illuminated books, such as *Songs of Innocence and of Experience* (1794), *The Marriage of Heaven and Hell* (1790), *America* (1793), *Europe* (1794), and *The Book of Urizen* (1794), which he printed himself. Copies were issued in small editions (probably of no more than ten). Conceived when Blake's prospects as an engraver seemed relatively positive, the project may have been designed as a supplement to his income which would also secure a public reputation. Production of the books was less innovative than is sometimes claimed, being more a variation on conventional graphic techniques. It involved drawing and writing backwards on copper, working directly on the metal plate so as to minimize the division between idea and execution (a notion essential to commercial reproductive engraving), then colouring the plates by hand afterwards. Blake's wife, Catherine, seems to have been largely responsible for this last part of the process, but her labour was essential to everything he produced.

Blake seems to have stopped printing illuminated books in about 1795 and did not print a new book until 1811. From 1795 to 1810 he worked primarily as a painter and illustrator. In 1795–6 he was commissioned to design and engrave illustrations to a deluxe edition of Edward Young's *Night Thoughts*, but the project foundered after the publication of a single volume in 1797. Thereafter he depended more and more on the commissions of loyal patrons like George Cumberland and Thomas Butts. He continued to write poetry, but *Vala or The Four Zoas* (c.1796–1803), *Milton* (c.1804–11), and *Jerusalem* (c.1804–20) were texts on which he worked intermittently for many years. Robert *Southey claimed to have seen 'a perfectly mad poem called Jerusalem' in 1811, but it was not first printed until 1820. *The Four Zoas* was never actually printed and may have been intended for conventional letterpress publication in the manner of the edition of *Night Thoughts*.

Such were the financial difficulties faced by Blake and his wife that in 1800 they accepted the patronage of William *Hayley and moved out of London to his estate in Sussex. Relations between Blake and Hayley deteriorated as the reality of the former's subservient situation became clearer. To make matters worse, Blake was arrested in 1803, accused of seditious words by a soldier he had thrown out of his garden. Acquitted with the support of Hayley, Blake returned to London. By the end of 1808 Blake was more involved in 'Designing & Printing' than producing illuminated books, but he was no more successful in finding a public for his painting or graphic art. The drawings he produced for a new edition of Robert Blair's *The Grave* were largely responsible for what little public reputation Blake ever gained, but when the job of engraving the drawings was given to another engraver in 1806 Blake was bitterly disappointed by the loss of income. When the same publisher commissioned Stothard to paint Chaucer's Canterbury Pilgrims, Blake felt that an idea of his own had been stolen. He decided to hold an exhibition centred on his version of the painting. The exhibition, which took place in his brother's hosiery shop in 1809, was a disastrous failure, bringing no sales and a review in *The Examiner* which described Blake as 'an unfortunate lunatic'. The disappointment was only compounded in 1812 when Blake took the Canterbury Pilgrims picture again, along with *The Spiritual Form of Pitt* (1809) and *The Spiritual Form of Nelson* (1809), to the annual show of the Associated Artists in Water-Colours which was another financial disaster [see *watercolour painting].

Milton was likely first printed in 1811, but Blake probably only began printing illuminated books again in earnest around 1818. His new friendship with John *Linnell played a part in this decision. Linnell claimed that when he first met Blake the artist had 'scarcely enough employment to live by'. The change of Blake's circumstances from the early 1790s is evident in the dramatic increase in price he asked for the books. Whereas originally the illuminated books were conceived of as books of poems which would be sold from stock, now he reprinted them as more highly ornamented collections of coloured prints for commissions on which he was depending for a living. Apart from the splendid copies of works first published in the 1790s, Blake's renewed interest in the illuminated book as a form led him to print *Jerusalem* for the first time in about 1820.

Linnell's friendship brought him work in other areas too. He commissioned a series of brilliant illustrations to the Book of Job in 1823 and secured a commission for woodcut illustrations for an edition of Virgil. It was also through Linnell that Blake came to know the group of young painters known as the *Shoreham Ancients, who looked to him as a mentor but misunderstood the radicalism of his visionary art. Despite Linnell's best endeavours, Blake died poor and in relative obscurity, finally unable to bridge the gap between artist and artisan in the eyes of the public. He was survived by Catherine, who proudly refused a royal pension. Only with the publication of Alexander Gilchrist's biography in 1863 did an interest in Blake begin to grow beyond the antiquarian collectors and fellow-artists who were his patrons.   JM

BLIGH, William (1754–1817), naval captain and colonial governor. Bligh participated in *Cook's second voyage of 1772–5 and was governor of New South Wales from 1805 until deposed in the 'Rum Rebellion' of 1808, but is most notorious for commanding the *Bounty* until the mutiny of 1789.

The *Bounty* voyage to Tahiti aimed to collect breadfruit trees that would be acclimatized in the West Indies (an object accomplished by a second voyage of 1791–3). It has been generally assumed that Bligh's tyrannical disposition, together with the crew's 'degeneration' in the course of a necessarily protracted stay in the voluptuous environment of Tahiti, sparked off the mutiny. Modern scholarship

has shown, however, that Bligh disciplined his men less harshly than many navigators, while the extent to which the crew really became ungovernable as a result of their immersion in Tahitian mores was exaggerated by a general preoccupation in the period with European degeneration in the tropics, and a more specific interest in Polynesian licentiousness.

After the mutiny Bligh and a number of the crew made an extraordinary journey of some 6,300 km in an open boat to Timor, from where they returned eventually to Britain. Although a number of the mutineers were later captured and executed, and Bligh's conduct officially vindicated, he became an exemplar of despotism within the navy, and the mutiny remained controversial.   NT

BLOOMFIELD, Robert (1766–1823), see *peasant poets.

bluestockings, an informal group of intellectual,   *71* artistic, and sociable women, which met in London at the homes of hostesses during the second half of the eighteenth century and flourished from 1770 to 1785. The bluestockings established the claim of polite women to the sociable ideal of conversation; pursued an active commitment to female accomplishment; cultivated aristocratic and middle-class forms of *philanthropy; and offered a significant contribution to late-eighteenth-century female epistolarity.

With a fluid and changing membership, composed predominantly but not exclusively of women, the group comprised several interlocking circles centred around the three main hostesses, Elizabeth Vesey (?1715–91), an Irish woman who started the gatherings in the early 1750s; Frances Boscawen (1719–1805); and Elizabeth Montagu (1720–1800), who started her 'Assemblies' in the 1760s in Hill Street before moving to Montagu House in Portman Square.

With Hannah *More, a prominent member and the most widely published, Elizabeth Montagu used her considerable influence and wealth as a patron and philanthropist to support the peasant poet Ann *Yearsley. After the success of *Evelina* (1778), Frances *Burney was introduced to these circles by her mentor, Hester Thrale *Piozzi. Other prominent participants included Hester Chapone (1727–1801) and Mary Delany (1700–88). Elizabeth *Carter, an accomplished linguist who knew Latin, Greek, Hebrew, Portuguese, and Arabic, represents the conventional (if somewhat misleading) idea of the bluestocking as a learned woman or scholar.

They fostered an ideal of sociability derived from the *Whig ideology of manners, politeness, or taste. This can be traced in turn to the civic and commercial humanism of the moral philosophers and political economists of the *Scottish Enlightenment, who modelled commercial exchange upon the free and civilized exchange of ideas through conversation. Sticklers for social form and *Anglican and feminine virtue, the bluestockings were scandalized by the marriages of Catharine *Macaulay to a younger man and of Hester Thrale to an Italian Catholic. Such actions gave ammunition to the many contemporary lampoons through which 'bluestocking' became a term of misogynist abuse. Hannah More's *The Bas Bleu; or, Conversation* (1786), a witty mock-heroic *ode to the skills of Elizabeth Vesey as a hostess and to the accomplishments and accoutrements of polite sociability, stresses the desirability of conversation over pedantry, in an attempt to counteract the stereotype of the bluestocking as the woman made masculine by too much education.

The participation of members of the Samuel *Johnson's 'Literary Club' (who traditionally retired to the homes of the bluestocking hostesses for dinner after their own meetings) was highly valued. Yet Johnson's thinly veiled scepticism about *female education and the claim of women to rational conversation (preferring them simply to listen) demonstrates the fragility of the bluestocking ideal of properly regulated egalitarian social intercourse between the sexes.

The bluestocking circle declined in the late 1780s: Elizabeth Vesey closed her house in 1785 upon the death of her husband, and Montagu House became diverted by continual renovations and additions, including a spectacular Angelica *Kauffman ceiling. With the gradual publication from the late 1800s of the long-standing correspondences that had sustained their relationships, the sociable bluestockings became an object of nostalgia for many younger women troubled by the growing influence of domestic evangelism.   CT

BONAPARTE, Napoleon, see *Napoleon Bonaparte.

BOSWELL, James (1740–95), biographer. Boswell is most famous as the author of the *Life of Johnson* (1791), which was preceded by his *Journal of a Tour to the Hebrides* (1785). The son of a Scottish judge and himself in the law, Boswell developed a new form of *biography, influenced by *Johnson's own theories, but far exceeding the latter's *Lives of the Poets* in detail, vividness, and intimacy.

Boswell combined a gift for contriving occasions in which his subject would 'perform' revealingly with the ability to capture the ensuing occasion and dialogue in a dramatic and informal transcription. The very candour with which Johnson was portrayed in the *Tour* led some of his contemporaries to refuse Boswell material for the *Life*. The discovery of manuscript diaries has revealed that Boswell edited, cut, and rewrote his material, and the *Life* should not be taken as a reliable, objective portrait. Boswell tends to attribute most of his own sexist prejudices, for example, to Johnson.

The diaries are themselves a fascinating and unselfconscious record of Boswell's turbulent emotional life, and his present reputation perhaps rests as much on these as on his formal works. They record his sexual adventures, his fraught relation to his father, his pursuit of literary celebrities, and his hypochondria. (His essays, *The Hypochondriac*, were published in 1777–9.) The diaries and the biographies are among the fullest and most candid records of late-eighteenth-century life we have.   JW

botany. Through its long-standing connection with *medicine [18] and agricultural improvement, botany was one of the most useful natural sciences during our period [see *land, 16 and *natural philosophy, 34]. It also had a wide cultural appeal, reflected in the growing interest in *landscape gardening and the cult of the *picturesque. Plants played a significant role in the life of the landed élite, who often possessed illustrated floras and synopses of classification schemes in their libraries. They also cultivated exotic plants and patronized plant collectors and landscape gardeners. Women were particularly prominent as authors of elementary textbooks, since botany was widely encouraged as a suitable science for genteel women to pursue. Indeed, it was one of the few sciences open to women.

Botany's greatest impact, however, came through geographical expeditions. These introduced a large number of new species, initiating a rage for choice specimens and providing the foundations of national herbaria and museum collections. Many of these exotics came from government voyages of *exploration [37] to Australia, the Cape, and the South Seas. Living plants could be seen at Kew Gardens (royal property until 1841), Chatsworth, or Syon Park near Chiswick. Enterprising private societies like the Royal Horticultural Society (founded in 1804) similarly sponsored collectors and ran gardens.

British prosperity overseas equally depended on the development of the plantation system in which staple crops like tea or sugar-cane were relocated for colonial purposes [see *empire, 5]. Naval officers, entrepreneurs, and government officials jointly opened up these routes to national expansion. The *East India Company took the lead in establishing botanic gardens in Saharanpore and Calcutta; and Kew Gardens, under Sir Joseph *Banks, became a hub of proto-imperial science.

Theoretical botany provided the foundations for these larger cultural exercises. The classification scheme of the Swedish naturalist Carolus Linnaeus (1707–78), for example, was immensely popular in Britain—simple enough for anyone among the widening reading public to grasp and supplying an easy method for naming the thousands of new species flooding into Europe. Botanists began to conceptualize plant distribution on a worldwide scale, formulating the local requirements which determined particular phylogeographical patterns. Based on counting the reproductive parts of the flower, Linnaeus's system generated the explicit sexual imagery of the poetry of Erasmus *Darwin.

After the death of Linnaeus in 1778, the botanist James Edward Smith (1759–1828) purchased his collections, originally offered to Joseph Banks. The Linnean Society of London was established in 1788, and soon became the premier botanical society in England. Smith was elected president at the first meeting, where he delivered an address entitled 'Introductory Discourse on the Rise and Progress of Natural History'. He later published *English Botany* (1790) and his most important work, *Flora Britannica* (1800–4). Smaller societies and specimen exchange clubs also proliferated, most of which used the Linnaean system of classification.

In specialist circles, botanists vigorously investigated physiology, reproduction, and anatomy, readily drawing parallels between animals and plants. Sensitive plants like the mimosa were thought to possess animal-like qualities such as irritability. Studies of 'breathing' in plants played a significant role in the discovery of oxygen and then photosynthesis; and the action of pollen in fertilization helped in understanding animal reproduction.   JBR

BOULTON, Matthew (1728–1809), pioneer of mechanized production of consumer goods and industrial machinery [see *consumerism, 19 and *industrialization, 14]. Born in Birmingham, Boulton was educated at the Revd John Hausted's school, before joining his father's local buckle-making business at the age of 14.

Throughout his life Boulton readily exploited the commercial potential of new materials and technologies. By the time his father died in 1760 he had diversified and enriched the family business through novel use of steel, enamels, and ceramics. In 1762 he built at Birmingham the Soho Manufactory, which soon became famous for innovative work practices and use of machines. Boulton favoured intensive training of young employees over traditional modes of apprenticeship, thereby giving the Soho works flexibility to respond to changes in consumer demand. He also established one of Britain's earliest mutual *friendly societies for its workforce.

Soho manufactured inexpensive plate and domestic furnishings, and later coins and commemorative medals, though in the late 1760s and early 1770s, Boulton employed machinery in making items of luxury furniture, including clocks, silver, and ormolu candelabra. However, sales were insufficient for him to profit from the venture, despite having acquaintances in various European centres to ensure that his *designs [25] mirrored élite fashions and taste. Those who could afford luxury wares still generally preferred to commission unique creations.

Boulton enjoyed greater success and widespread fame through his twenty-five-year partnership with James *Watt, constructing steam engines for mining and industry. By the mid-1780s over forty engines had been sold, half to Cornish mines, and the two men were honoured by election to the Royal Societies of Edinburgh and London.

Throughout his active life Boulton was a prominent spokesman for Birmingham's manufacturing interests, and supporter of reformist causes. He was active in local *literary and philosophical societies, a member of the Lunar Society, and sponsored Joseph *Priestley's scientific work.   PT

bowdlerism. Henrietta Maria Bowdler (1753–1830), woman of letters and *sermons, and her brother Thomas (1754–1825), physician and *philanthropist, contributed their surname to the English language. The Bowdlers famously expurgated the works of *Shakespeare, Henrietta producing four volumes in 1807, Thomas Bowdler, ten volumes of *Family Shakespeare* in 1818.

The verb 'to bowdlerize', associated with zealous, pious, and prudish literary censorship, means to edit and expunge offensive, sexual, or indelicate words and passages from literary and other texts. By his own account, Bowdler excised words and expressions 'which cannot be read aloud in a family'. Abridgements were 'made to exclude ... whatever is unfit to be read aloud by a gentleman to a company of ladies'.

The Bowdlers attacked writing they considered to be licentious, frivolous, irreligious, or immoral so as to prevent it contaminating the minds of the poor, young, and newly literate. Bowdlerism has been associated with the rise of *Evangelicalism and the aims of the Proclamation Society (later the *Society for the Suppression of Vice), of which Thomas Bowdler was an early member. Personally they were, however, cultured and educated individuals, friends of the *bluestockings as well as William *Wilberforce and the prominent Evangelical bishops Beilby Porteus (1731–1808) and John Hinchcliffe (1731–94). Henrietta Bowdler also edited poems of the popular religious poet and scholar, Elizabeth Smith (1776–1806), while Thomas expurgated Edward *Gibbon's *Decline and Fall of the Roman Empire* by removing chapters 'highly objectionable' in their hostility to early Christianity.   SR

BOWRING, Sir John (1792–1872), propagated and applied radical and Benthamite ideas across a wide range of public life, while his translations and advocacy significantly broadened English acquaintance with European folk literature.

Descended from an old Devon family in the woollen trade, Bowring's indifferent early education was redeemed by the informal tutelage of the *Unitarian minister, Lant Carpenter (1780–1840). Employed by firms trading to Spain, in Exeter, and after 1811 in London, Bowring mastered Spanish and became deeply involved in radical activity. In 1820 he entered the inner circle of Jeremy *Bentham, becoming co-editor of the *Westminster Review* and subsequently editor of Bentham's works.

After his own firm failed in 1827, Bowring was employed on official inquiries into European accounting practices and commercial circumstances in France, Egypt, and Syria. A radical MP in 1835–7 and 1841–8, he became consul in Canton and then governor of Hong Kong, where his insistence on freeing trade led (despite his long involvement in the peace movement) to bombarding Canton, the second Chinese War of 1856–60, and his recall.

Bowring gave his own Christian and Unitarian slant to Bentham's *utilitarianism, notably in the *Deontology* (1834). His compulsive versifying, deeply influenced by Mrs *Barbauld, found its outlet in many *hymns and other devotional literature. His wide acquaintance with languages made him rightly celebrated as a linguist, although many of the translations were done with the help of others.

Bowring made some famous enemies—George Borrow (1803–81) and John Stuart *Mill among them—so it is only recently that historians have arrived at a more just appreciation of his consistent radicalism, his signal contributions to free trade and the reform of government administration, the perceptiveness of his reports, and his achievements in East Asia, including the opening of Siam.   RKW

BOYDELL, John 'Alderman' (1719–1804), engraver, publisher, and patron of the arts. Boydell was born near Woore, Shropshire, one of three sons of Josiah Boydell, a land surveyor, and Mary Milnes. Although intended for his father's profession, Boydell apprenticed himself at 21 to the engraver W. H. Toms, and studied drawing at the academy in St Martin's Lane. He served six years of his apprenticeship, purchased back the remaining year of his term, and commenced living by his burin, chiefly on the proceeds of topographical engravings [see *prints, 22].

The success of his early graphic work enabled Boydell to establish himself as printseller and publisher at 90 Cheapside, London. When Boydell began his business in the early 1750s, Britain's print market was dominated by foreign imports, a situation he was determined to rectify through encouragement of a British school of engraving. To this end, he commissioned works from eminent engravers such as Basire (1730–1802), Woollett (1735–85), and *Sharp including highly successful engravings by Woollett after Richard *Wilson's *Niobe* and Benjamin *West's *Death of General Wolfe*. From 1773 Boydell worked in partnership with his nephew and successor, Josiah (1752–1817). After a lucrative career as a print publisher, Boydell proposed an edition of the works of *Shakespeare, illustrated by English artists, a project that led to the formation of his Shakespeare Gallery at 59 Pall Mall [see *viewing, 20 and *painting, 27]. Boydell was elected Alderman for the ward of Cheap in 1782, served as Sheriff in 1785, and was chosen Lord Mayor of London in 1790. Financial difficulties created by a decline in the export of prints during the continental *war [2] and lavish expenditure on the Shakespeare Gallery (which Boydell estimated at £350,000) forced the disposal of the Gallery by lottery in 1804.   CSM

BRAHAM, John (1774–1856), celebrated Anglo-Jewish tenor, composer, and impresario who performed mainly at London's *theatres [24], often composing *ballads and rousing patriotic songs for his own roles—'The Death of Nelson' written for *The Americans* (Lyceum, 1812) was particularly popular. He also appeared regularly at *concerts, provincial *music festivals, and briefly at the King's Theatre (1804–6).

A gifted, flexible singer with excellent diction, Braham played to his audiences whilst winning the respect of fellow musicians such as *Weber, who wrote the music of Huon for him in *Oberon* (1826). Braham retired rich, but lost money in two unsuccessful theatrical ventures—the Colosseum (1831) and St James's Theatre (1836). He therefore resumed singing, continuing well into his 70s.   RC

BRAND, John (1744–1806), antiquarian and chaplain. Educated at the Royal Grammar School, New-

castle, Brand was ordained in 1773. He acted as a teacher and curate in positions around Newcastle until 1784, when his friend and patron the Duke of Northumberland made him rector of the combined London parishes of St Mary-at-Hill and St Mary Hubbard. In 1786 he became one of the Duke's chaplains. On the basis of his 1777 edition of his *Observations on Popular Antiquities; Including the Whole of Mr. [Henry] Bourne's Antiquitates Vulgares*, he was elected president secretary of the Society of Antiquaries, a position he held from the year he moved to London until his death.

Brand published *The History and Antiquities of the Town and Country of Newcastle-upon-Tyne* (1789) and contributed frequently to the Society's journal *Archaeologia*, but his development of Henry Bourne's (1694–1733) researches was his most important contribution to the study of popular *antiquarianism [35]. The early editions were commentaries on Bourne's work. Brand's additions come in the form of compilations, drawing on the researches of Francis *Grose, Joseph *Strutt, and the suggestions of Francis *Douce. They implied that popular customs warranted serious antiquarian study as part of a national tradition rather than suppression as vulgar superstition [see *popular culture, 23]. Upon Brand's death (and making extensive use of Douce's notes), Sir Henry Ellis (1777–1869) edited and enlarged the compilation, which appeared as two volumes in 1813.   GAB

BREWSTER, Sir David (1781–1868), natural philosopher and Scottish Presbyterian divine. Born in a small Scottish town to the rector of the local grammar school, Brewster attended the University of Edinburgh at the early age of 12, where he became a close friend of Henry *Brougham and other *Scottish Enlightenment intellectuals. He was intended by his father for a career in the Church of Scotland, but despite receiving his licence never took up a living in the Church. From childhood he was interested in *natural philosophy [34], and he attended scientific *lectures during his university days.

For most of his life Brewster made a precarious living from a variety of sources. He was involved in a wide range of journalistic and editorial projects, including Blackwood's ambitious *Edinburgh Encyclopaedia*. At various times Brewster was editor of the *Edinburgh Philosophical Journal*, the *Edinburgh Journal of Science*, and the *Philosophical Magazine*, as well as being a constant contributor to a range of quarterlies. He used his journalism to mount a campaign against what he regarded as the corruption of the English scientific establishment.

Brewster regarded British science as being in a state of decline. He was a supporter of Charles *Babbage's attacks on the Royal Society and an early partisan of the British Association for the Advancement of Science (BAAS). He made several public attacks on the state of science at the universities of Cambridge and Oxford. As a reform *Whig, Brewster regarded science's decline as part of the corruption of an unreformed state.

7, 89

Well-known for his optical researches, Brewster was a vociferous opponent of the new undulatory theory of light, and he invented several optical instruments, including the kaleidoscope, which rapidly became one of the most popular of philosophical toys. Despite holding a patent, however, Brewster failed to profit from his invention. He interpreted his own experiences as examples of the failure of science and invention in Britain. IRM

British Museum, created in 1753 when parliament voted to purchase the books, manuscripts, and cabinet of 'natural and artificial curiosities' collected by the physician, antiquarian, and scientist Hans Sloane (1660–1753). Sloane's collection, together with the Cottonian and Harleian libraries, was the core of an institution that reflected *Enlightenment [32] theories of *natural philosophy [34] and human civilization. The bequests, donations, and purchases that formed the Museum's library and diverse collections of minerals, fossils, zoological and botanical specimens, antiquities, and art works are an index to the nation's political, military, and cultural history.

In 1757 George II donated a Royal Library founded in the fifteenth century; he also annexed the privilege of being supplied with a copy of every publication entered in the Stationers' Hall. Shortly after his succession, George III gave a collection of some 30,000 pamphlets and political papers relating to the events of the Civil War, 1640–61. Both *Cook and *Banks deposited natural specimens and artefacts culled from their Pacific voyages of *exploration [37]. William *Hamilton donated *geological samples from Mount Vesuvius and in 1772 sold the Museum his collection of classical vases and statuary. Charles Townley's (1737–1805) Greek and Roman *sculptures were purchased in 1805 and followed in 1814 by the Museum's acquisition of the Phigaleian Marbles. Sculpture salvaged from the Parthenon was displayed in temporary quarters in the Museum grounds between 1816 and 1831, when a permanent 'Elgin Gallery' was constructed [see *Elgin Marbles]. Many Egyptian artefacts, including the Rosetta Stone, passed into the Museum after the French surrender in 1801. From 1759 the Museum was housed in Montagu House, Great Russell Street, a refurbished seventeenth-century mansion that had been acquired and renovated with state lottery money. Robert *Smirke's design for a new building on the site was approved by the trustees in 1823 and completed in 1852. CSM

BRITTON, John (1771–1857), topographer, publisher, antiquarian. His topographical publications made detailed knowledge of Britain's medieval architectural heritage accessible to the reading public, raised the standards for contemporary *Gothic Revival design, and created popular support for the preservation of historic monuments.

The ill-educated son of a baker, Britton left Wiltshire for London at 16 to become an apprentice in the wine trade. Here he became acquainted with London's theatrical community, eventually quitting the trade and earning his living by a combination of *acting, public speaking, and hack journalism.

Britton's break came in 1798 when he received a commission to write and illustrate a guide to his native county, *The Beauties of Wiltshire* (1801). A consortium of publishers then engaged him and his friend Edward Wedlake Brayley (1773–1854) to undertake a topographical survey on a national scale. Proceeding alphabetically through the country, *The Beauties of England and Wales* was eventually completed in 1801, though by this time without Britton due to disagreements. Britton rejected the then popular *picturesque emphasis on scenic beauty and concentrated on the description and history of art and architectural artifacts [see *architecture, 28 and *antiquarianism, 35]. He illustrated his works with detailed engravings by some of the era's most talented artists.

Established as a publisher in 1805, Britton issued the first four volumes of *The Architectural Antiquities of Great Britain* between 1807 and 1814. Its success inspired him to undertake the first systematic historical and architectural survey of England's cathedrals. Fourteen volumes of *The Cathedral Antiquities of England* appeared between 1814 and 1835, several of which were collaborations with Brayley and A. C. *Pugin. They confirmed Britton's merits as a publisher, but their unprofitability initiated his financial decline, ensured by the failure of his subsequent publications. Throughout his later years Britton sustained himself with hack writing, and mobilized his antiquarian authority for the cause of the nascent national heritage movement. SS

BROOKE, Charlotte, (c.1740–93), translator and antiquarian scholar, a key figure in the late-eighteenth-century *Irish cultural revival, for which she provided widely respected and authentic translations of early Gaelic poems and legends.

The daughter of the celebrated novelist of *sensibility [11] Henry Brooke (c.1703–83), she was born in County Cavan and educated by her father in art, literature, and music. She became a keen student of the Irish language, and in 1786 was persuaded to publish anonymously a translation of a poem attributed to the famous harpist Carolan, in a collection by Joseph Walker (1761–1810) entitled *Historical Memoirs of the Irish Bards* (1785). Alone after the death of her father, bankrupted by a relative's unwise investments, and a recluse by nature, Brooke had to be pressured by Bishop *Percy and members of the newly founded Royal Irish Academy to publish a collection of her own. This eventually appeared in 1789 under the title *Reliques of Irish Poetry*. Containing heroic poems, songs, elegies, and *odes, and accompanied by scholarly notes, the *Reliques* was widely praised for its textual accuracy and lyrical beauty. Part of her motivation was to counter the forgeries and appropriations of James Macpherson, who had rendered the third-century Irish bard Oisin into the spurious Scottish figure of *Ossian.

A supporter of 'Patriot' Anglo-Irish liberalism in politics, Brooke also hoped to persuade the English of the value of early Gaelic civilization and culture. She died of fever in Longford soon after publishing a children's book and an edition of her father's works.

Two years later, in 1795, some of her poems were included in the *Gaelic Magazine* or *Bolg an tsolair*, notable because of its use of an Irish language title and its publication in the Belfast office of the United Irish republican newspaper, the *Northern Star*. Her translations were frequently reprinted, and were to exercise a powerful influence on W. B. Yeats and other figures in the Irish cultural renaissance at the end of the nineteenth century.   IMcC

BROTHERS, Richard (1757–1824), naval lieutenant, enthusiast, and a central figure in the London *millenarian circles of the 1790s. Known as 'the Great Prophet of Paddington Street', he established his reputation in 1794 with the publication of a work entitled *A Revealed Knowledge of the Prophecies and Times*, Part One, soon followed by Part Two. Brothers was neither a charismatic leader nor the founder of a new sect or cult, but he did encourage his readers to express in writing their own beliefs and dreams. The pamphlets written by his followers and their critics make up a significant body of popular millenarian literature.

Although Brothers's writings were chiefly drawn from apocalyptic biblical passages, they nevertheless contained opinions which had radical political and social implications. He wrote, for example, how God had commanded him to declare that radical reformers on trial for high treason were innocent, and that George III would lose his throne for making war on the French. Brothers also believed that he was a prince of the Hebrews, the nephew of the Almighty, and the ruler of the world; consequently the King should relinquish the Crown to him. Like many millenarian thinkers, Brothers looked forward with great anticipation to the return of the Jews to the Holy Land. He had an architect draw up plans for the restoration of Jerusalem with the Garden of Eden in the centre. In 1795 Brothers was arrested on suspicion of treasonable practices. He was examined before the Privy Council and subsequently confined as a criminal lunatic. He was later placed in a private *madhouse, where he remained for eleven years despite attempts by followers to have him released. Brothers's confinement and the government's continued association of millenarianism and radical political activity effectively discouraged all but a small group of his followers.   JM

BROUGHAM, Henry Peter, first Baron Brougham and Vaux (1778–1868), lawyer, reviewer, publicist, and politician. Brougham was also an indefatigable campaigner in speech and writing for numerous legal and social reforms. Educated in Scotland, he entered parliament in 1810, becoming unofficial spokesman in Commons for the 'Mountain' or radical wing of the *Whig party before being elected to Earl Grey's ministry as Lord Chancellor in 1830.

A formidable speaker, Brougham probably had more celebrated successes than any other politician of the period. In 1810 he expedited the *abolition of slave trading by having it reclassified as a crime punishable by transportation, an achievement followed two years later by the revocation of the Orders in Council that were crippling British trade during the Napoleonic wars. In 1832 his tactical intimidation of the *Tory peers was instrumental in forcing the passage of the *Reform Bill. Likewise in the courtroom he achieved such sensational defences as that of John and Leigh *Hunt in February 1811 against the charge of seditious libel for an article published in the *Examiner* against flogging in the army.

A parliamentary reputation for indiscretion and ambition was spectacularly confirmed by the one *cause célèbre* with which Brougham's name is still identified: the *Queen Caroline affair. Yet his tireless campaigning for legal and social reforms cannot be written off simply as ambition. Even without his abrasive handling, many of his causes (like universal *education [17], first assayed in a failed bill of 1820) were offensive to powerful members of both parties, although they gained considerable extraparliamentary support. Brougham's objective—'the re-establishment of the ancient intercourse between the Whigs and the people'—may have combined myth with illusion, but the gratification that he derived from popularity was real enough, sustained by his skills as a self-publicist. Little that he did was not heralded by a timely pamphlet, extensively distributed, or justified at length by an article in the *Edinburgh Review*, the *Morning Chronicle*, or *The Times*—all, with few exceptions, written by himself. None hitherto had used the press and periodical literature to such effect. While government exerted itself to contain the press and public opinion, Brougham exploited them, urging reforms which included, not surprisingly, *freedom of the press.

Though Brougham was dissatisfied both with the Whig party (often contemplating a third or 'liberal' party before its time) and the party system (actively encouraging a coalition with the Tory *Canning in 1825, for example), his maverick tendencies were less a matter of policy than of impatience with conformity, and contempt for a timorous and exclusive Whig aristocracy.   WC

BROWN, Lancelot 'Capability' (1716–83), landscape gardener and architect, whose natural style of landscaping revolutionized British *landscape gardening and consolidated the practice and discourse of 'improvement' that was such a central feature of the *agricultural revolution [see *land, 16].

After acquiring practical gardening skills on the estate of Sir William Loraine, Brown worked as kitchen-gardener at Lord Cobham's Stowe from 1739, where he assisted William Kent in designing and constructing *pleasure gardens. In 1748 he moved to the Duke of Grafton's Wakefield, where he adapted Hogarth's serpentine 'line of beauty' in the modelling of lake shores, river courses, skirts of woods, and lawn edges.

Brown was given the nickname 'Capability' after his habit of referring to the inherent capability or natural potential of his commissioned sites. Despite an emphasis on bringing out the naturally undulating lines of the landscape, certain features of his style became so standardized in the hands of imitators that he became identified with the most modernizing and destructive aspects of improvement. Brown's emphasis on improving the vista or prospect, which in practice dictated vast lawns, meant that many great houses became cut off from the neighbouring village people (who could even be moved out of their houses if these houses spoiled the view). Such an uncomfortable aesthetic reminder of social division belied the organic view of the village community, exemplified in Jane *Austen's *Mansfield Park* (1814), which fostered the illusion of common access to land. Followers of Brown included Humphry *Repton and Uvedale *Price.   CT

BRUCE, James (1730–94). Born in Scotland, Bruce briefly studied law, but turned to *oriental languages and antiquities, and then to archaeological research, while consul in Algiers in 1763–5. After resigning this post, he conducted a series of studies of ruins in North Africa, Crete, Syria, and Egypt, and became increasingly preoccupied with the idea of discovering the source of the Nile. In 1770 he involved himself in the turbulent politics of Ethiopia and secured rights to travel through the upper reaches of the Blue Nile, reaching springs which he later asserted represented the source of the great river itself. He spent more time in Ethiopia, Tigre, and Egypt, and travelled to Marseilles in March 1773.

When he returned to Britain some eighteen months later, Bruce encountered a fascinated, but rapidly incredulous, audience for his accounts of his travels. His *Travels to Discover the Source of the Nile* appeared in five volumes in 1790; rich in dramatic anecdotes and poorly organized antiquarian disquisitions, the book was immediately controversial. Suspicions of *travel literature as a genre were heightened in Bruce's case by his spurious claim to have discovered the source of the Nile, when he had in reality explored an inferior branch. Succeeding travellers in the region such as Lord Valentia (1769–1844) and Henry Salt (1780–1827) also took Bruce to task for many particular fancies and distortions. Bruce's *Travels*, however, retain great importance, not only for the extravagance of their evocation of barbaric yet anomalously Christian societies of north-east Africa, but also for the peculiar poignancy and reflexivity with which Bruce relates the alleged discovery of the springs. The admission that his sense of triumph was accompanied by a melancholic sense of futility is rare in the writings of imperial *exploration [37].   NT

BRUMMELL, George Bryan 'Beau', see *dandyism.

BRUNEL, Isambard Kingdom (1806–59). A highly innovative designer of railways, ships, and bridges, Brunel combined *engineering flair and theory with aesthetic sensitivity to achieve technical feats which captured the public imagination [see *transport].

Brunel was the protégé of his father, Marc Isambard Brunel (1769–1849), who fled revolutionary France in 1793, settling in England six years later and inventing machinery to mass-produce ships' blocks in Portsmouth royal dockyard. Isambard Kingdom was educated at a progressive *Unitarian school in Sussex and at the Lycée Henri IV, Paris. He returned

to Britain in 1822 to train with his father, who was preparing to drive a tunnel beneath the River Thames, using his patented mechanical shield. Despite dangerous and unpleasant conditions, half the tunnel had been constructed under the younger Brunel's supervision when financial stringency halted work in 1828; it was completed in 1842.

Clifton Suspension Bridge, in Bristol, was Brunel's first independent commission. His ambitious scheme offered the longest single span yet constructed. Financial difficulties again intervened: begun in 1836, work stopped in 1842, and was resumed only after Brunel's death. Appointed to remodel Bristol docks in 1833, he also became Engineer of the Great Western Railway. He masterminded its construction over six years and 118 miles of track from London to Bristol (and subsequently beyond), designing everything from rails, bridges, and signalling system to station lampposts. Opened in 1841, it was a technical triumph but costly in both lives and, at more than twice his estimate, money.

Brunel's vision extended across the Atlantic: at Bristol, rail passengers would board the company's ocean liners. His SS *Great Western* made the first transatlantic steam crossing in 1838, in under fifteen days. The iron-hulled SS *Great Britain* (1844) and the gigantic SS *Great Eastern* (1858) followed. Brunel's strengths were also his weaknesses. His vaulting technical ambition often achieved the unthinkable; it could also produce expensive failures, such as the South Devon atmospheric railway and the protracted launch of the SS *Great Eastern*. Elected to the Royal Society in 1830, he preferred the society of the Institution of Civil Engineers, which he served as vice-president from 1850 to 1859. He enthusiastically promoted the Great Exhibition of 1851, but disapproved of its medals and prizes as much as he did the patent system and all forms of state regulation.   CMacL

BRUNTON, Mary (1778–1818), wrote *novels [31] of moral etiquette in the tradition of Frances *Burney's *Evelina* (1778). Born the daughter of Colonel Thomas Balfour and Frances Lingonier on the island of Barra in Orkney, Brunton grew up in relative isolation with little formal education. At the age of 19 she married Alexander Brunton, a scholarly Calvinist minister who fostered her creative reading and writing. In 1803 the couple moved to Edinburgh, where the Reverend took a new parish and became professor of oriental languages at the university.

Brunton's first and most successful novel, *Self-Control*, was published in 1810: it was dedicated to fellow Scot Joanna *Baillie, and became an immediate bestseller. Jane *Austen proclaimed it an 'excellently-meant' and 'elegantly-written work'. *Self-Control* reveals many similarities with Austen's more subversive ideas about women and novels. Despite the overt prefatory intention of inculcating 'the triumph of RELIGION' and stressing heroinely restraint, the novel is clearly concerned with the difficulty of a woman earning her own living and with the importance of female financial independence. Like Austen's *Northanger Abbey* (1818), Brunton's fiction self-consciously defends its own genre, asserting the utility of novels to potential detractors. In her hope that the work might be 'in some degree useful', Brunton pleads: 'Let not the term so implied provoke a smile! . . . When the vitiated appetite refuses its proper food, the alternative may be administered in a sweetmeat.' In the text itself, Brunton claims the value of specifically female-authored fiction, making her exemplary heroine, Laura, cite a preference for novels written by women and choose as her fictional ideal the hero of Jane *Porter's *Thaddeus of Warsaw* (1803).

In 1815 Brunton published *Discipline*, quite different in plot from her previous novel yet recapitulating themes such as womanly fortitude in the face of rakish unreliability. She later planned to write a sequence of domestic tales, but finished only *Emmeline* (1819) before dying from puerperal infection at the age of 40.   KF

BULWER-LYTTON, Edward George Earle Lytton, first Baron Lytton (1803–73), novelist and parliamentarian. Though little read today, he was extremely influential during the latter part of our period and played a key role in disseminating popular images of *Byronic Romanticism and *dandyism, as well as in pioneering new literary genres such as *silver fork novels and *Newgate crime novels.

The youngest of three children, Edward Bulwer was educated at home with his mother (whose name, Lytton, he added in 1843), then in a variety of small private schools, before taking a BA at Cambridge in 1825. Besotted with the works of Byron and *Scott from an early age, he produced a series of juvenile poems in imitation of the former, and read avidly in history and romance like the latter. Bulwer also self-consciously imitated Byron's raffish, romantic life. This included undertaking brooding tours of the Lake District and Scotland, leading a reckless social life in London and Paris, taking up daring masculine sports such as pugilism and fencing, flirting with Lady Caroline *Lamb, and embarking on a destructive marriage in 1827 with Rosina Doyle Wheeler (1802–82), mother of Anna *Wheeler.

Needing to support an extravagant style of living, Bulwer wrote prolifically, both miscellaneous journalism for periodicals like the *Quarterly Review*, and a string of **novels [31]** beginning with the morbid *Falkland* (1827) modelled on Goethe's *Sorrows of Werther*. However, his most influential works during our period were *Pelham* (1828), the half-ironic tale of a Byronic dandy based on himself and friends, and the two Newgate novels, *Paul Clifford* (1830) and *Eugene Aram* (1832). Though these last two purported to promote reform of *prisons, they were severely attacked, especially by John Gibson *Lockhart, for their immoral idealization of criminality. Elected MP for the seat of St Ives in 1831, Bulwer supported the *Reform Act (1832) and a variety of other *Whig-liberal causes, including *copyright protection for authors. He was a close friend of John Stuart *Mill, who contributed a study of *Bentham to Bulwer's *England and the English* (1830). Though he was later to make important contributions to the development of occult, horror, and science fiction

novels, these achievements belonged to his later life as a Victorian colonial administrator.   IMcC

BUNTING, Edward (1773–1843), Irish folk-song collector. Bunting was involved in the Belfast Harp Festival of 1792, a gathering designed to recuperate and preserve traditional Irish music and poetry [see *Irish cultural revival]. The event contributed to the mobilization of national consciousness associated with the United Irish movement. Following the Festival Bunting toured Ireland, collecting airs published in 1796 (later volumes appeared in 1809 and 1840), referred to as 'sounds that might make Pitt melt for the poor Irish' by one contemporary. Bunting's work formed the basis for Thomas *Moore's *Melodies*, the greater success of that project causing resentment among Bunting's supporters.   GR

BURDETT, Sir Francis (1770–1844), aristocratic reformer. The most prominent radical reformer of the Napoleonic war years, he reappropriated much of the traditional popular association between *patriotism and political opposition which had been lost in the 1790s.

Of aristocratic background and education, Burdett made a name for himself after 1803 as a political reformer independent of the *Whigs, who was willing to work with and campaign for radical state prisoners, former Irish rebels, and mutineers incarcerated in Cold Bath Fields prison [see *prisons]. After winning the relatively democratic parliamentary seat of Westminster in 1807, he campaigned in and out of parliament, with the help of popular journalist William *Cobbett, to associate successive ministries with financial and moral scandals such as the Mary Anne *Clarke affair of 1808–9, with torture and repression in Ireland, with military corruption and carnage at Walcheren in 1810–11, and with the suppression of traditional English liberties such as freedom of speech and opinion.

He became a national celebrity when taken to the Tower for contempt of parliament in 1810, having been arrested while theatrically reading Magna Carta to his son. Serious 'Burdett and Liberty' riots followed in London, signalling a shift of popular sympathies away from *loyalism towards reform [see *riots and disturbances]. During the postwar years Burdett's popular reputation declined when he became alienated from artisan radical reformers. Though eventually a *Tory, he remained sympathetic to libertarian causes such as *Catholic emancipation, one of his major achievements having been to swing radical political sympathies away from antipopery and towards Catholic and Irish causes.   IMcC

BURKE, Edmund (1729–97), statesman, political thinker, and writer. His fame rests, despite wide interests and talents, on the *Reflections on the Revolution in France* (1790), which constituted a major work of opposition to the *French Revolution and articulated the foundations of modern British conservatism.

Educated in Dublin, Trinity College, and the Temple, Burke first pursued a literary career with *A Philosophical Enquiry into the Origin of our Ideas*

of the Sublime and Beautiful (1757), a formulation of the distinction between the aesthetic principles of the *sublime and the beautiful, which achieved international recognition. Burke entered politics in 1765 as the secretary to Lord Rockingham (1765–82), becoming MP for Wendover (1765–74), Bristol (1774–80), and Malton (1780–94), and Paymaster-General in 1782.

As Rockinghamite spokesman and pamphleteer, he defended party and loyal opposition with Thoughts on the Cause of the Present Discontents (1770); articulated the relationship of MPs to constituents in Speech to the Electors of Bristol on being Elected (1774); argued for the reform of national finances in Conciliation with America (1775); and sought the reform of the colonial administration of India through legislation and his unsuccessful impeachment of Warren *Hastings, Governor-General of Bengal (1788–95). He also worked inconspicuously for *Catholic emancipation in England and Ireland, and retained a persistent sympathy for the economic, political, and religious travails of the Irish Catholic.

The French Revolution reinspired British reformers already galvanized by the *American Revolution. Burke's first aim in the Reflections (1790) was to denounce the image of 1688 presented by Richard *Price in his sermon A Discourse on the Love of our Country (1789), which linked the French Revolution with the *Glorious Revolution on the basis of the principles of the rights 'to chuse our own governors, to cashier them for misconduct, and to frame a government for ourselves'. Burke's conservative interpretation of 1688 was argued more fully in his Appeal from the New to the Old Whigs (1791), which was seen by many as an aged reformer's apostasy. At issue was not only the interpretation of English history, but the very conception of *revolution [1], which hitherto had implied the restoration of a lost constitutional purity. Burke emphasized the contrasting innovatory character of French revolutionary rhetoric, on which view 1688 was very different—'a revolution prevented', not one accomplished.

As well as offering a conservative critique of the philosophical views behind the revolution, which it did episodically, in images and epigrammatic asides, rather than systematically, the Reflections offers a socio-economic analysis. Burke saw the revolution as a class-based revolt, that of enterprise against land, precipitated by a moneyed interest anxious to secure debts owed them by an insolvent ancien régime and in league with *Enlightenment [32] intellectuals. The subsequent appropriation of church lands served both an ideological and material function, in undermining the Christian religion and its support of the traditional order, and in the sale of lands which would secure the financiers' debts.

Burke saw the revolution as producing a volatile mix of new and inexperienced political actors—the 'country attorneys' in the National Assembly and the mob in the streets of Paris. Of the conditions of liberty desired by this alliance he predicted a destruction of deference, which would ultimately render all politics coercive whilst dismantling independent political establishments, and the rise of an unrestrained and possibly military absolutism.

Burke identified the ideology of the *natural rights of man as the central revolutionary credo. Identifying this with the Hobbesian spectre of an individualism of competing claims, he denied that natural rights could form the basis of a new society. This attack on natural rights evoked numerous responses, the most strenuous being that of Thomas *Paine. Burke also rejected the radicals' identification of nature with virtue and simplicity in opposition to social decadence and artifice, claiming instead that 'Art is man's nature'. Thus nature required for its realization a providentially guided and continuous history, which could be served by no discontinuous, secularly inspired reform.

In response to the radical use of social contract theory, Burke argued that society involved a contract not simply between present rulers and ruled, but one extending across the generations 'between those who are living those who are dead and those who are to be born'. This contract formed the very stuff of civilization, and people were simply not at liberty to abrogate it.

Pointing to the need for institutional continuity to support unaided reason, Burke sought to discomfit radical arguments by stressing the inadequacy of individual reason and the dangers of rational argument dissociated from experience. He contrasted individual reason, especially uneducated, unsocialized reason, with both custom and institutions. He believed ordinary people—the 'swinish multitude'—were especially susceptible to innovation and speciously simple projects for social or political reform. Reason also undermined natural, especially familial, affection, which Burke sought to recruit for the conservative political cause. Individuals performed best within traditions of habit and custom, and through social institutions which provided them with ready and predictable responses to life's problems. Destabilized expectations left individuals uncertain, and liable to be duped by the unscrupulous.

Burke's thoroughgoing empiricism led him to deny the possibility of knowing the practical properties of abstract, rational arguments for reform. Only actual, experienced institutions could be properly judged; all reform therefore should be cautious and piecemeal. Like the common law tradition to which he also owed much, Burke saw custom and institutions embodying the historical experience of a society, although their value might not be apparent to individual reason [see *laws, 8]. Institutions, being in principle immortal, were vehicles of culture through time and were essential to political survival. Their preservation required engaging the affections of a newly-politicized public. Burke thus set an

60. James Barry, Portraits of Barry and Burke in the Characters of Ulysses and his Companions fleeing from the Cave of Polyphemus, c.1776. Barry included in this history painting the image of his sometime patron and fellow Irishman Edmund Burke.

agenda for the conservative idealization of the past so enthusiastically pursued by some first-generation Romantics.   IH-M

BURNETT, James, Lord Monboddo (1714–99), Scottish advocate, judge, and writer on *language [40], *evolution, and philosophy. Burnett was notorious for his view that orang-utans were part of the human species. This assertion, widely ridiculed by his contemporaries, together with other eccentricities, such as a refusal to ride in carriages on the grounds that they manifested modern effeminacy and idleness, have obscured the significance of his writings. He was associated with naturalists and scientists such as William Smellie (1740–95), and with other *Scottish Enlightenment figures including William *Robertson and Adam *Smith. Although he was a passionate advocate of the classics, and frequently disparaged modern thinking, the vocabulary and the concerns of his major writings are consistent with those of many contemporaries.

Burnett's most significant work was *Of the Origin and Progress of Language*, published in six volumes between 1773 and 1792. He argued that language was not natural to humanity, but rather an art that evolved with the progress of society. Like Lord Kames (1696–1782) and others, he illustrated remarks on men in the 'brutish state' or in 'early' societies both from classical sources and from *travel literature concerning Africa, the Americas, and the Pacific. And like Kames, especially, he understood progress to be dogged by cyclical tendencies and corruption, explaining why even seminal Roman literature had degenerated. While the book ranged over many particular topics, including grammar and the history of style and rhetoric, its unifying emphasis was upon the varying states of language through the history of human society. Though Burnett was concerned above all to vindicate the classical age, he did so in a peculiarly modern way.
                                                        NT

BURNEY, Charles (1727–1814), historian of *music [26]. The foremost music critic of this period, Burney was a man of the *Enlightenment [32] who travelled Europe, listening to music, talking to musicians, and gathering first-hand the books and scores out of which he compiled his groundbreaking work, the *General History of Music from the Earliest Ages to the Present Period* (1776–89).

He had no university education, but his charm and abilities earned him an apprenticeship with the composer Thomas Arne (1710–78) in 1744. Through Fulke Greville, who purchased his indentures from Arne, Burney became a companion of 'great folk'. As he wrote, 'Though only a musician, I was never sent to the second table.' He became organist at King's Lynn before settling in London as a fashionable music teacher, associated with the court, and, for a long period, with George III's passion for *Handel. By the time of the Handel Commemoration of 1784, however, Burney was exasperated with the narrowness of the King's taste. A member of the circle around Mrs Hester Thrale *Piozzi and Samuel

*Johnson, he was accepted as gentleman and man of letters despite his profession.

Burney began research for his project in the 1760s, and in 1770 travelled to France and Italy, and in 1772 to the Low Countries, Austria, and Germany. His *Tours* give a lively account of travelling as well as social conditions, and they convey a vivid impression of his energy and persistence in uncovering sources. Like Johnson's *Lives of the Poets*, the *History* regards its subject as reaching a peak of 'polish' in the present age. Burney too interweaves criticism with anecdote and personal reminiscence ('My father, who was nineteen years of age when Purcell died, remembered his person very well').

The book's longest chapter is on the 'Origins of the Italian opera in England, and its progress there during the present century', a year-by-year chronicle of performances and singers. Though a modernist in musical taste, Burney made several discoveries in the course of his research, and the *History* gives high praise to early composers including Josquin des Prés, Tallis, and Byrd. Responsive to new music, he was one of *Haydn's earliest champions: in 1770 he called the 14-year-old *Mozart 'the little great wonder', and by 1804 had linked Haydn, Mozart, and *Beethoven ('that gigantic youth') together.

Dutifully prefacing his *History* with a chapter on ancient music, Burney complains that his researches on this 'were sometimes so unsuccessful, that I seemed to resemble a wretch in the street, raking the kennels for a rusty nail'. He was intelligently interested in folk music, but, despite his plans, this was not included in the *History*. The commitment to first-hand materials, the frank expression of his personal taste, and the unaffected liveliness of his style accounts for Burney's European reputation, and make his letters and books eminently readable. His MS autobiography, including much material on Haydn, was censored by his daughter, Frances *Burney, who cared little for music and was ashamed of the family's humble origins.   JW

BURNEY, Frances, Madame d'Arblay (1752–1840), novelist and diarist, whose *Evelina* was one of the most influential novels of the late eighteenth century.

Frances ('Fanny') Burney's first novel, *Evelina* (1778), dedicated to her father, Charles *Burney, was published anonymously and by stealth. It initates the themes of modesty, secrecy, and decorum which prevail in all Burney's novels and *autobiographical writings. Subtitled 'The History of a Young Lady's Entrance into the World', *Evelina* is not autobiographical, although the freshness of the character has led many readers to assume, wrongly, that Burney was as artless as the heroine she depicts. The novel is partly a study in genteel manners, influenced by Samuel Richardson's *Sir Charles Grandison* (1754), punctuated by comic episodes of violence and horseplay, derived from Tobias Smollett.

The situation of the young woman whose naïvety offers a device for exposing the artificiality of manners in society, and who is continually embarrassed by the results of her own ignorance, provided a model for later novelists, notably Jane *Austen.

Following the financial and social success of *Evelina*, which saw her taken up by Mrs Hester Thrale *Piozzi and become a favourite of the *Johnson circle, Burney wrote three other novels, *Cecilia* (1782), *Camilla, or, a Picture of Youth* (1796), and *The Wanderer* (1814). All of these novels thematize social misunderstanding, embarrassment, and *sensibility [11].

Burney began keeping a journal at the age of 14. Her early letters and journals display her talent for dramatic representation and the lively reporting of dialogue. Throughout the rest of her life she continued to write autobiographically, sometimes in the form of long journal letters to members of her family. They record her experience of many historic events, such as the trial of Warren *Hastings, and are interestingly skewed by Burney's highly coloured and self-centred view of events around her.

In 1786 Burney was appointed Underdresser to Queen Charlotte at the court, a position secured for her by her father and other well-wishers, including Edmund *Burke, but which she took up reluctantly. The job proved to be a five-year ordeal, requiring her to spend many hours each day dressing, standing stock-still, being a surrogate friend to the Queen, and dealing with other members of the court. Nevertheless, through the long years of her time at court, she kept writing. Her letters describe the anguish of her personal situation, intrigues among the courtiers, and events in the royal family, including the scenes of George III's 'madness', to which she was an intimate witness.

Eventually Burney fell seriously ill with a psychosomatic condition that ultimately made it possible for her to extricate herself from the court. Soon afterwards she met the expatriate French aristocrat Alexandre d'Arblay, and the two (both aged 40) fell in love. Marriage to the penniless d'Arblay in 1793 was followed by the birth of a son, Alexander, in 1794, and the building of a house called 'Camilla Cottage' after the novel that Burney was writing to fund its construction and support the family.

During the Peace of *Amiens of the Napoleonic wars the d'Arblays travelled to France in an attempt to recover d'Arblay's property, but when hostilities resumed they were trapped. These experiences are reworked in *The Wanderer*, set in England during the *French Revolution, which Burney had begun writing in the late 1790s. Years living quietly in Paris followed. Though the d'Arblays were poor, Fanny's reputation as a novelist of sensibility secured them highly placed friends. This was to prove important when in 1810 she began to experience pains in her right breast, for in September 1811 she underwent a total mastectomy. The operation, with no sedative but a wine cordial, was performed by *Napoleon's surgeons Dubois and Dominique-Jean Larrey. Burney's account of this occasion is her most memorable piece of writing—an extraordinarily harrowing, detailed, and lucid document.

This was followed by a series of other journal letters dedicated to special occasions in her long life. Their moderate length and restricted focus enable Burney to control her material more effectively than in her later novels. In much of her writing, interminable complications, contrived misunderstandings, and a breathlessly intense style test the patience of readers, though Burney was willing to take her characters into regions—*madness, suicide, breakdown—not normally entered by a lady novelist.

In 1815 she found herself near *Waterloo, from where d'Arblay departed to hold the fort against Napoleon at Trèves. Fleeing ahead of the Napoleonic army, she gave a vivid account of the panic and trauma of the events in her 'Waterloo Journal'. After Napoleon's defeat, Burney more or less hitchhiked across France to find her husband, a journey whose adventures, again, she recorded graphically.

The d'Arblays retired to Bath, where the General's health soon began to decline. Devastated by his death in 1818, Burney composed a long journal account of his last months as a 'Narrative of the Last Illness and Death of General D'Arblay' (1820), in which she celebrates his nobility of character and once again deploys the themes of intense sensibility and romantic devotion that prevail in her earlier work.

Various other brief narratives followed in her widowhood, but her only publication was the edited *Memoirs* of her father (1832). Surrounded by thousands of letters and documents, Madame d'Arblay set herself to cut and paste them, preserving secrets, and hiding the family's humble origins. The reassemblage of the original letters has become a major work of modern scholarship, and the *Journals and Letters* will eventually fill some twenty-four volumes. They display an extraordinary mixture of obsessive gentility with exceptional courage, of intense snobbery with acute sensibility, of conventional ideology and a totally unconventional life.

JW

BURNS, Robert (1759–96), poet. If Thomas *Chatterton forged his texts, Burns's self-promoting 'Preface' to the 1786 Kilmarnock edition of his poems seized public attention with a similar fabrication. Its depiction of a ploughman poet absorbed in the poetical minutiae of a local, rural world was a nonsense. Ironically, the London-published *newspaper was often for Burns a primary poetic source. Central to his art was his power to make revealing and satirical connection between local and international worlds. From the outset Burns was formally, thematically, and intellectually a poet of the highest sophistication and historical awareness. He not only grasped the complex, mature possibilities of eighteenth-century Scottish vernacular poetry but also fused them with a wittily allusive knowledge of classic English *poetry [29] and of the poetic means and public concerns of his English contemporaries. While he spoke for the common people in increasingly radical ways, it was often in the voice of a high-art poetry.

This paradox quickly and inevitably eroded the initial patriotic enthusiasm of his sentimental middle-class audience which, even in the palmy early days, never quite managed to put its money where its mouth was. *Whiggish Edinburgh, deeply disturbed by the *American Revolution and horrified by the *French one, simply could not countenance a social inferior who declaimed a Scottish brand of Paineite politics in irony-laden tones. While personal foibles contributed to the relatively rapid downward spiral of his career as poet, the increasingly fraught politics of the late eighteenth century compounded his growing social marginalization and fiscal anxiety. Despite the extraordinary excitement generated by the 1786 *Poems, Chiefly in the Scottish Dialect*, he published only two other volumes of poetry, in 1787 and in 1793, from which the meretricious book trade was the primary gainer. Burns's early Ayrshire farming experience took place on under-resourced, over-rented land, replicated at Ellisland, Dumfriesshire, where he lived from 1791 until his death. His creative work there, mainly song-writing, was met largely with miscomprehension, and he gained little return from his two collaborators, James Johnson (d. 1811) and George *Thomson. To augment his income he became an efficient excise officer, enduring the shame of the radical masquerading in government uniform. Given the peremptory harshness of the Scottish courts towards alleged treason in the early 1790s, he could not expose his political beliefs. The subsequent brilliance of his poetical strategies and the ironic role-playing of his letters thus had much to do with self-preservation.

Burns was also sustained in part by a preceding vernacular poetry of subtle political dissent. His debt to Scottish eighteenth-century vernacular predecessors Allan Ramsay (1686–1758) and Robert Fergusson (1750–74) is still seriously underestimated. Burns himself constantly emphasized his admiration for Ramsay and his empathy for the 'bauld and slee' Fergusson. Sir Walter *Scott put this down to false modesty, for, unlike Burns, he had little sense of the abundant linguistic and formal riches present in Ramsay and Fergusson. Such blindness had its roots in politics. The eighteenth-century Scottish vernacular tradition not only was anti-Union but can also be seen as a mode of Romantic nationalism before the event. Burns was the grateful recipient of Ramsay's retrieval of vernacular language and forms, especially the Dissenting, anti-clerical, carnivalesque, medieval 'brawl' poetry and folk-song, that identifies the spirit of the nation with the vitality of the common people. To Ramsay's and Fergusson's foundation of an anti-Unionist political satire, where Jacobitism is fused with a democratic impulse, Burns brought other native elements, principally the resurrected cult of William Wallace, the early-fourteenth-century Scottish warrior-martyr of the anti-English independence wars. To this he added imported forms of English radical dissent located in enlightened *freemasonry, as well as in the writings of Richard *Price and Thomas *Paine. From such an Anglo-Scottish fusion came his democratic poetry celebrating both individual and nation.

Burns was also deeply influenced by a more catholic range of English poetry. Like Ramsay's, his anti-Unionism was never an obstacle to an enthusiastic grasp of English poetic creativity. Indeed, it is arguable that the vigour of eighteenth-century vernacular Scottish poetry stems from its emulative awareness of contemporaneous English achievements. The sombre, erotic Pope figures prominently in Burns's thoughts. With William *Cowper and Oliver Goldsmith (?1730–74) he shared common themes: aristocratic-provoked national decline, expressed in the dissolution of traditional *agrarian society; empathy extended to the creaturely world; the often-thwarted aspiration of the common man to appear on the stage of world history; and, not least, the displacement of the true poet in this disturbing, new, patron-bereft, market-driven world.

Indeed, Burns is not only profoundly symptomatic of the catastrophic lives led by so many poets in the late eighteenth century but also a remarkably self-aware commentator on the fate of the 'Rhyming tribe'. To the bad taste and poor returns of the new capitalism he could add his own particular pains. The trauma of his father's debt always haunted him and neurotically conditioned his behaviour. Typically, he combined this neurosis with reckless generosity. Life as marginal farmer, underpaid exciseman, and, latterly, unrewarded poet was never less than difficult. He identified deeply with *Johnson's *Lives*, which he defined as 'Martyrologies'. Yet Burns's own incisive, personally anguished account of poets and poetry remains underexplored by scholars of Romanticism. Partly owing to his initial strategies for self-advancement and his subsequent strategies for fiscal and political survival, the sheer power of his intelligence and the full range of his poetry has been obscured. AN

BURY, Lady Charlotte Susan Maria (1775–1861), author of seventeen *silver fork novels, Bury is best known for her *Diary Illustrative of the Times of George IV* (1838), an anonymously published and highly successful scandalous memoir of her years (1810–15) as lady-in-waiting to Caroline, Princess of Wales [see *Queen Caroline affair].

Bury was the younger daughter of John Campbell, fifth Duke of Argyll and Elizabeth Gunning, widow of James Hamilton, sixth Duke of Hamilton. Educated in part in France and Italy, she was presented at court in 1790, and became hostess to a Scottish literary circle which included Walter *Scott, Susan *Ferrier, and Matthew 'Monk' *Lewis. She published an anonymous volume of poems in 1797. Her marriage to an indigent cousin, Colonel Jack Campbell, produced nine children, and his death in 1809 left her in straitened circumstances.

She accepted a post with the Princess of Wales, and published the first of her *novels [31]. The majority of these, however, were written during her marriage (1818–32) to her son's tutor, the Revd Edward Bury. Charlotte's characters were largely drawn from the upper and middle classes, but her romantic narratives emphasize the universality of women's experiences and predicaments.

Having edited the memoirs of two of her social peers, Bury published her own memoirs, which provided an intimate view of life at Queen Caroline's court and of contemporary literary and political life. In addition, it included Bury's reflections on her own emotional and intellectual life. The *Diary Illustrative of the Times of George IV* was widely recognized as hers and provoked much criticism of her apparent breach of trust. However, its insider's view of the court and immediacy have resulted in its subsequent use by most historians of the period. Along with other scandalous memoirs, such as those of Lady Ann Hamilton and Joseph Nightingale, Bury's *Diary* did much to establish an enduring image of *Regency hedonism. RCA

BYRON, George Gordon, sixth Baron Byron (1788–1824), the most popular, famous, and influential of English poets during the Romantic period. His early commercial success created a style's in itself, Byronism, associated with brooding profundity and ennui-stricken superiority, widely copied by young men all over Britain and Europe. For all his aristocratic self-consciousness, he was a master of *satire and combined these skills with a biting critique of contemporary politics and society in his unfinished comic *epic *Don Juan*. Whereas his early success was largely confined to an élite market, *Don Juan*, in part through cheap pirated editions, gained for Byron a popular readership perhaps only exceeded in the period by Thomas *Paine.

Unexpectedly succeeding to his title in 1798, Byron was subsequently educated at Harrow and Cambridge. His first book of *poetry [29], *Fugitive*

Pieces (1806), was a privately printed collection of extremely self-conscious verse. The subsequently revised edition, *Hours of Idleness* (1807), while filling out the autobiographical nature of the poetry, was more ambitious of public celebrity. The result was a scathing attack in the *Edinburgh Review* (January 1808) by Henry *Brougham. Byron responded with *English Bards and Scotch Reviewers* (1809), in which he showed off his satirical skills in a wide-ranging critique of the state of British letters.

With the publication of his satire, Byron set off on the tour of Spain and Greece which provided the basis of the first two cantos of *Childe Harold's Pilgrimage*, the publication of which in 1812 made him famous and secured a very large readership among the most fashionable sections of the reading public. From 1812 to 1816, the so-called 'years of fame', when he left Britain permanently, Byron was at the centre of fashionable *Regency society. His literary reputation was sustained by the development of the Byronic hero in the *Tales* (1812–14) and *Manfred* (1816), a morally ambiguous melancholic whose appearance combined the author's own physiognomy with those of the heroes of popular *Gothic novels. Although the autobiographical origins of this gloomy figure may lie in his unease over the homosexual tastes that he maintained from his schooldays or guilt at the incestuous affair with his half-sister Augusta, the unprecedented integration of a

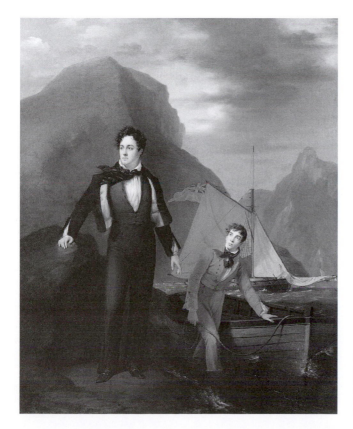

61. George Sander's posthumous portrait of *George Gordon, Sixth Lord Byron* (1788–1824), 1831, was one of many which evoked the poet as a figure of natural sublimity and manly action.

suspense-packed narrative, daring insights into the life of a member of England's noble élite, and unorthodox politics characterized by *ad hominem* attack generated sufficient praise and outrage in the reviews to continue his commercial successes.

It was the political element of the poetry that was responsible for Byron's widest impact in Europe. As a student member of the Cambridge University Whig Club, the young Byron had been as ambitious of political success as he had of poetic fame. Although the *Whig press initially responded angrily to the self-conscious aristocratism of his juvenilia, he became reconciled to *Holland House and consulted Lord *Holland before making his maiden speech in the House of Lords in February 1812. Yet even at this early stage his sympathy for the *Luddites was prophetic of a move towards more radical forms of opposition politics. Byron is frequently interpreted as retaining a life-long allegiance to aristocratic Whiggism, but it is unlikely that his short parliamentary career strayed much to the right of the left-wing 'Mountain' Whigs associated with Samuel Whitbread (1758–1815). The revolutionary narratives of the *Tales*, the explicitly political Italian dramas of 1821, and the politically motivated use in such later works as *Don Juan* and *Cain* of the anticlerical satire commonly associated with radicals such as William *Hone can be seen as milestones on a path towards the left wing of British politics.

This movement was accelerated by his exile from England, under a cloud of gossip and newspaper scandal, after the breakup of his marriage in 1816 (he had married Anne Isabelle Milbanke at the beginning of the previous year), which damaged his reputation as a poet of love and fidelity and inaugurated a significant decline in *copyright sales of his books. Byron's exile took him first to Switzerland, where he began his friendship with Percy *Shelley, and then on to Italy, where he lived for most of the rest of his life. By the early 1820s his work rivalled Shelley's in its attractions for radical pirate publishers back in England. *Don Juan*, begun in July 1818, with its sustained attack on the politicized morality of the *Tories and its combination of politics, blasphemy, and 'obscenity', has striking similarities with the popular radical literature of the time. The first two cantos were published to a storm of outrage in 1819, with Byron's publisher, John Murray (1778–1843),

who had been against the poem from the beginning, withholding both his own name and that of his author. Although in private he expressed disgust at the 'blackguard' radicals, Byron was impatient with Murray's unwillingness to publish in cheap enough editions to exploit the new market catered for by the pirates [see *publishing, 21]. Breaking with Murray at the end of 1822, Byron turned to the radical publisher John Hunt (1775–1848), who brought out subsequent cantos in cheaper editions, starting with Cantos VI–VIII in July 1823, including one of no fewer than 17,000 copies priced at a shilling. Even so, despite rapid sales, Hunt could not defend himself against the pirate editions, which remained immensely popular and easier to obtain when, in 1823, the court injunction was lifted and the copyright declared invalid on the grounds that the book was immoral.

During the controversy surrounding *Don Juan* Byron remained in Europe, disappointed by the public reception of his plays. In the middle of 1820 he became involved in the secret societies working for Italian freedom and 1821 began making plans with Shelley and Leigh *Hunt to contribute to literary and political affairs back in Britain through the pages of the *Liberal*. From the latter year he began discussing with his Italian friends the possibility of contributing to the struggle for Greek independence. He finally left for Greece in 1823. His death from fever in Missolonghi sealed his popular reputation as the poet laureate of liberty.

With few exceptions, Byron's posthumous influence was more strongly felt in continental Europe than in Britain, where for a variety of reasons writers like *Scott and *Hazlitt founded a tradition of regarding his social and political thought as superficial. This interpretation was to be reflected by a decline in posthumous sales of the poetry, as readers from the upper and middle classes shunned its disreputable morality and politics, and readers from the lower classes turned to Shelley for a more sympathetic statement of radical political objectives. Where his reputation was maintained, as in the case of Matthew Arnold (1822–88), he was valued above all as a poet of feeling and sentiment. It was a view whose consequences manifested themselves well into the twentieth century in a reluctance on the part of critics to accord to the later, more explicitly political poems and plays the attention the earlier works have claimed.　CWH

C

CAMPBELL, Thomas (1777–1844), Scottish poet and journalist. Capitalizing on the recognition gained for his early poem *The Pleasures of Hope* (1799), Campbell left Edinburgh for London in 1803 to become an exemplary 'man of letters' of the early nineteenth century.

An entry in Walter *Scott's journal for 1826 wonders why 'Tom Campbell, with so much real genius, has not maintained a greater figure in the public eye'. Campbell had never fulfilled the promise of *The Pleasures of Hope* (1799), his first publication and an accomplished if hardly audacious exercise in a then popular mode. The lengthy narratives *Gertrude of Wyoming* (1809) and *Theodoric* (1824) at best master rather than explore their pathos and conventions. His aspiration for the *New Monthly Magazine*, which he edited from 1821 to 1830—a 'calm spot in the world of periodical literature where all minds of common charity and candour may meet'—may solve Scott's puzzle.

Like Robert *Southey, Campbell's career testifies to the new respectability available to a writer who, without *patronage or private means, built a livelihood out of reputable literary activities: original *poetry [29]; contributions of 'learned' articles to *encyclopedias and *reviews; verse and criticism to magazines; the editorship (for a generous £500 per year); *lectures on poetry at the Surrey Institution in 1820; historical *Annals of Great Britain from George II to the Peace of Amiens* (1807); a biography of Sarah *Siddons (1834); and *Specimens of the British Poets* in seven volumes (1819). This last, a judiciously edited anthology justly successful in a crowded market, along with the instigation of the University of London in the 1820s, represents his most important cultural contribution.

Despite Scott's sense of anti-climax, Campbell's literary reputation secured him a burial in Westminster Abbey.

WC

CANNING, George (1770–1827), *satirist and statesman. A protégé of William *Pitt and a prominent satirist associated with the *Anti-Jacobin* in the 1790s, Canning gained a reputation as a *liberal Tory and held a number of ministerial positions from 1796, including Prime Minister for a few months before his death.

Originally associated with the *Whigs, Canning's gravitation towards the *Tories in the 1790s has been ascribed to opportunism, to an animus towards the exclusiveness of the great Whig families, and to a genuine sense of alarm at the impact of the *French Revolution on Britain. An internal critic of *Castlereagh's war policy during the Duke of *Portland's administration, Canning's involvement in plots against Castlereagh resulted in a notorious but not fatal duel between the two protagonists in 1809, following which Canning resigned from the foreign secretaryship. In the postwar period Canning's political and economic views aligned him with liberal Tory elements in his party.

An implacable opponent of *parliamentary reform, Canning was a firm but cautious supporter of *Catholic emancipation and of the *abolition of the slave trade. As Foreign Secretary from 1821 he supported the popular party in Portugal and recognized the independence of Spain's American possessions. These initiatives were related to Canning's interest in eradicating slavery but they also reflected his realism, his concern to offset the effect of France's occupation of Spain, and his wish to promote international trade and commerce.

Canning's obvious ambition, his political pragmatism, his oratorical skills, his tendency to rate his own abilities highly and to deprecate those of others, earned him the distrust of many of his ministerial colleagues. However, his support for Catholic emancipation won him favour 'out of doors'. His speeches and poetry (published in 1823) were accomplished and highly polished but were criticized by *Brougham, *Hazlitt, *Holland, and *Landor for being deficient in depth of feeling and understanding, though Hazlitt saw him as a key embodiment of the spirit of the age.

JMo

CARLETON, William (1794–1869), novelist. Though primarily a Victorian writer, Carleton produced several *novels [31] in our period which display an unparalleled personal knowledge of Catholic rural life and folk ways.

Carleton was born in County Tyrone, the youngest of fourteen children; his father was a small farmer fluent in Irish and English, with an abundant knowledge of folklore. After attending a hedge school (a small, rural, private school for Catholics specializing in the classics and Gaelic culture), William abandoned his early aspirations to join the church and worked as tutor in Louth and Dublin. In 1830 he published *Traits and Stories of the Irish Peasantry* which gave an intimate, unvarnished picture of the world of craftsmen, peasants, and small farmers at a time of mounting economic and political tension. The violence of agrarian outrage and the menace of secret societies gave Carleton's work a naturalistic bleakness which anticipates the work of Émile Zola in France. In 1834 he published further *Tales of Ireland*, and in 1839 a grim, emotive novel, *Fardorougha the Miser*. Carleton struggled to live on his proceeds as a writer and tutor, but was eventually assisted by a civil list pension obtained with the help of Maria *Edgeworth.

IMcC

CARLILE, Richard (1790–1843), popular radical journalist, publisher, and freethinker. Chiefly responsible for the early-nineteenth-century revival of Thomas *Paine's political and theological works, he became Britain's most notorious popular exponent of *republicanism, *Deism, feminism, and press freedom.

Of humble Devon origins, Carlile worked as a journeyman, tinmaker, and apothecary's assistant before moving to London to become a self-taught radical journalist and publisher in 1817. He was convicted in 1819 on multiple counts of blasphemous and seditious libel for republishing Paine's long-suppressed political and theological works, as well as those of other English, American, and French freethinkers. From Dorchester gaol Carlile mounted a six-year campaign for press freedom against both the *Tory government and *loyalist prosecuting societies. Using his periodical, the *Republican*, as an intellectual and organizational nucleus, he recruited volunteers—his wife, sister, and numerous artisan men and women from the provinces—to endure prison sentences for publishing and selling radical freethinking or 'infidel' works, including pirated editions of Percy *Shelley's *Queen Mab* and *Byron's *Cain*. By 1825 prosecutions ceased, marking a major victory for popular press freedom.

Carlile's followers also formed a nationwide 'Zetetic' or radical knowledge movement comprising autodidact reading and *debating circles. For a minority of men and women this included a commitment to materialist science, **women's [4] rights, and free love. In 1826 Carlile published *Everywoman's Book*, the first popular birth control pamphlet, which was attacked by both radicals and conservatives. Soon after, Carlile separated from his wife and children to form a free-love relationship, or 'new moral marriage', with a young middle-class follower, Eliza Sharples, who in 1830–1, while he was again imprisoned, preached political and theological feminism from the Blackfriars Rotunda. This theatre became a celebrated forum for radical freethought, sectarian Deism, *millenarianism, and reform politics, including the performances of Carlile's partner, Revd Robert Taylor (1784–1844), a flamboyant ex-clergyman doctor nicknamed 'the Devil's Chaplain', who preached a particularly successful blend of Deism based on astronomical myths, vitalist science, Romantic poetry, and theatrical burlesque. By the time of his death Carlile's obsessively individualistic, quarrelsome, and self-righteous personality had made him an isolated figure amongst the emergent *Chartist and *Owenite movements of the 1830s, but his former disciples became leaders of the Victorian republican and secularist movements.

IMcC

CARLYLE, Thomas (1795–1881), man of letters, often see as embodying the transition from Romantic to Victorian outlooks. Educated locally near his birthplace in Ecclefechan and at the University of Edinburgh, Carlyle's increasingly unorthodox religious views frustrated parental expectations that he would enter the Presbyterian ministry. After brief spells as a school master and private tutor, he embarked upon a literary career which raised him to the pinnacle of nineteenth-century letters.

From the late 1820s Carlyle enjoyed a rapidly expanding reputation as a thinker and writer of great force and originality. A correspondent of Goethe, he was an important early translator of his works and those of Musaeus, Richter, and Tieck. Carlyle hoped that German literature would furnish his British contemporaries with an understanding of the spiritual dimensions of human experience, a theme explored in his semi-autobiographical novel *Sartor Resartus* (1831), but prior to the appearance of this work Carlyle had already embarked on a trenchant critique of the modern mind. 'Signs of the Times' (1829) exposed the mechanical and dehumanizing tendencies of *utilitarianism; it developed a sharp contrast between the 'science of mechanics' and that of 'dynamics' which took account of the spiritual requirements of humanity as expressed in art, poetry, and religion. Subsequent writings, notably *Chartism* (1839), *Past and Present* (1843), and *Latter-Day Pamphlets* (1850), applied this conception in vivid and increasingly shrill criticisms of *political economy [33], *laissez-faire*, and conventional parliamentary government. Carlyle regarded these ideas and institutions as dangerous and inadequate substitutes for moribund tradition. In their place, he proposed an essentially authoritarian form of government which would address humanity's deep-seated need for integration in a new order embodying the infinite forces previously encompassed within the imagery and institutions of orthodox Christianity. From the 1830s he became increasingly concerned with the need for heroic leadership. In *On Heroes, Hero-Worship, and the Heroic in History* (1841), his views on leadership were developed into a comprehensive theory which embraced politics, religion, science, and literature.

Carlyle's involvement in the early 1830s with a group of 'mystico-radicals' which included the young John Stuart *Mill is indicative of the self-consciously progressive nature of his perspective, one that was reinforced by his major historical writings. The epic history *The French Revolution* (1837) portrayed this event as a historical necessity, and *Oliver Cromwell's Letters and Speeches* (1845) presented a similar view of the English Revolution. His reservations on the social and spiritual implications of industrialization, his images of violent revolutionary change, and his distinctive language were significant influences on the Victorian novel.

JMo

CAROLINE, Princess Amelia Elizabeth, see *Queen Caroline affair.

CARTER, Elizabeth (1717–1806), scholar, linguist, poet, and the most learned of the circle known as the *bluestockings. Taught at home in Kent by her father, a clergyman, she became proficient in both classical and modern European languages: Latin, Greek, Hebrew, French, Italian, German, Portuguese, and Arabic. As a young woman she contributed verses to the *Gentleman's Magazine*, whose editor, Edmund Cave, published her *Poems* in 1739. Her most famous poem, the 'Ode to Wisdom' (1737) was used, without her permission, in Richardson's *Clarissa*.

In 1739 Carter published translations from French and of Algarotti's Italian version of *Newton's *Optics* for a female readership. She contributed to Johnson's *Rambler* in 1750–1, and issued by subscription her most important work, a translation from the classical Greek of *All the Works of Epictetus*, in 1758. There were 894 subscribers to this translation, a third of them women, which remained in print for over 200 years. It includes a critical introduction comparing Stoic philosophy with Christianity, and displays a lucid, sceptical, balanced quality of mind.

The success of the *Epictetus* helped her to purchase her own home in Deal, but she spent several months in London each year, frequenting the circles of Elizabeth Montagu (1720–1800) and Elizabeth Vesey (*c*.1715–91) until their dissolution in the 1790s. She took a prominent role in an informal Anglican organization, the Ladies' Charitable Society. Her correspondence with another 'learned lady', Catherine Talbot (1721–70), published posthumously, and later with Lady Spenser, demonstrates her strong but temperate and always cogent interpretations of Christian doctrine and belief.   JW

CARTER, John (1748–1817), artist and architect. A skilled topographical artist and pioneer preservationist, Carter is credited, together with John *Britton and A. C. *Pugin, with setting the *Gothic revival on a solid archaeological footing. Son of a mason, Carter developed his draughting skills in the offices of Henry *Holland and James *Wyatt. He published his own designs in *Builder's Magazine* from 1774 to 1786.

Carter's greatest contribution to British *architecture [28], however, was his precise drawings of medieval antiquities. In 1795, he was named Fellow of the Society of Antiquaries and commenced *Ancient Architecture of England* (1796–1814). In his writings he sought to fix an English origin for Gothic architecture, and criticized the destruction and careless restoration of medieval antiquities by modern architects such as Wyatt.   SS

CARTWRIGHT, John (1740–1824), gentleman reformer. Towards the end of his long political career Cartwright began to be called 'father of reform', a title that well sums up his contribution to popular radicalism in this period.

Born into a small gentry family, Cartwright served in the *navy and then became a major in the Nottingham militia. A narrow but intense student of politics, Cartwright was influenced by the contemporary Saxon *constitutionalism of writers such as James Burgh (1714–75), and his best-known publication, *Take Your Choice* (1776), was written as a defence of the *American Revolution. Essentially Cartwright made a strong but rather formulaic appeal to the ancient democratic constitution of the Saxon King Alfred, an idea fashioned by seventeenth-century critics of monarchical tyranny. However, his enduring source of fame derived from an associated six-point reform programme—annual parliaments, equal-sized constituencies, payment of members, abolition of property qualifications for parliament, and, most daringly, universal male suffrage.

This was to become the platform of *Chartism, though it is doubtful whether the patrician Cartwright fully realized its democratic implications. For the remainder of his life he pursued this programme unceasingly; in a variety of prolix political pamphlets, as a member of the *Society for Constitutional Information during the 1780s, as a founder of the influential Hampden Club reform movement advanced through lecture tours of the provinces in 1812–16, and, finally, through the pages of T. J. *Wooler's influential postwar popular radical periodical, *Black Dwarf*.   IMcC

CASTLEREAGH, Viscount (Robert Stewart) (1739–1822). From the mid-1790s to his suicide in 1822, Castlereagh was a leading figure both in generating the resolve to fight on against Napoleonic France in the face of mounting opposition in Britain and in contributing to the European peace accord which followed the allied victory.

In 1789 Castlereagh was in Paris at the onset of the *French Revolution. This was profoundly to affect his later political dispositions. He learnt his public administration in Ireland as Chief Secretary during the Irish *Rebellion of 1798. Being part of the County Down establishment, Castlereagh was blamed by patriots for excesses committed by the Irish militia in the suppression of the rebels. His relative leniency with the captured rebels is remembered by Irish patriots less than his 'efficient' response to the revolutionary threat, a response echoed in his enduring nickname deriving from this period—'Derry Down Triangle', referring to the *flogging triangle used against Irish rebels after 1798. The Union of Great Britain and Ireland was part of this response, because the French threatened in 1798 to exploit Irish unrest by landing in Ireland [see *insurrections].

As Secretary at War, first in *Pitt's last administration (1805–6) and then in the Duke of *Portland's ministry (1807–9), Castlereagh presided over an army reorganization crucial to the country's ability to defeat the French. However, his attempts at strategy against *Napoleon brought his temporary downfall. He approved the unpopular Convention of Cintra and was closely associated with the disaster of the Walcheren expedition, in which a large British force failed to take Napoleon's massive naval establishment on the island of Walcheren in the Low Countries. The resulting fallout included his resignation, and a futile duel with George *Canning, then the Foreign Secretary.

In 1812 Castlereagh returned to the Government as Foreign Secretary in Lord *Liverpool's government, and remained so until his death in 1822. He was also Leader of the House of Commons and was consequently associated with many of the Liverpool ministry's unpopular measures. His occasional bluntness—he spoke of 'an ignorant impatience of

Taxation' in 1816—in speeches did not help his personal popularity.

As one of the architects of the Versailles peace settlement in 1815, Castlereagh sought to re-establish the balance of power in Europe through a policy of disinterestedness on the part of the United Kingdom. He was instrumental in including the French in this international diplomacy, having resisted the temptation to subject France to an abject settlement. He also manœuvred to check the growing power of Russia. After the initial settlement, he steered British foreign policy away from intervention in the internal affairs of other countries, and attempted to play a mediating role amongst the major powers. The Congress system gradually collapsed as Russia and Austria in particular sought to put down any revolutionary spirit which might show itself in Piedmont, Spain, or elsewhere.

Canning developed what Castlereagh started, and became popular in Britain as a result; Castlereagh was doomed to unpopularity through his association with Irish repression and the old order. He committed suicide by cutting his throat in 1822, his mental derangement possibly exacerbated by the activities of a group of criminals who were blackmailing him on the grounds of his alleged *homosexuality.   JF

CATALANI, Angelica (1780–1849), Italian bravura soprano and impresario. Catalani came to London from Lisbon in December 1806 to sing at the King's Theatre, which she subsequently dominated. Beautiful and charismatic, she displayed remarkable vocal power and agility, ornamenting melodies to a degree which thrilled some but offended others [see *singing]. Composers such as Pucitta and Portogallo wrote showpiece arias especially for her, which became favourite items at London *concerts, her own subscription series (Hanover Square, 1809), and her engagements throughout Britain.

Admired and romanticized particularly amongst the *bon ton*, Catalani, and her husband/manager, Paul Valabregue, commanded extravagant fees, provoking xenophobic hostility from some quarters. Her engagement at Covent Garden *theatre [24] in 1809 for £75 a night was one of the catalysts for the Old Price riots. She left England in 1814 to direct the Théâtre Italien, Paris, returning briefly in 1824.   RC

Catholic emancipation. The Test and Corporation Acts required government officers to take the sacrament in the Church of England. Catholics were specifically prevented from entering parliament, voting, or serving in the armed forces. From the late eighteenth century, recognition of Catholic rights and privileges was of major symbolic importance to the development of nationhood in Britain, and was arguably the political catalyst for the Great *Reform Act of 1832 and the destruction of the *Anglican confessional state.

The first major reform was the 1778 Catholic Relief Act, which removed serious restrictions on Catholic worship, including that which prevented Catholics from acquiring new property and which made their priests technically guilty of felony. Partially motivated by the desire also to increase the size of the armies in America, it removed the prohibitive oaths which prevented Catholics from serving in the armed forces, by requiring that recruits simply take an oath of fidelity to the Crown. The 1791 Relief Act replaced the oaths of supremacy and declaration against transubstantiation with an oath by which Catholics declared their secular allegiance to the Hanoverian dynasty.

The movement for Catholic emancipation developed against the troubled background of Ireland. Seeking a united Ireland and England to respond to the threat of revolutionary France, *Pitt's government steered the Irish Catholic Relief Act of 1793, which allowed Irish Catholics to vote and to hold minor civil posts, and enfranchised the Irish Catholic 40s. freeholders. Pitt regarded emancipation as the necessary consequence of the *Act of Union. When George III resisted, Pitt resigned in 1801. The monarchy continued to resist measures for Catholic emancipation, forcing *Grenville's resignation over the issue in 1807.

During George IV's reign, despite the continuing personal hostility of the monarch, opinion among the *Tories began to move in favour of concession, which resulted in the passage of four relief motions in the Commons between 1821 and 1828. Between 1823 and 1826, Daniel *O'Connell developed the Catholic Association, the first mass democratic movement, using the Catholic clergy as electoral organizers and the votes of 40s. freeholders to break the back of Protestant landlord power. In 1828, he was elected to the House of Commons for County Clare, despite being technically disqualified. The prospect of other Catholics being elected, backed by popular agitation and the threat of civil war in Ireland forced the Tory administration to pass the Roman Catholic Relief Act of 1829, which allowed Catholics to sit in both houses of parliament.   JF

CAVENDISH, Georgiana (1757–1806), see Duchess of *Devonshire.

caves were a conspicuous part of the British intellectual and geographical landscape during the Romantic period. From 1776, when Joseph *Banks produced his widely circulated account of Fingal's Cave on the Scottish island of Staffa, dozens of travellers made their way across choppy seas to experience what was proclaimed as one of nature's wonders [see domestic *tourism]. Fingal's Cave was, and remains, spectacular: a vault some 70 ft high, 40 ft wide, and 200 ft long, composed almost entirely of brown basalt columns standing on a base of solid, unformed rock.

Banks, a veteran traveller, spent twelve hours in and around the Cave and was overawed. So, too, were Dr *Johnson, on his tour through Scotland with *Boswell, and the poets Thomas Campbell (1800–48), James *Hogg, and Walter *Scott. Their accounts helped to popularize caves, and before long a stream of famous figures visited the island, amongst them Humphry *Davy, John *Keats, and William

*Wordsworth. The painter J. M. W. *Turner arrived at Fingal's Cave with his sketchbook, while Felix *Mendelssohn, on a tour from Germany, was sufficiently inspired by the scene to compose there the opening theme of his 'Hebrides Overture', one of the landmarks of Romantic music.

Other, more accessible, areas of Britain were a magnet to cave hunters, many of whom came primed with travel guides, books of cave verse, and geological hammers. The Peak District was rich in caves, amongst them St Anne's Well, Poole's Hole, and Peak Cavern. In London caves appeared, improbably, in a massive *panorama established in Leicester Square, as well as in theatrical *melodrama. Scientists, meanwhile, explored caves for fossil remains and in the hope that their preserved records would throw light on such perplexities as the age of the earth, human ancestry, and the origins of life. One of the most important geological treatises of the period was William Buckland's (1784–1856) *Reliquiae diluvianae* (1823), an enthusiastic account of the author's discovery of the bone caves at Kirkdale in Yorkshire and his subsequent efforts to account for these in terms of the Noachian Flood.　　　　MSH

CHADWICK, Sir Edwin (1800–90), Benthamite reformer and administrator, with a major influence on the expansion of central government into issues of social welfare and social control. Chadwick qualified as a barrister in London, but never practised. His formative influence was as Jeremy *Bentham's secretary for the last two years of Bentham's life. To his acceptance of *political economy [33], Chadwick added a *utilitarian belief in the virtues of the tutelary state and the preventive principle. His forte was manipulating royal commissions, with 'scientific' questionnaires and *statistics, to gain his ends. As Commissioner on the investigation into child labour in *factories, he helped to produce a Factory Act (1833) which avoided the radical ten-hour day, while enacting some controls on children's hours and conditions, and creating factory inspectors.

Chadwick was the major influence on the New *Poor Law. He wrote most of the *Poor Law Report* (1834), and introduced the principles of 'less eligibility' and the workhouse test, to deter people from applying for relief. The Act set up a national Poor Law Commission; he hoped for a Comissionership, but had to settle for being Secretary [see *poverty, 12].

His *Constabulary Commission Report* (1839) applied principles first set out in his article 'Preventive Police' (1829) to recommend a national professional *police force for the counties outside London [see *policing, 7]. He claimed that this was needed to deter crime—caused not by poverty but by the temptations of an easy life—and to crush *trade unions and strikes. To his annoyance, the resultant legislation of 1839 was merely permissive—allowing, but not compelling, the establishment of separate county forces.

His masterpiece was the *Sanitary Report* (1842), offering detailed, disgusting, and fascinating evidence of the appalling and dangerous sanitary conditions in the rapidly growing towns and cities. He advocated state-run systems to supply running water and sewerage to all houses, especially in working-class districts. Though the eventual Public Health Act (1848) fell short of Chadwick's hopes, it was an important step in eventual central government responsibility in this area. Chadwick was a dynamic, dogmatic, obsessive, and difficult man, who alienated as many people as he impressed. He never received the power or recognition he thought he deserved; he tried, but failed, to get into parliament—even his knighthood came only a year before his death. His career illustrated the tension inherent in Benthamite ideas between freedom and authority, between state action and *laissez-faire*. He is seen at his most authoritarian on the issues of poor law and police, and at his most sympathetic on public health, though even here his dominant concern was to curb the waste of human and economic resources caused by insanitary conditions. This archetypal Benthamite can also be viewed as a 'moral entrepreneur'—one who made his career from arousing public alarm on issues, advocating reforms to deal with them, and offering himself as the person to implement them.　　　　DP

CHAMBERS, Sir William (1723–96), architect. Surveyor-General and Comptroller of the King's Works, first Treasurer of the *Royal Academy, and author of the principal British treatise on the classical Orders, Chambers shaped public *architecture [28] in Britain from the 1760s into the 1790s. As the foremost authority on *oriental design, he also played a significant role in the development of British *landscape gardening.

Son of a Scottish merchant attached to the Swedish East India Company, Chambers travelled to the Far East three times during the 1740s. This experience paid for his subsequent architectural studies at Jacques-François Blondel's École des Arts in Paris. Within two years of settling in London in 1755 Chambers was named architect to Augusta, Dowager Princess of Wales, and architectural tutor to the future George III. He capitalized upon his Asian travels by designing numerous oriental structures at Kew Gardens (1757–62) and publishing *Designs of Chinese Buildings, Furniture, Dresses, Machines, and Utensils* (1757). He demonstrated his classical training and validated his professional standing by publishing his *Treatise on Civil Architecture* (1759), long regarded as the authorative work on classical *design [25] and ornamentation.

As one of the pre-eminent neoclassical architects in Britain, Chambers was often in direct competition with his fellow Scotsman, Robert *Adam. In 1761 they were both appointed as the Attached Architects to the Office of Works. However, Chambers remained the dominant force in royal and public architecture, becoming Surveyor-General as well as Comptroller during Edmund *Burke's administrative reorganization in 1782. One result was his most important architectural work, Somerset House, London (1776–96).

Chambers displayed great originality, particularly in the planning of houses such as Roehampton, Surrey (1760–8), Duddington House, Midlothian (1763–8), and Melbourne House, Piccadilly (1771–4). The purest expression of his tastes was in the casino for Lord Charlemont at Marino House, Dublin (1758–76).

A partisan of Roman taste, Chambers had no affinity for either the Greek or *Gothic revivals and was similarly conservative in his approach to landscape design. His *Dissertation on Oriental Gardening* (1772) argued for imaginative artifice in garden design against Lancelot 'Capability' *Brown's ascetic naturalism, but was literally interpreted as advocating Chinese gardening [see *chinoiserie].

ss

Chartism, the culmination of some eighty years of radical activism, generated the largest political movement of the working class in modern British history, and a remarkably rich and tenacious *class [15] culture.

Technically Chartism originated in June 1837, when a joint committee of six parliamentary radicals (including Daniel *O'Connell) and six working men (prominent figures in the London Working Men's Association) met to draft a text of the Charter. Its six major planks, originally formulated in the 1780s by Major John *Cartwright, were: universal suffrage for males over 21, secret ballot, annual elections, payment of parliamentary members, equalization of electoral districts, and abolition of property qualifications for MPs. The document underwent further drafting at the hands of William Lovett (1800–77), with advice from Francis *Place. It was published in May 1838 and endorsed by mass meetings at Glasgow in May and Birmingham in August. Other key impulses included the foundation of what was to become Chartism's mass organ, the *Northern Star*, in November 1837; the anti-poor law lecturing tours in 1835–6 of Chartism's future leader, Feargus O'Connor (1794–1855); and the activities of the popular political unions and the *unstamped press in the 1830s. Chartism undoubtedly also embodied a deep-seated popular disillusionment both with the *Reform Act of 1832, which had excluded all waged labourers, and with the interventionist 'reform' programme of the *Whig government between 1832 and 1837. The chief Chartist tactic between 1837 and 1842 consisted of the *constitutional, but intimidatory, process of gathering a mass *petition, supported by a National Convention, to present to parliament. A series of 'ulterior' measures, including a general strike and armed *insurrections, were also attempted at various times up until 1848.

Historians have generally attributed the ultimate failure of the Chartist movement to poor leadership, as well as to divisions between exponents of moral and physical force, or between metropolitan and provincial supporters. Above all, the movement's diversity of goals has been seen as a major weakness. Chartist newspapers reveal a broad participatory culture that encompassed schools, nurseries, tea parties, dances, trade societies, and women's groups.

Chartists also campaigned against flogging, long factory hours, capital punishment, and workhouse abuses. However, asking why Chartism failed is not necessarily the most apt question. It may be more pertinent to investigate the movement's extraordinary success in encompassing the diverse cultural aspirations of the bulk of the British working people for more than a decade.

IMcC

CHATTERTON, Thomas (1752–70), poet. Chatterton's Rowley poems were, with the *Ossian poems, the most important literary forgeries of the age. They answered a taste that celebrated a provincial English tradition against courtly classicism. Chatterton's early death provided an important model of the Romantic cult of *genius.

Born in Bristol, Chatterton began to write *poetry [29] at a very early age. In 1768 a local journal published a fragment of prose from a medieval manuscript that Chatterton claimed to have discovered in a church. Interested local antiquarians, by whose researches Chatterton had been inspired in the first place, were soon supplied with other fake medieval documents supposedly from the same source [see *antiquarianism, 35].

By this time he had already written some of the poems which he claimed had been authored by the medieval monk Thomas Rowley. At the end of 1768 he unsuccessfully offered some of these poems to Dodsley, the publisher of Thomas *Percy's *Reliques*. The following year he sent an essay on painting, purporting to be by Rowley, to Horace *Walpole, whose initial interest soon turned to suspicion. Several prose pieces in the style of Ossian and the only Rowley poem published during Chatterton's lifetime, 'Elinoure and Juga', were published in the *Town and Country Magazine* in 1769. Encouraged by this success he left for London, but within four months he was dead of an arsenic overdose. Literary legend regards his death as suicide in the face of poverty and despair, but he seems to have been quite successful in London, publishing several anti-ministerial *satires as well as antiquarian pieces in the capital's journals. Whatever the reasons behind his death, the garret where he died soon became a literary tourist attraction.

The collected Rowley poems were published in 1777, provoking a controversy which lasted into the 1780s and beyond. Chatterton's poems met the developing taste for the antique in poetry, and many of those who recognized that they were forgeries still admired his achievement. His death also provided an important model of vulnerable genius much celebrated by later poets: *Wordsworth called him 'the marvellous Boy' and *Keats dedicated his poem *Endymion* to him. However, this Romantic version of his importance has to be weighed against his role in extending contemporary interest in medieval and Elizabethan verse forms, including the *ballad and *Spenserianism, and in advancing the notion of a robust, local English cultural heritage against courtly and classical traditions.

JM

Cheap Repository Tracts, a series of popular *ballads and tales designed to improve the working

62. John Flaxman's *Thomas Chatterton taking the Bowl of Poison from the Spirit of Despair, c.*1780. Chatterton's notorious suicide at 18, together with his posthumous role as a subject of antiquarian controversy, stamped his reputation as a tragic Romantic genius.

classes, in circulation from March 1795 until 1798. Initiated by the *Evangelical writer Hannah *More, who wrote approximately 50 of the total 115 tracts produced, the tracts were designed to counter the radical and popular forms of literature which had become widely available in the 1790s, such as the writings of Thomas *Paine, and *street literature genres including *romances, *prophecies, *fairy tales, bawdy jokes, anticlerical humorous tales, and accounts of criminal trials. Prominent Evangelicals distributed the tracts to the rural poor, booksellers and hawkers, charity children, and *Sunday schools. Modelled on the popular genres of the *ballad, fable, and tale, the tracts emphasized *patriotism, *domesticity [13], and the *Anglican virtues of industry, honesty, and self-reliance. Whilst the tracts censured aspects of community life and *popular culture [23], such as *fortune-telling, and whilst some tracts, such as the ballads 'The Riot' and 'The Loyal Sailor; Or, No Mutineering', forbade crowd action and political revolt, most were not explicitly didactic. Within a year, the sales in England alone reached well over two million.   CT

chemistry at the turn of the eighteenth century investigated the changes in the fundamental states of bodies: fluid, solid, and gaseous. In the early eighteenth century, Georg Stahl (1660–1734) proposed that when a substance burned, a certain amount of phlogiston was released which determined the degree of combustion and the weight of the final element. Between the 1770s and 1790s, investigations employing new instruments such as the 'pneumatic trough' and the 'eudiometer', which isolated 'airs', led to the identification of different varieties of airs which had unique experimental effects when mixed with liquids. Pursuing this line of inquiry, the British chemists Joseph Black (1728–99) and Joseph *Priestley attributed different chemical properties to these airs. The French chemist Antoine Lavoisier (1743–94) contributed to these theoretical and instrumental developments and proposed a new theory of combustion, suggesting that burning substances absorbed an atmospheric gas which he termed 'oxygen'. Accompanying his new theory, Lavoisier and his colleagues developed a new descriptive nomenclature, an ambitious programme which historians have referred to as the 'chemical revolution'.

The properties of these newly identified gases were further elaborated in the 1790s by the British meteorologist and chemist John *Dalton, who proposed that the proportions of gases mixed in the atmosphere were determined by their ultimate 'atomic weights', which likewise formed the constitution of all elements. The importance placed on instrumentation, calculation, and precision measurement in chemical reactions soon extended to the analysis of the forces holding chemical compounds together, redefining the traditional notions of 'sympathy' and 'antipathy', or of 'chemical affinity'.

This analysis was expounded by the Italian physicist Alessandro Volta, in an 1800 description of the 'voltaic pile', or battery, published by the Royal Society. Chemists thus had an apparatus deploying electric current for the process of separating matter into its chemical constituents. The chief pioneers of this form of analysis in the early nineteenth century were Humphry *Davy in England and Jons Jacob Berzelius in Sweden.

Throughout our period, chemical theory underwent radical changes as the authority of analytical procedures attained social acceptance, largely as a result of new developments in instrumentation. While chemistry was widely supported for its *utilitarian applications to the arts and manufactures of an industrializing Continent, its metaphysical undercurrents allowed for radical interpretations of chemical knowledge, potentially productive of religious and political criticism. In a period of political and social instability in the aftermath of the *French Revolution, demonstrations of popular science *lecturers furnished radicals like Richard *Carlile with ammunition to expose and denounce kingcraft and priestcraft [see *natural philosophy, 34].   BPD

childhood. A long-dominant modern historiographical view that childhood did not exist as a concept before the seventeenth century, and that children during our period were merely small adults, has undergone major recent revision. Where once parents were alleged to have been indifferent or harsh to their children, many historians now believe that parental love and caring was little different from that in the western world today.

Childhood mortality was once thought to have been so high that parents insulated themselves emotionally against the death of their offspring. Infant mortality did rise in the Romantic age, and approximately one child in four died before the age of 9. Nevertheless, three children survived, and there is increasing evidence to suggest that parents concentrated not on the dead, but on the living children. The levels of mortality cannot, therefore, be used to explain the nature and pattern of parental affection and child-rearing.

Ever more evidence suggests that parents in the eighteenth and nineteenth centuries were alert to the needs and well-being of their offspring, caring for them throughout childhood's crises, mourning for them in death, worrying about how to discipline and train them, and anxious to educate or rear them in the most appropriate way for their sex and social rank. Family structure was one explanation for this. An old assumption about the prevalence of the extended family no longer holds. Instead, we know that, despite some variations according to class and geography, children typically grew up in homes with their parents, siblings (and sometimes servants)—and in smaller families than was previously claimed—4.57 being the average in the eighteenth century.

Childhood and child rearing were also influenced positively by the ideas of John *Locke and Jean Jacques *Rousseau, each of which helped in different ways to erode earlier medieval concepts of the child as an imp mired in original sin. Locke had emphasized the importance of the parental environment and *education [17] in moulding the blank sheet of the child's mind at birth, while Rousseau had stressed that children's natural innocence and purity needed to be protected from the corruptions of decadent adult civilization. Such ideas were widely disseminated through novels and writings of *sensibility [11], particularly the popular works of Thomas *Day and Maria *Edgeworth. They contributed to the growing idealization of childhood evident in the *poetry [29] of William *Blake and William *Wordsworth, and to an increasing emphasis on the importance of maternity and *domesticity [13]. From the rather different direction of *Evangelicalism, Hannah *More's equally influential publications stressed the need to protect the children of the poor from grinding labour, and from exposure to vice or violence. The burgeoning *Sunday school movement, as well as the myriad channels of *popular education and *self-improvement in the early nineteenth century, suggest that the poor and labouring classes were not exempt from this increasing concern with the well-being of children.

Literary and biographical evidence suggests that parents in our period experienced the whole gamut of reactions towards their children, from intense affection to weary exasperation. But they taught them, by example and precept, the risks and dangers of the world at large. Whether via illness or accident, the agony of parental bereavement was acute, and provides no evidence of parental coolness to the death of a child. The pleasures of childhood were provided both by the imagination of children themselves—absorbing then bequeathing the games, stories, rhymes, riddles, and inventions of traditional culture—and by products of commercial interests. There was a vast—and increasing—range of commercial toys available for both sexes; of hand-me-downs for poorer children; or home-made versions for the very poor. It was a world of childhood which is instantly recognizable because so familiar today—and from one society to another. The extraordinary growth in volume, range, and imaginativeness of *children's literature also testified to the interest in and preoccupation with the nurturing of children's minds and morals.

Of course we should not exaggerate the modernity of Romantic age responses to, or experiences of, childhood. Boys and girls were nearly always raised differently, and that difference seems to have become more stark in the course of the nineteenth century. Though fathers played their part in child-rearing and were not always aloof, distant figures, they nevertheless tended to concentrate more heavily on the eldest son, leaving daughters to be guided by the mother. Mothers were regarded as crucial in inculcating the habits and values of a lifetime. Corporal punishment was common, accepted, and generally unquestioned (within limits), yet it did not mean indifference. Punishments and reprimands were doled out, rarely from cruelty, but from a wish to inculcate responsibility and discipline. It is, today, too easy to misinterpret this aspect of childcare and rearing. Schooling in the early nineteenth century, however, did ascribe excessive importance to corporal punishment. More commonplace were the homilies—generally religious—designed to encourage obedience and morality. This was thought to be critical for the development of a good character. Internal discipline was widely seen as more important than the obvious lessons of physical punishments, and both boys and girls of all classes were frequently instructed in biblical tales and examples.

Pregnancy and conception were not fully understood (medically) until the late eighteenth century. As a result childbirth was often a fearful experience—dreaded in prospect—by most women. Until the mid-nineteenth century there was no available pain relief, and few ways of predicting or preventing many of childbirth's dangerous consequences. Childbirth remained a leading cause of death among women of childbearing years. Until 1800, it was also almost always a uniquely all-women affair; with a midwife, women friends, and neighbours—men absent from the room except, in a difficult birth, when a doctor was called in. But by the end of our period pregnancy and childbirth were being treated less like an illness. The first Caesarian operation was performed in 1793 in England, but it was not really a safe procedure until the 1830s. With the rise of formal and technical *medicine [18] in the early nineteenth century, men became more commonplace at deliveries.

Literary and biographical evidence also suggests that the arrival of a baby was, contrary to older arguments, greeted with pleasure—and relief—by men and women alike. Boys were, it is true, generally more welcomed than girls, especially among the propertied orders—with all the consequent pressures on the mother to produce a boy. Many parents did not want large families—if only to avoid the agonies of childbirth—and there were various efforts at primitive birth control, reaching from the aristocracy into the middling classes. Feeding of infants was also notoriously difficult, but the use of wet nurses was very restricted and has been far too glibly criticized. Then, as now, the weaning of children proved troublesome (by depriving them of their mothers' immunities). Babies had long been swaddled, but changes in styles of clothing of children, accentuated by the late eighteenth century, saw marked differences emerging between boys and girls, both eventually wearing clothing similar to adults. There is nothing to suggest, however, that this trend was interpreted as signifying the end of childhood.   JWA

children's literature. During the eighteenth century, factors such as the primary schooling of children, the spread of literacy in standard English, cheap paper, and the growth of London, Edinburgh, and Dublin *publishing companies expanded the market for books written for young people. At the start of the century, Christian devotional works and clerical authors were prominent in *publishing [21] and sales figures: by mid-century *novels [31] and *travel literature were overtaking them. The reading of fiction was comprehensively endorsed as a necessary prelude to adult cultural competence. Critics

and educators perceived a new constituency among child readers, and hurried to promulgate official prescriptions for segmenting it [see *education, 17].

The upsurge in books authored by women and the growth of a female readership served by *circulating libraries were complemented by an increase in books aimed at the juvenile market. In 1744 the publisher John Newbery (1713–67) started to specialize in children's literature, such as the perennial favourite *The History of Little Goody Two Shoes* (c.1765). The bookseller John Marshall listed no fewer than seventy books for children between 1780 and 1790. In the 1780s Maria *Edgeworth read Stéphanie de Genlis and other French pioneers of children's domestic instruction through storytelling, and translated Madame de Genlis's *Adèle et Théodore; ou, lettres sur l'éducation* (1782).

In 1808, during his mid-life career as an author and publisher of children's books, William *Godwin wrote, 'It is children who read children's books . . . but it is parents that choose them.' To succeed with the adult buyers of books for children, writers and booksellers had to avoid controversy or challenges to church, state, and paternal authority. 'The age we live in discovers a laudable anxiety for the improvement of the rising generation,' wrote one reviewer of *A Mirror for the Female Sex: designed principally for the Use of Ladies' Schools* (1798). The sententious rhetoric of improvement fitted with the aim of middle-class parents to see sons financially established and daughters advantageously married within their own lifetime. The *Encyclopaedia Britannica*, launched in the 1770s, became a staple of home and school curricula, combining the museum repository of general knowledge with the didactic unfolding of expert opinion [see *encyclopedias]. Natural and physical sciences were scooped up for the juvenile bookshelf, and history and ethnography merged with sentimental biography of Great Men to yield narratives of British progress, imperialist civilizing mission, and entrepreneurial verve. World geography with colourful maps demonstrating the global spread of English place-names was the lucrative speciality of the publisher Richard Phillips (1767–1840). Ethnographic *orientalism in the work of Edward Tyson (1650–1708) and others generated the graphic image of the Borneo orang-utan (ape-man) as an object of child-dread and child-solicitude, and forced new questions about human diversity even before the dissemination of Charles Darwin's *evolutionary theory. The child reader became a particular target as nineteenth-century Britain extended the imperialist project. Physiology and anatomy, especially genital and reproductive anatomy, were banned, and whereas the schoolboy reader was often initiated into sexual smut and the gender double standard by classroom texts of Latin and Greek authors, the classical languages and literature were generally closed to girls.

Books designed (or 'calculated') for 'the Instruction and Amusement of Youth' often had female youth in mind, since the small private girls' school was a likely buyer [see *female education]. Priscilla Wakefield, author of *Mental Improvement* (1794), and *Juvenile Anecdotes, founded on Facts; calculated for the Amusement of Children* (c.1797), also published pamphlets 'on the duties of women in the superior classes', 'the preservation of morals of female parish apprentices', and 'the state of infants in the work-house'. In this miscellany of good causes, the writing of books for children was a petty perquisite, delegated to female literature or reclaimed on occasion by men.

Traditional stories were modernized and *bowdlerized: *Gulliver's Travels* (only the voyages to Lilliput and Brobdingnag); *Shakespeare's romance comedies paraphrased as *Tales From Shakespeare* by Charles and Mary *Lamb; the Arabian Nights turned to moral allegory by Maria Edgeworth; and the Robinson Crusoe imitation, *Swiss Family Robinson*, translated by William Godwin under a pseudonym. Godwin's *Bible Stories* (1802) offered a liberal theological alternative to the repressive puritanism which led the market. His *Pantheon: or Ancient History of the Gods of Greece and Rome* (1806) was also used as a classroom text at Charles Burney's (1757–1817) grammar school, but only in its revised edition, with fig-leaves added to the illustrations of classical sculpture.

Brother and sister team Charles and Mary Lamb were flagbearers for a new generation of specialist authors of children's books. M. J. Godwin & Co. commissioned jointly authored *Mrs Leicester's School: or, The History of several Young Ladies, Related by Themselves* (1809). Seven of its ten original stories were written by Mary Lamb, and contain episodes where young girls have disturbing or shaming reading experiences. Translations also imported improving morals into the text, but foreign ideas like physical education, and co-education for boys and girls, were contraband. German-language texts were thought safer than French-language once the anti-Jacobin reaction of the 1790s set in, although popular French classics, like Perrault's *Mother Goose*, Antoine Galland's *Les Mille et Une Nuits*, Bernardin de St Pierre's *Paul et Virginie*, and Fénelon's *Télémaque*, were already naturalized in English. In 1789 the progressive publisher Joseph *Johnson commissioned Mary *Wollstonecraft's translation from the German of G. C. Salzmann's *Elements of Morality*, with designs adapted and engraved by William *Blake. Citing Salzmann in 1792, Wollstonecraft argued that parents should 'speak to children of the organs of generation as freely as we speak of the other parts of the body'. However, when Richard *Polwhele attacked Wollstonecraft in *The Unsex'd Females* (1798), he cited her Salzmann translation with particular viciousness, and accused book illustrator Angelica *Kauffman of exhibiting 'Priapic' images to young readers.

Illustrations have obvious appeal to very young children, and as they became cheaper with improvements in steel-engraving, Sarah *Trimmer pioneered their educational use, and later the publishing firm of Dalziel Bros. commissioned original artwork. Sisters Ann Gilbert (1782–1866) and Jane Taylor (1783–1824) accompanied their *Original Poems for Infant Minds* (1804–5) with accurate drawings in contemporary costume. Hannah *More's generation of women, who had taken cautious steps to secure male clerical approval for the expansion of children's literature, were overtaken by the upcoming generation of male writers, eager to recover market share for boys' tales of adventure, chivalry, and leadership. The moralistic and didactic aims of Sarah Trimmer and Mary Martha Sherwood (1775–1851) were formulated within a Lockean empiricism, based on the quotidian realities of childish dependence on higher authority. Imaginative fantasy, and the exploration of childhood's ideal spaces of garden, village, and home, once thought of as distinguishing traits of women's writing, were recuperated for antidomestic polemic by male authors and critics moving into the field [see *sensibility, 11]. Thomas *Day had been a pioneer in this regard. Employment opportunities thus opened for men as legislators of literary culture: S. T. *Coleridge argued for the 'Creative Imagination', ostensibly gender-free but certainly free from the daily physical care of children, as the essential prerequisite for authoring children's literature.

The education of schoolboys by having them take part in amateur theatrical performances began with Thomas Sheridan (grandfather of R. B. *Sheridan) and Jonathan Swift in Dublin in the 1720s, and was adapted by Hannah More for the girl pupils in her sisters' school at Bristol. More published her *Sacred Dramas* (1782) for use in private schools, and Anne Hughes (*fl.* 1784–90) followed with *Moral Dramas Intended for Private Representation* (1790).

The reading matter available to young females was under constant surveillance, and the young girl as solitary reader was a target for anxious speculation and prurient fantasy. This was recoded censoriously in *conduct books, like those of Dr Gregory and Mrs Chapone. The association of women with children was often selectively invoked to constrain them as a combined audience for male teachers and preachers, and to inhibit women's writing from attempting serious intellectual debate. Reviewers praised women-authored children's literature only if the writer's personal conduct was up for judgement about her book. Anna Laetitia *Barbauld, author of 'The Mouse's Petition' (1773), *Lessons for Children* (1778), and *Hymns in Prose for Children* (1781), won tight-lipped approval from the *Ladies' Monthly Museum* in September 1798: 'It has been pretty generally conceived of female literature, that it sometimes alienates its votaries from many important duties of life: several who have cultivated a talent for study have kept themselves single . . . Mrs Barbauld is an eminent exception to this foolish prejudice.' But her *Female Speaker* (1811), an anthology of elocution pieces for girls, and her antiwar poem *Eighteen Hundred and Eleven* (1812) drew her into controversy, because her market niche with a young female audience dictated that she self-censor any strong opinions, and preserve an anodyne reader identification with conduct book morality.   JB

chinoiserie describes the fashion for Chinese style in *design [25], *architecture [28], and the visual arts. It flourished in Britain in the eighteenth century and reached dizzying heights under the *Regency and the reign of George IV, but its roots were in the continental Europe of the seventeenth century. Inspired by fabulous accounts of the Far East as much as by the high quality of Chinese craft manufacture, in particular porcelain and lacquerware, the taste for the oriental became less an imitation of imported products than an imaginative recreation of the East. Two forms of chinoiserie in Britain should be distinguished: an earlier eighteenth-century restrained style and a later nineteenth-century rococo version.

As Prince Regent in 1792, George had a Chinese drawing-room installed in Carlton House by Henry *Holland and, most famously, remodelled the Royal Pavilion at Brighton. Completed in 1822 after the Prince had become George IV, its architecture owes most to John *Nash.

Sir William *Chambers was responsible for the work that served as the major source for chinoiserie in our period, namely *Designs of Chinese Buildings, Furniture, Dresses, Machines and Utensils* (1757). He was also the most notable writer on the Chinese style in garden design with *A Dissertation on Oriental Gardening* (1772) which gained a degree of fame despite his lack of real acquaintance with Chinese gardens. Royal patronage of chinoiserie faded with George's death. However, its importance was later superseded by the acquisition in the 1840s of a more thorough knowledge of genuine Chinese design.

BP

CHRISTIAN, Fletcher (1764–93), the most famous of the mutineers who put William *Bligh of the *Bounty* and a number of his officers and crew into an open boat on 28 April 1789.

As the mutiny has conventionally been narrated, Christian was the primary butt of Bligh's tyrannical conduct, which became steadily more onerous, after a stay on Tahiti during which Christian and others were tattooed and formed relations with local women. Christian allegedly proposed to abandon the ship alone, but instead seized an unexpected opportunity to take command. After Bligh and those officers loyal to him had been set adrift, Christian and the remainder of the crew sought an isolated place to settle, collecting provisions and local men and women at Tahiti—where some mutineers remained—before moving to Pitcairn. There, oppressive treatment of the Polynesians led to violence, and Christian and others were killed in October 1793.

Back in Britain, however, Christian's polite familial connections fostered the sense that Bligh's overbearing command rather than the mutiny itself was unjust, and this theme remained prominent in the many popular accounts of the events. Bligh said that Christian perspired so violently that he soiled anything he handled. The public—including *Byron—preferred to romanticize Christian's inner goodness, to indulge rumours that he had returned to Britain, and to read an apocryphal set of 'his' letters concerning the mutiny and subsequent travels. NT

Church of England, see *Anglicanism; *religion [10].

church music. Music featured in many different ways in the worship of the major denominations during the period 1776–1832, according to the distinctive practices of each denomination and the resources available at individual churches and chapels.

Choral music played its traditionally important part in Church of England services at cathedrals, collegiate chapels, and the Chapel Royal. However, for much of the period many choral foundations were in decline or moribund: choirs were under-strength, negligent in their duties, or incompetent, and little new music of consequence was being composed. In the parish churches the congregation was often involved in the music of the services, led by a choir and accompanied either by an organ or by a small band of instrumentalists. A revival of church music at both cathedral and parish church level took place in the 1830s and 1840s as part of a more general pattern of church reforms.

Music had a central place in worship within the *Methodist and *Evangelical movements. John *Wesley was quick to recognize the power of *hymn-singing as a 'heartfelt and spontaneous act' in which all the congregation could join, and Methodists readily adapted popular secular melodies to new, religious texts, many of them by John's brother Charles *Wesley. Congregational singing continued to be an essential component of Methodist worship throughout the period.

For the Baptists and Congregationalists, the value of congregational singing of hymns and psalm paraphrases was also recognized, and each denomination published its own collections: the principal Baptist collection was John Rippon's *A Selection of Hymns* (1787), while for the Congregationalists Stephen Addington's *Collection of Psalm Tunes* (1777), based largely on the work of Isaac Watts (1674–1748), ran to no fewer than fifteen editions.

The most complex church music to be heard was within the Roman Catholic church, which during our period moved from proscription to complete *Catholic emancipation. Until the passing of the second Catholic Relief Act in 1791, mass could not legally be celebrated in public. Because of their extraterritorial status, the chapels of the London embassies of Catholic powers were exempt from this prohibition, and became important centres for Catholic worship. At the Sardinian and Portuguese chapels under Samuel *Webbe the elder in the 1770s and 1780s, a tradition of church music developed which surpassed in elaborateness anything to be heard within *Anglican establishments, and was later to be continued by Vincent *Novello and Samuel *Wesley. The cause of Catholic church music was further advanced by an increasing number of publications: three volumes of church music edited by Webbe in the 1780s and early 1790s, the six-volume *Selection of Sacred Music* (1806–20) edited by C. I. *Latrobe, and various collections edited by Novello (from 1811). PO

circulating libraries, commercial libraries (sometimes known as subscription libraries), commonly with a few hundred volumes on offer, whose proliferation from the mid-eighteenth century encouraged the growth of reading generally and female readership and authorship in particular.

Established retailers in London, such as the *Minerva Press, and the provinces (especially in recreational centres and *spa towns like Bath) would purchase commercial libraries of between about 100 and, by 1791, 10,000 volumes, from which subscribers could borrow for an annual fee of between 10s. 6d. and one guinea, non-subscribers for a set price per volume. The access that this suddenly gave to many who could not afford the high prices of books not only expanded readership but also encouraged the production of reading material, especially of sentimental novels [see *sensibility, 11]. Hence there developed a protracted campaign against fiction by the classically educated élite, reflecting on the continuing debate about the value of literacy per se [see *language, 40]. By 1775, when R. B. *Sheridan's Sir Anthony Absolute in The Rivals denounced the circulating library as 'an evergreen tree of diabolical knowledge!', many voices had been raised against its agency in the spread of a corruption called 'the *novel' [31] amongst the feminine and lower orders of a burgeoning 'reading public'.

How wide that audience was is difficult to say; subscription fees still excluded the bulk of the population, though the post-Napoleonic period saw numerous cheaper counterparts. Two concomitants, if not consequences, were evident: first, the prominence of women amongst those liberated into the reading public, hence of women writers by the demand they created; and second, the progressively stricter class division of that public according to choice of reading material.   wc

CLAIRMONT, Clara Mary Jane (known as Claire) (1798–1879), teacher, lover of the poets *Byron and *Shelley, and mother of Byron's daughter Allegra (1817–22). Jane, as she was initially called, never knew her father, and shortly after her third birthday in 1801 her mother, Mary Jane, married William *Godwin as his second wife. Mary *Wollstonecraft's daughters Fanny Imlay and Mary Godwin (later Mary *Shelley) thus became slightly older stepsisters. Claire immediately began cultivating the legend of Mary Wollstonecraft, adopting Wollstonecraft's birth date of 27 April, and emulating Wollstonecraft's intellectual independence and eagerness for experience. She also qualified as a teacher, studied music and singing, perfected her French, and refashioned her name to 'Claire' to match the Franco-Swiss ancestry and feminist aspirations of her personal romance.

She abetted the furtive wooing of Mary Godwin and the married poet Percy Shelley on the site of Wollstonecraft's grave in St Pancras churchyard. When Mary and Shelley subsequently eloped to France in July 1814, Claire went with them, perhaps imagining herself replicating Mary Wollstonecraft's attempted relationship with Sophia and Henry *Fuseli in the 1790s. Mary Jane tracked the three to an inn at Calais, but was legally powerless to force her daughter to come home. On the day they eloped, 28 July 1814, Mary Godwin had begun a journal which she coaxed Shelley to co-write with her. Claire, not to be outdone, began her own somewhat livelier journal on 14 August.

By 1815 Claire found herself the unwanted outsider in the Shelley family plot. Now seventeen, she was a vivid brunette with a beautiful singing voice. Shelley had written a love poem to her ('To Constantia Singing'). She decided to try her luck and talents as an actress, and solicited the attentions of Lord Byron, a director at Drury Lane theatre. Byron obliged her in a brief sexual encounter which made her pregnant. She nagged Shelley into following Byron to Switzerland in the rainy summer of 1816, hoping with his support to persuade Byron to acknowledge her and the coming child, but this plan failed dismally. Shelley removed both Claire and Mary from Byron's vicinity to return in disarray to England.

Claire gave birth in concealment in Bath on 12 January 1817, to a daughter she named Alba, changed later at Byron's insistence to Allegra. Her journal and letters of this time reveal a frank delight in the intimate contact between mother and baby. In March 1818 Clara Allegra Byron was baptised in St Giles-in-the-Fields, London. The now married Shelleys, together with Claire and the infant children of both women, then embarked again for Europe to seek out Byron. Mary was adamant that Claire's child should go to Byron, and Claire herself depart from the Shelley household. Claire hoped that Allegra's appeal and Shelley's intercession would soften Byron's heart towards her but he made it plain that once he took the child he would permit no rights to Claire. On Byron's terms, the anguished Claire relinquished Allegra, who was sent to Byron in his Venetian palazzo on 28 April 1818. At Byron's holiday villa in Este, Claire was briefly reunited with Allegra in August 1818.

Claire and the Shelleys were intermittently together and apart for the next three years. In Naples in December 1818 Shelley registered the birth of a female infant, Elena Adelaide Shelley, naming Mary as the mother. Gossip reached Byron that Claire was the mother and Shelley the father of this infant, who was apparently left in a foundling home in Naples. Byron used this to damage Claire's reputation, and speculation about Claire's involvement continues, although material evidence is scanty.

Early in 1821, tiring of his child and loathing the child's mother, Byron consigned Allegra into the keeping of the nuns at Bagnacavallo, where he neither visited her nor permitted Claire even to communicate with her daughter. By February 1822 Claire was 'haunted by the belief that I shall never see her any more'. In April 1822 Allegra, aged 5, died of typhus. Shelley drowned that same year on 8 July and Mary resumed a warily flirtatious relationship with Byron, which excluded Claire.

Claire rallied, travelled to Vienna to stay with her brother Charles, then spent the years 1825 to 1828 as a governess to the daughters of wealthy families in

Tsarist Russia. In 1828, she was briefly reunited with the Godwin family in London, and from there went to Dresden as a companion-housekeeper. She returned to England after Godwin's death in 1836, and taught music while she nursed Mary Jane in her final illness in 1841. After her mother's death, she was next in Pisa, living with Mary Wollstonecraft's former pupil Lady Margaret Mount Cashell (known as Mrs Mason). Her correspondence with Mary Shelley, often stormy and bitter on both sides, lasted until Mary Shelley's death in 1851. Mary Shelley was generous enough to praise Claire deservedly as a superb letter-writer.

Shelley had made a will in Claire's favour for £12,000, and her legacy was paid by Sir Percy Florence Shelley in 1844. She converted to the Roman Catholic church, perhaps to console the ghost of Allegra, and lived on in the English expatriate colony in Florence in company with her daughter Paulina. In 1878 she provided information for Edward Trelawny's *Records of Shelley, Byron, and the Author*, which maligned the long-dead Mary Shelley and distressed the Shelley heirs.   JB

CLARE, John (1793–1864). Presented as 'the Northamptonshire Peasant Poet', Clare was a distinctive writer of the natural world, its people and politics, and later, during his confinement in asylums, a poet of remarkable visionary intensity [see *peasant poets].

His problematic place in the modern literary canon is a reflection of his own anxieties—and those of his contemporaries—as to his place in the literary world of his day. Born in Helpstone, Northamptonshire, he began writing verse in 1806 while working as a ploughboy. He later attracted attention from local booksellers J. B. Henson of Market Deeping and Edward Drury of Stamford, which led eventually to contact with the London publisher John Taylor (1781–1864). His *Poems Descriptive of Rural Life and Scenery* was published in 1820, during which year he visited London for the first time [see *popular culture, 23]. He was introduced to Taylor's literary circle, later meeting *Hazlitt and *Lamb, among others. Clare's return from London to Helpstone in 1824 was to confront the truth that his spiritual home was in neither place, in that he was a poet with ambitions above his station, surrounded by 'clowns' who could not read. His major *poetry [29] draws its strength from this tension, this uncertainty as to his identity and 'place'.

The particularities of his poetry are intimately linked to the peculiarities of his circumstances. As in *The Village Minstrel* (1821), so in *The Shepherd's Calendar* (1827), he constructs a poem that is personal elegy and social protest, in which the monthly 'descriptions' provide a nineteenth-century version of James Thomson's *Seasons* (the poem which made his heart 'twitter with joy'). The original plan for *The Shepherd's Calendar* had been to alternate the monthly sections with narrative tales; the importance of this lies in Clare's recognition that he was writing a political, polemical type of verse, in which people at work both defined the landscape and were defined

by it [see *land, 16]. Both here and in *The Parish*, written at the same time but never published in his lifetime because of its satirical tone, Clare's verse is anything but 'homespun' as he claimed. Whilst aiming, like *Crabbe and like *Byron, to voice 'the truth', Clare recognizes that the literary tradition, as much as the oral, provides the sounding-board for such a voice.

By the mid-1820s his voice was clear and distinctive, most readily discernible in the magnificent manuscript *The Midsummer Cushion*, which he hoped to get published in 1832, but which appeared, less magisterially and considerably reduced, in 1835, as *The Rural Muse*. It was in the early 1830s, when he moved three miles from Helpstone to Northborough, that this voice was put to one of its sternest tests, as he confronted his own displacement. Clare's crisis of identity was manifested in increasing illness and mental breakdown. In June 1837 he was confined in the asylum at Epping Forest under the care of Dr Matthew Allen, a proponent of the more humanitarian treatment of *madness, who encouraged Clare to continue writing. In 1841 he escaped from the Epping asylum, walking eighty miles to Peterborough with no food and little to drink: his narrative of the 'Journey out of Essex' is a powerful and moving account of the experience. In December 1841 he entered Northampton General Lunatic Asylum, where another interested keeper, W. F. Knight, transcribed his poems. At Epping Forest and at Northampton, Clare clung on to his own identity by imagining himself to be many people, most especially *Burns and Byron. Certainly in Northampton he cried, 'I am—yet what I am none cares or knows', but he also affirmed, with stubborn clarity, that he had left the physical world and its constraints behind: 'I gave my name immortal birth / And kept my spirit with the free'. What distinguishes all his work (and the sheer range and extent must be registered) is the extraordinary integrity of his vision, his hard-won knowledge that he was a poet, in his own words 'as great a bard as Byron'.   MS

Clarke, Mary Anne, affair. Though short-lived, this scandal of 1808–9 marked a turning-point in the fortunes of British oppositionists labouring under the taint of French Jacobinism. Aided by an entourage of journalists, *street literature publishers, and radical pamphleteers, Mary Anne Clarke (1776–1852) helped the opposition to reconquer the lofty peaks of *patriotism against a government which had seemingly squandered the *war [2] effort through sexual and moral corruption.

Born Mary Anne Thompson in the Bowl and Pin Skittle Alley, Fleet Street, her father was unknown, her stepfather was a printer, and her first husband a stonemason. A brief boarding-school education, courtesy of an early lover, gave her a measure of social polish and literary skill. She probably met the Duke of York, Commander-in-Chief and royal prince, at the London theatre. As his mistress in the early 1800s she boasted a lavish Gloucester Place establishment, a grand carriage, and liveried servants, but accusations surfaced in the radical press of 1808 that she had been using her influence with the Duke to run a military promotions racket. A former United Movement journalist, Peter Finnerty, wrote a widely selling pamphlet which aired the claims of an aggrieved soldier, Brevet Major Hogan, that he had been passed over for promotion in favour of one of her candidates. As a result, Mary Anne quickly found herself pitted against the full force of the state. However, *Whig and radical oppositionists, itching for a way to embarrass the government, seized the opportunity to rocket her to political prominence. Reformers Gwyllym Lloyd Wardle (?1762–1833) and Sir Francis *Burdett championed her cause in and out of parliament, and were successful in forcing the Duke's resignation.

Mary Anne also proved to be an adept political operator in her own right. She was bold, sarcastic, and quick-witted when interrogated before 600 men at a House of Commons Select Committee. A bevy of satirical *prints [22] celebrated her energy and wit, often depicting her as a carnivalian woman of misrule delightedly turning the ministerial and royal worlds upside down. Nicknamed 'the Pandora of Pamphleteers' by Grub Street scribe W. H. *Ireland, she produced her own bestselling memoirs and skilfully orchestrated a number of radical hacks to promote her cause. She was generally represented in the political prints as a victimized woman of the people, exploited by aristocratic and royal libertines whom she now exposed in concert with the forces of reform. Privately, she proclaimed her rights to receive healthy payments from the government in return for withholding her memoirs. Although she proved a fickle champion of radicalism, her image in popular literature as a wronged woman and champion of liberty helped pave the way for the *Queen Caroline affair.   IMcC

CLARKSON, Thomas (1760–1846), *abolitionist and *philanthropist. Serious-minded son of a curate schoolmaster, Clarkson won the University of Cambridge prize in Latin for an essay on *slavery [6] in 1785. From this time onwards he was like a man possessed, earning S. T. *Coleridge's ambivalent accolade of 'the Moral Steam-Engine, or the Giant with one idea'. Believing himself called to the task of ending Britain's involvement in slavery, Clarkson joined his prodigious labours to those, such as the *Quakers, who were already making their protests heard. For nine years, from 1786 to 1794, he was one of abolitionism's foremost campaigners, writing scores of tracts, pamphlets, and books, organizing committees, corresponding with hundreds of people, gathering *petitions, and spearheading reform innovations such as the popular sugar boycott. He also visited Britain's major ports, accumulating a mass of evidence about the trade's high mortality rates amongst seamen as well as slaves. Personally endangered by this task, he was also obliged to support those few witnesses courageous enough to give the evidence needed by William *Wilberforce to get the abolitionist bill passed by parliament. An enthusiast of the *French Revolution, Clarkson travelled to Paris in 1789 in the hope of achieving an Anglo-French ban on the trade. Despite many reverses, he remained for the rest of his long life 'a slave to the slaves', advising Henry Christophe, King of Haiti, joining the anti-slavery movement in 1823, and even, at the age of 81, believing himself called to address slavery in America. He is best known for his *History of the Abolition of the Slave Trade* (1808), and his *Portraiture of Quakerism* (1806). Although often described as a Quaker, Clarkson never joined the society.   DC

classics, rise of the. The first European canon of great musical works from the past arose in England during the eighteenth century. Traditionally, few pieces were performed long after the deaths of their composers. However, by 1785 a clearly defined repertory of widely revered old works, from the Elizabethan masters to Purcell and *Handel, became established in English *concerts and churches. This movement had its deepest roots in the succession of crises that overwhelmed *church music, from the reconstruction of the liturgy in the *Anglican Reformation to the abolition of sung services during the Civil War.

After the Restoration, a far larger body of works from the sixteenth century remained in use in England than anywhere else in Europe, providing a performing tradition by which sixteenth-century music was called 'ancient music'. The notion grew up chiefly among Oxford High Churchmen, in the musical meetings of the Revd Henry Aldrich, Dean of Christ Church and chief patron of the cathedral choir. Viewing with alarm the commercialization of musical life by *music publishers and theatre musicians, he and his colleagues called for works by the Elizabethan masters to be seen as models to prevent the degeneration of taste.

While the repertories of ancient music grew up in Tory surroundings, mainly in the cathedrals of the West Country, the movement took on a highly inclusive, much less partisan character. The annual music meetings where Purcell's and Handel's settings of the *Te Deum* were regularly performed expanded in scale during the 1750s with the production of Handel's *oratorios, and continued strong after his death in 1759. These works and the cathedral meetings retained powerful political meaning. The oratorios established in both textual and musical terms a theological and political middle ground that escaped the partisan conflicts of the previous century. The *music festivals helped to turn that achievement into national celebration. Both Anglicans and Dissenters of varying stripes subscribed to these performances. By the end of the century, for example, the subscribers to the Norwich meetings included members of leading families of Quakers and Unitarians as much as Anglicans. One could argue, then, that wounds opened up in the Civil War were healed within the Handelian tradition.

The Crown took full advantage of the national implications of the taste for ancient music. In 1776 the Concert of Ancient Music was established, with a repertory which redefined 'ancient music' as all works over twenty years old, but which was focused upon those of Handel (still known as a German trained in Italy). Led by the Earl of Sandwich, the concert drew a varied political clientele but came under the sway of the royal house. When in 1784 its directors sponsored the Handel Commemoration in Westminster Abbey and the Pantheon, George III attended all the performances and proceeded to attach himself so closely to Handelian taste in general that the series became known as the King's Concert. A German musician and a Germanic monarchy thus paradoxically worked to naturalize each other into epitomes of English national patriotism.   ww

CLEMENTI, Muzio (1752–1832), *pianist, composer, and businessman, a leading member of the London Pianoforte School and one of the founders of modern piano-playing.

As a child he was brought to England from Italy by Peter Beckford (cousin to the author of *Vathek*) and kept in virtual confinement in Dorset. Released in the mid-1770s, Clementi soon made an impact as a harpsichordist and pianist, the celebrated Op. 2 sonatas reaching new heights of *keyboard brilliance. During a continental tour he competed with *Mozart (who thought him a 'mere mechanicus'), before returning to London a fully-fledged piano virtuoso. Here in the late 1780s he wrote numerous piano sonatas, the genre on which his reputation principally rests. Developing a more profound and dramatic sonata style, he united the English piano's capacity for bold contrasts with expressive dissonance and rich counterpoint derived from J. S. Bach. These traits set his music apart from the earlier *galant* idiom, and were highly influential on *Beethoven. In particular, the powerful tension of the F minor sonata Op. 13 strongly foreshadows Beethoven.

After the 1790 season Clementi abruptly abandoned the career of piano virtuoso. He continued to compose expansive sonatas, such as *Didone abbandonata*: the title and operatic connotations suggest incipient Romanticism, fully borne out by the passionate sweep of the music and its agonized dissonances. He also had aspirations as a symphonic composer, but had the misfortune to come up against *Haydn at his zenith. Instead his career took a different turn. First he established himself as London's leading piano teacher, publishing a famous tutor in 1801 and some elementary sonatinas [see *music teaching]. Among his professional students were such successful figures as *Cramer and *Field. He then moved into the commercial world of piano manufacture and *music publishing, in which capacity he travelled throughout Europe from 1802 to 1810, persuading Beethoven to grant him the English rights to many major works.

Back in London Clementi continued his commercial activities, while enjoying an Indian summer as composer and revered master. In 1813 he was appointed a director of the new Philharmonic Society, conducting concerts from the piano until 1824 and successfully returning to symphonic composition. He also put together a compendium of piano studies, both technical and contrapuntal, entitled

Gradus ad Parnassum. Clementi received the rare distinction, for a musician, of a funeral in Westminster Abbey.   SMcV

closet drama, a term which refers to plays that are unperformed or unperformable, was not current in our period but in fact dates from experimentation in dramatic form in the late nineteenth and early twentieth centuries. 'Closet drama' was used in post-Second World War studies of Romanticism to define what was seen as distinctively 'Romantic' about the drama and theatrical culture of the period: that is, the withdrawal, particularly by the canonical poets, from active engagement with the *theatre [24] into an alternative internalized or 'mental theatre' of the *imagination. In that its use often endorsed the antitheatricalism of what it purported to describe, 'closet drama' is a highly problematic term which needs to be used with some caution.

That contemporaries preferred the term 'dramatic poem' tellingly illustrates the desire to redeem the authority of the genre of drama, debased by its connection with the theatre, by accruing to it some of the cachet of *poetry [29]. But not all dramatic poems entail an explicit or implicit rejection of theatrical representation, nor does 'dramatic poem' adequately encompass the range of what might be described as 'closet' plays, some of which are prose works or comedies. The term 'closet' itself was used widely in the period as a way of signifying the relationship between the act of reading, conceived as private and individualized (the closet was historically a room for private religious devotion), and the communal experience of theatre. A substantial readership for printed plays (often sold within the theatre itself) was stimulated by the *publishing [21] industry and a well-established interest in drama as one of the key genres of literature, making the relationship between text and performance a central consideration for theatrical and literary criticism. Elizabeth *Inchbald's prefaces to her *British Theatre*, for example, represent an extended disquisition on the relationship between text and performance.

The perception of the relationship between stage and closet as problematic is apparent in a wide variety of plays, both performed and unperformed— poems, tragedies, comedies, so-called 'German dramas', even serialized plays in periodicals—that resist rigid classification as a particular genre but can be said to be linked by a sense that the theatre was in cultural decline. These plays reflected concerns that theatrical representation was aesthetically, politically, and morally compromised by the increasing emphasis on spectacle after the innovations of de *Loutherbourg, the elaboration of forms such as *pantomime and *panorama which subordinated the word to the visual image, and the building of larger patent theatres after 1794. These anxieties were reinforced by the enhanced role in public culture after 1769 of *Shakespeare, the embodiment of the dramatic poet. Shakespeare was joined in a pantheon by John Ford, John Webster, and Philip Massinger, whose work was republished in the 1800s and excerpted in collections such as *Lamb's

Specimens of English Dramatic Poets (1808). This rediscovery of Jacobean drama had an important influence on dramatic poems such as *Beddoes's *The Bride's Tragedy* (1821). 'Closet' plays also served as a channnel for the period's profound antitheatricalism (exemplified by Hannah *More's *Sacred Dramas*).

Finally, 'closet' plays also emerged as a response to changing configurations of private and public, influenced by *sensibility [11] and ideologies of *domesticity [13]. The most interesting manifestation of this is Joanna *Baillie's *Series of Plays on the Passions* and the prefaces to the 1798 and 1812 editions of the same. Baillie's 1798 preface made it clear that she was not opposed to theatrical representation *per se*, and indeed regarded the theatre as a potentially more democratic medium than the book because it was accessible to those who could not read. Nevertheless, the book offered her the kind of artistic autonomy and control that would be denied her in the theatre, where the script could be interpreted by managers, actors, and scene-designers. So it is because authorial control was essential to Baillie's literary persona that the *Series of Plays* can be described as a Romantic or 'closet' text, not because they are antitheatrical. Baillie's characterization of Jane de Monfort in her play of the same name, later staged by John Philip *Kemble, was profoundly influenced by the acting of Sarah *Siddons who realized the part, as well as by the tradition of domestic tragedy which Siddons had made her forte. The scene in which the heroine of Rowe's *The Fair Penitent* (1703), Calista, finds herself alone in a closet-like cell with the corpse of her murdered lover, was a prototype for Baillie's attempt in her *Plays* to use dramatic literature to penetrate the deepest recesses of the self, revealing that privacy as theatrical. Baillie's endeavours represent, therefore, a continuum between theatre practice and the experimentation of 'closet' drama, not a disjunction between the two.

GR

COADE, Eleanor (1733–1821), manufacturer of the artificial stone known as Coade Stone, came to London from Lyme Regis to open a factory, the Coade Artificial Stone Manufactory, in Lambeth from about 1769 until 1820.

The manufacture of a sort of artificial stone was carried on as early as 1722, when Richard Holt took out a patent in partnership with the architect Thomas Ripley (*c.*1683–1758). What had been a dwindling business was then taken over by Eleanor Coade, who was reputed to be the daughter of the person who discovered the composition for the stone. Coade secured the services of the sculptor John Bacon (1740–99), and the business became an immediate success. She later took her cousin John Sealy (1749–1813) into partnership. Coade stone was popular as a convenient substitute for ashlar masonry and carved stone, and was used for figure *sculpture, monuments, and decorative work [see *architecture, 28 and *design, 25]. From 1774 most of the architectural ornaments in the West End of London, and many church monuments around Britain, came from the Lambeth factory. CT

COBBETT, William (1763–1835), radical leader and journalist whose weekly *Political Register* profoundly influenced the language, ideology, and aspirations of the *parliamentary reform movement, extending its impact and the range of its support.

Raised as an agricultural labourer in Sussex, Cobbett received little formal education, but taught himself English and French grammar and mathematics after enlisting in the army. He served six years in New Brunswick, Canada, and was discharged upon his return to England in 1791. When an attempt to charge his superiors with misconduct went astray, Cobbett fled to France and then to the United States, becoming an influential anti-French journalist in Philadelphia with the nickname of 'Peter Porcupine' and establishing his vigorous prose style and contentious habits. However, legal and financial difficulties related to his writing prompted his return to London, where he was welcomed by *loyalists and members of the government, including William *Pitt.

Cobbett immediately set himself up as a loyalist bookseller and journalist, and established the *Political Register* in 1802 with the support of his new friends. Yet he soon grew disillusioned with the Pitt regime, and by 1804 was attaching himself and his *Register* to Sir Francis *Burdett and his associates. The brief and unsatisfying tenure of the *Ministry of All the Talents confirmed his political disaffection and his commitment to radical parliamentary reform, a 'change of system' rather than of men. Drawing upon England's rich oppositional traditions, Cobbett developed a remarkably single-minded critique of what he called the 'system' of Old Corruption based on the manipulation of pensions and sinecures, the *national debt and taxation, paper currency, an expansive commercial economy, and the electoral practices of an unreformed parliament. His hatreds, personally directed against men like Pitt and *Castlereagh, had a profound impact on English radicalism, as did his faith in parliamentary reform and his idealization of the stable economic order of his childhood.

Political opposition was for Cobbett as personal as political corruption. His sense of his own heroic resistance intensified in 1810, when he was convicted of seditious libel and sentenced to two years in Newgate prison. Cobbett has often drawn praise for the levelling impact of his democratic tone and undeferential manner. Yet the weakness of early-nineteenth-century radical organization has also been traced to his personal vanity, his feuds with other reformers, and his suspicion of formal political clubs. He was also charged with inconsistency and contradiction, his enemies often embarrassing him by republishing his early attacks on reform. Marx called him 'the purest incarnation of Old England and the most audacious initiator of Young England', and commentators today still struggle to resolve his reactionary and progressive impulses.

Cobbett insisted that his political judgements were grounded in the impoverishment of the ordinary labourer, especially the agricultural labourer [see *land, 16]. (He was less interested in industrial conditions.) In this sense, his celebrated address 'To the Journeymen and Labourers' on 2 November 1816 was a significant departure for him and for the radical reform movement. Familiar arguments were now directed to working-class readers, who were treated to a flattering derivation of the nation's strength from 'the labour of its people'. Cobbett facilitated the circulation of the address by also reprinting it on a single, untaxed sheet, which he sold for two pence. The continued weekly appearance of his 'Two-Penny Trash' set the pattern for the radical *unstamped press. Having begun to address labourers as political agents, he was converted by Major John *Cartwright to universal manhood suffrage without any property requirement.

The unstamped *Register* appeared in a phase of widespread agricultural distress and popular unrest after 1815. When the government suspended habeas corpus in March 1817, Cobbett left England for America, convinced that prison was his only alternative. Other radicals criticized his decision, and the *Register* soon lost its timeliness and its leading role in the reform movement. Yet the perspective of exile served Cobbett well in two successful books: *A Year's Residence in the United States of America* (1818–19), which traced the fortunes of its author as farmer and agricultural improver, and *A Grammar of the English Language* (1818), which promoted the radical ideal of verbal clarity against the interference of corrupt power, and sought to make an empowering written vernacular available to 'Soldiers, Sailors, Apprentices, and Plough-boys' [see *language, 40].

Cobbett returned to England in November 1819, immediately after *Peterloo and in time for the prohibition of unstamped publication by the 'Six Acts'. He was briefly a champion and adviser of *Queen Caroline during her celebrated divorce trial. His activity in the 1820s was then dominated by a regular circuit of rural tours and *lectures, devoted to the linked issues of agricultural distress, high taxation, national debt, and currency reform. In the end, Cobbett's dire predictions of financial catastrophe were not realized. But he found sympathetic audiences through a decade of intermittent economic crisis, and was able to mobilize rural protest. The *Rural Rides*, published serially in the *Register* from 1822 to 1826 and reissued as a book in 1830, record the intensity of his political vision and activity in this period. As the heroic rural rider, Cobbett exposed the damage done to the English countryside, and launched a series of polemical campaigns against his lifelong enemies. Although he lost his farm at Botley to bankruptcy in 1820, he never gave up his habit of agricultural experiment. His *Cottage Economy* (1821–2) was a handbook of domestic and agricultural techniques intended to shield the rural household from commerce and corruption.

In his last years, Cobbett campaigned for parliamentary reform and *Catholic emancipation, and lived to see the success of both causes. In 1832, in the first election conducted under the new *Reform Act, he was elected MP for Oldham. By this time, however, poor health limited his effectiveness, and radical initiative was passing to a new generation of writers and agitators he had influenced. KG

coffeehouses catered for a heterogeneous clientele from aristocrats to labourers, and performed functions beyond their obvious business as victualling establishments, becoming important centres of commerce, learning, politics, sociability, and entertainment.

Coffeehouses first rose to prominence in the first half of the eighteenth century, declining after 1750 due to the rising popularity of private clubs and tea-drinking, to re-emerge in the early nineteenth century as a favoured rendezvous for the working and middle classes, largely because of their relative freedom from licensing controls.

In its most basic form, the coffeehouse was simply a place of recreation and refreshment, offering drink and sometimes food. However, as a gathering-place it maintained a versatile and complex cultural significance. Coffeehouses served as convenient and fashionable places to transact the type of mercantile and business deals which saw the proliferation of such establishments near the Royal Exchange.

The longest-serving function of coffeehouses was their role in the dissemination of news and their harbouring of political inquiry. Drawing clients from a wide social range, coffeehouses were places in which *newspapers were readily accessible and free discussion encouraged amongst an ever-expanding and politically alert reading public. In this way they promoted the expansion of the political nation, providing a regular forum for radicals and freethinkers from the seventeenth century through to the *Chartists and beyond. Although women participated in more respectable commercial *debating clubs, there is little evidence for their involvement in coffeehouse equivalents. Even so, coffeehouses, like *taverns and alehouses, helped to transmit a radical tradition from one generation to the next, becoming one of the most enduring and important social institutions in British history. MD

COLERIDGE, Hartley (1796–1849), eldest son of S. T. *Coleridge. Named after the philosopher David Hartley (1705–57), he was, as a child, perceived to share both his father's remarkable talents and his faults. He was brought up in Robert *Southey's household after his parents separated, his intellectual promise leading him to Oxford, where he was elected to a fellowship in 1819 only to be removed on the grounds of intemperance within a year.

After two years in London trying to make his way as a man of letters, he attempted to start a school in the Lake District. The failure of this project led to a move to Leeds, where he lodged with a publisher for whom he had promised to write biographical sketches of local figures. These were eventually published as *Biographia Borealis* (1833) and *Worthies of Yorkshire and Lancashire* (1836). A small book of poems was printed in 1833, the *sonnets proving especially successful, but a literary career continued to elude him and he moved back to a life of aimless wandering and occasional dissipation in the Lakes, where he died of bronchitis in 1849. Two volumes of poetry and prose were edited by his brother, Derwent (1800–83) in 1851.   JM

COLERIDGE, Samuel Taylor (1772–1834), poet, philosopher, and literary critic. The youngest of a vicar's ten children, Coleridge was only 9 years old when his father's sudden death led to his institutionalization at Christ's Hospital as a charity boy. At school, he fashioned for himself a *Chatterton-like persona, and was regarded by his peers as an eccentric genius. His brilliance as a classicist won him a scholarship to Cambridge in 1791, where he came under the influence of the *Unitarian and radical don William *Frend. Embroiled in debt, and with no prospect of gaining a Fellowship, he eventually left the University in 1794 without taking a degree. From this point until 1798, Coleridge was, intermittently, a democrat and outspoken radical, the disorienting effects of which can still be seen in his later, conservative apologias.

The difficulty of sustaining a deeply religious outlook simultaneously with radical politics during the turbulent mid-1790s resulted in a rich, if sometimes bewildering and contradictory, array of polemical prose, and a cluster of extraordinary poems for which he is chiefly remembered today. In the summer of 1794 he met Oxford undergraduate Robert *Southey, a Bristolian who shared his disaffection, restlessness, and radicalism, and together they planned to emigrate to rural America and establish *Pantisocracy, an experimental colony in which property and labour were to be equally shared by all. In 1795 in Bristol, one of Britain's largest slaving ports, Coleridge honed his anti-establishment and anti-Trinitarian polemics in order to finance this *utopia [9] in America. He delivered a number of *lectures on religion and politics, covering *inter alia* the slave trade, the war against France, and the government's repressive treason and sedition bills. Although some of his poems had been published individually, his first volume, *Poems on Various Subjects*, appeared in 1796, opening with 'Monody on the Death of Chatterton' and concluding with his *millenarian poem, 'Religious Musings'. This was also the year of the *Watchman*, his first attempt at running a *newspaper. The midlands tour undertaken by Coleridge to sign up subscribers was in part financed and organized by admiring Unitarian connections, and of the many career options open to him at this time—poet, philosopher, translator, schoolteacher, private tutor, political journalist, public speaker, lay preacher—the Unitarian ministry seemed the securest, if not the most exciting, choice for a recently married man about to become a father.

A ministry at Shrewsbury was organized for him with the help of Mrs *Barbauld, a poet he greatly admired, but the *Wedgwood family intervened at the start of 1798 with an annuity which saved him for his preferred activities of poetry, philosophy, and politics. His ardour for Southey cooled by the latter's desertion of Pantisocracy, he was soon transferring his hero-worship to another rising star, William

*Wordsworth. Their most important collaborative work, begun in 1797 and later consolidated by the annuity, was the anonymous *Lyrical Ballads* (1798), comprising four poems by Coleridge and nineteen poems by Wordsworth. Shortly after its publication the two poets left for Germany, accompanied by Wordsworth's sister, Dorothy *Wordsworth. Whereas the Wordsworths travelled with no clear purpose, Coleridge spent a year improving his understanding of German philosophy, theology, and literature, and he was later to become an important conduit for German ideas in pre-Victorian England. Back in England, the predominance of Wordsworth's contributions to *Lyrical Ballads* led to his claim of sole authorship when volume II appeared in 1800. Wordsworth also wrote the controversial 1800 'Preface', now regarded as an important poetic manifesto. Many years later, exasperated by the ongoing Jacobinical reputation of the 'Preface', Wordsworth claimed it was a task foisted on him by Coleridge, and certainly the latter's influence can be seen, particularly in some of the manifesto's propositions about *language [40]. Coleridge's other ambiguous gift to Wordsworth was the impossibly huge design for a philosophical poem entitled *The Recluse*, comprising thoughts on man, on nature, and on human life. So ambitious was the plan for this work that the hope of realizing it created for Wordsworth many guilty years of intellectual dependence on his less productive partner. The first part of *The Recluse* is Wordsworth's long autobiographical 'Poem to Coleridge', better known now as *The Prelude*.

Although there have recently been a number of attempts to establish the importance of Coleridge's poetry after 1802, it can still be argued that his loss of confidence during the collaboration with Wordsworth effectively terminated his brilliant poetical career. After 1800, with his marriage in difficulties and his dependence upon opium increasing, the rift which had begun to open up in his relationship with Wordsworth took the form of an irreconcilable difference in their poetical opinions, a difference later elaborated in political as well as literary terms in *Biographia Literaria* (1817). In 1804 Coleridge escaped his miserable domestic situation by taking up an administrative post in Malta, his chief qualification being his experience as a political journalist on the *Morning Post* and the *Courier* (1797–1804). The health cure of a two-year stay in Malta did not eventuate, and Coleridge returned to England so ill with opium abuse that he was almost unrecognizable to his friends. In 1808 he delivered the first of what would be many lecture series, often erratic, sometimes plagiarized, occasionally electrifying, and at other times dull. He then went north to the Wordsworths, with whom he stayed for two years, writing twenty-six numbers of his second newspaper, the *Friend*, a venture which he initially hoped would be supported by wealthy *Quaker subscribers. Despite some brilliant passages, the work is marred by its uneven style and uncertain subject-matter, ranging from the impossibly abstruse to a more accommodating readability, an oscillation which can be attributed to intense anxieties about the marketplace and the reading public. These anxieties dominate his later works too, for instance the three *Lay Sermons* (1816–17), the first of which is pitched at the learned and aristocratic class, the second to the higher and middle classes, and the third (never written) to the lower and labouring classes. It is in the second of these that Coleridge begins to formulate his notion of a 'clerisy', an ideally learned and philosophic readership which would value his ruminations on church and state matters. His increasing conservatism led to much obfuscation of his earlier career, provoking derision from former radical associates. In particular he displayed a good deal of animus against Dissent, dubbing Unitarianism the 'Sans cullotterie of Religion'. The influence of Coleridge's later prose writings can be seen in a range of Victorian politicians, educationalists, social theorists, and theologians.   DC

COLMAN, George, the younger (1762–1836), playwright, *theatre [24] manager, writer, and censor. Colman was the son of George Colman the elder, a prominent mid-eighteenth-century dramatist, author of *The Clandestine Marriage* (1766) and other comedies, and manager of the Haymarket theatre in London. Destined initially for the Bar, Colman's career inexorably gravitated towards the theatre, for which he wrote numerous pieces in a variety of genres, chiefly comedy and musical drama. He was also a notable exponent of *Gothic drama, producing *The Battle of Hexham* (1789), *Blue-Beard* (1798), and *Feudal Times* (1799). The plays for which he was best known included *Inkle and Yarico* (1787), *The Heir at Law* (1797), *John Bull* (1803), and *The Iron Chest* (1796)—his adaptation of *Godwin's novel *Caleb Williams*. The first performance of the latter at Drury Lane was not a success, for which Colman, in a testy preface to the published edition, blamed the actor John Philip *Kemble. However in a revised version *The Iron Chest* went on to become a repertory piece at the Haymarket. Colman's irascibility was also evident in his challenge to Elizabeth *Inchbald's remarks on his work in her *British Theatre*: he claimed that her gender disqualified her as a critic.

Colman succeeded his father as manager of the Haymarket in 1789 and at one stage managed the theatre from the King's Bench Prison, to which he had been confined for debt. Deeply immersed in the clubbable masculinist sociability of the theatre and literary worlds, Colman's circle included the Duke of York, the Prince Regent, and *Byron. In addition to playwriting, he also produced often risqué comic poems in the style of John *Wolcot (Peter Pindar). However, on being appointed Examiner of Plays by George IV in 1824, a post which he held until his death in 1836, Colman took to the role of moral guardian with relish, and with an insouciant disregard of charges of hypocrisy. As censor of scripts submitted to him prior to performance, Colman was cavalier with the blue pencil, excising even vaguely religious allusions, oaths (including 'demme'), and anything that could be interpreted as a comment on politics, both past and present. In this respect he played a part in the increasingly regulated climate

that attempted to discipline both audience behaviour and theatrical product in the 1820s and 1830s.   GR

COLQUHOUN, Patrick (1745–1820). Born in Dumbarton, Scotland, Colquhoun was a textile merchant and later Lord Provost of Glasgow between 1782 and 1784, during which time he established a chamber of commerce and promoted the region's cotton trade in London and Europe. He moved to London, and was appointed stipendiary magistrate in Middlesex in 1792. A tireless social reformer who was influenced by the ideas of the *Scottish Enlightenment, Cesare Beccaria (1738–94, Italian moral and legal reformer and political economist), and *Bentham, Colquhoun used the print media to advocate change in a number of spheres—poor relief, the *police and administration of the *law [8] in general, *education [17], and the *empire [5] (promoting emigration as a solution to the *population crisis identified by Thomas *Malthus). His *A Treatise on the Police of the Metropolis* (1795), a work of social theory as well as a handbook for change, disseminated *utilitarianism to a wider audience. Equally influential was his work as London agent for West Indian planters, which led to the establishment of a Thames police and increased *class [15] tensions in the London dockland.   GR

COMBE, William (1741–1823), versatile and prolific hack writer. After an early career as a flamboyant man of *fashion he turned to writing for his living, exploiting voracious contemporary interest and his personal knowledge of élite society to produce *satires and scandal pieces on Lord Irnham (whose mistress Combe married in return for a pension which was not forthcoming), the Duchess of *Devonshire, and Lord Lyttleton. Combe worked in a range of genres, usually anonymously and often as a ghost writer. In the late 1780s he began working for *Pitt as a ministerial hack on *The Times*, and in 1809 became associated with the publisher and entrepreneur Rudolph *Ackermann, for whom he worked as a house writer. Combe produced the text for the Tours of Dr Syntax, illustrated by Thomas *Rowlandson, with whom he also collaborated on *The English Dance of Death* (1815–16) and on topographical works such as *Microcosm of London* (1809–10).   GR

Common Pleas, court of, one of the central common law courts which sat in Westminster Hall, was normally a quiet backwater for private suits in the eighteenth and nineteenth centuries, although it achieved brief celebrity for its rulings during the controversy over John Wilkes and the arrest of opposition printers on general warrants [see *Wilkites].   DL

concerts and music societies. Already in the late seventeenth century British musicians had realized the commercial potential of the concert, formerly the private preserve of the aristocracy and of amateur music societies. The first public concerts—professional performances, for a ticket-buying audience— were promoted by John Banister at his Whitefriars music school in 1672. But apart from *Handel's oratorio seasons, London's concerts remained sporadic and insecure until the 1760s, when Mrs Teresa Cornelys incorporated subscription concerts into her fashionable programme at Carlisle House in Soho. These weekly events rivalled the snobbish allure of the Italian opera, their exclusive audience ensured by high prices and careful social screening. Another attraction was the new German symphony: dynamic and melodious, with vivid contrasts of orchestral colour. Mrs Cornelys's two composers, J. C. *Bach and C. F. Abel (1723–87), were at the forefront of these developments, inaugurating one of the most vibrant phases in London's concert life.

Bach and Abel went their own way in 1768, promoting concerts first at Almack's assembly-room and later at a new hall in Hanover Square. Their success prompted competition, notably at the Pantheon, James *Wyatt's splendid basilica of pleasure on Oxford Street. Impresarios vied to promote the latest virtuosi from abroad in innovative programmes, and May was crowded with alluring benefit concerts promoted by individual musicians. Nevertheless, there was much here that we would scarcely recognize. Bach and Abel still addressed the nobility and gentry, imposing social exclusivity by a system of ladies' lists. Their hall seated only 500, the sofas and gilded ornament recalling a large aristocratic drawing-room. Audiences wandered around and talked during concerts, occasionally lauding a favourite with indiscriminate bursts of applause. Programmes contained ten or more items, alternating symphonies and concertos with bravura opera arias and chamber music.

The death of J. C. Bach in 1782 left a vacuum in the instrumental field, but ultimately this was turned to advantage. The next two decades were dominated by the symphonies of another foreigner, Joseph *Haydn: indeed, a concert programme was scarcely complete without one. Haydn sent much new music to the Professional Concert in Hanover Square, and in 1791 he arrived in person, lured by a rebel violinist, Johann Peter Salomon (1745–1815). The star of Salomon's subscription series in 1791–2 and 1794, and of the 1795 Opera Concert, Haydn wrote not only the ever-inventive twelve 'London' symphonies, but also six brilliant quartets for Salomon and some striking vocal music.

A conviction that whilst novelty could be fruitful it could also lead to triviality and sensationalism inspired a return to older music. Handel's *oratorios were still performed at the playhouses during Lent, while the Academy of Ancient Music (founded in 1726) and the patrician Concert of Ancient Music (1776) were devoted to the cause of older music. The latter sought to preserve traditional values by reasserting the learned qualities of older music: their massive Handel Commemoration of 1784, attended by the entire royal family, became a public celebration of national unity, and the following year George III began to attend the Ancient Concerts regularly.

None of these series gave much attention to new British music, which could be heard only in more lowly venues. Occasionally a new oratorio was performed during Lent, but the summer *pleasure gardens provided the best outlet for British composers, who contributed sentimental *ballads, often in Scots idiom, and less refined comic songs. (James *Hook is said to have played an organ concerto at Vauxhall every summer evening for half a century.) During the 1780s a new opportunity emerged, with the transfer of the catch and *glee from the dinner table to the concert platform. In 1792 Samuel *Harrison and Charles Knyvett (1752–1822) founded their Vocal Concert, specifically to promote English songs and glees.

The decade from 1784 was one of intense musical activity in London, with Haydn dominating modern concerts and Handel venerated at gigantic festivals at Westminster Abbey. But the same enthusiasms could not be sustained. The Concert of Ancient Music lumbered on as a kind of court activity (eventually expiring in 1848), but regular symphonic concerts languished soon after Haydn's departure. The emphasis switched to vocal music. The Vocal Concert continued until 1822, when it was succeeded by the British Concerts and other similar organizations. Concerts were also promoted by opera stars, including Mrs *Billington and Angelica *Catalani, whose displays of vocal pyrotechnics became an end in themselves. Programmes increasingly featured opera ensembles and finales, by *Mozart, Rossini, and *Weber (Der Freischütz even reached the Lenten 'oratorio concerts' in 1826). Serious English songs were finally admitted to fashionable concert programmes, and conversely Italian *singers began to court more popular adoration by appearing at the oratorios.

Ever more surprising feats of virtuosity by singers and instrumentalists alike (culminating in *Paganini's arrival in 1831) led to accusations that modern music had become debased by vulgar mechanical display. In 1813 a group of musicians set up the Philharmonic Society with high artistic aims and a determination to exclude from the audience those without genuine musical interests (few of the nobility were among the subscribers). Vocal solos and even concertos were supplanted by a canon of continental symphonic repertoire, based around the works of Haydn, Mozart, and *Beethoven. The Society also commissioned new music from Beethoven himself, and from Cherubini and Spohr, who visited in 1815 and 1820 respectively. Resident composers such as *Clementi, *Ries, and *Potter achieved modest success in a more derivative vein. Eventually the new Romantic orchestral style arrived, urgent, impassioned and picturesque: the supernatural horrors of the Freischütz overture and the elfin evocation of A Midsummer Night's Dream made an immediate impact. *Weber himself came to London in 1826, the young *Mendelssohn in 1829 (beginning a long and influential association), and both were inspired by their British experiences: Weber to his own fairy evocation (Oberon, for Covent Garden), Mendelssohn to his atmospheric Fingal's Cave (The Hebrides), after a visit to Scotland.

There were also social changes in the offing. Aristocratic patronage of public concerts, inconvenient and increasingly open to mixed company, was beginning to wane. Instead the upper classes vied with each other to present opulent salon concerts with the latest divas and *pianists. Some of the *nouveau riche* bourgeoisie outflanked the nobility in displays of extravagance, but other middle-class amateurs were credited with more artistic discernment: at one of their societies *Don Giovanni* and Beethoven's 'Pastoral' Symphony were first performed in London in 1808. Ten years later a major city series was founded, at which amateurs were joined by top professional soloists. Lenten oratorios and even some benefits were increasingly aimed at a diverse and less critical audience: the way was prepared for new structures and a widening of the concert public in the 1830s and 1840s.

Outside London, few towns could sustain fully professional concerts. Bath was a special case, since its temporary clientele could afford and expect London standards, and entrepreneurs like Rauzzini had all the right connections. Much more typical were gentlemen's amateur societies, often based around cathedral musicians with a few professional principals. Sometimes the arrangements were rather haphazard: John Marsh (1752–1828) records travelling to Winchester on a concert night and simply joining in the orchestra. Increasingly, however, such societies were more formally organised: Edinburgh's music society at St Cecilia's Hall was a long-lived and ambitious example, attracting some prominent foreigners on a semi-permanent basis. New industrial towns like Manchester and Birmingham soon followed suit, while at a much more local level we read of societies even in the smaller villages of Norfolk and Cornwall. In Lancashire the handloom weavers known as the 'Larks of Dean' made music with untutored enthusiasm, even making their own instruments—apparently, they were so fond of 'singing and fiddling' that they worked day and night to indulge their hobby at weekends. With *industrialization [14], such freedoms evaporated, but the enthusiasm was channelled into more organized and socially engineered brass bands and choral societies.

SMcV

conduct books. Between 1785 and 1820 many books on female conduct were published, giving advice on the proper behaviour of ladies, and the disciplines for forming the moral character of young women and girls. Also termed 'advice books' and 'courtesy books', they were mostly written by evangelically minded men and women, and were aimed at, and imposed upon, young female readers. They promulgated a conservative ideology of women's subordination and dependence, and presupposed family and religious sanctions which made young girls confessionally open to their parents, especially their mothers. Favourite topics were modesty in dress, avoiding vanity and 'show', and the dangers of unsupervised reading and writing or receiving letters.

63. 'How often have I seen a girl, preparing for a ball, unable to satisfy her own vanity', illustration by Charles Rolls after Richard Westall to the 1822 edition of Hester Chapone's conduct book, *Letters on the Improvement of the Mind.*

Women authors of conduct books frequently apologized for daring to appear in print, and the advice they gave to young ladies, if strictly followed, would deter them from ever writing and publishing.

In Thomas Gisborne's *An Enquiry into the Duties of the Female Sex* (1797), class differences between genteel women and their servants and the labouring poor are elided, not in order to educate poor women through books, but to exert downward pressure on the aspirations of educated women, and to discourage alliances of common interests across the calibrations of rank. Hester Chapone's (1727–1801) *Letters on the Improvement of the Mind* (1773), lectured her niece on the perniciousness of novel reading. Dr James Fordyce concurred: 'There are very few novels that can be read with safety'; a woman who reads unsuitable novels 'must in her soul be a prostitute'. In qualified agreement with these strictures on novel-reading, Mary *Wollstonecraft's *Thoughts on the Education of Daughters: with Reflections on Female Conduct* (1787) appropriates James Burgh's progressive ideas about boys to the upbringing of girls, and her *Vindication of the Rights of Woman* (1792) argues for the moral and intellectual self-discipline of the female reader. It juxtaposes the standard conduct books of Dr Fordyce, Lord Chesterfield, and Dr Gregory's *A Father's Legacy to his Daughters* (1774), with texts of Jean Jacques *Rousseau, showing how the ideology of gender is disseminated through models of the fictional heroine. Wollstonecraft pays tribute to the writings and example of Catharine *Macaulay, and argues for women as professional educators and active role models for other women and girls.   JB

CONSTABLE, John (1776–1837), landscape painter. Widely thought to have represented the quintessential English landscape, Constable claimed a naturalism for his art. Uniquely prolific in painting oil studies of scenery and skies, he remained a semi-detached member of the English school of *landscape painting. Insulated against market forces by private means, Constable alone specialized in landscapes of the valley of the Suffolk Stour, his native countryside.

Constable's father, a wealthy miller and businessman, saw John, the second son, as his successor. But after meeting the connoisseur Sir George Beaumont (1753–1827) in 1795, John Constable developed artistic ambitions, and by 1799 had won permission to study at the *Royal Academy Schools. Despite lofty ambitions Constable progressed slowly, and professional recognition was belated. He became an associate of the Royal Academy in 1819 and a full member only in 1829, despite the award of a gold medal by the French for *The Hay Wain* (1821), exhibited in Paris in 1824.

In May 1802 Constable wrote a letter, in language adapted from Joshua Reynolds's *Discourses*, explaining his decision to profess *painting [27] rather than become a drawing-master in a military academy. Without irony, it set out his agenda—to strive towards producing a landscape of high moral seriousness that could serve as public art—for he understood nature to be inherently moral, and its representation capable of communicating truths more effectively than *history painting. In 1802 he worked to realize this ambition in a number of small, painstaking oil studies, which attempted to catch something of the ever-changing appearances of actual scenes. As his exhibits at the Royal Academy made little impact, he subsequently resorted to *watercolour and graphic media. *Portrait painting, at which he excelled by the 1820s, earned him a little.

Constable was strongly attached to places and people: in 1806 his uncle financed a trip to the Lake District, where he made studies and landscapes which he subsequently exhibited. By 1808 he was sketching in and around East Bergholt, and for the next eight years he concentrated on East Anglian subjects.

In 1809 he fell in love with Maria Bicknell, granddaughter of Dr Rhudde, the East Bergholt rector: to appear an eligible suitor he needed professional success. Consequently he began intensive sketching and painting in the Stour Valley. While others, such as John *Linnell or J. M. W. *Turner, practised oil sketching, Constable was more deeply committed than these to the medium, developing varieties of touches and paint textures to create highly direct studies. His frequent lack of compositional structuring and sharpness of colouring imbued these sketches with a modernity which continued through the sky studies from 1815 to the early 1820s, and through the Brighton sketches, for which he used small palette knives as well as brushes. On these studies were based landscapes like *Dedham Vale, Morning* (1811), a vista composed in the manner of Claude Lorrain presenting the Stour Valley as a modern Arcadia [see *picturesque]. Rhudde's opposition to Constable's courting his granddaughter drove the relationship underground and Constable to more intensive work. By 1814 he was painting exhibition pictures on the Arcadian motif. These landscapes were microcosms of a timeless England, presenting agricultural subjects in a georgic mode, untouched by *enclosure, a place whose virtues were embodied in a countryside of fields, woods, churches, and villages [see *land, 16].

The death of Constable's father in 1816 ensured sufficient financial independence for him to marry. The honeymoon, which the couple spent in Dorset with Constable's friend the Revd John Fisher, introduced a new region to his repertoire. Similarly, taking a house at Hampstead in 1819 (for his tubercular wife's health) inspired pictures of Hampstead Heath, and an unprecedented series of quasi-scientific sky studies.

After moving to London he maintained his working landscapes, but, significantly, shifted to the large scale with *The White Horse* (1819), the first of the 'canal scenes', culminating in *The Leaping Horse* (1825). Exposure to urban culture and to leisure on Hampstead Heath, together with changes in perceptions of nature prompted by studying skies, moved his art away from apparently unmediated reportage; socio-economic changes so evident in London rendered a Georgic view of Suffolk untenable. Believing

64. John Constable, *Study of Cirrus Clouds* (*c*.1822), one of many studies of atmospheric effects informed by his knowledge of contemporary scientific ideas about light.

that artists were visionaries, Constable strove to communicate the sensations of being in nature, thus bypassing contemplation on the moral meanings of landscape subjects. His great *Chain Pier, Brighton* (1827), vilified by some critics, incorporated an alien modernity into a work where natural forces represented a more enduring reality. *Salisbury Cathedral from the Meadows* (1831) incongruously accommodated Suffolk motifs like the cart from *The Hay Wain*, and showed the church steadfast in the vortex of a storm, rendered with wildly handled paint.

Based in London, Constable attempted metropolitan subjects, notably *The Opening of Waterloo Bridge* (1832) which occupied him from 1819–32. However, he exhibited mainly East Anglian scenes. From 1824 his wife began sojourning in Brighton for sea air, and Constable started picturing coastal and downland scenes. After her death in 1828 he kept mainly to London, developing an abstracted and expressionistic style, and creating works which came to act as a retrospect of his career.

With Turner, Constable believed landscape capable of achieving the greatest aspirations of a modern public art. By the 1820s he was recognized as one of the foremost British landscape painters, but later in the decade he came in for harsh criticism. Although active in the Royal Academy and a popular teacher at the life class, his tendency to sarcasm, and bleak estimate of his own and others' achievements, alienated many colleagues. Though deeply conservative, Constable was capable of navigating his way through an unstable modern world where the values embodied in institutions like Salisbury Cathedral were threatened by reform of church and parliament. His work

shows an artist confronting a period of rapid change so that the world which had shaped him came to seem estranging and alien.   MR

constitutionalism was the dominant political language or rhetoric during the reigns of George III and IV. At root it was a language which sought to justify political action by reference to the spirit and 'letter' of the unwritten British Constitution, harking back to a historicism [see *history, 38] of real or mythical libertarian events ranging from Saxon democratic practices to Magna Carta and the *Glorious Revolution of 1688.

Constitutionalism was a contested but shared terrain of politics during this period. Its ideology or rhetoric often comprised an amalgam of intellectual traditions, including civic humanist and 'real Whig' *republican theory, Paineite *natural rights arguments, elements of the customary rights of the freeborn Englishman, and the Saxon historicism of the Norman Yoke. Reference to an unwritten British constitution endowed political action in this period with a degree of flexibility in modes of political legitimation. At certain key moments constitutionalism could be a very powerful means of harnessing political discontent, such as *Wilkite electoral campaigns at Middlesex, the *Treason Trials in 1793–4, the scandals over the Duke of York and the Walcheren Expedition in 1809, and the political agitation after the end of the Napoleonic wars, 1815–20.

Constitutionalism should not, however, be understood as a monolithic language or a fixed and consistent body of theory. As a contested if broadly shared language, it was understood differently by opposing political actors, who struggled to fix and impose their various interpretations amid changing times and circumstances. Thus constitutionalist language needs to be examined with careful attention to context. The use of constitutionalism by radicals, for example, cannot be understood without explicating the rival versions of *Tories, *loyalists, and *Whigs [see *class, 15]. Radicalism and loyalism, for instance, gave different meanings to common constitutionalist terms, such as 'the people', 'patriotism', 'liberty', 'loyalty', 'revolution', 'resistance', 'property', 'labour', 'independence', 'the constitution', 'corruption', 'influence', 'reform', and so on. Most political groups explicitly sought to define these terms in opposition to each other, in order to recruit a public enlarged in size and political consciousness by the Napoleonic wars. Thus constitutionalist ideas could be deployed by radical agitators like Henry *Hunt and William *Cobbett to advocate reform and even *revolution [1]. Conversely this was also the language and terminology of loyalists in popular opposition to Gallic ideas and influences during the French wars.   JF

conversation piece, a genre of group portrait of two or more friends or family members engaged in some sort of informal interaction. Combining characteristics of both Dutch genre painting and the French *commedia dell'arte* scenes of Watteau and his followers, this type of painting was popularized in England in the 1720s and 1730s by William Hogarth (1697–1764), and its most influential practitioners were Arthur Devis (1711–87) and Johann *Zoffany. By the 1760s, conversation pieces had fallen out of fashion, but some of their characteristics remained common in English art until the end of the nineteenth century.

Conversation pieces could be set either indoors or outdoors, exploiting features of the home or estate to project images of leisure, family happiness, and prosperity. Arthur Devis's patrons were mainly merchants or country squires, whom he depicted in homes or on their estates, in detailed but slightly formal conversation pieces. Zoffany animated the genre with crowded canvases of lively figures in more sociable contexts.

In the last decades of the eighteenth century, conversation pieces by Joseph *Wright of Derby, Francis *Wheatley, and others used outdoor settings to reflect fashionable ideas of natural man [see *Rousseauism]. The informality of conversation pieces was also used in portraits of children to stress their childlike qualities. Scenes of children playing became the most common subjects for conversation pieces at the turn of the century.   SW

52, 81   **COOK,** James (1728–79), naval captain and explorer. Cook was born in Yorkshire and joined the navy in 1755. He served in Canada between 1758 and 1762 and subsequently surveyed around Newfoundland. However, he became famous for the three Pacific voyages of 1768–71, 1772–5, and 1776–80. On the first, accompanied by Joseph *Banks, he observed the transit of Venus from Tahiti and

charted the eastern Australian coast. His second voyage aimed to establish whether or not a great southern continent existed, and the third sought a north-west passage. The findings with respect to both the continent and the passage were negative, but the voyages were enormously important culturally for exposing European audiences to the exotic sociality of the Polynesians.

The three voyages dramatically extended European geographical knowledge, but Cook's personal importance lay in the degree to which he came to personify the enlightened and rational face of *exploration [37] and *empire [5], an image sustained since his death in popular biographies, monuments, and visual, literary, and dramatic art. In Australia and New Zealand his role in paving the way for white settlement made him a more conspicuous figure in national histories than the actual colonists. Cook did indeed handle encounters with *indigenous peoples with sensitivity. On the last voyage, however, he became increasingly injudicious, and it was aggressive behaviour, combined with the confounded expectations of Hawaiians who had identified him with the god Lono, that led to his death at Kealakekua Bay on 14 February 1779.   NT

copyright. In the eighteenth century it was customary for authors to sell ownership in a printed text which they had produced to the bookseller who published and sold the work. Copyrights in the work of marketable authors such as *Shakespeare or Samuel Richardson (1689–1761) were highly valued commodities, often traded in auctions or handed on after the death of a bookseller to his successors. The first Copyright Act (1710) protected rights in a published work for a period of twenty-one years in the case of dead writers and fourteen if the writer was still alive. In spite of this measure, London booksellers continued to claim that books had the same property status as goods or land, and that they were therefore entitled to perpetual copyright under common, as opposed to statutory, *law [8]. These claims were challenged in successive years by competitors in Ireland and Scotland, resulting in two significant law cases, *Millar* v. *Taylor* (1769) which ruled, in support of the London trade, that the author had a common law right of perpetual ownership in literary property, and *Donaldson* v. *Becket* (1774) which overturned *Millar* v. *Taylor* to assert the precedence of the 1710 Act.

The struggle over copyright law was therefore a struggle between London and other competing cultural centres in the British Isles and its colonies: while in the short term the 1774 case went against the London trade, the stimulus to printing and publishing which it gave ultimately benefited the capital's position at the hub of the *publishing [21] industry. The debate associated with copyright, while fundamentally a trade dispute between booksellers, was also formative in Romantic ideas of authorship. Samuel *Johnson's claim that a play or poem was not an author's by right of 'occupancy', but conferred a 'metaphysical right, a right . . . of creation, which should from its nature be perpetual', contributed to the increasing emphasis on *originality and *genius as constitutive of both the 'true' authorial voice and literary value. At the same time, the debate was also important in articulating an idea of literature as a group of significant texts to which the public deserved access and which increased in cultural value through circulation. One of the arguments which featured in *Donaldson* v. *Becket* was that intellectual property was not like other forms of property and could not be 'owned' in perpetuity by either the writer or the bookseller. The debate over copyright was therefore formative in the development of the idea of a literary canon and the reading public.

After 1808 the debate was revived when booksellers began lobbying parliament in opposition to the requirement of the 1710 Act that they submit copies of books and other printed material to nine libraries in England and Scotland. In 1814 the deposit requirement was clarified and the period of copyright extended from fourteen to twenty-eight years in the case of a living author. By an Act of 1842 this period was further extended to forty-two years or, if the author lived longer than this, to the duration of his or her life plus seven years. A prominent figure in the debate at this period was William *Wordsworth, who lobbied parliament and wrote poems in support of perpetual copyright, which he claimed was the recognition which society owed to writers of genius (what he described as 'men of real power, who go before their age') as opposed to the 'useful drudges of Literature', the hack writers of the *Grub Street market-place. One of Wordsworth's opponents was Thomas Tegg (1776–1845), the radical publisher of cheap reprints and abridgements, who put his case in terms of a contest between competing rights: those of the public as opposed to the individual writer, the man of literary property. Such rhetoric, with its differentiation between true and false literary value (and true and false men), was inevitably politically inflected by the contexts of post-1815 radicalism.   GR

corn laws, parliamentary legislation designed to protect the profits of English landlords by artificially imposing a minimum price for corn. In the seventeenth and eighteenth centuries provision was made for the protection of British agriculture, chiefly in the form of subsidies in the event of imports falling below a certain price. During the late eighteenth century the price of corn was relatively low. During the Napoleonic *wars [2], however, the interruption to trade, combined with the imposition of a high duty, forced the price up. A collapse of corn prices would inevitably follow peace and, consequently, legislation was introduced into a parliament dominated by landowners in 1815 to secure artificially a high price for corn. It did this by prohibiting all imports of grain if the domestic price fell below 80s. a quarter, a figure higher than the average price of the war year of 1814.

In a time of significant social dislocation attending the parliamentary *enclosures of the early nineteenth century, the corn laws attracted widespread opprobrium by ensuring a high price of bread, the 'No Corn Laws' slogan being widely displayed on banners at *Peterloo. The rigidity of the laws, together with their inability to generate government revenue, resulted in the introduction of a sliding scale of duties in 1828, which was amended in 1842.

While political economists such as *Malthus, who supported the corn laws, and *Ricardo, who opposed them, argued the issue from an economic perspective, radical pamphleteers such as *Spence and *Cobbett invoked the corn laws in arguments against aristocratic landlordism and 'Old Corruption'. Political opposition remained extra-parliamentary and tended to be excluded from the major journals and *newspapers during the 1820s, but it grew significantly during the 1830s as *parliamentary reform in 1832 changed the political landscape and the introduction of the *Poor Law Amendment Act of 1834 ensured the availability of wage labour at lower prices. The Anti-Corn Law League was formed in Manchester in 1838 under the leadership of Richard Cobden (1804–65), a cotton textile manufacturer. Drawing its support from the numerically small but highly vocal and articulate urban middle class, the League launched a concerted campaign for the introduction of free trade, ultimately leading to Robert *Peel's successful conversion of the *Tory party on the question and the abolition of the corn laws in 1846.   ARB

CORNWALL, Barry, pseudonym of the lawyer Bryan Waller Procter (1787–1874). His literary career began in 1815 with his contributions to the *London Gazette*, which drew him into the orbit of London's literary world. He formed important friendships with Leigh *Hunt and Charles *Lamb, and his sociability and hospitality caused him frequent financial difficulties at this time. With George Darley (1795–1846) he became the leader of a new generation of poets in the early 1820s whose *Hellenism and interest in **mythology [36]**, though keen, lacked the depth and ideological bite of *Byron and *Shelley's work in that vein. His ottava rima poem 'Diego de Montilla', for instance, was described by Francis *Jeffrey as a wholesome *Don Juan*. After about 1824 his literary productivity dried up as he devoted himself more to the **law [8]**, although in 1832 his popular *English Songs*, written a decade earlier, were published.   JM

corresponding societies, a term used, along with 'radical societies' and 'Jacobin clubs', to denote some forty *parliamentary reform organizations formed in London and provincial cities in the 1790s, which sought to correspond with other national and international groups on the model of *American Revolutionary societies. A notional appeal to 'membership unlimited' and modest joining fees enabled artisan membership, making them forerunners of democratic politics.

Among the best known was the London Corresponding Society, founded by Thomas *Hardy in January 1792, which at its peak in autumn 1795 numbered 3,000–5,000 members. Of these around 1,500 were activists, organized into divisions which met in *taverns to debate and circulate reading and other propaganda. They also called large open-air meetings to petition for reform. The LCS recruited mainly articulate artisans and small shopkeepers suffering wartime erosion of real wages, as well as marginal or frustrated lesser professionals such as medical men, law clerks, attorneys, publishers, printers, preachers, and journalists. Similarly, the Sheffield Society for Constitutional Information, founded by half-a-dozen mechanics in December 1791, drew most of its 2,500 members from skilled journeymen and small masters in cutlery and steel trade workshops. By contrast, the vigorous Manchester Constitutional Society tended to be a more middle-class affair with its roots in Dissenting congregations. Typically, its first president and leading activist was a cotton manufacturer, Thomas Walker (1749–1817).

Some corresponding societies favoured moderate reform, others espoused more radical principles such as manhood suffrage, annual elections, and equal constituencies. Most were committed to 'moral force' methods such as education and propaganda, but prepared also to contemplate physical force as a last resort. Members were drawn to Thomas *Paine's writings which debunked rule by a monarchical, clerical, and aristocratic élite, attacked government warmongering and taxation, and asserted the rights of citizens to sovereignty based on their *natural rights to life, liberty, property, and the pursuit of happiness. Such ideas were generally joined to an older *constitutionalist idiom and tactical repertoire which appealed to a lost Saxon democracy and asserted English 'freeborn' rights to elect a national convention to petition the King for redress of wrongs. Most of these radicals believed that social and economic inequalities derived from an unjust political system which fostered grinding taxation and poverty, and should thus be remedied by parliamentary reform. IMcC

CORRI family. Domenico Corri (1746–1825), Italian composer, *music publisher, singer, and teacher, established a remarkable musical dynasty with his wife, the soprano and miniature-painter Signorina Bacchelli.

Coming from Rome to conduct the Edinburgh Music Society's concerts in 1771, Domenico Corri lived in Edinburgh for eighteen years, spending a brief period in London during the production of his opera *Alessandro nell'Indie* (King's Theatre, 3 December 1774). Domenico became manager of Edinburgh's Vauxhall *pleasure gardens and Theatre Royal. When the latter failed in 1779 he set up the family music publishing business, which, on moving to London in 1790, he entrusted to his brother Natale Corri (1765–1822), composer, guitarist, singing-master, music publisher, and concert promoter. Domenico established a sister firm in Soho (c.1789–c.1806), and in 1794 was joined by his son-in-law, the pianist J. L. *Dussek, who fled abroad when the business faced financial crisis (c.1800). About the same time Natale was declared bankrupt, following the failure of his Edinburgh concert rooms, though he soon resumed his enterprises.

Domenico's daughter, Sophia Corri (1775–c.1830), had appeared in Edinburgh as a child pianist, but made her London debut as a *singer in 1791. She sang in the London premiere of *Mozart's *Requiem* (1801), at the King's Theatre (1808), and around the country, whilst continuing to perform on piano and harp. Her brother Philip Corri (c.1784–1832), composer, singer, teacher, and a founding member of London's Philharmonic Society, emigrated to America (1817), and Haydn Corri (1785–1860) moved to Dublin in 1821.

Montague Corri (c.1784–1849) ran the London business (1804–7) and composed or arranged scores for Astley's, the Surrey, and the Cobourg theatres. Natale engaged him to manage the Edinburgh Pantheon (1817), from where he moved to a series of theatrical posts around the country. Natale's daughter Frances Corri (1795 or 1801–c.1833), a mezzo-soprano, studied in London with John *Braham and Angelica *Catalani, toured the Continent with the latter (1815–16), and sang at the King's Theatre (1818–21). With her sister and father, she left for Europe in 1821. RC

COTTLE, Joseph (1770–1853), Bristol bookseller, publisher, author, and poet. Cottle's various enterprises reflect the increasing contribution to British culture made by an enlightened provincial booktrade [see *publishing, 21].

Remembered as the provincial publisher and patron of young radical poets *Coleridge, *Southey, and *Wordsworth in the mid- to late 1790s, Cottle was a prolific poet in his own right with an assured if ambiguous contemporary reputation. Following the publication of *Malvern Hills* and his retirement from bookselling, both in 1798, when he published Wordsworth's and Coleridge's *Lyrical Ballads*, he produced a handful of *epic poems: *Alfred* and *John the Baptist* (both 1801), *The Fall of Cambria* (1809), and *Messiah* (1815). According to Southey, a 'habitual preparation for an enduring inheritance' prompted Cottle's controversial *Early Recollections, Chiefly Relating to Samuel Taylor Coleridge* of 1837 (revised and expanded to become *Reminiscences of Samuel Taylor Coleridge and Robert Southey* in 1847). Though eulogistic on Southey, the work failed to do justice to Coleridge, treating his opium addiction without sympathy or understanding. More foolish than malicious, Cottle's misdirected moralizing and sanctimony often obscures the book's virtues—its liveliness and evocativeness—as an essay in *biography.

For most of Cottle's endeavours the epithet 'well-meaning' seems especially appropriate. While the biographies exaggerated his entrepreneurial role, his encouragement of talent was genuine and generous: Southey's *Joan of Arc* (1796) and Coleridge's *Watchman* (1796) would never have appeared without his assistance. Considered alongside such ventures as his and Southey's edition of Thomas *Chatterton in 1803, it confirms the social and geographical decentralization of literary culture in Britain in the later eighteenth century. WC

COWLEY, Hannah (1743–1809), dramatist and poet. Born Hannah Parkhouse in Tiverton, Devon, the daughter of a bookseller who encouraged her literary aspirations, she achieved fame with her first comedy, *The Runaway* (1776), performed at Drury Lane under the tutelage of David Garrick (1717–79). She was adept at theatrically effective plotting and dialogue and the creation of dynamic and witty comic heroines, revealing the influence of earlier woman dramatists Aphra Behn and Susannah Centlevre. Cowley worked in a range of dramatic genres, including comedies (*The Belle's Stratagem*, 1780, *A Bold Stroke for a Husband*, 1783, and *A School for Greybeards*, 1786); farce (the highly successful *Who's the Dupe?*, 1779); and tragedy (*Albina*, 1779, and *The Fate of Sparta*, 1788). The publication of *Albina* was accompanied by a paper war with R. B. *Sheridan and Hannah *More, whom Cowley accused of plagiarizing *Albina* in her 1779 tragedy *The Fatal Falsehood*.

Keeping her distance from day-to-day engagement with the *theatre [24] in order to preserve a reputation as a respectable dramatist, Cowley learnt how to use print culture to establish an identity as a professional woman writer (who after the departure of her husband for India in 1783 was responsible for the family income). She later withdrew from active involvement in metropolitan cultural life and returned to Devon. In 1780 she published a metrical tale, *The Maid of Arragon*, and became involved in the literary circle known as the *Della Cruscans, publishing poems of *sensibility [11] in the *World* newspaper (collected as *Poetry* by Anna Matilda in 1788) and establishing a sentimental correspondence with Robert *Merry. She was one of the targets of William *Gifford's satirical assault on Della Cruscanism. In the 1790s she became disaffected with the increasing emphasis on spectacle in the theatre and the decline in the popularity of the comedy of manners which had been her forte, renouncing the stage in the preface to her comedy, *The Town Before You* (1795). In 1801 she produced an *epic poem, *The Siege of Acre*, chronicling the resistance of the British forces under Sir Sidney Smith against Napoleon. It is the only poetic response to the *wars [2] with France in this period to take the epic form. Her collected *Works* appeared in 1813.   GR

COWPER, William (1731–1800), poet, memoirist, leading devotional poet of the *Evangelical revival, who as the author of the first *autobiographical narrative poem, *The Task* (1785), was a significant influence on *Wordsworth and *Coleridge, and whose confessional *poetry [29] elaborates a version of masculine *sensibility [11] as victimhood with an often startling, masochistic, and violent corporeality.

Cowper was the eldest son of a clergyman. His mother, Anne Donne, who died when he was 6, is celebrated in the elegiac 'On the Receipt of My Mother's Picture' (*c*.1790, pub. 1798). He was educated at Dr Putnam's private school in Bedfordshire before moving to the more enlightened Westminster, where the children were merely shamed rather than flogged for misbehaviour.

After being trained for the law and taking chambers in the Middle Temple in 1752, Cowper was overcome by depression. Moving to Southampton for a change of scene, he converted to Evangelicalism after an intense conversion experience. This is recounted in his posthumously published *Memoir* (*c*.1767, pub. 1816), a conversion narrative of unusual pathos, which scandalized contemporaries for its frank account of *madness and repeated suicide attempts. Despite this conversion, Cowper was dogged by depression for the rest of his life, fuelled by the belief—elaborated in his final poem *The Castaway* (1799)—that he was an outcast of salvation.

After three suicide attempts from 1763, and a period at St Albans asylum, he moved to Huntingdon in 1765. Here he came under the influence of John Newton (1725–1807), the reformed slaver and Evangelical curate, with whom he wrote *Olney Hymns* (1779), published by Joseph *Johnson.

John Gilpin (1782), a comic poem which quickly became a national favourite, was followed by his best-known and most popular poem, *The Task*, a blank verse *epic modelled on *Milton's *Paradise Lost*, hailed as a masterpiece by reviewers. Incorporating a more muted and less sententious voice of moral satire than that given free rein in *The Progress of Error* (1782), *The Task* portrays Cowper's retreat from the world using the figure of the 'stricken deer'; his recovery from mental distress; conversion to Evangelicalism; and search for rural retirement and companionship.

In *Tirocinium* (1785), which drew on memories of the horrors inflicted at Dr Putnam's, Cowper offers a critique of institutional *education [17], and recommends to the middling classes private education at home from the (boy) child's father or a clergyman.

A self-described 'Old Whig', who combined vaguely *republican sympathies with a Burkean reverence for the patrilineal mystique of *monarchy, Cowper composed a number of Georgic allegories. *Yardley Oak* (1804), for example, adapts the Augustan tropes of decline and decay to the current Georgian house and its succession crises. 'Annus Memorabilis, 1789' offers a tactful, fellow-sufferer's celebration of the recovery of George III from his bout of insanity (later diagnosed as porphyria) of 1788–9. From the late 1780s, when discussion over *slavery [6] came to a head, Cowper wrote a number of public anti-slavery poems: 'Pity for Poor Africans' (1788); 'The Morning Dream' (1788); 'The Negro's Complaint' (1789); and a 1792 *sonnet addressed to William *Wilberforce.

Celebrated by Coleridge as 'one of the first to combine natural thoughts with natural diction', Cowper offered an early version of the conversational style which Coleridge and Wordsworth later developed. In 1790, he rejected an offer to be nominated poet laureate. Despite such celebration and popularity, however, Cowper's position in a male *lyric tradition has always been ambivalent and fraught with the stigma of effeminacy. This is manifest, for example, in the mixed responses to his work by Francis *Jeffrey, who applauded his 'feminine gentleness, and delicacy of nature', and his 'minute and correct painting of home scenes and private feelings', and William *Hazlitt, who detected a 'sickly sensibility' and 'an effeminacy about him, which shrinks from and repels common and hearty sympathy'.

The *Memoir*'s primary autobiographical trope of the bullied schoolboy, weeping in 'melancholy recollection' of sufferings at the hands of strong tormentors, offers a trope of Cowper's posthumous reputation as the weak poet, falling short of sublimity through gushing sentimental excess. Indeed, it is a French writer, Sainte-Beuve, who offers probably the most sympathetic Romantic reception of Cowper on this score. In *Vie, Poésies et Pensées de Joseph Delorme* (1829), Sainte-Beuve uses Cowper's 'poetry of domesticity' and the biographical Cowper as a model of his own poetry of 'intimacy' and of the melancholy poet-hero who is the subject of this fictional posthumous editorial memoir and autobiography. And in *William Cowper, ou de la poésie domestique* (1854), Sainte-Beuve defends Cowper from the slights of the more 'bold and tempestuous' British Romantics, such as *Byron, who thought him 'coddled'. Instead, Sainte-Beuve offers a whimsical formulation of the enigma of Cowper's celibacy and poetry of *domesticity [13]: 'Cowper is the poet of the family, although he has never been a husband or a father'.

This issue of Cowper's 'effeminacy' has been complicated by posthumous rumours first put into circulation in 1834, by Robert *Southey, during the preparation of his *Life of Cowper* (1835-7), which suggest that Cowper may have suffered from a genital malformation. He is posthumously rumoured to have referred to himself as an androgyne and an hermaphrodite, or to have suffered from a genital disorder known as spadism. Some such condition could account for the two occasions on which he broke off marriage engagements, and for his tormented self-figuring in the *Memoir* as a barren fig-tree.

Cowper's female readers did not generally manifest the ambivalence that marks his reception by some contemporary male readers. Indeed, his work often undergoes further effeminizing in the process of quotation and allusion at the hands of female writers, such as Charlotte *Smith, who dedicated *The Emigrants* (1793) to Cowper. Throughout the correspondence and novels of Jane *Austen, especially, Cowper occupies pride of place in an extremely selective, polemically British intertextual canon. Austen's reworking of Cowper's Georgic within her own Napoleonic Georgic of the country-house novel also situates him within a burgeoning heritage and domestic *tourism industry. This is further manifested in a genre of topographic Cowperiana of works such as *Cowper Illustrated by a Series of Views in or near the Park of Weston-Underwood* (1803); *The Rural Walks of Cowper* (1822); *Cowper's Rose-Bushes* (1829) and Jane Taylor's (1783-1824) 'Lines On Visiting Cowper's Garden and Summerhouse'.

After the poet's death, his friend William *Hayley published a *Life* (1803-6), together with other works of Cowper's such as *Adelphi* (1802), a conversion narrative and recollection of the last illness of Cowper's brother.   CT

CRABBE, George (1754–1832). The leading anti-Romantic poet of the period, Crabbe saw himself as working in the realist tradition of Chaucer and *Shakespeare. He was widely read in his day, but his true stature has been obscured by the subsequent prestige of writers such as *Wordsworth and *Coleridge.

His father, a minor customs official, attempted on limited resources to educate Crabbe for a professional career. Inadequate medical apprenticeships were followed by labouring on the quays at Aldeburgh, Suffolk, and unsuccessful practice as an apothecary and surgeon. *Inebriety* (1775), in the style of Pope, was published anonymously at Ipswich. Crabbe improved his Latin to read *botanical books and *poetry [29]. In 1780 he moved to London to make a career as a poet. He associated with mathematicians and scientists, and witnessed the *Gordon riots. Rejected by publishers and aristocratic patrons, he recorded his poverty and desperation in a 'Poet's Journal' addressed to his future wife, Sarah Elmy. In 1781, Edmund *Burke befriended him and helped persuade James Dodsley to publish *The Library* (1781) and *The Village* (1783).

Burke's influence also enabled Crabbe to embark on a career in the church. He was curate at Aldeburgh (1781-2), domestic chaplain to the Duke of Rutland at Belvoir Castle (1782-4), and curate or vicar of various rural parishes in Leicestershire and Suffolk (1784-1814). From 1814 he was rector of the expanding industrial centre of Trowbridge, in Wiltshire, a living in the gift of the Duke of Rutland.

Crabbe's career had two distinct phases. His brief eighteenth-century career reached its climax with the bitter attack on *pastoral idealizations of rural poverty in book I of *The Village*. His nineteenth-century literary career, beginning with *Poems* (1807), was longer, more prolific, and more successful, producing two overlapping bodies of remarkable and original work. 'The Parish Register' (published in *Poems*) and *The Borough* (1810) are studies of provincial communities. 'The Parish Register' anxiously explores the relation between poverty and sexuality in a series of portraits of individuals, couples, and social groups. *The Borough, a Poem in Twenty-Four Letters* describes the life of a contemporary seaport. An imaginary place, it is nevertheless closely based on Crabbe's knowledge of a number of Suffolk towns and villages. As well as descriptions of activities and institutions, the poem contains some life stories of individuals (including 'Ellen Orford' and 'Peter Grimes').

The life story was subsequently his staple, in the great *Tales* (1812), *Tales of the Hall* (1819), and *Posthumous Tales* (1834). *Tales* was Crabbe's most popular volume in his lifetime; its success enabled him to sell his next volume, and his existing *copyrights, to the publisher John Murray for £3000. The individual tales are linked by similarities and contrasts, and by their Shakespearean epigraphs, but are otherwise independent. The Preface—Crabbe's major statement of intention as a poet—argues that his own talents and contemporary social reality preclude the neat integration of tales into a story about their tellers achieved by Boccaccio or Chaucer. *Tales of the Hall*, which attempts such an integration, is sometimes thought contrived and prolix, though it contains a masterpiece ('Delay Has Danger').

Crabbe experimented with other kinds of writing, much of which does not survive. He wrote and destroyed three novels and a treatise on botanical classification in English. His medically prescribed use of opium and his wife's mental disorder are probable influences on a group of poems, distinct from his other work in form and feeling, that dramatize *madness and hallucination. Of these only 'Sir Eustace Grey', a *closet drama set in a *madhouse, was published in his lifetime (in *Poems*).

Crabbe was not part of a literary movement. For twenty-two years in middle life he worked principally as a village clergyman, publishing some botanical studies but no poetry. He normally used the predominant verse form of the previous century, the heroic couplet. However, his poetry was both popular and fully engaged with contemporary social and cultural issues.

He shared his Romantic contemporaries' interest in social isolation and the workings of the *imagination. But he tried, sometimes with difficulty, to maintain a critical distance from these things, believing that they were usually sources of delusion rather than of special insight. He was a subtle rhymer, and had close affinities in his own time with novelists, especially William *Godwin, Jane *Austen, and Walter *Scott. *Mansfield Park* (1814) and *The Heart of Midlothian* (1819) define their own purposes partly through allusions to Crabbe. 'The Parish Register' is a struggle between identifiable contemporary attitudes to poverty (Burke and *Malthus on the one hand, Godwin and *Fox on the other). The protagonists of his verse tales are frequently people like himself and, no doubt, like many of his readers: people placed—often precariously—in Crabbe's own words 'between the humble and the great'. Among them are struggling tradesmen and professionals, freethinking intellectuals and would-be geniuses, religious Dissenters, apprentices, and women educated above their station. Crabbe writes the life stories of such people with laconic passion. He explores their attempts—which are normally, but not always, fruitless—to establish secure positions within or outside the bonds of patronage and dependence.

Crabbe claimed that his characters were based on actual individuals. John *Thelwall is a source for Hammond in 'The Dumb Orators' (1812), James *Lackington for John Dighton in 'The Convert' (1812), and Crabbe's own brother William for Allen Booth in 'The Parting Hour' (1812). However, Crabbe is subtly aware of the ways in which storytelling can influence as well as reflect reality. His tales are full of people whose lives are altered by the stories they tell to one another.   GE

CRAMER, Johann (John) Baptist (1771–1858), pianist, composer, publisher, and leading member of the London Pianoforte School. Eldest son of the *violinist Wilhelm Cramer (1745–99), he came to London at the age of 3 and was subsequently taught the piano by *Clementi. During the 1780s he frequently appeared as a prodigy at his father's concerts, including the Professional Concert series. From 1788 to 1791 he toured the Continent, returning to London as one of the principal virtuosi of his day. Cramer was particularly renowned for his interpretation of *Mozart's concertos. In his own music he combined an elegant and limpid expression derived from Mozart with the most modern pianism, exploring new virtuosic figurations and evocative sonorities on the instrument. His earlier works include large-scale concertos and sonatas, not strikingly original but worthy of revival. Increasingly drawn to writing for the amateur market, his name subsequently became a byword for innumerable fantasies and rondos on popular airs.

Cramer was a well-known teacher, and his didactic *Studio per il pianoforte* (recommended by *Beethoven) has lasted better than his own music. Cramer's style of legato melodic playing was particularly forward-looking. *Moscheles described his 'silk-smooth fingers' gliding across the keyboard in emulation of the human voice. Like his teacher, Cramer went into *music publishing, and the firm that bore his name continues to this day.   SMcV

CRISTALL, Ann Batten (1768/9?–after 1816), poet, born in Cornwall, later based in Rotherhithe and Blackheath, London. Her brother was the artist Joshua Cristall (1767–1847), founding member of the Society of Painters in Water-Colours [see *watercolour painting]. A. B. Cristall published *Poetical Sketches* (1795) with Joseph *Johnson, and associated with his circle which included Mary *Wollstonecraft. She supported herself through teaching.   GR

CROTCH, William (1775–1847), composer, organist, theorist, teacher, and painter. The son of a Norwich master carpenter, Crotch was perhaps the most precocious child prodigy in the history of *music [26]. His exceptional musical gifts, apparent by the time he was 18 months old, were exploited by his mother in a series of tours which began in 1778 and included Cambridge and London, where he played before George III in January 1779.

Crotch was appointed organist at Christ Church, Oxford, at the age of 15 in 1790, and professor of music at Oxford at the age of 21 in 1797. Between 1800 and 1804 he delivered a course of lectures on music at the university, revised versions of which were subsequently given at the Royal Institution and elsewhere in London. In late 1805 he left Oxford and moved to London, where he became well known as a lecturer, teacher, and scholar, and as an occasional performer. He was a member of the Philharmonic Society, 1814–19 and 1828–32, and was from 1822 to 1832 the first principal of the Royal Academy of Music. He was an associate of Samuel *Wesley and Benjamin Jacob (1778–1829) in the English *Bach movement.

Despite the fame of his oratorio *Palestine* (1812), described by one writer as 'the first even moderately successful oratorio composed in England since

Handel's day', Crotch's significance lies mostly in his lectures on music, his theoretical writings, and the central role he played in London musical affairs in the early nineteenth century.　　　　PO

CROUCH, Anna Maria (1763–1805), English soprano and actress. Crouch made her debut as Mandane in Arne's *Artaxerxes* in 1780, whilst still articled to Thomas *Linley. She appeared regularly at Drury Lane until her retirement in 1801, touring Ireland and the provinces during the summer. Crouch's voice lacked power but was praised for its 'delicacy and melting softness'. She created several of Stephen *Storace's heroines, including the title-role of *Lodoiska* (1794).

In 1785 Crouch married a naval lieutenant, but moved in with the tenor Michael *Kelly shortly after they met in 1787, often appearing with him in *concerts, *oratorios, and stage works.　　　　RC

12, 29, 33,
46, 68

CRUIKSHANK, George (1792–1878), engraver, etcher, illustrator, and satiric printmaker. One of the greatest print *satirists and illustrators of the early nineteenth century, the 'golden age' of English **print [22]** satire, Cruikshank reworked his inheritance from his precursor, James *Gillray, to develop print satire in the areas of wood-engraving and etching in the second decade of the nineteenth century.

Born in London, the son of Scottish artisan parents, Cruikshank rightly claimed to be 'cradled in caricature'. Trained as a *watercolourist, Cruikshank's father, Isaac, gained commissions after moving to London from Scotland, for caricatures, song heads, theatrical portraits, and illustrations to chapbooks. Cruikshank's mother also worked in the home studio, colouring and lettering the prints her husband produced. It was here that George gained his first experience as a colourist.

Despite a haphazard formal education, and a preference for street life over school, Cruikshank was an avid reader. He devoured the staple classics of *children's literature, particularly *Robinson Crusoe* (which he illustrated in 1830), as well as the *fairy tales first told to him by the family maids. In 1804 George's older brother, Robert, a *volunteer in the Napoleonic wars, was lost at sea in the St Helena campaign. George then became his father's chief assistant in the studio. Within a few years George was creating designs for craftsmen to turn into wood-engravings, before producing his own etchings and wood-engravings.

Cruikshank matured to become the leading print satirist in England from about 1811 to 1813, just when James Gillray became hopelessly insane. After the latter's death in 1815 Cruikshank not only purchased Gillray's work table but took on his mantle in terms of the stylistic complexity and moral nihilism of Gillray's etchings. The examples of details, symbols, and whole compositional structures reworked from Gillray's prints are legion. Nonetheless, Cruikshank developed his own style, narratively less complicated but graphically bolder than that of his precursor.

Cruikshank's attitude as a satirist is as self-contradictory as that of Gillray. He was a satiric mercenary who, throughout his early career, would produce work for whoever paid him. He became renowned for his radical satires, yet accepted government payments in return for a pledge to stop portraying the Prince Regent in any immoral context—a bind for which he found increasingly ingenious solutions.

Perhaps it was only in his anti-Gallicism that Cruikshank's attitudes were entirely consistent. He reworked Gillray's vision of the French republic as a state of chaos, and of *Napoleon as a crazed child, in attacks which produced some of the most remarkable images of the Napoleonic era. He could invoke the stiff narrative techniques of earlier print satire, as in *The Fox and the Goose* (1815), which uses group animalization within a framework that is diagrammatic, cartographic, and fabular, whilst simultaneously producing a print such as *A Radical Reformer or a Neck or Nothing Man* (1819), which combines caricature with abstract personification. This is one of the last great evocations of the image of the guillotine in English print satire. It came out in September 1819, a month after the massacre of *Peterloo, and uses the old *loyalist device of identifying radicalism with the excesses of the Terror. Here the guillotine is metamorphosed into a devouring creature, with a womblike space for the victim's head that holds a death's head grinning inside it, while blood runs in a menstrual stream between the creature's legs.

While Cruikshank continued to use the etching medium between the period 1813 and 1822, he increasingly turned to the mass-produced wood-engraving. Arguably his most influential political satires were those he made for the illustrated pamphlets of the radical publisher William *Hone from 1816 to 1822. These not only took the nation by storm, selling in hundreds of thousands of copies, but also pointed the way for the future development of illustrated journalism. His work for Hone showed the refinement of which the mass-produced wood-engraving was capable, and the richness with which it could extend the tradition of the satiric etching. Despite Thomas *Bewick's remarkable achievements with the wood-engraving in Newcastle, its use as a commercial print form in London was still relatively unrefined by 1820. Cruikshank's illustrations to pamphlets such as *The Political House that Jack Built* (1819) and *The Queen's Matrimonial Ladder* (1820) demonstrate a technical mastery of the medium that is unique for a popular pamphlet of this period. Cruikshank maintained the narrative directness of the crude woodcuts which traditionally adorned chapbooks and children's books yet introduced descriptive subtleties, particularly in the area of facial caricature, which relied on the capability of end-grain engraving to sustain detail.

With the demise of the single-sheet satiric etching in the 1820s and the rise of Victorian illustrated journalism, the supremely adaptable Cruikshank turned to book and periodical illustration and went on to become a leading Victorian illustrator. His first major success in this field came in 1823, with the tiny etched vignettes for the first English translation of *German Popular Stories* by the Brothers Grimm. He developed a style combining melodramatic violence and gentle humour, which made him an apt illustrator for Charles *Dickens's early works *Sketches by Boz* (1836) and *Oliver Twist* (1836). In succeeding decades, however, Cruikshank lost his ribald edge in favour of Victorian whimsy.   MW

CUBITT, Thomas (1788–1855). A carpenter by trade, Cubitt was the pre-eminent builder and developer of late Georgian London. He introduced innovative business methods by concentrating all trades under one roof as wage labour rather than contracting out. Instead of waiting for business to come to him, he launched his own development schemes, beginning with Highbury, Stoke Newington, and Barnsbury. He was responsible for the development of the Bloomsbury area in the 1820s and exploited John *Nash's building of Buckingham Palace to establish the fashionable estates of Belgravia and Pimlico. Cubitt's developments included modern infrastructure such as sewerage and lighting, and were renowned for their use of quality materials and attention to detail.   GR

CUMBERLAND, Richard (1732–1811), prolific dramatist and writer. The son of a cleric, who through *Whig connections was eventually appointed to an Irish bishopric, Cumberland had ambitions for a political career but achieved greater success in the *theatre [24] as a writer, mainly of comedies. He first gained notice with his comedy *The Brothers* (1769). Two years later the hit of the London season was his *The West Indian*, a sentimental comedy which sympathetically represents the planter scions of the West Indies slave trade. A self-conscious man of letters who cultivated the circles of *Johnson and *Reynolds, Cumberland had a finely developed sense of his own importance: he was famously satirized in R. B. *Sheridan's *The Critic* (1779) as the tellingly named Sir Fretful Plagiary. Cumberland's attempt at a historical tragedy allegorizing contemporary politics, *The Battle of Hastings* (1778), was also a comic target in *The Critic*. However, Cumberland's plays continued to be frequently performed and widely read, as suggested by numerous reprints of his works. His *The Jew* (1794), sub-

titled in some editions the 'Benevolent Hebrew', and *The Wheel of Fortune* (1794), which provided a famous role for John Philip *Kemble as the moody Penruddock, show how he could adapt to changing tastes for the *Gothic and for *sensibility [11]. Apart from his plays, he produced two novels, *Arundel* (1789) and *Henry* (1795), a periodical, the *Observer* (1785), and his 1807 *Memoirs*.   GR

CUNNINGHAM, Allan (1784–1842), Scots writer of dialect *ballads and poems, historian, biographer, and critic. Cunningham was educated at a dame school and as an apprentice stonemason to his brother, James (b. 1765). This training was to provide him with employment after an initial attempt, with the assistance of Eugenius Roche (1786–1829) and William Jerdan (1782–1869), to establish himself as a journalist in London, where he lived from April 1810. He worked as foreman and secretary to the *sculptor Sir Francis Chantrey (1781–1841) from 1814 until 1841, a mutually advantageous partnership which provided Cunningham with a steady income and Chantrey with the writer's promotional skills, evident in articles in *Blackwood's Magazine* and the *Quarterly Review*. Cunningham also helped Chantrey through shrewd business acumen.

Cunningham's ambition was literary renown and his output was prolific. His poems were first published in *Literary Recreations* (1807) under the *Ossianic pseudonym of 'Hidallan', followed by *Songs, Chiefly in the Rural Dialect of Scotland* (1813). Further songs and poems were published which show his indebtedness to Robert *Burns, whom he had met when living in Dalswinton. Cunningham was a mourner at Burns's funeral and in 1834 published an eight-volume edition of the poet's work. He was encouraged by James *Hogg and Walter *Scott, and his circle of acquaintance also included Joanna *Baillie. Cunningham wrote *romances as well, but arguably his most influential work was as a historian of the British school, with his seminal six-volume *Lives of the Most Eminent British Painters, Sculptors and Architects* appearing between 1829 and 1833 and a biography of David *Wilkie published posthumously.   AWY

D

DACRE, Charlotte (c.1772–c.1825), later Byrne, pseud. 'Rosa Matilda', widely published *Gothic novelist, journalist, poet, and songwriter. Charlotte was daughter of the notorious money-broker Jonathan 'Jew' *King (Jacob Rey) and his first wife, Deborah Lara, and was sister of Sophia King, later Fortnum, who also became a Gothic novelist, mostly with the highly commercial *Minerva Press. The two sisters seem to have been well educated and travelled, probably imbibing much of their early literary inspiration from the ardently sentimental and libertarian *Della Cruscan poetic circles around the radical Robert *Merry, a close friend of their father. In 1798, the two sisters published a collection of poems, *Trifles from Helicon*, which thanked their father for his commitment to their education and defended him against a public charge of sexual violence brought by two prostitutes, probably at the instigation of the government.

Adopting the pseudonym 'Rosa Matilda' in accordance with Della Cruscan practice, Charlotte wrote occasionally for the *Morning Herald* during the 1790s, and published another collection of poems, *Hours of Solitude*, in 1805. In the same year she published her first Gothic novel, *The Confessions of the Nun of St Omer*. Strongly indebted to the style of Matthew 'Monk' *Lewis and the ideas of Mary *Wollstonecraft, it was well received at the time, and has attracted praise from modern critics as an expression of the female Gothic *sublime. The following year she published her best-known and erotically charged Gothic novel, *Zofloya; or The Moor*. This imitated but inverted Lewis's *The Monk* (1795) from a female perspective, and it strongly influenced Percy *Shelley's juvenile attempt at Gothic writing, *Zastrozzi* (1810). *Zofloya* also appeared in chapbook form as the *Daemon of Venice* (1810), a testimony to Charlotte's contemporary popularity; she was also becoming known as a composer of *ballads.

Although the early writings of both Charlotte and Sophia King show the liberal and radical influences of their upbringing, both began to move towards conservative and even counter-revolutionary positions during the mid-1800s. As early as 1798 Sophia had quarrelled with her friend and sometime literary mentor William *Godwin over what he saw as a hostile portrait of himself and his ideas in her *Waldorf, or the Dangers of Philosophy*. Charlotte's marriage around 1815 to Nicholas Byrne, proprietor and editor of the then government-funded *Morning Post*, placed her squarely in the ministerial and anti-radical camp. Disillusionment that her father had abandoned her Jewish mother to live with the rakish Lady Lanesborough might also have contributed to Charlotte's repudiation of radical *Enlightenment [32] ideas and circles; and there are hostile portraits resembling 'Jew' King and his mistress in several of Charlotte's *novels [31].

By the early *Regency years 'Rosa Matilda' had become firmly identified through her writings in the *Morning Post* with attacks on *Whigs and radicals such as Francis *Burdett and William *Cobbett, with anti-Napoleon scurrility, and with praise of the Prince Regent. Even before producing her rhapsodic tribute—accompanied by musical lyrics—*George the Fourth* (1822), she had attracted *Byron's venom in *English Bards and Scotch Reviewers* (1809) as an archetypal ministerial hack, snivelling Matilda.

IMcC

DALTON, John (1766–1844), *chemist and meteorologist, whose scientific reputation is attributed to the development of his laws of proportion, expansion, and constitution of atmospheric gases, and to his 'atomic weight' theory which calculated fixed weights to the ultimate particles of matter.

Dalton's education in natural philosophical pursuits embraced the *Evangelical and *philanthropic activities of the *Quaker community in which he was raised. At 15 he moved from Cumberland to assist his brother in the administration of a school in Kendal. In 1785, when Dalton turned 19, he became co-principal with his brother and commenced his first *lectures in **natural philosophy [34]**, promoting subjects such as mechanics, optics, and astronomy. It was also in Kendal that Dalton initiated his lifelong pursuit of meteorology under the encouragement of his mentor, the blind scientific writer John Gough (1757–1825).

In 1793 Dalton was appointed professor of mathematics and natural philosophy at New College in Manchester. That same year saw the publication of his *Meteorological Observations and Essays*. Along with standard but meticulous data on daily temperatures, barometric pressure, and rainfall were his earliest theoretical statements regarding the absorption of water vapour in specific measures of air. His theory was that aqueous and atmospheric gases were not attracted by chemical affinity, which would thus result in chemical combination. Rather, Dalton maintained a mechanical view that water vapour as an independent entity mixed, or 'diffused', in air at quantities determined by temperature. Investigations surrounding the principles of evaporation were pursued throughout the next decade by Dalton. The sounding-board for his developing ideas was the Manchester Literary and Philosophical Society, to which he was elected in 1794, one year after moving to Manchester [see *literary and philosophical societies].

Major socio-economic changes that took place with the mechanization of the textile industry and the development of the *factory system make Manchester an important context for scientific development during the first few decades of the nineteenth century. The foundation of the 'Lit and Phil' in 1781 forged a variety of allegiances between scientific organization and practice with technical and industrial, as well as social concerns. Diverse social applications of scientific knowledge which shared patronage and pedagogical resources in a local context were not peculiar to Dalton's Manchester. Indeed, his involvement in the Society and its sponsorship of publications in the *Manchester Memoirs* occasioned research links between individuals across Britain.

Dalton's publications which developed his theory of water vapour included papers on steam pressure, which provided tables for changing evaporation rates at varying temperatures, and papers on the constitution of mixed gases, which elucidated his theory that gases remained independent entities and were reducible to vaporous particles. In these themes Dalton was reaffirming his premise that atmospheric gases were not chemically combined, a position which met with early criticism from chemists such as Humphry *Davy and Thomas Thomson (1773–1852). In response, Dalton directed his efforts to demonstrating that the proportion of gases in the atmosphere was based on the calculated weight of their ultimate particles, culminating in his *New System of Chemical Philosophy* (parts I and II, 1808–10; vol. II, 1827). Whilst Dalton's theories were rejected because of ontological objections, his heuristic concepts of the 'atom' and his reliance on quantifiable and measurable models which blurred analytical boundaries between physics and chemistry provided major contributions to science. **BPD**

DAMER, Anne Seymour (1748–1828), sculptor and novelist. Working at a time when few women were able to practice *sculpture professionally, Damer was recognized by contemporaries as an 'amateur' whose seriousness of purpose differentiated her from women practising 'accomplishment' art.

The only child of Field Marshal Henry Seymour (1717–97) and Caroline Campbell, Countess of Ailesbury, Damer was cared for by her godfather, Horace *Walpole, during her parents' sojourns abroad, and he promoted her interest in sculpture. As his executrix and residuary legatee, she lived at Strawberry Hill from 1797 until 1811. Her education enabled her to become proficient in Latin, Greek, French, Portuguese, and Italian. David *Hume, her father's secretary, is reputed to have first challenged her to attempt sculpture, and subsequently John Bacon (1740–99) and Guiseppe Ceracchi (1751–1801) were employed to instruct her in modelling and carving, while William Cruikshank (1745–1800) taught her anatomy.

Damer moved in the highest circles of society, but following marriage in 1767 she spent protracted periods away from her husband, including a *Grand Tour of the Continent in 1772 and a winter stay in Paris in 1774–5. Their separations were followed by his suicide in 1776, leaving her childless and with

debts of £70,000. However, her widow's jointure allowed her financial and personal freedom. She devoted herself to sculpture and, in a lesser degree, to literature and *theatre [24], while still continuing to administer Walpole's estate. Her close friendships with women, including Elizabeth *Farren, were represented in scandalmongering literature as *sapphic. Damer also travelled extensively—particularly to Italy, France, and Portugal—setting up her studio in each location. Politically, she was a *Whig, devoted to Charles James *Fox and campaigning in the Westminster *election of 1780 with the Duchess of *Devonshire.

Her close friendship with Mary Berry (1763–1852), dating from 1788, stimulated her literary and theatrical interests, the major outcome of which was her Romantic novel, *Belmour* (1801). She also produced Berry's play, *Fashionable Friends* (1801), for which their mutual friend Joanna *Baillie provided the prologue and epilogue. In 1802 Damer visited France with Berry and presented *Napoleon with her plaster bust of Fox.

Despite antipathy from some members of the *Royal Academy, she exhibited thirty-two works in a variety of media at its annual exhibitions between 1784 and 1818, and she was praised in the *Morning Post* by Thomas *Hope for her bust of *Nelson. Other exhibited works included ideal portrait busts (including a series of theatrical sitters), designs for public sculpture, and animal statuary. Sculptures for the public domain included two terracotta reliefs for *Boydell's Shakespeare Gallery, a bronze statue of Joseph I of Portugal, and a marble statue of George III for Register House, Edinburgh. Damer is also reputed to have made a colossal statue of Apollo for Drury Lane Theatre. **AWY**

88

DANBY, Francis (1793–1861), painter. A specialist in *landscape painting particularly around the Bristol area, he also helped to pioneer a fashionable genre of grand apocalyptic paintings.

Danby was born in Wexford, Ireland, of a small landowner family who moved to Dublin, having being disrupted by the sectarian fighting in the aftermath of the *Irish Rebellion of 1798. Young Francis learned drawing at the Dublin Society, and became friendly with James Arthur O'Connor (1792–1841), destined to become one of Ireland's leading landscape artists. It is possible that both men were influenced by the *Irish cultural revival, for, despite subsequent separation, their work developed along convergent lines, particularly in a use of strong colour and contemporary social landscape themes. Danby certainly claimed that his painting reflected the 'beautiful imaginings and rich, poetic feelings' characteristic of the Irish genius.

After exhibiting his first landscape in Dublin in 1813 and being dazzled in the same year by seeing Joseph *Turner's *Frosty Morning* at a Royal Academy exhibition in London, Danby tramped to Bristol intent on returning to Ireland. However, a modest success in selling watercolours and portraits induced him to stay. Over the next decade he became a prominent figure in what is now known as the 'Bristol school' of painters, dominated by Edward Bird (1772–1819) and the rakish radical Edward Rippingille (1798–1859). This lively group of landscape artists, who sketched together in Leigh Woods outside Bristol, intersected with a febrile urban culture of young intellectual writers, scientists, and experimenters, including the surgeon-engraver John King (1760–1846), the painter-writer George Cumberland (1754–1848), Robert *Southey, Thomas *De Quincey, and the Pneumatic Institute circle around Thomas *Beddoes and Humphry *Davy. Danby's powerful *Upas Tree* of 1820, with its echoes of *orientalist and radical themes, perhaps reflects the influence of this heterodox culture.

After fleeing in poverty to London in 1824, Danby entered into his period of greatest artistic success, aided by a generous and faithful Bristol patron, iron-founder John Gibbons (1777–1851). Danby's *Attempt to Illustrate the Opening of the Grand Seal*, begun around 1825, may well have initiated a vogue for vast apocalyptic paintings on biblical themes: certainly his Bristol friends believed that John *Martin plagiarized Danby's work-in-progress to produce his own more celebrated British Institute painting, *The Deluge* (1826). Nevertheless Danby was elected an associate of the British Academy in 1825 and came within one vote of gaining full membership in 1829, being defeated by John *Constable. The following year Danby's life become mired in scandal when he left an unhappy marriage to live on the Continent with his mistress, Ellen Evans. Though he continued painting, and eventually returned to England in the 1840s to produce some fine melancholy landscapes, he never recovered his reputation with the art establishment.   IMcC

DANCE, George, the younger (1741–1825). One of the most innovative neoclassical architects in Britain, Dance drew upon the contributions of theorists such as Marc-Antoine Laugier (1713–69) and talented peers such as Robert *Adam, James *Wyatt, and John Wood the younger (1728–82), but always allowed utility, not fashion, to direct his design efforts.

Dance built his career on that of his father, also George, who was clerk of the works for the City of London from 1735 to 1768. Six years of travel and study in Italy grounded the younger Dance in a knowledge of classical *architecture [28] from antiquity through to the contemporary work of French and Italian proponents of neoclassicism. He returned to London in 1764 and demonstrated his learning and practical abilities in the rebuilding of All Hallows Church, London Wall (1765–7). In 1768 he inherited his father's appointment, a position which provided him with a steady succession of major projects. His greatest success was the rebuilding of Newgate Prison (1770–80) as a massive, windowless bastion of retributive justice [see *prisons]. His other city works at the Guildhall, together with his Shakespeare Gallery (1788–9) for John *Boydell, were particularly influential for John *Soane, Dance's most notable pupil.

As clerk of the city works, Dance was also a major force in city planning and development schemes. His small-scale Minories development (1767–8) introduced the crescent and circus of John Wood's Bath to London. His boldest schemes were for the Port of London and were largely unrealized, except for the West India Docks, which opened in 1802. Together with Sir Robert *Taylor, Dance drafted the Building Act of 1774, which established unambiguous and uniform building codes for London.

Dance was a prominent member of London's professional society. He was an original member of the *Royal Academy, a Fellow of the Royal Society and of the Society of Antiquaries, and in 1794 Master of the Merchant Taylors' Company.   SS

dandyism, a style of masculine dress, code of values, and behaviour which originated in early-nineteenth-century London and is associated particularly with George 'Beau' Brummell (1778–1840).

Thomas *Carlyle in *Sartor Resartus* (1831) defined the dandy as 'a man whose trade, office and existence consists in the wearing of clothes', and he linked the rise of this 'sect' with the influence of Brummell—'others dress to live, he lives to dress'. The phenomenon of fashionable young men dressing and parading themselves as objects of display was not new; it had been associated with a cult of 'macaronis' in the 1770s, mainly young aristocratic men who flaunted elaborate dress *fashions and affected foreign manners in opposition to the *patriotism of their fathers. Fashionable men of this kind were also known as beaus, bucks, bloods, or blades, in accordance with specialist proclivities. But especially with the onset of peace in 1815 and the rise to fashion dominance of Brummell came a new label of dandy—from the French *dandin*—to describe those who modelled themselves on his particular dress-style and code of behaviour.

As defined by Brummell, dandyism eschewed the elaborate dress pretensions and masculine heroics of precursor fashion cults. Deriving his dress ideas from simplified and practical modes of country clothing worn by English aristocrats like Coke of Norfolk, Brummell inaugurated a new costume for the fashionable urban male. It comprised a well-cut blue or black coat with tails, buff waistcoat, pure linen cravat, and tight-fitting trousers tucked into highly polished Hessian boots. He stressed the need for cleanliness rather than powder and perfumes, and he practised a code of restraint and emotional detachment rather than the displays of feeling associated with the sentimental movement [see *sensibility, 11]. Though he was of middle-class origins Brummell's arrogant confidence and cult of exclusivity spoke to the insecurities of young aristocrats facing challenges from commercial and professional classes. He also appealed to an expanding urban reading market eager for sensation and entertainment. Brummell was imitated in Paris, befriended by the Prince Regent, welcomed by fashionable hostesses, and courted by tailors as a trademark of quality; and his doings, sayings, and dressings were eagerly followed through the fashion caricatures of Robert Dighton (?1752–1814), George

*Cruikshank, and others. However, Brummell's social pre-eminence ended abruptly when *gambling debts forced him in 1816 to flee to France, where he declined into a ragged oddity during twenty years of exile.

Despite his squalid end, Brummell left lasting cultural legacies: *Byron thought him one of the three most important men of the age. Brummell's dress-style became an enduring hallmark of modernity and masculine good taste, and his dandy code gained new inflections under early Victorian successors such as writers Edward *Bulwer Lytton and Benjamin Disraeli (1808–81) and painter-sculptor Count Alfred 'Blessington' d'Orsay (1801–52). Lytton's bestselling novel *Pelham* (1828), for example, helped to make the dandy into a more Byronic figure, an outsider characterized by brooding insolence and sexual exoticism. With the shrewd encouragement of its publisher Henry Colburn (d. 1852), *Pelham* also inaugurated a more domestic and feminine genre of *silver fork novels, in which the dandy featured within a *roman à clef* dissection of fashionable society. The wit, sociability, and aestheticism of Disraeli and d'Orsay were further legacies which dandyism transmitted to the bohemian literary and art movements of late-nineteenth-century France and Britain. IMcC

D'ARBLAY, Madame, see *Frances Burney.

49 **DARWIN,** Erasmus (1731–1802), physician, poet, and theorist of *evolution, *medicine [18], agriculture, and *female education. The son of a lawyer, Darwin was educated at Cambridge and studied medicine at the University of Edinburgh before practising in Nottingham, Lichfield, and Derby.

A key figure in the Lunar Society, which brought *Enlightenment [32] ideas to the British midlands and encouraged the application of science to industry, Darwin celebrated in *poetry [29] the accomplishments of its industrialists and natural philosophers—including James *Watt, Matthew *Boulton, Joseph *Priestley, Thomas *Day, and Richard Lovell *Edgeworth.

Having undertaken translations of Linnaeus, Darwin used the Linnaean classificatory system in *The Loves of the Plants* (1789), a poetic representation of the sex lives of plants, later parodied for the radical views of sexual equality it presented by George *Canning in the *Anti-Jacobin Review*. 65 Despite this conservative reaction, *Loves of the Plants and The Economy of Vegetation* (1791), published together as *The Botanic Garden* (1791), met with great popular success. Darwin's persistent poetic quest to 'inlist the imagination under the banner of science' was evident in his posthumous work, *The Temple of Nature* (1803), a full-blown vision of organic and social progress. However, didactic poetry in heroic couplets had by this time become unfashionable.

Offering a comprehensive nosology and theory of disease, the prose poem *Zoonomia* (1794–6) used the theory of associationism, the *natural philosophy [34] of Buffon, Linnaeus, and *Hutton, and the

*political economy [33] of Adam *Smith, to construct an account of physiological and organic development. Darwin's *Plan for the Conduct of Female Education in Boarding Schools* (1797) responded to contemporary interest in a distinctive education for young middle-class women.

Influenced by agricultural improvers in Scotland and England, Darwin produced a substantial treatise on agricultural and nutritional theory, *Phytologia* (1800) [see *land, 16]. A keen experimenter, prolific inventor, and Enlightenment thinker, Darwin was the progenitor of many twentieth-century ideas and artefacts. His complex and ambivalent legacy is also evident in Mary Shelley's *Frankenstein* (1818), and theories of evolution, particularly as formulated by his grandson, Charles Darwin (1809–82). MMcN

DAVENPORT, Allen (1775–1846), shoemaker turned literary aspirant, came from a rural labouring background, later becoming a dragoon and *trade unionist and an early co-operative activist. His remarkable *Life and Literary Pursuits* (1845) reveals a likeable, highly positive individual afflicted by hard work, poverty, and ardent literary ambition. An early convert to Thomas *Spence's brand of agrarian, parochial *socialism, he was by 1819 a prominent figure in London's ultra-radical circles, frequently speaking under an alias in *taverns, *debating clubs, and blasphemous chapels (Dissenting chapels in which the preacher gave freethinking, and often blasphemous, political sermons). He delivered an elegy on Spence at the Navy Coffee House in 1819 and, though an acquaintance of Arthur Thistlewood (1770–1820), managed to avoid implication in the ultra-radical Cato Street conspiracy to assassinate the Cabinet in early 1820.

Some of Davenport's earliest poems appeared in *Sherwin's Political Register* (1818) and the *Theological Comet* (1819), while his separately issued *The Kings* (1819), *Claremont*, and *Queen of the Isles* (1820) reveal standard postwar radical sentiments, although by the mid-1820s his verse began to reflect the influence of *Coleridge and *Shelley. In prose, he debated *agrarianism in Richard *Carlile's *Republican* (1824), as well as outlining a wage scale linked to bread prices in the *Trades Newspaper* (1825). A selection of writings appeared as *The Muses Wreath* (1827), including excerpts from his play *The Social Age*, performed for Robert *Owen in 1835.

From 1822 to 1828 Davenport worked as a caretaker, which provided him with a prestigious address from which to negotiate the 'impossibilities' of printers' charges which impeded his *Life . . . of Spence* (1836) and his short-lived poetry magazine, *Urania* (1838–40). From 1830 he was associated with several co-operative and mutual improvement groups, but felt most at home amongst veteran radicals in the Cornish Coffee House. In 1839 his shoemaking skills were not needed by the Manea Fen agrarianist project but, typically undaunted, Davenport continued to support them.

Davenport's place in radical historiography lies in his artisan origins and activist/intellectual transition from Spenceanism, through Owenite socialism to

*Chartist agrarianism. In literary history, he embodies communitarianism before its attenuation into Romantic individualism.   DW

DAVY, Sir Humphry (1778–1829), chemist and scientific *lecturer, the most publicly influential and controversial scientific figure in early-nineteenth-century Britain. As a lecturer at London's Royal Institution in the early 1800s, Davy turned *chemistry and *geology into a fashionable attraction for the London élite, and as an innovative professor of chemistry he used his institutional setting to concentrate the resources of experiment and proof in the hands of aristocratic sponsors who were changing the cultural force and direction of the burgeoning scientific disciplines.

In 1798 Davy, then a 20-year-old surgeon's apprentice, was recruited to supervise Thomas *Beddoes's medical laboratory in Bristol. There he experimented with pneumatic *medicine [18], especially nitrous oxide (or laughing-gas), and taught himself the latest chemical and medical knowledge. He became connected briefly with Beddoes's circle of radical intellectuals—William *Godwin, Joseph *Priestley, Erasmus *Darwin, and S. T. *Coleridge—at a time when the *anti-Jacobin media campaign was beginning to discredit the discourse and procedures of Britain's radical provincial science.

Davy alone emerged unscathed from the conservatives' critique of progressive *Enlightenment [32] science. In 1799 he published *Researches, Chemical and Philosophical: Chiefly Concerning Nitrous Oxide and its Respiration*, which established his scientific credentials and led to his appointment as assistant lecturer in chemistry at the new Royal Institution in 1801. There he quickly adapted himself to the aristocratic ethos of the Royal Institution's founders, and was soon promoted to professor of chemistry. In his inaugural lecture of 1802, he declared to his listeners that 'civilized life' was dependent on social and economic inequalities. His research, lavishly funded by his providers, expanded into work on chemical galvanism, electrolysis, the decomposition of fixed alkalis, the discovery of benzene, and eventually the invention of a safety lamp for mining.

Meanwhile, Davy's compelling public lectures drew upper-class audiences to London's gentrified West End, a spectatorship that unexpectedly included large numbers of women who found the new lecturing institution a substitute for the British universities they were barred from attending. Davy hailed his female audience as mothers of the techno-scientific revolution, transmitters of scientific knowledge through the intimate realm of the family.

More broadly, his rapturous lectures on chemistry and geology infused scientific discourse with the languages of *sensibility [11] and *sublimity. He had written *poetry [29] in the 1790s and helped *Wordsworth edit the second edition of *Lyrical Ballads* in 1800. His more intimate relationship with Coleridge led to the latter lecturing on English poetry at the Royal Institution in 1808, an appearance which launched the poet's public career as literary and cultural critic. Eventually the Davy–Coleridge association amplified both Davy's resonance as a cultural voice and the legitimacy of Coleridge's pronouncements on philosophy and poetry. Both men believed that the languages of chemistry and poetry could mutually resist the advances of French scientific and political rhetorics in the age of Napoleonic *war [2]. Together they forged a lasting myth of British 'Romantic science' as a kind of 'poetry realized in nature', the voice of a vitalist 'active universe'. In fact, as Coleridge eventually recognized, Davy's science was not a British version of Germany's *Naturphilosophie*, but instead a brilliantly effective rhetoric that cemented *Locke's empiricism and *Newton's mechanical universe to a new world order.

For though he invoked a literary sublime, Davy was actually uncoupling *natural philosophy [34] from other cultural discourses of the time. Lavish funding by the Royal Institution permitted him to stage his experiments on the basis of an unprecedentedly expensive apparatus of demonstration and proof. Unlike the small-scale scenes of provincial experiment where Joseph Priestley and others had worked to widen participation in replicating experiments, as the historian Jan Golinski has shown, Davy and his aristocratic patrons elaborated spectacular demonstrations of scientific experiment before the stares and applause of rapt lay audiences. This concentration of resources also allowed him to compete with French chemists for authority over the naming of elements such as chlorine, or for the decisive establishment of electrochemistry. He could use such instruments as the recently invented Voltaic battery in 1806–7, making his elaborate experiments increasingly difficult to replicate elsewhere. Between 1801 and 1812, Davy and the Royal Institution were decisive actors in transforming the sphere of British experimental science from the artisanal mode of Priestley into the institutionally centred 'big chemistry' of the new metropolitan science.

Davy's 1807 lecture publicizing his advances in *electricity and chemistry helped make him famous across the scientific circles of Europe. Knighted by the Prince Regent in 1812, then granted a baronetcy in 1818, he ascended to the presidency of the Royal Society in 1820. The latter event marked the acceptance of Britain's institutional, disciplinary transformation of modern science by the oldest representative of the seventeenth-century scientific revolution. During these years his successor at the Royal Institution, Michael *Faraday, introduced a more professionalized model of the new scientist than Davy himself, flaunting power and nationalist ambition, could ever achieve. Davy's final text, published posthumously in 1830 as *Consolations in Travel*, gave his career as England's most acclaimed scientific genius a chilling social legacy. The chemical revolution his own brilliance had helped achieve,

65. Pen and wash preparatory drawing by William Blake (after a design by Henry Fuseli) for his engraving *Fertilization of Egypt*, one of the illustrations to Erasmus Darwin's *The Economy of Vegetation* (1791).

he wrote there, would itself empower the 'transmission of hereditary qualities' by which Europe could finally drive back the 'negro race' and make 'extinct' the 'red men, aborigines of America'.   JK

DAY, Thomas (1748–89), radical, novelist, and one of England's most influential exponents and practitioners of *Rousseauism in *education [17], literature, and politics. Having inherited a moderate landed estate from his father, Thomas Day possessed sufficient means to devote his life to social, educational, literary, and political experiment inspired by the primitivist ideals of Jean Jacques Rousseau and the contemporary British cult of *sensibility [11]. Though he showed signs of marked asceticism during his school days at Charterhouse, particularly in his admiration of Spartan classical ideals, he seems to have imbibed his Rousseauist enthusiasm mainly at Oxford, where he developed an enduring friendship with Richard Lovell *Edgeworth, another ardent educational experimenter. Day gained a fervent belief in the rustic virtues of honesty, manliness, and independence, and a commensurate dislike of luxury, corruption, and aristocratic polish.

These principles fuelled Day's dubious experiment of seeking a perfect spouse through raising two young orphaned girls according to the stern ideals of Rousseau's Émile. Similar ideas underpinned his two highly didactic works of *children's literature, The History of Sandford and Merton (1783–9) and The History of Little Jack (1788). The former, one of the most widely read children's books of this period, tells how a simple, honest farmer's son manages to re-educate a young aristocrat to abandon his fashionable French manners in favour of a manly, patriotic English moral code.

Day's anti-aristocratic and sentimental ideals also manifested themselves in his political thought. His first published poem, The Dying Negro (1773), became a staple of *abolitionist propaganda, while his political radicalism surfaced in a series of tracts attacking the *American Revolution and espousing a wider suffrage. Though steeped in seventeenth-century *Whig constitutionalist principles, he disliked the Whig politicians of his day and supported the reforming programme of the *Wyvillites, the *Society for Constitutional Information, and the younger *Pitt. From the mid-1780s Day spent most of the last years of his life on an estate in Surrey, attempting with his wife, Esther Milnes, to practise and disseminate ideals of natural living and social benevolence.   IMcC

debating clubs or societies. Social gatherings centred around a debate which could range from small private functions to, more commonly after 1750, commercial ventures, advertised in *newspapers and costing between 6d. and 2s. for admittance. Debate in these clubs was eclectic, encompassing politics, history, philosophy, religion, literature, and theatre, as well as relations between men and women. It could be formal or informal, but offered an opportunity for people of all classes to exercise oratorical skills and reflected contemporary interest in the practice and theory of elocution. Though the admittance of women to debating clubs was limited from the 1750s, in the late 1770s there was a fashion for female orators and for clubs oriented towards women such as the Belle Assemblée and the Female Parliament at the University of Rational Amusement. Though there was a subsequent decline in the popularity of these clubs after 1781, their articulation of topics such as the rights of *women [4] to education and political representation was formative in the development of *Wollstonecraftian feminism. In the 1790s links between debating clubs and radical organizations such as the London Corresponding Society—John *Thelwall, John Binns, and John Gale Jones were managers of debating societies—led to their activities being monitored by government spies and suppressed by the Two Acts of 1795 [see *corresponding societies]. Although most prominent in London, debating clubs were also to be found in towns such as Birmingham, Norwich, and, in particular, Edinburgh, where debating societies were the training ground for the *Scottish Enlightenment.   GR

Deism, often equated loosely with freethought in general, underwent a significant revival and transformation in our period from being a relatively patrician philosophical or religious tendency into becoming a substrand of popular radical politics, usually known to contemporaries as 'infidelism'.

The term 'Deism' had been used in the early eighteenth century in an eclectic way to designate a variety of beliefs of a minimalist and universal kind to which all denominations and all humankind could supposedly subscribe. It tended to encompass belief in a supreme being and a commitment to natural moral laws or ethical principles. It eschewed revelation, dogma, and superstition, and criticized any elements of Christianity and Scripture thought to be incompatible with reason. In the hands of French intellectual philosophes such as Voltaire, d'Holbach, and *Rousseau, Deism took on the character of a powerful critical movement deeply implicated in attacks on the Catholic church and in defences of *toleration. In Britain for most of the eighteenth century, however, Deistic impulses tended to be more diffuse, often being absorbed by Latitudinarian *Anglicanism or by Rational Dissent. There were a few signs in the 1760s and 1770s that Deism was beginning to reach artisan radicals through schoolmaster Peter Annet's (1693–1769) Robin Hood tavern *debating club in the Strand and through David *Williams's Margaret Street chapel *lectures, but it was still far from being a sustained popular movement.

In the wake of the *French Revolution, however, Deism, or popular radical freethought, was rapidly labelled 'infidelism' by enemies and adherents alike, and soon boasted a series of enduringly influential foundation texts: notably Voltaire's Philosophical Dictionary, Mirabaud's (Baron d'Holbach) System of Nature, *Volney's The Ruins, or Revolutions of Empire, and Law of Nature, and, above all, Thomas *Paine's Age of Reason, parts I and II. All these works were translated by members of radical *corresponding societies and sold in cheap editions during the mid-1790s. Their intellectual appeal lay primarily in a deconstructive promise to expose the machinations and mystifications of the church as an agent of ruling-class exploitation. Even so, the impact of Deism was often profoundly divisive, leading to the secession of some prominent Christian radicals from London Corresponding Society sections. And, although Deism was widely associated with adherence to *republican principles in politics, it did not necessarily follow that Deist radicals were practical revolutionaries. Radicals like the *Spenceans who adhered to Christian *millenarian views were often more attracted to violent and apocalyptic underground politics than were rationalist-minded Deist counterparts like Francis *Place. Nevertheless, both government law officials and private prosecuting societies quickly established that it was easier to persuade juries and *judges to convict radicals on charges of blasphemy than of sedition, a tendency which encouraged an indiscriminate tarring of radicals with the infidel brush. Publisher-bookseller Daniel Isaac *Eaton, for example, was prosecuted twice in 1793 for publishing Paine's *Age of Reason*, forcing him to flee to America to escape a lengthy gaol sentence.

Although the *gagging acts and the anti-Gallican *loyalism of the French *wars [2] temporarily halted the spread of popular Deism, it flared back into life during the postwar years thanks mainly to the publications and activism of former tinmaker Richard *Carlile. Even before this, the shady Spencean lawyer George Cannon (1789–1854) had in a periodical of 1815 launched the first popular version of what was soon destined to become a major infidel text, Percy *Shelley's youthful poem *Queen Mab*. Carlile republished and sold this work in the 1820s along with a plethora of canonical freethinking texts from Britain, France, and America. Such popular Deism constituted one of the most important agencies for the popularization and transmission of *Enlightenment [32] ideas. Jailed on nine counts of blasphemous libel between 1819 and 1825, Carlile orchestrated a popular freethinking campaign from Dorchester prison, defying the government, the Constitutional Association, and the *Society for the Suppression of Vice by enrolling volunteer shopmen and women to keep publishing and selling Deistic material from his London shop. For a brief period Carlile and some of his more ardent radical followers also moved beyond Deism to embrace a fully-fledged atheist position based on the materialist theories of d'Holbach.

By the end of the 1820s Carlile was persuaded under the influence of his future wife, Eliza Sharples, and the flamboyant former Anglican cleric the Revd Robert Taylor (1784–1844) to abandon his atheism in favour of a quasi-Romantic view of Christianity as personified, mystical forces of nature. Taylor teamed with Carlile on several tours of the north and staged a series of extraordinarily well-attended lectures at Carlile's Blackfriars Rotunda in 1830–1. He elaborated the theories of Volney to argue, with spectacular theatrical demonstrations, that Christianity was only one of a series of world religions derived from zodiacal myths. Nicknamed 'the Devil's Chaplain', Taylor also reflected a typical trend of the later 1820s by adopting the structure and ritual of a Christian sect in order to conduct infidel 'services' attacking Christianity and espousing radical political reform. In doing so, he and Carlile also paved the way for the communitarian versions of Deism which were adopted by many of the followers of Robert *Owen during the 1830s and 1840s. Steeped in the language of rational religion, Owenite *socialism looked forward to a millennium of reason, based not on Christian Revelation but on the co-operative restructuring of social and economic relations.   IMcC

Della Cruscanism, a poetic movement characterized by self-conscious displays of emotion and celebration of liberal political opinions, features which influenced much of the magazine verse of the 1790s. Rather than the neoclassical forms usually cited, Della Cruscanism offers the most immediate poetic style against which the work of *Wordsworth and *Coleridge reacts.

The name 'Della Cruscan' has its origins among the British literati resident in Florence in the early 1780s. Together with a number of Italian patriots, Bertie Greatheed (1759–1826), Robert *Merry, William Parsons (1764–1828), and Hester Thrale *Piozzi privately published *The Florence Miscellany* in 1785. Piozzi's 'Preface' stresses the affective nature of the verse, downplaying the liberal sentiments which provided an important focus for the other contributors. The Accademia della Crusca had been closed by the Habsburg Grand Duke Leopold in 1783 to the anger of Italian patriots who saw it as a repository of national culture. That culture is deliberately celebrated in *The Florence Miscellany* as it was in an earlier collection, *Arno Miscellany* (1784), to which Merry had also contributed.

As the decade progressed the contents of the volume began to be known in Britain, especially through selections published in the *European Magazine* from 1786. Merry and the others had meanwhile left Italy and begun to build independent literary careers. It was an approach made to Merry by an old Cambridge friend, Major Edward Topham (1751–1820), to provide *poetry [29] for the *World* which marks the emergence of the idea of Della Cruscanism as an explicit movement in English literary culture.

Merry's poem 'Adieu and Recall to Love', signed 'Della Crusca', was published in June 1788. A reply, under the name of 'Anna Matilda', quickly followed. The author was Hannah *Cowley, whose identity was kept from Merry. A passionate poetic correspondence developed in the pages of the *World* to which others contributed, including 'Benedict' (Edward Jerningham), 'Reuben' (Greatheed), 'Arly' (Miles Peter Andrews), and 'Laura Maria' (Mary *Robinson). John Bell published a selection as *The Poetry of the World*, in 1788 (additional volumes were later published by James Ridgway, c.1782–1838). More Della Cruscan poetry was published in *The British Album* (1790).

Merry finally met 'Anna Matilda' in March 1789. Disappointed in her real identity, he signalled the end of their correspondence in 'The Interview', published in June 1789. The *French Revolution was soon taking up more and more of Merry's attention. The phenomenon of Della Cruscanism was effectively over. Nevertheless, it was still to receive a smarting attack in William *Gifford's *The Baviad* (1790). Gifford's primary concern was not the literary merit of Della Cruscanism but its ideological significance. He saw the movement as the sign of a creeping feminization of culture which brought with it dangerous political opinions and provincial tastes, a not unreasonable inference given the enthusiastic response of Merry and Robinson to the French Revolution. Gifford's response was itself a relatively early sign of the conservative reaction which was to sweep through literary culture in response to the French Revolution. The Della Cruscans remained convenient targets in his *Maeviad* (1795) while T. J. *Mathias contributed another notable attack in *The Pursuits of Literature* (1794–7). Despite these attacks, the influence of the Della Cruscans persisted well into the 1830s in the poetry of John *Keats and Thomas *Moore.   JM

DE LOUTHERBOURG, Philippe Jacques, see Philippe Jacques de *Loutherbourg.

dentistry. Modern British dentistry has its origins in the guild that united barbers and surgeons. When the guild separated in 1745, a group of barbers maintained their connections to the surgeons and sought to professionalize their activities as dentistry. Among the procedures offered were tooth extraction, transplantation, replantation, filling with gold or lead, realignment of crooked teeth, and the fitting and manufacture of false teeth.

John *Hunter made a significant contribution to the development of dental anatomy and practice with two influential works, *The Natural History of the Mouth and Jaws* (1771) and *A Practical Treatise on the Diseases of the Teeth* (1778). Hunter's dental science had its basis in human anatomy, and like most surgeons of his day he relied on cadavers supplied to him by grave-robbers or 'resurrection men' [see *Anatomy Act]. During the years he practised dentistry, he experimented unsuccessfully with the transplantation of teeth. In a procedure harshly satirized by Thomas *Rowlandson, he removed teeth from poor but healthy young donors and transferred them directly to the sockets of his wealthy patients.

Like the rising class of scientific surgeons in general, dental surgeons increasingly strove to play down the manual aspects of their craft. Hunter's association with prominent London dentist Martin Van Butchell (1735–?1812) brought harsh condemnation from his contemporary biographer and fellow physician Jesse Foot (1744–1826). With his flamboyant garb, long beard, and white pony with purple and black painted spots, Van Butchell exemplified the old style empiric and a tradition of advertisement no longer compatible with the changing self-image of a new profession.   LH

DE QUINCEY, Thomas (1785–1859), autobiographer, essayist, editor, novelist. Drawing consistently and sensationally upon autobiographical material, De Quincey was one of the first writers to offer the middle-class reader a portrait of the artist as one whose superior gifts entailed deracination and debauchery.

Born in Manchester and educated at schools in Bath and Winkfield, De Quincey attended Manchester Grammar from 1801, running away in 1802 to wander through Wales and London. A period in Oxford from 1804 to 1808 left him with a moderate opium habit and the acquaintance of *Coleridge and *Wordsworth. By 1813 he had developed a serious opium addiction, which he battled for the rest of his life. In 1809 he settled at Grasmere in the cottage formerly occupied by the Wordsworths, marrying the local farmer's daughter, Margaret Simpson, in 1817.

Having exhausted his private income he turned to journalism, editing the *Westmorland Gazette* in 1818–19 before being dismissed. Like so many of the professional writers of the early nineteenth century who took full advantage of the opportunities made available by the plethora of contemporary *reviews, *newspapers, and magazines, De Quincey's output was as various as it was prolific. Tales and pieces on *literary theory [41], such as 'On the Knocking on the Gate in Macbeth' (1823), appeared mainly in *Blackwood's* and *Tait's* magazines. He published occasional *essays on topics ranging from 'On Murder as one of the Fine Arts' (1827) through history, classics, philosophy, and linguistics to 'The Logic of Political Economy' (1844). His literary and sociological anecdotes were collected as *Recollections of the Lakes and the Lake Poets* (1834–9). He also published a novel, *Klosterheim* (1832), translated German texts, and wrote the long essay 'The Last Days of Immanuel Kant' (1827). De Quincey's more characteristic and original works are the stylized meditation on dreaming *Suspiria de Profundis* (1845), the sociological nightmare 'The English Mail-Coach' (1849), and *Confessions of an English Opium Eater* (1822)—his masterpiece of autobiographical indirection.

Begun as articles in the *London Magazine* in 1821—De Quincey having moved back to London in 1821—the *Confessions* came early in a career born of the poverty of his mid-thirties from which he never escaped. Readers were fascinated and De Quincey quick to revise and combine them in 1822, revising them again substantially in 1856 and converting a creative commentary on his mental life into a textual commentary on his career.

Ostensibly a self-vindication, they remain morally and imaginatively ambivalent about 'opium eating'. De Quincey was to make an art form of the haunting of unexplained or inexplicable guilt of the kind that impels the *Confessions*—though the stomach, ironically and comically figuring the unconscious, is often blamed. The opium passages subtly disqualify the opium dreamer as a reliable commentator on his own life, and his understanding remains spectacularly indeterminate. Marked by an ebullient literariness and stylistic heterogeneity, these highly stylized passages of the *Confessions* demonstrate the artifice of *autobiography and are anything but confessional.

WC

DERMODY, Thomas (1775–1802), poet. Known as 'the Irish *Chatterton', Dermody became celebrated in Britain as a further exemplary case of a young man of potential Romantic *genius drawn into premature death by the snares of *patronage and the pressures of commercialism.

Born in Ennis, County Clare, Dermody was employed at the age of 9 to teach classics in the school of his drunken father. The following year he ran away to Dublin, where his charm and precocity rapidly attracted a succession of patrons eager to display the talents of a ragged young prodigy. Such patronage included becoming a playmate for the future Irish writer Sydney *Owenson (Lady Morgan), and being sent to a boarding-school whose headmaster privately published the 14-year-old boy's first collection of poems. However, Dermody early revealed an incorrigible taste for drink and low life, as well as a tendency to satirize and alienate his patrons. His first biographer later claimed that the boy liked to boast: 'I am vicious because I like it.' The same rebellious temperament led Dermody to welcome the *French Revolution in a fiery pamphlet, *The Rights of Justice*, published in 1793.

Crossing the Irish Sea in 1794, he enlisted in the army and over the next four years distinguished himself as an officer and fighter. Pensioned on half-pay in London, he rapidly resumed his career of obsequious dependence on literary patrons interspersed with bouts of hack writing and drunkenness. Although briefly fêted after a further collection of his poems was published in 1800, he died in 1802 from a combination of alcoholism and malnutrition. His *poetry [29] and tragic life were publicized in the mid-1800s by a literary patron, J. G. Raymond.

IMcC

DESTAËL, Madame, see Madame de *Staël.

DEVONSHIRE, Duchess of (Georgiana Cavendish) (1757–1806), woman of *fashion, hostess, writer, and patron, the most celebrated aristocratic woman of her time. Cavendish was the daughter of the first Earl Spencer and Georgiana Poyntz. Her marriage in 1774 to Henry Cavendish, fifth Duke of Devonshire, placed her at the apex of *Whig society, which she commanded from Devonshire House in London and from Chatsworth in Derbyshire.

66. Anonymous caricature of the Duchess of Devonshire and Charles James Fox, 1784. This was one of many squibs produced during the controversy over the Duchess's public support of Fox in the 1784 election campaign: she was accused of having traded kisses for votes.

Her appearances at military reviews, court occasions, and at fashionable entertainments, her taste in dress and, later, her behaviour as a mother, said to be influenced by *Rousseauist sensibility, were widely reported in the print media. The dissemination in this way of news of the Duchess's activities made her a truly public figure, illustrating the capacity of a commercial print culture to fashion aristocrats as celebrities, an opportunity which aristocrats themselves were not reluctant to exploit.

As intimate of the Prince of Wales, *Fox, and *Sheridan, the Duchess was closely involved in politics, most notoriously as canvasser for Fox in the 1784 Westminster election. Her role in that affair caused a storm of controversy: *prints [22], squibs, broadsides, and pamphlets represented her canvass as evidence of loose sexual morality, as a compromise of her proper role as wife and mother—she was abandoning the Duke for Fox and the public—and, in her solicitation of the plebeian vote, as a transgression of the boundaries of class. The Duchess's participation in the election indicated a dangerous female influence on public culture which could even extend to Fox himself: caricatures such as 'Cheek by Joul' suggest that inasmuch as the Duchess was performing a masculine role, Fox was commensurately effeminized.

Her vilification in 1784 caused the Duchess to withdraw from political involvement of this kind, though she retained a role behind the scenes as hostess and confidante of the Prince of Wales. She also played an important covert role in negotiations to suppress scandalous memoirs of Queen Marie-Antoinette, written by French *émigrés in London. Her private life, which was never explicitly discussed in the press, was complex. She lived in a *ménage à trois* with the Duke and his mistress, Lady Elizabeth Foster, who remained close friends with the Duchess while bearing the Duke two children. The Duchess had an affair with the Whig politician Charles Grey (1764–1845), by whom she had a child in 1792.

Throughout her life she was interested in imaginative literature, producing numerous unpublished pieces as well as a novel, *The Sylph* (1779), and a poem, 'The Passage of the Mountain of St. Gothard' (written 1790s, formally pub. 1816), the subject of a response by *Coleridge in 1799 ('Ode to Georgiana'). She performed and composed *music [26], commenting on a march of hers being performed at the opera in 1784. The Duchess was well known as a patron of aspiring and indigent writers with radical or even ultra-radical sympathies, giving support to Mary *Robinson and Charles *Pigott, among others. The dominant passion of her life, however, was *gambling. She became addicted at an early age and the tremendous debts she accrued, amounting to £100,000 at one stage, affected all areas of her life. In spite of this, however, her reputation was never completely overshadowed by scandal: on her death in 1806 she was widely eulogized as one of the outstanding women of her age.   GR

DIBDIN, Charles (1745–1814), dramatist, *theatre [24] entrepreneur, music composer and song-writer,

and miscellaneous writer. Dibdin was the twelfth child of a Southampton silversmith, who, as a child, sang at Winchester Cathedral and at subscription *concerts in the same city. He later became an actor, achieving initial fame in 1765 as Ralph in Isaac Bickerstaffe's comic opera *The Maid of the Mill*, and later as Mungo in the same author's *The Padlock* (1768), for which Dibdin also composed the music. He arranged and wrote music for David Garrick's Shakespeare Jubilee in 1769, during which he quarrelled with the actor-manager. Acquiring a reputation as a temperamental collaborator, Dibdin was too ambitious to subordinate himself to figures such as Garrick and to the dominance by Covent Garden and Drury Lane of the London theatre, and he therefore set himself up as an entrepreneur. He staged puppet shows satirizing Garrick at Exeter Change (1775), and in 1782 went into partnership with the equestrian Charles Hughes and with the father of Joseph *Grimaldi to form 'The Royal Circus and Equestrian Philharmonic Academy'. Dibdin had failed to secure a licence from the Surrey magistrates and when they closed down the Circus the partnership broke up in acrimony. In the late 1780s he devised a successful one-man show, his 'entertainments sans souci', which consisted of songs, repartee, topical jokes, and satire.

Dibdin's lasting importance resides in his *ballads and sea-songs which, especially during wartime, did much to ameliorate threatening impressions of the navy created by the *press-gangs and *naval mutinies, and fostered the image of the 'jolly jack tar' as good-hearted, loyal, and true to both his sweetheart and country. Sung in theatres, *taverns, and on street corners as well as in drawing-rooms, distributed as cheap chapbooks or in more lavish volumes designed for the middling orders, Dibdin's songs penetrated the consciousness of the period. Their political role in concentrating *patriotic feeling on the figure of the ordinary sailor and making that figure politically uncontentious was recognized by a government annuity to Dibdin of £200, made in 1803. After his death, he was commemorated by a monument at the Royal Naval Hospital at Greenwich, highly unusual for a a man of the theatre.

Dibdin's published work included a *History of the Stage* (1800); a work of *travel literature and social commentary, *Observations of a Tour through Scotland and England* (1801–2) and his *Professional Life* (1803), containing the words of 600 songs. Two of his sons were also prominent in the British theatre. Charles Isaac Mungo Dibdin (1768–1833) was an inventor of spectacles, *melodramas, and *pantomimes and manager at Astley's amphitheatre, Sadler's Wells, and the Surrey theatre. Like his father, the actor, dramatist, and composer Thomas Dibdin (1771–1841) was a prolific writer of patriotic songs, as well as author of numerous afterpieces and entertainments for the London theatres.   GR

DICKENS, Charles (1812–70), novelist and writer, arguably the greatest novelist of the Victorian age. His early writings drew on and reshaped several Romantic age genres, including the *Newgate novel,

66

the miscellaneous *essay, and the picaresque cockney travelogue-cum-sporting chronicle.

Dickens's preoccupation with Newgate as a prison fortress, a symbol of the *ancien régime*, and a mode of literature derived in part from the humiliating boyhood trauma of witnessing his father, a feckless navy clerk, being imprisoned in the Marshalsea prison for debt. Young Charles's sympathy for pauper and street waifs also dates from the same period when, at the age of 12, he was forced to take lodgings away from his family and to undertake menial work in Warren's blacking factory. His later apprenticeship as a reporter and writer coincided, too, with a flowering of crime journalism, with heated parliamentary debates about the reduction of capital punishment, and with a vogue for Newgate literature—manifested especially in a series of bestselling novels of the 1820s and 1830s by Edward Bulwer Lytton (1803–73) and Harrison Ainsworth (1805–32). Typically, Dickens visited Newgate himself while researching the series of miscellaneous documentary essays of urban life which became his first book, *Sketches by Boz* (1836–7), illustrated by George *Cruikshank.

Dickens's early novels, *The Posthumous Papers of the Pickwick Club* (1836–7), and, still more, *Oliver Twist* (1837), borrowed something from Newgate novelistic predecessors, but he introduced a new moral seriousness into a genre which was under severe attack for promoting an unhealthy interest in vice, low life, and crime. *Barnaby Rudge*, projected in 1836 but not completed until 1841, showed Dickens's familiarity with *popular culture [23] as well as with *historiography: his sources included Thomas *Holcroft's eyewitness account of the *Gordon riots, the influential historical novels of Sir Walter *Scott, and the inspiration of Punch and Judy puppet theatre for his portrayal of Ned Dennis, the hangman. While the novel displayed a consistent hostility to the brutality of English *law [8] and *prisons, it also used the failed revolution of 1780 as a political exemplar for the ruling class of the 1830s in their dealings with the threat of *Chartism. But the foundations of his early success were built on comedy rather than drama. *The Pickwick Papers*, inspired by the comic sporting journalism and travelogues of Pierce *Egan and Robert Surtees (1805–64) and the cockney *prints [22] of Robert Seymour (d. 1836), rapidly became one of the publishing sensations of the nineteenth century, when Dickens was still only 25. Appearing in serial form, the first number sold 400 copies, the fifteenth, 40,000. The cockney servant Sam Weller, derived in part from a contemporary comic actor, Sam Vale, rapidly became a household name. By the early 1840s Dickens was not only editor of his own literary periodical, *Master Humphrey's Clock*, but was also called on to undertake a lecture tour of America during which he campaigned against *slavery [6] and the flouting of *copyright.   IMcC

D'ISRAELI, Isaac (1766–1848), literary historian and novelist, father of Benjamin Disraeli (1804–81). Born in London into a prosperous merchant family of Levantine *Jews who had emigrated from Italy in 1748, Isaac D'Israeli received a freethinking education in Amsterdam before returning to Britain, determined to become a poet. Despite the support of the then poet laureate, H. J. Pye (1745–1813), he failed in his ambition, but soon created a career for himself as a chronicler of the literary world. His best-known publication was the six-volume *Curiosities of Literature* (1791–1834), the first of several collections of literary anecdotes and essays. D'Israeli also tried his hand at writing *novels [31] and in 1797 published the anti-Jacobin *Vaurien* which memorably parodies *Thelwall in the person of 'Citizen Rant'. Like his close friend Francis *Douce, D'Israeli was an avid collector, and acquired several of *Blake's illuminated books, probably through auctions and private sales rather than directly from the artist.

D'Israeli withdrew from the London congregation of the Spanish and Portuguese Jews in 1817 and had his children baptized in the *Anglican church. Nevertheless, in 1833 he issued anonymously *The Genius of Judaism*, which celebrated Jewish history while criticizing its religious institutions. His proroyalist *Commentaries on the Life and Reign of Charles I* (1828–30) was an advance in historical research methods for its assiduous use of documentary records. Throughout his life he stayed close to literary celebrities: *Byron, *Scott, *Southey, and *Bulwer-Lytton all remained loyal friends and admirers of his scholarship.   JM

Dissenting academies. Excluded from the grammar schools and from the two universities, Dissenters developed in their own 'academies' an educational system that exploited their want of charter and encouraged vigorous, independent-minded speculation [see *education, 17].

Dissenting academies varied considerably, remaining an extension of their instituting principals and independent of the church elders whose sons they educated. As it happens, those principals included some of the most progressive intellects of their respective periods, from John Jennings at Kibworth, through Phillip Doddridge at Northampton and James Burgh at Stoke Newington, to Joseph *Priestley (tutor) at the second Warrington Academy.

Academies such as those at Hackney and Hoxton became, at different times, extreme in their Rational Dissent, entertaining the *Arian, Socinian, even *Unitarian 'heresies'. Some were also too freethinking for many Calvinist elders seeking training for their sons as Nonconformist ministers, forcing the closure of several of the more prestigious later in the century, as Dissent became synonomous with Jacobinism. Edmund *Burke described the Hackney Academy as 'the new arsenal in which subversive doctrines and arguments were forged', and it went into decline after being raided for republican sympathies in 1793.

In less controversial areas, their syllabuses were at once extensive and comprehensive. They encompassed French and Italian; history and political theory; geography and shorthand, which was compulsory and used to write *sermons; a version of

English literature; and, most notably, the new experimental sciences—all added to the classics with which establishment institutions remained preoccupied. From an academy, students would often proceed to universities in Scotland or Holland where its innovative knowledge and critical methods could be further developed.   WC

DOUCE, Francis (1757–1834), antiquarian and book collector, chiefly remembered for the valuable collection of books and manuscripts which he bequeathed to the Bodleian Library, Oxford.

Douce was trained as an attorney and entered Gray's Inn in 1779, but his real interest was collecting, to which he devoted most of his time and money. In 1779 he was elected a Fellow of the Society of Antiquaries and contributed regularly to its journal, *Archaeologia*. His most significant publication was *Illustrations of Shakespeare* (1807), which was primarily concerned with presenting *Shakespeare as a dramatist in touch with the culture of the people. Douce's view of Shakespeare was shared with fellow antiquarians such as Francis *Grose and Joseph *Ritson, and stands in stark contrast to the more Romantic version of the dramatist soon to be in the ascendant in the literary criticism of *Coleridge, *Hazlitt, and *Lamb. Francis *Jeffrey's review in the *Edinburgh Review* poured scorn on the pedantry of Douce's scholarship.

Douce also played a key part in the revival of interest in *romance. Both Ritson and George Ellis (1783–1815) used material lent by him for their editions of metrical romances, and Sir Walter *Scott used a Douce manuscript for his *Sir Tristram* (1804). Douce was also a friend of James *Barry, who drew his portrait in 1803, and he remained close to Isaac *D'Israeli, who influenced him in his decision to bequeath his collection to the Bodleian. He shared with D'Israeli and other antiquarians an interest in *Blake's illuminated books, and may have bought a copy of *The Gates of Paradise* as early as 1794.

For all his reclusiveness, Douce was a *Deist in religion and a radical in politics who worshipped *Napoleon. Like Ritson and the other antiquarians with whom he was associated, Douce's interest in *popular culture [23] was closely related to his political opinions. He encouraged William *Hone in his *antiquarianism [35], and showed an equal interest in his political pamphlets. In 1822 Douce anonymously attacked the government in the pamphlet *The Case of the Fundholders Maintained and Defended*.

In 1807 he was appointed Keeper of the Department of Manuscripts at the *British Museum, where he worked on the Lansdowne and Harleian collections, but he found it hard to conform to the demands of the institution and resigned in 1811, at odds with the trustees. A bequest from the sculptor Joseph *Nollekens, made in 1823, allowed him to indulge his collecting tastes more freely for the last ten years of his life.   JM

dower was a right of feudal origin which under English law accorded to widows one-third of their husband's property above and beyond any other settlement made upon them.

Over the centuries, however, dower was evaded by complex conveyancing procedures. By the early nineteenth century dower was seen to impede the commercial opportunities attendant upon the changing role of landed property associated with the *agricultural revolution. Following the recommendations of a parliamentary commission, the legal expenses and uncertainty of evading dower were resolved to the landowners' benefit when the Dower Act of 1833 allowed a husband to extricate himself from the 'burden' of dower by simply stating this wish in his will.   ARB

DOYLE, John (1797–1868), painter, caricaturist, leading political cartoonist of the late 1820s and 1830s, particularly on the issues of the *Reform Act of 1832, the *corn laws, and *Catholic emancipation.

Born in Dublin, Doyle came to London in 1821, exhibiting occasionally with the *Royal Academy. In 1827–8 he began the lithograph *prints [22] known as *Political Sketches*, using the initials 'H. B.' Numbering 917 in all, and continuing to appear until 1851, these sketches appeared at irregular intervals in batches of four or five, usually once a month during the parliamentary session. Their realism, decorousness, and light satiric touch offered a marked contrast to the extravagantly vitriolic and scurrilous caricatures of earlier figures such as Thomas *Rowlandson and James *Gillray. Indeed, the almost complete absence of exaggeration suggests they are better described as cartoons than as caricatures. Full of shadowy, subtly elongated masculine figures, Doyle's cartoons offer a brooding, mordant political irony, as in his representation of Daniel *O'Connell as the *Whigs' 'Political Frankenstein'. Doyle cartooned such leading figures as George IV, *Peel, and *Wellington.

Doyle's second son, Richard (1824–83), was a regular contributor to *Punch* magazine from 1843 until 1850.   CT

DRAGONETTI, Domenico Carlo Maria (1763–1846), known as 'Il Drago', Italian double-bass player, composer, collector. A musician of unique talent whose career in Britain was far-reaching and extraordinary, he transformed the function and status of the double-bass as an orchestral, chamber, and solo instrument.

Dragonetti arrived in London in the autumn of 1794: it was the beginning of a period of dominance. During the 1790s he became a famed virtuoso soloist, performing his compositions to widespread acclaim and astonishment. After 1815 his income was mainly derived from orchestral engagements. His diary included work for the King's Theatre, the Ancient Concerts, the Philharmonic Society, and provincial *music festivals. The performance of chamber music consolidated his reputation. Works by *Beethoven, Hummel, Neukomm, Spohr, *Moscheles, *Potter, and *Cramer were standard repertoire. Arrangements of works by Corelli and *Handel enabled Dragonetti to respond to the taste of audiences. His outwardly curved bow gave a characteristic strength to performances on his three-stringed instrument. An astute businessman, often aided by his close friend Vincent *Novello, he commanded high fees. His wrangles with the Philharmonic Society resulted both in his absence from the premiere of Beethoven's ninth symphony in 1825 and in the remarkable fact that he was the highest-paid member of the Philharmonic Society orchestra from 1831 to 1842.

The pomp and popularity of Dragonetti's funeral testifies to the niche that this musician had carved for himself at the heart of British *music [26]. His talent had changed the expectations of the musical world.

FMP

DRUMMOND, Henry (1786–1860), MP (Plympton Earls 1810–12; West Surrey 1847–60), *philanthropist, landowner, and self-confessed 'Tory of the Old School'. Drummond was a leading supporter of the religious congregation gathered around the charismatic Scottish preacher Edward Irving (1792–1834) in London.

Drummond's religious commitments and political affiliations were closely related. Believing that divine providence was an active, interventionist force in the world, he thought of government as an essentially paternalistic agency with a duty to regulate and succour its subjects. These beliefs placed him in direct opposition to *liberal Toryism. In 1825 he endowed the chair of political economy at Oxford which bears his name to counter the 'ignorance prevalent with respect to [its] true principles' and to oppose the baleful influence of what he disdainfully called the 'Scotch school of economists' [see *political economy, 33].

Drummond was a noted horticulturalist, who developed a splendid park at his property at Hartswood in Surrey, featured in William *Cobbett's *Rural Rides* (1830). In recounting a detour to admire Drummond's estate, Cobbett claimed that Drummond's philanthropic attitude towards the labouring classes gave him a surer claim to enjoy his estate than that possessed by any other landholder in England.

JMo

DRUMMOND, Sir William (?1770–1828) MP, diplomat, and antiquarian. His researches into comparative *mythology [36] and, especially, his sceptical opinions on the *Bible influenced a generation of freethinkers, including Percy *Shelley.

Drummond was the son of an old Scottish family and member of parliament for seats in the *Tory interest from 1795 to 1802. From 1801 to 1809 he was a diplomat at the courts of Naples and Constantinople (the latter granted him his knighthood), but his real interest lay with his antiquarian researches into comparative mythology and his philosophical inquiries [see *antiquarianism, 35]. The latter were best known through his *Academical Questions* (1805), a sceptical account of recent developments in philosophy, and several controversial reviews written for the *Edinburgh Review*. The treatise received a respectful review from Francis *Jeffrey, but Drummond's own scurrilous review of Hannah *More's

Hints toward Forming the Character of a Young Princess (1805) outraged many contemporaries. *Academical Questions* soon attracted a strong following among anti-Christian intellectuals such as Shelley and Thomas Love *Peacock. In the Preface to Laon and Cynthia (1818), Shelley described it as 'a volume of very acute and powerful metaphysical criticism'. The anti-Christian bent of Drummond's metaphysics is reflected in his antiquarian researches: *Herculanesia, or Archaeological and Philological Dissertations* (1810), *Oedipus Judaicus* (1811), and *Origines, or Remarks on the Origin of Several Empires* (1824–9). Printed for private circulation, *Oedipus Judaicus* soon joined texts such as *Volney's *Ruins* as part of the freethinking canon for its claim, adopted from Charles Dupuis (1742–1809), that much of the Old Testament was made up of allegories derived from worship of the sun. For much of the latter part of his life, clearly at odds with the British establishment, Drummond lived abroad. He died in Rome.

JM

duelling. The modern duel with its code of honour and elaborate etiquette emerged in sixteenth-century Italy, whence it spread to the rest of Europe. It denoted the armed conflict between two gentlemen, one of whom demanded 'satisfaction' for a perceived harm or insult, being ready to risk his life rather than see honour or reputation compromised.

Throughout our period, the duel was proscribed by church and state and vigorously opposed by a host of prominent legal writers, moralists, and novelists. In his *Commentaries on the Laws of England* (1765–9) the jurist William *Blackstone described duelling as an act of premeditated murder, and thus a capital offence. William *Paley complained in his influential *Moral and Political Philosophy* (1785) that the duellist's code of honour was not a genuine ethics but merely a set of rules to regulate the relationships among the ruling classes. The patrician code did not address the 'whole duty of man', and was a serious threat to public morals because of its preparedness to breach a gentleman's duty to God and to his social inferiors.

Duelling was also attacked by novelists, poets, and men and women of letters whose leading characters often embodied a very different set of moral ideals. Unlike the suave and ruthless heroes of the past, the new gentleman was an exemplary Christian and a good citizen, who displayed his superior courage by declining to duel from motives of reason and duty. Increasingly, fictional characters possessed non-martial virtues which reflected the new emphasis on politeness and *sensibility [11].

Yet despite this powerful *Enlightenment [32] critique of duelling and associated condemnation of other feudal and aristocratic ideals, the practice flourished. Sensibility was not necessarily at odds with the older ideals of courtly love and chivalry, and the age of revolution also celebrated physical courage, *patriotism, and blood sacrifice. Moreover, as Jeremy *Bentham noted in his treatise on *Morals and Legislation* (1789), traditional notions of honour were also compatible with modern notions of property. If a man's professional reputation was a kind of 'fictitious object of property', he could legitimately defend it as the law did his property. More typical was Walter *Scott, who discerned a tension between modern commercial ideals of person and property and those of the aristocratic and chivalrous past; he thus admired and respected some aspects of the code of honour but was, nevertheless, highly critical of it.

Duelling continued unabated until the second half of the nineteenth century. Gentlemen from all walks of life, soldiers, politicians, and even doctors fell, as Thomas *Carlyle put it, 'mutually skewered through with iron'. To the end, however, the duel remained the prerogative of the upper classes, and few duellists ever met the legal fate assigned to them by Blackstone.   LH

DUNDAS, Henry, first Viscount Melville (1742–1811), statesman (MP, Midlothian 1774–90; Newton 1780; Edinburgh 1790–1802), close political associate of the younger William *Pitt, patron, and leading figure among Edinburgh literati in the 1770s and early 1780s.

Dundas was accused of fostering his Scottish compatriots' interests as a member of the India Board of Control in 1785 and as First Lord of the Admiralty in 1804–5, though his distribution of patronage was relatively even-handed and his energetic attention to detail significantly improved the quality of administration. Skilled at managing men, he was far less adept in financial management, a failing which bedevilled his treasurership of the navy (1784–1800) and allowed his opponents to move for his impeachment before the House of Lords in 1806. This trial, the last of its kind in Britain, aroused great interest in political circles—especially among oppositionist pamphleteers—and resulted in Dundas's acquittal on charges of malverzation. A lack of executive and military ability marred Dundas's period as Secretary of War from 1794 to 1801, but as Home Secretary between 1791 and 1794 his pursuit of the propagators of revolutionary and reformist principles was notoriously energetic.

Despite a contemporary reputation for opportunism, Dundas possessed a genuine if complacent attachment to the traditional constitution, and excelled at the political management appropriate to pre-reform politics. During the course of his public career he cultivated both major and minor members of the landed classes in Scotland, and built up an interest which influenced the electoral politics of his native country until the passage of the *Reform Act in 1832.   JMo

DUSSEK, Jan Ladislav (1760–1812), Bohemian *pianist and composer, an important figure in the London Pianoforte School during the 1790s. Educated in Prague, Dussek was living in Paris under the patronage of Marie-Antoinette when the *French Revolution forced him to flee to London. From 1789

to 1799 he was London's principal virtuoso pianist; he also played a major part in the development of the piano itself, advising John Broadwood on technical matters, and in his own music experimenting with a range of colouristic textures [see London *keyboards]. His fine sonatas and concertos, unjustly neglected today, develop a pre-Romantic expressive vein, through a lyrical use of the keyboard and an unusual richness of harmonic palette. These characteristics were influential not only on local composers such as John Field (1782–1837) but also on Schubert and *Mendelssohn. Some of Dussek's best-known pieces also anticipate the new Romantic aesthetic in their use of titles: the programmatic *Sufferings of the Queen of France* (1793) is little more than a curiosity, but in its passionate intensity and exquisite poetry the 'Farewell' Sonata (1800) is one of the most profound works of its time. It reflected Dussek's feelings on his enforced departure from England, bankrupt on account of a publishing venture with Domenico *Corri.   SMcV

DYER, George (1755–1841), political pamphleteer, poet, scholar, and editor. Dyer attended Christ's Hospital from 1762, and subsequently Emmanuel College, Cambridge, meeting William Taylor (William *Wordsworth's schoolmaster at Hawkshead) and the classical scholar Gilbert Wakefield (1756–1801). After graduating BA in 1778, Dyer taught at Dedham Grammar School and John Ryland's baptist school at Northampton, where John Clarke (later John *Keats's schoolmaster) also taught. In the 1780s he tutored the family of Robert Robinson, the baptist minister whose *Memoirs* Dyer published in 1796.

Cambridge Dissent influenced his intellectual life and publications in the 1790s; he welcomed the *French Revolution, and encouraged political and social reforms in Britain. His pamphlets *The Complaints of the Poor People of England* (1793) and *A Dissertation on Benevolence* (1795) placed him at the forefront of the democratic reform movement. He was an important London contact for S. T. *Coleridge and Robert *Southey, distributing copies of their *Fall of Robespierre* and also, in May 1796, helping to offset Coleridge's losses after the failure of the *Watchman*. Dyer's verses and critical writings appeared widely in magazines and journals, and in his collected volumes *Poems* (1792), *The Poet's Fate* (1797), *Poems* (1801), *Poems and Critical Essays* (1802), and *Poetics* (1812). His later years were devoted to scholarly researches; see for example his *History of the University and Colleges of Cambridge* (1814) and *The Privileges of the University of Cambridge* (1824). He also worked as editor on Valpy's extensive edition of the classical authors. Often viewed as an eccentric, Dyer was a central figure in radical political and literary circles of the 1790s, and his later publications remain valuable, if often neglected, references.   NR

67. Augustus Earle, *Solitude. Watching the horizon at sunset in the hopes of seeing a vessel—Tristan D'Acunha, in the South Atlantic*, watercolour, 1824. The stranded painter represents himself as a solitary exile.

E

EARLE, Augustus (1793–1838), Anglo-American painter of *landscape, *portrait, and genre scenes. Probably the first freelance artist to tour the world [see *painting, 27 and *exploration, 37].

Earle exhibited at the *Royal Academy from 1806 and travelled to Europe, North Africa, and North America before sailing to Rio de Janeiro in 1820 for what was to be an absence of ten years. The *water-colours made on this world tour are his most notable achievement and were undoubtedly intended for publication before his premature death in 1838 pre-vented this. In 1824 he left Rio bound for the Cape of Good Hope. Cast away on the remote island of Tristan da Cunha, Earle put his time to good use, making watercolours of the island scenery and inhabitants and writing an engaging account of his residence there, together with a narrative of his later residence in New Zealand in 1827, both of which were published in 1832.

In Sydney from 1825 Earle established a litho-graphic press, painted eight views which Burford used for his *panorama of Sydney, and made por-traits of local worthies. He went on to visit Penang, Malacca, Guam, and St Helena before returning to London in 1830. In 1831 he was offered a position as draughtsman on the *Beagle*, sharing a cabin with Charles Darwin.

Earle is valued for his ability to adapt to different circumstances and surroundings and for his acute ob-servations of colonists, convicts, and native peoples in a number of continents. He resisted the use of standard European conventions of representation. More recently his work has been appreciated for its unusual and original representation of the complex relations between settlers and *indigenous peoples.

JH-J

East India Company, which began as a commercial venture, became the instrument for Britain's con-quest of India and more generally a vehicle for the dissemination of British economic, strategic, and cultural influence throughout monsoon Asia [see *empire, 5; Warren *Hastings].

Launched in 1600 by a group of London mer-chants, the Company won a royal charter giving it exclusive rights over the Asian trade. This was one pillar of its commercial success. The other was its financial structure. The East India Company was one of the first of the new joint-stock concerns, which revolutionized commerce in the early seventeenth century by tapping into the savings of a multiplicity of small stockholders. With an initial working capital of £3,200,000 it was, by the standards of the time, a corporate giant. Where a smaller enterprise would

probably have succumbed to the hazards which attended the Eastern trade in that period (shipwreck, political anarchy, rapacious rulers), the Company survived and prospered, returning a steady dividend to its shareholders in the early eighteenth century of around 10 per cent from sales of spices, cotton piece-goods, and China tea.

Left to their own devices, the Company's directors would have been quite content to continue in this vein, but circumstances dictated otherwise. The crumbling of state structures and the resultant rise of internecine warfare and banditry in India began seriously to inhibit its textile trade, as did competition from the French, who in the 1740s hit upon the idea of bribing local rajas to expel the English from their dominions. Reluctantly, though not without a sense of destiny, the Company raised an army and embarked on a forward policy of diplomacy backed increasingly by military campaigns: first against the French and their allies in the Carnatic, then against the Nawab of Bengal, and finally against Mysore and the Maratha confederacy. By 1765 it controlled, in effect, much of eastern India.

Mesmerized as it was with making money, however, the Company only gradually awoke to the political responsibilities which its military power conferred. Not until the 1770s did it begin to administer Bengal in its own right and not until the 1790s, under Lord Cornwallis (1738–1805), did its administration start to take on a mature colonial form. In the meantime it exploited Bengal mercilessly, triggering a terrible famine in which perhaps a third of the population perished. Ironically, though, while Bengal's taxes helped to swell the Company's investments, the resultant profits were eaten up by the costs of its military operations to the point where it was forced in 1772 to seek a loan from the Crown to meet its debts. All this led to calls in England for the Company to be brought to heel, and in 1773 the first of several Acts was passed to this purpose. The portentous East India Act of 1784 gave the Company a new and powerfully centralized administrative shape. But while the *Whigs were eventually accepting of this, others were not, and in the early nineteenth century the Company came under further attack from free-traders and *Evangelicals opposed to its ban on Christian missionizing. In 1813 parliament deprived the Company of its monopoly on trade with India, and forced it to accept *missionaries. In 1833 it lost its China monopoly, and in 1858 it was ignominiously wound up by a government intent on finding a scapegoat for British losses in the Sepoy Rebellion of 1857.   IC

EATON, Daniel Isaac (pseuds. 'Ebenezer Verax', 'Antitype') (1753–1814), radical publisher, bookseller, and propagandist. Providing unwavering support to leading radical writers and activists through his trade as a stationer, Eaton dedicated his life to political reform.

Educated in France and apprenticed as a stationer, Eaton displayed little interest in politics before he met Dr James *Parkinson. Trading in Hoxton, he came into contact with Parkinson's circle and was persuaded in 1792 to move his business to Bishopsgate Street. Immediately he joined the London Corresponding Society and supported the Friends to the Liberty of the Press [see *corresponding societies]. He became renowned for his courageous *publishing [21] ventures, including the works of Parkinson, John *Thelwall, and Charles *Pigott. With two acquittals in 1793 for publishing seditious libels in works by Thomas *Paine, Eaton's trials became pillars in the fight for liberty.

As a pamphleteer Eaton displayed infrequent skills. Issuing his first tract in 1793, he wrote just four more during his entire career, assailing issues like the *war [2] with France, encroachments on the *freedom of the press, and civil liberties. He found more success as a radical journalist, editing and publishing two radical weeklies in the 1790s [see *prose, 30]. *Politics for the People* (1793–5) was his first and most progressive weekly, running for eighteen months with regular contributions from Thelwall and Parkinson. The ideas he delivered in this journal were continued and developed in the *Philanthropist* (1795–6), a project in which William *Wordsworth apparently expressed an initial interest.

Eaton exhibited a brave and tenacious character as a radical activist. Involved closely with the LCS, his bookshop became a harbour for reformers and was renowned throughout England. Eight times prosecuted, outlawed, and exiled, he earned the respect of colleagues and the attention of *anti-Jacobins.

Late in 1797, Eaton fled to Philadelphia to avoid imprisonment, returning in 1802 to be incarcerated and declared bankrupt. After receiving a royal pardon in 1805, he quietly traded for five years at Stratford Green, before again moving his business to London. Entering the volatile world where freethought and political radicalism overlapped, Eaton became involved with a group of *Spenceans in the publication of extreme freethinking works. In 1812 he was tried and found guilty of publishing a blasphemous libel in Paine's *Age of Reason: Part the Third* (1811). Sentenced to stand in the pillory and to eighteen months' confinement, he penned his last pamphlet on the *Extortions and Abuses of Newgate* (1813). Late in 1813 he was released from prison and immediately apprehended for information about the publication of Baron d'Holbach's (1723–89) *Ecce Homo* (1813). He submitted to the pressure by May 1814, offering the name of the publisher and was subsequently granted immunity.

Eaton did not live much longer. Suffering from ill health, he spent his last months at his sister's house in Deptford, and died on 22 August 1814. The hardships he had endured and the headstrong courage he displayed in the course of his career bear testimony to the often maligned tenacity of many British Jacobins.   MD

EDEN, Sir Frederick Morton (1766–1809), social investigator and commentator on the condition of the poor. Eden's major work, *The State of the Poor*

(1797), is a detailed history and analysis of poor relief from 1066 to the 1790s. Using *statistics and case studies, Eden aimed to survey *poverty [12] systematically by measuring wages, prices, and expenditure on the poor in 181 parishes throughout England and Wales. He established domestic economy as central to the management of poverty. Eden argued against extensive public provision for the poor, preferring the principles of self-help and insurance. Eden's vast work was a significant intervention into debate on *poor law reform and a notable early contribution to a sociology of poverty. SL

EDGEWORTH, Maria (1767/8–1849), novelist, children's writer, and educationalist. As the initiator of the Anglo-Irish regional novel, the first writer to establish a significant readership for *novels [31] of Irish life, and the most celebrated and successful of practising British novelists during the 1800s and early 1810s, Edgeworth is a key figure in the development of British fiction.

After an intermittent education at home from her stepmother and at school in Derby and London, she moved to the estate of her father, Richard Lovell *Edgeworth, in Edgeworthstown, County Longford, in 1782, the year of the establishment of an independent Irish parliament. Here, she assisted her father in running the estate and educating the younger Edgeworth children. The fullest account of their educational methods is found in *Practical Education* (1798), an empirical development of *Rousseau, and the first product of a continuing collaborative relationship. Edgeworth's first fictional work, *Letters for Literary Ladies* (1795), offers a spirited defence of *female education. The earliest of her fictional works for children, which offer some of the earliest innovations in the burgeoning genre of *children's literature, *The Parent's Assistant* (1796–1800), also co-written with her father, was an influential advocate of the new, enlightened domestic patriarchy [see *domesticity, 13].

Edgeworth's four Irish novels, more accurately described as tales or novellas, are *Castle Rackrent* (1800), *Ennui* (1809), *The Absentee* (1812), and *Ormond* (1817). They manifest an informed awareness of the existence of the centuries-old near-continuous crisis in Ireland through a necessarily divided Anglo-Irish perspective and ironic self-consciousness. Coinciding with the approval of the 1800 *Act of Union, and set before the 1782 parliamentary independence, *Castle Rackrent* is a chronicle of the decline of the house of Rackrent narrated in the first person by the family retainer, Thady Quirk, whose attorney son eventually assumes control of the property. *Castle Rackrent* was the first novel to feature a narrator who speaks dialect. Whilst the use of actual Irish dialect is minimal, and the narrative depends more on the stylistic rather than strictly linguistic resources of Irish English, the striking characterization and complex ironic perspective developed through the persona of Thady Quirk marked a significant departure in the representation of the Irish from the conventional caricature of the English stage-Irish tradition. For this reason, and on account of its atten-

tion to social and historical detail and focus on common Irish life, *Castle Rackrent* was enthusiastically received by critics such as Francis *Jeffrey and by Sir Walter *Scott (who was greatly indebted to Edgeworth), and has been regarded as the first regional novel. Arguably Edgeworth's most innovative and complex fiction, *The Absentee* (1812) traces the consequences of the Union, focusing on the removal of a newly titled Anglo-Irish élite to London and the resulting deterioration of their Irish estates. Suggesting the development into novelistic technique of what Edgeworth had noted in Edmund *Burke's oratorical style as 'allusions by a single word', *The Absentee* is exceptional amongst contemporary domestic realist texts in its sophisticated allusive use of local detail. Worked into the story of the return to Ireland of an absentee family are fragmented yet highly charged allegories of Jewish and classical exile (it offers an early Anglo-Irish version of the Ulysses legend); Jacobite conflict; the relation of the Catholic question to French, English, and Irish Jacobinism; British imperialism in the Caribbean; and Edgeworth's own Anglo-Irish ascendancy family history. In its characterization of the allegorically named heroine, Grace Nugent, *The Absentee* samples and allegorizes the Irish aisling or vision-poem, an earlier-eighteenth-century Jacobite genre that superimposes historical narrative upon poetic reverie. Jacobite allusions are to some extent defused through the conservative paradigm of responsible landlordism, later given such a formidable Burkean ideological contour in Jane *Austen's *Mansfield Park* (1814). Grace Nugent comes to represent a domesticated Ireland, and lengthy revisions to the 1832 edition emphasize her domesticity. Edgeworth's calculated fictions distance themselves from the more sentimentalizing forms of contemporary Romantic *antiquarianism [35], such as the lavish novels of Sydney *Owenson (Lady Morgan) which she saw as politically naïve and indiscriminate idealizations of Irish traditions. Published in the series entitled *Tales of Fashionable Life*, and full of piquant social satire, *The Absentee* also exemplifies the contemporary satire on courtly or fashionable society life, a major post-revolutionary genre amongst women novelists such as Mary *Brunton. Edgeworth's English society novels, or novels of manners, *Belinda* (1801), *Leonora* (1806), *Patronage* (1814), and *Helen* (1834), tend toward generalizing, schematic moralism, despite a deft *silver fork touch. Subsequent editions of *Belinda* in 1803 and 1810 which occluded two controversial marriages between English women and a black servant and Creole master reflected the contemporary anxieties about intermarriage that accompanied the *abolitionism debate. They also tone down the sexually ambiguous, cross-dressing Harriet Freke and her support of *women's [4] rights. The *Memoirs of Richard Lovell Edgeworth* (1820), begun by her father, was completed by Maria after his death in 1817. The *Memoirs* manifest a paternalistic ascendancy perspective towards property, class relations, and the native Irish. However, its account of the 1798 riots in Edgeworthstown, when the Edgeworth family was threatened both by invading French troops and by a Protestant militia that suspected the liberal Edgeworth of siding with the rebel troops, provides an important example of the insecure and compromised historical position of the Anglo-Irish ascendancy class during the post-revolutionary years.   CT

EDGEWORTH, Richard Lovell (1744–1817), inventor and educational theorist. Richard Lovell Edgeworth's Protestant Anglo-Irish family were landlords of an estate confiscated from Irish Catholics by James I. Sent to study law at Oxford, he made a runaway match with the daughter of an impoverished English barrister. Maria *Edgeworth was their eldest daughter. Richard Lovell was to marry three more times, each wife younger than her predecessor, fathering altogether twenty-two children.

In 1766, while living in the English midlands, Edgeworth was introduced by Thomas *Day into the Lunar Society, along with Joseph *Priestley, Erasmus *Darwin, the engineer James *Watt, the potter and philanthropist Josiah *Wedgwood, and the reformist physician Thomas *Beddoes [see also *literary and philosophical societies]. The circle shared Edgeworth's enthusiasm for mechanical inventions and schemes of improvement. Edgeworth was particularly concerned with schemes regarding *children's literature and early childhood training. In some respects influenced by *Rousseau and perhaps more directly by *Locke and David Hartley (1705–57), Edgeworth believed in letting children learn by experiment, and emphasized applied science over the traditional classics. However, his schemes left little room for imaginative literature and, while he claimed with Rousseau to defer to the opinion of children, his theories had a *utilitarian stress on 'useful knowledge'. In 1780 he co-wrote *Practical Education* with his second wife, drawing extensively on her notes. Later, he and Maria collaborated under the same title for their first publication, *Practical Education* (2 vols., 1798). The second *Practical Education* heralds a theoretical shift towards the nuclear family unit as the primary socializer of the child. The failure of the text to find a role for religious instruction made Edgeworth notorious to *Tory journalists, who brought the matter up in reviews of his posthumous memoir.

The year 1798 saw the French invasion of County Mayo in support of the Irish *Rebellion. The Edgeworthstown estate workers rose against their landlord, but were put down after a sharp struggle during which Edgeworth and his children were forced to flee to the county capital. Edgeworth was subsequently elected to the Irish parliament for a rotten borough. The uprising shocked the family out of proprietorial complacency, and Edgeworth turned off the estate those of his tenants who had supported Wolfe *Tone, never permitting them to return. As an Irish MP Edgeworth campaigned for government control of *popular education and in 1799 brought in a bill in the Irish House of Commons 'for the improvement of the education of the people of Ireland'. Between 1806 and 1811 he was one of the Commissioners appointed by the United Kingdom government to inquire into public education in Ireland.

From 1805, Edgeworth corresponded with Étienne Dumont (1759–1829), a French commentator on Jeremy *Bentham and Samuel *Romilly, who offered him editorial advice and assistance. For Maria's next educational treatise, *Professional Education* (1809), Edgeworth no longer joined in the actual writing, though his name alone appeared on the cover. After Edgeworth's death in 1817, Maria was quick to repudiate Dumont's surveillance of her continuation of her father's *Memoirs*. In spite of Maria's labours on his behalf for thirty-five years, Edgeworth's will cut her out of any further role in running the estate.   JB

EGAN, Pierce, the elder (*c*.1774–1849), the foremost sports and crime journalist of the *Regency period, and a popular writer whose works exercised an enormous, but now largely forgotten, influence.

Egan grew up in London, where his Irish migrant father worked as a road labourer. Pierce was initially apprenticed to Bloomsbury printer Lockington Johnson, then worked as a compositor for the Smeeton brothers, printer-stationers of St Martin's Lane. Here Egan educated himself in every facet of the *publishing [21] trade, as well as in the convivial habitats and popular pursuits of cockney London. After writing chapbooks and other forms of ephemeral *street literature, his first great literary and commercial success was to produce an illustrated history of pugilism for Smeeton in 1812. *Boxiana* eventually ran to five volumes; its success reflected Egan's unique knowledge of the sport, the advent of a faster, more attractive style of fighting perfected by Daniel Mendoza (1763–1836), and the emergence of new commercial markets for the consumption of *popular culture [23]. By extolling the masculine and patriotic qualities of the ring, Egan also reflected and expressed the racy style of the Prince of Wales's set during the wartime years.

After working for some years as a crime and sports reporter on Robert Bell's lively populist newspaper the *Weekly Dispatch* (later *Bell's Weekly*), and producing a typical squib *satire in 1814 on the promiscuity of the Regent, Egan wrote one of the publishing sensations of the nineteenth century. *Life in London* was first issued in weekly parts in September 1820, with coloured illustrations by Robert and George *Cruikshank, and it immediately took Britain by storm. Drawing on an established genre of picaresque and sensational low-life explorations, Egan recounted the adventures of a young urban swell, Corinthian Tom, his sporty rural friend, Jerry Hawthorn, and the feckless Oxonian, Bob Logic [see *dandyism]. Readers were introduced with vivid particularity to the exuberant nightlife haunts and strange underworld patois of characters such as 'Black Sal', 'Flashy Nance', and 'Nasty Bob'. Published in full in 1821, *Life in London* was massively plagiarized and imitated; it also generated numbers of popular theatrical adaptations, most notably by

33

68. Illustration to Pierce Egan's *Life in London* (1821) by George and Robert Cruikshank. The three male protagonists dance with the prostitute Corinthian Kate.

Charles *Dibdin and W. T. Moncrieff (1794–1857). Its influence on the *Newgate literature of Victorians such as *Bulwer-Lytton, *Dickens, and *Thackeray was profound. Egan's last great success as a popular writer and journalist consisted of biographical studies in this same Newgate crime vein, the best-known being his *Recollections of John Thurtell* (1824), the account of a sometime boxing promoter and murderer whom Egan knew personally. Towards the end of his life Egan began collaborating with his son Pierce junior (1814–80), who became a prolific popular novelist. Arguably Pierce Egan senior did for urban plebeian culture what Walter *Scott did for the rural Scottish peasantry, inaugurating a brand of popular Romanticism which William *Hazlitt and the young Charles Dickens were to perfect.   IMcC

Egyptology. By the end of the eighteenth century British travellers had described many of the ancient monuments of ancient Egypt, both on site and in Rome where many obelisks had been re-erected in the late sixteenth century. At this time, private collectors and amateur archaeologists were publishing papers on ancient Egyptian culture in such journals as *Archaeologia* (established 1770), the organ of the Society of Antiquaries, while various scholars sought to clarify the chronology of Egyptian history. These attempts were based on flawed Latin and Greek sources and on the *Bible. Access to Egyptian sources had to await the deciphering of hieroglyphics.

The prevailing understanding of hieroglyphics, enunciated first by Athanasius Kircher (1602–80), was that they were not a language as we would recognize it but a direct visual expression of thought.

Progress on the deciphering of the Egyptian script was made possible by the discovery by the Napoleonic army in 1798 of the Rosetta Stone, later sequestered by the British in 1801. The Rosetta Stone is inscribed in parallel in Greek, hieroglyphs, and demotic Egyptian. Serious attempts to read the hieroglyphic inscription were made in 1815–16 by Thomas *Young, who published his findings in the 1819 edition of the *Encyclopaedia Britannica*. However, real clarity only came with the discoveries of the French scholar Jean-François Champollion (1790–1832), published in *Summary of the Hieroglyphic System of the Ancient Egyptians* of 1824.

The early nineteenth century also took a keen interest in the collection of Egyptian antiquities, including mummies. Henry Salt (1780–1827), British consul-general in Egypt from 1815 to 1827, was responsible for selling significant collections of Egyptian goods to the *British Museum. At the same time, Egyptian style fed the taste for the exotic in *architecture [28] and *design [25], paralleling the enthusiasm for *chinoiserie.   BP

36

eisteddfod, the competitive gathering of poets and musicians which came to play a central role in the *Welsh cultural revival. Its roots go back at least to the twelfth century and probably earlier. After the decline of the Bardic Order in the sixteenth century, poets and musicians still gathered in taverns to discuss poetry and versify, and in the early eighteenth century such meetings were advertised beforehand in *almanacs. They were small affairs of a dozen at most and there were no prizes. The 1790s saw the expansion of the eisteddfod into a centre of literary life through the backing of patriotic London Welshmen such as William Owen *Pughe. Definite conditions were set for competitions which attracted poets, harpers, and singers, and audiences included the gentry and a number of literary Welsh clerics.

These clerics wished to promote Welsh history, poetry, *antiquarianism [35], and *music [26] and were the chief patrons of the Carmarthen Eisteddfod in 1819, which introduced two important innovations: in addition to the bardic competitions there were evening musical concerts which attracted the non-Welsh speakers among the gentry; and for the first time Edward *Williams's Gorsedd of Bards, trailing druidic glory, met in conjunction with the eisteddfod. A subsequent meeting which included the Bishop of St David's and Lord Dynevor passed a number of resolutions to promote Welsh history and literature by copying and cataloging Welsh manuscripts. They also established the principle of the regional eisteddfod to spread the benefits of Welsh history and literature to all parts of the country, and these were held fairly regularly until 1834.   PK

ELDON, first Earl of (John Scott) (1751–1838), Lord Chancellor. Despite his modest beginnings, Eldon's technical mastery of the *law [8] and his service as the legal instrument of government repression in the 1790s made him the natural choice as Lord Chancellor in all the *Tory ministries between 1801 and 1827—a position from which he resisted all attempts at *constitutional or legal reform and exasperated litigants by his indecisiveness in the court of Chancery, while refining the principles of equity. His tendency to moralizing and his emotional outbursts of paternal sympathy in court were condemned by Percy *Shelley as mere crocodile tears in the context of the government's reaction to public distress and disorder in 1817 and 1819.   DL

elections. It is too easily assumed that in the unreformed electoral system parliamentary elections were entirely dominated by the landed classes: with the candidates selected by the local élite, elected by small electorates in constituencies that rarely went to the polls, chosen by submissive or venal electors, and not concerned to take a stand on a matter of principle or a national issue. There is some truth in all of these assumptions, but by no means represent the whole picture. The electoral system was more open and elections had to be more carefully managed than this stereotype implies. Some 558 MPs were elected to the Westminster parliament from Great Britain, and another 100 were elected from Ireland after the *Union of 1801. MPs were required by law to possess real estate worth £600 or £300 p.a. if they wished to represent a county or borough constituency respectively. As a result, the largest social group (at least half of all MPs) elected to the House of Commons was drawn from the landed élite. But by the early nineteenth century about half of all MPs were drawn from the professional, commercial, and manufacturing classes.

Candidates were sometimes nominated by a single individual, particularly in the small 'pocket' or 'rotten' boroughs, but more often they were selected by agreement between several competing local families and interests, who tried where possible to avoid an expensive contested election. In a very small number of constituencies (notably Westminster and Bristol) the voters tried to put up their own candidates. Despite the natural desire of the élite to avoid a rancorous and expensive contest, between a fifth and a third of English constituencies went to the polls in each general election. Parliaments were allowed by law to last seven years, but very few went to the full term and general elections were held on average about every five years.

The franchise varied from constituency to constituency, but in almost all cases it was attached to the ownership of relatively small amounts of property. The total electorate in Scotland and Ireland was quite small, but it was much larger in England and Wales—about 338,000 men in the late eighteenth century and about 439,200 in 1831 (17.2 per cent and 14.4 per cent of all adult males respectively). About 14 per cent of English electors were drawn from the landed and professional classes, and about the same percentage were labourers. The rest, the overwhelming majority of voters, were drawn from the middling classes (merchants, retailers, craftsmen, etc.).

Some constituencies were very small and results there were often heavily influenced by the Crown, great aristocrats, or the borough corporation. Other constituencies had several hundred electors, and influence was shared among several interests. In such cases electors needed to be persuaded how to vote. A significant number of the larger counties and larger boroughs (such as London, Westminster, Southwark, Bristol, and Liverpool) had quite substantial electorates of many thousands. These more open constituencies needed to be carefully managed if success were to be assured. In almost all constituencies, those seeking to influence elections generally had to show an interest in the local community and had to spend money in the constituency (contributing to the expense of local assembly-halls, schools, hospitals, and charities or spending money in local inns, retail shops, and workshops. In the more open constituencies the interests seeking to secure the election of their candidates had to spend considerable time, energy, and money: they frequently employed electoral agents, canvassed the voters assiduously, and paid their expenses so that they would make the journey to the polls.

Nearly all constituencies in England (though not elsewhere) were two-member constituencies (London had four MPs), and each voter therefore had two (or four) votes. Very few voters were openly bribed or were simply ordered by their landlord or employer how to vote. Even though there was no secret ballot and elections were held in the open air, patrons rarely expected more than one vote from their tenants or clients, and voters in the more open constituencies had some say in how they voted. Contested elections could be very boisterous affairs, involving speeches, music, marches, celebrations, and even violent riots. These activities could draw the non-voters into the proceedings of elections.

Most elections were about local issues, but, in the

more open constituencies and at times of political crisis, national issues could affect the results of general elections. It seems clear, for example, that public opinion did influence the overall results of the general elections of 1784, which gave the younger William *Pitt a clear majority, and of 1831, which ensured the subsequent passage of the *Reform Act.

HD

electricity in the late eighteenth century was a relatively new and exciting topic of *natural philosophy [34]. During the first half of the century new devices such as the plate and cylinder electrical machines and the Leyden jar had been developed. With these instruments the mysterious effluvium, or fluid, could be called forth to produce shocks, sparks, and strange attractions. Such electrical experiments were a staple of the popular natural philosophical *lecturers who mounted shows in *coffeehouses and rented halls. In the work of radical philosophers such as Joseph *Priestley, electricity could have revolutionary connotations. Electrical experiments provided a means of gaining access to the providential divine economy. Many of Priestley's works, such as his *History and Present State of Electricity* (1767), were deliberately written for a large market with the aim of making the divine economy accessible to all.

When the Italian Luigi Galvani drew electricity from frogs' legs, many hailed his work as providing evidence of the electric fluid's relationship to the life force. In 1802–3 Galvani's nephew, Giovanni Aldini, visited London to defend his uncle's work. In experiments before the Royal Society he used the dissected frogs and the heads of slaughtered oxen to produce the electrical fluid. The climax of his visit was the electrical demonstration on the corpse of a hanged murderer, fresh from Newgate.

In 1800 Galvani's fellow Italian Alessandro Volta devised the first electric battery to refute his fellow-countryman's claims. It provided a powerful new tool for electricians. Humphry *Davy in his flamboyant lectures at the newly founded Royal Institution used electricity in spectacular shows that dazzled his aristocratic audience. In his laboratory at the Royal Institution, Davy used massive electrical batteries to break down matter. New elements such as chlorine, produced by electricity, could be used to confound the French followers of the chemist Antoine Lavoisier (1743–94). Electricity's capacity to break down matter suggested to many that this was the force which held the universe together.

Davy's disciple Michael *Faraday made his career with electricity. Following Hans Christian Oersted's discovery in 1820 of the long-sought link between electricity and the equally mysterious force of magnetism, Faraday soon found a way of making an electric wire rotate around a magnet. Such philosophical toys proliferated during the 1820s. Faraday's competitor William Sturgeon (1783–1850) produced a whole range of new devices, winning the Society of Arts silver medal for his portable electrical laboratory. One of his instruments was the electromagnet, which used electricity to magnify the magnetic force. When electricity became a commercial

product a few decades later, this was to be a crucial piece of apparatus.

Electricity long retained its radical connotations. In the 1830s the *Owenite Thomas Simmons Mackintosh (*fl.* 1830s) could use his *Electrical Theory of the Universe* (*c.*1838) to call for the establishment of a new social order. The relationship between electricity and life was inevitably contentious. This became clear with the furore following the inadvertent production of insects by electricity in the laboratory of country gentleman Andrew Crosse. Speculations concerning electricity and life could still be dismissed as symptoms of the same revolutionary mania that had spawned mesmerism in France a few decades previously [see *animal magnetism]. Neither did electricity lose its capacity to dazzle. At the popular shows of the Adelaide Gallery or the Polytechnic Institution throughout the 1830s, electricity was central to displays of man's power over nature and its commercial application.

IRM

Elgin Marbles, Athenian friezes and sculptures collected by Thomas Bruce (1766–1841), seventh Earl of Elgin, during his tenure as ambassador in Constantinople between 1799 and 1803. In Britain, the Marbles generated much controversy. Although Elgin's collections were much admired, the publication and success of *Byron's *Childe Harold's Pilgrimage* in 1812 raised questions about the propriety of Elgin's acquisitions, although homages by (among others) Benjamin *Haydon and John *Keats suggest that Elgin's original ambition to introduce new standards of artistic excellence to Britain met with some success [see *Hellenism]. The enterprise proved very costly for Elgin. In 1810, and again in 1815, he petitioned the government to purchase his collections, although their sale in 1816 did little to restore his fortunes.

LT

ELLENBOROUGH, Earl (Edward Law) (1750–1818), judge. After considerable success as a barrister in the common law courts, Ellenborough made his public reputation as Edmund *Burke's principal opponent at the impeachment of Warren *Hastings. Like Burke and many of his contemporaries, his *Whiggism was overcome by fear of *revolution [1] after 1789; he subsequently became a supporter of the *Tory reaction, and in the House of Lords he used his authority as Lord Chief Justice of *King's Bench from 1802 to 1818 to oppose any reform in the criminal law. He also resisted *Catholic emancipation, and opposed the amelioration of arrest and imprisonment on suit for debt at common law, a system by which thousands of insolvent debtors were committed to prison every year.

DL

émigré journalists and publishers. Political and literary journalism flourished in London's French émigré community between 1792 and 1815, facilitated by a number of specialist printers and publishers. Émigré *newspapers and periodicals were important sources of information for the émigrés, merchants, foreign élites, and the British government [see *prose, 30]. They also helped the French émigrés form a sense of identity and maintain a public profile while in exile. Deeply reactionary from 1802 onwards, émigré journals helped to disseminate the 'Black Legend' of *Napoleon Bonaparte to an international audience and served as British propaganda. However, they failed to develop a positive rationale for Bourbonism, and thus contributed to the ideological failure of the restoration in France.

French exiles published pamphlet and journal literature from London throughout the eighteenth century. By 1789 there were several printers specializing in French in the metropolis: Edward Cox (fl. 1769–1809), printer of the Courier de Londres, in Great Queen Street, Thomas Baylis (fl. 1799–1809) of Greville Street, and Charles Spilsbury (fl. 1796–1810) of Snow Hill. Bookseller-publishers such as Joseph de Boffe and Thomas Boosey also enjoyed a thriving trade in *publishing [21]. In the 1790s the émigré community put out vast amounts of books, pamphlets, and other ephemera, and several émigrés entered the book trade, notably l'Homme, de Conchy, Peltier, and above all A. B. Dulau. These booksellers developed links with continental publishers, notably the house of Fauché and Lamaison-fort based at Hamburg and Brunswick.

The most significant French journal published in London in the eighteenth century was the twice-weekly Courier de Londres, founded in 1776. In April 1789 the former French finance minister Charles-Alexandre de Calonne bought a 50 per cent share in the paper, and in March 1793 he appointed an émigré named Verduisant as its editor. Subsequently the paper's editors included Calonne's brother, the abbé Jacques Ladislas Joseph de Calonne, and several other émigrés. The paper survived until 1826.

Jean-Gabriel Peltier (1760–1825), an experienced royalist journalist, produced a succession of titles between October 1792 and November 1818: Dernier Tableau de Paris (1792–3), Correspondance Politique (1793–4), Paris Pendant l'Année (1795–1802), and the notorious Ambigu (1802–18). Other émigré journals included Montlosier's Journal de France et d'Angleterre (January to July 1797), Jacques Mallet Du Pan's Mercure Britannique (1798–1800), a Mercure de France published in 1800–1 by an anonymous literary society, and Régnier's Courier d'Angleterre (1805–15).

In the 1790s such journals served a wide émigré audience, based primarily in London, where they perpetuated the factional strife of the early *French Revolution. After Napoleon's Brumaire coup on 9 November 1799, Peltier and Régnier campaigned against the consular regime, attempting to obstruct the return of the émigrés to France and the restoration of normal peaceful relations between France and Britain; in contrast, Mallet Du Pan and Montlosier supported the new regime. Peltier and Régnier soon resorted to satirical invective and personal attacks on Napoleon. Even before the Peace of *Amiens their tirades provoked repeated diplomatic complaints from the French ministry, and demands that Peltier be tried. Finally, the British government acceded. Peltier was found guilty of criminal libel and inciting

assassination, but the dispute had already intensified antagonisms between the two countries. Both Talleyrand and Whitworth, the British ambassador to Paris, agreed that the press and libel issues helped precipitate *war [2] in May 1803.

From 1803 to 1814 the British government increasingly used émigré papers to wage an international propaganda campaign, targeting governments and French-speaking political élites in Germany, Russia, Sweden, Spain, and Portugal, as well as in several former French colonies. The émigré press was to provide information as well as to influence opinion, for Napoleonic censorship and control over ports and mail services was severely hampering the flow of reliable information to governments. The émigré journals were thus an important point of contact between British and foreign governments.

The cultural goal of the London journals was to define and preserve uncorrupted literary forms and standards of taste that represented the 'legitimate' cultural heritage of a monarchist France in exile, in the hope that revolutionary contagion might be expunged from literature and the language in the wake of a Bourbon restoration. Thus the London émigré journals did little to serve the spread of Romanticism. Most of their literary articles were copied from the Parisian press and few favoured Romantic authors. However, there were partial exceptions for fellow exiles and friends such as Chateaubriand.   SBu

enclosure, the conversion of commons and the strip-based open-field system into compact, enclosed holdings to increase efficiency. Originating in the late medieval period, the process witnessed a surge in the late eighteenth century, particularly in the years from 1793 to 1815 [see *land, 16].

Enclosure lay at the heart of England's agricultural achievement and thus of economic change generally. However, it was achieved only at the cost of massive social dislocation. The economic gains enclosure brought were exaggerated and distributed unevenly. Larger farmers benefited, more so landlords whose rentals increased with the growth in farm productivity. Smallholders survived, and may even have increased in the short term, but thenceforth their holdings were increasingly marginal. Large sections of rural society were made vulnerable to pauperization, as seasonal unemployment increased and opportunities for female and child labour diminished. Most critical of all, the customary access of the landless to grazing, firewood, and game (crucial in the contemporary context of low and declining real wages) was extinguished at enclosure [see *poaching].

Because enclosure, even at its peak, was a piecemeal process, opposition to it was inevitably local and rarely concerted beyond one or two adjacent parishes. Radicals hotly attacked it, while *agrarianism articulated an alternative vision, but the progressive capitalization of rural society ground on remorselessly. The poetry of John *Clare conveys the simultaneous sense of impassioned hostility and futility that followed in enclosure's wake for the rural poor.   MC

encyclopedias. Encyclopedic reference works proliferated during the second half of the eighteenth century. This proliferation has often been seen as a French phenomenon alone, due to the fame of the *Encyclopédie* (17 vols., 11 vols. of plates, 1751–72), edited by Denis Diderot and Jean D'Alembert. It was, however, a European one. The *Encyclopédie* began as a translation of Ephraim Chambers's two-volume *Cyclopaedia* of 1728. This 'dictionary of arts and sciences' set the mould for encyclopedias that sought to cover a range of subjects, in contrast with *language [40] dictionaries concerned with the definition and usage of words. However, the line between encyclopedias and dictionaries was often blurred, not least because works such as Chambers's were, in part, dictionaries of scientific and technical terms.

The *Encyclopaedia Britannica*, issued in 100 instalments from 1768 and published in three volumes in 1771, deliberately presented the main bodies of knowledge as 'systems', devoting separate treatises (at least twenty-five pages) to subjects such as 'Astronomy', 'Chemistry', and 'Law' [see *natural philosophy, 34]. These were compiled from various sources by William Smellie (1740–95), the main editor; but from the third edition (18 vols., 1788–97) the *Britannica* began to recruit specialists to write scholarly articles on the scientific disciplines. By the sixth edition of 1823 (20 vols.) it had sold some 30,000 copies; it reached a seventh edition of twenty-one volumes in 1842. There were competitors, especially after 1800—for example, David *Brewster's *Edinburgh Encyclopaedia* (18 vols., 1809–18) and the *London Encyclopaedia* (22 vols., 1829)—but these and several others did not go beyond one edition. More threatening was Abraham Rees's (1743–1825) *Cyclopaedia*, completed in forty-five volumes between 1802 and 1819. All these encyclopedias were alphabetically arranged. Only the unsuccessful *Encyclopaedia Metropolitana* adopted a systematic organization of contents, devised by S. T. *Coleridge. Begun in 1817, it finally completed the 'circle of sciences' in twenty-eight volumes in 1845.

RY

ENFIELD, William (1741–97), Dissenting minister and man of letters. At the age of 17 he was sent to the liberal *Dissenting academy at Daventry as a theological student. He was ordained in November 1763 as minister of Benn's Garden Presbyterian chapel, Liverpool. In 1770 he became minister at the Sankey Street Chapel, Warrington, tutor in belles-lettres, Secretary to the Trustees, and rector of the Warrington Academy. His intellectual distinction was recognized in 1774 when the University of Edinburgh awarded him an LL D. A gentle, modest man, he lacked the iron qualities to cope with the disciplinary problems which beset the Academy. On its closure in 1783 he continued his ministry at Sankey Street for another two years, before accepting a call to the Octagon Chapel, Norwich. He died at the comparatively young age of 56 in 1797.

Enfield was a conscientious teacher, with considerable gifts of exposition, and many of his publications arose from his wide-ranging obligations as a teacher. He claimed no originality for his writings, but he made a significant contribution to thinking in a number of areas. He helped to shape taste by his numerous contributions to Ralph Griffiths's *Monthly Review* from 1774 to the year of his death. Equally influential was his work on elocution, the *Speaker*, which remained popular well into the nineteenth century, being reprinted as late as 1858 [see *language, 40]. This work comprised introductory essays 'On Elocution' and 'On Reading Works of Taste', followed by a selection of prose and verse intended to provide practical spoken exercises for improving speech. Passages were to be read aloud and, where possible, memorized. The aim was to create a natural way of speaking yet one free of rough, provincial dialects. Enfield produced a sequel in 1780, *Exercises in Elocution*, hoping also to shape the literary taste of the young, as well as impressing upon their minds 'sentiments of honour and virtue'. Indeed, he was a tireless provider of instruction and knowledge. His nine-volume edition of *sermons, *The English Preacher, or Sermons on the Principal Subjects of Religion and Morality* (1773–9), no doubt influenced pulpit oratory for a generation. His *Institutes of Philosophy* (1785) provided a very clear account of *Newtonian science, giving examples and experiments to enable students to understand the principles outlined.

Enfield's life and thought can be understood in terms of a determination to maintain unorthodox and unpopular views, but at the same time to practise the values of moderation and to remain broadly sympathetic to those with whom he disagreed. Temperamentally, he disliked conflict, and he was tolerant and ecumenical in spirit. He believed in practical, moral discourses, not pulpit controversy. This left him out of step with more radical compatriots, most notably Joseph *Priestley, with whom he clashed when Priestley was calling for Dissent to become more assertive. Enfield thought that many aspects of *religion [10] were open to doubt and indeed always would be. Errors and prejudice were best left to atrophy; it was safer to ignore than to confront them. He was, nonetheless, a convinced *Unitarian, holding the typical Rational Dissenting belief that the early church had been corrupted by pagan ideas, and that traditional churches perpetuated this tainted inheritance.

Enfield's politics similarly was a combination of firm principle and moderate application. Typically, he refused to allow the *French Revolution to upset his adherence to moderate reform; but he could change his mind on such subjects as *slavery [6]. Though once indifferent on the subject, he preached a sermon in 1788 calling for the emancipation of the slaves as 'a universal obligation of natural justice'. That sermon demonstrated his commitment to the doctrine of the sovereignty of the people and his belief that the greatest good was their wellbeing, as well as his concern that change should occur within the law, and his acceptance of the value of hereditary monarchy in providing stability and security. Thus, although Enfield's ideas have their roots in

Renaissance scepticism and irenicism, his blend of politics and principle also makes him a prototype of a nineteenth-century progressive *Whig. In his modest way, he did much to shape ideas and sensibilities in our period, and ultimately to ease the path of reform.   MF

engineering. Comprising a wide range of functions, from the construction of a *transport infrastructure to land drainage and machine-making, engineering rose to a new position of importance during *industrialization [14] and began to enjoy professional status.

The rapid expansion of trade (both inland and overseas) and the demand for faster communication put pressure on Britain's rudimentary transport network. Harbours needed to be enlarged, and docks constructed to allow the loading and unloading of ships irrespective of the tide. River improvements and canal-building extended the hinterland of ports and reduced freight costs. The construction of bridges to replace ferry crossings, combined with rerouting and improved surfacing, made road transport faster and safer. Meanwhile, the mechanization of industrial and agricultural processes and the deepening of mines stimulated the emergence of a specialist sector to build power-generating and production machinery, increasingly of iron. The demand mounted for more powerful watermills, more reliable windmills, and, increasingly, steam engines. To manufacture these things accurately and in greater quantity, machine tools were markedly improved.

At first craftsmen, such as millwrights, blacksmiths, carpenters, masons, and clock-makers, were called upon to expand their skills and to invent novel solutions to unprecedented design problems. Only military engineers received any formal training. Their civilian counterparts continued to learn their skills through apprenticeship, dignified increasingly by the professional term 'pupillage'. A knowledge of mathematics was becoming more important, but a body of theory concerning the structural behaviour of materials was accumulated only slowly, through direct experience and experimental researches such as those of John Smeaton (1724–92), on hydraulics and mechanical efficiency, and Thomas *Telford, on wrought iron for bridges.

Such engineers began to differentiate themselves from craftsmen by assuming design and supervisory roles, and by seeking professional status. By the late eighteenth century, a consulting engineer would draw up a scheme for his client, hire a contractor to implement it, then, leaving his resident engineer to supervise the construction, move on to design the next project. Leading machine-makers established *factories, but withdrew from the shop-floor to design their products. Their employees were designated by new skills, as, for example, pattern-makers, fitters, and turners. Even so, there was as yet little specialization among top engineers: Smeaton, James *Watt, and John Rennie (1761–1821) all combined canal and dock construction with engine-making; *Brunel designed ships as well as railways.

John Smeaton led the way to professional association, forming a select but diverse group of friends into the Society of Civil Engineers in 1771. Essentially an élite learned society, meeting in London to discuss matters of common interest over dinner, the Society never aspired to represent the emergent profession. In 1818, however, a younger group, aiming to promote professional education and interchange of expertise, formed the Institution of Civil Engineers. With Thomas Telford as its president, the Institution grew to 134 members by 1828, when it secured the charter that bolstered its claim to speak for the entire profession. Thus legally recognized and possessing its own premises and library, it was able to recruit a growing proportion of practising engineers.   CMacL

entail was a conveyancing practice designed to preserve landed estates through generations. The purpose of the entail was to remove the power to sell the land from the owner of the estate, placing it in trust for his eldest son. This was achieved by placing the legal interest in the estate in the hands of trustees. When the son obtained his inheritance, usually at 21, he was persuaded to resettle the estate, placing it in trust for his (perhaps unborn) eldest son. The practice of entail, complemented by the custom of *primogeniture, together secured for the English landed aristocracy what historian E. P. Thompson has called 'corporate inheritance—the means by which a social group has extended its historical tenure of status and privilege'.   ARB

enthusiasm. Although the term's opprobrious mid-seventeenth-century connotations of religious and political fanaticism were frequently applied to *Methodists, radicals, and *millenarians in our period, it was also reworked and secularized by Romantic poets to signify the *sublime inward inspiration necessary for true *poetry [29].

John *Locke, writing at the end of the seventeenth century, had castigated enthusiasm as 'the conceits of a warmed or overheated brain', and had denied its connection with either reason or the divine spirit. Nevertheless he had conceded its powerful persuasive force in influencing human actions. Dr *Johnson, even more famously, defined it in his *Dictionary* as 'a vain belief in private revelation'. In practice, enthusiasm tended to be associated with a wide spectrum of religious and political views: these included belief in free grace, in freedom from the moral law (antinomianism), in special spiritual insight, in divine personal favour or salvation, in direct spiritual communication, in ecstatic experience, and in emotional rather than rational religious or political impulses. Enthusiasm's associations with seventeenth-century sectarianism added a resonance of social and political subversion, widely thought to have been revived by the *Gordon rioters in 1780 and by supporters of the *French Revolution in the 1790s. Women and children were thought to be peculiarly susceptible to its lure because of their emotional *sensibility [11] and undeveloped rationality. However, *Enlightenment [32] theory, especially *psychology [39], tended to be ambivalent about the term, suspicious of its political and religious associations but supportive of its inspirational, imaginative, and illuminative capacities. It was these last three qualities that attracted Romantic poets and *literary theorists [41]. S. T. *Coleridge and William *Wordsworth, in particular, divested enthusiasm of its public and political dimensions, reconstituting it as a personal and divinely imaginative attribute of poetic *genius.   JMcC

epic, a heroic narrative, adapting or constructing a public *mythology [36] in and for a specific culture, which reflected the rise of national self-consciousness throughout our period. It also provoked revised formulations by many of its major poets.

John *Thelwall wrote in 1801 of a 'press teeming, and, perhaps the public already satiated with NATIONAL HEROICS', that 'desideratum in English Poesy'. The national epic was in terms of sheer numbers the period's most striking contribution to the genre. The title of John Ogilvie's (1733–1813) Britannia: A National Epic Poem in Twenty Books, also of 1801, says it all. A nation embattled within and without, found a surfeit of more or less talented bards willing to create a more or less spurious history and mythology. King Alfred was a popular choice (the poet laureate Henry Pye's effort of 1801 followed hard on the heels of Joseph *Cottle's Alfred of the previous year), as was Richard Cœur de Lion.

Not all these quasi-historical narratives had epic pretensions. Richard Payne *Knight's Alfred of 1823, for example, was subtitled A Romance, raising the issue of whether the epic and *romance should be distinguished. The 'heroic' narratives that captivated the reading public—from Macpherson's *Ossianic 'forgeries' (1761–5), through Robert *Southey's Madoc (1805) and *Scott's Marmion (1808), to *Byron's Childe Harold's Pilgrimage (1811; again, subtitled A Romaunt)—all arguably offer tendentious refractions of 'history' and certainly aspire to *Milton's definition of epic as 'doctrinal and exemplary to a nation' [see *history, 38].

Many poets attempted to adapt to their own period and purposes the numerous conventions making up the genre. These included a descent into the underworld; declamatory debates of gods or men in council; a self-consciously 'high' style; sonorous genealogies and contrived tests of heroic endurance, often involving the secular use of divine machinery or the use of extensive battle scenes.

These awkward accommodations invoke the more ambitious engagements with the epic during the period, in which the 'HEROICS' that the epic poet celebrates are often what *Blake called the artist's own 'mental fight' to generate cultural and political renewal as a form of creative *prophecy. The poets of the period saw Milton as the great model for this kind of revisionism and, in turn, set out to adapt or subvert his example. Blake sought to wrest the epic spirit from the dead letter of the epic tradition and to rescue Milton from his classical predecessors. *Keats's Hyperion had to be abandoned as too Miltonic, and its mythopoeic narrative reincorporated in The Fall

of Hyperion as the 'knowledge enormous' of a lyric quest. *Wordsworth's The Prelude completes this internalization of the genre. It represented a 'heroic' quest to discover and vindicate the poetic voice, representing the quest as the very stuff of epic.

The Prelude looks like the fulfillment of *Coleridge's belief that narrative in poetry should seek to convert a series into a whole; but Byron produced a completely different kind of revisionist epic in Don Juan. Where Coleridge envisaged ten years to prepare and another ten to write an epic, Byron's poem, 'acted on by what is nearest' (Canto XVI), flaunted the virtues of its own sporadic history of composition and publication. Its episodic structure and sheer stylistic variety modernized the genre from a perspective which judged Wordsworth's interiorization of it as fatally 'narrow'.   WC

EQUIANO, Olaudah (1745–97), slave, seaman, author, and abolitionist. Equiano was captured as a child by slave-traders and sold to a British sea-captain who named him 'Gustavus Vasa' after the sixteenth-century Swedish King who re-established his country's independence of Denmark. Sold again to a *Quaker merchant, Equiano became the first mate on his master's ship, and eventually purchased his freedom with the capital accumulated from various trading ventures. In his early 20s he returned to England, but later resumed life as a sailor. He made voyages to Asia Minor, southern Europe, the United States, the West Indies, and the North Pole. He acted as a plantation overseer on the Mosquito Coast, played a role in the abortive scheme to recolonize Sierra Leone, and fought with Wolfe's fleet in Quebec and Boscawen's in the Mediterranean. At sea and in England he was introduced to Christianity and received an informal education.

In 1789, at the height of the *abolitionist controversy in Britain, Equiano, now free, prosperous, and middle-aged, published his autobiography, The Interesting Narrative of the Life of Olaudah Equiano or Gustavus Vasa the African, Written by Himself. The first part of the work is a colourful account of his capture and bondage which depicts the journey from idyllic freedom in Africa to the horrors of the middle passage, servitude in the West Indies, and, finally, return to a new freedom [see *slavery, 6]. In the second part Equiano portrays himself as a man reborn and free to pursue his spiritual and material goals. His brilliant exposition of the cruelties and inhumanity of an institution created by ostensible Christians was well received by Britain's leading abolitionists. The Narrative, which went through numerous editions in Britain, the United States, and Europe, played an important part in the attempt by William *Wilberforce to introduce a bill in parliament for the abolition of the slave trade. His friends in the movement included the young shoemaker-radical Thomas *Hardy, through whom Equiano was drawn into British radicalism, becoming a member of the London Corresponding Society [see *corresponding societies]. He also joined with other 'sons of Africa' such as Cugoano (b. 1757) to promote the interests of the black communities in Britain.   JM

ERSKINE, Thomas, first Baron Erskine (1750–1823), lawyer and politician. A brilliant barrister, he numbered Lord George Gordon (1751–93), Thomas *Paine, and Thomas *Hardy among his clients, and was a close friend of Charles James *Fox and the Prince of Wales. These friendships were to influence his career. Erskine's speech in a libel case was instrumental in the passing of Fox's libel bill in 1792, which by allowing the jury to determine the fact of libel afforded protection to radicals in the years to come. Erskine's decision to call the Prime Minister, William *Pitt, to testify about his own earlier reforming activities helped to secure Thomas Hardy's acquittal of high treason in 1794. In 1806 Erskine was made a peer and Lord Chancellor in the *Ministry of All the Talents. Then and later, his closeness to the Prince of Wales seemed to dilute his radical *Whiggism. He failed, however, to gain office in the negotiations of 1812, and thereafter in retirement he became a leading radical in Westminster, often crossing swords with John Cam *Hobhouse. Like him, Erskine became a keen friend of the Greeks [see *Hellenism]. He also published an interesting South Seas *utopia [9] called *Armata* (1817), inspired by the voyages of *exploration [37] of *Cook and *Bligh.

RWD

essay, a contained piece of informal *prose [30], meditating and illustrating a single idea or social phenomenon, which became more experimental and more intensely self-conscious during our period. However, the many forms of periodical publication available entailed as many different forms of 'essay'—from technical contributions to the empirical sciences to grotesque comic and satirical flourishes.

Where *newspapers, annals, *reviews, and *encyclopedias offered in condensed form information and polemic otherwise available only in protracted works, the essay offered summary, personal reflections on politics or culture, or illustrative anecdotes and licensed musing on aspects of social or individual behaviour. As its root meaning of an 'attempt' suggests, it required only a tentative authority; indeed, it implicitly suggested that authority could only ever be tentative—a characteristic encouraged by the phenomenological bias of idealist, associationist, and sceptical philosophy. The Romantic essay was an 'attempt' by an educated intellect to comprehend new experiences in a specific environment or society by using the sensory self as primary mediator and interpreter. Hence the frequently 'impressionistic' nature of the essay's reading of ideas and events, its preoccupation with responsive consciousness, linked it with the poetry of *Wordsworth and anticipated the aestheticism of Walter Pater later in the century. This, also, explains the preponderance of overtly or covertly *autobiographical essays in the period, especially after 1800. The essayists, which included Charles *Lamb, William *Hazlitt, Thomas *De Quincey, Leigh *Hunt, William *Cobbett, James *Hogg, and 'Christopher North' (John *Wilson), all in their own idiosyncratic ways exploit confessional techniques and take the 'familiarity' of the essay to new extremes

of subject-matter, often focusing on apparently trivial details of everyday life and personal concerns, by indulging nostalgias, anxieties, or obsessions.

The venue for the 'occasional' or 'familiar' essay was most often the magazine, with which the market was amply supplied in the late eighteenth century (led by the *Gentleman's*, 1731–1914) and glutted by the 1820s. *Blackwood's Edinburgh Magazine* (1817–1980) and the *London Magazine* (1820–9) stand out, the latter for publishing Lamb's *Essays of Elia*, De Quincey's *Confessions of an English Opium Eater*, and much of Hazlitt's *Table Talk*. The very persistence with which new magazines were launched, in spite of the short life of most of them, suggests how (potentially) lucrative they must have been for the publisher. The essayist had certainly never had such opportunities, though payments varied dramatically and were never as generous as those for reviewing. Despite the brevity of the genre and the limits of the magazine, the essay was rather verbose than concise: rambling and arbitrarily or associatively digressive and periphrastic. Less surprisingly, it was self-consciously stylized or mannered—as much an exhibition of style as of the essayist's opinions and sensibility.　　　WC

Evangelicalism, a renewed confidence in the efficacy of a specifically Gospel-based Christianity, was first experienced by a small but influential number of Christians in the 1730s. Their conviction that the Word should be preached to all ensured that within a century their message permeated all parts of the Protestant church. The initial impulse was generated by a sense of the failure of an ethically based *religion [10] to address man's fallen and essentially sinful nature. Nature, the divine Book of Deeds, from which the *Deists felt that God could be rationally deduced, was replaced by the Bible as the sole means of Revelation. Its offer of Christ's sacrifice upon the Cross as the unique guarantee of salvation could be fully apprehended only by those who first admitted their need of the Holy Spirit to reveal their helplessness. The credal simplicity which emphasized a personal relationship with God, freely available to all, gave the laity a greater role and appeared to diminish the significance of sectarian division in favour of a Church Invisible composed of all true believers.

The first generation of converts were heirs of the *Enlightenment [32], relying upon the practical evidence of an individual's daily life to offer proof of conversion, and discouraging the abstract theological dispute that had characterized England before the 1689 Act of *Toleration. The movement's missionary impulse, however, meant that it was also capable of being affected by the changing ideologies it encountered. The sense of being held accountable for the spiritual welfare of one's immediate milieu resulted in according the family an importance as an organic unit favoured by God. It also encouraged charitable endeavours that offered a core of resistance to *laissez-faire* economics. Nevertheless, a bedrock conviction of original sin divided Evangelicalism from all philosophies conceiving of man as born innocent. Even those Evangelicals, such as

Wesleyan *Methodists, who adopted some form of belief in man's ability to achieve perfection, saw this as dependent upon the grace of God and as the reward of eternity rather than the result of secular change.

This subordination of the secular to the divine, combined with an emphasis upon the individual guidance provided by the Holy Spirit, meant that it was difficult to predict where Evangelicals would align themselves politically. However, once adopted, they would pursue such causes as the abolition of *slavery [6] with customary wholehearted- ness. The Clapham Sect, gathered around the focal figure of William *Wilberforce, exerted a powerful influence upon the mores of the governing circles of English upper-class society that was partly respon- sible for shaking off the decadence of *Regency society.

By the 1830s the apocalyptic mood detectable in politics and literature saw its Evangelical equivalent in a renewed interest in prophetic studies, debate among contending views of the impending millen- nium, and a renewed desire to search for apostolic purity [see *millenarianism].   EJ

EVANS, Evan (Ieuan Fardd) (1731–88), clergyman and scholar. The outstanding Welsh scholar of his generation, Evans adopted the bardic name 'Ieuan Fardd' (Ieuan the Poet), though his contemporaries more often referred to him as 'Ieuan Brydydd Hir' (Ieuan the Tall Poet). An unusually tall, angular man, Evans was born and raised at Cynhawdref farm in the parish of Lledrod, Cardiganshire, and educated at Merton College, Oxford. From the time he entered the *Anglican ministry in 1755 he lived his life on the very edge of self-destruction. A penurious, unkempt manic-depressive, he set himself the task of recover- ing and celebrating Wales's cultural identity and in particular its glorious poetic tradition [see *Welsh cultural revival]. But, apart from the period from 1771 to 1778, when Sir Watkin Williams Wynn II (1772–1840) of Wynnstay gave him the security of patronage, he was never able to engage the support of men of authority.

Evans was preoccupied by two burning issues— the anglicization of the established church in Wales and the indifference or enmity displayed by Welsh landowners towards the native culture. His attempts to secure a decent preferment were constantly rebuffed, and he served as a curate in a remarkable number of different parishes in England and Wales. As his gloom deepened he became, according to Samuel *Johnson, 'incorrigibly addicted to drink'. He came to despise the 'Anglo Bishops' who snubbed deserving Welsh-born clergymen in favour of pliant English time-servers, and his essay 'The Grievances of the Principality of Wales in the Church considered' (1765; remains unpublished) was the most sweeping indictment of the established church written in eighteenth-century Wales.

Convinced that Hanoverian bishops looked upon him 'with an evil eye', Evans found solace in schol- arly labour. He established contacts with ardent col- lectors of old Welsh manuscripts, corresponded

with the likes of Thomas Gray (1716–71) and Thomas *Percy, and discovered a number of key texts by visiting libraries and private collections [see *antiquarianism, 35]. Bursting with a new sense of pride and confidence, he believed that unearthing a mouldering Welsh manuscript like Y Gododdin was as great a discovery as that of America by Columbus. His knowledge of the contents of Welsh manuscripts was second to none and his major publication, Some Specimens of the Poetry of the Antient Welsh Bards (1764), was a work of high scholarship.

As Evans failed to win the financial support of affluent landowners he became increasingly disillu- sioned and aggressive. He denounced tithe-grabbing landlords for worshipping the 'Great Self' and aban- doning their duty to succour Welsh poets. In his best-known stanzas, Englynion i Lys Ifor Hael, com- posed at the ruins of Ifor ap Llywelyn at Bassaleg in Monmouthshire in 1779, he mourned the passing of old shrines of patronage which had generously fêted Welsh bards in late medieval times. His celebrated English poem—'The Love of Our Country'—was a deliberate attempt to instil into his fellow- countrymen, especially those in authority, a more public and strident pride in their national and cultural heritage.

Evans's waspish tongue and cultural nationalism did not endear him to the establishment, and until his death in 1788, in the remote farmhouse where he had been born, he remained impoverished, unfulfilled, and at odds with the world around him. But as a scholar and a guardian of the Welsh literary heritage he was a man of considerable distinction.   GHJ

EVANS, Thomas (Tomos Glyn Cothi) (1764–1833), the first *Unitarian minister in Wales and one of the most active and determined champions of liberty and *toleration in radical circles. A flannel-weaver by trade, he imbibed a rich fund of ideas and arguments at *fairs and markets. He also read voraciously, and fell heavily under the influence of the theological and political ideas of Theophilus Lindsey (1723–1808) and in particular Joseph *Priestley, so much so that he became known as 'Priestley bach' (little Priestley). He even named one of his sons Joseph Priestley Evans.

In 1792 Evans published Amddiffyniad o Bennad- wriaeth y Tad, the first Unitarian *sermon ever pub- lished in Welsh. Two years later he was elected minister of Cwm Cothi Meeting House in Car- marthenshire, the first Unitarian chapel in Wales, and began to preach radical Unitarian principles in communities where Calvinism had traditionally been dominant and where intellectual rigour was generally frowned upon. A gifted poet and hymnolo- gist, and a frequenter of the radical gorseddau insti- tuted by Edward *Williams (Iolo Morganwg), Evans was an outspoken critic of *Pitt's 'Reign of Terror'. In The Miscellaneous Repository or Y Drysorfa Gymmysgedig (1795) he flayed monarchs, courtiers, landowners, tax-collectors, and clerics with consid- erable relish.

In August 1801 Evans was brought before the Court of Great Sessions on a charge of sedition. It was claimed (by one of his own deacons) that he had uttered seditious words and declaimed inflammatory revolutionary songs at a *cwrw bach* (a bid ale) held at Brechfa in March of that year. Evans vigorously denied the charge, but was sentenced to two years' imprisonment and a visit to the Carmarthen pillory on two occasions. His incarceration failed to quench his zeal on behalf of political liberty, anti-slavery, and pacifism, and he spent his time in prison compiling an English–Welsh dictionary which was eventually published in 1809 [see *language, 40]. Unlike many fellow Welsh Dissenters, on his release from Carmarthen prison he renewed the struggle for liberty and continued to publicize his deeply held *republican and pacifist convictions at a time when the virtues of deference, submission, and obedience were being drummed into the heads of the Welsh people.

In Evans's view, the cause of Unitarianism and rational inquiry went hand in hand. In 1811 he was appointed minister of the Unitarian Meeting House at Aberdare in the swiftly industrializing county of Glamorgan, and in the same year he published a collection of 100 hymns—*Cyfansoddiad o Hymnau*—for the benefit of anti-Trinitarian congregations. With dogged persistence he preached against the 'vital religion' of *Methodism and encouraged lively radical spirits in the burgeoning industrial communities of south Wales to read and discuss rationalist and liberal ideas. Tomos Glyn Cothi lived long enough to witness—and celebrate—the first working-class rising by Welsh people at Merthyr in the summer of 1831. In Unitarian circles he is revered as a sturdy Welsh republican and an apostle of freedom.   GHJ

evolutionary theories. Until well into the nineteenth century, orthodox scientific opinion understood earth's myriad life-forms to constitute a purposefully designed economy, regulated by natural laws. Christian tradition generally also held the number of life-forms, and their apparent ordering into groups with common bodily characteristics, to have been fixed at the time of creation. However, by the late eighteenth century doubts mounted as to the immutability of life-forms because of the unearthing of fossils bearing only vague similarities to living fauna and flora, and the discovery of numerous strange new organisms in the course of colonial *exploration [37]. Nature now seemed a more dynamic system, with the potential to produce new forms of life.

Nature was seen as evolutionary, in the sense that the creator had determined the blueprint for species while allowing natural processes to affect the reproductive organs of individual organisms, so that over time a species might come to exhibit great variety. Transformation of species could occur, but only within divinely predetermined limits. The great taxonomist Carl von Linné, or Linnaeus (1707–78), believed that species generally bred true to type, but also that cross-breeding leading to fertile hybrids was a means by which the divine mind could bring new species into existence to perfect the animate economy. In his profoundly influential *Histoire Naturelle* (1749–89), the French naturalist Buffon (1708–88) took a more materialist stance, eventually concluding

that a single ancestor might give rise to new species, as nutrition and climate influenced reproduction. But he held that the new species could take only a limited number of forms.

During the course of the eighteenth century, some theorists explained change using older theories of preformation. Albrecht von Haller (1708–77) and Charles Bonnet (1720–93) held that all species existed from the moment of creation as elementary principles, or germs, from which distinct species were formed at different eras in the history of the earth. Nature could thus be understood as a hierarchy or chain, in which each species carried deep within it the potential to ascend towards perfection by giving rise to a higher form.

In Parisian intellectual circles from the mid-decades of the eighteenth century, natural theodicies became the target of thoroughgoing materialist critiques. Especially in the works of the *philosophes* D'Holbach, de la Mettrie, and Diderot, nature was conceptualized as having the potential to create life and to transform organisms randomly. The writings of these French materialists profoundly influenced early-nineteenth-century naturalists, notably Jean Baptiste Lamarck (1744–1829), who rejected atheism but eventually concluded that organisms were capable of open-ended transformation as their bodily structures became modified so as to ensure their survival in specific environments.

In Britain, materialism was challenged by thinkers such as David Hartley (1705–1757) and Joseph *Priestley, who blended *Unitarian Christianity with experimental science. Hartley appears to have inspired Erasmus *Darwin, grandfather of Charles Darwin, to share with Lamarck the view that organisms could adapt themselves flexibly to environmental needs.

However, the vision of nature as a freely evolving continuum gained little acceptance in established British scientific circles, especially during the conservative political climate of the post-revolutionary era. It was not until the 1820s that evolutionary ideas found a new audience amongst younger and socially aspiring medical students, a number of whom became influential teachers in British biomedical institutions. Even so, greater credence was given to theories reasserting that the divine mind left nothing to chance.

By far the most influential of such theories was that propounded by the French comparative anatomist Georges Cuvier (1769–1832). Drawing upon a wealth of clinical example, Cuvier held that all vertebrate animals took one of several preconceived basic forms, with bodily structures of distinct species being infinitely adaptable to environmental conditions. As the modern theorist Michel Foucault tantalizingly suggested, Cuvier's stress upon the adaptive evolution of basic forms can be viewed as a necessary cognitive precondition for Darwin's theory of natural selection.   PT

Exchequer, court of, the least important of the central Westminster courts, but having a special equity jurisdiction arising out of its concern with Crown revenue.   DL

F

factory system. Often regarded as the archetypal symbol of Britain's industrial revolution, the factory system is neither easily categorized nor explained [see *industrialization, 14]. As centralized locations of manufacturing, diverse in both scale and function, factories were common to many industries.

The conspicuous phenomenon of this period was the mechanized textile factory. Cotton-spinning factories proliferated from the 1780s, power-loom weaving from the 1820s. Flax and worsted mechanized production intensified at the same time, while mechanized processing of wool occurred several decades later. By 1835 only 40 per cent of textile workers were factory-based: outwork in homes and small workshops, known as the 'domestic system', expanded to complement mechanized production.

child and female attendants it would dispense entirely with skilled, male labour.

Marxist historians continue to emphasize the factory system's disciplinary and exploitative role, despite the enduring contests for control of work between operatives and employers. They also usefully challenge the common, determinist assumption that textile mechanization demanded factory organization. They suggest rather that the factory determined the shape of machine technology by channelling inventive effort into meeting its needs. An alternative, 'transaction costs' theory, suggests that, by concentrating production, factories offered lower running costs and greater quality control than outwork processes. The persistent expansion of the domestic system casts some doubt on this. Since

69. Richard Arkwright's mill at Cromford, built in 1785.

Contemporary commentators disputed the factory system's purpose. For Charles *Babbage it offered efficiency through intensive use of machinery and an extreme division of labour and skill. Andrew Ure (1778–1857) claimed in *Philosophy of Manufactures* (1835), as did Marx subsequently, that as powered machinery required only cheap, docile

these explanations are hard to test, and not always incompatible, the debate continues.   CMacL

fairs, public gatherings (usually open-air) for purposes of buying and selling goods and labour, often combined with entertainment. Some fairs were exclusively for pleasure.

Rural fairs were linked with the rhythms of the agricultural and liturgical year and were held in late spring and early summer (Easter and Whitsuntide), and in early autumn (Michaelmas). As occasions for unsupervised sociability, especially for rural youth, these fairs were often subject to criticism from the clergy and to regulation by the magistracy. The most famous London fair, held annually in September in Smithfield, was Bartholomew Fair. For its duration, Smithfield was crowded with booths selling ale and food, especially sweetmeats, and others housing puppet shows, dramas, acrobatics, human freaks, animals, exhibitions, peep shows, and waxworks. Since medieval times the fair had been identified as licentious, disorderly, and as a front for criminality. As one of the largest open-air gatherings in the metropolis, geographically close to the centres of parliamentary and royal power, Bartholomew Fair was always regarded with suspicion by the authorities: attempts were made to suppress it in 1761, 1762, 1798, 1816, and 1825–6, coinciding with periods of radical political activity. The fair's combination of carnival and market-place was also regarded as a threat to cultural hierarchy and stability, exemplified by *Wordsworth's attack on it as a 'Parliament of Monsters' in *The Prelude*, book VII. The subject of studies of *popular culture [23] by Joseph *Strutt (1801) and William *Hone (1826–7), Bartholomew Fair was ended by an act of the Corporation of London in 1854. For a time the locus of fair activity moved eastward to Greenwich, to which patrons could travel by the new steamships and railway. The metropolitan fairs were remarkably resilient in the face of attempts to neutralize their cultural and political impact; they remained important dates in the calendar of working people until well into the nineteenth century.   GR

fairy tales, a literary form, should be distinguished from oral folk tales. The term probably originated in the eighteenth century, appearing for the first time in print on the cover of a 1752 translation of the *Contes des fées* of Madame d'Aulnoy (first published in 1698).

From the late seventeenth century several collections of fairy tales became influential. Foremost among these was *Histoires ou Contes du Temps Passé* (1697) by Charles Perrault, translated as *Histories, or Tales of Past Times* in 1729. These included *Sleeping Beauty, Little Red Ridinghood, Puss in Boots*, and *Cinderella*, all of which became enormously popular in chapbook form [see *street literature]. In the early eighteenth century several English translations of the *Thousand and One Nights* (or *Arabian Nights*) also became popular as chapbooks, especially *Aladdin* and *Sinbad*. However, rational disapproval of the fantasies promoted by fairy tales was still widely expressed until Edgar Taylor's (1793–1839) translation in 1823 of Jacob and Wilhelm Grimm's *Kinder- und Hausmärchen* (first published in Berlin, 1812). The Grimm's book was a scholarly approach that managed to win support for the potential of fairy tales as antiquarian research at the same time as capturing a popular readership. It included *Snow White,*

70. Illustration to the chapbook *Cinderella* (c.1820). Cinderella became a popular fairy tale in the nineteenth century, retold variously in penny chapbooks, pantomimes, and an opera by Rossini.

Rapunzel, Rumpelstiltskin, and *Hansel and Gretel*. No doubt the success of Taylor's translation (*German Popular Stories*) was helped by George *Cruikshank's illustrations.

The rediscovery of *imagination and the role of fantasy was an important theme in the discussion of *childhood during this period. S. T. *Coleridge wrote in 1797 that because of his early reading of fairy tales and the *Thousand and One Nights* his mind had become 'habituated to the Vast'. However, a didactic tone in *children's literature remained dominant until the popularity of Hans Christian Andersen in the 1840s.   MP

famine. Aside from Ireland, Britain in the late eighteenth and early nineteenth centuries is often thought to have become immune to famine. Historians customarily assume that the industrial and *agricultural revolutions terminated the historic pattern of recurrent major subsistence crises accompanying demographic disaster.

Yet increased productivity in the *agrarian sector did not eradicate this pattern. The masses' customary diet was overwhelmingly cereal-based, and in the late eighteenth century Britain became a net importer of cereals, thereby supplementing indigenous produce. Required imports fluctuated considerably from year to year, depending on productivity of home yields. Obtaining stocks in overseas markets proved essentially unproblematic in years of peace, but difficulties surfaced during the French wars owing to disruptions of markets and trade routes. Crises following consecutive substandard harvests in 1794–5, 1799–1800, 1810–11 developed into famine conditions because of problems in buying adequate compensatory stocks overseas, aggravated by food price inflation out of proportion to the scale of the physical deficiency.

Marked inflation meant that most working-class

families spent an increasing proportion of incomes on securing food alone. Decline in purchasing power radically reduced demand for manufactured goods, and services, thereby severely compromising large sectors of the non-agrarian economy. Loss of overseas markets owing to military operations, trade embargoes, and the erosion of *mercantile confidence, caused further reductions in demand for industrial products, notwithstanding the government's military requirements. These difficulties were compounded in 1810–12, owing to the Orders in Council, aimed at denying British manufactured articles to the enemy, and aggravated by the United States's entry into the war against Britain.

Government responses proved critical. When famine conditions intensified over the severe winter of 1794–5, *Pitt's surprised ministry entered belatedly into the global cereal market, only to experience severe political problems over the internal distribution of stocks. Thereafter it depended on mercantile speculation, aided by various so-called 'bounty schemes'. None worked as envisaged. Initiatives ranged from much-publicized, patriotic promises on the part of the wealthy to reduce wheat consumption to advocacy of charities funding soup kitchens rather than traditional expenditure on subsidizing the poor's normal diet [see *poverty, 12]. Workers were encouraged by propaganda, bounties, and by *poor law and charitable provisions to switch to cheaper cereals, notably barley, oats, maize, and rice. Finally, governments insisted that the internal trade in provisions was governed by *laissez-faire principles.

Systematic analysis of these famines is restricted to those of 1794–6, and 1799–1801, partly because *population data remain defective. Yet even crude aggregate compilations reveal demographic distortions, with peaks in the death rate occurring in 1795, 1800–1, and 1810, and further peaks in the immediate aftermath, especially in 1802–4 and 1814–16. Baptismal figures, though ambiguous, decline markedly in 1801. More accurate local and regional figures show increased death and decreased birth rate, with delayed marriage in places as widespread as rural Devon, industrial Wiltshire, Somerset, West Yorkshire, and urban centres including Norwich and to a lesser extent London. Each famine was accompanied by severe outbreaks in malnutrition-related disease; dysentery, typhus, and what was denominated 'aliopathetic disease'. Observers recorded the 'wretched' physical appearances of workers and their families. Hungry miners collapsed at work. Rioters complained of 'dying by inches' and of the cries of their starving children [see *riots]. Fortunately, the English (and Welsh) poor law system averted large-scale death from starvation. Charities also played a major role. Even so, children swarmed over rubbish tips searching for potato parings, while others importuned kitchen staff at affluent homes for bones. Thousands of families were reduced to eating nettles and other foods normally reserved for animals. One senior official, who had served in India, concluded in 1800 that conditions 'would be called a famine in any other country but this'.   RW

FARADAY, Michael (1791–1867), natural philosopher and public *lecturer on science. The son of a blacksmith who served an apprenticeship to a bookbinder, Faraday's background was relatively unusual for a member of the élite philosophical community. He worked as Sir Humphry *Davy's laboratory assistant at the Royal Institution in London, and attended him on his Grand Tour of France and Italy in 1815. In 1825 he became director of the laboratory at the Royal Institution and in 1833 was appointed to the newly endowed Fullerian professorship of chemistry there. He was a member of the small and obscure religious sect of Sandemanians.

In 1820, Faraday followed up Hans Christian Oersted's discovery of a link between *electricity and magnetism by demonstrating the rotation of a current-carrying wire around a magnet. He was accused of having plagiarized William Hyde Wollaston (1766–1828), and as a result his nomination to a Fellowship in the Royal Society was almost blackballed. During the 1830s he embarked on an ambitious series of electromagnetic researches, the *Experimental Researches in Electricity*, first published in the *Philosophical Transactions of the Royal Society*. In the first series he demonstrated the production of electricity from magnetism.

His lectures at the Royal Institution's Friday Evening Discourses made him the scientific doyen of fashionable London. Crowds flocked to his performances and his services as a consultant were widely sought after. He advised the government on a range of matters, most notoriously following the Haswell Colliery disaster, where his evidence exonerated the owners from the charge of negligence. Faraday was portrayed by his contemporaries as the epitome of the humble philosopher, seeking nature's truths with no thought of personal gain.   IRM

FARREN, Elizabeth, Countess of Derby (1762–1829), actress and singer. Born into a struggling acting family, Farren rose to become one of the most famous performers of her generation, specializing in 'fine lady' roles such as that of Lady Teazle in *Sheridan's *The School for Scandal* (1777). Her success in these parts gave her entrée into élite circles in real life, highlighting the blurred lines of distinction between the worlds of *theatre [24] and *fashion. In 1785, following an affair with Charles James *Fox, she formed a liaison with the Earl of Derby, who was then married. The relationship was public knowledge, the subject of pamphlet and graphic *satire, as well as Thomas *Lawrence's *Portrait of an Actress*, painted for the Earl and exhibited at the *Royal Academy in 1790. However, rumours of a *sapphic friendship with Anne Seymour *Damer were regarded as more potentially dangerous to her reputation, the Earl forbidding an association between the two women. In 1797 the Countess of Derby died and Farren was able to play the fine lady in earnest, by leaving the stage to marry the Earl. Her career therefore followed a very different trajectory to that of her contemporary, Mary *Robinson, with whom, as an actress, she had much in common.   GR

fashion. For most of the eighteenth century, to be a man or woman of fashion implied an attention not only to dress but also to social position, political affiliation (usually *Whiggish), public prominence, even a London address. Far beyond its numerical size, the fashionable world exerted a fascination upon contemporary society that was fuelled by the reporting of its activities in the print media. In the eighteenth century the scale and extent of commercialization made entertainments and styles of dress increasingly accessible to those who had the capacity to pay, thus making fashion even less reliable as a badge of rank, and even more of a focus for disquiet at the apparent blurring of social distinctions, than it had been in earlier periods [see *consumerism, 19]. Linked with this uneasiness was a sense that fashionable society was undermining British strength by its self-indulgence, its taste for the foreign, its effeminate attention to detail and display. In spite of such criticism, the potency of fashion remained undiminished and was even intensified by commercialism. The drive towards excess, the transience of style, and the capacity to repackage the past as novelty made fashion entirely suited to the imperatives of the marketplace. Aristocratic women such as the Duchess of *Devonshire also used the opportunities of the commercialization of fashion to exert influence by means of a new force in society, that of media celebrity.

According to one commentator, 'a fondness for Dress' was 'the characteristic folly of the age'. Our period represented a sea-change in dress styles. A sign of the increasing informality of male dress was the fact that the sword was gradually replaced by the umbrella. There was also a greater differentiation between the sexes as male dress became more sober and less subject to fashionable change. For both men and women, the trend in dress styles was to emphasize, rather than disguise, the body. Wigs concealing and extending the hair, exaggerated hoop skirts, and tight lacing gave way to dress that enhanced body shape.

Such changes reflected the political and social upheavals of the period. The 1760s and 1770s were notable for the flamboyant 'macaroni' fashions of the young male aristocracy consisting of exaggerated wigs and hair extensions, decorated dress in the continental style, and high heels. Such theatricality announced the arrival of a new generation, influenced by the *Grand Tour and a profitable period in India, that was less staid and parochial than its elders. 'Macaroni' fashion—the term derived from the taste of these young men for Italian pasta, new to British palates—was significant for the way that the trend was seized upon and magnified by the print media, including caricaturists such as Matthew and Mary Darly. In its complex relations between highly theatricalized public behaviour and the print media, the macaroni craze marked the nexus between fashion, celebrity, and print culture that is the distinguishing feature of the modern consumer society.

For women, the confidence of the 1760s and 1770s was apparent in a mimicking of male dress in the adoption of riding habits and quasi-military uniform and a craze for highly elaborate and fantastic hair design. In 1777 Hannah *More was paid a visit by a group of women who 'had amongst them, on their heads, an acre and a half of shrubbery, besides slopes, garden plots, tulip beds, clumps of peonies, kitchen gardens and greenhouses'. Himself a leader in macaroni fashion, Charles James *Fox initiated the sobering of male dress when, around 1778, he began to appear unshaven and unpowdered, dressed in the plain blue coat and buff breeches of the American revolutionaries. The *French Revolution made the coded meanings of dress more highly charged than ever: cropped hair was a badge of Whig and radical politics, apparent in Thomas *Lawrence's sketch of the appearance of *Godwin and *Holcroft at the *Treason Trials of 1794, and in 1795 fashion became a political issue when, in order to alleviate shortages in flour, *Pitt taxed the use of hair powder. The revolutionary ideology of *natural rights and transparency was manifested in dress codes that rejected disguise and ostentation in order to reveal the 'natural' man or woman. The forces of fashion appropriated and redefined such a politics, for women in particular, in the form of the high-waisted, diaphanous dresses of the post-1789 period. Such styles, influenced by the fashions of the French Directory and Empire that were indebted to the paintings of David and antique statuary, revealed the form of the female body. This form of dress was less constricting and more 'natural' than the hoops and tight-lacing of the 1770s and 1780s, but it was not necessarily emancipatory as it stressed the sexual objectification, and often reproductive functions, of the female body. The post-1815 period witnessed another upheaval in fashion styles as the influence of Paris design was restored. British women favoured the huge bonnets, narrow waists, balloon sleeves, and projecting skirts that were the vogue in France. For men, there was a revival of fashion awareness as the returning officers of the Napoleonic wars expressed their newly anomalous position in the postwar world in the form of *dandyism. Dandy fashion, with its echoes of the fine cut and *élan* of the military uniform, was one way in which these men negotiated their assimilation into civilian sobriety.

The impact of these changes was communicated and commodified by increasingly sophisticated forms of retailing and marketing, augmented by the *newspapers. Larger emporiums opened in London in the 1780s and 1790s, offering fashion as yet another of the spectacles of the metropolis. Travelling salesmen and hawkers brought the new fashions to the provinces, while the rise of the fashion plate and magazine, exemplified by *Ackermann's *Repository of Arts*, publicized London and Paris innovations. No less significant in communicating trends were servants, who were renowned for emulating their masters and mistresses in dress as well as in behaviour. The economic impact of fashion was considerable: the man or woman of fashion was served by a network of tradespeople and servants including tailors, shopkeepers, weavers, stitchers, shoemakers, hatters, staymakers, mantua-makers, hairdressers, maids, valets, and washerwomen whose

103

livelihoods were dependent on the tides of fashion and circumstance. Beyond this economy of clothing, fashionable dress and the material used to make it sustained an extensive criminal network of thieves, receivers, and their customers, many of whom were women. While commercialization might have extended the ambit of fashion beyond the sphere of the 'great', fashionable dress remained a much-coveted index of wealth and privilege, the illegal possession of which condemned many to transportation or death.   GR

female education. The end of the eighteenth century witnessed convergence between the political agenda of reform and the cultural agenda of *self-improvement. For landless, urban, bourgeois men, and especially for the high proportion of Dissenters among that class, *education [17] opened the door to economic development and political enfranchisement. Male educational institutions negotiated between settled class interests and rising expectations, devising career paths, regulating competition, and expanding self-government by learned societies and professional bodies.

Augustan pedagogy had supposed the male pupil to be the social superior of his teacher, since in classical culture superior men did not stoop to nurturing and training the young. In the work of Robert *Merry and William *Godwin in the 1790s, the *Télémaque* of Fénelon, a pseudo-classical fiction of boys' education, was converted to an icon of progressive educational values, a move which blurred this class distinction between teacher and taught, substituting a new social contract between the like-minded bearers of reform across generations. This improved the career prospects of middle-class men, as gentlemen could now teach tradesmen's sons without loss of status.

Liberal ideas were much slower to penetrate the systems of education of *women [4]. The education of girls was entirely in the charge of their parents and guardians up to marriageable age, at which point it was assumed that formal schooling ended. It was inconceivable for women to undertake independent careers in the public sphere, or to train girls to do so. The very qualities of mind and will which distinguished a man of the ruling class were anathema to custodians of female morality. Female bodies and women's experiences were not illuminated by the widely disseminated values of the *Enlightenment [32]. Male theology was resistant to the pressures for change which were at work in other institutions of national culture, and the protection of young females from irreligious scepticism also sheltered exclusively male institutions such as the old universities from the public attentions of the censors. There were no professional standards, no public examinations, and no path of preferment for talents if women wished to pursue teaching and scholarship. On the other hand, female education was a topic intensively canvassed. The very dearth of public policies, or of any acknowledgment of women's prerogatives in their education, provoked contention. Furthermore, an oversupply of male university graduates laid the field

of infant and female education open to takeover by educationalists like Richard Lovell *Edgeworth, writers of *conduct books and moral tracts such as John Gregory, littérateurs of liberal sympathies like George *Dyer and Samuel *Rogers, medical doctors like Erasmus *Darwin and Thomas *Beddoes, and clerical pundits like Richard *Polwhele. The Lunar philosopher Thomas *Day, who adopted two orphan girls with the intention of forming himself one wife on *Rousseauist principles, is an egregious instance of this trend. The historic partnership of father and daughter Richard Lovell Edgeworth and Maria *Edgeworth as pioneers of early education for both boys and girls yielded sparse gains for adult women's education.

In Protestant England there were no self-governing female communities, and no lifelong vocations or disciplines accessible to women. No women's enterprise could prolong its existence beyond its present incumbents, and little or no intellectual distinction accrued to women's work in this field. The double bind of propriety confined teaching by women to private establishments, where they could only supervise and have the direction of the very young and the servant class, and this sequestering in turn weakened their claims to professional acknowledgement. The faintest whiff of scandal would depress a school's reputation, and women with a position to protect had to shun compromised sisters.

Genteel periodicals, such as the *Lady's Monthly Museum*, published biographical sketches of women writers whose personal lives were approved as role models. Enlightenment ideology of rational improvement carried separate gender meanings. The moral improvement of children was the duty of female teachers, but the market for *children's literature was closed to female-authored texts, which were deemed to be not sufficiently edifying.

Female educators operated on narrow financial margins, unable to delegate or appoint successors, obliged to carry supernumary male advisers, liable to lose their entire investment if they fell ill or took leave, as Mary *Wollstonecraft found. Prospects remained bleak for a woman teacher past first youth, unable to retreat to extended family home or to less arduous work with adults. The *More sisters and the *Lee sisters, whose schools in Bristol and Bath made profits, were able to close them once they had established themselves as authors. Claire *Clairmont worked as a governess and English tutor in Europe until retiring on a windfall legacy from Percy *Shelley at the age of 46. Frances *Burney's novel *The Wanderer; or Female Difficulties*, written but not published in the 1790s, depicted the miseries of 'toad-eating', the employment offered to respectable unmarried women as paid companion and childminder in moneyed families.

Cautionary conduct books warned against educating girls above their station, not just for the threat posed by progressive education to class distinctions but because the gentrification of middle-class households precluded acquisition of the feminine skills required to manage the domestic economy [see *domesticity, 13]. The aspirations of women for a wider social role and greater autonomy in their domestic and sexual relationships had to negotiate with the reality that female domestic labour and childbirth impeded professional authorship, public representation, and cultural advocacy.

In the immediate pre-revolutionary era, women who published their proposals for female education had mostly been established authors in other genres, such as Clara *Reeve, Sarah Scott (1723–95), Elizabeth Montagu (1720–1800), and Anna Laetitia *Barbauld. The Whig historian Catharine *Macaulay's *Letters on Education* (1790) denied that a liberal education for girls would necessarily lead to questioning Scripture, but cautioned educators not to outstrip the limits of female education, and never to pry into the deepest recesses of science. Macaulay glided over access to the knowledge of sexual reproduction, repeated traditional advice against coquetry and flattery, and endorsed the strict chaperonage of girls.

Two key texts of the 1790s, Mary Wollstonecraft's *Vindication of the Rights of Woman* (1792) and William Godwin's *Enquiry concerning Political Just-*

ice (1793), each had a chapter on 'A National Education'. Wollstonecraft speaks for a nascent feminism claiming a franchise and a public voice. For her, 'National Education' was universal education. She wanted to consider infant instruction as the formative milieu of culture itself, and she emphasized women's access and gender equity in education. She paid tribute to the work of Macaulay, whose *Letters on Education* she had recently reviewed for the *Analytical Review*, but was less generous to the pedagogical texts of Stéphanie de Genlis and Anna Laetitia Barbauld, where the overlaps of utopian project and theoretical exposition seemed problematic. The core of Wollstonecraft's own education was in English literature, and she imaginatively identified with the male-authored fictions of women, especially *Shakespeare's heroines. Her reading response to Rousseau, in particular, stressed the issue of the erotics of pedagogy, which her theory of education overruled.

A self-appointed spokeswoman 'on behalf of her own sex', as Mary *Shelley described Wollstonecraft in 1831, faced problems of consensus and representativeness in calling on women as a homogeneous

group. A utopian element was carried over from the *sapphist tradition of female communities and adapted in Wollstonecraft's prospectus to the co-education of boys and girls. The spotlight was focused on the child group, which was to form a future community not segregated by gender or class. The hierarchical divisions in the boys' schools, between masters and pupils and among boys of different status, were vigorously rejected, but the ideal child of the future was conceived in apolitical, non-gender-specific terms, and discussion of intimate relations among women, and between adult women and young girls was waived without debate. Misogynist tracts like Polwhele's *The Unsex'd Females* (1798) and William Beloe's *The Sexagenarian* (1817) allude to women's writings on the topics of schoolgirl lesbianism and sapphic schoolmistresses, carefully hedged elsewhere. The same-sex bonding to which none of the published texts by women dared lay claim was thrust upon women as a group by their detractors. Polwhele sniffed out a female pedagogical conspiracy spreading a radical contagion among girls and women, singling out Mary Wollstonecraft and Mary Robinson, both mothers of young daughters.

At the end of the 1790s, women who produced specialist texts attempting a comprehensive pedagogy included Hannah More, Jane *West, and Sarah *Trimmer. The year 1798 was one of reaction, in the aftermath of William Godwin's revelations about Mary Wollstonecraft's freethinking sex life. Mary *Hays's *Appeal to the Men of Great Britain in Behalf of the Women* (1798) was published anonymously by Joseph *Johnson following Mary Wollstonecraft's death. The poet Mary Robinson, writing as Anne-Frances Randall, complained against the mental subordination of women, her protest powering self-revelation from behind the flimsy mask of a pseudonym. Priscilla Wakefield's *Reflections on the Present Condition of the Female Sex* (1798), the Edgeworths' *Practical Education* (1798), and Mary Anne Radcliffe's *Female Advocate, or an Attempt to Recover the Rights of Women from Male Usurpation* (1799) each defended recent advances in educational and employment opportunities for women against a reactionary backlash.

At the close of the century, the Tory *Evangelical Hannah More was the leading female educationist. More's *Strictures on the Modern System of Female Education* (1799) closed off the prospectus advanced by Wollstonecraft, curtailing female pedagogy. She urged strenuous study on female students but held out no rewards, least of all genuine intellectual pre-eminence.   JB

FENWICK, Elizabeth (Eliza) (*c*.1766–1840), novelist and writer of *children's literature. Friend and correspondent of Mary *Wollstonecraft and Mary *Hays, Fenwick associated with radical writers of the 1790s and entered, through her literary works, contemporary debates over the value of *sensibility [11] and the virtues of *female education.

Her only novel for adults, *Secresy, Or, The Ruin on the Rock*, was first published in 1795 with the ascription, 'By a Woman'. Like Jane *Austen's *Sense and Sensibility* (1811), it used the popular device of pairing heroines in order to explore issues surrounding women's nature and rationality. Yet also like Austen's novel, and like Wollstonecraft's earlier writings, *Secresy* remained ambivalent about its subjects. Both Sibella, natural enthusiast, and Caroline, self-disciplined rationalist, meet tragic disappointments. Neither woman, each educated in very different yet similarly unconventional ways, can fully engage with, or defy, a male-centred society bound and driven by secrets. The only avenue for free female expression in the novel is found in the epistolary relationship between the two women.

Letters from female friends also perhaps served as the chief solace in Fenwick's own increasingly difficult life after the publication of *Secresy*. She separated from her radical husband, John Fenwick (d. 1820), soon after he fled London with debts in 1799. She struggled to support her family by writing books for children from 1804, by managing William *Godwin's Juvenile Library in 1807–8, and by taking various positions as teacher and governess before joining her actress daughter in Barbados in 1814. Hardship, obscurity, and the loss of both her children befell Fenwick before she died in Rhode Island in 1840.   KF

FERGUSON, Adam (1723–1816), clergyman-soldier in the 'Black Watch' (1745–54), professor of natural philosophy (1759–64), then of pneumatics and moral philosophy (1764–85) at Edinburgh. Ferguson was born where Highlands slide into Lowlands, and his main contribution to eighteenth-century thought was a distinctive interpretation of cultural differences such as those between the Gaelic tribe and the commercial society of the British state.

Despite his proclaimed dependence upon Montesquieu and his association with *Hume and *Smith, Ferguson rejected the idea that institutional arrangements, such as a modern system of justice, could secure liberty and the pursuit of wealth [see *political economy, 33]. At the same time, despite his intense use of the Roman republican tradition and associated neo-Stoicism, Ferguson did not reject commerce as inherently evil. He argued that the two could be combined but required a constant cultivation of active citizenship. This civility applied to any

71. *The Nine Living Muses of Great Britain* by Richard Samuel, 1777. Standing from left to right are Elizabeth Carter, Anna Laetitia Barbauld, Elizabeth Sheridan, singer, Hannah More, and Charlotte Lennox, author of *The Female Quixote* (1752). Seated from left to right are Angelica Kauffman, Catharine Macaulay, the intellectual and wit Elizabeth Montagu, and Elizabeth Griffith, playwright and novelist. On first seeing the print Elizabeth Carter remarked, 'Your Virgils and Horaces may talk what they will of posterity, but I think it is much better to be celebrated by the men, women, and children, among whom one is actually living and looking.'

stage of economic development, and in Scotland after the Union with England the first need was to establish a citizen militia and to promote regard for the culture of the community. For Ferguson, politics, economy, and communal life were intertwined; civil society could not be separated from the state. Moreover, modern society was not the unqualified achievement of progress. If wealth had been gained, public virtue—especially martial courage—and thus freedom were in danger of being lost. The stadial theory of society was, in Ferguson's hands, more a theory of change and diversity than an account of unequivocal improvement. Just as he maintained a subtle balance of acceptance without triumph in his contemplation of the modern world, so he combined proper social explanations (such as the idea of unintended consequences) with room for political action. But despite all his emphasis on active politics, Ferguson held the Hanoverian constitution as so valuable that attacks on it by disaffected colonists had to be firmly rejected.

The grand general picture was developed in Ferguson's bestselling *Essay on Civil Society* (1766). The local interventions occurred in lively pamphlets urging the establishment of a Scottish militia, arguing for the usefulness of stage plays (in defence of John Home's *Douglas* [see *theatre, 24]), defending the poems of *Ossian as authentic expressions of the Gaelic soul, and so on. The republican background was set out in *The History of . . . the Roman Republic* (1783), and a moral-philosophical foundation, in many ways pioneering 'Common Sense' ideas independently of Thomas *Reid, was laid down in textbooks and lectures, the *Institutes of Moral Philosophy* (1772), and the *Principles of Moral and Political Science* (1792). Ferguson was prominent in Edinburgh *Scottish Enlightenment circles, a member of the Select Society, and involved in the foundation of the Poker Club and in the Royal Society of Edinburgh. His books brought him European fame; the interest of Hegel, Marx, Sombart, and others secured a distinguished posthumous reputation. He is now honoured in his native land as one of the founding fathers of social theory.   KH

FERRIER, Susan Edmonstone (1782–1854), novelist. A pioneer of Scottish female *satirical and moral fiction (with Elizabeth *Hamilton and Mary *Brunton), Ferrier was its most notable exponent. Her three anonymously published novels are progressively didactic, but remarkable for their originality, wit, and comic characterizations of snobs, *bluestockings, and idiosyncratic Highlanders. Her letters provide a lively commentary on Scottish social and literary figures. The youngest of ten children and the only unmarried daughter of Helen Coutts and James Ferrier, Clerk of Sessions and agent for the fifth Duke of Argyll, she kept house for her widowed father from the age of 15.

Encouraged to write by Lady *Bury, she initially collaborated with Bury's cousin, Charlotte Clavering, in *Marriage* (1818), but completed it alone after rejecting Clavering's *Gothic emphasis. Incorporating many lightly disguised portraits of Ferrier's acquaintances, *Marriage* dramatizes late-eighteenth-century upper-class attitudes towards filial duty and personal inclination in women's marriage choices. *The Inheritance* (1824) also has proto-feminist elements, depicting parental tyranny and the options for women in Scottish landed society. It acknowledges a debt to Jane *Austen in its opening echo of *Pride and Prejudice* (1813).

Her novels, admired by Walter *Scott (a family friend), continued the vogue for Scottish material and were sought after by publishers. However, disliking publicity and with failing eyesight, she published no more fiction after *Destiny* (1831), in which social satire is overshadowed by moral concerns. In her later years Ferrier joined the Free Church and became active in temperance and *abolitionist causes.   RCA

field preaching. The tradition of open-air preaching went back to Bunyan and beyond, but *Methodism gave that tradition a new impetus in the middle of the eighteenth century. John *Wesley, who had originally regarded it as sinful to preach outside a church, responded to George *Whitefield's example and preached his first open-air *sermon in April 1739. To Wesley's dismay the practice was always viewed with suspicion, especially by *Anglican clergymen but also by some Methodists, who saw it as a potential source of public disorder. This suspicion became acute in the politically troubled years after the *French Revolution. W. H. Reid (d. 1826) accused populist field preachers of aiding the Jacobin cause by bringing *religion [10] into disrepute. For the next decade, Methodist freedom of worship and field preaching more generally was endangered. Under the *Toleration Act of 1689 Dissenters who took the oath of allegiance were exempt from the penalties of the Conventicle Act of 1670 and the Five Mile Act of 1665 if they obtained a licence from magistrates. Lord Sidmouth (1757–1844) believed that the licensing system was being abused to allow 'cobblers, tailors, pig drovers, and chimney sweepers' to preach. In 1811 he proposed legislation which would have restricted applicants for Dissenting minister's licences to 'respectable householders', but the bill was defeated in the House of Lords after a national campaign by Methodists joined with Old Dissent. The following year Dissenters went on to gain a new Toleration Act which repealed the Five Mile Act and the Conventicle Act, and took discretion away from magistrates in administering oaths to preachers. The latter no longer had to demonstrate their affiliation to the congregation of a registered place of worship. In effect, the act broadened the Toleration Act of 1689 to include field preaching and preaching in private dwelling-places and other unsanctified buildings.

EJ

FITZGERALD, Lord Edward (1753–98), revolutionary, ex-army officer, and MP for Kildare who, despairing of effecting *parliamentary reform in Ireland by *constitutional means, became the leading military strategist of the Society of United Irishmen and planned the *Rebellion of 1798 [see *United societies].

Having excelled at military studies in France until 1779, Fitzgerald joined the Sussex militia commanded by his uncle, the Duke of Richmond. A brief stint in the 26th regiment was followed by service with the 19th in which he fought with distinction during the *American Revolution. His political career commenced in 1783 when he was returned for Athy, County Kildare, where he derived an income from his Kilrush estate. In 1786 he entered the Military College, Woolwich, and two years later joined the 54th regiment stationed in Canada with the rank of major. A period of exploration in North America preceded his return to Ireland, where his liberal politics and army career proved irreconcilable. His condemnation of a crackdown on the patriotic *volunteer movement and comments he made arising out of a meeting with Thomas *Paine in Paris led to his being cashiered in 1792.

Increasingly critical of government for its enactment of coercive legislation in 1793 and 1796, its failure to grant *Catholic emancipation or to review the oppressive tithe system, Fitzgerald gravitated towards the extremist Society of United Irishmen. In June 1796 he and Arthur O'Connor (1763–1852) travelled to the Continent to press the French Directory to mount an *invasion of Ireland in support of an *insurrection, a mission which helped secure the abortive French invasion attempt at Bantry Bay in December 1796 [see Roger *O'Connor].

In July 1797 Fitzgerald, then a member of the United Irish Executive Directory, protested government policy by refusing to contest the seat for County Kildare which he had held for seven years. His experience of and flair for planning military operations ideally suited him to devising the sophisticated plan of insurrection the United Irishmen adopted, and he was also closely involved in building up their formidable secret paramilitary organization in Kildare. A fugitive from 12 March 1798, his betrayal and arrest in Dublin on 19 May contributed greatly to the failure of the Rebellion, which broke out prematurely four days later. Lord Edward Fitzgerald died in Newgate prison, Dublin, on 4 June 1798 from a mortal wound received while resisting arrest.   RO'D

FLAXMAN, John (1755–1826), sculptor, illustrator, and designer who, by replacing courtly allegory with sentimental bourgeois serenity, effected a significant shift in taste in the decorative arts [see *design, 25].

Flaxman learnt to read, draw, and model in his father's London workshop, which provided casts for sculptors. He entered the *Royal Academy in 1769 to study *sculpture and successfully exhibited a wax figure at the Academy as early as 1770. He completed his artistic training in Italy (1787–94). First employed as a designer for Josiah *Wedgwood in 1775, Flaxman's approach to sculpture and literary illustration was strongly influenced by his acquaintance with semi-industrial processes of manufacture. The outline engravings of 1793 to 1795, after his illustrations to Homer, Aeschylus, and Dante, earned him an international reputation unmatched by any contemporary British artist. At home, however, the scarcity of commissions for public monuments and the

strong competition in the lucrative market for portrait busts forced Flaxman to specialize in memorial sculptures which were soon filling the churches of England. Readily prepared alternative designs and a later gallery of small-scale models allowed customers to choose from a number of basic motifs which could be recombined in a variety of ways to suit a range of pockets.

While the demands of his market combined with his own inclinations led him to combine Christian piety with mythological material, Flaxman's style nevertheless represents the epitome of British classicism. Linear 'abstraction' and an extreme reduction of the illusion of space and volume were used to express often intimate domestic and religious feelings. The sinuous rhythm of his swelling outlines leaves sufficient room for the spectator's own emotional 'colouring', and the elegant compositions generally succeed in telling a simple story with even simpler means. Yet Flaxman combined stylistic historicism with the most advanced production strategies then available to the sculptor. His workshop relied on a proto-industrial division of labour, although the execution of his large-scale works by studio assistants resulted in some glaring distortions. His contribution to the empire's patriotic iconography is evident in the monument to Lord *Mansfield in Westminster Abbey, his designs for the 'Trafalgar Vase', his *Nelson memorial, and his statue of William *Pitt.

An Associate of the Royal Academy by 1797, Flaxman was elected a full member in 1800 and, in 1810, its first professor of sculpture. In this capacity he ingeniously rewrote the history of his art, proclaiming that the 'English School' had only now entered its Renaissance phase and would soon triumph over the competing continental schools. In the more private medium of his drawings, Flaxman favoured subjects from the *Bible, *Milton, Bunyan, or his own Christian allegory, 'The Knight of the Blazing Cross'. Sympathetic to *Swedenborgianism from an early age, he later produced a series of drawings illustrating the latter's *Arcana Coelestia*. Though not generally known to his contemporaries (except where isolated motifs were recycled for some church monument), these demonstrate that Flaxman apparently did not object to the growing conservatism of Swedenborgianism (unlike his friend William *Blake), preferring it over more radical forms of religious enthusiasm.   DWD

FORSTER, Johann Reinhold (1729–98), naturalist, travel writer, and publisher. Forster was born near Danzig and educated in Berlin and at the University of Halle. Initially a pastor with wide interests in languages and natural history, he undertook a survey of the Volga colonies in Russia in 1765–6 with his son George (1754–94), who was later a major figure of the German Enlightenment. Forster's report was critical of the management of the colonies, and the pair left Russia for Britain without payment.

In London, Forster became actively involved in the Royal Society, the Society of Antiquaries, and the Society of Arts. He made the acquaintance of men

2, 102

with interests in natural history, taught at the *Dissenting Academy at Warrington, and published many translations of Bougainville's *Voyage Round the World* (1772), as well as works by pupils of Linnaeus, and his own *Introduction to Mineralogy* (1768). He was offered the place of naturalist on *Cook's second voyage of *exploration [37] in 1772–5, after Joseph *Banks and his party had withdrawn. The voyage produced rich contacts with Oceanic peoples, which Forster 'methodized' in his remarkable synthetic work, *Observations Made During a Voyage Round the World* (1778). This book, however, was a byproduct of post-voyage acrimony: in the course of the expedition, Forster had quarrelled with many fellow participants, and after abortive negotiations was prevented from writing a voyage narrative.

Without prospects in Britain, Forster returned to Germany in 1780 and secured a professorship at the University of Halle, where he taught and published extensively until his death. The notoriety of his fractious character has often hindered proper assessment of his intellectual accomplishments.   NT

fortune-telling. Our period saw increasing public condemnation of claims to foretell the future which can be seen as part of a proliferation of areas of control and discipline over the mind and public behaviour. The Vagrancy Act of 1824 made it an offence to defraud by charging money for predictions, suggesting a fundamental dishonesty in any such attempt. The charge of pretence had been in place since 1736, when legislation against witchcraft was replaced by penalties for those who 'pretend to exercise or use any kind of witchcraft, sorcery, inchantment [*sic*], or conjuration, or undertake to tell fortunes'. The crime was closely connected with vagrancy and begging, and, through several subsequent versions of the Act, parliament suggested that fortune-tellers were likely to be idle and disorderly. The prominence of fortune-telling in the Vagrancy Act of 1824 was also connected with attempts at the time to control gypsy travellers.

However, fortune-telling was by no means limited to gypsies. Chapbooks such as *Napoleon's Book of Fate*, which gave instructions on the interpretation of oracles, were amongst the wares of any pedlar [see *street literature]. Such chapbooks, aimed largely at women readers, could also include palmistry, interpretations of omens in the natural world, interpretations of dreams, physiognomy, and lists of lucky and unlucky days in the year.   MP

3, 66 **FOX,** Charles James (1749–1806), MP, leader, and mentor of liberal *Whigs, who held office briefly under the *Tory Lord North (1732–92) before leading the Whig opposition, mainly against William *Pitt, through a long political life during which he championed America, Ireland, and India, as well as various domestic liberties and reforms.

In spite of thirty-eight often controversial years in the Commons and, from 1782, effective leadership of an admittedly fragmented and shrunken Whig party, Fox's major contributions to British politics were symbolic and ideological rather than legislative. His person and memory were treated with reverence by

the ideological faction of the Whigs that bore his name and wore his colours (buff and blue). During the long years in opposition to 1830, annual Fox dinners were held, his opinions authoritatively quoted, and his name and principles invoked to contain dissent. And yet no one reform originated with Fox or was carried by him through parliament. (His Libel Act of 1792, securing the right of trial by jury for the accused, is exceptional.)

The illusory but jealously defended party identity of the Foxite Whigs took no account of Fox's preference for broad-based administrations. Nor did it take account of his promiscuous entry into coalitions like that with Lord North in 1782. That it was the only way Fox could circumvent George III's proscription on his entering the ministry failed to absolve him in the eyes of politicians of all persuasions, or of the nation itself. Satirical activity in the press exploded, as it would again in 1788 when Fox, champion of parliament against the Royal prerogative, affirmed the prerogative of his friend the Prince of Wales over parliamentary deliberations about the conditions of regency during the King's illness.

Yet his undertaking to the Westminster electorate in 1790 to ensure the preservation of democratic liberty was neither meretricious nor empty. Admitting the cause of liberty to be incapable of strict definition, Fox campaigned energetically for religious liberty, the *abolition of the slave trade, and Irish and American independence. Freed by various defections from the obligation to appease both wings of the remaining Rockingham Whigs, he offered from 1794 less equivocal support for *parliamentary reform and an honestly indignant resistance to the revocations of various personal and civil liberties introduced by Pitt. While his singular and principled agitation for peace with France was unpopular and sometimes naïve, his support for the middle classes and his understanding that certain reforms would be effected through violence if ignored by parliament was deeply prophetic.   WC

freedom of the press meant freedom from government harassment and prosecution, on the assumption of a right to know and criticize what passed in parliament. In one sense it was secured as early as 1695, when government licensing officially lapsed. The freedom to print without requiring a licence meant a press subject not to censorship but to the consequences of law. At issue, after 1695, was how the law was applied and what constituted seditious, blasphemous, obscene, and defamatory libel (from the Latin *libellus*, 'a book or writing').

When, under interrogation from a burgeoning press, government acted jealously to preserve its prerogative over information and critical commentary, radicals and 'liberals' alike demanded freedom of the press as a political right. In Scotland in the 1790s, for example, the notorious judge Lord Braxfield operated on the declared assumption that, the constitution being perfect, any criticism of the government in the press was prima facie an act of treason; in 1811 the judge Sir George Wood insisted that 'parliament was the place for the discussion of the laws of the country, not newspapers'. The Attorney-General could charge any publisher on the strength of his own 'ex officio information' (circumventing a grand jury), and arrest any publisher against whom 'informations' were filed—proceedings often involving specially selected juries. In practice the government and associated conservative interests were also able to limit press freedom by a variety of other means. These included systematic campaigns of prosecution such as that instigated in the early 1820s against radical freethinker Richard *Carlile and his 'corps' of volunteer shop attendants by two conservative private societies known as the Constitutional Association for Opposing the Progress of Disloyal and Seditious Principles and the *Society for the Suppression of Vice. Government persecution of vendors was also widespread, particularly after Lord Sidmouth's (1757–1844) famous Circular of Letter of March 1817 urging rural magistrates to arrest persons judged to be selling seditious material, since, in law, the seller was deemed to be the publisher. Further harassment was exercised by withdrawing licences from *taverns known to carry radical *newspapers. Still more effective were revenue measures such as the Stamp Acts, which aimed to make newspapers too expensive for popular consumption. This was widely resented as a check on popular knowledge, and radicals such as William *Cobbett, William *Hone, and Henry Hetherington (1792–1849) responded by developing the *unstamped press. The demand for 'freedom of the press' thus ranged from the abstract 'right' to criticize government policy in print to specific and extensive reforms such as the abolition of the stamp and advertising taxes.

WC

freemasonry. Although European freemasonry has been seen as deeply implicated in the growth of *Deism, pre-revolutionary radical politics, and Romantic *literary theory [41], it appears to have been less subversive in Britain. Nevertheless, the British movement was significant as a vehicle of middle-class sociability, of occult-scientific speculation, and of conservative paranoia.

Although freemasonry is thought to have originated amongst stonemasons in Scotland at the beginning of the seventeenth century, it underwent extraordinary transmission and transformation throughout Europe in the eighteenth century. Its protean and eclectic beliefs make generalization difficult, but most masonic organizations seem to have used a form of secret initiation and ritual centred on the symbolism of King Solomon's Temple. Many also espoused *Enlightenment [32] universalism, committed themselves to moral and political regeneration, and dabbled in mystical metaphysical traditions derived from Renaissance Neoplatonism. However, judging by the comments of Horace *Walpole, British freemasonry had by the mid-eighteenth century become better known for its brand of masculine *tavern sociability. Even so, there is some sketchy evidence of connections with European-style illuminism. When the mesmerist-magician Count Alessandro di Cagliostro (1743–95) fled

France to London in 1786, he attempted to build on foundations laid by expatriate illuminati such as the Polish Count Grabianka in order to establish a new, more revolutionary, occultist masonic order based around his own invented Egyptian rite [see *animal magnetism]. Supported by prominent metropolitan figures such as 'Mad' Lord George Gordon (1751–93) and Philippe Jacques de *Loutherbourg, he encouraged the order through his wife, Seraphina, to admit women, as was the practice amongst French freemasons but rarely elsewhere. Although this society foundered when Cagliostro had once again to flee abroad, the radical artisan W. H. Reid (d. 1826) reported in his authoritative exposé of London radicalism, *The Rise and Fall of the Infidel Societies in this Metropolis* (1800), that groups of artisan freemasons and mystics flocked to join radical *corresponding societies in the early 1790s.

During the early nineteenth century, however, freemasonry appears to have had greatest cultural significance in Britain either as a spectre used by conservatives to blacken political opponents or as a source of *frisson* in *Gothic novels. Abbé Barruel's four-volume *Memoirs of Jacobinism* (trans. 1798) ascribed the *French Revolution to a conspiracy of revolutionaries, freethinkers, and masonic illuminati masterminded by the Bavarian law professor and former Jesuit Adam Weishaupt (1748–1830). The work had considerable impact in Britain: influential translations and local adaptations were produced by Robison in Scotland and Clifford in Ireland, and the government's Committee of Secrecy *Report* of 1817 appears to have applied Barruel's thesis to *Spencean tavern clubs. The *Shelleys were riveted by the idea of a European mystical-scientific conspiracy: Percy saw it as a model to be replicated by British intellectuals, but Mary's response was more ambivalent—as indicated by the fact that Dr Frankenstein is given his early education at the University of Ingolstadt, where Weishaupt taught. Bavarian freemasonry was also an inspiration for William *Godwin's *St Leon* (1799) and for several of the counter-revolutionary Gothic novels of his one-time friends Sophia King and Charlotte *Dacre. By the end of our period, however, the Inquisition seems to have supplanted the masonic secret society as a source of Gothic titillation and terror.

IMcC

freethought, see *Deism.

French Revolution refers both to the 1787–9 overthrow of the *ancien régime* or absolute monarchy of France marked by the storming of the Bastille on 14 July 1789 and to the revolutionary governments of the next decade.

The Revolution comprised a number of interrelated but relatively autonomous transformations: the aristocratic and bourgeois political revolution that centred on the National Assembly, the popular revolution in the streets of Paris and in the provincial townships, and the peasant-based agrarian revolt. Aristocratic attacks on the monarchy from 1787–8 paved the way for popular revolution through the convocation of the Estates-General in 1789 and the establishment of the National Assembly on 17 June 1789, by which non-clerical and non-noble representatives declared themselves to be the people's elected and legitimate representatives. The National Assembly was the effective national government of France until it dissolved itself on 30 September 1791.

The Revolution is conventionally seen as divided into three main phases. First was the period of constitutional monarchy from 1789 to 1792, when the 1791 *Declaration of the Rights of Man* established liberal freedoms, and when the Constituent Assembly introduced major legislative reforms, including administrative and church reform, the abolition of feudalism, and economic freedom. The Assembly was marked by the struggle for power between its two factions, the Girondists, headed by Brissot, and the Jacobins, headed by Robespierre, Marat, and Danton. The second, more radical, phase came with the rise to power of the Jacobin Convention, which operated from the overthrow of King Louis XVI on 10 August 1792 until the establishment of the Directory on 26 October 1795. This is conventionally known as the Reign of Terror, in reference to the repressive and intimidatory measures initiated to resist the threat of counter-revolution.

The overthrow of the Jacobin faction within the Thermidor coup of 27 July 1794 inaugurated the third phase of the Revolution, the Thermidorian Convention and then, from October 1795, the Directory, which attempted to re-establish the liberal, constitutional values of 1789–92. The Directory fell to a military coup in November 1799 engineered by *Napoleon Bonaparte, the conventional marker of the end of the Revolution.   CT

FREND, William (1757–1841), mathematician, university don, *Unitarian, and inveterate reformer. A pupil of William *Paley at Christ's College, where he entered in 1775, Frend became a Cambridge Latitudinarian when the movement was already in decline. Elected a fellow of Jesus College in 1781, he threw himself enthusiastically into teaching and into good works (including the founding of a *Sunday school) in the nearby parish of Madingley, where he served as curate.

By the mid-1780s Frend's awareness of abuses in the Church, his own theological inquiry, and his close friendship with the Unitarian don Robert Tyrwhitt (1735–1817) led him into Unitarianism, to which he in turn helped convert S. T. *Coleridge. Frend gave up holy orders in 1787, and the next year published an open avowal of his new beliefs that led to his removal as a tutor. He was closely associated with the London Unitarians, headed by Theophilus Lindsey (1723–1808), and in Cambridge with the liberal Baptist minister Robert Robinson (1735–90), the family of the radical squire Richard Reynolds (1730–1814), and the radical publisher Benjamin Flower (1755–1829).

In 1793 Frend published *Peace and Union*, a pamphlet urging moderate *constitutional reform and more thoroughgoing changes in the Church, including an abolition of doctrinal tests. An appendix deploring the *war [2] with France constituted

the last straw for powerful Cambridge enemies, chief among them Isaac Milner (1750–1820), the *Evangelical Vice-Chancellor. The ensuing trial banished Frend from the University, though (fellowships being freeholds) he continued to enjoy his collegiate income until he married the granddaughter of Archdeacon Francis *Blackburne in 1808.

In London Frend undertook private teaching, his most famous pupil being Anne Isabella Milbanke, later Lady Byron (1792–1860). Between 1804 and 1822 he also published a series of popular guides to astronomical observation. In 1806 he became chief actuary of the Rock Life Assurance Company. He had long opposed the slave trade and enlisted, with unflagging enthusiasm, in every phase of radicalism, linking the age of revolution to the age of *Peel.
                                                    RKW

friendly societies. The friendly or benefit society developed out of drinking clubs in *taverns, convivial societies, and *debating clubs of the eighteenth century. Men and women met once or twice a week in a public house or rented room to socialize, administer funds submitted to provide insurance against sickness or death, and, perhaps, to engage in political or social debate. By 1815, it has been estimated that nearly 10 per cent of the population was associated in friendly societies. They imposed upon themselves a high level of regulation through rules on almost every conceivable aspect of their interaction, particularly the financial arrangements. These centred on the 'box', where the subscriptions to the society were kept under lock and key.

Because of their largely artisanal and generally low socio-economic membership profile, these societies attracted the attention of the authorities from at least 1793, when the first Friendly Societies Act was passed. The purpose of the rules was to enable a society to be registered under the legislation. In return for legal recognition, societies opened themselves up to scrutiny by the state of their accounts and proceedings.

Debate about friendly societies has centred on the 'class collaborative' or robustly working-class nature of the culture of self-help and respectability fostered by them. Too much is liable to be made of their role as engines of working-class consciousness, if their social composition is emphasized at the expense of their wide-ranging utility to their members.   JF

FRY, Elizabeth, see *Quakers.

FUSELI, Henry (Johann Heinrich Füssli) (1741–1825), painter, book illustrator, and critic. The most learned painter of his generation, deeply read in the classics, the *Bible, Italian, British, French, and German literature and history alike, Fuseli devised a unique generic class of poetic or epic *history painting. Taken at face value, his works most often illustrated scenes from *Shakespeare or *Milton, and had the look of literary subject paintings. However, the artist's peculiar approach to literary materials enabled him to give expression to the refined humour and, especially, the subtle socio-psychological fears and horrors of a distinct group among Britain's upper class. In a sense, Fuseli's paintings function as an elaborate visual allegory of the economically and emotionally unstable position of his clientele under the threatening prospect of revolutionary change [see *painting, 27].

The young Fuseli, born in Switzerland into a dynasty of Zurich painters, was trained nonetheless to become a Zwinglian minister. As a student he immersed himself in the writings not only of Homer, Virgil, Ovid, and Dante, but also of Shakespeare and Milton, and was much impressed by British liberal political theory. Though he was ordained in 1761, his protest against a corrupt magistrate led to the end of his short-lived career in the church and to his semi-voluntary emigration in 1763.

In 1764 he first travelled to London, where he was to mediate between English and German literary circles. He translated Johann Joachim Winckelmann's (1717–68) Reflections (1765), and an acquaintance with *Rousseau while staying in Paris in 1766 prompted his Remarks on the Writings and Conduct of J. J. Rousseau (1767). Though Fuseli criticized Rousseau's concepts for political reform as *utopian [9], Rousseau influenced Fuseli's later argument concerning the 'moral usefulness' of the arts as 'at best accidental and negative'.

Having worked as a translator, writer, and critic in London for several years with only moderate success, Fuseli decided to become a painter and in 1770 went to Italy. At Rome, Michelangelo's Sistine Ceiling served as his principal model for figure drawing. Reinterpreting Baroque theories concerning the vocabulary of meaningful gestures and facial expressions, Fuseli began to assemble the elements of an 'elevated' style, and his approach to the human figure henceforth seldom failed to invoke his Italian High Renaissance and mannerist models. With fellow artists like Thomas Banks (1735–1803), the painter moved in a libertine circle; his work cultivated a highly expressive and simplified grammar of figural composition and narrative grouping. As a means of intensifying the emotional impact of the dramatic actions he depicted, Fuseli's style began to rely on contortions of the limbs and other anatomical exaggerations in the attitudes of the figures, charging their energetic and often violent movements with wildly expressive gesturing. Similarly, despite being scorned by contemporaries for the deficiencies of his painting techniques, Fuseli developed an approach to colour and chiaroscuro which today seems entirely in keeping with his dark and awe-inspiring subject-matter.

Attempting to visualize the menace of human existence in tragic and extreme conditions, to make 'philosophical ideas intuitive', and to personify sentiment, Fuseli left the depiction of national history to others and concentrated instead on private and individualized emotions such as love and hate, jealousy, revenge, and desolation. His breed of male heroes, all muscle and Michelangelo, and his femmes fatales, seemingly fragile women who entrap and manipulate the feelings of their male victims, are continually engaged in a struggle for power on the gendered battlefield of the supernatural *sublime.

Fuseli's mixture of intellectually complex and demanding themes with a menacing brand of eroticism appealed to a comparatively small but wealthy and powerful art- and book-buying public.

Upon leaving Italy, Fuseli stayed at Zurich for the last time during 1778 and then settled permanently in London, where among painters and intellectuals he soon rose to some eminence. When exhibited at the *Royal Academy, The Nightmare (1781) attracted much public attention [see *viewing, 20]. It is the first of a series of subject pictures in which Fuseli explored the realm of psychological experiences, then a relatively recent bourgeois interest. During the 1780s and 1790s he was closely affiliated with the radical members of the Joseph *Johnson circle, assisted William *Cowper in the translation of Homer, was a friend of Mary *Wollstonecraft, and supervised the publication of a sumptuous edition of the Essays on Physiognomy (1789–98) written by his friend Johann Casper Lavater (1741–1801). He also developed contacts with the nobility, and with rich art collectors such as William *Roscoe. As well as producing commissioned book illustrations for the publishers, he henceforth catered to this élitist audience for the sale of his large-scale paintings.

Fuseli's Roman sketches for a series of Shakespearean subjects, modelled on sixteenth- and seventeenth-century mural paintings, made him a natural choice for the execution of some of the more sensational contributions to *Boydell's Shakespeare Gallery. With the help of his patrons he next attempted to emulate Boydell as an entrepreneur by launching a Milton Gallery, furnished entirely with his own paintings. However, when the gallery finally opened in 1799 the public remained largely indifferent, dashing Fuseli's hopes for large financial gains from the sale of engraved reproductions of his paintings. Afterwards, his attempt to reach a larger public than was possible within the medium of oil paintings, and to gain control over the graphic reproductions of his designs, led to a particularly close association with a single engraver, Moses Haughton. Never a particularly popular artist, it is mostly through the circulation of the large-scale prints produced by Haughton, as a member of the Fuseli household from 1803, that the painter's 'epic' and 'dramatic' inventions were known to his contemporaries.

Made an associate member of the Royal Academy in 1788, Fuseli was elected to full membership only sixteen months later, in February 1790. From 1799 to 1805, and again from 1810 until his death, Fuseli acted as the Academy's professor of painting. When in 1804 he also became keeper, he had reached a social and economic position which largely freed him from dependence on the sales of his paintings. As the teacher of a whole generation of young artists, ranging from *Lawrence to *Constable to *Haydon, Fuseli gained considerable influence in the British art world. As well as advancing an original theory of artistic invention, composition, design, proportion, colouring, and chiaroscuro, his Lectures (the first three of which were published in 1801) gave an account of the history and changing social functions of the fine arts. Contrasting the conditions for the

27

production of works of art in antiquity and during the Renaissance with those in post-revolutionary Europe, Fuseli offered a lucid exposition of the dilemma of the academic system of the arts, fore-shadowing William *Hazlitt's critique. Fuseli's scepticism, combined with the experience of emigration and with an extensive knowledge of European cultural history, made him question most of the standard contemporary claims made for the future pre-eminence of British art. His sensitivity to the growing privatization of art prompted a cynical definition of the painter's role as merely furnishing 'the most innocent amusement for those nations to whom luxury is become as necessary as existence'.   DWD

G

gagging acts, a series of legislative enactments, beginning in the 1790s and ending with the Six Acts of 1819, designed to control popular radical political activity. In 1795 and 1817 habeas corpus was suspended, enabling suspected radicals to be imprisoned without trial. The main thrust of these acts, however, was directed against printed materials and public meetings, and they became increasingly more repressive as the scale and intensity of reform activity increased.

The Treasonable Practices Act 1795 made outspoken criticism of the government into a high misdemeanour. A similar measure, passed in 1817, laid even more stringent penalties on those uttering treasonable or seditious words. The corresponding legislation in the Six Acts of 1819 stiffened these penalties yet again, and added a 4d. tax on periodical publications, by then the favoured vehicle for radical opinions. In addition, magistrates in 1819 were given fresh powers of summary conviction, the power to search private as well as public houses, and authorization to suppress all training and drilling. This legislation also allowed transportation for those publishers twice convicted of seditious libel.

The government tried to control public meetings in 1795, 1812, and 1817 by restricting the numbers who could attend and by licensing meeting-places and itinerant preachers. The Seditious Meetings Act 1819 is significant for its definition of who was entitled to attend a political meeting, a first in British law. The Combination Acts of 1799 and 1800, though primarily aimed at controlling seditious assemblies, were to exercise far-reaching restrictions on the growth and shape of *trade unions.   JF

GAINSBOROUGH, Thomas (1727–1788), painter of landscape, portraits, and 'fancy pictures', whose representations of rural life responded to the changes effected by the *agricultural revolution.

Gainsborough's training in London in the 1740s brought him into contact with artists painting in the rococo mode and gave him access to seventeenth-century Dutch landscape paintings. He balanced these two somewhat opposing tendencies in a series of landscapes painted after his return to Suffolk in 1748. Works such as *Cornard Wood* ('Gainsborough's Forest') (c.1748) represented the few patches of untamed nature that still existed in that part of Suffolk, despite the effects of *enclosure.

Gainsborough shifted his emphasis when he moved to Bath in 1759 and began specializing in society *portraits. His popularity there made him a potent rival to Joshua *Reynolds and paved the way for eventual success in London. His portraits avoided allegorical trappings and symbols of status in favour of direct representations of the sitter. His use of natural settings in portraits such as *Mr. and Mrs. William Hallett* ('The Morning Walk') (1785) evoked *Rousseauian ideas of uncorrupted humanity.

Gainsborough's popularity was not undermined by public feuds with the *Royal Academy which prevented him from exhibiting in 1784. While continuing to accept portrait commissions until the end of his career, he undertook *landscape painting for personal pleasure. He also produced 'fancy pictures' of poor rural children in the style of Murillo, reflecting his nostalgia for a lost rural ideal.   SW

GALT, John (1770–1839), novelist, journalist, and entrepreneur, chiefly remembered for his studies of Scottish life, especially *Annals of the Parish* (1821). Galt regarded his *novels [31] as 'theoretical histories', taking the phrase from the historiographers of the *Scottish Enlightenment, many of whose ideas of the relationship between human society and historical change are reflected in his fiction.

The son of a Scottish shipmaster, born in Irvine, Ayrshire, Galt left his job as a clerk to go to London in 1804. His many subsequent attempts to combine literary and commercial interests were never entirely successful, and he was frequently forced to write for his economic survival. His first fictional work, *The Majolo*, was published in 1815–16, but success came only in the 1820s with his Scottish novels, some of which were serialized in *Blackwood's* before appearing in book form.

72. Thomas Gainsborough, *Sophia Charlotte, Lady Sheffield*, *c*.1785.

Around this time Galt began to develop business connections with North America as the parliamentary lobbyist for a group of Canadians seeking compensation for war losses. He originated the idea of a colonizing venture which eventually became the Canada Company. Galt was in Canada from 1826 to 1829, where he was involved in the foundation of the town of Guelph. He was never reconciled to his early recall by the company's directors, and in his *Autobiography* (1833) and *Literary Life* (1834) argued that he would eventually be remembered more for his efforts as a nation-builder than as a novelist. His experiences in Canada provided the material for his New World novels, *Lawrie Todd* (1830) and *Bogle Corbet* (1831), which deal with the struggle of migrants to adapt to the new kind of society developing in America. JM

gambling crossed class and gender boundaries and was often represented by social commentators as the most pernicious 'vice' of the age, the source of moral and national decline, family breakdown, and suicide. It took place in a wide range of social contexts including clubs, *taverns, and the private home, and was intrinsic to the development of sports such as horse-racing, cricket, and boxing, as well as to long-established and increasingly stigmatized activities such as cock-fighting [see *popular culture, 23]. Gambling was a conspicuous dimension of the lifestyle of *Whigs such as Charles James *Fox, who bet, flamboyantly and to excess, in *gentlemen's clubs such as White's and Brooks's which formed the social and political nerve centres of the male political élite. Fox's female counterpart, the Duchess of *Devonshire, staged gambling parties at Devonshire House (depicted by *Rowlandson in 1791), and frequented the 'faro' tables of prominent ladies of *fashion such as Albinia Hobart, later Countess of Buckinghamshire (1738–1816), and Lady Sarah Archer (1741–1801). Card-playing was also popular among middling-order women: its presence in the private home was represented, for example, in *conduct books as a distraction from family responsibilities and as an insidious threat to domestic order.

The map of gambling in London extended from the gentlemen's clubs of St James's Street and Pall Mall to the night cellars and 'hells' (gambling dens) of Leicester Square and Covent Garden, frequented by lower-class men and women. Patrick *Colquhoun estimated that in the 1790s there were forty-three gaming houses in the metropolis with an annual turnover of £7.25 million. Gambling was one of a number of metropolitan subcultures, including those of the criminal underworld and prostitution, with which it shared key players and a 'canting' language. This subculture, as represented by the ex-fishmonger William Crockford (1775–1844), baron of the famous gambling club of the 1820s, and by the 'flash' Johnnies in the work of Pierce *Egan, later became an intrinsic element of *Regency raffishness and excess.

Gambling had been a target for moral campaigners throughout the eighteenth century, but the attack on it intensified during the general climate of political instability of the 1790s. Upper-class gambling, believed to set a dangerous example to the lower orders, was a particular focus for the *Society for the Suppression of Vice: Fox curbed his gambling excesses, partly through necessity, and in 1796 the 'faro' ladies were threatened with the pillory by Lord Chief Justice Kenyon. The threat was not realized, though the ladies were fined in 1797: their already compromised reputations, however, never recovered from a public savaging in the print-shops and newspapers. According to common law, gaming houses could be prosecuted as public nuisances and there was also a plethora of statutes that could be used against them, but magistrates and police were often bought off by owners of dens. The extent of this corruption was highlighted in 1824 by evidence given in the notorious case of the murder by Thurtell, Hunt, and Probert of swindler and gambler William Weare—evidence which only intensified public concern that gambling was a dangerously destabilizing force in society.   GR

game laws, see *poaching.

GANDON, James (1742–1823), pre-eminent architect in Ireland from his removal there in 1781 to his retirement in 1808. Gandon's career reflects the cultural dominance of an English-educated élite in Ireland, and his civic buildings were the most tangible signs of English political and economic control [see *architecture, 28].

At the age of 15 Gandon was apprenticed to Sir William *Chambers, in whose office he remained until 1765. During the 1770s he built a viable London-based practice. In competition with more established and innovative architects such as Chambers, Robert *Adam, and James *Wyatt, Gandon's best chance for professional and social advancement lay in offers of patronage from St Petersburg and Dublin.

Gandon's Irish patrons, Lord Carlow, Lord Charlemont, and the Earl of Portarlington, handed him the choice commission to design a new Custom House (1781–91). Subsequently, he executed major additions to the Parliament House (1784–7, now the Bank of Ireland) and completed the judicial complex known as the Four Courts (1786–1802). These major civic works elevated Gandon to the top of his profession within Ireland, but also imbued the banks of the Liffey with an aura of neoclassical magnificence that echoed Chambers's Somerset House (1776–96) as well as the more distant Baroque grandeur of Christopher Wren's (1632–1723) Royal Hospital for Seamen at Greenwich (1696–1716).

A talented but conservative designer, Gandon consolidated Chambers's academic neoclassicism, adding to its Roman foundations and francophile tendencies an appreciation of the compositional genius of English architects such as Wren and Adam.

SS

GANDY, Joseph Michael (1771–1843), architect, artist. An idiosyncratic architect and talented perspectivist, Gandy is chiefly remembered for his renderings of John *Soane's works and his own visionary architectural fantasies akin to the work of William *Blake and J. M. W. *Turner [see *architecture, 28].   42

The youthful Gandy enjoyed the patronage of fashionable society, notably of the architect James *Wyatt, which enabled him to attend the *Royal Academy schools and travel to Italy from 1794 to 1797. Upon returning to London, he became a draughtsman in Soane's office but also practised independently from 1801. He completed only a handful of works, most notably the Phoenix Fire and Pelican Life Insurance Offices, Charing Cross (1804–5), and the so-called 'Doric House', Bath (1818). More significant were his unbuilt and strikingly original *Designs for Cottages, Cottage Farms, and Other Rural Buildings*, published in 1805, which rejected the fake rusticity of the *cottage ornée* and foreshadowed the planarity and functionalism of early-twentieth-century architecture.

Gandy's commissioned renderings of Soane's work enhanced their spatial complexity and dramatic lighting effects. They also intermittently lifted him out of the desperate poverty that twice led to his imprisonment. He exhibited his own *watercolours, often fantasies on literary themes, at the Royal Academy from 1789 to 1838.   SS

genius. In the *Edinburgh Review* for October 1802, Francis *Jeffrey complained of a new '*sect*' of poets who had 'reasserted the independence of genius'. Far from being original, he wrote, the poets of this school drew their doctrines from Germany. Jeffrey was alluding to the celebration of genius in the *Sturm und Drang* of the 1770s and to the Romantic literature of the 1790s [see *literary theory, 41]. He was also, possibly, referring to the philosophy of Kant, who in his *Critique of Judgement* (1790) defined *Genius* as 'the innate mental aptitude (*ingenium*) *through which* nature gives the rule to art'. In Kant's influential account, genius is aligned with *originality and the productive *imagination. As such, genius breaks with neoclassical accounts of art based on imitation and convention, for according to Kant it is not possible to create fine art (as opposed to craft) without genius.

In the first years of the nineteenth century, genius was not as foreign to British sensibilities as Jeffrey seemed to imply. In fact, German interest in genius was strongly influenced by writers such as Richard Hurd (1720–1808), Thomas *Warton, Edward Young (1683–1765), William Duff (1732–1815), and Alexander Gerard (1728–95). Of the texts produced by these writers, the most influential in Germany were Young's *Conjectures on Original Composition* (translated in 1760, the year after it was first published) and Duff's *Essay on Original Genius* (1767). This extensive literature was in part inspired by the sometimes uneasy realization that the plays of *Shakespeare—the quintessential original genius—were not bound by, and in fact transcended, Aristotelian literary conventions.

In Romanticism, drawing on both German and English traditions of thought, 'genius' moved to the centre of both literary practice and aesthetic speculation. As a term which identifies a private source of art in the individual artist, an origin beyond the reach of conscious thought, genius underwrites a criticism focused on the relation between the work of art and the author. At the same time it was believed that, as a source which is natural and spontaneous, the Romantic genius transcends the subjective, bridging the gap between subject and object, thought and thing. In so doing, genius promises, *Coleridge wrote in *Biographia Literaria* (1817), 'the union and reconciliation of that which is nature with that which is exclusively human'.

Even within the discourse of Romanticism, the concept of genius encounters certain difficulties. First, one can doubt whether genius achieves the reconciliation it proclaims. John *Keats's phrase 'the egotistical sublime', used to describe *Wordsworth's poetry, nicely suggests an infinite that remains within the orbit of the self. Second, as both Wordsworth and Kant recognized, insofar as genius does give the 'rule to art' and its products *are* original, it is likely to be received with incomprehension. A writer must therefore, wrote Wordsworth, 'create the taste with which he is to be enjoyed'. That popular taste might resist reformation is implied by the frequent depiction of the genius as an alienated and tortured soul, a Prometheus or Satan, at odds with the status quo. This stereotype in turn suggests an affinity between genius and *madness, popularly linked throughout the nineteenth century. Third, as these remarks might suggest, genius raises the problem of morality. How is one to judge productions that by their nature exceed received categories? This is an urgent question for the category of genius described by Coleridge as 'COMMANDING', a category which includes Napoleon. Finally, rather than speaking for all of humanity, the Romantic genius is marked by gender. Indeed as Mary *Shelley's *Frankenstein* (1818) suggests, and recent critics have argued, the Romantic genius appropriates for male creators qualities (imagination, emotion, spontan-

eity) usually associated with the feminine. This creative androgyny is, however, with very few exceptions, reserved for men.   POt

gentlemen's clubs. A variety of formal and informal clubs catering to the sociable, commercial, and convivial needs of upper- and middle-class urban males had long been a feature of British metropolitan and provincial life; however, such clubs became increasingly specialized venues for professionals, and particularly associated with literature, *gambling, and politics.

Dr Samuel *Johnson commented on the compulsive clubbability of the English, and himself hosted a legendary Georgian literary club. Indeed, the forming of clubs and associations of all kinds was often viewed as part of the libertarian heritage of male political and social civility. Female counterparts, usually called 'assemblies', were regarded as having a more purely convivial and genteel function, though the 1780s witnessed a brief flowering of mixed sex or women-only *debating clubs which canvassed a range of serious social topics.

Georgian gentlemen's clubs were usually venues for wining, dining, gambling and informal political scheming. Allmack's, satirized for its rakish *dandyism in Pierce *Egan's *Life in London* (1821), had been founded in Pall Mall in 1764 by a Scottish proprietor, William McCall. In 1778 it moved to a *Henry Holland building in St James and changed its name to Brooks's, quickly becoming a magnet for fast-living Whigs, such as Charles James *Fox, in search of 'deep play'. Here, and at the rival Tory club, White's, vast sums were nightly bet and lost.

During the French and Napoleonic wars these clubs began to assume an increasingly important role in political lobbying, stimulated after 1806 by the country-wide proliferation of Fox and *Pitt clubs, founded to perpetuate the principles of their respective and recently deceased political heroes. However, it was not until the 1830s that first the Tories, then the Whigs and radicals, founded clubs given over exclusively to party political functions such as mobilizing and registering party voters and disseminating press propaganda. Established in the immediate wake of electoral failures, the Tory Carlton Club, founded in 1832, and its rival Reform Club of 1836 are sometimes said to have introduced a new era of 'club government' to Britain, but this was really an extension of activities pursued in the racy gentlemen's clubs of the late Georgian era. Even so, the clubs of the 1830s, with their purpose-built premises situated near parliament, as well as their party-political governing bodies, carried a new air of professionalism, seen also in the imposing Athenaeum literary club founded by the conservative *reviewer John Wilson Croker (1780–1857) in 1824.   IMcC

geology was new, exciting, and fashionable in the decades around 1800. Focused on the structure and history of the earth, it was created from traditions of biblical theorizing, speculative cosmology, mineral collecting, mining lore, and *travel literature. These diverse origins made geology exceptionally contro-versial, and put the science at the centre of public debates about *natural philosophy [34], *religion [10], and morality in the wake of the *French Revolution.

Late-*Enlightenment [32] authors, notably the Scottish natural philosopher James *Hutton, the poet Erasmus *Darwin, and the physician George Hoggart Toulmin (1754–1817), had elaborated a cyclical vision of the terrestrial economy which demanded a time-scale far beyond the few thousand years traditionally assigned to the early history of the earth. This potentially threatened biblical accounts of the Creation, as did rationalist attacks on the reality of the biblical Flood. Such anti-scriptural polemics became the stock in trade of *Deists and atheists, notably Richard *Carlile, and other authors in the illegal *unstamped press. On the other side, a vast apologetic literature grew up around these issues, notably the Oxford geologist William Buck-land's (1784–1856) *Reliquiae diluvianae* (1823) which suggested that *cave fossils were 'relics of the Flood'.

During the early decades of the century, Buckland and other geologists throughout Europe unveiled an extraordinary sequence of 'lost worlds', distinctive assemblages of animals and plants which had formerly inhabited the planet. The leading figure in these discoveries was the French comparative anatomist Georges Cuvier (1769–1832), famous for his reconstructions of extinct and often bizarre crea-tures. The global, progressive history which was developed from these findings originated in Enlight-enment parallels between the history of life, the his-tory of the earth, and individual development. The emphasis in Britain was on adaptation—to show how earlier creations were perfectly fitted by a divine Creator for prevailing environmental circumstances. Even the gigantic reptiles discovered in the decade after 1814, such as the remains of ichthyosaurs and plesiosaurs along the Dorset coast, were represented as part of the divine plan.

Geological practice was soon distanced from potentially contentious theological issues. By the end of the 1820s nearly all geologists assumed that the Flood was local and that earth history was unimagin-ably long. The key project became an empiricist one, to determine 'the mineral structure' of the globe. The Geological Society of London (1807), one of the first scientific organizations to break away from the long-established Royal Society of London, became a lead-ing centre for collaborative research, publishing in 1820 a map of the strata of England and Wales. The independently wealthy gentlemen who dominated the Society imported practices of *mapping, mineral analysis, and classification developed in France, Sweden, and the German-speaking lands, notably at the Freiburg Mining Academy in Saxony under Abraham Gottlob Werner. In the British context, geologists stressed fieldwork and empirical research precisely because of the ideological risks of un-restrained speculation.

Despite Britain's dependence on iron, coal, and other mineral resources needed for *industrializa-tion [14], there was no mining school in Britain until 1851. Geologists could, with some reason, claim to have potentially valuable knowledge for mine-owners and the landed gentry. A small but expert group of practical men—including the canal engineer William Smith (1769–1839)—attempted to make careers in mineral surveying; Smith's map of the English and Welsh strata appeared five years before that of the Geological Society. But professional science was low in status and fraught with dif-ficulties. Teaching at Oxford and Cambridge did not aim to produce paid careerists, but presented geo-logical science as a suitable activity for Christian gentlemen.

As a field science, geology offered opportunities for manly exertion among the grand scenes of nature. Studies of erupting volcanoes conducted by Sir William *Hamilton, published in his *Campi Phle-graei* in 1776, put southern Italy onto the scientific travellers' map. Within Britain, pilgrimages to the *picturesque wonders of the Lake District, the Scot-tish Highlands, the Welsh mountains, and the Peak District could readily be combined with an interest in natural history features. Fingal's Cave on the island of Staffa in the Hebrides, first described by Joseph *Banks in 1776, could be celebrated not only for its associations with *Ossianic legend, but as a monu-ment of even more remote events in the history of the earth. After *Napoleon's final defeat in 1815, renewed possibilities for continental travel led many to visit the complex rocks of the Alps, the fossil-rich deposits of the Paris Basin, the extinct volca-noes of southern France, and other celebrated localities.

Visitors to these sites often aimed to contribute to the solution of puzzling features of earth history. Controversy raged, for example, over whether rocks such as granite and basalt had been formed by fire—as Hutton and his followers claimed—or as deposits from a universal ocean, as Werner (and his leading Scottish disciple, the natural history professor at the University of Edinburgh Robert Jameson, 1774–1854) argued. At the heart of such disputes were significant questions about what the shape of geology was to be, and who could legitimately practise it.

In his *Principles of Geology* (1830–3), Charles Lyell (1797–1875) attempted to articulate new and more secure foundations for the science. He claimed that visible causes acting at the present day were the only legitimate basis for interpreting earth history—no catastrophes had to be invoked. In his view, the widely accepted narrative of progress was an unphilosophical assumption. Many contempo-raries, however, complained that Lyell ignored a wealth of empirical evidence for the progressive his-tory of the earth and life upon it.

The concept of a progressive creation culminating in the appearance of the human race thus became central to public presentations of geology, most notably in the Tory chemist Humphry *Davy's posthumous *Consolations in Travel* (1831), in the work of Gideon *Mantell, and in the *Penny Magazine* and other popular 'useful knowledge' periodicals that emerged in the 1830s. Ideas of geological progress were also used to underwrite Christian versions of Malthusian *political economy [33], as in J. B. Sumner's (1780–1862) *Treatise on the Records of Creation* (1816) and Thomas Chalmers's (1780–1847) *Evidence and Authority of the Christian Revelation* (1814).

The profound engagement of contemporaries with geological questions can also be seen in paintings by Francis *Danby, Alexander Nasmyth, J. M. W. *Turner, and other *landscape artists. The apocalyptic visionary John *Martin created some of the earliest images of 'lost worlds' in scientific texts; the startling discoveries of geology, especially in relation to the Deluge, also provided subjects for epic verse, notoriously in *Byron's unperformed drama *Cain* (1821) and *Shelley's *Prometheus Unbound* (1820). Contemporary doggerel tellingly portrayed a geologist (Buckland) in a subterranean dialogue with Lucifer, who was brewing up:

> A drink to madden Byron's brain,
> To nonsense madder still than Cain,
> To fire mad Shelley's impious pride
> To final crisis, suicide.

JAS

George III, see *monarchy.

George IV, see *monarchy and *Regency.

GERRALD, Joseph (1763–96), celebrated radical reformer and political transportee. Son of a wealthy West Indian planter and later educated at a Hammersmith boarding-school under the close tutelage of the *Whig man of letters Samuel Parr (1747–1825), Gerrald became a prominent orator and activist in the *Society for Constitutional Information and the London Corresponding Society during the early 1790s [see *corresponding societies]. His best-known publication, *A Convention the Only Means of Saving Us from Ruin* (1793), advocated an ambiguous popular convention as the best means of restoring the ancient democratic Anglo-Saxon heritage on the basis of indirect manhood suffrage and equal electoral districts. Both the latter were also aims of the 'British Convention of the Friends of the People', summoned by Scottish reformers in Edinburgh in December 1793, to which Gerrald and Maurice Margarot were elected as English delegates. Given the punitive reputation of the Scottish legal system, delegates knew themselves to be courting great danger, especially since they took delight in employing French Jacobin modes. Arrest, prosecution and sentence of several of the ringleaders to fourteen years' transportation rapidly followed. Though the prospect of such a sentence meant likely death for Gerrald given his fragile health, he refused to take the advice of friends who urged him to skip bail.

His trial in Edinburgh in March 1794 was a self-conscious act of political martyrdom in which Gerrald used a French-style of dress and deportment, as well as brilliant oratorical skills, to publicize the arbitrary nature of the proceedings. Following his sentence and conviction, he spent a lengthy time in both Edinburgh and Newgate gaols prior to transportation, becoming a focal point for radical visitations. From then until his death from consumption in New South Wales five months after arriving on the convict ship *Sovereign*, everything combined to make Gerrald an exemplary radical martyr and symbol of resistance. Speeches, songs, and idealized portraits circulated in radical milieux all over the country. Intellectuals such as *Godwin and Parr publicized his virtues and ordeals, which included leaving behind two orphaned children to whom he had been devoted and rejecting a supposed pardon from the government in exchange for relinquishing his reformist principles.

IMcC

GIBBON, Edward (1737–94), philosophical historian and author of the *History of the Decline and Fall of the Roman Empire* (1776–88). Gibbon was the only son of a financially inept country gentleman to survive infancy. Intellectually precocious but sickly, he received limited formal schooling at Kingston Grammar and Westminster School. In 1752, at the age of 15, he entered Magdalen College, Oxford, as a 'Gentleman Commoner', only be to expelled eighteen months later for secretly journeying to London and receiving conditional baptism in the Roman Catholic faith. His father reacted angrily to the conversion, which jeopardized efforts since 1745 to align the family with Hanoverian and *Whig interests. Within a fortnight Gibbon was sent into Swiss exile under threat of disinheritance.

Gibbon spent five years in the rarified Protestant atmosphere of Lausanne, under the guardianship of Jean Daniel Pavilliard, a local pastor and professor of civil history at the Académie de Lausanne. By late 1754 he was formally reconciled to Protestantism, but was ordered to continue his studies until eventually being allowed to return home on turning 21 in early 1758.

In his last months at Lausanne, Gibbon began his first book, the *Essai sur l'Étude de la Littérature* (1761). Initially conceived as a spirited defence of antiquarian studies of ancient literature, the *Essai* soon became a more ambitious project. Greatly influenced by *Hume, Giannone, and Montesquieu, Gibbon championed a 'philosophical' approach to the study of history, in which the findings of erudite scholarship were appraised by the experiential and probabilistic modes of reasoning advocated by John *Locke and Pierre Bayle (1647–1706). By critically contextualizing ancient literature the 'philosophical historian' could show the profound influence of custom and manners in shaping the fortune of nations [see *history, 38].

From the early 1760s Gibbon was convinced that his own genius qualified him for the pursuit of this philosophical approach to the study of history. He was later to claim being inspired to write his monumental history of the decline of Rome in October 1764, while musing amidst the ruins of the Roman forum as vespers were being sung in the nearby church of Aracheoli. However, it was not until some years after abandoning a projected history of the liberties of the Swiss in 1767 that he commenced work on the *Decline and Fall*.

Essentially a secular universal history, the *Decline and Fall* was concerned with examining the power of *religion [10] as a factor in the destruction of pagan Rome, the emergence of Christian Europe, the rise of Islam, and the Reformation. The first volume also sparked a religious controversy that irreparably damaged Gibbon's literary reputation and moral character. Gibbon maintained that he sought to elucidate the purely historical causes of the rise of Christianity, but critics took his rigorous empiricism and bitterly ironic descriptions of early church devotees and martyrs to be a reaffirmation of the *Deism of earlier generations or worse. Gibbon responded to critics by way of careful ironic utterances, to the effect that he was innocent of infidelity.

Reduced financial circumstances led Gibbon to settle in Lausanne in 1783. In 1789 he commenced work on an autobiography, which remained unfinished at the time of his death from post-operative infection, in early 1794.   PT

GIFFORD, William (1756–1826). From the mid-1790s until the mid-1820s Gifford was Britain's most implacably conservative *satirist and critic of *Whig, liberal, or radical literary circles and ideas.

Gifford's early career reads like a Dickensian novel: physically disabled, he was orphaned by poor and drunken parents, mistreated by his guardian, and apprenticed to a rough shoemaker who impeded his strenuous efforts at self-education. Rescue came from both middle-class and aristocratic patrons who enabled him to attend Oxford, where he showed promise as a translator of Juvenal's satires. *Tory political patronage followed in 1797, when *Canning and *Pitt appointed him editor of the projected *Anti-Jacobin* newspaper. Beginning in the mid-1790s, when his satires, *The Baviad* (1790) and *Maeviad* (1795), lashed *Della Cruscan poetry of *sensibility [11], Gifford manifested his gratitude towards the Georgian social and political establishment by a lifelong support of Tory causes and an inveterate hostility to any form of liberal culture. In 1809 this brought the further reward of editorship of the *Quarterly Review*, a Tory attempt to counter the success of the Whig *Edinburgh Review*. Gifford quickly became legendary for subjecting all contributions to close political censorship, and for his own virulent criticism of all forms of literary or political innovation. He was widely assumed to have hastened *Keats's death with a rabid anonymous review of *Endymion* in 1818.

Inevitably Gifford became the target of counter-satire, most notably from John *Williams, John *Wolcot, Leigh *Hunt, and William *Hazlitt, all of whom stressed his sycophancy. Hazlitt's *Spirit of the Age* (1825) accused Gifford and the *Quarterly Review* of being imbued with 'the slime of hypocrisy, the varnish of the courts, the cant of pedantry, the cobwebs of law, the iron hand of power'. Gifford's ultimate reward for a lifetime of conservative service was to be buried in Westminster Abbey.   IMcC

GILLRAY, James (1757–1815), caricaturist, the greatest and most ambitious of the English graphic *satirists of the period. His work displays metaphoric extravagance, incisive political commentary, a precision in its deployment of personal caricature, and a ferocious irony.

Gillray was a Londoner, raised in the unconventional Dissenting atmosphere of a *Moravian family with its emphasis on the necessity of suffering and the inevitability of death as the reward of sin. All four of his brothers and sisters died before he was an adult. After a brief training as an apprentice to a writing engraver, he joined a travelling circus and toured the country. He returned to London at a moment when political *print [22] satire was about to take off as an organized commercial concern on an entirely new scale. By the early 1770s large publishing concerns such as those of Darly and Humphrey were well established, and there was a healthy and growing market for social satires. The beautifully executed mezzotints of Carington Bowles (*fl.* 1771–83) were also introducing a new technical refinement to the form.

It was Gillray's satiric experimentation during the *American Revolution which provided him with the technical resources for the dense stylistic and methodological fusions which typify the great prints from the mid-1780s until 1810. The majority of earlier political prints reflect the prevailing tides of opinion: initially anti-state, then anti-military, they finally attack members of the royal family, ending with the King himself. By the end of the American War Gillray had mastered a formidably varied graphic vocabulary. He had developed the stiff ideographic conventions of the mid-eighteenth century into his own fluid style of personal caricature, based on a glorious and confident line, and a mastery of academic conventions of figure drawing. 'The Thunderer', for example, a damning portrait of vainglorious Captain Banastre Tarleton, just back from America, shows the young etcher's skill in personal caricature and figure drawing, while 'Liberty of the Subject', a powerful indictment of the *press-gang system, demonstrates his ability to handle crowd scenes and the exactitude of his observation. Gillray's American War prints also testify to his ambitious ability to represent complicated political situations in strikingly immediate visual metaphors.

If the American Revolution provided the catalyst for the formation of Gillray's style, the *French Revolution was the historical framework responsible for his mature expression. It provided him with an ideal environment for the exploration of his morally decentred vision. He stands outside the irreducibly positive elements which appear to underlie the satire of Thomas *Rowlandson, especially in relation to representations of sexuality. For Gillray, sexual behaviour, like politics, was tainted by moral corruption. His drawing style during his mature period ranged from the high academicism of a design such as 'The Apotheosis of Hoche' (1798) to a deliberate infantile primitivism. 'Billy Playing Johnny a Dirty Trick' (1796) shows William *Pitt as a child sitting in a tree, eating a crown, and excreting into a sleeping

14, 17
50, 7.

73. 'The Hopes of the Party.' James Gillray's populist satire often made his political affinities difficult to fix: here he caricatures both Whigs and their supposed victims. William Pitt and Queen Charlotte hang helplessly in the background, while the masked executioner Charles James Fox is poised to decapitate the bovine King, spurred on by gloating and sodomitical 'Crown & Anchor' Whigs and oppositionists: John Horne Tooke, Joseph Priestley, Richard Sheridan, and Sir Cecil Wray.

John Bull's mouth. The design not only presents politicians as children but is drawn with the crudity, and innocent fervour, of the mischievous child.

The virulence of Gillray's satire in the 1790s took a variety of forms. There were the straightforward examples of defamatory attacks on the King and Queen. 'Sin, Death and the Devil' (1792), which depicts the Queen as an ugly hag, is perhaps the most notorious. Gillray was eventually recruited to the government cause, accepting a pension in 1797, yet even his concentrated assaults on the English radicals in the 1790s were as subversive of authority as they were unambiguous attacks on royalty. His favourite method for warning of the dangers of *revolution [1] was to create visions of the country overrun by the leading radicals and members of the *Whig opposition. The French are frequently an incidental addition. A successful revolution is carried through in the caricaturist's imagination in the most fantastic and extreme forms. As early as 1791 Gillray produced such an image of the violent overthrow of the state in 'The Hopes of the Party, prior to July 14'. The subtitle, in the form of a mock litany, 'From such wicked Crown and Anchor Dreams good Lord Deliver Us', refers to a notorious radical tavern and establishes the print's *loyalist credentials. Yet it is the extremity of the outrages committed against the King and Queen, leaving them without a vestige of regal mystique, which is the dominant impression of this print, overshadowing its warning

against the Foxite Whigs. Later prints such as 'Promis'd Horrors of the French Invasion,—or—Forcible Reasons for negociating a Regicide Peace' (1796) develop the theme of Gillray's delight in the destruction of the English system. There are heads everywhere, on plates, in baskets, even floating down the gutter. Gillray's fury is beyond the call of duty.

Gillray lived with the print-seller Hannah Humphrey at her shop in various London locations, most famously in St James's Street, close to Westminster and gentlemen's clubs such as Brooks's and White's, which he represented in 'Promis'd Horrors'. After 1811 he was diagnosed as insane and confined in a room in Mrs Humphrey's shop; he died in 1815. Fusing earlier and diffuse elements of print culture into forms which rapidly became paradigmatic, Gillray's work dominated the work of lesser contemporaries such as George Woodward, Henry Bunbury, Isaac Cruikshank, James Sayers, and Richard Newton. It provided a heritage and a satiric vocabulary which has had a bearing on virtually all subsequent attempts in the field. MW

GILPIN, William (1724–1800), clergyman, religious writer, schoolmaster, travel writer, and theorist of the *picturesque. Extremely influential across the fields of literature, art, and *landscape gardening, Gilpin's writings created a vernacular of British landscape writing which contributed to the nationalist *antiquarian [35] rediscovery of the British Isles, by emphasizing natural beauty of tracts of land unrecovered and untamed by *enclosure.

After graduating from Oxford in 1744 and being ordained in 1746, Gilpin became a teacher and vicar in Surrey, where he remained for thirty years. An enlightened schoolmaster, he replaced corporal punishment with fines spent on the improvement of the school library, encouraged a love of gardening, and participated in the burgeoning opposition to the conventional emphasis on classical languages by stressing the importance of the English *language [40].

During summer vacations Gilpin undertook sketching tours that produced his famous works on the picturesque. The first of these, *Observations on the River Wye . . . Relative Chiefly to Picturesque Beauty* (1782), went into five editions before 1800. This initiated a series of five similar works on different regional districts, including tours of the Lake District (1789), *Picturesque Remarks on the Western Parts of England and the Isle of Wight* (1798), and tours of the Highlands (1800), writings which established a new genre of domestic *tourism in Britain. The defining characteristics of Gilpin's idea of the picturesque, which he developed as an elaboration of Edmund *Burke's category of the beautiful [see *sublime], are theorized in *Three Essays: On Picturesque Beauty; On Picturesque Travel; and on Sketching Landscape* (1792). The foundations of this theory were laid in Gilpin's early anonymously published *Dialogue upon the Gardens* (1748) on the gardens at Lord Cobham's Stowe. Gilpin's work was parodied by William *Combe in *The Tours of Dr Syntax*.   CT

glee, a short piece of unaccompanied vocal *music [26] normally written for three or four solo male voices. Glees were primarily intended for largely amateur performance at the many catch and glee clubs which met for dinner and convivial singing at *taverns in London and in the larger provincial centres; they were also performed in the home and at public *concerts.

The glee may have arisen partly in reaction against the vulgarity and frequent bawdiness of the older catch tradition, and is distinguished from it by the respectability and gentility of its texts. In style and ethos it owes much to the English madrigal, examples of which were beginning to be known in the mid-eighteenth century. The subject-matter is frequently love, often in a pastoral context, but there are also glees on the joys of food and drink, and others with patriotic or moralistic subjects.

Very large numbers of glees were written and published, either singly or in collections. Almost every composer of the period wrote examples; those particularly associated with the form were Samuel *Webbe the elder, John Wall Callcott (1766–1821), Stephen Paxton (1735–87), John Stafford Smith (1750–1836), and R. J. S. Stephens (1757–1837), whose *Recollections* are a particularly valuable source of information on the subject. Principal glee clubs were the Noblemen and Gentlemen's Catch and Glee Club (1761), the Anacreontic Society (1762), and the Glee Club (1787).   PO

Glorious Revolution refers to the events which led to the replacement of James II by his son-in-law and nephew William of Orange in 1688 and the accompanying constitutional changes which established parliamentary *monarchy in Britain.

In response to opposition aroused by James's Catholicism and autocratic style, William landed with an invasion force at Devon on 5 November 1688. The Bill of Rights (1689) declared James's subsequent flight to France to be a desertion of the throne, and offered the throne jointly to William and his wife, Mary. This was followed by the Triennial Act (1694), which provided for the holding of elections every three years, and the Act of Settlement (1701), which secured the independence of the judiciary and provided for the ultimate succession of the Protestant Hanoverians by barring Roman Catholics from the throne.

By mid-century, 1688 was widely imagined not as a rebellion but as a limited resistance to extreme circumstances and as a renewal of the ancient constitution retrospectively justified by the stability of the Hanoverian establishment [see *constitutionalism]. Central to the legitimacy of the Hanoverian succession and to the self-image of eighteenth-century political, religious, and social establishments, the Glorious Revolution became a major reference point in the pamphlet wars from the 1770s, where it underwent a fierce battle of reinterpretation as radicals and *loyalists each used it to legitimate their cause.

For reformers over the next thirty years, the blandness and ecumenical nature of the Revolution's celebration pointed to the need for its reclamation, reinterpretation, or refutation. They believed that the settlement of 1688–9 had established political and religious liberties eroded or discarded by subsequent governments; consideration of 1688 thus became part and parcel of the campaign for economical and *parliamentary reform and for upholding the rights of the American colonists.

The centenary of 1788, celebrated by revolutionary gatherings, dinners, and, most notably, *sermons, marked the pinnacle of this revived interest. The succession of 1688 was given added political relevance by the Regency Crisis of 1788, precipitated by George III's first bout of insanity, as was the issue of religious *toleration by the renewed Nonconformist campaign for the repeal of the Test and Corporation Acts. But it was the revival of contract theory—stimulated by the supposed example of the *French Revolution—which dominated attention. In his famous sermon of 4 November 1789, *A Discourse on the Love of Our Country*, Richard *Price asserted that 1688 had established a general right of people to choose their own forms and members of government and to dismiss them if they proved oppressive or corrupt.

Conservative interpreters had always resisted such appeals to general principle. Edmund *Burke's *Reflections on the Revolution in France* (1791) worked with some success to sever the link between 1688 and

1789 and to reassert the conservative and restorative character of the Glorious Revolution. By 1808, the *Edinburgh Review* was to lament that even in *Whig circles 1688 could not be mentioned without seeming to give encouragement to the French Revolution.

As the central issue of politics in the nineteenth century became no longer aristocratic resistance to royal tyranny but the extension of the franchise and the political and social influence of the middling ranks, the Glorious Revolution assumed a less mythic status within political rhetoric and historical imagination. AMacL

GODWIN, Mary Jane (?1765–1841), author and publisher of *children's literature, mother and stepmother to William *Godwin's children. An English woman who had been forced to flee wartime Europe calling herself 'Mrs Clairmont', Mary Jane may have met Godwin at Mary *Robinson's funeral in December 1800. Her French émigré acquaintance countenanced a certain mystery about her past, coupled with the chance to employ her skills in French language and culture. In 1801 she took lodgings next door to Godwin for herself and her son, Charles, and daughter, Mary Jane (Claire) *Clairmont. Soon after, she married Godwin and bore William Godwin Jr. (1803–32).

As Godwin's second wife, she shared Godwin's plunging political fortunes after the demise of the English Jacobin movement. She was strong-willed and could be loud, but no self-assertions on her part could dint the mutual ascendancy in the family of Godwin and his daughter (later Mary *Shelley). Before her marriage, Mary Jane worked as a French translator and wrote children's books. When his ambitions as a serious dramatist failed in 1801, Godwin installed himself in Mary Jane's field of operations. In 1805 he took over the direction of a children's *publishing company, the Juvenile Library of M. J. Godwin & Co. Godwin published his books for children as 'Edward J. Baldwin', to disguise his identity from the *anti-Jacobin reviewers and Christian censors of *education [17], and to maintain a dignified distance from commerce and children. Mary Jane ran the shop and dealt with the customers. Her publications appeared anonymously, including *Dramas for Children*, advertised as 'by the editor of Tabart's Popular Stories'. She wrote only one book for the adult reader, a stately guidebook to Herne Bay, in 1835.

After *Waterloo, when many small businesses failed, the Godwins lost their house and livelihood, and until Godwin died in 1836 they lived in a pensioner's flat granted by parliament. From 1836 until her death in 1841, the widowed Mary Jane collaborated with Mary Shelley on editing Godwin's correspondence, for a 'Life of William Godwin', which remained unpublished at Mary Shelley's death in 1851. Mary Jane was buried beside Godwin and Wollstonecraft in St Pancras' Churchyard, which did not reject Roman Catholic corpses, but her grave was abandoned to the railway developers by the Shelley family when they reinterred Mary Shelley's biological parents in Bournemouth. JB

GODWIN, William (1756–1836), political theorist, novelist, writer, and influential radical. Godwin was born into a family tradition of religious Dissent and from an early age conceived a vocation for the ministry. One of his first works was a set of sermons delivered to his congregation in Beaconsfield. His last, posthumously published, work, *The Genius of Christianity Unveiled* (1873), was an unstinting attack on Christianity. Theological controversies framed Godwin's life, and profoundly influenced his political philosophy.

When he lost his vocation, a year or so after graduating from the Hoxton *Dissenting Academy, he made his living mainly by writing contemporary history. His *History of the Life of William Pitt Earl of Chatham* (1783), the first biography of William Pitt the elder, which brought Godwin to the attention of *Whig circles, shows a considerable grasp of contemporary politics, as does his authorship of the British and foreign history section for the *New Annual Register* from 1784 to 1791. From 1824 to 1828, he produced a four-volume *History of the Commonwealth*, together with other historical works, both for adults and children.

Godwin's educational writings also span his career, from a *Plan of a Seminary* in 1784, through *The Enquirer* (1797), to his *Letters of Advice to a Young American* (1818). Here, and in his activities as a teacher in the 1780s, Godwin sought to foster younger, not always tractable, minds, a preoccupation apparent in his roles as mentor to a range of young men and women from the 1790s to his death (most notably to his daughter Mary *Shelley and his eventual son-in-law Percy *Shelley), and as a publisher, commissioner, and writer of children's books throughout the first three decades of the nineteenth century [see *children's literature].

Political Justice and *The Enquirer* inspired Thomas *Malthus's attempted rebuttal of theories of progress in his *Essay on the Principle of Population* (1798). Godwin's replies, in part in his *Thoughts occasioned by . . . Dr Parr* (1801), but more fully in his *Of Population* (1820), and various letters, provide some of the earliest critical commentary on Malthus's essay.

Yet, for all Godwin's range, there is a basic thematic unity to his work. *Political Justice*, written in the wake of the opening stages of the French Revolution and published a matter of weeks after the execution of the King of France, crystallizes a sense among British radicals that the *American and *French Revolutions were inaugurating a new era of world peace, prosperity, and progress. The book's rationalism, its conviction of the sanctity of private judgment, and its sense that each individual can be brought to act motivated wholly by reason to secure the maximum benefit for fellow human beings, epitomize a *millennial optimism derived partly from the *philosophes*, but more directly from the writings of Dissenting theologians and philosophers, especially Richard *Price and Joseph *Priestley. The result is a moral theory mixing *utilitarianism (act so as to maximize the benefit you give) with an indefeasible constraint of right (each individual is to be sole judge, through the rigorous exercise of private judgement and via candid public discussion, of how he or she should act). Moreover, Godwin's utilitarianism becomes idealized by his conviction that the life of the mind and of benevolence are the greatest possible sources of happiness: utility thus becomes inseparable from the progress of mind. Although there are changes in the extent of Godwin's optimism (later editions of *Political Justice* tone down the original's speculations as to the prospects of immortality) and in the language in which he couches his arguments, his commitment to the value of a life of benevolent action remains as unshakeable in his last philosophical work, *Thoughts on Man* (1831), as it is in the first edition of *Political Justice*.

Godwin's *utopianism [9] in *Political Justice* might suggest political naïvety, but his letters and pamphlets from the 1780s to 1815 show an acute grasp of contemporary politics. His most renowned pamphlet, *Cursory Strictures*, was written against a Grand Jury verdict indicting several of his radical friends in the *Treason Trials of 1794. John Horne *Tooke, the most prominent of them, certainly believed he owed his life to the piece.

Given the optimism of *Political Justice*, Godwin's six mature novels, *Caleb Williams* (1794), *St Leon* (1799), *Fleetwood* (1805), *Mandeville* (1817), *Cloudesley* (1830), and *Deloraine* (1833), can surprise readers by their apparent pessimism revealed in the tragic fates to which his eponymous heroes generally succumb [see *novels, 31]. The essay 'Of History and Romance' (1798) offers a rationale for the novels, arguing that fictional history can be truer than real history. By portraying the part which political and social institutions play in the formation of character, Godwin attempted to show that the culture of aristocracy and inequality impels individuals into corruption and decline. His polemical design is shrewdly executed by forgoing the omniscience of a third-person narrator and working through a first-person narrator whose grasp of his situation, we gradually discover, is deeply flawed. Without the intrusions of the authoritative narrator, the reader is free to form their own judgement as to the characters' contributions to their fate.

A victim of the *loyalist reaction against France, Godwin was attacked throughout the 1790s in pamphlets, prints, poems, and novels. After the publication of the *Memoirs of the Author of a Vindication of the Rights of Woman* (1798), a frank account of the life of his deceased wife, Mary *Wollstonecraft, he became so tainted that he published his children's books under pseudonyms. Although forced to exchange fame for notoriety, and in debt for much of the last thirty years of his life, he exerted a powerful influence on the radicals and literati of the 1790s and on the generation which followed.   MPH

Gordon riots, 2–10 June 1780. Eighteenth-century Britain's most serious *riots, leading to more property damage in London than Paris suffered throughout the *French Revolution.

Variously attributed by historians to anti-Protestant bigotry, criminal looting, or anti-capitalist protest, the Gordon riots grew out of the religious politics of the *American Revolution. Their origins lay in Scottish antipapal agitations of 1778–9 against a mild measure of Catholic liberalization introduced by the North government in order to recruit Highlander and Irish Catholics to fight against the rebellious American colonists. As elected leader of the Protestant Association, Lord George Gordon (1751–93), volatile younger son of the Duke of Athol, developed an apocalyptic national Protestant mission against the supposedly repressive forces of international popery. His Puritan rhetoric and radical politico-economic programme attracted support both in London and in larger provincial towns, inspiring City radicals, Dissenters, and *millenarian artisans like William *Blake. When parliament refused to repeal the pro-Catholic legislation in England, London rioters attacked Catholic chapels, property owners, and eminent sympathizers. Contemporary pictorial and literary accounts show the mob ransacking houses, burning down prisons—including the newly rebuilt Newgate—and cremating themselves as they lap blazing alcohol from outside the gutters of Langdale's distillery.

The subsequent impact of the French Revolution has tended to obscure the contemporary trauma caused by the riots. Intellectuals such as the *Burneys, *Gibbon, and *Burke saw them as an eruption of seventeenth-century enthusiasm which threw doubt on rational achievements of the *Enlightenment [32]; they also deplored the failure of City officials to resist the mob, and applauded George III's initiation of martial action. The riots began a turn towards conservatism generally associated with the later reaction against the French Revolution. Some *Whigs now saw the strengthening of the *monarchy and standing army as less dangerous than social anarchy, triggering moves to improve urban *policing [7] and to suppress popular *debating societies. Burke's early and extreme hostility to the French Revolution owed much to his personal experiences of popular violence in 1780. Both he and Charles Dickens in his retrospective historical novel of 1841, *Barnaby Rudge*, represented the riots as Britain's counterpart of the Parisian revolutionary violence of the 1790s.   IMcC

Gothic began as a term of abuse, turned into a fashion, and gave rise to a modern sense of history, influencing on the way every branch of the arts from *architecture [28], to *painting [27], *sculpture, and literature.

'Gothic' (or 'Gothick') first appears in the seventeenth century as a derogatory term. The original meaning, 'pertaining to the Goths (or Germans) and their language', was synonymous with the barbarous and uncouth. Its most common use was in writings on architecture, where we find it applied as a blanket term of dislike to almost all medieval works of art up to the early eighteenth century.

Even when unfashionable, Gothic architecture never ceased to be built in Britain. It is debatable whether St John's College Library, Cambridge, built of brick in the late seventeenth century—supposedly at the height of neoclassicism—is the last genuinely Gothic building or the first example of the Gothic revival. Certainly, within half a century Gothic buildings were once again appearing, though of quite a new kind. Among the most striking were the Whig Lord Cobham's 'Gothic Temple' at Stowe (c.1740), symbolically the Temple of Liberty, and Horace *Walpole's modestly proportioned lath-and-plaster exercise in domesticized nostalgia at Strawberry Hill, near Twickenham. Walpole's famous Long Gallery was only 56 ft long and 15 ft wide, but the ceiling was a miniaturized copy from the Henry VII Chapel in Westminster Abbey. William *Beckford's vast extravaganza at Fonthill Abbey (1796–1807) was on the opposite scale. His architect, James *Wyatt, had begun as a stage designer (adapting the London Pantheon) and then restored Lichfield Cathedral on similarly theatrical lines. At Fonthill the hammer-beamed dining room was 80 ft high, and proved impossible to heat on virtually the only occasion when it was used; the 260-ft tower was unstable, and collapsed within a few years. By the nineteenth century a more scholarly and substantial Gothic architecture was associated with a revival of *medievalism, as in the Houses of Parliament (1840–60) or Glasgow University (1866–70).

For architects like A. W. *Pugin, a convert to Roman Catholicism, the Gothic style was essentially 'Christian', and expressive of Christian values, in contrast with the inherent paganism of neoclassicism. His influential book, Contrasts (1836), juxtaposes a series of pictures of contemporary and medieval life with the explicit aim of showing that pre-Reformation life was more kindly, more spiritual, and infinitely more beautiful than contemporary England, and foreshadowed the arguments of Victorian critics like Thomas *Carlyle and John Ruskin (1819–1900).

The Gothic *novel [31], also inaugurated by Walpole, was similarly eclectic. His Castle of Otranto (1764) was inspired by a dream of 'a gigantic hand in armour' on the banister of the staircase at Strawberry Hill. Improbably, it was a runaway success, and attracted numerous imitators. In poetry, works like S. T. *Coleridge's 'Christabel' (1798) and John *Keats's 'The Eve of St Agnes' (1818) combine Gothic architecture with moods of fear and suspense.

Such works helped to arouse a sense of the past, and were to lead towards the more painstakingly 'historical' novels of writers like Walter *Scott [see *history, 38]. They also offered the Romantics a symbolism and a language for expressing kinds of experience for which no alternative conceptual framework was then available, and often uncannily anticipate and illustrate the theories of later psychologists like Freud. The prevailing empiricist psychology of John *Locke and David Hartley (1705–57) allowed no room for theories of the unconscious, irrational deeds, and feelings of guilt, or the mysteries of pain and suffering. Later Gothic novels, such as James *Hogg's Private Memoirs and Confessions of a Justified Sinner (1824), show increasing psychological complexity.   SP

Gothic drama is a twentieth-century generic category for a number of plays which engage similar conventions and themes to those of the *Gothic novel, and the *Gothic effect in *landscape gardening, *landscape painting, and **architecture [28]**. However, contemporaries did not label these plays as such, generic definitions and boundaries in drama being particularly hybrid and in flux: for example, Matthew 'Monk' *Lewis's The Castle Spectre (performed 1797, published 1798) was described as 'a drama of a mingled nature, Operatic, Comical and Tragical'.

The 'Gothic' quality of a drama was primarily signalled to contemporaries by distinctive and often spectacular scenic locales such as the cliff-top castle, the prison, the convent, the forest; by lighting and music effects suggesting gloom and foreboding; and by themes involving threat and imprisonment, often of a vulnerable woman, at the hands of a male authority figure. Examples from the period include Hannah *More's The Fatal Falsehood (1779), Hannah *Cowley's Albina (1779), Robert Jephson's The Count of Narbonne (1781, based on Horace *Walpole's Castle of Otranto), John Philip *Kemble's Lodoiska (1794), George *Colman's The Iron Chest (1796, based on *Godwin's Caleb Williams) and his Blue-Beard (1798), Joanna *Baillie's De Monfort (1800), S. T. *Coleridge's Remorse (1813), Charles *Maturin's Bertram (1816), and Robert Lalor Sheil's Evadne (1819).

Gothic drama did not necessarily entail a tragic outcome: like *melodrama, its plots often hinged on the possibility of either tragic or comic resolutions. Walpole's incest tragedy, The Mysterious Mother (1768), has often been described as initiating the genre, but its genealogy can be traced to an earlier *romance tradition and contemporary romance theory of Clara *Reeve and others, as well as to the 'Gothic' elements of pathetic tragedies such as John Home's Douglas, the plays of Rowe and Otway, and the work of *Shakespeare, whose pre-eminent 'Gothic' drama was Macbeth. The 1790s saw a Gothic craze in the theatre, partly inspired by the success of Ann *Radcliffe's novels which were adapted for the stage by the dramatist and biographer James Boaden (1762–1839) and by Sarah *Siddons's son Henry. Matthew 'Monk' Lewis made the transition from notorious Gothic novelist to orchestrator of Gothic terror in the theatre with The Castle Spectre, the highlight of which was the appearance (twice) of the ghost of the heroine's murdered mother, 'her white and flowing garments spotted with blood'. While Radcliffe's novels had offered rational explanations for supernatural events, The Castle Spectre exploited to the hilt the Gothic fascination with the uncanny and the unexplicable. Embodying, so terrifyingly, the ghosts that in Gothic fiction existed in the imagination of the reader, the appeal of Gothic drama can be related to the preoccupation with the representational power of theatre, in relation to that of the literary text, exemplified by the Shakespearean criticism of *Lamb, *Hazlitt, and Coleridge. The contemporary descriptions of Lewis as 'horror-breeding' and 'spectre-mongering' suggest apprehensions of theatrical supernaturalism as more than mere stage effect but instead as a contaminating influence that violated the necessary aesthetic boundaries between performance and audience, and between author and literary creation. In the context of the 1790s these concerns also had a political dimension: in their prevailing atmospheres of insidious unease and disease, the Gothic drama was on the one hand interpreted by radicals as a harbinger of revolutionary change and on the other castigated as a sign of cultural decline and dissolution. (For Coleridge, writing in 1798, the keynote of 'the modern jacobinical drama', as he called it, was 'the confusion and subversion of the natural order of things'.) In 1816 Coleridge renewed his attack on such drama in the context of the success of Maturin's *Bertram*, focusing in particular on the adulterous relationship between the eponymous villain-hero and the heroine as evidence of the play's moral and political decadence. However, sexual and familial relations had always been key Gothic concerns. In their representations of families in conflict, of taboo relations and desires, of eruptions of internecine and intranecine violence, of women as both innocent victims and catalysts of male violence and jealousy, Gothic plays countered the valorization of *domesticity [13] in the work of writers such as *Burke and Coleridge with a darker image of the family as a site of conflict and, increasingly, of ontological uncertainty.

GR

Gothic novel. By 1830 the literary tradition of the *Gothic had developed two distinct forms, what we might call the 'male Gothic' and the 'female Gothic'. Both forms shared a concern with excavating what was buried beneath the façade of a supposedly 'happy' bourgeois capitalist society. To reveal what was repressed or hidden, these literary works relied on tropes of historical pastness or barbarism or even savagery. As the term Gothic implies, they dug up the ancient or medieval past, the unruly or unsocialized passions of the Goths, in order to suggest—in ways that Freud has led us to recognize—that such passions remain present in even the most 'civilized' of nations.

The leading representatives of the male Gothic novel—Horace *Walpole's *The Castle of Otranto* (1764), William *Beckford's *Vathek* (1786), Matthew *Lewis's *The Monk* (1796)—focus on male fears and anxieties, especially sexual anxieties. Their works figure the primal conflicts between sons and fathers, and between sons and mothers. In these Oedipal narratives, sons wrestle with fathers for control over women, wealth, and social status, but in the male Gothic novel the sons are usually destroyed by their fathers. In *The Castle of Otranto*, for example, the father both marries his son's fiancée and murders his son.

Sometimes sons are destroyed by all-powerful mothers or mother-figures. The hero of Beckford's *Vathek* is compelled by his sorceress mother to seek wealth, murder children, and violate virgins, all of which damns him to the eternal service of the devil Eblis. Lewis's *The Monk* is grounded on the trope of

Oedipal desire—Father Ambrosio breaks his vows of celibacy in order to have sex with the Madonna (in actuality Matilda, the girl who has both entered his monastery disguised as a novitiate and given him the self-portrait he worships as the Virgin). He is then seduced by that Virgin mother, Matilda, into sexual liaisons with his own sister and mother, whom he then murders. The male Gothic novel thus uncovers the taboo desires and anxieties of the bourgeois family romance, representing them as the very foundation of capitalist culture and recording a profound horror of such desires. Significantly, the authors of the male Gothic tradition were for the most part *homosexual: men who found the ramifications of compulsory heterosexuality terrifying.

The female Gothic novel focused on the same sexual structures of middle-class patriarchy, but with a difference. From the female point of view, patriarchal heterosexuality was no different from incest. The bourgeois family romance licensed the patriarch to desire and to possess his daughters. Mary *Wollstonecraft argued in *A Vindication of the Rights of Woman* (1792) that the women of her day were 'kept in a state of perpetual childhood', innocent, uneducated, and obsessed only with their personal appearance and with getting 'good' husbands—husbands who were older, wiser, richer, and thus infinitely more powerful than they. This meant that men typically married women young enough to be their daughters whom they treated in the same way that they treated their daughters.

That father–daughter incest is everywhere most monstrous and most ordinary is the argument of the leading writers of the female Gothic novel, Ann *Radcliffe, Charlotte *Dacre, and Mary *Shelley. In their novels, the female protagonist is desired either by her biological father, by her priestly 'Father', or by the man whom society defines as her legal father (her guardian, her uncle, her stepfather). While she typically escapes actual sexual violation, this is usually effected only by her death or, more troubling, by her 'rescue' by another man, her lover or husband, who is often troped as uncannily similar to her rapist-father.

The female Gothic novel goes one step further in its critique of contemporary gender relations. Not only is the heroine sexually pursued and psychologically molested by her father-figures; she also comes to *desire* such molestation. These novels sought to expose the ways in which girls were taught to map their erotic fantasies upon their own submission, to become the voluntary slaves and victims of the all-powerful, sadistic father. Ellena Rosalba, in Ann Radcliffe's *The Italian* (1797), emblematically expresses her 'gratitude' to the father-rapist Schedoni for his 'protection'. In a similar pattern, Shelley's Mathilda in the novel of the same name desires only to become 'the bride of death' in which she can enjoy a perpetual 'union' with her dead, incestuous father. Such patterns of female masochism and grateful submission to patriarchal power underlie even the 'realistic' female-authored novels of this period: Elizabeth Bennet's 'gratitude' to Darcy for marrying her in Jane *Austen's *Pride and Prejudice* (1813) encodes the same submission of a vivacious, intelligent woman to the financial and psychological control of a man of greater wealth and power.   AM

Grand Tour. Making a tour of Europe for *self-improvement was already a familiar intellectual and social feature of aristocratic *education [17] by the early eighteenth century, when advancements in roads and other *transport conditions fostered a travel boom.

The typical Grand Tour consisted in a journey to Venice, Florence, Rome, and Naples, via Paris and Switzerland; others involved periods of residence in the Netherlands and Germany, or extensions to Sicily and Greece. Not all travellers wrote, but those who did frequently combined a sentimental account of petty hardships with observations upon local customs that were occasionally elaborated into more systematic accounts of government and history [see *travel literature].

The Grand Tour was, above all, a literary phenomenon. Travellers were steeped in well-known earlier narratives, among which Joseph Addison's *Remarks on Several Parts of Italy* (1705) might be singled out. Though not all travellers regarded continental religious and political life censoriously, Bishop Burnet's book, usually published in the eighteenth century under the title of *Travels through Switzerland and Italy* (1686), set the tone for sustained attacks on Catholicism and attendant political conditions.

Many guidebooks such as Thomas Nugent's *The Grand Tour* (1749, 1756) also provided practical information about routes, and cultivated the sense of how foreign objects and people were to be regarded. Writers usually adopted an epistolary form, often claiming that narratives composed after return to Britain were written on the spot. Previous Grand Tour books were frequently plagiarized; stereotypic observations on such subjects as the sublime crossing of the Alps, the physical deformities of certain Swiss, the morality of Venetian women, and the onerous character of papal government were frequently reiterated. The hasty and partial character of many such accounts was evident to readers and writers at home, leading to an extensive critical and parodic literature that undermined supposedly authoritative claims and sometimes suggested that the whole venture was gratuitous.

It has frequently been presumed that promiscuity and good living were the most prominent elements of the Grand Tour experiences of men; and transgression and licence were indeed preoccupations of travellers themselves. It is, however, easy to neglect the political and aesthetic reflection prompted by travel. Experience of other forms of government generated observations ranging from self-congratulatory or ironic reflections upon English liberty to more sharply divided views after the *French Revolution. Many were prompted not just to compare, but also to inquire, albeit often cursorily, into whether climate, mode of life, or government was responsible for the happiness of people in one place and their despondency or poverty elsewhere.

The succession of contrasting scenes thus afforded matter for an intra-European 'anthropological' reflection that enabled Britons to deepen a sense of their own distinctiveness.   NT

GRANT, Robert Edmond (1793–1874), anatomy teacher and advocate of medical reform. The seventh son of Alexander Grant of Edinburgh, Writer to the Signet, Grant attended the Edinburgh High School before studying *medicine [18] at the University of Edinburgh. After taking his MD in 1814, he studied in Paris and other leading continental medical institutions, before returning to practise in Edinburgh in the early 1820s. By then he had become deeply interested in the comparative anatomy of invertebrates. Largely on the strength of pioneering research on sponges, he was appointed professor of zoology and comparative anatomy at the new University of London in 1827, a post he held until his death in 1874.

Grant was a fervent admirer of contemporary French *evolutionary theories, and became a prominent figure in medical reform circles during the 1830s. 'Dry and formal in manner', Grant was nonetheless an open and passionate critic of the Colleges of Physicians and Surgeons. He joined with Thomas *Wakley in condemning the corporations' exclusive right to license medical practitioners, representing their rejection of French developments in biological thought as symptomatic of their intellectual mediocrity. Conservatives responded by accusing Grant of being a pander to godless French materialism. He was elected to the Royal Society in 1836, but published little new scientific work in the four-and-a-half decades he lectured at University College. He died in poverty, a marginal figure in British science.

Grant decried Britain's failure to capitalize on its colonial supremacy through state sponsorship of comparative anatomy. However, many of the small number of students he attracted each year came to practise medicine in the colonial sphere, and few failed to send him rare natural history specimens. Though his evolutionary views found little favour in British scientific circles, the museum he eventually bequeathed to University College figured prominently in later Darwinian evolutionary theorizing.   PT

GRENVILLE, William Wyndham, Baron Grenville (1759–1834), statesman. William Wyndham Grenville was the youngest son of George, Prime Minister in 1763–5, at the beginning of the troubles with America. Like his cousin William *Pitt, young Grenville supported Lord *Shelburne's government in 1782–3. His eldest brother George, Lord Temple and later Marquis of Buckingham, served as George III's intermediary in the House of Lords and thus helped to secure the defeat and dismissal in 1783 of the Fox–North Coalition which had supplanted Shelburne's ministry the previous year. The brothers then went on to support their cousin on his appointment as Prime Minister. W. W. Grenville became Pitt's invaluable lieutenant, and in 1790 he went to the House of Lords as leader. From 1791 to 1801, when he resigned with Pitt after the King's refusal to countenance *Catholic emancipation, Grenville was also Foreign Secretary. A strong advocate of the *war [2] with France, Grenville broke with Pitt over the latter's failure to press hard against the weak ministry of Henry Addington (1757–1844) which followed.

Grenville, his brother Lord Buckingham, and their party, the 'Grenvillites', subsequently joined with the Foxite *Whigs, ostensibly over their joint criticism of the war, though the basis of the Whig objection was that there was a war at all. They also mutually agreed on a strong advocacy of Catholic emancipation. Despite Pitt's return to office in 1804, Grenville remained loyal to his Foxite friends; and he joined them in the *Ministry of All the Talents in 1806, resigning with them in 1807, when the King refused to consent even to a mild extension of religious liberty to Catholics and Dissenters. Relations in opposition with the former Foxites, now led by Lord Grey (1764–1845), were strained, over the continuing wars, and over *parliamentary reform, which the Grenvillites opposed. Grenville's support of the *Liverpool Cabinet's repressive policies after 1816 brought the relationship to an effective end, though there was never a definitive breach and a number of the younger Grenvillites maintained their Whig connection. In 1821 Grenville acquiesced in the rest of his party, under his nephew Richard (1776–1839), allying themselves with Liverpool's government. Grenville himself largely retired from politics, though he was always prepared to promote the cause of Catholic emancipation. RWD

GRIFFIN, Gerald (1803–40), Irish novelist and dramatist. As a contributor to the Irish regional and historical *novel [31] who provided an unparalleled fictional depiction of peasant mores and alienation, he is still widely underestimated.

Born and educated in County Limerick to Catholic middle-class parents, Griffin knew no Irish but was fascinated with the impact of social and linguistic change on the peasantry. After struggling between 1823 and 1827, with the assistance of the expatriate Irish playwright John Banim (1798–1842), to launch a writing career in London, he returned to Ireland to produce his grittily realistic *Tales of the Munster Festivals* (1827). Two years later he published his most successful novel, *The Collegians* (1829), an ardently Romantic but darkly violent tale set against the *sublime mountain scenery of Kerry and Wicklow, and based on a notorious contemporary murder trial. This was followed in 1832 by his most significant and undervalued work, *The Invasion*, a historical novel set in the pre-colonial Gaelic period and as rich in antiquarian detail as anything written by Walter *Scott [see *Irish cultural revival]. A play, *Gissipus*, was not produced in his own lifetime but gained a respectful reception at Drury Lane in 1842. In 1838 Griffin suddenly abandoned the writing life to join a Christian Brothers monastery in Cork, where he remained until his death in June 1840. IMcC

GRIMALDI, Joseph (1778–1837), actor and dancer, the outstanding clown of the British *theatre [24], whose acrobatic skills and comic inventiveness sustained the *pantomime as a popular and financially lucrative dramatic form. Son of the Italian-born Giuseppe Grimaldi (d. 1788), he came from a long line of dancer-performers; his mother, Rebecca Brooker (d. 1819), was also a dancer, who had performed since childhood at Drury Lane. Trained by his eccentric and sometimes cruel father and supervised by his mother, Grimaldi began his stage career while still a toddler, probably in 1781. By the early 1800s his innovations in the role of pantomime clown, involving more elaborate costuming and makeup and technically sophisticated comic spectacle, made his acting the centrepiece of the pantomime entertainments at the patent theatres and Sadler's Wells. Grimaldi's appeal crossed class barriers and cultural hierarchies, combining the anarchic folk traditions of the carnivalesque with a distinctively contemporary and urban sensibility. In their references to new exhibitions, shops, street characters, and innovations such as gaslight, his performances formed an index to a changing metropolis. He burlesqued the excesses of *Regency fashion including the *dandyism of the military élite, but the highly physical and often violent nature of his acting, like the worlds of *Rowlandson and *Egan, was itself very much of the era he anatomized. His *Memoirs* (1838) were edited by 'Boz' (Charles *Dickens) and illustrated by George *Cruikshank. GR

GROSE, Francis (?1731–91), antiquarian, lexicographer, and artist. Grose was born to Ann Bennett and Francis Grose, a well-established Swiss jeweller. He studied art rather than proceed to university, later exhibiting his drawings of antiquarian subjects at the *Royal Academy, and went on to serve for many years in the militia. Grose became a Fellow of the Society of Antiquaries in 1757 [see *antiquarianism, 35]. His interests in the military resulted in *Military Antiquities* (1786–8), *Treatise on Ancient Armour* (1786–9), and the earlier, humorous *Advice to the Officers of the British Army* (1782). Simultaneously, he worked on *A Classical Dictionary of the Vulgar Tongue* (1785; reissued in 1811 as *Lexicon Balatronicum*, edited by Pierce *Egan), and *A Provincial Glossary* (1787). His major work was the six volumes of *Antiquities of England and Wales* (1773–87). While on a walking tour in 1789, collecting materials for his *Antiquities of Scotland* (1789–91), he met Robert *Burns, who was impressed, as were many others, by his witty and warm personality as well as his physical bulk. Burns sent him 'Tam O'Shanter' for inclusion in the volume of Scottish antiquities and wrote verses to commemorate his new friend. *Antiquities of Ireland* (1791–5) remained unfinished at Grose's death, but appeared posthumously through his friend Edward Ledwich's (1738–1823) editorship. The miscellaneous essays collected together in *The Grumbler* (1791) were also published after his death and later supplemented with anecdotes, biographical sketches, and epigrams in *The Olio* (1792).

Grose routinely accepted that provincial and underworld speech deserved record rather than reform. His interest in contemporary *popular culture [23] even extended to publishing a collection of newspaper advertisements, *A Guide to Health, Beauty, Riches, and Honour* (1785). Like other antiquarians, he depended on bibliographic research, but was exemplary as an early collector in the field, whether the barracks, university colleges, or the countryside inn.   GAB

Grub Street, a street in London's Cripplegate Ward associated since the seventeenth century with London's community of hack writers and the popular and gutter press [see *prose, 30]. During the eighteenth century the proliferation of Grub Street publications made it the target of the *satirical writings of Pope and Swift. In *The Dunciad* (1729, 1742) Pope attacked the Grub Street 'Dunces', men such as John Dunton and Edmund Curll, and their overtly commercial appropriation of literature, as the signs of an impending cultural collapse. Although the street itself, as Johnson's *Dictionary* suggests, was actually 'much inhabited by writers of small histories, dictionaries, and temporary poems', the resonance of the term 'Grub Street' has become more figurative than literal, connoting popular and commercial writing in general. With reference to the late eighteenth and early nineteenth centuries, the term is associated less with the actual street than with mercenary writing of the sort excoriated in *Byron's *English Bards and Scottish Reviewers* (1809) and the popular and radical presses, as well as with bawdy or *pornographic literature. During the 1820s, established radicals such as William *Benbow, George Cannon (1789–1854), and William Dugdale (c.1815–68) published obscene literature, blurring the distinction between the culture of political radicalism and the broader 'mass' culture of the reading public. Radicalism and Grub Street shared a spirit of resistance to authority, and the convergence of libertarianism and libertinism in which the Grub Street radicals of the 1820s participated forged a link between political theory and popular practice.   LT

H

HAMILTON, Elizabeth (1758–1816), novelist, poet, *philanthropist, and writer on *education [17] and morals. Her experiments across a range of mixed fictional genres mark a sophisticated contribution to counter-revolutionary debate and to the burgeoning post-revolutionary forms of historical fiction and the regional *novel [31].

Born in Belfast and raised in Scotland, Hamilton settled in London in 1788 with her brother, Charles Hamilton, the *orientalist and colonial reformer in India. Her first novel, *Letters of a Hindoo Rajah* (1796), commemorates her recently dead brother and offers a sustained *Enlightenment [32] critique of the British *empire [5]. Using the orientalist convention of the mediating perspective of a foreign visitor to England, the *Letters* satirize English Jacobinism, reflecting contemporary debate on *Paine's *Age of Reason* (1794–5) and *Burke's *Letter to a Noble Lord* (1796). This counter-revolutionary *satire is developed in *Memoirs of Modern Philosophers* (1800), a parodic *roman à clef* about the *Godwin circle.

The quasi-historical *Memoirs of the Life of Agrippina, the Wife of Germanicus* (1804) involves a Christian reading of the fall of Rome that allegorizes 1790s French revolutionary history and the British decline from the virtuous *constitutionalism of the *Glorious Revolution. With *The Cottagers of Glenburnie* (1808), widely praised for its convincing fictional handling of Scots dialect, Hamilton is credited with initiating the Scottish regional novel. In this capacity she is often compared with Maria *Edgeworth, who praised her work highly, and with whom she corresponded.   CT

HAMILTON, Lady Emma (1765–1815), celebrated beauty, hostess, performer, and artist's model, who exploited her physical attractiveness, personal vitality, and skill as a performer to achieve fame, initially as Emma Hart and later as Emma Hamilton.

Born Amy Lyon, the daughter of a Cheshire blacksmith, she began her career in London as a domestic servant at the age of 14 and later moved in the less respectable fringes of the theatrical and art worlds [see *theatre, 24]. As Emma Hart she was mistress of Charles Greville for four years, and she is also alleged to have worked for the flamboyant showman and *quack James Graham (1745–94). In 1786 Greville ended the relationship by conveying her to his uncle Sir William *Hamilton, then plenipotentiary at the court of Naples. Emma, who later married Hamilton in 1791, became hostess and an attraction for visitors, including Goethe, in the performance of her 'attitudes'—dramatic poses in which she realized mythological, historical, and literary figures. Before leaving London she was already the favourite model of George *Romney and while in Italy was painted by a number of artists including Gavin Hamilton

(1723–98), Elisabeth Vigée-Lebrun (1755–1842), and Angelica *Kauffman. James *Gillray's representation of Emma as the disfigured bust of Laïs (a Greek courtesan), the object of Hamilton's icy scrutiny in his *A Cognocenti*, captures some of the complications of her role and reception in Britain. She was undoubtedly objectified as one of Hamilton's beautiful possessions who, in her attitudes and self-transformation, embodied an idea of the feminine as multiple role-playing. However, she was also able to exploit her talent for mimicry and her culture's theatrical construction of gender for her own advantage.

By 1801, the date of Gillray's caricature, Emma Hamilton was also notorious for her liaison with Admiral *Nelson, whom she met in Naples in 1793. He escorted her and Sir William with the Neapolitan royal family to Palermo in 1798 and his excesses in putting down the Neapolitan revolutionaries were blamed on her influence. The Hamilton–Nelson *ménage à trois* became a European-wide scandal, but its various constructions as heroic affair or sordid liaison have only served to enhance, rather than diminish, the aura of Nelson. Hamilton died in 1803 and after Nelson's death at the Battle of Trafalgar Emma Hamilton struggled to survive; she was arrested for debt in 1813 and died in penury in Calais two years later.   GR

HAMILTON, Sir William (1730–1803), MP, diplomat, antiquarian, collector, and patron of the arts;

influenced the development of the neoclassical movement in Britain. A disciple of Johann Joachim Winckelmann (1717–68), he was among the first to collect and appreciate the antiquities of Greece and Rome. His remarkable collection, which included Greek vases, terracottas, ancient glass, coins, and bronzes, was sold in 1772 to the *British Museum and laid the foundation for the Museum's present department of Greek and Roman antiquities.

Hamilton was British ambassador to the court of Naples from 1764 to 1800, a position which allowed him to pursue his artistic and antiquarian interests as well as developing his research into vulcanology. He was a patron of Pierre François Hugues D'Hancarville (1719–1805), whose theories about the origins of religion influenced Hamilton's letter on the remains of priapic cults in Italy published by Richard Payne *Knight in 1786. The association of these kinds of researches with immorality, reflected in James *Gillray's caricature of Hamilton, *A Cognocenti* (1801), was confirmed for many observers by the open affair carried on between his wife, Emma *Hamilton, and Admiral *Nelson.   JM

HANDEL, George Frideric (1685–1759), naturalized British composer of German birth. He was generally regarded throughout the period as England's greatest composer, and his **music [26]** was extensively performed both in London and the provinces.

75

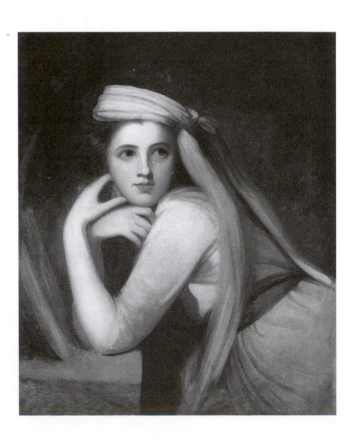

74. George Romney, *Emma Hamilton*, oil on canvas, 1785. The famed beauty before the commencement of her notorious relationship with Lord Nelson.

A COGNOCENTI contemplating ỹ Beauties of ỹ Antique.

75. James Gillray's 1801 caricature of William Hamilton scrutinizing the ruined bust of his wife Emma, represented here as a Greek courtesan.

After an early career in Halle, Hamburg, and in Italy, Handel arrived in England in late 1710. Italian opera, a recently introduced and fashionable novelty in London, was initially his main area of activity, and he had an immediate success with *Rinaldo* (February 1711). As its popularity waned during the 1730s, he increasingly turned his attention to the *oratorio, the distinctively English form of which was his creation, with such works as *Esther* (1718, rev. 1732), *Athalia* (1733), *Saul* (1739), and *Israel in Egypt* (1739). After the failure of *Deidamia* (1741) he abandoned opera composition entirely, and his remaining large-scale compositions are all oratorios, including *Messiah* (Dublin 1742, London 1743), *Samson* (1743), *Belshazzar* (1745), *Solomon* (1749), and *Jephtha* (1752). In addition to opera and oratorio, he wrote large quantities of instrumental and keyboard music and a number of important works for official occasions.

Handel quickly established links with the English court. In 1713 he wrote the *Ode for the Birthday of Queen Anne*, and settings of the Te Deum and Jubilate to celebrate the Peace of Utrecht. For these he was awarded an annual pension of £200, later doubled by George I. Mastery of the grand ceremonial style displayed his awareness of English seventeenth-century traditions and in particular of the music of Henry Purcell (1659–95), making him the natural choice to compose the four anthems for the coronation of George II in 1727. Subsequent examples of his official music are 'The Ways of Zion Do Mourn' for the funeral of Queen Caroline in December 1737, the Dettingen Te Deum (1743), and the *Music for the Royal Fireworks* (1749), written to celebrate the Peace of Aix-la-Chapelle. The success and wide exposure of these works at subsequent *concerts helped to consolidate Handel's reputation as an English composer whose music unfailingly caught the mood of the moment, whether of national rejoicing, triumph, or mourning. This patriotic flavour was further enhanced by the subject-matter of many of the oratorios: most obviously in the overtly nationalistic *Judas Maccabaeus* (1747), written to celebrate the defeat of the Jacobites at Culloden, but also to be seen in other oratorios on Old Testament subjects, where an identification of Britain with Israel would readily have been made by contemporary audiences.

In its setting of biblical words and its sacred subject-matter, *Messiah* stands apart from Handel's other oratorios. Largely because of its sacred text, it had been 'but indifferently relish'd' at its first London performances in 1743. However, its widespread popularity can be dated from 1750, when Handel began to give annual performances for the benefit of the Foundling Hospital, his favourite charity. Thereafter, *Messiah* soon came to occupy the uniquely popular position that it retains today, and the work became an invariable component both of the London seasons of oratorio concerts and of provincial *music festivals.

By the time of his death in 1759 Handel was a national institution, acclaimed as the greatest composer of his age, and his music had long achieved classic status [see rise of the *classics]. The operas with which he had first made his reputation had long disappeared, but *Messiah*, the other oratorios, and such favourites as the coronation anthems continued to be performed.

Handel's posthumous popularity was unprecedented in the history of music, where the more usual practice had been to discard 'old' music in favour of newer compositions. In London, the seasons of Lenten oratorio concerts begun by Handel continued, and when the Concert of Ancient Music was founded in 1776 with the express intention of performing only music more than twenty years old, his music formed the backbone of its programmes. In the provinces, and particularly at music festivals, the cult of Handel was equally pronounced.

Veneration for Handel and his music reached its peak with the Commemoration concerts of 1784, organized to mark the twenty-fifth anniversary of his death and what was thought, erroneously, to be the hundredth anniversary of his birth. The Commemoration attracted the whole-hearted support of George III and was conceived on an exceptionally large scale, with numbers of performers unheard of in Handel's own lifetime. The main performances at Westminster Abbey (of *Messiah*, *Israel in Egypt*, and miscellaneous selections of favourite pieces) involved over 500 *singers and instrumentalists, amateur and professional, from London and the provinces. This enterprise was commemorated by Charles *Burney's *An Account of the Musical Performances in the Commemoration of Handel* (1785). Similar festivals, with even larger forces, were held in London in 1785–7 and in 1790–1.

The Commemoration concerts had far-reaching effects. They consolidated Handel's canonical status as national composer, became potent public rituals in reinforcing national identity, and were a powerful stimulus to activity in the provinces. They also inaugurated a tradition of large-scale performance of Handel which continued throughout the nineteenth and well into the twentieth century.

Meanwhile, the public perception of Handel's music had been changing. Partly because of the growing concentration on *Messiah* at the expense of the other oratorios, as well as the practice at provincial festivals of performing oratorio concerts in church, Handel had increasingly come to be regarded as essentially a composer of sacred music. This view became central to nineteenth-century attitudes to Handel and his work.   PO

HARDY, Thomas (1752–1832), shoemaker and radical political organizer. Regarded as an exemplary artisan radical, he was founder and early leader of the London Corresponding Society [see *corresponding societies].

Born in Stirlingshire, Scotland, Hardy was converted to political reform by reading Richard *Price's *Observations on Civil Liberty* (1776) and by hardships incurred while working as a shoemaker in London during the *American Revolution. On 25 January 1792 he and seven friends met at the Bell *tavern on the Strand to found the London

Corresponding Society, with membership open to all willing to pay 1s. entrance fee and 1d. weekly subscription. Dedicated to *parliamentary reform and employing a divisional structure based on Methodist, trades society, and *freemasonic models, the Society proved especially attractive to urban artisans, lesser professionals, and shopkeepers, who met weekly in small tavern groups and elected delegates to a central executive of which Hardy became secretary and treasurer. By 1793 the Society numbered many thousands and was corresponding with the French National Convention, as well as sending delegates to the British Convention in Edinburgh.

A quiet, hard-working organizer who advocated educative LCS activities such as reading, debating, publishing, and dissemination of the Society's periodical, the *Moral and Political Reformer*, Hardy has been seen by labour historians as an exemplar of the moderate, peaceable, *self-improving radical artisanate. Yet he was a friend of the wild prophetic revolutionary Lord George Gordon, and flirted with insurrectionary schemes on several occasions [see *Gordon riots]. He also gained an aura of martyrdom after his imprisonment in the Tower on a treason charge, during which time his pregnant wife was harassed by a *loyalist mob and died soon after in childbirth. He was acquitted on 5 November, a day thereafter commemorated by British radicals. After receiving a pension from well-to-do radical admirers, Hardy largely withdrew from the political limelight, dying in the year of the 1832 *Reform Act which was largely brought about by popular radical and corresponding societies modelled on the LCS.   IMcC

HARRISON, Samuel (1760–1812), English tenor and impresario who specialized in sacred, 'ancient' song even as a boy, whose tenor voice perfect for this repertory; somewhat limited in range, power, and animation, it was pure in tone, taste, and intonation. He sang at the 1784 *Handel Commemoration, as principal tenor at the Ancient *concerts (1785–91), and as principal singer and director of the Covent Garden *oratorios (1789–92). Detecting a swing in public taste away from instrumental music, Harrison established the vocal concerts with Charles Knyvett (1752–1822) in 1792–5, presenting vocal solos, *glees, and catches, with only occasional Italian arias or instrumental pieces. He revived the concert series twice, with different partners (1801–3, 1804–12).   RC

HARRISON, Thomas (1744–1829), Yorkshire-born architect, most notable for his bridges at Lancaster and Chester and public buildings in the north-west of England. Commissions such as the Lyceum (1800–3) at Liverpool and the Exchange (1806–9) and Theatre Royal (1806) at Manchester reflected the wealth and self-confidence of these rapidly expanding urban centres [see *architecture, 28]. A concomitant development was the modernization of penal institutions in an area of Britain prone to civil disturbance [see *prisons]. Harrison was responsible for the redesign of the castles at Lancaster and Chester as formidable administrative

centres, incorporating prison and court facilities as well as armouries. Chester Castle was the first prison in Britain to be modelled on Jeremy *Bentham's panopticon. Harrison was also involved in the design of a number of private dwellings for the upper class throughout Britain. As architect of Lord Elgin's mansion at Broomhall, Scotland (1796–9), Harrison drew his patron's attention to the possibility of obtaining casts of the sculptures at Athens and was thus indirectly involved in the import of the *Elgin Marbles to Britain.   GR

HASTINGS, Warren (1732–1818), Governor-General of Bengal, whose trial and impeachment by the House of Commons was one of the *causes célèbres* of the age, lasting for over seven years (1788–95) and providing a platform for Edmund *Burke to deliver some of his most memorable speeches on the responsibilities owed by conquering powers to subject peoples.

Hastings epitomized the luck, spirit, and ruthlessness on which the British *empire [5] in India was built. Arriving in India in 1750 at the tender age of 17 and managing, unlike so many of his contemporaries, to survive the climate, Hastings rose swiftly through the ranks of the *East India Company. In 1758 he was elevated to a seat on the Bengal council and in 1772, still only 39, he succeeded to the governor-generalship. Despite his relative youth he proved an effective leader, consolidating the Company's possessions in the face of threats from Mysore and the Maratha confederacy and regularizing the chaotic administration of Bengal. Most historians now regard Hastings as a very considerable statesman.

Some contemporaries, though, notably Burke and Philip Francis (1740–1818), who served with Hastings for a time in Bengal until wounded by him in a duel, thought differently, and together they mounted a parliamentary attack on Hasting's methods and morals. Specifically, they charged him with misappropriating moneys and ordering the judicial murder of a native official, Nandakumar. This persuaded the Commons in 1787 to order his impeachment before the House of Lords. However the prosecution failed for lack of hard evidence, the Lords rejecting Burke's argument that the amorality of Hastings's actions was enough to warrant a conviction. Burke had to be content with a propaganda victory, the sweeter in that it left the accused almost penniless, while prompting the Company seriously to rethink its governing philosophy.   IC

HAWKESWORTH, John (1715–73), miscellaneous and travel writer. Born in humble circumstances, he began his career as an attorney's clerk but rose to be a collaborator with Samuel *Johnson and Joseph Warton (1722–1800) on the well-known periodical the *Adventurer* (1752–4). His interests in travel and exotica were evident in the essays he contributed to the paper, as well as in his later literary work: a rewriting of Southern's play *Oroonoko*, based on Aphra Behn's novella (1759), an *oriental tale, *Almoran* *and Hamet* (1761), and a translation of Fénelon's *Télémaque* (1768).

David Garrick (1717–79) recommended him to Lord Sandwich (1718–92) as a person fit to revise and publish the journals of the British expeditions to the South Seas during the 1760s [see *exploration, 37]. In 1773 appeared *An Account of the Voyages and Discoveries in the Southern Hemisphere*, recording the voyages of Wallis, Carteret, Byron, and *Cook, for which Hawkesworth was paid the fabulous sum of £6,000. He adopted from the French compiler Charles de Brosses the technique of delivering the narratives in the first person singular, in order, as he said, to bring 'the Adventurer and the Reader nearer together'. Hawkesworth appears not to have succeeded in this attempt, for his compilation of Cook's first voyage was roundly condemned as lubricious, inaccurate, and blasphemous. He was blamed for representing a scene of public copulation that had been described originally by Cook and Joseph *Banks. Cook said that Hawkesworth had made so free with his journal that the published account bore scant relation to the facts of the voyage, a charge enthusiastically seconded in print by Alexander Dalrymple (1737–1808), who thought the compiler was somehow responsible for Cook's failure to discover the Great Southern Continent. Elizabeth *Carter, James *Boswell, and Hester Chapone (1727–1801) were among the many who thought Hawkesworth's rejection of a particular providence in the account of the *Endeavour's* escape from the coral of the Great Barrier Reef was a godless rehearsal of the doctrines of *Hume and Bolingbroke (1678–1751). A few months after publication Hawkesworth died, quite broken-hearted according to Frances *Burney and Hester Thrale *Piozzi.   JL

HAYDN, Joseph (1732–1809), leading Austrian composer of his generation, whose visits to England in the 1790s represented a climactic point in his own career and in London's early *concert life.

Most of Haydn's life was spent in the service of the Esterházy family near Vienna. His symphonies and string quartets became popular in England in the early 1780s, their novelty and energy displacing the elegant lyricism of J. C. *Bach. Scarcely a concert programme lacked a Haydn symphony, his music apparently better appreciated in England than on the Continent. London audiences relished the unpredictable and bizarre elements: the unexpected silences and modulations, the incongruous juxtapositions of the humorous and the *sublime. Haydn's use of folk idioms was not new, but the symphonic context and the sheer orchestral exuberance were radical.

Not content with the stream of symphonies arriving by post, concert promoters vied to entice Haydn to London. It was only after the death of his patron that Haydn agreed to an offer from the *violinist J. P. Salomon (1745–1815). His years in London (1791–2 and 1794–5) were the most brilliantly successful of his career. Lionized as 'the Shakespeare of music', he made a handsome fortune and wrote some of his most enduring works, the 'London' symphonies and

quartets, an opera on the Orpheus legend, and piano music inspired by the sonorous instruments of Broadwood. The freshness of invention continued undiminished: the dramatic manipulation of engaging melodies, the moments of profound contemplation, the colourful orchestration, and the ever-ingenious solutions to formal problems. Haydn even recalled the contemporary taste for the *Gothic in his chorus *The Storm* (1792). One of the highlights of Haydn's second visit to London was his series of *English Canzonettas*, published in 1794 and 1795. The songs of the first group are settings of poems by Anne Hunter, the widow of the surgeon John *Hunter, while the second group includes a setting of a poem by Shakespeare.

Haydn's departure in 1795 did not end his connection with England. He contributed numerous harmonizations to George *Thomson's folk collections, and the two late *oratorios were inspired by his experience of *Handel's music in London. The libretto of *The Creation* drew directly upon *Milton, while *The Seasons* was adapted from the poetry of James Thomson (1700–48). In 1798 he composed the *Missa in angustiis* (Mass in straitened times, taken to refer to the Napoleonic threat) and known to contemporary audiences as the 'Nelson Mass', after Admiral *Nelson.

Haydn's music presents several paradoxes. Regarded now as the height of classicism, it seemed at the time unconventional and eccentric—Charles *Dibdin referred to his 'effusions of genius turned into frenzy'. It developed norms, while constantly questioning them; it appears witty and refined, yet draws on overtly popular thematic material. Haydn succeeded in appealing both to the connoisseur at the Hanover Square Rooms and to the least educated listener at the London *pleasure gardens. If his London music does not reach the tragic heights of *Mozart, it has a heart-warming appeal as well as extraordinary drama and sublimity. However, these qualities were less appreciated in the early nineteenth century, and only a few of the 'London' symphonies and *The Creation* remained in the repertoire.   SMcV

HAYDON, Benjamin Robert (1786–1846), self-taught artist whose obsession with *history painting was the root of a notoriety more lasting than the works he produced [see *painting, 27]. His involvement with Romantic literary circles, his voluminous and anguished diaries, and his suicide earned him the label 'Romantic genius'.

Like James *Barry, Haydon had aspirations to be a history painter, but his single-mindedness in pursuing this goal was far greater. In 1804 he moved to London from his birthplace, Plymouth, and insinuated himself into the art world through force of will and charisma. A series of disputes with the *Royal Academy over lack of recognition—he was never elected member—led to his eventual ostracism. He exhibited his own paintings, such as the *The Flight into Egypt* (1806), *The Death of Dentatus* (1806–9), and *Christ's Triumphal Entry into Jerusalem* (1815–21) privately, attempting to encourage *patronage for himself and for history painting. More influential were his efforts to support history painting through his public enthusiasm for the *Elgin Marbles, his teaching, and his lobbying for government support of the arts. He was also admired by *Wordsworth and friendly with *Keats.

His zeal did not match his income, and he was imprisoned for debt in 1828. Afterwards, he was forced to earn income by painting genre scenes and *portraits, and he succumbed to despair and suicide in 1846 when a final private exhibition of his historical pictures proved a commercial and artistic failure.

SW

HAYLEY, William (1745–1820), poet and biographer. Often disparaged by critics of the time for sentimentality and affectation, he was nevertheless widely read, and played an important part in the revival of the *epic.

The best-known of Hayley's poems was *The Triumphs of Temper* (1781), which went through twenty-four editions by 1817. His verse *Essay on Epic Poetry* (1782) urged British poets to return to the grandest of poetic forms as part of a revival of national culture. Although he habitually presented himself as a poet of retirement, the 'Hermit' of Felpham, Hayley's model for the true patriot poet, *Milton, was one of engagement with politics rather than withdrawal. His 'Life of Milton' (1794) vigorously defended his hero from the *Tory strictures of Samuel *Johnson. Published with an edition of Milton's poetry, the 'Life' seems to have suffered censorship at the hands of Hayley's nervous publishers, Messrs *Boydell and Nicol. It appeared alone in an expanded edition in 1796, but its politics seem more *Whiggish than the violent *republicanism feared by its original publishers.

Hayley devoted much of his later career to biography, producing lives of his friends the poet *Cowper (1803) and the artist *Romney (1809), but he is now best known as a patron of *Blake, to whom he was probably introduced by *Flaxman. Blake stayed with Hayley in Felpham from 1800 to 1803. *Ballads Founded on Anecdotes of Animals* (1805) seems to have been published for the benefit of Blake, who supplied engravings, but their relationship ended unhappily, with Blake feeling that he was treated as a dependent by his genteel patron.   JM

HAYS, Mary (1760–1843), novelist and critic, whose unique blend of Rational Dissent, *sensibility [11], materialist philosophy, and feminism made a fiery and passionate contribution to intellectual, radical culture of the 1790s.

Raised in a large middle-class Dissenting family in Southwark, London, Hays was brought up a member of a Baptist congregation and later corresponded with leading Dissenters such as William *Frend, Theophilus Lindsey (1723–1808), and George *Dyer. Unusual for a woman, she made her first entrée into the public world of letters through theological debate, a response to Gilbert Wakefield's *Enquiry into Public Worship* (1791) entitled *Cursory Remarks on an Enquiry into Public Worship*, pub-

lished under the pseudonym 'Eusebia'. Criticizing Wakefield for ignoring the influence of the *French Revolution in disseminating the spirit of freedom, *Cursory Remarks* defended public worship against Wakefield's attack, while arguing against established religion. Anna Laetitia *Barbauld, amongst others, had also published responses to Wakefield, but it was Hays who caught the public's attention.

Hays's immersion in a Dissenting tradition hostile to received prejudice laid the ground work for her thinking on *women's [4] rights and *female education. After reading Mary *Wollstonecraft's *Vindication of the Rights of Woman* (1792), Hays and her sister collaborated on *Letters and Essay, Moral, and Miscellaneous* (1793), with the advice of Wollstonecraft, who became a friend. Ranging over a variety of issues such as civil liberty and materialist philosophy, *Letters* carried a more feminist edge, calling for improved female education and elaborating the pathos of the situation by which women were prevented from progressing by a lack of educational opportunities.

In 1796–7 Hays contributed several pieces to the *Monthly Magazine* on Helvetius, the French materialist philosopher who stressed *education [17] and environment as determining factors of individual development. Helvetian materialism had an important influence on Hays's formulation of gender, which saw sexual distinctions not as natural but as socially constructed categories. While William *Godwin encouraged her first novel, *Memoirs of Emma Courtney* (1796), the work implicitly attacked Godwin's own compromised position on female sexuality and exaltation of depersonalized Reason in *Political Justice* (1793). Like Helen Maria *Williams, another radical woman attacked by the arch-anti-Jacobin Richard *Polwhele, Hays's support for the French Revolution was tempered by a belief that Jacobinism failed to incorporate the agenda of female equality. Her second novel, *The Victim of Prejudice* (1799), further pursues this feminist agenda.

Hays's version of sensibility, developed in opposition to Reason, emphasized charity, self-sacrifice, passionate individualism, and a belief in the truth of suffering and its capacity for *self-improvement: all these derived from her Nonconformist background. Her biography of Wollstonecraft was published in 1800 in Richard Phillips's *Annual Necrology, for 1797–8*. This formed part of Hays's larger feminist biographical history of women, *Female Biography* (1803). The later work, characterized by a less tolerant attitude to political agitation and religious freedom, comprises improving juvenile moral tales and religious tracts.   CT

HAZLITT, William (1778–1830), literary and political *essayist, critic of *painting [27] and *theatre [24], *lecturer, metaphysician, controversialist, and Romantic theorist of the *imagination; both a trenchant critic and sensitive interpreter of his age.

Early experiences and disappointments had a profound impact on his later work. The son of a *Unitarian minister, he was educated for the ministry at the *Dissenting academy at Hackney, but left school and his intended career in 1795. While never pious, he remained fiercely loyal to the Dissenting tradition. He subsequently pursued a career in painting, and his inability to distinguish himself by industry alone no doubt contributed to the privilege he later accorded *genius. His training as an artist left traces in his vivid prose style, and his essays on painting.

Hazlitt's first book, *An Essay on the Principles of Human Action* (1805), elaborated what he claimed to be an important 'metaphysical discovery'. Neglected in his lifetime, it has figured prominently in recent accounts of his work. Against the mechanical doctrine of innate selfishness, Hazlitt argued that our interest in our own future involves an act of imagination, a going outside of self, no different in kind from sympathy with others. The mind was therefore naturally disinterested and sympathetic. Yet Hazlitt recognized that any implied capacity for benevolence was easily frustrated, as self-interest hardened into habit. This anxiety lay at the heart of his lifelong hesitation between reformist optimism and bitter political despair.

The *Essay*'s challenge to personal identity ('I am not the same thing, but many different things') informed the content and style of Hazlitt's later writing. His restless intelligence expressed itself in a loosely structured, paradoxical, and densely allusive prose; bold epigrams and dramatic reversals punctuate long sentences and paragraphs. Though fond of dialectical thinking, Hazlitt disliked Samuel *Johnson's antithetical style, and was more willing to test extremes and play out contradictions. His flexible intellect became a professional asset. He often recycled elements of his own *prose [30], and published in an impressive range of periodicals, including the *Political Register*, *The Times*, the *Edinburgh Review*, and the *London Magazine*.

Despite his commitment to mental sympathy and diversity, Hazlitt often expressed himself in a more personal and idiosyncratic manner. Politically, he was proud of his consistent radicalism. Montaigne was a literary hero, and Hazlitt contributed to the English development of the familiar essay, especially in *Table Talk* (1821–2) and *The Plain Speaker* (1826). While *Liber Amoris* (1823), the scandalous memoir of his obsession with his landlady's daughter, Sarah Walker, was an extreme experiment in *Rousseau's confessional mode, emotion and passion were consistent co-ordinates of Hazlitt's writing. A commitment to controversy and to personal enmities made him a distinctive literary voice, and reinforced his reputation for misanthropy.

Politics was a leading passion. In an era of reaction, Hazlitt did not conceal his 'jacobin' enthusiasm for the *French Revolution. His *Political Essays* (1819) record his outrage at the revival of divine right monarchy after 1815 under the cloak of 'Legitimacy'. He treated *Napoleon as the heroic enemy of inherited privilege, an attitude that culminated in his four-volume *Life of Napoleon Buonaparte* (1828, 1830). Yet even politics could not escape Hazlitt's mental flexibility. He was fascinated with power, especially in the arts, and a meritocratic faith in the standards of genius complicated his democratic commitments. His progressivism was often undermined by a tragic sense of the ease with which public opinion and the press were corrupted. As incisive a critic of reform as of reaction, Hazlitt complained that radical theorists like *Godwin disseminated airy abstractions without regard for human passion or experience.

Hazlitt's mixed political impulses converged on the figure of Edmund *Burke, whom he praised for a powerful prose and sure grasp of habit and natural affection but held responsible for reaction at home and abroad. This troubled radical allies, but did little to appease political enemies. The *Tory assault on Hazlitt culminated in 1817 and 1818 with hostile reviews in the *Quarterly*, and a share in the *Blackwood's* assault on 'Cockney' vulgarity and licentiousness. Hazlitt's responses in 'A Reply to "Z" ' (1818, pub. 1923) and *A Letter to William Gifford* (1819) demonstrated his strength as a polemicist, and his sensitivity to personal criticism.

Politics informed Hazlitt's aesthetic judgements, and he may be best remembered as a critic for his attacks on the 'political apostasy' of the Lake School. Yet he could be a generous adversary. 'My First Acquaintance with the Poets' (1823) is for the most part a warm tribute to *Coleridge's genius, viewed through the charitable filter of youthful hope and memory. His 1814 review of the *Excursion* praised Wordsworth's strength and simplicity, while disparaging his egotism and idealization of rural life. Although Hazlitt resisted theoretical systems, his criticism combined an expressive interest in imaginative genius with more traditional ideas of art as an imitation of nature (though never abstract, general nature). The essay 'On Gusto' (1816) insisted that this 'power or passion defining any object' was to be found not only in 'expression' but also 'in what relates to things without expression, to the natural appearances of objects'.

In *Shakespeare Hazlitt found rich evidence of an active and disinterested imagination, and a welcome refuge from the self-absorption of Wordsworth and *Byron. His *Characters of Shakespeare's Plays* (1817) and *Lectures on the English Poets* (1818) had a profound influence on *Keats, and on the subsequent course of Shakespeare criticism. Hazlitt also produced important accounts of the contemporary theatre, gathered in *A View of the English Stage* (1818) and his enthusiastic reviews helped establish the reputation of Edmund *Kean.

The Spirit of the Age (1825) was Hazlitt's crowning achievement. Though sometimes taken to ratify the straightforward idea of a 'Romantic period', this series of essays offers a remarkably broad account of a complex and internally divided era. Alongside Coleridge, Byron, Wordsworth, and friends like Leigh Hunt and Charles Lamb, Hazlitt places Thomas *Malthus and Jeremy *Bentham, the preacher Edward Irving (1792–1834), and such politicians as Sir Francis *Burdett, Henry *Brougham, and Lord *Eldon. Reactionary and progressive impulses collide throughout the book, and disappointment and unfulfilled promise become ironic keynotes.   KG

Hellenism. After 1750 there was a revival of interest in Grecian culture (in architectural contexts more commonly referred to as *neoclassicism) that paralleled the developing taste for the *Gothic. Although they would seem to represent very different aesthetic principles, the Grecian and Gothic movements shared a nostalgia for an ideal of simplicity and liberty. The significance of this ideal was to be contested across a wide range of cultural endeavour including imaginative literature, *antiquarianism [35], the visual and plastic arts, *architecture [28], *design [25], and *fashion. Hellenism also had its political dimension—the issue of the fate of contemporary Greece as a vassal of the Ottoman empire. Supporters of Greek independence, which included *Byron, were known as 'philhellenes'.

The leading figure in the Hellenic revival of the mid-eighteenth century was the German art historian Johann Joachim Winckelmann (1717–78) whose work was translated into English by Henry *Fuseli. Winckelmann inspired a new understanding of the principles of Greek art and, especially, *sculpture, which presented ancient Greece as a society of 'noble simplicity and sedate grandeur'. This grandeur was illustrated in impressive detail in studies such as James Stuart and Nicholas Revett's *Antiquities of Athens* (5 vols., 1762–1830). Interest in antiquities was supplemented by accounts in *travel literature, which reflected the increased popularity of Greece when the Napoleonic *wars [2] barred travellers on the *Grand Tour from other parts of Europe. Writing in 1814, Byron's friend J. C. *Hobhouse commented; 'Attica . . . swarms with travellers.' This phenomenon received its most public literary statement in Byron's *Childe Harold's Pilgrimage* (1812), which makes great play of combining a sense of Greek history with an acute local knowledge of contemporary realities.

Although Winckelmann promoted an image of Greece as a culture of serenity, later commentators were inclined to emphasize the *sublimity and power of the Grecian relationship with nature; thus the change in taste which saw George Chapman's rugged seventeenth-century translations of Homer preferred to the mannered, polite style of Pope's versions. The primitive vitality of Greek culture was sometimes represented as incapable of imitation by the late-eighteenth-century artist. Fuseli's *The Artist in Despair over the Magnitude of Antique Fragments* (*c*.1778–80) suggests the overwhelming and disabling sublimity of Greek monumental art, while Thomas Love *Peacock's 'The Four Ages of Poetry' (1820) placed the *epic achievement of Homer beyond the grasp of modern society. William *Cowper could criticize the 'Christian meekness' of Pope's translation of Homer, but his own attempt of 1791 was scarcely more successful in capturing the heroic genius of an earlier age which was in any case felt to be too savage and too martially oriented for a modern commercial culture to emulate uncritically.

In 1816 the acquisition of the *Elgin Marbles by parliament for £35,000 spectacularly reinforced the identification of Greek art with natural strength and vigour. Previous models of Hellenistic culture, such as the Apollo Belvedere, were judged inadequate in comparison by commentators such as John *Flaxman, Benjamin *Haydon, and William *Hazlitt. Seeing the Marbles in 1817 probably influenced *Keats's shift towards 'a more naked and grecian manner' in *Hyperion* (1820). The rediscovery of Greek mythology in the work of Keats and *Shelley, along with

76. *The Sibyl's Temple at Tivoli*, pencil drawing, 1819, by Maria Graham, whose extensive travel writings, children's books, and art works did much to popularize the connoisseur's cult of Hellenism.

Leigh *Hunt, Barry *Cornwall, and Peacock, represented a celebration of the naturalness of southern, Mediterranean culture against the grim monotheism of northern Europe. In part this classical literary revival was building on inquiries into the origins of mythology undertaken by writers such as Erasmus *Darwin and Richard Payne *Knight at the end of the eighteenth century.

Among the previous generation of poets, *Wordsworth and *Coleridge were resistant to this aspect of Romantic Hellenism. Coleridge perceived in the Greek imagination a shallow anthropomorphism which fell short of the Judaeo-Christian desire for the infinite. When Wordsworth famously dismissed Keats's *Endymion* (1818) as 'a Very pretty piece of paganism', he voiced his disapproval of a Hellenism that seemed subversive of Christian values. Underlying such criticism was an implication that the Greek tradition had fallen into unsuitable hands. Although much-expanded and reissued books such as John Lemprière's *Bibliotheca Classica* (1788) and John Bell's *New Pantheon* (1790) made a knowledge of Greek mythology available to general readers without a classical education, the classics remained the preserve of a male élite. The deficiencies in Keats's second-hand knowledge were not easily overlooked by even liberal-minded reviewers of his poetry. Elizabeth *Carter was one of very few women with a command of Greek.

A parallel, though very differently derived, suspicion of 'Greek or Roman models' was voiced by William *Blake, for whom the *Bible remained the 'the Great Code of Art', in part because it was the tradition most closely intertwined with the vernacular. Blake's attitude to Hellenism was not without ambivalences, however, since he also responded positively to the idea of a culture of natural simplicity and liberty of manners which had a sacred place for the naked human body. The Hellenism of Shelley was based similarly on an ideal of 'republican Art' which Blake had located in the Bible. Like Byron, Shelley's Hellenism also had its political dimension in a strong commitment to the cause of Greek independence, most explicitly stated in the preface to *Hellas* (1822).

However, the enthusiasm for things Greek in the early nineteenth century did not always denote a *republican or radical politics. Nor was it confined to literature and the visual arts. Greek influence was to be seen in the architecture of *Smirke, *Wilkins, and *Gandy, among others, as well as the interior decoration of Thomas *Hope, the ceramics of *Wedgwood, and the high-waisted, clinging dresses of the *Regency lady that imitated classical statuary. Faced with the threat of French *invasion, the English were apt to see themselves as the defenders of civilized values in the face of continental imperialism. Their enthusiasm for Greece was one manifestation of this role as guardian of the core values of European life. The commercial success of Byron's *Childe Harold's Pilgrimage* and the 'Turkish Tales' (1813–14), whatever the political identification of their author, had a great deal to do with the fact that these texts were open to different kinds of appropriation by the English reader and not necessarily subversive ones.　　JM

HEMANS, Felicia Dorothea Browne (1793–1835), poet and dramatist, the most popular poet in England between 1820 and 1835, second only—if that—to *Byron. Born on 25 September 1793 in Liverpool, she spent a happy childhood in north Wales, where she learnt Latin and modern languages at home from a tutor, and was known as a child prodigy for her phenomenal memory. After her father emigrated to Quebec, effectively abandoning his wife and six children, she began writing *poetry [29] to help defray household expenses. Her first volume of poetry was published when she was 14, initiating a deep-rooted psychological connection for Hemans between male desertion and female literary creativity.

Rejecting Percy *Shelley's requests for a correspondence, she published her second volume of poetry, *The Domestic Affections and Other Poems* in 1812. That same year she married Captain Alfred Hemans of the Fourth or King's Own Regiment, a survivor of the *Peninsular Campaign who was, according to her sister, 'by no means destitute of advantages, either of person or education'. Within the next six years she produced five sons and four more volumes of poetry, including her celebrations of heroic military valor, *Tales and Historic Scenes* (1819) and 'Songs of the Cid' (1822). Shortly before the birth of his last son in 1819, Captain Hemans set sail for Italy, either for reasons of health (the public explanation) or because of a profound domestic 'incompatibility' (as friends and later biographers surmised). Felicia Hemans never saw her husband again, and while she never complained of him, resolutely upholding the decorum of the proper lady and devoted wife, she referred to their separation as 'un grand chagrin'.

Thereafter, her mother raised Hemans's five sons while she wrote to earn the family income, publishing a volume a year, including plays, poems, essays, and literary criticism. Her nineteen volumes of poetry and two dramas sold thousands of copies. Her tragedy, *The Vespers of Palermo*, was produced at Covent Garden in 1823, and in Edinburgh the following year. Hemans regularly contributed to the periodicals, annual gift-books, and keepsakes of her day. Her poetry was especially well received in America, where she was offered an annual salary of $1,500 to accept the sinecure of a nominal editorship of a literary magazine.

Her most successful volumes were *The Siege of Valencia* (1823); *The Forest Sanctuary* (1826), which included her own favorite poem, *Lays of Many Lands*; *Songs of the Affections* (1830); and above all, *Records of Woman* (1828). She won numerous prizes and was widely celebrated, praised by *Wordsworth and befriended by several other successful female writers, most notably Maria Jane Jewsbury (1800–33) and Joanna *Baillie. However, Felicia Hemans was devastated by her mother's death in 1827, going into a physical decline which brought on her early death at the age of 41.

Throughout her writing, Hemans reveals the tensions between her society's definition of the proper lady as the devoted daughter, wife, and mother and her own experience of domestic disintegration. While overtly celebrating the primacy of the home and the domestic affections as the source of enduring human fulfilment, her poetry nonetheless records all the ways in which the values of hearth and home are betrayed: by men who prefer fame and fortune to love, reject their female lovers for another, or follow a chivalric code of honour that willingly sacrifices the good of the family to the needs of the state. By inhabiting the private sphere or advocating the ideology of *domesticity [13] conventionally assigned to the feminine gender, Hemans shows all the ways in which that sphere fails to support the women and children it supposedly protects. The recurrent figure of her poetry—the filled circle of the happy family— is repeatedly emptied out, reduced to nought, while patterns of exile, displacement, and the estranged heart come to predominate.

Her finest work, *The Siege of Valencia*, a play that was never performed, stages the conflict between the values of the private feminine realm of maternal love and the public masculine realm of chivalric honour and heroism, only to reveal their mutual destruction. At stake in this play is the control both of language and of nature. Gonzalez, embracing a Judaeo-Christian code of duty, writes the sacrifice of his sons as Abraham's willingness to sacrifice Isaac, as heroic 'steadfastness'. His devotion to his city is endorsed by his 'heroic child', Ximena, who re-enacts the script for the female warrior of the medieval epic *romance *El Cid*. The Catholic church, represented here by Father Hernandez, further insists upon the sacred necessity for the deaths of Alphonse and Carlos to preserve a Christian city from heathen Muslims. But Elmina rewrites the story of Abraham and Isaac as cruelty, child abuse, and infanticide, redefining the word 'Father' to mean 'steadfast'. Elmina's narrative of a universal and natural maternal devotion which would save her sons' lives at no matter what social cost is subtly endorsed by Hemans's undermining of her opponents: Ximena dies of a heart broken for domestic love; Hernandez has murdered his own son in battle; the city of Valencia will fall in three days anyway; and Gonzalez receives his death-wound in a futile effort to save his sons. Despite the *deus ex machina*, the arrival of the troops of the King of Castile, that ends the play, the final stage image is one of 'desolation'. When the state sacrifices its own children, all civilized values collapse and only Elmina is left to say the last word, a word that memorializes a 'love' forever lost.

Although Hemans died in 1835, her popularity continued unabated through the nineteenth century, when she outdid all other poets in appearances in American and British anthologies of poetry, even Tennyson. In the twentieth century, during the Second World War, her poems—particularly 'Casabianca', 'The Homes of England', and 'The Graves of a Household'—were memorized by many British and American schoolchildren and were regularly recited in elocution competitions.   AM

HERSCHEL, Caroline Lucretia (1750–1848), astronomer, who worked as an apprentice to her famous brother, William *Herschel, for many years before receiving recognition as a scientist and scholar in her own right. By the end of her life Caroline had discovered eight comets, completed a catalogue of over 2,000 nebulae found by William and herself, and accepted royal honours both in Britain and in her homeland of Germany.

Born in Hanover, Caroline contracted typhus at an early age, which stunted her physical growth and development. Considered malformed and unmarriageable by her own family, Caroline seemed destined to live with her parents as a domestic servant. In 1772, however, William invited her to join him in Bath, where he was working as an organist and conductor. Although she acted as his full-time housekeeper, Caroline shared William's passion for *music [26] and became a prominent *singer in the fashionable *spa town.

William later turned to astronomy after receiving a pension from George III for his work in building telescopes. At first, Caroline helped only with the maintenance of William's instruments and business, but she soon became knowledgeable in the science: detecting nebulae herself, calculating their positions, and amassing joint discoveries into a publication. She, too, gained royal attention and became the first woman in Britain to receive a pension for scientific achievement. After William married and moved away, Caroline continued to work as a prominent astronomer, earning an honorary membership to the Royal Astronomical Society and fostering the endeavours of her nephew, John *Herschel. She returned to Hanover in 1822 and died at the age of 98.

KF

HERSCHEL, Sir John Frederick William (1792–1871), astronomer, mathematician, and poet; considered England's leading man of science for much of the nineteenth century.

He inherited a considerable intellectual fortune in the shape of his father's work. William *Herschel was a household name through his astronomical exploits, which included the 'discovery' of the planet Uranus and his novel cosmology. John's qualifications were boosted by becoming Senior Wrangler and first Smith's Prizeman at Cambridge University in 1813. During this period he teamed up with his intellectual partner, Charles *Babbage, in an attempt to propagate a continental form of mathematics in opposition to the entrenched British geometry.

Although he published several articles on mathematics and *chemistry, he was ultimately committed to the business of astronomy. In 1820 he helped form the Astronomical Society with Babbage, the stockbroker Francis Baily, and a number of other commercially orientated men. Throughout the 1820s Herschel sought intellectual and institutional reform, culminating in his reluctant stand for presidency of the Royal Society in 1830. In public his apparent political moderation enabled him to tread a middle path in which he was canvassed by both conservative and radical figures. His actual views seem to have ranged from a private radicalism during the 1810s and 1820s to one of Burkean conservatism from the early 1830s.

In October 1833 he embarked on a journey to the Cape in South Africa, and there spent four years plotting the heavens in the southern hemisphere, reforming colonial education, and instigating meterological surveys. During the 1840s he was active in attempting to reform the classification of the stellar constellations, and also helped mobilize a state sponsored survey of terrestrial magnetism. Between 1838 and 1843 he sat on a Royal Commission to examine the possibility of introducing a metric system of weights and measures. During the early 1850s he was appointed Master of the Mint by Lord John *Russell, in which he was expected to add his scientific authority to both staff and possible currency reform.

His reputation as England's leading man of science was consolidated in his popular writings, particularly his *Preliminary Discourse on Natural Philosophy* (1830), which appeared at a key moment of definitional confusion about the nature and role of science.   WJA

HERSCHEL, Sir William (1738–1822), Hanoverian refugee, musician, and astronomer who established a new astronomical practice and view of the universe. Herschel broke with traditional positional and cometary astronomy by adopting the classificatory techniques of natural history [see *natural philosophy, 34].

His father, Isaac Herschel, was an oboe player in the Hanoverian Foot Guards, and William consequently received his education at the Garrison school. He in turn also became a musician with the regimental band, and first visited England in 1756 on a posting with his father and brother Jacob. William was initially employed copying *music [26] in London, and later worked throughout the north of England, both as a freelance musician and as organist of the parish church at Halifax. In 1767 he was appointed organist for the Octagon Chapel in Bath and became a prominent figure in the musical culture of the *spa town, as teacher, director of *concerts and *oratorios, and as composer. While at Bath Herschel was enrolled into the short-lived Philosophical Society, where he encountered an active natural history community. His experience with this group informed the content and techniques which characterized his developing astronomical practice. Through powerful reflecting telescopes which he designed and manufactured himself, Herschel worked tirelessly on the observation of double stars and nebulae. As he wrote in 1791: 'I was in the situation of a natural philosopher who follows the various species of animals and insects from the height of their perfection down to the lowest ebb of life.' Through his vast telescopic sweeps Herschel detected what he first thought was a comet but later came to be heralded as the 'discovery' of the planet Uranus, a significant cultural as well as scientific event in late Georgian Britain. His chief patron was Sir Joseph *Banks, and it was through a combination of Banks's support and the 'discovery' of Uranus that Herschel

gained a pension of £200 per annum. This ensured further royal support for the remainder of his career.

With the assistance of his sister, Caroline *Herschel, who was also an astronomer, Herschel defined three species of nebulae between 1783 and 1791—the Orion Nebula, the 'resolved' star clusters, and planetary nebulae—all of which he claimed were connected through vast periods of time by gravity. He suggested that gravity could destroy individual systems in order to preserve the stability of a whole temporal cycle of systems. At certain moments the destruction of a star could be 'the means by which the whole is preserved and renewed. The clusters may be the *Laboratories* of the universe, if I may so express myself, wherein the most salutary remedies for the decay of the whole are prepared.' Herschel's construction of the heavens—especially its temporal economy—was informed by his acquaintance with the Scottish geologist James *Hutton. Through gravity, Herschel claimed, an almost uniform distribution of nebula material (such as the Orion) slowly condensed into planetary nebulae, which then imploded to form star clusters. The famous French savant Pierre-Simon Laplace (1749–1827) used the 'nebular hypothesis' to explain the origin of the solar system. Herschel's 'great laboratory' was both a product of gravity and *chemistry. His cosmology also provided the means to explain how life could be produced and sustained through power and matter, which in turn fed his arguments on the habitability of the sun and the moon.   WJA

historiography. Between the histories of David *Hume, William *Robertson, and Edward *Gibbon and those of the Victorians, there are scarcely any that are known today. In the field of history writing proper, the period witnessed the ending of an *Enlightenment [32] historiography, whose continuing vigour was attested by the phenomenal popularity of Hume's *History of Great Britain* (1754–62), and the first stirrings of a new emphasis on historiography as both a science and a Romantic art. The period was nonetheless remarkable in three respects: for the enormous expansion and in some instances the establishment of scholarly materials and standards; for the clear articulation and growing differentiation of a radical and conservative as well as a *Whig perspective on the English past; and for the halting emergence, less visible in historical writing proper than in political philosophy, poetry, and fiction—of a native historicism [see *history, 38].

Perhaps the most notable feature of the period was the sheer quantity and range of historical writing. Between the 1780s and the 1830s many thousand works of formal history—often in many volumes—were published, chiefly in London and Edinburgh. A growing public demand for historical subjects was fed particularly by the journals and reviews, and by astute publishers. Hume's *History* ran to eighteen editions by 1832, plus numerous excerpted or plagiarized versions, including such curiosities as *Hume's History of Great Britain revised for Family Use*. John Lingard's (1771–1851) eight-volume *History of England* (1819–30) ran to six editions in twenty years, Sharon Turner's (1768–1847) *History of England from the Earliest Period to the Norman Conquest* (1799–1805) to five. For the historical writer, there was money to be made and there were pensions to be won. Robertson's *Charles V* (1769) brought the author a princely £4,500, Lingard's *History* over £8,000 and a grant from the government; Charles James *Fox was paid nearly £20 a page for his *History of the Early Part of the Reign of James II* (pub. posthumously 1808)—little wonder that four Whig leaders over the next twenty years became part-time historians. Even such seemingly undigestible collections as James Macpherson's (1736–96) *Original Papers* (1775), William *Cobbett's *Parliamentary History* (1806–20), and William Coxe's (1747–1828) various aristocratic memoirs did surprisingly well. Indeed, readership often seemed disproportionate to the quality or accessibility of the work—something which occasioned the famous complaint from Jane *Austen (herself the author of an unpublished *History of England*, *c*.1792) that she thought it odd that history should be so dull since a great deal of it must be invention.

In truth, however, the period saw a considerable change in the attitude to sources and was crucial to the conversion of history into a fact-controlling discipline. Pride of place went to the publication of parliamentary records—notably the series of parliamentary diaries and debates which culminated in the thirty-six volumes of the *Parliamentary History of England*; but collections of private papers—including the Clarendon and Hardwicke State Papers, the Somers Tracts, the Harleian Miscellany, and the correspondence of the Walpoles, the Pelhams, the Talbots, and the Churchills—were also notable. So too were the first gleanings by *Mackintosh, Macpherson, and the various clerical contacts of Lingard from the Quai d'Orsay, from Jacobite and Hanoverian collections, and from the Italian and Spanish archives. Most important of all, however, were the various efforts made to collate and catalogue the deposits of the *British Museum, and to organize the public records through the work of a series of Record Commissioners from 1802, culminating in the Public Record Office Act of 1838. Thanks to this and to the activities of new *antiquarian [35] societies and clubs, the study of the past in the scientific mode of the later nineteenth century must have appeared within reach.

Nevertheless the research of most historians was selective and sporadic. Even Lingard, whose work on Tudor England was drawn, so he claimed, entirely from original diplomatic sources, used only an accidental selection of manuscript materials sent him by well-placed European friends. Fox's *History of James II* was yet more typical of the period: didactic in intent, and bolstered by a selection of proof texts supplied by his Whig colleagues and by one brief foray into the Paris archives. In their working habits, as in so much else, the historians of the age were transitional figures. True, there were notable exceptions to the rule of polemic: Sharon Turner placed the study of Anglo-Saxon history on a new footing; and Henry Hallam (1777–1859) produced in his *View of the State of Europe during the Middle Ages* (1818) what could be described as an early example of cultural history.

Much of the history of the period was, none the less, party history. Contemporary political debate was conducted through historical analogy and precedent—indeed, the Oxford and Cambridge Unions specifically limited public topics to those of previous centuries. And the great issues of the age—*parliamentary reform, *Catholic emancipation, the nature and meaning of the *American and *French Revolutions—inevitably triggered research and controversy on such issues as 'the Ancient Constitution', Tudor 'despotism', and seventeenth-century conflicts. In some instances—as in Thomas Oldfield's (1755–1822) *Representative History of Great Britain and Ireland* (1816)—the scholarship was unaffected by the inspirational polemic which usually lay at its core. The new radical historiography written in the 1770s and 1780s by Catharine *Macaulay and others was determinedly polemical in its celebration of seventeenth-century rebellion and its exhumation of the myth of the Norman Yoke which had obscured ancient Saxon liberties. In the first decades of the nineteenth century there developed a new *Tory perspective on the English and European past, typified by Isaac *D'Israeli's *Commentaries on the Life and Reign of Charles I* (1828–30) (from which his son, Benjamin Disraeli, drew inspiration for his novels), William Napier's (1785–1860) colourful but hugely partisan *History of the Peninsular War* (1828–40), and Archibald Alison's (1792–1867) *History of Europe from the Commencement of the French Revolution to the Restoration of the Bourbons* (1833–44).

These historiographical wars did lead to more detailed knowledge and more dispassionate judgement, but the real challenge to ahistorical assumptions and the growing sense of cultural development and relativity came from outside history-writing proper: from the historical consciousness disseminated by Edmund *Burke, S. T. *Coleridge, Lord *Byron, and, above all others, Walter *Scott. For it was Scott, less as formal historian than as historical novelist, who taught his contemporaries to see history as more than a narrative or a political record, and rather as a transformative process which encompassed the lives and circumstances of ordinary people. AMacL

history painting, a stylistic and thematic category of *painting [27] in which subject-matter drawn from the *Bible and classical literature is presented in an elevated and morally edifying manner.

The importance of history painting is part ideological, part conceptual. The focus of the continental academies on classical learning, correct drawing, a respect for decorum, and imitation of the art of the past all served to buttress the pretensions of the academicians to pre-eminence. They were also qualities which were best demonstrated through a mastery of history painting.

History painting never flourished in Britain. Neither artists nor their patrons, who seemed to resent the genre's moralizing and rather abstract tone, offered significant support. Unlike their continental counterparts, neither James Thornhill (1675–1734), who decorated Greenwich Hospital in the grand manner, nor his son-in-law William Hogarth (1697–1764), whose early attempts in the genre ended in failure, succeeded in establishing it as a significant genre in Britain. Joshua *Reynolds was the pre-eminent British history painter of the late eighteenth century, if only because his conceptual understanding of the theory of painting, expounded with admirable clarity in the *Discourses* (1769–90), was so far in advance of that of his contemporaries.

Important painters in Britain did not automatically adopt the genre. J. M. W. *Turner, for example, while sometimes working in the genre, tended to use it as an opportunity to represent the effects of nature. This British interest in nature stood in the same structural relation to the other genres as history painting did *vis-à-vis* the lesser genres on the Continent. While ambitious, innovative British painters like Turner and John *Constable found a ready market for their studies after nature with a public who had never shown much enthusiasm for the historical genre, those of their compatriots who maintained the primacy of the figure in artistic creation, such as George *Morland, were forced to adopt the less elevated themes of sentimental narrative paintings, such as orphaned children, fallen women, and soldiers departing for the wars.   PD

HOBHOUSE, John Cam, Baron Broughton (1786–1869), statesman and literary figure. Hobhouse is perhaps best remembered as Lord *Byron's college friend, travelling companion, and executor; but he was also a politician of some importance. Like Byron, he was a radical and something of a *dandy, but, save in the cause of Greek independence, he was more active politically than his friend [see *Hellenism]. A *Unitarian by birth and early education, and always by conviction, Hobhouse had the sort of radical credentials that recommended him to a metropolitan electorate. He was first elected to parliament in 1820, from Westminster, one of the earliest constituencies to see the emergence of non-aristocratic politics, under the leadership of such people as Francis *Place. The year before his election Hobhouse had displayed his radicalism with a pamphlet bitterly denouncing a political system that had just produced the Six Acts, aimed at silencing the expression of discontent [see *gagging acts].

But, though radical, Hobhouse was by birth and education a *Whig, and when he was elected to parliament it did not take him long to gravitate to Whig circles. He saw himself as a bridge between Whigs and radicals, who desired many of the same reforms, though differing as to the degree. His radical constituents, however, were not as anxious as he was to bridge the gap, and they ultimately parted over the question. Secretary at War in Grey's government from 1832, in 1833 Hobhouse was made Chief Secretary for Ireland; but he almost immediately resigned when the government proposed a window tax strongly opposed by his Westminster supporters. This, however, did not save him, and in 1834 he was defeated in the election. Thereafter Hobhouse settled into a comfortable career as a Whig officeholder and figure in literary circles. He was created a peer in 1851, and died in 1869.   RWD

HODGES, William (1744–97), *landscape painter and pupil of Richard *Wilson. Though he travelled and painted extensively within Britain and Europe, and visited India, Hodges's most renowned work derives from his appointment to Cook's second voyage of *exploration [37].

During the voyage, which incorporated Antarctic cruises in search of a great southern land, as well as visits to Tahiti, Tonga, New Zealand, and many other Pacific islands, he produced a remarkable corpus of sketches, *watercolours, and oils. Hodges departed substantially from classical conventions to engage with the specificities of Oceanic light and atmosphere, as well as with the singular features of *indigenous peoples and practices. The local specificity of his handling of human bodies was diminished in many of the classically idealized works produced after the voyage. In other respects an empirical strand in his art enhanced *picturesque and *sublime effects, for instance in the dramatic *View of Cape Stephens ... With Waterspout* (1775–6), which incorporates the precisely defined but daunting atmospheric phenomenon in an imaginative scene with classical associations. His magnificent Tahitian paintings evoked the feminized opulence of the climate and mode of life that was elsewhere described in some of the voyage writings.

Hodges engaged further with exotic environments during his tour to India, after which he published a travel narrative and a set of views. His views of the Ganges, then in the collection of Warren *Hastings, were later cited by Alexander von Humboldt as one of his principal inspirations to visit the tropics and study natural history.   NT

HOGG, James (1770–1835), antiquarian, poet, magazine editor, novelist, whose *Confessions of a Justified Sinner* (1824), in its probing of Scotland's self-inflicted wounds, is arguably the seminal Scottish *novel [31].

Together with his immediate predecessor, Robert *Burns, and his partial contemporary John *Clare, Hogg was a rural labouring-class poet whose authorial career was dictated by the social codes of an anxiously class-conscious metropolitan literary establishment [see *peasant poets]. Rural poets who bore bawdy sexual witness or revealed the pain of country labour, a pain grossly intensified in an age of *agricultural revolution and *enclosure, were unacceptable. Similarly, despite the enthusiasm for ancestral primitivism, the highest poetry could not come from the present lower orders. William *Wordsworth personally slighted Hogg's claim to be a brother poet. Such rejection and displacement, especially within a creative culture preoccupied with the problematic stability of the self, had extreme personal and creative consequences. Hogg's major theme is the fearful dynamic of self-division and dissolution.

Like Burns, Hogg lived a mainly marginal existence derived from inadequate publishing reward and failed sallies into farming projects. He worked as a shepherd from childhood until his mid-30s. However, he contrived a far longer Edinburgh career than Burns, as ballad collector, poet, editor of his own magazine (the *Spy*, 1810–11), and novelist. He contrived a partly mythical past and Rabelaisian persona, and so persisted as ambivalent jester at both the courts of Sir Walter *Scott, whom he befriended in 1802, and *Blackwood's Edinburgh Magazine*, founded in 1817, where he published many early stories and poems. None of this would have been possible, however, had he shared Burns's radical politics. His later experience of Napoleonic imperialism converted this Jacobite sympathizer into British patriot; and his home-grown Burkeanism engendered in him a conservative, compassionate sense of all mankind's fallen fallibility. The corollary of this was that he perceived political radicalism, especially in Calvinist Scotland, as a demonic, destructive claim to infallibility and omnipotence.

Given a background steeped in folklore but light on formal education and access to books, the fashionable notion that the greatest *poetry [29] belonged to the primitive genesis of human culture exerted a powerful appeal for him. His relatively rare poetic successes were all achieved within the restraining conventions of traditional Scottish forms. However, his greatest literary powers were both sophisticated and almost wholly contemporary. This late-developing Scottish peasant was a parodist of genius. In the anonymously published *Poetic Mirror* (1816), he parodied English peers such as Wordsworth, *Coleridge, and *Byron. He wrote two long novels: the parodic *The Three Perils of Man* (1822) and the more serious *The Three Perils of Women* (1823), sympathetically dealing with female prostitution, which excited furious, censorious critical rejection. Hogg's deep erotic honesty was increasingly alien to the age, and quickly led to his Victorian *bowdlerization.

Hogg's one prose masterpiece, *The Private Memoirs and Confessions of a Justified Sinner* (1824), came late. Pursuing his earlier portrayal of prostitution in a satire of religious fanaticism, it combined multiple voices and a tripartite narrative structure with a hallucinatory visual quality. It also blended folk myth with contemporary psychology. The comic side of Hogg had a late triumph, as a central participant in the *Noctes Ambrosianae* (1822–35), a series of Scottish vernacular dialogues which appeared in *Blackwood's*.   AN

HOLCROFT, Thomas (1745–1809), dramatist, novelist, journalist, translator. The self-educated son of a shoemaker, Holcroft was a stable-boy at Newmarket and a strolling player before trying his fortune in the London literary world. He soon published a novel, *Alwyn* (1780), based on his experiences as an actor, and journalist, including an eyewitness account of the *Gordon riots, as well as a well-received comedy, *Duplicity* (1781) [see *theatre, 24]. During the 1780s he translated works by Voltaire, de

Genlis, and Lavater which furthered the dissemination of the ideas of the *Enlightenment [32] in Britain.

A notable success in this field was his version of Beaumarchais' *Le Mariage de Figaro* (1784). Prevented from obtaining a copy of the play by orthodox means Holcroft committed it to memory on repeated visits to the theatre in Paris, producing a text, *The Follies of Fashion* (1785). In 1786 Holcroft met William *Godwin, establishing a friendship which was to be mutually influential. Holcroft's ideas informed the writing of *An Enquiry Concerning Political Justice* (1793), while Godwin was in turn a significant presence in Holcroft's political fiction, *Anna St Ives* (1792), *Hugh Trevor* (1794, 1797), and *Bryan Perdue* (1805). At the same time Holcroft continued a successful and lucrative career as a playwright. His comedy *The Road to Ruin*, which satirized the *gambling habits of the fashionable élite, was the hit of the 1792–3 season. Holcroft's associations with the Godwin circle, the social critique apparent in his literary work, and his activism—he was a member of the *Society for Constitutional Information and instrumental in the publication of Thomas *Paine's *Rights of Man*—made him increasingly suspect in the eyes of the government. In 1794 he was indicted for high treason: after voluntarily surrendering himself he was committed to Newgate prison and eventually released after the acquittal of Thomas *Hardy and others in the *Treason Trials. Stigmatized as a Jacobin, Holcroft found it difficult to pursue his career in the theatre. He diversified into dealing in *paintings [27] and tried to develop a polygraphic writing machine before leaving for Germany in 1799. On his return to Britain he quarrelled with Godwin over what Holcroft felt was a slur on his character in Godwin's *Fleetwood*. He began writing his autobiography on becoming gravely ill in 1809. After his death the manuscript was entrusted to William *Hazlitt who, after some interference from Godwin, eventually published a text in 1816. Holcroft's *Memoirs* are among the most significant accounts of plebeian life in the period.

Highly active in London cultural and sociable circles, Holcroft's range of contacts was enormous, including influential French intellectuals such as J. F. Brissot and L. S. Mercier, to whom he was related by marriage. His influence was as much felt in conversation and at the dinner table as it was in his published works. Godwin described him as one of 'his principal oral instructors'; S. T. *Coleridge, whose involvement in *Pantisocracy was influenced by Holcroft, claimed that his conversation 'absolutely infests you with *Atheism*'. An Enlightenment polymath, who was interested in *music [26] (he was a lifelong friend of William *Shield), the visual arts, and *natural philosophy [34], Holcroft also crossed national borders, apparent in his translation work, his involvement with the French theatre (he was responsible for introducing *melodrama to Britain), and his attempt to establish a journal, the *European Repository*.   GR

Holland House. From the late 1790s until 1840 Holland House was a focus of intellectual and social

103

activity for established and aspiring Foxite *Whigs, established and aspiring artists and writers, foreign diplomats, and political refugees, as well as becoming a venue for impromptu party and Cabinet meetings when the Whigs gained office in 1830.

Henry Richard Fox, third Baron *Holland, and his wife, Elizabeth (née Vassal, 1770–1845), Lady Holland, moved into Holland House, then just outside London, after returning from the Continent to a parliamentary inquiry into the minor scandal of their marriage. According to Henry *Brougham, Holland enjoyed the power of patronage conferred upon him as a birthright and 'like his uncle', Charles James *Fox, 'was always desirous of bringing forward the "young ones"'—amongst them Francis Horner (1778–1817), John Whishaw (?1764–1840), Thomas *Macaulay, and Brougham himself.

The Hollands also enjoyed genuine friendships and good company, and Holland House the presence of established reputations—in the party, Lord Grey and George Tierney; in literature, Samuel *Rogers, Walter *Scott, and the expatriate Ugo Foscolo (1778–1827); for wit and gourmandizing, Sydney *Smith; in all these areas, Richard Brinsley *Sheridan. Under Lady Holland's imperious orchestration, every meal was an occasion.

The 'culture' of Holland House was primarily a political one, however, Holland's literary tastes being not so much reactionary as perfunctory; *Byron received more assistance for his maiden speech in Lords than for his poetry.   WC

HOLLAND, Henry (1745–1806), architect. A relative of Lancelot 'Capability' *Brown, who was instrumental in his early career, Holland followed the conventional path of the fashionable architect, designing and remodelling the mansions and social centres of the *Whig élite, including Brooks's *gentlemen's club (1776–8). He is chiefly known for his association with the Prince of Wales which began in 1786 with a commission for the Marine Pavilion at Brighton (later remodelled by John *Nash) and culminated with extensive alterations on classical lines to Carlton House at Pall Mall (1783–96), for a long time the de facto headquarters of the Foxite Whigs. In the 1790s Holland was involved in rebuilding Drury Lane Theatre (1791–4) and altering Covent Garden (1792). Holland was a developer as well as an architect of London: during the 1770s he bought land in Chelsea and subsequently laid out Sloane Street, Cadogan Place, and Hans Place.   GR

HOLLAND, third Baron (Henry Richard Vassal Fox) (1773–1840), *Whig statesman and patron. Holland's life at the centre of the Whig party and of a renowned circle of talented politicians and artists was punctuated only by his and Lady Holland's other passion—touring Europe.

Holland was a faithful protégé of Charles James *Fox—the paternal uncle who, in an undisguised bid for personal immortality, undertook his cultural and political education. The Foxite demand for civil and religious liberties under the constitution became the leitmotif of Holland's political career in the Lords.

He most distinguished himself, however, at *Holland House, where he and his wife, Elizabeth, maintained a lively and talented salon.

After Eton and Oxford Holland embarked on a *Grand Tour, in the typical eighteenth-century mode. Here he confirmed a Foxite enthusiasm for *constitutionalism and foreigners, though he was never trusted to use his considerable diplomatic abilities and connections—with Lafayette and Talleyrand in France, or with Jovellanos in Spain. As cabinet minister in the 1830s with the minor post of Chancellor of the Duchy of Lancaster, his unsolicited meddling only embarrassed the government, as had his francophilia in the 1820s.   WC

Holy Alliance. In September 1815 in Paris, Tsar Alexander of Russia presented a Treaty of Holy Alliance to his fellow monarchs, the Emperor of Austria and the King of Prussia. By this document the autocratic rulers of three of Europe's major powers sought a mechanism for ensuring the permanence of the Settlement agreed upon in 1815.

Each monarch undertook to prosecute his foreign and domestic policy according to the precepts of 'justice, Christian charity, and peace', and in an air of false modesty declared that they looked upon themselves as 'merely delegated by Providence to govern the three branches of one family, namely, Austria, Prussia and Russia'. Christianity was the common ground which was supposed to unify the nations of Europe under the paternal rule of their monarchs. Conservatism was the basis on which the self-interest of each signatory was founded.

In terms of foreign relations, the Quadruple Alliance of November 1815, including as it did the United Kingdom, was the more important product of the deliberations in Paris. But the symbolic significance of the Holy Alliance as an indicator of the change of mood in Europe after the dramatic events and radical change of the Napoleonic period ought not to be underestimated. Initially signed in secret and only by rulers, the Holy Alliance heralded to some 'a world restored'; to others, it came to represent a period of conservative backlash and oppression. 'Legitimacy' became the byword for interference in the internal affairs of other European states.   JF

homosexuality. Our period saw the completion of a major transformation in the conception of male homosexuality towards identifiably modern norms, including the emergence of distinctive 'sodomitical' subcultures.

Prior to the beginning of the eighteenth century British attitudes to homosexuality seem to have been largely reflected in Tudor legislation, which rendered illegal acts of buggery and sodomy, thought to be sinful and unnatural, but did not relate such acts to any distinctive types of person. Statutes of 1563, in particular, outlawed behaviour of this kind, whether between males, males and females, or males and animals. Sodomy was often imprecisely defined and was seen to be implicated in a wider range of taboo, non-procreative sexual actions. Moreover, in late-seventeenth-century Britain—as in Italy and France—sexual relations between patrician males and younger adolescent boys were often tolerated and seem to have carried no particular implications for conceptions of masculinity. Same-sex relations were part of the spectrum of libertine sexuality enjoyed by Restoration wits and courtiers such as John Wilmot, Earl of Rochester. The German traveller Johan Wilhelm von Archenholtz commented on the existence of male homosexual 'Anandrinic clubs' and on the prevalence of lesbianism in late-eighteenth-century London. At much the same time Queen Marie-Antoinette of France was being accused of such 'unnatural' partialities in scandalous memoirs produced by *émigré hack writers centred in London. Even so, lesbianism had no presence in English law, and close liaisons between women seem rarely to have been publicly treated as having any sexual dimension [see *sapphism]. This was still true of the later relationship of the 'Ladies of Llangollen,' Lady Eleanor Butler and Lady Sarah Ponsonby, whose intimate amatory friendship presented no barrier to their respectability.

By the mid- to late eighteenth century, however, there was increasing evidence of changing attitudes towards male homosexuality. On the one hand it became more difficult, after a case in 1781, to convict for sodomy, since both anal penetration and the emission of seed had to be proved. Yet, when obtained, convictions seem to have led more invariably to execution, and the offence seems also to have become an increasingly conspicuous target for the morality campaigns of organizations such as the *Society for the Suppression of Vice. The lengthy duration of *war [2] during our period may have been one important trigger for the growth of such anxieties and suppression campaigns. The armed services, and particularly the navy, were deemed highly vulnerable to the development of sodomitical practices which endangered the maintenance of proper discipline and order. Smollett has a realistic portrait in his seafaring novel *Roderick Random* (1748), and there were several naval scandals involving homosexual acts during both the American and French wars. By the end of the eighteenth century the climate of tolerance had so changed that even extraordinarily wealthy patricians such as William *Beckford were forced to flee abroad in order to avoid threatened charges.

The appearance of opprobrious words like 'mollie', 'marianne', and 'madge-cull' to denote distinctive types of male, who affected feminine styles of dress and speech, indicated that homosexuality was now being associated with categories of persons as well as with unorthodox sexual acts. For a man to desire anyone other than a woman was now regarded as deviant. New conceptions of childhood as a distinctively pure and innocent state also increased anxieties over masturbation which might in turn have homosexual implications. Terms such as 'mollie' denoted, too, the emergence of homosexual subcultures in the cities. Low-life guides to urban life produced by hacks like Ned Ward reported the existence of transvestite homosexual brothels

around the Strand or in garrison towns and ports (an especially notorious one in Vere Street, London, was said in 1812 to hold transvestite marriage services conducted by an ex-Methodist parson called John Church). They also recorded the meeting-places, clubs, and distinctive argot, or 'parlare', of male homosexuals.

Increased social stigma exposed middle- and upper-class homosexuals to blackmail and persecution. Percy Jocelyn, Bishop of Clogher, had to assume a new and secret identity after being caught in 1822 in a compromising position with a guardsman in a *tavern, and in the same year Lord *Castlereagh's suicide was thought to have been precipitated by blackmailers who were accusing him of homosexual liaisons in Hyde Park. Jeremy *Bentham wrote a lengthy tract in the early nineteenth century describing homosexuality as 'an imaginary offence' dependent on changing codes of morality. He also called for the abolition or liberalization of homosexual laws. Significantly, however, Bentham was persuaded by friends to withhold publication: it lay amongst his voluminous papers until his death, a testimony to the mounting climate of intolerance in Britain.

IMcC

HONE, William (1780–1842), radical journalist, *satirist, parodist, folklorist, and *antiquarian [35]. Hone was one of the most ingenious and effective radical propagandists to attack Lord *Liverpool's administration during the resurgence of radical activism between 1816 and 1822.

By 1817, after several years publishing sensational pamphlet material in London, Hone had become an accomplished political publicist. He maintained a phenomenal rate of pamphlet publication and established the *Reformist's Register*, a journal designed to fill the gap created by the temporary absence of the *Political Register* after William *Cobbett's flight to America. In 1817 Hone produced a series of parodies based on various forms of *Anglican instructional text—the catechism, litany, and creed—three of which resulted in his prosecution by the government for blasphemous and seditious libel. He based his defence on the citation of a plethora of earlier political parodies which used religious forms, none of which had previously been prosecuted. Citing the satirical work of George *Canning, a member of the Liverpool Cabinet, Hone implicated a hypocritical state, causing a sensation. What S. T. *Coleridge described as the government's justified humiliation was largely responsible for the virtual cessation of state prosecutions for libel in 1818. Hone's triumphant acquittal made him a national celebrity.

The majority of Hone's subsequent political satires appropriated popular publishing forms such as *almanacs, press advertisements, chapbooks, children's books, nursery rhymes, games, poems, songs, last wills, dying confessions, playbills, showman's notices, and even bank notes [see *street literature]. In 1819 Hone published a number of pamphlets with wood-engravings by the politically freewheeling George *Cruikshank. The most successful of these, *The Political House that Jack Built*, inspired by the recent *Peterloo massacre, sold an unprecedented 100,000 copies in a few weeks. Hone continued to produce immensely popular satiric squibs until 1822. His other bestselling satiric squibs, *Non mi Ricordo* and *The Queen's Matrimonial Ladder*, savaged the Prince Regent and the Liverpool administration during the agitation surrounding the *Queen Caroline affair of 1820–1.

Converting to Nonconformist Christianity in the early 1820s, Hone produced pioneering publications on the early history of church festivals and church drama in England. He also became a respected antiquarian anthologist. His widely successful *Every Day Book* (1825–6), *Table Book* (1827), and *Year Book* (1832) consistently emphasized his knowledge of the ideological and formal inheritance of anti-state agitation in the context of folklore and *popular culture [23].   MW

HOOD, Thomas (1799–1845), writer, editor, and illustrator. Born near Fleet Street, son of a bookseller, Hood began work as an engraver at the age of 15 but soon turned to writing. He became sub-editor of the *London Magazine* in 1821, meeting *Coleridge, *De Quincey, *Lamb (an important mentor), and the poet John Hamilton Reynolds (1794–1852), whose sister he married. Hood's poetry during the 1820s includes lyrics, among the first to pay imitative homage to *Keats, and comic verses exploring social and domestic themes, often with the fantastical and macabre humour reminiscent of the popular *ballad. Poems such as 'The Last Man' expose Romantic subjects to a deflating popular register. *Odes and Addresses to Great People* (1825), written with Reynolds, was followed by *Whims and Oddities* (1826–7), two collections of self-illustrated comic poems accented by punning word-play which set the tone for his popular and widely imitated *Comic Annual* (1830–9, 1842). A three-decker novel, *Tylney Hall*, appeared in 1834, the year in which Hood's always precarious finances collapsed. He accepted self-imposed exile in Germany and Holland (1835–40), whence he conducted the *Comic* and wrote a travelogue, *Up the Rhine* (1839). Returning to England, he edited the *New Monthly Magazine* (1841–3) and *Hood's Magazine* (1844–5), publishing poems which, increasingly, protested against an age of exploitative capitalism. These included 'Miss Kilmansegg and her Precious Leg', 'The Bridge of Sighs', and, most famously, 'The Song of the Shirt'. Hood met Charles *Dickens in 1840 and campaigned with him for protective *copyright laws. Their literary work also shares a love of the ludic grotesque, fascination with the multiplicity of London street life, a concern about social issues, and an interest in literature as a commodity. Hood died in 1845, after a life of persistent ill health.   SLo

HOOK, James (1746–1827). A prolific composer of light songs, Hook composed and played the organ for the *pleasure gardens for half a century. He established himself as a musician in London by the age of 20 and, after working for Samuel *Arnold at Marylebone Gardens, went on to dominate the musical scene at Vauxhall until 1820. At Marylebone he was able to stage short dramatic pieces during the nightly entertainments; at Vauxhall, which had a smaller stage, only gestures were possible from the singers. Although he failed to obtain permanent employment at Drury Lane, Hook contributed occasional works to the winter theatres, including one of his most successful operas, *The Double Disguise* (Drury Lane, 1784). Hook wrote over 2,000 songs, typically in light melodious *galant* style and including many *ballads. His pleasure garden songs, published individually and in annual collections, were popular with amateur performers and domestic *music-makers. The best known is 'The Lass of Richmond Hill'. His instrumental music includes organ concertos, chamber works, and several orchestral works. A reputable piano teacher, Hook wrote an instruction book, *Guida di Musica*, in three parts between 1785 and 1796. His second son was the writer Theodore Edward Hook (1788–1841), who composed librettos for his father.   JG

HOPE, Thomas (1769–1831), antiquarian and designer. Part of a Dutch banking family who had fled to London in 1794 after the French invasion of Holland, Hope was an avid student of the classical and oriental world, amassing artefacts which he displayed in his houses in London and Surrey. In addition to collecting, he designed his own furniture, ceramics, wallpaper, and paint schemes. These were publicized in his book, *Household Furniture and Interior Decoration* (1807), which was influential in promoting Greek and especially Egyptian models as the epitome of fashionable style [see *Hellenism]. His other publications included *Costume of the Ancients* (1809) and *Designs of Modern Costume* (1812), and a *romance, *Anastasius, or Memoirs of a Greek written at the close of the Eighteenth Century* (anon., 1819).   GR

HORSLEY, Samuel (1733–1806), *Anglican divine, scientist, parliamentarian, and man of letters. One of the Church of England's leading exponents of High Church orthodoxy in the era of the *French Revolution, Horsley was the religious heir of the Caroline divines; he bridged the gap between the Anglican *Toryism of Sacheverell and the apostolic vision of the Tractarians. A theological giant in his day, nicknamed the 'Grand Mufti', Horsley's career and High Church Tory beliefs have been until recently overshadowed and marginalized by a flawed historical emphasis on the Latitudinarianism of the eighteenth-century Church of England.

Horsley came from Protestant Dissenting stock. After graduating LL B from Trinity Hall, Cambridge, Samuel was ordained in 1759; curacies, private tutorships, and livings followed. In 1767 he was incorporated at Christ Church, Oxford, receiving a DCL from the university in 1774. The Royal Society, to which Horsley was elected fellow in 1767 and to membership of its council in 1771, became the principal arena of his activities. Horsley attempted to collate and edit a heterogeneous body of Sir Isaac

*Newton's unpublished papers; Horsley's Latin edition of Newton's works, the *Opera Omnia*, finally appeared in five volumes between 1779 and 1785.

In the later 1770s, as his commitments to the Royal Society slackened, promotion in the Church started to come Horsley's way. In 1777 he was appointed chaplain to the Bishop of London, Robert Lowth (1710–87), and in 1782 he was made archdeacon of St Albans. In 1793 he was translated to Rochester and in 1802 to the see at St Asaph. Horsley's change from prominent scientist to prominent ecclesiastic coincided with his theological transformation from devotee of the European *Enlightenment [32] into a conservative and combative theological opponent of rationalism. His theological reputation was made by his assault on Joseph *Priestley's *History of the Corruptions of Christianity* (1782).

As a diocesan, Horsley was conscientious and a genuine proponent of church reform, doing much to improve the condition of his clergy. He became a celebrated champion of the Church and implacable opponent of Dissent and political radicalism. Yet while the hammer of Protestant Dissenters, Horsley was eirenic towards Roman Catholics, partly owing to sympathy for the beleaguered French émigré clergy. He played a leading role in the provision of Roman Catholic Relief (1791) and in a relief act for another hitherto persecuted minority, Scottish Episcopalians (1792).

In the 1770s Horsley had belonged to the world of scientific curiosity. The controversy with Priestley and the revolutionary upheaval in Europe set him on a new course. Cursing the name of Voltaire, whom he had once praised, Horsley regarded the French Revolution and its philosophical antecedents as part of a conspiracy to subvert revealed Christianity. In response, he turned not only to the Tory political weapons provided by the union of church and state but also to the theological armoury of the High Church Anglican tradition and to an exposition of scriptural prophecies, in which he branded Jacobinism with the mark of Antichrist. Horsley was a conservative *constitutionalist, rather than mere reactionary. In spite of his genuinely High Church credentials, he was a unifying force within the Church of England; his emphasis on doctrinal preaching, prophetical interpretation of Scripture, anti-rationalism, and treatment of the Calvinist controversy as an open question, earned him the regard of Anglican *Evangelicals. For all his political and parliamentary skills and acumen, his abiding legacy was a re-evaluation of Anglican High Churchmanship in more spiritual terms.   PBN

HOWARD, John (?1726–90), *prison reformer and *philanthropist. Howard had a Nonconformist education and inherited sufficient wealth from his father, a prosperous upholsterer, to spend early adult life as an improving landlord and traveller. Appointed sheriff of Bedfordshire in 1773, Howard inspected local gaols and then embarked on an investigation of *prisons throughout England and Wales, recording abuse, neglect, and disease. This project gave form and purpose to his life. In 1785 he extended his research to quarantine hospitals. Howard inspected English gaols and bridewells four times, visited institutions in Scotland, Ireland, the Continent, and Scandinavia, and went as far as Constantinople and southern Russia, where he died. These self-funded journeys covered over 50,000 miles. Howard subsidized the publication of his *State of the Prisons* (1777) and *Account of the Principal Lazarettos in Europe* (1789; vol. II, 1791). Fêted as a great humanitarian, he was twice called to give evidence to House of Commons committees, and his work was used by prison reformers such as Samuel *Romilly. He advocated sanitary improvements through the proper location, construction, and management of gaols, and recommended solitary confinement as conducive to reflection and repentance. He criticized the moral effects of mixing what he identified as different categories of inmates, including men and women. Howard's work was significant for systematically describing British prison conditions and setting them in an international context.

Howard was once regarded as a central and unique figure in progressive prison reform, but historians have since reassessed his influence. He contributed to eighteenth-century interest in penitentiaries which promoted efficient moral discipline as the means to social order.   SL

HUGHES, Hugh (1790–1863), painter, engraver, writer. Hughes was the most prolific *portrait and *landscape painter in Wales in his period, the pioneer of illustration in Welsh *language [40] publications, and a controversial public figure in religious debate.   *107*

Hughes was trained as a wood-engraver, but in all other respects he was self-educated. As a young man he absorbed or rejected elements of the great ideas of the past as they seemed to him consistent with the Calvinistic *Methodism that was the basis of his thought. He witnessed the formation of a new denomination, unique to Wales, by the secession of the sect from the Church of England at the ordination of ministers at Bala in 1811. The identification of the Welsh nation with Calvinistic Methodism, crystallized in this event, was of great importance to Hughes, who set about painting the leaders of the movement. These portraits may be considered the first self-consciously national series painted in Wales. In the form of popular *prints [22], his images of Thomas Charles (1755–1814) and Thomas Jones (1756–1820), both in about 1812, became icons of the culture [see *Welsh artisan painters].

By extension of his belief in the word of the Bible as the key to the knowledge of God, Hughes developed an intense respect for written words of all sorts as the means to *self-improvement, often reflected in the imagery of his engravings and paintings. He regarded self-education as superior to the *education [17] of universities (which he detested) and a characteristic virtue of his nation and his class. Between 1816 and 1832 he pioneered the illustration of popular Welsh language texts on music, science, religion, history, and current affairs, and of *children's literature. Unlike many of his generation, he espoused the Welsh language, rather than English, as the appropriate medium for the improvement of his compatriots.

Hughes's work not only exemplifies the importance of Methodism in Welsh identity, but also of Celtic *antiquarianism [35] and reverence for the national landscape. He published a highly successful series of sixty wood-engravings of *The Beauties of Cambria* (1819–23) and found himself welcome, for a time, in the liberal and patriotic *Anglican circles that revived the *eisteddfod movement. He painted his second national series of portraits, depicting some of the leaders of this movement, in 1825–7.

Though he hated papism, in 1828 Hughes's rationalism and belief in the authority of conscience lead him publicly to support *Catholic emancipation. As a consequence he was excommunicated from his Methodist church. He published the relevant documents of this event, along with a virulent personal attack on the conservative leader, John Elias (1774–1841), and the incident became a *cause célèbre*. Politicized and embittered, Hughes involved himself in the propagation of radical ideas, leading eventually to the establishment of the first weekly Welsh language newspaper, *Y Papyr Newydd Cymraeg* (1836). He came to despise the professional ministry, which he regarded as indistinguishable from the priesthood, and attacked it in the period of its greatest respectability with a biting sarcasm for which he became notorious. He found himself marginalized by the establishment, and his pioneering contributions to the *Welsh cultural revival and Welsh radicalism were forgotten.   PL

HUME, David (1711–76), Scottish philosopher and historian; arguably no single writer so greatly influenced the course of British thought in the era of Romanticism. Hume's controversial *Treatise on Human Nature* (1739), essays on religious themes, and the multi-volume *History of Great Britain* (1754–62) all changed in diverse ways the thinking of radical, moderate, and conservative intellectuals.

Well-read in the Graeco-Roman sceptics and modern empiricist traditions, Hume sought to investigate the human condition in a rigorously inductive fashion, modelled on Isaac *Newton's procedures when seeking to disclose the workings of the natural world. As Hume saw it, the truth of any proposition could only be as certain as the probability of it being experienced. Even then, the causal relationship observed was contingent upon the customary outlook of the observer. Hence he believed that the likelihood of a miracle being experienced was so small that it would be near-miraculous to find anyone who believed in the occurrence purely on the strength of having witnessed it.

This 'very sceptical' reasoning naturally outraged clerics and many pious contemporaries, and cost Hume dearly through lost patronage. Yet he continued to refine his arguments, convinced by the reaction of religious critics that metaphysical controversies were not simply empty words, but by their nature emotionally charged forms of discourse that could easily excite human passions to the point of endangering civil society. Religious discourse and its dangers were explored in depth by Hume in the *Natural History of Religion* (1757), and became a significant theme in the Stuart volumes of his *History of Great Britain*. However, it was Edward *Gibbon who methodically applied Hume's critique of *religion [10], in reinterpreting the history of Christianity.

With few notable exceptions, Hume's theological critics vigorously condemned him for perverting his literary skills to snare young and impressionable readers into infidelity. During the early 1790s, his posthumously published essays on suicide and the immortality of the soul (1777), the *Dialogues Concerning Natural Religion* (1779), and accounts of his having maintained scepticism about the existence of an after-life to the grave, were all readily reinterpreted by conservative clerical and court circles. The works were seen as evidence that he had been part of a deep-rooted infidel conspiracy which had done much to foster revolutionary upheaval in France and had sought the overthrow of the British constitution.

However, Hume's philosophical conclusions were essentially conservative, as thinkers as diverse in outlook as Jeremy *Bentham, Edmund *Burke, and William *Godwin were quick to appreciate. Defenders of the old regime were well disposed to Hume's verdict, in *History of Great Britain*, that the liberties of the British constitution were the unforeseen consequences of economic and religious events, and in no way the product of reasoned statecraft [see *constitutionalism]. On the other hand, his sceptical assessments of key aspects of Stuart churchmanship gave little comfort to would-be defenders of the religious establishment in the half-century or so after 1792. During the course of the nineteenth century, the *History* generally came to be regarded as a masterpiece flawed only by its author's antagonism to Christianity.   PT

HUNT, (James Henry) Leigh (1784–1859), a leading editor of political and literary periodicals for the reformist middle class, Hunt is remembered less for his own *poetry [29] and *prose [30] than for his support of younger writers, especially *Keats and *Shelley.

Educated as a charity boy at Christ's Hospital, Hunt was a precocious poet, and in 1801 published his first volume of poetry, *Juvenilia*. Four years later he became theatre critic for the *News*, where he established his critical independence and personal style, as well as his reputation for vanity.

In 1808 he and his brother John (1775–1848) founded the *Examiner*, with Leigh as editor and principal political writer. Vigorously independent, aggressive on the attack, and *constitutionalist rather than *republican in principle, this reformist weekly was distinguished for its polished style and literary content. Keats, Shelley, *Lamb, and *Hazlitt were all published and favourably reviewed. The paper soon drew the government's attention, and a string of libel charges culminated in 1812 with a successful prosecution for disparaging remarks on the

Prince Regent [see *Regency]. The brothers were sentenced to two years in prison and fined £500 each. They continued to produce the *Examiner* from prison, but its political energy diminished after their release. Leigh Hunt also set up a series of more strictly literary periodicals, including the *Reflector* (1810–12), the *Indicator* (1819–21), and the *Companion* (1828), but he continued to edit the *Examiner* until 1822, when he departed for Italy to join Shelley and *Byron on the *Liberal* (1822–3). Despite some brilliant moments, including Byron's 'Vision of Judgment' and Hazlitt's 'My First Acquaintance with the Poets', this latter project dissolved acrimoniously after Shelley's death amid Hunt's usual financial embarrassments.

Though modern anthologies tend to reprint his later sonnets, Hunt's most ambitious poem, and the most successful in his own lifetime, was *The Story of the Rimini* (1816), based on Dante's tale of Paolo and Francesca. Other narrative poems on mythological subjects followed, including *Hero and Leander* (1819) and *Bacchus and Ariadne* (1819). While critics praise his vivid description and metrical fluidity, most agree that his verse is too loose, mannered, and familiar. His colloquial style, radical politics, and petty bourgeois pretensions earned him the abuse of John Gibson *Lockhart in *Blackwood's* notorious series 'On the Cockney School of Poetry' (1817–19). Keats, whose early poetry betrays Hunt's influence, was found guilty by association.

Hunt's informal style and affectionate nature fare better in his prose. He became a master of the Romantic familiar essay, with an appealing personal voice and a fine sense of the ordinary. As a critic, he is remembered less as a theorist than an advocate. His appreciative essays reflect catholic tastes, and a good eye for the telling detail. Through his translations, anthologies, and prefaces, he introduced middle-class audiences to continental (especially Italian) literature, and to the English tradition from Chaucer and Spenser to Keats, and later Tennyson and Browning. His introduction to *Imagination and Fancy*, 'An Answer to the Question, "What Is Poetry?"' (1844), popularized Romantic ideas for Victorian readers. His well-regarded *Autobiography* appeared in 1850.   KG

HUNT, Henry (1773–1835), farmer, Bristol merchant, and the most celebrated radical orator and agitator of the postwar popular reform movement, 1815–21. Hunt rose to fame as an orator who developed the menacing tactics of the mass platform through addressing a series of meetings at Smithfield in November and December 1816 to petition the King for the claimed *constitutionalist demand of *parliamentary reform based on universal male suffrage. His reform campaign culminated in the legendary *Peterloo massacre of 16 August 1819, during which members of a peaceable crowd at St Peter's Field, Manchester, were sabred and trampled by militia yeomanry sent to arrest Hunt for sedition. He was sentenced to two and a half years' imprisonment in Ilchester gaol, from which he produced an acrimonious memoir attacking other popu-

lar radical leaders. He was elected to the seat of Preston in 1830, but was less effective in parliament than as a platform demagogue.

With his burly frame, stentorian voice, rakish reputation, theatrical flamboyance, and blunt farmer's idiom, Hunt managed to project the image of a John Bull-like radical patriot whose white top hat remained a radical icon long after his own eclipse.
                                                        IMcC

HUNTER, John (1728–93), anatomist and surgeon. The youngest child of a grain merchant and minor landholder, Hunter experienced limited schooling. In 1748 he took employment assisting his elder brother, William (1718–83), the leading 'man-midwife' and anatomy teacher in London. In 1756 John gained the post of house surgeon at St George's Hospital. By the mid-1760s he was a popular teacher of anatomy and surgery and practitioner of *dentistry, whose diagnostic skills and surgical dexterity had attracted a wealthy clientele. Hunter struck medical grandees as coarse in speech and demeanour, money-hungry, and possibly irreligious. At the time of his death in 1793 he had collected over 14,000 'rare and curious' bones and soft tissue structures, the bulk of which remained uncatalogued.

Within two decades of his death, Hunter had become an almost legendary figure in established medical circles. This apotheosis was the product of astute manipulation of his specimens by London's surgical élite. In 1799 the collections were purchased by parliament. The following year they were entrusted to the newly constituted Royal College of Surgeons, on condition that two courses of lectures on comparative anatomy illustrated by the specimens were given annually. Together with Hunter's manuscripts, the specimens became the basis of the most influential museum of comparative anatomy until well into the latter half of the nineteenth century. From 1814 the Hunterian Oration, a lecture honouring the memory and achievements of the great man, became the principal event of the College calendar. By the 1830s Joshua *Reynolds's portrait of Hunter had come to serve as a foundation icon, under which panels of examiners sat to assess candidates seeking admission to the College.

During the first half of the nineteenth century, the Hunterian lectures and orations served to reaffirm a collegiate self-image of a select company of gentlemen, respectfully intent on knowing the divine mind as expressed in regularities underlying the growth and reproduction of earth's myriad life-forms. In ways which now seem to mirror the political conservatism of the College, these discourses generally represented the animate creation as an immutable hierarchy of organisms.   PT

HUTTON, James (1726–97), geological thinker, often hailed as the father of modern empirical *geology, who inaugurated the concept of 'deep' geological time, pioneered uniformitarian theories which held that the earth's changes were brought about by gradual rather than catastrophic forces, and established the 'Vulcanist' interpretation of the

77

77. Detail of Joshua Reynolds's portrait of the physician *John Hunter* (*c*.1787), which presided regally over candidates for the Royal College of Surgeons.

primacy of volcanic activity in elevating new land masses as opposed to the 'Neptunist', retreating-ocean model.

Hutton's reputation in the late nineteenth century as a hero of modern science was fostered by narrow-minded attacks from some of his scientific contemporaries. Conservative Neptunists such as J. A. Deluc (1727–1817) and Richard Kirwan (1733–1812) castigated Hutton's paper, *The Theory of the Earth* (1788), and his subsequent book of the same name (1795), as a godless denial of Genesis and the Flood which fostered the atheism of the *French Revolution. However, modern historians of science have argued that this attack led to a subsequent anachronistic misunderstanding of Hutton's achievement and an undervaluing of rival contributions to geological theory.

A polymathic product of the *Scottish Enlightenment attracted to geology largely through an interest in erosion on his landed estates, Hutton based his famous theory of volcanic elevation not on empirical evidence but on a priori speculations about final causation. He viewed the earth as a providentially influenced machine which produced new elevated land masses in order to balance the forces of erosion. He thus had no real interest in the history of geological change; achievements in this area came much more from subtler contemporary 'Neptunists' such as the Edinburgh University professor Robert Jameson (1774–1854). Moreover, Hutton's work was almost unreadable; his ideas might have passed unnoticed had he not possessed a Boswellian friend and admirer in the Scottish mathematician John Playfair (1748–1815). As brilliant a stylist as Hutton was poor, Playfair published his *Illustrations of the Huttonian Theory of the Earth* in 1802, purging the original of its theology, strengthening the argument with empirical evidence, and emphasizing the uniformitarian aspects of geological change. It was in this form that Huttonianism came to exercise a profound influence on nineteenth-century geological and evolutionary thought. IMcC

hymnody. The *Evangelical revival and upsurge in domestic and foreign *missionary activity heralded a burst of *Anglican hymnody in the late eighteenth century. Until then, congregational hymn singing, though an essential part of Nonconformist worship, was virtually unknown in Anglican communions. In private, orthodox Anglicans sang closet and chamber hymns; in public, listened to choral *music [26] and *oratorios.

Hymnodists' inspiration was drawn primarily from the Gospel and Psalms, combining stoic themes of death, suffering, punishment, and atonement with those of *sensibility [11], fortitude, compassion, and nature's *sublime power. Particular hymns, such as *Amazing Grace*, by Revd John Newton (1725–1807), and *Oh, Worship the King*, by Robert Grant (1779–1838), were credited with revitalizing religious services and increasing congregations, and were swiftly incorporated into Church of England services. William *Cowper's *Olney Hymns* (1779), written in collaboration with Newton, received instant approval. *Methodists George *Whitefield and John and Charles *Wesley, and Anglican Bishop Reginald Heber (1783–1826), author of the missionary hymn 'From Greenland's Icy Mountains', were similarly successful.

Hymnody also provided a theological genre for women writers, such as Anna Steele (1717–81), whose hymns were published in 1760 under the pseudonym 'Theodosia'; Selina, Countess of Huntingdon (1707–91); Anna Laetitia *Barbauld; Hannah *More; Helen Maria *Williams; Cowper's aunt, Judith Madan (1702–81), and her daughter, Maria Frances Cecilia Cowper (1726–97); Jane and Ann Taylor [see *children's literature]; Harriet Auber, who wrote the popular *The Spirit of the Psalms* (1829), and Felicia *Hemans, who dedicated *Scenes and Hymns of Life* to *Wordsworth. SR

I

illuminism, see *freemasonry.

imagination. In his *Letters*, John *Keats replied to Benjamin Bailey's (1791–1853) doubts about the authenticity of the imagination by affirming that 'The Imagination may be compared to Adam's dream—he awoke and found it truth.' As described by *Milton in *Paradise Lost*, Adam's dream is of Eve, and the truth he discovers is the 'real' counterpart to the form he had imagined. This startling coincidence of human and divine creative powers supports Keats's view that 'What the imagination seizes as Beauty must be truth—whether it existed before or not.'

Keats's analogy and its remarkable application are emblematic of an imagination no longer confined, as was common in earlier thinking, to the representation or combination of ideas and images drawn from experience [see *literary theory, 41]. It evokes, to adopt Kant's terminology, a productive rather than merely reproductive faculty. Moreover, by correlating divine and human acts of creation, Keats makes the imagination the vehicle of a knowledge more profound than that available to reason. Residing at a level too deep to be scrutinized by the conscious mind, the imagination in its various guises (human and divine) is nevertheless identified as the ultimate source of both nature and the self.

Keats was certainly not alone in this estimation of the imagination: William *Blake personified 'The Human Imagination' as 'the Saviour, the True Vine of Eternity.' S. T. *Coleridge correlated the productive, unifying, human imagination (evident in art and perception) with God's creative power. Indeed, although there was little agreement on its precise nature or scope, the term was fundamental to Romanticism, where it took on ethical, political, and even therapeutic roles: the imagination is 'the great instrument of moral good' because, as Percy *Shelley wrote, thanks to its powers we are able to put ourselves 'in the place of another'; as a faculty whose work transcends historical determination, it served as rallying-cry for a variety of conservative and progressive groups; and it was therapeutic because (in poems such as *The Prelude*) it offered an antidote to the dislocations and artifice of modernity.

The Romantic ideology of imagination establishes literature as a privileged index to the imagination and therefore as a source of secular salvation. It underwrites a set of hierarchies (imagination/fancy, *genius/talent, organic/mechanical), generic divisions (*poetry [29], *prose [30]) and values (spontaneity, intensity, unity) which for literary criticism have proved remarkably influential. The key to the fascination this term exerts on Romanticism is, however, found in the links between this term and individuality, *originality, and freedom. Crucial to these connections is the ability of the imagination to create a heterocosm or alternate world: in Shelley's words, 'Forms more real than living man, / Nurslings of immortality.'

The idealizing view of the imagination sketched above was not shared by all the Romantics. In Keats's long poems, the subject of his letter to Benjamin Bailey is displaced by an imagination that operates as a compensation for irremediable loss. *De Quincey draws a scandalous correspondence between the idealizing and unifying capacities of imagination and opium. And *Byron is sharply critical of a Romantic ideology of the imagination. Moreover, the Romantic imagination was not thought to be equally available to all. William Duff (1732–1815) writes, in *Letters on the Intellectual and Moral Character of Women* (1807), that he cannot recall any instances of a 'powerful imagination' in the fair sex. In a commonplace Romantic trope, the female appears as matter to be shaped or the ideal that is sought by the male imagination. This is in part why writers such as Mary *Wollstonecraft and Mary *Shelley are frequently ambivalent about or critical of this faculty.

Although the history of imagination is often told as a heroic story in which the democratic and humanist self is gradually uncovered, as criticism moves further from its Romantic roots attention has shifted to the ways in which this term is inflected by both politics and gender.   POT

INCHBALD, Elizabeth (1753–1821), actress, dramatist, novelist, critic. Born in Bury St Edmunds to a Roman Catholic farming family as Elizabeth Simpson, she was first employed as an actress in 1772. With her husband, Joseph Inchbald, she spent several seasons in strolling companies touring Scotland and Yorkshire. In 1776 she began to write stage farces, and in 1777 the first sketch of a novel to be titled *A Simple Story*. Joseph Inchbald died suddenly in 1779.

She played with leading stars of *theatre [24] Sarah *Siddons and her brother, John Philip *Kemble, with whom she was said to be in love. In 1781–2 they acted together in Dublin, and the sexual sparring of the romantic leads in Restoration comedy features in *A Simple Story* with the added father–daughter sadism of the *Gothic novel. Back in London she read widely, translated from the French and German, cultivated literary acquaintants, and carefully studied the market and her audience. In 1784 her farce *The Mogul Tale* began a playwriting career that lasted twenty-one years, her final comedy, *To Marry, or Not to Marry*, opening at Covent Garden in 1805.

On retiring from acting in 1789, she had recommenced work on *A Simple Story*, combining the father–daughter romance of Lady Matilda and Lord Elmwood and the courtship comedy of Miss Milner and Dorriforth. As an established dramatist but tyro novelist, she sought advice from her colleague at Covent Garden, Thomas *Holcroft, and from William *Godwin. In *A Simple Story* (1791) the spoiled priest Dorriforth, later Lord Elmwood, remodels the St Preux character of *Rousseau, while Rousseau's two heroines are anglicized in Miss Milner the spirited heiress, and Matilda the neglected daughter of Lord Elmwood. Dorriforth was widely believed to represent Kemble, who had been educated for the priesthood; Miss Milner (the character has no first name) is a paler version of Congreve's Millamant. A second novel, *Nature and Art* (1796), based on the Faust and Marguerite tale of a seduced girl forced into crime, was less successful, and was followed by a theatre piece, a translation of Kotzebue's *Lovers' Vows* (1798), the play rehearsed by the amateur coterie in Jane *Austen's *Mansfield Park* (1814).

In the biographical and critical prefaces she wrote on commission for her collection of *British Theatre* (25 vols., 1808), Inchbald uses the prefaces to her own plays to establish vital liaisons of writing, performing, censoring, and producing the feminine self. George *Colman the younger publicly ridiculed these prefaces for lapses in trivial matters of fact and for the original presumption of female publication. Inchbald replied with a spirited defence of her critical practice which exposed the gender bias of his attack. She continued to receive well-paid commissions from the *Edinburgh Review*, and compiled a *Collection of Farces* (1809) and a second anthology, *The Modern Theatre* (1811), which included plays by Sophia and Harriet *Lee.

In later life Inchbald became increasingly reclusive, straitlaced, and devout; she died in a Roman Catholic hospice for women in Kensington, London. She maintained her friendships with *women [4] writers and the Kemble–Siddons circle to the end. She had lived frugally, and invested her earnings, and her will contained many bequests to poor relations and charities. The manuscript of her *Memoirs* was burnt under the provisions of her will, reportedly drawn up on the orders of her priest. This is a real loss, and James Boaden's *Memoirs of Mrs Inchbald* (1833), a prudish and pedestrian account, is no compensation.   JB

income tax was introduced by William *Pitt in 1798–9 to boost annual revenue to a level capable of meeting the exigencies of wartime expenditure. The tax was proposed to meet the expectations of the public credit within an overall policy of debt redemption, while the country borrowed millions to fund the *war [2]. It was also designed to offset the effects of fraud practised on the assessed tax system.

Pitt sought to levy a tax of two shillings in the pound on all annual incomes of £200 or more. People earning between £60 and £200 were to be taxed on a graduated scale. The system was based on self-assessment sworn on oath. Crown commissioners were empowered to investigate anyone unprepared to make an assessment voluntarily.

Some MPs were implacable in their opposition to this tax. Pointed comparisons were made with French taxation practices under the Directory. In the end, however, the measures were passed because the government made appeals to *patriotism.

By 1815, the income tax provided £14,000,000 of revenue. In peacetime, the clamour for an easing of the tax burden could not be met with patriotic appeals. The Commons rejected the *Liverpool government's proposal for its continuation. The change marked a move away from debt redemption to tax remission, putting revenue pressure back squarely on taxes on consumption. These became the target of a postwar radical movement keen to enlarge its constituency by appealing to those who felt aggrieved at having to pay tax on basic items of consumption such as tea and coffee.   JF

Indian music. A brief but intense vogue for Indian music among the British residents of Calcutta was characterized by the performance of 'Hindostanie' airs at *concert parties, the commissioning of paintings of Indian musicians, and the quasi-scientific investigation of Indian instruments. The fashion, which reached a peak during the governorship of Warren *Hastings, represents the first serious attempt by the British to come to terms with indigenous musical cultures in their eastern *empire [5].

The interest in Indian music which swept through Calcutta society in the 1780s had its origins in the cult of the *picturesque, the most striking musical manifestation of which was the vogue for 'national' airs, popularized by collectors such as Edward *Jones, Edward *Bunting, George *Thomson, and Thomas *Moore. That airs could in some sense express national identity went without question; that airs when arranged as parlour pieces for pianoforte lost much of their local flavour went without comment. Scottish and Irish airs in particular were published in large numbers, but interest was growing in musical cultures from further afield. Following the expansion of the *East India Company's interests in the second half of the eighteenth century, the rich musical cultures of India started to come to the attention of the substantial British population of Bengal, closely related to the arrival in India of significant numbers of middle-class women. Until mid-century few Englishwomen travelled out to India; but from the 1770s many career civil servants and officers of the Indian Army brought their wives and daughters with them, leading to the development of a vigorous expatriate culture. By the 1780s Calcutta, like most provincial British cities, could boast an annual subscription series, benefit concerts, and *Handel oratorio performances. Fashionable music from London poured into the colony on the Company's ships. Among the most enthusiastic amateur musicians of this generation of Calcutta residents were Sophia Plowden (a singer) and Margaret Fowke (a pianoforte player), both of whom played an important part in promoting the fashion for 'Hindostanie' airs.

Although Calcutta was the stage on which Indian airs were presented to fashionable Anglo-Indian

Within the image:
POOR Mr BULL IN A PRETTY SITUATION — *For the Rain it Raineth everyday*

RAINING · CATS · DOGS · & · PITCHFORKS with the PRONGS DOWNWARD
It must be the fault of the Weather — for when it rains · it rains Taxes · & when it shines · it shines Taxes —
Pub. March 20 1830 by T. McLean 26 Haymarket London

78. This 1830 print of a beleaguered John Bull by engraver William Heath formed part of the radical attack on burdensome indirect and income taxes in the early nineteenth century.

society, the city, a recognizably British creation, was of little use to collectors. To experience truly 'authentic' Indian music—authenticity was an important objective of the picturesque movement—a visit to the interior was deemed essential. There was an ideal location—the Kingdom of Oudh, where the East India Company had already assumed administrative control. Contacts between the nawab Asuf-ud-daulah and the British resident were frequent. The Indian ruler listened to harpsichord music, while the British party experienced the exotic delights of cock-fighting, tiger-hunting, and the Indian dancing of the nautch groups. At this period, any reputation that nautch dancers had as courtesans was overshadowed by their status as fashionable artists. In the British cantonments at Lucknow, Benares, and Cawnpore, leading nautch singers, notably a Kashmiri woman known as Khanam, enjoyed a remarkable following. Indian musicians regularly sat for artists such as *Zoffany, and musical miniatures were highly prized by English collectors. Khanam and other 'star' nautch performers regularly visited English homes to enable songs to be transcribed. Once the desired melodies had been notated in a form comprehensible to Europeans, they were performed at fashionable concert parties. Plowden described a masquerade at Calcutta at which she and a few friends wore Indian dress, played some simple tunes on Indian instruments, and presented themselves to the assembled company as a nautch group. Much attention was devoted to getting the costumes and accessories right, and on this occasion the British performers smoked hookahs and chewed betel.

Given the fundamentally different rhythmic and melodic systems of Indian music, any attempt to produce a version of an Indian tune for a European instrument such as a pianoforte was doomed to fail. Quite apart from the technical impossibility of such a transfer, the problem was to reconcile the conflicting demands of Indian authenticity with those of European taste. In practice, when faced with the 'wildness' of Indian music, European arrangers tended to remove it. William Hamilton Bird, author of the first published collection of Indian airs, *The Oriental Miscellany* (1789), described Indian music as 'wild' but 'pleasing when understood', in other words, when arranged in an appropriate European idiom. In the preface to *Indian Melodies* (1813) Charles Edward Horn, notwithstanding his strong conviction that 'the Music of Hindostan was of a value far beyond that which had been affixed to it by the report of Europeans in general', excused his transformation of the 'wild and sometimes intricate' airs with which he had been presented, on the grounds that they must have been garbled in the process of transmission by 'some unskilful hand'. The necessarily Eurocentric approach adopted by transcribers is paralleled in quasi-scientific accounts of Indian instruments which begin to appear about this time. Francis Fowke, whose competent account of the Indian *vina* was published by the Asiatick Society of Bengal, had to ask his informant, an eminent Indian musician, to tune his instrument to a harpsichord in order to describe it. Hastings was presented with an affidavit, signed by several Englishmen, which describes the results of their investigation into the circular breathing techniques of a flute player from Bhutan. The musician was asked to demonstrate on a French horn, while a feather was held under his nose to establish the direction of his breath.

By the early nineteenth century the fashion for Indian music among the inhabitants of Calcutta had declined sharply, and attitudes to Indian culture in general were becoming steadily more dismissive. In London, however, 'Hindostanie' airs were still published, both in popular collections such those by Bird and Horn and in large scholarly compilations such as Edward Jones's *Lyric Airs* (1804) and William *Crotch's *Specimens of Various Styles* (1808–15). To a public increasingly aware of India, these collections seemed to represent something of the exotic lure of the *Orient. It was a spurious claim. Later versions of 'Hindostanie' airs, arranged as *glees, part songs, or operatic numbers, usually contain few traces of the Indian originals, and it was but a short step to the wholly counterfeit Indian melodies of the late nineteenth century. Also lost from view was the important contribution made by women such as Plowden and Fowke to the development of the genre.   IW

indigenous peoples and theories of race. During the course of the seventeenth and eighteenth centuries, colonial *exploration [37] changed profoundly the lives of hunter-gatherer peoples and small-scale garden agriculturists in America, Africa, and the Pacific. Explorers, traders, and settlers unwittingly introduced diseases to which such peoples had little or no immunity. Where colonies based on cash-crop agriculture and pastoralism were established, competition for water and the depletion of native fauna led frequently to conflict and war. European weaponry and personnel came to be employed in long-standing indigenous conflicts, often with disastrous consequences. Where communities survived the ravages of disease and colonialist designs on their lands, they could not avoid becoming entangled in modes of trade and exchange which greatly altered the fabric of traditional life.

By the early nineteenth century the display of indigenous people at circuses, *fairs, and scientific *lectures was a frequent and popular form of entertainment. Yet the 'savages' displayed for the edification and amusement of metropolitan crowds were often women and men who had previously been skilled workers in the colonial economy.

The fate of indigenous societies was generally understood by the British in providentialist terms. Disease, warfare, and famine were taken as signs that 'savage' life was destined to be supplanted by Christian civilization with its superior agrarian regimes and manufacturing technologies. However, in representing the demise of indigenous ways of life as realization of the divine will, colonialist discourses generally reaffirmed the scriptural vision of humanity as sharing a common ancestry.

Theories of race generally took the form of

conjectural histories in which the survivors of the deluge recorded in Genesis were represented as gradually forming distinct tribes reliant upon pastoralism. In time, some peoples were forced to seek new grazing lands, with the result that they migrated far beyond the lands of Shinar. Some adopted agriculture; others eventually found themselves in country so inhospitable as to force them to abandon pastoralism for hunting and gathering. The savage 'life of the chase' had left these peoples neither time nor resources to preserve other than the barest rudiments of civilization and true religion.

Until the last third of the eighteenth century, physical and customary differences amongst the 'tribes' or 'races' of humanity were explained in environmentalist terms. Climate, food, life-ways, and disease were variously assumed to have changed 'bodily constitution, stature, and colour', to the extent that over time some peoples had become distinct 'nations' or 'races'. From the 1760s, however, the extent and origins of human difference came to be reappraised in metropolitan scientific circles in the light of new theories of human physiology and reproduction. The sites of reappraisal were the university medical faculties—particularly in Scotland—and the growing number of extramural anatomy schools and medical societies patronized by the middle classes [see *medicine, 18].

By the early nineteenth century there had emerged a new anthropology grounded in contemporary anatomical and physiological investigations of the circulatory and reproductive systems. It conceptualized the human body as a complex economy of interdependent structures, all of which were sustained and regulated by a vital principle, or life force, possibly destined to remain forever beyond empirical detection. This vital principle not only governed the bodily economy but was in turn susceptible to modification as bodily structures were altered by nutrition, climate, or other environmental forces. Modifications were transmitted to offspring, so that over the course of several generations, structures within an individual could come to differ markedly from those of their ancestors. Thus heads, for example, could be influenced by common modes of life or cultural practices, so that over time particular nations could come to exhibit a common shape of skull.

From the end of the eighteenth century until Darwinistic modes of thought revolutionized anthropological discourse from the early 1860s, explanations of racial difference in terms of environmental modification of human physiology and intellect commanded the assent of most educated Britons in the metropolis and the colonies. The most influential environmentalist writings were the encyclopedic and overtly Christian works of Bristol physician James Cowles Prichard (1786–1840). For many, the modifications to the 'vital department' experienced by Britons appeared to have so strengthened their 'animal department' as to render them destined by interbreeding to supplant all other varieties of the human race. As the Norwich physician John Greene Crosse (1790–1850) bluntly concluded in 1817, 'the white

man, in virtue of his superiority in all corporeal and mental powers, is lord of the world'. However, not all authorities who embraced environmentalism were so optimistic. For if the factors such as nutrition and climate were indeed responsible for the physiological and intellectual inferiorities of indigenous people, what guarantee was there that settler communities would escape a similar fate?

Monogenist environmentalism never enjoyed universal assent in our period. From the mid-decades of the eighteenth century various theories circulated in which physical and mental differences amongst the peoples of the earth were represented as the immutable legacies of separate creations. These 'polygenist' theories gained a favourable reception in the British sugar colonies of the Caribbean, and in the pro-*slavery [6] American states. They also found a receptive metropolitan audience amongst critics of colonialism, who argued that Europeans were physiologically incapable of withstanding the rigours of life in the tropics.

From the late 1820s key elements of the transmutationist biology of Jean-Baptiste Lamarck (1744–1829) and Geoffroy Saint-Hilaire (1772–1844) also came to inform discourse on the extent and origin of human racial characteristics. These theorists conceptualized matter as generating and co-ordinating life through a process in which organisms metamorphosed into increasingly sophisticated forms. Humanity came to be represented as having ascended from a less sophisticated ancestor, who in turn had ascended from a lower animate form, and so on. Physical and intellectual differences became apparent as races or nations realized full expression of what appeared to be their predetermined potential for bodily and mental sophistication.

Irrespective of whether racial difference was conceptualized as resulting from environmental modification, separate creation, or gradual transmutation, there was broad agreement that the extent and origins of racial difference were explicable only so far as careful observation of the current state, or recent history, of the earth's peoples allowed the establishment of indisputable fact. For those who favoured polygenist theories, it was important to trace the supposed lines of distinction between the various races, and then describe the principal characteristics of a race. Environmentalists and transmutationists sought to substantiate beyond question the differences which had emerged between the principal nations or races of humanity as they had developed, and then perhaps reconstruct something of the history and pace of change through which the natural history of man had become a story of gradual diversity.

Universal endorsement of the primacy of close empirical scrutiny of the bodily differences of indigenous peoples understandably made anthropological inquiry an attractive field for teachers of anatomy and their pupils, many of whom intended careers as naval and military surgeons in the colonial sphere [see *empire, 5]. It privileged the anatomically trained eye over that of travellers in earlier generations. It also rendered the bones and soft tissue of indigenous people objects of immense scientific value, and led to widespread desecration of burial places and trafficking in bodily remains.

For the indigenous peoples of what were once British settler colonies, the knowledge that remains continue to be preserved as specimens in metropolitan scientific institutions is often a source of great anguish.   PT

insurrection. The question of why Britain did not experience *revolution [1] in the age of revolutions still troubles modern historiography. Though few historians would now subscribe to Élie Halévy's proposition that revolution was somehow avoided through the strength of the conservative force of *Methodism among the poorer strata of society, most still underestimate the revolutionary potential represented by proposals for the reform of the late-eighteenth-century state on democratic principles [see *democracy, 3]. The implications of the restructuring of parliamentary constituencies so that each contained roughly equal numbers of electors, combined with the creation of manhood suffrage, were revolutionary. Other issues raised by advanced thinkers and writers, including the fiscally driven redistribution of wealth proposed by Thomas *Paine, and the *land [16] nationalization propaganda of Thomas *Spence, also had far-reaching ramifications. Given the revolutionary implications of this democratic political ideology, the state's repressive response to the birth of the first popular movement for political reform in the 1790s should cause little surprise. Insurrectionary movements developed partially in response.

However, the context created by other significant features of the 1790s was also crucial. This included not only *French revolutionary political ideology—liberty, fraternity, and equality—but most significantly the apparent foreign policy of the revolutionary French. The 1792 promise that the oppressed peoples labouring under the yoke of European *ancien régimes* were to be liberated, through the imposition of democracies by force of French arms, was paramount. It had two fold significance by 1793 when Britain became the paymaster of the allied *ancien régimes'* forces against the French. First, many of the ambitious popular organizations for political reform openly demonstrated their Francophilia and attacked the war, even if this proved divisive [see *corresponding societies]. Secondly, their Irish counterparts, the United Irishmen, not only developed a parallel reform programme but, once they experienced severe repression, also became nationalist and entered into negotiations for French aid to achieve independence forcibly [see *United societies].

The short period from 1794 to 1797 proved seminal, especially because of threats of *invasion by France of either Ireland, strategically and militarily the weakest link in Britain's defence, and/or Britain, where the French were perceived by some as potential liberators. In Ireland, hopes of *Catholic emancipation—which might have headed off militant nationalism—were dashed in 1795 with the recall of Lord Lieutenant Fitzwilliam, who had stoked anticipations of emancipation despite his short tenure of office. His departure stimulated resort to arms, which inevitably fostered sectarian conflict, and by 1796–7 parts of the country were gripped by civil war as the United Irishmen and their allies, notably the Catholic Secret Society of Defenders, organized their underground army. In Britain, the passage of the *gagging acts of 1795 served to drive popular politics underground, and a distinct minority of activists into revolutionary plotting, arming, and drilling. This meant that English, Scottish, and Irish radicals saw a common enemy in *Pitt's government, and perceived a common liberator in the French.

Some form of alliance between these diverse groups seems to have eventually materialized in 1797. The Irish, in particular, enjoyed large-scale support, in addition to their diplomatic relationships with ministers in the French government. The actions of Irish authorities in sending thousands of suspects to serve in the British navy also gave nationalists opportunities to organize to undermine the fleet. Here they met disaffected British sailors, some of whom had been involved in popular politics or driven into the navy by poverty. The notorious *naval mutinies of 1797 revealed both elements, who survived their belated suppression, and the heavy punishments meted out after the second mutiny at the Nore. The Irish seem to have been principally concerned with sabotaging their ships in the event of engaging a French invasion force, while the British primarily aimed to strike in order to force a peace and improve conditions of service. From 1797, the total reliability of the navy could never be taken for granted.

After the mutinies, Ireland became the principal insurrectionary theatre, with the main aim of a rising either in support of a French invasion or to encourage French intervention once a rising started. The strategy of their British counterparts, known as the United Englishmen and the United Scotsmen (or sometimes the United Britons), was to rise in support of an Irish insurrection and to tie down the British army on the mainland, thus preventing—or at least compromising—reinforcements being despatched to Ireland. Provincial groupings were to attack Pitt's new barracks, erected in many towns, while conspirators in London were to paralyse the government. But all these subversive organizations were penetrated by informers. Secret intelligence played some part in ensuring the chaotic and ill-timed Irish rising of May 1798, as well as the arrest of leaders in British centres of strength, notably in Lancashire and especially in London. British groupings were thus paralysed at the critical moment when insurrection intensified in Ireland. However, engagement with the French invader never materialized, and the rising in Ireland was effectively contained by the time a French expeditionary force reached shore in the far west.

Military repression, the trial, execution, imprisonment, and exile of United Irish leaders and others, together with a ferocious sectarianism unleashed by the insurrection, seriously compromised the United Irish capacity to reorganize. French allies had also proved both diplomatically and militarily untrustworthy. Yet Ireland retained its explosive potential, especially since the situation across Britain worsened dramatically with the devastating *famine of 1799–1801, which eventually produced a very broad-based war-weariness and disaffection. Famine conditions stimulated some resurgence of insurrectionary plotting, in which British groupings appear to have been much more vigorous than their erstwhile Irish allies. Intelligence sources on the United Englishmen show links between London and the provinces, though there is less evidence about Scottish developments. In England the United Englishmen had several strongholds principally, but not exclusively, in midland and northern industrial regions and the towns. A joint British–Irish head committee convened in London, and in 1801 was principally concerned to ensure that socio-economic conditions did not spark a premature *jacquerie*, in increasing expectation that a French invasion force would arrive on the mainland.

Ironically, the ephemeral Peace of *Amiens embraced 1802, the year the so-called Despard plot was exposed. In essence, Edward Marcus Despard (1751–1803)—an Irishman and ex-colonel in the British army—planned to commence a revolution by assassinating the King during the state procession to open parliament, seize key government institutions, including the Tower and the Bank of England, and take control of London. His forces included ten-cell units of armed men, plus similar groupings in sectors of the army, including guards regiments. Despard was also in touch with the French government, and his strategy was linked with *Napoleon's intention to restart the war. However, Despard's organization was penetrated by informants who facilitated a pre-emptive strike, followed by treason trials, and the execution of Despard and six co-conspirators. When Napoleon declared war in May 1803, he assembled a massive invasion force on the Channel coasts, though it never sailed.

Subsequent revolutionary plotting and insurrectionary conspiracies include the shadowy organizations which appear to have played some role in the intense midland and northern *Luddite explosion of 1811–13, in which earlier metropolitan/provincial linkages recurred. These were used by the notorious government agent 'Oliver the Spy' (W. J. Richards), not only instrumental in giving the Home Office critical intelligence about the maintenance of insurrectionary plotting during the economically depressed immediate postwar years, but possibly also an *agent provocateur* responsible for the premature Pentridge rising of 1817 in the midlands [see *spies]. This failure did not terminate physical-force politics. Metropolitan activists included the celebrated Cato Street conspirators of 1820, whose strategy seems to have echoed Despard's, except that their target comprised the members of the Cabinet, whom they hoped to assassinate. Once again London Irish revolutionaries were to be involved, along with *Spencean groups in the metropolis, and the conspirators maintained provincial links. Penetration by informers ensured their failure, and the subsequent execution of five leaders. The Scottish Bonnymuir rising of 1820, which saw supportive thrusts in at least two west Yorkshire locations, appears to have been a badly organized, and equally poorly timed, attempt to reverse the standard strategy, with provincial risings followed by insurrection in the capital.

It is easy to belittle this entire tradition, despite its recrudescence in *Chartist times, on any number of grounds. Only a minority from within a minority of politicized working people were involved, and few—except in Ireland—came from more elevated social ranks, from which it might be argued leaders would have to be drawn if such enterprises stood any chance of success. Yet minorities make revolutions, and there can be no disputing that war, poverty, and hatred of the state did at critical moments generate great volatility among strategically powerful working-class communities.   RW

invasions and invasion scares. In the late eighteenth century, during *wars [2] with France, there were a number of occasions when French invasion of Britain was a serious threat—1778, 1796–8, and 1803. Governments responded by assembling military forces (usually in the south of England), by recruiting *volunteers, and by defensive measures such as the building of Martello towers to protect the vulnerable coastline. These consisted of circular, 30-ft reinforced towers built on salient points and armed with swivel guns or howitzers. Actual invasion attempts by the French took place in Ireland in 1796 and 1798, and in Wales in 1797 [see *United societies]. While they were unsuccessful, they had an important psychological impact on the populace. Unidentified ships off the coast, fear of spies, the presence of foreigners, the large numbers of French prisoners of war on English soil, and poor communications all allowed the climate of fear to intensify. Many of those on the peripheries previously untouched by or indifferent to the war flocked to join the volunteers in these years. The invasion scare of 1796–8 also produced a financial crisis. A run on the country banks as people sought to realize cash for the impending chaos led to the suspension of cash payments by the Bank of England, a 'temporary' measure which lasted until 1821.

Long-established Francophobia meant that there was a ready audience for the squibs, caricatures, handbills, broadsheets, and song-bills that were produced in unprecedented numbers around the invasion scare of 1803 [see *prints, 22]. Representing the French as bloodthirsty marauders, such *street literature heightened the atmosphere of panic and contributed to the counter-revolution within Britain. The heroic figures of invasion propaganda—John Bull, Jack Tar, the volunteer—temporarily united the country, the real possibility of French attack from without proving a better social and national glue than any perceived commonality within. Even after the threat subsided, folk memories of invasion fears persisted.   JF

IRELAND, William Henry (1777–1835), literary hack and notorious forger of *Shakespeare. The illegitimate son of Samuel Ireland (d. 1800), a self-made engraver, antiquarian, and book collector, young Ireland was well educated at private schools in London and France. Inheriting his father's enthusiasm for literary antiquities, especially the works of *Percy and *Grose, and the Romantic story of young forger-poet *Chatterton, William began using old parchments acquired while working in a law office to forge documents, letters, and even whole plays supposed to have been composed by Shakespeare [see *antiquarianism, 35]. In so doing both Ireland father and son found themselves at the centre of a political struggle between scholars of liberal leanings, who wished to construct Britain's pre-eminent cultural icon as a radical people's bard and those, led by the scholarly critic and editor Edmond *Malone, who wished to cast Shakespeare as a pro-monarchical and Burkean conservative. Although Ireland's forgeries gained widespread early acceptance, gradually Malone's superior claims to critical authenticity prevailed. Ireland's bogus play *Vortigern*, supported by an epilogue from the radical poet Robert *Merry, was actually performed at Drury Lane on 2 April 1796 with John Philip *Kemble in the lead role, but it was already a subject of widespread satire, and both performers and audience treated it with ridicule.

Disgraced, William Ireland spent the remainder of his career working in Britain, Ireland, and France as a literary hack and journalist, composing a plethora of antiquarian mimicries, *romances, and juvenalian political satires. One of his last publications, *Scribblomania* (1815), was a lively *Dunciad*-style satirical typology of current popular literary culture, which deliberately inverted the *loyalist tendencies of T. J. *Mathias's *Pursuits of Literature* (1795). IMcC

Irish cultural revival, a diverse and politicized intellectual movement to recover, or sometimes invent, ancient Gaelic civilization and culture; it paved the way for Irish Romanticism and for a new hybrid sense of Irish nationality.

Although the fashionable *antiquarian [35] cultural revivals elsewhere in eighteenth-century Europe usually possessed a political dimension, nowhere was this as overt as in Ireland, where Gaelic scholarship sometimes anticipated, displaced, or shaped public discourse. Within our period two broad phases may be distinguished: a 'Patriot' cultural revival of the 1770s and 1780s, when Anglo-Irish and Catholic historians, linguists, antiquarians, and poets showed a tendency towards intellectual convergence; and a polarized phase from the 1790s to the 1830s, during which Gaelic revivalism resumed a more typically sectarian form.

By the 1770s the long shadow of the penal laws was beginning to recede. Eighty years of peace, combined with the spread of *Enlightenment [32] and *American revolutionary ideals, had begun to soften Ascendancy (the Anglo-Irish ruling-class) attitudes towards supposed Catholic peasant savagery. Politically, this inaugurated a tolerant phase where many Protestant landlords and parliamentarians espoused a patriotic identification with the land of Ireland, a brand of meliorative Whig-liberal paternalism towards the majority of Catholic inhabitants, and a keen interest in recovering Ireland's ancient Gaelic culture and history. For the Anglo-Irish, this ancient civilization offered a pre-British, and sometimes pre-Christian, source of cultural identity with the country they began to call Erin. A vogue for the harp music of the bard Carolan, and the holding of several harp festivals in the 1780s, was one such patriotic manifestation. Catholic scholars, however, found in Gaelic culture and history a means of countering Protestant condescension and of asserting claims to political citizenship. Charles O'Conor (1710–91) and Dr John Curry (d. 1780), for example, began to produce histories defending the role of Catholics in the Ulster Rebellion of 1641, managing to influence even bitter Protestant historians like Walter Harris (1686–1761) to adopt more consensual interpretations of this controversial event.

A further impetus for Irish scholarly convergence derived from widespread anger at James Macpherson's appropriation of the *Ossian legends for Scotland. From the late 1760s such unlikely allies as John O'Brien, Bishop of Cloyne (d. 1767), and Sylvester O'Halloran (1728–1807), a fiery young Catholic intellectual, issued strong claims for the authentic and antecedent third-century Irish bardic legends of Oisín, son of Fionn mac Cumhaill. Oisín, like Ossian, was presented as an original genius, steeped in primitive, natural values of bravery, *sublimity, and melancholy. Under the urging of the Protestant antiquarians, the brilliant but reclusive Charlotte *Brooke was also persuaded to provide some translations of early bardic poems for Joseph Walker's *Historical Memoirs of the Irish Bards* (1785), which she followed up with her own much more influential *Reliques of Irish Poetry* (1789). This sense of participating in a common cultural mission also stimulated scholarly co-operation in a series of antiquarian societies. Here the enthusiastic, if often erroneous, Gaelicist Charles Vallencey (1721–1812) led the way. Vallencey, the son of a Hugenot Irish army officer, not only published pioneering philological works such as his *Grammar of the Iberno-Celtic or Irish Language* (1773) and the antiquarian periodical *Collectanea de Rebus Hibernicus*, but also in 1779 helped found the Select Committee of the Dublin Society, which soon evolved into the Royal Irish Academy (1782).

By the beginning of the 1790s, however, there were signs that this ecumenical spirit was beginning to break down. Anglo-Irish from all walks of life were increasingly alarmed at the growth of Catholic assertiveness—manifested in land struggles, in sectarian warfare around the border counties of the North, and in the winning of franchise concessions from Westminster. Evidence of renewed tension surfaced with the publication in 1790 of the *Antiquities of Ireland* by the distinguished Protestant historian Revd Edward Ledwich (1738–1823). By reasserting a traditional hard-line interpretation of the Catholic role in the Ulster Rebellion and by attacking the Romanticism of Gaelic scholarship, Ledwich signalled his suspicion that men like O'Conor were making cultural revival a handmaiden of Catholic Committee political radicalism. With the terrible watershed of the 1798 *Rebellion, mutual suspicion flared into a new era of scholarly sectarianism. This was compounded by the *Act of Union of 1801 which, in an effort to halt the spread of *French revolutionary principles, established Ireland formally as a metropolitan colony of Britain. For the next three to four decades Anglo-Irish studies tended to attribute the rebellions of 1641 and 1798 to a common popish atavism and to display a profound ambivalence over the character and implications of early Gaelic culture. James Hardiman (?1790–1855) typified a new, militant generation of Catholic scholars and antiquarians with his *Irish Minstrelsy* (1831), which blamed historical atrocities and cultural degeneration on the British.

The flowering of the Irish *novel [31] in this period through the writings of Anglo-Irish liberals and Whigs like Sydney *Owenson (Lady Morgan) and Maria *Edgeworth, or Tories like Charles *Maturin, showed a common tendency to romanticize Irish landscape and aspects of Gaelic culture, yet also to criticize peasant barbarity and irresponsible Catholic antiquarianism. Against a background of endemic agrarian outrage, the pro-Catholic, Gaelic-inspired poetry, songs, and histories of Thomas *Moore, and the regional novels of William *Carleton and Gerald *Griffin, warned of the growing lawlessness and alienation of the peasantry for which they blamed absentee landlords and corrupt British administrators. As Ascendancy confidence ebbed still further with the successes of Daniel *O'Connell's mass politicization of the peasantry and the winning of *Catholic emancipation in 1829, Anglo-Irish intellectuals found themselves increas-ingly reliant on identification with ancient Gaelic culture as a means of justifying their social and economic dominance.

Ironically, it was thus the Anglo-Irish who most championed the preservation and revival of the Irish *language [40]. By the early nineteenth century, Catholic peasants were rapidly abandoning their native tongue because of its association with poverty and Protestant proselytizing, and because of the powerful appeal of English as a language of administration, business, and political agitation. Studies in Irish philology were centred mainly at the Ascendancy-dominated university, Trinity College, Dublin. In the 1830s and 1840s an Anglo-Irish graduate of this institution, Thomas Davis (1814–45) also elaborated a fully Romantic defence of the Irish language as a source of communal consciousness and wild, natural lyricism, as well as a bastion against arid English rationalism. After his death in 1845, Davis's Young Ireland movement fostered a brand of Romantic cultural nationalism which was to culminate in an abortive attempted revolution in 1848. Significantly, Davis's university rival, an Ulster Scottish and Tory lawyer, Samuel Ferguson (1810–86), eschewed his republicanism but endorsed his commitment to Gaelic cultural revival. In 1834 Ferguson published a series of influential articles in the *Dublin University Magazine* which called on wealthy and intelligent Protestants to acknowledge the ancient genius and sensibility of Catholics by helping to revive Gaelic scholarship and culture. Only thus, he argued, could the Anglo-Irish lead Ireland into becoming a moderate, modern, and culturally hybrid political state.   IMcC

Irish Rebellion, see *Rebellion of 1798.

J

Jacobin novel, the term often used to describe the fiction written in the service of social and political reform during the 1790s and early 1800s by novelists such as Robert *Bage, William *Godwin, Mary *Hays, Thomas *Holcroft, and Elizabeth *Inchbald. Although several of the novelists had produced fiction before the *French Revolution, anti-Jacobin writers habitually represented them as subverting church and state in the interests of French republicanism and atheism; but, if a single issue could be said to unite this diverse collection of novels, it would be their interest in the relationship between individuals and their social environment.

The first of the group to publish an explicitly revolutionary novel was Thomas Holcroft with *Anna St Ives* (1792), quickly followed by *The Adventures of Hugh Trevor* (1794–7). His friend William Godwin responded with *Caleb Williams* in 1794. Other Jacobin novels of the period include Inchbald's *Nature and Art* (1796) and Bage's *Hermsprong* (1796). Most of the plots involve an innocent individual pursued and often imprisoned by an unjust social system. Godwin and Inchbald presented memorable scenes in which a person speaks out at a trial against tyranny and in favour of the individual's right to liberty.

The strong sense of the individual trapped by an unjust society suggests the influence of *Rousseau, but nearly all these novels are critical of sentimentalism and show little of the interest in psychological processes found in the novel of *sensibility [11] of the preceding decades. The advocacy of reason and restraint seems indicative of the middle-class, Dissenting backgrounds from which most of these novelists came. Women in particular are shown as likely to be duped and ensnared by their emotions, but several of the Jacobin novels do also contain some kind of picture of the practical woman, emancipated from her passions by reason. Holcroft declared that the purpose of *Anna St Ives* was 'to teach fortitude to females', and a similar intention can be found, for instance, in Hays's *Memoirs of Emma Courtney* (1796).   JM

JEBB, John (1736–86), university don, doctor, Dissenting reformer, and political thinker. Jebb was the eldest son of John Jebb, Dean of Cashel. Before he entered Trinity College, Dublin, in July 1753, Jebb junior had attended no fewer than seven schools in England and Ireland. He moved to Peterhouse, Cambridge, in the following November, graduating in 1757. He remained in Cambridge, as a private tutor, proceeded to his MA, and was admitted a Fellow of Peterhouse in 1761. Ordained in 1762 (deacon), he was presented to a university living, the rectory of Ovington, in 1764. He became a university lecturer in mathematics and in November 1768 began to lecture on the Greek Testament. He soon became a controversial figure; in 1770 the university, fearful of his heterodoxy, banned all students from attending his lectures. He responded characteristically by publishing them. With a growing reputation as a reformer, Jebb became closely involved in the movement for the abolition of clerical subscription to the thirty-nine articles and of lay subscription in the universities. The campaign culminated in the unsuccessful Feathers Tavern Petition to the House of Commons in 1772 and again in 1774. A minor victory was achieved in that Cambridge abolished the subscription requirement for Bachelor of Arts in June 1772. Jebb, however, was defeated in his attempt to reform the university by the introduction of annual public examinations for all undergraduates.

Jebb also supported the American colonies in their dispute with Britain [see *American Revolution]. By the time he resigned his livings on conscientious grounds in 1775 and given up his fellowship, he had achieved prominence as a reformer. He now took the opportunity to change his career entirely, and to pursue one which would allow his political concerns a free rein. Having trained to become a medical doctor, he entered practice in 1778. In 1779, he was elected a Fellow of the Royal Society. Before his premature death in 1786, Jebb was exceptionally active in a variety of reform movements. He was a founder member of the *Society for Constitutional Information and was one of the first advocates of universal male suffrage. He thus helped to set the agenda for radical reform up to and including the *Chartists, foreshadowing the Charter itself. The SCI agenda was exclusively masculine, though Jebb himself believed that women should be equal before the law. Indeed, after his death his wife, Ann (1753–1812), kept in touch with political and religious radicals; she

wrote articles and pamphlets and proved to be a campaigner in her own right.

In the 1780s, her husband's interests came to embrace *prison reform, while his early passion for religious reform never waned. He was a founder member of the Society for Promoting Knowledge of the Scriptures. His politics were a mixture of old Whig *republicanism and of the democratic *natural rights radicalism of the late eighteenth century. As a political tactician he was, like John *Cartwright, inflexible. In Jebb's case, his belief in the ultimate success of radical reform derived from an intertwining of religious and scientific convictions common amongst fellow Rational Dissenters. He was confident that truth would prevail, that the *Newtonian system provided 'the only rational demonstration of the deity', that revelation was another form of reason, and that *religion [10] should be considered as 'a science, which has for its proper object the cultivation of the human heart'.   MF

JEFFREY, Francis, or Lord Jeffrey (1773–1850). Scottish advocate and judge, editor, critic, effectively the founding editor of the leading *Whig periodical, the *Edinburgh Review*, and one of the most prolific contributors to any *review, Jeffrey encouraged in the Whig party a more popular politics, and helped to form a reading public characterized by a socially conscious mode of critical reading [see *prose, 30].

As a young man Jeffrey attended the universities of Glasgow and Edinburgh. A year at Oxford in between served to inspire his defence of Scottish *education [17] against the encroachments of Oxonian priorities mooted by the Royal Commission into the Scottish Universities of 1826 and 1830. The *Edinburgh Review*, which Jeffrey established with undergraduate enthusiasm along with Sydney *Smith, Francis Horner (1778–1817), and Henry *Brougham in 1802, was a child of the broad and critically inquiring Scottish educational system and of Edinburgh's agonistic *debating societies. Though Jeffrey reviewed in most areas, the bulk of his substantial contribution (15–40 per cent of each number) was in politics, philosophy, and original literature.

As an editor he was disorganized—often relying on contributors to tell him how much he owed them—but ideologically and stylistically scrupulous, often writing and editing at high speed into the early hours. Though Brougham, because he probably contributed more even than Jeffrey, seems to have been allowed to impose on him, the *Edinburgh* remained very much Jeffrey's own throughout the twenty-six years of his editorship (1803–29). During that time the *Edinburgh's* popularity and influence remained impressively consistent.

For Jeffrey, the associations of those he called 'the ordinary run of sensible, kind people' coincided to form a politico-legalistic *consensus gentium*. This mass coincidence of unconstrained particularities he identified, in accordance with Whiggism, as 'public opinion'—the opinion, that is, of the 'middling ranks' or 'classes' of society. From a paradoxical consensuality of unique responses, Jeffrey derived his authority on critical, ethical, and political issues. The 'affectation of singularity' in an author offered a perverse challenge to this consensual ideal. In order to counteract tendencies of originality which he interpreted as socially divisive, Jeffrey adopted a position sometimes extreme in *its* affectation—of confusion or lack of sympathy. His infamous attacks upon *Wordsworth and those he dubbed 'the Lake Poets' are illustrative of this tendency, with some defensible only as good business. Yet it is equally indefensible in modern scholars to recognize Jeffrey *only* as the author of those attacks.

Self-elected spokesman for what he referred to as the 'virtual aristocracy', Jeffrey had dedicated his *Review* to 'guiding' public opinion toward the reform he ultimately helped to engineer when in 1832, as Lord Advocate of Scotland, Jeffrey was responsible for the Scottish Reform Bill which increased the franchise to fourteen times its original size (from 4,500 to 65,000).   WC

Jews. Conventionally British Jews are thought to have exercised relatively little intellectual impact during this period both because of their overall poverty and their generally liberal treatment, a view which underestimates both the level of discrimination they encountered and the wider Jewish contribution to British social life and culture.

Partly because of worsening social and economic conditions in Europe, Britain experienced a substantial immigration of Jews between 1750 and 1815. Patrick *Colquhoun estimated around 20,000 living in London and 6,000 in the provinces at the end of the eighteenth century. These comprised a majority of poor Ashkenazim from Germany, Poland, and Holland, and a lesser proportion of slightly better-off Sephardim from Spain, Portugal, France, and Italy. Settling mainly in London's East End, Jews rapidly became associated with street trades such as peddling old clothes and with criminal activities such as swindling. The notorious fence 'Ikey' Solomons (1785–1850) is supposed to have been the inspiration for Fagin in *Dickens's *Oliver Twist*, and Jewish convert Manasseh Masseh Lopes (1755–1831), a parliamentarian from 1802 to 1829 who was also jailed for electoral corruption, is thought to have influenced Trollope's hostile portraits. Yet poverty also generated a more positive image through the Jewish contribution to pugilism. This period produced some thirty acclaimed Jewish boxers, including the renowned Dutch Sam (1775–1816) and the legendary champion Daniel Mendoza (1763–1836), who pioneered a scientific style of fighting. Because of their tough reputation, Jewish fighters were recruited to control rioting crowds during the Old Price theatre riots of 1809 [see *theatre, 24].

Lack of an education amongst British Jewry hampered the emergence of an enlightened Jewish literati comparable to that centred on Moses Mendelssohn in Berlin. In an essay on this subject of 1798 and in his novel *Vaurien* (1797), British-born Sephardi author Isaac *D'Israeli attacked local Jewish culture for its rigid and parochial character. German-born Solomon Hirschell, Chief Rabbi in Britain from 1802, complained conversely about the debased and secular character of Jewish worship at London's Great Synagogue in Duke's Place. Yet the metropolitan Jewish artisanate more than compensated for any intellectual hiatus in the world of polite letters. The Jewish hevrot, or study group, became one of the many conduits of London's vibrant artisan intellectual culture. Out of such milieux came engraver-pamphleteer Solomon Bennett (1761–1838); teacher and later Hebrew professor Hyman Hurwitz (1775–1844) whom *Coleridge called the Luther of Judaism; moneylender, banker, and radical pamphleteer Jonathan *King; and hatter-scholar David Levi (1742–1801), who in the 1780s wrote a series of learned tracts disputing *Priestley's views on Judaism, Christianity, and *prophecy.

Priestley's philosemitic advocacy in the 1780s of a mutual *Unitarian conversion of Jews and Christians in anticipation of the impending millennium illustrates one way in which Judaism exerted a disproportionate impact on Georgian culture during the revolutionary period. In the mid-seventeenth century radical Puritans had frequently identified with the biblical promise of restoring a suffering people to the literal or spiritual new Jerusalem. Resurgent strains of such radical restorationism can be seen in the apocalyptic prophecies of Richard *Brothers, the British Israelite theories of John Wroe (1782–1863), and the prophetic poetry of William *Blake. More conservative versions of philosemitism were manifested in the foundation in 1809 of the London Society for the Promotion of Christianity among the Jews, an *Evangelical missionary movement triggered by concern that *Napoleon would pre-empt British *millennial leadership through his wooing of European Jewry with promises of civil emancipation.

In Britain, non-Jewish liberals with philosemitic leanings generally proved more active in pursuing measures of Jewish emancipation than British Jews themselves. Though restricted from full political rights and from operating businesses within London, British Jewry faced few legal disabilities compared with their European counterparts. Many of the most wealthy Anglo-Jewish families such as the Gideons, Rothschilds, and Goldsmids, who all contributed major loans to finance the British *war [2] effort, showed themselves anxious through intermarriage, education, and charitable activities to assimilate into the landed and commercial élite. Yet public liberality did not necessarily lessen private discrimination. Anti-semitic *prints [22], *ballads, plays, pranks, and jokes indicate the persistence of substantial levels of prejudice, confirmed in the testimonies of even thoroughly anglicized and educated figures such as D'Israeli and David *Ricardo. William *Cobbett's pronounced antisemitism, for example, revealed a darker, xenonophobic strain within British radical populism. When, following the passage of *Catholic emancipation, wealthy public figures such as Isaac Lyon Goldsmid and Nathan Rothschild mounted a successful campaign for full emancipation in 1833 they were nevertheless disturbed at the level of prejudice aroused. However, at least one ancient anti-semitic theme, the legend of the Wandering Jew, underwent positive reformulation during this period. The pervasive medieval European myth of the Jew, Ahasuerus, cursed with agonized immortality through his ill-treatment of Christ, was transformed by poets such as *Shelley, *Byron, *Wordsworth, and Coleridge into an affirmative figure around which to explore Romantic conceptions of history, travel, *orientalism, occult science, and the alienated self.   IMcC

Johnson circle. Joseph *Johnson is now chiefly known for the circle of intellectuals that gathered around his bookshop and met at his home (and later in the *King's Bench prison) for supper. Often Johnson either published their books or recruited them as contributors to the *Analytical Review*. The circle became a crucial centre of the *Enlightenment [32] in England and in the 1790s was a focus of radical and reformist opinion, though Johnson played host to intellectuals drawn from across the spectrum of political opinion, publishing most of the replies to *Burke's *Reflections on the Revolution in France* (1790). However, political tensions broke up the group later in the decade [see *publishing, 21].

The Johnson circle comprised those London friends whom Johnson saw regularly, including Henry *Fuseli, Alexander Geddes (1737–1802), John Horne *Tooke, Gilbert Wakefield (1756–1801), and Mary *Wollstonecraft, as well as more sporadically William *Blake, William *Godwin, Thomas *Paine, and William *Wordsworth. His contacts as publisher and correspondent with important figures outside the capital, including John *Aikin, Anna Laetitia *Barbauld, Erasmus *Darwin, William *Enfield, and Joseph *Priestley, made Johnson an important point of contact between the metropolitan and provincial Enlightenments.   JM

JOHNSON, Joseph (1738–1809), bookseller, kept a shop in St Paul's Churchyard till the year of his death [see *Johnson circle]. Born into a Baptist family near Liverpool, he was drawn to *Unitarianism after moving to London, where he remained for the rest of his life, to serve an apprenticeship. He was closely involved with Theophilus Lindsey (1723–1808) in establishing the capital's first Unitarian chapel in 1774 and became the official bookseller of the Unitarian Society in the 1780s. His publications reflected the broad political and scientific interests of Rational Dissent. Medical material, including the writings of William and John *Hunter, was a particular speciality. Johnson was also the major publisher of scholarly works on *prophecy and shared the *millenarian interests of his authors. All of these interests were also represented in the pages of the *Analytical Review*, the periodical which Johnson founded with Thomas Christie (1761–96) and which ran from 1788 to 1799. Johnson himself was a member of the *Society for Constitutional Information, and his opinions and contacts brought him into conflict with the government. He was questioned during the *Treason Trials of 1794 and arrested in 1798 for selling Gilbert Wakefield's *Address to the People of Great Britain*. Found guilty, he was incarcerated while in ill health in the *King's Bench prison for six months.   JM

JOHNSON, Samuel (1709–84), poet, essayist, and man of letters. Perhaps the dominant arbiter of literary taste at the outset of our period, by the early nineteenth century his view of the history of English *poetry [29] had been largely superseded. He still remained a figure of immense cultural authority, not least on the basis of his *Dictionary* (1755) [see *language, 40].

During the last two decades of his life Johnson's authority was exercised in part through the 'Literary Club', set up in 1763–4, in which such notable figures as Joshua *Reynolds, Edmund *Burke, David Garrick, and James *Boswell participated. Although Boswell's celebrated biography of Johnson depicted him as the epitome of patriarchal attitudes of his time, he was also a key figure for the *bluestockings. The crowning work of his old age was his *Lives of the Poets* (1779–81) which provided for the first time a critical history of the English poetry of the previous century or so. Nevertheless, its perspective was already being challenged. Thomas *Warton's *History of English Poetry*, completed in the same year as Johnson's *Lives*, goes back as far as the fifteenth century for its models. Warton's taste for the *sublimity and grandeur of the older poets was well established by the time of *Wordsworth's 'Essay Supplementary to the Preface' (1815), which regarded the *Lives* as wasted on 'metrical writers utterly worthless and useless'. Two years later, in the *Biographia Literaria* (1817), S. T. *Coleridge carefully distinguished between 'the School of Warton and the School of Johnson'.

Notwithstanding these changes in literary tastes, Johnson's stature as a literary monument was reinforced soon after his death by a spate of biographies. Although Boswell's *Life of Johnson* (1791) is the best known, it was preceded by Hester Thrale *Piozzi's *Anecdotes of the Late Samuel Johnson* (1786) and the *Life* (1787) by Sir John Hawkins (1719–89). 'Johnsonian', an adjective which first appears in Boswell's biography, became a term denoting, for some, authority and moral conviction, and for others—like the Romantics—bigotry and pompousness. The most Johnsonian quality of this famous style is, however, the fusing together of impersonal authority with the ring of private suffering and testimony which in many ways could be seen as anticipating Romantic taste.   JW

JONES, Edward (Bardd-y-brenin) (1752–1824), antiquarian and harpist to the Prince of Wales, and the most important collector of traditional Welsh *music [26]. Born into a well-to-do farming family in rural Wales with a strong musical tradition, he was a notable performer on the harp. The patronage of local gentry eased his path when he left for London for a career as professional harpist, teacher of the gentry, and *music publisher.

Although almost half Jones's published arrangements are of music from Europe and the East, his antiquarian Welsh contribution is the more significant [see *Welsh cultural revival]. In the two volumes of *Musical and Poetical Relicks of the Welsh Bards* (1784, 1794), in *The Bardic Museum* (1802), and in *Hen Ganiadau* (1820, 1825) he noted over 200 tunes, most of which are Welsh. Some were sent to him by his numerous correspondents and others he may have noted from oral tradition, while others he found in manuscripts in the homes of the gentry and in tune-books of harpers and fiddlers. He was also the first collector to note Welsh words to Welsh folksongs, as early as 1784.

Jones's collection served as a quarry for later arrangers such as George *Thomson, J. M. F. Dovaston (1782–1854), and John Parry (1786–1825) who set English words to Welsh tunes, often forcing them into an alien metre.   PK

JONES, John (Jac Glan-y-gors) (1766–1821), publican, *satirist, and pamphleteer. An unusually gifted and popular satirical writer and propagandist, Jones was the first to popularize the ideas of Thomas *Paine in Welsh. He migrated to London in the year of the *French Revolution, probably in order to seek a new life in the metropolis.

By 1793 Jones was manager of the Canterbury Arms at Southwark, where his witty and comical songs entertained Welsh expatriates. He was one of the leading members of the Society of Gwyneddigion (Men of Gwynedd), a society founded in 1770 for the benefit of migrants from north Wales [see *Welsh cultural revival]. Warm conviviality was the keynote of the meetings of the Gwyneddigion and, although promoting Welsh language, literature, and history was prominent among the aims of members of the Society, there was also much heavy drinking, ragging, mock *duels, and leg-pulling in the *taverns which they frequented. For a time, Jones served as secretary of the Society, as its official bard, and as vice-president in 1801 and 1813. He was also instrumental in founding another London-based society— the Cymreigyddion—in 1795.

John Jones was a committed *republican and pacifist, and the principal feature of his published tracts and songs was bitter hatred of corrupt monarchical government, punitive taxes, alien landownership, and oppressive tithes. His most celebrated pamphlets, *Seren Tan Gwmmwl* (Star under a Cloud, 1795) and *Toriad y Dydd* (Break of Dawn, 1797), both written in forthright and attractive Welsh prose, were deliberately designed to breathe new life into the cause of political and religious reform in Wales, following the *Treason Trials of 1794. Both works were, in essence, paraphrases of Paine's *Rights of Man*. In *Seren Tan Gwmmwl*, the star obscured by a cloud represented the light of the liberty which Jones cherished and which he believed all free and equal Welshmen should be allowed to enjoy; while in *Toriad y Dydd*, he reaffirmed Paine's trenchant opposition to the doctrine of prescription. Both works earned Jones the undying hatred of Calvinistic *Methodists in Wales, and 10,000 copies of a conservative antidote entitled *Gair yn ei Amser* (A Word in Season) were distributed in 1797.

Jones's iconoclastic wit, satirical songs, and lampoons also earnt him notoriety, and he reserved his most scathing invective for the *Dic Siôn Dafydd*, the expatriate Welshman who abandoned his native tongue and affected an English accent in the futile hope that this would render him more socially acceptable. His most memorable satirical work, *Hanes y Sesiwn yng Nghymru* (History of the Session in Wales), mercilessly exposed the inequalities, abuses, and confusions of the legal system in Wales.

For the last three years of his life John Jones was the convivial host of the King's Head tavern in Ludgate Street, London, where he was at pains to remind all his customers that a just society could only be based on the doctrines of popular sovereignty. No Welshman sang 'God Save Great Thomas Paine' with greater gusto than Jac Glan-y-gors.   GHJ

JONES, William (1726–95), the 'Welsh Voltaire'. Like many self-educated Welshmen in the late eighteenth century, Jones was a man of wide accomplishments: he was a farmer, a country healer (who cured himself of scrofula), a poet, a fiddler, an astronomer, a collector of manuscripts and pedigrees, and, above all, an ardent admirer of the political ideas of Voltaire.

His career gives the lie to the notion that only Welsh Dissenters and intellectuals who dwelt in London were receptive to the cause of egalitarianism and social justice. Jones spent virtually the whole of his life eking out a bare living in a boggy upland farm in mid-Wales; but he corresponded regularly with leading Welsh radicals, read the work of *Paine and Voltaire avidly, and familiarized himself with the terrain, social mores, and politics of America. Known as 'the rural Voltaire', he resembled his hero as much in physiognomy as in ideology and his correspondence, especially from 1789 onwards, is littered with barbed references to tyrants, fleecers, and oppressors, and celebratory praise for Jacobins, *sans-culottes*, and Painites. The rector of Llangadfan denounced him as 'a rank Republican [and] a Leveller' and threatened to pepper him with gunshot. Local *Methodists deplored his Ranter-like fondness for adultery, blasphemy, and beer, and it is perhaps significant that his most bawdy poem—'The enraptur'd lover to the Tune of Jack ye Latin'—has never been published.

When the *French Revolution broke out, Jones flung himself into letter-writing with demonic energy, even though he knew that his subversive views invited close surveillance. He composed odes on freedom and oppression, condemned arbitrary government and *Evangelical religion, and, in language redolent of his mentor Voltaire, declared that Welsh society was composed of 'Shearers' and 'Feeders', 'Oppressors and Slaves'. Few writers in the 1790s could match him for polemical vigour and satirical barbs, and a contemporary admiringly described him as 'the hottest-arsed' Welshman he had ever met.

In a bid to stiffen the Welshman's sense of national identity, Jones sought to establish cultural institutions which would champion the cause of Welsh

language and literature [see *Welsh cultural revival].
He was the first Welshman to advocate that efforts
should be directed towards establishing a national
library to house precious Welsh manuscripts. He
also waged a one-man crusade on behalf of a truly
national *eisteddfod of Wales, and as an antidote to
'God Save the King' and 'Rule Britannia', he composed a robust Welsh national anthem—the first of
its kind in the modern period—which was sung to the
refrain 'And join in joyful song on the fair break of
dawn'.

Economic hardship and political constraints
eventually persuaded him that social and economic
salvation could only be achieved in America. At the
Llanrwst eisteddfod in 1791 he distributed copies of
an eloquent address, bearing the title 'To all Indigenous Cambro-Britons', the gist of which was that
oppressed tenant farmers should quit Wales and sail
for the Promised Land. His own dream of buying
cheap and fruitful land in Kentucky remained unfulfilled and he died, aged 69, in late November 1795. It
was entirely characteristic of this Voltairean heretic
that he should have insisted on being buried in
unconsecrated ground on the northern side of the
graveyard of Llangadfan parish church.   GHJ

JONES, Sir William (1746–94), the leading British
*orientalist of the period, who founded the Asiatic
Society of Bengal in 1784, and was also its first president. His discovery of the affinity of Sanskrit with
Greek and Latin laid the foundations of historical
and comparative linguistics, and his work on Hindu
and Muslim law in India had an important bearing
on historical and comparative legal studies [see
*language, 40 and *law, 8]. With the help of his
colleagues in the Asiatic society, he also evolved the
basis of a methodology, to be improved by later
scholars, for the study of ancient Indian history.

Before Jones arrived in Calcutta in 1783 as a judge
to the Bengal Supreme Court, he had already
achieved a reputation as a leading European orient-
ist. His work was remarkable for its stress on fidelity
to sources. This, combined with his knowledge of
Arabic and Persian, set it apart from such fashionable
pseudo-translations of the eighteenth century as
Montesquieu's *Lettres persanes* (1721), Lord Lyttleton's *Persian Letters* (1735), Horace *Walpole's
Letter from Xo-Ho (1757), and Goldsmith's *Citizen of
the World* (1762). Jones himself felt it necessary to
draw attention to the fact that his translations in
*Poems Consisting Chiefly of Translations from the
Asiatick Languages* (1772) were of 'genuine compositions of *Arabia* and *Persia*'. They were not like the
'inventions' which had been offered to the public as
'genuine translations from the languages of Asia'. In
his essay 'On the Poetry of the Eastern Nations',
which was included in this volume of translations,
Jones argued for the revivification of European literature through a 'new set of images and similitudes'
drawn from the 'principal writings of the *Asiaticks*
and the 'language of the Eastern nations'. This plea
was influential in shaping the intellectual background to the 'oriental' *epics of such poets as
Robert *Southey and Thomas *Moore. It was on the

basis of a scrupulous regard for original sources that
Jones argued for a clear distinction between 'fables'
and history in *An Introduction to the History of the
Life of Nader Shah* (1773). Similarly, another of his
pre-India works, *The Mahomedan Law of Succession*
(1782), which was written for the use of the Bengal
government's judicial administration, was a verbal
translation of the Arabic treatise on which it was
based. Although Jones's knowledge of Arabic and
Persian might not match modern standards, in the
context of his age it was remarkable, especially given
the poor provision for teaching these languages at the
universities.

It was Jones's knowledge, however exploratory, of
Arabic and Persian, combined with a commitment to
remain as faithful as possible to sources, which left its
stamp on his legal, literary, and historical work
before he left for India. Here he showed a similar
concern for linguistic fidelity. His 'Third Anniversary Discourse' to the Asiatic Society on 2 February
1786 argued that affinities between Sanskrit, Greek,
and Latin pointed to the languages having 'sprung
from some common source'. In contrast to the etymological method of such works as Jacob Bryant's
Analysis of Ancient Mythology (1775), Jones stressed
the innovative importance of studying grammatical
structure when investigating relationships of kinship
between languages. It was this, more than anything
else, which paved the way for the historical method
of nineteenth-century linguistics. Jones had already
made frequent intercultural comparisons in his earlier writings on literature and history. His thesis of the
Indo-European family of languages now enabled
such comparisons between cultures to be made on a
firmer foundation.

However, Jones himself considered his most
important work in India to be a project for a digest of
Hindu and Muslim laws. Its fruition was the publication of *Al Sirajiyyah: or the Mohamedan Law of
Inheritance* in 1792, and the *Institutes of Hindu Law,
or the ordinances of Menu* in 1796. The latter text was
the basis on which judicial interpretation of this
branch of law in British India was built. These
works, together with the earlier *The Speeches of
Isaeus* (1779) and *An Essay on the Law of Bailments*
(1782), made Jones a forerunner of the historical and
comparative school of legal philosophy, as represented by such later texts as Sir Henry Maine's
Ancient Law (1883). Jones's project for a digest of
Indian laws partly reflected the character of the judicial system operating in the *East India Company
territories in this period. This generally administered British law for British subjects, Hindu and
Muslim law for civil cases involving Indians, and
Muslim law for criminal law. Such a policy in relation
to Indian laws was in turn part of the Company's
larger attempt to legitimize itself in a variety of Indian
idioms. But Jones's project was also based on his
own often-expressed conviction that the purpose of
the Supreme Court in Bengal was to ensure that 'the
natives of these important provinces be indulged in
their own prejudices, civil and religious, and suffered
to enjoy their own customs unmolested'. It is here
that his linguistic and legal work connected; Jones's

original reason for learning Sanskrit was to compose a reliable digest of Hindu law in order to check the power of pandits in Company courts.

Jones had stressed the importance of empirical historical research in such earlier works as *An Introduction to the History of the Life of Nader Shah* (1773). As president of the Asiatic Society, he developed this contribution to modern *historiography. The Society was the first European body to draw attention to the early period of Indian history and to Indian historical traditions. His 'Third Anniversary Discourse' to the Society in 1786 listed four 'general media of satisfying our curiosity' about ancient India: 'namely, first their *Languages* and *Letters*; secondly, their *Philosophy* and *Religion*; thirdly, the actual remains of their old *Sculpture* and *Architecture*; and fourthly, the written memorials of their *Science* and *Arts*'. While Jones was anxious to distinguish between 'fables' and history, arguing that the blending together of the two in 'Asiatick' narratives could be unravelled, this distinction sometimes collapsed in his own historiographical essays. Such inconsistency was particularly marked where his own historical and philological methodology conflicted with the Mosaic chronology of the Christian scriptures. Nonetheless, the methodology which he formulated in his historiographical essays, especially in relation to the study of ancient India, was to be the basis of much subsequent work.

Jones's work represents the beginnings of modern European scholarly interest in India, and of the larger academic disciplines which universities now call 'oriental studies'. He played a crucial role in opening up the world of Sanskrit to European scholarship and imaginations, and also in systematizing methods of comparing and contrasting different cultures. JMA

JORDAN, Dorothy (1761–1816), actress and singer. Born Dorothy Bland, she made her stage debut in 1779 at the Crow Street Theatre in Dublin. She left Ireland in 1782 to escape her liaison with the Dublin theatre manager, Richard Daly, which had left her pregnant and in considerable financial debt to her lover. The Yorkshire theatre manager Tate Wilkinson employed her for three years in his travelling company, and in 1785 she moved to London, where she established herself as the leading actress in comedy. (Wilkinson claimed to have been responsible for giving her the name of Jordan: 'You have crossed the water, my dear,' he said, 'so I'll call you Jordan.') Contemporaries lauded her as Thalia (the muse of comedy), counterposed to Sarah *Siddons's Melpomene (the muse of tragedy). Her many roles, both comic and serious, included Miss Peggy in *The Country Girl* (Garrick's adaptation of Congreve's *The Country Wife*), Viola in *Twelfth Night*, Hippolita in *She Wou'd and She Wou'd Not*, Ophelia in *Hamlet*, and Cora in *Sheridan's *Pizarro*. An exuberant and instinctive actor, she was at her most successful in parts, often involving cross-dressing, which confused gender roles and suggested sexual availability to both men and women: parts such as Viola, Priscilla Tomboy in *The Romp*, Little Pickle in

The Spoiled Child, and Sir Harry Wildair in *The Constant Couple*.

She formed a liaison with the barrister Richard Ford, by whom she had three children between 1787 and 1789. In 1790 she left Ford, with his agreement, to become the lover of the Duke of Clarence, then Royal Prince, who later became King William IV. Dorothy Jordan continued to act during long periods of her relationship with the Duke, supporting him and her large family, which included her own offspring—she had ten children by the Duke—as well as her mother and siblings. (In 1811 she claimed that she had earnt by her acting £100,000, a sum which should have made her very wealthy by contemporary standards, but which had gone to sustain those who depended on her.) Her liaison with the Duke, the object of *satire by *Gillray, among others, was well known to the theatre-going public, but did not diminish her popularity with audiences. In 1811, pressed by financial demands which Jordan's exhausting provincial tours could not satisfy, the Duke ended their relationship. She died in lonely exile in Paris in July 1816, having fled debts accrued on her behalf by her son-in-law, the husband of her daughter by Richard Ford. GR

judges. A tiny judicial élite dominated the administration of English *law [8] in the late Hanoverian courts. It comprised the 'twelve men in scarlet' who presided in the three common law jurisdictions (increased to fifteen after 1830, and consisting of one chief and three or four 'puisnes' or juniors for each court), and the equity judges of the court of Chancery (the Lord Chancellor and his assistant, the Master of the Rolls, plus one Vice-Chancellor from 1813, and two more after 1841). They were all recruited from among the senior ranks of the bar and, apart from the Chancellor, all held office during 'good behaviour', which meant a judiciary of middle-aged and elderly men who were never obliged to retire, short of death.

The Stuarts' intimidation and removal of intransigent common law judges for unpopular ends had rendered relations between the judiciary and the Crown sensitive, and the constitutional adjustments made after 1689 reduced royal prerogative power over them. But even after 1761, when the judges' tenure of office was secured against the demise of the Crown, there is considerable doubt as to whether the judiciary was, or even expected to be, fully independent of government influence. Nevertheless, ritual claims for their impartiality were commonplace.

Eighteenth-century government relied on the common law judiciary, and ministries of various persuasions clearly appointed judges whom they thought would be politically congenial—a process which was facilitated by the concentration of prejudicial legal patronage on the House of Commons after 1689, and the development of a tradition by which chief justices and lord chancellors were chosen from experienced parliamentary politicians and Crown counsel who were naturally intimate with ministers. The accidents of survival, combined with the independence of George III and political instability between 1760 and 1784, meant that no ministry could depend on a bench of pet judges when partisan issues arose in the courts. Even so, the élite *lawyers who became senior judges were nurtured within a broad governing culture which at least predisposed them towards the interests of order and authority, despite the libertarian implications of the common law tradition. Lord Chesterfield (1694–1773) probably exaggerated in 1758 when he wrote of state trials: 'there is hardly an instance of any person prosecuted by the Crown, whom the judges have not very partially tried, and, if they could bring it about with the jury, condemned right or wrong.' Nevertheless, Lord *Mansfield, a long-time servant of the Crown and the current Chief Justice of England, subsequently demonstrated considerable flexibility in extending the law against *Wilkite rioters.

So although judges who were considered favourable to government on appointment did not necessarily follow the current ministerial line in sensitive political cases—as shown by the behaviour of Mansfield over general warrants and of Chief Justice Eyre (1734–99) in the trials of *Hardy, *Tooke and *Thelwall—a high measure of consanguinity between judiciary and executive was clearly the norm before 1832. Indeed, it probably increased between 1784 and 1830, when appointments were generally in the hands of one party only, and was especially strong after 1791, when many public men clearly agreed with the government's *raison d'être*—that firm measures were necessary if revolution was to be avoided. During this period the ultra-conservative Lord *Eldon was Lord Chancellor for twenty-five years, and in 1818 he advised the Prime Minister that he believed senior judgeships should be confined to men who had 'been uniformly acting upon the principles of your Administration'. He had himself become Lord Chief Justice of *Common Pleas in 1799 after serving the government as solicitor and Attorney-General, on condition that he would accept a peerage and continue to support the *Pitt government from the Lords.

In these circumstances, it is hardly surprising that reformist lawyers who were adherents of the *Whig opposition were largely excluded from the upper reaches of the judicial bench until Eldon's retirement in 1827. Meanwhile his colleague Lord *Ellenborough, Lord Chief Justice of *King's Bench from 1802–18, had no inhibitions about becoming a member of the Cabinet in 1806–7 (as Mansfield had in 1757–60). On the Bench he also manifested an instinctive partiality for the establishment in church and state during the crisis of public disaffection after the end of the French *wars [2], even offering his resignation upon failing to browbeat a jury into convicting William *Hone for seditious libel in 1817. Like Eldon and virtually every English judge appointed in the age of *Wilberforce and *Peel, Ellenborough was personally incorruptible; but his firm convictions of a judge's place and duties in relation to the government and the Crown had been developed in an age when conscious judicial 'independence' was exercised within a concept of governance which placed the judiciary at its core. DL

K

KATTERFELTO, Gustavus (*c.*1740–99), itinerant popular *lecturer. Probably born in Prussia, Katterfelto had arrived in England by 1777 and was briefly fashionable in London in 1782–3. Most of his working life was spent touring provincial towns displaying entertaining experiments in *natural philosophy [34]. He competed with rival lecturers by combining the fascination of occult masonic mysteries [see *freemasonry] with the vogue for rational *self-improvement. Satirists, often bracketing him with the sexual therapist James Graham (1745–94), rendered him the epitome of *quackery.

Frequently styling himself 'Doctor' Katterfelto, he initially leapt to fame during the London influenza epidemic of 1782, when he marketed his patent *medicine [18] by using his solar microscope (which projected magnified displays) to reveal thousands of 'insects' writhing in a drop of water. Performing at Cox's former Museum (a celebrated collection of automata, gems, and timepieces in Leicester Square) and in Piccadilly, Katterfelto subsequently gave three-hour didactic shows which attracted large audiences, allegedly including members of the royal family. Although a caricature shows him clutching bags of gold, his appeal actually plummeted and he lived an arduous life—including spells in jail—supporting his family as an itinerant provincial entertainer before settling in Yorkshire, where he died.

Mocked for his Germanic accent and his advertisements headed 'Wonders! Wonders! Wonders!', Katterfelto's two renowned props were his necromantic black cat and his solar microscope. His diverse equipment included standard natural philosophical apparatus such as an orrery, an air pump, and an electrical machine, as well as more exotic devices such as a perpetual motion machine and a magnetic copying apparatus.

79. Angelica Kauffman, *Cornelia, the Mother of the Gracchi, Pointing to her Children as her Treasures, c.*1785.

As well as appearing in political cartoons, Katterfelto was mentioned by the poets William *Cowper and John *Wolcot, and, given his practice of charging people to watch him ascending in a hydrogen balloon, he was probably the model for William *Blake's 'Inflammable Gass the Windfinder'. PF

71 **KAUFFMAN,** Angelica (1741–1807), painter, one of the few female artists to excel in *history painting and to achieve a significant pan-European reputation. Born in Switzerland, talented in both music and painting, Kauffman chose the latter career and travelled with her father throughout Switzerland and Italy, copying Old Masters and making important contacts. Her relationship with the English community in Rome inspired her to come to London in 1766, where she participated in the circle of Joshua *Reynolds. Her reputation for *portraiture and history painting led to her appointment as a foundation member of the *Royal Academy in 1768. However, as a woman, she was excluded from the life class and prevented from attending meetings and voting.

Most of her portraits represent women, for whom she probably provided a refreshing alternative to the male-dominated art establishment of London. Wall paintings and decorative schemes based on her designs became popular in country and town houses, and were adopted by Robert *Adam for some of his interiors, such as Kenwood House, London. Her wide contemporary fame rested on her historical and literary subjects, painted in a muted neoclassical manner, and disseminated through engravings.

In 1781 she left England to return to Italy with her husband, the artist Antonio Zucchi (1726–95). Whilst her interest in history painting and her contemporary fame remained until her death, her posthumous reputation was diminished by biographies which concentrated more on her private life than her artistic influence. SW

KEAN, Edmund (1787/9–1833), actor. Kean was the son of a minor actress, Nancy Carey, and Edmund Kean, an ex-tailor turned actor who may have had *Jewish origins. The facts of his early life are uncertain, but the broad picture is undisputed: he was brought up on the fringes of the London **theatre** [24] world in unstable family circumstances, and acted in circuses and fairground booths, where he learned his tumbling and improvisational skills before gravitating in early adulthood to the roving life of the provincial actor. He appeared on stages from Derry to Dumfries, from Guernsey to Glasgow, and struggled for years to gain the notice of the metropolitan managers.

Finally, in 1813, having accepted an offer from one of the London minor theatres, the Olympic, he was approached by Drury Lane theatre while playing at Dorchester. Seizing the opportunity, Kean renounced his agreement with the Olympic management and insisted on a major part at Drury Lane, which was initially interested in his playing secondary roles. The part was that of Shylock in *The Merchant of Venice*, and Kean's appearance in the role on 26 January 1814 has entered the annals of cultural history as the defining moment in Romantic theatre. Rejecting the traditional interpretation of Shylock as a grotesquely comic figure, Kean played him as an embittered villain with the intense energy that also characterized his Richard III, just a few weeks later. For William *Hazlitt, whose accounts of Kean's performances are among the most significant works of dramatic criticism in the period, the actor's Richard 'had a preternatural and terrific grandeur', combining *sublimity with a beguiling dynamism: 'he filled every part of the stage'; 'there was . . . a sort of tip-toe elevation, an enthusiastic rapture in his expectations of obtaining the crown.' Kean was perceived as the antithesis of *Kemble and *Siddons, not only in his more emotionally expressive acting style, but also in his radical politics and unrespectability. He relished parts which allowed him to express the anger of the outsider, beleagured and desperate, roles such as Shylock, Richard, the eponymous hero of Maturin's *Bertram*, Oroonoko in a revival of Southerne's tragedy, and Sir Giles Overreach in Massinger's *A New Way to Pay Old Debts*. His descent into *madness in the latter play caused *Byron, for one, to faint with shock.

Kean never transcended his strolling origins, as the Kembles had done, and conducted a flamboyantly rakish personal life, founding the notorious Wolves club, associating with low-lifes and prostitutes, and, after a visit to Canada, receiving guests dressed as a Huron chief, Alanieouidet. Walter *Scott lambasted him in 1819 as 'a copper-laced twopenny learmouth rendered mad by conceit and success' while *Coleridge claimed that he was not 'thorough-bred gentleman enough to play Othello'. (The latter's more often quoted remark that seeing Kean act was like 'reading Shakespeare by flashes of lightning' has been convincingly reassessed by the theatre historian Tracy C. Davis as a subtly deprecating comment: 'flashes of lightning' was contemporary slang for gin drinking.) In 1824 Kean was named as an adulterer in a criminal conversation case involving the wife of Alderman Cox, and his career never recovered from the ensuing scandal.   GR

KEATS, John (1795–1821), poet. He was born in London at the sign of the Swan and Hoop, Moorfields; his father managed a prosperous livery stable there, while young John Keats attended the Clarke school at Enfield. Keats has always been placed in the first rank of the younger Romantic poets, and he is regarded as one of the best letter-writers in the English language. Most of the poems which are best known to the wider public were written in the space of just one year, 1819.

Keats suffered more than his fair share of loss. He was orphaned by the age of 14, and had lost five close relatives by the time he was 19. When he was 23 he watched his younger brother, Tom, die of the tuberculosis which was to claim him just two years later. He was long separated from his fiancée Fanny Brawne, knowing that 'death is the great divorcer for ever'. No wonder his *poetry [29] is shot through with death-consciousness, the pains of love as loss, and sharp melancholy at the transience of living things.

Nevertheless he had a keen sense of the pleasures of the senses and a deep attachment to the natural world. Such attachments were served, while he was healthy, by recreational travel, then fashionable for the middle class. Although always a Londoner, Keats went on a walking tour of the Lakes and Scotland with Charles Brown (1786–1842), visited rainy Devonshire, and spent time writing on the Isle of Wight and in Winchester [see domestic *tourism].

Keats's first choice of a career was *medicine [18]. In 1810 he was apprenticed to a surgeon, and on turning 19 entered Guy's Hospital as a student. In 1816 he qualified to practice as apothecary, physician, and surgeon. For five crucial years Keats maintained a commitment to a medical career and was apprenticed to top surgeons; since Guy's was an experimental hospital for incurables, he witnessed great suffering. In his letters and in many of his poems, particularly *The Fall of Hyperion*, he referred to the true poet as a healer, consoler, and physician to the mind and emotions. His constant 'great provider' was *Shakespeare, to whom he attributed the altruism and 'disinterestedness' of Socrates and Jesus.

Keats never gave up the idea of practising as a doctor. Financial problems and a lack of sympathy from the family's guardian, Richard Abbey, a tea merchant, meant that he could hardly afford to do so. But he made a very conscious decision just before he qualified in medicine to take the far riskier path of professional poet. His first volume, *Poems*, was published in 1817. His trial by fire in every way was *Endymion*. He began this *epic poem on the Isle of Wight in April 1817, setting himself the task of writing 4,000 lines as a 'test, a trial of [his] Powers of Imagination and chiefly of [his] invention'. Constantly beset by family creditors and debts, he was at least lucky in his publishers, Taylor and Hessey (and later his 'patron', the lawyer Richard Woodhouse) who showed dogged faith in Keats and continued to advance him money and lend him books.

Endymion received some favourable reviews, but ever since *Poems* (1817), Tory reviewers such as *Lockhart for *Blackwood's Edinburgh Magazine* and Croker (1780–1857) for the *Quarterly Magazine* had been circling the upstart 'cockney' poet like vultures.

He had signalled his liberal leanings by publishing in Leigh *Hunt's radical journal the *Examiner*, and by dedicating his first volume to Hunt. Keats was used as a stalking-horse for his publishers and for radicals like Hunt and William *Hazlitt (who was to become a firm friend), but the ferocity and personal tone of the reviews deeply hurt him. He did, however, continue to see himself as a 'Rebel Angel' speaking 'on the liberal side', commenting in his letters on contemporary affairs at the time when the British government was becoming increasingly repressive. At least obliquely and sometimes overtly, politics entered his mature poems such as *Isabella* (1820), where capitalism is briefly condemned, to the later satisfaction of Bernard Shaw, and the *Hyperion* fragments, where revolution is seen as 'Nature's law'.

More characteristically, Keats was restrained by an 'aristocratic temper' from political interventions as direct as those of *Shelley (who admired Keats and canonized him in *Adonais*), and of *Byron (who despised the 'voluptuousness' of Keats's language and probably his petty bourgeois class origins). Memory and the past held his attention more than any utopian future. Keats's great *odes, read alongside passages from his letters, can be interpreted as strenuous attempts to withdraw from contemporary strife into a classical calm and 'disinterested' stance, although the poems can still be read as veiled comments on his age's tensions. Even the serene 'To Autumn' (1820), when read against a historical context of violent corn riots, becomes an elegy for the loss of the days when communities were based on *agrarian labour, and when the world appeared more socially integrated, abundant, and in harmony with natural rhythms. *The Fall of Hyperion* can be read conservatively as a sympathetic lament for the defeated and decadent monarchy of the Titans, or radically as a celebration of revolution. Memory, personified by the goddess Moneta (in the first version Mnemosyne, the ancient Greek goddess of memory), stands in tragic impotence observing changing regimes.

Keats's love poetry, which influenced Victorian literature and pre-Raphaelite art, is never unequivocally happy or fulfilled. His masterpiece in this genre, 'The Eve of St Agnes' (1820), presents love as the escape of a dreaming maiden from a corrupt, feudal castle, but the explicitness of sex itself represents a painful awakening. Although 'Lamia' (1820) could be read as a fable of reason killing love, this simple pattern is undermined by the deception of the snakewoman, and the tantalizingly short 'La Belle Dame Sans Merci' (1820) can be read either as a condemnation of knightly males for fetishizing women or as condemnation of women as fatal temptresses. In Keats, love always has its victims, and joy is short-lived.

Pain and pleasure are paradoxically fused for Keats. Ultimately it is his capacity to use the music of language, to 'load every rift with ore'—as Shelley wrote—which makes this bracing and nostalgic refrain so powerful and memorable, as well as typical of the poetry of our period.   RSW

KELLY, Michael William (1762–1826), Irish tenor, composer, *music publisher, stage manager, and wine merchant. Kelly made his operatic debut in Dublin, but left the city in 1779 to study in Naples. Perhaps the high point of his singing career was his appointment to Joseph II's Italian opera company in Vienna (1783–7), during which he worked closely with *Mozart.

Arriving in England in 1787, Kelly performed at London's English theatres for over three decades, and composed or compiled some sixty theatrical scores, including *Bluebeard* (1798), which ran for twenty-six years. Kelly was stage manager at the King's Theatre (1792–c.1820), and published mainly vocal music from premises nearby until bankruptcy struck in 1811. An avid socialite, he published some vivacious memoirs in 1826.   RC

KEMBLE, John Philip (1757–1823), actor, theatre manager, and antiquarian. Kemble was the first son of Roger Kemble and Sarah Ward, managers of a theatre company which acted in the north and west of England and in Wales, and younger brother to Sarah *Siddons. Intended by his father for the Catholic priesthood, Kemble studied in the English College at Douai, France, between 1771 and 1775 before returning to England to join the stage. He spent a period acting in the provinces, where he met and formed a close friendship with Elizabeth *Inchbald, and in 1783 he followed his sister to Drury Lane theatre in London. Often supported by Siddons in a formidable acting partnership, Kemble's notable roles included Hamlet, Macbeth, King John, Cato, and Coriolanus. The latter role in particular, depicted by Thomas *Lawrence, was the perfect vehicle for the actor's commanding physical presence and imperious manner. What Leigh *Hunt described as Kemble's 'studious and important preciseness' also contributed to his successful roles in new plays, including Octavian in *The Mountaineers* by George *Colman the younger (1793), Penruddock in *Cumberland's *The Wheel of Fortune* (1795), and Rolla in *Sheridan's *Pizarro* (1799).

Kemble's ambitions were not confined to acting: in 1788 he became manager (effectively artistic director) of Drury Lane, under R. B. Sheridan, whose ineptitude and deviousness in financial matters eventually led both Kemble and Siddons to defect to Covent Garden. Kemble bought a one-sixth share in Covent Garden in addition to receiving a salary as manager. His career at this theatre was disastrously interrupted by the 1808 fire, which killed twenty-two people as well as destroying valuable property, and by the ensuing Old Price riots of 1809 [see **theatre, 24**]. Most of the animus of the rioters was personally directed at Kemble, whose autocratic response to the disturbances echoed Coriolanus's haughty disdain for the people.

In addition to theatre management, Kemble sought to establish a reputation as a gentleman scholar, particularly of *Shakespeare. He possessed a substantial library of manuscripts, printed plays, and theatrical ephemera, and published a critical work on Macbeth (1786), dedicated to Edmund

*Malone. From an early stage in his career Kemble's scholarly interests were manifested in his attempts at historical realism through costuming and scenic design, the latter influenced by the taste for the *Gothic and by *landscape gardening. His major contribution, however, was in cementing the pre-eminent position of Shakespeare in British theatrical culture, through revivals and adaptations. Productions such as *Henry VIII* (1788), *Henry V* (1789), *The Tempest* (1789), and his 1794 *Macbeth* introduced previously unsurpassed levels of pomp and pageantry which allied Shakespeare with enhanced royal ceremonial [see *monarchy] and the forces of counter-revolution.   GR

keyboards, London. London manufacture of keyboard instruments in the late eighteenth century saw a change from harpsichord to piano. The leading firms of John Broadwood (1732–1812) and Jacob Kirkman (1710–92) both switched as the new instrument, capable of an expressiveness not possible on the harpsichord, gained in popularity. Broadwood began by making square pianos like those of Johannes Zumpe (*fl.* 1735–83). Oblong in shape and with a simple action and feeble tone, the square piano was first popularized by the fashionable composer J. C. *Bach, and remained the staple for several decades, ceasing production in 1863. Compact in size and relatively easy to maintain, it found a ready market among musical amateurs, who bought and performed the many published solo and chamber pieces intended for it [see *music publishing]. The rapid growth of the London piano industry provided strong competition for continental makers, notably those in Vienna and Paris. By 1813 Broadwood was producing over 1,000 square pianos per year; by 1825 the figure had risen to over 1,500, though by this time the square, now equipped with a standard six-octave compass, faced competition from other types of piano.

The English grand piano, intended primarily for professional pianists, was 'invented' by Americus Backers (*fl.* 1763–78) in 1772 with his apprentices Robert Stodart (1748–1831), and John Broadwood. The latter began producing them in 1783, the earliest surviving example dating from 1787. With a heavier action, louder tone, and less efficient damping than its Viennese counterpart, the London grand was equipped with two pedals: one lifting the dampers; the other 'soft' or *una corda* shifting the keyboard so that hammers hit only two out of three strings per key. Square pianos had only a sustaining pedal. New features were introduced on the grand piano before the square; its compass increased first to five and a half octaves then to six in the 1790s, partly at the instigation of Jan Ladislav *Dussek, whose virtuoso piano concertos made use of the 'additional keys'. The six-and-a-half-octave grand was rare until after 1820, about the time iron bracing was added to strengthen the wooden frame.

'Upright grand' pianos were introduced by Stodart in 1795, and Broadwood sold them from 1805 to 1831. Unwieldy, they failed to sell satisfactorily and were supplanted by the 'cabinet' pianos: shorter uprights with strings extended down to the floor. Even smaller uprights, known as 'pianino' or 'cottage' pianos, were developed by Robert Wornum (1780–1852) in 1811. His improved action was patented in 1828. Such instruments competed with the square for the amateur market.

Broadwood was for a time probably the world's biggest producer of pianos and exported many of them abroad, but he had many competitors. Among them was the Paris-based Sébastien Érard (1752–1831), who opened a branch in London in 1792. He made important improvements on the basic English action, notably the double escapement of 1821. The virtuoso pianist and composer Muzio *Clementi turned to piano manufacture and music publishing in 1798, when he took over the firm of Longman & Broderip, *music publishers and sellers, who commissioned pianos by makers such as Thomas Culliford (1750–?1800) and John Geib (1744–1819). Clementi began in partnership with John Longman, who left in 1800, and then took on various partners, the most important of whom were the Collard brothers, whose name was added to that of Clementi in 1822. Like Broadwood, the mainstay of Clementi's manufacture was the square piano, but he also produced fine grand, upright, and cabinet pianos, exporting many to the Continent. His quality was matched by the prolific Thomas Tomkison (*fl.* 1798–1851), who built more than 9,000 instruments during his career.

London keyboard makers were notable for their enterprise and innovation during this early period of piano-making. The London industry attracted custom from a large amateur market as well as many notable composers and performers. Its variety, quantity, and quality are evidence of unqualified success at a crucial stage of the piano's development
                                                                 DDEV

KING, John or Jonathan, born Jacob Rey, known as 'Jew King' (*c.*1753–1824). Moneylender, radical, and father of *Gothic novelists Charlotte *Dacre and Sophia King (b. *c.*1782), he exemplifies the social, political, and religious ambiguities of an ambitious *Jewish intellectual of humble origins seeking to make his way in late Georgian London.

King's father was a London street trader of probable North African origins who made enough money to send his son to a Spanish and Portuguese Sephardim charity school, where he evidently received a basic religious and secular education. After working as a clerk and attorney's assistant, he opened up a business as a money broker. His social ambition is indicated in his anglicization of his name, his lavish entertainment of aristocrats and literati, and his abandonment of his Jewish wife, Sara Nunes Lara, around 1784 to live the remainder of his life with Lady Lanesborough, the racy daughter of an Irish Protestant earl. At the same time, King's occupation ensured his lifelong social unease. He specialized in procuring money for fast-living sons of nobility, a high-risk occupation which embroiled him in continuous litigation and led to several forced periods of exile in Europe. He seems, in fact, to have lived always on the edge of legality. Some of his more dubious moneymaking enterprises included the financing of *gambling dens and blackmailing introduction agencies, and the practising of various forms of extortion, most famously when he threatened to publish love letters from Mary *Robinson in 1781. Both he and his son, Charles, also a moneylender, were often castigated in print as swindlers, including King's appearance as the criminal moneylender 'Old Mordecai' in Pierce *Egan's *Finish to the Adventures of Tom, Jerry and Logic* (1830).

King's marginality probably also inclined him towards radical and *millenarian causes and milieux. As a schoolboy he had strongly impressed and befriended Thomas *Paine, and in 1783 King published a typical oppositionist reform pamphlet, *Thoughts on the Difficulties and Distresses in which the Peace of 1783 has involved the people of England*. A later public recantation from Paine's views, in an exchange of newspaper letters and pamphlets between the two men from 1792 to 1795, seems to have been an expedient response to government blackmail. Privately he continued to support anti-establishment causes, and he remained a close friend and patron both of radical intellectuals like *Holcroft and *Godwin, and of more plebeian and openly seditious radical activists like the *Spenceans. He also helped to finance ultra-radical newspapers, notably the *Argus* in the early 1790s and the *British Patriot* during the Mary Anne *Clarke affair of 1808–9.

King never converted to Christianity, and his early writings show an inclination common in *Enlightenment [32]-influenced European Jewry to represent Judaism as a rationalist or Deistical religion. He was also drawn to movements such as that of Joanna *Southcott, which posited an imminent restoration of the Jews to their spiritual or geographical homeland. Towards the end of his life, however, he began to reassert his orthodox rabbinical faith and to attack Christianity with a degree of bitterness, most explicitly in a long introduction to a new 1817 edition of David Levi's (1740–99) *Dissertations on the Prophecies of the Old Testament*. When he died in 1824 he left money to the London Sephardi congregation to sponsor an annual prayer in his memory.   IMcC

King's Bench, court of, the principal common law court in England, having original jurisdiction over pleas of the Crown, and also an important jurisdiction in private pleas by legal fiction.   DL

80   **KNIGHT,** Richard Payne, (1751–1824), Foxite MP, antiquarian, aesthetician, and mythographer. Heir to

landed estates acquired through ironmaking, Knight was a well-travelled, self-taught connoisseur renowned for his *antiquarian [35] knowledge and lucid aesthetic writings. He designed his country seat, Downton Castle, near Ludlow (1774–8), in a so-called 'mixed style', castellated on the exterior and neoclassical on the interior. As the first asymmetrically planned country house, Downton influenced generations of architects, in particular John *Nash. As the founder of the British Institution, and a mainstay of the Society of Dilettanti, Knight was also frequently involved in public controversy.

Knight first came to public attention with the *Discourse on the Worship of Priapus* (1786), which he published privately together with a letter from Sir William *Hamilton on Priapic remains in Italy. The pamphlet was distributed only to various members of the Society of Dilettanti and other interested gentlemen, including the Prince of Wales, but its contents soon became widely known and were attacked as immoral by anti-Jacobin commentators such as T. J. *Mathias. Despite a provocatively libertine tone, Knight's pamphlet argued seriously that sexual symbols found in many religions were not evidence of pagan licentiousness but rather proof of the origins of religious faith in the worship of procreation. His long didactic poem, *The Progress of Civil Society* (1796), was denounced in the *anti-Jacobin press for its defence of the *Discourse*. Eventually a modified version of his thesis was published for the general public under the title *An Inquiry into the Symbolic Language of Ancient Art and Mythology* (1818).

Knight's first commercially published work was *The Landscape* (1794), the poetical counterpart to *An Essay on the Picturesque* (vol. 1, 1794) by Uvedale *Price, a friend and neighbour to whom Knight dedicated his poem. Knight shared Price's enthusiasm for the *picturesque and his disdain for the broad, clipped vistas of Lancelot 'Capability' *Brown's *landscape gardening. However, in *An Analytical Inquiry into the Principles of Taste* (1805), Knight applied associationist theories to question Price's location of the picturesque in the physical appearance of objects. Knight rather insisted that the picturesque was a largely subjective concept determined by an individual's education and sensibilities. Though his reputation survived these hiccups, it was considerably tarnished after 1816, when he became the only parliamentary committee member to vote against the purchase of the *Elgin Marbles.   SS

L

LACKINGTON, James (1746–1815), bookseller and *autobiographer. A commercially innovative and successful London bookseller, Lackington publicized his own life as a self-made man in his *Memoirs* (1791) and *Confessions* (1804) [see *publishing, 21].

Lackington established himself in the London retail book trade in 1774. He sold books at low prices, for ready money only, and successfully challenged existing practice by selling publishers' remainders at a marginal profit. Lackington read widely. His marketing techniques included (from 1779) large catalogues, with each book described by himself, and (from 1789) a grandiose purpose-built shop, 'The Temple of the Muses', in Finsbury Square. The largest bookshop in London, possibly in the world, it may have had half a million volumes normally on sale. His *Memoirs of the First Forty-Five Years of the Life of James Lackington* tells a story of frugality, intermittent piety, and entrepreneurial skill: the son of poor parents progresses from itinerant meat-pieman to apprentice and journeyman shoemaker and then, with the help of an initial loan of five pounds from 'Mr Wesley's people', to successful metropolitan bookseller.

In 1798 he retired from Lackington, Allen, & Co. to live in retirement in the West Country, erecting chapels (and calling them 'Temples') for the Wesleyan *Methodists, and acting as lay preacher. *The Confessions of J. Lackington* recants the sceptical and mildly scurrilous picture of Methodist social life presented in the *Memoirs*. Lackington had passed through a period of infidelity, or *Deism, induced by reading Thomas Amory's (?1691–1788) *John Buncle*, and by the influence of an obscure oilman-mystic John Denis. He also recounted his involvement with mystical and virtuosi artisan circles which included influential artisan intellectuals such as journalist W. H. Reid (d. 1826) and rabbinical scholar David Levi (1740–99) [see *Jews]. George *Crabbe's poem 'The Convert' (in his *Tales*, 1812) draws on the *Memoirs* to present an ironic analysis of the relations between religious conversion, commercial acumen, and social mobility.   GE

laissez-faire, lit. 'leave to do', seems to have been coined as an economic doctrine by the French physiocrat Gournay in the eighteenth century, and to have reached Britain around 1825, when it was used by the Marquess of Normanby in *England in Italy*. During our period it denoted a policy in which individuals should be allowed to pursue their economic and, to a lesser extent, political interests with minimal interference from the state. Early proponents, who were often *utilitarian social reformers, usually wished to confine the role of the state to protecting property and persons, and to providing national

defence and a few related public activities. As such, the doctrine tended to be associated retrospectively with the writings of Adam *Smith, particularly with his supposed advocacy of the naturally benign workings of the free market. However, Smith, like John Stuart *Mill after him, employed the idea only with very careful qualifications. *Laissez-faire* did not become a ruling political or economic dogma until well into the Victorian period.   IMcC

LAMB, Lady Caroline (1785–1828), novelist and poet. She was the daughter of Frederick Ponsonby, third Earl of Bessborough, and Henrietta Ponsonby, and niece of Georgiana Cavendish, Duchess of *Devonshire, in whose household she spent her childhood. In 1805 she married William Lamb (later Lord Melbourne).

She first encountered *Byron at a ball in 1812, and although their love affair was brief, they continued a complex public and textual relationship that endured beyond their deaths. Lamb revealed a flair for publicity and the manipulation of performative personas that mimicked and occasionally excelled Byron's skill in self-fashioning. She claimed to have written her *roman-à-clef* of the affair, *Glenarvon* (1816), in the course of a night while dressed as a pageboy. Set largely in Ireland during the *Rebellion of 1798, the novel combines elements of the *Gothic, the 'national tale' in the manner of *Owenson and *Maturin, and *satire on fashionable metropolitan life. It includes thinly veiled attacks on Lady Holland [see *Holland House], caricatured as the grotesque Lady Madagascar, and on Samuel *Rogers. The character of Glenarvon, libertine and trans-European revolutionary, fanned the flames of the Byron legend, but the hero also resembles another *Whig rebel, Lord Edward *Fitzgerald, whose role in the 1798 rebellion is split between Glenarvon and a female character, Elinor St Clare, who commands a band of revolutionaries dressed as a man before leaping off a cliff to her death. Lamb's impersonation of the Byronic role and voice continued in her *New Canto* (1819) which successfully ventriloquizes Don Juan and anticipates later developments of Byron's epic. She also notoriously appeared at a *masquerade in the guise of Don Juan in the company of devils. Later works included the novels *Graham Hamilton* (1822) which concerns a fine lady *gambler, and *Ada Reis* (1823), and lyrics published with Byron's *Fugitive Pieces* (1829) by her friend Isaac Nathan (?1791–1864).   GR

LAMB, Charles (1775–1834), poet, essayist, writer of *children's literature, who brought an idiosyncratic voice and oblique rhetorical strategy to the *essay of the period. He cultivated an anachronistic eccentricity to explore questions of continuity and consciousness in the face of dehumanizing commercial and technological developments.

Born in London, Lamb committed his life to the care of his sister, Mary Anne *Lamb, subsequent to her bout of insanity in 1796 during which she killed their mother. In 1823 they moved from London to Islington, Enfield, and, finally, Edmonton. The pathetic story of their subsequent walks together to the asylum, complete with straitjacket, following intimations of her progressively more frequent relapses, is well known. Part of that commitment was the protracted tedium of a clerical job: Lamb worked for thirty-three years as a clerk with the *East India Company.

In 1800 Lamb entered journalism to supplement his income, writing jokes and occasional pieces for the *Morning Post*. Between 1805 and 1811, he wrote several works of children's literature for William *Godwin's Juvenile Library. Among these were *Tales from Shakespeare* (1807) and *Mrs Leicester's School* (1809), on which he collaborated with his sister [see *Shakespeare]. An autobiographical fragment of 1827 betrays a rare pride in having edited unfashionable sixteenth- and seventeenth-century authors (*Specimens of the English Dramatic Poets who Lived about the Time of Shakespeare*, 1808).

However, Lamb's taste for earlier English literature was more than a hobby-horse cultivated in retreat from the mundanity of clerical work, it also expressed an oblique but stubborn resistance to the *utilitarian spirit which he saw as threatening to convert society into the mindless drudgery of a self-auditing commercial enterprise. As critic, Lamb sought to communicate and exploit 'the beauty of the world of words in that age'. He was attracted to a rich, heterogeneous literature, full of puns, allusions, and neologisms; a sceptical, anti-authoritarian challenge to the 'definite', the 'fixed', and the 'petrified'.

Lamb's comic *Spenserian allegorization of his clerical job as 'the damn'd Day-hag *business*' itself reflects the strategy in the 'familiar' *Essays of Elia* (1823) and *Last Essays of Elia* (1833) of ironizing and defamiliarizing the ordinary with a characteristic if not mannered archaism, a self-conscious literariness comparable to the private games and eccentric rituals developed to obviate the threat of the everyday. As life is ritualized, so people are 'characterized' and Elia's past is rendered old—remote and mythical; recollection becomes a kind of genteel archaeology in which images and moments are conjured, savoured, and enfolded for preservation. Though 45 when he began contributing essays to John Scott's (1783–1821) *London Magazine*, writing under the pen-name of 'Elia', his most famous lyric, 'The Old Familiar Faces', is an exercise in nostalgia written at the age of only 20.

Lamb's resistance to the dehumanization of commerce, though less visionary and Miltonic than, say, *Wordsworth's, less speculative and polemical than *Coleridge's, less sensational than *Dickens's, may indeed be more resolute precisely for being a habit of mind cultivated out of the necessity to preserve his personal sanity. WC

LAMB, Mary Anne (1764–1847), writer of *children's literature. Trained to needlework and largely self-educated, Mary Lamb collaborated with her brother Charles *Lamb on stories and poetry for children. Only Charles's name appeared on *Tales from Shakespeare* (1807), though Mary contributed stories from all but the tragedies—fourteen of the twenty in all. Of the ten stories in *Mrs Leicester's School* (1809), all but three were written by Mary, as were between one and two thirds of the *Poetry for Children* (1809). Both were published anonymously.

That none of the three collaborative works, all published by Mary Jane *Godwin, was attributed to Mary Lamb may have been due to a desire to preserve her privacy after she killed her mother while temporarily insane in 1796 and received extensive publicity. Mary's ideal of femininity—to 'be accounted the helpmates of *men*'—also subscribed to a radical anonymity. In the article 'On Needlework' (the *British Lady's Magazine*, 1815), Lamb advocated needlework as a way out of the distress women were suffering from reduced employment opportunities.

Mary's moderate success with *Mrs Leicester's School, or The History of several Young Ladies, Related by Themselves* (running into eight editions by 1823) reflects an established market for children's writing as surely as the steady growth in popularity of the *Tales from Shakespeare* reflects how a familiarity with *Shakespeare was fast becoming a national cultural imperative. *Mrs Leicester's School* also represents the growing concern with policing reading matter for young females [see *female education]. In 1823 Mary and Charles co-adopted an orphaned child called Emma Isola. WC

LANDON, Laetitia Elizabeth, later Maclean, known as L.E.L. (1802–38), poet and novelist, one of the most popular and prolific writers of the 1820s and 1830s. Landon achieved early fame when she published the poem 'Rome' in her neighbour William Jerdan's *Literary Gazette* (1820). Her first collection of poetry was *The Fate of Adelaide* (1821), followed by *The Improvisatrice* (1824), *The Troubadour* (1825), *The Golden Violet* (1827), and *The Venetian Bracelet* (1829). She also published four novels, the first of which, *Romance and Reality* (1831), was a *roman-à-clef* which fuelled rumours linking her name with Edward *Bulwer-Lytton. She penned *reviews, numerous short stories, and over a thousand miscellaneous verses for literary journals and annual gift-books, one of which, *Heath's Book of Beauty* (1833), she wrote and edited entirely by herself.

In her *poetry [29] she often assumed the persona of the innocent but rejected female lover, elaborating Edmund *Burke's identification of the 'beautiful' with a certain kind of femininity: soft, delicate, tender, submissive, devoted to others, and yet tinged with melancholy. In the process, she correctly gauged the taste of her time to become one of the bestselling authors of her day. Her editor, William Jerdan, estimated her income at £250 per annum and £2,585 in her lifetime, a fortune by nineteenth-century standards. After her father's death in 1825, she used her income to support separate London establishments for herself and her mother as well as to send her beloved brother, Whittington, to the University of Oxford and subsequently to purchase him a clerical living.

Landon paid a heavy price for her popularity. After rumours forced her to break off an engagement, she married George Maclean, Governor of the British slave-trade outpost at Cape Coast, West Africa, in a desperate attempt to salvage her reputation. Within seven months of her marriage and emigration to Africa, she was dead of a self-administered overdose of prussic acid, whether accidentally or intentionally we shall never know.   AM

LANDOR, Walter Savage (1775–1864), poet and prose writer. His frequently obscure writing never achieved significant sales, but deeply influenced the classical and *orientalist tastes of younger writers such as Thomas *De Quincey and Percy *Shelley.

Expelled from Rugby at the age of 16, then suspended from Oxford in 1794 for discharging a gun at the window of a fellow student, Landor never finished his degree. His temper brought him into legal difficulties throughout his life. Politically his independence of spirit expressed itself in an aristocratic *republicanism disdainful both of the British establishment and of democratic principles. His *Poems* of 1795 was followed in the same year by an anonymous twenty-page verse *satire, *Moral Epistle to Lord Stanhope*, condemning *Pitt's government.

Landor's most influential poem was probably the seven-book *epic *Gebir* (1798) which tells the story of an Iberian prince's ill-fated colonial expedition to ancient Egypt. Although far from accessible, Landor's poem is full of topical allusions and, especially, praise for *Napoleon, whose expedition to Egypt it commends while condemning British imperialism. Landor was later to repudiate Napoleon as a tyrant and to fight against him as a volunteer in the *Peninsular War in 1808. *Gebir* played an important part in developing the taste for orientalism in poetry after Sir William *Jones's translations, though Landor himself dismissed Persian poetry as the 'high-seasoned garbage of barbarians' in his own volume of translations, *Poems from the Arabic & Persian* (1800). Robert *Southey acknowledged the influence of *Gebir* on his own orientalist epic, *Thalabar* (1801), and dedicated *The Curse of Kehama* (1810) to Landor.

If the *Gebir* was his most influential poem, the much-anthologized 'Rose Aylmer', published with other love poems in *Simonidea* (1806), became his best-known. For his contemporary public, however, Landor's slender literary reputation rested mainly on his experiments with prose in *Imaginary Conversations of Literary Men and Statesmen* (1824–9). These dialogues, which mixed fiction with historical facts, were written in Florence, where Landor had settled in 1821. He had gone into exile on the Continent in 1814, pursued by court cases arising out of attempts to modernize the estate he had bought in 1805 at Llanthony in Wales with an inheritance from his father.

Abandoning his family in Italy in 1835, Landor returned to Britain and settled in Bath, where he became a much-visited literary celebrity, providing *Dickens with the basis of Boythorn in *Bleak House*. However, his taste for controversy remained: entangled in a libel case at the age of 82, he fled back to Florence. He died there having been taken in by Robert Browning (1812–89) after his family refused to have him back.   JM

landscape gardening, a term which Humphry *Repton claimed to have introduced as a replacement for what had previously been called English gardening. Like country house *architecture [28], landscape gardening was a recognized form not merely of aesthetic but also social and political statement. Whereas earlier neoclassical landscape architects often aimed for symbolic meanings in their designs, and distinguished the cultivated garden from the 'wilderness', the open park, or the surrounding countryside, later-eighteenth-century designers sought to fuse garden and landscape into a continuous aesthetic whole to be interpreted subjectively.   95–6

Until the mid-eighteenth century gardens recreated an ancient arcady or biblical paradise, a hermitage, a haven of solitude, or they acted as a setting for theatre and display. Classical mythology, filtered through writings on rural life by Virgil, Pliny, and Cicero, was balanced by biblical and Christian imagery. However, the Christian idea of topography as a mirror of the moral life persisted into the late eighteenth century. It is exemplified in an English sampler of 1799 which pictures the 'happy man' in his garden, each part of which corresponds to a particular Christian virtue.

Many popular seventeenth- and eighteenth-century poems celebrated particular gardens. Addison, Shaftsbury, and Pope compared the art of gardening with *painting [27]. It was also explicitly likened to the theatre. The words 'scene' and 'scenery', were first applied to landscape during the eighteenth century as direct metaphors from the stage. William Kent (1685–1748), the greatest garden designer of the early century, had been first a successful stage designer.

Pope, an associate of Kent, and Lord Burlington (1694–1753), creator of the great garden at Chiswick, also had his own garden, on a miniature scale, complete with a (widely imitated) grotto, at his Twickenham villa. Kent's design for Rousham in Oxfordshire brought the Renaissance ideal of an allegorical garden into the eighteenth-century landscape. Buildings and the order in which they were encountered were equally important. The same was true at Stowe, where Kent altered Bridgeman's layout, and at Stourhead—a joint creation of Henry Flitcroft, a Kent associate, and the owner, Henry Hoare, who cites Milton, Pope, Akenside, Virgil, and Ovid in his design. As in *history painting, or a historical drama, landscape gardening was part of a continuous cultural and moral dialogue with the past.

From the 1760s ideas of picturing a landscape would be transformed under the influence of new aesthetic ideas championed by Edmund *Burke in his *A Philosophical Enquiry into the Origin of our Ideas of the Sublime and Beautiful* (1757). Burke stressed the subjective response to landscape; beauty he associated with a pleasurable response to harmony and order, and the sublime with fear and horror evoked by wild scenes. These had their painterly counterparts respectively in the landscapes of Claude Lorrain and Salvator Rosa. The tradition of landscape gardening established by William Kent would also be challenged by a new generation of landscape architects who in different ways combined elements of the sublime and the beautiful in their works. Lancelot 'Capability' *Brown and his successor, Humphry Repton, developed the 'capabilities' of many existing gardens and landscapes by sweeping away avenues, fences, and even formal flower arrangements in favour of open landscapes where (discreetly broken by the ha-ha, or concealed ditch) the park appeared to come right up to the steps of the house. Others, like Richard Payne *Knight and Uvedale *Price, extended associations with painting by the concept of the *picturesque, recreating wilder and rugged scenery (often influenced by the paintings of Salvator Rosa). In his *Observations on Modern Gardening* (1770) Thomas Whately (d. 1772) distinguished between 'emblematic' and 'expressive' gardens—the former with the allusiveness of history painting, the latter providing space for observers' personal meanings. Such a distinction is paralleled in the symbolism of Jane *Austen's *Mansfield Park* (1814). Whately believed that 'a semblance of an antient British monument' was more 'agreeable to a wild view' than a classical temple. Humphrey Repton was in agreement with the Gothicizing trend. In the early 1800s, in collaboration with the architect John *Nash, he designed a number of asymetrical Gothic houses, such as Luscombe in Devon, which he believed to be natural buildings for a natural landscape. Nonetheless he feared the abandonment of sensible rules of gardening by more extreme adherents of the picturesque. The latter was a fairly plastic concept, but even a moderate adherent like Uvedale Price regretted that in the immediate vicinity of the country house, picturesque beauty needed to be sacrificed to neatness.

The general trend in the late eighteenth century was indeed to place houses within an overall parkland setting of nature, and *Gothic style architectural forms were felt to fit into this pattern of enhancing nature. These trends were exemplified when Lowther Hall, Westmorland, was rebuilt by George *Dance the younger and his pupil Robert *Smirke, and renamed Lowther Castle (begun 1802–14). This was accompanied by John Webb's magnificent landscaping of the surrounding parkland. Finally the castle and landscape were painted by J. M. W. *Turner in (as described by a contemporary magazine) 'a most transcendent style of effect'. This was the consequence not only of viewing nature as a garden but also of regarding gardening as *landscape painting.

The Romantic age landscape garden's exaltation of nature opened the way for the Victorian garden tradition in which the landscape element was drastically reduced. The Victorians drew on distinct elements of eighteenth-century horticultural practice which had been under-represented in the picturesque landscape garden. The eighteenth-century grand garden tradition had been preserved and practised by 'florists', artisans usually of Huguenot origins. Also from *c*.1760 conservatories had been attached to houses with access from within, and there was a growing vogue for exotic plants, of the sort which Sir Joseph *Banks collected at Kew. Victorians were able to meld these elements in smaller upper-middle-class gardens of a few acres where conservatories and greenhouses, and formal beds, coexisted with the informal planting of individual plants amongst shrubs and trees. This latter trend began under Repton but was especially associated with his successor, J. C. *Loudon, who named it 'gardenesque'. We may thus detect a general sequence in the Romantic age whereby first the terrors of the sublime landscape were tamed by the picturesque landscape garden and then the pleasures of the picturesque landscape garden were domesticated by the gardenesque.

SP and MF

landscape painting burgeoned during this period, but its history is complex, confused, and largely unwritten. It includes paintings not only of Italy but also of popular sites, the exotic, and colonial holdings. Encompassing both aesthetic debates and social tensions, its study is central to understanding the development of the British rural environment and of urban modernity.

In the 1770s activity in landscape painting was lively, if undirected. Alexander Cozens (1717–86), pioneer with Richard *Wilson of ambitious historical landscapes, published *The Various Species of Composition of Landscape, in Nature* (1770s) which claimed landscape to be expressive of any sentiment or ideal, while Joseph *Wright was selling precise and experimental British and Italian scenes. In due course Richard Wilson's pupil William *Hodges would distinguish himself with paintings developed out of studies made in *explorations [37] of the South Pacific with Captain James *Cook in 1772–5. William *Gilpin published the first of his profoundly influential *picturesque guidebooks, *Observations on the River Wye* in 1782, while Thomas Gainsborough's canvases, like *The Market Cart* (1786–7), elevated a forest scene with travelling peasants by references to Rubens. In addition, Gainsborough and Paul *Sandby were expanding the capabilities of water-based pigments, while Francis Towne (*c*.1739–1816) developed abstract linear compositions and Thomas Jones (1743–1803) made accurate oil sketches. Jones's development of such study into historical landscapes like *The Bard* (1774) demonstrated the dominance of academic conventions of practice, in an environment where landscape painting lacked focus.

By the 1790s circumstances had changed. Touring to view famous landscapes in the Lake District, north Wales, or the Derbyshire Peaks had become fashionable for the élite and middle orders [see domestic *tourism]. The death of Sir Joshua *Reynolds in 1792—the pre-eminent exponent of *history painting—removed one barrier against landscape developing high academic ambitions, while debate on the picturesque by Uvedale *Price, Richard Payne *Knight, and others both captured popular interest and placed landscape in the foreground of fashionable intellectual concerns. A new generation was also emerging, including such artists as *Turner and *Constable, who would depict landscape by choice and who were as conscious of the precedents of Wilson or Gainsborough as of the continuing practice of Wright, Sandby, or John Robert Cozens (1752–97). Crucially, the closure of the Continent because of the French *wars [2] meant that tourists who would have visited Italy for their cultural education stayed at home. Great historical landscapes from French or Italian collections (for instance, the Altieri Claudes) were also sent for sale in Britain. Moreover, the British countryside itself came to represent what stood to be lost were France to triumph.

Drawing, an essential polite accomplishment, normally focused on landscape, and specialist drawing-masters proliferated, including notable practitioners like John Sell Cotman (1782–1842) and David Cox (1783–1859). The fact that provincial societies of art, initially at Norwich (from 1803) and subsequently at Bristol and elsewhere, also produced landscape predominantly suggests that it had become a fashionable and widespread taste. There was, however, no formal and easily identifiable 'movement'. Sporting pictures had to feature landscapes, but were held in low esteem because of the socially dubious nature of their subjects. At the other end of the spectrum were the fantastically theatrical landscapes of John *Martin, while landscape could also appear on the scale of life in the form of *panoramas or in intimate *watercolours which had high academic pretensions. The experimental brilliance of Thomas Girtin (1775–1802) fired many others, including Turner, Cotman, and John Varley (1778–1842), so that landscape watercolour painting also began to lay claims to a high status. The Society of Painters in Water-Colours was founded in 1804 expressly to challenge the claims of painters in oil (a project rendered the more ambiguous as William *Blake attempted to reclaim water-based media for historical subjects).

Taste for landscape was catholic. Originals by Turner, Richard Westall (1765–1836), William Collins (1788–1842), Peter de Wint (1784–1849), and others were published as *Picturesque Views of the Southern Coasts of England* between 1814 and 1826. These were complemented by Joseph Lycett's *Views in Australia* (1824–5) and Thomas and William Daniell's *Oriental Scenery* (1795–1808). In contrast to this exoticism, Constable and the Norwich painters concentrated on local landscapes, representing them in a variety of ways from the antiquarian to the 'Dutch'. Turner took advantage of the Peace of *Amiens in 1802 to reach Switzerland and subsequently to paint French and Swiss subjects, the latter forcefully conveying the overwhelming grandeur of Alpine scenery. At home Turner had been painting Thames scenes based on intensive study along the valley from the mid-1800s, developing work from oil sketches. The latter practice had been introduced into England from France by Richard Wilson, who regarded it as the preliminary stage in the production of academic landscapes, a status it retained for Turner. But for others, like John *Linnell, it formed the basis for a landscape which aimed to convey a plausible representation of actual appearances. Linnell's *Kensington Gravel Pits* (1813) represented a working landscape where industry was shown to be underpinning British society morally, as with Constable's landscapes of the Stour Valley, or George Robert Lewis's *Hereford from the Haywood Lodge* (1815), a fine topographical scene showing the final stages of corn harvest, with harvesters drinking cider. These paintings celebrate Britain in Georgic terms analogous to some of Turner's Thames landscapes of the 1800s. Along with studies of farmyard scenes by Robert Hills (1769–1844), or of labourers by Thomas Barker (1769–1847), such work shows how in the 1810s, under the particular pressures of wartime, the labouring poor could claim a brief place in art [see *land, 16 and *poverty, 12]. Nevertheless, such subjects papered over manifest social tensions. The Lake District, for example, was often pictured as the unchanging environment of eternal human values, in part because its relative proximity to the industrializing regions of the North West allowed it to serve as an antidote to and retreat from those regions. Industrial subjects themselves, save for Philippe Jacques de *Loutherbourg's *Coalbrookdale by Night* (1801), were generally ignored, as was much of the urban modernity increasingly becoming the daily experience of those who generally formed the audience and market for landscape painting.

Sublimity was not an attribute of the city but was to be found rather in paintings like William Ward's (1766–1826) enormous rural landscape *Gordale Scar* (1814). There were likewise far more paintings or watercolours of ruined than of contemporary churches, and artists sometimes dealt with contemporary issues obliquely. In *Dido Building Carthage* (1815) and *The Decline of the Carthaginian Empire* (1817) Turner's theme, though classical, was nonetheless germane both to the fate of *Napoleon and to the future of Britain. His overt concessions to the contemporary were, however, confined to the use of modern paint—pigments developed by improved technology were able to communicate startling effects—and perspective, which was more scientifically correct than in the paintings of Claude Lorrain on which many works were modelled. Even so, these works met with a controversial reception, exposing tensions in the cultivated world which liked to use its appreciation of art to display its sense of taste. The landscape of Turner and other 'white' painters like Augustus Wall Callcott (1779–1844) was hated by Sir George Beaumont (1753–1827) and the influential connoisseurs of the British Institution, for whom this art manifested a technical modernity which invalidated a landscape tradition based on Old Master techniques. Beaumont's antipathy to such landscapes led to a stand-off between the

Institution and the *Royal Academy which high-lighted how aesthetic disputes could be incorporated into and reflect *class [15] tensions.

Not all landscapists were as concerned with the contemporary as Turner, who relished the bustle of the Pool of London or the industrial glamour of Dudley in the west midlands. During the 1820s, however, Constable, for one, retreated from the documentary working scenes of the 1810s, to create dramatic landscapes of broken surfaces meant to detach them from particular time and place. At Shoreham, Samuel Palmer (1805–81) transformed Kent into a fruitful place of retreat and contemplation [see *Shoreham Ancients], his very distortions pointing to an alienation from actuality in an odd parallel to his contemporary Augustus *Earle, who represented Australia as a place where the European foothold was eerily unstable. By now the culture which had accommodated the plurality of landscape expression was narrowing, in accordance with urban bourgeois tastes. For this reason, both Turner and Constable came in for abuse and incomprehension from the press in the mid-1820s. While William Collins could make a good living from anodyne confections of rural and coastal scenes, Cotman, who continued to engage in formal experimentation, struggled to make any kind of a living. The coming generation of painters, the Mulreadys, Landseers, and Maclises, was now more interested in an affecting subject than in the power of its setting. Landscapists, like the short-lived Richard Parkes Bonington (1802–28), Thomas Shotter Boys (1803–74), or Samuel Prout (1783–1852), were tending increasingly to work in watercolour, with lithographic reproduction as the projected aim. By the 1820s the British landscape school, though recognized by both domestic and continental critics as pre-eminent in Europe, was on the brink of rapid decline.   MR

LATROBE, Christian Ignatius (1758–1836), *Moravian minister, composer, and editor of music, significant for his role in introducing continental Catholic *church music to English audiences. His most influential musical publication was the six-volume *Selection of Sacred Music* (1806–20), the early volumes of which anticipated the publications of Vincent *Novello, and contained music by such composers as Graun, Hasse, Pergolesi, *Haydn, and *Mozart.   PO

LAWRENCE, James Henry (1773–1840), author of a feminist and freelove theory which exercised considerable influence on both literary intellectuals and working-class radicals. Born of Jamaican colonist stock and educated at Eton and in Germany, Lawrence came to literary notice in Britain in 1811 when he published a four-volume romance, *The Empire of the Nairs*, which illustrated and advocated the matriarchal and freelove practices of the Nair people of the Malabar coast in Kerala. A noble caste of Hindus, the Nairs had come under the rulership of the *East India Company in 1792: their matrilineal and matrilocal practices inspired Lawrence to publish in the following year an essay in German for

Wieland advocating the Nair system. Schiller, too, was intrigued by Lawrence's suggestions.

By the time his novel appeared in English, Lawrence had elaborated his freelove and feminist ideas through acquaintance with William *Godwin and Mary *Wollstonecraft in the Newton–Boinville freethinking circle. Young Percy *Shelley wrote to Lawrence from Lynmouth in 1812 declaring himself 'a complete convert' to his doctrines which called for the abolition of marriage as a form of licensed prostitution, and for inheritance and child-raising to be the responsibility of the mother. Shelley was to adapt and incorporate this critique of Christian marriage in his poems *Queen Mab* and *Laon and Cythna*. Mary *Shelley also read Lawrence but was less impressed by his *utopian [9] programme, which she partially parodied in *Frankenstein*. Lawrence's feminist and freelove ideas passed into working-class radical circles in the late 1820s, when they were elaborated and disseminated through the journalism and birth-control tracts of Richard *Carlile.   IMcC

LAWRENCE, Sir Thomas (1769–1830), painter, whose virtuosity and idiosyncratic style earned him the label of 'the first Romantic portrait painter'. Lawrence's prodigious ability as a draughtsman was apparent from early pastels produced while he was resident in Bath. His provincial reputation preceded him to London, where he became a student at the *Royal Academy schools from 1787. His portrait of Queen Charlotte (1789) was praised for its likeness, and criticized for indecorous informality, but the subject and manner of the painting earned him instant attention in the London art world. Lawrence progressed steadily through the institutional hierarchy, becoming a Royal Academician in 1794 and president of the Royal Academy in 1820, following a knighthood in 1815.

His portraits were characterized by an attention to mood. Many of them were set outdoors and dominated by stormy skies, and his several paintings of the actor John Philip *Kemble in roles such as Coriolanus (1799) and Hamlet (1801) were deliberately designed to have some of the qualities of *history painting. In 1818 he was sent by the Prince Regent to paint the Allied heads of state in the aftermath of the wars with *Napoleon. He travelled throughout Europe to prepare this gallery of heroes for the 'Waterloo Chamber' at Windsor Castle, and these works established his position as the portraitist of high society, royalty, the military, and élite society in general.   SW

LAWRENCE, Sir William (1783–1865), anatomist, anthropologist, and medical reformer. The son of a leading provincial surgeon, he was educated at Elmore School near Gloucester, then apprenticed to John *Abernethy. He became a licentiate of the College of Surgeons in 1805, shortly afterwards establishing his critical reputation with work on hernia and eye diseases [see *medicine, 18]. Through Abernethy he gained the post of assistant surgeon at St Bartholomew's and election to the Royal Society in 1813. Within two years he had gained sinecures at

80, 103

80. Thomas Lawrence's portrait of the antiquarian, aesthetician, and erotic theorist Richard Payne Knight, 1794.

the Royal Bridewell and Bethlehem hospitals, and the prestigious Hunterian professorship of Anatomy and Surgery at the College of Surgeons.

Lawrence used his two inaugural *lectures to challenge the orthodox belief that life was a vital principle or power divinely bestowed on matter. Inspired by the Parisian anatomist Cuvier, Lawrence argued that life was the product of the organization of matter. The following year he directly attacked Abernethy on the issue, and a public controversy ensued which forms part of the intellectual background to Mary *Shelley's *Frankenstein* (1818). A survey of the controversy published in the *Quarterly Review* in November 1819 denounced Lawrence for his materialism and accused him of blasphemy. The College subsequently suspended Lawrence and called on him to suppress his lectures. Lawrence complied, but the lectures were pirated by a radical printer named Smith and serialized by Richard *Carlile in 1822–3. Lawrence subsequently threw himself into Thomas *Wakley's campaign for reform of the Colleges of Physicians and Surgeons, contributing numerous articles to the *Lancet* and chairing meetings in the name of medical reform. Then, in 1827, Lawrence shocked fellow reformists by gaining election to the Council of the College of Surgeons. His manœuvres culminated in 1831, when he had Wakley physically removed from the college lecture theatre. During the next two decades Lawrence built up a lucrative practice and ingratiated himself with various establishment figures, eventually becoming sergeant-surgeon to Queen Victoria and dying a baronet.   PT

lawyers. Despite the prominence of creative radicals and liberals like Thomas *Erskine, Samuel *Romilly, and Henry *Brougham, late Georgian lawyers earned a public reputation for conservatism in the face of demands for change. Writing of the *law [8] and its practitioners in 1792, Jeremy *Bentham said 'Not an atom of this rubbish will they ever suffer to be cleared away. How can you expect they should? It serves them as a fence to keep out interlopers.' Certainly the Bar (numbering fewer than 600 practitioners in 1798, and maybe reaching 1,300 by the mid-1830s) proved generally reluctant to countenance law reform, and had to be prodded by parliamentarians, journalists, and scholars, many of whom ultimately agreed that the majority of barristers put their own material and cultural interests before the cause of efficient administration of justice. Their backwardness may have been fostered by a diet of do-it-yourself legal education which entirely neglected jurisprudence for practice. And as Bentham suggested, it is even possible that 'Judge & Co.' had encouraged the elaboration of litigation procedure in order to protect their livelihood, for the essence of their professional work—advising and representing civil litigants in the Westminster courts and assizes—was in very short supply before 1800, and confidence did not return until the 1850s.

The more numerous attorneys and solicitors of the legal profession's 'lower branch' (amounting to at least 5,000 around 1800) had a more elastic supply of work, and generally improved their standing in the late eighteenth and early nineteenth centuries. Unlike the barristers (who tended to concentrate in London), the majority were spread out over the country, and were therefore available for a host of grass-roots clerical, business, and administrative functions, including estate management and land-broking, moneylending, and basic conveyancing, besides the initiation and general conduct of litigation (per specialist firms in the capital). Their traditionally poor reputation as unlearned and corrupt pettifoggers was ameliorated from the mid-eighteenth century through the efforts of several provincial law societies and the 'Society of Gentleman Practisers in Law and Equity'—a campaigning body which blazed the trail taken up by the Law Society in 1823.

Like individual barristers, members of the lower branch of lawyers (who increasingly preferred to be called 'solicitors') assisted in the transformation of British society, in their case especially as agents for *enclosure schemes, turnpike trusts, and canal and railway projects [see *transport]. But despite the criticism of the Bar, they continued to be regarded as socially inferior to the barristers. The latter were all gentlemen by definition and members of the 'Honourable' (and moribund) inns of court; although it is remarkable that the Old Bailey practitioner—a new growth amidst the general depression of Bar practice in the late eighteenth century—came to be regarded as 'a by-word for disgrace and infamy'. Given that defence counsel were largely responsible for improving the rights of defendants in criminal trials, this may stand as an ironic judgement on the prevailing attitudes and interests of the Bar as a whole.   DL

lecturing institutions complemented the increasing cultural authority of literary *reviews and were important venues for the dissemination of new developments in moral and *natural philosophy [34], and literature.

In 1800 fifty aristocrats, led by Count Benjamin Rumford (1753–1814) and Sir Joseph *Banks, set out to wed science to commerce, philosophy to technology, and literary traditions to the newest frameworks of modernity by establishing the Royal Institution in London's West End. Equipped with a public auditorium, laboratories, reading-rooms, and a library, the Royal was followed over the next thirty years by the London Institution (*fl.* 1806), the Surrey Institution (*fl.* 1807), the Russell Institution (*fl.* 1809), and many others.

As an emerging third arm of Britain's culture industry, in addition to the *publishing houses and the periodical press, the London lecturing empire developed an audience of well-heeled 'fashionables' who beheld spectacular demonstrations of the new technological science by dazzling lecturers such as Sir Humphry *Davy and Michael *Faraday. When Sydney *Smith lectured on moral philosophy and S. T. *Coleridge on English *poetry [29] at the Royal, the scientific enterprise became a wider campaign to mould the shape of public discourse across the categories of knowledge. Women, excluded from Britain's universities, were conspicuous students of the scientific, moral, and literary lecturers.

A faction of the Royal Institution's proprietors—mainly bankers and colonialists—broke away to found the more lavishly financed and commercially aggressive London Institution in 1806, though its full lecturing programmes did not begin until 1820. Orientated to wealth derived from colonization rather than from the agricultural improvement promoted by the Royal Institution, the London Institution emphasized lectures in biology, palaeontology, and, for the non-scientific part of its programme, an early form of popular anthropology [see *exploration, 37]. The Leverian Natural History Museum was founded in 1787. It operated as the Surrey Institution in Blackfriars Road for some time, when *Hazlitt and Coleridge lectured on literature to an audience composed partly of *Quakers and Dissenters, then in 1830 became the famous radical and freethinking forum, the Blackfriars Rotunda.

The overall impact of London's lecturing empire is hard to overestimate. *Utilitarians adopted its model to found the *Mechanics' Institutes in the mid-1820s and, on a less scientific and more commercial basis, the lyceum movement in the United States. Cross-Atlantic intellectual traffic occurred between the British and American lecturing worlds, and the audience-building begun in England was vastly amplified by the popular lecture circuits and institutions of the United States.   JK

LEE, Sophia (1750–1824) and **Harriet** (1757–1851), novelists, playwrights, schoolmistresses, whose writings see a convergence of the waning Restoration stage play, historical costume *romance, *Gothic melodrama, and fashionable *roman-à-clef* novel.

They were the daughters of the actor John Lee. Their mother died early, so Sophia kept house for her father, and held the family together. The two sisters worked in close collaboration, sometimes wrote joint letters to their friends, and developed similar handwriting. Neither Sophia nor Harriet ever married, Harriet rejecting a proposal of marriage from William *Godwin in 1798, with Sophia's collaboration. Together they lived and wrote, first in Bath and later at Clifton, near Bristol, which was, like Bath, a provincial centre hospitable to literary females.

On the death of their father in 1781 the sisters established a school for young ladies at Belvidere House, Bath [see *female education], with the proceeds of Sophia's first play, *A Chapter of Accidents* (1780). Based on Diderot's *Le Père de Famille* (1760), it was produced at the Haymarket Theatre, ran into many editions, stayed long in the repertoire, and was reprinted in many collections including Elizabeth *Inchbald's *The Modern Theatre* (1811). For twenty years the sisters prospered, frequently visiting

London, where they had many friends in literary and theatrical circles, while Bath in the season, as the marriage mart of England, drew many pupils to their school and visitors to their stately evening parties.

As Miss Lee, the elder unmarried sister, Sophia assumed the headmistress's position, and the heroine protagonists of her plays and *novels [31] show a command of the domestic hierarchy of mistress over servant, teacher over pupil, and between elder and younger sister. Her novel The Recess (1783–5) adapted the Stuart dynastic allegiances of *Toryism to courtship romance, and was influential for the novels of Ann *Radcliffe (who as Miss Ann Ward was a pupil of Sophia Lee), and Walter *Scott. A cavalier mix of historical personages with fictitious characters detours recorded history into imaginary alternatives, and projects the current unpopularity of the Hanoverian and Bourbon monarchs onto a witchified Queen Elizabeth I.

Sophia Lee's blank-verse tragedy set in Moorish Spain, Almeyda, Queen of Granada, opened at Drury Lane on 20 April 1796, with Sarah *Siddons and her brother, John Philip *Kemble, as the ill-fated lovers, Almeyda and Alonzo. According to Siddons's biographer, the Prologue and Epilogue were written by Harriet Lee. The morganatic Celtic dynasty of The Recess reappears in oriental dress. Queen Almeyda's sacrifice of inclination to duty is an edifying spectacle to the Muslim rulers of Spain, but these genuflections stop short of the programmatic conversion of Islamic rulers to Western Christianity. Harriet Lee's first novel The Errors of Inocence (1786) used the epistolary style of Richardson; her second novel was Clara Lennox (1797). Harriet's first stage comedy was The New Peerage (1787), and another play in 1798 was published but not performed.

However, it was their jointly authored volumes of short stories, Canterbury Tales (1797–1805), which won the sisters most acclaim. Ten of the twelve were by Harriet, including 'Kruitzner or the German's Tale', an acknowledged influence on *Byron, a story of two men locked in pursuit and flight. Sophia's was the minor contribution, but in the spirit of sisterly collaboration she contributed to all but one of five volumes over the seven years of publication.

In 1803 they decided to close the school, and Sophia published a six-volume semi-autobiographical novel, The Life of a Lover (1804). However, by this date, their most successful works were behind them, and neither sister published new work in old age, although Harriet's The Three Strangers, a dramatization of 'Kruitzner or the German's Tale', in Canterbury Tales (1801) appeared in 1825.   JB

lesbianism, see *Sapphism.

LEWIS, Matthew Gregory 'Monk' (1775–1818), MP, novelist, playwright, and poet who became one of the most widely recognized literary figures of the 1790s following the scandalous success of his *Gothic novel, The Monk (1796).

The first son of Matthew Lewis and Frances Maria Sewell, Matthew Gregory Lewis's home life was privileged, albeit somewhat unconventional. Lewis's

parents separated permanently in 1781, although his father's bill for divorce was ultimately denied. After his mother left the family, Lewis continued to live with his father, who was prominent in the War Office. He remained close to his mother, however, offering her emotional and financial support throughout his life, and frequently acting as a mediator between his parents. Lewis was educated at Westminster School and Oxford; his father intended him for a diplomatic career, and so he became remarkably fluent in modern languages, including French, Spanish, and German.

While still in his teens, Lewis coveted a literary career as a route to celebrity and fame as well as a way to earn money to supplement his mother's allowance. He achieved that goal early; when he was 21, his first published novel brought him great praise and even greater censure. By The Monk's anonymous initial appearance in 1796, the Gothic novel had already gained a reputation as the province of hack writers who catered to *circulating library patrons' taste for terror and immorality. Early reviewers treated Lewis's anonymous novel as just another clever example of the debased Gothic genre, until the second edition revealed that 'M. G. Lewis, Esq., MP' was the novel's author. This revelation enabled contemporary reviewers and moralists to focus their anti-Gothic rhetoric on a particular author: Matthew 'Monk' Lewis. Reviewers like S. T. *Coleridge claimed to be shocked that a British legislator would stoop to purveying vice-ridden and blasphemous circulating library 'trash', thereby implying that Lewis's identities as a politician and a hack writer were grossly incompatible.

Such attitudes reveal the extent to which authors were coming to be held personally responsible for the harmful effects their literary works might have on public morals. For example, Lewis himself was apparently threatened with prosecution over The Monk, rather than his publisher or bookseller—the usual targets for such legal proceedings. In the face of such threats, Lewis undertook a revised fourth edition, and charges were never formally lodged against him. This censored edition did little to satisfy his critics' objections, however, and only increased the public's interest in the uncensored early editions, and in the man who created them.

Lewis's celebrity and notoriety resulted from the reading public's insistence on identifying him with his novel's transgressive title-character, Ambrosio, 'The Monk'. The character's exploits include murdering a woman who turns out to be his mother, lusting after a woman who turns out to be his sister, and having an illicit affair with a young woman whom he at first believes to be a male novice, but who may be a disguised demon. By equating Ambrosio, 'The Monk', with his creator, 'Monk' Lewis, Lewis's audience constructed the author's desires as similarly perverse. Even before Byronism cemented cultural links between literary fame and sexual notoriety, gossip about Lewis's erotic attraction to men became a similarly 'open secret' that played a key role in establishing him as a literary lion. Instead of hurting his literary career, this scandalous identification of

Lewis with 'The Monk' seemed further to whet the general reading public's appetite for his work.

Lewis never seriously returned to novel-writing following his initial success with *The Monk*. Instead he turned his attention to the stage, writing both tragedies and comedies for R. B. *Sheridan at Drury Lane, and later for Thomas Harris (d. 1820), who managed Covent Garden. Lewis was a prolific playwright, writing, adapting, or translating more than ten plays between 1797 and 1812. The plays secured Lewis's reputation as a clever hack whose mastery of Gothic conventions proved as successful with contemporary *theatre [24] audiences as it had with the novel-reading public. Although Lewis proved a versatile playwright, his most successful efforts were Gothic *melodramas attended with spectacular stage effects, for many of which Lewis himself provided detailed stage directions. *The Castle Spectre* (performed 1797, published 1798), Lewis's first play to be produced, delighted audiences with such dramatic effects as the fortuitous appearance of the ghost of the heroine's mother, and the discovery of the heroine's long-lost father in a ghastly castle dungeon. Lewis's celebrity as 'the author of *The Monk*' both helped and hurt his theatrical career. While reviewers continued to scrutinize his plays for hints of immorality, Harris valued Lewis as a draw for new productions, and defied convention by featuring the playwright's celebrated name prominently on his playbills.

Lewis's contemporaries like Walter *Scott and Lord *Byron were both fascinated and repelled by Lewis's celebrity. They generally admired his poetry (and its commercial success), even if they did not find much to praise in his novels or plays. Even reviewers who generally disliked *The Monk* praised Lewis's poetry, especially *ballads like 'Alonzo the Brave and the Fair Imogene', which were frequently reprinted separately. Lewis might be said to have launched Scott's poetic career in his capacity as editor of *Tales of Wonder* (1801), a collection of imitations and translations of ancient ballads. Although the collection was scornfully dubbed 'Tales of Plunder' because of its low proportion of original poems and its high price, Lewis's and Scott's ballad imitations found their adherents, even at a time when the ballad form's cultural authority was on the wane. Although Lewis's successors to literary fame may have publicly scorned his commercial success, his career undoubtedly provided a model of the rewards and pitfalls of popular authorship in the Romantic period.   LW

liberal, used in the late eighteenth and early nineteenth centuries as a generic epithet to characterize those concerned to maintain or secure for the individual citizen various liberties or rights under law. In this sense, 'the individual citizen' referred either to an abstract universal—'all men', according to the American *Declaration of Independence* (1776), being entitled to 'Life, Liberty, and the pursuit of Happiness'—or to one who, by virtue of property, possessed an interest in the conduct of the affairs of the nation.

Although it was 1859 before Britain had an acknowledged Liberal Party, liberalism had been around at least since John *Locke's *Two Treatises on Government* (1698). However, liberal thinking was divided on certain issues—for example, liberal *Whigs and, later, philosophical radicals like Jeremy *Bentham, rejected the Lockean assumption of natural, inalienable rights under God. Liberalism is thus best thought of as a reticulated system of changing policies unified by the assumption of certain freedoms of person, property, conscience, and opinion. Such freedoms aimed progressively to minimize the constraints imposed by government, whose authority supposedly derived exclusively from the people to protect the people [see *laissez-faire*].

Prominent amongst the freedoms coveted by liberalism in the period were those of speech, assembly, worship, and (persistently denied to Catholics and Nonconformists) advance within the establishment. The basic freedom from arbitrary arrest or imprisonment (habeas corpus) was taken for granted, at least until the 1790s when, under *Pitt, even that was more honoured in the breach than the observance. Consequently, liberalism during the war with France often presents as opposition to legislative oppressions.   WC

liberal Toryism was an important feature of postwar administrations from Lord *Liverpool's of 1812, and is associated particularly with Liverpool, George *Canning, William Huskisson (1770–1830), and Sir Robert *Peel. Its proponents accepted the conventional constitutional nostrums of the *Tory party but were advocates of a liberal approach to economic policy in both the domestic and international spheres. Liberal Tories were closely identified with moves to reduce protectionism in international trade (illustrated by modifications to the Navigation Code in 1822, and by the review of the *corn laws between 1825 and 1828 and in the 1840s). They also aspired to end both unsound speculation and manipulated uncertainty by a return to the gold standard; to promote economic growth through an adoption of direct rather than indirect *income taxation; and to reform administration so as to make government an efficient but restricted mechanism [see *parliamentary reform].

These policies aroused considerable resentment from more traditionalist elements within the party. Liberal Tories were accused by both orthodox and radical Tories of being converts to the superficially beguiling but divisive and ungodly doctrines of modern *political economy [33]. Such charges are understandable given that the economic and social policies of liberal Tories foreshadowed *laissez-faire* ideologies of the Victorian era. The refocusing of Tory economic policy has been attributed both to a change in the party's most important constituency from landed to non-landed interests and to the impact of ethical concerns which reflected a deep-seated religiosity. The abandonment of interventionism treasured by conventional Tories was thought necessary to restore a 'natural' system of order in which the disciplines of the market expressed the workings of Providence.   JMo

Linley family. Thomas Linley (1733–95), composer and harpsichordist, established himself in Bath as a singing-master, and directed the city's Lenten oratorios and concerts (c.1755–75). He and his wife, Mary Johnson (1729–1820), a wardrobe mistress, had twelve children, eight of whom were exceptionally gifted musically and performed in their father's concerts from a young age. The eldest, Elizabeth Ann (1754–92), was soon idolized as the finest soprano of the day, but following her marriage to R. B. *Sheridan in 1773 she sang only in private. Thomas junior (1756–88), a precocious violinist and composer, was sent to Florence (c.1768–71) to study with Nardini, where he befriended the young *Mozart. Mary (1758–87) was a gifted soprano who married the dramatist Richard Tickell in 1780.

Despite growing prestige and prosperity, Linley considered his family's horizons limited in Bath, so he extended their London contacts. Elizabeth and Mary both appeared in the capital's oratorios; shortly afterwards, Linley became joint director of the oratorios at Drury Lane (1774), where he did much to rehabilitate *Handel's music. Following the success of *The Duenna* (Covent Garden, 1775), his collaboration with Sheridan and Thomas junior, Linley bought a share in Drury Lane theatre and moved his family to London (1776). He acted as music director at the theatre, composing and arranging scores for plays, *pantomimes, and operas. His songs were thought to uphold the 'pure English school' against the voguish Italian style.

Linley's later years were tinged with tragedy, all but three of his children predeceasing him. Perhaps the most distressing was the drowning of Thomas junior in a boating accident, just as he was beginning to realize his great potential as a composer.

Others of the eight musical children include Samuel (1760–78), oboist; Maria (1763–1784), an oratorio soprano; and William (1771–1835), a theatrical composer, musical director, and author. Famed for beauty as well as talent, the family became favourite subjects with artists, including *Gainsborough and *Reynolds. RC

LINNELL, John (1792–1882), *landscape painter. The son of a print-seller who showed early talent as a draughtsman, he was employed by his father to copy fashionable watercolours. Linnell entered the *Royal Academy schools in 1805, while Henry *Fuseli was still keeper, and proceeded to earn his living mainly as a *portrait painter until 1845, after which time he devoted himself to landscapes or historical landscapes with a religious flavour.

In 1811 Linnell became a Baptist and maintained the radicalism in his political opinions traditionally associated with Nonconformity. This, together with his taste for the grand, primitive style of Dürer and Michelangelo, explains why Linnell became such a firm friend and supporter of William *Blake from 1818 onwards, despite a concern that '[Blake] said many things tending to the corruption of Christian morals'. Most of the commissions of Blake's last decade were obtained with the help of Linnell, who also introduced the poet-painter to the *Shoreham

Ancients (though Linnell himself was not well disposed to the rather pious mysticism of the group). JM

LISTER, Anne (1791–1840), scholar, heiress, traveller, diarist, and lesbian. Lister's diaries offer a fascinating case study of Romantic female *autobiography and an unprecedented and startlingly self-conscious early modern elaboration of lesbian identity, sexual practice, and performative style [see *sapphism].

Born in Halifax, west Yorkshire, the eldest surviving child of Captain Jeremy Lister, Anne Lister inherited the estate of Shibden Hall after the death of her unmarried paternal uncle, James Lister. After a rural East Riding childhood, Lister was educated at boarding-school in York before moving back to Halifax in 1806, to live with her uncle and aunt. Here she remained for the rest of her life, when not travelling abroad. She educated herself in languages and natural philosophy, and ran the estate with its farms, tenancies, and mining and quarrying interests.

From 1806 Lister began keeping a brief journal, which she conducted from 1817 until her death. This vast diary (approximately 6,000 pages) was not systematically edited and published until the late 1980s, and most of it remains unpublished. Written largely in code, the journals speak the pathos of Lister's desire for a lifelong female companion, while presenting in witty and fulsome detail her schoolgirl romances, adult flirtations, casual affairs, and long-term sexual relationships with women, predominantly from the lower gentry and upper-middle-class neighbouring circles of provincial Yorkshire. Her most cherished long-term lover was the doctor's daughter Marianna Belcombe (later Lawton), from whom she contracted venereal disease and with whom she pledged vows and hatched schemes of domestic bliss in the event of the fantasized early death of Marianna's husband—sadly for the two women unrealized.

In 1824, during the Bourbon Restoration, when post-revolutionary France reopened the *Grand Tour to a new breed of English tourist, Lister stayed in Paris in a modest pension, 'sauntered' habitually down the Champs-Elysées, and conducted a series of brief but complicated affairs. Travelling in Russia, she contracted a fever and died at the foot of the Caucasian mountains in 1840. Her then lover, the neighbouring heiress Ann Walker, who had been living and travelling with Lister (but who was none the less never to be for Lister the grand passion that Marianna had been), transported her body, together with her diaries, back to Shibden Hall. CT

literary and philosophical societies. The eighteenth century was an age when societies flourished. They ranged from informal circles or coteries, through secret masonic or masonic-style societies [see *freemasonry], to publicly organized societies with regulated or open membership. Their purposes varied from the cultivation of the latest ideas and patronage of high-minded *Enlightenment [32] endeavours in the arts and sciences to *debating

48

societies and convivial drinking clubs: they were almost exclusively masculine. The development of the literary and philosophical societies in the mid- to late eighteenth century combined different aspects of Enlightenment virtue: the pursuit of science in an active way, including its commercial exploitation; keeping up to date with the latest knowledge, through meetings, correspondence, and the creation of good libraries, laboratories, and museums; the deliberate fostering of civic pride; the cultivation of gentlemanly virtue; and the attempt to use the latest ideas to improve municipal life, not least public health. Rational Dissenters featured strongly amongst their members, which is indicative of their eminence in the late Enlightenment world, of their desire to demonstrate that they were good citizens despite their unorthodox ideas and also to re-shape the very notion of good citizenship for the emerging middle class of the industrial revolution.

At their inception, literary and philosophical societies were usually a recognition and formalization of existing circles of Enlightenment cultivation, and were especially important in the growing cities of the midlands and the north. The exemplar and most distinguished of these societies was the Lunar Society of Birmingham, which had a relatively short life from about 1765 until around 1800. It owed its name to the fact that its members met formally on the Monday afternoon nearest the full moon. No other society had such a distinguished membership, which included Matthew *Boulton, Erasmus *Darwin, Thomas *Day, Richard Lovell *Edgeworth, Joseph *Priestley, James *Watt, and Josiah *Wedgwood. Its total membership was only fourteen, yet this represented a microcosm of distinction in *natural philosophy [34], *medicine [18], the arts, and industry. Next in importance was the Manchester Literary and Philosophical Society, established in 1781. It was a more substantial society than the Lunar, having twenty-four founder-members. Thomas Percival (1740–1804), physician and Rational Dissenter, was the most eminent of its founders, and was president for nineteen of its first twenty-five years. John *Dalton was also an early member, and his presence was indicative of the attractions of the society which survives to this day. Other cities followed the Manchester example, including Derby in 1783, Newcastle upon Tyne in 1793, Liverpool in 1812, and Leeds in 1820.

Such enlightened and public-minded, though élitist, enterprises are important reminders not only of an Enlightenment legacy but of the adaptation of Enlightenment aspirations to industrial society. In due course some key features of these private initiatives, such as libraries and museums, would be taken over by municipal authorities and become an integral part of Victorian civic mindedness. If, as the nineteenth century wore on, the societies themselves bred liberal respectability, becoming *gentlemen's clubs whose members basked in Victorian civility, there were still individuals associated with them who retained the desire to make the world a better place through the active application of knowledge—an Enlightenment inheritance which caused them ever-increasing anxiety.   MF

Liverpool Cabinet. From 1790 to 1832, when eighteenth-century methods of managing parliament were no longer so effective and yet party discipline had not yet developed, the role of parliament was peculiarly important as a decider of major policy issues. In this context, Lord Liverpool (1770–1828) developed a strategy for organizing the executive arm of government which produced an unusually uncontroversial Cabinet and the subsequent perception of the Liverpool administration's mediocrity.

Cabinet under Liverpool was filled with 'politicians'—men who had significant electoral influence. Those who influenced policymaking on tariffs, currency, and finance were as far as possible kept out of Cabinet. The reason for this demarcation between policymaking and politics, or 'men of business' and 'politicians', was to avoid attacks on the government from a parliamentary back bench unusually independent of executive influence. Most major policy initiatives resulted from careful management of parliamentary select committees. This management of political business was Liverpool's executive reformulation of a broadly eighteenth-century governing ethos.

Liverpool's Cabinet had three main objectives. First, in the years 1812 to 1815, the overwhelming aim was to defeat *Napoleon. From 1816 to 1823, Liverpool sought to manage the transition from *war [2] to peace. Third, the years from 1823 to 1827 saw the demise of Liverpool's largely successful executive strategy of keeping policy out of the political arena, due mainly to the advent to the Cabinet of George *Canning and William Huskisson (1770–1830). As career politicians, it was in their interest to connect day-to-day politics with the status of the Cabinet.

                                                                                  JF

LLANDAFF, Bishop of, see Richard *Watson.

LOCKE, John (1632–1704), philosopher, one of the first and leading figures of the European *Enlightenment [32]. Locke's main writings are *An Essay Concerning Human Understanding* (1690) and *Two Treatises of Government* (1689); the former contains mainly what is now called epistemology and philosophy of science, the latter his political theory. However, the *Essay* also discusses issues in ethics and metaphysics. Locke became interested in philosophy by reading Descartes, whose writings were not part of the curriculum at Oxford when he was a student. He had a strong interest in the developing experimental sciences, and for some time worked with Robert Boyle (1627–91), the founder of modern *chemistry. Locke's thinking in ethics and political theory was influenced by the natural law tradition, and he was particularly impressed by the seventeenth-century German natural-law theorist Samuel Pufendorf.

In dealing with the problem of knowledge, the *Essay* is concerned with (among other things) the respective roles of reason and experience. According to Locke, all 'ideas' (mental contents) are in the last analysis derived from experience. He rejects the view, common in the seventeenth century, that there are innate ideas and principles. Because of this emphasis on the experiential basis of knowledge, Locke is often said to be the father of modern empiricism. But 'empiricism' can be a misleading term to describe his philosophical position. For Locke does not say that knowledge is directly derived from experience; rather, he claims that knowledge is constructed by the understanding which makes use of the experience-based 'ideas'. Moreover, he argues that we cannot attain knowledge of the real essence of natural objects. At best we can arrive at 'probable beliefs' about them, and there can be no 'science of nature'. For Locke, knowledge is characterized by absolute certainty, and this can be had only in those areas where reason is able to discover a priori, necessary truths—in disciplines such as mathematics and (as Locke thought) ethics. Thus, his position in epistemology is now often (and rightly) described as a form of 'mitigated scepticism'.

Two Treatises was written in 1680–2, and contains Locke's now famous theory of property in terms of the notion of labour. But his main concern is with the legitimization and function of political authority. Locke argues that each individual has a right to life, liberty, and property, and that it is the function of political authority to protect these rights. He emphasizes that the people have a right to resistance and even revolution when the political authority no longer fulfils its proper function—that is, when it no longer protects the rights of the individual citizens.

Other important writings include *The Reasonableness of Christianity* (1695), where he argues that Christians need to subscribe only to a few fundamental articles of faith; *A Letter Concerning Toleration* (1689), which calls for the toleration of Protestant Dissenters; and *Some Thoughts Concerning Education* (1693), according to which the main aim of education is to instil the motivation in the child to live rationally and virtuously. In general, Locke emphasizes the primacy of critical reason in all areas of human theory and practice.

The impact of Locke's thought has been immense. In Britain, the *Essay* was reprinted about every three years up to 1830, and many further editions have appeared since. Several abridgements of the book also contributed significantly to the spread of Locke's influence. In the eighteenth century, his thought was at the centre of philosophical discussions. Contemporaries compared his role with that of Aristotle in the Middle Ages, and his theoretical philosophy impressed (among many others) David *Hume in Scotland, Étienne Bonnot de Condillac in France, and Immanuel Kant in Germany. Kant, although very critical of Locke, took over from him the idea of a critical epistemology. Locke also influenced the developing discipline of *psychology [39] and contemporary theories of *education [17]. In psychology, for example, David Hartley (1705–57) in his *Observations on Man* (1749) put forward a mechanistic theory of the mind, based on the notion of the association of ideas which Locke had pioneered in a chapter added to the fourth edition of his *Essay* (1700). Many of his ideas also became common knowledge and were taken up in the literature of the time, for example in the works of Richardson, Swift, Sterne, and Addison. More generally, it has been argued that Locke's account of the self—which abandons the traditional view that an immaterial thinking substance is essential to personal identity—has had a decisive impact on the development of modern literature.

The ideas of *Two Treatises* became so well known thay they had an impact even where the text itself was not studied in any detail. Arguments and ideas from Locke were used by the Irish Nationalists: William Molyneux's *The Case of Ireland* (1698) became a standard text of the movement. And although the importance of the *Two Treatises* for the independence movement in the *American Revolution has been overestimated, it remains true that many leading intellectuals of that movement were very familiar with the principles of Locke's work. This is also true of some of the ideologues of the *French Revolution.

UT

LOCKHART, John Gibson (1794–1854), novelist, *reviewer, editor, biographer. 'The Scorpion which delighteth to sting men's faces' was Lockhart's own choice of persona; John Scott (1783–1821) named him 'Emperor of the Mohocks' after the upper-class hooligans of the early eighteenth century. A devoted *Tory who became intimate with Cabinet ministers during his editorship of the *Quarterly Review* from 1825 to his 1853, Lockhart was of the Scottish professional middle class, educated at Glasgow University and Balliol College, Oxford, with a law degree from Edinburgh. A 'Scorpion' he could be, however; a reviewer and *satirist whose cruelty—tempered by time and his father-in-law, Walter *Scott—accompanied an impressive critical intelligence and social and psychological insight.

His treatment of the sexually repressive religiosity of the Presbyterian temperament in *Some Passages in the Life of Mr Adam Blair* (1822) ultimately forsakes that insight, however, seeking atonement like its eponymous hero. The novel falls victim to the fear of sensual abandon that inspired Lockhart's political and religious conservatism and notorious sneering in *Blackwood's Edinburgh Magazine* at what he called 'the Cockney School of Poetry'—amongst them Leigh *Hunt, John *Keats, and William *Hazlitt—as well as a regime of abstinence in old age through which he nearly starved himself to death.

It was not in the novel that Lockhart achieved his ambition to record 'the Caledonian humours' of his own age, therefore, but in social and cultural documentary like *Peter's Letters to His Kinsfolk* (1819)—a perceptive if partial study of Edinburgh life and letters—and, pre-eminently, in his biography of Scott. Limited by conventional set-pieces and an ultimate concern with 'character' rather than personality, his seven-volume *Memoirs of the Life of Sir Walter Scott, Bart* (1837–8) is otherwise innovative and strong in its detailed, critical re-creation of social and physical conditions and its construction of an internal 'logic' of personal and professional development through different phases—priorities inherited from *Scottish Enlightenment historiography.

WC

London Corresponding Society, see *corresponding societies.

London Revolution Society. At the outset of the *French Revolution, the London Revolution Society enjoyed a brief period of fame and notoriety. The society predominantly comprised Dissenters, and existed to perpetuate what it conceived to be the ideals enshrined in the *Glorious Revolution of 1688. It first came to prominence in 1788 by organizing a major celebratory dinner to commemorate the centenary of the Glorious Revolution. This was held on 4 November, King William's birthday. Gradually, the society began to act more like a reform society than a convivial club. Extant records begin on 16 June 1788, and for the next few years it met at least once a month and worked to proclaim its principles. Set out by Earl Stanhope (1753–1816) in a report presented to a commemoratory meeting on 4 November, these asserted that all civil and political authority is derived from the people; that the abuse of power justifies resistance; and that the right of private judgement, liberty of conscience, trial by jury, the *freedom of the press, and the freedom of *elections ought ever to be held sacred and inviolable.

Such principles formed the basis of Richard *Price's *Discourse on the Love of Our Country*, preached the following year. By portraying the French as the embodiment of the principles of the Glorious Revolution, he generalized British revolutionary principles and associated them with those of the *Enlightenment [32]. The idea of an international enlightened confraternity was given credibility by the active correspondence between the society and leading French figures, the National Assembly, and revolutionary societies early in the French Revolution. Congratulatory addresses were exchanged, French delegates were received, and for a year or so a wave of euphoria swept over its members, who believed that enlightened cosmopolitan principles were triumphing and that the *millennial vision of a warless world was on the way to being established. However, this vision rapidly dimmed as the French Revolution failed to stabilize itself, as the drift into future international conflict was signalled by the flight of émigrés from France, and as its members were confronted by more radical and programmatic proposals for reform.

The last recorded meeting of the society was its anniversary meeting on 4 November 1791. Although its prominence had been short-lived, the LRS helped frame the terms and tone of discussion of the French Revolution. Edmund *Burke's *Reflections on the Revolution in France* (1790) attacked not only the notion that the Glorious Revolution had established universal principles but also the whole idea of applying 'abstract' ideas to particular situations. Burke linked the society with a specific historic revolution and its revolutionary principles, namely that which executed Charles I and established a Commonwealth in England.   MF

LOUDON, John Claudius (1783–1843), landscape gardener and horticultural writer. Born in Scotland,

Loudon's practice as a landscape gardener was influenced by the *picturesque theory of Richard *Payne Knight and Uvedale *Price, but his chief impact was as a prolific writer and editor of books and journals concerning horticulture, *landscape gardening, and domestic *architecture [28]. Loudon was a pioneer in the development of the aboretum, thereby assimilating interest in *botany to the picturesque aesthetics of landscape gardening. His wife, Jane Loudon (1807–58), with whom he closely collaborated, was also a prolific writer of horticultural texts, aimed particularly at women.

Works such as *Encyclopaedia of Gardening* (1822), *Encyclopaedia of Agriculture* (1825), *Encyclopaedia of Plants* (1829), and *Encyclopaedia of Cottage, Farm and Villa Architecture and Furniture* (1833), in addition to his magazines, the *Gardener's Magazine* (1826–42), the *Magazine of Natural History* (1829–36), and the *Architectural Magazine* (1834–8), extended the audience for what had previously been the preserve of the landed élite. These works were design and lifestyle manuals for the middling orders, formative in the development of early Victorian urban and domestic space.   GR

LOUTHERBOURG, Philippe Jacques de (1740–1812), painter, stage and costume designer, faith healer. Born in Strasburg, Loutherbourg established himself as a painter in Paris before moving to London in 1771. Under David Garrick (1717–79) and later R. B. *Sheridan, he worked at Drury Lane theatre as its chief stage designer and was responsible for far-reaching innovations in perspective and lighting effects. His most notable productions included *The Camp* (1778) and *The Critic* (1779) for Sheridan; *The Wonders of Derbyshire* (1779), influenced by *Gilpin's theory of the *picturesque; and *Omai* (1785) [see *theatre, 24].

Loutherbourg's costume designs for *Omai* were based on paintings made by John Webber (1750–93) during his voyage with *Cook, and they contributed significantly to the fashion for historical and ethnographic authenticity in stage costuming. In 1781 Loutherbourg established the Eidophusikon, a miniature scenic illusion combining lighting effects and mechanically operated models, accompanied by music. The innovations of the Eidophusikon anticipated the development of the *panorama and diorama, and, ultimately, of cinema.

Loutherbourg was interested in alchemy and *fringe medicine and was probably a *freemason. In 1786 he met the magician and freemason Count Cagliostro (1743–95), whom he sponsored and protected in London, following him in 1787 to Switzerland where a dispute between the two men ended in a *duel. On returning to London Loutherbourg set himself up as a faith healer, with little success: in 1789 his home was attacked by an irate mob.

As a painter, he worked in variety of genres—*landscape, *history, and battle—his most famous works being *A Midsummer Afternoon with a Methodist Preacher* (1777), *The Battle of Valenciennes* (1794), and *Coalbrookdale by Night* (1801). The latter work interpreted Britain's *industrialization [14] as   *19*

81. *The Apotheosis of Captain Cook* (1794), an engraving based on Philippe Jacques de Loutherbourg's design for the concluding scene of John O'Keeffe's popular pantomime of 1785, *Omai*. Loutherbourg designed the stage scenery from drawings made by John Webber during Cook's second Pacific voyage.

The APOTHEOSIS of CAPTAIN COOK.

From a Design of P.J.De Loutherbourg. R.A. The View of KARAKAKOOA BAY
& Is from a Drawing by John Webber. R.A (the last he made) in the Collection of Mr G.Baker.

London. Pubd. Jany. 20. 1794. by J. Thane. Spur Street. Leicester Square.

spectacular, alchemical theatre, and exemplifies the cross-fertilization of the various media and fields in which Loutherbourg worked.   GR

loyalism and loyalist associations. Loyalism was a set of political values and practices, in opposition to radicalism, which interpreted the constitution and the social order as divinely ordained and natural, and not to be tampered with by man on the basis of abstract principle or innovation. Its bastions were respect for the *monarchy, the *Anglican Church, and property, and its high theorist was Edmund *Burke, especially in *Reflections on the Revolution in France* (1790).

The formation in November 1792 of John *Reeves's *Association for the Protection of Liberty and Property Against Republicans and Levellers was followed by numerous loyalist associations throughout the country. Their activities, modelled to some extent on the radical constitutional societies, included correspondence with each other and with local and central authorities, the organization of addresses and petitions, public meetings and disturbances (as in the Thomas *Paine effigy burnings and the Church and King *riots), the monitoring of

radicals, and, after 1793, support of the *war [2] effort—especially the *volunteers. Alarmed by the influence of Paine's *Rights of Man* (1791), the associations were also involved in the dissemination of loyalist propaganda to the lower orders in the form of chapbooks, broadsides, and handbills [see *street literature]. Their activities abated somewhat in the late 1790s, but an intensified radicalism after 1815 led to a revival in loyalist associations such as the Brunswick clubs.   JF

Luddism. In 1811–12 the east midlands hosiery trade centred on Nottingham, the west Yorkshire woollen trade, and the Lancashire cotton trade experienced the destruction of machinery on an unprecedented scale. The term 'Luddism' derives from the name (taken from a pseudonym in an anonymous letter) of the mythical leader of the Nottingham machine-breakers, General Ned Ludd.

The causes of Luddism included threats to artisans' livelihood, work patterns, and status through the cyclical unemployment of the *war [2] years, the inability to trade with Europe due to the Napoleonic blockade, and the introduction of machinery and manufacturing techniques which made hard-earnt skills obsolete [see *industrialization, 14]. Conditions in the hosiery and woollen trades in particular were also influenced by the vagaries of *fashion, while the prohibition on trade with the United States after the 1811 Orders in council badly affected the cotton trade. Systematic machine-breaking arose in the aftermath of the passing of the anti-trade union Combination Acts of 1799–1800, the culmination of a decade-long struggle to have the Elizabethan Statute of Artificers enforced in the hosiery, woollen, and cotton trades. (The statute made it illegal to employ a man who had not served the requisite apprenticeship.) After campaigns for a minimum wage and appeals to parliament were rejected by politicians convinced by the arguments of *political economy [33], artisans sought to extort concessions from employers by using direct action. Machine-breaking was not indiscriminate: particular factories and workshops were targeted because of changes in production standards, harsh employers, the use of new machinery, or a combination of these factors. The government regarded the Luddite threat so seriously that by the summer of 1812 over 12,000 soldiers were deployed in the affected areas, more than the force that the Duke of *Wellington had with him in the *Peninsular War. In 1811 a bill was passed to make frame-breaking a capital offence: *Byron was among those who spoke against the measure in parliament.

Historians have long debated the connections between Luddism as a movement of economic protest and the radicalism of the early 1800s, a problem compounded by regional variations and strong traditions of secrecy. Most now agree, however, on the existence of a fluctuating but persistent overlap between the movement's industrial and political aspirations. While little was achieved in the long term as far as raising wages or banning new machines was concerned, Luddism provided the organizational impetus and strategic direction to the postwar radical movement. Major John *Cartwright's tour of the manufacturing districts in 1812 had some success in channelling Luddite insurrectionary discontent into constitutional forms. The importance of Luddite protest for early-nineteenth-century popular radical culture ought not to be underestimated.

JF

Lunar Society, see *literary and philosophical societies.

lyric, the most common form of *poetry [29] throughout the period, also came to be seen more abstractly as its purest or quintessential form. Lyric is a form of poem that imitates musical structure and evokes an experience undergone by a characteristic *sensibility [11]. Subsuming innumerable specific configurations—from the inherited *sonnet, *ode, and so forth, to the innovative 'greater Romantic lyric' identified by M. H. Abrams—the lyric was the most common genre of our period. *Wordsworth, for example, wrote more sonnets than any other British poet.

The lyric was encouraged by a number of related phenomena: a primitivism and *antiquarianism [35] seeking to recuperate as 'spontaneous' and more 'sincere' unsophisticated poetry from the past or the geographically and/or socially remote; a conception of 'poetry' as a mode of apprehension, rather than artistic construction; and the dismantling of a classical and neoclassical hierarchy of genres only reluctantly accommodating certain kinds of lyric.

Beyond this, a more symbolic 'lyric spirit' or 'lyricism', frequently characterized as feminine, is envisioned as supervening upon the genres of *epic and tragedy—masculinist, agonistic, complicit with authoritarianism—in a prophetic celebration of the fulfilment of the human spirit. The fourth act of *Shelley's *Prometheus Unbound* (1820) involves a version of this myth of poetic genre.

WC

M

McADAM, John Loudon (1756–1836), road surveyor. The eponymous inventor of a durable, smooth road surface, McAdam helped take long-distance road *transport in Britain to a peak of speed and efficiency in the 1820s and 1830s.

Born into the Scots minor gentry, McAdam was an unlikely recruit to the lowly occupation of road-making. He left for New York in 1770, and became a merchant. As a convinced loyalist during the *American Revolution, he returned in 1783 to Scotland, resuming the life of a country gentleman at Sauchrie in Ayrshire. However, involvement in the projects of his inventive cousin, Archibald Cochrane (1749–1831), brought financial disaster. Only the sale of his estate averted bankruptcy. In 1798 he moved south to rebuild his fortune; by 1801 he was resident in Bristol, his occupation unknown.

Prompted perhaps by his weary journey south, McAdam began an extensive investigation of England's roads. He travelled the country, observing the passage of vehicles, questioning turnpike trustees, surveyors, and workers. By 1811 he could confidently diagnose the problem and offer his remedy to a parliamentary select committee. During the eighteenth century Britain's main roads, under pressure from increasing commercial traffic, had been privatized: turnpike trusts were established, authorized to collect tolls for their maintenance from travellers. Most trustees acted conscientiously, McAdam argued, but they ignorantly wasted money on constant, futile repairs of easily rutted surfaces. McAdam prescribed a composition of small stones, broken to a maximum diameter of one inch and laid to a depth of one foot directly onto the subsoil, with no added sand or earth; the camber should be minimized. Under the weight of passing traffic the stones would coalesce into a smooth, solid, dust-free surface. Reuse of the large stones that had been dumped ineffectually by earlier menders, combined with fewer repairs in future, would guarantee lower costs. The committee seemed impressed, but no action followed.

In 1816 the opportunity to implement his ideas finally arrived. Appointed surveyor of Bristol's roads, McAdam imposed a reformed hierarchy of management. With all subordinates trained in his surfacing technique, he soon returned Bristol's turnpikes to repair and profitability. The demand for McAdam's services rose so swiftly that his three sons (and subsequently other kin) were drawn in as consultants and resident surveyors: they supervised the widespread improvement of road surfacing and administration throughout lowland Britain (the Scottish Highlands were Thomas *Telford's territory). By 1825 such roads were popularly described as 'macadamized'. Coaches travelled faster, regardless of all but the severest weather; passengers enjoyed greater comfort and safety; mail arrived more regularly; freight rates fell.

Parliament rewarded McAdam with grants totalling £6,000. His third son, Sir James McAdam, continued to prosper, principally as surveyor general of London's roads from 1827 to 1852. However, the family's business as a whole, so flourishing in the 1820s and 1830s, declined quickly in tandem with Britain's highways: long-distance road transport (and turnpike trusts) could not withstand the competition of the railways.   CMacL

Macartney's embassy to China (1792–4) was the first official mission sent from Britain and is of central importance to the history of diplomacy, trade, and cultural contact with China.

Most of the trade from China in the eighteenth century consisted of tea, silks, lacquerware, and porcelain. The *East India Company had been trading at Canton under what it regarded as restrictive regulation and corrupt administration. The idea of a direct representation to the Chinese court was put forward in mid-century to improve conditions at Canton as well as to open up trade, including the selling of English woollen goods, in other more northerly ports.

Henry *Dundas first appointed Lieutenant-Colonel Charles Cathcart ambassador in 1787, but he was an advanced consumptive and died *en route*. Dundas then appointed the diplomat George Macartney (1737–1806), who set out in 1792 with two ships, two Chinese interpreters who had trained as priests at the Chinese College in Naples, a natural philosopher, a botanist, and a five-piece German band, as well as the usual complement of sailors, painters, and officials. An enormous volume of records flowed from the embassy in the form of journals, accounts, observations, paintings, charts, and treatises.

The embassy failed in all its aims. The Chinese court would not receive diplomats from any country on equal terms, only accepting foreign emissaries as tribute missions who bowed down before the Emperor, figuratively and literally. (One of the contentious issues in the Macartney mission was precisely whether he would perform the kowtow or triple prostration or follow the rituals of the British court.) There was no perception on the Chinese part that any change in relations between the two countries was desirable or necessary.

Macartney's embassy features in caricatures by James *Gillray as well as in *satirical verse, notably *A Pair of Lyric Epistles to Lord Macartney and his Ship* (1792) by John *Wolcot.   BP

MACAULAY, Catharine (1731–91), republican historian, polemicist, writer on philosophy, ethics, and *education [17]. Her pamphlets and *History of England from the Accession of James I* (8 vols., 1763–83) were highly effective polemical interventions on behalf of a radical *Whig programme for *parliamentary reform, providing one of the most authoritative demonstrations of the significance of seventeenth-century English history for eighteenth-century radical politics [see *historiography].

Macaulay's *History* was initially welcomed as the first radical Whig reply to David *Hume's Tory *History of Great Britain* (1754–62) and its attack on the parliamentary leaders of the seventeenth century. Later volumes dealing with events after 1640 demonstrated the strength of her *republicanism and commitment to commonwealthman ideology which espoused cheap, efficient government sustained by a citizen militia. Macaulay moved in circles that included *Wilkites, Real Whigs, and members of the Society of the Supporters of the Bill of Rights—co-founded by her brother John Sawbridge. A prescient, early opponent of Edmund *Burke, Macaulay attacked his moderate Whig use of the *Glorious Revolution and patriot language in her *Observations on . . . Thoughts on the Cause of the Present Discontents* (1770) and *Observations on the Reflections of the Rt. Hon. Edmund Burke* (1790). Her *Address to the People of England, Scotland, and Ireland* (1775) attacked the Quebec Act for establishing a popish government in Canada, and blamed parliamentary corruption and excessive taxes for the pending *American Revolution. Mary *Wollstonecraft greatly admired Macaulay, praising her final work, *Letters on Education* (1790), for its views on *female education.   CT

82. Statue of Catharine Macaulay, 1772, by the wax modeller (and American spy) Patience Wright, erected by a fervent admirer, the Revd Dr Thomas Wilson, in the church of St Stephen's Walbrook, London. In the elevated inscription he states: 'once in every age I could wish such a Woman to appear, As a proof that Genius is not confined to Sex.'

MACAULAY, Thomas Babington, Baron Macaulay (1800–59). Lawyer, politician, and civil servant, Macaulay achieved widespread and lasting fame as a critic, essayist, and, in the last decade of his life, historian of England. He was the eldest child of prominent Clapham *Evangelicals, Zachary Macaulay (1768–1838) and Selina Mills Macaulay (1767–1831). Highly intelligent and precocious, Macaulay was greatly influenced through the course of his childhood by his parents and their intimate friends amongst the men and women who constituted the so-called 'Clapham Sect' of religious and social reformers.

By the time he arrived at Trinity College, Cambridge, in 1818, Macaulay had still not experienced the personal call to Christ that Evangelicals held as essential to true faith. He was strongly attracted to literature and politics, and became an active and popular participant in Cambridge Union debates. This led to tensions and unhappiness between Macaulay and his father, especially as Zachary realized that his son still shared his reformist ambitions but now generally viewed the affairs of the world in a secular light.

By 1824 the collapse of the family's finances left Macaulay with no option but to seek a career in *law [8]. By the time he joined the Northern Circuit as a barrister in early 1826, he was an active member of John Stuart *Mill's London Debating Society, and had established his literary fame, as well as *Whig political patronage, by articles published in the *Edinburgh Review* on West Indian *slavery [6] and on John *Milton.

Macaulay was elected to parliament as a reform-minded Whig in 1830. In 1834 political and financial circumstances led him to accept a seat on the Supreme Council of India, in Calcutta, where he continued to write for leading British journals until his return to London in 1838. He was famed in his time as one of Britain's leading men of letters, and his letters, essays, and *History of England* (1848–61) remain invaluable sources for understanding the intellectual and social history of Britain in our period.   PT

MACKENZIE, Henry (1745–1831), lawyer, novelist, and Scottish man of letters who wrote perhaps the most influential British novel of sentiment. Born and educated in Edinburgh, Mackenzie published his first novel, *The Man of Feeling*, in 1771, which quickly earnt him comparison with Laurence Sterne and *Rousseau. The novel emulated the work of the former in its episodic, fragmentary structure, and of the latter in its portrayal of an innocent, rural hero whose blend of *sensibility [11], benevolence, and true virtue was exemplified by tenderness towards lunatics and prostitutes. An implicit Scottish nationalism can also be detected in his espousal of primitive and nativist motifs against the decadence and corruption of urban aristocrats, leading Robert *Burns to prize the book 'next to the Bible'.

Though Mackenzie's later novels and plays were less successful, he established himself as a major literary figure in Scotland through his editing of two literary journals, the *Mirror* (1779–80) and the *Lounger* (1785–7), as well as through his championing of Burns and his adjudication on the controversial authorship of the *Ossian poems. Like his friend Walter *Scott, Mackenzie combined Scottish cultural pride with generally conservative political views, being rewarded in 1804 for his pro-Pittite writings with a lucrative post as comptroller of taxes for Scotland.   IMcC

MACKINTOSH, Sir James (1765–1832), recorder at Bombay, *Whig MP, professor of law and politics at the East India College at Haileybury. Known mainly as one of the great turncoats and talented failures in British public life, he is of interest, however, because his life involves so many representative aspects of his age.

Born in Scotland, he attended the University of Aberdeen, where the professor of humanity, William Ogilvie, initiated him into his theory of agrarian reform. While studying medicine at Edinburgh, Mackintosh picked up Dugald *Stewart's version of Scottish moral philosophy and philosophical history as well as his rhetorical style as a public philosopher. These ideas combined with a vague *Rousseauist *natural rights doctrine to form Mackintosh's very public stand against Edmund *Burke's *Reflections*, namely *Vindiciae Gallicae* (1791).

Along with many liberal Whigs, Mackintosh saw the *French Revolution as a more complete English one, and like them, he soon realized his mistake, as he first proclaimed in his 'Lectures on the Law of Nature and Nations' at Lincoln's Inn (1799–1800). Natural rights here reverted to traditional natural law, *republicanism gave way to traditional *constitutionalism, philosophical history shaded into Burkean traditionalism—a sensational performance underscored by Mackintosh's mean and arrogant public dismissal of his friend from radical days, William *Godwin.

After eight years in India, reading German philosophy, studying linguistics, and yearning for the great and unattainable philosophical synthesis (cf. *Progress of Ethical Philosophy*, 1830), Mackintosh settled into a life of falling short of his own and others' expectations, while writing usefully and intelligently on a huge variety of political, literary, philosophical, and historical subjects, mainly for his old friends at the *Edinburgh Review*. Not least, he developed the traditionalist and constitutional themes of earlier work into an articulate Whig history and theory of government in *The History of England* (1830–1). KH

MACPHERSON, James, see *Ossianism.

54 **madhouses.** In 1800 Bethlem Hospital, London, was the only public asylum in Britain that admitted the pauper insane, and although it restricted entry to the 'curable' it provided only confinement, not care. During the eighteenth century such cities as Norwich, Manchester, York, and Liverpool established subscription hospitals for paying patients. The pauper insane who attracted official attention were sent to workhouses, bridewells, poorhouses, and *prisons. In addition to the public hospitals of varying size, many small private madhouses took in boarders [see *medicine, 18].

Often owned by doctors, madhouses were profit-making businesses that offered a wide range of care and accommodation, the impoverished being paid for by the *poor laws. Made subject to licensing and cursory inspection by the 1774 Madhouse Act, madhouses were otherwise unregulated until 1828. They held about 1,000 inmates in 1800, much the same number as that held in the public asylums. The 1828 Act required madhouse inmates to have a medical certificate of insanity and a detention order from a Justice, but adequate record-keeping and appropriate standards of care were not demanded until 1845, when a new Act compelled all counties to provide asylums for the pauper insane. The many asylums that were then built tried to segregate the different types of patient so as to prevent unwelcome influences, and also tried to offer in-house work for inmates. These asylums made it possible for doctors and medical students to study large numbers of mental patients under hospital conditions, and to maintain systematic records of treatment. Sources of such information prior to 1845 are scanty.

Until the eighteenth century *madness was commonly regarded as a natural sign of human sinfulness, and only dangerous lunatics were legally confined. With the extensive development of lunatic asylums and madhouses in the mid-eighteenth century, and control of them by medical practitioners, punitive methods of subduing the unruly passions of inmates became easier to apply: beating, starvation, physical restriction, and isolation were commonly used to create fear and restore reason. Bloodletting, purges, immersion, electric shocks, and drugs were employed, as in other forms of illness, to stimulate or pacify body and mind, and were given various kinds of theoretical justification. The obvious failure of these methods coincided with visible social misery. The consequent wave of *philanthropy toward the poor and oppressed also ameliorated the treatment of the insane. Increasingly after 1800 the insane were regarded as medical cases who needed, not punishment for wickedness, but a gentle and healthy regimen that would teach them to control themselves. Although theories about the nature of insanity altered with these changes in public attitude, and were first expressed in the mild treatment given at St Luke's hospital in mid-century, and most prominently in the 1790s at the *Quakers' York Retreat, the theories themselves were as much the effect as the cause of the new regimen. RB

madness. The half-century between 1775 and 1832 began in Britain with one set of views held by the educated concerning insanity and its treatment, and ended with a quite different set. This change occurred despite the fact that little scientific progress was made during the period either in the aetiology of mental disturbances or in their effective therapy. Long-held views about the sinful causes of insanity were abandoned, and new notions of human malleability, and with them the gentler treatment of mental 'management', were accepted. These changes resulted from cumulative changes in public sentiment, not from advances in systematic knowledge [see *medicine, 18 and *psychology, 39].

The chief problem faced by mad-doctors during the eighteenth century, and for most of the nineteenth, was their almost total ignorance of the nature and causes of mental illness and hence of suitable therapy. In his *Treatise on Madness* (1758) William Battie (1704–76), the *physician at St Luke's hospital for the insane, who later became the owner of a private hospital, wrote: 'This distemper is as little understood as any that ever afflicted mankind.' Throughout the period there were three common views concerning the causes of mental illness: that the causes were organic and located in the brain; that they were mental but distinguishable from the psychological symptoms created by physical diseases; that the causes were sometimes physical and sometimes mental. The majority of medical men favoured the first view. The *phrenologists added the belief that, although insanity had physical causes in the brain, these could be either structural defects or functional disorders. This explained why a postmortem often revealed no structural defect in the brain of a mentally ill person. The originator of phrenology, J. F. Gall (1758–1828), argued that the brain was a set of organs, each one of which influenced a specific mental property. Inactivity or hypoactivity of a particular area would produce a specific mental disturbance, and the phrenologists claimed to have discovered many of those correlations.

Although medical practitioners commonly agreed that insanity resulted from disharmony among the brain areas, they disagreed as to how the nerves conveyed impulses or vibrations from the sense organs to the brain, and whether they were hollow pipes or wires along which vibratory motions passed. There was constant debate also as to how harmonious agitation of brain areas was to be maintained or restored. Medical confusion concerning the difference between symptoms of illness and the patients' unsuccessful attempts to explain, and protect themselves against, those symptoms made classification of illnesses difficult. In turn, this confusion encouraged the use of the term 'insanity' to refer either to a mysterious single ailment or to the conditions of groups such as the senile, alcoholics, epileptics, psychotics, eccentrics, and vagrant paupers. Both usages obstructed medical and psychological investigation; neither usage could suggest effective therapy.   RB

Madoc controversy. The celebrated Madoc Legend excited greater interest in the 1790s than at any other time in history. Poets, scholars, and radicals immersed themselves in the extraordinary tale of the exploits of Madoc, son of Owain, Prince of Gwynedd, who abandoned strife-torn Wales in 1170 and sailed with eight ships westwards to the continent which came to be known as America.

The legend was first popularized in the Elizabethan period, when Dr John Dee argued, on the basis of Madoc's feat, that the claim of the Queen of England upon the treasures of the New World was immeasurably stronger than that of the King of Spain. During the seventeenth century, however, the tale lay dormant and was not awakened until the publication of a second edition of *Drych y Prif Oesoedd* (A Mirror of the First Ages) in 1740 by Theophilus Evans (1693–1767), an *Anglican clergyman whose contempt for Spanish popery knew no bounds. Evans published an alleged statement by Morgan Jones (1768–1835), a Dissenting minister who had been captured by an Indian tribe and whose life had been spared at the eleventh hour only when he was recognized by some of the braves as being a Welsh-speaker. Here was clear evidence not only that the descendants of Madoc, in the form of a tribe of Welsh-speaking Indians, were alive and well, but

that, in the period when the War of Jenkins' Ear was raging, Britain's claim to America was more valid than that of Spain.

A similar case was argued when war broke out with Spain in 1789 and interest in the Madoc legend reached fever pitch when Dr John Williams (1727–98) published *An Enquiry into the Truth of the Tradition Concerning the Discovery of America by Prince Madog ab Owen Gwynedd about the year 1170.* The Welsh literati in London were captivated by the tale and the arrival of 'General' William Augustus Bowles, a plausible rogue clad in the garb of a Red Indian chief, caused a great stir in taverns frequented by members of the Gwyneddigion Society. One of them, David *Samwell, was moved to compose ninety-six stanzas entitled 'The Padouca Hunt' (1799) and plans were laid for an expedition to America in search of the Madogwys, the Lost Brothers. Edward *Williams (Iolo Morganwg) embarked on a rigorous fitness programme in preparation for the great adventure but was eventually forced to abandon his plans as personal and domestic crises overtook him.

It was left to John Evans (1770–99), the 22-year-old son of a *Methodist exhorter from Waunfawr, Caernarfonshire, to cross the Atlantic in 1792 and undertake an epic, life-threatening journey of 2,000 miles up the Missouri river, where he was received by white-skinned Mandan Indians. None of them, unfortunately, spoke Welsh, and in a disconsolate letter addressed to his Baptist friend, Dr Samuel Jones (1728–97), in July 1797, Evans admitted: 'I am able to inform you that there is no such People as the Welsh Indians.' Heartbroken, Evans drowned his sorrows in alcohol and died in New Orleans in May 1799.

By the turn of the eighteenth century the Padouca Hunt had lost its meaning and relevance, but even in our days there are those who believe that America was discovered long before the days of Columbus and that the legend of Madoc cannot and will not die.

GHJ

MALONE, Edmund (1741–1812), critic and editor. Born in Dublin, Malone trained as a lawyer before settling permanently in London in 1777. His literary and political associates included *Johnson, *Boswell, *Reynolds, *Walpole, *Blackstone, and *Burke. He made his name as an editor of *Shakespeare, beginning in 1778 with his *Attempt to Ascertain the Order in which the Plays of Shakespeare were Written.* This was followed two years later by a *Supplement* in two volumes to the 1778 Johnson–Steevens edition which included the first critical edition of the sonnets and some apocryphal plays. His major achievement in Shakespeare studies was his ten-volume edition of the plays and poems (1790), later revised by James Boswell the younger (1778–1822) in 1821. This edition was the first to make a claim for authority on the basis of textual and historical authenticity (although it had a precedent in Edward Capell's 1768 edition). In its emphasis on the authority of the original and historically verifiable Shakespeare, ignoring modern accretions, Malone's

594 · MALONE

edition had its corollary in Burke's view of the respect due to tradition and custom. Indeed Burke praised his fellow Irishman's achievement, describing the *Plays and Poems* as 'gold' to the 'brass' of his own *Reflections on the Revolution in France* (1790). Joseph *Ritson was less enthusiastic on scholarly as well as on political grounds, attacking Malone's 'profound ignorance'.

Malone's application of a 'scientific' method to literary history, that is the idea of authorship as an objective truth that can be factually demonstrated, was also apparent in his interventions in the *Chatterton and *Ireland controversies [see **antiquarianism, 35**]. His editorial work and cultural polemic reflects the emerging Romantic ideal of the author, embodied by Shakespeare, as an autonomous subject, historically verifiable, but also capable of transcending history.   GR

48   **MALTHUS,** Thomas Robert (1766–1834), political economist and clergyman. Born in Wotton, Surrey, he was educated primarily by the Unitarian Gilbert Wakefield near Nottingham, and then at Jesus College, Cambridge. Arguably the best-known social theorist in nineteenth-century Britain, Malthus influenced economic theories, political philosophy, and social policy [see **political economy, 33**].

Son of Daniel Malthus, *Rousseau's executor, Malthus's intellectual development can be read to some extent as a rejection of his father's embrace of the perfectibilist notions of Rousseau, Condorcet, and *Godwin. His singular education included residence with the Revd Richard Graves (1715–1804), the author of an anti-Methodist satire, enrolment in the *Dissenting academy at Warrington, and the private tutorship of the *Unitarian minister Gilbert Wakefield (1756–1801). He attended Cambridge University between 1784 and 1788, graduating in mathematics. Malthus was educated, therefore, in a social context of religious Dissent and political turmoil. Those tumultuous issues provided the setting of his intellectual output.

In 1789 Malthus was ordained, and through his father's influence he was granted a curacy—with stipend—at the chapel of Okewood in Surrey. His career in the church lasted forty-five years, including the positions of Rector of Walesby, Lincolnshire, in 1803, and the perpetual curacy at Okewood in 1824.

Malthus's reputation was established with his first (anonymously) published work, *Essay on the Principle of Population* (1798). Written in response to radical arguments favouring redistribution and equality, and to Godwin's *Political Justice* (1793) in particular, Malthus attempted to refute the *Enlightenment [32] belief in the 'perfectibility of mankind'. Malthus argued that such views were based on false principles, in that *utopian [9] hope ignored the immutability of the laws of nature, by which he meant the biblical reference of God's admonition to Adam and Eve on the unavoidability of work and death.

At the core of Malthus's argument lay a striking proposition: that *population will, if unchecked, increase in a geometric ratio, while the food supply can only ever increase in an arithmetical ratio. This,

Malthus argued, was the immutable law of nature, and this, rather than social institutions or economic regimes, was the cause of immiseration. The political and policy implications of Malthus's argument were profound.

Malthus's *Essay* contributed forcefully to the debate over the existing *poor law, particularly the Speenhamland system of poor relief introduced in 1795 which tied the level of assistance to food prices and family size. His population thesis asserted that government intervention in the form of relief would exacerbate *poverty [12], the cause of and solution to which lay with the sexual passions of the poor. His policy prescription was thus the abolition of poor relief. If a labourer could not support his children, Malthus argued, 'they must starve'. Malthus's *Essay* went through a number of editions, and was influential on the passage of the Poor Law Amendment Act of 1834, which led to the growth of the workhouse system. The policy influence of Malthus's argument spread beyond the borders of Britain as a result of his appointment as professor of political economy at the *East India Company's Haileybury College in 1805. From the College were sent a large number of administrators to deal with the problems of Indian famine after instruction from Malthus in the 'laws' of political economy.

The political implications of Malthus's *Essay* require an appreciation of the times when it was composed. Habeas corpus had been suspended in 1794, and many democratic *corresponding societies were suppressed. Britain was at *war [2] with revolutionary France. Radical pamphlets had been produced by Godwin, *Paine, and *Spence favouring *democracy [3] and egalitarianism. Malthus provided a powerful critique of these calls for equality. He believed that mankind was basically selfish and motivated primarily by the sexual passions. The implication of such an argument was that inequality in the existing order of property was 'natural'. 'All cannot share alike the bounties of nature,' he argued, for without 'the established administration of property . . . [s]elfishness would be triumphant.' To interfere with the operation of the market, therefore, would be to destroy 'those stimulants to exertion which can alone overcome the natural indolence of man'.

Malthus's argument also has important implications for prevailing conceptions of property. It followed from the population principle that 'the cause of poverty', Malthus argued, 'had little or no direct relation to forms of government, or the unequal division of property'; and therefore the poor had no 'claim of right on society for subsistence'. This argument denied the legitimacy of prevailing Christian conceptions of property, entailing rights and obligations which had hitherto justified charity as a duty.

The political implications of Malthus's writings are also revealed in his famous dispute with *Ricardo over the question of the *corn laws in 1814 and 1815. Malthus, like Adam *Smith, whose intellectual legacy he saw himself continuing, accorded priority, both economic and political, to the agricultural rather than the manufacturing interest [see **land,**

16]. While Malthus articulated an economic argument in favour of agricultural protection, important political implications underlie his economic defence of protection. Arguing that the capital investments in agriculture during the Napoleonic wars had to be consolidated, Malthus drew upon arguments for agricultural self-sufficiency during times of war, together with the claim that manufactures, unlike agriculture, are vulnerable to both fashion and war. Consequently, agriculture, he argued, brought stability to the nation in a way that manufacturing could not, and for this reason required protection. In this way, his economic arguments, from his attack on poor relief to his defence of agricultural protection, can be seen to provide a political defence of the landed interest.

In his *Principles of Political Economy* (1820), for example, Malthus argued that the surplus produced by labour cannot be consumed by that labour, as the fact that its price exceeds the cost of the labour reveals its nature as surplus. Nor will the capitalist consume the surplus, he argued, as the capitalist will need to reinvest. Consequently, there is required an unproductive class, that will consume the surplus without adding to it. 'In this case the landlords no doubt stand pre-eminent,' he argued. The political implications of his economic arguments were thus inextricably intertwined.

Malthus's influence exceeded his originality as a thinker, as the relationship between population growth and food supply, for which he is chiefly remembered, had been noted before he wrote. His importance lies in the degree to which he represents an important 'moment' in the decline of what E. P. Thompson referred to as the 'moral economy' of the eighteenth century, which stressed social values of culture and custom, in the face of a rising 'political economy' of the nineteenth century, which accorded priority to the economic calculus of the profit system [see *class, 15]. ARB

MANSFIELD, first Earl (William Murray) (1705–93), *judge and politician. Mansfield was the pre-eminent judge of his day, celebrated by many contemporary lawyers for his liberal and legal learning, which he used to develop the rules of commercial *law [8] during thirty years as Lord Chief Justice of the *King's Bench (1756–88). To the *Wilkite radicals, on the other hand, his creativity and political influence represented the sinister intrusion of arbitrary Scottish principles, and his *Enlightenment [32] attitudes inspired popular distrust. He was condemned by Junius for adulterating English law with Roman ideas, and in 1780 the *Gordon rioters burnt his London house and books for his support of Catholic relief. His critics also rejected Mansfield's strict interpretation of the law of libel, which restricted the jury to questions of fact only, a position which was overturned by Charles James *Fox in 1792. Even his immediate and more cautious judicial successors repudiated what they discerned as Mansfield's tendency to work for a *rapprochement* between the systems of law and equity. Yet although it is possible to interpret Mansfield's generally flexi-

ble attitude to the law as a derogation from the common law tradition of the 'Englishman's birthright', which was typical of a *lawyer brought up in government service, his ruling in *Somerset's Case* (1772) insisted on a restricted construction of *slavery [6] in England and gave a great stimulant to the *abolitionist cause. DL

MANTELL, Gideon Algernon (1790–1852), geologist, medical practitioner, discoverer of dinosaur fossils. The son of a cordwainer, Mantell studied *medicine [18] in London before returning to his birthplace of Lewes in 1811 to practise surgery. It was here that he made his spectacular discoveries of dinosaur fossils, such as *Iguanodon* and *Hylaeosaurus*, and acquired an unquenchable enthusiasm for *geology. In 1816 Mantell married Mary Ann Woodhouse, and in 1833 he moved with his family of four children to fashionable Brighton. By this time his geological and palaeontological reputation had grown so great that his qualifications as a surgeon were eclipsed, and his Brighton practice proved a failure. Mantell's house, now bursting with fossils and rock specimens, was turned into the Mantellian Museum. In 1838 Mantell sold his collection to the *British Museum for £5,000 and bought a medical practice in London. Here he was able to attend meetings of the various learned societies to which he belonged (he was elected a Fellow of the Royal Society in 1825 and became vice-president of the Geological Society of London in 1848), and to throw himself into a flourish of social and scientific activity. He established himself as a popular *lecturer on science and a sharp antagonist in geological controversies. His wife and son Walter left him shortly after his move to London, each driven out by Mantell's querulous and occasionally paranoid nature, and by his complete absorption in science.

Mantell's prolific writings, over sixty books, exhibit broad interests in medicine, *natural philosophy [34], archaeology, and geology, as well as indomitable energy and enthusiasm. Such notable and popular books as *The Wonders of Geology* (1838) and *The Medals of Creation* (1844) went through many editions, as did a charming children's work, *Thoughts on a Pebble* (1836). Mantell also prepared catalogues such as *The Fossils of the South Downs* (1822), with illustrations by Mrs Mantell, and *The Geology of the South-east of England* (1833), which together display a discipline and care not always evident in his later work.

Mantell died following an overdose of opium taken to relieve the pain of a spinal disorder; he had in his last years alienated many colleagues and friends, and his funeral drew not one scientific or public figure. MSH

mapping. Maps shaped the geographical and cultural imagination of Britons in the Romantic age. As the work of parish and county surveyors illustrates, landowning patricians were keen sponsors of maps, often taking as much pleasure in them as in commissioned *paintings [27] of their estates. In parliamentary and naval circles high priority was given to the production of accurate sea charts, especially after the loss of the American colonies ensured that colonial *exploration [37] in Asia and the Pacific acquired new commercial and strategic significance. Mapping the Americas and the Pacific also expanded cultural horizons through the opportunities it provided for the creation of visual and written accounts of 'other' landscapes and peoples. In Canada, Australia, and New Zealand, for example, surveyors were often the principal source of knowledge about the life-ways and cultures of indigenous peoples.

Maps were also instrumental in the coalescence of national identity in Britain and Ireland. The Jacobite uprisings of 1745–6 demonstrated with frightening clarity the Hanoverian state's need for topographically accurate maps, if its small land-based military forces were to meet threats of French *invasion or civil unrest. The Peace of Paris likewise intensified calls for a comprehensive state sponsored survey of Britain. However, it was not until the early 1780s that surveying began in earnest, largely due to the enthusiasm of Charles Lennox, third Duke of Richmond (d. 1806), and the Council of the Royal Society under Joseph *Banks. The first one-inch ordnance survey map, of the strategically vulnerable county of Kent, was completed in 1801.

Between 1825 and 1838 ordnance survey resources were diverted to Ireland, ostensibly with the aim of reducing tensions caused by antiquated rate records and maps being used to assess land taxes. Survey parties were unarmed and the military value of their efforts downplayed, though work was greatly hindered by community resistance such as the theft of survey polls.

Contemporary advances in reproductive technologies ensured that maps of Britain and its colonies entered the national imagination. They became powerful symbols used for differing political ends, notably in *prints [22] and broadsheets which visually equated 'Britishness' with loyalty, or opposition, to the established political order.   PT

MARA, Gertrud Elisabeth (1749–1833), German bravura soprano and impresario. Mara appeared in London initially as a violin prodigy (1759–65), but later returned as a singer (1784–1802, 1819). She performed at the 1784 *Handel Commemoration, sporadically at the King's Theatre (1786–91), and then at London's English theatres. She also sang at the *oratorios, the *concerts (promoting her own subscription series in 1787–8), and provincial *music festivals.

Mara's voice was florid and wide-ranging, with a rich tone. Her Handel interpretations were particularly acclaimed, but she apparently lacked stage presence. Headstrong and impulsive, she had a turbulent relationship with the public, exacerbated by flamboyant extramarital liaisons with singers Samuel *Harrison and Charles Florio (d. 1820).   RC

MARTIN, John (1789–1854), painter, etcher, engraver, *engineer, and reformer. As a painter of a technologically modernized apocalypse and as the author of numerous projects for urban improvement, Martin offered a thoroughly industrialized version of the Protestant *millenarianism of the 1790s and early nineteenth century. It was through his mother that he had become acquainted with the millenarian tradition, a tradition which also had a powerful influence on his brothers, most notoriously Jonathan Martin, the religious enthusiast and incendiary of York Minster.

Trained in Newcastle upon Tyne, John Martin came to London in 1806, where he worked as a china and glass painter. He first exhibited at the *Royal Academy in 1811, at the British Institution in 1813, and he soon became a popular rival to J. M. W. *Turner. Though remaining an outsider to academically approved artistic conventions, his career reached a first peak during the 1820s when he exhibited Belshazzar's Feast (1826) and published his mezzotint illustrations to John *Milton's Paradise Lost (1827). He achieved rapid fame in continental Europe, where he always had a more appreciative audience and stronger following than in Britain [see *painting, 27].

In style and content Martin's art presents an eclectic yet highly effective combination of two distinct traditions. Colossal landscapes and architectural phantasmagorias in the manner of Philippe Jacques de *Loutherbourg and Turner supplied the setting for his paintings, which are generally populated with tiny figures, seen from a great distance, who mimic the emphatic gesturing of the *sublime mode as popularized by Henry *Fuseli or Benjamin *West. Both elements were unified by 'scientific' means (perspective and geography), which allowed for complete control over scale, as well as by the use of strong contrasts of darkness and light, and by the dominance of a single colour (preferably a glaring red).

Whether turning to the *Bible, Milton, or Roman history, Martin generally preferred subjects touching on the first and last things in the existence of nature or human society. Pamphlets containing his descriptive commentaries made the paintings' complicated iconography accessible to a large audience.

The funds he earned as a painter and illustrator allowed Martin to indulge in numerous engineering and town planning projects. Without being discouraged by recurring financial crises, much of his time was occupied by inventive schemes for water supply and sewage disposal systems, for railway construction, or for the building of iron ships. His ambitious plans for the improvement of living conditions in the metropolis and for safer technologies in the mining industry or the navy inform his painted biblical or historical catastrophes with a didactic or reforming impulse. These apocalyptic works were apparently intended as a warning to the inhabitants of modern-day Babylon, and were fuelled by the artist's conviction that reform was badly needed in order at least to postpone the apocalypse they envisioned.   DWD

83. Mezzotint of The Fall of Babylon (1831) by John Martin, the most successful of a group of early-nineteenth-century painters of the apocalyptic sublime.

MARTINEAU, Harriet (1802–76), radical writer, has been called both the first woman journalist in England and the first woman sociologist. The sixth of eight children of Thomas Martineau, a textile manufacturer, she grew up in a widely connected, predominantly *Unitarian intellectual circle, though her childhood and youth were often unhappy, owing to ill health and the early onset of deafness. Following excellent early schooling and rigorous self-education, she became an enthusiastic adherent of *Necessarianism. In 1822 she began to publish devotional essays and tales, and after the family business failed earnt her living as a writer, mostly for the Unitarian *Monthly Repository*, then edited by W. J. Fox (1786–1864). *Illustrations of Political Economy* (1832–4), a series of tales to demonstrate the doctrines of the newly fashionable science, brought her fame and entry into the London literary world.

With broad interests and firm opinions—she eventually gave up Unitarianism for freethought but never abandoned Necessarianism—she crusaded for anti-slavery and women's causes, free trade, and a wide variety of reforms. To extensive travel writing (notably on a two-year visit to the United States in 1834–6) she added two novels, some durable children's tales, much *reviewing, an influential abridgement and translation of Auguste Comte's *Cours de philosophie positive* (1853), and more than 1,600 leading articles for the *Daily News* between 1852 and 1866.

Bedridden in her early 40s from the effects of an ovarian cyst, she insisted she was cured by mesmerism [see *animal magnetism] and resumed a strenuous life, including a visit to the Near East. Settled in the Lake District, she spent her last twenty years in expectation of imminent death, ever active, generous, and controversial. She splendidly illustrates the continuity of eighteenth-century modes of thought into the mid-Victorian generation.

Her recollections of famous contemporaries in her correspondence, in biographical sketches for the *Daily News* (reprinted 1869), and in her notoriously candid *Autobiography* (1877) are invaluable, as is her *History of the Thirty Years Peace* (1849–50), the finest contemporary narrative covering the first half of the century. RKW

masquerades, entertainments, involving music, dancing, and eating. Participants dressed in disguise, most commonly the Italian-derived 'domino', or cloak and some form of mask concealing the face. Masquerades were introduced to England in 1710 by the Swiss Count Heidegger and always retained an exotic, foreign allure. They were identified as the playground of the fashionable aristocracy and had an important political function of mediating the theatricality of the 'great'. However, admission prices, especially in the *pleasure gardens of Ranelagh and Vauxhall, also made them within the reach of the middling orders. In the 1760s and 1770s new masquerade venues were opened by the enterprising Teresa Cornelys at Carlisle House, Soho, and at the opulent Pantheon in Oxford Street, designed by James *Wyatt [see *concerts]. A topos in numerous plays, poems, and novels, including Frances *Burney's *Evelina*, Hannah *Cowley's *The Belle's Stratagem*, and *Byron's *Don Juan*, the masquerade signified transformatory excess as well as sexual licence. In the 1790s and after, in the work of Thomas *Rowlandson and John *Williams (Anthony

598 · MASQUERADES

Pasquin), the masquerade was represented as a scene of ruling-class decadence. It seems also to have functioned as a means of reflecting on the historicity of the immediate past: that is, the transition from an eighteenth century to Romantic *sensibility [11]. The entertainment itself enjoyed a revival at the height of the *Regency (Harriette *Wilson describes one in her *Memoirs*), but its cultural and political resonance was never as powerful as it had been in the eighteenth century.   GR

MATHIAS, T[homas] J[ames] (?1754–1835), *satirist and Italian scholar; his fame rests on a single satirical poem of the 1790s, which helped to launch and shape the conservative attack on liberal and radical intellectuals.

Educated at Eton and at Trinity College, Cambridge, where he gained a reputation in the 1770s as a Latin scholar, Mathias made good use of his family connections with the court and his own *Tory friendships to inherit his father's former position as sub-treasurer to the Queen, and then in 1812 to gain an appointment as librarian to Buckingham Palace. In 1764 he published anonymously the first part of *The Pursuits of Literature*, a vicious poetic satire with elaborate footnotes modelled on Pope's *Dunciad*. Mathias's chief target was market-dependent writers of *Whig, liberal, or radical disposition such as William *Godwin, Richard Payne *Knight, and Matthew 'Monk' *Lewis. The poem's enthusiastic reception with the political and cultural establishment prompted Mathias to publish several further parts in the late 1790s. By the early nineteenth century, however, the poem's reputation had slumped: Thomas *De Quincey probably reflected typical literary opinion in castigating it as pedantic, self-aggrandizing, and impotently spiteful.   IMcC

MATURIN, Charles Robert (1782–1824), novelist and dramatist who, although an *Anglican clergyman, produced *Gothic tales which met popular tastes of the early nineteenth century. Born into an Anglo-Irish family in Dublin, Maturin was educated at Trinity College, Dublin, and ordained an Anglican minister. Appointed curate to a Dublin church, he began his literary career in 1807 with the publication, at his own expense, of *The Fatal Revenge*, followed by *The Wild Irish Boy* (1808), an attempt to profit from the success of Sydney *Owenson's *Wild Irish Girl* (1806), and *The Milesian Chief* (1812). In 1809, for reasons which remain unclear, his father was disgraced, losing his bureaucratic position at the Post Office. Reliant on his father's support, Charles never recovered financially from the setback.

Certainly Maturin never achieved the advancement in the Church which would secure him anything more lucrative than his original curateship (possibly because of the taboo subjects raised in his novels and plays). He did secure the patronage of Sir Walter *Scott, who admired the early historical *novels [31]. Scott also succeeded in having *Byron place the manuscript of Maturin's play, *Bertram*, at Drury Lane in 1816. Produced by *Kean, the play

was a great success, although attacked by *Coleridge as an example of the degeneracy of Gothic taste [see *theatre, 24]. For Maturin himself public acclaim was a double-edged sword, which encouraged expensive habits his income could not sustain. None of the plays which followed was successful. By 1818 he was deeply in debt, and decided to return to novel writing. *Women, or Pour et Contre* appeared in 1818, followed by one of the great Gothic novels of the 1820s, *Melmoth the Wanderer* (1820), in which the orthodoxy of its attack on Catholic superstition is often swamped by a general sense of horror and despair. The novel's preface acknowledges that writing Gothic novels may be at odds with a religious profession, but justifies it by complaining of the lack of professional remuneration. Maturin died in poverty in 1824, the year in which his final novel, *The Albigenses*, appeared.   JM

Mechanics' Institutes, see *popular education.

medicine, fringe, a term used to denote a disparate body of health ideas, practices, and movements which functioned outside the often imprecise and transitional boundaries of orthodox *medicine [18]. It served as a vector of heterodox and radical-Romantic social ideals, especially those stressing the importance of holistic, spiritual, and naturalistic health remedies.

Alternative or fringe medicine embraced a spectrum of practices: these included the highly commercial sale of patent medicines by unlicensed *quacks; the still widespread use of traditional domestic medicines or self-health remedies passed on by folklore and popular manuals [see *popular culture, 23]; and the crop of popular healing movements or cults which sprang up in the British provinces during the 1820s and 1830s. Within the last there was also considerable diversity; some were indigenous mystical cults possessing health dimensions, such as the *Swedenborgians; some were European-influenced popular science movements such as *phrenology and *mesmerism; and some were imported American popular health movements spawned in a less-regulated medical market. Whatever their origins, most early-nineteenth-century fringe medical movements were characterized by an intense hostility to the use of drugs, purgatives, or bleeding, and by their advocacy of democratic and naturalistic epistemologies. Romantics like Percy *Shelley, for example, became ardent *vegetarians and mesmerists. Some forms of alternative or fringe medicine also proved attractive to political radicals, and many *Chartist groups developed their own dispensaries.

In 1858 a liberal Scottish doctor and medical journalist, Samuel Brown, coined the term 'Physical Puritanism' to describe this kindred collection of fringe health movements and practices, which he claimed to have originated in ancient Paracelsian vitalist, alchemical, and atomic speculations. He cited hydropathy, vegetarianism, *botany, spiritualism, mesmerism, and phrenology as constituting a revolutionary movement that would sweep through Britain engulfing medical and social orthodoxy.

Although this did not eventuate, fringe medicine retained a tenacious minority hold on the working classes throughout the nineteenth century, and also possessed close intellectual affinities with strands of Romantic science espoused by S. T. *Coleridge and others. IMcC

medievalism. Romantic medievalism was to some extent a reaction against neoclassical canons of good taste and decorum, but, together with the associated cult of the *Gothic, it rapidly opened up a new sense of history that was to pervade every area of nineteenth-century culture.

The word 'medieval' is first recorded by the *OED* in 1827. It tends to replace the word 'Gothic', a general and largely ahistorical term of abuse for works of an earlier period that did not fit eighteenth-century critical canons and which by the early nineteenth century had acquired sensationalist literary overtones. The implied concept of the 'Middle Ages', coming between the classical world of antiquity and self-conscious standards of contemporary civilization, rapidly gained ground in nineteenth-century thought and achieved further definition in contradistinction to the ideas of the 'Renaissance' (which entered circulation shortly afterwards). It forms part of a new sense of history that was to be further strengthened by the work of von Ranke and Niebuhr (significantly, the English translation of the latter's *History of Rome* was begun in 1827).

Architecturally, medievalism began early with Batty Langley's (1696–1751) *Gothic Architecture, Improved by Rules and Proportions* (1742). Significant literary statements of this new sense of the worth of the Gothic past came with Richard Hurd's (1720–1808) *Letters on Chivalry and Romance* (1762) and Thomas *Percy's *Reliques of Ancient English Poetry* (1765). The latter's influence can be seen in poems as different as *Wordsworth's 'White Doe of Rhylstone', *Coleridge's 'Christabel', and *Scott's 'Marmion'. In the novel, the break with the sensationalism of the Gothic is clearly signalled by the sophisticated **history** [38] of Scott's *Ivanhoe* (1819). Medievalism also fed the genre of *history painting and the associated vogue for medieval costume events such as the 'Mischianza' in Philadelphia in 1778, and the Eglinton Tournament (1839), which extended even to the redesigned rituals of Queen Victoria's coronation and statues of Prince Albert in full armour.

In politics, medievalism came to offer a new way of interpreting the social order, stressing the interdependence of the different classes and emphasizing that the relationship between landowner and tenant was more than merely economic. The five volumes of Kenelm Digby's (1800–80) *The Broadstone of Honour* (1822) gave this view perhaps its fullest expression, but the most influential statement of the idea of medieval society as an organic whole remained Coleridge's *Lay Sermons* (1816–17). SP

melodrama. The first notable use of this term, dating from Thomas *Holcroft's 1802 adaptation of Pixérécourt's *Coelina, ou L'Enfant du Mystère* as *The Tale of Mystery*, referred specifically to the use of music to enhance the expressiveness of actors at particular moments of dramatic significance—hence 'mélo-drame', 'music drama' [see *theatre, 24]. But the term was soon much more broadly interpreted to refer to a form of sensational drama, in which a victimized figure of good is pitted against the forces of injustice, a scenario which could result in either tragic or comic resolution. The origins of the melodrama can be traced back to Elizabethan domestic tragedy; to the sentimental tragedies and comedies of the eighteenth century such as Lillo's *The London Merchant* (1731) and the 'she-tragedies' of Rowe and Otway; to the novels of Samuel Richardson, especially *Clarissa*; and to the impact in the 1790s of contemporary German drama and the traditions of the *Gothic and *romance. Melodrama also had much in common with the struggle between 'good' and 'evil' that structured the *pantomime, from which it borrowed some elements such as the emphasis on gesture, the body, and the thrill of the chase. Generally speaking, melodrama was an extremely hybrid and fluid form in which can be identified the traces of non-dramatic cultural forms and events—popular song, legend, the folk-tale, the *novel [31] (such as those of *Radcliffe and *Scott), topical and historical events, and even *paintings [27] (such as Jerrold's *The Rent Day* (1831), based on the painting by *Wilkie)—thereby illustrating the interpenetration of élite and *popular culture [23] and of oral and print traditions. Melodrama was also technically sophisticated, making the most of innovations such as the *panorama and diorama, and improvements in lighting techniques, in ways which emphasized spectacular effect. In its reliance on tableaux or 'situation', as contemporaries described it, for dramatic climaxes, melodrama exemplified the increased pictorialism of the early-nineteenth-century theatre, making playgoing much more of a visual experience than an aural one.

For these reasons—its generic hybridity and emphasis on the visual, on gesture, and on the body—melodrama, a 'modern anomaly' as Scott described it, was seen to threaten the cultural authority of tragedy, the novel, and the patent theatres. A caricature of 1807 in the journal the *Satirist* depicted 'Melo-drama' as a monstrous hybrid animal, with the heads of *Sheridan, *Kemble, and *Grimaldi—contemporary dramatists—sucking at its teats, while it tramples the 'regular drama' of *Shakespeare, Congreve, and Beaumont and Fletcher. Such an image makes it clear that the patent theatres of Covent Garden and Drury Lane had an investment in the development of the genre; but melodrama was most often identified as an illegitimate form, the progeny of the minor theatres such as the Surrey/Royal Circus, Adelphi, Olympic, Coburg, and the Royalty that were increasingly dominating London's theatrical culture.

Three broad types of melodrama have been distinguished—'outlaw' plays dealing with renegade figures or *banditti*, the nautical melodrama, and domestic melodrama—but these subgenres often overlap. As in *Gothic drama, the family suggests loss and uncertainty, indicated by the recurrence of orphans, bastards, adultery (both past and present), and narratives involving restitution and reconstitution of these fractured family units that in some cases represent society or the nation as a whole. Melodrama can also be seen to deal with issues such as the emergence into the political sphere after 1789 of the lower orders (embodied by the sailor or the factory worker). It also explored how loyalty to the family, as stressed by ideologies of *domesticity [13], might conflict with other obligations to class or military hierarchy (primarily a problem for men rather than for women); and how the emerging disciplines of *medicine [18] and *law [8] had created a new politics of the body and the social body in general, involving constraint, disciplining, and surveillance, especially of the underclass. In dramatizing these concerns, melodrama can be said to deal in fantasies of restoration and retribution which, however tragic the outcome, had the effect of endorsing the audiences' sense of moral and social justice.   GR

MELVILLE, Viscount, see Henry *Dundas.

MENDELSSOHN, Felix (1809–47), German composer, pianist, and a leading figure of early Romantic *music [26]. He made several visits to Britain, which he came to regard as his second home and where his music had a lasting influence.

In 1829 he quickly became absorbed in the whirl of metropolitan life, making a strong impression with his passionate First Symphony and the airy and fantastical *Midsummer Night's Dream* overture. He was immediately elected an honorary member of the Philharmonic Society and in July set off for Scotland, meeting Walter *Scott and travelling as far as the Hebrides. He showed no interest in the local music, but the wild loneliness of the Scottish countryside made a powerful impact on him, captured in the *Hebrides* overture (*Fingal's Cave*); the visit also inspired the 'Scottish' Symphony, not completed until 1842. During this period he also wrote the first book of *Songs without Words*, mainstay of the Victorian piano album. Returning to London in 1832 he was even more successful, with performances of *Hebrides* and the new G minor Piano Concerto. This led to another commission from the Philharmonic Society—the 'Italian' Symphony, inspired by his southern travels, which was first performed at the Hanover Square Rooms in May 1833.

Mendelssohn's early Romanticism—passionate, sentimental, and *picturesque, yet always within classical bounds—was immediately seen as the acceptable face of modern music (by contrast with Berlioz, for example). If his influence ultimately proved enervating for British music, that should not eclipse the creative importance of his first visits to Britain.   SMcV

mercantilism, a set of commercial policies and ideals emphasizing state intervention to ensure trade surpluses and the influx of bullion. British foreign policy in the eighteenth century was mercantilist in that it pursued trade monopolies through force, most notably in the Seven Years War (1756–63) which was fought to exclude French merchants from North America and other British trade spheres [see *war, 2]. Mercantilist policy became untenable towards the end of the eighteenth century as the great financial costs of military intervention to maintain an exclusive trade empire became apparent.

After 1776, mercantilism featured as the object of criticism by a diverse group of social thinkers. In advocating a *laissez-faire* economy, Adam *Smith's *Wealth of Nations* (1776) refuted the mercantilist equation of economic prosperity with 'money, or . . . gold and silver', and also attacked the 'force or constraint' which was so often the basis for international trade. In the *Watchman* (1796), S. T. *Coleridge criticized the mercantilist ideal of a perpetually favourable balance of trade, arguing that this constituted a threat to the 'health' of the nation. Coleridge's envisioned commercial system based on 'reciprocity of advantage' was conceived as the antithesis of mercantilism's narrow self-interestedness. Thomas *Paine, whose *Rights of Man* (1791) criticizes commerce based on dominion and enforced by large navies, proposed a new world order characterized by friendly commercial relationships between nations.

Mercantilist prejudices about protectionism and the balance of trade declined as *political economy [33] developed scientific aspirations and its emphasis shifted to methodical laws of production and distribution.   RG

MERRY, Robert (1755–98), poet, dramatist, the chief proponent of *Della Cruscan poetry, and an important radical journalist in the 1790s, who produced inventive squibs and *satires.

He was educated at Eton and Cambridge. *Gambling debts forced him to leave for the Continent, and he finally settled in Florence in 1784, where he edited and contributed to *The Florence Miscellany* (1785). It was after his move to Brussels in 1787 that Merry established his reputation as 'Della Crusca'. His subsequent exchange of verses with Anna Matilda (Hannah *Cowley) attracted a number of imitators who corresponded in the pages of the *World* and other *newspapers. Merry's energies were soon taken up by an enthusiasm for the *French Revolution. Rushing to Paris at the news of the fall of the Bastille, he subsequently became involved in radical circles both in Paris and London and only narrowly avoided being stranded in the French capital on the outbreak of war in 1793. He contributed both *poetry [29] and newspaper satires and squibs to the radical cause. His 'Ode for the Fourteenth of July' was read before a large audience at the Crown and Anchor *tavern in London in 1791, while a series of savage epigrammatic attacks on *Pitt appeared in newspapers such as the *Argus*, run by his friend Sampson Perry (1747–1823). His mock advertisement parodying Pitt as 'Signor Gulielmo Pittachio' was widely copied and circulated in numerous cheap forms.

Merry also wrote for the *theatre [24]. In 1791 his tragedy *Lorenzo* was performed at Covent Garden, where he met and married Anne Brunton (1768–1808), a leading actress. His next play, *The Magician No Conjuror* (1792), a veiled attack on Pitt, was withdrawn after two nights. Government harassment made it increasingly impossible for Merry to pursue a career as a playwright. Unable to get his play *Fenelon* performed, he did manage to publish *The Wounded Soldier* (*c*.1795), a long sentimental poem on the effects of the war. Deeply in debt, he emigrated in 1796 with his wife to the United States, leaving behind *The Pains of Memory*, a poem reflecting on the vicissitudes of his life.   JM

mesmerism, see *animal magnetism.

Methodism, an *Evangelical religious movement, whose origins in *Anglican Oxford were slowly submerged, under the direction of its best-known member, John *Wesley, until it became an organization distinct in doctrine and discipline from the Church of England, with a strong following abroad, particularly in America. Wesley's *Complete English Dictionary* (1753) defined 'A Methodist' as 'one that lives according to the method laid down in the Bible'. The mutually supportive group of students, meeting in Oxford in the 1720s, known either as 'Methodists' or 'the Holy Club', sought to follow the ordinances of the Church and exercised a practical ministry by charitable work and *prison visiting. Methodism always sought to promote the immediate experience of *religion [10] and its sense of the vital importance of establishing small, mutually responsible, religious communities continued to dominate its organizational thinking.

Although Methodist 'bands' and 'classes' began as a supplementary aid to church worship, Methodists who sought to preach a salvation freely offered to all inevitably found themselves contravening parish boundaries and antagonizing the combined authority of squire and parson in rural areas. Until his death in 1791 John Wesley supervised every part of Methodism's evolving machinery. Parallel developments in the Calvinist wing of Methodism, under the leadership of George *Whitefield and Selina, Countess of Huntingdon (1707–91), failed largely because they lacked Wesley's foresight, and his meticulous attention to detail. Although Wesley was the final arbiter in all matters, his organization epitomized the Evangelical trait of allowing the laity a new importance in religious matters: Methodism not only made use of lay preachers from social classes who could never have sought ordination, but in its early days also even authorized occasional female preaching.

By 1791, however, Methodism found itself having to take account of a changed economic and political landscape. It found itself changing from Wesley's vision of an organization capable, through its members' diligence and frugality, of ministering to all in need into a more inward-looking and prosperous denomination. A new generation of Methodists feared to lose the wealth and respectability their industrious sobriety had won them by being seen to distribute indiscriminate charity to beggars: for the increasing numbers of the dispossessed were being

reconstituted as a threat to public order rather than being viewed as merely indigent [see *poverty, 12].

As these implicit tensions with Methodism's originating impulses developed, fissiparous tendencies developed at the organizational level. Those who felt that the centralized power held by the annual conference of Methodist itinerant preachers was out of kilter with the egalitarian ideas popularized by the *French Revolution pressed for greater powers for the laity and for local groups. Others believed that Methodism had departed from its search for the apostolic purity of the early church. The first group seceded to form the Methodist New Connexion in 1797, and the second radical tendency threw up two movements: the Primitive Methodists, founded in 1811, and the Bible Christians, established as a new sect in 1819. Meanwhile the main body of the movement, under the leadership of Jabez Bunting (1779–1858), interpreted their role as Wesley's heirs in terms that favoured obedience to ministerial leadership over fostering the autonomous development of local chapels. These different trajectories enabled Methodists to be reviled by the religious establishment as potential 'Jacobin' demagogues, while radicals often depicted them as collaborating with the forces of *Tory repression.

Methodism had also proved popular in America: its links with *Moravian pietism, its high estimate of the *Bible, and its recognition of the unique importance of each individual soul found a ready hearing in the land tilled by the Pilgrim Fathers. In 1784, though still maintaining his allegiance to Anglicanism, Wesley had ordained men for the American ministry, so laying the groundwork for the Methodist Episcopal Church. In America race was eventually to provide the divisive issue, as evidenced by the formation in 1816 of the African Methodist Episcopal Church.

This diversity of Methodism's membership makes its cultural impact hard to categorize definitively. Least contentious would be its claim to have contributed to the inroads upon illiteracy made by the Evangelical movement in its endeavour to allow all humanity access to the Gospel. John Wesley fostered the reading habit among his less educated followers by providing them with a veritable library of abridged books such as Edward Young's *Night Thoughts* (1742–5). Methodist tracts and magazines, with their formulaic tales of conversions and examples of God's providential intervention, found their way even into the staunchly Anglican Brontë parsonage. Methodist conversions were popularly associated with scenes of wild emotionalism, yet the spread of 'religion of the heart' had been overseen by a man of an otherwise typically eighteenth-century cast of mind, prone to tabulate and rationalize and be suspicious of 'enthusiasm'. Nevertheless, Wesley's conviction that the sudden change needful was the instant gift of God, and that neither God nor His creation, man, could be satisfactorily accounted for by mechanistic explanations, were to find secular counterparts in Romantic theories of inspiration and in man's sense of himself located within an ultimately mysterious universe. The sense of community provided by a local Methodist chapel, the conviction of every man's importance before God, and the philosophical conviction of a prophet like Thomas *Carlyle that the fellowship of man should be conscious of the dynamic religious drama against which political and economic life unfolded, all contributed to the protest against the dehumanizing aspects of the industrial revolution. By the mid-nineteenth century the tensions inherent in the history of Methodism's development were frequently reduced, by outsiders, to the aesthetic paradox of a new, squat, redbrick chapel, from which issued heartfelt singing and impassioned preaching.   EJ

military bands were ensembles of wind musicians attached to a branch of the army. Their primary military role was to raise the morale of troops going into battle and to intimidate the enemy: at home military bands contributed to both military and civilian ceremonial occasions as well as to private music-making. Several regular army regiments formed bands from the 1760s, and later in the century commanding officers of volunteer and militia units started to employ bands privately, leading to the establishment of a wide, decentralized network of musically literate instrumentalists who sustained musical activity in general, particularly in the provinces.

Foreigners, especially Germans such as the *Herschels, were prominent as performers and leaders in London and county bands, introducing continental practices: it was through German military musicians that the trombone was reintroduced into England after being obsolete for almost a century. Bands performed at various public and private functions, playing marches and popular, often patriotic, tunes, but many also imitated the repertory and instrumentation known in Germany as 'harmoniemusik'. Joseph *Haydn and J. C. *Bach wrote for British military bands, as did a number of English-born musicians such as Thomas Attwood (1765–1838) and Charles *Dibdin.   TH

MILL, James (1773–1836), philosopher, economist, and radical controversialist. One of the leading exponents of *utilitarianism, Mill played an important role in popularizing Jeremy *Bentham's ideas and acted as a teacher and guide to a younger generation of philosophical radicals, which included his own son, John Stuart *Mill, as well as such figures as David *Ricardo and Francis *Place.

Mill was trained at Edinburgh as a Presbyterian minister, but agnosticism led him to give up the clergy. He became a freelance writer in London, facing financial difficulties until he secured a position with the *East India Company. Mill's most significant work was his 'Essay on Government', which first appeared in 1820 in the Supplement to the fifth edition of the *Encyclopaedia Britannica*. This essay was widely perceived as defining the ideology of philosophical radicalism and its alliance with utilitarianism. As in the rest of his work, Mill rooted his argument in what he called 'the whole science of human nature'. Mill argued that the hedonistic calculus of utilitarianism had to form the basis for any conception of the nature of politics and government. His

argument for a representative *democracy [3] dominated by the virtues of the middle classes as the best system of government was supposedly logically 'deduced' from these first principles of utilitarianism, which he articulated in his essay. Thomas *Macaulay wrote his famous rejoinder, 'Utilitarian Logic and Politics', in the *Edinburgh Review* of March 1829, ridiculing Mill's use of deductive reasoning in political argument.

Mill's commitment to utilitarianism was outlined in other essays contributed to the *Encyclopaedia* on subjects as diverse as *education [17], jurisprudence, the *freedom of the press, and the law of nations. The commitment to associationist *psychology [39] which underpinned his philosophy was later set out in his *Analysis of the Phenomena of the Human Mind* (1828). His status as the leading publicist of philosophical radicalism was cemented by his *Elements of Political Economy* (1821), intended as a summary of Ricardo's *Principles of Political Economy* (1817), but Mill's own *magnum opus* was the three-volume *History of British India* (1817) which brought him the appointment in 1819 to the East India Company and hence provided him with financial security for the rest of his life.

Mill's *History* was influential in its attempt to use British India as a testing-ground for utilitarianism. It also played a role in strengthening the increasing influence of utilitarianism as a school of thought on British Indian administration [see history, 38 and *mythology, 36]. But it would be misplaced to see the *History* as only an attempt to apply utilitarianism to British India. The *History* also fashioned a critique of British society itself and its own dominant ideologies, and established an idiom in which cultures could not only be compared and contrasted, but criticized as well. Given the increasingly heterogeneous nature of the British *empire [5] in this period, and the problems this raised regarding *law [8] and government, this was a significant venture in itself.   JMA

MILL, John Stuart (1806–73), social philosopher, political and economic theorist. A writer of astonishing range and versatility, Mill both popularized and influenced social thought and political action in fields as diverse as utilitarian philosophy, *political economy [33], feminism, *democracy [3], and *socialism.

Son of James *Mill, he was shaped by a singular education which began with the study of Greek at the age of 3, followed by Latin, algebra, the differential calculus, and syllogistic logic before the age of 12. At 13 he began a study of political economy which allowed him to assist his father in the writing of *Elements of Political Economy* (1821). In 1820 his father arranged for him to spend a year in France as the guest of Jeremy *Bentham's brother, Sir Samuel. In France he absorbed Benthamite ideas through a reading of Étienne Dumont's *Traités de Législation Civile et Pénale* (1802). His study of Benthamite *utilitarianism was supplemented by reading *law [8] under John Austin on his return from France. At 16 he formed a Benthamite discussion group, 'The

Utilitarian Society', through which he both propagated and studied utilitarian philosophy.

In 1823, through the intervention of his father, he took up a position with the *East India Company, with which he served until 1858. In the late 1820s, while holding this clerical position, he also acted as secretary to Bentham while the latter was preparing his *Rationale of Judicial Evidence* (1827). This experience led to a personal and intellectual crisis which profoundly affected his subsequent views and writing.

Mill's education under his father's guidance had eschewed nature and the senses in favour of the intellect. He had mastered syllogism but not been exposed to *Shakespeare. The tensions dormant in such a one-sided development coalesced in Mill's realization of a certain intellectual sterility in the natural law assumptions of Benthamite utilitarianism. His reading of Guizet and Michelet and his acquaintance with Thomas *Carlyle awaked in Mill an acknowledgement of the importance of history. The problem, he felt, with Benthamite utilitarianism was the unhistorical character of its method, building on a narrow and essentialist view of human nature. Mill did not, however, abandon the methodological assumption of the philosophical radicals that it was possible to construct a science of society based on the natural sciences, but attempted rather to broaden the utilitarian agenda through the incorporation of historical and social context. As a result, he took utilitarianism to questions of social concern such as property ownership, political reform, and the place of *women [4] in society.

The other profound influence on Mill's intellectual and political development was undoubtedly his meeting, partnership, and finally marriage to Harriet Taylor (1807–58). They met in 1830 while she was still married, forming a deep personal and intellectual partnership. Only after the death of her husband did they marry in 1851. In his *Autobiography* (1873) Mill claimed that when the thoughts of two people are completely in common 'it is of little consequence in respect to the question of originality, which of them holds the pen . . . In this wide sense, not only during the years of our married life, but during many of the years of confidential friendship which preceded, all my public writings were as much her work as mine.' Most subsequent scholars have dismissed Mill's own words, ignoring Taylor in their study of Mill's writings, although there is now some acceptance of his claim. Irrespective of authorship, Mill's public feminism, evident both in his writings and in his attempt to secure female suffrage during the parliamentary debates over political reform in 1867, was almost unique among the social philosophers and political economists of nineteenth-century England, matched, perhaps, only by the socialist William *Thompson.

The bulk of Mill's writings was produced from the mid-nineteenth century and his short parliamentary career as member for Westminster (1865–8) places his importance and influence in the second half of the nineteenth century. Yet an understanding of his most influential writings—on economics,

Principles of Political Economy (1848), on social philosophy, *Utilitarianism* (1861), on politics, *Considerations on Representative Government* (1861), and on feminism, *The Subjection of Women* (1869)—requires an appreciation of his formative intellectual influences. Of these, his education in utilitarian thought, his crisis of belief in the methodological foundations of Benthamite utilitarianism, his attempt to bring an understanding of social and historical context to a science of society modelled on the social sciences, and last, but by no means least, his partnership with Harriet Taylor are the most important.

Mill may finally be read as a template against which to measure the development of English social and political thought from the late eighteenth to the late nineteenth century. Seen in this light, there is a beguiling symmetry in the fact that this intellectual 'child' of Jeremy Bentham, should, a year before his death in 1873, be appointed godfather to Bertrand Russell. ARB

MILLAR, John (1735–1801), professor of law at Glasgow (1761–1801) and the most talented of Adam *Smith's students. His *Origin of the Distinction of Ranks* (1771) developed a striking historico-sociological theory of power relations that is notable for its pioneering discussion of the changing status of women [see *exploration, 37]. In *An Historical View of the English Government* (1787), Millar wrote *Whig history tempered by the influence of David *Hume and Smith. More overt than Hume and Smith in his political commitments, he welcomed both American independence and the early, constitutionalist phase of the *French Revolution, and argued for reform of property law and *parliamentary reform and against the slave trade. Millar became a famous teacher who influenced a generation of law students and gave prominence to the Glasgow law school. KH

millenarianism. The expectation of the Second Coming of Christ as prophesied in the *Bible is usually known by modern scholars as millenarianism, or millennialism. Such expectations were widespread in our period, especially in response to natural disasters or political upheavals such as the *French Revolution, reaching a crescendo at the turn of the century.

In modern discussions of this phenomenon, a distinction is often made between premillennialism and postmillennialism. The former is the belief that the 1,000-year period prophesied in Revelation 20: 1–8 will see the literal return of Christ to rule the world before it comes to an end with the Apocalypse and the Last Judgement. Such a view often went hand in hand with the expectation of sudden, violent, and apocalyptic events. Postmillennialists generally believed that the millennium would precede the Second Coming, a view usually associated with a more gradualist and progressive belief in the spread of Christian principles.

Premillennialism is often identified with the popular tradition which produced prophets like Richard *Brothers and Joanna *Southcott. Within this tradition both the Bible and the visionary experiences of individual believers continued to be credited with providing signs of the times which signalled the imminence of the last days. Such views provoked deep social and political anxieties among the British ruling classes because of memories of the violent sectarians of Cromwell's time, because of the notorious assassination attempts on George III by 'fanatics' such as Margaret Nicholson (1786) and James Hadfield (1800), and because prophetic roles were frequently espoused by individuals from the most humble and unlettered backgrounds.

However, millenarianism did not simply remain part of the *popular culture [23] in the period. Joseph *Johnson alone published over thirty books on *prophecy. His output reflects the market for such books and the interest in millenarianism within Rational Dissent. Joseph *Priestley and Richard *Price were devoted millenarians who believed that the diffusion of knowledge and political reform were moving the world towards the millennium. Such a faith in a providential, general progress of *Enlightenment [32] seems easily transmuted into something like William *Godwin's secularized faith in perfectibility, yet both Price and Priestley also looked forward to the literal return of Christ and the cataclysms and upheavals that were to accompany it. Neither fits neatly into the premillennialist or postmillennialist category. Similarly, the distinctly unrespectable radical Thomas *Spence could blend what seems a postmillennialist faith in the human agency of revolutionary reason with rhetoric full of apocalyptic resonance that appealed to the popular, millenarian tradition.

Perhaps because of the associations between the millenarian tradition and radical ideas, millenarianism was not a common feature of *Anglican discourse. In the 1790s Bishop Samuel *Horsley was one exception, and some attempts were made by *Pitt to sponsor a literature seeking to identify the French Revolution with the Beast of Apocalypse, but the identification of the Catholic monarchy of France with Antichrist was too strong a part of the English Protestant tradition to provide much scope here. More common was the idea, to which Richard Brothers owed his brief bout of public notoriety, that the Revolution was a sign of the onset of the last days and perhaps even itself the beginning of the figurative rule of Christ. Not until the rise of *Napoleon were loyalist caricaturists and writers successfully able to demonize the Revolution by association with ideas of the Antichrist. Napoleon's invasion of Egypt and promise to restore the Jews to Palestine in 1798, followed later by his wooing of European Jewry at the Paris Sanhedrin in 1806–7, triggered an intensive bout of prophetic analysis from English loyalists who feared that Napoleon was fulfilling the signs promised in biblical prophecy. The Anglican scholar Henry Kett (1761–1825) and the Dissenter James Bicheno (d. 1831) were typical in their concern to redefine England's providential role within the coming millennium in the face of the threat posed by Napoleon.

Throughout the period, millenarianism exerted a strong presence in literature and the visual arts, especially the latter because of the visionary nature of the Book of Revelation. This was also the period when poetry was increasingly being redefined as above all a visionary activity. The powerful hold of millenarian ideas on the imagination of the period is perhaps best illustrated in the work of artists like James *Barry, William *Blake, Philippe Jacques de *Loutherbourg, Benjamin *West, and, later, John *Martin.

JM and IMcC

MILLER, Hugh (1802–56), stonemason, newspaper editor, essayist, popular geological writer, and Presbyterian intellectual. From an early age Miller exhibited a volatile, sometimes aggressive, character (he stabbed a fellow pupil at school), and against the advice of his uncles he took up an apprenticeship as a stonemason rather than following university studies. In the time snatched from hewing rocks, Miller collected fossils, wrote verses, and gathered folktales from the environs of Cromarty, on the east coast of Scotland. His anonymously published *Poems* (1829) received a mixed and generally subdued reception, but his *Scenes and Legends of the North of Scotland* (1835) was recognized, and has been since, as a pioneering example of popular *antiquarianism [35]. But Miller's fame came to rest on his *geological work and on his ability to write more vividly and evocatively about fossils and the earth's history than any other in Britain. Such books as *The Old Red Sandstone* (1841), *Footprints of the Creator* (1849), and *The Testimony of the Rocks* (1857) were in print throughout the nineteenth century and sold tens of thousands of copies.

Miller's name first came to public attention with his powerful polemic against efforts to 'intrude' ministers into Scottish parishes, against the tradition of popular election. His fiery *Letter to Lord Brougham* (1839) drew the notice of powerful political and religious figures in Edinburgh, who invited Miller to edit a newspaper launched to promote the cause of non-intrusion. The *Witness* appeared under Miller's editorship in January 1840; within five years it rivalled the *Scotsman* in sales north of the English border, and was a powerful voice in the events leading up to the Disruption which tore apart the Church of Scotland in 1843.

Miller wrote prolifically for his newspaper, on ecclesiastical and political matters, as well as on art and literature, and on such matters as *Catholic emancipation, Scottish nationalism, and English effeminacy. His columns in the *Witness* won to his circle of admirers figures as diverse as Charles *Dickens, Thomas *Carlyle, and Charles Darwin. His beautifully composed autobiography, *Schools and Schoolmasters* (1854), is a classic narrative of autodidacticism and has remained in print almost continuously since its first appearance [see *popular education]. Miller's suicide, incited by terrifying and bloody visions, added mystery to an extraordinary life already full of enigma. MSH

MILTON, John (1608–74), a major icon of English culture in our period, although he remained a specifically *republican hero (or villain) for some, as in

Samuel *Johnson's representation of him as a 'surly republican' in *Lives of the Poets* (1779–81). However, changing aesthetics and a more nuanced appreciation of his political situation was already in the process of altering the general estimation of the poet's reputation. This process was helped and reflected in the growth of Milton scholarship in the eighteenth century and in the multiplication of different editions of his poetry—*Paradise Lost* (1667) in particular (including a Welsh translation by William Owen *Pughe in 1819). Most of the valuable commentary from the preceding century was included in H. J. Todd's (1763–1845) edition of the poetical works (1801) which was to become canonical for the nineteenth century.

By the end of our period, Milton was firmly enshrined as the hero of English liberty in the *Whig tradition, with texts such as *Areopagitica* admired across the political spectrum for its defence of *freedom of the press. Thomas *Macaulay's laudatory review in the *Edinburgh Review* (1825) of a translation of the recently discovered statement of Milton's religious beliefs, *De Doctrina Christiana*, may be taken as the culmination of this tradition, but respect for the poet did not necessarily presuppose political sympathy. By the middle of the eighteenth century, *Paradise Lost* had become the prime example of the *sublime in English letters, and it was in this mode that Milton was also frequently evoked. Indeed as an *epic poet he made a more appropriate guiding deity for English letters than *Shakespeare, who was frequently still regarded as an untutored *genius.

During the 1790s the struggle for Milton's name became particularly intense. An important blow against Johnson's Tory strictures was struck by William *Hayley in his 'Life of Milton' (1794), which nominated Milton 'the great English author'. Others sympathetic to the *French Revolution invoked Milton's name as the paradigmatic revolutionary poet-prophet. Joseph *Johnson was particularly involved in publishing Milton, reflecting the political interests of his circle across the spectrum of reformist and radical opinion. Johnson was one of the original sponsors of Henry *Fuseli's plan for an extended series of paintings on Miltonic subjects, although the original idea of a de luxe illustrated edition was abandoned for economic reasons and because of the illness of the proposed editor, William *Cowper, another devoted admirer of the patriot poet. Fuseli went on alone and opened a Milton Gallery in 1799, but failed to garner the public interest he had expected [see *viewing, 20].

Fuseli's financial failure notwithstanding, the period after 1795 witnessed a remarkable increase in visual representations of Milton's poetry, often influenced, as in Fuseli's case, by the increasing demand for illustrated books. Two currents can be identified in paintings and illustrations of Miltonic subjects: an elegant one associated with Thomas *Stothard's many illustrations, and the more sublime or 'Romantic' vein found in Fuseli. The latter tradition is present in the poetry as well as the painting of Fuseli's friend William *Blake, who returned obsessively to

Miltonic subjects throughout his career. The promise in *Areopagitica* that England could become a nation of prophets remained an inspiring force behind the *millenarianism of Blake's poetry, culminating in the direct but critical treatment of his hero in the epic *Milton*. Blake was also a regular illustrator of the poems (though typically in terms of his own highly original interpretations). John *Martin represents perhaps the last exponent of the Miltonic sublime, the majority of English painters after 1800 preferring conventional adaptations in a classical manner.

It was in poetry, predictably enough, that Milton's influence and example was most directly felt. Thomas *Warton's 1785 edition of the minor poems played an important part in establishing Milton as 'an old English poet', the representative of a native sublimity and warmth which was coming to be valued over neoclassical tastes. By the late eighteenth century Milton was increasingly represented as a key figure in an authentically English literary tradition which Warton identified with 'picturesque description and romantic imagery' rather than 'polished numbers, sparkling couplets, and pointed periods'. Writing in August and September 1802, *Wordsworth produced a series of 'Sonnets dedicated to Liberty' which invoked the figure of Milton as the patriot poet, though whether this Milton is a republican hero is a matter of debate. Wordsworth's own epic, *The Prelude*, is in many ways an attempt to rewrite *Paradise Lost* for a modern age. Percy *Shelley is representative of the wave of young intellectuals for whom Milton remained a political and poetical hero, reminding readers in his *Defence of Poetry* (1821) that 'the sacred Milton was . . . a republican and a bold inquirer into morals and religion', but by this time the iconic status of the great poet-prophet was already firmly established. The 'glory of English literature', as Macaulay called him, was regarded by the majority of his readers in the nineteenth century as a *patriot in a newer sense which privileged national pride over any particular political principles. JM

Minerva Press, a publishing house established by William Lane (?1745–1814) in 1773, operating under this name from 1790 to 1820, in Leadenhall Street, London, which pioneered the mass production of popular fiction and its distribution in *circulating libraries throughout Britain and the colonies.

Instrumental in the spread of the circulating library to the provinces, where it flourished in seaside resorts and health *spas, the Minerva Press contributed significantly to the development of a new conception of reading as a leisured, recuperative, and sociable recreation. The Minerva's development of the lending library as a profitable sideline of engravers, picture-framers, perfumers, jewellers, and confectioners expanded the possibilities of the book as an object of consumer desire [see *consumerism, 19]. In pioneering new technologies of mass book production, the Minerva Press also became a focus of *copyright issues.

The exuberant capacity of the Minerva Press

novel for self-parody and self-advertisement attested to its pre-eminent status as a synonym for *novel [31] and *romance genres. A major publisher of the *Gothic novel, Minerva published each of the representative Gothic novels that Jane *Austen parodied in *Northanger Abbey* (1817). Minerva provided an important avenue for *women [4] writers, publishing twice as many works by women as by men. Notable authors with works first published (usually anonymously) by Minerva include Amelia *Opie, Robert *Bage, William *Godwin, Sydney *Owenson (Lady Morgan), and Jane *West.   CT

Ministry of All the Talents, formed in 1806 when Lord *Grenville succeeded William *Pitt the younger as Prime Minister. The members of Pitt's former ministry hoped to be retained, but most of them were rejected by Grenville in favour of a coalition which contained Charles James *Fox and a number of the *Whig oppositionists, including R. B. *Sheridan, as well as some prominent ultra-Tories such as Lord Sidmouth (1757–1844). This political diversity earnt it the title of 'All the Talents', which quickly became ironic, especially after an influential *satire by that name had been produced by the talented hack writer Eaton Stannard Barrett (1786–1820). The radicals William *Cobbett and Sir Francis *Burdett regarded Fox's joining of the coalition as a betrayal of reforming principles, and they began publicly to air their disillusionment with the Whigs. Fox's death in 1806 weakened the shaky coalition further, and on 18 March 1807 the remnants of the ministry resigned after failing to persuade the King to accede to a mild measure of reform for Catholics in Ireland.   IMcC

missionaries and missionary societies became prominent in Britain from the mid-eighteenth century with the formation of societies devoted to domestic and foreign *Evangelical missionary crusades. The *Methodists began mission work amongst West Indian slaves before the 1760s and *Anglicans and Dissenters also formed missionary societies from the 1760s onwards. These Christian denominations worked separately to bring the message of salvation and eternal life, establish the primacy of Christian theology, and extend their congregations in foreign lands. Anglicans, for example, worked to establish an indigenous church in India and Africa and eventually confirmed and ordained 'Native Christians'.

Evangelicalism accelerated the missionary impulse in Britain from the 1780s and was linked directly with the dissemination of the printed gospel and active missionary work undertaken abroad. Domestic missions were usually conducted under the auspices of benevolent charitable institutions, through societies such as the Society for the Promotion of Christian Knowledge, through local missions, and through *Sunday schools. Under the inspired leadership of John Ryland (1753–1825) the first modern society, the Baptist Missionary Society, was formed in 1792 (originally founded as the Particular Baptist Missionary Society for Propagating the Gospel among the Heathen). John Ryland and others, including William Carey (1761–1834), the Society's first missionary to Serampore in India in 1792, instituted specific training for missionaries. David Bogue (1750–1825), one of the founders of the inter-denominational Missionary Society formed in 1795 (later the London Missionary Society), influenced by George *Whitefield and the Countess of Huntingdon's Connexion, introduced similar vocational training in the Gosport Academy and Missionary Seminary. The Church of Scotland's Foreign Mission and the Glasgow Missionary Society were both formed in 1796, followed in 1797 by the Society for Missions to Africa and the East established by Charles Simeon (1759–1836) and other Anglican Evangelical churchmen. The Society for Missions was renamed the Church Missionary Society in 1799.

British missionary societies and individual missionaries sought to bring the gospel to expatriate men and women, but the chief purpose of all foreign missionaries remained to evangelize and proselytize amongst native populations. Missionaries distributed illustrated religious tracts and free bibles; many learned to speak fluently in native languages and wrote vernacular texts. Interdenominational societies such as the Religious Tract Society (1799) and the British and Foreign Bible Society (1804) were founded for the propagation of Christian knowledge, translating the Bible and other Christian works into many languages and dialects for use in Europe and the Far East.

Congregations of all classes and denominations in Britain collected large sums to support the missionary cause. Overseas and domestic missionaries were drawn chiefly from the clerical profession, but many able men were attracted to missionary endeavours from other professions and respectable trades. Missionary work also provided an important outlet for the idealism and creative energies of middle-class women.

Evangelical missionaries established extensive networks and native churches in India, China, the Pacific, Australia, and New Zealand throughout this period, and many were instrumental in the long campaign leading to the abolition of *slavery [6]. This achieved, missionaries redoubled their efforts to Christianize Africa, and crusades were organized to convert the *Jews and Catholics in Britain and on the Continent. By the 1830s and 1840s, Evangelicals looked critically at the state of the domestic church and the growing numbers of 'home heathen' and renewed their efforts to encourage religious conversion. City missions formed in Britain's industrial and metropolitan conurbations encouraged a revival of missionary and Evangelical enthusiasm within the nation.   SR

monarchy in Britain operated under the provisions and conventions established during and after the *Glorious Revolution. Actual limitations on the Crown were still few: monarchs could still make war and peace, call and dissolve parliament, appoint and dismiss ministers from amongst their Protestant subjects, and exercise their extensive patronage in the army, navy, church, and diplomatic corps. As independent and autocratic German rulers in an age of personal monarchy, aided by a political élite anxious not to undermine a dynasty that served them well, the Georges played a significant role in foreign and domestic affairs. Indeed, recent scholarship has done much to close the gap between the constitutionally limited but often truly executive kingship of the Hanoverians and the theoretically absolutist but personally and conventionally constrained administrative monarchy of their Bourbon counterparts.

Yet, as continental observers invariably remarked, there were also profound differences, the most obvious being money. Parliamentary provision for the monarchy in the form of the civil list was quite insufficient for effective sovereignty. Then there were the political constraints of a parliamentary system in which the monarch's business had to be done by ministers who needed to work with both the Crown and the Commons. Added to this was the corrosive effect on the personal authority of middle-aged monarchs of a divided and self-interested court. Most important of all were the invisible constraints of perception and attitude. To many, the Hanoverians were intractably foreign and lacked legitimacy. How much legitimist allure still attached to the exiled House of Stuart is difficult to gauge, but their succes-

sors were never allowed to forget that they were monarchs of religious and constitutional convenience, the dubious beneficiaries of an era which had seen one king executed and another expelled.

George III was different. When he ascended the throne in 1760 at the age of 22 he was the first of his dynasty to be native born and bred, and on his own account he gloried in the name of Briton. For the first time, he was able to attach to the dynasty some of the loyalties and the personnel hitherto proscribed as Jacobite. Deeply religious, priggish, conscientious to a fault, victim of a genetic blood disorder which later gave rise to his supposed *madness, George appeared to be an interventionist monarch to a degree that his immediate predecessors were not. The political significance of this activity—whether it was to restore balance to a constitution long monopolized by a narrow *Whig oligarchy or, as his critics maintained, to subvert the system of government established by the Glorious Revolution—was a matter of intense contemporary and subsequent historiographical dispute. Be that as it may, after twenty years of seemingly active kingship, George had little to show for his efforts. Widely credited with the persecution of Wilkes and his followers [see *Wilkites] and the loss of America, he was deeply unpopular, unable to retain his favoured ministers or to defend

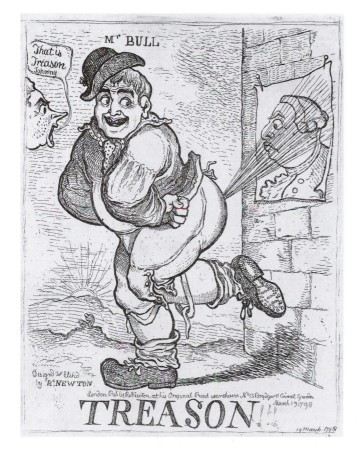

84. *Treason!!!* by Richard Newton, 1798. John Bull targets George III.

himself from the play of political cliques ready to gang up against the titular head of government. Little wonder that the buffeted and humiliated king contemplated abdication.

Many contemporaries and most historians regard 1784 as a turning-point. George's successful coup when he replaced the ministry of *Fox and Lord North (1732–92) with that of young William *Pitt commanded widespread popular support, since this alliance of two former enemies was seen as predatory and corrupt. Thereafter, George was the indirect beneficiary of nearly twenty years of political stability, administrative reform, and wartime *patriotism under Pitt. Even the Regency Crisis of 1788—when he temporarily succumbed to 'the flying gout', and the Prince of Wales and his supporters jockeyed for the spoils of office with untoward alacrity—rebounded to his advantage. For the first time, the injured King became the object of sympathy and respect. He was able to keep the hated Fox out of the wartime ministry and to block *Catholic emancipation for a generation, even at the price of Pitt's leadership and unrest in Ireland. And since his prejudices mirrored those of his subjects, his intervention did the monarchy no harm. Yet personal monarchy was nevertheless on the wane, the outcome of the King's age and illness, the shrinkage of royal patronage, and the gradual emergence—or re-emergence—of party.

The very decline of direct royal influence, however, contributed to a growing mystique of monarchy. Attempts to depict it as a survival and transformation of traditional divine-right ideology do not convince. Rather, the idiom was new. George's intensely moral private life, his hobbies, and horticultural interests were celebrated after his recovery in 1789 as never before. And the paterfamilias, 'Farmer George', was complemented by Queen Charlotte, mother and nurturer of a score of much-painted princesses and princelings, a paragon of wifely duty. But it was the assault on kingship in Revolutionary France which was most responsible for the monarchy's growing popularity. Patriotic Gallophobia, once characterized by a bluff anti-absolutism bordering on *republicanism, was now charged with the celebration of British 'majesty': after 1793, kingship, as refurbished by Edmund *Burke, could seem like virtue, or at least chivalry.

The new cult of monarchy took many forms, such as the renovation of Windsor Castle, Carlton House, and Buckingham House, and the building of new palaces at Brighton and Kew [see *architecture, 28]. There was a flurry of invented royal traditions: garter ceremonies, thanksgivings—the first since Queen Anne's time—for British victories; mass celebrations of the King's own Jubilee in 1809, and five years later of the centenary of the Hanoverian accession. There was also the upsurge in popularity of what was now unproblematically called the national anthem. Celebration of nationhood merged with that of monarchy which somehow, for the first time in modern British history, combined homeliness and grandeur.

For most Britons, however, the magic of monarchy did not extend to the monarchical principle *tout court*. After 1800, the struggle against French republican tyranny was replaced by one against Napoleonic monarchical tyranny. In the aftermath of *Waterloo, tolerance of dynastic monarchy was also tested by the antics of the restored Bourbons in France, Naples, and Spain. Even at home the celebration of monarchy was a brittle affair, dependent, as such cults invariably are, on the propriety of family members. As the old King drifted into mental oblivion after 1810, so the focus shifted to the Prince Regent (see *Regency) and his unsavoury brothers. Politically reactionary, personally extravagant, and domestically scandalous, the royal dukes did little to enhance the dynasty's popularity: between 1812 and 1830 formal monarchy was held in widespread contempt. The obloquy heaped on George IV was due partly to his political clumsiness, monumental debts, regal self-indulgence, and outrageous marital affairs, and partly to the escapades of his brothers. But it was also an indication of the fragility of patriotic monarchy itself. There were plenty of radicals for whom the royals' unedifying, parasitical lives highlighted the fraudulence of the whole enterprise.

George's personal popularity—save in Hanover and Scotland—never fully recovered from the *Queen Caroline affair. Politically, he usually contrived to make the worst of both worlds, as when he filibustered but failed to prevent Catholic emancipation and with it the gradual dissolution of the Tory-Anglican establishment. His inability to control ministers like *Wellington, and his habitual indolence, contributed to a serious decline in monarchical influence, culminating in the act of Catholic Emancipation which helped to smash the old British confessional state. Politically less maladroit, his brother William IV managed—at the eleventh hour—to associate the Crown with limited parliamentary reform, and to recover its popularity once more. But the new symbolism of monarchy did not waver. Monarchy was sublimated, transmuted into the theatre of royal visits and excursions, oriental buildings, kilts, and battlements. It was also feminized, finding its outlet in the unlikely defence of Queen Caroline, in the cult of Great Britain's 'favourite child', Princess Charlotte, and eventually, in 1837, in the mystique of the 18-year-old Queen Victoria.   AMacL

MONBODDO, Lord, see James *Burnett.

monitorial system, the term used to encompass the separate systems of *popular education introduced into Britain independently by Dr Andrew Bell (1753–1832) and Joseph Lancaster (1778–1838), whereby pupils or monitors were used to teach elementary instruction to groups of their peers under overall supervision from a schoolteacher.

When Samuel Whitbread (1758–1815) introduced his unsuccessful national *education [17] bill based on monitorial principles in 1807, he attributed the monitorial system jointly to Bell and Lancaster. Their schemes, though arrived at independently, had much in common. Bell's founding treatise, *An Experiment in Education*, was published in 1797,

Lancaster's *Improvements in Education* in 1803. Both had been influenced by associations with the armed services and by attempts to teach indigenous people in the *empire [5] cheaply. Bell had worked with half-caste children of soldiers in Madras (hence his was sometimes called the Madras system) and Lancaster had combined a naval career with attempts to teach black children in the West Indies. Above all, both systems drew explicit inspiration from *factory models, borrowing particularly the idea of the division and co-operation of labour, and the need for exemplary surveillance. Using mechanistic methods, though without corporal punishment, they sought to inculcate moral discipline in labouring-class children while also providing them with cheap, minimal instruction in reading and writing.

However, during the early decades of the nineteenth century both the two systems and their advocates became embroiled in political and religious controversy. Bell, whose system emphasized scriptural catechism, was championed by officials of the established Church, by Christian propagandists such as Sarah *Trimmer, and by conservative Romantics such as *Southey, *Coleridge, and *Wordsworth. Wordsworth sought to introduce monitorial teaching at Grasmere, though Bell disconcertingly recruited the local teacher for elsewhere. Coleridge and Southey supported Bell in articles and tracts of 1808–11, comparing his *philanthropic influence to that of the great abolitionist Thomas *Clarkson and his Madras educational system to the revolutionary invention of print as an agency for bringing morality and social stability to

Britain. They also attacked the *Quaker Joseph Lancaster's rival monitorial system for endangering the traditional link between church and state and for disseminating poisonous irreligion amongst the working classes.

Though supported by influential Nonconformists, *utilitarian liberals, and radicals, Lancaster succumbed to this barrage of attacks and migrated to America in 1814. His financial ineptitude, unorthodox methods of discipline based on shaming, his *Deist sympathies, and, some claimed, his *homosexuality, forced the reformulation of his monitorial programme, first as the Royal Lancastrian Society in 1808, then as the British and Foreign Schools Society from 1810. The latter extended its mission from the labouring classes to the colonies, as did the rival National Society for the Education of the Poor, an *Anglican organization partly founded by Wordsworth's brother Christopher in 1811 in order to promote Bell's methods and message. Ironically, as the National Society flourished in the early 1830s, Wordsworth began to express increasing doubts about its mechanistic methods and stiflingly unimaginative, non-literary curriculum. In 1833 the government gave formal recognition to the monitorial system by granting £20,000 and a small inspectorate in order to extend its network of primary schools throughout Britain.   IMcC

MOORE, Thomas (1779–1852), Irish writer. Born in Dublin, the son of a Catholic grocer, Moore was educated at Trinity College, where he was a contemporary of the United Irishman Robert Emmet

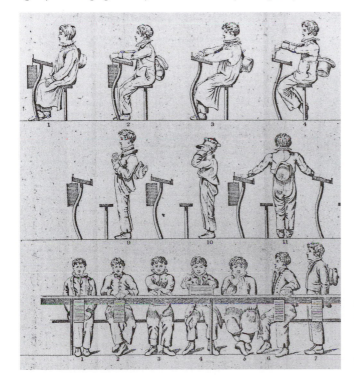

85. Detail of *British System of Education, Positions of the Scholars,* from *Manual of the System of Primary Instruction* (1831), an illustrated guide to the monitorial principles of the British and Foreign Schools Society.

(1778–1803). He achieved early success with *Odes of Anacreon* (1800) and *The Poetical Works of Thomas Little, Jr.* (1801). In 1803 he was offered a government position in Bermuda. After a brief stay he appointed a deputy in his stead and returned to England. Using the resources of the literary marketplace and a talent for self-promotion, Moore exploited his Irishness to establish a position for himself among the *Whig literati. He became associated with the *Holland House circle, with *Byron, Leigh *Hunt, and Samuel *Rogers. An attack by Francis *Jeffrey on Moore's *Epistles, Odes and Other Poems* (1806) led to a notoriously farcical *duel between Jeffrey and Moore in which neither of the protagonists managed to fire a shot. They later became friends.

In 1806, recognizing the commercial potential of the folk-song collections of Edward *Jones and Edward *Bunting, the Dublin music sellers William and James Power invited Moore to provide English lyrics to traditional Irish airs, some of which were derived from Bunting's *General Collection of Ancient Irish Music* (1796). The musical arrangements were by Sir John Stevenson (?1760–1833). The *Irish Melodies*, published between 1807–8 and 1834, turned what had been the preserve of *antiquarians [35] into a European phenomenon. While Moore was criticized by some for prettifying the original airs (William *Hazlitt claimed that he 'converts the wild harp of Erin into a music snuff-box'), the *Melodies* were significant for a romanticization of Irish identity which, however sentimentalized, became an important focus for national expression in the nineteenth century. The *Melodies* made Moore a heroic figure to stand with Emmet, *Fitzgerald, and the martyrs of the 1798 *Rebellion. Identified as an Irish nationalist by the Tory press in London, Moore continued to write on Irish themes for the rest of his career, including *Memoirs of Captain Rock* (1824), a satire on British rule of the island from the perspective of an agrarian Whiteboy; *The Life and Death of Edward Fitzgerald* (1831); and *The History of Ireland* (1845).

Apart from the *Melodies*, Moore's other significant commercial success was his narrative poem *Lalla Rookh* (1817), set in the Near East, which exploited interest in *orientalism. He was also an effective political satirist, attacking the Prince Regent and his ministries in squibs and topical verse such as *Intercepted Letters, or the Twopenny Post Bag* (1813), a work which became a fertile source for *print [22] caricaturists. In 1819 Moore's deputy in Bermuda absconded with £6,000, forcing Moore into a three-year exile on the Continent in order to avoid debt. In 1824 he became involved in a struggle over the memoirs of Byron, which the latter had given to Moore in 1819. Moore had sold the memoirs to John Murray in 1821 for 2,000 guineas with the proviso that the text could be redeemed, but after Byron's death in 1824 a complicated argument ensued between Murray, Moore, and the representatives of Lady Byron and Augusta Leigh. At stake in this dispute was a symbolic struggle over proprietorial rights to Byron's reputation which conflated the poet and his text: it ended with the burning of the memoirs in Murray's

office. Moore did, however, eventually produce his own version of the life of Byron (1830), the first significant biography of the poet.   GR

Moravianism. The Moravian Brethren were a Protestant community uprooted from their original heartlands in Moravia and Bohemia by the religious wars of the seventeenth century. Resettled in Saxony under the patronage of Count Zinzendorf in the 1720s, the sect became a centre of popular revivalism and a model community for various satellites. By the end of the 1730s there were missions in the West Indies, North America, and South Africa. The congregation in London, which James *Gillray's father joined in 1753, was the focal point for this expansion. Count Zinzendorf himself arrived in London in 1751 to direct the building of the model town of Sharon. A group of Moravians encountered on their voyage out to America in the winter of 1735–6 contributed to the conversion experience of John and Charles *Wesley, though John was later to suspect their emphasis on salvation by faith as having antinomian tendencies.
                                                     JM

MORE, Hannah (1745–1833), female educator, conservative propagandist, and *Evangelical religious writer. The fourth of five daughters of a High Church Tory headmaster married to a farmer's daughter, Hannah More reproduced in her career and writings the class and gender preconceptions normative to that family background, especially as regards the mother's lesser cultural and intellectual status.

Her father was her earliest mentor until he withdrew tuition because she outclassed his paying boy pupils in mathematics. Hannah excelled in the school run by her elder sisters for young ladies at College Green, Bristol, and later became its principal. Her first literary production was 'The Search after Happiness' (1762, published 1773), a pastoral drama in verse, for performance by 'female friends in private parties'. An Evangelical reformer, she hereafter busied herself to secure the conservative ideology of her origins, and to put out the brush fires of feminism and secular democratic *republicanism which had agitated and inspired the England of her prime. Her lifelong celibacy and piety recommended her to the powerful middle class as a preceptress to thier daughters, who were destined to bypass their teacher as they became matrons and mothers. Her engagement was announced in 1767 to a man twenty years her senior who, to the indignation of More's supporters, kept postponing the marriage and died still a bachelor in 1822, leaving her an annuity as heart-balm. More's writings reproduced her father's ambivalence about female self-assertion, and channelled her anxiety about usurping masculine prerogatives by displaying a quasi-maternal solicitude towards her female readers and girl pupils. Her essays, plays, and fictions are cautionary moralities, gesturing towards the abyss of masculine rejection which awaited women who transgressed gender barriers, and schooling them to accept the role of self-effacing mediators of male desire and ambition.

On More's first visit to London in 1774, a letter of

introduction from the family physician generated meetings with David Garrick (1717–79), Samuel *Johnson, Edmund *Burke, and Joshua *Reynolds, among the first of many male mentors. *Essays on Various Subjects, Principally Designed for Young Ladies* (1777), dedicated to Elizabeth Montagu (1720–1800), preaches the gendered aesthetics of Burke's *A Philosophical Enquiry into the Origin of our Ideas of the Sublime and Beautiful* (1757), and More attempted to perpetuate Johnson's legacy in *Florio: A Poetical Tale for Fine Gentlemen and Fine Ladies*, and *The Bas Bleu: or Conversation*, two mildly sententious vignettes of the London literary scene.

In 1777 *Percy: A Tragedy* and *The Fatal Falsehood* (written for Garrick in his last retirement) show the deleterious effects of unsuccessful Shakespearean imitation. *The Fatal Falsehood* was denounced in 1779 by Hannah *Cowley for plagiarizing Cowley's own tragedy, *Albina*, and this combined with the death of Garrick to turn More against the stage and the sophistication of London manners. This incident was prophetic of a later contretemps in 1784 between More and Ann *Yearsley, the plebeian woman poet who indignantly threw off More's patronage when More tried to isolate Yearsley from her husband and sons. After 1779 More gave up her stage ambitions and turned to the adaptation of Bible stories for performance by children. The didactic *Sacred Dramas* (1782), dedicated to Mrs Boscawen, indicated her public aversion to metropolitan literary and artistic circles, a gesture anticipating the Romantic turn against the city by William *Wordsworth in *Tintern Abbey* (1798).

In 1787 the More sisters closed the Bristol school, and Hannah now assumed a wider scope for her public activities, loyally supported and tended by her sisters. In 1789 she started Anglican *Sunday schools for poor village girls, and in 1793 her propaganda efforts on behalf of the anti-revolutionary cause earned her an invitation to preside over a ladies' committee for the relief of the emigrant French clergy set up by Dr Charles *Burney.

An early champion of *abolitionism, More published *Slavery: A Poem* in 1788, and in old age she celebrated in verse the official relinquishing of *slavery [6] by the British colonial rulers of Ceylon (Sri Lanka). The 1792 pamphlet 'Village Politics, By Will Chip', if not exactly commissioned by the *Pitt regime on the eve of declaring war on France, was eagerly promoted by it. This inspired a series of *Cheap Repository Tracts, which readily found official sponsors in the Church of England, notably Archdeacon *Paley. The village wiseacre Will Chip is a white Anglican forerunner of Harriet Beecher Stowe's black African slave, Uncle Tom. More's 1799 *Strictures on Female Education* confirms the backlash against the campaign for *women's [4] rights and education by Catharine *Macaulay and Mary *Wollstonecraft, and consummates her repudiation of the London stage, where she had failed to draw an audience.

After meeting William *Wilberforce in 1787, More gravitated towards the Clapham group of Evangel-ical Anglicans, where Wilberforce was the acclaimed leader of anti-slavery reform, but here she incurred powerful enemies on the religious Right (notably William Windham, 1750–1810), and was attacked in the press, chiefly by Windham's ally William *Cobbett, who had previously promoted her. She was a scapegoat for the *Anti-Jacobin Review*, for Croker ('John Wilson') of the *Quarterly Review*, and even the Walter *Scott/John *Lockhart faction at the *Edinburgh Review*. Perhaps the worst setback was her bitter feud with the curate at Blagdon, who in 1800 temporarily forced the closure of More's network of Sunday charity schools by spreading allegations of her *Methodist leanings, which insulted her self-image as a true daughter of the established Church. More appealed to higher clerical authorities, and the Bishop of Bath and Wells duly supported her, but she was fatigued and harried by the crisis, and convinced that God was punishing her. Still surrounded by her sisters, she retired to a country cottage near Bristol. *Hints Towards Forming the Character of a Princess* (1805) was dedicated to the Bishop of Exeter and looked wistfully to the infant Hanoverian, Princess Charlotte of Wales, as ideal object of More's pedagogical aspirations. More's bestselling work *Coelebs in Search of a Wife* was published in 1809, and sold particularly well in the growing American book market. All More's sisters died before her, and she lived on till 1833, dying in the same year as her erstwhile leader, Wilberforce.   JB

MORGAN, Lady, see Sydney *Owenson.

MORGANWG, Iolo, see Edward *Williams.

MORLAND, George (1763–1804), painter, well-known for his prolific production of rustic genre scenes which reveal sympathy for the rural poor. Morland worked for his father, the painter Henry Morland (*c.*1719–97), and began making copies of pictures while still in his teens. A dispute with his father led him to work for a picture dealer in 1784–5, but he soon struck out on his own by producing scenes of country life. Unlike many of his contemporaries, Morland was not a member of the *Royal Academy and did not earn money by painting *portraits. Instead, he produced rustic scenes as speculations and sold them through dealers and other middlemen. This disdain for *patronage liberated him from the constraints of contemporary taste, but his works were popular nevertheless. His country scenes became known through engravings by his brother-in-law William Ward (1766–1826), and he also exhibited at the Royal Academy.

A self-professed 'drunken dog', Morland was infamous for his dissolution, and financial difficulties led him to be arrested for debt in 1799. He eventually died in prison. His contemporary reputation for moral laxity has overshadowed subsequent appreciation of the radical nature of some of his paintings. In the wake of the *French Revolution, some observers were disturbed by the disruptive potential of Morland's representation of the rural poor who were shown drinking, talking, or wasting time, rather than labouring and producing [see *poverty, 12]. Although such leisure scenes could be construed as merely *picturesque, they were also disturbing for conservative observers who felt threatened by the spectre of revolution in Britain.   SW

MOSCHELES, Ignaz (1794–1870), the leading early Romantic *pianist before Chopin, resident in London from 1826 until 1846. Trained in Prague and Vienna, Moscheles was already a renowned virtuoso when he appeared in London in 1821. The brilliant passage-work and sheer bravura of his *Fall of Paris* variations caused a sensation when he performed at the Philharmonic Society. Elsewhere he delighted audiences by improvising on 'My lodging is on the cold ground'. Clearly this was playing of a different order from that of J. B. *Cramer, and in many ways Moscheles typifies the Romantic virtuoso. In constant demand at public *concerts and salons, he published innumerable display pieces, as well as arrangements of popular melodies for the amateur market.

Though he perhaps never recaptured the level of his earlier music, Moscheles's diaries reveal a sensitive and serious musician. In 1832, for example, he directed the first London performance of Beethoven's *Missa Solemnis*. In the virtuoso *Allegro di bravura* (1828), dedicated to Mendelssohn, he brings an impressive urgency and drive to the expected keyboard trickery. And even such an obvious crowd-pleaser as the *Recollections of Ireland* (originally improvised in Dublin in 1826) climaxes with a *tour de force*, combining 'The Last Rose of Summer', 'Garry Owen', and 'St Patrick's Day' in grandiose counterpoint.   SMcV

MOZART, Wolfgang Amadeus (1756–91), Austrian composer and pianist. Following his visit to London as a child from 1764–5, Mozart never returned, despite associating closely in Vienna with several prominent British musicians, such as Michael *Kelly and Nancy *Storace, who sang in the premiere of *Le nozze di Figaro* (1786), and composer Stephen *Storace. Mozart's plans to accompany these friends to London in 1787 fell through, but they perhaps engineered the offer he received to compose two Italian operas for the short-lived Pantheon company (1790). J. P. Salomon (1745–1815) and Lorenzo Da Ponte (1749–1838) also invited Mozart to England, without success.

Access to Mozart's music in England during his lifetime was limited. Editions of his keyboard sonatas (K.309–11, for example) reached London in 1784, the year in which unspecified Mozart orchestral works began to appear sporadically on London *concert bills. Isolated operatic numbers by Mozart were performed as concert items only after his death, from 1792.

Mozart's style was described as 'scientific' and 'learned'—epithets which praised or attacked depending on the critic's bias. Although *Haydn enhanced his posthumous reputation, Mozart's operas were slow to reach the King's Theatre, mainly because of the partisanship of Italian singers like

Angelica *Catalani. Frustrated musical amateurs therefore resorted to their own private performances (c.1808–12).

Generally speaking, the King's Theatre managers produced a Mozart opera only after a singer's benefit night had proved it viable; thus, Elizabeth *Billington introduced *La clemenza di Tito* (1806) and Teresa Bertinotti-Radicati pioneered *Così fan tutte* (1811). *Figaro* was staged sumptuously in response to a rival company's production of Acts I and II at the Pantheon (1812), but it was not until William Ayrton's production of *Don Giovanni* (1817) that Mozart's music truly caught the popular taste. The English theatres presented bowdlerized versions of these operas in the vernacular, the music adapted by Henry *Bishop. Leigh *Hunt and William *Hazlitt were amongst the first English critics to appreciate Mozart's dramatic and musical genius.   RC

music, domestic. Modes of participation in domestic music and amateur performance differed significantly according to gender. While the performance of music was generally not considered suitable for gentlemen, the aristocracy did include some enthusiastic instrumentalists. The Earl of Mornington, for example, was a fanatical *violinist, and the Prince of Wales organized serious chamber-music parties at which he himself played the cello. Devotees like James Harris of Salisbury kept music going in provincial orchestral societies, more meetings of dedicated amateurs than public *concerts. Undemanding duets for the flute or violin were published in great numbers. Despite these examples, it was far more fitting for a man to take part in a convivial after-dinner *glee, and this remained the principal form of male domestic music, whether at home or in more formal glee clubs.

For women, on the other hand, music played quite a different role—an accomplishment designed to attract a husband, and a pastime after marriage [see *women musicians]. Young ladies practised their *singing or the piano in solitary confinement for hours on end, so that they could occasionally be displayed to family and guests. Jane *Austen used music to elucidate character and for social comment: the plain Mary Bennet in *Pride and Prejudice* played a long concerto with 'a pedantic air and conceited manner', while the much less diligent Elizabeth delighted through her natural and unaffected taste; Lady Catherine de Bourgh merely listened to half a song before resuming her conversation.

Music was a prime vehicle of middle-class aspiration, and few homes with serious social pretensions lacked a piano. Some viewed this as a laudable spread of culture and polite entertainment, but others criticized it as time-wasting vanity. The figure of the farmer's daughter, raucously entertaining the neighbours, was mercilessly caricatured by James *Gillray; while in *Thackeray's *Vanity Fair* (1847–8) the vulgarity of the self-made city merchant Mr Osborne was revealed by his ostentatiously carved grand piano.

The amateur market of *music publishing prompted the publication of vast numbers of songs, ranging from Italian opera and *Handel oratorio, to English *ballads and favourite Scottish and Irish tunes. Many ballads derived from the *pleasure gardens (such as *Hook's 'The Lass of Richmond Hill') or English *operas (Horn's 'Cherry Ripe'), whilst others were featured at the vocal concert or *oratorios, a valuable incentive to middle-class consumption. Many sentimentally evoke a lost world of simple country virtues: thus Henry *Bishop's 'Home, Sweet Home' embodies a reassuring vision of English country life and family stability. This same nostalgia informed the continuing vogue for Celtic airs in George *Thomson's collections and Thomas *Moore's *Irish Melodies*. Generally the melodies are smoothed out, their poignancy and Celtic melancholy restrained by respectably tonal harmonizations.

Amateur *pianists could become highly proficient through long hours of practice: by the 1820s, we read, *Clementi's difficult Op. 2 sonatas were routinely mastered by lady pianists, for whom the latest virtuosi published their concertos, concert sonatas, and fantasies. But for a more popular market less taxing music was required, and publishers' catalogues were increasingly filled with all kinds of variations, rondos, and even sonatas based on operatic melodies or national airs; cotillions, waltzes, and quadrilles; and descriptive battle-pieces. The *Harmonicon*, a monthly journal, published a supplement of such pieces: *Moscheles pointedly refused to allocate opus numbers to such trifles, but did not disdain to write a gigue for five guineas. Much the most popular amateur piece was *The Battle of Prague* by Kotzwara, on every piano-stand until the mid-nineteenth century.   SMcV

music festivals, concentrated series of concerts, usually for the benefit of charity, based on performances of *oratorios and other choral music, which were an important component of provincial musical and social life in the period [see rise of the *classics]. The origins of the music festival can be traced back to the late seventeenth century and to annual sermons and musical celebrations to mark the feast day of St Cecilia, patron saint of music. The oldest festival was the Three Choirs, which by 1716 or 1717 was being held on an annual basis, rotating between the cathedral towns of Hereford, Gloucester, and Worcester. By 1800 almost every major centre had its festival—annual, biennial, triennial, or on an occasional basis—and the festival movement continued to grow during the first half of the nineteenth century. Its development can be linked to the expansion of towns and the general increase in leisure activities. Other contributory factors were improvements in road transport, leading to increased mobility and comfort for performers and audiences alike, and the popularity of the music of *Handel, which soon came to dominate festival programmes.

A further increase in the number both of festivals and of those involved followed the large-scale performances of the Handel Commemoration in 1784 and of the even larger London Handel festivals of 1785–7 and 1790–1. Press advertisements for the

Birmingham Festival, for example, claimed 'upwards of a hundred' performers in 1802 and 'nearly two hundred' in 1808, when it was proudly stated that 'the band [the orchestra and chorus] will be the largest ever assembled on such an occasion out of London'. At the same time, audience numbers, receipts, and profits also increased dramatically. Festivals formed an important part of the social calendar of the late Georgian town. A typical festival would be held in late summer or early autumn and would be of three days' duration, opening with a church service and continuing with concerts in the mornings and evenings of subsequent days. The main concerts were the oratorio performances, usually held in the mornings in the principal church or cathedral. Handel's *Messiah* was almost invariably performed at one of these concerts, the other consisting of a miscellaneous selection of Handel extracts, or another oratorio. Evening concerts took place in the local assembly rooms or theatre; they would frequently include more modern items and be of a lighter character, followed by a ball.

The music festival provided provincial audiences with their only opportunities to hear large-scale performances of choral and orchestral music. It also brought to them the leading vocal and instrumental performers in the country, in concerts which equalled anything to be heard in London. Local input was usually small, even in those cases where the town had its own musical culture. The principal vocal and instrumental soloists, most of the orchestra, and usually some of the chorus were from London, engaged *en bloc* by a local organizing committee through such orchestral contractors as the various members of the *Ashley family. To these would be added a contingent, usually small, of more local professionals. The greatest attractions were invariably the singers, both for their roles in the oratorio performances and in solo items in the evening concerts: successive Birmingham festivals featured Madame *Mara, Elizabeth *Billington, John *Braham, and Angelica *Catalani, the most celebrated operatic soloists of their day. Leading instrumental players were also engaged, both to play in the orchestra and to perform as soloists in the evening concerts.

Although festivals were usually found in large centres of population, they could also be viable in much smaller places. In 1809, for example, a two-day festival for the benefit of church funds was held at Tamworth, a market town of some 3,000 inhabitants on the Warwickshire–Staffordshire border thirteen miles from Birmingham. Four concerts given by leading performers, including *Messiah* and *Haydn's *The Creation*, resulted in takings of £1,660 and profits of £326. The success of festivals in such small places points to a strong demand for large-scale concerts, and suggests that a favourable position, good communications, and the presence of wealthy patrons within easy travelling distance were as important as a large-town or city location.   PO

music historians. In the late eighteenth century British writers began to address the history of music in a systematic way, reflecting not only a general spirit of historical inquiry and wider dispersal of knowledge but also the antiquarian interest of societies like the Academy of Ancient Music. Two major histories stand out: the *General History of the Science and Practice of Music* by Sir John Hawkins (1776) and Charles *Burney's *General History of Music* (1776–89). Hawkins maintained the more scholarly and measured approach, though there is no mistaking his passionate advocacy of the subtlety of older music. Burney wrote more empirically, with an underlying conviction of progress in musical history: he highlighted the 'crudities' of John Blow, and even Purcell, while devoting inordinate attention to now-forgotten Italian operas of his own day. Burney's *History* was more successful with the reading public, and it formed the basis of subsequent histories by Thomas Busby (1819) and William Hogarth (1835).

Music was also beginning to figure in aesthetic treatises. The *sublime was readily identified with the awesome effect of *Handel's choruses, the beautiful with the charm and simplicity of Italian opera melodies. More difficult was the challenge posed by the unpredictable and irregular drama of *Haydn's symphonies. An important contribution to music theory was made by William *Crotch, who, in his lectures to the Royal Institution (*Substance of Several Courses of Lectures*, 1831), appropriated the term *'picturesque' from Uvedale *Price's theory of *landscape gardening.   SMcV

music publishing. By the 1780s, numbers of music publishers and printers were competing in the growing market led by the middle-class demand for cheap music. Interest in music-making was spurred on by the increasing availability of public *concerts and, in the environs of London, the presence of *pleasure gardens and their open-air concerts. As a result, by the close of the eighteenth century numbers of major music publishers were established, including John Preston (established mid-1770s); John Bland (established by 1776); Robert Birchall (in business by the early 1780s); and active outside London: Robert Bremner, Edinburgh (established 1754); Robert Purdie, Edinburgh (established 1809); James Aird, Glasgow (established 1778); and Smollet Holden, Dublin (established c.1807).

The early nineteenth century saw music publishing become a major financial endeavour, catering to the growing demand for music-making. In amateur groups such as choral societies, vocal scores, especially of sacred music, were the dominant format, while for *domestic music performance small ensemble works, for flute, piano, violin, or solo instruments, were favoured. Among the firms catering for these requirements the most notable were Novello's, founded by Vincent *Novello in 1811; J. B. *Cramer and Co. (founded as Cramer, Addison, and Beale, in London in 1824); and Robert Cocks and Co. (London, established 1823). Novello's primarily provided piano–vocal scores, mostly from the traditional repertoire, while Cramer offered music of more contemporary composers such as *Beethoven and Johan Nepomuk Hummel (1778–1837). The London publisher Christian Rudolph Wessel

(founded as Wessel and Stodart, 1823) became well known in later years as an important publisher of Chopin, but established its reputation on Schubert, Schumann, and, later, *Mendelssohn.

The rapid increase in the number of publishers was aided by innovations in music printing, allowing for larger print runs, cheaper costs, and lower prices. The development of lithography (invented by the German Alois Senefelder, 1771–1834, at the end of the eighteenth century) proved a major breakthrough. Stereotyping, also utilized in the eighteenth century, was now adopted and used by music publishers such as Novello's. Movable type was also employed, and J. Alfred Novello, son of the founder, designed new typefaces for movable type which he used for his own printing and for outside commissions.

Printing presses also developed with innovations in music-setting. The Columbia Press, invented by George Clymer (1754–1834), was one of the earliest nineteenth-century presses to be manufactured in great numbers. This iron handpress, sold throughout the New England region of the United States and patented in England in 1817, could produce 250 impressions per hour. An alternative was the Albion Press, invented c.1820, by Richard Cope, with the advantages of simplified mechanisms, lighter weight, and quicker pull of sheets. As steam power developed, so too did the presses, becoming more mechanized and efficient.

This flourishing industry was hampered, however, by the restrictions of myriad taxes and duties on printed material as well as by inadequate copyright legislation. Although some *copyright protection was provided during the 1830s it was not comprehensive, and it remained until 1842 for an amendment act to ensure greater safety.   VLC

music teaching. Music was occasionally used in the education of the working classes, for benevolent improvement or as a diversion from the *tavern. A few factory owners actively encouraged musical instruction: the children at Robert *Owen's New Lanark were taught from large wall-charts. By 1830 Mechanics' Institutes were beginning to offer classes in music [see *popular education]. However, it remained a largely élite pastime until new methods of teaching singing developed in the 1840s.

Aristocratic young ladies usually took piano and singing lessons at their own homes, paying as much as one guinea for the most prestigious masters. Music lessons also formed an essential part of the curriculum at girls' boarding-schools [see *female education], becoming a touchstone of middle-class aspiration. *Music publishers' catalogues began to overflow with ever-optimistic piano tutors and elementary sonatinas, in addition to advanced studies by J. C. *Cramer and others. In the late 1810s J. B. Logier (1777–1846) ingeniously exploited this expanding market with a system of group teaching using ten or more pianos simultaneously, and a mechanical aid he called the 'Chiroplast'.

For professional training the traditional route was apprenticeship. But many apprentices learnt more by music-copying and deputizing than by systematic instruction. It was to remedy the shortcomings of British musicians that the Royal Academy of Music was opened in 1823, under the guidance of a noble amateur, John Fane, known as Lord Burghersh (1784–1859). Though idealism was blunted by a lack of professionalism, poor practice conditions, and financial crises, the Academy did educate such important figures of the Victorian era as William Sterndale Bennett and George Macfarren.   SMcV

musical press, collective term for writing on music in the general press and in some dozen periodicals devoted exclusively to music and musical literature. As a literary phenomenon it developed from commercial *publishing [21] initiatives in the mid-eighteenth century, stimulating activity and discussion among music professionals and fostering musical literacy among the wider reading public.

From the 1760s, books about music came under review in the higher literary journals, at first in the *Monthly Review* and the *Critical Review* (Charles *Burney contributed to both), then later in the *Analytical Review* (for which Mary *Wollstonecraft wrote music book reviews, 1789–92) and the *British Critic*. From the 1780s new music itself, in printed editions, began to be surveyed in the *European Magazine* (originally by Samuel *Arnold, then in 1814–16 by Samuel *Wesley), and from the 1790s in the *Monthly Magazine*, later also in the *Gentleman's*. Notices of public and private concerts and of opera performances appeared sporadically in newspapers.

In the early nineteenth century review journals continued to publish the most erudite music articles available, but the quarterly interval inaugurated by the *Edinburgh Review* allowed even more scope for extended, occasional music essays—in that journal as well as in the *Westminster Review* and the *Foreign Quarterly Review*. The review function of earlier monthly magazines was partly taken over by incisive new political and arts weeklies, such as the *Examiner* (with opera reviews by Leigh *Hunt), *Atlas*, and *Spectator*. Magazines—new ones receptive to musical topics were *Ackermann's *Repository of Arts*, Robert Baldwin's *London Magazine*, and the *New Monthly Magazine*—also continued to publish a huge variety of miscellaneous pieces. Daily papers such as *The Times* and the *Morning Chronicle* devoted greater and more regular space to performance-reviewing from the late 1810s.

The periodical designed especially for people wanting sheet music and music information was a new concept in 1760, when two such journals appeared—the *Musical Magazine or Monthly Orpheus* and the *Monthly Melody*. The *New Musical and Universal Magazine*, with a literary supplement edited probably by Charles *Dibdin, followed in 1774–6. All were issued by general booksellers trying to create a specialist corner in the profitable magazine market. In the 1780s music publishers attempted similar projects. the *New Musical Magazine*, edited by Samuel *Arnold and Thomas Busby, and *Musical Miscellanies*: and in the 1810s a few private individuals launched journals of self-promotion, notably A. F. C. Kollmann with the *Quarterly Musical Register* (1812). However, none of these works matched the scope and critical standard of the two most important titles of all: the *Quarterly Musical Magazine and Review* (1818–30), edited and produced in Norwich by the newspaperman and amateur musician Richard Mackenzie Bacon, and the *Harmonicon* (1823–33), edited by William Ayrton, produced by the printer William Clowes, and supported by a consortium of London music sellers.

Generalizations from this wide range of material are hazardous, but certain trends are clear. Music discussion was usually embedded in a literary or liberal-arts framework, included with articles on other topics, addressed by non-specialist writers, and circumscribed by press conventions. At the same time, prominent musical writers including Burney, Arnold, Busby, Bacon, Ayrton, and Edward Holmes (1799–1859) contributed to both specialist and general publications, working in the real world of London journalism as much as courting a high literary status unavailable to mere musicians.

Generically, favoured forms were the book or music review, the biography, the history of a musical institution, the 'current state of music' report, the pseudonymous polemical essay (often disguised as a letter to the editor), and the lexicon or musical dictionary feature; all drew on precedents in history, literature, and philology. Advocacy writers sometimes hit important targets: R. M. Bacon campaigned tirelessly for serious all-sung opera, and his journal's impetus to the provincial *music festival movement and to the founding of the Royal Academy of Music was widely acknowledged.

Judging by the two-year, two-month average lifespan of specialized titles between 1760 and 1840, the audience for musical journals was small and unpredictable. Yet the vigorous competition in music printing and marketing begun in the 1820s helped lower prices and raise curiosity, so that within a few years music and music information were available to a vastly increased buying audience.   LL

mutual improvement societies, see *popular education.

N

nabobs, a term derived from the Persian word for ruler (*nawab*), was applied in the late eighteenth century to those newly rich members of élite society whose fortunes had been made in India.

In part, establishment disapproval of the nabobs rested on sheer snobbery, for they were overwhelmingly self-made men from middle-class or Celtic backgounds. But there was also a large measure of envy. The rapid rise of British military power and the breakdown of indigenous ruling structures in late-eighteenth-century India produced an environment in which bold and lucky *East India Company servants, on the surface quite poorly remunerated, were able to amass huge fortunes from presents, kickbacks, and collusive private trading. Robert Clive (1725–74), for example, retired in 1767 with £400,000 in cash, bonds, and jewels and the title to a *jagir* worth £30,000 a year; while Thomas Rumbold (1736–91) is reputed to have garnered as much as £1 million while serving as governor of Madras between 1778 and 1780. Nonetheless, the nabobs' conduct back in Britain did not help their cause. They tended to dress tastelessly; their manners were often coarse; they purchased or built enormous country houses, such as the dazzling onion-domed 'Sezincote' in Gloucestershire, thereby pushing up the price of real estate; they bought into the peerage; and they pushed their way into parliament by throwing money at electors in rotten boroughs, which encouraged the perception that these inordinately wealthy and ambitious men posed a real danger to the constitution.

Recent research suggests that the harsh contemporary view of the nabobs mirrored in Samuel Foote's (1720–77) popular *satirical play of that name (1772) was to some extent unwarranted. Of the 900-odd Company servants who went out to India between 1760 and 1790, about half perished from disease, and of those who did survive only a small minority accumulated in excess of £10,000. Furthermore, only a handful of these returnees actually made it into parliament: from twelve in 1761, their numbers increased slowly to a peak of twenty-seven after the election of 1780. And their immediate impact as a pressure group, except perhaps on India, where they typically used their influence to stave off attempts to inquire into their pecuniary affairs, was minor. On the other hand, lingering perceptions of nabob corruption provided a spur to the attacks of Edmund *Burke and others on British rapacity in Bengal, which culminated in the trial of a former governor-general, Warren *Hastings, and legislation bringing the Company under closer parliamentary scrutiny. Paradoxically, too, the nabobs helped cultivate in England a fashion for Indian domestic culture not unlike the contemporary French enthusiasm for *chinoiserie. Although to some extent a passing fad, aspects of this cultural borrowing, such as the wearing of *pyjamas*, the smoking of *cheroots*, the taking of *showers*, and the building of houses in the *bungalow* (or Bengali) style, have left an indelible mark on British society.   IC

NAPOLEON BONAPARTE (1769–1821), soldier and politician, Emperor of France 1804–15. Admired by many as the 'great man' and 'genius' of the age, Napoleon dominated European political and military affairs during his extraordinary career, and acted as a focus for central political and cultural debates in Britain.

Rising from relatively obscure origins in Corsica to become First Consul of France in 1799, Consul for Life in 1802, and Emperor in 1804, Napoleon was seen to embody the idea of the career open to talent. His relationship to the *French Revolution was much debated, often along party lines. Some British observers, often *Whigs or radicals, saw him as the champion of the Revolution, consolidating its gains in a civil code and defending it against the counter-revolutionary aggression of the European monarchs. Others, such as the increasingly Tory William *Wordsworth, saw Napoleon's coronation as part of his betrayal of revolutionary promise, also enacted through his gagging of the press, reimposition of slavery in France's colonies, aggressive imperialism, and restoration of the old regime through the establishment of his own dynastic empire. Napoleon's diplomatic trickery and expansionist policy during the *Peninsular War turned many of his former British supporters against him. However, some Whigs and radicals, such as *Byron, *Hazlitt, and *Hone, continued to use Napoleon as a symbol of opposition to the Tory government, up to and beyond his final defeat at Waterloo and exile to St Helena in 1815.

As the subject of innumerable pamphlets and caricatures, Napoleon occupied a central place in popular *print [22] culture. Produced in an increasingly bellicose atmosphere, these propagandist pieces tended to represent Napoleon in one of two ways. On the one hand, he was portrayed reductively and comically as the diminutive yet overreaching figure, as in James *Gillray's 'Little Boney' caricatures or S. T. *Coleridge's 'Upstart Corsican' in the *Morning Post* (1802). On the other, he was presented as a monstrous object of terror: the Corsican Ogre, the Corsican Bugaboo, and the Beast of the Apocalypse. Napoleon became increasingly demonized in British culture, portrayed as an associate or favourite of the Devil. In texts aimed at an educated readership, he was often represented in terms of *Milton's Satan, as in Coleridge's journalistic and philosophical

86. *Napoleon* by Thomas Rowlandson after the German engraver Votz, published by Rudolph Ackermann in 1813. This emblematic 'corpse head' with its naked figures signifying the Napoleonic lust for conquest, and with the providential hand of the allies poised to rip away the cobweb star on the Emperor's breast, was one of the most widely disseminated pieces of anti-Napoleonic propaganda in Europe.

writings, George *Cruikshank's caricature 'Boney's Meditations on the Island of St Helena' (1815), and Hazlitt's lecture 'On Shakespeare and Milton' (1818).

Napoleon was important to the self-conception and self-representation of several writers. In his sonnets of 1802–4, Wordsworth contrasted his own education and status as a poet with that of Napoleon, the man of action. Coleridge used Napoleon as an example of 'Commanding Genius' which he opposed to 'Original Genius' in *Biographia Literaria* (1817). Whereas Wordsworth and Coleridge thereby defined themselves through opposition to Napoleon, Byron controversially conceived himself in Napoleonic terms, acting out a lifelong identification with Napoleon and hailing himself in Canto XI of *Don Juan* (1823) as the 'grand Napoleon of the realms of rhyme'. SB

NASH, John (1752–1835). Renowned for the design of London's Regent's Park and Regent Street

(1811–26), Nash was the pre-eminent *Regency architect. Shrewd in his business dealings and a skilled practitioner of the dramatic visual effects of the *picturesque, Nash developed a highly successful practice that culminated in the reconstruction of Buckingham House.

A degree of mystery surrounds Nash's early life. The son of a millwright in Lambeth, he was employed in 1766 by Sir Robert *Taylor, one of the capital's leading architects. Nash seems to have been interested in *architecture [28] more as a business than as an intellectual enterprise. Without any academic training, he left Taylor's office in 1774 to design speculative developments in Bloomsbury. Although several townhouses mimicking Taylor's robust neo-Palladian style were built, this venture failed and Nash was declared bankrupt in 1783. After his marriage to a surgeon's daughter also failed, Nash retreated to his ancestral Wales.

Based in Carmarthen, Nash cultivated minor

architectural commissions and social contacts among the local gentry. Through the 1790s he established himself as the region's leading architect, building new gaols in Carmarthen (1789–92), Cardigan (1792–3), and Hereford (1793–6). His ventures into the West Country brought him into contact with the leading lights of the picturesque school, Richard Payne *Knight and Uvedale *Price. Nash designed a castellated seaside villa for Price at Aberystwyth, Cardiganshire (c.1795).

Ambition led Nash to resettle in London, where he formed a partnership in 1796 with the landscape designer Humphry *Repton. The heir to Lancelot 'Capability' *Brown's practice, Repton possessed extensive social and professional contacts and secured numerous commissions for which Nash claimed the majority of both fees and acclamation.

By the time the partnership dissolved in 1802 Nash had achieved success on a national scale as a country house architect. His approach to design emphasized the picturesque concern for visual effect and variety in plan and elevation. Within this system, Nash's designs consisted principally of four stylistic categories: a decorative neoclassicism reminiscent of the work of Robert *Adam, as employed at Southgate Grove, Middlesex, (1797); a castellated *Gothic, as at Luscombe Castle, Devonshire, (1800–4); an Italianate vernacular idiom, as at Cronkhill, Shrewsbury, (c.1802), which derived from the buildings represented in seventeenth-century *landscape painting; and a highly detailed English vernacular cottage. This last was his most original stylistic contribution, and was employed with exuberance at Blaise Hamlet (1810–11), a picturesque assemblage of pensioners' residences near Bristol.

In 1798 Nash was introduced to the Prince of Wales by Repton, then employed at the Royal Pavilion. The two developed a mutually rewarding relationship. In 1806 Nash was appointed Architect to the Office of Woods and Forests, the position that led to his design of Regent's Park and Regent Street. As the Prince's personal architect, he completed several significant projects, including additions to Carlton House (1813), the remodelling of the Royal Pavilion at Brighton (1815–22) into the *oriental extravagance it is today, and the transformation of Buckingham House into a palace (1825–30) after George IV's accession.

This last commission placed Nash in the unenviable position of having to satisfy both parliament's fiscal concerns and George IV's grandiloquent vision of his reign. Unable to manage both costs and the King, Nash allowed the project to exceed its budget and saw it widely ridiculed for its air of false majesty. Exonerated from accusations of professional misconduct by a Select Committee in 1829, Nash was summarily dismissed without his promised baronetcy upon the King's death in January 1830.

His reputation destroyed, Nash retreated from the capital once again. He enjoyed several years of retirement at his castellated villa, East Cowes Castle, on the Isle of Wight, which he had begun in 1798. He left his practice to his ward, James Pennethorne

(1801–71). The ranks of Nash's large office also included several other significant young talents, including Anthony *Salvin and A. C. *Pugin, whose archaeological interest in Gothic architecture was encouraged although not shared by his employer.

Nash made innovative improvements in new building technologies and the planning and financing of urban development. His earliest speculative buildings utilized a new stucco patented by the Adam brothers, and Nash used such durable stuccoes extensively in Regent Street and the Park terraces. During his years in the ironmaking regions of Wales and the West Country, he developed an enthusiasm for the structural use of iron. He incorporated iron columns and staircases in the Royal Pavilion and iron girders in Buckingham Palace.

Nash's chief claim to fame, however, lay in the unparalleled scale and inventiveness of the Regent's Park and Regent Street developments. As Architect to the Office of Woods and Forests, he was presented with this opportunity due to the Prince Regent's enthusiasm for architecture and emphatic need for revenue, and the timely expiry of the Duke of Portland's lease on the 500-acre Marylebone Park. Nash and Thomas Leverton (1743–1824), Architect to the Office of Land Revenue, both submitted plans for the speculative development of Marylebone. Unlike Leverton's straightforward extension of the existing street pattern, Nash boldly proposed erecting distinctively shaped terraces within a park-like setting and connecting them to the commercial and governmental centres via a broad new street. The Regent's Park plan constituted an adaptation of Bath's system of circus and crescents to a landscaped setting.

A prime rationale of Nash's scheme for Regent Street was to create a dignified and income-generating boundary between working-class Soho and chic Mayfair. Nash displayed his greatest talents in the execution of this scheme. Converting logistical adversities into aesthetic advantages, he transformed the original straight run of Regent Street into a snaking sequence of picturesque urban vistas. Having completed Regent Street, he went on to plan the development of Trafalgar Square as a monumental component of the grandest and most systematic redevelopment London has seen. ss

national debt was a political obsession in Britain for much of this period, since the Seven Years War sent it spiralling from less than £80 million in 1757 to £240 million in 1783. During wartime, public borrowing was the main source of revenue. This money came from a relatively large cross-section of the better off, and provided an important source of social cohesion among the propertied classes. Nevertheless, by the time *Pitt came to power in 1783 it was widely perceived that there was a debt crisis. Pitt adopted the solution proposed by Richard *Price of a 'sinking fund' which would have the first claim on tax revenues in order to pay off the debt. As it was, the revolutionary and Napoleonic *wars [2] made the fund unworkable and forced the government to take the previously politically unacceptable step of introducing an *income tax in the crisis year of 1798. By the

87. *John Bull and the National Debt*, sculpture by Charles Waterton. Best known as a naturalist who developed new techniques of taxidermy, Waterton also practised an idiosyncratic art which blended animal and human forms. This preserved porcupine with human face and tortoiseshell carries on its back a lizard representing the burden of national debt on the people of Britain, and probably dates from the 1820s.

end of the French wars the burden stood at £900 million, and interest repayments amounted to about one third of total government expenditure in 1815.

Concern about the debt was not the province of any particular political ideology. *Tories like David *Hume were as alarmed as commonwealth men like Price by its growth. After the resumption of the Napoleonic wars in 1803, William *Cobbett brought the issue to the centre of popular radical ideology. The national debt was at the heart of 'Old Corruption' for Cobbett. He called several times for the suspension of payments on loans, believing that the broader public interest was being sacrificed to parasitic stockholders and money-jobbers.   JM

National Gallery, established in Britain in 1824 when parliament agreed to purchase a collection of thirty-eight pictures formed by the late philanthropist and merchant John Julius Angerstein (1735–1823). The foundation of this *viewing [20] institution followed many decades of speculation amongst artists, connoisseurs, and politicians over the aesthetic effects, social benefits, and civic implications of a permanent public art repository in the nation's capital. Both the mode of the Gallery's inception (through the nation's purchase of a small core collection rather than evolution from a noble or royal cabinet) and the relative lateness of the event in Britain are significant features. In his *Picture Galleries in England* (1824), William *Hazlitt stated approvingly that the founding collection was 'not a bazaar, a raree show, a Noah's ark of all the Schools, marching out in endless procession; but a sanctuary, a holy of holies, collected by taste, sacred to fame, enriched by the rarest products of genius'. Under the administration of the Gallery's first keeper, William Seguier (1771–1843), the sixteenth- and seventeenth-century Old Master paintings and a selection of works by *Reynolds, Hogarth, and *Wilkie were displayed to the public at Angerstein's residence, 100 Pall Mall. The collection

grew in 1826 with a bequest of sixteen pictures from George Beaumont (1753–1827), who had been instrumental in the institution's foundation, and thereafter with many smaller purchases, donations, and bequests. In 1834 the collection was removed from its original quarters to an equally insufficient space at 105 Pall Mall, before being transferred in 1837 to a gallery purpose-built by William *Wilkins in Trafalgar Square.   CSM

natural rights, more commonly known as human rights, refers to inalienable rights possessed by persons as human beings, in their natural or pre-political condition. Though compatible with the advocacy of absolutist government, as in the work of Thomas Hobbes (1588–1679), whereby natural rights are surrendered upon entering civil society, a more radical sense of natural rights, as those entitlements which could be appealed to by a people against an oppressive government, was instituted with the English Civil War of the 1640s and the *Glorious Revolution of 1688. This more radical interpretation, which found its most influential expression at the end of the seventeenth century in the writings of John *Locke, became the dominant theory of natural rights during the eighteenth and early nineteenth centuries.   CT

naval mutinies of 1797, together with the *invasion scare of 1803, were the most serious threat to the security of Britain during the *wars [2] with France, 1793–1815.

The first mutiny of the Channel Fleet began at Spithead, Portsmouth, on 16 April 1797 with petitions for improved pay and conditions. Limited concessions were made by the government, and the mutiny ended on 23 April. However, a delay in the ratification of the agreement led to a second mutiny on 7 May, as a result of which the government pushed through the bill to increase pay and sent the popular Lord Howe to conciliate. His agreement to withdraw unpopular ships' officers represented a victory for the sailors, who ended the mutiny on 15 May.

Following the precedent of Spithead, the North Sea fleet at the Nore, near Yarmouth, mutinied on 12 May. Their demands were similar, but also included more radical proposals such as the introduction of jurors at the court martial. After a blockade of the Thames on 2 June, the government sought special powers to deal with the mutiny, blaming insidious Jacobin elements, and so contributing to a reaction against the perceived militancy of the Nore mutineers. Internal divisions eventually led to the mutineers' surrender on 14 June. Their leader, Richard Parker, was court-martialled and hanged with thirty-six others.

Whether the mutinies were politically motivated or exclusively economic continues to be debated, but the election of delegates and committees, the language of their demands, and the ritual of oath-taking suggest, at the very least, the influence of radical organization in the 1790s. The United Irishmen, who had been instrumental in fomenting and sustaining the mutinies [see *United societies], hoped that the fleet would desert to the French, while more moderate groups such as the London Corresponding Society tried to use the mutinies to further demands for peace [see *corresponding societies]. Though the failure of the mutinies damaged radical politics, the events of May–June 1797 shocked the wider community deeply by emphasizing how dependent Britain was on the loyalty of its armed forces.   GR

Necessarianism (also Necessitarianism), a deterministic philosophical theology that underlay much radical understanding and activity. First fully formulated by the physician and theologian David Hartley (1705–57) in his *Observations on Man* (1749), Necessarianism was rooted in associationist *psychology [39] and emphasized the invariable succession of cause and effect and the determining power of motives.

Attacked for denying freewill, Necessarians insisted that if the motives present to the mind remained unchanged, consequent action would always be the same: they thus denied (in their phraseology) 'philosophical liberty', while leaving individuals a full sense of practical autonomy. The parallel accusation of fatalism was, they believed, negated by providence and divine foreknowledge, while they escaped the arbitrariness of Calvinism through the possibility of changing motives—by the working of institutions, education, experience, and personal example—thus bringing human action into conformity with the laws proclaimed by a beneficent God. Necessarians denied divine interposition in everyday life or in the affairs of nations, rejected the substitutionary view of atonement, and were convinced that salvation, and even perfection, lay within human grasp.

Joseph *Priestley published an abridged version of Hartley's system in 1775. Holding that neither Hartley's theory that sense impressions were recorded on the brain through vibration of the nerves nor his own materialist view of mind–body relations were essential to the Necessarian scheme, Priestley helped to ensure its persuasiveness. Among its most notable later advocates were Thomas *Belsham, William *Godwin, Harriet *Martineau, and the eminent Victorian physician and sanitary reformer Thomas Southwood Smith (1786–1861).

S. T. *Coleridge, an early convert—he named his eldest son David Hartley Coleridge—was among the earliest to abandon it, and in time others under the impress of Romanticism came to question or reject a scheme that seemed to diminish individual freedom and to reduce the soul to mechanism. But Necessarianism remained a powerful stimulus to rational analysis, self-knowledge, and reform.   RKW

NELSON, Horatio, Viscount Nelson (1758–1805), Vice-Admiral. A naval commander of genius, Nelson's victories during the *wars [2] with France gripped the popular imagination, transforming him into an enduring icon of Englishness.

He was born in comparatively obscure circumstances, the son of the rector of Burnham Thorpe in Norfolk, but a combination of talent and family connections secured a rapid ascent in the navy. On the outbreak of the war with France in 1793 Nelson was sent to the Mediterranean, where he was involved in the attack on Corsica, losing an eye in the successful siege of Calvi. It was at this period that Nelson first met Sir William *Hamilton, then ambassador to Naples, and his wife, Emma *Hamilton, with whom he later had a scandalous affair.

His growing celebrity was confirmed by his role in the battle of Cape St Vincent (1797), as a result of which he gained the first of many awards, the Order of the Bath. In the same year he led an unsuccessful attack on Santa Cruz in the Canary Islands, during which he lost an arm. After recovering in England he rejoined the Mediterranean fleet and, revealing his strategic and tactical acumen, pursued the French to Aboukir Bay, believing that their object was Egypt with the ultimate goal of access to India. His leadership of what he described in Shakespearean terms as his 'band of brothers' led to an overwhelming victory which was a turning-point in the war, restoring national morale at a time of political crisis. The 'Hero of the Nile' was celebrated throughout Britain with bonfires, illuminations, and dinners, his image adorning the newspaper press, broadsides, commemorative medals, and ceramics, his name ringing out in songs in the theatres, assemblies, the parlour, and the street.

However, the triumph of the Nile was followed by the most controversial episode in his career. In December 1798 the French overran Naples, establishing the Vesuvian or Parthenopeian Republic. Nelson evacuated the royal family and the Hamiltons to Sicily, where he stayed while a blockade was conducted against Naples which eventually secured an armistice with the revolutionaries. Nelson subsequently annulled the treaty, and as the centrepiece of the punishment of the rebels court-martialled and hanged Prince Carracioli, a Neapolitan noble who had joined the revolution. Even Robert *Southey,

His state funeral at St Paul's Cathedral was the occasion for an outpouring of national grief. But even before his death a Nelson cult had emerged, sustained by the hero himself, who revealed a flair for showmanship and an ability to exploit the various forums offered him by a commericalized public culture. The Nelson of popular imagination was a humane commander with the common touch who represented the quintessential national character that transcended the divisions of rank or faction. His concern for the welfare of his men and his acting as character witness at the treason trial of Colonel Edward Despard (1751–1803) in 1803 made him a popular figure with radicals and an object of some suspicion to the monarchy and the government, who were apprehensive of the political role he might exert. The response of James *Gillray, who alternatively celebrated and lampooned him, is indicative of the manœuvres that the government had to make in order to exploit Nelson's popularity while at the same time keeping it in check. The struggle over Nelson's 'immortal memory' in visual and printed texts was in effect a struggle for the meaning of *patriotism, the Nelson phenomenon playing a significant role in the diminution of patriotism's oppositional tendencies.   GR

88. Anne Damer's highly praised sculpture of Lord Nelson (1801) formed part of the popular acclaim to which the Admiral returned in 1800.

whose *Life of Nelson* (1813) generally lauded the hero as an example to Englishmen, baulked at the episode, interpreting it as the result of his 'baneful passion' for Emma Hamilton, who had close links with the Neapolitan queen. Even more serious was his refusal at this time to leave Naples in order to defend Minorca III. Believing his career at an end, he returned to England in November 1800 to be greeted with popular acclaim.

In 1801, as second-in-command of the Channel fleet, Nelson sailed to the Baltic against the combined forces of Russia, Denmark, and Sweden, then allied in the Northern Confederacy against Britain. In the battle of Copenhagen Nelson famously disregarded the signal of his commander-in-chief to discontinue the action by claiming that he could not see it. Adding the title of Viscount to his numerous honours, he toured England with the Hamiltons during the Peace of *Amiens in 1802, gaining a reception which was said to outrival that given to the *monarchy. On the renewal of the war he was given responsibility for the blockade of the French fleet at Toulon, which, however, succeeded in breaking out in an attempt to rendezvous with other elements of the French navy in the West Indies. Nelson chased the Toulon fleet across the Atlantic and back, finally encountering the combined French and Spanish forces in a decisive engagement off Cape Trafalgar on 21 October 1805. The *Victory* became the stage for one of the seminal events in the English national consciousness as Nelson was mortally wounded by a French sniper, surviving long enough to learn that a decisive victory had been won.

neoclassical revival, an aesthetic movement and style of the romantic age which sought to replicate directly the spirit and forms of classical antiquity, particularly of Greece, and which derived much of its inspiration from mid-eighteenth-century archaeological discoveries and their subsequent publicization in works such as James Stuart and Nicholas Revett's *Antiquities of Athens* (1762).

In Britain the revival's greatest achievements were expressed through *architecture [28], especially in the elegant public buildings of Robert *Adam's Edinburgh, and—though sparer and less ornamented—in the works of Sir John *Soane. In Britain, unlike Europe, neoclassicism did not become deeply fashionable in *painting [27] circles, but it did exert a considerable literary influence on young Romantic intellectuals such as P. B. *Shelley, who knew it under the alternative label of *Hellenism.   IMcC

Newgate literature, a generic term covering a proliferation of literary forms in our period, which had the life and fate of the criminal as their chief focus.

Interest in sensational crimes and criminals, particularly the imprisonment, execution, and dying speeches of murderers, is apparent in the earliest forms of British *street literature. Romanticized versions of the lives of highwaymen and escapees such as Dick Turpin, Claude Duval, and Jack Sheppard were deeply embedded in urban *popular culture [23]. The ubiquitous puppet theatre, Punch and Judy, further introduced generations of children to the bloody spectre of Newgate prison and its cretinous executioner, Jack Ketch. With the growth of the reading public during the later eighteenth century, specialist chapbook publishers such as Jem Catnach and popular journalists like Pierce *Egan were able to make large sums from particularly lurid and bestselling accounts of criminal trials, the most celebrated being that of prize fight promoter John Thurtell in 1824.

From 1773 collections of criminal biographies also began appearing under the title of *Newgate Calendar*. Three years later Newgate Ordinary John Villette inaugurated an associated and long-lasting tradition by issuing his own collection, *Annals of Newgate*, which included personal reminiscences. The most influential and exhaustive of such collections, however, was published in 1826–8 by attornies Andrew Knapp and William Baldwin as the *New Newgate Calendar* (6 vols.). Collections of this kind also became an important background source for a new genre of fiction which emerged in the 1820s and 1830s, rapidly acquiring the opprobrious label of 'the Newgate novel'. Although fictional interest in criminal psychology and picaresque deeds had been pioneered by writers such as Defoe, Fielding, and William *Godwin, a new trend of exploring and sometimes celebrating topical crimes and underworld culture was inaugurated by Edward *Bulwer-Lytton's novels *Pelham* (1828), *Paul Clifford* (1830), and *Eugene Aram* (1832). At a time when *Peel was pursuing reform of the criminal code in parliament, Bulwer-Lytton's novels established a trend of social criticism which attacked the class bias of the legal system, the harshness of the penal code, and the brutality of punishments in *prisons such as Newgate. W. H. Ainsworth's (1805–82) *Rookwood* (1834) and *Jack Sheppard* (1839) took the Newgate novel into the realms of the bestseller, inspiring numerous *melodramas in unlicensed penny gaff theatres (cheap, small-scale theatres mainly for boys and girls) and becoming a staple of the Victorian penny blood serial.

However, from the outset the Newgate novel was viewed with ambivalence or hostility even by writers such as Charles *Dickens, William Maginn (1793–1842), and William *Thackeray, whose own early works owed much to the genre. The latter two in particular used the pages of the Tory periodical *Fraser's Magazine* to lambast Bulwer-Lytton and the Newgate school for glamorizing vice and for feeding sensationalist popular appetites. By the 1840s periodical *reviews were already drawing a line between the morally valid explorations of crime such as Dickens's *Oliver Twist* (1837) and the unhealthy sensationalism of Newgate literature.   IMcC

newspapers, though inhibited by taxes and political interference, developed rapidly in this period until, by its end, they were essential to the formation of middle-class opinion on a national scale and on the verge of attaining mass circulation.

At the beginning of the eighteenth century newspapers were dominated by information concerning trade and commerce, but they later made greater room for general news and commentary. Nevertheless *advertising remained crucial to the economics of the press, sales alone almost never being sufficient for financial survival. Blackmail, payment for personal puffs, and government subsidies also provided funds for the less scrupulous editors [see *publishing, 21].

Prior to 1700 all newspapers were printed in London, but thereafter a provincial press grew up, largely dependent on metropolitan sources, though from around the 1780s there was an expansion in the coverage of local affairs. Access to the London papers improved with the introduction of the mail coach in 1784, while from 1792 the Post Office delivered newspapers free of charge. By the early nineteenth century, the provincial press had become a powerful and self-confident voice, and local newspapers in cities such as Leeds and Manchester competed fiercely in debates about reform.

The wider the circulation gained by newspapers, the more it was in the interest of governments to limit the *freedom of the press. Indeed, taxes on newspapers (stamp duty), advertising, and paper had been introduced early in the eighteenth century to limit circulation. The stamp duty was increased regularly, William *Pitt bringing government control to new heights in the 1780s and 1790s, when he effectively bought newspapers through the Treasury funds. The *Whig interest funded its own papers, but the weight of financial power remained on the Treasury's side. Interfering with distribution, increasing taxes, harassing printers and editors with prosecution, and forcing papers into bankruptcy were all means used to silence the opposition press.

Despite these obstacles the newspaper press established itself as a national institution. London had fourteen dailies by 1790. The *Morning Chronicle* and *Morning Post* were founded in 1769 and 1772 respectively. *The Times* followed in 1788, and by 1820 had established itself as the pre-eminent metropolitan daily. Its sales reached 7,000 by that year, and during the *Queen Caroline affair rose for a short time to more than 15,000. The principal mouthpiece of middle-class reform, the paper's pre-eminence also depended on its technological leadership. The first steam printing machine in the world was used to publish *The Times* in 1814.

By the early nineteenth century the foreign and domestic press had established the ubiquitous presence for which it has become renowned. Government was soon intercepting 'packets' sent by journalists from the battlefields in Europe to keep itself up to date, and letters of contemporary politicians are full of marvelling over events first brought to their attention by the newspapers, as well as of indignation at journalistic breaches of confidentiality.

Despite these achievements, a genuinely popular readership was not achieved for newspapers in this period, though signs of its emergence were apparent. The first Sunday newspaper appeared in 1779 and after the Napoleonic wars the Sunday paper began to reach a working-class public for whom stamp duty made the daily papers too expensive. A radical *unstamped press developed from 1816 with the publication of William *Cobbett's cheap edition of his *Political Register* in response to the increase in duty to 4d. *Bell's Weekly*, *Reynolds Newspaper*, and the *Chartist *Northern Star* all attained circulations in the early Victorian years that made them forerunners of the modern mass press. Nevertheless it was not until 1855, when the newspaper tax was finally abolished, that the newspaper could begin to develop into the feature of all literate households that it finally became at the turn of the twentieth century.   WC

Newtonianism. Although Isaac Newton (1642–1727) wrote far more about theology, ancient chronology, and alchemy than about *natural philosophy [34], by the late eighteenth century he was established as both a scientific and national hero. Newtonianism embraced diverse doctrines, and had come to stand for scientific rationality and an experimental approach towards elucidating nature rather than for any specific model of the physical world. Different interpreters of Newton's work defined themselves as Newtonians to help legitimate their theories, in a context in which views on natural phenomena were enmeshed within wider cultural debates about political and religious issues. Newton himself epitomized the solitary genius dispassionately elucidating ruthless natural laws, whether critically portrayed by William *Blake as imprisoning nature with his mathematical dividers or revered by William *Wordsworth for 'his prism and silent face' in the statue at Trinity College, Cambridge.

Newton wrote two especially influential scientific texts. The Latin *Philosophiae Naturalis Principia Mathematica* (1687), was a mathematical treatise on gravitational astronomy and mechanics. The far more accessible English *Opticks* (1704) covered his optical work and also set a wide-ranging agenda for experimental philosophy, including *chemistry. Throughout the eighteenth century, natural philosophers invoked Newton to supplant earlier rival theories such as French Cartesianism, and to suppress contemporary criticisms levelled mainly by High Church Tories. As scientific knowledge became an essential component of polite culture, expositions labelled as Newtonian appeared not only in learned texts, but also in poems, journals, and popular *lectures. Newton's conversion into a household name contributed to the construction of disciplinary science as a publicly beneficial activity.

Despite this wide appeal, the internal inconsistencies of Newton's writings facilitated contradictory interpretations which served particular local interests. For example, natural philosophers cited the *Opticks* to validate various versions of a subtle Newtonian aether explaining light, electricity, and heat which were imbued with contrasting theological significances. Thomas *Young was amongst those embracing a wave theory of light rather than Newton's corpuscular model. The reforming *Unitarian, Joseph *Priestley, proposed a Newtonian ontology in which matter was inherently attractive, a view strongly attacked by *Anglican Newtonians both for its materialistic removal of God and its implicit pantheism. In Paris, the Laplacian school formulated a Newtonian celestial mechanics whereby inert particles were propelled through a vacuum by law-governed forces, a model open to theological criticism for its determinism. Reacting against the perceived revolutionary threats to religious and political order presented by such reformulations of Newtonianism, scientific writers such as John Robison (1739–1805)—popularizer of Abbé de Barruel's conspiratorial *Memoirs of Jacobinism* and professor of natural philosophy at Edinburgh University 1773–83—and David *Brewster argued for a return to the original corpus. They insisted that Newtonians should concentrate on analysing observable systems, reinstating Newton's vision of gravity as the consequence of direct divine action, and defending the corpuscular theory of light.

As nineteenth-century historians created exemplary scientific biographies, the Newtonian ideology changed in character but retained its polemical vigour despite challenges to Newton's theories, scientific methodology, and moral character.   PF

NOLLEKENS, Joseph (1737–1823), the foremost *sculptor of his generation to build his artistic reputation upon the production of portrait busts. The second son of an artist who had come to Britain from Antwerp, Nollekens was baptized a Roman Catholic. After rudimentary schooling he attended Shipley's school in the Strand and at the age of thirteen was apprenticed to Peter Scheemakers (1691–1781). In Italy throughout the 1760s, Nollekens developed his sculptural practice, absorbing and combining his study of classical antiquity with that of the Baroque. The effectiveness of his busts of Charles James *Fox (1791, 1803) and William *Pitt (1807) provided him with a regular income from the sale of copies. Recognition of his artistic status came with election to the *Royal Academy as Associate in 1771 and as Academician one year later.

Apart from busts, Nollekens also produced some notable ideal works in his fashionable Mortimer Street studio, including four statues of goddesses made for Wentworth House in the early 1770s. He executed public monuments for Westminster Abbey and St Paul's Cathedral, and established a brisk trade in smaller church monuments. He had a more questionable reputation as a dealer in fake and restored antique statuary. Some of his most spirited works were executed in terracotta, and a number of his sketches in this medium survive at the Victoria & Albert Museum.   AWY

NORTH, Christopher, see John *Wilson.

NOVELLO, Vincent (1781–1861), organist, music publisher, editor, conductor, composer, who was an important figure in English musical life in the first half of the nineteenth century. He began his musical career as a choirboy and organ student at the Sardinian embassy, Lincoln's Inn Fields, under the direction of Samuel *Webbe the elder. At 16 Novello became a professional organist in his own right with his first appointment at the Catholic chapel of the Portuguese embassy, where he introduced a repertoire of relatively unknown works including English music from earlier periods.

In an effort to make more of this music available, Novello produced his first collection of edited works in 1811 and was soon publishing other collections to serve professional organists and skilled amateurs. Among his numerous editions were *Purcell's Sacred Music* (5 vols., 1828–32), *The Fitzwilliam Music* (1825), an edition of sacred music from the collection of the Fitzwilliam Museum, University of Cambridge, and editions of the sacred music of *Haydn and *Mozart. Novello and his family were prominent in musical and literary London life, and included in their circle Leigh *Hunt, Charles *Lamb, and Percy *Shelley. Not only did Novello establish what would become a leading music publishing house which continues to this day, he also brought to light an important and neglected repertoire of music to entertain and educate the growing English middle class.

VLC

O

O'CONNELL, Daniel (1775–1847), lawyer and politician. Daniel O'Connell was the pioneer of Irish popular politics, which eventually secured the Roman Catholic Relief Act of 1829 and inspired liberal Catholicism on the Continent. He was at once ideologue and pragmatist. Born into a Catholic landholding family whose income was sustained by trade, licit and illicit alike, he grew up in the shadow of the anti-popish 'penal laws', with a lifelong resentment of the civil and social inferiorities which these imposed on him and his co-religionists. His initial conservatism (tempered by schoolboy enthusiasm for Washington's achievements and Earl Grattan's part in securing Irish parliamentary 'independence' in 1782) was confirmed by his later schooling in the continental seminaries of Douai and St Omer up to January 1793, when he escaped from France. He was a fervent anti-revolutionist who had observed mob power at first hand and come to fear and loathe it.

O'Connell's removal to London, where he read law from 1793 to 1796, transformed him into a radical. He became a *Deist; and it was to be at least fifteen years before, initially under his wife's influence, he returned to the Catholicism of his youth. William *Godwin's *Political Justice* (1793) completed, in 1795, his conversion to the radical cause, which had begun to attract him seriously in the preceding year. From Godwin he derived the general political principles which governed, to a remarkable degree, his long and varied career: that violence in pursuit of a political cause was never justifiable, and that the key to every beneficial change lay in the enlistment of public opinion and its effective canalization.

O'Connell's applied, as against his universalist, ideology centred on formal civil liberation and equality for all persons and peoples, and, most immediately, on the abolition of Catholic disabilities and Ireland's legislative independence. It was personal and institutional parity that he sought, not change in the social order. Later, he proclaimed himself, for a time, a Benthamite; at least, he concurred with Jeremy *Bentham in his lifelong passion for rational legal reform and in the individualist basis of his radicalism.

If O'Connell was a more or less faithful disciple of various contemporary ideologies, he was extraordinarily original and inventive in both his amalgam of purposes and the means that he designed to realize them. He was the pioneer of liberal Catholicism. As early as 1815 he forced the Irish episcopate, largely by dint of the popular pressure that he mounted, into an anti-Roman stance in rejecting any sentiment of the Irish Catholic question which gave the British government a veto over higher ecclesiastical appointments. Again, between 1824 and 1828, he secured the prelates' support, virtually *en bloc*, for his mass movement designed to weaken the government's resistance to *Catholic emancipation by the sheer force of numbers and by the ultimate threat of civil war. These were practical demonstrations of his belief not only that there was no incompatibility between Catholicism and *democracy [3] but also that the future of the Church depended on just such an alliance. Together, his theory and practice had a profound influence in the emergence of a left wing among European Catholics, especially in France and Germany. With a similar boldness, he defended his nationalism in terms of individual rights and insisted that it was both compatible with and dependent on constitutionality.

O'Connell led the Irish Catholic movement, beating off 'respectable' and demagogic challenges alike, from 1808 until its final triumph in the Roman Catholic Relief Act of 1829. In his hands, the movement took many forms, in general tending in an increasingly democratic direction. Its final manifestation, the Catholic Association, set up in 1823, attempted to mobilize and politicize the entire Irish Catholic population in a systematic challenge to and defiance of the Protestant Ascendancy. After nearly two decades of trial and error, O'Connell had finally developed a thoroughly modern extra-parliamentary party, built around his person by a continuing and concentrated agitation. Once he had won entry into the House of Commons in 1830 he extended his organizations accordingly and orchestrated agitation to a hitherto unprecedented scale in 1842–3, in the course of his last major but unsuccessful campaign for repeal of the *Act of Union.

In all this, O'Connell was a remarkable innovator, the first European cartographer of the then unknown continent of mass constitutional politics. He was also a tireless gadgeteer and inventor in the field of political machinery, never daunted by failed organizational experiments. Nor was he daunted by failed campaigns. He was always pragmatic in action, ready to compromise or set off upon new courses. Yet his ultimate goals never changed. He was a Fabius among demagogues; an ethnogogue (Gladstone's word for him) among democrats. His form of leadership was to present himself as popular apotheosis while maintaining a tight control upon mass action. Even taking Charles Stewart Parnell (1846–91) into the calculation, O'Connell was the giant of nineteenth-century Irish politics—as well as a very considerable figure in nineteenth-century British radicalism and parliamentary development.

He was shaped by more than his Catholic heritage, late *Enlightenment [32] ideas, and innate political genius. Dependence on a rich, ambitious, and exacting uncle from childhood onwards bred habits of concealment, duplicity, and ready flattery in O'Connell. It may also have contributed to the gross financial irresponsibility that left him vulnerable to attack and, worse still, ridicule, especially after 1830. His wife and children also deeply influenced his career—his wife as confidante-cum-keeper of conscience, his sons both as reminders of the career disadvantages under which Catholics laboured and as obstacles to the establishment of an effective lieutenancy outside the O'Connell ranks. Most of all did his thirty-one years of unremitting practice at the Bar determine his form of politics, from the vast variety of his types of advocacy to his eagerness to settle for lesser gains in doubtful issues and his obsession with the limits of legality.

In his repeal campaign of 1843 he perfected the techniques of mass mobilization and deployment that he had begun to explore in 1808. Immediately, his own imprisonment in 1844 marked the failure of his last great exertion; and indeed he himself never recovered fully in confidence, health, or, perhaps, judgement after his release at the age of 69. But, in the long run, the ideas which he had crystallized, and the pressures which had been built up by and in 1843, set in motion the process of 'killing Home Rule with kindness' that ultimately undermined the Act of Union. In almost every aspect of Irish constitutional politics, O'Connell was the pioneer; scarcely a single later development is without its precedent in the course of his complex and lengthy struggle.

OMacD

O'CONNOR, Roger (1762–1834). United Irishman, radical, author, and friend of Sir Francis *Burdett, O'Connor was associated with several secret societies and political organizations between the 1790s and 1830s which sought social and *parliamentary reform in Ireland [see *United societies].

Although an admirer of Voltaire and notoriously anticlerical, O'Connor espoused conservative politics in early life and was called to the English Bar in 1784. In 1786–7 he helped suppress the agrarian terrorist 'Whiteboy' movement as a magistrate and member of the Muskerry volunteers but his views changed in the early 1790s, when he joined the revolutionary United Irishmen. He fled to England in early 1797 to avoid arrest for sedition, but returned under an amnesty in July which he promptly breached by defending United Irish prisoners at Cork assizes. Branded an 'arch-traitor', he was re-arrested on a charge of high treason on 27 September 1797 and imprisoned until brought to trial and acquitted in April 1798. He returned immediately to London, but was soon detained and committed to Dublin's Newgate prison on 2 June 1798. O'Connor was held with the United Irish state prisoners, including his brother Arthur (1763–1852), who were removed to Fort George, Scotland, in April 1799 and released after June 1802.

Upon his return to Ireland in 1803, O'Connor gained a reputation for eccentricity and financial recklessness. He netted £5,000 insurance in 1809 for the burning under suspicious circumstances of his Dangan Castle residence in County Meath, ruined Arthur's estate which he held in trust, and eloped with a married lady. In October 1812 he robbed the Galway mail coach in an apparent attempt to recover incriminating love letters written by his close friend Francis Burdett, and was fortunate to be acquitted of the crime and the murder of a guard when the case was tried in 1817. He was also cleared of administering an illegal oath, but his practice of signing himself Richard O'Connor, King (ROCK), and publication of *Captain Rock's Letter to the King* (c.1825) which criticized the nobility, signalled his sympathies with the violent agrarian 'rockite' movement. More certain is his proprietorship of the seditious newspaper the *Harp of Erin*, to which he was the main contributor.

O'Connor's pseudo-historical *The Chronicles of Eri* (1822), dedicated to Burdett, attempted to trace Ireland's ancient lineage, and he also gained a reputation as a brilliant conversationalist before his death in 1834. The *Chartist leader Feargus O'Connor (1794–1855) was his son by his second wife.

RO'D

odes. By the late eighteenth century the English ode had become both the vehicle of bombastic effusions and, alternatively, a fertile ground of experimentation, in which the elevated and dramatic style of the Pindaric form was combined with the more meditative movement of the Horatian ode.

Of the two major classical models for the English ode, the odes of Pindar are thought to have been designed for the Greek chorus, with a triadic structure comprising strophe, antistrophe, and epode. By contrast, the Greek origins of Horace's odes are the lyrics of Sappho and Alcaeus; their character is, consequently, more contemplative and less dramatic, their form usually monostrophic. Common to both is their formal, occasional character and elevated tone and diction. Enlightenment *antiquarianism [35] added the songs of the Old Testament to the category, so that the 'sacred ode' ousted classical models in the hierarchy of lyric modes.

Abraham Cowley (1618–67) promulgated an irregular Pindaric ode which became the dominant form of public, celebratory poetry in our period. The ode flourished as the chief mode of the *sublime, and the proliferation of odes to a variety of personified abstractions made it a much-parodied form. Nonetheless, in the hands of William Collins (1721–59) and Thomas Gray (1716–71) it became the stage for dramas of both nationhood and selfhood, as in Collins' 'Ode to Liberty' (1747) and 'Ode on the Poetical Character' (1747) and Gray's 'The Bard' (1757). As titles like these suggest, the ode became the most self-reflexive of forms, the pre-eminent medium for investigating the nature and role of poetic vocation in the modern state.

This feature was taken even further in the odes of the Romantics. By the 1790s the ode was firmly established as the radical poet's vehicle of choice, subverting the traditional triumphalism of the ode form. Its dramatic and dialectical character was increasingly exploited for expressions of ambivalence, both personal and political. Amelia Anderson's [see Amelia *Opie] 'Ode on the Present Times, 27th January 1795' bemoans the tyranny of poverty at home and of Europe's despotic regimes, but also the bloody price of freedom. By the decade's end the radical poet's growing misgivings are famously expressed in *Coleridge's 'France: An Ode' (1798). Coleridge retreats further into doubt and self-scrutiny in 'Dejection: An Ode' (1802), begun as a reply to the earliest version of *Wordsworth's 'Intimations Ode' (written 1802–4; pub. 1815). Both of these poems are based on the irregular Pindaric ode, Wordsworth's more strictly so, yet they exploit the form's dialectical progression for the purposes of Horatian-style contemplation and philosophical inquiry. The conversational style of Wordsworth's 'Lines Written a Few Miles Above Tintern Abbey' (1798) made its author shy of naming it an ode, but in his 1800 note to the poem he claims that 'it was written with a hope that in the transitions, and the impassioned music of the versification would be found the principle requisites' of the form.

Later poets resumed the ode's promotion of progressive nationalist politics, such as *Byron in 'Ode to Napoleon Buonaparte' (1814) and 'Venice: An Ode' (1818) and *Shelley in 'Ode to Liberty' (1820), 'Ode to Naples' (1820) and 'Ode to the West Wind' (1820), the latter reviving in particular the ode as vehicle of the sublime, yet even less tied to classical models than earlier Romantics. *Keats's odes can be read as the culmination of the period's experimentation in the ode form, an experimentation which ultimately signalled the end of the ode as a viable genre. While indebted to the popular ode of *sensibility [11]—such as Mary *Robinson's two poems entitled 'Ode to the Nightingale' (1791)—Keats's odes are monostrophic and incorporate features of the *sonnet. Accordingly, the dramatic and dialectical character of the ode form is maintained as much through intertextual relations as intratextual ones, as these odes challenge and rework generic expectations.   SC

operas, English, shared the stage with plays at Covent Garden and Drury Lane during the winter theatre season, and at the Little Theatre in the Haymarket during the summers. They appealed to a more socially diverse audience than Italian operas, which were overwhelmingly patronized by the upper classes. Like spoken dramas, English operas were also performed on the provincial circuit (including Dublin) during the summers, and in America.

English opera developed its characteristics during the 1760s in works such as Thomas Arne's (1710–78) *Love in a Village* (1762) and Samuel *Arnold's *The Maid of the Mill* (1765). Both had comic, *pastoral plots, with spoken dialogue to carry the action, and a mixture of newly composed and borrowed *music [26], most of it simple enough for actors to sing. In 1775 Thomas *Linley achieved success with his setting of *The Duenna* with words by his son-in-law, R. B. *Sheridan. When David Garrick (1717–79) retired the following year, Sheridan and Linley took over Drury Lane, and Linley reluctantly became house composer. In 1777, Arnold was appointed as house composer at the Little Theatre, followed by the appointment of William *Shield to Covent Garden in 1782 which firmly established the presence of English opera in the playhouses. All three composers continued the tradition of keeping drama and music separate, with musical numbers comprising simple ensembles and solo songs. For the few professional *singers, they composed virtuoso airs in Italianate style; Shield and Arnold often borrowed folk-songs and composed in folk style.

In 1788, Stephen *Storace joined the Drury Lane company and soon took over informally as house composer. Storace introduced the first real innovations to the genre, gradually integrating music and drama in the Italian style, most notably in the multi-section finales of *The Pirates* (1792). He had the advantage of composing for singers such as his sister Nancy *Storace and the tenor Michael *Kelly. All the principal composers of the last decade of the century exploited and encouraged contemporary taste, introducing *Gothic elements, for example, as in Storace's *The Haunted Tower* (1789), fashionable crazes such as female archery (Shield's *The Woodman* (1791), and the exotic, as in Arnold's *The Siege of Curzola* (1786).

After Storace's death in 1796 and Shield's retirement in 1797, no lasting successors emerged. Arnold made only one unsuccessful attempt to follow Storace's innovations in *The Shipwreck* (Drury Lane, 1796). He died in 1802. Linley's son William proved a failure at Drury Lane, which left Kelly to take over operatic production and direction. Kelly's and John *Braham's pieces (often collaborative) typically consisted of an overture plus isolated songs and ensembles that were limited in scope. Patriotic texts reflected the bellicose times. When writing solos for themselves or another prominent soloist—such as, in Braham's case, Nancy Storace—they exhibited more virtuosity; elsewhere their style was extremely restricted. In the work of *Mozart's pupil Thomas Attwood (1765–1838) and other better-trained composers, the idiom of English opera contended with a more substantial musical vein (couched in late-eighteenth-century techniques) that promised greater dramatic effectiveness yet could not break free of constraints.

The popularity of melodies in a folk idiom gained further impetus from dramatizations of *Scott's novels. John Davy's (1763–1824) *Rob Roy Macgregor* (1818), for instance, was compiled from Scottish airs. But by now the leading composer of several years' standing was Henry *Bishop, who wrote music for many productions, mostly at Covent Garden and Drury Lane (at various times he was director of music at each). The plots of his operas were loosely based on Scott, *Shakespeare, and popular *melodramatic themes. His versions of Mozart's and Rossini's operas, drastically different from the originals, were tailored to prevailing circumstances, but they also indicate his unwillingness to venture beyond established public taste. *Weber's *Der Freischutz* and *Oberon* (1826), composed for Covent Garden, revealed a quality of musical drama and a compositional technique, notably as regards orchestration, that no British musician could equal—as Bishop's rival production, *Aladdin* (1826), showed to its cost. Thereafter Bishop largely retreated into arranging existing works. English opera emerged from its ensuing fallow period a decade later when the generation of Barnett, Balfe, and others, with suitable managerial support, brought it new fame.   JG and GB

OPIE, Amelia (1769–1853), novelist and poet. Opie grew up in radical circles in Norwich, the daughter of James Alderson, a locally prominent *Unitarian physician. Her precocious literary talents resulted in published verse by her teenage years and a first novel, *The Dangers of Coquetry*, by 1790. During the early 1790s Opie visited London and made the acquaintance of radicals such as William *Godwin, Thomas *Holcroft, and Mary *Wollstonecraft. In 1798 she wed the 'Cornish wonder', painter John *Opie, but enjoyed only nine years of marriage before he died in 1807.

Opie's most successful novel was *The Father and Daughter* (1801), which spawned an opera, a play, and reputedly buckets of tears from Sir Walter *Scott. Perhaps her work of most enduring interest is *Adeline Mowbray, or The Mother and Daughter* (1804). It was based loosely on the life of Wollstonecraft, who was apparently the only thing, together with the Lake District, which had impressed Opie at first sight. The novel remains ambiguous in its political sympathies. The heroine Adeline adopts fashionable freethinking opposition to wedlock, to the horror of her poseur mother and to the undoing of her own reputation. Adeline's ultimate reconciliation to religious duty and worldly convention represents a rejection of the Wollstonecraftian feminism that had struck Opie so forcefully in the 1790s.

Upon her husband's death Opie returned to Norwich, where she continued writing poems, tracts, and fiction. After attending occasional Friends' meetings for more than a decade, she became a *Quaker in 1825 and consequently gave up novel-writing. Her new commitment to visit workhouses, hospitals, and *prisons was interspersed throughout the rest of her life with regular trips to London and brief sojourns in Paris's café society.   KF

OPIE, John (1761–1807), painter of *portraits, genre scenes, and fancy pictures, who overcame the obstacles of a modest rural background to become professor of perspective at the *Royal Academy [see *painting, 27].

Opie was initially apprenticed to his father, a carpenter, but a natural scholarly and artistic aptitude brought him to the attention of Dr John *Wolcot (Peter Pindar) at Truro. He encouraged Opie and introduced him to London society as the 'Cornish wonder' in 1781. Opie's early paintings were of beggars and elderly men and women, and these representations of poverty and age inspired comparisons with Rembrandt and Caravaggio. He soon gained aristocratic and royal *patronage and transferred his energies to portraiture. He also produced *history paintings for *Boydell's Shakespeare Gallery in 1786, including the *Assassination of Rizzio*, which was attacked for its anachronistic detail. In 1787 he became a Royal Academician.

After a first disastrous marriage, Opie married the authoress Amelia Alderson [see Amelia *Opie] in 1797, and they travelled together to Paris in 1802 to view *Napoleon's spoils. They also made contact with Charles James *Fox while there. In 1805 Opie was appointed professor of perspective, and gave lectures on design, invention, chiaroscuro, and colour. Despite his unconventional background and associations with radical circles, he thus became one of the most important members of the Royal Academy establishment.   SW

oratorio had four meanings: first, the large-scale musical form of soloists, chorus, and orchestra developed by *Handel in London from the early 1730s; secondly, a concert consisting of a performance of a single oratorio, or of extracts from oratorios and other choral and vocal music; thirdly, a *music festival, where the principal concerts were oratorios in the first two senses; and fourthly, in the plural, the seasons of Lenten concerts given at Covent Garden and Drury Lane theatres from the late 1730s until 1840 [see rise of the *classics].

The oratorio as conceived by Handel was a large-scale work in English, synthesizing elements of the Italian opera with the older English traditions of the masque and the anthem. In three acts, for soloists, chorus, and orchestra, it was usually dramatic in form, on a biblical subject, and intended for performance in the theatre but without scenery, costumes, or action. But the term was frequently loosely applied, and there are notable exceptions to this definition, including, for example, *Messiah*, which is not dramatic.

Although originally conceived by Handel as a secular entertainment, the oratorio soon came to be regarded by audiences and commentators as a sacred form. The biblical subjects of most of the oratorios and the tradition of Lenten performances

89. An engraving of John Opie's *The Assassination of David Rizzio* (1786, destroyed in the Second World War). Although criticized when first exhibited in John Boydell's Shakespeare Gallery, which published the engraving, the work became Opie's most famous history painting.

encouraged this view, and it was further reinforced by the growing popularity from around 1750 of *Messiah*, Handel's only unambiguously sacred oratorio. Although received at the time of its first London performances with little enthusiasm in some quarters and outright hostility in others on account of its sacred subject-matter, from the 1750s *Messiah* came to be seen as the archetypal oratorio. Later, while complete performances of the other oratorios grew ever more infrequent, *Messiah* became a national institution, the work by which Handel was chiefly remembered, and with which all other oratorios were compared. Thus was the oratorio reinterpreted as a sacred genre, a process accelerated by the increasingly frequent practice of performing Handel's oratorios in church.

In London, the Lenten oratorio seasons inaugurated by Handel continued after his death. Their survival until as late as 1840 owed much initially to the seemingly limitless appeal of his music, but latterly more to tradition and the need to fill the theatres on the two nights a week during Lent on which operas were prohibited. The move (begun in Handel's lifetime) away from complete performances of oratorios towards programmes of extracts and compilations continued, and by the 1790s *Messiah* was the only

Handel oratorio regularly to be performed in its entirety. Increasingly, the original character of the Lenten oratorio concerts came to be diluted by the inclusion of instrumental and operatic items. In the provinces, performances of oratorios dominated music festivals, to the extent that the festival as a whole was frequently referred to as 'an oratorio'.

Handel made the oratorio form so completely his own that few examples by other composers had any degree of success, either in his lifetime or after: even such popular works as *Redemption* (1786) by Samuel *Arnold were compilations to new words of favourite music by Handel. A notable exception was *Haydn's *The Creation* (Vienna, 1798; London, 1800), a work conceived on Handelian principles which rapidly became second in popularity only to *Messiah*. Another was William *Crotch's *Palestine* (1812).   PO

ordnance surveys, see *mapping.

orientalism refers in the main to the scholarly, literary, and artistic works on the Middle East and South Asia, produced in the wake of European colonial expansion [see *empire, 5]. As such, 'orientalism' is a key area in helping us to understand the variety of relationships which were developing between Britain and its colonial territories in non-European parts of the world in the Romantic period.

Biblical criticism formed one important strand of orientalism. The treatment of the Scriptures as oriental literature was initiated by Robert Lowth's *Lectures on the Sacred Poetry of the Hebrews* (1753). This approach was subsequently developed by German biblical critics, whose work had an important influence on the *Unitarian movement in the 1780s and 1790s. However, the most important scholarly influences were the publication of Anquetil-Duperron's *Zend-Avesta* (1771), and the opening up of the worlds of Sanskrit and ancient India in the works of Sir William *Jones and the Asiatic Society of Bengal. These works revealed worlds of learning that were independent of both biblical and Graeco-Roman traditions, whose genealogies in some cases extended further back historically than those of Europe. This alone was to have an important influence in some circles on European self-perceptions.

The impact of oriental scholarship of this kind is evident in such popular and self-consciously exotic literary texts as Robert *Southey's *Thalaba* (1810) and *Kehama* (1810), as well as Thomas *Moore's *Lalla Rookh* (1817). The care which both poets took to refer to their sources in the copious footnotes to their texts indicates the breadth and quantity of scholarship and *travel literature on the 'orient'. Such texts are also indicative of the complex ways in which imagined 'orients' interacted with political and religious positions. Artistic interest in the *picturesque and the *sublime produced a re-evaluation of Indian art and architecture in accounts such as William *Hodges's *Travels in India* (1793), Thomas Maurice's *Indian Antiquities* (7 vols., 1793–1800), Thomas and William Daniell's *Oriental Scenery* (1808), Edwin Moor's *The Hindu Pantheon* (1810), and James Forbes's *Oriental Memoirs* (1813). Musically, too, the taste for the picturesque turned to the orient and a vogue for *Indian music and 'Hindostanie' airs was evident both in the colonies and in Britain.

Although India remained the key sphere of British orientalism, European interest in Egypt had received a new lease of life with the French *invasion of 1798. Vivant Denon's *Voyage dans la Basse et la Haute Égypte* (1802) was translated into both English and German, but it was Giovanni Battista Belzoni's (1778–1823) record of his outstanding discoveries which captured the imagination of the British public. Belzoni was encouraged by Henry Salt (1780–1827), the British Consul-General in Egypt, who gave him his first *Egyptological commission. Belzoni's *Narrative of the Operations and Recent Discoveries within the Pyramids* was published in 1820, and an exhibition of his casts, finds, and drawings was held in the Egyptian Hall, Piccadilly, in May 1821, to much popular acclaim. Thomas Maurice's *Observations on the Remains of Ancient Egyptian Grandeur and Superstition* (1818) also inspired Thomas Moore to write *The Epicurean* (1827), a novel evocative of

the diversity of orientalist perceptions of Egypt, with its depictions of Alexandria and Memphis, and its fascination with early Christianity and the Egyptian mysteries.

It is clear that orientalism had a number of strands, some of them conflicting, which need to be understood in the context of the variety of religious and political positions of orientalist authors. Perhaps more important, though, was the way in which orientalism began to have an impact on cultural self-definitions. However, the precise relationship between orientalism and the growing colonial power of Britain and other European states as a whole remains complex and controversial.   JMA

originality. In its earliest usage, 'original' refers to the source or earliest state of a person or thing. The word implies a glance back in time to the beginning. By the eighteenth century, 'original' is used in discussions of works of art to describe the new [see *literary theory, 41]. Pope writes, for example, 'If ever any Author deserved the name of an *Original*, it was Shakespear.' This accolade is bestowed, however, because *Shakespeare was thought to be an original *imitator*. Rather than deriving his subjects from previous writers, he draws on life to find new topics for art; in Pope's words, he draws 'his art . . . immediately from the fountains of Nature'. Although the eighteenth century noted and often celebrated Shakespeare's ability to *create* things not found in art or nature, *neoclassical literary practice was centred on imitation rather than creation. In Romanticism this hierarchy is reversed. Originality, a word which enters common currency only in the last third of the century, registers this change in emphasis.

In Romantic aesthetics, the concept of originality has a number of threads. First, it describes a work of art which breaks free from literary precursors, but this quality is now understood primarily in relation to the artist's creativity. As Edward Young (?1683–1765) writes in his *Conjectures* (1759), often described as the *locus classicus* of the new ethos of originality, 'An *Original* may be said to be of a *vegetable* nature; it rises spontaneously from the vital root of genius.' Originality is therefore closely aligned with individuality. Second, as Young suggests, rather than relying on extrinsic models, originality is organic, governed by laws which are intrinsic to its nature. An original work is therefore unified, autonomous, and self-governing: it forms a heterocosm or world in itself. Third, its evocation of the individual as origin of the work transfers to the artist some of the aura previously reserved for the divine creator. As *Hazlitt writes of *Wordsworth, 'his mind is . . . coeval with the primary forms of things'. This association lends authority to the work of art. Fourth, and somewhat paradoxically, by proclaiming the indivisibility and particularity of the work of art, and by tying it to individuality, originality associates art and property. An original belongs by a species of natural right to its originator, the author.

The concept of originality draws on and is in part determined by the tradition of possessive individualism inaugurated by *Locke; the development of *copyright laws which recognized the author as proprietor of the work of art; the decline of *patronage; the growth of the reading public; and the appearance of literary professionals who depend on this public for their livelihood. On the one hand, originality is a key term in the development of Romantic reading practices which value qualities such as intensity, spontaneity, vitality, authenticity, and unity; which privilege the relation between author and text; and which are preoccupied by the division of the organic from the mechanical, creation from convention, the original from the copy. On the other hand, this same term ensures that Romanticism will be haunted by the premonition that the boundary between one work and another, authors and their precursors, cannot finally be drawn. It is deeply ironic that texts which seemed exemplary products of original genius, *Fingal* (1762) and *Temora* (1763), supposedly by the ancient bard *Ossian, were fashioned by James Macpherson. Not the originals they purported to be; yet not copies, because when asked to produce the originals he had translated Macpherson had to forge them; these poems are original counterfeits, an oxymoron which suggests something of the tangled history of originality which they precede.   POT

Ossianism. James Macpherson's (1736–96) supposed translations of the poetry of Ossian, a third-century bard of the Scottish Highlands, are now chiefly known as the most spectacular literary forgeries of the eighteenth century. Based on collections of Gaelic *ballads and old manuscripts made on tours of the Highlands, Macpherson reworked the material he collected as *Fragments of Ancient Poetry* (1760), *Fingal* (1762), and *Temora* (1763). The last two volumes were *epic poems, a form he believed would meet the polite literary tastes of Edinburgh and London.

Contemporary suspicions about the authenticity of the poems, voiced by David *Hume and Samuel *Johnson among others, were confirmed by the Highland Society's *Report of 1805*. The committee, chaired by Henry *Mackenzie, concluded that Macpherson had over-zealously edited his original and had inserted passages, but the findings did not seriously damage the cult status of the poems. Macpherson had adapted his material to fit widespread assumptions about the nature of primitive societies and their literatures. Hugh *Blair, Macpherson's chief supporter, took the Ossianic style to epitomize the 'wild, harsh and irregular' nature of ancient poetry. The authenticity of the poems was validated primarily against the model of the Old Testament, defined by contemporaries as the archetypal primitive text, and they met the growing taste for the *sublime both in Britain and on the Continent, where the poems were highly valued.

The image of sturdy national independence available in the poem ensured Ossian's popularity not only with Scottish patriots but also with nationalist sentiment throughout Europe well into the nineteenth century. Few were as influenced as William *Blake by what he insisted were the genuine effu-

sions of an ancient bard, but many writers, including *Coleridge in 1793, composed their own Ossianic fragment. Others like *Gibbon and *Byron, whatever their reservations about the authenticity of the poems, celebrated the vigorous liberty of Macpherson's ancient Caledonia. Nevertheless the patriotic aspects of Macpherson's writing and influence need to be weighed against his concern to make the poems acceptable for a British reading public. His subsequent work as a historian and government propagandist during the *American Revolution suggests that he was convinced of the identity of interests between England and Scotland.

Not all the readers who thrilled to descriptions of a primitive state of liberty viewed them as the foundation of a *republican art in the present. It was perhaps the melancholia of Macpherson's bard, who himself mourns the passing of the heroic age described in the poems, which represented the foundation of Ossian's popular success. Many readers, like William *Hazlitt, saw in Ossian a 'recollection and regret of the past' which anticipated a modern sense of inadequacy in the face of the sublimity of antiquity.   JM

OWEN, Sir Richard (1804–92), comparative anatomist, palaeontologist, and scientific grandee. The son of a West India merchant, Owen was educated at Lancaster's New Grammar School, then apprenticed to local surgeons. After medical training at the University of Edinburgh, Owen was recommended to John *Abernethy, who in 1827 secured him the post of assistant to William Clift (1775–1849), college conservator [see *medicine, 18]. Thus began Owen's long association with the college, which led to appointment as Hunterian professor of comparative anatomy in 1836 and college conservator in 1842.

Between 1837 and 1855 Owen gave a series of annual *lectures on comparative anatomy and physiology attended not just by medical students but by politicians, literary figures, clergy, and a host of genteel scientific amateurs. The attraction of Owen's lectures lay in his skilful use of specimens from the vast collections of the College of Surgeons to represent vertebrate structures as expressions of a divine 'archetype or primal pattern' on which all boned animals had been constructed. Owen's idealist theorizing owed much to the influence of German *natural philosophy [34], and especially the work of the Swedish naturalist Carl Gustav von Carus.   PT

Owen, Robert (1771–1858), industrialist and founder of British *socialism. Owen's career can be divided into two main phases: before and after 1817. Owen's life until 1817 was one of the great success stories of his day. His origins were obscure, but after serving an apprenticeship as a shop assistant, he became a pioneer in the field of cotton-spinning, beginning in Manchester in the early 1790s and then most famously at the New Lanark cotton mills built up by the *philanthropic industrialist David Dale, whose management he assumed in 1800. From his earliest experience in managing a cotton factory, Owen demonstrated a flair for both technical innovation and human management. He never sought, however, to introduce the former at the expense of the workforce. And it was this commitment to the welfare of his workers which produced one of the most extraordinary volte-faces of his age: in 1817, at the age of 46, after a lengthy period of criticizing fellow factory managers for refusing to countenance laws restricting child and female labour and ameliorating factory conditions, Owen proclaimed his opposition to the *factory system, individual competition, and the private ownership of property.

'Socialism' had certainly not been Owen's aim at New Lanark, where he sought to eradicate vice and improve conditions for the workforce while increasing discipline and output. By reducing the price of goods in the company store, and paying wages during an American cotton embargo, Owen gradually won the confidence of the workforce. By 1816 he was able to reduce hours of labour from eleven and three-quarters to ten and three-quarters daily. Using his great profits, he opened his 'Institute for the Formation of Character', and is still often associated with the founding of the infant education movement [see *education, 17].

By 1815 New Lanark was famous throughout Europe, receiving over 2,000 visitors annually from 1815 to 1825. Owen planned to introduce public kitchens and dining-rooms in order to reduce his employees' living expenses still further, but found his efforts blocked by his pious Quaker partner, William *Allen, who objected to Owen's *Deism. About this time, Owen published *A New View of Society; or, Essays on the Principle of the Formation of the Human Character* (1813–14), and began to extend his ideas of moral reform, national education, and the relief of the poor [see *poor laws]. His broad principles met with considerable sympathy in an era of Evangelical moral reform; his specific application of them met with almost universal resistance.

The ending of the Napoleonic wars transformed the environment of poor relief proposals. Tens of thousands of demobilized soldiers and sailors roamed the country, while the introduction of new machinery displaced thousands of other industrial workers. The predominant view was that the supply of and demand for labour would balance each other eventually. Owen found this a cruel condemnation of the deserving poor. In *Observations on the Effects of the Manufacturing System* (1815) he condemned 'buying cheap and selling dear', the 'spirit of competition', as the cause of widespread displacement. He warned that the working population was quickly being reduced to a state 'infinitely more degraded and miserable than they were before the introduction of those manufactories'. As opposition mounted to his ideas, Owen's plans became increasingly elaborate. By 1817 he proposed that the poor be housed in co-operative colonies where labour and goods would be in common, and suggested that eventually the entire population would prosper in such an environment, free from the degrading cities, *famines, and factories of the existing urban system. His mission now clearly assumed an overtly religious character; his aim was no longer 'the relief of the poor' but 'the

emancipation of mankind'. He condemned the priesthood as his greatest enemy, for offering its nearly unanimous moral support to the existing social and economic system.

The second half of Owen's life was one continuous effort to realize these ideals. In the *Report to the County of Lanark* (1820), he explicitly committed himself to 'the Principle of united labour, expenditure, and property, and equal privileges'. He condemned the existing system of exchange, proposing instead a medium of notes based upon labour time. Against Adam *Smith he argued that 'the most minute division of mental power and manual labour in the individuals of the working classes led private interests to be placed perpetually at variance with the public good'. The new system, however, would combine 'extensive mental and manual powers in the individuals of the working classes [and] a complete identity of private and public interest.'

Soon after 1820 practical efforts to found Owenite communities began, first at Orbiston south of Glasgow, then at New Harmony in Indiana, and most impressively at Queenwood in Hampshire between 1839 and 1845. Schemes to raise funds for a community through consumer co-operative stores also date from the early 1820s. Owen attempted in the mid-1830s to establish labour exchanges, where artisans could exchange their produce directly without paying middlemen and shopkeepers. For a time in 1833–4, he was also briefly leader of the Grand National Consolidated Trades Union, the first effort to found a national union of all trades [see *trade unions]. All of Owen's communities failed, however. This was due to a number of factors: the difficulty of recruiting correctly trained members, the recurring absence of markets for agricultural products, and the fact that large debts were often incurred in beginning communities. At Queenwood, Owen's grandiose designs for building and decoration proved ruinously expensive. His communitarian ideals thus met widespread failure in practice. His writings, however, inspired a generation of socialist economists like William *Thompson. And his plea for moral reform and co-operation left a notable mark on Victorian attitudes towards the poor, the working classes, and factory reform. GC

OWENSON, Sydney, Lady Morgan (?1776–1859), Irish novelist and nationalist. A celebrated political, literary, and social figure in her day and popular advocate of Irish nationalism and *Catholic emancipation, Owenson wrote nine *novels [31], a comic *opera, *essays, memoirs, a biography of Salvator Rosa, poems, and *travel literature.

The elder daughter of Jane Hill and Irish actor Robert Owenson (originally MacOwen), she was probably born in 1776, according to family tradition, at sea between Ireland and England. She spent much of her childhood backstage in Dublin theatres, later at boarding-school or on tour with her father. For a time she was the playmate of the young poet-prodigy Thomas *Dermody. Between 1798 and 1800 she was a governess.

Her third and most influential novel, *The Wild*

Irish Girl: A National Tale (1806), dramatized the relationship between England and Ireland, blending propaganda with romance and with her characteristic footnotes, here detailing Irish history and customs. Recurrent themes in her novels are the position of women and colonization (in Ireland, Greece, and India). In a later preface she remarks that 'a novel is especially adapted to enable the advocate of any cause to steal upon the public'. Owenson's Irish nationalism made her fashionable in *Whig circles in London but a target for the *Tory press, with John Wilson Croker's onslaughts in the *Quarterly Review* including an inquiry into her age.

In 1809 she joined the household of John Hamilton, Marquis of Abercorn, and on 20 January 1812 married his physician, Sir Thomas Morgan. The marriage may have provided protection for her next novel, *O'Donnel* (1814), published by Henry Colburn (d. 1855), which was more radically Irish Catholic than its predecessors. Subsidized by Colburn, Owenson visited France between 1815 and 1817, writing a travel-book in 1817 in which she voiced strongly pro-revolutionary sentiments, and provoked accusations of ignorance and Jacobinism in the *Quarterly Review*. As in *Italy* (1821), the first commissioned travel account of that country, she remarked on literature, religion, and politics, and was one of the most observant of contemporary travel writers.

Her lifelong concern for women is reflected in *Woman and her Master: A History of the Female Sex from the Earliest Period* (1840), the first part of a projected series on the social position of women throughout history. In 1837 Owenson was granted a civil list annual pension of £300. She published a selection of her memoirs shortly before her death in 1859.   RCA

P

PAGANINI, Niccolò (1782–1840), supreme Italian violin virtuoso of the nineteenth century. At the height of his reputation when he arrived in London in 1831, Paganini astonished everyone with his showmanship—the cascading arpeggios and sensational harmonics, the left-hand pizzicato and flying bowings, the pieces on the G-string alone—and also with the poetry and feeling he brought to slow movements. But he also cut a Romantic figure, as a solitary genius surrounded by guilty legends—a mystique he encouraged by his spectral appearance on stage, which was almost as thrilling as the music. The haunted absorption of his performances magnetized audiences everywhere, and he undoubtedly nurtured his demonic reputation by playing such pieces as the *Witches' Dance*.

More than anyone before him Paganini exploited virtuosity for the utmost financial gain, his exorbitant fees contributing to his legendary reputation. After eighteen concerts in London had earnt him over £10,000, he embarked on a six-month tour of Ireland, Scotland, and provincial England, successfully overcoming resistance to high ticket prices. Ultimately he suffered both from the gruelling exertions of touring and from an increasingly hostile press: a final British tour in 1834 was a failure, yet his image as a tormented artist endured, extending far beyond the sphere of violin-playing.   SMcV

PAINE, Thomas (1737–1809), radical pamphleteer and international revolutionary. At the age of 37 he sailed for America, a failed exciseman, staymaker, tobacconist, sometime teacher, and husband. Thirty-five years later, he died in obscurity on a small piece of property in New York State. Between these two events he became one of the most famous and infamous revolutionaries of his day, both in America and Europe.

Paine's revolutionary career began in Pennsylvania in 1775 when, as a writer and editor for the *Pennsylvania Magazine*, he moved in Philadelphia's radical circles while hostilities with Britain were reaching a head. His *Common Sense* (1776) was the first pamphlet to urge independence from Britain. Written in blunt, unpretentious prose, it became the most widely read pamphlet of the *American Revolution. It opens with a swingeing attack on *monarchy and hereditary rule, arguing that government is an adjunct to society and should be organized wholly with a view to minimum expense and maximum benefit. Hereditary government is an absurdity, condemned by the Bible and by experience alike; only republican rule can ensure that the people are given proper weight and consideration. America, therefore, could not be subject by right to the English king, and whatever ties of affection and kinship had once existed had been forever expunged by the violent and predatory attacks of the English on their colonies. America must seize the time, unite in defence, and establish its own government so as to secure her freedom.

Paine's success with *Common Sense* was repeated with his *American Crisis* letters, written throughout the Revolution. His personal fortunes, however, fluctuated. He was appointed secretary to the Foreign Affairs Committee of the Continental Congress, but was forced to resign for betraying confidences concerning the activities of Congress's agents in France. Subsequently vindicated, he went on to act as clerk to the Pennsylvania Assembly.

After the Revolution, having been rewarded by Congress and several state governments for his services, Paine turned his energies to science. He designed a single-span bridge which he decided to take to Europe in the hope of finding funding for its development. He returned to England in 1787 and also visited Paris, where Thomas Jefferson was the American Minister. He took an active interest in the opening stages of the *French Revolution, meeting with Lafayette's circle at Jefferson's house, and communicating information received from Jefferson to opposition circles in England (notably to Edmund *Burke). When Burke's *Reflections on the Revolution in France* was published in November 1790 Paine responded with *Rights of Man* (1791), in which he refuted Burke's account of events in France in 1789 and argued for the *natural rights of man and the sovereignty of each generation over its affairs, against Burke's doctrine of prescriptive right and the utility of established institutions.

The second part of *Rights of Man*, published a year later, contained Paine's most radical innovations. The opening chapters outline a theory of government founded almost entirely on the American, as opposed to the French, experience. American republicanism is avowed as the true republican form, and the American revolution is hailed as having inaugurated a revolution in the principles of government throughout the world. The final chapter of the work, turning to the finances of the British state, proposes a series of reforms to substitute progressive taxation for direct taxation and to establish a welfare support for the indigent, aged, and sick.

Rights of Man circulated on an unprecedented scale throughout Britain and helped prompt demands for political reform, especially in extra-parliamentary circles and among the artisan classes. Alarmed by its success, the government initiated a libel prosecution against Paine, outlawing him in 1792. By this time he was in France, sitting as the elected member of the National Convention for Calais, and involved in the drafting of a new constitution for France. But his association with the Girondins, and his plea against the execution of the King, identified him as an enemy of the Jacobins. After the purging and execution of his Girondin associates in the summer of 1793, Paine was an increasingly isolated and vulnerable figure. Expecting the worst, he attempted to write about his other great concern, religion. He finished his *Age of Reason*—an eloquent attack on Christianity and defence of *Deism—in December 1793, shortly before being arrested and imprisoned in the Luxembourg.

Paine survived both illness and intended execution, and the indifference of the American minister, to emerge bitter and sick in the winter of 1794. The new Minister, James Monroe, cared for him and curtailed his worst excesses, but once out of Monroe's supervision, he published his *Letter to George Washington* (1796), accusing his former friend of betrayal.

Paine was welcomed back in the Convention, but he played little active role although he continued to write, notably his *Dissertation on the First Principles of Government* (1795), which attacked the 1795 constitution for failing to endorse universal manhood suffrage; *The Decline and Fall of the English System of Finance* (1796), which predicted a fiscal crisis for the British state; and *Agrarian Justice* (1796) which expanded his welfarist claims to endorse a basic entitlement to a natural inheritance on the age of majority. Although he had begun his career arguing for minimal government interference, he ended it with a firm belief that the European systems of government had been instrumental in exacerbating poverty and inequality, and that some basic compensation for the loss of original rights to common property was required. Returning to America in 1803, he was anathematized as an atheist and leveller: outlawed in his country of origin, and dissatisfied with the new order in France, Paine became an outcast. Yet he remains an icon for the period. A self-made man, turned radical and revolutionary, indebted to the languages of eighteenth-century English liberal and opposition thought, but never wholly dependent on them, he developed a radical *republicanism which found the answer to the inequities of the hereditary regimes of Europe in an interpretation of the American Revolution as fundamentally egalitarian, rights-based, and democratic.   MPH

PALEY, William (1743–1805), cleric, university teacher, *Anglican apologist. A systematic and clear expositor, Paley was the author of textbooks of enduring influence in politics, ethics, Christian apologetics, and natural theology. A major theoretician of late-eighteenth-century Latitudinarianism, his *utilitarianism proved to be the theological counterpart of Benthamism.

The son of a cleric and teacher, Paley was educated at his father's school, Giggleswick Grammar School, and then at Christ's College, Cambridge, where he was elected Fellow in June 1766. Subsequently ordained, he collected, over a long career, a number of benefices, the most notable (though not the most lucrative) being the archdeaconry of Carlisle (1782), which was a sinecure. Paley was of Yorkshire stock, and retained a North Country bluffness throughout his life. He was also one of a number of distinguished Cambridge Latitudinarian clerics who came from the north of England including Edmund (1703–78) and John Law (1745–1810) and Richard *Watson. Like them he favoured the aims of the Feathers Tavern petitioners, but did not openly support their goal, notoriously quipping that he could not afford to keep a conscience. He did however, support the movement anonymously in print. Paley favoured a more liberal, comprehensive church establishment which would reduce the need for dissent to a minimum, and complete *toleration for those who continued to dissent exclusively for religious reasons.

Paley's politics were of a pragmatic reformism. He

actively supported the movement for the *abolition of the slave trade, and described *slavery [6] as 'this odious institution'. He favoured practical help to the poor and noted that 'the care of the poor ought to be the principal object of our laws' [see *poverty, 12]. The rich he believed could look after themselves. He opposed tithes on the ground that they discouraged agricultural improvement and he approved proposals for graduated taxation. But he was radical neither in practice nor in theory. Thus, for example, the representative system, although a 'flagrant incongruity', could be justified on utilitarian grounds; and claims for equality of representation based on *natural rights theory were fallacious, for logically they should embrace the franchise for women. Paley was socially conservative and paternalistic in attitude, and his utilitarianism had a key theological and metaphysical dimension which enabled him to view the world as one in which God maximized happiness for all his creatures. He provided the most thorough exposition of the argument from design since the damaging attacks on the theory by David *Hume in the mid-century. In particular he argued that there were many examples of God's beneficent design which, cumulatively, were convincing. He avoided the anthropocentricism common amongst those who deployed the design argument while developing the argument that a design presupposed a designer, using the familiar analogy of a watch and watchmaker. Indeed, he viewed the world as populated by many little mechanisms all exhibiting God's purpose. However, he did not avoid a rather naïve anthropomorphism in his view of the animal kingdom: in his *Natural Theology* (1802) he enthused on the individual happiness of young shrimps 'bounding into the air from the shallow margin of the water'.

Paley was one of the first to realize the need to counteract the appeal of Thomas *Paine's *Rights of Man*, especially Part II (1792), by simple, direct arguments addressed to the lower classes. In his *Reasons for Contentment Addressed to the Labouring Part of the British Public* (1792) he translated his metaphysical and theological views into arguments for social conservatism suggesting both that 'some of the necessities which poverty . . . imposes, are not hardships but pleasures' and that 'religion smooths all inequalities, because it unfolds a prospect which makes all earthly distinctions nothing'. Later his *Evidences of Christianity* (1794) appeared opportunely to counter Paine's *Deistic *Age of Reason* (1795), although it was intended as a defence against the earlier onslaught of Hume.

Paley's major works went into many editions, and his *Moral and Political Philosophy* remained a key textbook in nineteenth-century Cambridge. His systematic theological utilitarianism assisted the transition of Latitudinarianism into the Broad Church movement, which retained its irenic ideals and an ethically focused Christianity. Yet for others he was a suspect figure. Many churchmen believed his views on the Trinity to be unorthodox. Moreover, it was not difficult for radicals to harness many of arguments and memorable observations to support more far-reaching reforms than those which he would have accepted. In many ways these were consequences of Paley's fair-mindedness and his willingness to concede that it is not erroneous ideas but poor conduct and bad practice which should be the focus of our attention.   MF

panorama, or the 'all-embracing view', a 360-degree *painting [27] housed in a rotunda structure, was originated by an Irish-born painter, Robert Barker (1739–1806), first in Edinburgh in 1785–7 and then in London. Barker's Leicester Square Panorama, opened in 1793, was a landmark until the 1860s under his son, Henry Aston Barker, and later the Burford family. The exhibition, part of London's proliferating culture of spectacles, combined the roles of the art gallery, the peep-show of the traditional *fairs, and the didactic function of the *lecture [see *viewing, 20]. It attracted a middle-class clientele and soon spread to many provincial towns and cities, as well as to Europe and the United States. The subjects of panorama paintings, undertaken by the Barkers and Burfords themselves, as well as by artists such as David Roberts (1796–1864) and Augustus *Earle, included urban landscapes—especially of London—battles, and exotic foreign locations such as New Zealand and the polar regions. The panorama played a significant part in the growing consciousness of London as a great imperial centre, a metropolis of historic importance to compare with Constantinople or Cairo (both panorama subjects), as well as suggesting that the 'all-embracing view' of the British subject could extend to all corners of the globe [see *empire, 5]. Indeed, later panorama entertainments acted as recruiting material for emigration to the Antipodes and elsewhere. In its representation of battles such as Trafalgar and *Waterloo, the panorama also catered to voracious domestic interest in Britain's *wars [2]. The scale of the paintings and the attention to detail—the Barkers made much of their use of officers who had taken part in the actual battles—used the conventions of a new kind of pictorial realism, anticipating the later development of cinema, to enhance a vision of British patriotic endeavour.

The verisimilitude of the panorama was extended through innovations such as the moving panorama, used in the London theatres and in exhibitions such as the Marshalls' 'Coronation of His Majesty George IV' (1823) which featured 10,000 figures. In 1823 the Frenchman L. J. M. Daguerre opened a diorama in a building in Regent's Park designed by Augustus Charles *Pugin. Influenced by Philippe Jacques de *Loutherbourg's *Eidophusikon*, Daguerre's diorama used lighting and transparency effects to suggest diurnal, seasonal, and atmospheric changes to images, culminating in a revolution of the auditorium to suggest movement. The competing 'British diorama' of 1828, with paintings by David Roberts Stanfield (1793–1867), was less technically ambitious, moving its images on rollers. Other variations on the panorama included the cosmorama, a room of images individually viewed through magnifying lenses. Cosmoramas were located as adjuncts to new shopping emporia, highlighting the link between visuality and the *consumerism [19] of the period. For some contemporary artists the verisimilitude of the panorama-type exhibitions went too far: *Constable claimed that the diorama could not be described as art 'because its object is deception', while for *Wordsworth, writing in Book VII of *The Prelude*, the 'all-embracing view' of the panorama artist signified the power of artistic representation to destabilize a sense of the autonomy of the self.   GR

Pantisocracy. The scheme to establish a 'Pantisocratic' community based on shared property and social equality on the banks of the Susquehanna river in Pennsylvania was jointly conceived by S. T. *Coleridge and Robert *Southey in mid-1794, when the two poets were still undergraduates at Cambridge and Oxford. By mid-August 1794 they planned to assemble twelve couples of like-minded individuals who would embark from Bristol to America the following April. Each man would provide a capital of £125 and would (in theory) only need to labour for two or three hours a day on commonly held land, passing the rest of the time in study and 'philosophical' conversation. From the start the project had strong links with radical education theory; Coleridge, writing in his journal, the *Friend* (1809), asserted that 'our little Society, in its second Generation, [would] have combined the innocence of the patriarchal Age with the knowledge and genuine refinements of European culture'. But Coleridge's account here misrepresents Pantisocracy as a visionary and *utopian [9] project related to the political enthusiasm of the 1790s.

Although the Pantisocracy plan would seem to have originated in Southey's circle in Oxford, in the mid-1790s American land agents were active in both England and France, selling off plots in Pennsylvania and Kentucky. The settlement of the émigré *Unitarian leader Joseph *Priestley and his son-in-law Thomas Cooper (1759–1840) in Northumberland, Pennsylvania (also on the banks of the Susquehanna), provided an additional incentive to Coleridge, who even hoped that Priestley might join their settlement. Shifting from the universities, the plan was subsequently centred upon the Dissenting culture of Bristol, where the two men moved in 1795, convenient as a western seaport offering easy access to America. Loyalist aggravation, mounting war taxes, and the perceived failure of republican politics in France and Britain made emigration to America an attractive option for Dissenters and radicals in 1794.

Although Coleridge and Southey were agreed that the purpose of the community was to be the 'aspheterization' (or abolition) of private property, their conceptions of the aims of the scheme were somewhat different. For Southey, Pantisocracy appears to have been the point upon which he could place William *Godwin's fulcrum for reforming mankind as outlined in *Political Justice* (1793). The Unitarian Coleridge's conception of Pantisocracy seems rather to have been based on James Harrington's (1611–77) republican account of the Jewish Commonwealth, based on equal division of prop-

erty, in *The Art of Lawgiving* (1659). Coleridge described this Mosaic theocracy in his *Lectures on Revealed Religion*, given at Bristol in 1795 to raise funds to lease land in Pennsylvania. The anti-Godwinian basis of his plan is made very clear in a letter written to Southey in October 1794: 'The leading idea of Pantisocracy is to make men *necessarily* virtuous by removing all Motives to Evil—all possible Temptations . . . It is each Individual's *duty* to be just, because it is in his *interest*.'

The Pantisocracy scheme never materialized. Land prices in America rocketed in the mid-1790s, and the Jay–Grenville trade treaty of 1794 represented a new *rapprochement* between the American and the British governments, so that America ceased to be a land of milk and honey for English radicals. Coleridge wrote dismissively in 1796 that 'the Americans love freedom because their ledgers furnish irrefragable arguments in favour of it'. Money raised by Coleridge and Southey from *lecturing and journalism was insufficient to meet the high capital input required. They also quarrelled in late 1795 about the feasibility of taking servants to America, Coleridge accusing Southey (now eager to marry Edith Fricker and pursue a professional career) of backsliding. Yet far from being a utopian or 'visionary' scheme, as Coleridge later maintained, the principles of Pantisocracy remained an important element of his political thought long after the American scheme was abandoned.   NL

pantomime, in one sense gesture without speech, was a form of dramatic entertainment, derived from the Italian *commedia dell'arte*, which became popular in the English *theatre [24] and *fairs in the early eighteenth century under the influence of the dancer and manager John Rich. It consisted of two parts: the first, an introduction or opening based on classical legend or, later, *fairy tales, nursery rhymes, *novels [31] such as *Gulliver's Travels* (1726), topical events and trends. During these scenes the actors would customarily wear carnival masks and costumes which would be removed to reveal the stock characters of Harlequin, Columbine, Pantaloon, and Clown. The second part consisted of a chase in which Pantaloon attempted to thwart Harlequin's romance with Columbine. Harlequin often endured a particular ordeal or 'dark scene' during which he was lost in a wood or *Gothic dungeon, before the climactic reconciliation with Columbine and the triumph of the forces of good. Within this broad framework the pantomime form was extremely flexible, combining elements of song, music, dialogue, dancing, knockabout physical comedy, and complicated scenic design.

The success of Joseph *Grimaldi as Clown had the effect of enhancing the importance of the harlequinade and the clown role with it. During the *Regency, the pantomime became a vehicle not only for Grimaldi's virtuoso comic skills but also for a sophisticated satire on the foibles of *fashion, urbanization, and *consumerism [19]. It could also be used as a commentary on the *poor laws and events such as the passing of the *Reform Bill and *Catholic emancipation, though the extent of that commentary was always constrained by the vigilance of censors such as George *Colman. The pantomime was a holiday entertainment, staged at Covent Garden and Drury Lane between Christmas and mid-February and at the minor theatres such as Sadler's Wells at Easter, Whitsun, and in the summer. It attracted audiences from all social classes, but was increasingly deprecated by polite opinion as a form of popular or low entertainment. Those who felt that the status of dramatic literature was under threat from the increasing emphasis on spectacle and the body often used pantomime as a focus for criticism and as a shorthand for cultural degeneration. Thus William *Hazlitt, discussing the theatre's inadequate measure of *Shakespeare's greatness, commented that it was only 'the *pantomime* part of tragedy . . . which is sure to tell, and tell completely on the stage'.

GR

PARK, Mungo (1771–1806), natural historian, traveller, explorer, and writer [see *exploration, 37]. Park was born near Selkirk, and educated locally and at Edinburgh University. Through the influence of Sir Joseph *Banks, he secured a medical appointment on an *East India Company vessel, visiting Sumatra in 1792–3, as well as a subsequent commission from the African Association to establish the course of the Niger. The latter quest amounted to a continental equivalent of that of the north-west passage: it was hoped that the river might be followed sufficiently far east towards the Nile as to open another route to the Mediterranean, and that a lucrative commerce might be opened up with African trading civilizations of the interior.

In late 1795 Park moved inland from the Gambia river, where he had already resided for five months, and acquired some proficiency in the Mandingo language. Unable to organize a full expedition party, he eventually departed accompanied only by two indigenous servants. He arrived at Sego on the Niger in July 1796; the fact that the river flowed east at this point pointed to the possibility of a link with the Nile, and hence fuelled interest in further exploration. His journey was astonishing for its difficulties. Seemingly never the master of circumstances around him, Park was robbed and held prisoner; fell ill and starved; and was frequently reliant upon the goodwill of individual Africans, who were for the most part hostile. The narrative Park wrote after his return to Britain in late 1797 is notable for its sentimentality, which can be seen to foreshadow and condition the emphases on suffering and empathy in *Evangelical *missionary writings which were to become popular in the nineteenth century.

NT

PARKINSON, James (1755–1824), apothecary, surgeon, radical, and medical writer. As a hard-hitting London Corresponding Society pamphleteer of the 1790s, then a major medical popularizer, reformer, diagnostician, and pioneering palaeontologist, Parkinson illustrates the range, talent, and complex continuities of the popular radical *Enlightenment [32] in the Romantic age.

Shoreditch, especially Hoxton, was Parkinson's cultural crucible; here he followed his father's footsteps as a surgeon-apothecary, imbibed liberal reforming principles of a Dissenting stamp, and learned a sympathy for the artisan poor amongst whom he practised all his life. His early publications showed a pronounced hostility to medical élitism and a fascination with *electricity. Influenced by American and French revolutionary ideas, he first joined the *Society for Constitutional Information, then in 1792 the LCS [see *corresponding societies], becoming an influential organizer, debater, songwriter, pamphleteer, and *satirist. Under the pseudonym 'Old Hubert' he produced a series of cheap works with radical publishers *Eaton, *Spence, and John Smith. These lampooned Edmund *Burke, defended LCS radicals against *spying and persecution, and advocated *Revolutions without Bloodshed, or Reformation Preferable to Revolt* (1794). Despite its practical moderation, this last brought him to the attention of the Privy Council, which in October 1794 also interrogated him over the 'Pop-gun' plot, an alleged attempt to assassinate George III with a dart-gun. Parkinson's testimony was trenchant and courageous, a pattern repeated when defending John *Thelwall at the *Treason Trials, and when attending sick political prisoners in Newgate and demanding improvement in their living conditions.

From the turn of the century he diverted his energies into social, and particularly medical, reforms. Utilizing the radical publisher H. D. Symonds, he produced numbers of influential tracts, books, broadsides, and other forms of *street literature aimed at disseminating rational medical information to the poor. These works castigated *quackery and mercenary doctors who shrouded their nostrums in secrecy. Against the commercialism and corruption of the free medical market, Parkinson asserted the ideal of the medical man as a rational prophet committed to disseminating Enlightenment knowledge and to reforming the health and social well-being of the public. As well as writing and practising medicine, he worked in Hoxton to promote *Sunday school education and practical employment assistance for the parish poor. In 1810–11 he campaigned to reform the laws governing private *madhouses after having himself been accused of improper practice.

Parkinson's depth of experience, broad education in the principles of *natural philosophy [34], and practised powers of exposition led him in 1817 to make a brilliantly original nosological description of the shaking palsy which came to be known as Parkinson's Disease. The same abilities produced a three-volume study of British palaeontology which Victorians hailed as a pioneering classic. With typical moderation Parkinson's work on *geology reconciled traditional and modern theory by positing a series of long-term catastrophic stages of creation, an idea which deeply impressed *Shelley amongst others. Towards the end of his life Parkinson became a founder of both the Chirurgical Society of London and the Royal Geological Society.

IMcC

PARLIAMENT AND PARTIES · 637

parliament and parties. Technically, there were three elements in parliament; the *monarch, and the two Houses, Lords and Commons. The Crown's formal powers of veto and creation of peers to overcome opposition were never exercised after the Hanoverian succession in 1714, though the latter prerogative was still recognized in 1832 when the threat of a creation broke *Tory opposition to the *Reform Bill. Like the power of dissolution, however, this prerogative was exercised only in the interest of the government of the day and at its behest, not by the monarch in his individual capacity.

This is not to suggest, however, that the monarch was by any means a political cipher; until 1832 he or she could wield decisive influence. In the eighteenth century, such influence rested partly on patronage and on the granting of titles and honours. Since all offices under the Crown, civil and military, as well as the higher and more desirable ecclesiastical appointments, and creations and promotions in the peerage, were a part of the monarch's patronage, the potential for influence was very great. But like the Crown's prerogative powers, there was a tendency for more and more of such patronage in fact to be exercised by the government. Yet, at least until the mental breakdown of George III in 1810, ministers could never be certain that patronage powers were really theirs.

By then, as far as the power to influence parliament was concerned, patronage was counting for less and less. The long and draining conflict with France made it necessary to squeeze as much waste as possible out of the budget. Military efficiency, as opposed to political dependability, became the basis for promotion of officers. Besides war, the *Evangelical revival further depleted the stocks of patronage. Political bishops became no more acceptable than political officers. The definition of corruption also became a good deal more exacting. With other forms of patronage shrinking to nothing, titles and honours became more important; but by the 1820s they had been utilized to such a degree that they were in danger of becoming cheapened to the point of uselessness.

Parliaments, however, did not appear to act much differently, even with the disappearance of what was once thought to have been the most important element in their management. The House of Lords had always been a reliable bastion of support for the King's ministers: in the 1820s it continued to be. The House of Commons was almost as reliable; usually only long persistence in disastrous policies, as in the case of Lord North's (1732–92) ministry of 1770–82, brought about the ousting of the King's government. Yet in 1830, contrary to all previous experience, the Duke of *Wellington's ministry did not win the general election. And almost as soon as parliament met, the Duke was forced from office by adverse votes in the House of Commons.

What had happened? The answer is that by the 1820s, in a momentous shift, ideology had come to take the place of interest. Two broad party groupings emerged, based on differences of principle. True, not all those who usually voted in one camp or the other would have admitted their adherence to party,

and there was little or no effective discipline. Still, parties based on principle were acknowledged; and as John Cam *Hobhouse named it in 1826, 'His Majesty's Opposition', which once would have been denounced as mere faction, became recognized as necessary and legitimate.

What had kept Lord *Liverpool's government in power from 1812 to 1827 was distrust of *Whiggism and its nostrums. A majority of members of parliament in both Houses did not want religious liberty, in the sense of the full admission to political rights, for Roman Catholics and Protestant Dissenters [see *toleration]. Neither did they want *parliamentary reform.

In the 1790s a majority of parliament, and of the nation, had rallied to the government of William *Pitt under banners that proclaimed that they wanted just the opposite: 'Church and King' and 'Friends of the existing establishment in Church and State'. In other words, while the Whigs wanted reform, the majority in parliament favoured the status quo. This was the majority that followed Pitt and his several successors; those who after the government dissolved in 1827 often referred to themselves as constituting 'the party of Lord Liverpool', and were referred to by others as the *Tories.

Yet the Tories were not a party as the Whigs were. For one thing a large, though diminishing, group would not have thought of themselves as a party at all, but as independent supporters of the King's government, whose inevitable head was Lord Liverpool. For another, though the Whigs suffered from divisions, they were united on the greatest domestic question of the first three decades of the nineteenth century, that of *Catholic emancipation. They could also refer their support to a unifying principle, the cause of 'Civil and Religious Liberty', though they also stressed emancipation's pragmatic urgency as the key to governing Ireland. The latter had been Pitt's position when he left the service of his royal and anti-emancipation master in 1801; but not after he returned as Prime Minister in 1804. His followers divided on the issue, some of them such as Liverpool becoming 'Protestant' Tories, opposing emancipation, and others such as George *Canning, 'Catholic' Tories, supporting it—but on pragmatic grounds alone, at least to begin with. The Tories could therefore only remain united so long as a Tory government, as such, took no stand on emancipation.

It was a situation that could not last. In the 1820s Daniel *O'Connell and his Catholic Association produced convincing evidence that, without emancipation, they would make Ireland ungovernable. Growing numbers of Liverpool's own followers took the 'Catholic' option. Early in 1827, when Liverpool was felled by a disabling stroke, his party dissolved. George IV appointed Canning Prime Minister; but most of the 'Protestant' Tories refused to serve with him, and he was forced to turn to the Whigs for support. Upon Canning's death in August, Lord Goderich (1782–1859) continued the coalition, but, unlike Liverpool and Canning, he could not handle George IV, and was forced from office by the King's machinations in January 1828.

George then turned to Wellington. The Duke tried to put 'the party of Lord Liverpool' back together again, but it fell apart early in May. The King, and almost everyone else, believed Wellington to be a pillar of 'Protestant' Toryism. But to George's dismay, and the blind fury of the 'Protestant' party, that proved not to be the case. Faced with the challenge of O'Connell's election for County Clare—either to concede emancipation or see Ireland dissolve into chaos—the Duke did what he had meant to do from the beginning of his ministry, and took the lead in carrying emancipation.

Several important results followed from the events of 1827–9. The Whigs and the former followers of Canning learned to work together; and, with Canning himself removed, the Canningites embraced the broader doctrine of religious liberty, and even parliamentary reform. Their leading members joined Lord Grey's (1764–1845) government, to work for both causes, in 1830. Shocked by the passage of emancipation into the belief that parliament must indeed be corrupt, even some of the 'Protestant' Tories, or ultras as they became known, also for a while became converts to reform. And it was the ultra hatred of Wellington that forced him from office, thus clearing the way for Grey and reform. But, shocked in their turn by the sweeping reform proposed by the Whigs, the ultras soon returned to the Tory fold. For forty years the Tories had been the King's government. Now Tory *election managers wrested from the King's ministers things the latter had always had—control of the election of Scottish and Irish representative peers, for example; and Tory majorities in the House of Lords temporarily threw out the *Reform Bill and mauled other legislation of the King's government. Opposition had made a party out of the Whigs. Now it made a party out of the Tories.

RWD

parliamentary reform. The reform of franchise and representation began to be discussed during the *Wilkite agitations after 1768, but did not gain wide support until the Economical Reform Movement of 1779–80.

The Economical Reform Movement focused mainly on the issue of expenditures that led to the supposed corruption of parliament: if one way to deal with corruption was to root it out, another was to make members of parliament (in this case, members of the House of Commons) less corruptible. Associations in support of economical and parliamentary reform were formed in several counties and in the metropolis. Members of the former aimed to secure more county members, already noted for their independence and resistance to corruption. The metropolitan bodies, particularly the *Society for Constitutional Information, had a more ambitious goal, including universal manhood suffrage and annually elected parliaments. In fact, their programme spelled out the aims that would later become the six foundational points of the Charter in the 1840s. Though the movement gained the support of perhaps a fourth of the existing electorate, the steam was effectively taken out of it by the *Gordon riots of

1780, which led to a sharp reaction against the campaign for parliamentary reform.

The next stage in parliamentary reform came with the formation of popular reform societies in the 1790s, such as the London Corresponding Society, founded in 1792 by Thomas *Hardy. Later in 1792, the future Earl Grey (1764–1845) formed his Society of the Friends of the People, which included the brilliant lawyer Thomas *Erskine. This society aimed to give the lead to, and thus moderate, lower-class organizations such as the LCS, but though *Whigs managed to temper the wind of prosecution, *Pitt's government successfully suppressed the reform campaign in the 1790s.

Thanks largely to Sir Francis *Burdett, parliamentary reform enjoyed a revival between 1809 and 1812. However, despite the indefatigable efforts of the veteran reformer, Major John *Cartwright, in founding the reforming Hampden Clubs during his lecture tours of 1811–12, the movement did not really swell until the end of the war. Between 1816 and 1820, under the impetus of economic recession and demobilization, reforming sentiments spread not only to skilled tradesmen in the older trades but to workers in newer industries centred in such mushrooming towns as Manchester. In 1819 workers constituted the majority of the protesters who turned out in their tens of thousands for a meeting in support of reforming the franchise, the length of parliamentary terms, and voting methods. This meeting was transformed into the *Peterloo massacre, after the magistrates of Lord *Liverpool's government used troops to disperse the crowd, resulting in a dozen deaths and numerous woundings.

Though shocked by these events, Liverpool's government had no sympathy with parliamentary reform and dared not repudiate the rudimentary local government. Lord Grey, though favourable to moderate reform at the right time, was hardly more comfortable with the threat of popular disorder. The popular disturbances surrounding *Queen Caroline whom the Whigs defended with varying degrees of distaste against a prosecution reluctantly pressed by the government, suggested to both parties that something needed to be done to curb the unrest.

Two kinds of response emerged. The *Tory liberal response, associated with such policies as a loosening of trade restrictions and penal reform, and carried out under the leadership of figures such as George *Canning and Robert *Peel, aimed to demonstrate that the existing system was capable of ruling wisely and justly without constitutional reform. The Whig response argued that constitutional reforms, designed to extend the franchise to new classes of people, were essential. In reawakening interest in such measures, young Whig members of the House of Commons, such as Lord John Russell and Lord Althorp, took the lead.

In the late 1820s a coalition of discontents prepared the way for the triumph of reform. Repeal of the Test Acts in 1828, removing political restrictions from Protestant Dissenters, released Dissenting energies for the cause of reform. Protestants angry at the passage of *Catholic emancipation the next year became convinced that parliament must be reformed. Both advocates and opponents of the *corn laws believed they might benefit, as did opponents of municipal as well as parliamentary corruption, and discontented working people. In 1830, with the resignation of the Duke of *Wellington's Tory government, Lord Grey stepped in to carry parliamentary reform.

Grey proceeded according to the best principles of Whiggism. He aimed to produce a respectable and independent middle-class electorate, and a sufficient redistribution of seats in the House of Commons to do away with irredeemably rotten boroughs, and to give new interests a clear voice in the legislature. He argued that only thus could aristocratic government regain the confidence of the people. The *Reform Act of 1832, which embodied these principles, was far from satisfying everybody, but it gave enough satisfaction to enough people to bring the desired stability. Even those who disliked it, such as working men, most of whom were excluded, never lost faith in the system's capability of further reforming itself.

RWD

PASQUIN, Anthony, see John *Williams.

pastoralism, in a general sense, denotes the representation of idealized rustic life in poetic, dramatic, or prose form. Its association with Arcadia, as the locale of ideal existence, began in classical literature; Virgil, for example, described the mountainous Peloponnesian region in these terms in the *Eclogues*. In Romantic writings, however, both pastoral and Arcadian references often had unspecified locations and could simply signal an imaginary paradise removed from the activities of *industrialization [14].

In its more specific sense, the pastoral has been claimed as an essentially urban product: a form of literature which relies on a sharp distinction between country life and city life, invariably written from the experience of the city, reflecting either nostalgically or hopefully on the moral superiority of the country. As such it is a relational concept, usually thought to begin in Britain with the Renaissance revival of the classical interest in pastoral themes, exemplified in texts such as *Spenser's *The Shepheardes Calender* (1579) and Sidney's *Arcadia* (1581). Pope's *Pastorals* (1709) illustrate the early-eighteenth-century interest in the form, but pastoralism is generally conceded to have declined in popularity as a kind of polite literature by the mid-decades, earning the scorn of Dr *Johnson, who thought it 'easy, vulgar, and therefore disgusting'. Nonetheless, James Thomson's version of the pastoral mode in his poem *The Seasons* (1726–30) remained immensely influential through the century and beyond. In the form of cheap editions it penetrated the households of rural labourers such as John *Clare.

The attempt to approach rural life from a more realistic perspective begun during the eighteenth century is sometimes said to augur the death of pastoralism in the Romantic age. The 'honest' work of *peasant poets or the nature verse of the Lake artists are not seen as pastoral because, it is argued, they lack insightful comparison with urban complexity or, as in *Wordsworth's poems, they are more interested in a Nature endowed with visionary power than in the social habitat of rural people. This view perhaps denies too much. The salience of the pastoral dynamic in our period—whether it is employed affirmatively, satirically, or antithetically—is evident in many forms. It is found in the moralizing *novels [31] of 'hearth and home', such as *Our Village* (1824) by Mary Russell Mitford (1786–1855); in the *Gothic polarity between urban and rural ways, in the *utopian [9] speculations about Antipodean lands, and in the complex anti-pastoralism of George *Crabbe.

KF

patriotism. A hybrid ideology traditionally compounded from myths of Protestant elect nationhood and immemorial English liberties, and from a set of beliefs about independence and civic virtue, patriotism was notoriously oppositional. In the early eighteenth century patriots inveighed against pensions, places, public debt, court dependence, corruption of parliaments, German mercenaries, and Hanoverian entanglements. The heightened national awareness of patriots—stunningly displayed in the xenophobic iconography of John Bull, Britannia, and 'Calais Gate or the Roast Beef of Old England'—was significantly deepened after 1750 by the revival of patriotic art and scholarship, the recovery of native literature and folk culture, and a rampant ideology of Saxonism. This last nostalgically extolled the virtues of an idealized democratic constitution under the Saxon 'people's king' Alfred, whose overthrow in 1066 with the Norman invasion was followed by a 'Norman Yoke' of absolutist monarchy and baronial aristocracy. Underpinning all this was a virulent Francophobia. To be a patriot was above all to be anti-French, and often anti-Scottish. What was striking was the way in which this now merged with the struggle against corruption, faction, and the loss of English liberty. Corrupt ministers were represented as hardened francophiles, sapping England's vital interests and destroying her native institutions.

However, as a result of the *American Revolution, the patriot programme began to lose its oppositional unity. Some, such as Thomas *Paine, increasingly identified true patriotism with *natural rights, whatever their provenance. Others supported the taxation and coercion of the American rebels, especially once the rebellion was supported and England threatened with invasion by the national Satan: absolutist, aristocratic, papist France. The process was repeated after 1789; the *French Revolution seemed to some radical patriots to embody the principles of national renewal they sought in England, while others rallied to the loyalist patriotism invoked by Edmund *Burke and William *Pitt in the war against the new Jacobin theology emanating from the old enemy. The Napoleonic period particularly saw a counter-revolution of political values in Britain—a partial appropriation of patriot ideology by a conservative ministry, and a radicalism now widely condemned as anti-patriotic.

But patriotism was too populist a brew for the political and religious establishment: even such seemingly uncomplicated icons as John Bull and Britannia carried a freight of malcontent and oppositional meanings. The eighteenth century marked the first period in which the English were forced to live with the effects of their imperial expansion: the Scots and Irish especially looked to a polity which was assimilative rather than fundamentalist or exclusive. Dissident patriotism also posed problems for an *Anglican Church whose practices were those of social and increasingly significantly regional exclusion, and for a *monarchy which aspired to be British but never could be wholly English. For the latter the dangerous associations and history of patriotism were supplanted by the altogether safer term *'loyalism'. AMacL

patronage. In relation to art, patronage has two meanings: the first refers to the private encouragement and support of the arts; the second concerns the granting of benefits or offices by a government or court. In both respects, British patronage was in a state of flux during this period, as industrial and political change led to new practices.

Art patronage had not been strong in England from the seventeenth century, when court circles encouraged primarily foreign artists and commissioned *portraiture above all other genres of art. Despite attempts by William Hogarth (1697–1764) to stimulate interest in contemporary art, the lack of an institutional base for artists hindered any progress until the foundation of the *Royal Academy in 1768 [see *viewing, 20]. The reluctance of the Hanoverian monarchs to extend patronage grew from their desire to distinguish themselves from the profligate Stuarts, and it was not until George III that the Crown showed an active interest in the arts. Church patronage was equally minimal, as the desire to avoid associations with the Catholic church prevented Anglicans from commissioning public religious works.

These tensions intensified in the 1780s and 1790s. James *Barry's *Inquiry into the Real and Imaginary Obstructions to the Acquisition of the Arts in England* (1775) made a strong argument for art patronage and attacked religious strictures against it. The entrepreneur John *Boydell invested a large part of his income in setting up a Shakespeare Gallery in 1786. His project provided major commissions for historical painting to many contemporary artists.

Barry's and Boydell's efforts to champion *history painting and to encourage patronage did not produce substantial results, as portraiture continued to be the principal means of livelihood for contemporary artists. In the nineteenth century, growing dissatisfaction with the Royal Academy's failure to promote patronage led to systematic attacks on that institution, the most vitriolic of which was by the engraver John Pye (1782–1874). Benjamin Robert *Haydon also condemned the Royal Academy, and in opposition to them launched solo exhibitions of his historical paintings as a lure for wealthy patrons. Although Haydon was ultimately unsuccessful,

some artists did continue to gain the attention of individual patrons. J. M. W. *Turner was encouraged by the third Earl of Egremont, and given his own studio at the Earl's home, Petworth. There were also provincial patrons in towns such as Norwich, who actively encouraged local art. In the early decades of the nineteenth century, wealthy industrialists formed a new breed of patron, but they favoured landscapes and genre scenes, rather than the elaborate historical subjects advocated by Barry and Haydon. SW

PEACOCK, Thomas Love (1785–1866), poet, *satirical novelist. As a poet, Peacock shared in the revisionary *Hellenism of the 1810s and 1820s; as satirical novelist, he stood good-naturedly opposed to a manifold of contemporary follies, 'progressive' as well as reactionary, writing in the Menippean tradition against the presumption of authority and knowledge.

Peacock's status as an eccentric—a classicist and satirist in a 'Romantic' period—is best used to explain his work, not explain it away, especially now that the commentary of literary historians like Mikhail Bahktin has recovered and theorized the classical genre of Menippean satire.

In *Headlong Hall* (1816), *Melincourt* (1817), *Nightmare Abbey* (1818), *Crotchet Castle* (1831), and *Gryll Grange* (1860)—his satirical *novels [31] and *romances—representatives of contemporary society, especially of its intelligentsia, meet in secluded retreats to begin a pattern of feasting, debate, and courtship. A succession of symposia, punctuated by brief and stylized comic action, allows for the play of the obsessive ideas or 'humours' figured by the various characters, with the emphasis on play: on linguistic play—neologisms and macaronics, pedantry, preciosity, and vulgarity, catalogues and cant; and on formal play—narrative, epistles, poems and songs, dialogues and lectures, prefatory inscriptions, and extensive footnotes. All voices are permitted utterance in the festive atmosphere. More significantly perhaps, the courting, with which the symposia alternate, moves towards a final marriage in which all participate.

Peacock characterized the serio-comic tradition in an essay on 'French Comic Romances' as one in which 'characters are abstractions or embodied classifications, and the implied or embodied opinions form the main matter of the work'. It is the tradition of Aristophanes, Petronius Arbiter, Rabelais, Swift, and Voltaire. To disembody those abstractions and opinions, however, by reading the satires only in terms of contemporary ideas and ideologies, or to identify them too exclusively with their 'originals', would be to disavow their formal heterogeneity and to fly in the face of that tradition. Impatient with the aggressive, partisan politics of the age, Peacock's works betray no strong political attitude.

Indeed, the assumption implicit in their heterogeneity, cynic if not cynical, is that there is no one way of perceiving or understanding the world; that ideas are pathological or 'humorous' and competition for the 'truth' absurd. But while the laughter derides and negates, it also celebrates and renews; the spirit of sociability and affirmation pervades, making the 'comic' vision of the ritual marriages in the novels less perfunctory than archetypal.

Peacock's reputation has suffered from his friend-ship with Percy *Shelley, rather as his tongue-in-cheek essay on 'The Four Ages of Poetry' (1820) is best known for having precipitated Shelley's now classic *Defence of Poetry* (1821). That the essay's iconoclastic wit should have robbed it of its interest as an early, often acute example of an historical ma-terialist theory of poetic production makes its fate in Romantic scholarship typical of Peacock's works generally. As so often, the comic has been read as frivolous, the frivolous as irrelevant. Peacock only stands to gain from a developing understanding of, and taste for, the comic—a mode, as Peacock himself suggests in *Nightmare Abbey*, vulnerable to a 'Romantic' self-consciousness devoid of self-irony.

WC

peasant poets. Under the influence of ideas about original *genius, the image of the peasant poet was a pervasive part of literary culture and the standard means for representing acceptable working-class literature. Poets such as Robert *Burns and John *Clare were encouraged by patrons keen to unearth authentic native genius, a process which may have had its origins in a nostalgia for vanishing rural cus-toms exploited by such educated poets as William *Wordsworth.

The role of patrons in this process was often exerted less by direct financial assistance than by gathering subscriptions or puffing the book in the right circles. In 1831 Robert *Southey was instru-mental in the publication of *Attempts in Verse, by John Jones, an Old Servant*, prefacing the volume with an essay on 'our Uneducated Poets', accom-panied by selections from their verse. The working-class writers who sent their products to literary men such as Southey, and who inundated the periodicals and *newspapers, often took the idea of the republic of letters at face value, assuming their right to partic-ipate in both its sociability and literary outlets on equal terms with well-to-do and well-connected literati. Indeed, some plebeian writers followed Burns, who somewhat disingenuously contrasted 'prostituted learning' with his own 'honest rusticity'. Of course, a great deal of working-class poetry had nothing at all to do with the representation of quotid-ian rustic experience. Religious poetry, for instance, flooded into periodicals such as the *Evangelical Review*, and Samuel Bamford (1788–1872), the weaver's boy, and Ebenezer Elliott (1781–1849), the *corn law rhymer, were just two among many who broached social and political issues in their verse.

Nevertheless both Bamford and Elliott took advantage of the image of the native genius which was the primary interest of the literati. Peasant poets were valued above all for the authenticity of their render-ing of rural life, and pretensions beyond that orbit were frequently discouraged by patrons. Southey complained that such poets too frequently ended up conforming to approved models after having begun writing 'expressing their own thoughts and feelings in their own language'. Hannah *More was rather more explicit in discouraging peasant poets from dreams of professionalism when she stressed that her patronage was not intended to distract Ann *Years-ley, the Bristol milkwoman, from her proper station.

Lower-class poets from a range of backgrounds were appropriated to the image of the peasant poet. Perhaps Robert Burns is the best-known example, but even the urban artisan William *Blake could be regarded by some as 'A Native poet' who 'sings his wood notes'. The poets themselves were often com-plicit in this process, realizing that there was much to be gained by styling themselves peasants. James *Hogg took the pose to the level of self-caricature, but perhaps the most successful was Robert Bloom-field (1766–1823), the so-called 'Farmer's Boy' who managed to bypass the process of subscription patronage and turn directly to the literary market-place. *The Farmer's Boy* (1800), Bloomfield's first volume of poetry, sold 40,000 copies, sales secured after two years of effort and the help of a patron who obtained him a publisher and woodcuts from Thomas *Bewick. Bloomfield was actually a shoe-maker when the volume was published, the poems celebrating a brief period twenty years earlier when he had worked as a farm labourer. Bloomfield can-nily used the profits from the work to set up his own shop, continuing in the trade to the end of his life. But, despite his early success, he died in the poverty which was the end expected by the 'myth' of the peasant poet.

JM

PEEL, Sir Robert (1788–1850), statesman. An MP from 1809 (Cashel 1809–17; Oxford University 1817–29; Westbury 1829; Tamworth 1830–3), Peel served as Irish Secretary (1812–18) and Home Secre-tary (1821–7, 1828–30) before leading a brief minority *Tory government in 1834. He was again Prime Min-ister from 1841 to 1846. This administration came to grief as a result of Peel's determination to repeal the *corn laws, but it was destroyed formally by an adverse vote on Irish policy.

Peel's ministerial career was closely connected to the development of *liberal Toryism in early-nineteenth-century British politics. Attracted to *laissez-faire* ideas, Peel exercised caution in apply-ing them. For example, in the 1840s he was prepared to use funds from central government to relieve chronic distress in Scotland and Ireland by promot-ing or reviving economic activity. The governments with which he was associated exhibited a determina-tion to abandon tariff barriers and other uses of state power which served and protected special interests; they also pursued extensive programmes of adminis-trative *parliamentary reform. As Home Secretary, Peel was identified with the establishment of a regu-lar *police force in London to replace the haphazard arrangements inherited from the past and the secret and irregular systems of informers and *spies favoured by recent governments [see *policing, 7].

Peel enjoyed an exalted posthumous reputation, but his contemporary standing was complex and paradoxical. His promotion of economic *liberalism (traceable to the Christian doctrine of atonement, rather than to any *utilitarian or even materialistic concerns) was accompanied by a deep attachment to the traditional constitution, Church, Crown, and aristocracy. Following the *Reform Act of 1832 Peel attempted to preserve and rejuvenate these institutions by an appeal to the newly enfranchised middle classes. The *Tamworth Manifesto* of 1834, outlining his past and future commitment to gradualism, was a landmark in the process by which the Tory party of the eighteenth and early nineteenth century was transformed into the Conservative party. Whilst the party developed a sophisticated and effective organizational structure under his leadership, Peel was hostile to party government. Adhering to an increasingly outmoded conception of ministerial responsibility towards the Crown, Peel believed it was the purpose of parties to support governments, not *vice versa*. The depth of his attachment to a statesmanlike ideal of good government was attested by his determination to repeal the corn laws at the cost of the unity of his party. Following his resignation in 1846 Peel vowed that he would 'take care . . . not again to burn my fingers by organising a party'.

While Daniel *O'Connell's quip that Peel had a smile 'like the silver plate on a coffin' represented a common judgement on his haughtiness and lack of personal warmth, he enjoyed emotionally close relationships with many of his ministerial colleagues. Execrated by large sections of the landed classes for 'betraying' their interests in 1845–6, his conduct won him the admiration and gratitude of many working-class radicals and spurred Thomas *Carlyle to cast him in the mould of a heroic statesman. Peel's noted collection of Dutch paintings provided the foundation of the Dutch holdings of the *National Gallery.

JMO

Peninsular War, 1807–14. The Spanish and Portuguese Peninsula was the setting for Britain's main land-based participation in the *war [2] against France. Termed by *Napoleon 'the Spanish ulcer', the Peninsular War sapped French resources and morale, playing a major part in the ultimate defeat of France.

The French *invasions of the Iberian Peninsula in late 1807 and 1808, and Napoleon's 'election' of his brother Joseph to the throne of Spain, was met with insurrections that began in May 1808 and led to six years of savage guerrilla warfare. British forces supported the Spanish. Sir John Moore's victory at Corunna (1809) and the Duke of *Wellington's victories at Vimiero (1808), Oporto, Talavera (1809), Salamanca (1812), and Vittoria (1813) were widely celebrated in Britain, often in the form of popular and patriotic poems such as Charles Wolfe's (1791–1823) 'The Burial of Sir John Moore at Corunna' (1817).

The events in the Peninsula prompted important shifts in the British conception of the war. A small number of radicals saw Napoleon's invasion positively, as an act of potential liberation of the Spanish from the tyranny of despotic monarchy and the Inquisition. The majority, however, were united in their condemnation of it. Many who had previously been supporters of Napoleon, such as Whitbread and Lord Holland, saw him for the first time as the aggressor. Support for the war was also strengthened by the representation of the Spanish cause as one driven by nationalism; Napoleon was now seen to be fighting against a 'People' rather than against the armies of the monarchs of the old regime. The defeat of Napoleon's forces at Baylen in 1808 marked the end of the popular myth of his invincibility which had grown out of his spectacular victories over the years such as Austerlitz (1805) and Jena (1806). Henceforth, the Spanish cause was used in Britain as a symbol of Napoleon's imminent defeat, often in prophetic and apocalyptic terms, as in James *Gillray's caricature 'The Valley of the Shadow of Death' (1808), in which Napoleon is confronted by Spain represented as Death astride a mule of 'True Royal Spanish-Breed'.

The general outcry in Britain over the Convention of Cintra of 1808, by which the French Marshal Junot was allowed to evacuate his defeated army from Portugal in British ships, illustrates the strength of feeling for the Spanish cause. The Convention was seen as an act of betrayal of the Spanish and public demand led to the British generals Dalrymple, Burrard, and Wellington being forced to face a court of inquiry which exonerated only Wellington.

William *Wordsworth's Miltonic tract on the Convention, published in 1809, and S. T. *Coleridge's articles on the Peninsular War for the *Courier* (1809–10) exemplify the increasingly polarized and elevated vision of the struggle against France as one of liberty against tyranny, good against evil, light against darkness. The war also became the subject of a number of long narrative poems such as *Scott's *The Vision of Don Roderick* (1811), *Landor's *Count Julian* (1812), and *Southey's *Roderick: The Last of the Goths* (1814). *Byron, who visited the Peninsula in 1809, provided the most famous poetic account of the war in the first Canto of *Childe Harold's Pilgrimage* (1812). SB

PENNANT, Thomas (1726–98), prominent naturalist, traveller, and prolific writer. Born at Downing in Flintshire, Wales, he made a series of tours in Wales, Ireland, Scotland, and the English counties. These became the basis of descriptive works in natural history in the broadest sense, including topography, *antiquarianism [35], *architecture [28], and economics. His generally impersonal and precise writing style no doubt recommended him to *Johnson, who found him to observe 'more things than anyone else does'. On the basis of his tours Pennant published *A Tour in Scotland* (1771), *A Tour in Wales* (1778–81), *London* (1790), and many similar works.

A friend of Joseph *Banks and Gilbert White (1720–93), Pennant had some contact with both Linnaeus and Buffon, and became a Fellow of the Royal Society in 1767. Though primarily concerned with the natural history of his own country, he was also interested in the zoology of more remote regions, and at times associated with Linnaean travellers such as Johann Reinhold *Forster. Pennant was important for developing Buffon's emphasis on animal behaviour, and for advocating a shift towards empirical art, part of a trend towards a naturalistic, scientific aesthetic. This was most conspicuously expressed in illustrations to works of *natural philosophy [34] such as his *British Zoology* (1766), *Synopsis of Quadrupeds* (1771; later *History of Quadrupeds*, 1781), *Indian Zoology* (1781), and many others.   NT

PERCY, Thomas, born Piercy (1719–1811), divine and antiquarian, whose *Reliques of Ancient English Poetry* (1765) was one of the most important antiquarian publications of the eighteenth century, influential on the Romantic revival of the *ballad [see *antiquarianism, 35]. Born into a family of Shropshire grocers and educated at Oxford, Percy claimed to be related to the noble Percy family of Northumberland, to whom he dedicated the *Reliques*. He was made tutor to the Percys' youngest son and subsequently rewarded with the bishopric of Dromore. The *Reliques* was widely read on publication and later appreciated by poets of the next generation such as *Coleridge, *Scott, and *Wordsworth.

However, it was Percy's own poetic pretensions which made his scholarship suspect to antiquarians, and especially to Joseph *Ritson, who waged a twenty-year war against him. Percy was apologetic about the roughness of the material presented in the *Reliques* and, at the end of each of the three volumes, added his own compositions as examples of ballads more suitable to modern tastes. Ritson voiced severe doubts about the authenticity of the original manuscript, which Percy claimed to have in his personal possession. He suggested that Percy had modified the supposedly authentic material. When the manuscript was published in 1867–8, Ritson's accusations were largely substantiated.

Nonetheless Percy's intellectual and antiquarian interests were broadly based. He published in 1761 (from a Portuguese version) the first English translation of a Chinese novel. Under the title of *Northern Antiquities* (1770), he later translated the Frenchman P. H. Mallet's collection of Norse poetry which was to have a deep influence on scholarship and *poetry [29] alike.   JM

Peterloo. The dispersal of an estimated 60,000 men and women on St Peter's Field in Manchester on 16 August 1819 as they met to call for a reform of parliament is universally regarded as a central event of modern British history. More than ten people were killed and several hundred were injured when the local magistrates ordered the Manchester yeomanry cavalry to arrest Henry *Hunt, the chief radical orator.

These events rapidly earnt the label 'Peterloo', in a deeply ironic reference to the victory over the French at *Waterloo four years before, which the government had represented as the defeat of French authoritarianism by Britain's free institutions. Four years later, radicals used the 'Peterloo massacre' to deny that British freedoms were safe in the hands of Lord *Liverpool's Tory government.

For radicals, Peterloo marked the culmination of a

battle with the government to secure fundamental reform in the franchise, the length of parliamentary terms, and voting methods. It proved the intransigence of the ruling élite in the face of sustained public pressure and produced a shift in the balance of political forces. Though not enough to topple the government in the short term, it changed the minds of several key *Whig politicians, such as Lord John *Russell and Earl Grey (1764–1845), who became key figures in the passing of the *Reform Act of 1832.
JF

petitions. Petitioning, both directly to the King or channelled through parliament, was already a widely established practice at the beginning of our period. Petitions embraced a vast range of concerns, from the local and particular to the national and even international. The *abolitionist petitioning movement at the end of the eighteenth century, which appealed mainly to the middle classes and aimed to end the slave trade, attracted signatures on a scale that was scarcely equalled even by the later, better-known petitioning movement of *Chartism.

Because the House of Commons refused any calls for radical reform of the representative system during our period, petitioning also gradually became a more working-class phenomenon as well, incorporating artisans, industrial operatives, labourers, and other middling sorts; all hoped to persuade or intimidate an unsympathetic parliament by marshalling countrywide support for their cause. Since many petitions 'lay on the table' in the Commons, however, it is difficult to gauge the influence they may have had on MPs. After 1815 a demobilized citizenry, told by their government throughout the *wars [2] that they had fought for liberty against French despotism, arrived home ripe for persuasion to the reform cause. Petitioning provided a very important means for their voices to be heard in parliament. During the campaign for *Catholic emancipation in 1829, and the agitations surrounding the passing of the *Reform Act of 1832, mass petitioning reached its zenith. Thousands were received both for and against each issue.

After 1832, as the more even distribution of representation helped to channel popular views, there was a sense in which petitions were a less effective tool of influence or even a rough guide of public opinion. A strengthened state could also afford to ignore any threat implied by large numbers of signatures. The massive Chartist petitions were dismissed as full of bogus signatures and therefore unrepresentative. The gradual development of party politics generated its own forms and strategies of influence, and the petition was increasingly relegated to smaller, more localized attempts to publicize specific issues.   JF

philanthropy, or the practice of voluntary charity to the poor, was extensive in our period. By 1796, over £6,000,000 was distributed annually as charity in England and Wales, a sum substantially greater than parish relief. The gap between charity and public relief was even wider in Scotland, where public relief was more restricted.

Acts of individual benevolence and contributions to organized charities were promoted as a Christian duty made necessary by social inequality. Few endorsed indiscriminate giving, although John *Wesley was a notable practitioner. Instead, clerics and philanthropists urged donors to ensure that charity's effects were beneficial to the recipient and to society in general. Both men and women had specific duties. Women's charity was a traditional element of household economy; for aristocratic women, personal charity was an obligation on property and an expression of their families' status and power. Late-eighteenth-century fears of institutional mismanagement encouraged a revival of personal charity to be disbursed only after investigation of the individual's needs.

Organized philanthropy overlapped with parish assistance, and always claimed to advance public interest and order. Thus in the 1810s various mendicity societies pioneered the systematic investigation of beggars, a group already covered by the vagrancy laws. *Evangelicals established moral reform as the prerequisite of social improvement. Legal status, not objectives, distinguished charitable from statutory activity.

Parliamentary interest in *poor law administration and in the statistical representation of *poverty [12] generated surveys of the country's charitable resources (the Gilbert Returns of 1786–8; the work of the Brougham Commissioners in the 1820s and 1830s) and legislation to protect charity funds.   SL

phrenology. The science of phrenology identified the human brain as a collection of organs, each the site of a specific quality, or 'faculty', of emotion or intellect. Phrenology held the contours of the outer surface of the skull to be an accurate indicator of the relative size of each organ, and thus of the strength of the corresponding mental 'faculty' in the operation of the mind. This mapping of head shape to disclose the strengths and weaknesses of personality earned phrenologists the scorn of contemporary critics as 'head-readers' and 'bumpologists'.

Phrenology was pioneered by Austrian anatomist and physician Franz Joseph Gall (1758–1828). Gall evolved his schema of cerebral localization more through correlating observed behaviour with head shape than by detailed clinical investigation. Critics seized upon this fact, arguing that phrenology was a pseudo-science. British interest in phrenology was aroused by Johann Caspar Spurzheim (1776–1832), Galls's student and collaborator, who undertook the first of several British lecture tours in 1813–14. However, the most influential British phrenologist was George Combe (1788–1858), a Scots notary and founder of the Edinburgh Phrenological Society (1820).

Phrenology initially gained converts amongst aspiring young medical and other professionals from non-establishment backgrounds [see *medicine, 18]. By the early 1820s the science had founded powerful critiques of various institutions in pre-reform Britain which favoured social rank over natural ability. Phrenology also gained a wide middle-class following during the 1820s and 1830s as an ingeniously simple means of achieving orderly social and moral progress in the emerging world of industrial capitalism. George Combe's *Constitution of Man* (1828) was probably the most popular non-fiction work in English in the middle third of the nineteenth century.

Constitution illustrates well how phrenology offered its adherents greater meaning and emotional satisfaction than established religion. It presented a cosmogony in which a rational creator revealed to humanity the means of improvement through knowing the strengths and weaknesses of cerebral inheritance. Familial duty, sobriety, and work discipline were all represented as means by which the individual could maximize psychic potential. More importantly, it rationalized *poverty [12], crime, and sickness within the emerging social order as resulting from individual refusal to acknowledge 'laws . . . plainly written in Nature for the direction of man'. Early critics condemned phrenology as thinly veiled materialism, although by the 1830s the science was in effect a secularized puritanism which many took to have refined the essential truths of Christianity.

As middle-class phrenological societies declined in the early 1840s, the science found a growing audience amongst urban artisans and skilled workers, many of whom by the 1840s had come to see themselves as constrained by an increasingly rigid and exploitative social order. During the latter half of the nineteenth century phrenology came to be incorporated into various proletarian institutions [see *fringe medicine].

Articulated within the context of new institutions resulting from the increasingly specialized intellectual needs of entrepreneurs and professionals, phrenology was extremely influential within the social sciences until the last decades of the nineteenth century.   PT

physicians. Until the Medical Act of 1858, physicians claimed superior status in the traditional tripartite division of their profession. Unlike the surgeons and apothecaries, who trained by apprenticeship, physicians received a liberal education and a university degree, being regarded as the gentlemen of the medical profession. According to critics, their education, with its emphasis on classical and theoretical learning, did not adequately prepare them for general practice, where practical skills and a broad knowledge of common diseases were required. Physicians generally practised among the wealthier parts of the population, but with the advent of the hospital and charitable movements in the late eighteenth century, their clientele was broadened as well as the practical basis of their medical knowledge.

By a royal charter in the early sixteenth century, the London College of Physicians was granted a monopoly on their class of practice in the metropolis and its precincts. College Fellows, who were exclusively graduates of Cambridge and Oxford, and licentiates were thus legally permitted to practise and oversee all branches of *medicine [18]. Custom, however, decreed that they restrict their practice to internal medicine, which included diagnosis, prognosis, and prescription. Ideally the physician did not practise medicine as a manual art, like the surgeon, or as a trade, like the apothecary. In reality this demarcation was honoured only in the cities and larger towns; provincial physicians were, by necessity, often general practitioners.

At the end of the eighteenth century, medical practice in Britain was dominated by graduates of Scottish universities, whose practical training and scientific education was generally superior to that of the Cambridge- and Oxford-educated physicians. Excluded from fellowship of the prestigious London College, the Scots and the rising surgeons and apothecaries clamoured for those reforms which, in 1858, helped to establish a more egalitarian and less divided profession.

Physicians viewed themselves as priests of the body and guardians of public health. As private clinicians their task was to recognize disability, reduce anxiety, and relieve suffering. As public men they designed, created, and staffed the new charity hospitals, and advised local authorities on the latest developments in ventilation, sewerage, and water systems for institutions. Physicians were also expected to pronounce upon the role of climate in the spread of disease. They held key positions in the armed forces, and increasingly they took responsibility for the management of the insane and mentally ill [see *madness]. From early in the nineteenth century, physicians also contributed to the shaping of forensic medicine.

Although the therapeutic arsenal of physicians was limited, and although folk wisdom retained a significant role in the treatment of disease, science played an increasingly important role in the practice of medicine. Edward Jenner's *vaccine for smallpox, James Lind's work on the prevention of scurvy, William Withering's digitalis, and William Heberden and John Fothergill's work on angina pectoris and its relation to heart disease were among the significant steps in the development of modern scientific medicine.

Physicians were also notable contributors to cultural life and often saw medicine in a wider philosophical, literary, and social perspective. In the earlier *Enlightenment [32] period, physicians such as John *Locke, Bernard Mandeville (?1670–1733), Bishop Berkeley (1685–1753), Oliver Goldsmith (?1730–74), and David Hartley (1705–57) were prominent members of the republic of letters; towards the end of the century, Erasmus *Darwin, William Hunter (1718–83), James *Hutton, John *Aikin, and Peter Mark Roget (1779–1869) were among the most influential literary physicians. LH

pianists. In 1776, the piano was still comparatively new, undeveloped mechanically, and under-exploited. By 1832, not only had the modern grand developed in most of its essentials, but virtuosi of the highest calibre were visiting Britain—fêted everywhere and central to public concert life. London played a major role in the technological and musical development of the piano, an instrument capable of the most brilliant execution and the most poetic expression. Piano-playing and composition were the city's most distinctive musical contribution [see London *keyboards].

London's first important pianist was J. C. *Bach, whose sonatas Op. 5 (1766) transformed the old harpsichord idiom through expressive variety of tone, singing melodies, and contrasts of orchestral origin. He played one such sonata in 1768 on a small square piano by Zumpe, Bach's first documented performance on the piano. The grand piano was developed soon after this, enabling Bach to pit soloist against orchestra in large-scale concertos [see *concerts and music societies].

Bach was succeeded in the 1780s by the brilliant young Muzio *Clementi, whose Op. 2 sonatas, especially the famous 'octave lesson', were regarded as virtually unplayable. More importantly, Clementi went on to develop a richly expressive pianistic idiom, exploiting the tonal characteristics of the weighty English piano—its resonance and full-bodied cantabile, its capacity for thick chords and extremes of volume. Although Clementi himself retired from the concert platform in 1790, he had laid the foundations for the 'London Pianoforte School', including *Dussek, *Cramer, and Steibelt, as well as the promising but short-lived George Frederick Pinto and, briefly, John Field (1782–1837). *Haydn, too, wrote several piano sonatas and trios in which the English influence is evident.

Here was a distinctive brand of pre-Romantic pianism that was highly influential on *Beethoven and Schubert, with its fluid textures and dramatic contrasts, its harmonic experiment and formal freedom. Even within the traditional sonata and concerto, descriptive works such as Clementi's *Didone abandonnata* (c.1805) looked to the future, as did Dussek's more populist *Naval Battle and Total Defeat of the Grand Dutch Fleet* (1797). Later, in St Petersburg, Field went on to create the poetic nocturne, one of Chopin's most evocative genres.

After 1800 only Cramer continued active in Britain, and his concerns gradually appeared old-fashioned. Instead, London attracted a new generation of pianists from abroad—Wölfl, *Ries, Kalkbrenner, *Moscheles, Hummel, *Mendelssohn, and the young Liszt—as British pianists such as Cipriani *Potter and Lucy Anderson attempted to keep pace. As well as a more Romantic bravura and passionate freedom of expression, these pianists imported new levels of virtuosity. The sonata was marginalized, as pianists introduced brilliant showpieces based on anything from English ballads to Rossini arias. Thus Moscheles might follow a concerto with his *Fantasy on Airs of the Scottish Bards* (1828) and later improvise on a popular melody from the audience. In response, the high-minded Philharmonic Society initially banned solos. Mozart and Beethoven concertos were re-admitted, and those of Mendelssohn could scarcely be refused for lack of artistic stature. Yet even as the restriction was lifted, there remained a resistance to what was perceived as virtuoso display for its own sake.

The piano was also the instrument of the conductor, though the *violinist remained the leader of the orchestra. Haydn conducted from the piano, and the tradition persisted into the 1830s, by which time baton conducting was well established on the Continent. The most famous pianist-conductor was Sir George Smart (1776–1867), whose dominance owed a great deal to his administrative abilities, although he did go to the trouble of consulting Beethoven about the speeds of the Ninth Symphony.   SMcV

picturesque, an eighteenth-century theory of landscape which had particular application in the fields of bucolic literature, *pastoral poetry, *landscape painting, and *landscape gardening [see **literary theory,** 41].

Situated midway, aesthetically and chronologically, between the historicizing landscapes of the seventeenth century and the later *sublime landscapes of the Romantic period, the picturesque is an aesthetic category with distinctive characteristics. Principal among these is the idea of variety in landscape, revealed through an interest in irregularity, ruggedness, rusticity, intricacy, singularity, and chiaroscuro. These are the qualities which the leading theorist of the visual picturesque, the

90 (*top*) and **91.** *Scene without Picturesque Adornment* and *Scene with Picturesque Adornment*, illustrations by William Gilpin in his *Three Essays* (1792).

Revd William *Gilpin, identified in his *Three Essays* (1792) as stimulating to the imagination, to reverie, or admiration.

However, Gilpin did not assume that such qualities occurred naturally. They needed to be combined by the artist into a pleasing composition. For the landscape was not in itself picturesque; rather, it contained picturesque potential. Thus whilst the qualities of the picturesque are in opposition to the ordered compositions of the historical landscape, the artist in search of the picturesque needed a receptive eye and a willing imagination.

One technical aid to the discovery of the picturesque was found in the Claude glass, a tinted convex mirror which was designed to render the scene like a picture. The device, so called because it imitated the compositional and tonal dispositions favoured by the seventeenth-century landscapist Claude Lorrain (1600–82), was used by both artists and tourists. Gilpin lauded its ability to transform nature into 'the brilliant landscapes of a dream'.

Landscape gardening was another way to improve nature on picturesque principles. By the later eighteenth century the English park was strewn with picturesque ruins in the *Gothic style complemented by cataracts of water and outcrops of rocks.

Uvedale *Price's *Essay on the Picturesque* (vol. I, 1794, vols. I–II, 1796–8) argued that the fashion for historicizing landscapes (here characterized as a continental import) had failed to acknowledge the inherent qualities of the English landscape. This celebration of nature after landscape's colonization by the followers of Claude Lorrain opened the way for the Romantic landscape to play on the emotions, and not, as hitherto, on reason.

Illustrations of the picturesque, such as those that adorn Richard Payne *Knight's poem, *The Landscape* (1794), show, in the manner of A. W. N. *Pugin's *Contrasts* (1836), the advantages of the 'native' style over continental imports. The Claudian parks of Lancelot 'Capability' *Brown give way to wilderness, and classicizing neo-Palladian mansions to Tudor Gothic piles. Thus the picturesque established local styles shorn of the classicizing ideals of continental theories of beauty. It inaugurated a native aesthetic leading to a celebration of the English countryside in the paintings of J. M. W. *Turner and John *Constable.　　　　PD

PIGOTT, Charles (d. 1794), radical writer. Brother of French Jacobin émigré Robert (1736–94) and uncle of the writer Harriet Pigott (1766–1846), Charles Pigott was an old Etonian who, after Cambridge, led a dissipated life in aristocratic *Whig circles which eventually resulted in imprisonment for debt. Pigott exploited his Whig connections, possibly using blackmail, by printing in *The Jockey Club* (1792) scurrilous biographies of the aristocrats who had been his friends. The pamphlet caused a sensation and quickly went into several editions. Other works in similar vein followed, including *The Female Jockey Club* (1794), *The Minor Jockey Club* (1794), and *The Whig Club* (1794).

Pigott's pamphleteering was politically as well as commercially motivated: he was a committed *republican who believed that 'a revolution in government, can alone bring about a revolution in morals', and was a member of the same division of the London Corresponding Society as Daniel Isaac *Eaton and John *Thelwall. The Prince of Wales, whose circle fared particularly badly in *The Jockey Club*, urged the government to prosecute the pamphlet 'as a libel upon the King, ourself and the constitution'. Within a fortnight prosecutions were under way against the publishers James Ridgway (*fl.* 1782–1838) and H. D. Symonds (d. 1816).

In September of 1793 Pigott considered fleeing to Switzerland with Robert *Merry on the advice of Samuel *Rogers, but the pair turned back at Harwich. At the end of that month Pigott was arrested for uttering seditious words after an incident in a London *coffeehouse with fellow LCS member Dr William Hodgson (1745–1851). Hodgson received two years for calling George III 'a German hog-butcher', while Pigott was held in prison for over a month before the charge against him was thrown out by the grand jury. His defence was published as *Persecution* (1793). He died in June of the following year, having been thrown in gaol once more. His *Political Dictionary* was published posthumously in 1795, becoming another radical classic, widely reprinted and anthologized. However, the scurrility of Pigott's often extremely amusing publications has ensured that he has never been regarded as a martyr in the history of radicalism.　　JM

PINDAR, Peter, see John *Wolcott.

pious perjury, the term applied by Sir William *Blackstone to the deliberate undervaluing of stolen goods by juries in criminal trials, thereby allowing relatively minor offences to be treated as noncapital.　　　　DL

PIOZZI, Hester Lynch Thrale (1741–1821), miscellaneous writer. Born Hester Lynch Salusbury of Welsh gentry stock, she wrote prolifically in her teenage years, publishing pseudonymously in various newspapers. In 1763 she married the brewer Henry Thrale, apparently against her inclinations. It proved an unsatisfactory partnership, plagued by his infidelities and financial crises, and by the death of seven of their eleven children. In 1764 the Thrales met Samuel *Johnson, who immediately became a close friend, staying with the family in their Streatham home for several months the following year. Mrs Thrale shared a special intimacy with Johnson through their literary interests, and they appear to have edited and translated works together. During this period, as Mrs Thrale, she also made the acquaintance of many *bluestockings. She patronized the young Frances *Burney, and greatly admired the achievements of Sarah *Siddons and Elizabeth *Carter.

Henry Thrale died in 1781, freeing his wealthy widow to develop her love for Italian musician Gabriel Piozzi, whom she had met the previous year. The association was strongly censured by her daughters and friends, particularly Johnson, who accused her of forfeiting her children, religion, fame, and country. Chief objections to Piozzi included his inferior social status, foreign birth, and Catholic faith—although in Johnson's case the Italian may have simply represented the bleakness of life without Hester's company. Mrs Thrale defiantly married Piozzi in 1784 and spent the next three years with him in Italy, where she contributed to the *Florence Miscellany* [see *Della Cruscanism]. She used her Italian experiences to produce a work of *travel literature, *Observations and Reflections* (1789).

Her most controversial work is *Anecdotes of the Late Samuel Johnson* (1786), published two years after her friend's death. This was followed by an edition of Johnson's letters in 1788, some indifferently received miscellanies in the 1790s, and her ambitious history of the world, *Retrospection* (1801). After Piozzi died in 1809, Hester moved to Bath. Upon her death she left her entire estate to her adopted son, Piozzi's nephew, who subsequently changed his name in her honour to John Piozzi Salusbury. Collections of her diaries, letters, and commonplace books appeared in *Piozziana* in 1833 and *Thraliana* in 1942. The latter is one of the most significant records of the personal, social, and professional life of a late Georgian woman of letters. KF

PITT, William, the younger (1759–1806), statesman. The second son of Pitt the elder was a scholastic and political prodigy; having entered Cambridge at the age of 14, he took a seat in parliament at 21 and formed his first administration at 23. He was Prime Minister from 1783 to 1801 and from 1804 until his death, first coming to office following the defeat of Charles James *Fox's India bills in the House of Lords in December 1783. Elevated to this position by the King and his advisers, Pitt's tenure was expected to be short-lived, but in the event he clung to office throughout the early months of 1784 before securing his position by routing the *Whigs in a general election. This success was due both to royal patronage and to popular support, a combination that sat well with Pitt's self-image as a patriot on the pattern of his father.

In the years that followed, Pitt settled the government of India on a new basis, giving the Crown a significant but not an overwhelming role in the administration of the subcontinent. He also tackled the burgeoning *national debt by increasing revenue, establishing a sinking fund to secure its eventual elimination, and overhauling the administration to make it less burdened by sinecure offices, examples of public prudence which contrast sharply with his reckless handling of his personal finances.

Before the *French Revolution Pitt's reforming zeal extended to a freeing of international trade, the *abolition of the slave trade, and the promotion of a modest cleansing of the electoral system. The first of these measures gave rise to a trade agreement with France, but the second and third were frustrated by opposition from his own colleagues and from the King. By relying on the support of the Crown to provide an alternative to party government, Pitt left himself at the mercy of the King's strongly conservative predilections; his reluctance to press his claims for fear of precipitating bouts of royal insanity became more marked following the crisis in George's mental stability in 1788–9 which raised the spectre of a Regency by a Whig-inclined Prince of Wales.

The outbreak of the French Revolution was greeted calmly by Pitt, who did not think that it signalled the arrival of a new age. This position was accompanied by a sanguine response to its strategic implications. As late as 1792 Pitt could see no reason to expect a disruption of peace, and when war broke out in 1793 he pursued a largely conventional war strategy—subsidies to continental allies; small-scale military expeditions on the Continent; the use of the navy to blockade France and to assist in the seizure of France's colonial possessions—in order to maintain a balance of power in Europe. At the same time, he sought to negate the impact of revolutionary ideas at home. By about 1797 an extensive network of *spies, the utilization of existing legal provisions supplemented by a few additional pieces of repressive legislation, and the manipulation of patriotic anti-French and anti-radical sentiment (expressed most notably in the *loyalist associations) had effectively discouraged open sedition within the United Kingdom. In Ireland the problem of internal order required a political rather than a merely penal solution. Pitt hoped that by unifying the United Kingdom and Irish parliaments he could remove provocative political penalties against Irish Roman Catholics without unduly alarming their Protestant compatriots. The first stage of this policy was achieved through the *Act of Union of 1801, but the King's opposition to *Catholic emancipation prevented Pitt from fulfilling his pledge to the Irish Catholics. Having first promised the King neither to oppose his new ministers nor to raise the emancipation issue again, he resigned from office on 14 March 1801.

The final stage of Pitt's political career began in May 1804, when he returned to office in response to a widespread feeling that the Addington administration was incapable of conducting the war with France. Pitt's 'broad-bottomed' ministry included many who had served under Addington, and eschewed the pursuit of those reforms which George III now openly deplored. Pitt's enemies attributed this compliance to ambition; a more sympathetic interpretation is that he placed attachment to the Crown and the effective conduct of the war above his impulses to reform.

In 1802 Pitt's friend and colleague George *Canning wrote a poem which celebrated Pitt as the 'pilot who had weathered the storm', an appreciation of Pitt's wartime conduct which was shared by many of his contemporaries; moreover, in his later guise as a *liberal Tory, Canning paid his old master the compliment of extending the processes of administrative and financial reform which had been a feature of Pitt's prewar administration. Pitt's turn away from the grand aristocracy, his utilization of the long-excluded, increasingly serious-minded gentry, and his sympathy towards commercial interests provided a model for subsequent *Tory and conservative administrations.

During his life Pitt was handled roughly by his opponents. When he first assumed office he was dubbed 'Master Billy' and was the subject of lampoons which exploited his youth and his lack of experience; with the dissolution of parliament in March 1784 the Whigs portrayed him as monster of constitutional impropriety; and in the 1790s his domestic policy earned him the visual and verbal condemnation of oppositionists. James *Gillray caricatured Pitt as a fungus on a dunghill, an image that was taken up by S. T. *Coleridge in his early, radical lectures. In an era which counted *Burke, Canning, Fox, and *Sheridan among its parliamentary luminaries, Pitt had the unusual distinction of leaving no artistic, historical, literary, or philosophical traces. Although he was accused of personal coldness, the press made much of Pitt's over-fondness for the bottle and boon companions; he was also the victim of homophobic innuendoes. Long after Pitt's death these images jostled with those presented by his Tory admirers, to whom he was an icon.   JMo

PLACE, Francis (1771–1854), tailor, radical organizer, and labour archivist. The political activity, intellectual effort, organizational talents, and archival legacy of the 'radical tailor of Charing Cross' were important elements of the reform cause over sixty years. Having risen from journeyman leather breeches-maker to prosperous master, Place has been accused by some social and labour historians of being a traitor to his *class [15], and of parroting rather than inquiring into *utilitarianism and classical *political economy [33]. Place's life has often been seen as a model example of the successful working-class person changing political orientation along with social position.

Place's career encompassed working as trade club organizer and London Corresponding Society class leader in the 1790s [see *corresponding societies], founding the Westminster Committee and masterminding the election of Sir Francis *Burdett in 1807, making important connections with Jeremy *Bentham and James *Mill, being intimately involved in London radicalism after 1815, and playing key roles in the repeal of the Combination Acts [see *trade unions], the *Reform Bill crisis of 1831–2, and *Chartism. He wrote countless tracts, pamphlets, and broadsides (many of which were anonymous) on subjects as diverse as trade union activity, *population growth, contraception, political economy, and financial, educational, and radical reform. The Place Collection in the British Library, Place's assemblage of books, papers, pamphlets, manuscripts, and printed ephemera, is an essential tool for the social historian of this period.

Criticism of Place has centred on his egotism, the emphasis in his archive on his own efforts and influence, his apparent bias towards *self-improving tradesmen and middle-class intellectuals like Bentham, and his inclination to prefer back-room manipulation to glory on the hustings and in the press. This impression of Place's life overlooks his

tenacity and consistency of effort at a time when the political danger of involvement with activists was still considerable.

Place believed throughout his life in gradualist change through ameliorative measures. The position of the working classes, he thought, was best improved by paying careful attention to the lessons of classical political economy, coupled with basic education to provide working-class people with the necessary capacity to exercise their citizenship effectively. He believed that radicalism had contributed in this period towards the reformation of artisan manners and morals, away from masculine blackguardism and brutality towards family-centred self-improvement and humanity. His arguments for the repeal of the Combination Acts in 1825 were based on a careful elucidation, according to current political economic tenets, of the effect an artificial regulation of the wages system would have on profits, and on his belief that the removal of such an adverse system would mean the disappearance of combinations.

Again, in the Reform Bill crisis of 1831–2, Place proved an artful strategist. His largely successful attempts simultaneously to marginalize the influence of physical-force extremists while using the unlikely spectre of *revolution [1] as a threat to frighten parliament helped the Reform Bill to become law.   JF

pleasure gardens. Public gardens, organized on a commercial basis which featured walks, facilities for eating and drinking, and venues for entertainments, including music, fireworks, and *masquerades. They sustained a wide range of artists and cultural workers, including composers, singers, musicians, painters, scene designers, pyrotechnicians, architects, and builders, and were an important conduit for cultural trends such as the *Gothic and *orientalism. The three main types in London were the large-scale gardens at Vauxhall and Ranelagh, established since the late seventeenth century, gardens associated with springs such as Bagnigge Wells (on the west side of King's Cross Road), and numerous smaller-scale tea gardens. Provincial towns such as Bath, Birmingham, Bristol, Coventry, Newcastle upon Tyne, and Norwich also had pleasure gardens emulating Ranelagh and Vauxhall.

Pleasure garden sociability occurred during the summer months and in the evening, when lanterns and decorations spectacularly transformed the often shabby daytime appearance of the walks. Access was determined by capacity to pay and, as in the case of other cultural activities, price of entry was used as a means of regulating the patron's social class. Vauxhall cost at least one shilling, while Ranelagh was more expensive, at 2s. 6d.; the tea gardens, which were cheaper, attracted men and women of the lower middle and artisanal class. In spite of attempts to promote an image of gentility, Vauxhall's clientele was socially diverse with an element of unrespectability: pleasure gardens were associated with prostitution, and in novels such as Frances *Burney's *Evelina* (1778) are represented as potentially dangerous,

92. Thomas Rowlandson's *Vauxhall Gardens* (1784) presented the London pleasure garden as a sociable space where both genteel and disreputable elements rubbed shoulders.

erotically charged spaces for the genteel woman. They are also frequently shown as the habitat of young masculine rakes—usually military officers with a propensity for gambling, whoring, and duelling. Thomas *Rowlandson's *Vauxhall Gardens* (1784) depicts the gardens' patrons as emblematic of Georgian society as a whole, a Hogarthian crush of duchesses and whores, princes and shop-boys.

Pleasure gardens were highly artificial environments, their aesthetic of the country in the city—*rus in urbe*—registering the fluidity of boundaries between the urban and the rural. The growth of the metropolis and the tendency in Romantic writing to erect a gulf between the country and the city made such highly artificial environments uncongenial to tastes which favoured the country in its pristine, 'natural' state. The Ranelagh rotunda was closed in 1805 and the famous Vauxhall cascade, a mechanically operated waterfall made of tin, was removed in 1816. Although Vauxhall survived into the Victorian period by staging mass spectacles such as the *Battle of Waterloo* (1827), its heyday was over. It eventually closed in 1859. GR

poaching. The traditional Romantic conception of the hungry farm labourer poaching game in order to provide his family with a periodic morsel of meat to supplement a monotonous diet of bread and a sliver of cheese—with the partial exception of rabbits and hares—is not substantiated by modern research. Game preservation meant game privatization, and for many more substantial landlords their sporting tradition was joined by business acumen, as letting

shooting rights became as significant for some as entertaining friends and relations. Hunting deer and shooting birds were protected by an increasingly draconian criminal law, underpinned by game licences introduced in 1784. Eligibility depended on landownership. A battery of existing statutes—already so complex that when William *Blackstone composed his voluminous legal *Commentaries* in 1764 he refused to burden his readers with them—was increased, notably by successive Night Poaching Acts with their transportation penalties for transgressors. Throughout our period until 1831, trading in game was illegal. The principal profile of poaching, and of poachers, was conditioned by that illegality, by the avaricious urban middle-class appetite for game, and by the *poverty [12] of the vast bulk of rural workers. Many others in small towns and industrializing villages, often abutting the countryside, were similarly poverty-stricken and also avid poachers.

Urban demand for game was the principal means for some mitigation of that poverty; the conduit was the well-organized black market, and the major agents for the transfer of poached game were the ubiquitous hucksters who toured rural regions dealing in perishable farm goods. To this legitimate trade they added game, which they collected at countryside rendezvous, notably the alehouse and from 1830 the new and principally proletarian beershops [see *taverns]. Their proprietors were commonly intermediaries between hucksters and the poachers themselves. Other poachers, notably those issuing forth from the towns, used urban fences, most of whom were legitimate business men anxious to inflate profits by dealing in game. Some game, especially rabbits, was raffled off in alehouses on Sundays, often along with stolen items including chickens and geese, revealing an overlap between widely popularly legitimated poaching and less broadly condoned criminality.

The gentry, equally anxious to preserve their game from incursions, resorted increasingly to spring guns and gamekeepers (there was an entire hierarchy on larger estates concerned not simply with protection but also breeding birds to maximize sporting provisions). They represented a growing threat to the poacher, further encouraging night poaching—itself favoured because birds were quiescent, easy targets at night—and the formation of poaching gangs to take on posses of keepers. This resulted in the notorious recurrent, and commonly bloody, even murderous, armed affrays between keepers and poachers, which appear to have attained a crescendo in the hard years from 1815. It could be argued that desperation deriving from under- and unemployment, rock-bottom wages, and parsimonious poor relief, combined with the severity of the penalties for those arrested, led to this state of rural affairs, a view taken by parliament when it repealed the Night Poaching Acts in 1828.

This reform still left plenty of statutes adequate to deal severely with poachers—and on occasion trigger-happy gamekeepers—who resorted to extreme violence. But the central fact remains that poaching was very profitable, and remained so despite the very small numbers of dealers licensed under the 1831 Act. Perhaps the most telling testimony of this—other than occasional press reports of men who made minor fortunes—was the rather more mundane capacity of poachers to pay off considerable fines, £5 per bird for possession of anything up to half a dozen brace. This reflected poachers' subscription organizations, whose collective funds enabled the payment of fines which kept the convicted out of prison.   RW

police acts, a series of acts, beginning with the Metropolitan Police Act of 1829 and later extending to the boroughs and counties, which laid the basis of the modern British police force as a national, centralized, and professional body [see *policing, 7]. Major controversy centres on whether these acts arose in response to the failure of the old local system to cope with the strains of urban and industrial growth or whether they were introduced by middle-class Benthamite reformers concerned to foster social and political discipline.

In the aftermath of the *American Revolution many contemporary observers such as Patrick *Colquhoun believed Britain to be in the grip of a crime wave, arguing that the patchwork of local, parish, voluntary, and private police forces could no longer manage the burgeoning growth of London and northern cities. Evidence of several select committees and a rising pattern of committals after 1806, when regular *statistics were recorded, seemed to bear out the efforts of liberal Tory Home Secretary Robert *Peel to introduce reforms. The Metropol-

itan Police Act of 1829 gave control of the London police to the Home Office and two salaried commissioners, and inaugurated a trained, uniformed, and salaried force of 3,500 constables paid for by a tax and organized into systematic divisions.

Modern revisionist historians have thrown doubt on the motives for this and subsequent countrywide police reform measures. They point out that much of the legislation was unnecessary and inappropriate for rural areas, and they find little evidence of increase in crime in highly industrialized areas like the Black Country. They locate the origins of such legislation rather in middle-class distrust of aristocratic paternalism, combined with fears of working-class political unrest and social disorder as in the reform and *Chartist agitations. Certainly, sections of the working classes in London and the north proved extremely hostile to the new police, as evidenced by strong support for rioters who killed a constable in a mêlée at Coldbath Fields in 1833—a pointer to continuing high levels of assaults against police officers. Equally, the new police seem to have been welcomed by the middle classes, not only for their role in controlling *riots and radical agitation, but also for providing such social services as protecting property, suppressing unruly sports and pastimes, enforcing drinking controls, and removing vagrants [see *popular culture, 23]. However, popular libertarian fears that the new police would act as continental-style agent of central despotism seem gradually to have abated, and acceptance of the protective functions of the local 'bobby' was more widespread by the mid-nineteenth century.   IMcC

POLIDORI, John William (1795–1821), liberal essayist, *physician, author of the *Gothic novel *The Vampyre* (1819). Polidori was of Italian-Scottish parentage and Roman Catholic religion. His father, Gaetano Polidori, had left the service of the Piedmontese dramatist Vittorio Alfieri to settle in London as a publisher and translator. John William was schooled by the Benedictines at Ampleforth, Yorkshire. A handsome, self-concerned young man with liberal ideas, Dr Polidori graduated in 1815 from Edinburgh Royal College of Physicians with a dissertation on sleepwalking, *De Morbo Oneirodynia*, which sketched a psychosexual analysis of nightmares, and hinted at a critique of the calculus of privilege and patronage which controlled the British medical profession [see *medicine, 18].

In 1816, when *Byron fled rumours of sodomy and incest into exile on the Continent, he hired Polidori as his personal physician. In Byron's rented Villa Diodati near Geneva, in the company of Matthew 'Monk' *Lewis, Percy *Shelley, Mary *Shelley, and Claire *Clairmont, Polidori wrote up a scandalous diary and experimented with fiction and pharmaceuticals, and Mary Shelley conceived the idea of *Frankenstein* (1818). While summer lasted, Polidori's manifest jealousy of Percy Shelley seems to have amused Byron, but he also quarrelled with the local Swiss, and more seriously with an officer from an Austrian regiment. In early autumn Polidori was sacked by Byron after his gaucheries had attracted the disfavour of Madame de *Staël's famous salon at neighbouring Coppet. He made a walking tour of Italy, where he was received in the home of the distinguished physician Andrea Vaccà Berlinghieri (1772–1826), before returning to England, still hovering between a literary and a scientific career. *The Vampyre: A Tale* was published by Henry Colburn's *New Monthly Magazine* in April 1819, touting Byron as its author. The Byronic *milord* Ruthven was lifted from Lady Caroline *Lamb's *Glenarvon* (1816), and the ingénu Aubrey is the upper-class Englishman which Polidori longed to be.

Under pressure from John Murray (1778–1843), Byron's publisher, Polidori retracted Byron's name and acknowledged his own authorship, but claimed in letters to the London papers and in the preface to his novel, *Ernestus Berchtold; or The Modern Oedipus* (1819), that Byron had proposed a ghost story-writing competition, and that Mary Shelley's *Frankenstein*, as well as his own fictions, originated in that suggestion. Gossip spread about the Geneva tourists as a 'League of Incest' with women in common, especially after the *Quarterly's* hostile review in April 1819 of Percy Shelley's *The Revolt of Islam*; while an anonymous pamphlet, *Don Juan* (1819), linking Lord Byron 'and Family' to 'a Sketch of the Vampire Family' launched the legend of 'vampiric' closeted collaboration among male Romantic writers, merging Polidori with his vampire fiction as a figure of *homosexual notoriety. In her 1831 introduction to the third edition of *Frankenstein*, Mary Shelley wrote condescendingly about Polidori's pretensions to be taken seriously by the English male poets, and banged the lid on the spectre of Polidori's wounded narcissism by deliberately omitting to mention *The Vampyre*.

Returned from Europe, Polidori sought out literary circles and tried to establish a medical practice near Norwich. He suffered severe head injuries in a carriage accident, and died in 1821 from a self-administered dose of prussic acid. A Miltonic pastiche, *The Fall of the Angels* (1821), was published posthumously. Polidori's younger sister Frances was later the wife of the Italian expatriate Gabriele Rossetti, and mother of Dante Gabriel, William Michael, and Christina Georgina Rossetti. In their childhood home, even the mention of John William's name was strictly forbidden.   JB

POLWHELE, Richard (1760–1838), *Anglican cleric, Oxford graduate, pamphleteer, antiquarian topographer of Devon and Cornwall. A quarrelsome curate with literary aspirations, Polwhele came to notice with a jeering misogynist pamphlet, *The Unsex'd Females: a Poem, dedicated to the Author of The Pursuits of Pleasure* (1798, 1800). He joined in the attack begun by the *Anti-Jacobin Review* on William *Godwin's 1798 *Memoirs of the Author of A Vindication of the Rights of Woman*. Mary *Wollstonecraft was Polwhele's principal target, and Godwin's *Memoirs* provided Polwhele with ammunition from her disreputable private life, and a link to the *French Revolution and 'Gallic licentiousness'.

Polwhele was particularly severe on women writers with male patrons such as Godwin and George *Dyer, who had praised Wollstonecraft, Catharine *Macaulay, Charlotte *Smith, and Helen Maria *Williams for writing 'on the side of Liberty'. Polwhele also appointed himself moral tutor of 'a groupe of female writers' of more conservative texts, including Anna *Seward, Elizabeth *Carter, Anna Laetitia *Barbauld, Elizabeth Montagu [see *bluestockings], and Polwhele's particular admiration, Hannah *More. Polwhele approved More's efforts as a moral educator of women, and praised her 'feminine delicacy and grace' in his memoirs, *Traditions and Recollections* (1826). From this vantage-point he also passed judgement on Mary *Robinson, Charlotte *Smith, Ann *Yearsley, Mary *Hays, and Angelica *Kauffman.

Polwhele's footnotes, twenty times the length of his verse text, draw on John Robinson's *Proofs of a Conspiracy Against All the Religions and Governments of Europe* (1797), a paranoid anti-Jacobin text, derived from the Abbé Barruel's influential conspiracy theory, *Histoire du Jacobinisme* (1797).   JB

poor laws, also known as the Old Poor Law, provided the legal framework for poor relief. Acts of 1598 and 1601 codified existing responses to *poverty [12] in England and Wales, establishing parishes' responsibility to relieve the helpless or 'impotent' poor, and to employ or discipline the able-bodied. This was funded by a compulsory, property-based rate levied on inhabitants of the parish and administered by overseers of the poor, supervised by Justices of the Peace. Scottish poor relief was based on an Act of 1579, widely interpreted in the early nineteenth century to preclude relief of the able-bodied; the sick and incapable were largely relieved from voluntary contributions. This distinctive system reflected Scotland's social structure and forms of government.

In England and Wales, settlement, an extremely complex area of law (1662, 1691, and subsequent modifications), determined which parish was responsible for an individual. The main methods of gaining a settlement were apprenticeship, yearly hiring, rental of £10 or more a year, payment of local rates, holding a parish office, or birthplace (if illegitimate). Wives acquired their husbands' settlement; children their fathers'. Parishes could 'remove' to their place of settlement those 'chargeable', or, until 1795, potentially burdensome, through application to a magistrate. Many poor lived away from their places of settlement: they held certificates from their home parish, were subsidized by it as non-resident poor, or simply escaped notice.

Settlement touched the lives of all poor people and influenced decisions about migration, employment, and application for relief. Settlement examinations record considerable information about the lives of the poor. Some had extensive knowledge of settlements and most knew their grounds of entitlement. By the late eighteenth century, changing employment patterns restricted opportunities to gain new settlements and an increasing proportion of men took their settlement from fathers and grandfathers.

Relationships with responsible parishes might therefore be quite tenuous.

Specific legal provisions covered the recalcitrant and disorderly poor—vagrants, those who refused to work, prostitutes, and the dissolute. After 1815, interest revived in bridewells and houses of correction, which were intended to deter, punish, and reform the poor [see *prisons].

Gilbert's Act (1782) confirmed the shift in poor law practice towards outdoor relief for the able-bodied poor, and allowed parishes to unite to establish a common workhouse for relief of the infirm. Select Vestries Acts (1818, 1819) also promoted administrative reform by concentrating power in small committees which supervised the work of full-time, paid officials. As permissive, non-compulsory legislation, these and local acts contributed to the varied character of relief in England and Wales.

In his *History of the Poor* (1793), Thomas Ruggles (?1737–1813) estimated that the poor laws regulated the conduct of over seven million people. More money was raised under them than any other form of local taxation and they required complex administrative arrangements. Although many pamphleteers urged the gentry to involve themselves in poor law business, offices were filled by men, and sometimes women, of the middling and lower ranks. Parliamentary interest was considerable. Comprehensive reforms failed in 1796 and 1807, and House of Commons Select Committees inquired into the system in 1817, 1824, and 1828: all this reflected a mounting sense of crisis at the escalating cost of poor relief.

The 1834 Poor Law Amendment Act, founded on a critique of dependence and pauperism, centralized the poor relief system, taking power away from the parish. It attempted to abolish outdoor relief by giving assistance only to those who entered the workhouse, which was provided as a last and unattractive resort.   SL

popular education. Unlike Scotland, which in our period already possessed nearly universal basic education through its parochial school system, and Ireland, where fears of the spread of Catholic education impelled the *Whig government to institute in 1831 a massive scheme of elementary national education, England and Wales continued to proffer a diverse non-governmental patchwork of popular educational programmes [see *education, 17].

A parliamentary committee survey of England and Wales in 1819 counted 4,176 endowed schools (700 of them grammar schools for teaching the classics), 14,282 private venture schools, including *Dissenting academies, and 5,162 *Sunday schools. Together these reached, albeit sporadically, around half the children in the country. To many middle-class educational reformers, however, these figures seemed alarmingly low, and the type of education provided extremely narrow or haphazard. As early as 1776 in the *Wealth of Nations* Adam *Smith had advocated a national system of primary education to improve working-class skill levels and morale. Followers of *Malthus had similarly supported a plan designed to lead to improved social stability and

reduced dependence on the *poor laws. Existing educational systems seemed inadequate for either purpose. Leigh *Hunt complained in the *Examiner* of 1808 that ancient endowed schools like his own school, Christ's Hospital, had abandoned their original obligations to provide some education for the poor and become openly élitist. As the century progressed, Sunday schools and charity schools under the control of the Society for the Promotion of Christian Knowledge had also lost a good deal of their original momentum. Their preoccupation with social discipline and the inculcation of catechism by rote also ran counter to *Lockean trends of imparting education through the use of dialectical methods and rational incentives. Private venture schools, mainly small, cheap dame schools akin to the hedge schools of Ireland, were equally suspected because of the teachers' low literacy skills, informal methods, and rudimentary facilities. However, the persistence of such schools in the face of later, more modern alternatives suggests that they often suited the culture, needs, and work rhythms of working-class families.

Despite the failure of national education bills proposed by Samuel Whitbread (1758–1815) in 1807 and Henry *Brougham in 1820, the first three decades of the nineteenth century brought a marked increase in the range and type of education available for the British poor and labouring classes. Between 1819 and 1833, for example, the number of children at non-endowed schools doubled to more than a million. The rivalry between the Anglican National Society and the Nonconformist British and Foreign School Society, both espousing cheap *monitorial systems of elementary education, produced a growing network of schools which were given governmental approval in 1833 with the provision of a grant of £20,000. The secular counterpart of this religious drive to enlighten and moralize the labouring classes centred on the Society for the Diffusion of Useful Knowledge (SDUK), a circle of philosophical radicals and liberal Whigs led by Brougham, Francis *Jeffrey, and Francis *Place. Their vision had been influenced by Jeremy *Bentham's *Chrestomathia* (1815), which had advocated a national, secular education system of useful learning aimed at generating a happy and productive citizenry. Drawing on his own experience as London tradesman, Place also believed that the dissemination of rational adult education would give systematic expression to the revolution in artisan morals and manners which earlier radical institutions such as the *corresponding societies had begun [see *reformation of manners].

Brougham had also been inspired by mechanics' classes run at Glasgow University by his friend of student days Dr George *Birkbeck. The two men thus launched the London Mechanics' Institute in February 1824, aiming to provide *lectures and classes in science and technology for self-improving artisans, skilled labourers, or 'mechanics'. The movement spread rapidly into provincial towns and, during the 1840s, into the countryside as well: by mid-century there were more than 700 mechanics institutes across the country. However, the retention

654 · P<small>OPULAR</small> E<small>DUCATION</small>

of financial and intellectual control by middle-class patrons tended to alienate mechanics and to attract instead a constituency of lower-middle-class clerks and shopkeepers. A more successful arm of the 'steam intellect society', as Thomas Love *Peacock dubbed the SDUK in his brilliant satire *Crochet Castle* (1831), was its popular publishing programme, largely masterminded by Charles Knight (1791–1873). In 1824 the self-made London publisher Knight had tried to initiate a 'national library' comprising cheap condensations of canonical works in science, *political economy [33], and technology. Though this scheme foundered, his subsequent superintendence of SDUK publishing activities from 1829 produced a 'Library of Entertaining Knowledge' and a series of widely selling useful knowledge works such as the *Penny Magazine* (1832–5), the *Penny Cyclopaedia* (1833–4), and eventually even a *Pictorial Shakespeare* (1838–41).

Eclipsing all such movements of educational provision *for* the people were those *of* the people, a diverse, vibrant culture of radical *self-improvement. This expressed itself through the publications and political campaigns of the *unstamped and radical press in the 1820s and 1830s, through the establishment of numerous, if short-lived, co-operative schools, lyceums, and reading circles associated both with *Owenite and *Chartist movements, and through often heroically self-disciplined individual quests for self-education attested in a growing number of working-class *autobiographies. Owen's *A New View of Society* (1813–14) had not only proclaimed a mission of extending rational consensual learning to the labouring masses, but also depicted co-operative education as revolutionary agency for transforming society and culture [see *socialism]. At a more mundane and practical level, however, the pre-eminent institutional expression of working-class self education in this period was the mutual improvement society, which generally took the form of an informal learning circle attached to chapel, *tavern, or Sunday school. Small subscriptions usually supported a basic library and a hired room where members could gather twice weekly in the evenings to read, discuss, and debate topics that spoke to their experience and aspirations. Significantly, during the 1820s and 1830s a substantial minority of working women, both artisan wives and independent factory workers, began for the first time to participate in this vital culture of self-improvement.   IMcC

population. One of the most dramatic turning-points in the history of population growth, the late eighteenth and early nineteenth centuries saw a rise in population of enormous magnitude. Between 1771 and 1831 the population of England more than doubled (from 6.4 million to 13 million). In Scotland average annual rates of population increase rose from 0.6 per cent between 1755 and 1801 to 1.5 per cent between 1801 and 1831, by which time the population of the country (2.4 million) was almost twice as large as in the mid-1750s (1.3 million).

In the 100 years or so prior to the middle of the eighteenth century the populations of Britain and each of its constituent countries had grown very little. In England, where the number of inhabitants rose from 5 million in 1670 to 5.7 million in 1750, rates of population growth averaged just 0.2 per cent a year. In Scotland, where the total population was probably no larger at the end of the seventeenth century than at the beginning, they remained as low as 0.25 per cent a year throughout the first half of the eighteenth century.

In the course of the second half of the eighteenth century the pace of population increase suddenly accelerated. From an annual average of 0.6 per cent between 1751 and 1771, rates of English population growth rose to around 1 per cent between 1771 and 1801 and to almost 2 per cent between 1801 and 1831. Albeit at slightly lower levels, high rates of population increase were maintained throughout the remainder of the nineteenth century.

Never before had the population risen so rapidly over so prolonged a period, and never before had the British economy been able to sustain such large numbers of people. For the first time, earlier and more obviously in Britain than anywhere else in Europe, many countries broke free from a demographic system in which periodic crises of mortality caused by *war [2], disease, and *famine imposed relatively modest upper limits on rates of long-term population increase.

The causes of this revolutionary increase in rates of population growth have long puzzled historians. In Scotland and the countries of continental Europe, falling mortality appears to have been the main causal mechanism at work. In England, whilst falling mortality played a part, rising fertility, itself largely due to a trend towards earlier marriage, was chiefly responsible.

Why mortality declined remains a matter of dispute; the search for an explanation is hampered by the fact that both within and between nations declining death rates seem to have occurred in economic, social, and political environments of widely differing type. Currently, all that can be safely concluded is that it was probably the result of a number of factors. Down to the 1830s perhaps the most important of these were autonomous changes in the virulence of certain infectious diseases or in human resistance towards them, medical innovations such as the spread of hospitals and dispensaries, inoculation and *vaccination against smallpox, and improvements in nutritional standards made possible by advances in agriculture and higher real incomes [see medicine, 18].

Historians are equally puzzled about the causes of earlier marriage and rising fertility. Some see it as a consequence of greater employment opportunities for men, women, and children. Some argue that it resulted from the increasing proletarianization of the labour force and reflected the fact that wage-earning labourers in agriculture and industry tended to marry sooner and conceive more regularly than the live-in farm servants and self-employed artisans they replaced. Others believe that it owed at least something to the introduction of temporarily more generous systems of poor relief. Which of these factors exerted the greatest influence it is not yet possible to say.

If the causes of the population revolution remain unclear, its consequences are less obscure. Through the effect it had on the size of the labour supply and levels of demand, the population growth had a considerable impact on the performance of the economy. On balance, the nature of this impact was beneficial, larger numbers of people helping to provide the markets and low-cost labour needed to initiate and sustain the world's first industrial revolution [see *industrialization, 14]. Together with the effects of economic development, the increase in rates of population growth also had dramatic cultural, political, and social implications, such as the rise of urbanization.

At the beginning of the 1770s about a quarter of the population of England and Wales and less than a fifth of the population of Scotland lived in urban communities. By 1801 the proportions had risen to over a third and more than a fifth; forty years later, to almost a half and around a third. In the 1750s London and Edinburgh were the only towns in Britain with more than 50,000 inhabitants. By 1801 the number of such places had risen to eight and by 1841 to twenty-six. By 1851, when one in every three people lived in settlements with a population of at least 50,000, over half of all residents in England and Wales were urban dwellers. Between the late eighteenth and mid-nineteenth centuries Britain became the world's first extensively urbanized society.

At least initially, the cultural, political, and social consequences of rising rates of population growth, and the transformation from rural to urban living which accompanied them, were highly disruptive and alarming. By making it more difficult to ensure adequate standards of public health, personal hygiene, basic *education [17], and *law [8] and order, and by undermining traditional codes of sexual conduct, provisions for sport and leisure, socio-occupational *class [15] structures, and household and family forms and relationships [see *domesticity, 13], the new demographic environment helped create a potential for social dislocation which contemporaries found deeply disturbing. Not until well into the second half of the nineteenth century did it gradually become apparent that their concerns were exaggerated, and that society had the capacity to respond successfully to the novel, cultural, political, and social requirements of a population that was larger, more mobile, and more densely congregated than ever before.   NLT

pornography. The word 'pornography' was not coined until the mid-nineteenth century, when it came into simultaneous use in Britain and France. However, a specialist category of literature which accords with modern definitions—literature depicting sexual acts aimed primarily at sexual arousal and/or the violation of existing taboos—had emerged in Britain by the end of our period.

Literature that was pornographic in the strictly etymological sense of 'writing about whores' had circulated in Britain and Europe since at least the six-

teenth century. These works usually took the form of fictional memoirs, or dialogues between veteran and newly initiated prostitutes, or descriptive guides of brothels. Pietro Aretino's famous *Ragionamenti* (1536) was probably the foundation work of the genre. Such books were often to be found in the locked cabinets or secret collections of eighteenth-century gentlemen, and were generally expensive, lavishly illustrated, and untranslated from Latin or French. Thomas *Rowlandson and other *print [22] caricaturists delighted in implying a connection between conoisseurship and sexual lechery—with some justification, given the elaborate erotic libraries gathered by *antiquarian [35] collectors such as Richard Payne *Knight and Francis *Douce.

Other more popular genres also depicted sexual acts or the doings of prostitutes: these might take the form of bawdy comic song-books and chapbooks, criminal conversations, trial reports for adultery, grotesque or comical sexual prints, and medical or pseudo-medical guides. Although no formal censorship prevailed in Britain, all forms of sexual material could be subject to trial at *King's Bench for obscene libel. Here the legal emphasis seemed to be on the tendency of the material to shock in a way conducive to violence or disorder. For much of the eighteenth century, however, it was difficult to distinguish obscene from blasphemous or seditious libel, since almost all sexual writing contained anticlerical or political dimensions as well. One strand of such literature looked back to the Puritan and anti-Puritan sexual satire of the seventeenth century.

Even more explicitly anticlerical or anti-religious elements informed most of the erotic literature which drew on the *Enlightenment [32] tradition of libertinism. Works such as *Thérèse Philosophe* (1748), written either by the Marquis d'Argens or Denis Diderot, typically attacked the hypocrisy of priests, disputed the authority of the church, and endorsed a materialist ontology [see *Deism]. In such 'philosophical books' (as they were known in France) freethought and free love became part of a common hedonistic calculus aimed at maximizing sexual pleasure and minimizing pain. With the almost sole exception of the indigenous libertinist classic *Fanny Hill, or Memoirs of a Woman of Pleasure* (1748–9) by John Cleland (1709–89), the bulk of such literature was throughout our period imported or plagiarized from the French. Although libertinist works generally purported to be written by women, most in reality were authored by men and purveyed male fantasies of boundless female voluptuousness. Nevertheless, some of their protagonists, especially a brand of proudly self-made and independent libertine whores, could convey feminist viewpoints that were at odds with social orthodoxy. Connections between political and sexual radicalism had also been cemented from the time of John *Wilkes's obscene parody, *An Essay on Women* (1763).

By the 1820s and 1830s, however, there were signs that such connections were shaking loose, and that a specialized literature of sexual arousal or shock was coming into being. Two of the pioneers of this new genre of pornography were former radical pressmen

George Cannon (1789–1854) and William Dugdale (c.1800–68). Both had been active in *Spencean and ultra-radical circles during the postwar years, and both had issued popular editions of notable free-thinking works, including Percy *Shelley's *Queen Mab* and Voltaire's *Philosophical Dictionary*. However, perhaps because of the reduced demand for radical and Deistic literature after the repressive *gagging acts of 1819, Cannon and Dugdale began to adapt the techniques of clandestine publication in order to sell expensive erotic literature. Cannon specialized particularly in the literature of flagellation, thought by continentals to be a peculiarly English vice, and Dugdale published or plagiarized every conceivable sexual genre. It was Dugdale's prolific output of pornography that eventually provoked the passage of the Obscene Publications Act of 1857. By this time the law aimed to proscribe sexual literature with a tendency to deprave and corrupt morals (especially those of women and minors): a new and peculiarly modern literary genre had come into being.   IMcC

PORTER, Jane (1776–1850), historical novelist and dramatist. Friend of the young Walter *Scott and other writers such as Hannah *More and Anna Laetitia *Barbauld, Porter wrote some of the earliest surviving examples of historical *romance. *Thaddeus of Warsaw* (1803) narrated a fictional saga against a background of the doomed Polish struggle for independence of the 1790s: it was highly successful, running to nine editions by 1810. *The Scottish Chiefs* (1804), based on the heroic career of William Wallace, was even more popular. Porter's later efforts at drama were less rewarding. One play, *Switzerland* (1819), starred Edmund *Kean but closed after a single performance. With her more prolific sister, Anna Maria Porter (1780–1832), she wrote *Tales Round a Winter Hearth* (1821), *Coming Out* (1828), and *The Field of Forty Footsteps* (1828).

Publishing some years before Scott, Porter was seen by many as an important pioneer of the historical romance. Joanna *Baillie acknowledged a debt to her and Mary Russell Mitford (1787–1855) also admired her novels. In her preface to an 1828 edition of *The Scottish Chiefs*, Porter claimed that 'what ballads were to the sixteenth century, romances are to ours; the constant companions of young people's leisure hours'.   KF

PORTLAND, third Duke of (William Henry Cavendish Bentinck) (1738–1809), statesman. Portland was twice Prime Minister, first in 1783 when he presided over the government resulting from the Fox–North coalition, and again from 1807 to 1809, following the dismissal of the *Ministry of All the Talents. He was a fine example of eighteenth-century *Whiggism, closely connected to the Pelhams and to Lord Rockingham, in both of whose ministries he served. In 1782 he was Lord-Lieutenant of Ireland, presiding over the ending of the formal predominance of the British over the Irish parliament.

After the fall of the Fox–North coalition, Portland loyally supported *Fox and refused to break with him until 1794, though his support was increasingly strained after 1792, when Fox countenanced Lord Grey's (1764–1845) reforming activities and continued to exhibit sympathy with an increasingly radical *French Revolution.

In 1794 Portland led a number of other conservative Whigs into an alliance with *Pitt, himself becoming Home Secretary. In that position, he continued to act with the same kind of tolerance and restraint that he had shown in his Whig incarnation, never, for example, conniving at the persecution of Protestant Dissent which became fairly frequent in those years. Nevertheless, Portland was a determined resister of the French threat after 1793 and gave his adherence to whatever government had the King's support, joining Addington's (1757–1844) administration after Pitt's resignation over *Catholic emancipation in 1801, and then rejoining Pitt when he returned to power in 1804. In 1807 Portland saved the King from the unacceptable demands of the Talents by agreeing to form a 'Protestant' government, and he resigned only on the approach of death in 1809. Though Portland was not the dominant figure in either of his administrations, the trust and respect he enjoyed made him much more than the mere cipher he is often held to have been.   RWD

portraiture. This was the most commonly practised genre of *painting [27] during the period, as well as the most lucrative: many artists were compelled to produce portraits in order to maintain their income. Portraiture was always in some respects a public art, as portraits painted for private houses were usually hung in state rooms where they could be seen by visitors; but with the foundation of the *Royal Academy in 1768 portraits became more obviously public works, and the practice of portrait painting changed dramatically. The display of portraits in Academy exhibitions, where the greatest attention was given to large portraits with unusual formats or poses, led artists to alter their style in order to gain the attention of potential *patrons. Sitters were anxious to be seen at their best by fashionable contemporaries. The new public display of portraits also led to an intensification of competition among portrait painters, who were expected to have their own studios in the West End of London, amidst fashionable society. Portrait painters competed for the most famous and noble patrons, and they sought good engravers to make copies of their work to be sold in *print [22] shops. The major portrait painters in London during the last two decades of the century were Sir Joshua *Reynolds, Thomas *Gainsborough, and George *Romney, each of whom had a different contribution to make to the practice of portraiture.

As first president of the Royal Academy and a portrait painter himself, Reynolds had the task of justifying the practice of portraiture to his contemporaries. The Royal Academy had been founded to promote British *history painting, and while Reynolds concentrated on this 'highest' form of art, he also advocated an elevated form of portraiture. In his fourth *Discourse* of 1771, he contrasted the 'Grand Style' and the 'ornamental style', and claimed that portraiture could be 'raised and improved' through idealization of facial features and costume. He practised this form of portraiture in such works as *Mrs Musters as Hebe* (1785) and *Mrs Siddons as the Tragic Muse* (1784), in which real individuals were cast in the guise of mythological, historical, or allegorical figures. In the portrait of Sarah *Siddons, he borrowed a pose from Michelangelo's Sistine Ceiling, thereby exalting his sitter.

Reynolds popularized this form of elevated historical portraiture, variations of which were practised by a number of his contemporaries. Romney's many portraits of Emma *Hamilton in character and Benjamin *West's epic group portrait, *The Death of General Wolfe* (1776), exemplified the grand style. In the form of engravings, such portraits were sometimes renamed to emphasize their historical character. For example, Reynolds's portrait of *Lady Cockburn and her Three Eldest Sons* (1773) was engraved by Charles Wilkin (1750–1814) with the title *Cornelia*, referring to the Roman matron who sacrificed everything for her children.

Gainsborough's portraits, with their emphasis on fashionable dress and hairstyles, offended Reynolds's precepts about historicizing portraiture.

Reynolds categorized them pejoratively as 'ornamental', but they attracted patronage nevertheless. Gainsborough's popularity in the fashionable *spa town of Bath was due to his ability to represent his sitters in a flattering light, without resorting to the allegorical trappings favoured by Reynolds. Thomas *Lawrence transformed the grand-style portrait into a more Romantic mode through his emphasis on pose, dress, and atmosphere. His *Lord Mountstuart* (1795) appears in Spanish dress under a stormy sky, while *La Penserosa* (1792) shows Emma Hamilton in a dramatic craggy setting, with dishevelled hair and vaguely classical garments.

Portraits of women and children were strongly affected by changing attitudes towards the family, *domesticity [13], and gender, inspired by ideas of education and family relationships current in the cult of *Rousseauism and by contemporary notions of *sensibility [11]. Family togetherness, the role of the mother in childhood development, and children's games were all dominant in late-eighteenth-century portraiture. Depictions of children were particularly popular, although they were sometimes shown as miniature adults in works such as Lawrence's *Sarah Barrett Moulton (Pinkie)* (1794). Men were also represented in novel poses and guises, at leisure or in the countryside. Joseph *Wright of Derby's portrait of

93. *Mr. Banks*, engraving by J. R. Smith after a portrait by Benjamin West, 1773. West emulated Reynolds's elevated style of portraiture, which sought the grandeur and cachet of history painting.

Sir Brooke Boothby (1781) represents the sitter reclining in a landscape with a copy of Rousseau's *Dialogues*. His feminine pose is unprecedented for a male portrait, but it is linked with a tradition of representing melancholy and thereby hints at Boothby's sympathy and sensibility.

Portrait painting and *sculpture were particularly important during the Napoleonic wars. In 1795, parliament contributed funds to public monuments to be erected in St Paul's Cathedral. Although the subsequent commissions commemorated dead war heroes, sculptors sought to obtain a faithful likeness of the individuals represented. The establishment of a gallery of heroes was also the aim of the Prince Regent, who commissioned Lawrence to paint the allied leaders after the defeat of *Napoleon. Grand-style portraiture was particularly appropriate for creating impressive images of military heroes.

The practice of portraiture continued unabated until the end of the nineteenth century, but by the 1820s other forms of art, principally *landscape and genre painting, had gained precedence. Although portraits were still commissioned, they were no longer the focus of attention at public exhibitions, and portraitists became more modest in their use of gesture, costume, and pose. SW

postal system. The speed, cost, and efficiency of British postal services underwent a dramatic transformation in our period, having far-reaching effects on *industrialization [14], *transportation, government, and cultural communications generally.

At the beginning of the Romantic age the British postal system had altered little since the late seventeenth century, when letter rates and speeds had been promulgated under the Stuarts. Given the rising commercial prosperity of the country, the post was inordinately expensive and slow. Postmasters, many of them innkeepers with vested commercial interests, enjoyed the benefits of monopolies, and the postboys who delivered the mail in extremes of weather often had to endure great hardship. Fashionable *sensibility [11] made the plight of such children and their horses a subject of concern. The pace of urbanization and of *population growth also exerted pressures on existing services. A sharp rise in postal revenues in 1776 led to the introduction of some local mail carts, but it was the entrepreneur John Palmer (1742–1818) who, with the active support of William *Pitt, transformed the future of the service in 1784 by establishing a mail coach service to Bath which promised to transport mail at the astonishing speed of nine miles per hour. Other coach routes quickly followed, capitalizing on the benefits of improved turnpike roads. Postal revenues quadrupled in the next fifteen years, reaching £500,000 by 1797.

Despite the increasing appointment of government officials as postmasters and the use of specialized contract mail coach services, the professionalization of the service was strenuously, and often effectively, resisted. Anthony Todd, who was both postmaster-general and responsible for intercepting mail for domestic and international surveillance (see *spies and spy system), blocked a number of potential improvements. It was with the greatest difficulty that Rowland Hill (1795–1879), a former schoolteacher and sometime commissioner to South Australia, introduced the second portentous reform in postal services in 1839. He instituted a scheme for a uniform penny post on letters weighing half an ounce, funded by prepaid adhesive stamps. This facilitated the transmission of cheap mail all over Britain irrespective of distance. By the 1840s British mail was famed for its speed and economy, enabling an unprecedented flow of news and information throughout the metropolitan and provincial arteries of the country. IMcC

POTTER, (Philip) Cipriani (Hambly) (1792–1871), influential English composer, pianist, teacher, and conductor, nicknamed 'Little Chip' because of his diminutive stature. Born into a family of musicians and instrument-makers, Potter studied with his father and several eminent masters including *Crotch (1808–9) and Salzburg-born Joseph Woelfl (1805–10). To Woelfl, Potter attributed his profound understanding of symphonic form and orchestration, and his sympathy with musical developments on the Continent: both were unusual in English musicians at this time.

Following his debut in 1816 as symphonist and pianist at the Philharmonic Concerts, Potter went to Vienna hoping, with Ferdinand *Ries's mediation, to study composition with *Beethoven. Beethoven advised Potter on scores, recommending him to Aloys Forster (1748–1823) for lessons. After returning to London (1819), Potter gave the English premières of several Beethoven and *Mozart piano concertos at the Philharmonic Concerts. In 1822 he was appointed piano teacher at the new Royal Academy of Music, initiating a long involvement which culminated in the Principalship (1832–59). A witty and engaging teacher, he influenced many British musicians, including George Macfarren (1813–77) and William Sterndale Bennett (1816–75), and consolidated a new school of pianism known as 'the English School' of *pianists or London Pianoforte School.

Recalling Woelfl's teachings, Potter encouraged appreciation of German instrumental music. In composition classes he placed new emphasis on proficiency in large-scale symphonic forms, in managing and developing musical materials, and in orchestration—qualities demonstrated in his own compositions. Despite the calibre of his symphonic writing, Potter gave up composition in 1837 to concentrate on teaching, administration, and editing. RC

PRAED, Winthrop Mackworth (1802–39), poet and MP. Educated at Eton, where he launched the college magazine, the *Etonian*, and Trinity College, Cambridge, where he moved in *Whiggish circles associated with Thomas *Macaulay, Praed's political views became increasingly conservative in the 1820s. He eventually bought a parliamentary seat in 1830 and was active in the opposition to the *Reform Bill. His seat was disenfranchised by the Bill, and

Praed was unsuccessful in the Cornish constituency for which he stood in ensuing *elections. He remained out of parliament until 1834.

During this period his output of *prose [30] and *poetry [29] increased, although his writing career was always confined to periodicals, *newspapers and 'keepsake' annuals such as *The Casket* (1829). His extremely popular verse tended towards either the refined sentiment of 'Beauty and Her Visitors' (1829) or the gentle satire of 'Chancery Morals' (1823). Praed was returned to parliament in the 1834 election and made secretary to the Board of Trade by Robert *Peel. He died of consumption in 1839. The first collection of his poetry was published in New York in 1844.   JM

prerogative writs, a species of executive writs issued by the common law courts (normally *King's Bench), and used to control the exercise of authority (e.g. the writs of *prohibition, quo warranto, mandamus,* and *certiorari*).   DL

press-gangs and crimping. The *American Revolution and the prolonged French *wars [2] posed massive recruitment problems for the armed services. In part this reflected the small peacetime establishment of both services, including relatively few professional naval ratings and soldiers. Though conscription was never politically viable, a number of statutory initiatives—notably with the militia—approached it. Navy and army service was unpopular except perhaps among adventurous young men. Endemic *poverty [12] rather than *patriotism proved the principal recruitment agent, yet even disasters of debt and bankruptcy for master craftsmen and petty entrepreneurs failed to generate adequate recruits amongst the competing services.

Resort to the press-gang was vital to procure experienced seamen to man the navy. Pressing was legal, but gangs were supposed to observe restrictions, including the critical one that only certain seafarers were eligible. Force was nevertheless central to operations, and generated notorious conflicts in the seaports. Crimping, whereby individuals were lured into service, depended as much on subterfuge as on violence. Many crimps were brothel-keepers and publicans, making money from bounties paid for recruits or from advanced wages. They often also functioned as loan sharks, entrapping their victims with debts, drink, or prostitution, combined if necessary with cudgelling. Not surprisingly, both press-gangs and crimps were deeply unpopular. Press-gangs were recurrent targets of crowd anger, and the fierce metropolitan anti-crimp riots of 1794 and 1795 showed that particularly scandalous activities would not be tolerated.   RW

PRICE, Richard (1723–91). Leading Dissenter and political pamphleteer, Price made important contributions in the fields of moral philosophy, theology, mathematics, the development of insurance, demography, and public finance. He was prominent in the defence of the American rebels and in the British

response to the opening events of the *French Revolution.

Price's first published work was *A Review of the Principal Questions and Difficulties in Morals* (1758), which, among other topics, defended the objectivity of moral judgement against the subjectivism of Francis Hutcheson (1694–1746) and David *Hume. In 1764 he established his reputation as a mathematician by editing and publishing Thomas Bayes's (1702–61) *An Essay towards Solving a Problem in the Doctrine of Chances,* for which he also supplied an introduction. As a result, Price was elected Fellow of the Royal Society in 1765, Benjamin Franklin being one of his sponsors. Intensive study of the actuarial and demographic problems of newly founded institutions such as the Society for Equitable Assurances (1762) led to his *Observations on Reversionary Payments* (1771), which ran to seven editions and became a classic in its field. At about the same time, Price developed an interest in the problems of public finance, in particular the size of the *national debt. In 1772 he drew attention to the threat of national bankruptcy and the measures that could be used to avert it in *An Appeal to the Public on the Subject of the National Debt.*

The work which brought Price national and indeed international fame was *Observations on the Nature of Civil Liberty* (1776), followed in 1777 by *Additional Observations.* In these he defended the cause of the American rebels by defining liberty as the right of every community to govern itself, arguing also the right of every individual male capable of independent judgement to participate in the government of his own community. However, Price's advocacy of self-government was not as radical as Thomas *Paine's. He still hoped that the break-up of the British *empire [5] could be averted by means of a confederation in which Britain and the United States would hold equal status. He also opposed universal male suffrage, arguing that the vote should not be given to those who were likely to sell it.

While he was engaging in the debate over the *American Revolution, Price also produced works on metaphysics (*A Free Discussion of the Doctrines of Materialism, and Philosophical Necessity,* 1778, which contained a series of letters to and from Joseph *Priestley) and *population. In *An Essay on the Population of England from the Revolution to the Present Time* (1780) he defended the thesis that the population of Britain was in decline. When the results of the 1801 census were published he was found to have been wrong, and this damaged his posthumous reputation even though Thomas *Malthus praised his argument. Price was also unfortunate to receive little credit when a popular measure to control the national debt, the Sinking Fund Bill, was passed in 1786, even though William *Pitt had received considerable help from him in preparing the ground. After the Napoleonic wars, however, when it was seen that the scheme set up by the Act had been mismanaged, much of the blame was laid at Price's door.

In *Observations on the Importance of the American Revolution* (1784) Price congratulated the Americans on achieving their independence and offered advice on how their success could be consolidated. In doing so he returned to the topics that he had been concerned with throughout his career: the need to establish religious freedom and the freedom of inquiry, the need to avoid the evils attending church establishments and a national debt. He also emphasized the need to emancipate the blacks and to ensure that the powers of the federal parliament were sufficient to secure effective government.

The initial events of the French Revolution were greeted by Price and his fellow members of the Revolution Society with great enthusiasm. In his sermon in celebration of the *Glorious Revolution of 1688, published under the title *A Discourse on the Love of Our Country* (1789), he identified the French Revolution as the legitimate successor of the Glorious Revolution and the American Revolution. Events in France, Price claimed, showed that the people were establishing the right to choose their own governors, the right to cashier them for misconduct, and the right to frame a government for themselves. In capturing the rapture with which the radicals greeted the opening events of the Revolution, Price aroused the wrath of Edmund *Burke, who attacked him unreservedly in *Reflections on the Revolution in France* (1790). When this appeared Price was in declining health and replied to Burke only briefly, yet effectively, in the preface to the fourth edition of *A Discourse*. In the eyes of many, the course of the Revolution served to justify Burke, and for a long time after Price's death in 1791 his reputation was deflated. However in this century, as bibliographical studies testify, scholarly interest in his work and significance has revived.   DOT

PRICE, Sir Uvedale (1747–1829), one of the principal theoreticians of the *picturesque aesthetic. Price's ideas were widely disseminated and greatly influenced both *landscape gardening and *architecture [28].

A former pupil at Eton and Christ Church, a Herefordshire landowner, and *Whig Member of Parliament, Price was companion to Charles James *Fox on their *Grand Tour of 1767. Price combined a knowledge of art and aesthetics with an interest in agricultural improvement and landscape design. His principal publication, *An Essay on the Picturesque* (vol. I, 1794, vols. I–II, 1796–8), argued that Edmund *Burke's delineation of the *sublime and the beautiful as the two principal aesthetic categories was valid but insufficient. Price established the picturesque as an intermediate aesthetic category especially appropriate to the appreciation of the landscape.

Sir Joshua *Reynolds and Revd William *Gilpin had preceded Price in discerning the picturesque in art and nature. However, Price systematized their observations and pinpointed 'the two opposite qualities of roughness and of sudden variation, joined to that of irregularity, as the most efficient causes of the picturesque'. The landscapes that Price and his colleague and neighbour, Richard Payne *Knight, designed on their estates of Foxley and Downton respectively, repudiated the drastic naturalism of Lancelot 'Capability' *Brown and his successor, Humphry *Repton. Instead, Price and Knight signalled a renewed appreciation of the formal and imaginative pleasure of artifice in the man-made landscape.   SS

PRIESTLEY, Joseph (1733–1804), perhaps the leading figure of the *Enlightenment [32] in England. His contributions to *natural philosophy [34], linguistics, and politics were all governed by a committed *Unitarianism. The destruction of his house in 1791 and his departure for exile in the United States in 1794 were key moments in the defeat of Enlightenment principles in the reaction against the *French Revolution.

Priestley was born near Leeds into the family of a cloth manufacturer of devout Dissenting beliefs. His mother died giving birth to her fifth child in the winter of 1739–40, and at the age of 9 Joseph was sent to stay with his uncle and aunt. He acquired a knowledge of *Newtonian mathematics and classical and modern languages locally, but as a Dissenter he could not complete a university education in England unless he was prepared at some stage to subscribe to the thirty-nine articles of the *Anglican Church. Since he opposed all religious tests, whether imposed by Churchmen or Dissenters, he entered the *Dissenting academy at Daventry.

By the time he left the vibrant social and intellectual atmosphere of the academy in 1755, he was well equipped to cope with advanced ideas in the whole range of subjects which concerned enlightened thinkers, although these accomplishments contributed to the problems he experienced when he took up his first position as assistant minister in Suffolk. Apart from the unorthodoxy of his theology, he suffered severely from a stammer, and the attempt to supplement his paltry income through teaching failed dismally. After three years of struggle he accepted a ministry in Cheshire, where, in contrast, his heterodoxy was accepted and the school he established proved a notable success.

Priestley stayed in Cheshire for three years, his renown as a teacher growing, especially after the publication of *The Rudiments of English Grammar* (1761) [see *language, 40]. In 1762 he became tutor in languages and belles-lettres at the recently revived Warrington Academy (1757–84), which was to become the most distinguished Dissenting academy in England. Priestley played an important part in building up its prestige, publishing *The Theory of Language and Universal Grammar* in the year of his arrival. When he left the academy in 1767, to take up a ministry back in Leeds, he took with him a reputation for immense energy, intellectual ability, and versatility. The University of Edinburgh had awarded him an honorary doctorate in law in 1764; two years later he was to be elected a Fellow of the Royal Society of London. While he was in Warrington, Priestley married Mary Wilkinson, daughter of Isaac Wilkinson, the ironmaster. A woman of great character, she proved to be a wonderful support for Joseph throughout a busy and eventful life. They had four children.

Priestley's genius for natural philosophy became apparent while at Leeds. He also gained a reputation as a radical, publicly supporting the cause of the rebellious colonies in the *American Revolution. In 1773 he took up a position as tutor and librarian to the Earl of *Shelburne, with whom, in the following year, he made his only visit to Europe. During his six years in the Earl's service, Priestley contained his radical tendencies and devoted himself to natural philosophy, until in 1780 he accepted a call to take up the ministry again, this time in Birmingham. He was happier than at any time in his life; he also resumed his radical career, advocating *parliamentary reform, universal *toleration, and the separation of church and state. He became embroiled in a fierce controversy, most notably with Archdeacon *Horsley, about the nature of the early church, which Priestley claimed to have been Unitarian. These views, expressed notably in his *An History of the Corruptions of Christianity* (1782), earned him the reputation as the leading enemy of the established church.

Priestley welcomed the French Revolution; this, coupled with his existing notoriety, explains why he was the first victim of the British reaction to the events in France. Local celebrations of the second anniversary of the fall of the Bastille on 14 July 1791 were used as the trigger for attacking Priestley. His house, laboratory, and library were destroyed, while he and his family were forced to flee to London, where he became co-pastor at Hackney and *lectured at the New College. He remained associated in the popular mind with *revolution [1], a view confirmed by his election as a Deputy to the French National Convention in September 1792, although he declined to accept the office. His situation remained fraught with danger until in 1794 he emigrated to the United States, setting up home in Pennsylvania, where he spent the rest of his days.

Priestley was a key figure in the later phase of the English Enlightenment. His contribution to a great range of subjects was outstanding, lending character and confidence to the movement. In his political philosophy, for example, he clarified the distinction between civil and political liberty. The latter he viewed as a safeguard for civil liberty but not essential to it. Equally important was his argument for intellectual liberty. He emphasized the candid expression of opinion, believing that prejudice and ignorance could be combated by open-minded inquiry and plain speaking. As a proponent of the associationist ideas of David Hartley (1705–57), he believed that the mind should be presented with a range of ideas so that true associations could be made, and that one would act rationally [see *psychology, 39].

Many aspects of his thought appear to be characterized by a freewheeling experimentalism, a willingness to welcome new ideas and change for change's sake. Dr *Johnson accused him of 'unsettling everything and settling nothing'. However, his ideas were held together by a profound belief in God's providential superintendence, in the conviction that it was our duty to pursue truth, that God had framed the world in such a way as to encourage man to seek truth through experimentation, even in government, and, finally, that the end result would be man's happiness, and a world 'paradisiacal beyond what we can conceive'.

Such ideas were the source of fear for those who clung to orthodoxy in *religion [10], opposed change in the constitution of church and state, and adhered to the status quo in government and society. At the same time Priestley's ideas inspired a whole range of thinkers. Jeremy *Bentham secularized Priestley's *utilitarianism, while liberal Dissenters were excited by his positive demonstration that the early church was Unitarian and that open inquiry led neither to *Deism nor atheism. Liberal Roman Catholics such as Father Joseph *Berington shared Priestley's anticlerical outlook and were grateful for his including Catholics in his argument for wider toleration. Utopian thinkers like William *Godwin were persuaded by his doctrine of philosophical necessity, and early Romantics were excited by his development of Hartley's associationism. S. T. *Coleridge hoped to join him in Pennsylvania by creating a pioneering utopian scheme or *Pantisocracy, and many political radicals in the 1790s were grateful for Priestley's refusal to renege on commitment to liberty. 'Violence is temporary, truth is eternal,' he declared following the Birmingham *riots.

Such beliefs and conduct were consistent with his scientific work, increasingly his main claim to fame. He was an amazingly fertile thinker and experimenter. He was a major participant in the chemical revolution, sharing with Scheele the credit for first isolating oxygen. He refused to go along with developments in quantitative *chemistry led by Antoine Lavoisier (1743–94), but his isolation of many gases, including nitrous oxide, nitrogen dioxide, hydrogen chloride, sulphur dioxide, and ammonia, and his important discovery of photosynthesis in 1772 contributed hugely to the growing knowledge of nature. Although by the time he died his ideas looked increasingly eccentric, this was not so much a result of his continued belief in the doctrine of phlogiston as of the fact that he was a representative of a dying tradition in natural philosophy. Science was becoming increasingly specialized, professional, and secular. As a theologian and an amateur chemist, Priestley remained a true exponent of the Baconian tradition in that his studies were intended to further man's understanding of eternal verities, to be of permanent benefit to mankind, and to transform the world.   MF

primogeniture, an inheritance practice whereby the whole of the landed estate passed to the eldest son. At law, primogeniture was invoked only on intestacy— that is, if no will had been made. As an inheritance custom, when written into the will, primogeniture was of particular importance to the landed aristocracy, as the devolution of the estate to the eldest son was complemented by the devolution of the aristocratic title to the eldest son, thereby securing a bond between landed status and titular authority. Primogeniture was fiercely protected from reform in the nineteenth century, only being abolished in 1925.
ARB

Prince Regent, see *Regency.

prison reformers. Systematic inspection of *prisons was rare until the mid-1770s. In parishes over the country, institutions for imprisonment—county gaols, houses of correction or bridewells, debtors' prisons, county boroughs, and corporations—were privately owned and administered by keepers generally more interested in profit than rehabilitation. Unsatisfactory conditions in houses of correction and, later, the infamous prison hulks were brought to the attention of authorities not by official inspectors but by interested individuals. Such men and women, often *philanthropists, were concerned with the failure of imprisonment as a deterrent to crime. They complained about the inconsistencies in punishments, the ill-effects of prison accommodation on the physical, moral, and spiritual condition of inmates, and the unchecked and undisciplined mingling of male and female debtors with convicted felons.

Prison reformers came from diverse intellectual and occupational backgrounds: they included magistrates, newspaper proprietors, lawyers, businessmen, bankers, politicians, humanitarians, philosophers, *utilitarians, disciplinarians, *Quakers, *Evangelicals, atheists, aristocrats, and educationalists. From the 1770s onwards the cause attracted numerous celebrities, including William *Allen, Jeremy *Bentham, Henry Fielding (1707–54), John Fothergill (1712–80), Elizabeth Fry (1780–1845), Jonas Hanway (1712–86), John *Howard, John Lettsome (1744–1815), James *Mill, John Neild (1744–1814), and Sir Samuel *Romilly, together with little-known local reformers such as Sarah Martin (1791–1843), a Yarmouth seamstress. Motives for reform were equally mixed. Some called for more punishment and discipline, some for separation, spiritual reformation, and improved morals, others for repentance and rehabilitation; all, however, hoped for reductions in crime and prison populations.

Under eighteenth-century penal *law [8], the 'bloody code', judges imposed capital punishment and transportation rather than long-term and costly imprisonment on grievous and habitual felons. Judicial authorities, juries, and the public often also preferred sentences which imposed public humiliation on major offenders—terms of banishment, whipping, and the pillory. Summary imprisonment was more frequently reserved for debtors and petty criminals convicted for non-capital felonies, such as vagrancy, minor misdemeanours, and insolvency. These offenders usually served sentences of between one and three years in small, overcrowded, and insanitary gaols and prison hulks.

When conducting the first comprehensive prison census of England and Wales in 1776, John Howard, then High Sheriff of Bedfordshire, counted 653 petty offenders in confinement, although prison numbers were growing rapidly. A year earlier Jonas Hanway, distressed by the indiscriminate crowding of prisoners, had argued for separate confinement of male and female felons and debtors in purpose-built 'proper prisons' to enable repentance and rehabilitation. Howard noted that prison inmates experienced disease, malnutrition, and physical violence, as well as the unruly, corrupt, and licentious behaviour of fellow inmates. Hard labour, corporal punishment, leg-irons, and chaining were often also used to restrain and discipline prisoners.

However, it was John Howard's investigations and influential *Prison Report on the State of the Prisons in England and Wales*, published in 1777, that provided the chief impetus for major reforms and legislation, the first being the Transportation Act (1776) covering the hulks and houses of correction, and the Penitentiary Act (1779), which set out a programme of prison building. His systematic prison visits between 1773 and 1789, his evidence to House of Commons committees in 1774 and again in 1778, his extensive knowledge of abuses in British, Irish, and continental prisons and lazarettos, and his subsequent published reports all paved the way to prison reforms in the early nineteenth century. Such concerted campaigns resulted notably in the passage of the Gaols Act (1823) under the instigation of Home Secretary Robert *Peel. This instituted the payment of gaolers, regular inspections and reports, the building of new penitentiaries, improvements in sanitation, dietary regulations, standardization of discipline, and regular medical attention for prisoners. An official prison inspectorate was finally instituted in 1835.   SR

prisons. During the Romantic period the prison began to be viewed less as a holding-pen for criminals prior to the infliction of retributive and spectacular forms of punishment than as a penitentiary which punished individuals as a means of achieving their moral and social reform.

Throughout our period Newgate gaol in London retained and even enhanced its formidable reputation as a bastion of old-regime methods of criminal punishment. Dating from the fifteenth century, it was completely rebuilt and refurbished between 1770 and 1779 under the direction of the architect George *Dance the younger. Within a year it had been destroyed in the *Gordon riots, an incident which was often compared subsequently to the storming of the Bastille in the *French Revolution. Though rebuilt once again by 1785, Newgate incorporated none of the new thinking about the functions and structure of prisons that was being disseminated in Europe by *Enlightenment [32] thinkers such as Beccaria, and which were evident in Gloucester prison completed the same year. Over the next fifty years Newgate's notoriety grew, stimulated by the sensationalist popular genre of *Newgate literature and by the influential tract, *State of the Prisons* (1777), produced by *Quaker philanthropist John *Howard. He and other *prison reformers criticized Newgate in particular for its overcrowding, its disease, its differential treatment of poor and rich prisoners, its control by a brutal inmate subculture, and its encouragement of bribery, gambling, drink, and prostitution. The prison also remained the residual site of old forms of punishment which, under the influence of *Evangelicalism and *sensibility [11], were coming to be seen as uncivilized and inhumane.

11 Executions were moved from Tyburn to outside Newgate's walls in 1783, and Newgate was the site of the last burning of a condemned woman in 1789 as well as of the last post-hanging decapitations in 1820. The carnivalian spectacle of public hangings also attracted increasing criticism, particularly after a large number of people were killed or hurt in a mob crush outside Newgate in 1807. Charles *Dickens and William *Thackeray both witnessed the execution of Courvoisier there in 1840, and both published influential attacks on capital punishment as a result.

Impulses towards the development of the new institution and regime of the penitentiary came from several quarters. The *American Revolution put a permanent halt to the flow of British convicts working as indentured labourers in the New World, and, although transportation was resumed to the fresh destination of Botany Bay in 1788, neither this system nor the use of prison hulks could cope with the burgeoning numbers of convicted felons. Coldbath Fields prison also gained the nickname 'Bastille', together with a series of searching early-nineteenth-century inquiries into prison conditions as a result of publicity generated by Sir Francis *Burdett's attempts to gain election in the constituency where the prison was located. At the same time John Howard and other Evangelical reformers, including the Quaker Elizabeth Fry (1780–1845), drew on European and American experience to recommend new, flexible prison buildings and punishment regimes where convicts could be brought to moral repentence and rehabilitation through isolation and hard labour. Jeremy *Bentham's tract *Panopticon* (1791) outlined a similar though more secular and *utilitarian trend in prison thinking. In it he devised a model prison capable of continual prisoner surveillance and of inculcating appropriate habits of social discipline. At least some of its features were later incorporated into the grim colonial prison at Port Arthur in Tasmania.

Both the influence of Bentham's theories and the degree to which they represented a new bourgeois drive to indoctrinate industrial work habits continues to be debated by modern historians. Although the government purchased land from Bentham in 1812 to build a penitentiary on the banks of the Thames at Pimlico, the resulting prison of Millbank which opened in June 1816 bore little resemblance to Bentham's panopticon. Incorporating the newly fashionable principles of prisoner isolation and paid work, it nevertheless proved to be an expensive rabbit-warren as susceptible to overcrowding and disease as its eighteenth-century predecessors.

IMcC

PROCTOR, Bryan Waller, see Barry *Cornwall.

prophecy, the prediction of the future by direct revelation, or the exposition of existing predictions, was a strong thread of continuity running through *popular culture [23], and became a frequent vehicle for the expression of political radicalism from the 1790s through to the 1830s.

The status of prophecy was ambivalent. In 1794 it was one of the evidences of Christianity cited by William *Paley, but it was also closely linked with *millenarianism, whose expectation of an end to earthly government was likely to be radical. The Church distinguished between the days of biblical prophecy, which it regarded as over, and modern visions, which were generally unacceptable. However, this did not avoid the problem of radical interpretations of biblical prophecy, which were increasingly widespread in the 1790s, when the *French Revolution acted as catalyst for the growth of millenarian groups and publications. Protestant England was familiar with the image of the Pope as Antichrist, the Beast of Revelation, whose destruction would herald the reign of saints. By overthrowing the papacy in France, the French Revolution signalled to those watching for such signs that the last days of earthly tyranny were approaching. Apocalyptic themes related to events in France were important in the work of such diverse radicals as Joseph *Priestley, Robert *Wedderburn, and Thomas *Spence.

Prophetic discourse was circulated widely by broadsheets, *almanacs, and other forms of *street literature which were not always millenarian. Some chapbook collections of prophecies included predictions of an imprecise kind, such as the very well-known prophecies of Mother Shipton and the collections of the seventeenth-century 'Cheshire prophet', Robert Nixon. The bestselling almanac was *Vox Stellarum*, whose yearly hieroglyphic, or pictorial representation of the future, usually underpinned a quietly reformist message. Among the most frequently quoted prophets were Nostradamus, Merlin, and Joachim of Fiore, though the images and terminology of the Bible (Ezekiel, Isaiah, Daniel, Revelation) were predominant.

New prophets claimed to be the recipients of fresh visions. From 1780 to 1789 a woman named Mary Evans (*c*.1745–89) led a movement in Wales which accepted her as the 'bride of Christ'; and in the 1780s a Scottish woman called 'Luckie' Buchan (*c*.1738–91) became the centre of a community that believed her to be the 'Woman clothed with the Sun' of Revelation. The movements that gathered around these new prophets were seen as threatening, even when, like the Buchanites, they withdrew from society. The role of the prophet as a critic of unjust rule was long established, and most likely to come to prominence at times of unrest and uncertainty. Richard *Brothers exemplified this role, and even Joanna *Southcott, despite her determination to remain non-political, aroused governmental fears.

William *Blake tapped into the popular culture of prophetic imagery, although he emphasized the mytho-poetic nature of prophecy rather than its predictive function. His use of biblical metaphor can be read more as a subversive critique of the Church than as an expression of millenarian expectation. The language of biblical prophecy was used throughout this period not only by visionaries who saw the end of earthly rule but also by those who incorporated popular millenarianism into a sceptical tradition whose aim was to begin a new era of just government.   MP

publishing companies. London's eighteenth-century booksellers and publishers were labelled by James *Boswell simply as 'the Trade'. Labouring under this commonplace rubric was a lively and closeknit community of specialist publishers, booksellers, and printers devoted to the production of Britain's books and reading matter. As a general rule, most celebrated publishing houses combined publishing, bookselling, and printing and it was exceptional to find a company able to confine its business exclusively to *publishing [21]. Later in the century, however, a number of companies split the functions of bookselling and publishing, while others abandoned bookselling and confined themselves solely to publishing. Others, more adept at retailing, moved from publishing *per se* and concentrated on wholesaling and the remaindering of books.

The majority of small eighteenth-century publishing companies were owned and run either by a single proprietor or by partners who monitored all the printing and publishing processes. Established companies active in literary publishing undertook everyday printing and regular reprints of popular works, usually to subsidize their fine-book publishing. Larger publishing firms with two or more active financial partners, such as Longman's, which was established in 1724, frequently owned a number of profitable *copyrights and maintained a list of favoured literary authors, as well as employing a number of printers and apprentices within the company. Under the succeeding proprietorships of Thomas Longman (1730–97), who inherited the Bristol company from his uncle (the founder, Thomas Longman (1699–1755)) and Thomas Longman's son, Thomas Norton Longman (1771–1842), the firm moved to Paternoster Row, then the geographical heart of London publishing. By the 1750s the company had developed into a large and profitable publishing business and employed a workforce of skilled editors, printers, and engravers to handle 'in-house' publishing, in addition to contract printing for academic presses and smaller publishers. With steady income derived from reprinting popular copyright works (Lesage's *Gil Blas*, *Johnson's *Rasselas*, Smollett's *Humphry Clinker*) Thomas Longman had, by 1794, almost £100,000 invested in various publications. For the most part, business was conducted by gentleman's agreement although formal written contracts were also registered, and publishers frequently launched writers and books from the Chapter Coffee Shop where publishers and writers fraternized.

London's publishing companies tended, through the organization of trade, to dominate the trades of printing and bookselling in England, and London firms also held the majority of valuable copyrights. Provincial towns had printers and booksellers who maintained retail outlets for the London trade, but as the century progressed they provided London with some healthy competition, particularly the Edinburgh firms of Blackwood and Ballantyne. The uni-

versity presses of Oxford, Cambridge, Glasgow, and Edinburgh specialized almost exclusively in publishing academic and scholarly works, but the demand for instructional and practical works, including primers and schoolbooks, works of non-fiction and, later, *novels [31] provided publishing companies in London and the provinces with growing markets. The *Minerva Press, under the roguish direction of William Lane, published popular novels, first *Gothic, and later *roman-à-clef* and *silver fork fiction. This path was followed in the 1820s by Henry Colburn (d. 1855), who also published *Burke's Peerage* and with characteristic perspicacity purchased the rights to Samuel Pepys's and John Evelyn's diaries.

Like a number of new publishing companies established in the mid-eighteenth century, the houses of Rivington and Murray were founded by men who came into publishing late. In the early days these ambitious publishers, without the benefit of valuable copyrights, began by purchasing saleable stock, acquiring shares in the copyrights of standard books held by the Stationers' Company, and buying manuscripts and full copyrights from writers of promise. Each proprietor invested personal and borrowed working capital and seized opportunities to modernize and specialize in particular genres. Rivington owned copyright shares in the works of *Shakespeare, *Milton, and *Locke, and concentrated on religious and educational publishing. In 1760 Rivington's was appointed publisher to the Society for the Propagation of Christian Knowledge (SPCK), which proved to be highly lucrative. Murray produced reference works, a dictionary, belles-lettres, *travel literature, and literary works including the works of *Byron, but eschewed novels. Longman's, who had acquired the profitable shares in Ephraim Chambers's *Cyclopaedia*, relied upon standard reference works, educational books, and, later, fiction. Under the directorships of John Rivington, John Murray, Thomas Longman, and their successors, these companies also branched out into periodicals. Rivington's produced the *British Critic* from 1793 and published the profitable *Annual Register* for a time; John Murray produced the *Quarterly Review* and owned a half-share in *Blackwood's Edinburgh Magazine* from 1817; and Longman owned a half share in the *Edinburgh Review* which, after Archibald Constable's (1774–1827) spectacular collapse in 1826, he purchased outright [see *prose, 30].

Significant alternative centres for publishing included Scotland, Ireland, and a number of English cities including Bristol, the home of Joseph *Cottle, who was closely associated with *Coleridge, *Southey, and *Wordsworth. The Leicester publisher Richard Phillips (1767–1840) was a friend of Joseph *Priestley, Henry 'Orator' *Hunt, and other contemporary radicals. Labelled 'the dirty little Jacobin', Phillips was imprisoned in 1792 for selling Thomas *Paine's *Rights of Man*. He moved from Leicester to St Paul's Churchyard in 1796, where he published inexpensive educational books and popular literature and—ironically, given his past—was later knighted for his services as Sheriff of London. Liverpool-born Joseph *Johnson was also a friend to Romantics and radicals, poets and philosophers. By the end of the eighteenth century, a number of Scottish firms had moved to London, including Archibald Constable, A. and C. Black, Collins, and William Strahan, the publisher of Adam *Smith's *Wealth of Nations* (1776) and Edward *Gibbon's *Decline and Fall of the Roman Empire* (1776). John Murray had established his business in London in 1768 and brought before the reading public writers such as Madame de *Staël, Jane *Austen, Henry Crabb *Robinson, Caroline Norton (1808–77), and Sir Walter *Scott. William *Gifford, J. W. *Croker, and the young Benjamin Disraeli (1804–81) were engaged as editors. Murray made a small fortune from Croker's edition of Boswell's *Life of Johnson*, the works of Byron, and two publications, Markham's *History of England* and Mrs Rundell's *Domestic Cookery*. In the elegant drawing room of No. 50 Albemarle Street, John Murray II (1778–1843) conducted business and attracted London's brightest literary writers and wits, who gathered there regularly for literary receptions and dinners.

At the opposite end of the publishing spectrum, catering exclusively to another eager market, William Dugdale (*c*.1815–68), the former *Quaker and radical who pirated Byron's *Don Juan*, published *pornography and other salacious texts in company with other marginalized publishers. Far removed from publishers like Dugdale, the Religious Tract Society, founded in 1799, and the non-denominational secular Society for the Diffusion of Useful Knowledge (SDUK) produced cheap fortnightly magazines for working people which encouraged another publisher, Charles Knight (1791–1873), to produce cheap instructional works on a massive scale [see *popular education]. *Missionary societies and the Society for the Propagation of Christian Knowledge published tracts, texts, and books for new readers. By 1832, secular and religious philanthropic societies vied for profits from the printed word with established publishing companies in a seemingly ever-expanding and highly competitive market-place.   SR

PUGHE, William Owen (Gwilyn Dawel) (1759–1835), lexicographer and grammarian. At the beginning of the nineteenth century Pughe's knowledge of early and medieval texts was unrivalled and his major publications established his name as an assiduous and prolific lexicographer, grammarian, and editor. His colleagues considered him the outstanding authority on Welsh *language [40] and *antiquarianism [35] and only of late have scholars exposed in full the calamitous effects of his idiosyncratic orthography on the *Welsh cultural revival.

Although he imbibed the rich poetic and literary traditions of Merioneth from an early age, by his own testimony Pughe was deeply impressed by the view of his kinsmen that the city of London was 'the primary point in the geography of the world'. He migrated to London in 1776 and remained there until 1825. He earned a precarious living as a private tutor and freelance writer, and endeared himself to the London Welsh as a modest, amiable, credulous man, known to all as 'Gwilym Dawel' (William the Silent). In 1806 a modest estate left to him by a distant relative, Rice Pughe, vicar of Nantglyn in Denbighshire, gave him a greater measure of security, and as a gesture of gratitude to his benefactor he adopted after his original birth-name, Owen, the surname 'Pughe'.

From 1783 onwards Pughe was a leading member of the Gwyneddigion Society and served as secretary (in 1784) and president on three occasions. This gave him access to a treasure trove of manuscripts acquired by the Society from members of the celebrated Morris Circle. An incorrigible Romantic, Pughe also succumbed to some of the more bizarre myths and theories concocted by the likes of Edward *Williams (Iolo Morganwg). According to Iolo, he used to entertain London Welsh radicals to tea in the 1790s to 'talk of Politics, republicanism, Jacobinism, Carmagnolism, Sans-culottism and a number of other wicked and trayterous *isms*'. The long and weary war against France soon cured him of his radicalism, but he then became besotted by the prophetic fantasies of Joanna *Southcott, whom he served as factotum from 1803 until 1814.

His major contribution, for good or ill, was to the cause of Welsh literature. He assisted Owen Jones (Owain Myfyr, 1741–1814) in editing the poetry of Dafydd ap Gwilym in 1789, and in 1792–4 he published (with an English translation) the poetry of Llywarch Hen. He was also chief editor of the much-acclaimed three-volume work known as *The Myvyrian Archaiology of Wales* (1801–7). His most controversial publications, however, were *A Grammar of the Welsh Language* (1803) and *A Welsh and English Dictionary* (1803). Pughe believed that all languages were combinations or permutations of abstract 'roots', and his etymological and orthographical quirks were so outlandish that he found it impossible to convince the ordinary Welshman, let alone educated scholars, that his interpretation of Welsh grammar reflected 'the language of Heaven'. Outsiders were rather more charitable: in 1822 Oxford awarded him a doctorate for a translation of *Milton's *Paradise Lost*, for which Iolo Morganwg aptly cried, 'Alas, how truly lost!' Most of Pughe's prose, too, was unreadable, and his extraordinarily Romantic notions, coupled with his bizarre orthography, served to poison the waters of the Welsh literary tradition for many generations.   GHJ

PUGIN, Augustus Charles (1768–1832), artist and publisher, who, together with John *Britton and John *Carter, was responsible for converting the taste for *Gothic architecture from a *picturesque fashion into an archaeological passion. He exercised a strong influence on his son, Augustus Welby Northmore *Pugin, initiator of the Victorian Gothic revival.

Established in Paris as an artist and designer, Pugin apparently left for London when the market for luxury goods collapsed in the early years of the *French Revolution. He became a principal draughtsman for the fashionable architect John *Nash. Pugin achieved success outside Nash's office as an illustrator for Rudolph *Ackermann's topographical publications. With Thomas *Rowlandson, he illustrated the popular *Microcosm of London* series (1808–10), and many of his illustrations appeared in *The Repository of Arts, Literature, Commerce, Manufactures, Fashions, and Politics*, a periodical Ackermann initiated in 1809. Pugin also contributed to Ackermann's illustrated surveys of England's medieval monuments.

Pugin's reputation for accurate and detailed illustrations of Gothic ornament was made with *Specimens of Gothic Architecture* (1821–3), published with Britton's assistance. Over the next decade, five more lavishly illustrated books on Gothic subjects followed.   SS

PUGIN, Augustus Welby Northmore (1812–52), architect, designer, and writer. Pugin dedicated his brief but passionate life to proselytizing his vision of the redemptive power of *design [25] that was *Gothic in form and Catholic in function. His belief that medieval art and *architecture [28] embodied Catholic faith remains the wellspring of the modern appreciation of the Gothic. Although most of his work belongs to the early Victorian era, its roots lie in the antiquarian accomplishments and polemics of late Georgian architects and publishers such as his father, Augustus Charles *Pugin.

A skilful draughtsman, Pugin was involved from a young age in his father's enterprises, and after his father's death he completed *Examples of Gothic Architecture* (1831–6). In 1827 he also designed Gothic style furnishings for Windsor Castle, rebuilt as a castellated country seat for George IV by Jeffry *Wyatville.

Pugin's most significant and successful collaboration was with the architect Charles *Barry. This relationship began with Pugin's design of Gothic interiors for Barry's King Edward VI Grammar School in Birmingham (1833–7) and culminated with their winning entry in the 1835 competition for the new Palace of Westminster.

Aside from collaborating with Barry, Pugin's other life-shaping decision of the mid-1830s was his conversion to Roman Catholicism. In Pugin's case faith followed art. His passion for medieval art and architecture worked a spiritual transformation, and it became his lifework to communicate this. In *Contrasts* (1836; repr. 1841) he juxtaposed examples of late medieval and late Georgian architecture in order to demonstrate the aesthetic and moral destitution of contemporary society.

These brilliant graphic polemics garnered him fame and prominent patrons among the Catholic laity, most notably Charles Scarisbrick and John Talbot, Earl of Shrewsbury, for whom he designed Scarisbrick Hall, Lancashire (1837–45) and Alton Castle, Staffordshire (c.1840), respectively. Pugin also exerted a powerful influence within the Catholic church itself. He designed dozens of churches and institutional structures, including the cathedrals of St Chad, Birmingham (1839–41), St George, Southwark (1840–8), and (with Joseph A. Harrison) St Mary's, Newcastle (1841–4). His ecclesiastical works in Ireland are particularly noteworthy.

During his brief but prolific career Pugin's convictions deepened and his tastes shifted. He began with a conventional *picturesque enthusiasm for highly decorative later medieval works, which continued to inform his purely decorative work as in the furnishing of the Palace of Westminster. However, in his work for the church he cultivated more fundamental principles of medieval design such as asymmetrical massing, structural and material truthfulness, and the expressive potential of light and space, which he elaborated in *The True Principles of Pointed or Christian Architecture* (1841).

During the last decade of his life Pugin increasingly tended to follow the forces of fashion, as both his health and Catholic patronage declined. He associated with J. G. Crace (1809–89), a decorator, in mass-producing his decorative designs, and was responsible for the immensely popular installation of Gothic revival furnishings and finery in the Medieval Court at the Great Exhibition of 1851.   SS

PYNE, William Henry (1769–1824), *watercolourist, illustrator, and writer who gained most success producing lavishly illustrated books in association with Rudolph *Ackermann.

94. Detail from *Gleaners* by W. H. Pyne, from his *Microcosm* (1803–6).

Pyne was the son of a London leather-seller, who apprenticed him to a draughtsman. He subsequently exhibited watercolours at the *Royal Academy between 1790 and 1796. He was an original member of the Old Water-Colour Society, set up in 1804, but resigned in 1809 and exhibited again at the Royal Academy in 1811. By this time he had already begun to work on the *Microcosm of London* (1803–6) and

Costume of Great Britain (1808). The former was written with William *Combe and illustrated with plates after A. C. *Pugin and Thomas *Rowlandson. Later in his life Pyne devoted himself more or less entirely to writing. He contributed a popular column of literary gossip to the *Literary Gazette* which was subsequently collected as *Wine and Walnuts* (1823).

JM

Q

quackery, used to denote the practices of uncredentialled and commercially mercenary medical hucksters, charlatans, mountebanks, or empirics, who sold proprietary medicines or nostrums which usually boasted secret recipes, grandiose labels, and wide-ranging curative claims, but had little or no therapeutic powers.

Though a common term of opprobrium, 'quackery' was in practice a fluid, ambiguous concept which highlights the uncertain status and limited efficacy of orthodox *medicine [18] in this period. Like the term hack within the literary world, it smacked of grubby and unprincipled commercialism but possessed no clear boundary at a time when the contours of professional science and medicine were being actively delineated and hotly contested. Some inventors, sellers, or manufacturers of nostrums did in fact possess orthodox medical degrees, and many proprietary medicines and untrained empirics gained such repute that they were resorted to by polite society, including orthodox medical practitioners. Martin Van Butchell (1735–?1812), the self-taught son of a Flemish tapestry maker, became one of the most notorious quacks of this period, practising as a *dentist, inventor of fashion girdles, and healer of fistulas, yet he also fraternized with Dr John *Hunter, attracted George III as a patient, made significant advances in the structure of false teeth, and commanded large fees for his non-abrasive techniques of fistula treatment.

Lacking the authority of professional credentials, however, quacks were often forced into developing innovative and extravagantly theatrical repertoires of personal and brand identity, publicity, and propaganda in order to carve niches in the boisterous medical market-place. Many quacks were pioneers of modern commercial *advertising techniques, as well as modes of self-fashioning. Van Butchell became notorious for his eccentric Jewish dress, flowing beard, painted pony, syntactically bizarre *newspaper advertisements, and an annual public display of his embalmed first wife. It is arguable, too, that as quacks were subjected to increasing social and

legislative attack from reform-minded or jealous medical practitioners, some became carriers of alternative medical ideas, recipes, and regimens, all of which continued to attract a following from those outside the formal knowledge system or unable to pay the fees of regular practitioners. Thomas *Carlyle identified quackery as a peculiarly restless and amoral condition of modernity ushered in by the hot apocalyptic forces of the *French Revolution and archetypally represented by the charlatan, seer, and magician Count Cagliostro (Guiseppe Balsamo, 1743–95).

IMcC

Quakers, members of the Society of Friends founded in 1648–50 by the prophet and mystic George Fox (1624–91), represented a small though influential group of 'Old Dissenters' in the eighteenth and nineteenth centuries. Quakers were required to live according to pacifist principles, to adopt quietism as a religious practice and use it as a political stance. By the late eighteenth century many Friends had reassimilated into 'the World', excelling particularly in the field of banking. However, from the ranks of eighteenth-century Quakers came articulate, industrious, prosperous, and skilled artisans, manufacturers, merchants, artists, craftsmen, bakers, brewers, *physicians, physicists, educationalists, painters, lawyers, botanists, scientists, apothecaries, printers, *prison reformers, and political lobbyists and Dissenters.

Like other Nonconformists, Quakers were refused admission to universities or political office until the removal of the Test and Corporations Act in 1828. In accordance with their religious principles, Quakers also refused to take oaths or register births, marriages, and deaths in parish registers, electing to keep their own detailed registers which required witnesses from within the Society of Friends. Without clergy and despising rank, the ministry consisted of testimony given by ordinary men and women; missionaries travelled the country preaching the concept of the 'light within men's hearts'. In the 1780s Sarah Lynes Grubb (1756–90) and Thomas Shillitoe

(1754–1836) were noted quietist missionaries whose writings and testimony remained influential until the 1830s. Quakerism produced some of the period's most remarkable individuals. Thomas *Paine, whose demand for social justice may be traced partly to the Quaker influence of his father, rebuked American Quaker loyalists in his 'An Address to the People called Quakers', published in 1776 with *Common Sense*. He accused American Friends of acting as a 'political body' and thus against traditional Quaker principles. Political quietism was regarded as an acceptable form of political activity, as were *petitioning and deputations. Ironically, Paine was denied the right to vote and speak at the Jacobins' National Convention in Paris in 1792 because of his Quaker background.

Benevolent and *philanthropic activity was also strongly associated with the Quakers. Wealthy physicians John Fothergill (1712–80) and John Coakley Lettsome (1744–1815) both became prominent medical reformers and philanthropists. Fothergill financed the collection of rare plants, donated large sums to the *British Museum, underwrote the publication of important scientific works, and helped establish the Ackworth school for Quaker children. Lettsome founded the General Dispensary in London, established the Royal Humane Society and the Medical Society, and assisted with founding the Society for General Innoculation. Also an enthusiastic botanist and collector, Lettsome's work was admired by Sir Joseph *Banks. He became physician to prisoners in the Wood Street Compter and was closely associated with the work of prison reformers John *Howard and James Neild (1744–1814).

Another prison reformer, Elizabeth Fry (1780–1845), née Gurney, was informed about conditions in Newgate prison by her cousin William *Allen and influenced by a Quaker preacher named Deborah Derby to take an active philanthropic role [see *prisons]. She began with a soup kitchen, later established a small 'Lancaster' school, and in 1812 began visiting women prisoners and their children at Newgate. She gave evidence to a House of Commons committee on prison conditions, the first woman to give advice to government officials. She, like other Friends, opposed capital punishment. The Frys were involved in banking, printing, cocoa, and chocolate manufacture, and publishing, and, later, development of the railways.

Many Quakers were associated with the *abolition of the slave trade, including Allen, a silk manufacturer's son, a member of the Africa Institution, and a supporter of Joseph Lancaster's British and Foreign School Society [see *monitorial system]. He and another Quaker, Stephen Grellet (1773–1855), undertook missions to royal heads of Europe, Russia, the Ottoman Empire, and the Vatican in the cause of the abolition of *slavery [6]. Allen, with Jeremy *Bentham, Robert *Owen, and others, bought New Lanark Mills in 1814 to continue the social improvement scheme envisaged by Owen.

By the mid-nineteenth century, Quakerism had split into liberal, 'worldly', and evangelical groups. Many had emigrated or resigned, and the number of 'plain' Quakers in Britain had diminished to under 17,000 members. They remained, however, an influential pressure group amongst *Whig politicians and sympathetic parliamentarians, and many later entered parliament.   SR

Queen Caroline affair, the period's greatest popular political mobilization, arose from the public accusations of adultery brought against Princess Caroline of Brunswick by her husband, George, Prince of Wales, over a period of years from around 1802, culminating in the so-called 'trial' of Queen Caroline in 1820 in an abortive attempt by the new King (now George IV) to prevent Caroline being crowned as Queen. The affair generated street marches, floods of *satirical literature, and an unprecedented feminist agitation when addresses and petitions in the Queen's favour were supported by large numbers of women of all classes.

After the arranged marriage of the Prince of Wales and Caroline of Brunswick in 1795, a long period of separation followed, prompted largely by George's widely satirized infidelities with the Countess of Hertford. In 1806 the Prince instigated the Delicate Investigation, a parliamentary inquiry into Caroline's conduct spurred by a claim that she had given birth to an illegitimate child. Her exoneration proved so embarrassing that George attempted unsuccessfully to suppress the report, known popularly as 'The Book'. Public sympathy for Caroline was also aroused by George's refusal to permit their only child, Princess Charlotte, to visit her mother. From 1814 Caroline thus undertook a lengthy series of travels in Europe and the East, which attracted scandalous gossip associated with her relationship with her valet, Count Bartholomew Bergami.

On the accession of George IV in January 1820 Caroline's name was removed from the Liturgy, provoking her to return to England to take up her crown. After trying to bribe her not to return, the government prepared to introduce into parliament a Bill of Pains and Penalties to legitimize a divorce. Caroline landed in Dover in June 1820 and was cheered by crowds all the way to London, where she was welcomed by a range of oppositionists. Both radicals and *Whigs, recently silenced by the repressive *gagging acts, relished the opportunity to reclaim the title of constitutional patriots defending the 'people's queen' against a corrupt *monarchy and government.

For the next four months a torrent of ribald satirical pamphlets, cartoons, speeches, chapbooks, and broadsides accompanied Caroline's parliamentary 'trial' in the House of Lords. Most publications treated the affair as a domestic melodrama, representing the Prince as a profligate libertine and Caroline as a wronged wife. Fearing widespread disorder, the Liverpool government chose to drop the Bill after it passed its second reading by only a slender majority. Country-wide celebrations followed on a scale unparalleled since the Peace of *Amiens.

After Caroline was persuaded in February 1821 to accept a large government pension, public support began to wane. At the coronation in July 1821 she was turned away from Westminster Abbey. It appeared that the populace had deserted her, but her death in August 1821 sparked a renewal of sympathy. Crowds mourning at her funeral procession from London to Harwich rioted when the Government attempted to steer the cortège into back streets, resulting in the deaths of two labourers killed by guardsmen. Caroline's funeral was thought, even at the time, to symbolize the death of an era of postwar popular radical protest.

JF and IMcC

R

RADCLIFFE, Ann (1764–1823), travel writer, poet, and pre-eminent *Gothic novelist of the 1790s. Educated at a boarding-school in Bath run by the novelist Sophia *Lee, Radcliffe was further inspired by her uncle Thomas Bentley (?1748–1831), a scientist, traveller, and friend of S. T. *Coleridge. In 1787 she married an impoverished journalist, William Radcliffe, who became the proprietor of the journal the *English Chronicle*, and urged his wife to write for money. In the next twelve years she published five novels, as well as *travel literature in the form of journals. Her first novel, *The Castles of Athlin and Dunbayne: A Highland Story* (1789), reflects contemporary popular antiquarian interest in the national customs of Scotland and in the theory of the *picturesque. This was followed by *A Sicilian Romance* (1790), her first venture into Catholic Europe as a site of political, personal, and sexual oppression. *The Romance of the Forest* (1791) was so popular that she received an unprecedented £500 advance for *The Mysteries of Udolpho* (1794), which earnt her the sobriquet 'The Great Enchantress'. *The Italian* (1797), the last work published during her lifetime, earned £800.

Through the emphasis on sexual oppression and predation, Radcliffe's novels defined the fundamental structure of what has come to be known as the 'female Gothic'. In this genre, the greatest evil that women must fear comes not from external or social forces but from forces inside the supposedly 'safe haven' of the aristocratic home. Radcliffe invokes the landscapes of the *sublime of Edmund *Burke, setting her novels among the mountains of the Italian Puglia or the French Pyrenees, in order to suggest that the true terror of the sublime is produced not by nature but by man. She powerfully locates the forces that most threaten her young, vulnerable heroines within the sanctified family of patriarchal aristocratic culture. Here they are systematically pursued, even threatened with death, by their fathers, guardians, uncles, and priests.

As Radcliffe maps this pattern of incestuous desire of the father for the daughter, her texts also suggest the daughter's ambivalent response, since her heroines marry supposedly virtuous young men who nonetheless eerily resemble the father-figures who have attempted to violate them. The ruined castles, convents, and huts in which her heroines are trapped become metaphors for the female body. The texts often suggest a process of desire and arousal on the part of the heroines as these corridors and doors are penetrated.

Though she outlined dichotomies for the male character—the priest versus the devil—and for the female—the virgin versus the whore—Radcliffe also implies that such binary distinctions are inherently unstable. In *Udolpho*, Valancourt, Emily St Aubert's desired lover, is disturbingly reminiscent of Montoni, her violator: both are gamblers who have spent time in prison, both are self-indulgent and headstrong. Only their own capacity for independent, rational action, and the sustenance they can derive from a consoling Mother Nature or an all-female community like the convent of Santa Pietà in *The Italian* can protect these young women from the aggressions of such men.

Radcliffe's travel writing was published as *A Journey Made in the Summer of 1794, Through Holland and the Western Frontier of Germany . . . To Which Are Added Observations During a Tour to the Lakes* (1795) [see domestic *tourism]. After receiving an inheritance after her parents' death in 1800, Radcliffe and her husband retired to the country; she wrote only one more novel, a romance, *Gaston de Blondeville*, published posthumously in 1826. This novel includes the essay 'On the Supernatural in Poetry', which was published in the *New Monthly Magazine* in 1826. She died in 1823.

AM

RAFFLES, Sir Thomas Stamford (1781–1826), travel writer and colonial administrator, journeyed to south-east Asia in 1805 as an employee of the *East India Company. He quickly became fluent in Malay and rapidly rose through the company ranks. Mainly in Penang over the following five years, he began linguistic and ethnological research: in 1811, after the British invasion of Java, he became Lieutenant-Governor. Influenced by Adam *Smith's political economy, and contemptuous of local rulers, whom he regarded as oriental despots, he drastically reformed the plantation structure. He abolished the local aristocrats' right to corvée labour and established a system of leases intended to open up markets for British exports and permit commercial expansion. Raffles was recalled in 1815 as Java was to be handed back to the Dutch, and he prepared his extensively illustrated *History of Java* in 1816–17. He took up the governorship of Sumatra in 1819 and acquired Singapore for the British that year. He oversaw the development of this port and conducted further research, amassing considerable anthropological and natural history collections, although these materials, together with a vast collection of drawings, maps, and manuscripts, were lost in a fire at sea in 1824. His death within two years of this tragedy meant that he never completed a long-projected study of Sumatra.

The importance of Raffles's *History of Java* lies in its elaboration of racial and cultural characterizations of the various insular south-east Asian peoples, and in its extension of the colonial antiquarianism that was already well established in India.   NT

Rebellion of 1798, the last concerted uprising involving both Catholics and Northern Irish Protestants, and the most serious armed domestic challenge faced by the British state throughout the long eighteenth century.

In 1798 the republican United Irishmen attempted to achieve by force the total independence of Ireland from Britain. In planning their Rebellion they envisaged a country-wide uprising to assist an invasion by their French allies, but severe coercion from March 1798 forced them to stage a premature outbreak on the night of 23–4 May 1798 in the counties adjoining Dublin. The city garrison was alerted in time to prevent an internal seizure of the capital, thus ending all hope of the Rebellion being a national effort. Fighting began nevertheless in Kildare, Carlow, and Wicklow on 23 May, with a wave of attacks on small garrisons and county towns which spread to most parts of Leinster in the ensuing days.

Armed with pikes and small quantities of muskets, the rebels enjoyed success in rural areas in east Leinster, but without cannon could not dislodge troops from stone barracks in the larger towns. Their efforts were further hampered by mobilization difficulties, the lack of a unified command structure, and munition shortages. Undeterred by heavy losses, the rebels took up positions in mountains and bogland within twenty miles of the capital and massed to attack the city.

An impressive turnout of Wexford insurgents on 26 May resulted in the fall of the county, and inspired neighbouring districts. Close defeats in the battles of Newtownbarry, New Ross, and Arklow on the borders of Wexford between 2 and 9 June prevented the rebels maintaining their momentum, and the assault on Dublin was postponed. On 6 June the largely Presbyterian United Irishmen of Antrim and Down rose: despite winning several minor engagements, they were prevented from forming a juncture with the Leinstermen before their defeat at Ballynahinch on 11 June.

As rebellion failed to take hold in the provinces of Munster or Connaught, the government was able to concentrate its forces in the critical sectors until early June, when they regained the initiative with reinforcements from Britain. Rebel-held areas were isolated and defeated piecemeal, with the main government counterattack commencing on 21 June at the camp of the rebel mainforce at Vinegar Hill in Wexford. However, a tactical error allowed the vast bulk of the rebels to escape into Wicklow and Kilkenny. The most effective anti-insurgent tactic proved to be Lord Cornwallis's liberal amnesty programme, which most rebels accepted.

A hard core of several thousand waged a guerrilla campaign in the Wicklow mountains, but fewer than a thousand were willing to fight on after a disastrous recruiting expedition to Kildare and Meath in mid-July. This small force was too weak to pose a grave threat to the capital when the long-awaited French invasion took place in Mayo on 22 August 1798.

A vanguard of 1,000 French troops under General Humbert, together with their Irish auxiliaries, was victorious in several battles against larger opposing forces. However, their defeat at Ballinamuck on 8 September was the last significant engagement of the Rebellion. The tenacity of the rebels, Humbert's good showing, and the last minute interception of another invasion fleet off the Donegal coast on 12 October underlined the narrow margin by which the government prevailed in 1798.   RO'D

REEVE, Clara (1729–1807), novelist, literary historian, writer on *education [17], translator, and poet, whose most important work, *The Progress of Romance* (1785), offers one of the first histories of prose fiction, and the first serious theoretical attempt to raise the status of the *novel [31].

Reeve's most popular work was the *The Old English Baron* (1778), notable for its historical accuracy and a genteel feminization of the *Gothic novel that anticipates Ann *Radcliffe. *The Progress of Romance*, cast in fictional dialogue form after Madame de Genlis's *Theatre of Education* (1785), pits Reeve's spokeswoman, Euphrasia, a connoisseur of prose fiction and defender of *romance, against a learned gentleman who announces a misogynist rhetoric of the novel genre. Reeve faults the literary histories of James *Beattie and Thomas *Warton for lack of detail and want of attention to minor works, and singles out for praise the historical work of the early-eighteenth-century writer Elizabeth Rowe (1674–1737) and her near-contemporary Susannah Dobson (d. 1795).

The *Progress* offers the first systematic distinction between the romance and the novel which demonstrates the arbitrary nature of the literary canon and opens the way for a substantial revision of the generic hierarchy. A denunciation of *circulating libraries and the dangers of novel reading for the young, rearticulated in Reeve's preface to *The School for Widows* (1791), voices the concern over the pedagogical effects of fiction that was common to radicals and conservatives alike.   CT

REEVES, John (1752–1829), barrister, loyalist, pamphleteer, and government appointee. Of obscure background, Reeves came to the notice of government in the 1780s. Best known as founder of the *Association for the Preservation of Property Against Republicans and Levellers, the most active of the *loyalist associations of the 1790s, his *Thoughts on the English Government* (1795) argued that the King was the pre-eminent authority in the state, to which parliament was completely subordinate. Interpreted as an attack on the *Glorious Revolution, the tract led to Reeves being prosecuted in 1796 for seditious libel against parliament. Although he was acquitted, the trial marked the end of Reeves's political career, and while he held a number of government positions, including superintendent of the Alien Office between 1808 and 1814, he still regarded himself as rejected by the establishment.   GR

Reform Act of 1832. With an economic crisis following the end of the Napoleonic wars in 1815 came renewed agitation for *parliamentary reform, the most contentious political issue from 1815 until 1832, when the Reform Bill became law, initiating the movement towards modern *democracy [3].

Up until that time an electorate little changed since 1430 gave a quarter of the Commons' 658 seats (some with only eleven or twelve voters) to powerful landowners—particularly in the south and east of England—and left another quarter under their unchallenged influence or secured through bribery and intimidation. The Reform Act dispensed with fifty-six English borough constituencies returning two members, and reduced representation in another thirty from two members to only one, while creating forty-one constituencies in previously un- or underrepresented areas.

Though shocking to parliament itself, the Act was cautious in the context of radical demands for universal manhood suffrage, annual parliaments, and a secret ballot. Restrictions on voting rights still left 70–80 per cent of adult males without a vote, and while urban industrial centres would return members for the first time, increases in county seats and boundary changes in the boroughs tended to strengthen the landowning interest.

With few exceptions, the *Whigs who forced the Bill through a recalcitrant Lords by threatening to create enough peers for a majority, were interested only in obviating glaring electoral iniquities and enfranchising the middle-class, property-owning interest—thus securing the sovereignty of parliament against the threat of *revolution [1].   WC

reformation of manners. The late-eighteenth-century campaign to improve morality and public decorum is one element in a longer history of changing social expectations and gender relations. It was shaped by *Evangelical perceptions of human corruption and by international and local events, including the loss of America, the *French Revolution, *war [2], social unrest, fear of crime, and the increasing distress and cost of the poor [see *poverty, 12]. Activists throughout Britain combined *religion [10] with *patriotism to promote moral reform as the means to national survival.

Following seventeenth-century precedents, William *Wilberforce obtained in 1787 a royal 'Proclamation for the Encouragement of Piety and Virtue, and for the Preventing and Punishing of Vice, Profaneness and Immorality', and founded a voluntary organization, the Proclamation Society, to enforce it through the courts. Aimed primarily at aristocratic vice, especially gambling, duelling, and libertinism, Wilberforce's campaign attracted substantial and influential support, benefiting from earlier attempts by those such as the Countess of Huntingdon (1707–91) to improve the morals of the upper class. The *Society for the Suppression of Vice also employed agents to secure prosecutions, but its members were predominantly middle class and, unlike the Proclamation Society, included women. The reform movement was strongest in urban areas, and set the intellectual framework for a range of social and cultural activity.

Although campaigners thought corruption ubiquitous, they directed particular effort after the 1790s to reforming the lower classes, and to eradicating sexual immorality: *pornography, masturbation, and prostitution. They aimed to teach the poor Christian morality and to enforce religious observation, by promoting *Sunday schools and purging the Sabbath from contaminating influences, notably drink and popular recreations [see **popular culture, 23**]. Using principles of scientific management, *philanthropists aimed to discipline the poor, giving material assistance only where it supported moral improvement.

The campaign was socially conservative, motivated in the 1790s by fears of *revolution [1]. Propagandists emphasized the need to restore social harmony and order between the classes, and to protect the institution of marriage.   SL

Regency. Constitutionally the Regency represents the period from 1811 until 1820, when George III's lapse into permanent insanity forced parliament to sanction the rule of his oldest son, George, Prince of Wales, as Regent. Though technically the Regency ended in 1820 when, on George III's death, his son was crowned King George IV, it has come to be associated more generally with the early decades of the nineteenth century when the personal scandals, fashionable lifestyles, and artistic tastes of George IV and his brothers were in the ascendant.

Soon after George IV's death in 1830, a spate of memoirs, histories, and novels began to look back on his reign as Regent and monarch as marked by unprecedented personal scandal, frivolity, and profligacy, inaugurating what has become an enduring historical interpretation of the period. Influential reflections on the Regency emanated from hack writers such as Joseph Nightingale, from former ladies-in-waiting of the estranged *Queen Caroline such as Lady Ann Hamilton (1766–1846) and Charlotte *Bury, and from the brilliant William Makepeace Thackeray (1811–63), especially in his first novel, *Vanity Fair* (1847). Although verse and graphic satire against the *monarchy had often sold in large quantities during earlier periods, the volume and intensity of lampoons, *satires, and attacks against the Regent are probably unequalled in British history. In part this stemmed from the marked contrast between the feckless, immoral, and extravagant lifestyle of George and his brothers when compared with the sobriety, seriousness, and decorum of the court under his father. More important, though, was the bitter disappointment that the Regent engendered when, on assuming power in 1811, he turned his back on former friends among the *Whigs and oppositionists who had long supported him. Over the next decade the Regent became the butt of savage verse squibs by neo-Pindarians [see John *Wolcot] such as George Daniel and John Agg, of satirical and sensationalist periodicals such as the *Scourge* and *Town Talk*, and of journalism and verse satire from young liberal intellectuals such as *Byron, *Moore, and *Hunt.

There is no doubting that the Regent made an ideal target for satire. In youth his charm and handsome figure had been likened to that of Adonis, but by the early nineteenth century he weighed more than 300 pounds, with a stomach that hung down to his knees. Even among courtiers he had become a byword for indolence, gluttony, and selfishness. His factotum, Sir William Knighton, called him 'the Great Beast'. His extravagance in dress (he once went through 72 waistcoats in two months); his much-publicized affairs with corpulent courtier wives such as Lady Hertford and Lady Conyngham; his constitutionally illegal marriage to the Catholic Mrs Fitzherbert in 1785; his fantastic pretensions to martial and equine glories: these all made for ridicule. Above all, the harsh and hypocritical treatment of his wife, Queen Caroline, provided a sustained focal point for anti-monarchical scurrility, commercial sensationalism, and political opposition throughout his rule. During the same period, moreover, his brothers, the Royal Princes, were often similarly mired in scandal, most notably in the affair of the Duke of York and Mary Anne *Clarke. The Regent also became strongly identified with political reaction, becoming a target of the radical press during the wave of postwar popular discontent between 1815 and 1820. William *Hone's bestselling verse squib, *The Political House that Jack Built* (1819), illustrated by George *Cruikshank, established an enduring icon of the Regent as the gross 'dandy of sixty' [see *dandyism]. He also presided over a serious decline in the constitutional influence of the *monarchy.

Only as a patron of the arts, *design [25], and *architecture [28] did the Prince Regent manage to attract a measure of contemporary admiration. Although his love of *chinoiserie was frequently ridiculed, and particularly his building of a fantastic oriental-style pleasure dome in Brighton, he did encourage the purchase of the *Elgin Marbles from the Parthenon, help sponsor the *Royal Literary Fund for impecunious writers, and stimulate interest in science by serving as president of the Royal Institution. Above all, it is his achievements in altering the physical shape of London that have made the Regency synonymous with distinction in architec-

ture. Working in close co-operation with John *Nash, George connected the royal estates and houses around Westminster to the new terraces and parkland at Regent's Park, from which ran the sweeping grandeur of Nash's new Regent Street. George also encouraged the state to embark on such major public buildings and monuments as the Law Courts, the *British Museum, the *Bank of England, and Trafalgar Square.

With the passage of time this positive legacy of the Regency has been increasingly stressed. Modern historians and novelists often now treat the era nostalgically, seeing it as a last pre-modern plateau of royal style, artistic taste, and sexual relaxation before the onset of the Victorian period, supposedly characterized by the moral seriousness of *Evangelicalism and *self-improvement, and by the social seriousness of *industrialization [14] and *class [15] struggle.

IMcC

REID, Thomas (1710–96), minister of New-Machar, 1737–51; regent at King's College, Aberdeen, 1751–64; professor of moral philosophy, in succession to Adam *Smith, at the University of Glasgow, 1764–80.

The philosophical tradition known as 'Scottish Common Sense philosophy', while closely linked with earlier moral sense theories such as those of Francis Hutcheson (1694–1746), arose from the comprehensive criticism that Reid levelled against David *Hume. Reid subsequently extended his attack to form a critical account of more or less the whole of modern philosophy in his three main works, *An Enquiry into the Human Mind on the Principles of Common Sense* (1764), *Essays on the Intellectual Powers of Man* (1785), and *Essays on the Active Powers of Man* (1788). Reid's philosophy formed the basis for a comprehensive *Enlightenment [32] agenda in practically all the arts and sciences, as well as for a humanist politics with *utopian [9] leanings. Supported by his disciple, Dugald *Stewart, Reid's philosophy gained a huge influence in America and France in the first half of the nineteenth century.

KH

REPTON, Humphry (1752–1818), *landscape gardener, acknowledged successor to Lancelot 'Capability' *Brown, and protagonist of the controversies on the *picturesque which followed the publication of Richard Payne *Knight's *The Landscape* (1794).

Repton was trained for business and worked in a textile firm before inheriting a modest income and purchasing a small estate at Sustead, Norfolk, in 1778. Here he devoted himself to the practical aspects of estate management, such as husbandry and horticulture. In 1783, after being forced to sell Sustead, he turned to art criticism, and produced a *catalogue raisonné* for *Boydell's Shakespeare Gallery.

In 1788 Repton began gaining landscape design commissions, and he soon established a successful landscaping practice. Early work followed Brown's serpentine line, but he also advocated a return to formality. Repton's success derived largely from his marketing flair, which included presenting designs to clients with movable flaps to show a before and after effect.

Knight's *The Landscape* (1794) attacked Repton as a plaything of the decadent landed élite, a line of criticism developed in Uvedale *Price's *Essay on the Picturesque* (vol. I, 1794; vols. I–II, 1796–8). Repton replied in his conciliatory *Letter to Uvedale Price, Esq.* (1794) that there was no real difference between himself and his predecessors. In Jane *Austen's Burkean country-house novel, *Mansfield Park* (1814), Repton is identified with a fashionable and recklessly modernizing style of improvement, opposed to a privileged sense of moral improvement that idealizes the past as heritage and the estate as a symbol of continuity.

Repton published *Sketches and Hints on Landscape Gardening* (1795), *Theory and Practice of Landscape Gardening* (1803), *Designs for the Brighton Pavilion* (1808), and *Fragments on the Theory and Practice of Landscape Gardening* (1816).

CT

republicanism. A republic is a form of government without a monarch, in which the supreme power rests with the people and their representatives. This formal definition, however, was frequently ignored in post-Restoration political theorists, many of whom believed that a mixed government, involving the combined rule of king, nobility, and commons, was the best form of republican government. Such writers contrasted republics to despotisms, rather than to monarchies. Republican government was a government of laws directed towards the common good of the people; despotism was arbitrary government, with the capricious will of a tyrant subordinating the political realm to his or her personal interests.

95 (*top*) and 96. Two views of Harleston House and Park, published in Humphry Repton's *Fragments on the Theory and Practice of Landscape Gardening* (1816). Repton's method of presenting 'before' and 'after' images—where 'before' is on a flap that folds back to reveal 'after'—proved a highly successful marketing ploy.

This deeper distinction raised the issue of the preconditions for stable republican government. Most writers claimed that political rule required a selfless commitment to the republic—a degree of civic virtue among both rulers and ruled. To explain how to generate and sustain this commitment they drew on a rich tradition of classical republican thought, beginning with the Greeks and Romans (and the examples of Sparta, Athens, and Rome) and revitalized within a European context by Machiavelli's *Discourses*, and subsequently in England by James Harrington (1611–77). Eighteenth-century writers found in this tradition a flexible political language with which to articulate their opposition to the dominance of the court. Where classical writers had condemned commerce and wealth as inevitably corrupting, these became gradually integrated into the ideal of a commercial republic (as celebrated by Montesquieu in a gloss on England in *L'Esprit des Lois*, 1748). Moreover, there was a growing emphasis in the British context on the importance of the liberty of the press and freedom of speech, on popular participation in elections and the achievement of a balance of class forces and interests within the state, and on institutional and constitutional safeguards against usurpation [see *democracy, 3]. Each case carries an increasing tolerance for the pursuit of individual interests and a tendency to interpret the common good of the commonwealth in terms of the protection of individual liberty and security.

Within both the *American and *French revolutions, however, more radical and classically inspired reinterpretations of republicanism took shape. *Rousseau's celebration of the republic of virtue in *Du Contrat Social* (1762) was invoked by revolutionary enthusiasts between 1791 and 1794 to legitimate the attempt to create a republic of virtue, in which citizens would subordinate their private and personal interests to the demands of active participation in the civil and military institutions of the state. The public festival and the *levée en masse* in France were inspired by this more Spartan, more virtue-oriented conception of the republic, which subsequently became anathematized as an integral part of the Jacobin Terror.

The revolutions also inspired attempts to transform the republican legacy into a defence of the principles of representative government. Despite some early and florid republican sentiments, by July 1791, when he proposed a republican constitution for France, Thomas *Paine was working with a very lean version of the doctrine: 'By republicanism . . . I understand simply a government by representation—a government founded upon the principles of the Declaration of Rights'. He had also come to see any form of monarchy as a usurpation of the sovereignty of the people, and in so far as a republican movement existed in Britain after 1789 it took this Paineite form: the demand for popular sovereignty exercised through representative institutions, unconstrained by hereditary institutions.

The two revolutions placed the issues of popular representation and democratic participation firmly on the republican agenda. Many eighteenth-century theorists followed Harrington and his successors in seeing landed property as a basic prerequisite for citizenship within a state. But from the beginning of the American Revolution there were increasing demands for universal suffrage (unattached to property—or where the ownership of one's own labour is seen as a property) as the necessary bulwark against élite tyranny. This gradually became a touchstone of political faith for British radicals. However, the French Revolution and the popular agitation in Britain in the 1790s ensured that early-nineteenth-century liberal and conservative political theory inverted these arguments, focusing less on the risk of despotism by the ruler and more on the despotism threatened by the involvement of the masses. The result was a widespread repudiation of the Jacobin republic-in-arms, and, instead, the emergence of proposals for a limited republic, in which participation was played down in favour of constitutional guarantees of basic liberties and security—most famously in Benjamin Constant's (1767–1830) 'The Liberty of the Ancients Compared with that of the Moderns' (1819). Similarly, in America the *Federalist Papers* (1788) attempted to distance the new American republic from its revolutionary past, and to curtail popular republican activism within constitutional constraints.

By the early nineteenth century the language of classical republicanism, in which so much of the political debates of the previous century had been conducted, had become marginalized. In part this was the result of the emergence of historicist and positivist theories of social change, which undercut the tradition's concern with virtue and corruption [see *history, 38]. Also, once mass politics was recognized as historically inevitable, the problem became one of integrating the mass into stable political institutions, for which the tiny, slave-owning Greek city states offered little guidance. Yet republicanism's eclipse also attests to its success. Monarchy may have persisted, but the real republican legacy was its offensive against arbitrary government. For a time at least, liberal *constitutionalism was established as the basic model for modern states—constraining both the ruler and the sovereign people. That model was always contested, however, and it became increasingly fragile in the second half of the century when confronted with dichotomous class conflicts between the working class and the bourgeoisie and aristocracy. In these conditions more positivist, élitist, and often authoritarian political theories emerged which appealed to elements of the classical tradition and which pretended to a commitment to the common good while displacing the classical emphasis on liberty and patriotism in favour of often virulent forms of populist nationalism.   MPH

reviewing. The cultural authority creatively assumed and enforced by the major reviews of the early nineteenth century confirms both the extent to which Britain had become a 'print culture' and the extent to which that culture had become politicized [see *prose, 30].

In the 1730s the London booksellers were obliged

by *copyright expiry actively to promote their material in the provinces, and periodicals like the *Gentleman's Magazine*, begun in 1732 with accurate and comprehensive lists of recent books and a wide circulation, played a crucial role. To make more informed choices, however, readers looked to reviewing. The *Monthly Review* was established in 1749, the *Tory *Critical Review* in 1756, partly in reaction to its success—setting a pattern for the early nineteenth century, when the Tory *Quarterly Review* (1809) would follow the *Whig *Edinburgh Review* (1802).

When a legal decision finally abolished any claim to 'perpetual copyright' in 1774, the living author became a more viable commercial proposition, publishers more reliant upon reviewing, and reviewing more integral to the network of ancilliary or supplementary genres that were proliferating throughout the eighteenth century (Goldsmith compared publishing's excrescences to the Persian army's going into battle with ten attendants for every soldier).

The endeavours of eighteenth-century reviews like the *Monthly* and the *Critical* to discuss or at least register as many publications as possible resulted in their remaining ancilliary or contingent. With the determination of the *Edinburgh* 'to be distinguished, rather for the selection, than for the number of its articles', reviewing as a form ceased to be simply a service industry entering 'no farther into the province of criticism, than just so far as may be indispensibly necessary to give some idea of such books as come under our consideration' (to quote the editorial policy of the *Monthly*, Ralph Griffiths (1720–1803)). Now it began to take priority over the publications under review, which became rather material for an inductive, reflective, and self-reflexive political and cultural production. So central to the official culture had the reviews made themselves by 1831 that Thomas *Carlyle looked with foreboding toward the day when 'all Literature has become one boundless self-devouring Review'.

Exploiting the new importance placed by a consolidating print culture on the need to be informed and to have opinions, reviewing offered readers a critical orientation. In a complicated symbiosis, reviewers in turn claimed that reviewing was a passive conduit: 'among the legitimate means by which the English public both instructs and expresses itself' (to quote Francis *Jeffrey, the *Edinburgh*'s longest and most successful editor). Reviewers often identified with and conscripted consumers against the pretensions of authorship.

The uneasy relationship subsisting between the reviewer and the professional author dates back to early entanglements in a rapidly enlarging booktrade. Contributors to the *Monthly* and the *Critical*, the *Analytical Review* (1788), and the *British Critic* (1793), however, still tended to be either practitioners or diffident extractors. With the *Edinburgh* reviewers we first witness the phenomenon of the specialist critic. The often antagonistic attitude taken by nineteenth-century reviewing also played a crucial role in reinforcing the self-consciousness of authorship. WC

REYNOLDS, Sir Joshua (1723–92), painter, author, and first president of the *Royal Academy of Arts, was born in Plympton, Devon, one of eleven children of Revd Samuel Reynolds, master of the local grammar school, and Theophilia Potter. Reynolds's education, directed by his father, was predominantly classical, but he manifested an early inclination for art, copying engravings in Plutarch's *Lives* and Catt's *Book of Emblems* and avidly reading treatises such as Debreuil's *Perspective Practical* (the 'Jesuit's Perspective') and Richardson's *An Essay on the Theory of Painting*.

In 1740 he was sent to London to study under Thomas Hudson, a former student of Richardson and a mediocre but successful portrait painter [see *painting, 27]. Reynolds left Hudson's establishment in 1742 and spent several fallow years in Devonshire. Although he later spoke regretfully of this period, he produced some competent, if conventional, portraits of the local gentry and naval officers of Plymouth, the notable *Self-Portrait with Shaded Eyes* (1746) and well-observed genre pieces such as the *Boy Reading* of 1747. Reynolds's acquaintance with Captain (later Commodore) Augustus Keppel brought an invitation to join a Mediterranean voyage in 1749. He visited Algiers, Gibraltar, Cadiz, and Lisbon before settling into a two-month stay in Minorca. From Minorca he made the ambitious artist's requisite pilgrimage to Italy, where he remained until 1753, living in Rome, travelling to Florence, Bologna, Naples, and Venice, establishing his judgement, and storing his memory with study of the great masters—as he later described to students at the Royal Academy. He also dabbled in caricature: a send-up of Raphael's *School of Athens*, in which the philosophers and disciples are replaced by swaggering English milords belongs to this period. An illness brought on by work in wintry Vatican chambers is said to have caused his deafness.

After his return to England in 1752, Reynolds took lodgings in St Martin's Lane and painted a series of works that established both his idiom as a *portraitist 77 and his claims to fashionable notice. Reynolds's full-length portrait of his patron, Keppel (1752), presents the commander striding ashore from the wreck of the *Maidstone*. Arrayed in his elegant, if anachronistic, naval uniform and *contrapposto* borrowed from classical statuary, Keppel is the embodiment of patrician calm and authority amidst the vindictive forces of storm and war. With the assistance of another patron, Lord Edgecumbe, Reynolds garnered important portrait commissions from figures such as the Duke of Devonshire, the Lord Chamberlain, and the Duke of Cumberland. Portraits, rather than the pure historical compositions he adjudged to be the highest form of painting, formed the bulk of his production and income; although in some of his finest works the boundaries between the genres blurred— 108 *Garrick Between Tragedy and Comedy* (1762) and *Mrs Siddons as the Tragic Muse* (1784) are significant in this respect. Reynolds's professional stature is frequently measured by the fees he came to command for portrait work. According to his executor and biographer, Edmund *Malone, Reynolds charged

12 guineas for a head around 1755, 24 for a half-length, and 48 for a full-length portrait. By the 1780s these fees had risen to 50 guineas for a head, 100 for a half-length, and 200 for a full-length portrait.

Although Reynolds functioned comfortably within the patrician circles of eighteenth-century art collection and connoisseurship, his career is closely tied to the gradual professionalization and institutionalization of the arts in this period [see *viewing, 20]. His name appears on a 1753 circular calling for the establishment of a national school and repository for art. He donated work to the Foundling Hospital and became a member of the Society of Artists, whose annual exhibitions provided a valuable showcase for contemporary art. In 1765 the Society of Artists received a royal charter of incorporation, which was later upgraded to the foundation of the Royal Academy of Arts. Conspicuous among his peers for his 'professional rank, his large fortune, the circle of society in which he moved', as his ex-student James Northcote (1746–1831) describes in the *Memoirs*, Reynolds was unanimously elected president of the Royal Academy in 1768, a position he held without interruption until 1790.

Reynolds's *Discourses* grew from lectures composed to mark the Academy's annual distribution of prizes. The first discourse was delivered in January 1769 to commemorate the opening of the institution and the fifteenth—in which Reynolds pronounced the name 'Michelangelo' as the final public statement on art—was delivered in December 1790. A collected edition of the first seven performances, with an introduction by Samuel *Johnson (falsely rumoured to be their real author), was published in 1778. The *Discourses* is a seminal treatise of British neoclassicism: Reynolds sets out rules for the study of art and cultivation of taste, examines the principles of beauty and notions of invention, expression and imitation, *genius and *imagination, and touches on the civic responsibilities of art. He is emphatic about the place of *history painting in the hierarchy of artistic production. Reynolds's own efforts in this branch included *Count Hugolino and His Children in the Dungeon*, exhibited at the Royal Academy in 1773, *Infant Hercules* (1788), a work admired by Henry *Fuseli and James *Barry for its *sublimity, and the figure of *Theory* adoring the ceiling of the Royal Academy library. John *Boydell commissioned five paintings from Reynolds for his Shakespeare Gallery, including the controversial *Death of Cardinal Beaufort*. Reynolds also executed works for Bowyer's Historic Gallery and Macklin's Poets' Gallery.

Reynolds's considerable energy found expression in sociability as well as in art. He founded the Literary Club and was a long-time member of the Dilettanti Society, well-heeled amateur collectors and connoisseurs whom he commemorated in a group portrait finished in 1780. He maintained a close friendship with Samuel Johnson for over thirty years (perhaps the best testament of his social stamina) and was a confidant of Edmund *Burke, David Garrick (1717–79), and Oliver Goldsmith (1728–74). The latter described Reynolds in a mock epitaph entitled 'Retaliation': 'his pencil was striking, restless, and grand / His manners were gentle, complying, and bland.' In 1781 and 1783 Reynolds made tours of Holland and Flanders, drawing up critical remarks on the paintings he viewed. He continued to work until 1789, when he lost sight in his left eye. He died of liver disease in February 1792 and was interred with great state in St Paul's Cathedral. His large collection of Old Master paintings and drawings was sold by auction in 1795 and 1798. The British institution took the novel step of mounting a retrospective of Reynolds's works in 1813, the first such exhibition held in the country. In the catalogue of this show, Reynolds is characterized as a painter who had raised himself and his profession through application and diligence: his finest pictures taught the connoisseur what to value and the artist what to follow, while his inferior or faded paintings (the result of unsuccessful experimentation with colour) taught the student not to despair.   CSM

RHYS, Morgan John (1760–1804), Baptist minister. Although he died at the relatively young age of 44, Rhys's career was highly eventful, and no historian would endorse his own description of himself as 'an insignificant Welsh Baptist'. A man of enormous energy and initiative, he was fired by the ideals of the *French Revolution during his period of office as Baptist minister of Pen-y-garn, near Pontypool. He resigned from the ministry in June 1791, went to London to establish a French Bible Society, and travelled to Paris to launch a crusade among the *sans-culottes* on behalf of Protestant Bible-reading and liberty of conscience. Rhys fervently believed that the revolution in France was the fulfilment of biblical *prophecies, and that the destruction of the Popish Antichrist would usher in an age governed by peace, harmony, and prosperity.

Inspired by his Parisian experiences, Rhys launched the first Welsh political journal. Entitled *Y Cylchgrawn Cynmraeg* (The Welsh Journal), it publicized the ideals of liberty, equality, and fraternity, and included Welsh translations of some of the works of *Volney, Voltaire, and the millenarian Bicheno. It also became a vehicle for propaganda against parliamentary corruption, crippling taxes, bribery, class privilege, the slave trade, and war. Only five numbers of the journal (at three different presses) were published in 1793–4, but Rhys's flinty radicalism continued to cause unease in government circles. Hounded by *spies, he began to urge his fellow countrymen to forsake the corrupt, ungodly, and illegitimate British state for the Land of the Free across the Atlantic. Bitter and disillusioned, he sailed from Liverpool in August 1794. Convinced that the 'Signs of the Times' betokened crisis years for the people of Wales, he was certain that God had singled him out to fulfil an age-old dream, namely the establishment of a *Gwladfa*, a national home in the American West for the despised and downtrodden Welsh.

In America Rhys embarked on extensive and exhausting preaching tours during which he championed the rights of black people, Red Indians, and slaves. His name became synonymous with liberty of conscience, pacifism, and anti-slavery. In 1798 he bought a substantial tract of land in the Allegheny mountains which he named Cambria. It was here that a Welsh settlement, appropriately christened Beulah, was established as an asylum for hundreds of Welsh emigrants. At Beulah Rhys published a radical newspaper called the *Western Sky*, launched a *missionary society for the Red Indians, and established a new denomination known as the Church of Christ. His model community, however, failed to live up to his expectations, and in 1799 he moved to Somerset County, USA, where he died five years later.

In an anti-slavery tract which he translated into Welsh and published in 1789, Rhys described himself as 'a Welshman opposed to all oppression'. In many ways, he was the epitome of the *citoyen du monde*, a man who boldly championed the cause of liberty on both sides of the Atlantic and who stood proudly on the ruins of the Bastille.   GHJ

RICARDO, David (1772–1823), political economist and MP. Through his publications and parliamentary speeches, Ricardo influenced government policy on such matters as the currency, *corn laws, *poor laws, and *income taxation. His theories attracted such prominent disciples as Thomas *De Quincey, James *Mill, John McCulloch (1789–1864), and John Stuart *Mill.

Son of a Dutch Jew who settled in England and prospered through the stock exchange, Ricardo's early career was also spent in the stock exchange, where he made a sufficiently large fortune to be able to retire in 1814. His interest in **political economy** [33], sparked by reading *Smith's *Wealth of Nations* (1776) in 1799, led him to write a number of letters to the *Morning Chronicle* on the bullion controversy which formed the basis of his 1810 pamphlet, *The High Price of Bullion*. Ricardo argued that the 1797 Order in Council suspending the convertibility of *Bank of England notes to bullion had led to inflated prices and the depreciation of the pound. He called for a regulation of money supply by an immediate resumption of convertibility.

In 1815 Ricardo addressed another controversy, the corn laws. His *Essay on the Influence of a Low Price of Corn on the Profits of Stock* argued that duties on imported corn effectively raised wages, and therefore reduced the profit margin for manufacturers. Ricardo's *Principles of Political Economy and Taxation* (1817) propounded the idea that agricultural capital and labour would yield progressively diminishing returns, since *population increase resulted in the use of *land [16] of an inferior quality. Ricardo's text also corroborated *Malthus's view of population, in emphasizing the need for checks to restrain the growth of the labouring classes.

In 1819 Ricardo entered parliament as the member for Portarlington, where his first significant act was to give evidence before a parliamentary committee on the bullion issue. His opinion prevailed with Lord *Liverpool's government despite the objections of commercial and manufacturing interests which believed that the resumption of convertibility would

depress trade. Ricardo's parliamentary speeches consistently advocated freedom of trade and the removal of government interventions. In addition to his criticism of the corn laws, he also spoke out against the poor laws, believing that they encouraged a redundant poor while taxing industry [see *poverty, 12]. He objected to a proposal to relieve large families by providing asylum for their children, on the grounds that this assurance would be an encouragement to population increase. He also supported William Huskisson's (1770–1830) proposal to repeal the Spitalfields acts, which empowered magistrates to fix the wages of silk weavers. Ricardo's *laissez-faire* doctrine went hand in hand with a *liberalism that supported *parliamentary reform, the introduction of the ballot, and freedom of expression.

Ricardo retired from parliament in 1823, due to illness, and died the same year. His influence continued long after his death, largely because of John Stuart Mill, who was perhaps his most widely read disciple and who also drew on the liberal heritage of Jeremy *Bentham. Mill's *Principles of Political Economy* (1848) utilizes such Ricardian doctrines as the declining marginal productivity of agricultural capital and the need for wages to be freely determined rather than influenced by government intervention.   RG

RIES, Ferdinand (1784–1838), virtuoso *pianist and composer, who contributed particularly to advances in pianism during his residence in London (1813–24). English audiences admired the power and technical assurance of his playing, praising its 'Romantic wildness' which was considered 'purely German'.

From 1814 Ries figured prominently in the Philharmonic Society *concerts, as soloist and composer of concertos, symphonies, and chamber works. He also served as principal link between the Society and *Beethoven, with whom he had studied piano for six years in Vienna; he was instrumental in their commissioning of the Ninth Symphony in 1822. His own compositions were highly regarded by many as products of the Beethoven school.   RC

riots and disturbances. The British propensity to demonstrate and riot was proverbial. The issues involved included electoral and populist politics, industrial relations, technological redundancy, the privatization of land and roads, recruitment of the armed services, and above all subsistence problems. In some senses these were national issues, but they were joined by a plethora of local matters.

The most common cause of mass mobilizations was recurrent subsistence problems. These became increasingly national, as opposed to regional, most notably in the three *famines during the prolonged French *wars [2]. During these crises Britain experienced intense rioting. If some of these riots manifested new symptoms of populist conviction in democratic political principles current after the *French Revolution, their principal features drew on an ancient ideological corpus which E. P. Thompson called the 'moral economy' of the crowd. That ideology hinged on two basic principles: that food prices should be affordable, and that traders should not profiteer by exploiting consumers through such practices as adulteration, withholding supplies, engrossing stocks, and market manipulations. In outbreaks of riot, market-place crowds arbitrarily fixed prices at popularly determined levels, deemed to be fair, often forcibly stopping consignments of food dispatched by roads, river, canal, and along the coast [see *transport]. They also insisted that farmers market their produce rather than speculate with prices. Magistrates and local élites were enjoined to use their ancient powers—in abeyance in normal years—to control markets, food supplies, and suppliers so as to protect consumers' interests. Magistrates commonly complied, at least to a degree, sometimes increasing the poor relief under the statutory system (at least in England and Wales) and organizing subscription charities to combat the exigency [see *poor laws].

Concepts of legitimacy almost invariably underpinned other objectives of the mobilized crowd—one reason for their frequently conservative, even reactionary cast, as in the anti-Catholic *Gordon riots of 1780. A parallel case is the Bristol riots of 1831, when a huge crowd mobilized initially to protest against the rejection of the First *Reform Bill by the House of Lords. What began as a demonstration against the Bishop, who had voted in the majority, escalated into an orgy of prolonged violence over several days, revealing deep-seated hostility to the state, local government, and upper classes. With the creation of turnpike trusts, which effectively privatized existing roads, the introduction of gates to facilitate the collection of tolls also provoked considerable resentment. If turnpike protests never achieved the intensity of food riots, this *class [15] antipathy survived and was expressed most notably in the Welsh Rebecca riots of the late 1830s and 1840s.

Parliamentary *enclosure attained its zenith during our period, generating varieties of rural protest [see *land, 16]. Taking their name from a mythical leader, the Captain Swing riots of 1830 were, however, the explosive product of the prolonged postwar agricultural depression which engulfed much of southern and eastern England. Hundreds of rural communities participated in this wave of mobilization and riot. The principal objectives reflected manifold grievances, including the low wages of rural workers; perennial exposure to under- and unemployment, aggravated by some technological redundancy; increasingly devalued levels of poor relief; taxes on items of mass consumption; and the exactions of tithe owners. Swing achieved *insurrectionary proportions in the autumn of 1830, additionally deploying tactics of incendiarism. Parish employers and ratepayers were forced to increase employment levels, wages, and poor law allowances, while tithe owners were compelled to reduce their exactions to enable employers to meet the protesters' demands. Landlords volunteered or were cajoled into rent reductions to the

same ends. Politically advanced Swing activists also articulated commitments to radical *parliamentary reform.

Some historians have identified a fundamental shift in patterns of riot during our period from concern with food price levels to that of wages, leading to an increasing reliance on workplace alliances—combinations—rather than on crowd action to achieve required incomes. However, despite the marked upsurge in collective tactics which responded to pronounced and apparently irreversible inflation in the 1790s, industrial relations nevertheless retained much of their violent, early-eighteenth-century characteristic. Rioting accompanied many disputes over the increasingly fraught issue of machinery and technological redundancy, sometimes linked with the threat to traditional cottage or domestic outwork organizations posed by experimentation with *factory systems [see *industrialization, 14].

As the eighteenth century progressed, disputes in textiles, printing, *engineering, papermaking, timber, and shipbuilding intensified. Machine-breaking was a long-established tradition, but in the disputes which eventually found expression in *Luddism, resort to violence was not immediate. In the anti-technology campaign in West Country and West Riding woollens at the turn of the century, prolonged but ultimately unsuccessful negotiation was followed by attempted legal moves and parliamentary *petitioning before violence was used. However, eventual violence in these regions, notably the nocturnal variety, again reached insurrectionary proportions, symbolized by the fact that more troops were committed to containing the Luddites than were available to the Duke of *Wellington in the critical *Peninsular phase of the war with France.

Rioters were drawn predominantly from relatively respectable and employed members of working-class communities, in some cases supported—if not led—by their womenfolk, together with children. Some cases witnessed the participation of those somewhat higher in the social pyramid, including smaller farmers in anti-enclosure mobilizations and in the Captain Swing riots, and those employers who reacted against industrial technologies and restructuring.

State reaction was influenced both by the lessons of the French Revolution and by sympathy with *laissez-faire economic principles. These last were insisted upon particularly strongly during the wartime famines, when government, backed by substantial parliamentary majorities, ordered the immediate suppression of food riots, supported by the army where necessary. Likewise, popular opposition to industrial developments was also resisted by the state, which viewed cheapening production as an individual employer right and as a national good. Thus governments usually unambiguously supported local authorities when deaths resulted from clashes between soldiers and the crowd, though they normally sought to prevent extensive capital retribution at the hands of the *judges after violent episodes. The notoriously savage British penal code remained basically intact during the Romantic age, not least because it embraced *revolution [1] too.   RW

RITSON, Joseph (1752–1803), antiquarian, critic, and *vegetarian who played a key role in the revival of interest in *ballads and popular antiquities and in the development of more accurate standards of editorship and criticism.

Born in the north-east of England, after education in a local school Ritson entered the law as a conveyancer, a profession which gave him ample opportunities to develop his interests in *antiquarianism [35], and he moved in the same vibrant provincial intellectual circles as *Bewick, *Holcroft, and *Spence. He shared Spence's interest in spelling reform, adopting an idiosyncratic phonetic system of his own in the 1780s [see *language, 40]. In 1775 he set up a successful conveyancing practice in London, being appointed bailiff of the liberty of the Savoy in 1784. Residence in London allowed him to expand his antiquarian work by pursuing an exhaustive course of reading in the *British Museum.

Ritson's taste for literary controversy revealed itself in his anonymous *Observations* (1782) on Thomas *Warton's *History of English Literature, 1100–1603*. Ritson questioned Warton's scholarly credentials in a way that was regarded as ungentlemanly, but his more fundamental objection was to the fact that Warton had not gone far enough in his revision of Samuel *Johnson's classically biased perspective on English literary history. Ritson's reputation for combativeness was compounded with his attacks on Johnson and George Steevens's (1736–1800) edition of *Shakespeare in 1783. In opposition to the latter's neoclassical tendencies, Ritson wanted to stress the vernacular Shakespeare, 'the poet of nature, addicted to no system of bigotry'. Ritson published sharp criticisms of most of the subsequent editors of Shakespeare and in 1795 detected William *Ireland's forgeries.

These controversies aside, Ritson's major claim to literary fame rested on his collections of popular antiquities. He had been a collector of local songs and ballads in the 1770s and 1780s, but reached national notice through his typically vigorous attack on Bishop Thomas *Percy in the preface to his *Select Collection of English Songs* (1783). The *Selection* was published by Joseph *Johnson with vignettes engraved by *Blake after *Stothard. It was followed by a series of other similar collections which continued and amplified the dispute with Percy, including *Pieces of Ancient Popular Poetry* (1791), illustrated by Bewick, *Ancient Songs* (1792), illustrated by Stothard, and *Robin Hood* (1795), which came with cuts by Bewick.

Ritson's argument with Percy was based on fundamentally different conceptions of cultural authority. He refuted Percy's view that the ballads which circulated in the *popular culture [23] of the eighteenth century were the degraded remains of aristocratic originals. Ritson, in contrast, saw a continuity in popular culture which preserved what amounted to an alternative tradition, replete with its own version of history enshrined in ballads and folklore. The differences between Percy and Ritson were also evident in their editing techniques. Percy strove to represent the songs and ballads of his collections in a polite

form, whereas Ritson delighted in the rougher qualities of his ballads, preserving the fact that they were 'extremely incorrect' and ran into the 'utmost licence of meter'. Most reviewers preferred Percy's manicured versions, the *British Critic* finding the Robin Hood ballads too close to the state 'in which they may be found in any vulgar copy of Robin Hood's Garland dangling on the walls of the poor ballad stationers'. By the mid-1790s such responses were increasingly informed by an antagonism to the *republicanism which Ritson displayed in his notes and prefaces. He associated with active members of the reform movement in London, such as, *Godwin, Holcroft, and *Thelwall, and his letters suggest he was also intimate with *Eaton and Spence, perhaps providing antiquarian material for their respective periodicals, *Politics for the People* and *Pig's Meat*.

Sir Walter *Scott, who admired Ritson's knowledge, if not his politics and temperament, consulted him while collecting material for his *Minstrelsy of the Scottish Border* (1802–3). After staying with Scott for a period in 1801, Ritson resumed his own writing with enthusiasm, publishing his *Abstinence from Animal Food as a Moral Duty* (1802) of which *Southey remarked: 'every page and almost every line ... teems with blasphemy'. His *Ancient English Metrical Romances* was published in the same year, but was largely neglected in favour of George Ellis's (1783–1815) *Specimens of Early Romances* (1805), despite Scott's attempt to do justice to Ritson's work in a review of the latter in 1806. Ritson gave way to insanity in 1803, barricading himself in his room in Gray's Inn and setting fire to many of his manuscripts. He died a few days later, remembered more as the crank shown in the cruel caricatures of him made by James Sayers (1748–1823) and James *Gillray than as someone who had made such important contributions to debates about the history of British culture over the preceding two decades.

JM

ROBERTSON, William (1721–93), historian and divine, friend of David *Hume, Adam *Smith, and Edward *Gibbon, was one of the ornaments of the *Scottish Enlightenment. He was best known for his immensely popular histories: *History of Scotland during the Reigns of Queen Mary and King James VI* (1759), *History of the Reign of the Emperor Charles V* (1769), and *History of America* (1777). Like Gibbon, he successfully married a philosophical interest in the development of societies and civilizations with the scholarly concerns of the *antiquarian [35]. His histories were remarkable both for their attention to comparative material and environmental factors and for the scope of what he referred to as their 'proofs and illustrations' [see *history, 38].

Unusually among his contemporaries, his interest in the sixteenth century was not so much concerned with the Renaissance and Reformation but rather with the origin of modern political structures—the conceptual starting-point of most nineteenth-century professional history—and with European exploration and conquest. Above all he provided his contemporaries with clear and vivid narratives of distinctive and exotic times and places. His account of Balboa beholding 'the South Seas stretching in endless prospect below him' was misremembered by John *Keats as Cortez staring at the Pacific 'upon a peak in Darien'.   AMACL

ROBINSON, Henry Crabb (1775–1867), whose diary comprises the longest, fullest, and most consistent record of intellectual life in London from 1811 to 1867. The son of a tanner, Robinson was educated at an inferior *Dissenting academy in Devizes, unprofitably articled to a Colchester attorney, and buried in a London clerkship from 1796 to 1798, when a legacy of £100 a year brought him independence. Like many orthodox Dissenters at the time, he had moved into *Unitarianism, and though his early Jacobin sympathies soon faded, he remained a radically tinged liberal, dedicated to the *abolitionist cause, and a long-time supporter of the secular University College, London. From 1800 to 1805 he lived in Germany, studying at the University of Jena, meeting the principal Romantic writers including Goethe and Madame de *Staël, and supplementing his Unitarian heritage from John *Locke, David Hartley (1705–57), and Joseph *Priestley with an intensive study of Kant.

A fixture in the radical intellectual circles of the London Unitarians, in 1807–9 he was a correspondent for *The Times* in Germany and Spain, alternating with work in the paper's London offices as 'a sort of foreign editor'. Called to the Bar in 1813, Robinson practised chiefly on the Norwich circuit until 1828. A wonderfully sociable bachelor and committed, like his early Norwich friend William *Taylor, to serving as a mediator and missionary for German culture, he knew intimately all the London writers, major and minor, over more than sixty years and was a careful observer of political, religious, and literary currents.

His early letters from Germany, the diary, and the travel journals have been extensively excerpted, but the many manuscript volumes, now in Dr Williams's Library, London, can still be profitably consulted for, among other subjects, reports of his assiduous theatregoing.   RKW

ROBINSON, Mary 'Perdita' (1758–1800), actress, courtesan, poet, novelist, and memoirist. Born Mary Darby in Bristol, she was at first genteelly educated at the school run by Hannah *More and her sisters. When Mary was 13 her father deserted his wife to hunt whales off the Labrador coast. With few resources, and three children, her mother moved to London. Mary was plucked out of the Misses More's school, which charged high fees, and sent to inferior schools, at one of which a lesbian teacher, Meribah Lorington, encouraged her to write love *poetry [29].

In 1774 David Garrick (1717–79) rehearsed her as the latest in a long line of Cordelias to his King Lear. But her stage debut was cancelled when she married Thomas Robinson, to whom she bore a daughter, Maria Elizabeth. In 1775, the Duchess of *Devonshire assisted Mary Robinson to publish a first volume of poems, and in 1776 she signed a contract for

the Drury Lane season under its incoming manager R. B. *Sheridan. In five years Robinson played most of *Shakespeare's romantic heroines, and was a great success in cross-dressed trouser roles [see *theatre, 24]. Her portrait was painted by leading painters, including Sir Joshua *Reynolds. Robinson's stage-work established the patterns of heterosexual relations, eroticized self-display, and competitive improvisation which she was to bring to her poetry. It was also decisive in separating her permanently from respectable female society.

In December 1779, aged 21, she played 'Perdita', in Garrick's adaptation of Shakespeare's *The Winter's Tale*, before the 18-year-old George, Prince of Wales (later George IV). Smitten, he sent her letters signed 'Florizel', and promised to settle £20,000 on her. Malicious gossip about the liaison decided Robinson to retire from the stage. In 1781 Perdita's carriage with its masculine entourage was the most fashionable spectacle in London, but by the end of the year the Prince had tired of his Player Princess. Abruptly facing destitution, she appealed to Charles James *Fox to make a bargain for her with the Prince, and he salvaged an annuity of £500.

Until the outbreak of *war [2] in 1792 she rusticated in France, and solaced her disappointments with poetry. In 1784 her legs became permanently paralysed, possibly when a pregnancy miscarried, for she was now the lover of a swashbuckling military man, Colonel (later General) Sir Banastre Tarleton, who eventually abandoned her in 1798 for a politically advantageous marriage. In 1788 Robinson had joined Hannah *Cowley, Hester *Piozzi, and Robert *Merry in the pages of the *World* newspaper as one of the *Della Cruscan circle. Her two-volume *Poems* appeared in 1791–3 and in 1796 a *sonnet sequence, *Sappho to Phaon*, invoked the Ovidian *Sappho in love with a young man. The very fine late *ballad 'The Haunted Beach' engaged in a transfusive correspondence with S. T. *Coleridge's *The Rime of the Ancient Mariner* (1798). Robinson also published novels which sold well, including *Walsingham; Or, The Pupil of Nature* (4 vols., 1797). From 1797 she contributed urban *pastorals of London life to Daniel Stuart's *Morning Post*. Her interlocutors now were the rising male poets on the liberal wing of politics, Robert *Southey and Coleridge. In 1799, after the death of her friend Mary *Wollstonecraft, and the fit of public morality which greeted William *Godwin's *Memoirs* of Wollstonecraft in 1798, she published (as 'Anne Frances Randall') *A Letter to the Women of England, on the Injustice of Mental Subordination* which was given a hostile review in the *Monthly Review*. Her last poems, *Lyrical Tales*, were published eight days before her death on 26 December 1800. Her daughter Maria Elizabeth completed and published Robinson's *Memoirs* in 1801, and her *Poetical Works* in 1806.   JB

ROGERS, Samuel (1763–1855), banker, poet, patron, art connoisseur. Rogers's indifference to either political party, along with the wealth he derived from his family's banking business and the phenomenal success of his fastidiously crafted *poetry [29], gave him the access he craved to most of the distinguished social and cultural groups of the day, where he could indulge a passion for gossip, art, and talented company. Few of the vast numbers of memoirs and diaries written by public figures of the period, male or female, are without some reference to Rogers, an habitué of *Holland House and other fashionable London gatherings and an inveterate 'caller-in' also renowned for his own breakfast parties at St James's Place. In a sociable period, Rogers was sociable to a fault, or to the detriment of his reputation, for he features so often as an acerbic gossip as to have become typecast.

Rogers was in fact a successful banker, before handing the family business over to his younger brother in 1802; a talented and successful poet (his *Pleasures of Memory* of 1792, written in polished rhyming couplets with a complex aural patterning, ran to nineteen editions by the turn of the century and by 1820 had sold around 25,000 copies); an art connoisseur with commitment and assured taste— upon both of which he was prepared to act, becoming a major figure in the establishment of the *National Gallery and contributing many of the finest works from his own collection, which was still valued at £150,000 on his death [see *viewing, 20].

Though discriminating, Rogers was equally generous with financial assistance to poets and painters (few went without his help with money, comment, or proofreading). And throughout 92 years he was more capable of genuine friendships than his reputation would suggest, with people of all ages and as different as William *Gilpin and Charles James *Fox (whose epitaph he wrote); Lord *Byron and the Duke of *Wellington; Lady Holland and Mary *Shelley; Thomas *Moore and William *Wordsworth; Ruskin and *Dickens.

Byron—who admittedly ran hot and cold—celebrated Rogers's *Pleasures of Memory* in *English Bards and Scotch Reviewers* (1809) as one of the redeeming literary features of the age, and published his *Lara* with Rogers's *Jacqueline* in 1814. Ruskin dedicated his *Stones of Venice* (1853) to Rogers as the author of *Italy*, the work on which Rogers lavished inordinate care in the 1820s and 1830s. He combined with his love of both poetry and art (scrupulously attending to the illustrations commissioned from *Turner and *Stothard) the political *liberalism and religious tolerance that he inherited from his Dissenting parents and the philosophical radicals amongst their friends. Joseph *Priestley was a familiar of his childhood, spending his last night with the Rogers family before his self-exile to America, and Richard *Price inspired him to wish to enter the ministry from which he was disqualified by a weak voice. Though neither radical nor populist himself, Rogers devoted the time not spent in gossip, composition, and touring France and Italy to many liberal causes of the day, promoting and subscribing heavily to the new University of London, for example.

When Rogers was offered the laureateship on the death of Wordsworth in 1850, sensitive to his 87 years and always diffident about his own talent, he recommended its award to Tennyson, another friend and a poet whose work he admired—as well as he might have, for it was heavily influenced by his own.   WC

romance, a term applied to various forms of verse and prose narrative displaying archaic or exotic subject-matter, imaginative freedom, and motifs or structural features derived form *medieval and Renaissance romances (collectively known as 'old Romance'). Such forms, which included allegorical poems, *Gothic and historical novels, verse tales on historical, **mythological** [36], and *oriental themes, and more experimental forms of psychological quest romance, acquired enormous popularity in the period, and subsequently contributed to the labelling of its dominant literary culture as 'Romantic'.

The re-emergence of romance in the secular, rationalist world of the late eighteenth century constituted a revolution in taste, reversing the critical assumptions of the previous two centuries. Condemned by the puritans for its supposed licentiousness and superstition, and by the neoclassicists for its irregularity and extravagance, romance had found few to defend it from the comprehensive satire of Cervantes's *Don Quixote* (1605), and had generally fallen into contempt and disuse. Its revival partly inspired by the work of *antiquarian [35] scholars such as Thomas *Percy, Richard Hurd (1720–1808), and Thomas *Warton, reflected reawakened interest in the chivalric Middle Ages, as well as a reaction against the perceived limitations of neoclassical generic theory. The publication and discussion of the medieval romances, and the reappraisal of later *epic romances of the European Renaissance by Tasso, Ariosto, and above all *Spenser, led modern writers to imitate and experiment with this highly versatile genre, which proved capable of an extraordinary range of transformations.

Romance was a major influence on the development of the *novel [31], both in its theory and its practice. In *poetry [29], one of the earliest forms was the Spenserian imitation, common from the 1730s. Thomas *Beattie's *Minstrel* (1771) transforms this static allegorical model by introducing the poet as hero, and by portraying, in a more naturalistic way, the progress of *genius. Variously modified, this new paradigm provides the basis of poems as diverse as *Wordsworth's *Prelude*, *Shelley's *Alastor* (1816), *Clare's *The Village Minstrel* (1821), and *Byron's 'Romaunt' of *Childe Harold's Pilgrimage* (1812–18), all of which display the introspective tendency and visionary patterns characteristic of Romantic quest romance (though Byron's also has a marked anti-romance element which at times borders on parody). Equally characteristic of the period is the combination of romance with other genres, as in *Blake's *Milton* (1804–8), *Keats's *Endymion* (1818), and Shelley's *Prometheus Unbound* (1820).

In contrast to the modernized versions of romance by Byron and Shelley, *Coleridge's fragment *Christabel* (1816) and Keats's *Eve of St Agnes* (1820) are fictitious narratives set in medieval times which are particularly striking for their creation of an atmosphere of romance, heavy with enchantment and ambiguous sexuality. Compelling, dreamlike, and mysterious, this vision of the medieval world, and of romance as pure imagination, later influenced Tennyson and the Pre-Raphaelites.

In the eyes of contemporaries, however, it was *Scott's historical verse romances, beginning with *The Lay of the Last Minstrel* (1805), which best captured the pace and pageantry of medieval narrative, creating a large, new readership for narrative poetry and a cultural vogue for chivalry. Of Scott's many imitators, the most successful was Byron, whose 'Turkish Tales' of 1813–14 extended the fashion for oriental romances already established by *Southey's *Thalaba the Destroyer* (1801) and *The Curse of Kehama* (1810). Later contributions to this important subgenre included *Moore's *Lalla Rookh* (1817), *Peacock's unpublished *Ahrimanes*, and Shelley's *Laon and Cythna* (1817).

Escapist, hierarchical, and aristocratic, yet also idealistic and potentially revolutionary, romance remained a controversial and politically ambivalent genre which at its most complex explored some of the deepest desires and anxieties of the age. Its polarizing, visionary quality also made it a suitable vehicle for polemic, metaphors of romance and chivalry frequently informing both *Burke's counter-revolutionary writings and those of his opponents.
DD

Romantic irony. The German philosopher Friedrich Schlegel (1772–1829) developed the theory of Romantic irony to characterize, both ontologically and rhetorically, an attitude of detached scepticism adopted by the highest 'modern' or post-classical art towards its own activity and/or material.

According to Schlegel's construction, ironic works of art are informed by an awareness that their own expressive or representational means are necessarily incommensurate with the transcendental Idea they strive to comprehend. In short, they are necessarily 'fictions'. Schlegel acknowledged as a paradigm of the human condition that noble beauty was created only to fail—and the more noble and beautiful the aspiring creation, the more acute the sense of failure and the deeper the irony.

One corollary of this awareness of the limits of human apprehension and creativity is that apprehension and creativity—the artist's and the reader's—become themselves the subject-matter of the work of art. Inadequate discourse (or fiction) is for critical purposes displaced by discourse about fictiveness and fiction-making.

While for German Romantic aestheticians such as Köpke 'Irony is not merely negative, it is rather through and through positive'—a version of the fortunate fall, in fact—the term 'irony' sometimes also designates Byronic pessimism about the self-sabotaging idealism of humanity. The concomitant awareness of its own fictiveness that art betrays thus becomes desperate, even nihilistic, and Romantic irony can be seen to anticipate recent forms of anti-humanist deconstruction.
WC

romanticism. Although the idea of the 'romantic' was certainly current in the period which we now normally characterize by its 'romanticism', and which is encompassed in this *Romantic Age Companion*, the poets and literary doctrines that have become definitively important parts of that 'ism' did not usually earn the epithet at the time. Complicating the issue further, the poets whom we customarily think of as 'romantic'—upholders of the romantic world-view or the 'romantic ideology'—did not typically consider themselves romantic, and most would not have been honoured to learn that others did. 'Romantic' at the time had a cluster of associated meanings which we know from its colloquial usage today: things associated with *romance, like medieval enchantments and wild scenery; the more sophisticated senses of the word, now uppermost, like 'organicism' or 'idealism', only find themselves gathered to the word in the later nineteenth century.

When we try to define what romanticism means, our instinct is to return to all the works gathered under the name and find out what they have in common; but if there are different uses of the word, we should be careful to compare like with like. William *Blake may be exemplarily 'romantic' thanks to a usage entirely distinct from that by which *Byron is self-evidently 'romantic'. We should be on our guard against this kind of pun: the critic René Wellek once mounted a stirring defence of the concept on the basis of the continuity of its semantic life, but the persistence of the mere *word* is really neither here nor there. For most literary scholars, S. T. *Coleridge is effectively—though unwittingly—*the* spokesman for English romantic theory because he propounds so vehemently doctrines of organic form, the *imagination, the precedence of 'mind' over 'nature', and so forth; but for his contemporaries he was a 'romantic' poet (when he was) because, unlike William *Wordsworth who wrote about everyday things in ordinary language, he wrote about wonders and mysteries, and events confounding reason, as in 'Christabel' (comp. 1797–1801) or 'The Ancient Mariner' (comp. 1797–8). The important literary categories for much of the nineteenth century, in their origins mostly journalistic, made the 'romantic' one movement among several: Wordsworth, Coleridge, and Robert *Southey formed a 'Lake School'; James Leigh *Hunt, John *Keats, William *Hazlitt, and others a 'Cockney School'; while the poets singled out as superlatively 'romantic' were Walter *Scott and Byron (in his oriental tales and *Childe Harold* (pub. 1812–18). Wordsworth, championing the language of men, was frequently cast as the very antithesis of everything romantic; for modern critics from M. H. Abrams to Jerome McGann, on the other hand, the romantic *Weltanschauung* is practically synonymous with Wordsworth.

'Romanticism', then, has its own history, and we should be aware of it. Any literary classification, like romanticism, depends upon—and in turn helps to define—a cluster of literary works which exemplify it; and the shape of the history of 'romanticism' can be discovered by watching the fluctuating canon of authors successively ranged beneath its flag. Taking a long view over the last 200 years, there appear to be three broad defining movements within the 'romantic' canon. First, the marginalization of Scott and Byron—implying, perhaps, a category increasingly determined by more abstract or philosophical concerns as opposed to one describing plots and settings of narrative: something more akin to 'realism', therefore, and less like (say) *Gothic. Second, we can track the growing dominance of Wordsworth, so that the figure who is the opposite of 'romantic' in the period is now usually seen its very quintessence, especially the author of that great epic of the self, *The Prelude* (comp. 1798–1839)—a poem which only becomes central to Wordsworth's *œuvre* in the twentieth century. Third, particularly since the early twentieth century, we can see the startling rise of Blake: for a historian of the early years of the century Blake would be a marginal figure, scarcely integral to a definition of romanticism; while for the modern critic Harold Bloom in *The Visionary Company* (1961) Blake is *the* definitive case, away from which the other poets shade.

Given the eminence of Blake, it is no surprise to find that foremost in most modern definitions of romanticism stands some brand of philosophical idealism, often derived from Kantian sources: for it was Blake (independent of Immanuel Kant, incidentally) who proclaimed that mental things alone are real; and we can find similarly enthusiastic idealisms in Coleridge and Percy *Shelley. This is what has come to be known as 'romantic ideology'; so that critics who complain of modern thinking about 'romanticism' as incorrigibly infected by 'romantic' habits might see the very creation by literary historians of a totalizing mental creation like 'romanticism' as a sign of the malaise. But the prominence of Wordsworth in the canon complicates things: the celebrant of mind as lord and master fits an idealist romanticism; but the poet keeping his eye steadily upon his subject (as he says in the Preface to *Lyrical Ballads* (1800)) evidently holds to a brand of realism quite contrary to it. (Blake's marginalia show that he clearly recognized Wordsworth's divided nature on this point.) If an idealist emphasis upon the mind is predisposed to value the unity that the mind is able to create from the given plurality of sense experience that it receives, then a countering realism is likely to stress the opposite: the worth and respectability of nature's ordinary, independent diversity. Close inquiry into Coleridge and Shelley may reveal similarly counter-idealist trends.

This does not mean that a division between idealism and realism should be seen as *really* definitive of romanticism; but it does imply the way that our methodological problems with the word are anticipated in some of the poets of the period themselves. For while 'romanticism' is indeed a mental creation, and so in some sense an act of imagination, its totalizing, classificatory ambitions are constantly frustrated by a return to the diversity of works that it sought to gather together; and in this intrinsic hesitation between the categorical claim of unity and a realist loyalty to diversity, the concept proceeds on its properly uncertain path.   SPP

ROMILLY, Sir Samuel (1757–1818), barrister and *law [8] reformer. A remarkable autodidact and early admirer of the European *philosophes*, Romilly conceived a horror for the cruelty and injustice of the criminal law. He published anonymously an early tract advocating penal reform (1786), but his views achieved little recognition until he became a leader at the Bar and entered parliament. His dogged campaign for *parliamentary reform after 1806 achieved only limited success in the unfavourable climate of *Tory domination, and his untimely suicide prevented any chance of accelerating the process.   DL

ROMNEY, George (1734–1802), English portrait and history painter associated with literary circles and well known for his many paintings of Emma *Hamilton. Like John *Opie, Romney was of modest rural origins, and trained under his father, a cabinet-maker. His facility in capturing likeness led to his apprenticeship to an itinerant artist, Christopher Steele, and he began painting portraits and copies of Old Masters. In 1762 he moved to London, followed in 1764 by a trip to Paris which fuelled his desire to be a history painter, reinforced by a visit to Italy in 1773–5. His reputation grew significantly after his meeting with Emma Hart, later Lady Hamilton, in 1782, his depictions of her blending qualities of *portraiture and *history painting. He showed her in numerous guises and poses, and as literary, mythological, and allegorical characters, such as Daphne, Hebe, Nature, a seamstress, a Bacchante, and Miranda from Shakespeare's *The Tempest*. He also used Lady Hamilton's face in history paintings produced for *Boydell's Shakespeare Gallery. Many of these paintings were engraved, thus enhancing Romney's popularity. He also made contact with writers through his friendship with the poet William *Hayley, and he spent much time at Hayley's Sussex home, Eartham, where he met William *Cowper and Charlotte *Smith. He made a number of sketches for literary and historical paintings, but his livelihood continued to depend on portraiture.   SW

ROSCOE, William (1753–1831), historian. Famous in his lifetime as the first British biographer of Lorenzo de' Medici, Roscoe also contributed as an intellectual and politician to the early movements for *abolition and *parliamentary reform. Self-educated from the age of 12, Roscoe worked for his father, a market gardener, and briefly for a bookseller, before taking articles with a solicitor in 1769. He benefited from the nearby *Dissenting academy, absorbing the liberal politics of its members as well as their knowledge of modern and classical languages.

A gradualist and moderate, Roscoe directed his early reformist sympathies toward public *education [17]. He helped to found the Liverpool Society for the Encouragement of the Arts, and his 'Ode on the Institution of a Society in Liverpool' (1774) impressed Joshua *Reynolds and inaugurated Roscoe's lifelong involvement with partisan verse. He praised the *French Revolution in the broadsheet 'Day-Star of Liberty', and lampooned the 'Life, Death, and Wonderful Achievements of Edmund

Burke' in a mock-heroic *ballad (both 1791). His 'Wrongs of Africa' (1787–8), a benefit for the Committee for the Abolition of the Slave Trade, inverted liberal cliché, condemning *slavery [6] for its resemblance to monarchical tyrannies long banished from Britain.

Roscoe subscribed to no other national reform organization, but his liberal circle was influential in Liverpool, organizing meetings to commemorate the *Glorious Revolution and the fall of the Bastille, and circulating radical texts, including Mary *Wollstonecraft's A Vindication of the Rights of Woman. Defying the May 1792 Proclamation against seditious publications, Roscoe's group continued to distribute handbills, and *petitioned the King on behalf of the people of Liverpool [see *gagging acts]. However, the mayor suppressed the petition, and *loyalist threats forced the group to disband in 1793.

Roscoe resumed his work for cultural access, helping to establish the Liverpool Athenaeum (1798), and prepared his two monumental historical biographies [see *history, 38]. The Life of Lorenzo de' Medici (1795), which linked Lorenzo's cultural policies to public freedom and order, won the praise of Horace *Walpole. His Life and Pontificate of Leo the Tenth (1805) was less well received, and the Edinburgh Review led a general attack on Roscoe's sympathy with Catholicism.

In 1806 Roscoe was elected to parliament, where he voted against the slave trade and for Dissenting rights and public education, but his support for abolition cost him his seat in 1807. Despite postwar financial failures, and bankruptcy in 1820, he helped to inaugurate the Liverpool Royal Institution (1817), which offered public *lectures in sciences and letters. Roscoe continued until his death to publish tracts on parliamentary and *prison reform, as well as *children's literature, a *botanical treatise, and a controversially respectful edition of Pope.   MB

ROUSSEAU, Jean Jacques (1712–78), Genevan philosopher and novelist. A major if controversial contributor to the European *Enlightenment [32], he was a central influence on the cult of *sensibility [11] as it developed in Britain from the 1750s onwards. His *republican advocacy of simplicity of manners against aristocratic corruption made him a hero in liberal middle-class circles, especially in relation to his ideas on *education [17]. The advent of the *French Revolution, with which he was closely identified in Britain, coming in the wake of revelations about his private life in the press and his own Confessions, led to the rapid contraction of the circle of his admirers, although he remained a venerated figure among British radicals.

The first English translation of Discours sur les Sciences et les Arts appeared only a few months after the first French edition in 1751, but the book which really established a British reputation was Lettre à d'Alembert sur les Spectacles, which repudiated the didactic potential of the *theatre [24] and denounced its role in encouraging aristocratic fashion and female display. Reviewed at length in the British journals in 1759, Rousseau's pamphlet

secured him a reputation as a defender of a simple, manly, republican virtue against a corrupt and effeminate aristocratic culture, though even at this stage his primitivism was regarded as admirable more for its ardour than for its practicality. This reputation as a moralist of primitive virtue against modern luxury was reinforced by the popularity of the novels Julie, ou La Nouvelle Héloïse (1761) and Émile (1762).

The fourth part of the latter, La Profession de Foi du Vicaire Savoyard, was regarded as one of the most influential statements of natural religion in the century. Intended to refute the scepticism of the French philosophes, its celebration of the inner light of faith offended the religious authorities, and Rousseau was forced to flee from France. In Britain, despite some ominous rumblings in the *Tory press, the continental condemnation of Rousseau as a *Deist, subversive of established *religion [10], served to sanctify his image as a prophet of middle-class morality suffering at the hands of a corrupt aristocratic establishment. Indeed, the title of the first English translation, Emilius and Sophia (1762), foregrounded the novel's interest in domestic relations and its denunciation of aristocratic child-rearing practices (in particular upper-class women who left their children in the care of servants or schoolmasters and practised birth control). The ideas on education put forward in Émile influenced middle-class reformers such as Thomas *Day and Richard Lovell *Edgworth in their advocacy of the middle-class virtues of self-sufficiency and practicality, although the gospel of nature alienated *Evangelicals such as Sarah *Trimmer, who abhorred its banishment of Christianity from the nursery. Mary *Wollstonecraft later denounced Rousseau's failure to extend his principles to *female education, confining himself rather to 'the study of men, and to the attainment of agreeable accomplishments'.

Nevertheless, for most of the 1760s Rousseau's image as a man of *genius and sensibility survived unimpaired; but as stories about his personal life entered the daily press, so more and more questions were asked about his personal morality and the more radical political implications of his writing. Public knowledge of the break with David *Hume, which led to him leaving his British exile to return to France in 1770, accelerated these criticisms. Even so, this criticism was still more often couched in terms of personal instability, the madness of the inspired man, rather than the kind of political and religious heresy with which he was identified on the Continent: his reputation as a man 'whose heart was made to feel the great, the good, the beautiful, and the affecting', as the Monthly Review put it, remained essential to the cult of sensibility in Britain throughout the 1780s.

The decisive break in Rousseau's reputation came with the French Revolution and in particular Edmund *Burke's treatment of him. Once the French Assembly decided to honour Rousseau by erecting his statue in December 1790, the personal revelations of the Confessions, published in two parts in 1782 and 1789, were used to traduce both the man and the Revolution with which for British readers he became increasingly synonymous. His sexual preference for aristocratic women, often his employers, and the fact he had placed his illegitimate children in a foundling hospital were returned to obsessively by anti-Jacobin writers. Burke played a major part in representing Rousseau's personality as the key to understanding the values of the Revolution as a whole. A large portion of his *Letter to a Member of the National Assembly* (1791) is given over to attacking Rousseau. In Burke's hands, the hero of sensibility becomes a sensualist who would have the servants of the *ancien régime* seduce their mistresses. Indeed, in the figure of Rousseau the whole cult of the feeling heart was revealed as a creed of self-absorption and depravity. In the light of this kind of attack even sympathizers with the Revolution, such as Joseph *Priestley, found themselves concurring with Burke's estimate of Rousseau. Although Rousseau remained a hero of the Revolution in some popular radical circles, which reprinted cheap translations of his writing for a new readership in the 1790s, only a few literary commentators, Madame de *Staël and William *Hazlitt among them, were afterwards able to see in his literary sensibility the seeds of a universal benevolence. JM

ROWLANDSON, Thomas (1756–1827), watercolour artist, etcher, illustrator, portraitist, and caricaturist, the foremost graphic social satirist of the period. The son of a prosperous London tradesman, Rowlandson trained in both figure-drawing and topography at the *Royal Academy and in Paris, where he was influenced by the sensuality and decorative exuberance of French rococo draughtsmanship. He began his fifty-year career in 1777 as a *portrait painter, and subsequently exercised his versatility as a draughtsman in a range of subjects and artistic media. His technical range in pencil, pen and ink, and *watercolour was enormous. He was an accomplished etcher, using line and aquatint with limpid force in many of his book illustrations, and also an adventurous eroticist and *pornographer.

Rowlandson's work in caricature, which began in the 1780s, does not show the rabid destructive energies characteristic of James *Gillray. Rowlandson produced little political satire or portrait caricature of distinction, and exhibited none of Gillray's fascination with the interrelationship of imagery and text [see *prints, 22].

Rowlandson was at his greatest as a social *satirist veering between a sentimental comedy of manners and a furious Hogarthian moral didacticism. The majority of his satires deal in generalized ways with physical pleasures and the sufferings which result from their over-indulgence. His *Vauxhall Gardens* (1784), exhibited at the Royal Academy and later engraved, was an early success in depicting late Georgian sociability: it was followed by representations of military reviews, races, *gambling tables, art exhibitions, inns, and theatres. In the latter part of his career Rowlandson concentrated on book illustration, principally for Rudolph *Ackermann. He collaborated with William *Combe on the *Tours of Doctor Syntax* (1812–21), which associated his name

with the rise of the comic *picturesque. A keen analyst of *agrarian life, he also explored the conventions employed in depicting the agricultural poor in *Harvesters Resting in a Cornfield* (c.1780s) and *The Cottage Door* (1805). He was a *landscape painter of genius, during a period which produced Cozens, Cotman, Girtin, and the early work of *Turner.

In many ways Rowlandson is the graphic essence of the *Regency, the artist technically and temperamentally most fitted to record and to celebrate the triumph of young love over cautious age, and staggering feats of intoxication, debauchery, and suffering. With his sinuous and sensuous line he elevated the fine leg of the Regency man about town, the exuberant hips and bust of the Regency beauty, and the bony shanks and bespectacled cadaverousness of the old 'dry-as-dust' into a graphic vocabulary for the society and culture of the time. His energized and egalitarian line appears as the ideal tool for representing the fusion of low and high life in the *tavern, the brothel, the public garden, the cockpit, and at the racecourse [see *popular culture, 23]. MW

Royal Academy of Arts, established by royal charter when George III signed its Instrument of Foundation on 10 December 1768. It was originally housed in Pall Mall, then Somerset House, and in 1837 moved into the *National Gallery in Trafalgar Square. While the precursors of the Royal Academy date back much further than 1768, its foundation was tardy in comparison to the academies of Florence (1563), Rome (1593), and Paris (1648).

Like its continental precursors, the Academy aimed to raise the status of the fine arts and foster a national school of art through the instruction of young artists, the provision of objective criteria governing the arts, veneration of the past, and the establishment of an annual exhibition of new art [see *viewing, 20]. It provided instruction in those liberal arts relevant to the education of the artist, and established professorships in *architecture [28], drawing, anatomy, perspective, and *painting [27]. It required of each new member an admission piece for the Academy collection.

The first president of the Royal Academy was Sir Joshua *Reynolds. His *Discourses*, originally delivered as a series of lectures from 1769 until 1790, articulated the Academy's aspirations to promote the fine arts as a reasoned, principled, and moral discipline, and to unite talent and provide a bulwark against the vagaries of fashion. However, it was not long before the Academy's cautious approach to change provoked the charge of conservatism, an attack that was also encouraged by the emergent Romantic ideals of novelty, intuition, emotion, and *originality. PD

Royal Literary Fund, a philanthropic fund and society set up at the urging of Revd David *Williams in 1790 to assist distressed writers or their dependents. The fund reflected both the full-blown *consumerism [19] of late-eighteenth-century authorship and also its fragility as a professional career at a

97. *The Vestibule at Somerset Place*, 1796. William Chambers's administrative and cultural complex, Somerset House, took nearly twenty years to build. The Royal Academy was located in its grand salon from 1796 until moving to the National Gallery at Trafalgar Square in 1837.

time when publishers still held great *copyright advantages and when pirating of publications was widespread [see *publishing, 21].

Although the fund was supported by the Prince Regent [see *Regency] and some influential literati, it was not well endowed and tended to give out relatively small sums. David Williams also had to survive attempts to oust him from the secretaryship because of his well-known radical and *Deistical views. Struggling authors were still less fortunate, and a number of worthy cases were turned down on flagrantly political grounds. Nevertheless, S. T. *Coleridge, John *Clare, James *Hogg, Thomas Love *Peacock, and Thomas *Dermody all benefited from grants. The Society was granted a Royal Charter in 1818 and became known as the Royal Literary Fund in 1845.   IMcC

RUSSELL, Lord John, first Earl Russell (1792–1878), statesman. Later twice Prime Minister, Lord John Russell's importance before 1832 was as one of the 'Young Whigs' who were mainly responsible for breathing new life into the *Whig party in the 1820s. Though receiving advice and sometimes encouragement from their elders in the party, such as Lord Grey (1764–1845) and Lord *Holland, it was the 'Young Whigs' in the House of Commons, the more

liberal of the two Houses, who made the running in the introduction of new issues. Others among the 'Young Whigs', such as Lord Althorp, heir to the Spencer earldom, might have had more weight and influence in the party, but it was Russell, third son of the sixth Duke of Bedford, who made more of a mark in carrying legislation. Thus it was Russell who moved the February 1828 motion that resulted in the repeal of the Test and Corporation Acts, making Lord John the great hero of the Protestant Dissenters, the Whigs' most reliable supporters in the country [see *toleration]. Russell was also largely responsible for reviving the question of parliamentary reform in the same decade. And it was Russell in 1831 who shepherded the *Reform Bill through the House of Commons. His later tendencies to petulance and flightiness would make him a difficult colleague, but up to 1832 he was perhaps the outstanding representative of resurgent Whiggism. In his studies of his own seventeenth-century ancestors and of Charles James *Fox, he was also the most important of its historians and myth-makers.   RWD

RYVES, Elizabeth (Eliza) (1750–97), poet, essayist, translator, and playwright. Born in Ireland, she moved to London in 1775 after losing property, through litigation, inherited from her father. Her first published work was *Poems on Several Occasions* (1777), which included *odes, *pastoral elegies, and a comic opera. Her plays *The Prude* and *The Debt of Honour* were accepted by a theatrical manager but never produced. Her novel *The Hermit of Snowden, or Memoirs of Albert and Lavinia* (1789) incorporated *Gothic and sentimental conventions.

During the 1780s Ryves wrote poems in support of the Foxite *Whigs, including a 1785 satirical piece on Warren *Hastings. In 1791 she translated *Rousseau's *Social Contract* and Abbé Raynal's 'Letter to the National Assembly', which accused the Assembly of betraying the ideals of the *French Revolution.   CT

S

Saint-Simonianism, the chief of several strains of French *utopian [9] socialism to reach Britain, contributed to advanced thinking on the rights of *women [4] in the early nineteenth century.

Although the Frenchman Henri de Saint-Simon (1760–1825) had little to say on the subject of feminism, women had featured as electors in his proposed scheme for world government led by members of learned professional élites. One of his chief successors, Prosper Enfantin (1796–1864), also advocated a form of mystical free love and committed the movement in 1829 to attaining the 'complete emancipation of women'. With the encouragement of activists such as Anna *Wheeler, these ideas began to move backward and forth across the Channel during the 1820s, to be followed in early 1831–2 by a mission to Britain of Saint-Simonian apostles dressed in striking red, white, and blue uniforms. Their intention, Robert *Southey recorded in the *Quarterly Review*, was to announce women's 'definite enfranchisement, their complete emancipation, not abolishing the holy law of marriage, but fulfilling it by giving it new sanction'. A programme was elaborated in *Saint-Simonianism in London* (1833), a pamphlet written by two of the leading apostles, Dr Prati and Signor Fontana. It attacked the orthodox marriage system and proposed liberal divorce, as well as the abolition of prostitution and bastardy, and the development of equal educational and employment opportunities for women.

Though Saint-Simonianism remained a minority movement in Britain, it exerted an important intellectual influence on British feminist thinkers, including Anna Wheeler, William *Thompson, Robert *Owen, and John Stuart *Mill.   IMcC

SALVIN, Anthony (1799–1881), architect. Salvin's work provided an essential link in architectural *medievalism between Robert *Adam's 'Castle Style' and later Victorian architectural styles. Salvin combined an interest in *antiquarianism [35] with moderate skill as a *picturesque designer to become a country-house architect and authority on medieval

*architecture [28], primarily serving the landed gentry.

Apprenticed in John *Nash's London office in the early 1820s, and made a Fellow of the Society of Antiquaries in 1824, Salvin grounded the Romantic and naïve late Georgian approach to medieval architecture in prevailing concerns for archaeological accuracy and picturesque effect. His most original work was Peckforton Castle, Cheshire (1844–52), but he was also responsible for the restoration of some of the country's most notable medieval monuments, including the Tower of London (*c.*1851).   ss

SAMWELL, David (Dafydd Ddu Feddyg) (1751–98), surgeon, travel writer, and radical Welsh antiquarian; a key contributor to the *Welsh cultural revival and to the cultural deification of James *Cook as Pacific voyager and **Enlightenment [32]** icon.

Born in Nantglyn, Wales, of a clerical family, Samwell trained as a surgeon and then moved to London, where he joined a lively circle of Welsh expatriate radicals and popular antiquarians, whose druidic and Celtic revivalism influenced both William *Blake and Robert *Southey [see *antiquarianism, 35]. Sympathetic to the *American and *French Revolutions, Samwell was informed by Enlightenment scepticism and sexual libertinism, but also moved by the Romantic quest to recover and disseminate the ancient religion, music, mythology, and literary achievements of the Welsh people. His poem 'The Padouca Hunt' (1799) was a witty evocation of the intense contemporary debate over claims that a pre-Columbian Welsh voyager, *Madoc, had discovered America and founded a tribe of Welsh-speaking American Indians. Samwell was an early member, and later secretary (1788) and vice-president (1797), of the Gwynediggion, a populist Welsh cultural society. He was a key figure in the revival of the *eisteddfod in Wales. He also helped to reinvent Welsh bardic traditions and presided at the Gorsedd of Bards held at Primose Hill, London, on 21 June 1792, along with its prime instigator, Edward *Williams (Iolo Morganwg).

Samwell's Welsh cultural nationalism seems to have given him a particular interest in recording the culture and language of Polynesian peoples, whom he encountered when serving as a ship's surgeon on Cook's third and last Pacific voyage of *exploration [37] between 1776 and 1780. For this reason, and because he was present at Cook's death, Samwell's published journal has exceptional value. A short separate account of Cook's death, published in 1786, also contains a lively discussion of the impact of venereal disease on the peoples of the Sandwich Isles, a subject of more than theoretical interest to the sexually predatory surgeon.   IMcC and MF

SANCHO, Ignatius (1729–80), musician and prose writer, the first African to publish in these fields in Britain. Sancho was born on a slave ship in the Atlantic and christened at sea shortly before his African mother died of disease and his father killed himself to escape a life of *slavery [6]. When still a young child he was given to three maiden sisters at Greenwich who called him Sancho after Don Quixote's squire but resisted his efforts at self-education. At the age of 20 he ran away to the nearby Blackheath residence of the Duke and Duchess of Montagu, who had earlier shown him some sympathy. For the next fourteen years he worked as a butler for the Duchess, while simultaneously acquiring the tastes and accomplishments of an enlightened gentleman, musical composer, and man-of-letters. He wrote poetry, several stage plays, and a treatise on the 'Theory of Music' which seems never to have been published. However, he did publish an anonymous collection of genteel and fashionable songs, minuets, and chamber pieces [see *music, 26]. An avid lover of food, *gambling, and the *theatre [24], Sancho aspired to play the African roles of Othello and Oronooko, but was too corpulent and lacked the voice. However, he cultivated literary and artistic friendships with David Garrick, Samuel *Johnson, and Laurence Sterne, whom he both imitated and attempted to recruit to the *abolitionist cause.

In 1773 Sancho, accompanied by his Caribbean wife, Anne, and six children, moved to Charles Street in Westminster, where he opened a grocery shop with the help of a small legacy from the Duchess of Montagu. Here he became something of a social celebrity, to such an extent that when his *Letters* were published two years after his death, they immediately attracted 1,200 subscribers and swiftly passed into several editions. The letters, written in the sentimental style of Sterne, show the outlook of an urbane British man of letters, but they also reveal a wry, good-humoured awareness of someone who felt he lived in Britain as a 'lodger' and was used to ridicule and condescension from white Europeans. Sancho died shortly after witnessing the *Gordon riots of June 1780, an outbreak of uncivilized 'madness' which made him glad he was an African.   IMcC

23, 105 **SANDBY, Paul** (1730–1809), painter of *landscape, satires, and genre scenes in *watercolour, gouache, and oil; military draughtsman; drawing teacher; printmaker; and publisher. Sandby was the first landscape artist to travel extensively in Scotland and Wales. His views of that scenery played a significant role in shaping the development of *picturesque and naturalistic landscape painting towards the end of the eighteenth century. After one year of training at the Board of Ordnance in London, in 1757 he became chief draughtsman of the ordnance survey of Scotland, established to provide the army with accurate information about Scottish topography [see *mapping].

From 1752 in London and Windsor, he established a reputation as an outstanding topographical artist. With his brother Thomas he played a key role in the establishment and promotion of artists' societies. Both were founder members of the Society of Artists and the *Royal Academy, thereby enhancing the status of landscape and *painting [27] in gouache and watercolour. During this period he expanded his range of subjects to produce satires attacking Hogarth, as well as a Hogarth-influenced series of etchings called *Twelve London Cries*.

In 1768 Sandby was made chief drawing-master of the Royal Military College at Woolwich. During the 1770s he made three tours of Wales, producing watercolours and gouaches of landscape, figurative, antiquarian, and industrial subjects. These are remarkable for his experimentation with media and for the range of landscape conventions and compositional approaches chosen to suit the subjects at hand. He was the first successful publisher of a series of views of Wales via the new medium of aquatint.   JH-J

Sapphism, the predominant term during the second half of the eighteenth century to refer to sexual relations between women, also functioned with reference to non-sexual relations to indicate intense emotional attachment and preference for the company of other women. Positioned within the prevalent social and discursive conventions of romantic friendship and sentimental letter-writing, Sapphism simultaneously elides and maintains the distinction between sexual and platonic relations.

An important component of the discourse of *sensibility [11], romantic or sentimental friendship involved the open expression of passionate emotional attachment, and was to varying degrees a respectable ideal of sociability. Eleanor Butler (?1739–1829) and Sarah Ponsonby (?1735–1831), two Irish women known as the Ladies of Llangollen, who eloped in 1778 to settle in a cottage in Wales, provide the most celebrated example of romantic friendship as a utopian practice. Visited by admiring men and women of the literati, they were also vilified as lesbians and Sapphists in the popular press and in the privacy of diaries by those who patronized them, such as Hester Thrale *Piozzi, whose diaries register a continual source of tension in the reception of intense female friendships. In the erotically charged journals of Butler, and in the correspondence of *bluestocking Elizabeth *Carter, the pervasive language of romantic friendship fails to uphold a stable distinction between friendship and sexual intimacy.

The epistles, *sonnets, and elegies of Anna

*Seward (an enthusiastic admirer of the Ladies of Llangollen) to her foster-sister Honora Sneyd, addressed as Lesbia, discreetly revise the gendering of the heterosexual Ovidian Sapphic triangle with an autobiographical love plot in which a woman laments the loss of a younger woman to an older man. These epistolary exchanges, poetic epistles, and elegies enact a fugitive yet specifically Sapphic textuality alienated from the mainstream of a male transvestite Sapphic tradition initiated by Pope and Addison. In the Ovidian tradition, explicit references to the lesbian Sappho are coy. Mary *Robinson's sonnet sequence *Sappho and Phaon* (1796) explains Sappho's passion for women in terms of the 'extreme sensibility' of the Greeks, where, by functioning as definitionally opposed to but indistinguishable from lesbian relations, sensibility exercises its notorious prerogative for instability of meaning and its generous capacity for euphemizing the unseemly associations it generates. Growing suspicion of such instability was registered in the anti-sensibility fictions of the 1790s, where *homosexual panic is figured in the parodic backlash against romantic friendship.

Among minor *pornographic genres, satirical and parodic guidebooks and sexual *almanacs sometimes map secret societies and meeting-places for sexual encounters between women. The *Covent-Garden Magazine; or, Amorous Repository* (1773), a guide to sexual underworlds of and around London, uses the phrase 'Sapphic Passion' to index a discussion of sex between women. Of the related genres of *chroniques scandaleuses*, mock-epitaphs, and the satirical pamphlet, *A Sapphic Epistle, from Jack Cavendish to . . . Mrs D***** (c.1782) uses an explicit invocation of the lesbian associations of the Sapphic epistle to address Anne *Damer as a well-known 'tommy'. ('Tommy', possibly from 'tomboy', a slang word for women who engage in lesbian practices, was in use from at least 1773.) This revision of the genre of the Sapphic epistle as pornographic misogynist slander effectively overrides the genre of the Ovidian tradition.

Linking criticism of the institution of marriage with the cultivation of female friendship and radical schemes for *female education is the late eighteenth-century separatist tradition of female communities. This develops and revises the campaign for Protestant nunneries that flourished earlier in the century. A key influence on such separatist activity and imagining was Sarah Scott's (1723–95) novel *Millennium Hall* (1762), a pedagogical *utopia [9]. This inspired separatist schemes well into the 1800s, as did Lady Mary Hamilton's (1739–after 1818) pedagogical utopia, *Munster Village* (1778). The late-eighteenth- and early-nineteenth-century development of a rhetoric of pedagogy as surveillance turns the spotlight on female education as a significant site of lesbian scandal. In her self-vindicatory pamphlet *Who Are the Swindlers?* (1801), Eliza Frances Robertson (1771–1805), who ran a school in Greenwich from 1795, responded to accusations of fraud, cross-dressing, and having improper relations with her colleague, Charlotte Sharp, by justifying their rela-

tionship in terms of the biblical model of Naomi and Ruth. In the 1811 case in Scotland of Marianne Woods and Jane Pirie against Helen Cumming Gordon, in which an Indian schoolgirl accused her two teachers of having sex together, the judges' decision that the 'imputed vice has been hitherto unknown in Britain' suggests race as a more significant contemporary determinant of sexuality than gender. It also establishes a precedent for the proverbial invisibility of lesbians during the nineteenth century.

The most explicit documentation of sexual relationships between women occurs in the recently discovered diaries of a young Yorkshire lesbian of the gentry class, Anne *Lister. Originally written in code, these *Diaries* (1988), which date from 1817 to 1826, detail Lister's numerous sexual fantasies, her intense masculine identification, and her bold and rakish pursuits of and physical encounters with other women. Drawing on Jean Jacques *Rousseau's *Confessions* (1781–8), Lister's diaries position themselves as a record of sexual development and an elaboration of a self-conscious sexual identity. They offer the earliest example of a woman who identifies explicitly as a female and who finds sexual and emotional fulfilment in other women. Developing a Rousseauean discourse of nature, Lister's critique of Sappho and 'Sapphic love' as 'inconsistent and artificial', to which she opposes her own feelings as 'the effect of nature', involves an early formulation of the biological argument that was so influential in late-nineteenth-century apologies for homosexuality. Lister's ironically compunctious reflections on the Ladies of Llangollen, 'I cannot help thinking that surely [their relationship] was not platonic. Heaven forgive me, but I look within myself & doubt', neatly interrogate the supposed asexuality of contemporary 'romantic friendships'. CT

satire. Although not usually associated with satire, the Romantic period opens with an efflorescence of political satire associated with the savaging of Lord North's ministry during the *American Revolution and ends with a flood of material covering the run up to the *Reform Bill of 1832. The highly polemical half-century in between generated an incredible range of satirical productions which refuse critical synthesis, but give the lie to notions that satire is not a Romantic genre.

Famous exponents of satirical poetry such as Peter Pindar (John *Wolcot), one of the most popular writers of the period, or George *Canning in the *Anti-Jacobin* were only the most salient features in a landscape which rested on a subterranean world of disreputable hacks and *pornographers. Opportunists like the seedy 'Anthony Pasquin' (John *Williams), for instance, came into their own in the context of public scandal and national outrage, not to mention major electoral contests. The 1784 election, in particular, produced an outpouring of satirical material, including the influential *Criticism on the Rolliad*, an anonymous collection of *Whig political satires directed against *Pitt, first published in the *Morning Herald*.

There was a corresponding proliferation of satire in the *print [22] trade. In the late 1770s James *Gillray was emerging as the major figure in this area. There followed half a century which saw the maturation and decline of the English political caricature. During the first decade of the nineteenth century Gillray was joined by Thomas *Rowlandson and Isaac and George *Cruikshank in the production of a mass of social and political satire. Although print satire went through a general decline from 1822 to 1832, it regained something of its vituperative edge prior to the Reform Bill, when the large, crude woodcuts of C. J. Grant (fl. 1830–46), in particular, forced aside the illustrational smoothnesses of incipient Victorianism to give the time-honoured icons of the political bestiary—fat bishops, corrupt Cabinet ministers, the Prime Minister, and the *monarchy—one last curtain call.

The period witnessed above all a tremendous loosening of the social and formal range of satire. This loosening itself has to be primarily located in the satirical struggle between the radical press and the *loyalist opponents in the 1790s. The radical press became increasingly powerful, experimental, and influential in the early 1790s and after a fallow period fought to reassert itself from 1815 to 1822. An explosion of radical propaganda directed against Lord *Liverpool's administration and the Prince Regent was unprecedented in its scale and diversity. Radical satirists and propagandists came from an impressive variety of social backgrounds and levels of political commitment. Charles *Lamb and Thomas Love *Peacock wrote occasional squibs and poetry supporting radical causes, as did *Byron and Thomas *Moore. Among the literary mainstream, William *Hazlitt and John and Leigh *Hunt maintained a more continual and polemical radical stance, although they were all careful to dissociate themselves from the more demotic satire published in bestselling journals such as William *Cobbett's *Political Register*, T. J. *Wooler's *Black Dwarf*, and Richard *Carlile's *Republican*.

While intellectual radicals did on occasion flirt with the forms of popular satire, and exceptionally, as in the case of Leigh Hunt, had to suffer imprisonment for what they wrote, it was frequently left to populist autodidacts who targeted the lower areas of the *publishing [21] market to exploit emergent print forms and to face the full force of government harassment. The three outstanding popular radical satirists of the post-Waterloo years were Cobbett, Wooler, and William *Hone. They dominated cheap polemical publication in the areas of the *newspaper, the journal, and the pamphlet, and were all hounded by the government as a result.

Radical satire used very diverse models and styles. Many radicals experimented with satires using methods which drew on recently developed areas of the *advertising industry both inside and outside the press. This process had began in the 1790s. Thomas *Spence and Daniel Isaac *Eaton, for instances, combined traditional forms of *street literature with new forms of publishing which advertising had developed. They also exploited burgeoning areas of the book and print trade. These included the markets for *children's literature, adult and children's toys, political caricatures, and *almanacs. The increase in the range and gusto of popular satire during our period results to a large extent from the ways in which it exploited expanding commercial publishing environments of the early nineteenth century.

Parody was also thriving as a satirical form in this period. The *Rejected Addresses* (1812) of Horace (1779–1849) and James Smith (1775–1839) cast its mimetic net wide, catching the stylistic essence of the major poets of the day alongside the prose of Cobbett. With 'Drury Lane Hustings, A New Halfpenny Ballad By a Nic Pic Poet', it even took up the typical form of the street *ballad. James *Hogg attempted to organize an anthology composed of contributions by his famous poetic contemporaries and, finding them reluctant, provided the absent verses himself. The resulting volume, *The Poetic Mirror* (1816), although uneven, produced some of the most delicate satire ever written. While these collections are undoubtedly indicative of a new vogue for literary satire, they indicate only one facet of far more general changes in the approach to parody, language, source, influence, and creativity during this period. William *Wordsworth viewed parody with especial contempt, regarding the form as a kind of plagiarism or forgery, which took away from him his property and identity. Ironically, he was perhaps the most parodied of major poets, J. H. Reynolds's (1796–1852) *Peter Bell* and Percy *Shelley's *Peter Bell the Third* being only the best known of several parodies of Wordsworth published in 1819.

Electoral contests were great showcases for popular parody of all sorts, and fed directly into the work of early-nineteenth-century radical publicists (figures such as Francis *Place and William Hone built up large personal collections of this material). The law and the church had also inspired a rich popular tradition of parody based on their language and rituals. Last dying speeches and a whole variety of trials and cross-examinations had been commonly travestied since the seventeenth century. At the heart of much political satire is the knowledge that to parody something is to disempower it. Parodies of trials and sacred texts ridiculed the official language of the courts and the church while simultaneously celebrating radical ideology. Radical satirists saw structures that could be parodied in all areas of life. The dress, habits, and behavioural codes of the aristocracy, state-backed art and monumental *sculpture, and even preferred styles of *architecture [28]—all were grist to the radical's satiric mill. Both the Prince Regent's enormous proportions and his bizarre building experiments, embodied in the Brighton Pavilion, were parodied in radical prints and writing as manifestations of the corruption and decadence of the nation's rulers [see *Regency]. Parody of this scale and diversity is not a tame phenomenon to be written off as imitative, ephemeral—a ridiculing outgrowth of serious literature. Parody was chipping away continually and uncontrollably at the notion that language reflected *class [15] and social position, that polite and literary forms of language could be set up above and separate from the language of the multitude.

This diverse world of popular parody fed directly into the work of the major writers of the period. Shelley's *Swellfoot the Tyrant* (1820) was an attempt to write a classical dramatic fragment attacking the Prince Regent during the *Queen Caroline affair. It is most profitably understood as an attempt to write in the spirit of the vulgar squibs which the scandal generated in the gutter press. Peacock was an obsessive parodist. His early mature novels are all built around various core parodic structures. The assault on the intellectual and stylistic constructs of leading literary figures in *Nightmare Abbey* (1818) developed into extended bursts of more populist parody in the most explicitly political of his longer works, *Melincourt* (1817). The parodic dialogue between Thomas *Malthus (Mr Fax) and the John Bullish Bridegroom which takes up the thirty-fifth chapter of *Melincourt* could be read as a particularly hilarious contribution to the mass of popular didactic dialogues between country bumpkins and their social superiors which mushroomed, at both extremes of the political spectrum, after the success of Hannah *More's *Village Politics*. The thirty-ninth chapter of *Melincourt*, the notorious attack on the Liverpool administration and on the apostasy of *Southey and Wordsworth, is chock-full of squibs and nicknames in the style of the radical pamphlet and journal satires of the post-Waterloo period.

The greatest monument to the satirical variety of the age is Byron's *Don Juan*. The parody of 'The Ten Commandments' in the first Canto is an unblushing testament to the influence of the kind of satire being published by Hone, Wooler, and others at the time. Hone sarcastically upbraided Byron's publisher, John Murray (1778–1843), 'strenuous supporter of orthodoxy and the Bible society', for bringing out a parody of precisely the sacred text for which he had been prosecuted in 1817. *Don John, or Don John Unmasked*, in which Hone's attack appeared, hastily written to exploit the success of Byron's poem, and the spurious *Don Juan, Canto the Third* are further evidence of the fact that radical publishers recognized a kindred spirit in Byron's poem. When Byron himself changed publishers from Tory Murray to John Hunt, he was acknowledging that his masterpiece was part of the literature of the multitude in a way which would have delighted Hone.   MW

schools, see *Dissenting academies; *education [17]; *monitorial system; *popular education; *Sunday schools.

scientific societies. The spread of scientific societies throughout eighteenth-century Britain reflected the cultural centrality of science in the value-system of the governing élite. The Royal Society (1660) had established that science could be a loyal servant of the ruling order, and a multitude of provincial centres emulated its example by setting up societies where scientific interests could be pursued in the ambience of a *gentleman's club. One such society, the Gentle-

man's Society in Peterborough (1730), for example, refused to allow tradesmen to become members.

By the late eighteenth century, the newer provincial centres and their attendant scientific societies— notably the Lunar Society of Birmingham and the Manchester Literary and Philosophical Society— provided something of a challenge to this association between science and established values by linking science more closely with religious Dissenters and the more politically suspect [see *literary and philosophical societies]. However, such associations largely faded with the onset of the *French Revolution—symptomatically, the Lunar Society of Birmingham was dissolved in the mid-1790s.

Under the long presidency of Sir Joseph *Banks from 1778 to 1820, the Royal Society further strengthened its ties with the established order during the age of revolution. However, even before his death in 1820 there were signs of increasing restiveness within the scientific old regime. The gentlemanly scientific culture which the Royal Society embodied emphasized utility and cultural breadth rather than the scientific specialization which was increasingly a feature of continental (and especially French) science. Hence Banks viewed the foundation of specialist scientific societies like the Geological Society of London (1807) and the Astronomical Society of London (1820) with considerable disfavour. He did, however, take a more indulgent view of the foundation of the Linnean Society of London in 1788 and the Royal Institution in 1799, since the goals of these societies were in harmony with the gentlemanly scientific culture promoted by the Royal Society. Both these organizations were naturally attuned to the values of a landed class, since the Linnean Society promoted natural history and the Royal Institution had as its object 'the application of science to the common purposes of life' [see *natural philosophy, 34].

Banks's successors as presidents of the Royal Society were more conciliatory in their attitude to the foundation of new specialist scientific societies such as the Zoological Society of London (1826), but the Royal Society continued to be regarded as too traditional in character and too London-centred to promote scientific culture at a national level—hence the foundation in 1831 of the British Association for the Advancement of Science with the avowed purpose of 'giving a stronger impulse and a more systematic direction to scientific enquiry'. The reforming impulse that transformed the constitution in church and state in the late 1820s and the 1830s also left its mark on the scientific establishment, with Charles *Babbage's *The Decline of Science in England* (1830) serving as the manifesto of the reformers. And in science, as in constitutional matters, the British old regime showed itself capable of reform and renewal as the Royal Society and other major scientific societies emerged from this decade better able to accommodate the increasing specialization and professionalization that nineteenth-century science demanded. These trends did, however, also concentrate the nation's major endeavours back in London, thus reversing the enhanced significance of provincial scientific societies that had been a feature of the late eighteenth century.   JGA

SCOTT, Sir Walter (1771–1832), novelist, poet, critic, biographer, antiquarian, and dramatist. One of the most important early practitioners of the historical and regional *novel [31], Scott has a complex relationship to Scottish literature and national identity.

Born and raised in Edinburgh, the son of a lawyer, and educated at Edinburgh University, where he studied classics and law, Scott inherited the intellectual traditions of the *Scottish Enlightenment. His education was interrupted by ill-health and several stays on his grandfather's farm in Roxburghshire, which inspired his lifelong attachment to the Border country between Scotland and England. In 1797 he married Charlotte Charpentier, the daughter of a French royalist family. In 1799 he was appointed Sheriff-depute of Selkirkshire and in 1806 a Clerk of the Court of Session (Edinburgh).

His first published *ballads appeared in 1796, when he was 25. His imaginative literature as a whole was to become preoccupied with the political, economic, and aesthetic values of Enlightenment Edinburgh, imbued as an undergraduate. His inherited project was to integrate Scotland into what was seen as the constitutional security, progressive prosperity, and civility of the post-1688 Anglo-British state. To an extent this placed him in opposition to the revolutionary predilections of late-eighteenth-century Romantic nationalism, manifested for Scott in cultural phenomena such as *Ossianism. He became increasingly anxious that an age of *revolution [1] held particularly dire dangers for Scotland, in that it would release the regressive, anarchic forces he believed were embodied in feudal Celticism and Covenanting or ultra-Protestant fanaticism. His consistent goal, across a number of literary genres, was to anatomize and neutralize such sinister energies of this past while at the same time commercially exploiting the appeal of that past to the reader.

These intentions are discernible even in Scott's first, apparently neutral, role as ballad collector in his own culturally rich Border region where, with assistance from James *Hogg and William Laidlaw (1780–1845), he collected from oral informants the folk-songs and *ballads that constituted *Minstrelsy of the Scottish Border* (1802–3). His *Tory vision could not accept, as Joseph *Ritson's counter-theory could, that the ballads were folk productions. For Scott, the common people were inherently recipients, not originators. All poetry was written by an elevated, munificently rewarded poet living near the top of a stable, hierarchical society—Scott's own desired self-image. In consequence, as a collector he ignored the bawdy, carnivalesque, irreverent sources beloved of Robert *Burns, and transcribed ballads much more concerned with making chivalrous war than love. Scott was equally deaf to the folk tone and anti-Union sentiments of the vernacular poetry of Ramsay, Fergusson, and Burns, especially when, as in Burns, the vernacular fused triumphantly with international revolutionary idealism.

Scott's first novel, *Waverley*, which deals with the Jacobite rebellion of 1745, met with immediate success upon its anonymous publication in 1814. His poetry and fiction shared the same thematic core: the chafing interaction between an archaic, even atavistic, culture and a modernizing, civilizing one. Mid-eighteenth-century Scotland was a unique laboratory for the first social scientists to study both a feudal and simultaneously a commercial, proto-industrial society. And, true to his *Enlightenment [32] inheritance in *historiography and sociology, Scott wanted to represent the evolution from the earlier society to the later one. His Scottish novels are respected as his most serious treatment of this problem, though his representation of the Highlands has been controversial, beginning with the response of his contemporary, the writer and historian Anne Grant of Laggan (1755–1838).

While Scott deals sympathetically with critical moments in Highland history, he does not fully develop his thesis to assess the destructive suffering which a Unionist, benevolent capitalism was causing in the Highlands. This is nowhere more apparent than in *Rob Roy* (1817), where, as opposed to the savage sadism of Rob's wife, the manufacturies and plantations of Baillie Nicol Jarvie cost nothing in sweat and blood. Moreover, Scott's Highland characters—Fergus McIvor, Mrs MacGregor, and Redgauntlet—are not simply fictive *Gothic villains but also embody the demonic energies Scott identified with past Jacobitism and contemporary Jacobinism.

Scott's middle period novels with English settings, particularly *Ivanhoe* (1819) and *Kenilworth* (1821), were hailed and imitated almost as widely as the Scottish romances. However, his final novels, *Anne of Geirstein* (1829), *Count Robert of Paris* (1831), and *Castle Dangerous* (1831), are markedly inferior to his Scottish novels, largely due to the haste caused by financial wounds after his publishing partner, James Ballantyne, incurred massive financial losses. At one level these novels nourish the often violent medieval fantasies of middle-class nineteenth-century England; at another they are his final Scottish ideological endorsement of the virtues and valour of the British state. Ironically, given his suspicion of the whole Scott cult, they point forward to the work of Thomas *Carlyle. Like Carlyle, too, Scott's literary reputation has risen in the latter part of the twentieth century after a lengthy post-Victorian trough.   AN

Scottish Enlightenment has now become the accepted label for the efflorescence of intellectual culture in Scotland in the eighteenth century. While Scotland displayed most of the central features of the common European *Enlightenment [32], its philosophers (especially Francis Hutcheson (1694–1746), George Turnbull (1698–1748), David *Hume, Adam *Smith, Thomas *Reid, and Dugald *Stewart) strove particularly to find a coherent philosophical basis for all human knowledge, theoretical and practical. This endeavour was intimately connected with significant developments of particular areas of knowledge—*natural philosophy [34] and mathematics; *medicine [18]; *law [8]; the arts; not to speak of new fields of sociological, economic, and linguistic study [see also *political economy, 33] and *language, 40]. Furthermore, in common with Enlightenment elsewhere, all this knowledge was ensconced in new or reformed institutions—universities, academies, *literary and philosophical societies, *publishing [21] ventures (first and second *Edinburgh Review*, the *Encyclopaedia Britannica*, etc.). Finally, in the hands of well-connected and highly sociable literati, dominated by moderate, literary-minded clergymen such as Hugh *Blair, John Home, George Campbell, and Alexander Carlyle, new knowledge and its institutionalization were made to serve a culture of mind and manners that would make society polite, progressive, and stable. Behind all this lay a more fundamental factor. Scottish Enlightenment intellectual culture was one way that the eighteenth century rejected the Augustinian notion of original sin and asserted the power of the human mind to shape life in the present world. Since this power had to be understood in the various situations of its exertion, nearly all Scottish philosophy had a contextualist aspect that commonly was, and is, seen as 'historical'.

This Enlightenment culture was lent its peculiarly Scots quality by two factors in particular: nationhood and religion. Scotland's Enlightenment was, at least in some measure, a nation's response to loss of statehood, and is identifiable as the phase between the politico-economic Union with England in 1707 and the formation of an inclusive British culture in the early nineteenth century. Not only did the disappearance of national politics concentrated in Edinburgh make culture, law, and church into a kind of ersatz politics, but the very need to redefine Scotland and Britain as polities concentrated the Scottish mind on ideas of rights, contracts, sovereignty, law, citizenship, and church and state. The result was a flourishing of political theory in which elements of neoclassical *republicanism and modern natural law theory were often combined. The same need led to a sharpened perception of Scotland as a unique national culture preserving continental European elements within a new British setting. It was thought that the way to understand the novelty of Britain as a commercial society in an extensive agrarian country—as opposed to a city-state—was through a new kind of history, that of civil society. Scottish Enlightenment preoccupation with [see *history, 38] was further nourished by debts to early modern humanists and to Calvinist scholars or preachers, particularly figures such as Hector Boece, John Mair, and George Buchanan. Both these long-standing Scottish traditions had granted history a privileged status—as a storehouse of human experience, a record of the workings of providence having predictive potential, and a means of inculcating private and public moral virtue.

All this, combined with the above-mentioned 'historical' method in abstract philosophy and theoretical science, meant that the legacy of the Scottish Enlightenment was that of a pre-Romantic historical

school. In fact, the division between Enlightenment and Romanticism is even more dubious in Scotland than elsewhere in Europe, a point epitomized, and by no means exhausted, by Sir Walter *Scott's profound debts to Scottish historicism.   KH

sculpture. The impact of *revolution [1] and the *war [2] against France created demand for temporary and permanent symbols of political dominance in which sculpture played a major role. In Britain there was unprecedented state *patronage for monuments to heroes such as *Nelson, a context which was acknowledged by John *Flaxman when he took up his appointment as the first professor of sculpture at the *Royal Academy in 1810. In France acts of iconoclasm during the Revolution had seen the destruction of large quantities of public and religious sculptures, the reuse of sculpture from the *ancien régime*, or its removal to the Musée des Monuments Français. Temporary and sometimes colossal statues were raised as the centrepieces of elaborate festivals, many designed by Jacques Louis David (1748–1825). At a less idealistic level the three-dimensional record of those executed during the revolutionary period in Paris was made by Marie Grosholtz (later Madame Tussaud, 1761–1850), who toured England, Scotland, and Ireland in 1802 with her historical waxworks exhibition that included over thirty wax heads of figures such as Marat. It was established as a permanent display at the Old London Bazaar in 1834. In a 'higher' mode of this popular art form, the final wax effigy to be placed in Westminster Abbey was that of Nelson (1806) by Catherine Andras (1775–1860), who was modeller in wax to Queen Charlotte. Although women were active in this popular area of sculptural activity, they were mostly excluded from the institutional structures which preserved sculpture as a 'high' art. A notable exception was Anne *Damer, who exhibited at the Royal Academy and was recognized as the leading amateur sculptor of her day.

In Britain proposals for 'sublime' national monuments to naval and military victory were put forward in 1799, 1805, 1814, and 1815, including Flaxman's *Britannia Triumphant* (1799)—a design for a 200-foot high statue of Britannia to stand at Greenwich, based upon the Athena Parthenos—and Major John *Cartwright's (1740–1824) *Hieronauticon* (1802). In a similar vein the artist James *Barry added to his completed painting, *Navigation, Triumph of the Thames* for the Royal Society of Arts, a utopian scheme for a 'naval pillar, mausoleum, observatory and lighthouse'. In London attempts to create large-scale and expensive 'national' monuments failed to raise sufficient funds through subscriptions, but Richard Westmacott's (1775–1856) colossal bronze statue of *Achilles* (1814–22), dedicated to the Duke of *Wellington by the ladies of England, was an exception. Nevertheless, monuments on a more modest scale were raised to individual heroes (notably Nelson) in the provinces where local attestations of national identity combined with civic pride to create permanent works as focal points within the rapidly expanding towns and cities.

Throughout the Romantic epoch Rome remained the centre of international artistic activity. Sculptors who wished to study from classical antiquity and work in the studios of leading proponents of modern sculpture, notably those of Antonio Canova (1757–1822) and Bertel Thorvaldsen (1770–1844), travelled to Italy. Several British sculptors were to establish their studios there, including John Gibson (1790–1866) and Richard Wyatt (1795–1850). Others such as Thomas Banks (1735–1805), Westmacott, and Flaxman returned home to practise their own interpretations of the 'true' or 'correct' style, in a manner that suited the demands of the market. Inevitably the emphasis was upon contour and discreetly modulated surfaces which took as a starting-point a canon of classical antiquity that, as defined in Winckelmann's writings, emphasized the erotic and imaginative charge of ancient Greek sculpture. Canonical works for modern sculptors included amongst others the *Belvedere Antinuous*, *Apollo Belvedere*, and the *Belvedere Torso*; the *Laocoön*, the *Medici Venus*, and *Niobe and her children*. The cultural significance of ancient sculptural works after 1789 was demonstrated by the terms of the Treaty of Tolentino (1797) in which Pope Pius VI ceded to *Napoleon and the Revolutionary Armies of France the ancient and modern art works from the Capitol and Vatican collections. Napoleon's supremacy over Europe was epitomized by the open, public display of such plunder in Paris, including the canonical *Medici Venus* and *Apollo Belvedere*.

In Europe there were several important public collections of ancient classical sculptures housed in museums devoted to their display and study. One such purpose-built 'temple' was Leo von Klenze's (1784–1864) Glyptothek (1816–30) in Munich where Thorvaldsen was employed to arrange the ancient sculptures, including the *Barberini Faun*. Important private collections were also formed in which 'Greek' sculpture was seen to be an indicator of refined taste [see *Hellenism]. Charles Townley (1739–1803) housed his famous collection of ancient marbles (sold in 1810 to the *British Museum) at No. 7 Park Street, London, restored to their 'original' state of perfection by Joseph *Nollekens and catalogued by Pierre François Hugues, Baron d'Harcanville (1729–1803). Other private collectors in England formed collections of modern and ancient sculpture, sometimes in purpose-built galleries such as the Duke of Bedford's at Woburn Abbey, with its two end temples dedicated to Liberty—centred upon Nollekens's *Bust of Charles James Fox*—and to Canova's *Three Graces*. Other important private collections included those of the Duke of Devonshire at Chatsworth, the Earl of Egremont at Petworth, Richard Payne *Knight, and Thomas *Hope, whose Flaxman Room at Duchess Street housed the sculptor's *Aurora and Cephalus* (1790–4). The acquisition, display, and appreciation of modern sculpture was an international activity, stimulated by the circulation of casts, copies, and engravings. Lord *Byron's admiration for Canova's ideal *Head of Helen* (1811) was prompted by his viewing of the original in Isabella Teotochi Albrizzi's residence in

Venice in 1816, and its fame spread through a further six copies made by the sculptor. British sculptors also profited from the circulation of copies and variants including the leading portraitists Joseph Nollekens and Francis Chantrey (1781–1841): Nollekens's bust of *Fox was in great demand, as was Chantrey's bust of George IV, first commissioned in 1822, with many copies being issued from his studio as well as an edition of plaster replicas.

The demand for casts after the antique flourished alongside the demand for modern sculpture. The 'acquisition' of the Parthenon sculptures by the seventh Earl of Elgin (housed in a temporary museum in Picadilly in 1807 and subsequently purchased by the state in 1816) was a significant episode in the history of British sculpture, marking a seismic shift within the dominant classical canon [see *Elgin Marbles]. Sculptors were thrilled by these unrestored ancient works, particularly admiring the pedimental sculptures that combined a heightened naturalism with the ideal in the interpretation of the human body. The most direct and obvious borrowings were found in architectural or decorative sculpture such as William Theed's *Hercules Taming the Thracian Horses* (1816) on the Royal Mews, Richard Westmacott's *Waterloo Vase* (c.1830), and Edward Hodges Bailey's frieze executed for the Marble Arch, London (1828). The classical ideal of the importance of pure white marble propounded by Falconet, Diderot, and Winckelmann continued to dominate sculptural production throughout Europe, with the use of bronze for major exterior sculpture. Throughout the period however, there was a growing recognition of the use of colour in ancient sculpture.

British sculptors, like history painters, found it difficult to sustain a career based upon a pursuit of the ideal, and the most financially successful were those who adapted to the demands of the market. Sculptors continued to provide designs for decorative works such as fireplaces, as well as designs for silver and ceramic ware for firms such as Rundell, Bridge and Rundell, and *Wedgwood [see **design, 25**]. Sculptors also worked for artificial stone manufacturers, such as Eleanor *Coade, and for makers of wax portrait medallions like James Tassie (1735–99) of Edinburgh. There was comparatively little demand for ideal gallery pieces, although there were many fine examples of works that represented epic and erotically charged subjects from classical mythology and history. Thomas Banks, a close friend of *Fuseli, created many highly-wrought pieces in tune with the artist's expressive style. Given the paucity of opportunity to practise their art at the highest level, sculptors found ways of integrating the ideal within the commercially viable mainstream of work; predominantly portrait busts, statues, and church monuments. Thomas Banks's *Monument to Penelope Boothby* (1793), Chantrey's *Monument to the Robinson Children (The Sleeping Children)* (1817), and *Resignation: Monument to Charlotte Digby* (1825) were put on public exhibition before being installed in their intended religious settings, and received much public acclaim. Their simplicity of form enshrining childlike innocence or feminine virtue was exactly suited to a public attuned to sentiment and melancholy [see *sensibility, 11]. Monuments to writers and poets also allowed the opportunity to explore literary themes, as in Flaxman's monument to Mary *Tighe, *Statue of a Lady, Authoress of 'Psyche'* (1814–15). The consolidation of the British school of sculpture was expressed definitively by Allan *Cunningham in his *Lives of the Most Eminent British . . . Sculptors* (1829–33).   AWY

self-improvement. During the 1820s, a spirit of intellectual, social, and moral advancement animated some sections of the urban working and middle classes. This movement, often characterized as 'the march of mind', generated an enthusiasm for autodidacticism and a flourishing informal educational infrastructure [see *education, 17]. Mutual improvement societies, reading groups, and mechanics' institutes offered opportunities for liberal education and self-improvement to sections of society which had little or no access to formal education [see *popular education]. Reformers such as Francis *Place, radicals such as T. J. Evans (b. 1763) and Allen *Davenport, and the pressman Richard *Carlile adopted self-improvement as a means of lending respectability to the radical movement. Carlile's Zetetic societies, for example, advocated intellectual and religious freedom at the same time as they held to an ethos of earnest and morally puritanical discipline. This drive for respectability generated a new mode of political reform and radicalism. A sober, intellectual culture, at home in the *coffeehouse, asserted itself against the rough, dangerous, and potentially violent radicalism of the *tavern. Many ultra-radicals, as the spy Abel Hall reported, seemed to have been 'converted', and adopted more respectable practices. The march of mind and its attendant developments also lent a strong intellectual aspect to the emergent working-class culture of the nineteenth century. The extent of this, however, remains debatable, as is the extent to which a respectable hegemony had been established in radical culture. Throughout this period of self-improvement, underground popular and radical practices persisted, belying the sober image projected by the march of mind: the shift from public house to coffeehouse, it has been suggested, was neither as profound nor as permanent as the respectables might have hoped. The 1830s saw an ultra-radical revival which did much to displace the respectable values of the 1820s.   LT

sermons were a major tool of the Protestant denominations, occupying a central place in religious services, revivalist campaigns, and political and social life. Buying, reading, and listening to sermons was widespread. Through exhortation and exposition, sermons offered a commentary on the *Bible, Christian doctrine, national history, government, and social relations. The genre was mobilized both at the centre and on the fringe of the British political establishment, and was part of an eighteenth-century economy of gesture and ritual in which performance and verbal content together constructed meaning.

*Anglican sermons were incorporated into the official, public calendar and advanced a version of British history distinguished by divine favour. In the ritual of the Assizes, sermons imbued events with religious authority. Prominent clerics opened proceedings, trotting out familiar lessons on the divine model of justice, co-operation between church and state, and the necessity of punishment. Four national feast or fast days commemorated key royal events and were the occasion for preachers to rehearse the arguments for political submission. Sermons delivered in times of national emergency, particularly the 1790s, stressed the religious duty of obedience and the dangers of lawlessness. Political topics were not, however, confined to the established Church. Richard *Price's sermon *A Discourse on the Love of our Country* (1789) goaded Edmund *Burke to reply, while radical *Spenceans borrowed the forms of organized religion to preach blasphemy and sedition.

Sermons were a mainstay of charity fundraising and often expressed a specific form of conviviality and male sociability. Successful preachers, both Anglican and Nonconformist, extolled the spiritual value of benevolence, its earthly pleasures, the national advantages arising from well-placed donations, and the merits of a particular charity. In the 1770s a fashion for sentimental sermons appealing to sympathy and the imagination encouraged displays of emotion. By the turn of the century, distrust of *sensibility [11] and changing attitudes to *poverty [12] were evident in sermons which asserted that charity should reform, not indulge, the poor.

Sermon composition and delivery were important elements of clerical duty. A generally conservative form, sermons offered a complex and malleable stock of themes and commonplaces which were adapted according to occasion and audience. Sermons on property and social order displayed the greatest uniformity; differences were most apparent on doctrinal matters. Nonconformists and *Evangelicals tended to stress faith and experience, while traditionalists emphasized reason and authority. Preaching manuals recommended elements of classical rhetoric: rational argument, practical applications, and plain expression. Although ardent outbursts and *field preaching were frequently regarded with suspicion, these were a hallmark of some practitioners.

Many preachers had a collection of their own and others' sermons which they repeated. Evangelicals, however, tended to extemporize, putting words on paper later. Publication was a source of income, especially for clerics' and ministers' widows. Individuals and institutions used an expanding print culture to attract patronage and circulate a successful sermon around a wider audience. The high proportion of Dissenters' sermons published suggests an assertion of a particular community identity in the period before the repeal of the Test and Corporation Acts. A 1783 text, compiled to aid preachers, listed over 23,000 sermons published since 1660, and sermons remained a substantial, if declining, slice of the *publishing [21] market.   SL

SEWARD, Anna (1742–1809), poet and letterwriter, acclaimed in her day as 'the Swan of Lichfield'.

She was the daughter of Elizabeth Hunter and the Revd Thomas Seward, Rector of Eyam and later Canon Residentiary of Lichfield, from then on Anna's home. Samuel *Johnson, a native of Lichfield, was a distant connection, but their mutual antagonism is reflected in her published letters, which included pseudonymous criticism of Johnson and acrimonious exchanges with James *Boswell.

Her correspondence records literary friendships with Hester Thrale *Piozzi; Thomas *Day; Lady Eleanor Butler and Sarah Ponsonby [see *Sapphism]; and Helen Maria *Williams, whose *French revolutionary sympathies Seward denounced in the *Gentleman's Magazine* in 1793.

Her early attempts at *poetry [29] were discouraged by her parents. Largely self-educated, she was confident of her own literary standing and her poetry attracted admirers despite its ornateness and sentimentalism. She denounced Charlotte *Smith's experimentation with the *sonnet form, but was praised for her *epic elegies, a form which Erasmus *Darwin, a friend, credited her with inventing. These included an *Elegy on Captain Cook* (1780) and her best-remembered poem, the *Monody on the Death of Major André* (1781). Written on the hanging of a friend as a spy during the *American Revolution, and containing an attack on George Washington, it had great success and led Washington himself to contact her in his own defence. In 1784 she published a verse novel, *Louisa*.   RCA

SHAKESPEARE, William (1564–1616). In 1769 at Stratford, David Garrick (1717–79) presented a Shakespeare Jubilee which marked the unique preeminence that Shakespeare had attained in British cultural life well before our period. During the eighteenth century, over 7,000 performances of Shakespeare were given in London alone; editors and scholars devoted much time to his plays, and a succession of new and cheaper editions made them widely read. Many of Shakespeare's coinages, maxims, and original turns of phrase had passed into common speech, while parody, satire, and political caricature relied heavily on recognizable Shakespearean allusions. Parliamentary debate included frequent Shakespeare quotations. Shakespearean subjects became popular in *painting [27], giving rise, for example to John *Boydell's ambitious, if rather unsuccessful, Shakespeare Gallery. In the *theatre [24], adaptations of Shakespeare's plays were giving way to more authentic, though much-abridged, versions. It became commonplace during this period to speak of Shakespeare as a god rather than a man, and while critical objections to his supposed violations of neoclassical rules and notions of decorum still lingered, they were being gradually displaced by celebrations of his *genius, truth to nature, and powers of character creation.

Interest in the man himself was also growing. Portraits were sought, fabricated, and disputed, and at Stratford, from the mid-century, a shrine for his devotees, stimulated a lively tourist industry. The paucity of biographical records gave rise to a number of forgeries, such as W. H. *Ireland's sensational

'discovery' of a collection of documents relating to Shakespeare, and even a couple of lost plays. By the end of the century Shakespeare had become an icon of English identity, a source of English history and patriotic pride. In short, the main elements of early-nineteenth-century Shakespeare idolatry had been solidly established by the last quarter of the eighteenth century.

There is substantial evidence that between 1782 and 1833, from the first success of Sarah *Siddons on the London stage to the death of Edmund *Kean, there was a sustained period of great acting and of audiences which came again and again to see Shakespeare represented. By contrast, many critics— among them Charles *Lamb, Leigh *Hunt, William *Hazlitt, and Thomas *Carlyle—expressed a fundamental objection to stage performances on the basis that material representations of the plays curtailed their imaginative freedom. S. T. *Coleridge claimed never to have seen the plays performed without pain. Some recent studies attribute this apparent antitheatricalism to broad underlying causes such as a reaction against revolution and political action, an élitist attempt to protect Shakespeare from vulgar popularization, or a misogynist response to women on the stage. Others blame the theatres of the period, with their emphasis on spectacle, their anachronisms, mutilations of Shakespeare's texts, unruly audiences, and submission to a popular taste for farce and burlesque. Nevertheless, Lamb, Coleridge, Hazlitt, and Hunt were all frequent theatregoers and testified to the power of performances of Shakespeare by John Philip *Kemble, Kean, and, above all, Siddons. For Lamb, the very intensity of theatrical experience was a drawback, substituting a painful sense of presence for the meditative delight derived from reading Shakespeare's words. The shift of attention from performance to reading gave new importance to Shakespeare's text.

Garrick's Shakespeare Jubilee, though not a complete success in England, was acclaimed in the Continent, where Shakespeare was similarly growing in stature. The German critic A. W. Schlegel (1767–1845) and his successors translated Shakespeare into modern German, making him more readily accessible. Schlegel's criticism formulated a theoretical approach based on the social function of *poetry [29] which exalted Shakespeare, characterizing him as the ideal conception of the poet. This theory crystallized much in the thinking of the time, and remained influential well into the twentieth century. More importantly, it paralleled and influenced Coleridge's definition of the poet 'described in ideal perfection' as well as his account of Shakespeare's imaginative powers in the narrative poems. Like Schlegel, Coleridge derided the view of Shakespeare as untutored genius, emphasizing instead his artistic judgment: 'he never introduces a word or a thought in vain or out of place: if we do not understand him, it is our own fault.' What made the Shakespeare criticism of Coleridge and Schlegel a significant advance on ideas already in circulation was that it was based on and permeated by conscious and elaborated theoretical principles: through them the ideas and associated critical practices took definitive form [see *literary theory, 41].

Coleridge's Shakespeare criticism revived appreciation of the non-dramatic poems and, by exploring the dramatic functions of imagery, metaphors, and verbal play, brought about a new understanding of the integral role of poetry in the plays. A scattering of remarks showed also his understanding of Shakespeare's theatre, though Coleridge still assumed that the right way to approach Shakespeare was through reading, not performance. He seems to have believed that Shakespeare addressed the plays to future readers, writing both for his own age and for all ages. Similarly, Coleridge insisted that Shakespeare was of no religion, party, or profession. Even his language was entirely his own. The effect was to take Shakespeare not only out of the theatre but also out of history. Dehistoricizing Shakespeare enabled Coleridge to present him as at once a detached observer of society and a staunchly traditional moralist and political conservative. Shakespeare, said Coleridge, displayed a wonderfully philosophical impartiality, and, at the same time, profoundly venerated the established institutions of society, delighted in distinctions of rank, and good-naturedly laughed at the mob. Coleridge presents all this not as paradoxical or self-contradictory but as evidence of Shakespeare's universality, his realization of the principles that hold a society together and bind one age to another.

Such counter-revolutionary views appealed to the higher and middle classes that Coleridge addressed. In several other ways, too, his Shakespeare criticism reflected the preconceptions and prejudices of that audience. Shakespeare's bawdiness and profanity, already toned down in the theatre by this time, began to trouble readers. As early as 1774 Bell's Shakespeare had attempted, haphazardly, to remove 'glaring indecencies'. Some commentators suggested that the offending passages were interpolated by other hands than Shakespeare's. Coleridge shared the new squeamishness, finding, for example, the Porter scene in Macbeth disgusting, but he argued nevertheless that Shakespeare was morally sound. Why Coleridge felt the need for such a defence may be suggested by the success of The Family Shakespeare, an edition by Thomas *Bowdler and, covertly, his sister Henrietta Maria. The first major expurgation of Shakespeare, it aimed to make his 'almost inexhaustible fund of instruction as well as pleasure' available for reading aloud in the family. First published in 1807, enlarged and revised in 1818, it became the bestselling edition of Shakespeare in its period and remained popular throughout the nineteenth century. Also published in 1807, Tales from Shakespeare by Charles Lamb and, also covertly, his sister, Mary *Lamb, transformed the plays into prose narratives. The Tales became immediately popular, and it has remained in print to the present, partly because it fulfils its aim of making the plays easy and attractive reading for young children [see *children's literature]. It also makes them innocent (the Porter scene simply disappears). The Preface states that the tales were written chiefly for girls, and invites young gentlemen to read passages of the originals to their sisters, carefully selecting what is proper for a young sister's ear. By 1822 another and more severely expurgated edition, by J. R. Pitman, was designed for schools, a signal that by then the study of Shakespeare was beginning to form part of formal *education [17] (though brief extracts from the plays had long been used in teaching rhetoric and in reading anthologies).

Hazlitt had heartily repudiated Bowdler's scruples. Such critics, he wrote in Characters of Shakespear's Plays (1817), confound modesty with hypocrisy. In contrast to Coleridge, Hazlitt declared Shakespeare to be no moralist at all—in the sense that he was not censorious. In another sense he was the greatest of moralists: he sympathized with all of human nature. This notion of Shakespearean sympathy was not new but Hazlitt put it to fresh critical use, making it the basis of overtly political, democratizing readings of the plays. Hazlitt thought of Shakespeare as protean, entering imaginatively into the situation of every character and identifying with them: he had only to think of anything to become that thing. Unlike others, however, Hazlitt gave to this capacity a moral as well as a psychological or aesthetic dimension. Shakespeare, he said, was the least possible egotist (implying a contrast with contemporary poets like *Wordsworth and *Byron), and such self-effacement enabled Shakespeare to see both sides of a question, according to the interests of the parties concerned. Coriolanus, for example, presents a political vision encompassing both *Burke and *Paine, arguments for and against aristocracy or democracy. Praising the play for its handling of opposing arguments, Hazlitt adds that 'perhaps from some feeling of contempt for his own origin', Shakespeare seems to have leaned to the patrician side 'and to have spared no occasion of baiting the rabble'. This of course undercuts Hazlitt's repeated assertions of Shakespeare's evenhanded impersonality, but it does reflect an ambivalence in the play that continues to vex its critics.

For Hazlitt, the bias he sees in the play derives primarily from what he regards as the nature of poetry itself: poetry, he suggests, is anti-levelling; its language falls in with the language of power; imagination is aristocratical, excited by inequality, because men naturally love power in themselves and admire it in others. This idea of poetic language seems at odds with Hazlitt's subtle and admiring account of Wordsworth's levelling muse and of the relation between poetry and the revolutionary movement of the age. It involved him in a bitter dispute with William *Gifford, editor of the Quarterly Review, in which paradoxically it was the *Tory, Gifford, who argued that Shakespeare did not lean to the aristocratic side.

Among theatre audiences in this period, political sentiment remained fundamentally conservative, anti-French, and anti-revolutionary, although levelling impulses appeared in the Old Price Theatre riots at Covent Garden in 1809. Theatre managements were similarly conservative, as their selection of Shakespeare's plays attests. The potentially subversive Julius Caesar, for example, was kept off the

London stage from 1780 to 1812, and after the fall of the Bastille, Kemble suspended performances of *Coriolanus* and did so again in 1792. In 1808 Elizabeth *Inchbald noted that the play had been withdrawn in recent years for 'reasons of state'—meaning it might inflame the lower orders. In October 1789, on the other hand, Kemble revived the patriotically appealing *Henry V* and ran it again for five successive seasons from 1790. *King John*, restored to the stage by Kemble in 1791, remained popular for similar reasons, especially when in 1803 anti-French additions were included from the version devised by Richard Valpy (1754–1836) for pupils at Reading School. Kemble produced it every year from 1804 to 1817.

In London, the two patent theatres, Drury Lane and Covent Garden had a near-monopoly on regular productions of Shakespeare. Successive rebuilding made them so large that they imposed special constraints on performance: actors could not be properly heard or seen from distant parts of the auditorium, and subtleties of expression tended to be lost. The size of the stage encouraged the use of lavish spectacle, and crowd scenes and processions grew huge. A strong influence on the theatre came from the growing interest in *antiquarianism [35], which combined with *patriotism to produce a desire for accurate representation of the national past. Kemble's brother Charles (1775–1854), for example, employed the antiquarian James Planché (1796–1880) to design costumes and scenery for the 1824 production of *King John*, with such success that Planché could boast of having made a complete reformation of dramatic costume inevitable from that moment.

The period was also marked by major transformations in acting style and stage presentation. Garrick's delivery had been rapid and varied, his gestures lively and graceful, and audiences in his time had looked for virtuosity in the performance of standard roles, while Sarah Siddons and her brother, John Philip Kemble, introduced a more heroic, elevated mode of acting, with a high degree of identification between performer and character. Kean's advent on the London stage in 1814, a few years before Kemble's retirement, was greeted by contemporaries as effecting a revolution; later commentators have described it as marking the triumph of Romanticism in the performance of Shakespeare. Kean's acting was dynamic and fitful, concentrating on moments of intensity. Unlike the consistent Kemble, whose style was thought by some too unchanging whatever part he played, Kean was uneven, his acting persona unsuited to some roles. Hazlitt thought his Hamlet too splenetic and rash, his Romeo leaden. His greatest performance was probably in *Othello*, where, according to Leigh Hunt, his rendering of the range of feeling in the title-role was as complete as an actor could make it: 'we never saw anything', wrote Hunt, 'that so completely held us suspended and heart-stricken.'

This emphasis on individual character, in the theatre as in criticism, combined with a developing interest—helped by the power of Siddons's acting—in female roles. When the period began, according to one commentator in 1772, the universally prevalent opinion held that Shakespeare treated women severely and rendered them as dramatically insignificant. At the period's end Anna Jameson (1794–1860) claimed to find this opinion still prevalent and constantly repeated. In between, however, William Richardson (1743–1814) in 1789 and Hartley *Coleridge as late as 1828 had attempted to refute it; leading male critics had written worshipfully about particular female characters, and a number of women writers, including Siddons herself, brought their own perspective to the topic.

Elizabeth Griffith (1727–93) in 1775 praised Shakespeare's power to express what none but a woman could possibly feel. Jameson's *Characteristics of Women* (1832), the first book devoted entirely to women in Shakespeare, speculated on how the heroines would have behaved in hypothetical situations or in each other's plays, and carried still further the exaltation of their virtues. Jameson praised Shakespeare for portraying the feminine character in its elementary principles of modesty, grace, and tenderness—inherent qualities which could be perverted but never wholly crushed out of a woman's soul [see *sensibility, 11]. She laid down as an invariable principle that the intellect of woman is inferior to man's, and different in kind, because in women intellect is less independent of sympathies and moral qualities. Nevertheless she repeatedly credited the heroines with impressive mental powers.

Towards the end of the eighteenth century a new attitude to Shakespeare's texts emerged. Objections to his word-play, diction, and usage persisted into the 1790s, but changing conceptions of literature and *language [40] emphasized the importance of Shakespeare's own words, and more scholarly editions helped to restore lost meanings. Edward Capell broke with the practice by which successive editors since Rowe had simply revised the text handed down by their predecessors. He based his 1768 edition on a painstaking collation of the early quartos and folios, and his three-volume commentary—published in 1783, after his death—made the first use of such important Elizabethan sources as the Stationers' Register, Holinshed, North, and Meres. The two other most notable editors of the period, George Steevens (1736–1800) and Edmund *Malone, were less thorough and systematic in collation (bringing on themselves fierce, accurate criticism from Joseph *Ritson). Their main contribution lay in amassing supplementary information to elucidate the texts. Steevens's early editions of the plays form the basis of the First Variorum, which was published in 1803 under the editorship of Isaac Reed (1742–1807). Malone wrote the first account of the Elizabethan theatre based on contemporary records, attempted to ascertain the chronology of the plays, and produced the first critical edition of the sonnets. His considerable knowledge of Shakespeare's period enabled him decisively to expose the Ireland forgeries. Malone's 1790 edition, including the non-dramatic poems, has been described as summing up the editorial work of the eighteenth century on

Shakespeare. After his death in 1812, the material he was preparing for a revised edition passed to James Boswell the younger (1778–1822), and became the basis of the monumental Third Variorum (also known as 'Boswell's Malone') of 1821.

On creative writers in the period, Shakespeare's influence was pervasive, at once inspiring and inhibiting. His example and his overwhelming reputation bore heavily on the psychology of authorship, on the process of composition, and on the aesthetic and social ambitions of writers in this age. His influence was particularly evident in poetic drama, a genre not usually numbered among the period's main achievements. Among authors now canonized, Coleridge alone enjoyed success on the public stage, and he with only one play, *Remorse* (1797). Yet *Blake, *Southey, *Scott, *Shelley, *Keats, *Beddoes, Wordsworth, Lamb, and Byron all attempted the form, as did others now less well remembered like Joanna *Baillie and Charles *Maturin. Most of their plays have been regarded as *closet drama and have drawn criticism for retreating from both the theatre and the historical conditions of their time; until recently, at least, their recourse to Shakespearean modes has been taken as a sign of regression. Shakespeare's influence, or the influence of the way he was read, can be seen in their preoccupation with individual consciousness, with problems of conscience, and with characters of moral ambiguity; though it is in their language that most of them fall obviously under Shakespeare's shadow, and in this respect the influence is usually not benign.

Matthew Arnold (1822–88) at mid-nineteenth century made a similar objection to Shakespeare's influence on the major poetry of the Romantic period. He thought it dangerous for young writers to model themselves on Shakespeare because they would be likely to absorb and attempt to reproduce his style and language, rather than develop forms of expression suited to their own times. Keats and Shelley, he thought, entered a false track by trying to reproduce the exuberant expressiveness and rich imagery of the Elizabethan poets. Modern critics see the matter as more complex, acknowledging that Shakespeare's example did in various ways prove damaging but pointing in detail to his creative influence on the poetry of the period. It needs to be remembered that other influences were also strongly at work—sometimes more strongly, as *Milton's was for Blake and Wordsworth, or Plato's for Shelley and Pope's for Byron. But as an abiding cultural influence, Shakespeare's presence was the most widely spread. FL

SHARP, William (1749–1824). The most eminent line-engraver of the period, Sharp also epitomizes much of the radicalism and the apocalyptic enthusiasm which inspired London's artisan culture in the years around 1800. Trained to decorate door-plates, pewter pots, or visiting-cards, he found employment as a writing engraver in the 1770s, was admitted to the *Royal Academy schools in 1771, and in the early 1780s began to earn a reputation as a competent reproductive engraver [see *prints, 22]. An active member of the *Society for Constitutional Information, he engraved a portrait of Washington in 1780, and a 'Declaration of Rights', dedicated to the SCI, in 1782. By 1790 he was in contact with William *Godwin, John Horne *Tooke, Thomas *Paine, and other London radicals, and was questioned before the Privy Council during 1794. While Sharp's precise role as a witness in the trial of Tooke remains difficult to determine, the production and publication of a substantial group of portraits, including the likenesses of Richard *Brothers, Francis *Burdett, Daniel Isaac *Eaton, Joanna *Southcott, Tooke, and Paine exemplify his radical sympathies and his important contribution to the visualization of radical London from the 1790s onward.

A follower of *Swedenborgianism in the 1780s and subsequently of Brothers, Sharp was later instrumental in the popularization of the cult of Southcott, with whom he was closely involved after 1801. He was given custody of her writings in 1802 and sponsored her move to London at this time. He later suspended his work as an engraver to promote her cause, and was involved in a shady financial deal with John 'Jew' *King in an attempt to finance her mission. Even after Southcott's failure to produce her son, Shiloh, and her death in 1814, Sharp remained a committed disciple. DWD

SHELBURNE, Earl of (William Petty, first Marquess of Lansdowne) (1737–1805), statesman. A leading (but often distrusted) figure in opposition circles in the late 1760s and 1770s, Shelburne took office as Southern Secretary in Rockingham's ministry of 1782. His short-lived ministry in 1783 (defeated by the Fox–North coalition) was responsible for concluding the *American Revolution. At this time Shelburne headed a party that was strong enough, so Jeremy *Bentham said, to tell 'in the balance against the great aristocracy of the country: it was as they say at Cricket, *Shelburne against England*'. An active proponent of administrative and financial reforms that were designed to reduce corrupt influences in parliament and government, and of open international trade, Shelburne was connected with many of the leading radical intellectuals of his day. A correspondent of *philosophes* in France, he was the patron of Richard *Price, Joseph *Priestley, and Bentham. These thinkers provided Shelburne with a *utilitarian framework for his reforming ideas; they also helped to satisfy his apparently insatiable appetite for information.

For his part, Shelburne infused a degree of political realism into the productions of his less experienced and more visionary intellectual associates. The antipathy of the King, the mistrust of his fellow politicians—Edmund *Burke hated him with a passion—and his incapacity to act as the member of a party kept him out of office for the last two decades of his life. Shelburne's extensive collection of antique statuary and manuscripts was acquired by the *British Museum after his death. JMo

SHELLEY, Mary Wollstonecraft (1797–1851), author of *Frankenstein; or, the Modern Prometheus*

and other fiction, and editor and biographer of Percy *Shelley. In her works of radical imagination, *Frankenstein, Mathilda*, and *The Last Man*, Mary Shelley redrew the borders between fabulation and intimate psychological realism, although she worked best in shorter fictional forms of novella, sketch, or tale, which were also popular with European contemporaries like John William *Polidori [see *novels, 31].

Mary *Wollstonecraft Godwin died twelve days after her second daughter, Mary, was born, and the widower, William *Godwin, registered the birth at Dr Williams' Library and passed the mother's name to the baby. With her half-sister, Fanny, she was cared for by nursemaids in her father's household until he remarried in 1801, and Mary Jane *Godwin, formerly Clairmont, took over the household. Mary was among the first generation of child readers of contemporary *children's literature, and Godwin and his friends were its authors and illustrators.

Mary's juvenile writings were lost on her trip to France and the Rhineland in 1814, when she eloped with Percy Shelley, whom she had met in her father's house. She began keeping a journal jointly with Shelley, and was to keep it until 1844. They returned to England to find the door of Godwin's home barred against them. Mary bore a baby girl in February 1815, tentatively named Mary, who survived only ten days. She quickly became pregnant again, and bore William Godwin Shelley in October 1815.

In summer 1816 Mary and Shelley, with baby William, and Mary Jane, calling herself Claire *Clairmont, travelled to Geneva, where they joined Lord *Byron and his party of summer visitors. Eagerly abetted by Shelley, she put part of every day into writing what was to be her masterpiece, *Frankenstein; or, the Modern Prometheus*. On return to England Mary drew on her journals of both European tours for her first publication, *History of a Six Weeks' Tour* (1817). As a woman and mother she controlled no separate time or space for her writing, and adapted by decanting her constant reading and the recurrent stresses of her life into the text in progress. During the prolonged gestation of *Frankenstein*, Percy Shelley composed 'Laon and Cythna'. It was euphemistically retitled *The Revolt of Islam* (1818), and dedicated to Mary Wollstonecraft Godwin, his 'Child of Light', Mary's name blended with her mother's as Shelley's secret feminine avatar. This fantasy of creative intersubjectivity was to be repossessed by Mary as Shelley's posthumous editor and biographer.

The Shelley name became legally hers on 30 December 1816 when she and Shelley married within weeks of two suicides, illegitimate sister Fanny Imlay and deserted wife Harriet Shelley. The first legitimate child of the Shelley marriage was born in September 1817, a daughter named Clara Everina, and ambivalent attitudes to legitimacy are inscribed in the births and deaths of children in *Frankenstein*.

In January 1818, *Frankenstein; or, the Modern Prometheus* was published anonymously by James *Lackington. It bore a dedication to Godwin as author of *Caleb Williams*, and a preface signed P.B.S., so reviewers, including Sir Walter *Scott, attributed authorship to Percy Shelley. The influence of *Caleb Williams* was demonstrable in the ambivalent relationship between the Demon and Victor. The Demon parallels Caleb as the man of the rising lower class and instructor of the waning aristocrat Falkland in the harsh realities of 'things as they are'.

In March the Shelleys and their two children, along with Claire Clairmont and her daughter, sailed for Italy and its freemasonry of expatriate writers. The great period of Percy Shelley's poetry commenced in Europe with the renewed relationship with the self-exiled Byron. But Mary Shelley was precipitated into anxiety, loneliness, and the sickness and death of her two children, Clara Everina dying in September 1818 in Venice, William in June 1819 in Rome.

In August 1819 the Shelley couple, now childless, moved from Rome to Leghorn and then to Florence for Mary to deliver her fourth child. Mary began a novella modelled on Wollstonecraft's posthumously published fable of female initiation, 'Cave of Fancy'. *Mathilda* is a tragic tale of father–daughter incest, blending the lyricism of Dante's *Purgatorio* with the fatal passions of Vittorio Alfieri's verse tragedy *Mirra*.

Percy Florence Shelley was born in November 1819, and in summer 1820 Mary Shelley sent the MS *Mathilda* with Maria Gisborne to Godwin in London. Godwin pronounced it a detestable failure, and refused to return the manuscript, which remained unpublished until 1959.

In 1820, living among the English community in Pisa, Mary entered more boldly into the intellectual and aesthetic experiences offered by Italy. She shared Shelley's intense attraction to *theatre [24] and collaborated with him on *Proserpine* and *Midas*, two plays suitable for child actors based on Ovid's fables. Their Italian acquaintances now included the celebrated *improvisatore* Tomasso Sgricci, and a flamboyant homosexual academic, Francesco Pacchiani. In defiance of English taste, which had rejected Shelley's Renaissance tragedy *The Cenci*, Mary declared that it was his best work. She had begun a historical novel set in the Italian Renaissance: this too was to raise money for Godwin, who had been made bankrupt and evicted from the Skinner Street house and shop. The commanding figure was to have been Castruccio, the egoistical grandee who uses sex as power, but Godwin intervened to change the title to *Valperga*, the name of the woman-inherited castle. A *romance, in Ann *Radcliffe's style, of the father-identified daughter who inherits the role of absented mother, this effectually gestured towards his own *St Leon*, published after Wollstonecraft's death.

The final chapter of Mary Shelley's Italian sojourn opened in spring 1822, with the dreadful misfortune of 5-year-old Allegra Byron's death. Shelley had moved their household to the coast at Lerici. On 8 July 1822 his boat capsized in a Mediterranean summer storm and he, Edward Williams, and a young sailor were drowned. After several days of agonized waiting, Mary and Jane Williams were informed that the bodies had washed ashore.

After the initial shock of Shelley's death, Mary Shelley showed her wounded feelings and disappointments only to her 'journal of sorrow'. She fortified herself to care for her child, Percy, and to keep the legacy of Shelley the poet intact. The unpublished manuscripts were in her keeping, and her own and Percy's future depended on her skill in negotiations with the world which waited to claim her back in England.

In 1823 a second edition of *Frankenstein* was called for, and she and Godwin together went to see *Presumption*, a *melodrama based on *Frankenstein* without the author's permission by R. B. Peake (1792–1847). Peake stigmatized Victor Frankenstein as the modern type of 'presumptuous' atheistical scientist, a definitive reading for the expanding American audience. In 1831 Mary Shelley's revised *Frankenstein* elaborated this verdict against scientific reason, converting the three brief volumes of 1818 into a monumental one volume, with the complaint of the Demon against Victor Frankenstein at its centre.

From 1823 she relied on publishing periodical fiction and *reviews as a steady source of income. In 1824 she published Percy Shelley's *Posthumous Poems*, omitting poems to Harriet Shelley and Claire Clairmont, and including her own arrangement of Shelley's drafts of *The Triumph of Life*. Her next novel, *The Last Man* (1826), is a future fable almost as original as *Frankenstein*, with recognizable portraits of Shelley and Byron, but contains no dynamic counterpart to the Demon-Creature of Frankenstein. In 1829 she published Shelley's *Essay on Love*, and some minor verses in *Keepsake*, a popular *silver fork annual.

The 1830s was Mary Shelley's most copious decade. It began in 1831 with a collaborative project of family memoirs and editing undertaken with Godwin for the publisher Henry Colburn (d. 1855), saw her multi-volumed *encyclopedia biographies for Lardner's *Cabinet Cyclopaedia*, and ended with the editorial apparatus and biographical commentary for six volumes of Percy Shelley's poetry and prose in 1839. Her lengthy introductions to the third edition of *Frankenstein* and to Godwin's reissued *Caleb Williams* were settings of family history shaped into decorous literary memoirs. She organized Godwin's increasingly untidy manuscripts for publication, and edited *Transfusion* (1835), a novel left in manuscript at the early death of her half-brother, William Godwin, Jr. Her latest novels, *Lodore* (1835), and *Falkner* (1837), return to the father-identified girl heroine of a Radcliffe romance, but the parochial stamina of Radcliffe in rehabilitating the father eludes Mary Shelley.

98. Frontispiece by W. Chevalier after T. Holst, in the 1831 edition of *Frankenstein*.

Godwin himself died in 1836, appointing her his literary executor, and for the next four years she laboured to produce a standard 'Life and Correspondence' from his huge archive of papers. If she appeared compliant with the constraints of her social position, her bitterly resentful short story 'The Parvenue', published in 1837, gives the lie to appearances. She declined Godwin's instructions to publish his apologia for leaving the church, 'The Genius of Christianity Unveiled', and concentrated on an account of his early manhood, for which she relied on the autobiographical notes that Godwin had compiled. She perused his daily journals of the 1790s and many bundles of letters, and organized a first volume covering Godwin's life and publications up to 1798, the year in which he published his *Memoirs and Posthumous Writings* of Mary Wollstonecraft. She discovered the correspondence between Godwin and the writer Harriet *Lee of Bath in 1798, in which Godwin tried to persuade Lee to marry him, less than six months after Wollstonecraft's death. This cast doubt on the biography's sentimental climax in the death of Wollstonecraft and Godwin's tributary *Memoirs*, but Mary Shelley did not record any decision not to publish Godwin's life story, simply allowing the momentum of work to tail off.

In 1840 she was frequently ill and pleading exhaustion. Nonetheless, she made several pleasant excursions in Europe with Percy, and published the successful *Rambles in Germany and Italy in 1840, 1842, and 1843*. Mary Shelley died from a brain tumour at the age of 53 after a period of debilitating pain. She had not been able to write or study for some time past. A lightning flash of the Romantic vision of selfhood, with all its terror of blood sacrifice, had produced *Frankenstein* before she was 20; Mary Shelley was afterwards to be the survivor and memorialist of that vision.   JB

SHELLEY, Percy Bysshe (1792–1822), poet. The eldest son of an MP (later a baronet), Shelley was educated at the family home, Field Place, then Eton before going up to Oxford. He sidestepped his father's ambitions for a parliamentary career by publishing *The Necessity of Atheism* (1811) at Oxford, written with his friend, T. J. Hogg, for which he was expelled from the University. The subsequent break with his father, which meant that he struggled for money through the rest of his life, was a crucial moment in terms of both his domestic relations and literary work. His writing often portrayed social tyrannies in terms of hateful father-figures such as Jupiter in *Prometheus Unbound* (1820) and the incestuous count in *The Cenci* (1819). After quarrelling violently with his father, Shelley eloped with the 16-year-old Harriet Westbrook in 1811. Shelley was later infamous for his views on the evils of marriage and the desirability of free love, and may have practised the latter with Harriet and Hogg, as well as in later relationships. The marriage broke down in 1814 and he subsequently eloped abroad with Mary Wollstonecraft Godwin (Mary *Shelley), together with her stepsister, Mary Jane 'Claire' *Clairmont,

to form what was to become an enduring but often tense domestic group. Harriet committed suicide in 1816 and Shelley was deprived of custody of their children. Nevertheless, through all these tribulations, the family unit remained the touchstone of his poetic vision of social harmony.

Shelley's thinking was profoundly indebted to the radical enlightenment (*Paine, *Rousseau, *Volney, and others), but his wide philosophical and political reading, encouraged by his tutors at Field Place and Eton, also included Plato and Spinoza. From an early age he maintained a strong interest in science (including early forms of *psychology [39]) which informed his philosophical materialism. Between 1811 and 1813 he corresponded vigorously with William *Godwin, but the latter was horrified when Shelley became involved in distributing pamphlets and addressing public meetings in Dublin in 1812, his remonstrances playing a part in Shelley's departure from Ireland. After travelling in Wales, Harriet and Shelley became involved in what would now be called an experiment in social ecology—the land reclamation project in the new town of Tremadoc. Pressure from the local squirearchy eventually drove them out. Since the summer of 1811 Shelley had been writing *Queen Mab*, which was eventually published privately in 1813. Disguised as a philosophical fairy story, it was a vision of past, present, and future society and an incitement to radical change. Shelley's ambivalent relations with the different circles in which he participated is well illustrated by the history of *Queen Mab*. The poem was initially presented to and then pirated by the radical underground in cheap, pocket-sized editions. Shelley later repudiated these connections, sometimes speaking of the popular radical press with aristocratic contempt. *Queen Mab* was a lasting influence on his later work which could be read as the ceaseless reworking of its central poetic figures, but he continually shied away from the popular audience whose enthusiasm for its contents (there were at least fourteen editions between 1821 and 1845) would have allowed him to have made a different kind of political intervention.

Meanwhile Shelley had been building contacts in liberal sections of literary society. While visiting London in the winter of 1812 he saw much of Godwin and his family and formed a lasting friendship with Thomas Love *Peacock. An important member of Godwin's circle was the vegetarian J. F. Newton (1767–1837) who arranged for Shelley to join the community of his sister-in-law, Harriet Boinville, at Bracknell in the late summer of 1813, after the flight from Wales. Shelley experimented with *vegetarianism there and met the materialist surgeon Sir William *Lawrence. During the subsequent time abroad, after his marriage with Harriet collapsed, Shelley made contact with Lord *Byron, who was also to be an important influence.

Shelley arrived back from the Continent amid the revival of the reform movement in 1816. Late in the year he made another important contact, Leigh *Hunt, whose journal the *Examiner* acknowledged him as one of a crop of promising young poets that included John *Keats. Through most of the next year, while living at Marlow near the Thames, this group, along with Godwin and Peacock, provided Shelley with perhaps the most settled environment he was ever to experience, but by March 1818 pressure from creditors, illness, and political hostility had driven Shelley permanently abroad.

Nevertheless Shelley continued to seek to intervene in the reform movement. On receiving news of *Peterloo, he wrote *The Mask of Anarchy* (1819), which Hunt refused to publish in the *Examiner* on the grounds that it might inflame 'the people at large'. Apart from maintaining an interest in popular politics in Britain, Shelley continued to speculate on large-scale social schemes. Discussions on agricultural reform with a G. W. Tighe in Italy in 1820 made use of Humphry *Davy's lectures to model a scientific approach to the problems set by *Malthusian social theory. The influence of both Davy and Malthus is clear in *A Philosophical View of Reform* (1820) and 'To Liberty' (1820), the latter combining its allegory of the progress of liberty with a discussion of the relationship between sustainable ecologies and economic demand. Shelley never segregated such matters from his poetry, and the notes from the reading recommended by Tighe were written in the same book in which he drafted 'Ode to the West Wind' during an extraordinary year of poetic creativity beginning in the summer of 1819. In this period he also finished *Prometheus Unbound*, wrote *The Cenci*, which he hoped to have produced at Covent Garden, and completed 'Julian and Maddalo'.

Even after the disappointment over *The Mask of Anarchy* and the failure to have *The Cenci* produced, Shelley continued to address public issues. He read widely in the cultural history of Italy and enthusiastically supported the insurrection in Naples in 1820. In 1821 he met Prince Alexander Mavrocordato, the leader of the Greek patriots, and dedicated his poem *Hellas* (1822) to him the following year. He was returning from a meeting with Hunt and Byron in Pisa to discuss their plans for launching the *Liberal*, a magazine devoted to issues of literature and politics, when his boat went down in a summer storm.

Shelley devoted his life to the exploration of two questions. What was the nature of historical and political change? And to whom should his ideas on these issues be addressed? They are questions which permeate not only the explicitly political writings, but also the great lyrics like 'The Ode to the West Wind'.   TBM

SHERIDAN, Richard Brinsley (1751–1816), dramatist, *theatre [24] manager, and politician. Sheridan's mother was the novelist and dramatist Frances Sheridan (1724–66); his father the redoubtable Thomas Sheridan (1719–88), actor, theatre manager, and writer on *language [40] and *education [17]. Born in Dublin, Sheridan left the Irish capital with his family for England in 1760. He was educated at Harrow school and in 1770 the Sheridan family moved to the *spa town of Bath where Thomas supplemented a pension from the government with *lecturing and tutoring. It was at Bath that the

Sheridans encountered the *Linleys, then the most celebrated musical family in the country. Richard Brinsley's friendship with the soprano daughter Elizabeth Linley led to their elopement to France in 1772 and, on their return, to two *duels with a thwarted admirer, Captain Thomas Mathews. The drama of the young couple's romance was played out in the *newspapers and public assemblies of Bath, Dublin, and London, creating a perception of their relationship as a model of *sensibility [11], and also establishing a public profile for Sheridan at an early stage of his career.

Sheridan's marriage to Elizabeth Linley in 1773 was strongly disapproved of by his father on the grounds of the unrespectability of the Linley sisters as public performers. Indeed, once married, Sheridan ensured that his wife never sang for money again, as his biographer Thomas *Moore put it, preferring 'the manlier resolution of seeking an independence by his own'. This 'independence' was sought in the law, in journalism, and most successfully in the theatre with which his father-in-law Thomas Linley was associated—Covent Garden. *The Rivals*, his comedy of sensibility, set in his old stamping-ground of Bath, was a failure when first staged at Covent Garden on 17 January 1775 but after revision went on to become a popular repertory piece. Sheridan is best known today for this work, and for *The School for Scandal* (1777), a comic satire on fashionable London. But he was adept in other genres, too, producing a farce *St Patrick's Day* (1775), a comic opera, *The Duenna* (1775), which was highly successful in its day, sophisticated topical afterpieces *The Camp* (1778) and *The Critic* (1779), as well as numerous witty prologues and epilogues. Like David Garrick (1717–79) before him, Sheridan's understanding of the arts of theatre embraced the visual, aural, and mechanical as well as the literary text: he encouraged and benefited from the work of Philippe Jacques de *Loutherbourg, whose ingenious designs for *The Camp* and *The Critic* were crucial to the success of these plays. The latter was a work which parodies theatrical bombast and in particular *Shakespearean heroic tragedy while at the same time celebrating Georgian *patriotism as intrinsically (and sometimes ludicrously) theatrical. More than *The Rivals* or *The School for Scandal*, it is Sheridan's comic masterpiece: in its spectacular modes *The Critic* epitomizes the complex interrelationship of theatre and politics at this period, as well as the confidence of its author at this stage in his career.

Complex financial negotiations led to Sheridan becoming part-owner and manager of Drury Lane theatre in 1776. As successor to Garrick and as the outstanding dramatic author of the time, much was expected of him which was never fully realized, largely because of Sheridan's simultaneous entry into the sphere of parliamentary politics. As was the case with his theatrical career, his marriage to Elizabeth Linley acted as a springboard: she introduced him to the Duchess of *Devonshire and the *Whig circle associated with Devonshire House, in particular the Prince of Wales and Charles James *Fox. The Duchess sponsored Sheridan's election to parliament in 1780 for the seat of Stafford. Identified with the Rockingham Whigs in the 1780s, Sheridan made his name as a stunningly effective parliamentary speaker and debater, reaching his apogee in the 'Begums speech' of February 1787, in which he argued, for nearly six hours, on the necessity for the impeachment of Warren *Hastings. He repeated this performance, before an audience of fashionable London, at the beginning of Hastings's trial in June 1788, collapsing into the arms of *Burke as he concluded. Sheridan was active in the extraparliamentary movement for reform, being involved in the Westminster Committee as early as 1780, and was a founding member of the *Society for Constitutional Information. After 1789 he expressed support for the principles of the *French Revolution, and sided with Fox in the split with Burke. He opposed Britain's entry into *war [2] with revolutionary France and *Pitt's *gagging acts of 1795, but later in the decade revised his position, refusing to join the Foxite secession from parliament in 1797 and urging patriotic support for the *volunteer movement against the threat of French *invasion. In 1799 his play *Pizarro*, an adaptation of Kotzebue's *Die Spanier in Peru*, attempted to capitalize on the popularity of the German author; it also negotiates Sheridan's changing relationship to both Fox and the *monarchy.

Sheridan's social origins and associations with the unrespectable worlds of theatre and music made him an incongruously successful figure in a parliament where aristocratic rank was the norm, making him an outsider even within his own faction. His success was due to the power of personality and the theatrical skills of debate and persuasion which were a constant reminder of his source of income. Increasingly that source was itself problematic: Drury Lane failed to make money and Sheridan's financial obligations became uncontrollable. His star actors, John Philip *Kemble and Sarah *Siddons, stuck by him, but after years of non-payment of salaries and broken promises they eventually left for Covent Garden. *Pizarro* was partly an attempt to recapture the galvanizing impetus which his early success as a dramatist had given to both his own career and the London theatre in general, but while an outstanding success, it was not enough to sustain him, financially or politically. The financial affairs of Drury Lane became a matter for the Court of Chancery in 1801–2, followed by the disastrous fire of 1809: Sheridan's ownership and management of the theatre were effectively wrested from him in 1811.

The decline in his theatrical fortunes was paralleled by disappointments in politics. In 1806 he was made Treasurer of the Navy in the *Ministry of All the Talents, a scant reward, he believed, for years of service to the Foxite faction. After the death of Fox in 1806, he succeeded him as member for Westminster but not, to his disappointment, as Whig leader; he lost the seat in 1807 and thereafter owed his position in parliament, as member for Ilchester, to the patronage of the Prince of Wales. His parliamentary career ended when he failed to win back his Stafford seat in 1812. Sheridan died four years later at his house in Savile Row, to which he had been confined

by his creditors in a desperate attempt to retrieve the sums he owed. His funeral, the scale of which exceeded those of both Pitt and Fox, was followed by burial at Westminster Abbey, significantly in Poets' Corner, rather than next to Fox, as he had wished.

Contemporary representations of Sheridan as Bardolph, the red-nosed and corrupt crony of the Prince of Wales, as Joseph Surface, the smooth-talking, attractive deceiver of his own *School for Scandal*, and as Harlequin, the *pantomime shapechanger, indicate his ambiguous status. By forging a place for himself in the political sphere he indicated what could be achieved by men of talent who exploited to the full the theatricality of élite political culture. But in doing so he threatened those who owed their position to rank and wealth, and also proved a disappointment to extraparliamentary radicalism because of his unrealized promise. When advising Thomas Moore about writing Sheridan's biography, *Byron highlighted how exceptional Sheridan had been in getting so far without money or connections, concluding: 'Recollect that he was an Irishman and a clever fellow, and that *we* have had some very pleasant days with him.'   GR

SHIELD, William (1748–1829). One of the leading composers of *English opera before 1800, Shield composed in a popular, often folkish, style. He studied with Charles Avison (1709–70) in Newcastle before settling in London, and in 1773 became principal viola with the Italian opera company at the King's Theatre, a position he held for eighteen years, during which he also composed about forty operas for the English stage. He became house composer at the Theatre Royal, Covent Garden in 1782, after his all-sung afterpiece *Rosina* proved popular. He travelled abroad in 1791, to observe the new political regime in Paris and to study the teaching of singing in Italy. On his return to Covent Garden he seems to have lost his enthusiasm for operatic composition, and had virtually stopped by 1797.

Shield followed the English operatic tradition of keeping drama and music separate. His songs (some newly composed, others borrowed) include both elaborate formal airs after Italian models for professional singers like Elizabeth *Billington and simple strophic ballads for the actors who played many of the operatic roles. His ensembles too are simple, often *glees. Shield incorporated fashionably exotic, *Gothic, and topical elements into many of his operas. He also helped Joseph *Ritson edit two volumes of English and Scottish songs, which sparked his interest in preserving the original qualities of folk-songs.   JG

Shoreham Ancients, a circle of earnest young early Victorian artists led by Samuel Palmer (1805–81), who often met in rural Shoreham. They revered William *Blake's early lyric poetry and woodengravings but were baffled by his prophetic and revolutionary writings. Their patronage and adulation mark the beginning of a long process of canonizing Blake by muffling his eighteenth-century artisan cultural origins and by transforming him into a depoliticized Romantic *genius.　　　　IMcC

99　**SIDDONS**, Sarah (1755–1831), leading actress, the subject of celebrity and controversy whose presence pervaded the journalism, letters, and visual art of the period.

The first child of Roger Kemble and Sarah Ward and sister of the actor John Philip *Kemble, she received her formative education in the barns, inns, and country theatres frequented by her family, who were managers of a touring provincial theatre company. She made her stage debut at the age of 11 as Ariel in *The Tempest* and, while performing in Cheltenham in 1774, gained the notice of David Garrick (1717–79), still the leading actor in Britain. Garrick encouraged her to join Drury Lane theatre in London, where she made her debut as Portia in *The Merchant of Venice* in December 1775. Her initial period at Drury Lane was not a success, due to her acting inexperience and lack of familiarity with the internal politics of Drury Lane. She later expressed her belief that Garrick was using her in order to frustrate the ambitions of other leading actresses. In 1776 she was dismissed while on tour in the provinces, a blow which she later claimed 'was very near destroying me'. She returned to the provincial theatre, basing herself at Bath, where she extended her repertoire of roles and gradually rebuilt her reputation.

On 10 October 1782 she made her reappearance at Drury Lane to tremendous acclaim in the title-role of Garrick's adaptation of Thomas Southerne's *Isabella: or, The Fatal Marriage*. This was followed by celebrated performances as Euphrasia in Arthur Murphy's *The Grecian Daughter*, Jane Shore in Nicholas Rowe's tragedy of the same name, Calista in *The Fair Penitent*, also by Rowe, Belvidera in Thomas Otway's *Venice Preserv'd*, Zara in William Congreve's *The Mourning Bride*, and Lady Randolph in *Douglas* by John Home. The greatest success of her career, however, was Lady Macbeth, which she first performed in London in 1785. Her notes on the role claimed that she envisaged Lady Macbeth as retaining her femininity while displaying a powerful political ambition. This more sympathetic response to the role was a significant contribution to the view that *Shakespeare's greatness lay in the complex inner life of his characters.

As the leading interpreter of Shakespeare, Rowe, and Otway, Sarah Siddons was a celebrated public figure, courted by the royal family, the nobility, politicians, and writers. Her performances became occasions for the expression of public *sensibility [11], drawing tears from figures such as Edmund *Burke and Charles James *Fox. She was lionized by the *bluestockings, including Anna *Seward, who wrote of her 'Siddonian idolatry': her social circle included Hester Thrale *Piozzi, Maria *Edgeworth, Elizabeth *Inchbald, Joanna *Baillie, and Anne *Damer, who instructed her in *sculpture. Displaying a decorous gravity which made her less suited to comic roles, she excelled in parts which allowed her to express a passionate intelligence as well as pathos. While many of the roles she played represented women as victims, her performances were such that she often transformed this victimhood into an assertion of strength. Many commentators noted the physicality of her acting—her leaps, the triumphal deliberation of her walk, the power of her stare, and, above all, the expressiveness of her arms which, according to one critic, lent a 'masculine ferocity' to her Lady Macbeth. As the embodiment of virtue and sensibility, qualities which were regarded as neither exclusively masculine nor feminine, she was much sought after by painters such as *Gainsborough, *Romney, *Opie and *Lawrence, and *Reynolds, for whom she famously sat in her own character as *The Tragic Muse* (1784).

Siddons was conscious of the notoriety surrounding the careers of other actresses such as Elizabeth *Farren and Dorothy *Jordan, and was careful to maintain a reputation for high standards of personal morality. She married Henry Siddons, an actor in the Kemble company, in 1773 and bore him seven children, only two of whom survived her. However, her career did not remain free of controversy. In 1784 she was hissed by a hostile audience in London after it was rumoured that she had demanded payment for charity performances in aid of other actors while on tour in Ireland. She survived this setback by publicly challenging her detractors from the stage, but her reputation for avarice and self-interest remained with her for the rest of her career. She was also rumoured to have been romantically involved with the painter Thomas Lawrence, and in 1809 the actress Catherine Galindo accused Siddons in print of committing adultery with her husband.

Siddons's formidable reputation for moral probity, derived largely from her acting, survived these controversies intact. As a woman she was disqualified from following her brother into the management of a patent theatre, but her acting remained vital to the commercial and artistic success of both patent theatres. She made significant contributions to new productions such as *Sheridan's *Pizarro* (1799) and Baillie's *De Monfort* (1800), and eventually retired in 1812. Appropriately, her last performance was the sleepwalking scene from *Macbeth*, the benchmark of tragic acting. For *Hazlitt she was the embodiment of sublimity, 'something above nature . . . the stateliest ornament of the public mind'.　　　　GR

silver fork novel. The label 'silver fork' designates *novels [31] of high life designed for a middle-class, largely feminine readership. The phrase is *Hazlitt's, writing of Theodore Hook's (1788–1841) magazine articles: 'Provided a few select persons eat fish with silver forks, he considers it a circumstance of no consequence if a whole country starves.' The majority of silver fork novels were published by Henry Colburn (d. 1855), who was adept at blurring the boundaries between scandalous memoirs and fiction in ways that made an author's private life and social position commodities which could be turned for profit. Colburn held the *copyright for *Burke's Peerage*, and advertised within it new titles like Edward *Bulwer-Lytton's *Paul Clifford* (1830), 'By

99. William Hamilton, *Sarah Siddons, c.*1784. The object of widespread 'Siddonian idolatry', Sarah Siddons sat for many acclaimed painters of the period.

the Author of "Pelham", "Devereux", etc.' Bulwer-Lytton gentrified the plots and protagonists of the older novelists *Godwin and *Holcroft, and his urbane heroes give off hints of Byronic freethinking.

Marguerite Power, Countess of Blessington (1789–1849), was a fashionable London hostess whose adventurous life, and proximity to social lions like *Byron, gave a certain cachet to her novel *The Magic Lantern, or Sketches of Scenes in the Metropolis* (1822). Poet and silver fork novelist Laetitia *Landon (L.E.L.) escalated the *romance stakes when she became infatuated with the wife and husband Rosina and Edward Bulwer-Lytton. The heroine of

Landon's *Romance and Reality* (1831), who 'looked the incarnation of her husband's genius', is a self-defeating icon of female spectatorship. Catherine Gore (1799–1861) was a market leader with *Women as They Are, or The Manners of the Day* (1830) and *Cecil, or The Adventures of A Coxcomb* (1841), as was Lady Charlotte *Bury. Benjamin Disraeli (1804–81) was unmasked as the pseudonymous author of another Colburn success, *Vivian Grey* (1826–7): his *The Young Duke—A Moral Tale, though Gay* (1831), sums up the silver fork genre in the year of Colburn and Bentley's *Novels and Romances* series of one-volume reprints.   JB singing was a much-applauded art at all levels of British society during our period. The profession's élite was engaged at London's King's Theatre—a satellite of the Italian opera industry which generally staged performances from December until July, to coincide with the fashionable season and the sitting of parliament. The annual engagement of this predominantly Italian company was the focus of much speculation and debate amongst critics and audiences. Feelings ran high among the champions of a particular prima donna: public excitement surrounding the appointment of Henriette Sontag (1806–54) reached an intensity which almost overwhelmed her at her debut in 1828, and when in May 1813 Angelica *Catalani refused to appear because she had not been paid, the audience rioted. The King's Theatre managers courted such devotion amongst their subscribers, though it led to inflated salaries and over-reliance on star singers.

Singers were also employed in the music dramas presented by London's English theatres, the most prominent of which were Covent Garden, Drury Lane, and the Lyceum [see English *opera]. There was surprisingly little interchange of personnel between these theatres and the Italian opera house. John *Braham and Maria Dickons (c.1770–1833) both came to the King's Theatre following successful appearances on the English stage, but a move in the opposite direction could arouse xenophobic discontent; Catalani's costly engagement at Covent Garden (September 1809) was a catalyst in the theatre's Old Price riots [see *theatre, 24].

Although often contractually barred from doing so, opera singers could supplement their salary by appearing at the subscription *concerts and *oratorios. Some singers specialized in these non-dramatic performances. Those with entrepreneurial flair, such as Samuel *Harrison, established their own subscription series, but a standard means of generating funds open to all singers was the annual benefit concert—a risky but potentially lucrative venture.

Singers toured the provinces usually in the summer, often covering large distances between city musical meetings, such as the Three Choirs Festival. In 1807, Catalani sang at Bath, Dublin, Cork, Edinburgh, Liverpool, York, Oxford, Manchester, and Birmingham. Summer also opened the *pleasure gardens, providing additional venues for vocal solos, ensembles and choral items.

Male singers obtained relatively secure employment in the choirs of cathedrals, collegiate parish churches, the Chapel Royal, and the 'royal peculiars' of Westminster Abbey and St George's Chapel, Windsor. However, the pay was low, and vicars-choral often took additional jobs to survive. In the absence of a central music school for most of our period, the nation's religious foundations also played a vital role in nurturing talent. Braham's first public appearances were as a treble chorister at the Great Synagogue, Aldgate, and the composer R. J. S. Stevens began his career as a chorister at St Paul's Cathedral [see *church music].

Amateur singing grew considerably in popularity amongst the wealthier classes during our period, mainly in the forms of *domestic music and, for men, the *glee. Upper-class children therefore enjoyed private tuition, but since they studied singing as a liberal art, they rarely entered the profession. Lower-class parents, if they could afford it, prepared their children for the profession by negotiating an apprenticeship with a singing-master. Both these trends made *music teaching a more reliable income for singers, with figures such as Thomas *Linley and Venanzio Rauzzini (1746–1810) deriving an increasingly high proportion of their earnings from this source.　　　　　　　　　　　　　　　　　　RC

sister arts, the arts of *poetry [29] and *painting [27]. Their supposed similarity is famously characterized in Horace's *Ars Poetica* by the dictum 'ut pictura poesis' ('as is painting, so is poetry'), which from the sixteenth to the nineteenth centuries legitimized painting, long considered as a mechanical art, through its association with the liberal art of poetry.

Both arts were seen to be concerned with the imitation of nature, but not of nature as it is, rather of nature perfected. The importance of the doctrine to both poet and painter was that, in the age of classicism, its antique provenance elevated practitioners away from being mere copyists of imperfect nature to exponents of the classical tradition. By the eighteenth century, however, some critics cast doubt on the closeness or utility of the association, and Gotthold Lessing in the *Laocoön* (1766) in particular argued for an imitation which respected the integrity of each art.

Unsurprisingly, the doctrine posed particular problems for Romanticism, not least because of a new-found faith in nature itself as the site of perfection. By the early nineteenth century both painting and poetry were, despite acknowledged affinities, seen to be concerned with finding means of expression proper to the medium. Thus a painter like John *Constable, while drawing subjects from nature, treated his themes expressively, emphasizing the painterly qualities of form, colour, and texture over those of narrative. Likewise, poets such as William *Wordsworth wrote of nature as not only a source of inspiration but also a horizon of artistic endeavour that could not be transcended.　　　　　　　　　　PD

slave narratives, life stories which were written or dictated testimonies by ex-slaves and fugitives of their experience of enslavement and struggle for freedom, a struggle whose success is often intimately connected to their acquisition of literacy, formerly denied to them under *slavery [6]. These narratives were extremely popular during the heyday of *abolitionism, with Olaudah *Equiano's *Interesting Narrative* (1789) reaching eight editions by 1794. Important historically for providing the slave's perspective on slavery, they were also crucial documents for those who argued that blacks were intellectual and emotional beings who shared a common humanity with whites. As a group the narratives often share certain sets of conventions, being for the most part chronological and episodic, and almost all were published with 'authenticating' documents, usually by white abolitionists anxious to pre-empt doubts about authorship or authenticity. For this reason, they often exhibit complex relations between oral and written forms of narrative, and on the whole are very difficult to classify, as either history, literature, autobiography, or polemic. Fewer than 12 per cent of the narratives are by women, the first in Britain being *The History of Mary Prince, A West Indian Slave* (1831). Although it is clear that Mary Prince was, like so many slave women, the victim of sexual abuse, her account is a veiled one in comparison to Harriet Jacobs's (1818–96) *Incidents in the Life of a Slave Girl* (Boston, 1861), a blistering exposé of sexual exploitation which concludes, 'Slavery is terrible for men; but it is far more terrible for women.' Recently, much interest has been shown in the influence of slave narratives on black *autobiography, and on the fictional forms of the contemporary African-American novel.   DC

SMIRKE, Sir Robert (1781–1867), probably the most successful and least inspired architect of the early nineteenth century. Smirke's technical reliability and mastery of a suitably impressive if predictable classical style earned him a string of commissions for the major public buildings of his day [see *architecture, 28].

He began his career in 1796 under John *Soane, leaving within a few months because of mutual antipathy. After a year travelling Italy and Greece, Smirke received his first important commission, Lowther Castle, for the Earl of Lonsdale, largely upon the recommendation of George *Dance. In 1807 he was appointed architect to the Board of Trade, and in 1813 he became one of the three official architects attached to the Board of Works, together with Soane and John *Nash. When the Board dissolved in 1832, Smirke received a knighthood in recognition of his services. Smirke's major works include Covent Garden Theatre (1808–9); the Royal College of Physicians (1822–5); the north-west corner of Somerset House (1817–19); the *British Museum (1823–46); and the General Post Office (1824–9).   CT

SMITH, Adam (1723–90), professor of logic (1751–2) then moral philosophy (1752–64) at Glasgow; private scholar (1764–77); Commissioner of Customs at Edinburgh (1777–90).

Although Smith was a great moral philosopher and social theorist in the vein of David *Hume, he is today principally seen as the father of modern economics and the patron of free-market politics. This distortion of Smith was largely accomplished during the period covered by the present volume. Smith was partly a victim of the success of *The Wealth of Nations* (1776), which completely overshadowed his *Theory of Moral Sentiments* (1759), and which Henry Buckle in his *History of Civilization in England* (1861) saw as 'probably the most important book which has ever been written'. But Smith was also needed as a victim for Romantics as they attempted to define themselves through contrast

with the preceding age. Indeed, the notion of the 'dismal science' of economics as a product of the eighteenth century, and especially of Smith, is the epitome of an anti-Enlightenment distortion of history that began in our period and endures today.

Despite these caricatures, Smith was a philosopher who constructed a general system of morals in which *political economy [33] was but one part. The philosophical foundation of his system was a theory of the imagination largely derived from Hume, but which encompassed a more sophisticated idea of sympathy. Smith saw sympathy as our ability to understand the situation of the other person, a form of knowledge that constitutes the basis for all assessment of the behaviour of others. Our spontaneous tendency to observe others is inevitably turned upon ourselves, and this became Smith's key to understanding how a person's moral identity is formed through social interaction. On this basis he suggested a theory of moral judgment as the judgment of an impartial spectator, which in turn leads us to pre-empt such judgments through an imaginative spectating of ourselves and through associated adjustments of behaviour. Differences in the judgments of spectators solidifies the ideal of the ideally impartial spectator, which, as it becomes our guiding ideal, endows us with a moral conscience and the ability to make moral judgment.

Within this system of morality, a few features of morality remain constant. First, there is the procedural 'virtue' of impartiality which seems unavoidable wherever any sort of human sociability has place; second, the human mind nearly always recognizes the infliction of harm as an evil and this is reflected in the universality of the 'negative' virtue of justice; and third, although all the other, 'positive' virtues vary enormously from culture to culture, many of them have sufficient family resemblance for empirical comparisons to be possible.

Smith also developed an original theory of jurisprudence centred on 'negative' justice as the protection of rights, and this is the key to his theory of government as, primarily, the upholder of justice. At the same time, he maintained the political significance of the 'positive' virtues; some might be the moral but 'imperfect duty' of the government, while many others were the moral task of the leaders in the public, non-governmental sphere. In other words, Smith had a theory of both government and of the conduct of policy, and it was only within such a framework that he saw the possibility of a market economy developing as an expression of humanity's prudent self-interest. Such self-interest, he argued, was a basic feature of human nature and therefore at work in any form of society, but only under special circumstances could it be efficiently expressed.

One of the other influential features of Smith's work was a historical and structural account of civil society and its governance, organized into four stages. This emphasized that the special attributes of commercial society arose from the compatibility of the pursuit of self-interest with that of individual liberty. His central point was that in the market the poor are not recognized dangers for the rich. At the same time, he recognized dangers in commercial society that needed careful institutional and political management.

Although Smith's basic philosophy was contained in *The Theory of Moral Sentiments*, he regarded a major part concerning law and government as imperfect and burnt the manuscript before he died. Consequently the connection to *The Wealth of Nations* can only be partially reconstructed from two sets of students' notes from his *Lectures on Jurisprudence at Glasgow* (1762–4). These writings are complemented by a volume of essays and student notes from lectures on rhetoric and belles-lettres.

A public philosopher, Smith nevertheless epitomized the Enlightenment ideal of privacy to a degree rarely achieved by his contemporaries. He left no autobiographical account and his surviving correspondence is meagre. Only a few portraits record his appearance, and there are no extensive accounts of his personality, except Dugald Stewart's retropective 'Life of Adam Smith' (1794), which aimed to assimilate him within the 'Common Sense' school of philosophy. While Smith was a fairly sociable man, his close friendships were few, aside from his one-time student, John *Millar, and the scientists Joseph Black (1728–99) and James *Hutton, whom he entrusted with burning his manuscript papers as he lay dying. KH

SMITH, Charlotte Turner (1749–1806), novelist and poet. Smith's experimentation with the *sonnet form in *Elegiac Sonnets* (1784) and her Romantic perception of nature influenced *Coleridge, *Keats, and *Wordsworth, but she is now primarily remembered for her ten novels, with their social criticism, concern for feminist questions, and dramatization of the political issues raised by the *American and *French Revolutions.

The eldest child of Sussex and Surrey landowner Nicholas Turner and Anna Towers, Smith was sent to boarding-school at 6, entered London society at 12, and in 1765 was, in her own words, 'sold into marriage' at 15 to Benjamin Smith, the violent and dissolute son of a West India merchant. In her twenty-two years of marriage Smith bore twelve children. Her husband's profligacy resulted, in 1783, in her spending seven months with him in debtors' prison. *Elegiac Sonnets* was initially published at her own expense at this time as a money-making venture. Dedicated to William *Hayley, patron of *Cowper and *Blake, the book was an immediate success, and ran to nine subsequent editions. Later, faced with legal battles and having separated from her husband in 1787, she depended on the income from her novels and children's books, mainly on natural history, to support her family.

Smith's novels often include sentimental and *Gothic elements but also draw upon her own experiences in depicting disastrous marriages and irresponsible male characters. An autobiographical element is apparent in a number of strong minor female characters such as Mrs Stafford in *Emmeline* (1788). Smith's increasingly polemical tone reflects not only her impetus towards social satire but her own continuing bitterness at being obliged to write fiction for her living. William *Godwin's diaries show that from the mid- to late 1790s her London house became a vital gathering-place for embattled Dissenting and radical intellectuals. At the time of her death, she was completing *Beachy Head with Other Poems* (1807), an 800-line evocation of childhood in the context of a closely observed study of local flora and fauna which has been compared with Wordsworth's 'Tintern Abbey'. RCA

SMITH, Sydney (1771–1845), reviewer and wit. The youngest son of a wealthy merchant family compelled to take holy orders by financial circumstances in 1797, Smith was a kind of fifth columnist in the Church, using the *Edinburgh Review*, which he help to found in 1802, and his best known work the *Letters of Peter Plymley* (1807–8), to attack its obstruction of the principles of 'enlightened' reform to which his *Whiggism committed him.

After becoming an important figure in Edinburgh literary circles from 1798, forming a lasting friendship with Francis *Jeffrey, Smith moved to London in 1803 where he preached, wrote, and especially talked with great success. He became a favourite at *Holland House and contributed to the London's *lecturing circuit, speaking on 'moral philosophy' to packed houses at the Royal Institution. Although he attacked the *Anglican Church and defended the rights of Catholics and Dissenters, he believed both of the latter had faults of their own. The anti-Catholic sentiments of the old Dissenters were for him 'the most intolerable circumstance' in the dispute over *Catholic emancipation, and he had a thoroughly Protestant attitude to Catholic 'superstition'.

Nevertheless, his public figure as an enlightened Whig cost him preferment in the Church and in 1808 he was recalled to his living in Yorkshire, a move which cut him off from the metropolitan society on which he thrived. Only towards the end of his life, when he was made canon-residentiary of St Paul's, did he gain any significant advancement in the Church of England. WC

SOANE, Sir John (1753–1837), architect whose innovative approach to design sought to assert *architecture's [28] relevance to contemporary society. The son of a bricklayer, Soane was briefly apprenticed in that trade before gaining a place in the office of George *Dance in 1768. A precocious but diligent youth, Soane transferred to Henry *Holland's office in 1772 and simultaneously attended the *Royal Academy schools. There he exhibited the tenacious competitiveness that would compel his professional success but also torment him. After gaining only a Silver Medal in the 1772 school competitions, he won the Gold Medal in 1776 with a design for a Triumphal Bridge.

This academic success attracted the attention of Sir William *Chambers, the Academy's Treasurer, who obtained the King's Travelling studentship for Soane for a period of three years beginning in 1778. Based in Rome, Soane made trips to Florence, Parma, Venice, Naples, Pompeii, Paestum, and

Sicily. While in Italy he not only studied the monuments of Antiquity and the Renaissance but also came into contact with the currents of international neoclassicism. These experiences inspired him to envision an architecture of antique magnificence and design a series of idealistic objects, most notably a British Senate House.

In Italy Soane also made important social contacts that were crucial to his later professional success. Indeed, he was perhaps over-eager to befriend and impress more aristocratic British travellers. One, the Bishop of Derry (later Earl of Bristol), convinced him to return to London a year early with the promise of significant patronage, but it never materialized. Nevertheless, Soane's Italian acquaintances provided him with a series of modest residential commissions that enabled him to establish himself professionally. These early works included Saxlingham Rectory, Norfolk, (1784–7); Tendring Hall, Suffolk, (1784–6); and alterations to Holwood, Kent (1786 and 1795) for William *Pitt, the Prime Minister.

Soane obtained the Holwood commission through one of his Italian acquaintances, Thomas Pitt, Lord Camelford. This connection proved to be the making of Soane's career, since the Prime Minister's consequent support was instrumental in his being appointed Architect to the *Bank of England in October 1788. Pitt's influence also facilitated Soane's commission to rebuild the House of Lords in 1794, although this project was subsequently aborted. Professional success together with a significant inheritance from his wife's uncle, the builder George Wyatt, gave Soane a freedom of purse and the independence of action to pursue his personal and professional inclinations.

In 1793 he began building himself a residence and office at No. 12 Lincoln's Inn Fields. In the course of a long life he expanded this to include Nos. 13 and 14, and filled it with collections of architectural fragments, drawings, *sculpture and *painting [27]. A private Act of Parliament established the premises as the Sir John Soane's Museum in 1833. The father of two sons who survived infancy, John and George, Soane also hoped to found a professional dynasty along the lines of the *Adams or *Wyatts. To this end he purchased Pitzhanger Hall, Ealing in September 1800 and transformed the small villa into a private architectural academy. As his sons rebelled against their father's wishes, this experiment failed and Soane sold Pitzhanger in 1810.

Meanwhile, the rebuilding of the Bank supplied Soane with both a steady source of income in the otherwise unpromising war years and an opportunity to develop the distinct architectural style that secured his status as a major figure in British architectural history. In the Bank Stock Office (1791–2) Soane distilled the formal, structural, and aesthetic principles of both classical and *Gothic architecture. The products of this effort also owed much to significant borrowings from the work of Dance, Soane's mentor and friend. Soane shared Dance's theoretical interests and read copiously, especially after being appointed professor of architecture at the Royal

Academy in 1806. From this point, Soane infused his work with a broad knowledge of contemporary French and British architectural and aesthetic theory, particularly that of the *picturesque.

The characteristics of Soane's idiom include the frequent use of shallow domes, segmental arches, cross-vaults and multi-storeyed spaces; ingenious and highly efficient planning, particularly where existing construction had to be accommodated; a concern for dramatic lighting effects, often accomplished through top-lighting; and the abstraction of the classical orders into a system of incised linear decoration. In addition to the Bank and his own residences, Soane's principal built works include renovations and additions to Wimpole Hall, Cambridgeshire (1791–4); Tyringham Hall, Buckinghamshire (1793–c.1800); the stables and infirmary at the Royal Hospital, Chelsea (1809–17); the Picture Gallery and Mausoleum at Dulwich College (1811–14); the Law Courts, Westminster (1822–5); the Royal Entrance to the House of Lords, Westminster (1822–4); and the Board of Trade and Privy Council Offices, Whitehall (1824–6).

Although Soane's idiosyncratic style occasioned notable criticism, he was regarded highly in architectural circles and beyond as a consummate professional. He was meticulous in the handling of his commissions and instructed a steady stream of pupils in the fifty years of his practice, most notably J. M. *Gandy. Soane published many of his designs, often with polemical intent, but contributed most to architectural discourse with his series of lectures delivered to the Royal Academy from 1809 to 1836. As an Academician, Soane had to refuse the presidency of the Institute of British Architects, which was offered to him upon its founding in 1834. However, he proudly accepted the knighthood conferred by William IV on 21 September 1831, the culmination of a distinguished and socially mobile life.   ss

socialism. The word 'socialist' first appears in print in Britain in 1827, and in manuscript about five years earlier; 'socialism' was in use commonly by 1835 to describe the views of Robert *Owen and his school of communitarianism. Both terms derive from Owen's description, even before 1820, of 'the social system' by contrast to 'the individual system'. The latter was shorthand for the central doctrines of classical and particularly Ricardian *political economy [33], encapsulated in the assumption that aggregate needs would be satisfied best by each individual following their own self-interest in an economy based upon 'individual' competition. By the mid-1830s Owenites condemned such views as 'individualism', meaning an exaggerated love of money, personal distinction, and privilege at the expense of others. The 'social system', by contrast, enjoined the principle of benevolence to others in order to harmonize individual and social needs. This was to be best accomplished, in Owen's view, by practising a 'religion of charity', which was essentially *Deist, and by reorganizing society along communitarian lines. In the belief that character was formed principally by the environment, Owen thought this would

42

allow a rising generation to supersede the impoverished ethical standards of the old society and to create a 'new moral world'. Once his idea of character was understood, Owen believed, it would no longer be possible to punish individuals for behavioural errors. By 1820 'the social system' had thus come to be contrasted to 'the individual system . . . of individual rewards, punishments, and competition.'

British socialism from 1820–50 was thenceforward almost exclusively Owenite in orientation. There was some interest in *Saint-Simonianism, especially its feminist component, in the 1830s; and in Fourierist communitarianism in the 1840s. After 1845 revolutionary forms of communism were present among mainly foreign refugees, some of whom found left-wing *Chartists like George Julian Harney (1817–97) sympathetic to the application of revolutionary means to socialist ends. The 1848 revolutions also witnessed the birth of Christian socialism in Britain. 'Socialism' in the preceding two decades, however, principally meant Owen's efforts to found a 'home colony' of about 2,000 persons, sharing labour and property in common, alternating between manufacturing and agricultural employment, and eliminating the sharply increasing problem of postwar unemployment.

No Owenite socialist community survived for longer than a few years. Efforts were made at Orbiston near Glasgow, at New Harmony in Indiana, and most impressively at Queenwood in Hampshire between 1839–45, as well as elsewhere. Each community, however, had problems raising funds, recruiting a skilled workforce, and competing in agricultural markets. From the early 1820s onwards, retail co-operative stores as a means of raising funds for communities were founded. During the mid-1830s labour exchanges, where artisans directly exchanged their produce upon a calculation of labour time and materials costs, were also attempted. In 1833–4 Owen also led the Grand National Consolidated Trades' Union, the first effort to create a national labour union [see *trade unions].

These efforts resulted in the wide diffusion of socialist ideas in Britain. (Some millions of tracts were disseminated at the height of the Owenite movement in the early 1840s.) Owen himself found many a sympathetic ear but the notion of a socialist transformation of Britain attracted a few thousand adherents at most. The legacy of socialism to 1850 was thus as a potent critique of 'individualism' and the gospel of Mammon, and as a plea for the more humane treatment of the working classes whose eventual issue was the twentieth-century welfare state.   GC

societies, see *corresponding; *debating; *friendly; *literary and philosophical.

Society for Constitutional Information, 1780–92, an influential middle-class reform association which propounded the basic principles and programmes adopted by the British popular reform movement until the late nineteenth century.

Modelled on earlier associations for moderate *parliamentary reform, the Society for Constitutional Information of 1780 eclipsed all former groups in the rigour of its principles based on seventeenth-century *natural rights theory, in the extremity of its political demands centred on annual parliaments and universal manhood suffrage, and in the range of its social programmes including religious toleration, *abolition of slavery, penal reform, and disestablishment of the Church of England. SCI-sponsored publications also advanced an appealing *constitutionalist historiography of Saxon democracy lost to Norman invaders, and compiled detailed listings of parliamentary corruption and influence.

Though high subscription rates confined members to middle and upper ranks, the SCI boasted some exceptionally trenchant theorists, including reforming Lincolnshire landlord Major John *Cartwright and Unitarian lawyer-doctor John *Jebb. After early success in recruiting Foxites and aristocratic Whigs, the Society's reform impetus faltered in the mid-1780s mainly through internal divisions, only to revive in 1788–9 under the stimulus of the Dissenting campaign for repeal of the Test and Corporation Acts, the advent of the *French Revolution, and the emergence of new leaders such as John Horne *Tooke. Like most 1790s reform associations, the SCI succumbed to the stifling influence of repressive government legislation, but its basic principles and programmes passed into the mass reform movements of the nineteenth century.   IMcC

Society for the Suppression of Vice, originated with a Royal Proclamation against Vice and Immorality which William *Wilberforce and fellow *Evangelicals obtained in 1787, and followed up with a supporting Proclamation Society. This organization was endorsed by most of the *Anglican bishops, and dedicated to reforming morals and manners. Particular goals included: ending clerical absenteeism, enforcing the Sabbath, proscribing literature of an immoral or infidel tendency [see *pornography], and eliminating *gambling, *duelling, and cruel or unruly pastimes [see *popular culture, 23].

From the outset the Society adopted aggressive tactics of legal prosecution and harassment, including the use of informers. However, it was not until after 1804, when it became the Society for the Suppression of Vice, that the organization began to gain both a substantial accession of aristocratic members and a measure of notoriety. In 1809 the Whig clerical wit Sydney *Smith launched a stinging attack on the Society in the *Edinburgh Review*, castigating the anonymity of its 1,000-strong membership, its unconstitutional supercession of law, *police, and parliamentary functions, and its hypocritical focus on the enjoyments of the poor. The parliamentary radical Joseph Hume (1777–1855) made an even stronger case in 1823, on the occasion of the Society's imprisonment of Richard *Carlile's sister, Mary, for selling freethinking literature [see *Deism]. Hume's nickname for the organization, 'the Society for the Promotion of Vice', was widely adopted in the radical and *unstamped press. By the end of our period, however, the Society had achieved considerable success in suppressing *fairs and blood sports, and, still more, in enforcing stricter public morality on senior clergy and parliamentarians.   IMcC

SOMERVILLE, Mary Fairfax Greig (1780–1872), an outstanding woman of *natural philosophy [34] and expositor of mathematical and scientific theories. Her life highlighted and even redefined the limits on women's participation in the natural sciences during her era. The descendant of established English and Scottish families, Somerville received her only formal education in a year at an expensive boarding-school. Self-educated through reading, she developed an early interest in mathematics.

During two marriages (both to cousins, Samuel Greig in 1804 and Dr William Somerville in 1812) and while a widow, Somerville pursued scientific interests living in London, travelling in continental Europe, and residing in Italy from 1838 to 1872. Her extensive network of prestigious scientific and literary contacts (including Charles *Babbage, Henry *Brougham, David *Brewster, Humphry *Davy, Maria *Edgeworth, Sir William *Herschel and Sir John *Herschel, and William *Whewell) was crucial in this pursuit. She translated and explicated Laplace's *Mécanique Céleste* in *The Mechanism of the Heavens* (1831) which greatly influenced British mathematical teaching and thought. *On the Connexion of the Physical Sciences* (1834) synthesized contemporary developments in the physical sciences for a wide readership. She published the well-received *Physical Geography* (1848) and papers on scientific experiments. Somerville tutored another outstanding woman in the history of mathematics, Ada Byron Lovelace (1815–52).

Presenting herself as a conventional woman with modest expectations about female contributions to science, she advocated improved educational provision and suffrage for women [see *female education]. Somerville's contributions to science were lauded by scientific institutions around the world.   MMcN

sonnets are short poems, usually in fourteen decasyllabic lines, rhyming according to different conventions, the main types of which are the Petrarchan and the Shakespearean. They are sometimes written in sequences in which each sonnet can function like a stanza. Originating in Italy in the thirteenth century, the sonnet became extremely popular in Britain in the sixteenth. The form was almost completely neglected in the eighteenth century and scorned by Dryden, Pope, and *Johnson. Johnson was not far from the truth when he stated in his *Dictionary* (1755) that the sonnet 'has not been used by any man of eminence since Milton'.

However, in the 1770s the sonnet enjoyed a revival. Thomas *Warton and Thomas Gray (1716–71) included sonnets in their collections. In the 1780s the sonnet of *sensibility [11] was in vogue, especially following the publication of William *Hayley's *Poetical Works* (1785) and Charlotte

*Smith's *Elegiac Sonnets* (1784), which went into eleven editions by 1851. The year 1789 saw the publication of sonnets by its foremost exponents; William Lisle Bowles (1762–1850), Charlotte Smith, Anna *Seward, and Sir Samuel Egerton Brydges (1762–1837).

In 1796–7, this assembly was joined by Mary *Robinson, Charles *Lamb, Robert *Southey, and S. T. *Coleridge. William *Wordsworth, John *Clare, Leigh *Hunt, John *Keats, Felicia *Hemans, *Shelley, and *Byron also all produced notable examples of the form. By 1821 the sonnet had become so fashionable that the *New Monthly Magazine and Literary Journal* warned of a dangerous disorder, 'Sonnettomania'.

The significance of the sonnet in the period between 1770 and 1800 derived from its formal complexity, self-consciousness, and emotional resonances. Its brevity appealed as a refuge from heroic or *epic poetry, and its closure provided an alternative to the more fragmentary shorter forms. The sonnets of the 1770s to the 1790s were largely melancholy and elegiac, and lacked the wit and argument of the Shakespearean sonnet whose form they most often imitated. *Lyric descriptions of loss were fused with moral reflection, both springing from *picturesque natural description.

There was some debate in the period as to the proper form of the sonnet, which was often viewed as an immigrant that had not been fully naturalized. Promoting the dignity of the sonnet by stressing its difficulty, some like Seward and Robinson defended the Petrarchan or 'legitimate' sonnet, as opposed to the 'illegitimate' or Shakespearean form. Many sonnets, notably those by Smith and Bowles, were formally so loose that they are best described as quatorzains.

Lines of influence may be traced from Warton to Bowles (who was Warton's pupil at Oxford) to the early poems of Coleridge, and from Smith to Wordsworth. Yet both Wordsworth and Coleridge later developed in different directions. Coleridge affectionately remembered Bowles in his *Biographia Literaria* (1817), though in 1797 he published the amusing parodies, *Sonnets attempted in the Manner of Contemporary Writers*, under the name of Nehemiah Higginbottom [see *satire].

Wordsworth published over 530 sonnets, more than any other English poet. His first published poem was the sentimental sonnet 'On seeing Miss Helen Maria Williams Weep at a Tale of Distress' (1787). Later though, he attributed his serious interest in the form to hearing his sister, Dorothy *Wordsworth, read *Milton's sonnets to him one day in 1802. The influence of the sonnet of sensibility may be felt on his ambulatory and descriptive sonnets, for example the *River Dudden* sequence (1820). Yet Wordsworth transformed the sonnet by combining the moral reflection of the arguably 'feminized' sonnet of sensibility with what he called the 'manly' political engagement and formal weight and unity of Milton's sonnets. He self-reflexively defended the form in 'Nuns fret not . . .', which prefaced his important first collection of sonnets in

Poems, in Two Volumes (1807). As well as powerful individual sonnets, he composed several groups and sequences, including those on public themes like 'Sonnets Dedicated to Liberty' (1807), and *Ecclesiastical Sketches* (1822; called *Ecclesiastical Sonnets* from 1837). He also published descriptive sequences combining sonnets and other poems, including *Memorials of a Tour on the Continent* (1822).

Wordsworth's influence was far-reaching. Byron's 'On Chillon' and Shelley's 'To Wordsworth' and 'England in 1819' engage antagonistically with Wordsworth's example. Keats, whose sonnets manifest the self-consciousness, hypersensitivity, and playfulness found in his other poetry, was influenced by the Italian and Shakespearean sonnet as well as the Wordsworthian. More generally, Wordsworth lent the sonnet a new status, an authority which was borrowed by, among others, Thomas Lovell *Beddoes and Thomas *Hood.   JH

SOUTHCOTT, Joanna (1750–1814), prophetess and leader of a movement based on a succession of *millenarian *prophecies revealed to her from 1792 to 1814. The Southcottian movement survives into the late twentieth century, with followers claiming that world peace will not be achieved until the prophecies left in a sealed box are opened and examined by twenty-four *Anglican bishops [see **popular culture, 23**].

Southcott was born in a Devonshire village called Tarford (or Taleford) near Exeter in Devon in 1750, and spent her early working life in domestic service; but in 1792 she began to hear voices telling her of coming events and ordering her to set the messages down in writing. The substance of these prophecies was a warning that Christ's second coming was imminent, and that it was to be preceded by war and famine. Such prophecies were not new, but *war [2] with France did indeed eventuate in 1793 and the harvests of the 1790s failed as she predicted they would [see *famine].

Her reputation grew locally and she was widely consulted as a wise woman. In 1801, using her own money, she published her first pamphlet, *The Strange Effects of Faith*, which spread her fame far beyond Devon. Several followers of Richard *Brothers, who was by now in prison, approached Southcott to invite her to London. Thus began a nationwide movement, with Joanna travelling extensively to set up congregations of believers.

At first she expected recognition and welcome from the *Methodist congregation to which she belonged, since she believed her prophecies to be simply an exposition of biblical teaching, but her hopes were disappointed. The Anglican clergy also responded with hostility, accusing her of sectarianism. However, for the rest of her life she continued to assert loyal membership of the Church of England. Similarly, she disavowed political radicalism, advocating a quietist approach; yet the movement aroused government concern. Southcott's visions pictured a Christ militant, sword in hand. In an attempt to reassure authorities that she posed no threat to stability, she declared the real enemy to be

*Napoleon, who was the Antichrist, and she urged her followers to join the war against him.

From 1804 Southcott began to issue paper declarations testifying to the salvation of the owner, signed by her and sealed with the letters I.C., standing for Jesus Christ. This was a development that brought much criticism, but she insisted that salvation was not dependent on receiving one of these seals, or even on becoming one of her followers. It has been estimated that by the time of her death there were perhaps 100,000 sealed members in London, with many thousands more in other centres.

Southcott saw herself as the woman of Revelation, 'the Woman Clothed with the Sun', and as the bride of Christ. At the end of 1813, aged 63, she announced that she was pregnant by her divine husband, and would give birth to a son, to be called Shiloh. Shiloh would rule an earthly kingdom and prepare the way for Christ's coming. Several prominent London physicians confirmed the pregnancy. However, the child did not arrive, and Southcott's physical condition deteriorated. She died on 27 December 1814.

It has been suggested that the Southcottian movement contributed to the emerging feminist *socialism of the 1830s and 1840s. There were indeed several Southcottians who took a radical political stand, advocating an end to *women's [4] subordination. In 1831 John 'Zion' Ward (1781–1837), a Devon shoemaker who believed himself to be Southcott's Shiloh, arrived in London and preached a libertarian sexual morality before being imprisoned for blasphemy. Another Southcottian, the Revd James Elishma Smith (1801–57) from Edinburgh, became editor of the *Owenite paper the *Crisis*, and contributed several articles on the doctrine of the female Messiah, the end of marriage, and women's superior moral power. In her mystical path to illumination, Joanna Southcott gave voice to a popular rhetoric of prophecy that continued to resonate through nineteenth-century radicalism.   MP

SOUTHEY, Robert (1774–1843), poet (appointed poet laureate 1813), historian, and essayist. Born the son of a respectable Bristol linen draper, he was expelled from Westminster school for producing a *satirical magazine, the *Flagellant*, in 1792. In a review of *Thalaba the Destroyer* published in the *Edinburgh Review* in 1802, Francis *Jeffrey attacked him as the leader of a 'sect of dissenters' from the poetic mainstream, which also comprised William *Wordsworth and S. T. *Coleridge. Southey had acquired a reputation for politically radical views, mainly through his early poems such as *Botany Bay Eclogues*, his association with the *Monthly Magazine* in the 1790s, and the interest in popular antiquities reflected in the many imitations of *ballads he published in 1797 and 1799 [see **antiquarianism, 35**]. In the mid-1790s he was also involved with Coleridge in the short-lived *Pantisocracy scheme at a time when both men were supporting themselves by *lecturing at Bristol. Southey's earlier enthusiasm for the *French Revolution, reflected in the plays *Wat Tyler* (1794), *The Fall of Robespierre* (1794, written with Coleridge), and *Joan of Arc* (1796), faltered as events in France took an increasingly violent turn, and with the rise to power of *Napoleon in 1799 he began to adopt an anti-Gallic stance.

Over the next decade or so, Southey's political ideas underwent changes. In 1807 he received a government pension, but it was his association with the *Quarterly Review* from 1810 onwards which really signalled the beginning of his role as a spokesman for conservative views. Some of his *essays for the *Quarterly* were collected as *Essays, Moral and Political* (1832). This, together with his *Sir Thomas More* (1829), are the most fully developed expressions of his later political views. Taken as a whole, Southey's conservative writings constituted a defence of the system of established institutions which existed before the 1829 *Catholic Emancipation Act opened the floodgates of reform. The original part of his argument lies in his analysis of the effects of the Reformation on the decline of both religious beliefs and a corresponding loyalty to the established institutions of the country. In response to what he perceived to be the consequences of the Reformation, Southey developed his role as a man of letters whose task was to defend the established order against the tide of radical rhetoric. This defence, he argued, could only be undertaken by reformulating the traditions of that order as the basis of a wider national culture. It was also in defence of the established order that Southey criticized—particularly in his pseudonymous *Letters from England* (1807)—the doctrine of *laissez-faire* which he believed was an inadequate response to the social and political problems that the 'manufacturing system' had brought in its wake. Southey believed that only the active intervention of the State (for example, in providing programmes of public works and welfare) would relieve these problems.

Southey's output was prolific, but as a poet his reputation rested in the main on his self-consciously 'exotic' epic poems. These were in part inspired by his interest in comparative *mythology [36], particularly by his reading of Picart's *Cérémonies et coutumes religieuses* (1723), but Sir William *Jones's plea, made in 1772, for 'a new set of images and similitudes' in European literature drawn from 'the principal writings of the *Asiaticks*' also played its part. Southey's many reviews for journals of the day included some on the *orientalist work of both the Asiatic Society of Bengal and of *missionaries in India, so that his youthful interest in mythology was later supplemented by a knowledge of the scholarly work of European orientalists.

Southey's scholarly and imaginative interest in the growing field of orientalism left its mark on the content and style of such epics as *Thalaba* (1801) and *The Curse of Kehama* (1810). These works combine an 'exotic' subject matter drawn from Middle Eastern and Hindu mythology, with careful annotations referring to the scholarly works and accounts from which he drew inspiration. Southey's interest in mythology and, in particular, the blending together of mythology and historicism [see *history, 38] was also evident in *Madoc* (1805), a work based on the Welsh legend of the discovery of America by a prince of Gwynedd in the twelfth century, as well as in his 1817 edition of Malory's *The Byrth, Lyf, and Actes of Kyng Arthur*, which was the first modern consideration of Malory and his sources [see *Madoc controversy]. *The Doctor* (1834–48) contained narratives gleaned from antiquarian sources, as well as such children's tales as 'The Three Bears'.

Southey's epics, as well as his many reviews of both scholarly and travel literature, reflect an exhilarating experimentation with different cultural material for works of the imagination. But this experimentation also found fruition in some of his scholarly work, such as his *Life of Nelson* (1813) which took biography onto a new plane of research. His *History of Brazil* (1810–19) was also the first comprehensive treatment of Brazil's colonial history in English. The background to this aspect of Southey's work was, in part at least, the expansion of Britain's overseas *empire [5] in the early nineteenth century. This brought in its wake an increasing number of publications, pitched at varying levels, on the range of cultures which the British empire was beginning to encompass. It is this background, together with the changing nature of Southey's political views and his lifelong interest in legend, myth, and history, which makes the variety of connections between different aspects of his work deserving of further study and elucidation.   JMᴀ

spa towns. Spas developed a distinctive cultural profile due to a combination of three particular defining characteristics: the presence of a spring or springs, which formed the foundation of a range of medical services; the provision of commercialized leisure facilities; and a substantial seasonal population of visitors.

By the late eighteenth century, there was an already well-established network of spas. Some centres were virgin settlements, others were bolted onto an established centre. Many were no bigger than villages or hamlets, though a number grew to be substantial towns. The leading centre was Bath, which mushroomed from a small town of 2,000 to 3,000 people in 1700 to a major city of some 33,000 inhabitants—about the tenth largest town in England and Wales—by 1801. From the middle of the eighteenth century the future of this network was challenged by the rise of the seaside resort. Many traditional spas, such as Tunbridge Wells and Epsom, were clearly passing their prime. However, competition did not initially lead to the demise of the inland watering-place. The years between the 1770s and the 1830s witnessed a new surge of creations and expansion, particularly in the midlands and north. Smaller centres like Malvern, Buxton, Matlock, and Harrogate all experienced phases of growth. The most dynamic settlements were Cheltenham, whose population increased from 3,000 to 36,000 between 1801 and 1841, and Leamington, from 500 to 12,600 between 1811 and 1841. Regional *industrialization [14] and economic growth, which created a prospering and rapidly enlarging middle class, largely facilitated this wave of expansion. Another significant factor was the short-term boost provided by the Napoleonic wars, which shut much of the Continent to British travellers. However, long-term prospects for the spa system were limited. Bath had peaked by the early 1800s and Leamington's leap forward was already faltering by the mid-1830s. Competition from the proliferating coastal resorts, and inherent flaws within spa development itself, undermined the future of the network.

Compared with other towns, watering-places were especially geared to élite cultural production and provision. In Bath, the Woods pioneered forms of high-status corporate urban architecture, culminating in the Royal Crescent (1767–75). These considerably influenced the design not only of other resorts, for example, the Crescent at Buxton (1780–90), and the Royal Crescent at Brighton (1798–1807), but also town planning in cities like Edinburgh and London. The concentration of wealthy visitors, who needed to fill the vacant hours of a workless day, led to a rich provision of assemblies, *circulating libraries, bookshops, drama, and *concerts. The Bath *theatre [24] reached its zenith between the late eighteenth and early nineteenth century, acquiring splendid new premises in 1805 and providing a nursery for the metropolitan stage. There were also theatres at Cheltenham and Leamington, the latter patronized by the renowned London actor-manager R. W. Elliston (1774–1831), who had spent the early years of his career on the Bath stage. A cornucopia of luxury retail outlets provided access to the pleasures of an explosive consumer culture [see *consumerism, 19]. In 1819 Pierce *Egan observed of Bath's legendary Milsom and Bond streets, 'the shops are tastefully laid out; capacious and elegant [and the streets] afford to the utmost extent every thing towards supplying the real or imaginary wants of the visitors.' Spas were also especially well endowed with *pleasure gardens and walks, many of which were elaborately contrived representations of nature, designed to satisfy the combined urban and rural sensibilities of their users.

Out of this range of facilities there emerged a distinctive spa culture, built around a corpus of ideals. Health was the primary goal of both sound and sick visitors. The spring waters were a premier symbol and source of healthiness [see *medicine, 18]. A salubrious environment—clean and airy streets, access to nature—and recreations were also major contributors. Vital to the image of spa life was the principle of sociability, embodied in the concept of 'the company', and encouraged by institutions like the assemblies, practices like the daily round of events, and communal housing and living conditions. However, status, and later *class [15], recognition were also fundamental criteria, and the endemic tensions between an open and an exclusive ethos were a destabilizing feature of resort culture. By the later eighteenth century Bath was working hard to shake off its earlier libertine sexual reputation, in pursuit of the model moral environment of charity, religion, and respectability. These characteristics formed the dominant moral agenda of the later Georgian resorts. Order was also given a high premium. Within the company, publicized codes of behaviour and the office of Master of Ceremonies

were means to achieve this. In the spa as a whole, good government and effective control of the poor, particularly vagrants, were the principal mechanisms. Together these ideals created an image of the spa, carefully cultivated in guidebooks, that influenced the attitudes of visitors. However, this culture and self-image was undermined by many inherent flaws and contradictions. The more successful a spa was, the more it attracted the sick, hoi polloi, and the poor; the bigger it became the larger working class it spawned, with the greater potential for *poverty [12] and disorder. Given these conditions, it was no coincidence that Bath became a centre of radicalism in the early nineteenth centry. Size exacerbated the inherent contradictions between sociability and exclusivity, encouraging more privatized modes of behaviour; and rapid growth implied a trend away from a visitor-led society to a residential one, which threatened the very existence of the spa as a type of settlement. Spa life and culture had, therefore, a tendency to self-destruct, which along with its close association with *fashion, contributed to the volatile fortunes of individual inland watering-places, and to the long-term vulnerability of the system as a whole.

PB

SPENCE, Thomas (1750–1814), *agrarian reformer and radical propagandist. A pioneering critic of private property in *land [16], he was also committed to the reform of the English *language [40], Spence made a seminal contribution to the revolutionary and reform movements in England.

His thought was a distinctive amalgam of seventeenth-century and *Enlightenment [32] ideas, iconoclastic Calvinism, and indigenous English radicalism with strong *millenarian overtones. He was introduced to radical politics by James Murray, a Tyneside Calvinist pastor and author of a pro-rebellion history of the *American Revolution. Spence's first publication, however, was a phonetic dictionary (1775), printed from type supplied by his friend the engraver Thomas *Bewick to a scheme of Spence's own. His lifetime's devotion to the cause of language reform was born of a profound conviction that it was want of *education [17] that held down the poor. This same belief impelled him to publish, in the manner of *street literature, the text of a lecture on property, 'The Rights of Man', that he gave to Newcastle Philosophical Society in 1775 (for which he was expelled).

Several times reprinted, the lecture remained the keystone of his political thought. Following John *Locke, Spence accepted as an axiom the equality of property in the state of nature; but he broke free from the dominant interpretation of Locke, that time conferred innocence on private property, and it is from this that the radical thrust of his thought derives. He argued that those who acquiesced in the privatization of land denied the rights they relinquished to posterity; but to deprive anything of the means of living supposed a right to deprive life itself, which was anathema. Any ascendancy over land was thus an ascendancy over people's lives, and therefore the nature of landownership lay at the root of all injustice, inequality, and economic exploitation.

The 1775 lecture predicted that *popular education would readily secure universal consent to agrarian equality (Spence was at this point a schoolteacher). Moving to London in 1788, Spence rapidly responded both to the *French Revolution and to the quickening of millenarian speculation that it stimulated. Henceforward his political writings assume an overtly revolutionary tone. He was an active member of the London Corresponding Society, and publisher of the most explicit statement of its principles in 1794 [see *corresponding societies]. He threw himself into radical propaganda, chalking walls with graffiti, bookselling, countermarking coins with radical slogans, and issuing his own highly politicized token currency.

In 1792 he began to publish his own works: editions of the 1775 lecture, a remarkable periodical *One Pennyworth of Pig's Meat*, and a series of pamphlets developing his ideas. In *The End of Oppression* (1795) he criticized Thomas *Paine for not embracing thoroughgoing land reform, and for attacking *monarchy whilst leaving the greater evil of private property intact. His *Rights of Infants* (1797) argued for female equality and suffrage [see *women, 4]. He continued to advocate his phonetic alphabet as an aid to popular learning, and published his most substantial and cogent work, *The Restorer of Society to its Natural State*, in both conventional and phonetic editions. His last significant work, *The Restorer*, developed the case in favour of armed rebellion, citing both the American and French revolutions and the *naval mutinies of 1797 as exemplars.

He was arrested at least eight times, and served two significant prison sentences. The first of these was in 1794 whilst awaiting trial for high treason. Charges were dropped after the acquittal of Spence's London Corresponding Society colleague Thomas *Hardy. The second in 1801–2 followed his conviction for seditious libel arising from the publication of *The Restorer*. It broke Spence financially and it was five years before he was able to resume bookselling on a permanent basis, and then only from a barrow. Yet this same period marked the consolidation of his reputation as a revolutionary theorist. From 1801 active conspirators in the capital were consistently associated with his name. The peak of Spencean revolutionary activity postdates his death, notably with the Spa Fields and Cato Street conspiracies of 1816 and 1820 [see *insurrections].

Spence's enduring influence, however, was as an agrarian theorist, whose ideas fed into the radicalism of subsequent decades through a small cadre of energetic followers [see *Spenceans]. The most notable, Thomas Evans, George Petrie, and Allen *Davenport, extended Spence's concept of public ownership to mines, shipping, and manufactories. It was Evans's version of Spenceanism that Thomas *Malthus targeted, along with Robert *Owen, in his attack on 'systems of equality' in the fifth edition of his *Essay on the Principle of Population* (1817). Robert *Southey did likewise in the *Quarterly Review* the previous year. A significant Spencean

presence is to be found in key radical organizations of the 1820s and 1830s, and even into the *Chartist era. Thus, though Spence's works went unpublished after his death until the 1880s, his thought remained a benchmark for later reformers. MC

Spenceans, followers of the agrarian reformer Thomas *Spence who grouped together in 1815 as the Society of Spencean Philanthropists. Spence's funeral in September 1814 announced his ideological survival: the shoemaker poet Robert Charles Fair, by then a convert to Percy *Shelley's *Queen Mab* (1813), attended the procession and the veteran London Corresponding Society radical William Snow 'made a very judicious harangue over the grave'. Within a few days Thomas John Evans, at the behest of his father Thomas Evans, baker, print-colourer, and braces-maker, was propagating the opinions and philosophy of Spence to United English exiles in Paris; he was accompanied by the surveyor and ex-army officer Arthur Thistlewood (1770–1820). By 1815 the Society of Spencean Philanthropists had instituted themselves in London. Evans (Snr.) was their librarian. At their peak before 1820, there may have been 200–300 committed London-based followers plus ten times that number of active sympathizers, all dogged by government *spies and informers.

Thomas Evans and Thistlewood exemplify the two main strands of postwar Spenceanism. Evans concerned himself with ideological dissemination, while Thistlewood, known as the Cato Street conspirator, carried out the concurrent interest in direct action. Evans's *Christian Policy The Salvation of the Empire* (1816) and *Christian Policy in Full Practice Among the People of Harmony* (1818) developed Spencean doctrine by combining the political theory of *agrarianism with the spiritual language of 'a political millennium' or 'jubilee' modelled on the *land [16] restoration in Leviticus 25. His son's editorship of the *Manchester Observer* in 1820 provided a broader, northern industrial outreach, while support amongst London pressmen included John Murray's *Byron printer, Thomas Davison. However, influential rationalists like Richard *Carlile remained lukewarm. Spencean propaganda, based upon 'free and easy' drinking clubs, included bill-posting, pamphleteering, wall-chalking, and convivial singing, together with *tavern and *debating room 'speechifying'.

Although Spencean land nationalization can never be fully separated from contemporary interests in tillage, anti-*enclosure and waste land movements, it was an ideology sufficiently well marked to be traceable back to the revolutionary plans of Colonel Despard (1751–1803) of 1802 as well as to the *insurrections of 1816 and 1817 at Spa Fields and Pentrich. While Thistlewood, the apothecary James Watson Snr. (1766–1828), the shoemaker Thomas Preston (1768–1850), and the black ex-slave, tailor, and editor Robert Wedderburn (c.1763–c.1835), veered towards physical force, others, such as the shoemaker Allen *Davenport and the musician, hairdresser, and poet Edward James Blandford, combined radical intellectualism with sedition. By

1817 the parliamentary *Report from the Committee of Secrecy* imagined Spenceanism widespread, and Thomas *Malthus's fifth edition of *An Essay on the Principle of Population* singled them out for attack, as did Robert *Southey in the same year. To answer them, Southey's *Wat Tyler* (1794) was pirated for its revolutionary resonances.

Arrests, surveillance, executions, death, the pro-*Queen Caroline agitation, and better harvests decisively deflected Spenceanism during the 1820s, but the economic and *natural rights basis of Spence's doctrine were later revived by incorporation (sometimes simply by swapping nouns) into aspects of the *socialism of Robert *Owen, the co-operative movement and Feargus O'Connor's *Chartist Land Plan of the 1830s and 1840s.   DW

Spenserianism. The poetry of Edmund Spenser (?1552–99) enjoyed a revival in the mid-eighteenth century as part of the more general rediscovery of *medieval and Elizabethan *romance, reflected in the work of antiquarians such as Richard Hurd (1720–1808), Thomas *Percy, and Thomas *Warton, particularly the latter's *Observations on the Faerie Queen* (1754). By the late eighteenth century, Spenser was firmly ensconced as a key representative of a distinctively English national tradition of verse which also included Chaucer, *Milton, and *Shakespeare. Few poets wishing to secure a place for themselves within this native tradition went without at least attempting an early imitation of Spenser. Examples include *Blake's 'An Imitation of Spenser' from his *Poetical Sketches* (1783) and *Coleridge's 'Lines in Imitation of Spenser' (1795). The early nineteenth century witnessed a spectacular efflorescence of Spenserian imitations, perhaps stimulated by H. J. Todd's (1763–1845) eight-volume variorum edition of 1805 and a new edition of Warton's *Observations* in 1807, as well as by the publication of Joseph *Ritson and George Ellis's researches on medieval metrical romances, popularized by Walter *Scott. Lord *Byron's reputation was made by *Childe Harold's Pilgrimage*, a poem which used the Spenserian stanza and pseudo-Spenserian questing hero. More typical of the influence of Spenser on the period was the extension of Warton's idea of him as a poet of 'fancy' into an emphasis on the luxurious and even erotic dimensions of his work. Mary *Tighe's allegory *Psyche* (1805), written in Spenserian stanzas, reflects this development. Perhaps the chief spokesman for this version of Spenser was Leigh *Hunt, who labelled himself a 'Spenser-ophilist'. The first poem *Keats ever wrote was also an imitation of Spenser. Influenced by Tighe's example and with the direct encouragement of Hunt, he went on to produce several other luxuriously Spenserian poems, including, most famously, 'The Eve of St Agnes' (1820). The idea of seductive appeal of the Bower of Bliss in *The Faerie Queene* remained a potent one for young poets such as Keats and *Shelley, but while they shared Spenser's sense of the dangerous allure of the palace of pleasure, they more often repudiated the Christian morality on which Spenser's allegory was based.   JM

spies and the spy system. In Britain in the eighteenth century, spying on the King's subjects was seen to be dishonourable, contrary to the rights of the freeborn Englishman as expressed by custom and the constitution of 1688–9 and redolent of French absolutism and popery. Needless to say, however, *raison d'état* ensured that some mechanisms for countering potential subversive elements existed throughout the century. A 'Private Office' within the Post Office, for instance, opened the mail of suspected Jacobites, and various government ministers employed their own agents to gather intelligence and penetrate suspicious groups. However, successive administrations failed to develop a permanent and systematic programme of spying, or preventative police, until the era of the *French Revolution. Even then, although the Alien Office, attached to the Home Office from 1793, acted as the nerve-centre of government counterintelligence activities, the source of much information continued to come gratuitously from public-spirited sources in the provinces, particularly from magistrates in disturbed areas, who sometimes organized their own networks of informers. Government, with few resources to follow up evidence of disaffection and wary of opportunistic informers, continued to rely on ad hoc means of confirmation: Bow Street runners, young law students, and government messengers were often used on a temporary basis.

The *Pitt government's greatest problem lay with collating and analysing the mass of information obtained from various sources. Fortunately, in the crisis years 1798–9 William Wickham (1761–1840) at the Alien Office established procedures which enabled the accurate assessment and cross-referencing of data to reach a high state of efficiency. Working closely with Lord *Castlereagh and Edward Cooke (1755–1820) in Dublin, Wickham produced the framework of a system of preventative police, which ensured that government was kept remarkably well informed of subversive activities in England, Ireland, and among radical expatriates on the Continent [see *policing, 7]. Access to reliable information from agents close to the United Irish leaders helped, as did the garrulousness of rebel prisoners. But as with previous counterintelligence measures, Wickham's organization lasted only as long as the apparent threat to the state existed. The surprise occasioned by Robert Emmet's (1778–1803) uprising in Dublin in July 1803 demonstrated that once Castlereagh, Cooke, and Wickham had moved on, counterintelligence practices began to decay. The idea of a permanent system of preventative police quietly disappeared, the product of a transient alarmism.

Thereafter, until the closure in 1844 of the Post Office's Secret Office marked the official rejection of intelligence-gathering, government relied on local magistrates' networks and individual informers for information on potentially subversive plebeian organizations. Divorced from the working-class culture of the new manufacturing towns, government was forced almost entirely to rely on informers who could blend in with these surroundings (and who were often of dubious character). Cross-checking of information became increasingly difficult; the line between gathering information and acting as an *agent provocateur* was frequently crossed. The misdeeds of the despised Edwards, Groves, and 'Oliver the Spy' hastened the demise of a British 'spy system' that had always been seen as a temporary expedient.   MDu

STAËL, (Anne-Louise) Germaine (Necker) de (1766–1817). A prolific French writer of works of philosophy, politics, and literary criticism, as well as of novels and plays, Staël is a major figure in the enmeshed political and literary relations of revolutionary Europe. While Germaine Necker's early desire to write was not encouraged by her parents, her precocity as a conversationalist was allowed to develop in the company of the famous and powerful who gathered at the home of her educated *salonnière* mother and Swiss banker father, finance minister under Louis XVI. Jacques Necker was exiled to Brussels on 11 July 1789, but his triumphant return to Paris after the fall of the Bastille—when he was fêted by thousands who lined the streets—was later described by his daughter who accompanied him as the high point of her life. In 1786 Germaine had married the Swedish ambassador to France, Eric-Magnus de Staël, and opened the doors of her own salon on the rue du Bac. Her salon here and later at the family estate, Coppet, near Geneva, was a meeting-place for important political and literary figures, some of whom became her companions over many years, such as A. W. Schlegel (1767–1845).

While her early works tried to stay within the bounds of the 'lady novelist' she quickly moved into genres more ambitious for a woman, writing political and philosophical pamphlets and books. Her major works of fiction are *Delphine* (1802) and *Corinne, or Italy* (1807), the latter an immediately successful work, part novel, part travel-writing. *Corinne's* portrait of the woman poet as doomed *improvisatrice* was extremely influential on some British women writers, including Felicia *Hemans and L. E. *Landon. Significant among her other writings are *On Literature Considered in its Relations with Social Institutions* (1800) and *On Germany* (1813). The latter, pulped by *Napoleon's troops, offered Germany as a model of Romantic nationalism for the emergent revolutionary nations of Europe and America.   SC

statistics. The first decades of the nineteenth century saw a dramatic increase in the scale and range of the commitment to the gathering of detailed quantitative data on demographic, economic, and social matters, so that by the early Victorian period the basis of the modern discipline of social statistics was firmly established.

The statistical movement began in 1662 with the publication of Captain John Graunt's *Natural and Political Observations on the Bills of Mortality*, followed by Gregory King's remarkably sophisticated attempt in the mid-1690s to estimate the size and age structure of the *population of England and Wales.

This momentum was not sustained into the eighteenth century, when the collection of social statistics temporarily diminished. Growing opposition to the gathering of personal statistical data on grounds of privacy was sufficiently powerful to defeat proposals for the introduction of a civil census in the 1750s. Nonetheless, detailed annual statistics on the volume and value of exports and imports, first extensively collected in 1697, continued to be compiled. Occasional, crude attempts at national income accounting were undertaken, most notably by Joseph Massie in 1759 and Arthur *Young in 1770. During the late eighteenth century, the number of private censuses of population steadily increased. These were carried out for local government or ecclesiastical purposes and, more commonly, to help resolve the controversy over whether the population was rising or falling. Also, men like Richard *Price, John Heysham (1753–1834) at Carlisle, John Haygarth (1740–1827) at Chester, and Thomas Percival (1740–1804) at Manchester, in their quest for more accurate information on standards of health and longevity, either as the basis for improved life insurance schemes or in the interests of public health reform, considerably extended the amount of data available on the rates and causes of mortality [see *medicine, 18]. More significantly, however, their demonstration of the inadequacies of the existing data on population and vital rates helped lay the foundation for the dramatic transformation in attitudes towards the provision of social statistics which occurred after 1800.

One of the most obvious manifestations of the growing interest in quantitative inquiry and analysis was the foundation of privately funded statistical societies in many of the country's largest towns. The first of these was established in Manchester and London in 1833. Numerous others soon followed, at Bristol and Glasgow in 1836, and at Belfast, Birmingham, Leeds, Liverpool, and Newcastle in 1838. Most were short-lived and, hindered by constraints of time and resources and a reluctance to take on what were thought to be functions more appropriate to the role of the state, the direct results of their labours were generally modest and disappointing.

By far the most significant and durable feature of the early-nineteenth-century statistical movement was the wholly unprecedented involvement of the state in the provision and publication of an increasingly wide range of social statistics. Decennial civil censuses were begun in 1801. Official annual returns on crime were regularly published for England and Wales from 1805 and for Scotland from 1832. Parliamentary committees of inquiry into standards of working-class education were undertaken in 1816, 1818, and 1833, presaging the more thorough and reliable survey of *education [17] conducted as part of the 1851 census. The amount of quantitative data on trade, industry, and other economic and social matters was considerably expanded by the establishment in 1832 of a Statistical Development at the Board of Trade. General Register Offices were instituted in England and Wales in 1836 and Scotland in 1855 to register and collate data on births, marriages, and deaths and causes of death. A Select Committee on the Health of Towns was set up in 1840. Two years later, under the aegis of the *Poor Law Commission, Edwin *Chadwick published his monumental *Report on the Sanitary Condition of the Labouring Population of Great Britain*. In 1843-4 a Royal Commission on the State of Large Towns and Populous Districts was established.

What underlay this sudden surge of private and public enthusiasm for quantification? In part, as earlier, it reflected a desire to improve the range and quality of the factual information required for good government at a time when such information was demonstrably lacking. Without adequate censuses, it was argued, governments could have little idea of the military and productive capabilities of a nation, no firm basis for their *income tax programmes, no clear idea of their food requirements, or basis for export and import policies. More so than ever before, however, the greatly enhanced interest in statistical compilation and analysis was rooted in a desire for social reform. For the majority of those involved, the provision of an extensive and unbiased body of factual information was seen as an essential prerequisite for the social and moral improvement of the lower orders, an improvement which would bind the social classes more closely together and lessen the risk of political upheaval. In a period of hitherto unparalleled demographic and economic change, when public health conditions were deteriorating under the impact of rapid urbanization and the incidence of *poverty [12], crime, and social disturbance apparently increasing, it was inevitable that vigorous attempts would be made to assess the scale and nature of the problems as a prelude to their possible solution. Even so, systematic national approaches to statistical collection were not instituted until the late nineteenth century.   NLT

STEDMAN, John Gabriel (1744-97), mercenary and adventurer who, as a captain in the Scots Brigade of the Dutch army, went out to Surinam (Dutch Guiana) in 1773-6 as part of a fruitless military expedition against the runaway slave communities of maroons. The diary he kept in these years formed the basis of his highly acclaimed *Narrative, of a Five Years' Expedition, against the Revolted Negroes of Surinam*, composed between 1778 and 1790 but not published until 1796, by which time it was extensively revised on the authority of the publisher, Joseph *Johnson. Although the revisions slanted the text away from cultural relativity and ameliorism towards a pro-slavery stance, the *Narrative* was hailed by supporters of *abolitionism as a blistering indictment of the opulence, decadence, and cruelty of Dutch plantation society. Also popular was Stedman's highly romanticized version of his 'marriage' to the mulatto slave Joanna and her rejection of his offer to take her back to Europe as his 'Lawfull wife'. The *Narrative* was lavishly produced in two volumes with eighty engravings, sixteen of which were executed by William *Blake, including the well-known 'Europe supported by Africa & America'.   DC

STEWART, Dugald (1753-1828), mathematician and influential philosopher during the later stages of the *Scottish Enlightenment. Educated at the University of Edinburgh, with a period at Glasgow University listening to Thomas *Reid, Stewart was professor of mathematics at Edinburgh from 1775 to 1785, then professor of moral philosophy at Edinburgh from 1785 to 1810 in succession to Adam *Ferguson.

While disliking the term 'Common Sense', Stewart rightly saw himself as an heir to Reid in his basic philosophical outlook, which held that philosophy depended upon *psychology [39] treated as an inductive science. However, he was an eclectic philosopher who was also much influenced by others especially the *political economy [33] of Adam *Smith.

Stewart was enormously influential in his own time, thanks to his popular lectures, his numerous works, including *Elements of the Philosophy of the Human Mind* (1792) and *Outlines of Moral Philosophy* (1793), and the prominence of many of his students, including the founders of the *Edinburgh Review*, Sir Walter *Scott and James *Mill, sons of *Whig grandees, and foreign luminaries such as novelist-politician Benjamin Constant (1767-1830). A Whig who sympathized with the *American Revolution and the early stages of the *French Revolution, Stewart was also immensely popular in America and France for a couple of generations. He was a member of the Speculative Society of Edinburgh from 1772 to 1775, to whom he delivered a paper on dreaming. The combined effect of his and Reid's philosophy led to the idea of a 'Common Sense School', often simply known as 'the Scottish School'.   KH

STORACE, Nancy (Anna or Ann Selina) (1765-1817), soprano. After singing Italian opera in Italy and Vienna (where she was the first Susanna in *Mozart's *Marriage of Figaro*), Nancy Storace settled in London in 1787, initially performing in Italian opera at the King's Theatre. She joined Drury Lane in 1789 as its most highly paid singer, specializing in comic roles composed by her brother, Stephen *Storace. She toured Europe from 1797 to 1801 with the tenor John *Braham, with whom she had an intimate relationship for seventeen years. Nancy Storace brought a strong dramatic sense to English *opera, her dynamic stage presence compensating for her sometimes harsh vocal tone. She retired a wealthy woman in 1808.   JG

STORACE, Stephen John Seymour (1762-96). The most innovative theatre composer of his day, Storace gradually integrated music and drama in his English *operas. Born of an Italian father and English mother, he studied in Naples, composed his first two Italian operas for Vienna, then returned to England in 1787 to become unofficial house composer at Drury Lane until his death.

In his main-piece English operas with spoken dialogue, Storace gradually modified the traditional separation between the action (in spoken dialogue)

8

and music. With the help of his librettist, James Cobb (1756–1818), he integrated music and drama in the manner (though not the scale) of *opera buffa*, particularly in multisection finales and dramatic ensembles. Storace's most Italianate opera is *The Pirates* (1792), which unfortunately suffers from weak dialogue. Other main-piece operas, including *The Haunted Tower* (1789) and *The Siege of Belgrade* (1790), exploit contemporary tastes for the *Gothic, exotic, and spectacular; some later works, such as *Lodoiska* (1794), use more serious, romantic plots. In his afterpiece operas, many of them settings of farcical librettos by Prince Hoare (1755–1834), Storace continued the English tradition of separating action and music. Most were first performed at benefit performances by Drury Lane's main singers; they include one of his most enduring works, *No Song, No Supper* (1790). Storace's operas dominated the operatic repertoire at Drury Lane for almost a decade and he achieved popular acceptance for his innovations, but his influence was short-lived.   JG

STOTHARD, Thomas (1755–1834), painter, book illustrator, and designer of silverware. Apprenticed to a designer of patterned silks, Stothard grew up in the radical neighbourhood of Spitalfields, but subsequently turned into a strong supporter of gendered middle-class ideologies. Much employed in book illustration from the early 1780s onward, Stothard also supplied *designs [25] for Josiah *Wedgwood's jasper ware or decorated silver dishes. Married to a Baptist and the friend of *Sharp, *Flaxman, and *Blake, Stothard moved in much the same radical circles as these fellow artists during the 1780s and 1790s. Apparently, the painter was in contact with Lord George Gordon's (1751–93) Protestant Association by 1780, and in 1782 he designed an emblematic 'Declaration of Rights' dedicated to the *Society for Constitutional Information. However, his achievement as a book illustrator and designer of 'furniture prints' made a much more lasting contribution to the cultural and sexual politics of the period by shaping its sentimentalized conceptions of innocent childhood, of leisurely *domesticity [13], and particularly of female 'grace, dignity, and elegance'.

As might be expected from a *Royal Academician (he was elected a full member in 1794), Stothard would dabble in the heroic and the military *sublime with an occasional battle piece. But it was in association with publishers of illustrated books that he catered to, and shaped the visual appetites of, a new middle-class public. Between 1778 and 1834 Stothard illustrated almost every title from the entire canon of fashionable literature. Though a few early works exhibit a mild eroticism, his skilfully arranged compositions prepared for the print and booksellers never give an 'impure suggestion' that might provoke public odium. The multitude of subjects delineated by his pen, and mostly engraved on small plates 'embellishing' the products of publishers such as Bell, Harrison, Cadell, and Sharpe, attracted a numerous audience. Contemporary characterizations of his imagery usually stress Stothard's concern with charm and tenderness, especially typical of his female figures, mostly seen in graceful action within an arcadian world. In marked contrast with Mary *Wollstonecraft, Stothard thus disseminated popular depictions of women as essentially pretty creatures entirely subject to their feelings and dependent on male 'protection'.   DWD

street literature. The distribution of literature by travelling pedlars and street sellers in towns had long been a feature of *popular culture [23], but our period witnessed a substantial increase in the volume and impact of such material. Middle-class reformers consciously modelled their publications and their distribution techniques on existing patterns of street literature in an attempt to counter its moral and political influence amongst the increasingly literate lower orders [see *Cheap Repository Tracts].

One of the factors contributing to increased output was the reduced cost of letterpress printers, numbers of which almost trebled between 1785 and 1824. Rate of production increased further with the newly developed iron press, first patented by Lord Stanhope in 1800, which could produce over 200 impressions in an hour. The appearance of broadsheets became more attractive as heavier types led to more varied print, while improvements in wood-engraving allowed more complex illustrations [see *prints, 22].

Street literature was considered ephemeral, printed on the cheapest-quality paper, often relying for its success on the speed with which it followed an event of notoriety. It is not surprising, then, that reliable sales figures should be unobtainable. The most popular broadsheets and broadsides (the latter printed only on one side) were probably those to do with crime, such as the famous 'Confession and execution of William Corder, the Murderer of Maria Marten', a broadside which sold over one and a half million copies. Supposed dying confessions were often sold at the public execution of the criminal concerned. Other sheets were 'cocks', far-fetched stories presented as if they were true, which appeared in both prose and *ballad form costing as little as a farthing. Chapbooks were small duodecimo books, often sold for a penny, which, in the words of the publisher William Chambers (1800–83), 'appealed to the popular love of the heroic, the marvellous, the pathetic, and the humorous. Many of them were nothing more than an embodiment of the legends, superstitions, ballads, and songs, which had been kept alive by oral tradition before the invention of printing.'

It was the circulation of cheap editions of the works of political radicals that middle-class educational reformers most feared, especially the satires of William *Hone, who imitated popular ballad and chapbook forms. Hone's parodies, such as *The Political House that Jack Built* (1819), illustrated by George *Cruikshank, were part of the appeal of the radical 'pauper press' to the widening body of literate plebeian readers.

However, both *Evangelical and radical publications were challenged by the commercial enterprises of publishers such as John Pitts (1765–1844) and

100. Notorious crime and lurid scandal were among the most enduring subjects of nineteenth-century street literature. This woodcut was reproduced in many broadside accounts of hangings published by John Pitts in the 1830s.

James Catnach (1792–1842), who made popular literature the mainstay of their businesses. From Seven Dials, the printing centre of London, Pitts and Catnach published broadside ballads, prose broadsheets, chapbooks, handbills, execution sheets, and *almanacs. The journalist Henry Mayhew (1812–87) looked back from the 1850s on the time of these two publishers as the heyday of street literature, reporting that 'Jemmy Catnach' was rumoured to have made more than £10,000 from his business, much of that deriving from broadsheets relating to the *Queen Caroline affair.

The Catnach press provides a valuable insight into the elusive issue of sales figures of popular literature, because if Catnach produced a penny or twopenny copy of a more expensive title, it suggests that there was considerable demand for the original. In the 1820s he produced a twopenny chapbook, *Life in London; or, the sprees of Tom and Jerry*, exploiting the popularity of the original *Life in London* by Pierce *Egan, and in the 1830s a sheet almanac called *The Prophetic Messenger*, echoing the subtitle of the new astrological almanac by Raphael. Such plagiarism speaks convincingly of success.

Provincial printers of street literature were also active, with Newcastle and Birmingham often mentioned by London printers as rival centres. From about 1801 to 1831 John Marshall of Newcastle was one of the largest publishers outside London. Dialect ballads and poems had appeared in Yorkshire and Lancashire from the late seventeenth century, but from the middle of the nineteenth century a more substantial dialect literature flourished, some of it in the form of street literature.

Anecdotal evidence from publishers and middle-class observers offers the main evidence of the importance and widespread influence of street literature. Accounts by working-class autodidacts of their childhood reading can be useful, but such self-improving memoirs often stress the superstitious nature of popular literature, suggesting that works expounding marvels, ghosts, and foolish folk beliefs were prevalent. Mayhew, writing in the 1850s but referring to the memories of earlier times, presents a more varied sense of material available, drawing distinctions according to the method of selling. 'Running patterers' would be continually on the move while calling out the attractions of their wares; 'standing patterers' would build up the amazement of a crowd in the 'wonders' described by their literature; public-house 'paper-workers', sellers of sealed packets of pornographic material, would hawk their goods in bars and taprooms. According to Mayhew, street hawkers thought themselves superior to other costers, perhaps because of the level of literacy and creativity required for their dramatic presentations. Functional items such as almanacs, pocket-books, and stationery were usually sold by women, who did not take part in the 'oral puffery' required by works of fiction and sensation.

The death of the broadside was hastened by the growth of *newspaper circulation in the second half of the nineteenth century. Ballad sheets could not compete with the popularity of songbooks filled with music-hall hits, while the chapbook gave way to the penny dreadful, and the almanac was replaced by the calendar. Street literature gradually gave way to new mass-industrial forms of entertainment and information.   MP

STRUTT, Joseph (1749–1802), engraver, antiquary, and author. Although an accomplished and recognized engraver, Strutt's significance rests on his research into *antiquarianism [35], begun in the *British Museum in 1771. This led to *The Regal and Ecclesiastical Antiquities of England* (1773), *Manners, Customs, Arms, Habits, &c., of the People of England* (1774–6), and *Chronicle of England* (1774–6). Strutt supplemented his bibliographical research with frequent expeditions to the sights depicted. After the death of his wife in 1778, he devoted seven years to painting, exhibiting nine works on classical subjects at the *Royal Academy. By the end of this period he had produced his *Biographical Dictionary of Engravers* (1785–6), which remains the basis for subsequent works of the kind.

In 1790 Strutt retired to Hertfordshire to regain his health and recover financially from the dishonest dealings of a relative. Returning to London in 1795, he brought out *Dresses and Habits of the English People* (1796–9), and *Sports and Pastimes of the People of England* (1801). Strutt's research on regal and ecclesiastical relics was the first of its sort published in Britain; his last two books were widely read, particularly that on sports and games, which ran to subsequent printings and was an influential text in the recording and reform of *popular culture [23].

GAB

STUBBS, George (1724–1806), painter of animals, *portraits, *conversation pieces, and rural scenes; etcher; anatomist. Stubbs had no formal artistic training: he worked briefly with the etcher Hamlet Winstanley (1698–1756) in his home town of Liverpool and earned a living by painting portraits in Leeds before moving to York in 1745 to study anatomy. He learned print-making techniques when requested to illustrate Dr John Burton's *Essay Towards a Complete New System of Midwifery* (1751), which resulted in eighteen copperplates of anatomical dissection.

In 1754 Stubbs travelled to Italy, where he reputedly met an African and gained invitation to his village near Morocco. There he witnessed a lion pounce on and savage a white Barbary horse, a scene which would profoundly influence his later equine pictures, through the story of its provenance has been doubted by some critics. In 1758, back in England, Stubbs began his *Anatomy of the Horse*. He performed all the dissections, drawings, and accounts himself over a period of eighteen months. The engravings of the plates took nearly eight years to complete, as Stubbs maintained his professional commitment to painting during the day, only working on the *Anatomy* at night. The book was finally published in 1766 to acclaim from both artists and scientists.

During the 1760s, Stubbs built his reputation as a painter of horses and their owners, as well as of their domestic habitats. He began his 'Lion and Horse' series in 1762 with *Horse Attacked by a Lion*, a fine example of his artistic balance between neoclassical proportion and Romantic *sublime. This motif also appeared in his enamel works. In order to procure tablets of pottery large enough to sustain his ambitions, Stubbs turned to Josiah *Wedgwood, who managed to produce the innovative canvases after much trouble and expense.

Stubbs was known for his accurate paintings of unusual as well as of familiar animals. The anatomist William Hunter (1718–83) declared that Mr Stubbs's representation of a Nylghau (1769) ensured that anyone would recognize the creature—an obscure

101. George Stubbs, *Horse Frightened by a Lion*, 1770. Stubbs explored this wild pairing of horse and lion in many settings of sublime landscape.

species of antelope from India—'wherever he may happen to meet with it'. Stubbs became an associate of the *Royal Academy in 1780 but was never elected member. He commenced *A Comparative Anatomical Exposition of the Structure of the Human Body with that of a Tiger and a Common Fowl* in 1795, but finished only fifteen of the projected thirty plates by the time he died in 1806.　　　　　　　KF

sublime. Amidst an extensive eighteenth-century literature on aesthetics, discussions of the sublime hold a prominent place [see *literary theory, 41]. This category is usually defined in opposition to the beautiful. As Edmund *Burke writes in his influential *A Philosophical Enquiry into the Origin of our Ideas of the Sublime and Beautiful* (1757), the sublime is provoked by great and terrible objects, while a sense of the beautiful is aroused by small and pleasing ones. The first arouses our admiration, the second our love; the one forces, the other flatters, us into compliance. This distinction is sharpened by a commonplace association of the former with men and the latter with women.

An experience of the sublime characteristically begins with the interposition of an overwhelming force, which shatters equanimity and produces a feeling of blockage. As this power takes hold of mind and emotions, inertia becomes transport: we are hurried on as if 'by an irresistible force'. As the experience recedes, it leaves behind a newly invigorated sense of identity and, frequently, admiration for the blocking power. It is as if the mind has appropriated to itself 'some part of the dignity and importance of the things which it contemplates'.

In England, widespread interest in sublimity dates from the publication in 1736 of French poet Nicolas Boileau's translation of *Peri Hypsous*, a first-century Greek text by Longinus. However, in its identification of sublimity with oratory, this treatise forms a point of departure rather than a blueprint for eighteenth-century thought on sublimity. In the work of writers such as Addison, Burke, Baillie, Gerard, and *Hume, interest shifts from the rhetorical to the natural sublime. Investigation of the effects of natural sublimity is critical to a consideration of the sublime in art.

In the late eighteenth and early nineteenth century, the natural sublime is in turn displaced by a Romantic sublime, anticipated in Kant's *Critique of Judgement* (1790), that has its source in and is revelatory of the individual's own powers. As S. T. *Coleridge writes, 'I meet, I *find* the Beautiful—but I give, contribute, or rather attribute the Sublime'. Great size and grandeur are therefore not necessary conditions for sublimity. Indeed, William *Blake is able to discover eternity in a grain of sand and, in *Wordsworth's 'The Ruined Cottage', the Pedlar reflects on a time when 'the least of things / seemed infinite'. As these passages suggest, the Romantic sublime is a moment of vision which, by providing an intuition of the absolute grounds of existence, claims to close the gap between subject and object.

This narrative, from the rhetorical to the natural and then the Romantic sublime, is often used to map the shift from neoclassicism to Romanticism. The Romantic sublime is identified with emotion, *genius, spontaneity, *imagination, the individual—all those things that exceed a literature based on rules and convention. By contrast, recent studies have argued that the sublime is a technique for producing the self discovered by Romanticism; a strategy for mastering excess; and a category which is deeply implicated in eighteenth-century ideologies of gender.　　　　　　　POT

Sunday schools. Educating children on Sunday was a widely accepted Sabbath practice by the late eighteenth century. It is estimated that by 1787, at the height of the *Evangelical revival, over 200 Sunday schools had been established in British parishes, with enrolments of over 250,000 children. By 1831, the Golden Jubilee of the Sunday school movement, more than one and half million pupils were counted in school registers.

Many Sunday schools had been established in the seventeenth century across the British Isles. Presbyterians, *Anglicans, and, later, *Methodists brought religious teaching and rudimentary instruction to children across the countryside in England, Scotland, and Ireland. However, Robert Raikes (1735–1811), a businessman of Gloucester, established the first systematized provincial Sunday schools in the 1780s. As editor of the *Gloucester Journal*, Raikes used his own newspaper to popularize the idea of Sunday schools as a constructive answer to the problems of juvenile delinquence, religious ignorance, and unemployment. His first school was opened in Sooty Alley, opposite the city gaol in Gloucester. Raikes engaged men and women to teach on Sundays, mixing clergy and laity in the process.

Raikes was already actively engaged in prison visiting, and had observed children running wild on the streets of Gloucester on Sundays [see *prison reformers]. He provided evidence to local *philanthropists, church leaders, and regular parishioners of the compelling need for free Sunday schools to provide the poor with a knowledge of the gospels and religious enlightenment, as well as an opportunity to learn to read. Widespread belief that crime was linked with idleness and illiteracy prompted interested individuals such as Sarah *Trimmer and Hannah *More to encourage schooling on Sunday in rural villages, as well as in populous manufacturing towns and the great cities. By the late 1780s, Sunday schooling was being viewed by religious reformers and philanthropists as an effective means of reducing crime and regulating behaviour. This led to the foundation of some non-denominational religious societies, including the Sunday School Society, the London-based Society for the Encouragement of Sunday Schools, and, in 1812, the non-denominational Sunday School Union.

Religious tracts, pamphlets, and religious tales were published cheaply for Sunday school scholars by the Religious Tract Society and the Society for the Propagation of Christian Knowledge. Raikes's own publication, *The Sunday Scholar's Companion*, appeared in 1785. Through the movement, hundreds of thousands of children and young adults without benefit of regular schooling were made literate, and Sunday schools often played a central role in the parochial and cultural life of working-class communities. By the 1830s, Sunday schools also provided elementary *education [17] and had achieved a formal organizational structure.   SR

SWEDENBORG, Emanuel (1688–1772). Though Swedenborg's posthumous cultural importance lies in his mystical religious writings, which were widely read by Romantics, he is also a major figure in the history and philosophy of science, making important contributions to algebra, anatomy, *chemistry, *engineering, linguistics, mineralogy, mining, physics, and physiology [see *natural philosophy, 34].

The son of a Swedish Lutheran bishop, Jesper Swedberg, Swedenborg was appointed in 1716 assessor extraordinary to the Royal College of Mines, a post he held for more than thirty years. His contri-

butions to mining technology include improvements in ventilation systems without which the deep coalmines essential to the British industrial revolution could never have been worked. His theoretical work in physics and physiology has been seen as anticipating twentieth-century discoveries.

From the late 1740s to the end of his life he describes, with the same meticulous scholarship as his scientific writings, a series of mystical or visionary experiences concerning the nature of God, the social organization of angels in heaven, and the interpretation of the *Bible, which he saw as inaugurating the Second Coming. His best-known work is probably *Heaven and Hell* (1758). Though he never sought to proselytize or to create any organization, followers in London, including for a time Catherine and William *Blake, inaugurated the New Jerusalem Church in 1784. S. T. *Coleridge was also fascinated by his writings, as much for the psychological state they describe as for their content.   SP

T

taverns and alehouses. At the beginning of the eighteenth century public drinking in Britain took place largely in three ancient and relatively distinct institutions—the inn, the tavern, and the alehouse, each having separate identities in both statute and common law. Broadly, inns were substantial establishments offering wine, beer, good-quality food, and lodging to prosperous locals and travellers. They were frequently centres for coach travel, for county local government, judicial and commercial business, and for aristocratic and gentry sociable rituals such as fox-hunting, feasts, and balls. The tavern appealed to a similar social clientele but specialized in drink, particularly wine, rather than accommodation. Alehouses were traditionally the neighbourhood and communal centres of the common people, ranging from artisans and middling sorts to labourers and criminals. Offering mainly beer, porter, spirits, and humble food, they developed from the seventeenth century a diverse and pivotal set of sociable, economic, cultural, and political functions. These included the supply of popular reading-matter as well as the provision of venues for the business meetings and convivial activities of *friendly societies, box clubs (small-scale co-operative insurance systems), trade societies, sporting and recreational groups, sectarian gatherings, political and *debating clubs, 'free-and-easies', and *glee clubs, prostitutes, criminal receivers, and theatrical performers [see *popular culture, 23].

During the Romantic period each of these institu-

tions experienced unprecedented challenge and change, especially the tavern and alehouse which began to converge. Politics provided one impetus for this transformation. During the counter-revolutionary climate of the French and Napoleonic wars, the association of *corresponding societies and *United movement conspirators with metropolitan alehouses heightened ruling-class fears that these institutions fostered plebeian sedition and disorder. A further concern derived from the growing tendency of both urban and village alehouses to provide customers with *newspapers, particularly *Cobbett's *Political Register*. In the 1790s various *gagging acts tightened control over alehouse gatherings, while magistrates all over the country began to withhold licences from publicans who encouraged radical meetings or reading-matter. By 1795 a group of London publicans was compelled to form a defensive association against such attacks. Nevertheless, in Manchester and other provincial cities it became commonplace until the mid-1820s for alehouses to display signs warning away Jacobins. Numbers of village alehouses were also closed down as potentially disorderly through the influence of select vestries or through *Evangelical-inspired attacks on their sporting and recreational functions. The emergence in the early nineteenth century of highly capitalized breweries and tied public houses also hastened a trend towards respectability, as did the growing retreat of the middling classes away from public drinking in favour of home entertainment or rival self-improving institutions such as mechanics' institutes [see *popular education], *Sunday schools, art galleries, reading circles, and *literary and philosophical societies. Other goads to specialization and respectability came from commercial developments; a drop in excise duties magnified the burgeoning challenge posed by tea and *coffee-houses. Cheaper alternatives to alehouse fare were also offered by dram houses, gin palaces, lodging-houses, chop houses, and a proliferation of illegal flash houses centred in urban slum areas.

With the fragmentation of the popular drinking market, taverns and alehouses tended to evolve into more elaborate, specialist-built, and capital-intensive institutions known as 'public houses'. These usually boasted distinctive façades and well-appointed saloons for genteel drinking and recreation, as well as taprooms for labouring-class males. In addition, public houses began to build associated club rooms, musical theatres, and games facilities in order to attract the patronage of middle-class families. However, the growing conservatism of the drink trade produced a corresponding pressure to liberalize what were seen as restrictive and mono-polistic regulations. The resulting Beer Act in 1830 virtually deregulated the drink trade, allowing the rapid emergence of small-scale beerhouses which took the place of illegal flash houses, and filled the cultural vacuum created by the gentrification of the public house. IMcC

TAYLOR, Thomas (1758–1835), known as 'the Platonist', translator of classical works, especially Plato, which were influential in disseminating an idealist philosophy. Taylor was most interested in the works of Proclus, a writer of the Athenian School, who reworked the philosophy of Plotinus into a system which in the nineteenth century came to be known as 'Neoplatonism'. This was a form of monism, in which it was posited that all creation emanated from an original unity. Neoplatonism taught that the necessary end of existence was a return to the one, but that most of humanity had forgotten its source, imagining that its separation into individuals was the natural order of things. The movement away from unity, with all its resulting frag-mentation—man from woman, man from nature—became a motif in the work of several writers who were influenced by Taylor's translations, such as William *Blake. The importance of love as the centripetal force reconnecting the fragments and drawing them back in a circle to their origin was also a recurring theme. Percy *Shelley, too, was greatly influenced by Neoplatonic thought, but he had first encountered this at Eton, reading Plato in the original Greek; and S. T. *Coleridge's monism likewise derived from his ability to read the original works.

Taylor received much scorn during his lifetime, on the basis of weaknesses in his translations and accusations of polytheism. He did not conform to the standard expected by some classical scholars, but his interest was more a passionate, devotional one. His translations made Neoplatonic ideas available to a wide array of Romantic writers, helping to shape the forms in which they could express their own disaffection with the contemporary scene. MP

TAYLOR, William (1765–1836), played an important role in introducing German literature and ideas into Britain, chiefly through the periodical press, for which he produced literally hundreds of *essays and *reviews, mainly in the *Monthly Review* and *Monthly Magazine*. Perhaps his most famous contribution was the translation of Bürger's *Lenore*, written in 1790, but published in the *Monthly Magazine* in 1796, a *ballad which became wildly popular and which directly influenced the *poetry [29] of *Coleridge and *Scott.

Taylor's interest in Germany reflected the *Enlightenment [32] principles of the Norwich Dissenting community into which he was born. A life-long *Unitarian, his opinions on Christianity, often expressed after 1796 in his reviews of biblical criticism for the *Monthly Magazine*, were widely regarded as blasphemous. Robert *Southey up-braided Taylor for giving such 'strong meats' to the 'weak stomachs' of the magazine's Dissenting readership. Nevertheless Southey remained a firm friend, recruiting him for the *Critical Review* for two brief periods in the early 1800s.

William *Hazlitt credited Taylor rather than the later *Edinburgh* reviewers with introducing 'the style of philosophical criticism', which transformed the review from a compendium of quotation and para-phrase into a vehicle for the discussion of larger issues. Many of these reviews were collected together into his *Historic Survey of German Poetry* (1828–30), the first English history of German literature. The book was reviewed sharply in the *Edinburgh* by Thomas *Carlyle, for whom German literature was equally important but for very different reasons. Car-lyle's antagonism was itself a sign that Taylor's con-ception of the significance of German culture had been largely displaced by the attitudes popularized by Mme de *Staël's *De l'Allemagne* (1813) and subse-quently by Coleridge and Thomas *De Quincey. JM

TELFORD, Thomas (1757–1834), civil engineer. Telford played a major role not only in creating the *transport infrastructure vital to Britain's *industri-alization [14] but also in enhancing the professional status of *engineering. Raised by his mother, a farm-worker widowed shortly after his birth, in Dum-friesshire, Scotland, Telford attended the parish school and was apprenticed to a local mason in 1770. He progressed quickly from mason to architect, undertaking commissions in Portsmouth Royal Dockyard, 1784–6, then in Shrewsbury (including the new gaol, with advice from the prison reformer John *Howard). Appointed Surveyor of Public Works for Shropshire in 1787, Telford turned to designing road bridges: he completed over 1,000 in his career, mostly of the masonry arch form and renowned for their elegance and durability [see *architecture, 28].

Telford extended the use of iron as a structural material. With cast-iron arches of novel, lighter design he spanned numerous rivers, but to bridge the Menai Straits and the Conway estuary in north Wales (both opened in 1826) he advanced the suspension principle, using wrought-iron chains. In conjunction with an associate, William Jessop (1745–1814), he introduced cast iron into the construction of aqueducts, making them watertight and lighter, and, as at Pont-Cysyllte on the Ellesmere Canal, spectacular.

With industrialization the demand for transport escalated. Telford was the last great builder of canals in Britain, before their eclipse by railways from the 1830s. The scale and terrain of two sea-to-sea routes, the Caledonian Canal (1804–22) through Scotland's Great Glen and the Gotha Canal (1808–32) in Sweden, tested his engineering prowess. Overtaken by coastal steam shipping, however, neither canal proved commercially successful, while the military rationale for the former had long disappeared.

Telford was also responsible for a major road-building programme in the Scottish Highlands, funded by the government, which vainly hoped that better communications would stem the tide of emigration. Simultaneously, he constructed new harbours along the eastern Scottish coast for the British Fisheries Society, and later deployed the knowledge gained there in the massive St Katharine's Dock project in London. Undoubtedly, Telford's greatest road was the London to Holyhead, begun in 1815 and intended to improve communications with Ireland. He substituted a wide, solid carriageway with smooth gradients for a dangerous and difficult track, and the Menai Suspension Bridge for a hazardous ferry crossing. In the 1830s he canvassed steam traction on roads rather than railways.

In 1820 Telford was invited to preside over the newly founded Institution of Civil Engineers, its prime function being to help raise the status of engineering from a trade to a profession. His reputation (enhanced by election to the Royal Society in 1827) and his enthusiastic promotion of the Institution stimulated its growth; his legacy of £2,000 and his library helped buttress its foundations. The Institution's insistence on his burial in Westminster Abbey (against his more modest wishes) further bolstered its prestige. Telford's genial nature and his interest in literature attracted a wide circle of friends, including Robert *Southey, who celebrated his achievement in his *Journal of a Tour in Scotland in 1819*.

CMacL

theatricals, private, amateur performances of plays, were highly popular in the period among all social classes. They were fashionable among the aristocracy, who staged lavish events, involving considerable expenditure on items such as the building of specially designed theatres and the recruitment of professional actors. Occasions such as the theatricals at Richmond House in 1787, for which so many *Whig luminaries had forsaken parliament that a motion had to be postponed, achieved wide publicity in the press. The pastime was also popular among the gentry and the professional middle classes, as indicated by accounts in the diaries of Frances *Burney. Jane *Austen's experience of family theatricals at Steventon in the 1780s was influential in her later fictional account of such an episode in *Mansfield Park* (1814). However, the craze was not confined to the upper classes. Young artisanal men, military subalterns, and clerks formed amateur acting societies or 'spouting clubs' where they could essay roles from *Shakespeare in the style of *Kemble or *Kean. Amateur acting was also an important part of the curriculum of public schools such as Westminster, well known for its annual production of a Greek or Latin drama, and was a distinctive aspect of military culture. Within Britain, officers hired theatres and staged their own productions, or improvised when on ship, on the battlefield, or in the colonies.

Private theatricals therefore represent a complex phenomenon which can be accounted for in a number of ways. First, in the case of the upper classes, they were part of a repertoire of highly theatrical behaviour, associated with other forms of public display that connoted power and status. Second, for all classes, 'getting up a play' had an important educative function, especially in the training of young people in the gendered roles they would perform as adults. Conducted within the walls of the 'private' home, they also explored the boundaries between public and private worlds—between self and society—that were being complicated by the contemporary discourses of *sensibility [11] and *domesticity [13]. Amateur acting allowed the denizens of the spouting clubs to explore the meanings of class and gender in terms of the performance of roles, as well as access to the culture's canonical texts. Private theatricals also entailed a relationship between amateur and professional cultural activity and therefore registered the commercialization of late Georgian society. The involvement of professional actors, the hiring of theatres, the news of theatricals in the press, the publication of plays specially written for amateur theatres, such as William *Hayley's *Plays of Three Acts* (1784), and the development of the monologic play-reading by which patrons paid to enter a 'private' home, indicate that the boundaries between amateur and professional were always blurred. Finally, in the military context, amateur theatricals were important in defining distinctions of rank, the relationship between often isolated and beleaguered military communities (such as the actors of *The Recruiting Officer* in New South Wales in 1788) and their domestic audience, and in expressing ideas of nationhood.

GR

THELWALL, John (1764–1834), political *lecturer, poet, journalist, and elocutionist; the foremost radical orator of the 1790s. After a basic school education, he worked in the family silk business, as a tailor, and also trained for a legal career. But literary ambitions held a stronger attraction for him. He edited the *Biographical and Imperial Magazine*, and from the 1780s his poems and essays were published widely in journals, *Poems on Various Subjects* appearing in 1787. At this period Thelwall gained experience as a public speaker in *debating clubs such as the Society for Free Debate. His interests included *natural philosophy [34]. He was a member of the Physical Society at Guy's Hospital, where in 1793 he presented a controversial lecture later published as *An Essay Towards a Definition of Animal Vitality*.

From the early 1790s Thelwall was prominent in reform societies such as the Friends of the People, the *Society for Constitutional Information, and the London Corresponding Society [see *corresponding societies]. His literary output flourished, and in 1793 he published his 'political-sentimental' collection of *prose [30] and verse, *The Peripatetic*. He was also establishing a name for himself as a powerful popular orator, his lectures appearing as separate pamphlets and, during 1795–6, in his journal, the *Tribune*. Arrested with other leaders of the reform movement in May 1794, he was brought to trial in December and acquitted of a charge of high treason [see *Treason Trials]. His *Poems Written in a Close Confinement* date from his imprisonment in the Tower and in Newgate prison.

After his release Thelwall resumed his lecturing career, but distanced himself from the London Corresponding Society. The two *gagging acts of December 1795 were intended, in part, to silence him. Undeterred, and at some personal risk, he continued his political lectures under the guise of talks on classical history. During 1796 he made a lecture tour in East Anglia, and was attacked by a *press-gang at Yarmouth. By this time the reform movement was in retreat. Like S. T. *Coleridge (with whom Thelwall corresponded from April 1796) and other former republicans and revolutionaries, Thelwall now projected a retired life of farming and literary pursuits. He visited Coleridge and William *Wordsworth at Nether Stowey in July 1797, and contemplated living there too, but he was not encouraged by the 'Lakers' and eventually settled on a farm at Llyswen on the banks of the River Wye in south Wales. While the farming enterprise failed to prosper, his literary output of this period, *Poems Written in Retirement* (1801), deserves favourable comparison with Coleridge's blank verse of the late 1790s.

After 1800 Thelwall resumed his career as a public lecturer, concentrating now on speech therapy and elocution (having suffered from a stammer in his early life) [see *language, 40]. In 1804 he returned to London, where he established a school of elocution at Lincoln's Inn Fields. With the revival of the reform movement after *Waterloo, Thelwall supported the cause as editor of the *Champion* newspaper, contributing powerful denunciations of the *Peterloo massacre in 1819. Nevertheless, his style of radicalism now seemed mild compared with the new breed of radical orators such as Henry *Hunt. Thelwall lectured widely on elocution and on literary topics right up to the end of his life.   NR

THOMPSON, William (1775–1833), socialist and feminist writer, a key intellectual influence on British *Owenism, on *trade union and labour economics, and on early-nineteenth-century thinking about the rights of *women [4].

Born into a wealthy landowning and merchant Protestant family in Cork, Thompson's early life typified the late-eighteenth-century *philanthropist and philosopher. Strongly influenced by *Rousseauian and early *French revolutionary principles, he was an active member of the Cork Literary and Philosophical Society and undertook experiments to improve the farming techniques, habitations, social life, and *education [17] of his tenantry [see *literary and philosophical societies]. Interest in Benthamite educational principles and a lengthy stay with *Bentham also generated intellectual and personal connections with Robert Owen and Anna *Wheeler, Thompson's future collaborator in feminist writing.

In addition to his pioneering contributions to feminism, most notably in *Appeal of One-Half the Human Race* (1825), Thompson spent much of the remainder of his life in Ireland applying and extending Owen's insights. In three works, *An Inquiry into the Distribution of Wealth Most Conducive to Human Happiness* (1824), *Labour Rewarded: The Claims of Labour and Capital Conciliated* (1827), and *Practical Directions for the Speedy and Economical Establishment of Communities* (1830), he significantly advanced contemporary socialist theory. While extending David *Ricardo's ideas on the value of labour in wealth, he advocated Owenite principles of economic and social co-operation in communities and labour exchanges, yet he untypically retained some belief in competitive incentives. Unlike Owen, too, he advocated the need for wedding economic to political reform; he proposed a system of communal-based and elected legislatures, a model which exercised enduring influence on trade union syndicalist thought and practice.   IMcC

THOMSON, George (1757–1851), song-collector who produced numerous volumes of Scottish, Welsh, and Irish songs between 1793 and 1846, an important part of both the *Irish and *Welsh cultural revivals. These volumes were unusual because they contained British folk melodies with new musical arrangements by European composers (including *Haydn and *Beethoven), thus embodying a marriage of two distinct musical cultures and languages.

Raised in Banff, the son of a schoolmaster, Thomson worked in Edinburgh as the Clerk to the Board of Trustees for the Encouragement of Arts and Manufactures in Scotland from 1780 until 1839. He successfully used his official connections with the diplomatic service and banking circles for his private *music publishing venture. During the 1780s he attended the concerts of the Edinburgh Musical Society, and was inspired by the new music of Europe and by renditions of Scots songs by visiting Italian singers. He decided to produce large, sophisticated volumes, and concentrated closely on the quality of both *music [26] and *poetry [29]. Famous composers were joined by many literary contributors, including Robert *Burns, Walter *Scott, and Joanna *Baillie. The musical arrangements for piano, voice, violin (or flute), and violoncello, were intended both for the home and the concert hall. Thomson's work was a precedent for similar ventures, most notably Thomas *Moore's *Irish Melodies*. KMcC

THRALE, Hester Lynch, see Hester Thrale *Piozzi.

TIGHE, Mary (Blachford) (1772–1810), Anglo-Irish poet, best known for *Psyche, or, The Legend of Love* (1805). Her father, William Blachford, was a wealthy *Anglican clergyman and librarian; her mother was a Tighe, from a Wicklow landed family. In 1793 Mary was married to a maternal cousin, Henry Tighe, MP for Wicklow from 1790 until the dissolution of the Irish Parliament in 1801. The marriage was apparently unhappy, and remained childless.

Tighe's career as a published poet began in 1805, with *Psyche, or, The Legend of Love*, a narrative poem in five cantos of *Spenserian stanzas, published in London, where she had moved to live apart from her husband. Her hospitality and minor repute as a fine poetic sensibility attracted the acquaintance of Thomas *Moore, like herself an Irish expatriate come to the metropolitan literary world. In 1811, the year after her death in Dublin, *Psyche . . . and Other Poems* was published by Longman, together with *Elegy to the Duke of Bedford*, by Amelia *Opie. The 1811 edition was read and admired by John *Keats while he was writing *Endymion*, and in 1812, when Percy *Shelley visited Dublin, *Psyche* was still the talk of the literary world.

Tighe's 1805 preface to *Psyche* takes pains to discriminate between the classical sources of her legend and its vulgar modern accretions and, under the rubrics of taste, sentiment, and edification, to bowdlerize Apuleius' erotic tale. She spins a wavering line between juvenile *romance and adult fantasy. The plot is circular, beginning and ending with an unconsummated marriage between the timid supplicant Psyche and the elusive Cupid figure. Psyche endures ordeals at the hands of her harsh mother-in-law Venus, and repels a satanic rapist in Canto III. Amid Tighe's borrowings from the stories of Proserpine, Arethusa, and Psyche, glimmers the Irish family romance: an abandoned mother, defaulting father, and obsessively overvalued son. Tighe skirts the puritan intensities of *Milton's *Comus*, mingling elements of the contemporary courtship novel with Milton's allegory of the Protestant soul as feminine aspect. JB

toleration in our period related primarily to the power of states through their own religious establishments to control the terms upon which other religions were tolerated. Confessional states of this kind were the norm in Europe. They claimed the right to control the religious adherence of their subjects, on the ground that there was a direct relationship between *religion [10] and good citizenship. Such beliefs and practices came under attack from *Enlightenment [32] thought and *French revolutionary action. States were to lose their power to dictate the terms upon which Dissenting religions were tolerated or not, and the era permanently altered the basis on which religious establishments functioned. In England the process would occur in a rather uneven way. First it would affect Old Protestant Dissenters, then Roman Catholics, ending eventually with both gaining full citizenship. But along the way basic questions concerning religious liberty and the liberty of thought would be raised in relation to *Methodists, *Deists, and eventually *Jews.

At the outset of this period Protestant Dissenters were very clearly second-class citizens. The Toleration Act of 1689 repealed no statutes, merely exempting Protestant Dissenters from the penalties of existing legislation. Dissent itself actually remained a crime until the Mansfield verdict of 1767, which ruled that the Toleration Act gave Dissenters not merely exemption from hostile legislation but also public protection for their Dissent. Chief Justice *Mansfield's opinion that persecution was 'against Natural Religion, Revealed Religion, and sound Policy' articulated ideas of toleration which would be increasingly accepted in this period. Encouraged by the confirmation of their status, Dissenters sought to gain relief from subscription to the thirty-nine articles of the Church of England for their ministers, schoolmasters, and tutors. Defeats in 1772 and 1773 were followed by success in 1779, when they were required only to declare that the Scriptures 'do contain the revealed will of God'.

It was typical of the eighteenth-century state to be more tolerant in practice than in theory, but some Dissenters, Richard *Price among them, sought a more complete freedom. Enthused in part by the spread of enlightened ideas concerning toleration in Europe and America, they resolved to apply for the repeal of the Test (1673) and Corporation Acts (1661). This legislation had been intended to exclude Dissenters from influence in local and central government, including military positions, by insisting on their taking the sacrament of the Church of England. Since then the legislation had been modified in detail, and Indemnity Acts were passed from 1727 on, annually from the mid-century, to protect Dissenters from the full impact of the law.

Despite vigorous campaigning, the Dissenters were defeated in 1787, 1789, and 1790 in their applications to the House of Commons for repeal. It remained one of their strongest grievances in this period, not least because the Irish Test Act had been repealed in 1779. Their Scottish compatriots were also unsuccessful in their application to parliament for relief from the Test Act in 1791. In the following year, the defeat of the petition for relief for *Unitarians ended attempts to extend the toleration available to Dissenters for two decades. During the turbulent years of the 1790s Dissenters, especially Rational Dissenters, were suspected not only of challenging the church establishment but also of seditious political ideas, and so suffered disproportionately from *loyalist persecution. In the longer term, they demonstrated their loyalty and sobriety. Their campaigns had, moreover, enjoyed the support of an influential group of MPs, mainly Foxite *Whigs, who would eventually carry the day in parliament. In 1828 the Test and Corporation Acts were finally repealed.

The English Catholic community had suffered more than Protestant Dissenters from persecution in the eighteenth century. Anti-Catholicism was a defining characteristic of the British state and society. It was a naturally prominent feature of politics in the first half of the century when the very real threat of Jacobitism was associated with the attempt to impose Catholicism on the nation. Anti-Catholicism began to lose its mythic centrality once this threat was perceived to have abated in the 1760s, and when enlightened ideas of toleration were of growing importance in élite circles. There began the slow and uncomfortable process by which the state rid itself of its anti-Catholic nature. The *Gordon riots occurred at the beginning of this process, and reflect popular resistance to the abandonment of this well-worn and comforting shibboleth. The riots failed to the extent that they did not in England frighten politicians into repealing the Catholic Relief Act (1788), though it was abandoned in Scotland. By the 1790s the threat posed by the French Revolution weakened popular prejudice against Roman Catholics. The traditional French enemy was now no longer identified with Catholicism, and considerable efforts were being made to help émigré priests exiled in Britain.

Of more concern to the government in the revolutionary years were the traditionally radical sympathies of Dissent. The suspicion of Nonconformism was reinforced by the development of Methodism into a Dissenting sect following John *Wesley's death in 1791. The Methodist practice of *field preaching in particular alarmed the establishment, but government attempts to introduce legislation against itinerant preachers were fought off in 1811. The result was the new Toleration Act of 1812. The price that the Methodists paid for firmly establishing their credentials as a powerful group within Dissent was a new emphasis upon their own social respectability and political loyalty. The 1812 Act was followed by the Unitarian Toleration Act of 1813 which legalized Unitarian worship. These two acts tolled the knell of the confessional state, but the extent of the new toleration was still to be worked out. It would soon become clear that freedom of worship did not amount to freedom of thought.

102. In John Flaxman's sculpture of Mary Tighe, completed in 1815 and erected at the Tighe Mausoleum at Inistioge in Ireland, the personification of her famous poem 'Psyche' kneels behind her head.

The initial draft of the Unitarian Toleration Act positively endorsed the right for free expression of opinion on all matters concerning religion, but this draft was dropped in favour of an act which simply repealed the English Blasphemy Act of 1697 and two Scottish Blasphemy Acts. The government was determined to protect the perceived religious foundations of the state against the more outspoken freethinkers. Lord Sidmouth (1757–1844) encouraged local magistrates to take action against both seditious and blasphemous literature. Fears were inflamed by the boldness both of Unitarian propagandists and of irreverent radical works. The popular radical freethinker Richard *Carlile was imprisoned for blasphemy in 1819. In retrospect, the determination to link freethinking and blasphemy with sedition appears paranoid, but given the underlying assumption of the relationship between religion and good citizenship it hardly needs explaining. Moreover, there was ample evidence to fortify such views. Some seventy-five prosecutions for blasphemous and seditious libels were initiated during the reform agitation of 1819 and the pressure was kept up on radical publicists in the following years, but the government ultimately failed to suppress heretical publications. If Carlile exaggerated his achievement in defence of toleration, it remains true that the government never again tried such systematic and ruthless suppression of opinion. The episode in its conclusion represents a move towards a pluralist state.

A much greater step in that direction occurred with *Catholic emancipation. Emancipation was eventually granted in 1829 for pragmatic political reasons, and because of a growing feeling that the requirements of citizenship, of allegiance to the state, should be secular. Those who argued against emancipation on religious grounds were undermined therefore not only by the conviction of those like George *Canning that the question was 'a practical political question', but also by many who accepted that religion was a moralizing force which worked best independently of the state. The basis of an argument for rejecting any sort of religious test for citizenship on pragmatic, utilitarian, and religious grounds had been laid many years earlier by Joseph *Priestley. In the debate in 1828 on the repeal of the Test and Corporation Acts, Lord John *Russell presented a version of Priestley's views. Religion and politics should be separated, he argued, as religion was a divisive element in politics and political interference in religious freedom was profane. Russell was laying the groundwork for Roman Catholic emancipation. Indeed, the Catholic grievances and their disruptive political effects supported his argument. Religious resentment at *Anglican supremacy had played a major role in the Irish *Rebellion of 1798. The failure to grant emancipation at the time of the *Act of Union meant that religion remained at the forefront of politics in the new United Kingdom.

Yet if that gave politicians cause for wanting the issue to be resolved, it could not be resolved without at the same time recognizing a growing conviction that Catholicism was compatible with good citizenship. The best indication of that came through the co-operation of the hierarchy of the Catholic church with the government. Since about 1810 the British government had been allowed an informal veto on appointments to the Catholic episcopate in the United Kingdom, and in 1815 Pope Pius VII, restored to Rome by the Duke of *Wellington, had assured the government that the clergy would not interfere in politics and confirmed a limited veto on appointments. In 1817 commissions and chaplaincies in the British *army and *navy were opened to Catholics, thus extending the relevant provisions of the Irish Relief Act of 1793 to Britain. Emancipation was once more on the political agenda, and had a strong measure of support in the House of Commons. After several emancipation bills had failed, Daniel *O'Connell's election to parliament in October 1828 finally convinced sufficient numbers of the die-hard opponents of emancipation, including the King, that principle had to give way to political expediency. Emancipation passed speedily through parliament in the spring of 1829. Anti-Catholicism remained a powerful force in British culture, but no longer a dangerous one, as it had been in 1780.

The extension of toleration was, however, not a smooth process. Political expediency played a major part in legislative changes, but the notion of what was expedient also changed. Benthamite utilitarianism fortified the trend in Enlightenment thought which separated matters concerning the church and the state and regarded persecution as useless as well as wrong. By 1830 the Test and Corporation Acts had been repealed and the Roman Catholics emancipated. Both Dissenters and Catholics could, in principle, therefore take a full role in politics and government. On mainland Britain, *Evangelical forms of religion appealed strongly to the lower and middle ranks of a society undergoing rapid *industrialization [14]. This meant that in England the Church of England's status as the religion of the majority was in jeopardy by the 1830s; in Scotland a third of the Protestants in the Lowlands were adherents of Dissenting churches, and the number was growing. Irish immigration also increased the Catholic presence, creating overall a picture of growing religious pluralism.

Though Britain as a whole might have become more Christian in this period, the consequence of the loss of authority of the established churches inevitably led to important developments in the secularization of the state. Nevertheless the Anglican Church would only slowly give way to pressure on most issues, and it did not relinquish its privileged position within the state, symbolized by the representation of the episcopate in the House of Lords and its pre-eminence on state occasions. It also retained immense social cachet. Those who did not belong to it remained 'Nonconformists'. Christianity would still be protected by laws against blasphemy. Non-Christian religions and atheists still had to fight the battle for legal toleration. And, while it is true that nothing as serious as the Gordon riots happened again, the transition to a secular state tolerant of all manner of beliefs did not happen. The British still saw themselves as a Christian nation, one which did not entirely embrace tolerance for those who were heterodox, non-Christian, or atheists.   MF

TONE, Theobald Wolfe (1763–98), revolutionary. Recognized as 'the father of Irish Republicanism', Tone founded the Society of United Irishmen in 1791 and induced the French Directory to make several attempts to invade Ireland between 1796 and 1798 to effect the country's full independence from Britain [see *invasions].

Although called to the Irish Bar in 1789, Tone had little interest in his chosen profession. Exposure to the political debates of the late 1780s, however, inspired him. His anti-government pamphlet *A Review of the Conduct of Administration Addressed to the Electors and Free People of Ireland* (1790) was well received by the Whig Club, and he joined the *Whigs in the circle of Henry Grattan's (1746–1820) Protestant 'patriot party', which favoured *parliamentary reform. Sir Lawrence Parsons (1758–1841), MP, convinced Tone at this time that British interference in Irish affairs was the root cause of many of the country's social ills, and his progression towards separatism and republicanism continued with a pamphlet which argued that Ireland should remain neutral if war broke out with Spain in 1790.

In the winter of 1790–1 Tone founded a political club in Dublin which attracted future radical thinkers, while his close collaborator, Thomas Russell (1767–1803), forged links with the patriotic *volunteer movement in Belfast. Lacking focus, Tone's society soon lapsed, but he elaborated his ideal under the influence of Thomas *Paine's *Rights of Man* in February 1791 and his own experience drafting resolutions for a meeting of the Belfast volunteers to commemorate the *French Revolution. Tone came to believe that it was necessary 'to break the connection with England, the never-failing source of all our political evils' by 'substituting the common name of Irishman, in place of the denominations of Protestant, Catholic, and Dissenter'.

To convince Presbyterian radicals in the north of Ireland that true reform must include political rights for Catholics, Tone wrote *An Argument on Behalf of the Catholics of Ireland* (1791), which resulted in the founding of the multi-denominational Society of United Irishmen in Belfast in October 1791 [see *United societies]. A Dublin club was founded the following month to debate and propagate Tone's ideas which soon contained most of the society's leading activists. The outbreak of war with France in February 1793 saw him contacted in April 1794 by an Irish-born agent of the Directory, Revd William Jackson (c.1736–95), to discuss a French invasion of Ireland in support of the United Irishmen. Jackson's arrest on 28 April implicated Tone in high treason and led to the suppression of the society. When it reorganized in mid-1795 it was a secret, oath-bound republican movement seeking foreign aid to overthrow the government. Tone was informed of this prior to leaving in June 1795 for Philadelphia where he was permitted to exile himself. Upon arrival he established contact with the French representative in Philadelphia and petitioned for military aid.

On 1 January 1796 he sailed for France to press the Directory to assist a rebellion in Ireland and conferred with Carnot on 24 February. He and other lesser United Irish agents persuaded the French to make four invasion attempts—in December 1796, July 1797, August 1798, and October 1798. Bad weather, ill luck, and British naval strength hampered each attempt, and Tone was captured during the last effort on 12 October. Sentenced to death for high treason, he attempted suicide on 11 November 1798 in protest at being ordered hanged rather than shot as soldier, and he died of his wound eight days later.   RO'D

TOOKE, John Horne (1736–1812), radical pamphleteer, political organizer, and philologist. The longevity of Tooke's career provided an important link between different generations of radicalism, while his gregarious nature enabled him to build contacts between radicals of different political opinions and varying social backgrounds. His importance as a broker of radical ideas can scarcely be overestimated.

Horne Tooke was born in Westminster to John Horne, a wealthy poulterer (he added the name Tooke in 1782 at the request of a patron, William Tooke). Educated at Westminster and Eton before going to Cambridge, he was ordained a priest in 1760 and took over the living at New Brentford, a decision he was later to regret. Tooke's clerical career was anyway little more than nominal, since he was something of a libertine.

During a tour of France as a tutor in 1765, he met and befriended John *Wilkes, then an outlaw for his attacks on George III in *The North Briton*. When the controversy over the Middlesex election broke out in 1768, Horne Tooke became his friend's staunchest public advocate. With Horne Tooke originated the idea of a Society of the Supporters of the Bill of Rights in 1769 to support Wilkes financially and to 'maintain and defend the legal, constitutional liberty of the subjects'. Much of the programme drawn up by the Society in 1771—including annual parliaments, 'full and equal' representation, and the elimination of placemen and pensioners from parliament—became fundamental to the radical reform movements of subsequent decades.

Horne Tooke's commitment was to reform rather than to Wilkes personally. When the latter showed no qualms about spending the Society's money, Tooke opposed him publicly and established a rival Constitutional Society (1771). The Wilkes controversy waned, but Horne Tooke soon became involved in the agitation surrounding the *American Revolution, arguing that the struggle in America had direct consequences for liberties in England. The Constitutional Society undertook to raise money for 'our beloved American fellow subjects' so 'inhumanly murdered' at Lexington in 1775. An advertisement for the fund published in the *newspapers brought about Tooke's arrest and conviction for libel in 1777. From the King's Bench prison he published *A Letter to Dunning* which, in the process of offering a defence against the charge of libel over the meaning of the word 'that', put the basic argument of the later and much more substantial *Diversions of Purley* (vol. I, 1786, rev. edn. 1798, vol. II, 1805). Widely admired, especially by radicals such as *Cobbett and *Hazlitt, Tooke's book advanced a materialist theory of the origins of *language [40] against the tradition which understood the parts of speech to be 'the genuine perceptions of pure mind'.

On his release from the King's Bench, Horne Tooke played a leading part in the agitation which followed the American War, forming important alliances with a number of important fellow radicals. He joined the *Society of Constitutional Information and subscribed to the idea, like Major *Cartwright, another SCI member, that England was blessed with an ancient Anglo-Saxon constitution (an idea which also underpinned his account of the history of the language). In 1780 he joined with Richard *Price in publishing details of the places and pensions which were essential to the Crown's management of politics. He also shared the proposals for economic reform put forward by *Burke and *Pitt.

Paradoxically, given similarities of temperament and even politics, one constant of Tooke's political positioning was a suspicion of *Fox's claims to be 'the man of the people'. He stood against Fox at the Westminster *elections of 1790 and 1796 and continued to prefer Pitt's over Fox's claims to be a reformer. Tooke's platform was one which denounced both *Whigs and *Tories for supposing that they alone had a right to office by virtue of rank and tradition regardless of the wishes of the people. The success of Sir Francis *Burdett and Lord *Cochrane in the 1807 Westminster election were the fruits of Horne Tooke's early efforts.

What was potentially more difficult for Horne Tooke and his like was squaring the older traditions of radicalism dating back to the Wilkes controversy and before with the ideas set in play by the *French Revolution. He distinguished himself from Thomas *Paine's *republican followers with the often-quoted remark that he would accompany them for part of their journey, but where they would go on to Windsor, he would get out at Hounslow. He saw himself as a *constitutionalist, opposed to universal suffrage, and no republican. In spite of his personal opinions however, he greatly facilitated the development of a popular radical movement in the 1790s. He supported the dissemination of Part II of Paine's *Rights of Man*, helped John *Thelwall develop his political career, and built contacts between the SCI and the more proletarian *corresponding societies. It was in the light of these activities that the *Quarterly Review* could look down on him as 'the principal ornament and support of the English Jacobins' in 1812.

It was an opinion shared by the government in the 1790s and, in consequence, he found himself in the dock at the *Treason Trials of 1794. The government tried to connect him with the popular politics of the corresponding societies, a strategy which Horne Tooke brilliantly parried by calling Pitt himself as a witness to attest that they had been members of the same reform associations in the 1780s. Nevertheless, the period of imprisonment in the Tower awaiting trial adversely affected Tooke's health, and in 1795 he announced his retirement from radical politics. The contradictions of his career are typified by the fact he stood again for parliament the very next year, and in fact remained influential in radical circles until his death.

Ironically, when Horne Tooke did finally enter parliament briefly in 1801 it was as an MP for the rotten borough of Old Sarum, which was under the control of his disciple Thomas Pitt, but he found himself frustrated by the government bringing in a bill declaring that clergymen were ineligible to sit in parliament. Thereafter he spent his years in retirement at Wimbledon, but partly through the influence of his weekly dinners never actually ceased his involvement in political affairs. The social gatherings there helped launch the careers of such key radicals for the next generation as Henry *Hunt and kept alive a radical intellectual climate during the dark days of the Napoleonic wars.   JM

Toryism was originally an opposition ideology espoused by Jacobites who questioned the legitimacy of the Hanoverian succession established with the *Glorious Revolution of 1688, and by 'Country party' figures who abhorred the putative growth of oligarchy under the first two Georges. Following the accession of the young George III in 1760, Tories reconciled themselves to the ruling house by expanding the aura of divinity with which they had previously endowed the Stuarts to embrace the prevailing political and social order.

Although the younger William *Pitt's supporters did not describe themselves as Tories until well into the nineteenth century, his first administration launched an ethos of efficient, supposedly national, non-sectional administration which was to become the watchword of early-nineteenth-century Tory governments. The 1820s witnessed growing tension between orthodox and more *liberal Tories. Moreover, accusations of neglect of traditional aristocratic responsibilities towards the poor in the early 1830s—focused on attempts to protect adult female and juvenile workers through legislative measures and on the reform of the *poor law—produced a variety of radical Toryism which divorced Tory values from the traditional structure of social and political power. Aspects of radical Toryism may be discerned in the postwar career of William *Cobbett, but the label is more usually applied to Richard Oastler (1789–1861). Despite these tensions, the parliamentary party thrived under the leadership of Sir Robert *Peel in the latter part of the 1830s; after the issue of the *Tamworth Manifesto* in 1834 espousing gradualist change the party was increasingly referred to as the 'Conservative party'. Having come into office in 1841 with a large majority the party was damaged irreparably by Peel's decision in 1845 to repeal the *corn laws.

After 1832 Peel cemented the attachment between the Tory Party and the commercial classes which had begun under Pitt. However, while Toryism and its successor were not the exclusive preserve of the landed classes, its frame of mind and many of its tenets drew upon values associated with the gentry. Tories staunchly defended property rights and endorsed the widely held belief that viable social orders were hierarchically structured. However, many Tories buttressed these claims by appeals to divine authority, stressed the social and political importance of the Church of England, and evoked bucolic images of deference and paternalism. Hierarchy was thought a 'natural' pattern of social organization, ordained by divine Providence and warranted both by the Scriptures and history. Although natural, hierarchy was not a spontaneous product of enlightened self-interest or of the workings of an automatic system of penalties and rewards. Orthodox Tories stressed the positive role of government, and upheld the traditional Protestant *constitution in church and state because of its capacity to harness the coercive and paternalistic energies of the country. They believed the primary role of government and of traditional élites was to moderate avoidable hardships leading to destabilizing and destructive popular outbursts, and to maintain order through coercion where this became necessary.

The Tory social vision, exemplified in its most extreme form by paternalists such as Henry *Drummond and Lord *Eldon, rested firmly on the principle of social hierarchy. Deference and élite responsibility at the local level restricted membership of the political nation to those whose position in the ecclesiastical and social hierarchy pointed to a capacity both to nurture and to control the population. Unlike 'grand' *Whigs, who regarded the aristocracy as the dominant partner in a relationship which gave some role to the forces of mass opinion, Tories favoured a passive population. During the 1790s the unease engendered by British responses to the *French Revolution produced a bifurcation within the political élite. The Whig grandees, whose instincts and intellectual interests were informed by *Enlightenment [32] ideas and who were proponents of civil and religious liberty, moved into more or less permanent opposition. Tories began to present themselves as the defenders of the traditional constitution. For the first three decades of the new century they resisted not only radical reform but also modest attempts to purge the electoral system of abuses and to consolidate the exclusively *Anglican character of the English state. They therefore opposed the repeal of the Test and Corporation Acts [see *toleration] and *Catholic emancipation when these issues became important in the late 1820s; they also resisted pressure for *parliamentary reform in the early 1830s. Tory attitudes can be illustrated by their response to Edmund *Burke's later writings: they admired his account of the traditional constitution but had reservations concerning his sympathy towards the aspirations of Irish Catholics.

After the onset of the French Revolution, Tory sentiments formed the staple of an important body of periodical literature. The cause was promoted, and its enemies were vilified, in the *Anti-Jacobin Review; the Quarterly Review (launched as an ideologically sound alternative to the Whiggish Edinburgh Review), and Blackwood's Edinburgh Magazine. In their later years both *Southey (a mainstay of the Quarterly) and *Wordsworth espoused Tory constitutional doctrines and resisted the insidious growth of political radicalism; so too did *Coleridge, but his position was more subtle and qualified. Walter *Scott's writings are also pervaded by robust Tory sentiments. A more subtle portrayal of the personal, domestic, and social implications of Tory values can be discerned in Jane *Austen's novels.   JMO

tourism, domestic, a cultural practice of visiting estates and *picturesque sites, as well as a set of genres including travel journals, guidebooks, treatises, and estate poems. Domestic tourism arose within the burgeoning heritage industry that marked the rise of British nationalism from the late eighteenth century. As a sociable practice, set of discursive genres, and form of *advertising, it marketed views and private property as both a national asset and a new commodity of consumer culture [see *viewing, 20 and *consumerism, 19].

Country-house tours enjoyed their greatest vogue in the first quarter of the nineteenth century, particularly during the French wars, when much of the Continent was closed off to travellers on the *Grand Tour. The rise in tourism can be attributed to increasing social mobility amongst the middle classes, as well as improvements in *transport. It was a direct consequence of changes in property relations and landownership which resulted from *enclosure. The greatest period of domestic tourism coincides with the greatest number of enclosure acts, which peaked in the war years, 1793 to 1815.

The genre of the country-house guidebook was initiated in England during the first half of the eighteenth century, with a number of guides to the gardens at Stowe in Buckinghamshire, and to Blenheim Palace and Chatsworth in Derbyshire. Horace *Walpole's 1774 Description of Strawberry Hill is probably the most famous example of the genre, which was characterized by a study of the genealogy of the family, a description of the gardens, then of the house, and a room-by-room account of the pictures. All of these generic features are incorporated in the country-house novel, arguably initiated by Jane *Austen in Pride and Prejudice (1811) and Mansfield Park (1814). Austen's country-house novels share the ideological strategies of domestic tourism which reinforce social hierarchy within a framework of limited social mobility by identifying private property as a national asset.

The writings of William *Gilpin, such as Forest Scenery (1790), Picturesque Remarks on the Western Parts of England and the Isle of Wight (1798), and Tours of the Highlands (1789) linked earlier eighteenth-century traditions of literary travel writing with later tourism and the theory of the picturesque (although the *sublime was also an important category for the experience of domestic tourism). William Hutchinson's Guide to the Lakes (1774, with ten editions by 1812) established the English Lake District as a prime tourist site. This was followed by Gilpin's tour of the Lakes (1789); by Ann *Radcliffe's *Journey Through Holland in 1794* (1795), which details a trip to Europe curtailed by the war and offers the Lake District as a second choice, 'faintly rivalling' the lakes of Geneva; and by *Wordsworth's *Guide to the Lakes* (1810). Wales and the Scottish Highlands also became popular destinations, reflecting the growing interest in *antiquarianism [35] and the rediscovery of regional cultural traditions.

The numbers of guidebooks declined in the 1820s, and the practice of country-house touring died out in the Victorian period as private houses began to be closed to the public.   CT

trade unions. Our period saw both an unprecedented growth and challenge to the existence of British trade unions, as well as their evolution to embrace new theoretical aspirations and institutional structures.

By 1776 trade unions were already a recognized institutional presence in British life. Writing in his *Wealth of Nations* of that year, Adam *Smith took both them and employer combinations for granted. Craft unions based mainly in the old skilled artisanal trades, such as weaving, shoemaking, and tailoring, were the most explicit institutional form of union, and by the mid-eighteenth century these were already working to defend and sometimes improve conditions of work and pay, and to maintain the well-being of members during strikes or illness. Historians estimate that by 1800 at least fifty such unions were in existence and some, like the London tailors, were—according to one-time member Francis *Place—'a perfect and perpetual combination'. Nevertheless the form and function of the trade union was in some ways still inchoate in the late eighteenth century, deriving in part from traditional forms of sociability such as box and benefit clubs and *friendly societies. Unions were often also transient and informal, depending for information and membership on itinerant artisans who undertook regular annual tramps in search of work. The selectively violent actions of *riots in towns and cities, the machine breaking of northern *Luddites, and the more systematic collective violence of secret agrarian societies in Ireland can all be seen as practising a form of incipient trade unionism. Employers often threatened, and more rarely undertook, prosecutions against unions as common law conspiracies.

The conservative reaction to the *French Revolution, however, brought mounting fears that trade unions were becoming implicated in democratic politics [see *democracy, 3]. The Combination Acts of 1799 and 1800, as part of the government's repertoire of *gagging acts, prohibited all forms of collective action and association in defence of common interests. These were followed in 1814 by a further serious erosion of the traditional rights and existence of skilled craftsmen when the clause of the Statute of Artificers of 1560, which required seven-year trade apprenticeships, was repealed. This, coupled with the growth in the use of sweated outworkers during the French *wars [2] and the explosion of unskilled

labour produced by the demobbing of soldiers and sailors in 1815, led to a series of bitter labour struggles involving shoemakers in London, mulespinners, shearmen, and croppers in Yorkshire, and frame-knitters in the east midlands.

By the mid-1820s improvements in trade conditions and the spread of *laissez-faire* economic principles instituted a new and dramatic change in the fortunes of British trade unions. In 1824 Francis Place, with the help of the Ricardian political economist John McCulloch (1789–1864) and radical parliamentarian Joseph Hume (1777–1855), skilfully orchestrated the repeal of the Combination Acts on the grounds that combinations of all kinds would wither away in a free labour market. Although a fightback from employers saw this legislation tightened again in the following year, trade unions were now legally entitled to combine and bargain over wages and hours, but were still subject to severe restrictions on picketing, conspiracy, and intimidation. In 1824–5 this liberalization, combined with a brief trade boom, led to a proliferation of both old craft and newly industrialized unions. However, numbers again declined during the remainder of the decade, when worsened economic conditions and a series of failed strike attempts exposed continuing legal and organizational fragilities [see *industrialization, 14].

The year 1834 highlighted the contradictory losses and gains in trade union strength and confidence since the eighteenth century. With the encouragement of Robert *Owen, the Grand National Consolidated Trades Union was formed in London. Though short-lived, this constituted an impressive national general organization covering more than twenty trades and attracting 16,000 members, a dramatic expression of new-found *class [15] pride and theoretical sophistication on the part of organized labour. However, 1834 also saw a harmless group of agricultural workers in Dorset, the Tolpuddle Martyrs, being successfully prosecuted under an obscure act against oath-taking and sentenced to fourteen years' transportation. Here was dramatic indication of the continuing fragility of trade unionism within British political life.   IMcC

transatlantic radicalism. Between Britain and America in this era there existed a genuine reciprocity of radical ideas based on a common ideological inheritance and a common political language. Allowing for individual interpretations and emphases, there were two broad radical traditions in the Anglo-American world. The first, which appealed most strongly to both societies' middle groups—*lawyers, merchants, heterodox intellectuals, and clergymen—was the Commonwealth tradition encompassing the writings of John *Locke, Algernon Sydney, Trenchard, Gordon, and their successors. The other, which matured more swiftly in America than in Britain in the years from 1766 to 1780, was the small producer tradition. Appealing to the middling classes—artisans, mechanics, shopkeepers, and journeymen—this stream of radicalism had its roots in the sectarianism of the *Quakers and the Leveller movement of the mid-seventeenth century.

In the years of the *American Revolution these traditions had enough in common for their adherents to act in concert in support of political reform and the protection of 'English' liberties. American patriots received the ideas of the Commonwealthmen from Britain, where they were circulating amongst a new, if small, generation of radicals who looked with suspicion and apprehension on the activities of the King and his ministers, who they thought were attempting—by undermining parliamentary independence, manipulating the financial system, and systematically attacking British liberties—to establish a new despotism. Fuelled by the Commonwealth belief that only a virtuous, self-denying, and independent citizenry could prevent the misuse of state power, British radicals feared that political corruption had undermined the constitutional gains achieved by the *Glorious Revolution.

The peak phase of Anglo-American radicalism began in the wake of the *French Revolution in about 1792 and lasted for the next decade. It was characterized by the emergence of popular radicalism in Britain, with its strong Paineite and small-producer influences, and by a significant British impact on the Jeffersonian party in America. Although only a handful of Americans participated in the radical movement in Britain, where they had but marginal influence in promoting republican values, the impact of Paine's *Rights of Man* (1791), especially Part the First, which was heavily reliant for its arguments on his understanding of American *republicanism, was undoubtedly profound. Of perhaps equal importance were the practical lessons which popular radicals in Britain, learned from the past activities of their American counterparts. *Corresponding societies, by which British radicals organized themselves throughout the country to create a powerful network of opposition, were an American innovation. So too was the potentially revolutionary idea of a convention, which Scottish and English radicals unsuccessfully employed as a way of maximizing external pressure on parliament.

In the reverse direction, the United States became an asylum for hundreds of British and Irish radicals, including many middle-class *Unitarians who had been involved in the radical movement in its earlier phase and who still adhered to the Commonwealth tradition. Many others were journalists and printers inspired by Paine and small-producer radicalism. Arriving in the United States in the 1790s, their expectations of a democratic, egalitarian, and republican society were swiftly confounded when they analysed Federalist policies. Jumping wholeheartedly into the political fray, their newspapers and pamphlets were the main conduits by which Jeffersonian republican policies reached a mass constituency. Radical exiles were particularly prominent in helping the Republicans adjust their political principles to the new circumstances of the 1790s. The key to their usefulness was their recognition that Federalist policies in America had close affinities with the policies of William *Pitt, from which they had recently escaped. Faced in America with the menace of excessive governmental power, of a financial system supported by the state, and of a corrupt officialdom, the exiled radicals responded with the same mix of political arguments they had used in Britain, infusing them into the Jeffersonian party.

Aiming its message primarily at urban mechanics, small masters, and shopkeepers, exiled radical activists promoted 'participatory democracy', an intermediate position between direct democracy, which was felt to be unworkable in a large republic, and representative democracy, which the radicals believed in its current form had reduced the influence of the people and allowed a 'natural' aristocracy to assume power. Influenced by their experiences in the popular societies in Britain, swayed also by the anti-Federalist arguments of 1788, in the name of the 'Spirit of '76' the exiles attempted to revive the small-producer radicalism of the 1770s. Committed to a democratic republicanism in which everyone was actively involved in politics, they added a radical wing to the Jeffersonian coalition, suggesting the need for constitutional revision, questioning the utility of the Senate, the mode of appointment to and tenure of the judiciary, and the powers of the President. However, though useful while the Federalists were powerful opponents, they were regarded as a nuisance when Republican policy aimed at conciliating the moderate Federalists. By the War of 1812 the radical vision of small-producer democracy in America had been defeated. Excluded from the Republican party's councils, the radicals were reduced to a rump.

Another generation of radicals, still believing the United States to be both asylum and elysium, were to exile themselves in the years after 1815, bringing with them communitarian *socialist ideas as well as further instalments of a Paineite version of small-producer radicalism, but they were not to have the influence of their predecessors. Fewer in number than in the 1790s, they nevertheless were amongst the leaders of the working men's political movement and involved in the resurgence of communitarianism in America, introducing a secular *millenarian strain to coexist with the indigenous religious millennial communities.   MDU

transport. The period between the middle of the eighteenth century and the early years of the nineteenth saw the beginnings of the modern transport revolution, with major improvements to transport services, particularly in the provision of road services and the system of inland waterways. These improvements emerged out of the quickening pace of economic activity, which exposed the inadequacy and high cost of transport provision, particularly away from good natural harbours. *Population expansion, together with increased migration and personal mobility, all associated with economic growth, similarly increased the demand for transport. The initiative for improvement and much of the necessary finance came from merchants, manufacturers, and landowners who had most to gain directly from improved transport services. While the most apparent aspect of this transport revolution lay in the technology of building and operating transport systems, it was accompanied by important organizational developments, particularly the growth of specialist operators both as private firms and joint stock companies.

By acts of 1555 and 1563 parishes were made liable for the maintenance of roads in their vicinity. However, this sometimes proved difficult to achieve, particularly in relation to main roads with significant amounts of through traffic. From 1618 a series of acts and proclamations attempted to control and limit road use, but this was unlikely to provide a long-term solution to demand pressures. The most important change occurred with the introduction of turnpike trusts, whereby responsibility for organizing the upkeep of the road was transferred to a group of trustees, and the cost to its users. The trusts consisted largely of local entrepreneurs, who had a strong vested interest in maintaining the quality of the roads. The first turnpike trust was established by act of parliament in 1663. However, after a slow start, the number of turnpikes increased rapidly with the economic expansion of the 1750s and 1760s, when around three-quarters of trust mileage was established. Further booms occurred during the French *wars [2] in the early 1790s and 1809–12, and then again in the mid-1820s. In the first of these booms turnpike trusts were established across many areas of Britain; in the second and third phases expansion was particularly linked with the port and dock activities of wartime; and in the final period the industrial expansion of Lancashire and Yorkshire provided a strong incentive. By the mid-1830s around 22,000 miles of roads had been turnpiked or entrusted to Improvement Commissioners, representing about one-fifth of all roads.

Accompanying these improved organizational arrangements were important developments in road-building and maintenance technology. Thomas *Telford and John *McAdam have been given much of the credit for the improved quality of roads from the later eighteenth century. Roads were strengthened by packing broken stones into them, and drainage was improved by developing convex surfaces. By 1829 concrete was also being used in roads. Many more tunnels and bridges were constructed in order to avoid steep gradients and long contours. The finance for road improvements was mostly provided by the private sector through toll revenues and loans on the security of future tolls, although there were occasional government grants, often for political or security reasons, such as £20,000 towards the improvement of the Great Irish Road in 1815.

These road improvements, together with enhanced coach designs and horse breeds, enabled higher speeds and longer continuous periods of travel, including overnight movements. Their major impact was upon passenger services. The number of passenger miles completed in England has been estimated to have increased very rapidly, from 183,000 in 1773 to 2,043,000 by 1816. Regular inter-city coach services expanded in the second half of the eighteenth century, particularly those linking London to the main regional centres. Between 1773

and 1796 the number of services operating from London grew fourfold. Specialist carriers, most notably Pickford's, emerged or expanded to provide such services. These included London to Manchester by 1754 and to Liverpool by 1757. By the end of the eighteenth century London was also connected to many smaller towns, although direct connections between provincial cities remained less common. The variety of services expanded, and included 'flying coaches' for rapid transit. Average travel times declined: the journey time from Edinburgh to London fell from ten to four days between 1754 and 1776 and that from London to Holyhead from forty-one to twenty-eight hours between 1815 and 1831. Although it remained relatively expensive to move anything but high-value goods over long distance land routes, freight transport also benefited from these efficiency improvements, which encouraged a substantial expansion in the number of services provided between the 1760s and the 1830s [see consumerism, 19].

As with roads, so with inland waterways: in the half century or so before 1750 various navigation improvements had been completed which generally modified existing rivers by cutting off winding bends or deepening shallow areas. However, from the second half of the eighteenth century there was heightened interest in the construction of manmade, deadwater navigations; that is, canals. The Sankey Brook Navigation, which was partly opened in 1757, connected the coalmines of St Helens with the river Mersey. The Bridgewater Canal, which was opened in 1761, joined the coalmines of the Duke of Bridgewater at Worsley with Manchester. These two canals are viewed as heralding the beginning of a period of intensive construction which lasted until the end of the French wars in 1815. In a similar fashion to the turnpike trusts, canal construction required the permission of a private act of parliament, and this provides us with a proxy for the intensity of waterway expansion. In the decade and a half from 1760 canal construction proceeded apace. This was then followed by a slowdown for about a decade, until expansion rose to a peak in the first half of the 1790s: between 1790 and 1796, 106 acts were passed sanctioning an expansion or improvement of the inland waterway system. There was a further flurry of activity between 1810 and 1815, after which the British canal network was all but completed. The major exception was the Manchester Ship Canal, which was finished in 1894. While the Bridgewater Canal was a short local canal, it was followed by longer trunk canals connecting different regions, including the Forth and Clyde Canal in 1790, which gave Edinburgh access to the commercial waterway of the River Clyde, and the Leeds and Liverpool Canal in 1816, which crossed the Pennines.

To a much greater extent than the development of road services in this period, waterway expansion was heavily oriented towards freight traffic, especially in high-bulk goods requiring only a low rate of dispersion in their delivery. Many of the earliest canals were promoted and financed by individual entrepreneurs to the direct benefit of their own firms. These were mostly connected with the industrializing regions of Lancashire, the west midlands, and south Wales. A leading engineer, John Rennie (1761–1821), built the Lancaster Canal in 1819 and the Royal Canal of Ireland in 1817. The Trent and Mersey Canal, which formed a link between the west and east coasts of England, was completed in 1777. Its promoter was Josiah *Wedgwood, who used the canal to ship his pottery to the ports of Hull and Liverpool and receive the raw materials of coal and clay. Canal construction in the 1790s, benefiting from a demonstration effect in response to the success of many of these early industrial canals, was much more widely focused in terms of geographical area and promoters. By the later years of the French wars there was a flurry of construction of small agricultural canals.

The construction of these canals confronted engineers with enormous natural obstacles which were uncommon in the less challenging tasks of improving existing rivers. The building of tunnels, cuttings, embankments, bridges, and aqueducts took many years, as evidenced by the long lag periods in completing the trunk canals. The Forth and Clyde was completed in 1790, twenty-two years after its Act was passed. While the Trent and Mersey took from 1770 to 1816. These technological challenges in turn generated financial challenges. Whilst leading entrepreneurs financed some of the pioneering canals, by the later years of the century a more active market in canal shares began to emerge. With denominations typically as high as £100, however, this expansion was restricted to the mercantile and landed élite. In the boom of the 1790s, however, denominations in some companies were reduced to around £20 or £30.

Waterway transport was largely undertaken in narrow boats pulled by horses from the towpath. There was little use of steam on canals before the middle of the nineteenth century, although fly boats became common during the early decades. Like the flying coaches on the roads, they used relays of horses, ran to regular timetables, and often worked all night. The canal companies ran some services but also competed with mercantile and manufacturing firms, who operated their own boats, and specialist carrier firms. Pickford's was again the leading specialist; by 1838 it owned 116 canal boats and provided services throughout most of the canal network.

For international transport, sail remained the dominant form. In the late eighteenth century copper sheathing was often applied to the hulls of wooden vessels to extend their life (although it was not until the middle of the nineteenth century that iron vessels were regularly built). Experiments with steam boats took place on the Clyde in the first years of the nineteenth century, and interest soon spread to the Humber, Mersey, and Thames. By the 1820s and 1830s steam vessels were being used in the coasting and near overseas trades. The General Steam Navigation Company was one of the first companies to run a fleet of steamers, but faced a constant battle to keep its vessels fully employed and to cover the high capital and running costs. The period also represents a major growth phase of the British shipping industry,

with its world leadership being extended under the stimulus of economic growth and intermittent warfare. British vessels began to voyage more frequently beyond Europe, including to the Americas, Australasia, and the East [see *exploration, 37]. The expansion of trade was fostered by the construction of docks at some of the major ports, particularly London and Liverpool. Besides introducing a more efficient system of cargo and ship handling, the docks also countered the growing problem of embezzlement. Organizationally, there began to emerge specialist, professional shipowners eager to take advantage of these opportunities, and committed to this single occupation rather than combining it with mercantile and related activities. Whilst the joint-stock company also penetrated the shipping industry, older forms of joint ownership, based on local connections and lacking limited liability, remained remarkably durable through much of the nineteenth century.

As with shipping, landed steam locomotion in this period remained more a portent than an actuality. The British railway network was built mostly in the middle decades of the nineteenth century. The completion of the Liverpool to Manchester line in 1830, however, is often seen as an important starting-point, representing the application of steam locomotion to long-distance rail travel. Many of the earliest railways, or wagonways, were built in the later years of the eighteenth century to connect coalmines in the north-east of England with local points of shipment, particularly on the Tyne. The increased demand for high-quality household coals and the need for deeper moorings in the lower reaches of the Tyne extended the distance between pithead and riverhead. Coal was moved down to the riverside staiths in trucks by force of gravity, and returned by the use of stationary engines or horses. Once more, much of the initial technology for the subsequent system was developed through a process of experimentation before 1830. The successful trial of Stephenson's 'Rocket' at Rainhill in 1829 was the culmination of such experiments and, in turn, was improved upon in the course of the nineteenth century.   SV

travel literature. Travel writing constituted one of the largest genres of Romantic-period publication. It included accounts of experience and *exploration [37] beyond Europe, descriptions of European peripheries as well as accounts from the more conventional *Grand Tour, and descriptions of scenery and journeys within Britain, sometimes primarily directed toward the discussion of aesthetics, political conditions, or methods of agricultural improvement. Travels to different regions entailed contact with diverse local populations and led to different sorts of knowledge, emphasizing *antiquarianism [35] and *architecture [28] in the case of Islamic and south Asian societies, spectacular horrors such as cannibalism among people regarded as savages in the Americas or the Pacific, and the appreciation of *paintings [27] and ruins in Italy. Travel narratives were extensively excerpted in periodicals, collected in anthologies, and synthesized in *encyclopedic compendia such as the *Modern Universal History* (1759).

Exploration beyond Europe by land and sea provided geographical and strategic information from which trade and settlement could follow. Encounters with exotic peoples, as well as accounts of unusual animals and scenery, provided the raw material for publications that were frequently well illustrated, popular, and influential. It is not surprising, then, that a fraudulent literature flourished, and that many accounts of actual journeys incorporated improbable material designed to arouse the wonder and excitement of the public. Although the element of the fantastic that was conspicuous in travel writing up to the mid-eighteenth century gradually diminished as regions became better documented, the genre remained one replete with stereotypes, mystifications, and exaggerations.   NT

Treason Trials, the proceedings in 1794 against Thomas *Hardy, John Horne *Tooke, and John *Thelwall for alleged treason. These marked both the most dramatic victory of the radical cause and the start of its retrogression, as well as a seminal point in the legal history of Britain.

Fearing domestic *revolution [1], the British government arrested Hardy, secretary of the London Corresponding Society [see *corresponding societies] and Daniel Adams, secretary of the *Society for Constitutional Information, on 12 May 1794, beginning a roundup in which the government, determined to cripple the radicals and their causes, at one stage drafted 800 warrants for the arrest of suspected revolutionaries.

With the suspension of habeas corpus at the end of May, the prisoners were detained in the Tower of London before Hardy was eventually brought before the Old Bailey on 25 October 1794. The trial lasted eight days, with public interest reaching fever pitch when the jury promptly returned a verdict of not guilty. Tooke was next to be tried, followed by Thelwall. Both were exonerated, forcing crown *lawyers to drop charges and release all remaining prisoners and drop the charges against them. The legal argument of the prosecution centred on the construction of treason as imagining the death of the King, while the rhetorical thrust of the successful defence aimed at turning the charge back against the government. The Treason Trials were a vital and important victory for the accused radical leaders and the reform movement, but also instigated a decline in their political careers and the slow but progressive dilapidation of the movement they had promoted and led. Thelwall, Hardy, and Tooke lost the greater part of their political energies and had to contend with increasing repression after the trials, marked most noticeably by

103. Sketch by Thomas Lawrence of Holcroft and Godwin—radical onlookers at the Treason Trials of 1794.

the two Acts of 1795 [see *gagging acts]. The reform movement was thus forced to look for new leaders and to begin a long journey underground for its survival.   MD

TRIMMER, Sarah (1741–1810), writer of *children's literature, religious educator. An adherent of the Church of England, author of *Sacred History* (1782) and *Fabulous Histories: The History of the Robins* (1786), and founding editor of an *anti-Jacobin periodical, the *Guardian of Education* (1802–6), Sarah Trimmer was a household name in children's literature.

Between 1778 and 1789, Trimmer ran *Family Magazine*, and meanwhile bore twelve children. She was actively involved in establishing the *Sunday school movement, and in her *missionary zeal to bear the word of Scripture condemned outright both progressive secular *education [17] and traditional children's story-books. She deplored the popularity of *Robinson Crusoe*, and reviewed favourably Lucy *Aikin's *Poetry for Children* (1801), which rebuked Romantic *sensibility [11] and its 'false picture of the real world'. She was particularly vehement against the influence of *Rousseau on the ideas of Thomas *Day, and on Maria and Richard Lovell *Edgeworth's *Practical Education* (1798). 'The true centre of education should be religion,' she argued; 'even geography, writing and arithmetic may be made in some measure subservient to religious instruction.'

Trimmer's instrumentality peaked in the 1790s, when she widened the attack against certain publications to a war against all Dissenting secularist freedoms. Her clergy mentors installed her as editor of the High Church publication *Guardian of Education* (1802–6), the opening number of which warned of 'A conspiracy against CHRISTIANITY and all SOCIAL ORDER . . . endeavouring to infect the minds of the rising generation, through the medium of books of Education and Children's Books'. Trimmer and the Society for the Reformation of Principles joined High Churchman John *Bowdler, William *Wilberforce, and Hannah *More to form the *Society for the Suppression of Vice, a coalition against the *popular education movements espoused by Joseph Lancaster and the non-denominational British and Foreign Bible Society and British and Foreign Schools Society.   JB

TURNER, Joseph Mallord William (1775–1851). Generally regarded as the most eminent practitioner of nineteenth-century English *landscape painting, Turner was born in Covent Garden, London, the son of a barber [see *painting, 27]. From this modest start he worked as a copyist in various engravers' shops throughout his early teens, and in 1789 entered the *Royal Academy schools to study with Thomas Malton, exhibiting a *watercolour of *The Archbishop's Palace, Lambeth* (1790) at the Academy the following year.

From 1792 Turner embarked on his first sketching tour, of north and central Wales. His habit of undertaking these tours, to gather material for his studio paintings or for engravings published after his work,

was to last until some six years before his death in 1851 (his last trip, to Dieppe, took place in 1845).

While continuing to work at copying and watercolours, Turner exhibited oil paintings from 1796, notably *Fishermen at Sea* (1796). While to this point he had been less innovative than his friend Thomas Girtin (1775–1802), he quickly arrived at a maturity through paintings such as *Buttermere Lake* (1798), although his claim that had Girtin lived, he, Turner, would have starved is perhaps apocryphal.

From the age of 24 Turner succeeded to the academic honours which lifted him beyond the reach of want or the vagaries of public opinion. His financial needs were in part met by his appointment to the post of professor of perspective in the Academy (1807); his membership of the institution had taken place some years before—he was made an associate member in 1799 and a full member in 1802.

In the same year, 1802, Turner extended the scope of his sketching trips to include continental Europe, visiting France and Switzerland and studying the art of the Old Masters in the Louvre (much of it looted by *Napoleon during his Italian campaign). In the mountains of Switzerland he had the opportunity to deepen his understanding of *sublime landscape, culminating in such paintings as *The Fall of an Avalanche in the Grisons* (1810). This interest in the effects of a violent nature—storm, plague, and natural disaster—is allied with a strong narrative content in paintings such as *Snow Storm: Hannibal and His Army Crossing the Alps* (1812), in which the diminutive army, exposed on a high pass in the Alps, is engulfed in a vortex of black clouds which are about to obliterate the sun.

This interest in narrative landscape, evidenced in paintings as widely spaced as *The Fifth Plague of Egypt* (1800) and *Ulysses deriding Polyphemus: Homer's Odyssey* (1829), separates Turner from many of his contemporaries who saw the genres of landscape and *history painting as mutually exclusive. Instead, such paintings place him within the European tradition of 'historical landscape' practised by Claude Lorrain (1600–82), and it is no surprise to find that Turner paid Claude the compliment of imitation in his *Dido Building Carthage* (1815), which is closely modelled on Claude's *Seaport with the Embarkation of the Queen of Sheba* (1648).

By mid-career Turner was established as the leading painter of his day. While some criticized his choice of violent and dramatic subject-matter and his increasingly painterly application of pigment, others were committed patrons, such as Lord Egremont of Petworth House and Walter Fawkes of Farnley Hall, Yorkshire, at whose houses Turner was frequently a guest [see *patronage]. He continued to make regular forays to the Continent, including a long trip to Italy in 1819–20. Likewise he continued to publish his work through engraving, notably the seventy plates (100 were projected) of his *Liber Studiorum* 31 (begun 1807) which, in another emulation of Claude, was based on the latter's *Liber Veritatis*, published in an engraved form in 1777.

By the 1830s Turner's technique, which had early

manifested the skills of an outstanding draughtsman, had matured through his Claudian phase into a far more personal and disturbing style, characterized by the use of colour dragged with a palette knife or brush over a rough underpainting, the texture being built up by these multiple layers of pigment. Indeed, Turner was famous for presenting his work in an 'unfinished' state. He used varnishing day at the Academy to complete his paintings—although many regarded the result as sketches, not finished paintings.

In paintings such as *Yacht Approaching the Coast* (*c*.1835–40), the yacht of the title has become one with the seascape. Marginalized on the left of the composition and counterbalanced by menacing dark shapes on the right, the yacht is shown without any accommodating detail which would provide succour to the inquiring viewer. Rather, the spectator must accept the totality of the scene which tunnels, vortex-like, into a white sun. Across this composition the paint has been dragged, rubbed, and scoured, leaving a surface on which no part contains detail, but no part is less highly worked than the rest.

Late in life Turner was still capable of producing a major new work. At the Academy of 1839 he exhibited *The Fighting Téméraire Tugged to Her Last Berth to Be Broken Up* (1838). This painting, which enjoyed immediate and popular success, showed the old warship, with sails furled, towed by a steam tug to the scrap yard. William Makepeace Thackeray

(1811–63), struggling to find an adequate description of the pathos of 'the brave old ship, with death, as it were, written on her', concludes that Turner's success lies in making 'you see and think a great deal more than the objects before you'.

Later paintings from the 1840s give new meaning to Thackeray's words, for in *Light and Colour (Goethe's Theory)—the Morning After the Deluge—Moses Writing the Book of Genesis* (1842), Turner abandoned representational painting to present a meditation on colour, perhaps influenced, as the title suggests, by Goethe's treatise, published in England in 1840. These late paintings leave one in no doubt that Turner has transcended representation to find in painting an equivalent to nature, where paint, by association, stands for ideas, actions or feelings.

In his last years Turner was championed by the art critic John Ruskin (1819–1900), whose *Modern Painters* sought to secure a lasting reputation for the artist. But Turner's achievements speak for themselves. He stands at the apex of the Romantic movement through his synthesis of expression and emotion, given form through a technique which allows the medium its full tactile qualities. His study of light, atmosphere, and colour placed him far above his rivals in England or Europe in his understanding of natural phenomena. On his death he left some 300 paintings and 20,000 drawings and watercolours to the nation.   PD

U

Union, see *Act of Union.

Unitarianism refers to both a theology that rejects the divinity of Christ and a key denomination of Dissent [see *religion, 10]. Dispute over the Trinity goes back to the first centuries of the Christian era, and regularly resurfaced in heretical movements. In the early modern period its most famous advocates were the Spanish theologian Michael Servetus (put to death by John Calvin in Geneva in 1553) and the Italian heretics Lelio and Fausto Sozzini, whose name gave rise to the word 'Socinian', which became a term of abuse and was supplanted by the less contentious 'Unitarian' in the mid-eighteenth century.

Known in Britain from the 1640s, Socinian ideas posed a challenge within the Restoration Church of England. In the early eighteenth century, the eminent *Anglican theologian Samuel Clarke (1675–1729) published an extensive scriptural analysis that brought him to the so-called Arian position, which held that Christ, while divine, was created of a lesser

divinity than God the Father. Attractive to rationally oriented and scripturally inclined thinkers, this view made considerable progress among Latitudinarians in the Church and in time among English Presbyterians, generally the wealthiest, best-educated, and socially most considerable of Dissenters. The gradual spread of Unitarianism, with its insistence on a fully human Christ, divided many Presbyterian congregations. The Unitarian denomination that absorbed what was left of the Presbyterians by about 1820 was small but still impressive in terms of position and influence.

The most important figure in the transition was the scientist and theologian Joseph *Priestley, who in many polemical works defended his new faith and the concurrent philosophy of *Necessarianism. Despite years of suspicion and even persecution during the period of the *French Revolution, Unitarians regained confidence and recruits early in the new century and were a significant presence in provincial England and among liberal intellectuals. From the

1830s Priestley's theology began to lose ground to the more Romantic, less scientific temper represented in the leader of the 'New School', James Martineau (1805–1900); but the denomination retained its social and intellectual importance throughout the century.   RKW

United societies, republican organizations founded in Ireland and Britain in the wake of the *French Revolution with the aim of reforming parliament by force of arms.

The Society of United Irishmen was established in October 1791 by Theobald Wolfe *Tone and other leading Irish radicals who initially espoused the legislative and economic independence of Ireland from Westminster by *parliamentary reform. The lawyers, pamphleteers, and intellectuals who constituted its early membership developed their theories in debate, using the popular press and other media, such as the *ballad, to disseminate their ideas. The Society made common cause with the French Jacobin Clubs, the Scottish Committee for Reform, the Manchester Constitutional Society, and other bodies who shared a commitment to the 'rights of man' and other democratic principles. Close contact with the Scottish Association of the Friends of the People and London Corresponding Society resulted in the exchange of delegates, addresses, and the identification of common ground [see *corresponding societies].

However, at its first convention in December 1792 the influential Scottish Association rejected an address sent by the Dublin United Irishmen lest endorsement of its extremist tone provide justification for government suppression. Nevertheless, at the 'British convention' in Edinburgh in November 1793 Scottish and English reformists strongly condemned Irish coercive measures. The implied threat of delegates to 'assert their rights' by force of arms led to a crackdown on the movement which dashed hopes of changing the nature of government by constitutional means. A small faction led by Robert Watt (d. 1794) was captured while plotting an *insurrection in the summer of 1794, resulting in Watt's execution in October.

The discovery in April 1794 of a suspected plot to overthrow the Irish administration led to the banning of the United Irishmen. Abandoned by its moderate wing, the society came under the control of militant republicans determined to effect armed revolution in Ireland with French help. The United Irishmen reorganized in mid-1795 as a secret, oath-bound, and armed force, and promoted the creation of sister organizations in Britain such as the United Scotsmen who adopted their constitution of 10 May 1795 within the year. The constitution provided the model for a sophisticated structure designed to enhance the security of grass-roots cells while maintaining an intricate chain of command with the leadership at local, county, provincial, and national level.

The arrival in Bantry Bay of a large French *invasion force in December 1796 proved that their undertakings to the United Irishmen were sincere, and highlighted the need for greater structural flexibility

to faciliate mobilization to fight. A new constitution was adopted in August 1797 which attempted to tighten the cellular structure, though this does not seem to have been adopted by the United Britons.

By September 1797 the United Scotsmen are said to have numbered almost 10,000 members, boosted by widespread opposition to the Militia Act of that year, which extended their influence into rural areas. The arrival of experienced Irish radicals fleeing martial law in Ulster in 1797 also bolstered revolutionary cadres in Scotland and the north-west of England. By the end of the year there were over eighty societies in Manchester and Lancashire, a sizeable presence in London, and societies in Birmingham, Leicester, Wolverhampton, and Nottingham.

Bantry Bay heightened the prospect of a French invasion of either or both Britain and Ireland. It moved the United Englishmen, formed in April 1797, and the United Scotsmen to commit themselves to armed support of the French wherever they landed. Thomas Muir (1765–99), leader of the United Scotsmen, unsuccessfully pressed the Directory in Paris to make Scotland its chief object, although he remained willing to sponsor a rising in his homeland to assist one in Ireland. United Irish agents based in Britain and on the Continent promoted sedition in the Royal Navy, playing a role in the critical *naval mutinies at Spithead and the Nore in 1797, but were less successful in their attempts to suborn the army, militia, and fencibles.

The arrests of key United Briton leaders in March/April 1798 and communications difficulties contributed to the failure of their organizations to support the rebellion in Ireland. Despite the bloody defeat of the United Irishmen, conspiratorial activity continued in Britain and Ireland, experiencing a revival after 1799 as a result of economic hardship and near-*famine conditions.

In the summer of 1802 Colonel Edward Despard's (1751–1803) plot to stage a *coup d'état* in London was narrowly averted, and a similiar attempt by Robert Emmet (1778–1803) in Dublin in July 1803 ended in disaster. It is significant that, as in the case of the *Rebellion of 1798, both plots were initially conceived as a joint enterprise by the new United Irish/British leadership. Emmet was at one point Despard's agent in Ireland. The totality of their failure caused the United societies to go into terminal decline and temporarily closed off physical-force nationalism as an avenue of radical expression in both islands.   RO'D

unstamped press. From its inception in 1816 through the postwar years of economic dislocation and popular unrest, the unstamped weekly newspaper was the leading mode of radical expression in print. Its capacity to reach and radicalize working-class readers worried the government, and the form was effectively proscribed by the Six Acts of 1819 [see *gagging acts].

Derived from early eighteenth-century revenue measures, the stamp duties on *newspapers became a way of limiting the circulation of news and political discussion. Set at 1*d.* per copy for most of the century, the stamp duty went up to threepence half-penny in 1797, and then to 4*d*. in 1815, amounting to most of the cost of a London newspaper. Readers learned to share subscriptions and to rely on public houses and reading-rooms that took papers; a single copy of an early-nineteenth-century newspaper had as many as thirty readers. These expedients had the effect of slowing the diffusion of political discourse, hampering a radical reform movement that relied on the press in matters of organization.

William *Cobbett introduced the unstamped weekly in 1816 when he heard of threats to the licences of public houses where his *Political Register* was being read. He discovered a legal loophole that exempted papers containing only news commentary from taxation, and began reprinting the lead essay of the *Register* on a single, unstamped sheet. The sheet cost only 2*d*., as opposed to a 1*s*. ½*d*. for the complete stamped *Register*. For the first number, his 2 November address 'To the Journeymen and Labourers', Cobbett claimed sales of 20,000 copies in the first two weeks, and 200,000 within two months. He then shifted the format to a nominally taxed octavo pamphlet, and regularly sold 30,000 or more each week, as opposed to perhaps 2,000 of the stamped version. Because the unstamped 'Two-Penny Trash' was not entitled to free postage, Cobbett had to improvise an elaborate network of local dealers. A host of imitators were encouraged by Cobbett's success in making the radical gospel of *parliamentary reform available to a new class of readers. While radical weeklies varied in price (from 1*d*. to 4*d*.), format, and ideological complexion, most were built around a lead 'editorial' essay, which could incorporate prohibited news content by way of commentary. The remaining pages were filled out with miscellaneous essays, reports, poetry, extracts, and correspondence. These aggressive campaigning newspapers helped organize meetings, *elections, boycotts, and *petitions, and were closely integrated with radical agitation through some of its headiest years.

T. J. *Wooler's *Black Dwarf* (1817–24) was the chief beneficiary of Cobbett's decision to leave England after the suspension of habeas corpus in 1817. Wooler, a printer turned editor and publisher, claimed a circulation of 12,000 by 1819. Though eclectic in his political principles, he supported the constitutional reformer Major John *Cartwright, who probably financed the paper. The *Black Dwarf* was distinguished by its literary character and fiercely satirical style. The government soon charged Wooler with seditious libel, and his 1817 trial became a popular sensation in London. Defending himself, he secured an acquittal on one charge and a disputed verdict on another, and went on to conduct a successful campaign against the use of special juries in London.

William *Hone edited *Hone's Reformists' Register* (1817) during the period leading up to his own celebrated prosecution for blasphemous libel. Less reckless than the *Black Dwarf*, this well-printed weekly attacked the *Whigs, and reported extensively on radical agitation and the treatment of reform in parliament. In early 1817 the Paineite republican

William Sherwin (b. 1799) set up *Sherwin's Weekly Political Register* (1817–19), which achieved its greatest impact after it was taken over by Richard *Carlile and renamed the *Republican* (1819–26). Carlile was uncompromising in his attacks on *monarchy and established religion, and enlisted the *Republican* in support of a parallel campaign of infidel publication. He and his shopkeepers and hawkers were relentlessly prosecuted by the government, and he spent most of his tenure as editor in court or in prison.

With financial support from Jeremy *Bentham and Francis *Place, John Wade (1788–1875), a former journeyman wool-sorter, was able to sell his *Gorgon* (1818–19) for one penny, though a halfpenny was added after several months to increase the profit to dealers. Wade joined other radicals in attacking corruption and supporting parliamentary reform, but his *Gorgon* was distinctive for its *utilitarian reasoning and evidence, and its campaign against the Combination Laws. In 1819 Wade began the anonymous publication in two-penny sheets of his *Black Book*, an encyclopedic exposure of corruption in church and state.

The *Peterloo massacre triggered a spate of new unstamped weeklies, including the *Briton* (1819), the *White Hat* (1819), the *Cap of Liberty* (1819–20), and the *London Alfred* (1819). The last two papers, along with the *Medusa* (1819–20), came from the press of the ultra-radical printer Thomas Davison (d. 1826). A Paineite republican and supporter of Carlile's infidel publications, Davison endorsed the popular right of armed resistance. The year 1819 also witnessed the appearance of cheap radical weeklies in several provincial cities, complementing the national circulation achieved by Cobbett, Wooler, and Carlile.

The government and the 'respectable' press viewed the unstamped weeklies as a leading source of popular unrest. Radical editors, publishers, and hawkers were harassed with libel prosecutions, and some effort was made to answer the radicals in kind, in papers like the government-subsidized *White Dwarf* (1817–18). But it was not until the passage of the Six Acts in 1819 that the government effectively contained the unstamped press. The Newspaper Stamp Duties Act extended the definition of a newspaper to works containing 'remarks or observations' on the news, and issued new controls on everything from price to the size of a sheet of paper. Radical editors were left with only two formats, a longer unstamped paper that could be sold for 6*d*. or a stamped edition costing 7*d*. or more but entitled to free postage. Only Cobbett's *Register*, the *Black Dwarf*, and the *Republican* survived the early months of 1820. The unstamped press did not return to prominence until the mid-1830s, when the 'war of the unstamped' forced the government to reduce the newspaper tax to 1*d*.   KG

utilitarianism. During the course of the eighteenth century, credence increasingly came to be given to utilitarian theories of human motivation and associated schemes for moral and social reform. Utilitarianism had at its core the idea that people were instinctively driven to seek pleasure or to avoid pain. Most who so conceptualized human nature and motivation believed that as people grew to maturity, their powers of reasoning became refined through experience. Even so, it was believed that no matter how intellectually sophisticated a person became, she or he would still act out of self-interest, in that they would seek to employ their powers of reasoning to bring about those conditions in which they might enjoy the greatest pleasure or suffer the least pain. Taking self-interest to be the fundamental determinant of human conduct, utilitarian thinkers generally regarded life-ways and social institutions as good to the degree that they were useful; that is, how far they contributed to the general happiness of society, either through increasing the sum of pleasures citizens enjoyed or by diminishing the pains they suffered.

However, utilitarians differed markedly in how they understood true happiness. From the late seventeenth century, successive generations of theologians and moral philosophers embraced utilitarian modes of reasoning. In general, they held that by far the greatest happiness was that arising from the *sublime pleasures of knowing the divine will as expressed in Scripture and the fabric of nature. Yet even among religious utilitarians there could be profound disagreement over whether the quota of human happiness could be enriched through schemes of religious and political reform. In the 1790s, for example, Anglican theologian William

*Paley harnessed for conservative ends much the same utilitarian reasoning that Joseph *Priestley used to justify the reform of church and state.

Utilitarianism could also be determinedly secular in outlook and aims, as is most clearly evidenced by the writings and influence of Jeremy *Bentham. While far from being the proponent of egoistic hedonism that contemporary antagonists charged, Bentham nonetheless regarded the comforts promised by religious traditions as having served actually to diminish human happiness. For Bentham, the only true path to greater happiness was through the rigorous empirical investigation of human nature. Indeed, what orthodox Christians derided as the grossest of sensual pleasures, he regarded as the most solid grounds on which to construct theories of morals and legislation resulting in greater human happiness.

The influence of utilitarianism in both its secular and religious variants has been the subject of extensive historical scrutiny in recent years. Little exists by way of consensus beyond agreement that utilitarianism, especially in its Benthamite formulation, greatly influenced the thinking of many men who played active roles in government and the creation of state agencies, especially during the middle decades of the nineteenth century. Even so, many were inclined to embrace utilitarian reasoning only so far as they understood it to be compatible with Christian belief in the essentially spiritual nature of humanity.

PT

V

vaccination (and anti-vaccination). Strictly speaking, vaccination, the artificial implantation of the living virus of cowpox to protect against smallpox, was discovered by Edward Jenner (1749–1823) in the late 1790s and superseded inoculation in the treatment of smallpox.

Jenner's discovery of vaccination, first publicized in his *Inquiry into the Causes and Effects of Variolae Vaccinae* (1798), had its basis in the lay belief that milkmaids who contracted cowpox, a benign eruptive disease, were immune to the deadly smallpox. Subsequent testing and research by supporters and critics of the technique demonstrated its advantages over inoculation, first popularized in Britain by Lady Mary Wortley Montagu (1689–1762) in 1721–2. The main disadvantage of inoculation, which involved introducing the smallpox virus itself, was the spread of the disease to the unprotected.

The anti-vaccinists, some of whom were disgruntled inoculators, deployed a potent mixture of genu-

ine criticism, scurrilous personal attack, and appeals to fear and superstition. Ironically, the experiments of such critics as the physicians William Woodville (1752–1805) and George Pearson (1751–1828) provided valuable evidence in the search for a safe technique. Others, like Dr William Rowley (1742–1806) and John Birch (c.1745–1815), argued that smallpox was a kind of 'poor man's friend' and vaccination the impious interference with God's will. Jenner's most inveterate critic, Dr Benjamin Moseley (1742–1819), issued public warnings about the dangers of inflicting on humans the diseases of animals. Moseley's remarks about a disease he called 'cow-mania' inspired James *Gillray's cartoon *The Cow Pock* (1788).

The debates between the Jennerians and anti-vaccinists highlight the increasing importance of the popular press as a forum for discussing medical ideas, as well as the ambiguous status of medical science in the early part of the nineteenth century [see *prose, 30 and *medicine, 18].

LH

104

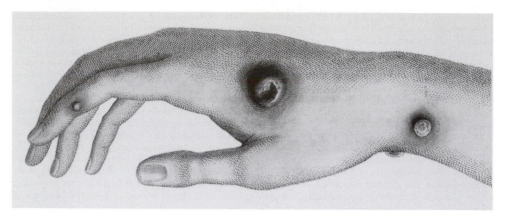

104. Coloured stipple engraving by William Skelton after Edward Pearce of cowpox pustules on a female hand, from Edward Jenner's *An Inquiry into the Causes and Effects of the Variolae Vaccinae* (1798).

vegetarianism. The word 'vegetarian' was not coined until 1847 (when the Vegetarian Society was founded), but there existed between 1770 and 1830 a burgeoning subculture centred on 'Pythagorean', 'Brahmin', or 'natural' diet (as it was then known). Vegetable diets (often associated with teetotalism) were both popular and politicized in the period. Two kinds of vegetarianism (countercultural and subcultural) were sustained by three kinds of discourse: asceticism, medicine, and animal rights. Eminent vegetarians included Percy and Mary *Shelley, John Oswald (*c.*1760–94), John Stewart (1747–1822), Sir Richard Phillips (1767–1846), Joseph *Ritson, John Frank Newton (1767–1837), William Lambe (1765–1847), and the young Benjamin Franklin (1706–90). Outside this diverse selection, vegetarianism was discussed in David Hartley's (1705–57) *Observations on Man* (1749), *Rousseau's *Émile* (1762) and *Monboddo's *Of the Origins and Progress of Language* (1773–92). The diet was practised by a large subculture, from the readers of vegetable recipe books like *On Food* (1802)—generally, members of literate and reasonably affluent classes who wanted to be frugal—to William Cowherd's (1763–1816) church of *Swedenborgians at Salford attended by Joseph Brotherton (1783–1857). Vegetables predominated in the working-class diets of the period, but meat and bread were commodities which were popularly demanded as symbols of status.

Vegetarianism had become a matter of popular asceticism, rather than simply a mystical practice, a medicinal procedure, or a fad. In Europe, vegetarianism had been practised by mystics in Greece (such as the Orphists), and later by Christian ascetics and mystics (e.g. Thomas Tryon, 1634–1703). The cardinal virtue of temperance persisted into a more spiritually diverse (not entirely secularized) and less hierarchical age as a means of balancing the body internally and externally according to axiomatics of harmony and homoeostasis. The vegetable or 'cooling' regimen was an aspect of *medicine [18] which persisted through medieval, early modern, and

eighteenth-century treatments. As one of the six non-naturals, food in 'diet' was important in earlier humoral theory, as well as air and exercise. For the countercultural vegetarians, other practices such as nudism or air baths sometimes accompanied their diets. By the eighteenth century, more mechanistic and fluid theories of the body had been developed: vegetarianism fared well in these discourses as a means of capitalizing on energy (e.g. in the writings of George Cheyne, 1671–1743). The discourse of animal rights developed in the writing of Latitudinarian divines (who wondered whether animals could get to heaven), and the radical politics of sympathy and *sensibility [11].

Vegetarian discourse had a wide orbit in the period. Debates over the game laws used arguments familiar to vegetarian writers [see *poaching]. The figurative presence of vegetarianism in the work of James Thomson (1700–48), William *Blake, Alexander Montgomery (*c.*1545–*c.*98), Samuel Pratt (1749–1814), William *Cowper, and Oliver Goldsmith (*c.*1730–74)—and later *Wordsworth and *Coleridge—reconfigured human relationships with the natural world. Questions about human rights (for workers, women, and slaves) were framed in terms of animal rights: the anti-slavery poetry of Pratt's *Humanity* (1788) involved vegetarian rhetoric. The counter-revolution imagined the radicals as a violent irruption of wild nature which intemperately consumed the social order (see the scenes of cannibalism in Edmund *Burke's *Reflections*). Progressive and conservative thinkers alike exploited cults of anti-luxury.   TBM

violinists. In the 1770s and 1780s the violinist held an unchallenged position in *concert life, both as soloist and as director of the orchestra. This dominance was, however, later threatened both by the increasing flamboyance of piano soloists and by the rise of the *pianist-conductor.

London's lucrative prospects attracted many of the finest continental violinists, including Felice Giardini, Wilhelm Cramer, and Johann Peter Salomon, all of whom played a prominent part in concert management. Salomon famously enticed *Haydn to London in 1791; in turn Haydn wrote the quartets Op. 71 and 74 in a vivid, public manner to show off Salomon's string quartet. During the 1790s younger virtuosi crossed the Channel, often to escape royalist connections in France. Giornovichi and Yaniewicz continued the graceful manner of their predecessors, but a new voice was provided by Giovanni Battista *Viotti in 1793, universally regarded as the greatest violinist of his age. After 1815 London hosted a new influx of continental virtuosi, such as Kiesewetter and De Beriot, who often preferred to play crowd-pleasing fantasies and variations, uniting popular operatic melodies with extravagances of violinistic trickery. All were eclipsed in 1831 by *Paganini, the ultimate showman on the violin and at the same time the embodiment of the Romantic supernatural.

One violinist resisted the trend towards ever more brilliant virtuosity for its own sake. Louis Spohr (1784–1859), who first visited London in 1820, stood out for higher artistic values. A composer of wide-ranging accomplishments, he dedicated a new symphony to the Philharmonic Society and also attempted to introduce baton-conducting, if only at a rehearsal. Spohr's symphonies and *oratorios became popular both in London and at provincial *music festivals, and he was a frequent visitor in later years.   SMcV

VIOTTI, Giovanni Battista (1755–1824), outstanding Italian *violinist, founder of the modern school of violin-playing, and an influential figure in London's concert life during the 1790s.

In 1782 Viotti arrived in Paris, becoming chamber musician to Marie Antoinette. Here he developed a grander style of violin-playing, which led directly into the nineteenth-century bravura manner. His violin concertos transformed the elegance of the *galant* style into a more intense, high-classical idiom: many are in the minor mode, with powerful orchestral writing and resolute melodies on the outer strings of the violin.

Eventually forced to leave France, Viotti was engaged by Salomon for his 1793 concert series. He was recognized as London's pre-eminent violinist until 1798, when he was suspected of Jacobinism on account of alleged contacts in France and again became a political refugee. In his London concertos he continued to favour minor keys, although the earlier boldness now gave way to a resigned melancholy—especially in the nostalgic A minor Concerto No. 22, which Brahms was to hold in special affection. Viotti's concertos are among the principal works of the classical repertoire, not only for the idiomatic violin writing (influential on *Beethoven) but also for their vivid invention and colourful orchestration.

Back in London by 1801, Viotti did not attempt to re-establish his reputation, preferring instead to go into the wine trade. Nevertheless he was a founding member of the Philharmonic Society in 1813, and occasionally led *concerts during its first three seasons.   SMcV

VOLNEY, Constantin François de Chasseboeuf, comte de (1757–1820), French traveller, philosopher, and member of the National Assembly whose *The Ruins, or a Survey of the Revolutions of Empires* (1791) was, with Thomas *Paine's *Age of Reason*, the most popular and influential of freethinking texts in nineteenth-century Britain.

The first of Volney's texts to reach a British readership was *Travels through Egypt and Syria* (trans. 1787), which went into several editions, but it was *The Ruins* which made his name. In 1826 a *republican periodical, the *Lion*, identified three different translations of Volney's tract in circulation. The first and perhaps best known, published by Joseph *Johnson in 1792, was translated by William *Godwin's friend James Marshall, although Godwin himself disliked the book immensely and Joseph *Priestley, a close friend of the Johnson circle, attacked its *Deism in *Letters to Mr Volney* (1791). An answer to Priestley from Volney was published in 1797. Volney himself apparently believed that the Marshall translation softened the radicalism of his views. A second translation was undertaken in Philadelphia, before being followed by the third, in Paris by Volney himself in collaboration with the American Joel Barlow (1754–1812).

Opening with the reflections of a traveller meditating on the ruins of the Syrian-Roman city Palmyra, who is then taken up to the heavens by the genius of the tombs, Volney's narrative offers a vision of the whole of human history which reveals religion (including Christianity) as a deception practised on the people to defraud them of their rights. Almost from the moment of its first translation Volney's book found an eager readership in popular radical circles and among sceptically minded intellectuals. In the 1790s it seems to have been read at branch meetings of the London Corresponding Society [see *corresponding societies], and parts appeared in periodicals associated with the Society such as Daniel Isaac *Eaton's *Politics for the People* and Thomas *Spence's *Pig's Meat*. The fifteenth chapter—offering a typology of *class [15]—and its vision of the 'new age' was especially popular and frequently circulated as a tract or appended to other radical publications. Richard *Carlile claimed that by 1820 it had already sold something like 30,000 copies.

The Ruins seems to have influenced William *Blake's *prophecies, but its most direct literary influence was on Percy *Shelley's *Queen Mab* (1813), itself destined to become a radical classic in cheap editions. Shelley's poem is indebted to Volney's book both for its visionary form and for its freethinking content, although Shelley distanced himself from Volney's view that 'self-love, the desire of happiness, and an aversion to pain' were the 'essential and primary laws' of human action. In Mary *Shelley's *Frankenstein* (1818), *The Ruins* figures as the book from which the Monster learns about human history.

Apart from *The Ruins*, Volney's *The Law of Nature* was published in French and English by Eaton in 1796. His *Lectures on History* (trans. 1800) and *New Researches into Ancient History* (1814, trans. 1819) also became sources of controversy for their infidel content. In 1830 the radical publisher James Watson (1799–1874) issued a *Brief Sketch of the Life of C. F. Volney* which was often appended to later nineteenth-century editions.　　　　　　JM

volunteers, an auxiliary armed force raised for temporary local defence, especially when *invasion was threatened in 1778–9, 1797–8, and 1803–5.

The social and cultural activities associated with volunteering—parades, drilling, and conviviality— made it particularly important in the mobilization of *patriotism during the revolutionary and Napoleonic *wars [2]. By 1803 the volunteer movement numbered 400,000 men, its social composition having been extended from the largely urban middle and upper class to include the lower orders. Its effectiveness as a counter-revolutionary force was often more potential than real: during the food short-ages of 1795–6 and 1800–1 some volunteers sided with popular protest. There were also certain material advantages to volunteering which makes it an unreliable indicator of unquestioning loyalty to authority. Conditions of service such as payment by the government after 1794, the fact that volunteers did not have to leave local communities as in the case of militia service, and exemption from compulsory military service as decreed by the Levy en Masse Act (1802), made volunteering more attractive than other branches of the armed services. After 1806 the gov-ernment ran down the movement because it was regarded as too expensive, too draining of manpower resources from the militia and regular army, and also militarily ineffective. There was also a degree of alarm at the fact that mass arming on such a scale might be translated into demands for political rights.　　　　　　JF and GR

W

WAKLEY, Thomas (1795–1862), politician, med-ical reformer, founder and editor of the *Lancet*. Wak-ley first achieved notoriety when, as a young surgeon, he was falsely accused of decapitating the bodies of the Cato Street conspirators on the scaffold [see *insurrection]. Friends of the hanged men assaulted him and burnt his house to the ground. His insurance company subsequently claimed that he was the arsonist, a charge he successfully defended in court. Wakley's sensational legal battle brought him into contact with William *Cobbett, who encour-aged him to embark on a career in medical journal-ism. In 1823 he founded the *Lancet*, a weekly newspaper which soon became a powerful vehicle for medical improvement and reform [see *medi-cine, 18].

Wakley's reformist agenda included the dissem-ination of new medical knowledge and the reforma-tion of medical teaching and licensing. He also saw as his task the exposure and eradication of monopoly, nepotism, and jobbery. His key targets were the Royal College of Physicians, the Royal College of Surgeons, and the Worshipful Company of Apoth-ecaries, whose exclusiveness he believed to be at odds with the interests of the general body of British medical practitioners.

In the *Lancet* Wakley published the *lectures of some of London's most distinguished medical teachers. He encouraged the publication of case reports and investigations into the efficacy of *quack medicines. Most controversially, he sought out and reported cases of malpractice and maladministration in the metropolitan hospitals. His tone was strident and his attacks on individuals and groups were vitri-olic. In the *Lancet*'s first ten years Wakley was brought to court ten times and he was once forcibly ejected from the theatre of the Royal College of Surgeons.

As a member of parliament for Finsbury (1835–52) he attempted to establish a uniform bill of medical registration in Britain and Ireland. Although the bill failed, it eventually culminated in the Medical Act of 1858, which defined the nature of medical qualifica-tion and brought the profession a semblance of unity. Wakley's parliamentary reforms included the reduc-tion of stamp duties on *newspapers in 1836. He sympathized with the *Chartists, opposed the *corn laws, and advocated the repeal of the Irish Union.

During his long term as coroner for Middlesex (1839–62), Wakley reformed the office and increased its power and status. He performed many controver-sial inquests on the inmates of *prisons, *mad-houses, and workhouses who he believed died under suspicious circumstances. His inquiry into the death of a soldier who died from the effects of a flogging effectively ended the practice in the army.

Wakley continued his reforming activities until the time of his death, when he was still engaged in an inquiry into the controversial *Poor Law Amend-ment Act of 1834.　　　　　　LH

WALPOLE, Horatio (Horace), first Baron Walpole (1717–97), author, letter-writer, antiquarian, polit-ician, and connoisseur. Walpole was born in London, the youngest son of Sir Robert Walpole, first Earl of Orford, and his first wife, Catherine Shorter. He was tutored by a son of the Bishop of

Exeter and sent to Eton at the age of 9. In 1735 he entered King's College, Cambridge. Two years later he was appointed by his Prime Minister father to the post of Inspector of Imports and Exports in the Custom House, and the following year to Usher of the *Exchequer. Further sinecures granted in 1738, and a subsequent appointment to the Collectorship of Customs, brought Walpole a comfortable income by the time he reached his late 20s.

Walpole left Cambridge in 1739 and for the next two years made the requisite *Grand Tour, visiting France, Switzerland, and Italy in the company of the poet Gray. In his absence from England, he was elected MP for the borough of Callington in Cornwall. This position was exchanged for a hereditary seat in Castle Rising in 1754 and later for a seat in the borough of King's Lynn. Walpole's involvement in the workings of parliament was minimal. Describing himself as a 'quiet Republican' and 'unadulterated *Whig', Walpole retired permanently from politics in 1768.

Walpole's contribution to the literary sphere is more substantial. His first published work, a treatise entitled the *Aedes Walpolianae* (1747), describes his father's collection of paintings at Houghton Hall, Norfolk, and forms an invaluable record of a cabinet subsequently sold to pay the debts of Orford's heir [see *viewing, 20]. This was followed in 1758 by a work of patrician literary criticism, *A Catalogue of Noble and Royal Authors*. Between 1762 and 1780, Walpole edited and expanded upon manuscripts of the antiquary George Vertue (purchased from Vertue's widow) to produce the *Anecdotes of Painting in England* and its companion *A Catalogue of Engravers*. Walpole's most ambitious work of scholarship, *Historic Doubts on the Life and Reign of King Richard the III* (1768), was praised by contemporaries for the liveliness of its argument but censured for its revisionist historical claims. He is better known for *An Essay on Modern Gardening*, written in 1770 but published in the last volume of *Anecdotes*.

Walpole also produced fiction, drama, verse, *essays, and a quantity of *satirical and political pamphlets. The latter range from the light-hearted *Letter from Xo Ho, A Chinese Philosopher in London* (1757) to a defence of his conduct in the affair of Thomas *Chatterton's suicide. Walpole is chiefly celebrated, however, as the author of the first *Gothic novel in England, *The Castle of Otranto*, which he wrote in under two months and published pseudonymously in 1764 as a translation of a sixteenth-century document. Walpole is regarded as one of the best letter-writers of the period; his self-conscious, sharply observed, lively prose and gift for matching correspondent with topic is evident throughout his surviving correspondence. The Yale edition of his collected letters runs to some forty volumes and illuminates the politics, intrigues, social mores, and literary and artistic developments of nearly half a century.

Walpole's mode of living must also be regarded as an aspect of his creative production. In 1748 he purchased Strawberry Hill, a small house with five acres of land in Twickenham. He gradually appended new rooms, a tower, battlements, a cloister, stained-glass windows, and interior fixtures that transformed a cottage within easy distance of London into a surprisingly potent Gothic fantasy—a modest country seat with an atmosphere worthy of *Otranto*. This structure, together with Walpole's extensive collection of art, bibelots, and curiosities became so popular with sightseers that its owner printed rules of admission and instituted a postal ticket system to regulate the flow of visitors. The house and its furnishings greatly advanced the fashion for Gothic *architecture [28] and *design [25] in the last decades of the century.

In his final decade Walpole, increasingly frail and severely afflicted with gout, divided his time between Twickenham and a house in Berkeley Square, London. When the death of his nephew brought him the title in 1791, he declined to assume his seat in the House of Lords. Walpole found consolation in his last years in the company of the sisters Agnes and Mary Berry, whom he installed, together with their father, in a cottage on the grounds of his estate. It was for their amusement that he wrote his *Reminiscences* (1788) of the courts of George I and George II, and to Mary Berry fell the task of editing his papers for publication. A five-volume edition of his works appeared in 1798. Walpole died unmarried and without issue at the age of 80 in March 1791, and was buried at Houghton. Strawberry Hill was left to the sculptress Anne *Damer. Walpole's *Memoirs of the Last Ten Years of the Reign of George the Second* and *Memoirs of George III* were published in 1822 and 1845. Thomas *Macaulay's attack on Walpole in the *Edinburgh Review*, October 1833, heralded the decline of Walpole's reputation in the nineteenth century. CSM

WARTON, Thomas (1728–90), poet, antiquarian, and literary historian. Along with his brother Joseph (1722–1800), Warton by his researches into the history of English *poetry [29], made an important contribution to the developing *Gothic taste for medieval and Renaissance literature and the revival of interest in associated forms such as *romances and *ballads [see *antiquarianism, 35].

Warton spent most of his life in Oxford, where he was professor of poetry (1757–67), and professor of history from 1785. He collected a famous miscellany of university verse as *The Oxford Sausage* (1764). The two editions of his *Observations on the Faerie Queen* (1754; enlarged 1762) were important in the revival of *Spenser's reputation. His subsequent antiquarian researches culminated in the three-volume *History of English Literature, 1100–1603* (1774–81), often regarded as the first example of English literary *historiography. Whereas Samuel *Johnson's *Lives of the Poets* (1779–81) ignored English literature prior to the mid-seventeenth century, Warton's *History* was dominated by an antiquarian relish for the 'warmth of fancy' found in earlier literature. A projected fourth volume of the *History* was never completed, perhaps because of Joseph *Ritson's criticisms in 1782 of Warton's scholarly methods. That same year Warton involved himself in the controversy over the Rowley poems, declaring Thomas *Chatterton to be their real author.

Although he celebrated the vigour and intensity of early English poetry, Warton's tastes were informed by a confidence that eighteenth-century Europe had 'advanced to the highest degree of refinement'. His own poetry certainly does not aspire to the Gothic grandeur he valued in his antiquarian researches. His appointment as poet laureate in 1785 was greeted with derision in the *satirical *Probationary Odes* published with *Criticism on the Rolliad*.   JM

watercolour painting in the period was associated with original naturalistic effects, modern subjects, and departures from the accepted academic hierarchies of subject and style. However, its history was mythologized almost from the moment it emerged as an independent category of artistic practice in the early nineteenth century with the setting up of separate watercolour exhibition bodies: the Society of Painters in Water-Colours in 1804, and the short-lived Associated Artists in Water-Colours in 1808. In 1812–13 a series of articles, 'Observations on the Rise and Progress of Painting in Water-colours', appeared in the fashionable magazine *Repository of Arts*, which declared watercolour 'almost . . . a new art'. The rich range of colouring and effect achieved with transparent washes on relatively large paper, which distinguished the best recent work in the medium, was said to elevate it from the category of mere drawing to that of *painting [27]. For contem-

poraries it was 'most interesting, if not wonderful, to see art accomplish so much with so scanty a material'. At the same time, with the abandonment of penned outline had come an increase in 'truth to nature' and new possibilities for individual expression. For the author of the *Repository*'s articles, this transition was represented by the difference between the works of Paul *Sandby, who had laid the foundations of the new art, and those of J. M. W. *Turner and Thomas Girtin (1775–1802), which were respectively admired for their 'sentiment' and 'boldness and spirit'. In contemporary criticism these terms had nationalistic connotations, since French art was widely represented as 'cold, unfeeling and heartless' (the counterpart to an inhuman Gallic rationalism in political matters), and Britain was claimed as 'the only place where there is anything like a poetic feeling in art'. The perceived uniqueness of British watercolour painting meant it could be hailed as 'strictly national', and 'a monument to the honour of the British nation'.

Actually this uniqueness was something of an illusion, and eighteenth-century British watercolourists had been influenced by a range of continental artists, including Marco Ricci, Jakob Hackert, and A. L. R. Ducros. The *Repository*'s history was also mythical in its essentially arbitrary demotion of opaque watercolour, and its rather slighting judgments on artists such as John Robert Cozens (1752–97), whose work

105. One of Paul Sandby's private pupils in watercolour painting, learning this relatively new art, *c*.1770. Her paints are contained in oyster-shells.

was no less pictorial than that of the generation of Turner and Girtin, on whom it had considerable influence. The *Repository*'s myth of origins and maturity indicates the increased ambitions of water-colour painters around 1800, which partly motivated the founding of the first watercolour society. But another factor behind this development was the need to advertise a distinctive product in the highly competitive London art market. Watercolour exhibitions were criticized in some contemporary reviews as being repetitive and dominated by 'worn out land-scapes' of the same subjects. There was an element of truth in this, in that the economic base of much watercolour art lay in the demand for views of well-known tourist sites in Britain and the Continent, and also in commissioned illustrations for topographical, *picturesque, and antiquarian publications. (Turner's illustrations for W. B. Cooke's *Picturesque Views on the Southern Coast of England* (1814–26) and for Charles Heath's *Picturesque Views in England and Wales* (1827–38) are among the best-known of these.) Although the medium was closely linked with *land-scape, the watercolours of the early nineteenth century which obtained the highest prices were probably the genre scenes of Thomas Heaphy (1775–1835) and Henry Richter (1772–1857), while another prominent practitioner, Joshua Cristall (1768–1847), made his reputation with scenes of rural types and classical subjects. Moreover, individual artists became known for their specialisms in particular subjects: Peter De Wint (1784–1849) for cornfields, Robert Hills (1769–1844) for farmyard scenes, and Samuel Prout (1783–1852) for continental picturesque architecture.

The work of such leading figures was also associated with a trademark style. In contemporary criticism, 'style' was understood as an index of individual and original creative power. But its repetition was also condemned as 'mannerism' and 'affectation', a charge frequently levelled at Prout among others. However, watercolour also had its defenders, particularly in the publications of entrepreneurs such as Rudolph *Ackermann, who published the *Repository of Arts*, and, as manufacturer and innovator in paints, had a direct interest in advancing the status of the medium and of modern topography. The link between watercolour and topography helps explain why watercolour became a vehicle for original subjects and effects, and why some of its leading practitioners, including Girtin and John Sell Cotman (1782–1842), experimented with colouring sketches on the spot.

As a form of art usually smaller in scale and in a higher key of colour than oil, and one which was practised by many female amateurs (at whom the *Repository* was particularly directed), watercolour was prone to being 'feminized'. The characterization of an exhibition of 1821 in the *Monthly Magazine* as having a 'cloying sweetness, like an entire meal of pastry, or a concert of flageolets, or musical snuff boxes' exemplifies this. Watercolour was also associated with domestic spaces: 'the parlour, the study, and the boudoir'. Moreover, its blatant commercialization through normally modest prices and direct

sales from the Water-colour Society's exhibition rooms meant that its practice could not signify the heroic self-sacrifice associated with *history painting—even if in reality that genre was no less market-oriented. Although its status as a polite female accomplishment helped make watercolour popular, the role of the drawing-master, on which many contemporary watercolourists depended for a livelihood, was widely regarded as reducing the artist to little more than a domestic servant. Despite the feminization of the medium, professional watercolour painting was entirely dominated by men. (The Associated Artists in Water-Colour Painting admitted women members, but they were only allowed to vote by proxy at its meetings.) In fact, the key criterion of achievement in watercolour as in other areas of art was 'imagination', identified as an essentially male province. As a result of their functions as teachers, watercolourists produced some of the most important treatises on landscape painting of the period—examples are David Cox's *A Treatise on Landscape Painting and Effect in Water Colours* (1814) and John Varley's *A Treatise on the Principles of Landscape Design* (1816–21)—which particularly stress the need for the artist to have 'a proper feeling of the subject'.   AH

Waterloo. The battle of Waterloo was fought between France and the allied powers of Britain and Prussia on 18 June 1815, and with the final defeat of *Napoleon ended twenty-three years of almost uninterrupted *war [2] in Europe. The British press reported the battle exaltingly, giving the credit for the victory to the British army and, above all, to the Duke of *Wellington. Belgians, Dutch, and Hanoverians, who accounted for almost two-thirds of the Allied force, often went unmentioned and the vital role of General Gebhard von Blücher's Prussians was often diminished. Wellington himself criticized the hyperbolic nature of reports of the battle.

Numerous contemporary accounts describe how individuals first heard news of the battle, which was met with euphoric public celebrations in Britain. London was spectacularly illuminated, with displays often taking the form of 'G.R.', 'G.P.R.', and 'Wellington and Blücher'. In Edinburgh, a public holiday was declared and nineteen cannons were fired in jubilation. On Skiddaw, Robert *Southey and William *Wordsworth danced round a huge bonfire singing 'God Save the King'. Soon after the battle commemorative medals were struck and plans announced for the erection of statues and the building of a pillar or triumphal arch. A few individuals, however, including *Byron and *Hazlitt, refused to join the national celebrations, seeing in Napoleon's defeat the triumph of the reactionary forces of the old regime.

The battlefield of Waterloo, south of Brussels, immediately became a tourist attraction, visited by Walter *Scott, Southey, and Byron, among others. The months after Waterloo produced a huge and varied body of writing on the battle, including personal accounts, works of history giving 'narratives' and 'circumstantial details', biographies of the main protagonists, topographical guides, and descriptions of tours to the battlefield. The most popular medium was verse. The battle was celebrated in numerous poems, amounting to 'hundreds' by December 1816, according to the critic Francis *Jeffrey. The publication of such pieces persisted well into the 1820s. The vast majority of these poems followed a familiar pattern, condemning Napoleon's 'atrocities', granting Britain the central and divinely ordained role in his defeat, and praising Wellington and the other British heroes of the battle such as Brunswick, Picton, and Ponsonby. The battle was constantly likened to Crécy, Agincourt, and Blenheim, and Wellington was compared to Edward the Black Prince, Henry V, and Marlborough.

Scott in *The Field of Waterloo* (1815) and Southey in *The Poet's Pilgrimage to Waterloo* (1816) both called upon these standard tropes, Southey elevating this already elevated subject through the use of a visionary framework that invokes *Spenser and *Milton. Wordsworth in his 'Ode: The Morning of the Day appointed for a General Thanksgiving' (1816) represented the battle as an apocalyptic event, though his infamous address to the Deity 'Yea, Carnage is thy daughter' was satirically alluded to by Byron, Hazlitt, and Percy *Shelley. Byron gave a celebrated account of the night before the battle in *Childe Harold's Pilgrimage* III (1816), though his self-projecting portrait of Napoleon and the absence of any praise of Wellington were strongly criticized by Scott in the *Quarterly Review* (1816).   SB

WATSON, Richard (1737–1816), successively professor of chemistry (1764–71) and then regius professor of divinity (1771–82) at Cambridge before becoming Bishop of Llandaff (1782–1816). A *Whig in politics and genuinely liberal by inclination, he aroused unsustainable radical expectations on being made a bishop, and when these were dashed, he was correspondingly vilified by many Romantics.

When Watson was made professor of *chemistry at the age of 27 he admitted that he had 'never read a syllable on the subject, nor seen a single experiment', but he was tired of mathematics and **natural philosophy [34]** and wanted to try something new. Immersing himself in the new subject—and blowing up his laboratory in the process—within three years he had produced course textbooks and published work on the solutions of salts distinguished enough to earn him unanimous election to the Royal Society (1769). In 1772 he invented the black-bulb thermometer, and in 1779 he made improvements to the manufacture of gunpowder that saved the government £100,000 per annum and assisted British forces in the coming *war [2] with France.

On election to the chair of divinity, of which he 'knew as much . . . as could reasonably be expected of a man whose course of studies had been directed to . . . other pursuits', he showed similar energy, publishing a series of theological books and pamphlets [see *religion, 10]. His sermon 'The Wisdom and Goodness of God in having made both Rich and Poor' provoked *Wordsworth's *Letter to the Bishop of Llandaff* (1793). His *Apology for the Bible* (1796)

was written against Thomas *Paine and went through many editions. Though *Coleridge described him as 'that beastly Bishop, that blundering fool', it is typical of Watson that he took out a subscription to Coleridge's own journal, the *Friend*.
                                                                SP

WATT, James (1736–1819), engineer, inventor. Renowned for his improvements to the steam engine, Watt was celebrated by his contemporaries as no inventor had been before.

Born in Greenock, Scotland, Watt trained as a scientific instrument maker in Glasgow and London, before establishing a workshop with several employees in the precincts of Glasgow College in 1757. At that time approximately 250 'atmospheric' engines, invented by Thomas Newcomen fifty years before, were then employed in Britain, primarily to drain coalmines. In 1763, when a model Newcomen engine was brought in for repair, Watt solved the problem of how to remedy the engine's chief defect, its high consumption of coal. His solution was the separate condenser, which avoided the repeated cooling of the piston chamber, thereby conserving heat and fuel. With financial backing from John Roebuck, owner of the Carron iron foundry, Watt began to experiment on full-scale engines and patented his invention in 1769 [see *industrialization, 14].

Further development was postponed, however, by the blossoming of Watt's career as a civil engineer. From 1767 he was regularly commissioned to survey the route of Scottish canals and river improvements, stimulated by burgeoning trade with England and the colonies [see *transportation]. In 1773 he supervised the implementation of his plans for Port Glasgow's harbour and Greenock's water supply, then left Scotland for Birmingham. Depressed by his wife's recent death and financially stalled by Roebuck's bankruptcy, he accepted the partnership offered by Birmingham hardware manufacturer Matthew *Boulton. Intensive experimentation on the steam engine followed, and commercial production began in 1776.

The Cornish tin industry, where economy of fuel in mines drainage was at a premium, provided many early customers. Watt's adaptation of the engine to rotative motion enlarged its potential market, not least in the fast-expanding cotton industry from the mid-1780s. In 1786 Boulton and Watt travelled to Paris to consider an offer from the French government to build steam engines in France under an exclusive patent, finally rejecting it on the grounds that it would not be in Britain's interests.

As success prompted other inventors and imitators to enter the field, Watt was preoccupied during the 1790s with protracted patent litigation. The original 1769 patent had been extended to 1800 by a controversial private act of parliament. His tight control over the engine combined with his anxiety concerning the safety of high-pressure steam probably delayed further development.

An active member of the Lunar Society, Watt shared the scientific interests of Joseph *Priestley, Erasmus *Darwin, Josiah *Wedgwood, and other midlands luminaries [see *literary and philosophical societies]. Elected to the Royal Society of Edinburgh in 1784 and, of London in 1785, he was honoured (rarely for a foreigner) in 1808 and 1814 by the Académie des Sciences. In 1800 Watt retired from Boulton and Watt, dividing his time between Handsworth, Staffordshire, his Welsh estate at Doldowlod, and continental travel. Regularly consulted on *engineering problems, he continued to exercise his inventive talents and to enjoy the company of scientists, statesmen, and literati. In life he refused a baronetcy; in death his name was widely perpetuated, with donations subscribed by all ranks of society to erect statues (including one in Westminster Abbey), and to found libraries, colleges, and scholarships. His son, James (1769–1848), studied science in Paris and became an ardent early supporter of the *French Revolution. However, he fell out with Robespierre and the Jacobin Club, and fled back to Britain in 1794, after which he became an active partner in his father's Soho business. CMacL

WEBBE, Samuel, the elder (1740–1816), Roman Catholic organist, teacher, and composer of *church music and *glees, the most important and influential figure in the small world of Roman Catholic church music in London in the years leading up to and immediately following the second Catholic Relief Act of 1791 [see *Catholic emancipation]. He wrote music for the chapels of the Portuguese and Sardinian embassies, where he was organist. He also gave lessons free of charge; among his pupils were Vincent *Novello and probably Samuel *Wesley. In the 1780s and early 1790s he was responsible for the publication of three volumes of Catholic service music, much of it by himself. He also wrote music for the *Anglican Church.

Webbe's other main area of activity was in the sociable world of the glee club, where he held a pre-eminent position both as a composer and as an official, demonstrating that Roman Catholicism was no bar to social acceptance in this area. His glees, which number well over 100, are distinguished by their tunefulness and superior technique. He was appointed librarian of the Glee Club on its establishment in 1787, and his glee 'Glorious Apollo' was performed at the beginning of every meeting during the club's history. He became secretary of the Catch Club in 1794, and was also a member of the Anacreontic Society and the Concentores Sodales, two other glee clubs. Webbe's son Samuel Webbe the younger (1768–1843) was also a composer of church music and glees. PO

WEBER, Carl Maria (Friedrich Ernst) von (1786–1826), composer, conductor, and pianist. Weber's works introduced the emerging German Romantic operatic style to Britain. *Der Freischütz* (Berlin, 1821) established his fame, with music of unusual dramatic coherence and a plot making melodramatic use of supernatural elements. Following the London performances of 1824 he was commissioned by Charles Kemble (1775–1854) to write an *opera for Covent Garden. The outcome was *Oberon*, premièred in

1826 with immense success. Though seriously hampered by a weak text, by English conventions such as non-singing roles, and by difficulties with the tenor, John *Braham, Weber's ability to distil drama in *music [26], particularly through imaginative orchestration, was undimmed in this piece. His death was hastened by the effort involved in mounting the production. GB

WEDGWOOD, Josiah (1730–95), potter and entrepreneur. By combining the art and science of ceramics with the niceties of marketing and *factory organization, Wedgwood raised both his firm and the English pottery industry from a *design [25] backwater to a position of international leadership.

Born into a clan of potters in the heart of the English industry, Wedgwood was apprenticed to his eldest brother, Thomas (c.1709–73). In 1759 he established his own business, making tableware in rococo fruit and vegetable shapes that gleamed with the translucent green lead glaze he had invented. Experimenting to find a clear glaze, by 1763 he developed a new earthenware body to rival porcelain. This was creamware, elevated in 1765 to the brandname of 'Queen's Ware' through the patronage of Queen Charlotte, which earned Wedgwood the title 'Potter to Her Majesty'. Creamware's apogee came with the commission in 1773 from Catherine the Great of Russia for a 952-piece dinner service, decorated with 1,244 different views of English country houses. Ever attentive to public relations, Wedgwood displayed it at his new London showroom. In 1774 he issued the industry's first catalogue (of Queen's Ware).

During the mid-1760s he entered separate partnerships with his cousin, Thomas Wedgwood, for 'useful ware' (tableware and sanitary ware), and with Thomas Bentley (1731–80), a Liverpool merchant, for 'ornamental ware' (vases, cameos, and figures). Bentley's presence in London society was invaluable: he courted aristocratic patronage and advised Wedgwood on shifts in fashion, encouraging him to reject rococo for the simplicity of neoclassical styles that became his hallmark. To exploit their essential elegance, Wedgwood experimented to improve the black 'basaltes' (a very dense stoneware) and to invent in 1775 a completely new ceramic body, 'jasper', which could be coloured throughout to contrast with the applied white bas-reliefs (designed by artists such as John *Flaxman). Copies of the Portland Vase, produced in black jasper in 1790 after four years of experimentation, crowned Wedgwood's international reputation.

Wedgwood opened a purpose-built factory in 1769, at 'Etruria', beside the 'Grand Trunk' Canal, which he had promoted. He was a pioneer of factory management. His workforce was well housed and well trained, but closely regulated, and specialized through extensive division of labour to meet long, standardized production runs. Work flow was built into the layout and a system of cost accounting devised [see *industrialization, 14].

Wedgwood benefited from close friendships with other innovative manufacturers, such as Matthew

106. A staunch opponent of slavery, Josiah Wedgwood fashioned this black basalt medallion with abolitionist inscription, 'Am I not a Man and a Brother?', in 1787. Half a century later its slogan was still popular, used by radicals concerned about a new slave economy forming in Britain along class lines.

*Boulton and James *Watt, and with leading *chemists. For Joseph *Priestley he developed ceramic apparatus, which burgeoned into an important new line, much appreciated by scientists and apothecaries. Wedgwood's own research into the chemistry of ceramics and the measurement of temperature in kilns (culminating in his invention of pyrometers) led to his election to the Royal Society in 1783. A zealous supporter of *abolitionism through the Anti-Slavery Society, he also sympathized with the *American, and early *French, revolutions. Despite Wedgwood's best efforts, none of his sons was interested in business, and the firm languished during the nineteenth century. However, one son, Thomas (1771–1805), was a close friend and patron of S. T. *Coleridge, providing the poet with an annual pension of £150 which freed him from dependence on the market or the *Royal Literary Fund. Thomas also initiated important experiments in early photographic technology, including the first production of unfixed photographs.   CMACL

WELLESLEY, Arthur, see Duke of *Wellington.

WELLINGTON, first Duke of (Arthur Wellesley) (1769–1852), field marshal and statesman. Hailed as a national military hero who defeated Napoleonic France, he later became equally famous in the political arena as a bastion of ultra-Tory and aristocratic values against the forces of liberal change.

Born to a poor but noble Irish Ascendancy family,

he was educated at Eton and at Angers military academy, beginning a political apprenticeship in the Irish parliament from 1790 and a military apprenticeship in India from 1798. Eight years of Indian service, including combat in the Second Mahratta War, trained him to command large armies in the field, schooled him in the hardships of campaigning, and taught him military diplomacy as well as the importance of meticulous logistical planning. In April 1809 he became Commander-in-Chief on the Iberian Penisula, campaigning almost continuously until his final defeat of *Napoleon at *Waterloo on 18 June 1815. During this period he fought more than 100 actions, won eleven major battles, and bested five of Napoleon's top generals. As a military commander he was as conservative as Napoleon was radical; Wellington avoided combat as much as possible, allowed the Spanish and Portuguese guerrillas to sap the French armies, and capitalized decisively on luck or French mistakes. Nicknamed 'the Iron Duke', he was respected by his men for coolness and courage, but he abjured personal popularity and deeply despised the moral and intellectual qualities of both his officers and troops. He was also suspicious of innovation in military education or weaponry, and supported the traditional aristocratic purchase of commissions. During the *Peninsular War he was showered with British and foreign honours, becoming as much a symbol of British national identification as *Nelson before him, and attracting a similar spate of gifts, heroic paintings, and public statuary.

National prestige ensured Wellington's prompt postwar elevation to the Tory Cabinet, although his relations with the Canningite liberal wing were always uneasy because of his opposition to liberal national revolt among Spain's South American colonies [see *liberal Toryism]. As Prime Minister in 1828–9 he had almost immediately to preside over 'the most painful act of a long life' when forced from fear of civil war in Ireland into passing *Catholic emancipation. Having broken the constitutional spine of the old regime, Wellington set himself resolutely to resist the measures of political reform introduced by Grey's (1764–1845) *Whig ministry in March 1831. His tenacious but ultimately unsuccessful attempts to prevent the passage of the *Reform Act of 1832 brought threats from the London mob and the smashing of his windows at Apsley House. Throughout his life, however, Wellington remained unmoved by swings in popularity; he disliked democracy and believed in strong, just government by a propertied, disinterested aristocracy. An eighteenth-century male aristocratic outlook was also revealed in his readiness to *duel, his reputation for religious indifference and sexual rakishness, and his indifference to the threat of public exposure in Harriette *Wilson's celebrated blackmailing memoirs of 1825. By the time of his death in 1852 Wellington's direct involvement in ultra-Tory politics had ceased, and he was given a splendid state funeral in St Paul's Cathedral before more than a million mourners.   IMcC

Welsh artisan painters created the images which both represented and contributed to the development of the national self-perception as a literate and religious people from the beginning of the nineteenth century.

As a nation without a state or any urban focus of economic and political power, Wales could not sustain academically trained resident painters in the period. Furthermore, the marginal position of the English-speaking gentry in national life meant that their *patronage, even when patriotically directed to the likes of Richard *Wilson and William Parry (*c*.1742–91), did not truly reflect the emergent forces that would drive the indigenous culture in the nineteenth century.

Some earlier artisan *portraits exemplify with striking directness the class-relatedness of this *painting [27]. While the gentry patronized society painters in England, their servants—such as those depicted in *Servants at Gwenynog celebrating the coming of age of Richard Myddleton of Chirk Castle* (1785)—were usually painted by artisans. The inscriptions on the face of this picture are of an archaism characteristic of artisan practice, and the fact that they are written in the Welsh *language [40] emphasizes the relationship between *class [15] and nationality in Welsh life. Between 1791 and 1796, John Walters of Denbigh (*fl.* 1791–6) painted the most remarkable artisan portraits of the period in a similar social context—six images of servants and tradespeople associated with the Erddig estate, near Wrexham. The plain style and visual narrative, reinforced by a painted text, in the portrait of Tom Jones, butcher and publican, make it an epitome of artisan painting.

'Artisan painter' is an imprecise term, but broadly speaking it refers to professional painters trained in a craft tradition rather than in an academy. Practitioners combined the painting of houses, signs, and carts with occasional commissions to paint religious images and portraits. As a substantial middle class emerged in Wales through the second half of the eighteenth century, a demand was created for portraits which enabled some artisans to specialize. In this respect, Wales was little different from other regions of Europe or from the United States, which also sustained a flourishing practice of artisan portraiture. However, the dominant position assumed by Welsh-speaking individuals drawn from this middle class and from *y werin* (the folk) in intellectual life in Wales gave these portraits of them an importance that they did not generally possess in other cultures. The elevation of some of these images to the status of icons of the culture through popular *prints [22] was a process that continued to develop well beyond the period of this survey. Nonetheless, many of the original paintings fall within our scope, reflecting in particular the coming to maturity of Calvinistic *Methodism and of the *Welsh cultural revival of the eighteenth century. The Nonconformist ministers and literati who lead Welsh public life were almost exclusively recorded by artisan painters.

The earliest prominent member of this intelligentsia to acquire an extensive artisan iconography was Thomas Edwards (Twm o'r Nant, 1739–1810). His satirical interludes made him a national celebrity. The earliest portrait of him is dated 1763 but images

painted by Edward Pugh (*c*.1761–1813) in about 1800 and the classic depiction of Twm done on his last public appearance in 1810, inscribed *Twm o'r Nant, the Cambrian Shakespeare*, were the most widely distributed as engravings. Prints were often published with the works of poets and the memoirs of preachers, but the custom soon developed for display in the home and also in chapel vestries, which sometimes exhibited substantial rows of images including both prints and original artisan portraits.

Some portraits painted by Hugh *Hughes are notable because they were frequently translated into prints and, unlike most artisans in other cultures, Hughes himself engraved. His powerful image of *John Evans of Bala, aged 90* (*c*.1812–19) is quite unlike the standardized translations produced by London engravers working for the *Evangelical Magazine*. Hughes's image of *Thomas Charles of Bala* (1812), leader of the Welsh Methodists, and William Roos's (1808–78) portrait of *Christmas Evans* (1835), the celebrated Baptist preacher, received the most complex iconographic development. They were the basis of a wide variety of engravings whose deep penetration into Welsh national consciousness is further attested by copies done from them both by naïve painters and by the artisans themselves. For example, William Roos copied from prints both of Thomas Charles (1755–1814) after Hugh Hughes and of John Elias (1774–1841) after

107. Hugh Hughes, frontispiece to *Alwedd Duwinyddiaeth (The Key to Theology)*, wood-engraving, 1823. Hughes engraved many of the popular prints that became icons of the Welsh cultural revival.

Hugh Jones (1800–*c*.1861). In addition to the proliferation of two-dimensional copies, the eventual appearance of public *sculpture further extended public familiarity with the images.

Roos was born in Anglesey and became the most technically sophisticated of the itinerant artisan painters. He wandered throughout Wales, and his sitters included many prominent religious figures and poets such as David Owen (Dewi Wyn o Eifion, 1784–1841). Individuals with a lower public profile, but who were, nonetheless, important in forming opinion in Wales, also often sat for Roos. His earliest surviving portrait is of the well-known teacher John Williams (yr Hen Syr, *c*.1745–1818), painted in 1827 after the sitter's death. Hughes also recorded such individuals. His masterpiece, *The Family of John Evans, Carmarthen, at Breakfast* (*c*.1823), depicts the proprietor of one of the earliest regional newspapers in Wales, the publisher of the radical periodical *Seren Gomer* and a prolific printer of books and pamphlets.

The consonance between Welsh-born artisan painters and Welsh patronage is striking. Both Hughes and Roos often worked in London and Liverpool, but even when in England their work was substantially done for Welsh patrons, underlining the peculiarly national characteristics of the phenomenon. Indeed, in a patriotic gesture Hughes attempted to establish the Cambrian Portrait Gallery in London in 1830. Among his first group of sitters were well-known intellectuals such as the radical Thomas Roberts (Llwyn'rhudol, *c*.1765–1841). Academic portrait painting on the other hand, even by Welsh-born painters with an artisan background such as Thomas Brigstocke (1809–81), rarely represented this core of national leadership. PL

Welsh cultural revival. The eighteenth century saw a revival of interest in Welsh history, literature, language, music, and traditions. For centuries the gentry and the bards had given cultural leadership. But by the early eighteenth century Welsh poets had only a feeble grasp of their ancient literary tradition, old Welsh music was forgotten, and the concept of a distinctive history of Wales lost, though the common people still preserved their ancient language, customs, folklore, and legend. The eighteenth-century success of vigorous movements of popular evangelism, such as *Methodism, threatened to destroy what remained of distinctively Welsh culture even amongst the common people.

The revival began as a movement of *antiquarianism [35] among the middle classes. They used new methods to preserve ancient oral and manuscript culture through the printing press (which first appeared in Wales in 1718), replacing noble patronage by book subscriptions, clubs, and societies, with amateur authors replacing professional bards. The antiquarians printed historical texts, general histories, bibliographies, grammars, and dictionaries. They set up societies, first in London, and then later in the century in Wales itself, such as the Honourable Society of Cymmrodorion (founded in London, 1751), to publicize Welsh history, literature, and language. The Cymmrodorion was overtaken after

1770 by the Gwyneddigion Society, also in London, which patronized the revived *eisteddfod as a focus of their patronage for literature and music in Wales. The eisteddfod, held intermittently and on a small scale from 1701, became a large, stage-managed exercise in publicity from 1789 onwards. After the return of peace in 1815, eisteddfod meetings were organized not so much in London as by cultural societies in Wales itself, several with patriotic names such as Cymreigyddion ('Welsh patriots').

The main fields of activity were language, literature, music, and history. Revivers of *language [40] around 1700 took advantage of the antiquarian movement's search for early Welsh history and of movements for popular literacy. Collections of manuscripts were scrutinized for vocabulary and for the correct basis for Welsh grammar. The enthusiasm of the Welsh scholars was fired by the work of the Oxford scientist Edward Lhuyd (1660–1709) and the Breton scholar Paul-Yves Pezron (1639–1706), showing that Welsh was descended from the language of the Celts, who had dominated much of prehistoric Europe. They thought they were reviving the language of the ancient druids, and even that Welsh was directly descended from the primeval language of the patriarchs. But lexicographers late in the century, such as John Walters (1721–97) and William Owen *Pughe, were also inventors of hundreds of new words, to show that Welsh had a more ample vocabulary than English, and that it could cope with the new worlds of *industrialization [14] and *sensibility [11].

The early-eighteenth-century antiquarians were dissatisfied with the trivial fare provided by the common people's literary diet of *ballads and (often bawdy) interludes. The almanackers Thomas Jones (?1648–1713) and John Roderick (1673–1735) raised popular taste by inserting snippets of classical Welsh verse in their *almanacs, and Roderick inserted in his grammar of 1728 instructions to help amateurs compose Welsh classical *odes. Welsh societies such as the Cymmrodorion discussed why Welsh poetry had died with Queen Elizabeth I, and congratulated their contemporaries on reviving the dead art. Goronwy Owen (1723–69) felt that Welsh lacked status because it lacked *epic poems, and attempted to supply Welsh with epic poems of *sublime grandeur. But Lewis Morris (Llewelyn Ddu o Fôn, 1710–65) and his protégé Evan *Evans discovered in 1755 the manuscript of a genuine Welsh epic, the Gododdin of Aneirin, describing an attack on Catterick Bridge in the sixth century. The antiquarians began the process of printing the great medieval literary corpus, such as the Welsh laws in 1730. The *Ossianic controversy spurred Evan Evans to publish *Some Specimens of Antient Welsh Poetry* (1764). As the century went on, more collections of early Welsh verse appeared, such as the poems of Dafydd ap Gwilym (1789), the poems then attributed to Llywarch the Old (1792), and an extensive collection of medieval prose and verse in *The Myvyrian Archaiology of Wales* (1801–7)—paid for by one of its editors, Owen Jones (Owain Myfyr, 1741–1814), a rich London currier. By 1789, however, the exact scholarship of earlier antiquarians did not satisfy the unquenchable thirst of the Welsh public for ancient literature, and many of the literary monuments of the period (such as the three mentioned above) were marred by the forgeries of Edward *Williams (Iolo Morganwg).

Wales was not yet known as the 'Land of Song' at the start of the eighteenth century. The traditional instruments of the Welsh were little used and much of the *music [26] played was imported from London. Manuscripts of harp music performed in the early seventeenth century seem to have been indecipherable by the early eighteenth, and *penillion* singing to accompany the harp was confined to the remotest fastnesses. The revival of interest in Welsh music was a deliberate campaign by three harpists, John Parry ('The Blind Harpist', ?1710–82) in the 1740s and 1750s, Edward *Jones (Bardd y Brenin) in the 1780s and 1790s, and John Parry (Bardd Alaw, 1776–1851) in the early nineteenth century. 'Blind' Parry's *Ancient British Music* (1742) claimed that the Welsh harp repertoire went back to the music of the ancient druids, and his concert at Cambridge in 1757 inspired Thomas Gray (1716–71) to complete his poem *The Bard*, itself a work which created a myth about the heroic martyrdom of Welsh bards at the hands of Edward I in 1282. Antiquarians drew attention to the vast corpus of *penillion* (stanzas) that the common people sang to the harp; the triple harp (possibly of early seventeenth-century Italian origins) was made out to be the Welsh national instrument; tunes with English titles were dressed up as ancient Welsh airs; and the eisteddfod gave prizes for harp playing and *penillion* singing. Edward Jones and Bardd Alaw wrote books on Welsh music and publicized it in *concerts, and their contemporaries founded societies to promote Welsh music such as the Canorion and the Welsh Minstrelsy Society.

Central to the whole process of revival was the gradual recovery of a Welsh historicism [see *history, 38]. The first stage of the revival, around 1700, was the discovery that the Welsh were descended from the ancient Celts, thus having their own distinctive prehistory and heroes such as the druids. Theophilus Evans (1693–1767) wrote a popular history of the Welsh (in Welsh) in 1716, a book frequently reprinted, and during the course of the century scholars put into print some of the manuscript materials of Welsh history. Several large-scale histories of Wales and several volumes of county histories were published, and much of the *travel literature of the period, such as the tours in north Wales by the scientist Thomas *Pennant, were in effect popular history books.

The common people could grasp a certain amount of their history through hearing of Welsh heroes, such as the druids. In 1792 Iolo Morganwg launched on an unsuspecting world his druidic moot, the Gorsedd of Bards, where he claimed to be the last successor of the ancient druids, and prepared to initiate supporters of things Welsh into the secrets of druidism. Other heroes were Caractacus and Boadicea from Roman times and Welsh medieval princes, such as Prince *Madoc of Gwynedd, who was believed to have discovered America about 1170, and Owen Glendower (Owain Glyndwr): Pennant played a crucial role in rehabilitating *Shakespeare's half-demented rebel as a fine upstanding national hero. Gray's bard who cursed King Edward I as he flung himself into the River Conway was mythical, but Iolo Morganwg's fourteenth-century chieftain Ifor Hael, a perfect patron of poets, had genuinely existed.

History was also made palpable for the Welsh by the new interest in Welsh landscape. In the early part of the century the Welsh took no pride in their mountainous landscape, while the English found it repellent. Early antiquarianism not only drew attention to prehistoric remains, usually labelled 'druidical', but also to ruined abbeys and castles. The movement drew travellers into remote, unvisited parts of Wales [see *tourism, domestic]. From the 1750s onwards the paintings of Richard *Wilson and his followers created an image of Wales as a *sublime setting for the monuments of prehistory and the middle ages. The *picturesque movement, led by William *Gilpin in the 1770s, created an attractive image of other, less mountainous, parts of Wales. In time, artists and travellers came to find inspiration in the wild landscape for its own sake, which gradually spread to the Welsh themselves, so that by the early nineteenth century the natives began to take an interest in their own land, seeing the mountains as a fortress against conquest or absorption, and a unique setting for the nation [see *Welsh artisan painters].

The first third of the nineteenth century is the period when revival reached its greatest height. Artists in this period also invented a range of national symbols or insignia for the Welsh which they could use on the title-pages of books, and on the medals or decorations of the eisteddfod ceremonial, what might be called a 'heraldry of culture'. These included the Welsh goat, the leek, the mistletoe, and the megalithic cromlech of the druids, to which Iolo Morganwg added the arcane symbolism of his Gorsedd of Bards, and a whole new Welsh runic alphabet.

Coming late in the revival was the symbol of the Welsh woman wearing her 'national costume' of red cloak and tall black hat. Late-eighteenth-century travellers remarked on the peculiar, picturesque costumes of Welsh women, the poverty and remoteness of the country keeping the costumes far behind the times. But the Welsh patriot who in the 1830s composed out of the varied female dresses a recognizable 'national costume' was Augusta Hall, Lady Llanover (1802–96). The cultural revival had been associated to some extent with radicals at the time of the *French Revolution, but from 1815 to the 1840s it was mainly in the hands of reactionaries, such as Lady Llanover and patriotic *Anglican clerics.

Despite all its successes, Welsh life changed so rapidly in the mid-nineteenth century that with the growth of Nonconformity, widespread involvement in politics, the rise of industry, the spread of scientific history, archaeology, and philology, and rapid Anglicization, the cultural revival faced a crisis in the 1840s and 1850s, and survived only as a rear-guard movement in Welsh life after that period.   PM

WESLEY, Charles (1707–88), founder *Methodist and *hymn-writer. The younger brother of John *Wesley, Charles was the first to attract the nick-name of 'Methodist' for being a member of the 'Holy Club', an informal study group attempting to live according to *Anglican notions of piety [see *religion, 10]. Converted a week before his brother, he too embarked upon an itinerant ministry, but desisted from this in 1756 when he could no longer assure himself that Methodism would remain within the Church of England, to which he remained faithful. This decision, and his refusal to lay personal claim to his contributions to the brothers' 'Hymns and Sacred Poems', resulted in his partial eclipse as a Methodist leader.

Charles used song and *sermon together in his evangelism, composing his meditations in verse, often upon a biblical theme or text, almost daily. Although the style of his hymn-writing reflected his classical education, he also strove for 'utmost simplicity and plainness, suited to every capacity'. His hymns differed from those of Augustan contemporaries in looking to the Bible and Christ's redemptive powers as God's means of revelation rather than to the creation. Their insistence on the 'joy' that resided at the heart of creativity presaged Romantic aesthetics and countered Charles's temperamental affinity with 'the graveside poets'. The continued widespread popularity of hymns such as 'Hark, the herald angels', or 'Jesu, lover of my soul' is a tribute to the antisectarian impulse that generated them.   EJ

WESLEY, John (1703–91), first leader of *Methodism. The fifteenth child of the rector of Epworth, John was the last of the children to be rescued from the fire which devastated Epworth rectory in 1709, and from this experience of being 'a brand plucked from out of the burning', as he wrote in his journal of 1753, stemmed Wesley's lifelong sense of a special Providence ruling over human affairs. The method his mother employed with her children 'to conquer their will and bring them to an obedient temper' has frequently been cited as a paradigm of eighteenth-century educational principles. His education continued as a 'poor scholar' at Charterhouse, and then at Christ Church, Oxford. After ordination Wesley's life was for several years pulled in two directions: exercising a parochial ministry as his father's curate, and pursuing the life of a scholar and tutor at Oxford as Fellow of Lincoln College. In 1729, deciding in favour of his Oxford duties, he found himself able to exercise his ministry by assuming leadership of the 'Holy Club' his younger brother Charles *Wesley had established. This small group's methodical pursuit of *Anglican piety and practical charitable activities in the surrounding community satisfied his sense of mission until he and two others from the group were offered a new field of spiritual *missionary opportunity in the American colony of Georgia.

Two years later Wesley left America, a virtual outlaw. Depressed and doubting his own commission, he fell in with a London group of the German *Moravians whose calm piety had impressed him during the rigours of the transatlantic sea voyage. At a meeting on 24 May 1738 Wesley felt his heart 'strangely warmed: I felt I did trust in Christ, Christ alone for salvation.' This emphasis upon a personal relationship with Christ, whose atonement upon the Cross had secured salvation for all who would receive it, remained the central plank of Wesley's preaching for the next fifty years. Nevertheless the simple language of this message was found to conceal radical possible differences in its interpretation. Acrimonious disputes arose about how far the doctrine of predestination might be said to limit the availability of Christ's sacrifice, whether it was always necessary to feel 'Assurance' (a personal conviction that one's sins had been forgiven), whether faith alone was necessary for salvation, or whether one's regenerate life became a place of probation and progress towards Perfection. Further, the insistence upon personal relationship, encoded in a language of feeling rather than a language of moral obligation, was to give rise to charges of emotional abandon in Wesley's hearers that ranged from accusations of *enthusiasm to the encouragement of sexual promiscuity. Whatever the excesses of some of his followers, the last charge showed a fundamental misunderstanding of Wesley, who was both temperamentally and educationally more inclined to eighteenth-century rationality than to the cult of *sensibility [11], and whose often-quoted advocacy of 'the religion of the heart' was not based upon any belief in the natural virtue of spontaneity but rather formed an appeal to a particular tradition of Christian piety, which he summed up in a letter as 'the religion which Kempis, Pascal, Fénelon enjoyed'. [See *religion, 10.]

Although Wesley continued to proclaim his allegiance to the Anglican Church until his dying day, and to claim that Methodism, in as much as it offered only a practical framework for faith, was compatible with other religious allegiances, he soon found himself in collision with the establishment. Less than a year after his conversion Wesley became a *field preacher, and during his travels throughout Britain, Ireland, and the Continent eventually delivered some 40,000 *sermons in his endeavour to ensure that the Gospel message might be made available to all. Since even his tireless efforts could not penetrate every corner, nor secure the continuous spiritual growth of widely dispersed converts, Wesley appointed lay preachers to assist in the work and established a network of mutually supportive classes and circuits, responsible to him through an annual conference, begun in 1744. In 1784 similar considerations led Wesley to ordain men for the American ministry, thus effectively establishing an alternative ecclesiastical hierarchy to that of the Church of England.

Despite the increasing sophistication of this organization, Wesley remained the chief authority in all matters. The conviction that had legitimated his transgression of parochial boundaries—'I look upon all the world as my parish'—underwrote every relationship, making it well-nigh impossible for Wesley to allow any of his co-adjutants to make his own mistakes. Even his brother Charles's writings were subject to John's editorial corrections.

In Wesley's case paternalist instincts coexisted with a desire to revive the early church's practice of sharing possessions. He advocated that Christians should 'Gain all you can . . . save all you can . . . give all you can'. Following his own dictum, Wesley dispensed the excess income he amassed from his own writings in spreading the Gospel and trying to train the artisan classes, among whom Methodism initially made its greatest inroads, into habits of self-sufficiency. A medical textbook for self-diagnosis and cure, for instance, was intended to lessen the burden of *physicians' and apothecaries' fees. Orphanages and *Sunday schools were established at his instigation. *Education [17] remained a life-long passion for Wesley. Reading continuously and eclectically wherever he rode, he abridged works for his followers, providing a library of tracts on subjects as diverse as history, physics, philology, theology, and literature. Both then and now Wesley has been demonized both as a rabble-rouser and as the leader who channelled the discontent of the disaffected away from radical politics, thus preventing an English revolution. While it is true that he expressed some initial sympathy with American grievances, he was always anxious to stress Methodist loyalty to the Crown, and to contribute his 'mite toward putting out the flame which rages all over the land', for, as he justly boasted, 'This I have more opportunity of observing than any other man in England.' As a guide to conditions throughout Britain between 1738 and 1790, Wesley's *Journal*, in which he provided for his scattered flock an account of his 250,000-mile Evangelical mission, remains unsurpassed.   EJ

WESLEY, Samuel (1766–1837), composer and organist, son of Charles *Wesley and nephew of John *Wesley. After early fame as a child prodigy, Wesley was between 1779 and 1785 involved as a composer and as a performer on organ and violin in a celebrated series of private subscription *concerts at the family home. At the same time he was attending Roman Catholic services at the Portuguese embassy chapel, and in 1784, much to his family's dismay, he converted to Roman Catholicism. Although his active involvement with Roman Catholicism does not seem to have lasted long, this period marked the beginning of an involvement with the *music [26] (if not the doctrines) of the Catholic church which lasted over forty years.

Wesley's adult career was patchy and uneven. He was generally recognized as the greatest English organist and, on the evidence of his best works, arguably the finest English composer of his age. The largest and most important part of Wesley's varied and diverse output is his *church music for the Roman Catholic rite, the latter part of it composed during the period c.1811–24, when he was unpaid assistant to Vincent *Novello at the Portuguese embassy chapel. He also wrote *Anglican church music, organ and piano music, chamber music, and orchestral music. For many years he was in demand

as an organist in London, where he played at the *oratorio concerts at Covent Garden, and at provincial *music festivals. He gave several lectures on music, at the Royal Institution, the Surrey Institution, and elsewhere, and contributed reviews of music to various periodicals of the *musical press. However, his maverick temperament and dislike of any sort of authority, his irregular private life, and his recurring bouts of mental illness all combined to place him outside the leading ranks of London musicians.

Perhaps Wesley's most significant contribution to the musical life of the period was in the role he played in the English *Bach movement. Although not the first in the field, he was the most energetic, or at any rate the most vociferous, of the small group of musicians who promoted the cause of Bach's music with almost religious zeal. He was responsible, with Benjamin Jacob (1778–1829), William *Crotch, Vincent *Novello, and others, for the first performances in England of many of Bach's works; in collaboration with C. F. Horn (1762–1830), he published the first English editions of Bach's organ *Trio Sonatas* (1809) and of the *Forty Eight Preludes and Fugues* (1810–13).

Amongst Samuel Wesley's many children was the organist and composer of Anglican church music Samuel Sebastian Wesley (1810–76), with whom he is often confused.   PO

WEST, Benjamin (1738–1820), American-born painter of religious and historical subjects and *portraits. West spent most of his career in England, achieved much fame in his own lifetime, and became the second president of the *Royal Academy (1792–1805, 1806–20).

Trained in America, West soon enjoyed substantial *patronage from local benefactors at the age of 22; he travelled to Italy in 1760 and then on to London in 1763. His Italian sojourn brought him into contact with leading neoclassical painters such as Gavin Hamilton and Anton Raphael Mengs, who influenced his own response to classical antiquity. At his London debut in 1766 he exhibited neoclassical works, and his adherence to the style continued with *Agrippina Landing at Brundisium with the Ashes of Germanicus* (1768), which made his career and ushered in many years of royal patronage.

The painting for which he is best known, *The Death of General Wolfe* (1771), created artistic controversy and materially affected the course of British *history painting because West clothed his figures in contemporary dress rather than in neoclassical attire. His later career was marked by some disappointment; his 'French sympathies' angered the *monarchy and he faced criticism within the Royal Academy, being forced to resign temporarily. Towards the end of his life he gained William *Beckford's patronage and began to work on large-scale religious subjects such as *Death on the Pale Horse* (1817) which has been compared with the work of French Romantic painters such as Delacroix. His portraits, too, seem to usher in the Romantic style in their dramatic presentation of mood.   SRP

WEST, Jane (1758–1852), writer of *novels [31], poems, plays, and *conduct books. West wrote popular works of anti-Jacobin rhetoric and Christian moralizing. Extraordinarily prolific, yet effacing literary ambition, West was admired by conservatives such as Jane *Austen, Sarah *Trimmer, and Bishop *Percy.

After publishing several volumes of poetry, West wrote her first novel *The Advantages of Education, or The History of Maria Williams* in 1793, an anti-sentimental tale tellingly ascribed to 'Prudentia Homespun'. *A Gossip's Story* followed in 1797 under the same pseudonym. West's political conservatism was evident in *A Tale of the Times* (1799), which presented a Godwinian philosopher as the rapist-villain, and in *Elegy on Edmund Burke* (1797), which mourned the loss of the Tory statesman.   KF

2 **WHEATLEY,** Francis (1747–1801), English painter of *portraits, *landscape, genre scenes, and *conversation pieces. Wheatley is best known today for his fourteen *Cries of London* (1792–5), which show itinerant street vendors hawking their wares and which achieved enormous success as engravings [see *prints, 22]. The style and sentiment of these and other genre works have rightly been compared to the work of Jean-Baptiste Greuze, feeding public demand for *sensibility [11] with decorative images of comely young women. Wheatley trained in London and visited France, the Low Countries, and Ireland in the 1760s. A liaison with the wife of the artist John Alexander Gresse led to a relocation to Dublin, where Wheatley was much in demand between 1779 and 1783 as a painter of fashionable society and events associated with the establishment of an independent Irish parliament. When his domestic arrangements became generally known in Dublin, Wheatley resumed his career in London. As a portraitist he painted competent if unassuming likenesses as well as conversation pieces, usually on a small scale. His landscapes, especially those in *watercolour, include accomplished examples of *picturesque tourism in England, Wales, and Ireland. Wheatley also attempted rustic genre, painting *The Harvest Wagon* (1774) in direct emulation of *Gainsborough's ambitious canvas of c.1767 but reducing its subject to a much more mundane scale.

Wheatley worked for the print publisher John *Boydell from the 1780s, contributing book illustrations as well as compositions to his Shakespeare Gallery. He achieved professional recognition in the London art world, becoming both a Fellow of the Society of Artists and a Royal Academician. In the range and technical competence of his production, Wheatley's practice typifies that undemanding art which circulated in polite circles at the close of the eighteenth century.   SSM

WHEELER, Anna Doyle (1785–1848), the most advanced but neglected feminist and socialist activist and thinker of the period after Mary *Wollstonecraft.

Born to a Protestant family in Limerick, Anna married disastrously at 15, then in 1812 fled her drunken landowner husband, taking her two eldest daughters to live successively in Guernsey, Dublin, Caen, and Paris before settling in London in the 1830s where she became an active writer in *Saint-Simonian and *Owenite circles. Her beauty, flamboyance, and unorthodox domestic life have obscured Wheeler's theoretical achievements and intellectual significance in the history of British *socialism and feminism [see *women, 4].

Her significance is, first, in acting as a carrier of French feminist and *utopian [9] socialist ideas to Britain: she introduced Robert Owen to Irish Fourierist Hugh Doherty (fl. 1830s) and French socialist-feminist Flora Tristan (1803–49), she translated and disseminated French Saint-Simonian articles in Owenite newspapers such as the *Crisis*, and she encouraged the careers of important British socialist-feminists such as the two Scots Frances Wright (1795–1852) and J. E. Smith (1801–57).

Secondly, through her powerful influence on William *Thompson, Anna Wheeler contributed to the most original and trenchant publication on feminism produced in our period. When publishing *Appeal of One-Half the Human Race, Women, against the pretensions of the Other Half, Men* in 1825 Thompson extolled her virtual co-authorship. The *Appeal* went beyond earlier feminist writing in attacking marriage as a form of domestic slavery, and in asserting the urgency of providing education, the vote, and alternatives to *domesticity [13] for women. Wheeler also expressed grave suspicion of arguments which endowed women with natural capacities for nurture and love. Her second daughter, Rosina (1802–82), became equally celebrated in later years for her passionate denunciations of her ex-husband, Edward *Bulwer-Lytton.   IMcC

WHEWELL, William (1794–1866), historian and philosopher of science. The eldest son of a carpenter, Whewell became master of Trinity College, Cambridge, and a robust participant in debates on the cultural status of science. He published mathematical textbooks and he coined many scientific terms including 'anode' and 'cathode', and the word 'scientist' itself.

The most influential of Whewell's many works appeared in the 1830s, at a time when the *natural philosophy [34] of the previous century was giving way to new scientific disciplines. *Astronomy and General Physics* (1833), a volume in the Bridgewater Treatises on natural theology, argued that the physical sciences, properly pursued, supported belief in a world designed by a benevolent Deity. His two major works, *History of the Inductive Sciences* (1837) and *The Philosophy of the Inductive Sciences* (1840) affirmed science as a noble pursuit requiring intellectual discipline and moral character. Whewell was sympathetic to the position of his friends Julius Hare (1795–1855) and Hugh J. Rose (1795–1838), who criticized the *utilitarian and materialist interpretations of science. He also agreed on the role of *imagination in the thought of great discoverers, but stressed that intuition had to be grounded in solid empirical research and methodological rigour.

Whewell is now recognized as a major contributor

to (and founder of) the philosophy of science, but this was not a specialist field when he wrote. Indeed, he can be viewed as a cultural critic, like *Coleridge and *Carlyle, commenting on the nature of science, its place in *education [17] and its relation with *religion [10] and philosophy, while at the same time forging the vocabulary of these discussions in *lectures, *sermons, and periodical *reviews. He did this at a time when the increasing specialization of the sciences threatened to make such public conversations untenable. RY

Whiggism refers to the political attitudes of the Whig party, which gradually emerged after 1760 in opposition to the person and policies of George III. Whiggism was first associated with those who followed Thomas Pelham-Holles (1693–1768), first Duke of Newcastle, out of office in 1762. The next leader of the party was the second Marquis of *Rockingham, Prime Minister in 1765–6 and 1782, who led it until his death in 1782.

During the years 1762 and 1782, spent mostly in opposition, the Rockinghamites developed a number of political positions, acting on several of them in Rockingham's brief ministry in 1782. However, having successfully set in train peace with America, granted legislative independence to Ireland, and managed to reduce royal patronage, principle seemed conspicuously absent in the party's actions. Charles James *Fox, its most prominent leader, shocked even former friends by his coalition with Lord North (1732–92) in 1783, by his grab for patronage in the Coalition's India Act of 1784, and by taking the high prerogative line in arguing for an unrestricted *Regency for his friend the Prince of Wales in 1787.

In 1787 Fox pursued the repeal of the Test and Corporation Acts, which excluded Dissenters from municipal government and office under the Crown. He had first championed the cause of religious liberty by his unswerving support for the Dissenters' successful effort in the 1770s to free themselves from the necessity of subscribing to the articles of the Church of England. Fox himself moved the last unsuccessful motion for repeal in 1790. The first stages of the *French Revolution coincided with the last stages of the Dissenters' campaign [see *toleration]. Fox recognized identical principles in the Dissenters' demands and the French Declaration of the Rights of Man and of the Citizen of 1789, with its endorsement of religious liberty and careers open to talent.

Though Fox and his Dissenting friends were repelled by the later excesses of the Revolution, they never renounced their approval. Reacting violently against events in France were Fox's old friend and colleague Edmund *Burke and the titular leader of the Whig party, the Duke of *Portland. In 1794 the majority of the Portland Whigs followed the Duke into an alliance with the Prime Minister, William *Pitt, to stand against the domestic and colonial threat posed by revolutionary challenges. Some of the Portland Whigs would later find their way back to the minority of the party which now became the

Foxite Whigs. Pitt, the son of Chatham, would always call himself a Whig, but most of his followers would become *Tories. It was the Foxite Whigs who soon became known as the Whigs.

Among those who remained loyal to Fox was Charles Grey (1764–1845), later, as the second Earl Grey, the Prime Minister who would carry the *Reform Act of 1832 [see *democracy, 3]. It was Grey, with the loyal though unenthusiastic support of Fox, who first associated the Whigs with the issue of *parliamentary reform by founding the Society of the Friends of the People in 1792. Though the franchise would be a good deal higher in 1832 than the householder franchise Grey proposed in the 1790s, the aim was the same: to create an independent borough electorate to join a county electorate deemed independent already. By 'independent' the Whigs meant electors who would not be susceptible either to crude bribery or to heavy-handed coercion. They had no objection to softer and more subtle forms of 'legitimate influence'.

In the 1790s, Pitt's large majority would hear of no sort of reform. Nor were many of Grey's own colleagues keen on it either. Therefore the Whigs' main efforts concentrated on advancing the aims summed up in the new motto, 'Civil and Religious Liberty'. However, they concentrated mainly on defensive efforts to save Dissenters and radical reformers from persecution.

Not until 1806, and then only in a *Ministry of All the Talents, would the Whigs have another crack at office. They were already allied with the Grenvillite party, headed by Lord *Grenville and his brother the Marquis of Buckingham. What made alliance possible in the first place was that both were critical of the *war [2] with France. Though this was not a very secure basis for co-operation—the Whigs were critical of the war and the Grenvillites thought it was being badly fought—it was enough to bring them together. This in turn brought to the fore other areas of more wholehearted agreement, especially on *Catholic emancipation, and the removal of tests which barred Catholics from municipal government, offices under the Crown, and parliament. Grenville was also ready to support another cause close to Fox's heart, the *abolition of the slave trade, which was carried in 1807.

Whilst the loyal support of the Grenvilles allowed the Whigs to override smaller parties in the coalition, most notably Lord Sidmouth's, one thing they could not override was the stubborn prejudice of George III. Grenvillites and Whigs agreed on the necessity of carrying a modest measure of emancipation, a proposal to allow Catholics to hold military offices from a colonelcy downwards. Whig principles secured the inclusion of the same right for Dissenters. The King would not hear of it, and when he also demanded a promise that similar proposals would never be put to him again, the Talents resigned in 1807.

The next twenty years would largely repeat the patterns of the previous fifteen. The Whigs would remain critical of the wars fought up to 1815, and of Britain's allies. The only exception was the Spanish, whom they saw as a people struggling to be free. Latin Americans, Greeks, and Poles would later be approved for the same reason. After 1811 there would be some secondary but significant gains in religious liberty, such as *Unitarian toleration and the removal of some of the anti-Dissenting statutes of the Restoration period. From 1816 to 1820, the Whigs would again defend the civil rights of radical reformers against government repression.

In the 1820s, however, the Whigs began to come into their own. Dissenters, whose numbers had been vastly increased since the last campaign by the impact of the *Evangelical revival [see *religion, 10], began to stir once again for repeal of the Test Acts. Their efforts were spurred on by the Irish, whose vigorous and determined efforts for emancipation were now directed by an organizer of genius, Daniel *O'Connell. In 1828 Lord John *Russell took charge of the Dissenters' repeal motion, hoping that by winning that battle first, he would undermine the foundations of the Protestant constitution itself. Success came quickly. Defeated by a substantial majority in the House of Commons, the Duke of *Wellington's government gave way and agreed to facilitate the passage of repeal. Shortly afterwards the Commons passed a motion for emancipation. O'Connell administered the *coup de grâce* by getting himself elected for County Clare. Rather than trying to refuse to seat the Catholic leader and thus having to deal with an uncertain majority in the Commons, and an aroused Ireland, Wellington decided to tackle emancipation himself. He carried it, but only with the strong and united support of the Whigs.

With their victory over the Test Acts, the Whigs had begun what they saw as a necessary shoring-up of the political system by bringing in the middle class. For, like the Dissenting leadership itself (and like the Tories, for that matter), the Whigs saw the Dissenters as the leading element in that class. It was necessary to bring such independent men within the pale of the Constitution in order to resist pressures from dangerous elements outside it. When Wellington refused to continue the task by proposing parliamentary reform in 1830, the Whigs did so. More aristocratic even than the Tories, Grey and his Cabinet would never have dreamt of relinquishing leadership into the hands of the middle class. What they believed was that free men, whose own opinions were treated with respect, would be content to follow aristocratic leaders.   RWD

WHITEFIELD, George (1714–70), leader of the Calvinistic *Methodists. Son of an innkeeper who paid his way through Oxford by waiting on genteel undergraduates, Whitefield joined the Methodists 'Holy Club' and experienced conversion in 1735. He spent much of 1737 preaching to large, emotional congregations in London and the West of England.

Whitefield devoted his life to itinerant evangelism which included regular tours of North America where he purchased a plantation and owned slaves. When the crowds grew too large or priests refused their churches to him, Whitefield took to *field preaching. A passionate and theatrical speaker, he

was the most populist preacher of the *Evangelical revival. Samuel *Johnson considered him a mob orator, little better than a huckster, and the *enthusiasm particularly associated with his brand of Methodism remained an object of suspicion for the religious establishment well into the nineteenth century.

What Whitefield lacked was John *Wesley's organizational ability, though his convert Selina, Countess of Huntington (1707–91), did try unsuccessfully to give Calvinistic Methodism some organizational structure among the upper classes. Partly as a result of this failing, the Arminian branch of Methodism associated with Wesley came to dominate the movement.   JM

WILBERFORCE, William (1759–1833), politician and *Evangelical reformer, instrumental in the *abolition of the slave trade [see *slavery, 6]. The son of a wealthy Yorkshire merchant in the Baltic trade, Wilberforce began his long and influential parliamentary career in 1780, spending nearly £8,000 to gain the seat of Kingston upon Hull. He was a close friend of William *Pitt before entering the House of Commons, and firmly supported Pitt's cautious pursuit of *parliamentary reform and peace with America. In 1784 Wilberforce was chosen country member for Yorkshire largely on the strength of his support of Pitt, and held that seat until 1812.

Towards the end of 1784, Wilberforce underwent a religious conversion marked by depression and guilt at having sought parliamentary distinction solely out of personal ambition. He gained spiritual comfort and advice from leading Evangelicals, and in particular John Newton (1725–1807), an Anglican cleric and anti-slavery campaigner, who in his youth had been a slave overseer on the Gold Coast. Wilberforce had been openly critical of the slave trade since early youth. By the end of 1786 he was convinced that Providence had set him the task of using his wealth and parliamentary influence to bring about 'the suppression of the slave trade and the reformation of manners.' For the remainder of his long parliamentary career, Wilberforce worked tirelessly to end the slave trade and championed various schemes for moral reformation. By the early 1790s he was Britain's most influential Evangelical lay spokesperson.

At various times through the era of revolution, Wilberforce was prepared to alienate the court and his *Tory parliamentary allies by aligning himself with opposition politicians and, on occasion, more radical critics of the old regime. This he did believing his independent action would best contribute to the moral regeneration of his fellow Britons. However, as Wilberforce's responses to poverty and popular unrest in the early years of the nineteenth century demonstrate, his reformism was essentially conservative. In common with most Evangelicals, he equated democratic radicalism with atheism, and regarded the stratified ordering of society as providentially ordained.   PT

WILKES, John (1725–97), see *Wilkites.

WILKIE, Sir David (1785–1841), Scottish painter, whose genre scenes contributed to a transformation of artistic taste, and whose historical subjects have been compared to Walter *Scott's novels [see *painting, 27].

Wilkie trained as an artist at the Trustees' Academy in Edinburgh, and produced his first major oil-painting, *Pitlessie Fair*, in 1804. This commemoration of a village festival in Fife contained all the elements which made Wilkie famous when he went to London the following year. London audiences were attracted to his interest in low life and to the subtleties of gesture and expression—qualities that Wilkie adopted from Dutch and Flemish genre painting. The focus on low life was against the grain of the *Royal Academy's emphasis on *history painting as the highest form of art, but Wilkie's popularity signalled a change in taste brought about by the expanding middle-class market for art.

In later works such as *The Village Politicians* (1806) and *The Blind Fiddler* (1807), Wilkie presented more detailed views of village sociability, which gained him *patronage from both aristocracy and royalty. Admiration of his works was based partly on their resemblance to old master paintings by Teniers and Ostade. Contemporary critics praised Wilkie for his 'truthful' views of village life, although his paintings could be more accurately described as nostalgic or droll visions of an imaginary rural existence. Walter Scott compared himself to Wilkie in *The Antiquary* (1816), in which he praised the painter for attempting to capture Scottish traditions under threat from modern *industrialization [14].

The next phase in Wilkie's career was influenced by Scott's attempts to combine anecdotal fiction with historical fact. His *Chelsea Pensioners Reading the Gazette of the Battle of Waterloo*, commissioned by the Duke of *Wellington and exhibited at the Royal Academy in 1822, depicts the imaginary scene of old soldiers reading news of the battle of *Waterloo as if it had actually happened, by including accurate depictions of regimental dress, as well as an identifiable setting near the Royal Hospital at Chelsea. The painting was so successful that a rail had to be erected to protect it at the Royal Academy exhibition.

Wilkie's ill health resulted in a trip to the Continent in 1826–7, during which he visited Italy, Germany, Central Europe, and Spain. Inspiration from continental, particularly Spanish, Old Masters transformed his style, and he became more interested in history painting after returning to England. His most ambitious work, *Sir David Baird Discovering the Body of Tipoo Sahib* (1834), revealed both historical imagination and accuracy of detail. He continued to gain respectability: he was appointed Painter-in-Ordinary to the King in 1830 and knighted in 1836, but he became less popular with the exhibition-going public, who still identified him with diverting genre scenes. In 1840 he took a trip to the Holy Land to gather information for paintings with biblical themes, but he died at sea.   SW

WILKINS, William (1778–1839), architect, theatre manager, scholar. The son of William Wilkins (1751–1815), who was also an architect and theatre manager, the younger Wilkins was educated at Caius College, Cambridge. After graduating he travelled in the Mediterranean and the Near East and on return to England became a leading exponent of the Greek revival [see *Hellenism]. He combined a career as an architect with interests in the East Anglian theatre circuit, owning playhouses at Norwich, Yarmouth, Bury St Edmunds, Colchester, Ipswich, and Cambridge. His theatre at Norwich (1825–6) is a fine example of late Georgian provincial theatre design. His significant buildings include Downing College, Cambridge (1807–20), University College, London (1827–8), and the National Gallery, London (1834–8). One unrealized project was a design with J. M. *Gandy for a commemorative monument to the battle of *Waterloo which was to have been sited at the northern end of Portland Place. Wilkins interpreted its rejection on the grounds of cost as symptomatic of the government's failure to endorse prestigious projects of national significance in the immediate postwar period. A scholar of classical *architecture [28], he published a number of works on the subject and in 1837 succeeded Sir John *Soane as professor of architecture at the *Royal Academy.   GR

Wilkites, the followers of John Wilkes (1725–97), a charismatic London distiller's son frequently hailed as the father of modern British radicalism. Wilkes was responsible for greatly expanding the boundaries of the eighteenth-century political public and for moulding a plethora of commercial energies and social discontents into an effective libertarian movement of political opposition. Wilkes's oppositional campaigns sprang from personal interests, yet he possessed considerable courage to defy the anger of George III and his ministers throughout the 1760s and 1770s. Though opportunistic, Wilkes generally adhered to a core of *Whig-liberal principles. His pungent anti-monarchical satires developed into wider defences of individual liberty and freedom of opinion, which included resistance to government use of general warrants, a campaign to open parliamentary debates to newspaper reporters, and an assertion of the rights of Middlesex voters to elect the member of their choice in defiance of legal and political coercion from parliament, Crown, and ministers. Though no democrat, he introduced the first formal motion for *parliamentary reform in 1776. His champions also formed the Society for the Supporters of the Bill of Rights, a pioneering political association which organized a successful nationwide petitioning campaign in 1769.

Wilkes's supporters included merchants angered by government war policies in America, Dissenters excluded from formal political participation, artisans suffering wartime inflation, and unenfranchised labourers schooled in the truculence of the eighteenth-century crowd. A master of political propaganda and theatricality, he skilfully exploited metropolitan and provincial *newspapers, *debating and singing clubs, *coffeehouses and *theatres, and he seized opportunities for novel political expression created by the commercial production of badges, tokens, coins, handkerchiefs, ceramics, and jewelry. His rakish wit also found common cause with a lively plebeian culture of anti-establishment raillery and saturnalia, expressed in *street literature, satirical *prints [22], *ballads, and processions. The popular catch-cry 'Wilkes and Liberty' heralded the arrival of the common people as an organized presence in Georgian public political life.

Ironically, Wilkes told George III towards the end of his life that he, Wilkes, 'was never a Wilkite'. Having been allowed to take his parliamentary seat in 1774, he became Lord Mayor, and his strong belief in toleration induced him to act vigorously against the *Gordon rioters in 1780, earning the monarch's gratitude for his firmness. Wilkes's support for *Pitt during the French and Napoleonic wars further confirmed his estrangement from earlier radical causes and his growing reputation for conservatism. IMcC

WILLIAMS, David (1738–1816), a neglected *Deist preacher and radical *Enlightenment [32] intellectual who acted as an important conduit between polite and plebeian culture in the late eighteenth century.

Born and brought up at Waunwaelod, near Caerphilly in south Wales, he followed the wishes of his father, who died when he was 14, in attending Carmarthen *Dissenting academy to be trained for the ministry. He left the academy in 1757, ministered at a Presbyterian chapel in Frome, Somerset, for four years, then moved to the Independent Mint Meeting, Exeter, until 1769. He left under a cloud with allegations of moral impropriety and theological laxity, having introduced the Liverpool liturgy which had minimal theological content. Williams moved from Exeter to London, serving for a while as a part-time minister at Highgate. Poorly paid, impatient with the theological differences between various brands of Christian orthodoxy and heterodoxy, and deeply critical of the intolerance, as he saw it, of the Dissenters, he soon made his own independent way as a natural religionist. However, he never relinquished his belief in the value of public worship, which he saw as essential to moral wellbeing and indispensable for the development of a science of politics and morality. This tension between belief in the value of social worship and in a moral code which was natural and individualistic remained a feature of most nineteenth-century ethical societies, and appeared in Williams's Essays on Public Worship (1773).

His views on *toleration, however, were more controversial. While accepting the need for an established church, Williams argued for complete religious and intellectual liberty in terms guaranteed to shock: he wrote in his The Nature and Extent of Intellectual Liberty (1779), 'I do not see why thieves should not be allowed to preach the principles of theft; murderers of murder; seducers of seduction; adulterers of adultery, and traitors of treason.'

Following his departure from Highgate, Williams attempted to implement his Deistic ideals by setting up a Deist chapel at Margaret Street, London, which lasted from 1776 to 1780. Known as 'The Priest of Nature' he attracted influential supporters, including Thomas Bentley (1731–80), Josiah *Wedgwood, James 'Athenian' Stuart (1713–88), Sir William *Jones, and Benjamin Franklin (1706–90). Williams publicized his ideas on the Continent, and both Voltaire and *Rousseau replied to his solicitations enthusiastically; the *Cook voyage naturalists Georg and Johann Rheinhold *Forster attended when in England. Williams used his own Deist liturgy, the Liturgy on Universal Principles (1776), which gives thanks to God for his beneficence, strictly avoids petitionary prayer, and could have been written for the inhabitants of Voltaire's Eldorado. For a variety of reasons, including Williams's chronic ill health, the enterprise failed, but his efforts helped to frame the outlook of radicals who favoured complete intellectual liberty, had roseate views of God's creation, and who liked to set up theophilanthropic societies and *lecture series.

For the rest of his career, Williams maintained himself though teaching and journalism. He had become a major figure in the literary world, and something of a guru to artisan intellectuals. He engaged briefly in a more active role in politics in 1792 when he accepted honorary French citizenship, though he declined to stand for the French Convention, notwithstanding a long-standing friendship with the Girondin pamphleteer J. P. Brissot. He had formulated his political philosophy in a number of works in the 1780s, which looked forward to a 'reformation' in France. In December 1792, on Brissot's invitation, he travelled to France to advise on the construction of a new French republican constitution, but was dismayed by the turbulence of the meetings of the Convention and by Brissot's disastrous foreign policy. Knowing French, he played a modest, intermediary role between Britain and France. However, months after the execution of Louis XVI in January 1793, Williams returned to England, having had little impact on French politics or constitutional thought, and disillusioned with the direction the Revolution had taken.

Williams did not relinquish his previous views—he had never been a conventional radical—but he now eschewed all involvement in reformist activity. He had shared with the radical reformers the belief in an original Anglo-Saxon constitution which could serve as the model for political reform [see *democracy, 3]. Yet he had been wary of a declaration of rights: he favoured equality before the law, educational equality, and equal voting rights, but in other matters he believed that equality was enervating. Instead he favoured 'a rigorous equity'. His contribution to political thought, however, was less programmatic than analytical. Unlike many radical thinkers, he understood the interconnection between political forms, public confidence, public morality, and economic and financial policy. In a polity founded upon political liberty, the government could pursue a relatively interventionist policy and allow the *national debt to grow, whereas in one where the people at best possessed civil liberty, it was desirable for the government not to interfere in economic life. Appropriately, he came gradually to see political liberty as an independent good superior to civil liberty. His *Letters on Political Liberty* (1782) defined political liberty in terms of the answerability of the executive to the legislature and that of the legislature to the people. In a state in which political liberty existed and the government could be seen as an expression of the will of the people, he suggested a series of appropriate institutional arrangements. These included, at the local level, groupings of 'hundreds' and 'tythings', based on putative Anglo-Saxon example, and, at the centre, a national convention to be elected quadrennially, and a constitutional council, annually elected by the whole of the electorate. Such ideas continued to influence radical thought in the 1790s, though Williams himself ceased to espouse them publicly.

By the 1790s Williams was sufficiently famous for a biographical memoir to be published, and he used his fame and connections to establish a project of lasting significance. In 1790 he set up a Literary Fund for indigent writers and worked ceaselessly to put it on firm foundations [see *Royal Literary Fund]. He saw it not simply as a charity but as a means of promoting intellectual liberty. Initially it relied on the subscription of its members and an annual celebratory dinner for raising funds, but in 1797 it created an endowment which would ensure permanence of the institution. Williams's own association with the fund was briefly placed in doubt when a conservative faction in the fund, led by Sir James Bland Burgess (1756–1824), took offence at Williams's *Claims of Literature* (1802), which was a defence of the fund and his literary ideals. Williams survived his censure and Burgess resigned. The fund itself has continued to the present day.

Williams's other achievements do not fit easily into a pattern. Though his aspiration for a science of morals and politics was not fulfilled, he came closer to establishing a genuine empirical basis for his thought in his educational ideas and experiments. These combined a concern for *education [17] responsive to individual needs and capacities which at the same time created a framework for the development of good citizenship crucial to general wellbeing and the flourishing of political liberty. Although an often difficult person with a libertinist streak, he was personally unselfish and benevolent. In 1774 he had to cope with the death of his wife while she was giving birth to his son, and he often sacrificed his own health to his work. He was convinced that a vegetarian remedy, Velno's Vegetable Syrup, had helped him recover from serious health problems, and he became a proselytizer for the medicine and a critic of 'chemical' medicines. This links him to the *vegetarianism of the radical world which has had a continuous if tortuous history through to the Greens today.

MF

WILLIAMS, Edward (Iolo Morganwg) (1747–1826), generally known by his bardic pseudonym, meaning 'Ned of Glamorgan'; stonemason, Welsh poet and antiquary, forger of Welsh medieval prose and poetry, and inventor of Welsh traditions, such as the Gorsedd of Bards.

In youth he was deeply influenced by the *Welsh cultural revival, becoming adept at imitating medieval bardic poetry, and assisting local clerics with Welsh lexicography. Working as a mason in London and Kent in the 1770s and 1790s, he was influenced by the political radicalism and historical enthusiasms of the London Welsh, notably the Gwyneddigion Society. In 1789 he contributed a collection of poems purporting to be by the fourteenth-century bard Dafydd ap Gwilym to the Society's edition of the bard's works. English literary movements such as neodruidism were conveyed to Iolo by friends such as *Southey, and in June 1792, on Primrose Hill, London, he organized the first meeting of the Gorsedd of Bards of the Isle of Britain, claiming to be one of the last surviving Welsh bards who had received their lore and wisdom from the ancient druids. At the same time he encouraged Welsh emigration to America by spreading propaganda about its discovery around 1170 by the Welsh prince *Madoc, and the possible survival of his followers as Welsh Red Indians. Many of Iolo's fantasies and obsessions are aired in *Poems Lyric and Pastoral*, his two-volume collection of English poems in 1794.

His political radicalism being muted during the Napoleonic wars, he gave his attention to *Unitarianism, helping to found the sect in south Wales in 1802, for which he wrote a huge collection of *hymns published in 1812. The return of peace in 1814–15 saw an outburst of cultural activity in Wales in which Iolo appeared as a central figure, succeeding in grafting his druidic moot or Gorsedd onto the *eisteddfod from 1819 onwards, and devoting much of the last decades of his life to inventing a vast quantity of historical lore, part of which he published in *The Myvyrian Archaiology of Wales* (1801–7), and part of which his son and other editors published from 1829 to the 1860s.

The lack of printed primary sources for Welsh history and letters, and the absence of scholarly institutions or criticism, allowed Iolo's fertile imagination (fevered by a lifelong addiction to laudanum) and many-sided artistic facility to produce literary forgeries of all kinds without detection. Because he was a manuscript copyist and collector with an unrivalled knowledge of sources, his inventions were usually also based on a grain of truth [see *antiquarianism, 35]. His motives were varied: he wished to prove (in the absence of satisfactory evidence) that his native Glamorgan was of central importance to Welsh history and literature, that the bards and druids represented the essential Welsh tradition since the dawn of history, that the Welsh had played an important part in world history, and that the Welsh were the primary people of the British Isles. It is possible that his neodruidism, with its pacifism and egalitarianism, was a coded political manifesto, the attempt of a radical to make converts at a time of political persecution and reaction.

The institution of the Gorsedd of Bards (a kind of league of supporters for Welsh *language [40] and history) helped to retain the Welshness of the national eisteddfod at a time of Anglicization of Welsh life in the nineteenth century. PM

WILLIAMS, Helen Maria (1761/2–1827), poet, novelist, and chronicler of the *French Revolution from 1790. One of two daughters born to a Welsh army officer and Scottish mother, Williams launched her literary career in 1782 with the publication of the verse tale *Edwin and Eltruda*. Her patron Dr Andrew Kippis (1725–95), an old family friend, introduced her to a circle of intellectuals and Dissenters which included Elizabeth Montagu (1720–1800), Anna *Seward, Frances *Burney, and Hester Thrale *Piozzi. When her collected *Poems* were published in two volumes in 1786, she could boast seventy-seven pages of subscribers. The influence of her first volume on the young William *Wordsworth can be clearly seen in his later 'Lucy' poems, while a more immediate response appeared in his sonnet to her, published in 1787. In 1790 she published her first and only novel, *Julia*. Intermixed with social satire is the *Rousseauist story of two cousins, Charlotte and Julia, whose close friendship is threatened by Charlotte's marriage and her husband's tragic infatuation with Julia. The novel, admired by Mary *Wollstonecraft, ends with the death of the husband on the birth of his heir, and the reunion and re-devotion of the cousins to each other and the child.

In 1790 Williams crossed to Paris, where her arrival in time for the Festival of the Federation confirmed her revolutionary sympathies and initiated her new persona as 'citizen of the world'. Her *Letters written in France* (1790) were enthusiastically received by a large home audience eager for eyewitness accounts of French affairs. As a foreigner and a woman she gained easy access to all the prime tourist locations, such as the Bastille and Versailles, and a front seat at the National Assembly. The epistolary form gave scope to her presentation of politics as an affair of the heart, the 1790 *Letters* concluding with the romance of the Du Fossé family, reunited in republican bliss after persecution by the *ancien régime*. Williams did not return to England after 1792 but remained in Paris, where she kept a salon which included, at different times, Wollstonecraft, *Paine, and leading Girondins. Believing that 'the existence of liberty in Europe is fixed on the fate of the French Republic', Williams continued chronicling French politics in narratives and sketches until 1819, but her early popularity declined, and, despite losing many friends to the guillotine, she was stigmatized as a Jacobin. Imprisoned by Robespierre, she translated Bernardin Saint Pierre's *Paul and Virginia*, a Rousseauist tale of an innocent way of life destroyed by corrupt civilization. In general her political views were liberal and compassionate. She argued against despotism and terror of all kinds, be it the royal terror of the counter-revolution in Naples or the Jacobin terror of Paris, and throughout her writings displayed sympathy for the dispossessed, such as negro slaves and the labouring poor. The lot of *women [4] was also a recurrent concern, although women's limited gains under the new ordinance somewhat tempered her generally optimistic view of the achievements of the French Republic.　　　　　　　　　　　　　　DC

WILLIAMS, John (1761–1818), pseud. 'Anthony Pasquin', one of the most feared and unscrupulous *satirists and critics of the age. Born in London, he was educated at the Merchant Taylors' school and then apprenticed to the Strand shop of engraver Matthew Darly (*fl.* 1782) where he showed early promise as a graphic caricaturist [see *prints, 22]. Around the age of 17 he also became a friend and informal secretary to the celebrated American waxwork artist, republican, and spy, Patience Wright (1725–86). Here he fell in with a glittering circle of artists and dramatists, including David Garrick (1717–79) and Benjamin *West. Links with dangerous American revolutionaries and Protestant enthusiasts [see *Gordon riots] may account for his sudden retreat to Dublin around 1781, where he worked as a journalist and began to write verse satire with an anti-government leaning. Two years later he recommenced his career as a London journalist, specializing in *theatre [24] criticism and working initially for the famous 'fighting parson' Henry Bate Dudley (1745–1824) on the *Morning Herald*.

As well as gaining a reputation for vicious satire and personal slovenliness, Anthony Pasquin, as he called himself, organized private theatricals and played the buffoon for the rakish circle of bloods who gathered at the Earl of Barrymore's Wargrave residence. Most of the rest of his life in Britain was spent alternating between London and the fashionable *spa town of Bath, where opportunities for scandalous satire and blackmail abounded. Pasquin's theatrical criticism and verse satire in works such as *The Children of Thespis* (1786–7) and the *Dramatic Censor* (1811) made him the terror of actors, but *A Looking Glass for the The Royal Family* (1796) showed he was not afraid to lampoon the *monarchy as well. By 1797 his reputation was so seedy that Lord Kenyon (1732–1802) scoffingly dismissed a libel suit which Pasquin brought against the anti-Jacobin satirist William *Gifford. The last few years of Pasquin's life were spent in New York writing local satires and editing a democratic newspaper called the *Federalist*.　　　　　IMcC

WILSON, Harriette (1786–1845), courtesan and autobiographer. Wilson (a pseudonym) was the most renowned courtesan in London high society in the early 1800s. Her autobiographical *Memoirs* (1825) describe a predominantly masculine world, inhabited by such figures as the Duke of *Wellington, Lord *Byron, Henry *Brougham, and Beau Brummell [see *dandyism], in which courtesans had transient power and independence.

She was one of several daughters of Amelia Cook (the natural child of a gentleman) and the Swiss-born John Dubochet, an irascible and violent man obsessed by mathematics. Mother and daughters supported the family by stocking-mending. Following the example of two sisters, she left home in her teens for a sexual career, as recorded in the memorable opening line of the *Memoirs*: 'I shall not say why and how I became, at the age of fifteen, the mistress of the Earl of Craven.'

Wilson had a series of titled protectors, but her success as a fashionable courtesan declined after 1812. In 1823 she married an indigent Irish officer, William Henry Rochfort. Impoverished, she wrote the *Memoirs*, recounting her liaisons and friendships with members of the British aristocracy, with Rochfort's encouragement, as an instrument of blackmail. Published by John Stockdale (?1749–1814), they were used to gain substantial exclusion fees from those who wished not to be featured, eliciting the famous phrase from the Duke of Wellington, 'Publish and be damned'. Numbers of opportunist radical publishers, such as the future pornographer William Dugdale (*c*.1815–68), pirated versions of the memoirs for commercial gain and because they embarrassed the government. The memoirs also became one of the literary foundation-stones of subsequent interpretations of the *Regency.   RCA

WILSON, John (1785–1854), poet, magazine *reviewer, and *satirist. Wilson's being better known by his pseudonym 'Christopher North' is a telling comment on a mercurial, probably disturbed personality whose criticism, like his personal relations, could turn unpredictably from warm admiration to derision. His cultural significance derives less from his sub-Wordsworthian *poetry [29] and mawkish *novels [31] than from high-spirited satire and occasional critical insight.

John Wilson taught moral philosophy at the University of Edinburgh subsequent to his appointment to the chair in 1820. As Christopher North, on the other hand, he was a various and energetic contributor to *Blackwood's Edinburgh Magazine* or 'Maga', a self-consciously miscellaneous and often scurrilous experiment in periodical 'familiarity'. Of his two personas, Professor Wilson was the fraud, accepting the politically inspired offer without qualifications, then constraining others to help out with lectures.

Though the pseudonym dates from 1822, North was central to 'Maga' from October 1817, when with James *Hogg and John Gibson *Lockhart he attacked Edinburgh's *Whig cultural establishment in a mock-'Translation of an Ancient Chaldee Manuscript', setting a tone of manic irreverence popular enough to justify numerous libel payments.

It was as orchestrator of the serialized symposium *Noctes Ambrosianæ* (1822–35), however, that North found his authentic voice(s). Taking the form of modified, often enriched 'transcriptions' of conversations between North, Lockhart, Hogg (as 'the Ettrick Shepherd'), William Maginn (1793–1842), and occasional others, the 'nights at Ambrose's [Tavern]' unapologetically exploits a broad Scottish culture. Without authorial, thematic, or textual centre, *Noctes* enacts a 'dialogic' process challenging origins, teleological form, and conceptual hierarchies; abuse, argument, and anecdote move promiscuously from ghosts to gossip and from poultry farming to poetry. While allowing North subtle arrogations as Lord of Misrule, *Noctes* was ideally suited to one constitutionally incapable of adopting a consistent, accountable position.   WC

WILSON, Richard (1713/14–82), Welsh painter of portraits, landscapes, and historical subjects; worked in Italy, England, and Wales. Although poor and overlooked in the last decade of his career, by the beginning of the nineteenth century he was commonly regarded as a misunderstood *genius and one of the founders of English *landscape painting.

Wilson's family was well connected, so his decision to become a professional artist was unusual. He worked initially as a *portraitist but during his sojourn in Italy (1750–6/7) he changed direction and henceforth devoted himself to landscape painting, combining observation with a grandeur derived from studying the works of Claude Lorrain and Gaspard Dughet. Back in London, his reputation was assured when he exhibited *The Destruction of Niobe's Children* (1760), and he rapidly built up a successful practice painting Italian scenes and classical subjects. He also depicted landed estates in England and Wales, using an idealized style far removed from tame topography. Many of these latter works can be understood as offering a comforting vision of paternalism and social harmony to their patrons at a time of increasing uncertainty around the time of the Seven Years War. In the 1770s, however, Wilson's reputation faded. His disdain for connoisseurs and his alcoholism provide some explanation for this, but equally his learned and socially exclusive art may have fared less well with the emergence of a more mercantile *patronage. His adherence to the Grand Style in landscape was also increasingly at odds with the cult of the *picturesque and the beginnings of a more naturalistic aesthetic in British *painting [27].
SSM

WOLCOT, John (1738–1819), pseud. 'Peter Pindar'. The most prolific, popular, and admired *satirist of the late Georgian period, he remains seriously underestimated by modern social historians and literary scholars.

A Devonshire surgeon's son, Wolcot attended a series of grammar schools where he acquired a considerable classical learning, as well as impressive accomplishments in *music [26] and *painting [27]. His early career as a doctor and curate, practising mainly in Cornwall and Jamaica, failed to satisfy a restless, Rabelaisian nature, and he soon began making a local name for himself as a writer of satirical verse and musical lyrics. Around 1781 he moved permanently to London, hoping to promote and share in the success of Cornish painting prodigy John *Opie, whose rough talents he had recognized and fostered. Though his career as Opie's agent proved short-lived, Wolcot achieved critical success with his scathing verse satire of the *Royal Academy's art exhibition, *Lyric Odes to the Royal Academicians for 1782* (1782). In 1785, using domestic detail gleaned from a friend among the royal servants, he wrote a hilariously irreverent satire, *The Lousiad*, from the perspective of a louse that had dropped off George III's head onto his eating-plate. Successive cantos followed each year until the mid-1790s, and it was this rich vein of anti-monarchical satire, above all, which was to make Wolcot, under the pseudonym of 'Peter Pindar', a household name in Britain and abroad.

By the late 1780s Wolcot had become a London literary identity, a low-life equivalent to Samuel *Johnson, whom he knew, admired, and burlesqued in several works, including *Bozzy and Piozzi* published in 1786. By this time Wolcot's satires were selling as many as 20,000 numbers in a single day, and passing through multiple editions. His fame was such that foreign celebrities like the Polish nationalist leader Taduesz Kosciuzkco (1746–1817) and the Austrian musical genius Franz Joseph *Hadyn eagerly sought his friendship and intellectual collaboration. By the early 1790s the *monarchy and William *Pitt—the target of persistently savage Wolcot lampoons—regarded his satires as so damaging that they tried to muzzle him through a pension. But Wolcot proved to be a temporary and unreliable ministerial ally. One of his last publications, the *Carlton Fete of 1811*, even turned against a long-time supporter, the Prince Regent, inaugurating a spate of similar satires on George's manners and morals by a new generation of Pindarian imitators and disciples, culminating in the bestselling postwar squibs of William *Hone.

Given Wolcot's enormous contemporary impact, his subsequent neglect at the hands of historians and literary critics is puzzling. The chief explanation seems to be that both his politics and literature resist easy categorization. Politically he was unquestionably a radical, a close friend of William *Godwin and the *Treason Trialists, a lifelong opponent of Pitt, and a favoured target of the *Anti-Jacobin Review*. Yet he did not hesitate to satirize Thomas *Paine, and he displayed a pugnacious English *patriotism and populist dislike of aristocracy and pretension (including *Whigs) which is reminiscent of James *Gillray and the younger William *Cobbett. His poetry and satire displayed a similarly ambiguous and populist character. Wolcot's admiration of Charles Churchill (1732–64), his frequent classical allusions, and his use of rhyming couplets in six-line stanzas clearly align him with Augustan satirists. At the same time his fondness for vernacular idiom, his libertine coarseness and personal scurrility, his celebration of commercialism and dislike of sensibility, his love of low burlesque forms and focus on public and political issues, his promiscuous genre borrowings including journalism and *street literature, and his pride in being a 'people's poet'—none of these sits easily with either Augustan or Romantic satirical traditions as commonly defined. Yet his disruption of classical forms, self-reflexivity, and bizarre rhyming clearly influenced both *Byron and the American Romantic-revolutionary poet Philip Morin Freneau (1752–1832), who hailed him as a formative influence.   IMcC

7 **WOLLSTONECRAFT,** Mary (1759–97), radical feminist writer. Wollstonecraft was the eldest girl of the seven children born to an Irish mother, Elizabeth Dixon [or Dickson], and an occasionally violent English father, Edward Wollstonecraft. This Anglo-Irish colonial family, with its personal pain and drive

to seek the metropolis as an arena for creative self-vindication, was an important context for Mary Wollstonecrafts' later career.

Her first love was at 14 for a neighbour's daughter, Jane Arden, and her second ardent friendship was also with a young woman, Fanny Blood, whose whole family Mary long supported. Her first job away from home was as nurse companion to an elderly widow in Bath. Called back in 1781 to attend her dying mother, she used the months of sickbed duty to salvage a semblance of mother–daughter intimacy from the crushing disappointment of her mother's preference for her brother Ned. Her first attempt at economic independence was to establish a school for girls at Islington, which united her sisters and Fanny Blood under her leadership. Wollstonecraft soon moved their base to the Dissenter neighbourhood at Newington Green, where Thomas *Day, the reformist schoolteacher, and Richard *Price, the liberal clergyman, were leading lights. Hannah Burgh, widow of educational writer, James Burgh, welcomed her, and Wollstonecraft crafted her anthology *The Female Reader* out of Burgh's *The Art of Speaking* (1772). Wollstonecraft's *Thoughts on the Education of Daughters* (1787), *Original Stories from Real Life* (1788), and *The Female Reader* (1789),   22 capitalized on the growing readership for topics of *female education and public cultural representation by *women [4]. In 1785, after Hugh Skeys and Fanny Blood had married in Lisbon, Wollstonecraft travelled there but arrived only in time for Fanny's and her baby's funeral. She returned, bereft, at New Year 1786, to find her sisters quarrelling, the school defunct and in debt. She threw herself into producing *Thoughts on the Education of Daughters*, which argued for the rights of women to education and to professional advancement as the acknowledged best educators of their own sex, and it was accepted for publication by the radical publisher Joseph *Johnson, a key supporter of her career.

With this confirmation of her future as a writer, she braced herself in November 1787 to work in Ireland as governess to the three eldest of the daughters of Lord and Lady Kingsborough. *Mary: A Fiction* (1788) is a *Rousseauist novel drawn from this episode. Soon, according to her letters, her girl pupils developed a crush on her, and she was dismissed by Lady Kingsborough in August 1788.

She returned to London and a rent-free house offered to her by Johnson, who also gave her work translating and reviewing for the *Analytical Review*, which stimulated her appetite for news and intellectual debate. When Edmund *Burke's *Reflections on the Revolution in France* was published in November 1790, Wollstonecraft's anonymous retort, *A Vindication of the Rights of Men*, appeared before the year was out. In 1791 the éclat of her name on the second edition of *Vindication* ushered her into radical intellectual company in London. She began her acquaintance with American expatriates circulating between London and Paris. In November 1791, Johnson introduced her to Thomas *Paine and William *Godwin at one of his dinner parties, and the conversation grew heated when as a woman she presumed too far on the priority of her own protest against anti-jacobin propagandists. She conceived a powerful attraction for the painter Henry *Fuseli, and during this affair wrote her major work, *A Vindication of the Rights of Woman* (1792). The women invoked in its pages are heroic peers and democratic allies, fearless to support and free to criticize each other, versions of Wollstonecraft's high-achieving contemporaries Catharine *Macaulay and Anna Laetitia *Barbauld, but removed to a disinterested plane where dependence on men and money was unknown. Once it was published, in the winter of 1792–3 Wollstonecraft travelled to Paris alone, to try to recover from her rejection by Fuseli. In Paris in the dark days of the Terror, Mary, pregnant for the first time, went into hiding with the Pennsylvanian land speculator and soldier of fortune Gilbert Imlay (1752–1828). The child Fanny was born in Le Havre in May 1794 after Imlay had arranged a certificate of cohabitation. Imlay's devotion had worn thin even before the birth; he persuaded Wollstonecraft to return to London but provided no home. Johnson published her *Historical and Moral View of the French Revolution* in 1794 as a first volume, which breaks off before the overthrow of the Girondists. Meanwhile, her efforts to win back Imlay continued doggedly: she made a half-hearted attempt at suicide with laudanum, and was rescued by a maidservant. Recovering, she agreed to travel to Scandinavia on business for Imlay, who was in financial difficulties, and made a great success with the book of the tour, *Letters written during a short residence in Sweden, Norway and Denmark* (1796). Imlay, openly living with another woman, did not respond to any of her overtures, and in October 1795 Wollstonecraft made a serious suicide attempt by jumping into the Thames, but was hauled out by wherrymen.

This time her recovery was assisted by Mary *Hays, who in January 1796 reintroduced her to William Godwin. Now that Godwin was a successful author and acknowledged spokesman on public policy he no longer reacted to her as a threat, and they became lovers, she having to lead the way for this prim bachelor of forty years. They exchanged letters, took Fanny for walks, and visited each other at odd hours, but she swiftly fell pregnant, ending the brief respite from anxiety and jealousy. They married at St Pancras's Church on 29 March 1797, apparently at her urging, to give this second child a name and Fanny a home, but Godwin maintained separate quarters for his daily writing and social life. The actress Sarah *Siddons and her circle hastily withdrew from their society because the marriage collapsed the polite fiction that Wollstonecraft was the legal, wronged wife, 'Mrs Imlay', though Mary *Robinson, Maria Reveley, and Amelia Alderson (later Amelia *Opie) remained personally loyal to Wollstonecraft. Godwin was demurely discouraging about Wollstonecraft's current writing, listing its faults and advising her to follow a regime of calculated progression, like his own. As the work was a *Gothic novel titled *The Wrongs of Woman*, which also fictionalized the affair with Godwin, first as an

antidote to the desperate failure with Imlay and then increasingly as a nightmare of its repetition, she disregarded his advice, and the manuscript grew ever more chaotic and unfinishable. She gave birth to her second daughter, the future Mary *Shelley, on 30 August 1797 and died on Sunday 10 September, infected during manual removement of the placenta by a physician. Only one woman was among the medical men at the deathbed, Eliza *Fenwick, wife of Godwin's friend John Fenwick. In the next four months Godwin produced *Memoirs and Posthumous Works*, the immediate reaction to which was scandalized outrage. A vicious caricature depicted Wollstonecraft as a bowler-hatted pipe-smoking Irish tinker, while George *Canning's anonymous attack on Wollstonecraft and Godwin in the *Anti-Jacobin* newspaper was swiftly followed by Richard *Polwhele's *The Unsex'd Females* (1798), damaging Wollstonecraft's reputation for years to come. After Godwin's death in 1836 Mary Shelley composed 'Life of William Godwin', containing an idealized portrait of Wollstonecraft, which was left unpublished. JB

women musicians and composers. Although most of the celebrated women musicians of our period attained fame as performers, many women also composed, and several achieved public recognition for their vocal and instrumental works. Like their male counterparts, women composers benefited from the strong demand for *domestic music that resulted from increased middle-class leisure and from an ideal of femininity in which musical accomplishment held an important place [see *domesticity, 13].

Most professionals who composed, whether male or female, did so alongside careers as performers or *music teachers, for while popular pieces written for the large, amateur market often brought in a substantial profit, much of that gain went to *music publishers. Composers of more serious and demanding works seldom received a significant level of reward for their labour. Maria Hester Reynolds (Mrs Park), most of whose works for harpsichord and piano were written during the 1790s, published for both market segments; she wrote easy music for the domestic market as well as several virtuosic works, including a piano concerto that she herself performed. As this example suggests, career patterns directly shaped the choice of musical genre. A renowned singer, such as Elizabeth *Billington, was likely to write songs whose sales would be enhanced by their author's fame, while a respected performer or teacher of harpsichord or piano would compose or write instructional books for performers and students of keyboard instruments.

The majority of women composers were born into families in which one or several members made their living in the musical world. The singer and pianist Ann Cantelo, student and protégée of J. C. *Bach, came from a noted family of Bath musicians. The Leicester family of Ann Valentine included five music professionals. Harriet Wainwright was probably one of the Cheshire Wainwrights, a family that included a composer, an organist, a music-seller, a

singer, and a double-bass player. Wainwright studied privately with the well-known organist and composer John Worgan. Her 1792 oratorio, 'Comala', was one of the few large-scale works composed by a woman during the period.

Instruction from a musician-parent gave an incalculably great advantage to a young woman whose access to musical training was otherwise far more limited than was the case for her male peers. There are numerous examples of this pattern of parental, especially paternal, pedagogy. The father of singer and pianist Maria Parke (Mrs Beardmore) was the eminent oboist John Parke. Robert Hudson, a noted singer and organist, was the father of organist and hymn writer Mary Hudson, while the songwriter Harriot Hague was the daughter of Cambridge professor Charles H. Hague, an organist and composer. Jane Savage, who wrote vocal and instrumental music, was the daughter of William Savage, a composer, organist, bass singer, and a friend of *Handel. The German wind player Carl Weichsell was the first instructor of both of his musically gifted children, the violinist Carl and the pianist and singer Elizabeth Billington.

A number of women composers had mothers who were professional musicians. Mrs Billington's mother was a noted singer who had studied with J. C. Bach. The mother of Sophia *Corri was also a professional singer; later, Sophia Corri Dussek became the teacher of her own daughter, the composer Olivia Dussek. The singer Polly Young Barthélemon and her violinist husband, François Hippolyte Barthélemon, often performed together and both wrote music; their daughter, Cecilia Maria Barthélemon, a composer of harpsichord sonatas, treasured memories of her parents' friendship with *Haydn, a frequent guest during his two London visits. Parental instruction often brought with it the possibility of important professional and social connections. And Maria Parke derived a highly visible advantage from her family's warm relationship with Haydn and his evident regard for her musicianship: the great composer played the piano at Parke's benefit concert in May of 1794, an event at which she both sang and performed one of her own piano works.

The girlhood talents of composers not born into families of professional musicians were often encouraged by musical amateurs and music teachers. Anna Maria *Crouch, one of England's most admired actress-singers, was the daughter of an attorney; she received early encouragement from the local chapel organist who was her music teacher, and she later attracted the patronage of the aristocratic wife of her father's employer. The talents of Jane Guest (later Miles), daughter of a Bath tailor, must have attracted the attention of a musically knowledgeable person in order for her to have performed publicly in that city before her 6th birthday. Occasionally, a gifted young singer would be 'discovered' by an enthusiastic listener with useful connections. Ann Catley, daughter of a coachman and a laundress, was discovered in the pubs where she sang as a young girl; the ballad singer Maria Theresa Bland began her career at the Royal Circus after her singing was overheard by a theatrical hairdresser.

Songs written for the theatre and performed by singer-actresses like Bland, Harriet Abrams, and Dorothy Jordan were enormously popular in the United States. Abrams's ballad 'Crazy Jane' was well known on both sides of the Atlantic as was Jordan's 'Blue Bells of Scotland'. The English woman composer best known in the early American republic was the singer Mary Ann Pownall; known to English theatregoers as Mrs Wrighten, she migrated to the United States and performed widely. Her varied programmes included excerpts from Handel, operatic selections, and her own songs, some of which ('Jenny of the Glen', 'Lavinia', and 'The Straw Bonnet') were among the most popular in turn-of-the-century America.

At least until the founding of the Royal Academy of Music in 1823, women born into non-musician families had limited access to a thorough programme of training in composition. Males of similar backgrounds began with the same disadvantage, but they were not barred, as women were, from the only English institutions that offered excellent professional music education at this time: London's two cathedrals and royal chapels whose chorister training provided a foundation for careers in both secular and *church music. Women were also barred from the more informal educational institution of the orchestra.

Female musicians were, however, greatly admired and often richly rewarded—as performers and as teachers to élite families. Serious private study with respected professionals was therefore considered appropriate for ambitious female singers, keyboard soloists, and harpists whose families could afford the expense. Elizabeth Billington studied privately with her mother's teacher, J. C. Bach, and later sought instruction from other eminent professionals; Jane Guest (Mrs Miles) was another of Bach's students. Since teaching was a high-status and often lucrative practice, professional musicians often devoted a large proportion of their time to it. Although female musical instruction was almost always focused on vocal or instrumental performance, a young woman interested in composing could easily have requested her mentor's guidance in the form of a critique of a song or sonata. This seems all the more likely, since women singers, from whose ranks came most women composers, usually studied with composers. J. C. Bach, Joseph Mazzinghi, Thomas *Linley, and Venanzio Rauzzini were the most prominent composer-teachers of successful female students.

Young women who could not afford private tuition could acquire musical education through the

---

108. Joshua Reynolds, *Mrs Billington as St. Cecilia*, 1786–9. Reynolds's work often blurred the generic boundaries between portraiture and history painting. Here the famous singer, actress, and social notoriety Elizabeth Billington is depicted as the ancient patroness of musicians.

traditional practice of apprenticeship according to which training would be give for a stipulated number of years upon payment, by parent or guardian, of an agreed fee. The master would receive a portion of the apprentice's earnings for the duration of the term of service. A number of women composers entered the profession by this route. Polly Young Barthélemon, for example, began her career as an apprentice to the composer Thomas Arne (1710–78) and to his wife, the singer Cecilia Young. Anna Maria Crouch was articled for a three-year period to Thomas Linley, music master of the Drury Lane theatre. Crouch's middle-class origins were unusual among female theatrical apprentices, since middle-class parents tended to be wary of a connection dangerous to their daughter's virtue and reputation. Their fears were not imaginary: one well-publicized, cautionary example was that of Ann Catley, whose master, the composer William Bates (fl. 1750–80), was convicted of attempting to gain money by prostituting her.

Occasionally, female apprenticeships were arranged outside the world of theatre. Such was the case with Ann Cantelo, who was articled to J. C. Bach and his wife, a professional singer. Bach, highly placed as music master to Queen Charlotte, did his best to advance Cantelo's career in upper-class circles, but the apprenticeship came to an early close with his death in 1782. Cantelo, then aged 16, returned to her native town of Bath and, after further study with the composer and singer, Rauzzini, developed a successful career as an oratorio singer. The connection with Bach was also helpful to the career of Cantelo's friend, Jane Guest Miles, whose keyboard sonatas were published with the prestigious support of several hundred subscribers and whose success both in teaching and performing led to her appointment as instructor to Princess Charlotte, daughter of the Prince of Wales. The *Monthly Musical Magazine* reviewed Mrs Miles's compositions and characterized her as a musician of taste and reputation.

In addition to songs and keyboard sonatas (the latter sometimes included optional accompaniment for violin or flute for male instrumentalists), Mrs Miles was one of a number of women who contributed to the pedagogical music literature so popular at this time. Ann Ford had set the precedent with a popular instruction book for English guitar, an instrument popular among women during the 1760s and 1770s; subsequently several women, including Harriet Wainwright and the ballad composer Clara Chatelain, published manuals for singers, the latter with an endorsement by the great opera singer Grisi.

Marriage often meant the interruption of a woman's professional musical career or, as was the case for Maria Parke, its termination. Marriage was less disruptive for amateur composers, since they had always worked apart from the pressures of public performance and were accustomed to writing as opportune time appeared. Many amateurs wrote *hymns and simple songs, but others were considerably more ambitious. Catherine Barlow, the first Lady Hamilton, composed music for the harpsi-

chord; her skill at that instrument was admired by Leopold Mozart and Charles *Burney. Another aristocrat-composer, Elizabeth Craven, Margravine of Anspach (1750–1828), wrote songs and contributed music to several operas. Anne Hunter, wife of the eminent surgeon John *Hunter, was a poet and singer, as well as a song-writer, whose poems were set by Haydn.

Although the Royal Academy of Music, from its 1823 opening, offered instruction in composition to all pupils, girls appear to have received a less rigorous course of study. According to the musician W. T. Parke (Maria Parke's uncle), whose memoirs were published in 1830, the boys' course of instruction at the Academy was designed to qualify them as singers, performers on various instruments, and composers, while the female curriculum prepared girls to be singers, harpists, and pianists. Such access as girl students had to the study of composition during the early years of the severely underfunded and poorly staffed Academy was not likely to compensate for the disadvantages that female students faced, both in the belief in their limited intellectual and creative powers and in the severely restricted roles open to them as music professionals.

Eliza Flower (1803–46), the musician often described as the foremost English woman composer of the 1830s and early 1840s, lacked even the superficial training in composition offered at the Royal Academy. The counterweight to this educational deficit, which severely restricted the scope of her talents, was the encouragement she received from a strongly feminist social circle. Flower, a charismatic and deeply religious woman whose formal musical instruction was limited to lessons from a village organist, was a prominent member of a politically radical circle that included J. S. *Mill, who wrote several admiring press reviews of her work.   PG

WOOLER, T[homas] J[onathan] (1785/6–1853), radical journalist, *satirist, printer, and publisher [see *publishing, 21]. An effective journalist, political organizer, and critic of the government during the post-Waterloo era of popular agitation, T. J. Wooler joined a festive satirical style with an inflexible commitment to the principles of radical reform.

Born in Yorkshire and apprenticed as a printer, Wooler began his political career after he moved to London and established himself as an articulate representative of plebeian radical aspirations, first in metropolitan *debating circles, then through his role as editor, *prose [30] writer, and publisher for a series of radical periodicals, including the *Republican* (1813), *Stage* (1814–16), *Black Dwarf* (1817–24), and *Wooler's British Gazette* (1819–23).

The *Black Dwarf* was Wooler's signature project. Launched in the heady climate of postwar economic dislocation and popular unrest, the four penny weekly was likely patronized by Major *Cartwright, whose version of *constitutional reform it tended to endorse. Wooler immediately established an independent radical voice, and a position for his paper, by criticizing William *Cobbett's decision to flee England for America after the suspension of habeas corpus; in Cobbett's absence, *Black Dwarf* super-seded the *Political Register* as London's leading radical periodical, with a peak circulation of perhaps 12,000 per week. Known for its unruly satire and furious attacks on government ministers and policies, *Black Dwarf* was also among the most comprehensive of the postwar *unstamped weeklies, and its pages regularly contained poetry, letters from readers, legal reports, and theatre reviews, in addition to regular coverage of reform politics.

The government was quick to respond to Wooler's challenge. He was arrested in May 1817, and subsequently charged for seditious libels contained in two early numbers of *Black Dwarf*. Though Wooler no doubt suffered during the period of his imprisonment, his success in the two trials that followed in June became his greatest public triumph. Conducting his own defence, and casting himself in the role of plain citizen and victim of a repressive regime, he used his very public trial to draw attention to a wide range of legal and constitutional issues, particularly the government's practice of packing juries with special jurors. He secured an acquittal on one charge, and while a disputed verdict on the other allowed the government to imprison him for several weeks after the trial, he emerged from prison a popular hero.

Wooler remained active as a radical journalist and orator through the *Peterloo crisis and beyond, and his periodicals were instrumental in publicizing radical strategy and organization. He was prosecuted by the government again in 1819, and this time convicted and sentenced to fifteen months in prison, for his participation in a political meeting held to elect Sir Charles Wolseley (1769–1846) as 'legislational attorney' for Birmingham. The fortunes of *Black Dwarf* declined after the introduction of the new controls on the cheap radical press contained in the Six Acts, and the paper folded in 1824.   KG

WORDSWORTH, Dorothy (1771–1855), writer of journals, letters, *travel literature, and *poetry [29]. Long famed as the devoted spinster sister of William *Wordsworth, Dorothy occupies a difficult place in modern Romanticist criticism. While some feminist scholars have tried to rescue her writings from the shadow of William's work, and even discerned a poetic of holistic domesticity in them, others have suggested that the interest in Dorothy is still conditioned by her familial proximity to the canonical poet.

After her mother died in 1778, Dorothy was separated from her four brothers and brought up by various relations in northern England. She was reunited with William in 1794, and the two siblings moved in together the following year, establishing a domestic arrangement which would survive numerous homes and disruptions. In 1797 they rented Alfoxden House to be near *Coleridge in Nether Stowey. Dorothy's writings of this time, including the remnants of *Alfoxden Journal* (1798), reveal important details about William's recovery from personal crisis, about the extraordinary poetic creativity of Wordsworth and Coleridge in their *annus mirabilis*, and about

the growth of that bond between the three friends which inspired each to develop their quintessential Romantic sensibilities. Her works also show the beginnings of an astute prose style which would flower in later accounts of local tours and daily life.

Dorothy was an ardent traveller, visiting the Continent a number of times and touring Britain with relatives, friends, and by herself. She accompanied Wordsworth and Coleridge during their brief German tour of 1798–9, and also joined them for a walking holiday in Scotland in 1803. The latter journey was recorded by Dorothy chiefly for friends, although *Recollections of a Tour made in Scotland* was circulated and admired widely, eventually finding publication in 1874. None of her writings was published in her lifetime; however, parts of *Excursion on the Banks of Ullswater 1805* and *Excursion up Scawfell Pike 1818* were evidently lifted by William for later editions of his popular *Guide to the Lakes* (first written 1810).

In 1799 the Wordsworths moved to Dove Cottage and Dorothy began her *Grasmere Journal* (1800–3). This is her better-known diary which uncovers the private world of a Romantic woman of letters and her apparently seamless existence of writing, cleaning, reading, baking, copying, walking, editing, gardening, and nursing. Through the course of subsequent moves to other homes and the expansion of the Wordsworth family, Dorothy continued to write prose and some poems. However, she mainly devoted herself to assisting William in his literary pursuits, and earned the expression of his deep affection in poems such as *An Evening Walk* (1793) and 'Tintern Abbey' (1798). Her demanding schedule and hidden talents were noted by some contemporaries. Both Samuel *Rogers and Thomas *De Quincey encouraged Dorothy to consider herself a publishable writer, the former also once airing his concern about 'the whole care' of domestic work which seemed to 'devolve . . . upon Miss Wordsworth', and the latter observing sadly how she carried 'an air of embarrassment and even self-conflict, that was sometimes distressing to witness'.

Her only attempt at prose narrative, *Concerning George and Sarah Green of the Parish at Grasmere* (1808), told the tragedy of a couple's death, and was sold locally in manuscript form to raise funds for their orphaned children. In 1829 Dorothy suffered severe intestinal difficulties and most probably a nervous breakdown. This inaugurated a pattern of illness and senility which would plague her body and writings until the end of her life.   KF

WORDSWORTH, William (1770–1850), still widely regarded as the pre-eminent poet of the period. Wordsworth's poetry is deeply concerned with responding to the disappointment of *utopian [9] expectations in the *French Revolution and their transference to the realm of *imagination. Argument continues about the exact chronology of his move from youthful *republicanism to more conservative values modelled after Edmund *Burke.

The Wordsworth children were orphaned when their father, legal agent to the Earl of Lonsdale, died in 1783. Their mother had died five years earlier. William went to the intellectually progressive Hawkshead grammar school, where his earliest writings were encouraged by a master. His first published poem, a sentimental *sonnet, appeared in the *European Magazine* (March 1787). In October 1787 Wordsworth went up to St John's College, Cambridge. Having made a promising start to his degree, he graduated without honours in January 1791. Any hopes of academic attainment had been sacrificed to a walking tour in the Alps the previous summer. The tour was his first encounter with the French Revolution, which he recalled in Book VI of *The Prelude* and the political sonnets of 1802.

The earliest of Wordsworth's poems to attract public notice, *An Evening Walk* and *Descriptive Sketches*, were composed during his undergraduate years and published in January 1793 by Joseph *Johnson. Both poems demonstrate his competence in the fashionable genre of topographic verse, and his skill in handling the rhyming couplet. The poems were elaborately literary, but also had a basis in the poet's own experience: *An Evening Walk* described Lake District scenes, and *Descriptive Sketches* drew upon the European tour of 1790. Wordsworth had returned to Europe to gain a closer acquaintance with events in France for a year over 1791–2. He visited the sights of Paris, including the ruins of the Bastille, then travelled south, where he met and fell in love with Annette Vallon (1766–1841). By March 1792 Annette was pregnant, and their daughter, Caroline (1792–1862), was born in December. Wordsworth's friendship at this time with Michel Beaupuy, an officer in the revolutionary army, encouraged his allegiance to the republican cause (recalled in *The Prelude*, Book IX). He returned to Paris just after the massacres of September 1792. He lingered in the city, meeting some of the leading revolutionaries, and seems to have returned to London by mid-December.

The commencement of the French wars was a severe blow to a man emotionally and intellectually committed to a revolution his own country now sought to destroy. Early in 1793 Wordsworth wrote, but did not publish, *A Letter to the Bishop of Llandaff*, a republican pamphlet justifying the recent execution of the French King Louis XVI and calling for an end to the war [see Richard *Watson]. His intellectual commitment to progressive change was encouraged by the appearance of William *Godwin's *Political Justice* and its assertion of human perfectibility. Godwin provided a vindication of progressive politics at a time when war and terror were making the French Revolution look a less attractive promise of the future of liberty. Those events provided the background for Wordsworth's *Salisbury Plain* (begun summer 1793; published 1842). Written in *Spenserian stanzas, the poem portrays human misery as a rallying-cause for political and social protest, a first step towards the more subtle analysis of suffering in his poems of 1797–8.

From mid-1795 Wordsworth's discontent with Godwin's neglect of human feeling initiated a period of self-examination, intellectual crisis, and recovery (see *The Prelude*, Book x). This accompanied Wordsworth's reunion with Dorothy *Wordsworth, his sister, and his early friendship with S. T. *Coleridge (whom he first met in Bristol, late August or September 1795). William and Dorothy now made their home at Racedown Lodge, Dorset, and during this period (1795–7), he composed his play *The Borderers* (published 1842) and his blank verse poem 'The Ruined Cottage'. *Lyrical Ballads* (1798, jointly authored with Coleridge) dates from the *annus mirabilis* which began in July 1797, when the Wordsworths moved to live at Alfoxden House, Somerset, near Coleridge's home at Nether Stowey. Written in an appropriately plain style, most of Wordsworth's ballads treat 'human passions, human characters, and human incidents'. In all of Wordsworth's poems in *Lyrical Ballads* 'kindness' is a vital word which recalls both the democratic principles of the French Revolution but also the mutual responsibilities of individuals as human beings and the conservative values which formed the basis of Burke's *Reflections on the Revolution in France* (1790).

From March 1798 Wordsworth projected a philosophical poem on 'Nature, Man, and Society', *The Recluse*, which he intended should 'do great good' after the failure of the revolutionary cause. Never formally completed, this scheme preoccupied Wordsworth until the end of his life; indeed, he thought of all his poems as contributing to its grand architecture. The plan encouraged his exploration of his poetic and intellectual powers, thus reinforcing the introspective tendency of the reflective memorial poem 'Tintern Abbey' (which concluded *Lyrical Ballads*). During the winter of 1798–9, when Wordsworth and Dorothy were living at Goslar, Germany, he composed the mysterious 'Lucy' poems and the first blank verse passages subsequently incorporated in *The Prelude*.

The earliest version of *The Prelude* (intended as a preliminary to *The Recluse*) was completed in two books by December 1799. This poem treated the formative experiences of childhood and adolescence, especially those unforgotten moments or 'spots of time' which quickened his imagination in later life. Wordsworth resumed intensive work on his poem in 1804 and had completed a thirteen-book version by May 1805. After extensive revisions over the next forty-five years, it was finally published in July 1850, three months after Wordsworth's death. His widow, Mary, titled it *The Prelude*.

Wordsworth and Dorothy settled at Dove Cottage in December 1799, a return to the site of their earliest childhood. Here, as in former years the wealth of observation in Dorothy's journals proved a vital resource for Wordsworth's poetry. In the following decade, Wordsworth married his childhood friend Mary Hutchinson (October 1802) and fathered four children. Many of his greatest lyrical poems date from the Dove Cottage years; the Lake District *pastorals, 'The Brothers' and 'Michael'; the lyrics of spring 1802, including 'Resolution and Independence', and 'Ode' ('Intimations of Immortality', completed 1804); the political sonnets of August–September 1802; and the powerful elegies for his brother, John, who had drowned at sea in 1805.

These poems define Wordsworth's 'great decade' and, with *The Prelude*, have for many years been taken to be the heart of his achievement as a poet. All had been composed by May 1808, when the Wordsworth family quitted Dove Cottage for a larger house in Grasmere. It was here, between autumn 1810 and 1812, that a series of misunderstandings permanently damaged Wordsworth's and Coleridge's friendship. In 1813, leaving behind the unhappy residence in Grasmere (two children, Catharine and Thomas, died) the Wordsworths settled at Rydal Mount, the poet's home until his death.

Wordsworth's later years were saddened by Dorothy's mental illness and by the death in 1843 of his daughter Dora. To the public, however, Wordsworth at Rydal Mount had become a national institution. From 1813 he had served the government as Distributor of Stamps for Westmorland. His public reputation as a poet was secured by his long dramatic poem *The Excursion* (1814) and the two-volume *Poems* (1815). He celebrated the defeat of *Napoleon at *Waterloo in a 'Thanksgiving Ode'. In the years immediately following the peace, the political and literary controversy surrounding the 'Cockney' writers Leigh *Hunt, William *Hazlitt, and John *Keats served to reinforce Wordsworth's stature as the champion of orthodox values [see *copyright]. His native place, the subject of many of his poems, was also treated in his popular *Guide Through the District of the Lakes* (1810). In 1843 he succeeded Robert *Southey as Poet Laureate. So the one-time republican, who had identified so closely with the French Revolution, ended his life as a revered member of the Victorian establishment.

NR

WRIGHT, Joseph, of Derby (1734–97), English *portrait and *landscape painter born into a middle-class Derby family of which the paterfamilias, John Wright, was town clerk.

In 1751 Joseph left Derby for London to study with the fashionable portraitist Thomas Hudson (1701–79) with whom he pursued a traditional training in the craft of *painting [27] while broadening his cultural horizons with studies after older art, particularly Italian examples and art in the manner of Caravaggio. Wright returned to Derby in 1753 and, after a further period of training with Hudson in London (1756–7), established himself among local industrialists and landowners as a portraitist of note. He exhibited in London at the Society of Artists from 1765, the year in which he showed two paintings including *Three Persons Viewing the Gladiator by Candle-Light*. This painting is an early example of his interest in the effects of candlelight, stylistically reminiscent of Georges de la Tour (1593–1652). His submission to the exhibition the following year, *A Philosopher Giving that Lecture on the Orrery, in which a lamp is put in place of the Sun*, displayed his fascination with the effects of artificial light in the context of an abiding interest in scientific and technological experimentation and *industrialization [14]. The scientific demonstration offered by the Orrery—which shows the movement of the planets around the sun—may be seen as an example of the intellectual and scientific interests of Wright's friends and patrons, made up of industrialists, professional men, and progressive landowners. The Lunar Society, a group of provincial philosophers, scientists, and industrialists, some of whose members (including Erasmus *Darwin) were painted by Wright, would have made such experiments familiar to the artist, and introduced him to a circle of patrons of similar interests [see *literary and philosophical societies].

Two years after the exhibition of the *Orrery*, Wright sent *An Experiment on a Bird in the Air-pump* to the 1768 exhibition. Combining tremendous compositional flair with telling psychological insights, prompted by the death of the bird in a vacuum, Wright's painting is a representation of the philosophy and practice of the *Enlightenment [32], based on scientific experimentation, rational inquiry, and demonstrable knowledge. In it a lecturer demonstrates to a group of family and friends the implacable laws of nature as the death of the oxygen-starved bird approaches. But Wright disrupts the spirit of scientific inquiry through his complex handling of the subject. The lecturer, for example, somewhat manic in appearance, presages the strictures of Mary *Shelley on the dangers of untrammelled experimentation. From the evidence of the *Air-pump* Wright may be considered a master of dramatic tension, a painter within the narrative tradition which leads from Hogarth (1697–1764) to *Wilkie. Likewise his painting may be properly considered a *history picture, that is, a painting in which a theme of universal significance is represented in a high moral tone.

Working in a town at the heart of the industrial revolution, it is unsurprising that Wright painted this new meritocracy, men like Sir Richard Arkwright, who is portrayed, in Wright's portrait of 1790, not as might be supposed as a wealthy gentleman, but with the spinning frame which made his fortune. Wright also painted Arkwright's mill at Cromford in Derbyshire, both as it looked by day and by night, for work went on around the clock. However, he did not spend his entire career in Derby. From 1768 to 1771 he worked in Liverpool, and between 1775 and 1777 he attempted to break into the fashionable portrait market in Bath. Between these sojourns he travelled to Italy (1774–5) which revivified his interest in history painting. Most notably he painted the eruption of Vesuvius at night—a sort of *sublime candlelight painting—in 1774, and continued to reproduce the image, of which some thirty variations exist, on his return to England.

Throughout his life, portraits were the basis for Wright's practice as a painter. While he painted landscape, this genre did not provide him with an income. Likewise his magnificent 'histories', such as the *Orrery*, were group portraits animated by sublime and universal themes. Today Wright's reputation is rightly on the ascent, for as a painter of his milieu he had no equal.

PD

WYATT, James (1746–1813), architect, best known for his design of the Pantheon Building in Oxford Street, London (1770–2). Influenced by Byzantine church *architecture [28], the Pantheon was a 'Winter Ranelagh' or fashionable assembly rooms and venue for *masquerades and musical *concerts.

Wyatt's work on the restoration of the cathedrals of Lichfield, Salisbury, and Westminster Abbey earned him the nickname 'the Destroyer'. It also enabled the development of his highly detailed *Gothic style, exemplified by Fonthill Abbey (1796–1812), erected for William *Beckford.

Exhibiting at the *Royal Academy between 1770 and 1799, Wyatt was elected associate of the Academy in 1770, becoming a fully-fledged Academician in 1785 and president temporarily in 1805. In 1796 he succeeded William *Chambers as surveyor-general to the board of works.   CT

WYATVILLE, Sir Jeffry (1766–1840), architect. A member of the Wyatt clan of builders and architects, Wyatville is best known for his work on Windsor Castle for George IV and William IV from 1824 to 1840 [see *architecture, 28]. The *picturesque triumph earned him a knighthood and permission to elaborate his surname.

Wyatville apprenticed with his uncles, Samuel (1737–1807), from 1784–91 and James *Wyatt from 1791–9. Methodical and cost-effective renovations of major aristocratic seats grounded his reputation, and led to his selection as architect for Windsor Castle over John *Soane, John *Nash, and Robert *Smirke.   SS

WYVILL, Christopher (1740–1822), see *Wyvillites.

Wyvillites, followers of Anglican clergyman and northern gentry landowner Revd Christopher Wyvill (1740–1822), who founded an extraparliamentary reform movement in the 1780s known as the Yorkshire Association or Associated Counties movement. This pioneered reform ideas and methods, and served as a prototype of the organized voluntary association that became a hallmark of late Georgian civil and political activism. [See *democracy, 3.]

Launched in December 1776 with the assistance of the Dissenting doctor John *Jebb, the Yorkshire Association gathered up many of the discontents of the American War, which Wyvill ascribed to the growth of unconstitutional political developments in Britain. He fanned the traditional animosities which independent landed freeholders in county seats felt towards 'court' policies such as war expenditure, high taxation, and the exercise of undue political influence through corrupt borough seats. The County reform movement grew until it eventually encompassed a central committee in London, representing more than a dozen mainly northern counties. Between 1780 and 1783 Wyvill's Association levied sizable fees from its members, organized resolutions and mass petitions to the King, and embarked on an intensive propaganda campaign in provincial newspapers. Its programme encompassed 'economical reform' aimed at trimming government expenditure and wastage, as well as the introduction of annual or triennial parliaments and an additional 100 independent county seats in the House of Commons.

Despite initial success, the movement was ultimately damaged by the conservative reaction to the *Gordon riots, as well as by internal divisions and the conflicting goals of allied reformers, especially Rational Dissenters, London City radicals, and oppositionist *Whigs.   IMcC

Y

YEARSLEY, Ann (1752–1806), poet, known as 'the Bristol Milkwoman', born Ann Cromartie. Her parents were rural labourers; her mother had a milk round which Ann later took over. Married to an illiterate labourer, John Yearsley, in 1774, she gave birth to six children, and struggled to support them, her mother, and her invalid (or feckless) husband. She had been taught to read and write by her brother, and her mother had borrowed books for her, so *Shakespeare and *Milton and their eighteenth-century imitators were embedded in her taste for *poetry [29]. Somehow she managed to fit the writing of poems into the evenings of the working day. In the bad winter of 1783–4 she and her brood were only

just short of starvation, and her mother in fact died. Yearsley's desperate circumstances were brought to Hannah *More's attention; More responded with strenuous charity, and enlisted Elizabeth Montagu (1720–1800) as another patron. Already in the 1760s Montagu had patronized James Woodhouse, the 'shoemaker poet', who had come to resent her treatment of him [see *peasant poets].

Yearsley appeared as living proof of More's thesis that literature is beneficial to morality, even or especially for women and the poor, and 'that reading and writing cou'd allay hunger and subdue calamity'. There was an extraordinary excitement in finding a woman who milked cows and fed hogs but still hungered after the refinements of literature, where More was the authority. Milk supplied the refrain to their intercourse, and 'Lactilla' was adopted by Yearsley as a poetic signature.

In the autumn of 1784 More's pastoral enthusiasm provided Yearsley with a grammar, a spelling-book, a dictionary, and 'a little Maid, to help her feed her pigs, and nurse the little ones, while she herself sells her Milk'. More campaigned to raise subscribers for a volume of poems, and was successful in gathering over 1,000 signatures for Yearsley's *Poems on Several Occasions*, published in June 1785, with a preface by More in the form of a letter to Elizabeth Montagu, dated from the November of 1784. In 'Soliloquy' and 'On Mrs Montagu', Yearsley drew on Shakespearean romance for vindication of women's poetry.

Already in June 1785 the relationship between Yearsley and More was rupturing, as More invested Yearsley's money ('lest her husband should spend it'), for the eventual benefit of the Yearsley children. The childless spinster Hannah More miscalculated the effect on Yearsley if her long-term future as well as her present were blocked out. By September 1785 More was publicly lamenting Yearsley's 'savage' ingratitude and Yearsley was writing up the experience in an 'Autobiographical Narrative', appended to the fourth edition of her *Poems* (1786). More's class allies rallied to her side of the story, Horace *Walpole calling Yearsley a 'parish Sappho'. Richard *Polwhele's *Unsex'd Females* (1798), included Yearsley, 'an untutored milk-woman', in its denunciation of 'amazonian writers'.

Yet Yearsley found supporters such as the poet Anna *Seward, and she published *Poems on Various Subjects* (1787), *Poem on the Inhumanity of the Slave Trade* (1788), *Stanzas of Woe* (1790), and a historical tragedy, a novel based on the story of the Man in the Iron Mask, and a last collection of verse *The Rural Lyre* (1796). After the break with More, the poems deal critically, in the Virgilian georgic manner, with social wrongs and the abuse of power. Yearsley's *Inhumanity of the Slave Trade* (1788) was obviously competing with More's *Slavery: A Poem* of the same year, but like other Yearsley poems, it is a secular satire of institutions, whereas More lectures from within the pale, like an *Evangelical missionary.

In the 1790s Yearsley opened a *circulating library in Bristol, and became known to the circle of writers about Joseph *Cottle's bookshop. One of these, Robert *Southey, joined her with Stephen Duck (1705–56) in *The Lives and Works of the Uneducated Poets* (1830). Alexander Dyce's anthology, *Specimens of the British Poetesses* (1825), included brief excerpts from Yearsley.

Yearsley's independence, which Anna Seward labelled 'Johnsonian', seems fortified by her claims of interdependence with her sons. This was compatible with her working-class culture, where Hannah More's all-women's world, and women writers' sponsorship, were an alien possibility for her.   JB

YOUNG, Arthur (1741–1820), agricultural and travel writer, is probably better known today as a selectively deployed witness to the *agricultural and *French revolutions than for the substance of his writings. However, because of his skill as a communicator—both in person and in print—he was widely admired in his lifetime.

He was a prolific writer: best known perhaps for his *Tours* of the southern counties (1768), the north (1771), the east (1771), and Ireland (1780), for his *Travels in France* (1794), and for his *General Views of Agriculture* in a variety of English counties. He was also celebrated in his day as the author of a huge range of specialized works on farming questions, including a number of the Board of Agriculture's *Reports*, a more general treatise on *Political Arithmetic* (1779), and above all as the editor and major contributor for over thirty years to the *Annals of Agriculture* (1784–1815). Though modern historians criticize his haphazard method of collecting material, and catalogue his many exaggerations, inaccuracies, and contradictions, Young saw himself more as a propagandist and a *philosophe* than as an accurate recorder of data. As rural investigator, pamphleteer, parliamentary reporter, estate steward, editor, correspondent, and secretary to the Board of Agriculture, his aim was to change the agrarian habits of the past.

His enthusiasm for agricultural improvement of every kind was characteristic of the contemporary passion for innovation. He was the most articulate spokesman for what he misrepresented as the 'new' Norfolk system of the flexible rotation, for the enclosure and cultivation of waste lands, the application of 'scientific' (especially chemical) knowledge, the introduction of new techniques and implements, the commutation of tithes, the removal of prohibition on wool exports, and a host of other measures which served the interests of the efficient large-scale farmer. Correspondingly, he was an unswerving critic of antiquated sharecropping and of 'the goths and vandals' of the common fields. He believed fervently that the open-field school of farming needed to die. Yet he was no enthusiast for improvement for its own sake, and he always provided detailed cost–benefit analyses of his proposals. Young thought the small farmer, working close to the margin, had to be persuaded that new techniques were serviceable and that they would pay.

Much honoured and fêted by the great, Young's advice and practical help was widely sought not just by improving English landlords like Egremont, Portland, and Rockingham, but also by correspondents from Russia, Poland, France, and America (Washington's *Letters* to him were published in 1801). His greatest achievement, the *Annals of Agriculture*, though limited in circulation, served as an influential forum for progressive views and for news of experiments and innovations. His advice of the Board of Agriculture also eventually bore fruit in *Pitt's legislation of 1793.   AMacL

YOUNG, Thomas (1773–1829), physician, natural philosopher, and *Egyptologist. A self-educated child prodigy, Young was a socially well-connected gentleman scholar highly regarded by his contemporaries for his expertise in many fields, although now most famous for his work in optics. His densely argued texts were not always influential, but he held important posts as a scientific administrator and published widely, often anonymously.

After qualifying as a physician, Young studied at Cambridge and then came to London in 1800, where—with limited success—he practised and taught *medicine [18], and *lectured on *natural philosophy [34] at the newly founded Royal Institution. Active at the Royal Society, he was employed as a consultant on diverse topics, including shipbuilding, public gas supplies, and life insurance, and served as secretary to the Royal Commission on Weights and Measures and the Board of Longitude. Following the discovery of the Rosetta stone, Young played a crucial role in deciphering hieroglyphic inscriptions and translating Egyptian texts.

Young's extensive medical publications included his innovatory studies on vision concerning lens accommodation and colour perception. Drawing analogies to sound, he opposed contemporary particle models of light, controversially reintroducing a wave theory in 1800. Young subsequently devised experiments to demonstrate that coloured fringes are caused by interference, and provided wave explanations of other optical phenomena such as crystal refraction. Strongly criticized for his ideas, he became involved in a priority dispute with French protagonists of wave theories, but was elected to the Parisian Académie des Sciences. Young also studied capillary action, tides, and heat; Young's modulus is still a fundamental measure of elasticity.

PF

Z

ZOFFANY, Johan (Johannes Josephus Zauffaly) (1733–1810), German painter of *conversation pieces, *portraits, and theatre scenes. Born near Frankfurt, Zoffany arrived in London in 1760 after an apprenticeship in his home country and a tour of Italy during the early 1750s. He retained a strong German accent and apparently struggled with English idioms all his life, one of which included the corruption of his name from Zauffaly to Zoffany. He found employment decorating clock-faces before the actor David Garrick (1717–79) commissioned him to paint theatrical scenes and family portraits. The exhibition of these conversation pieces in 1762 made Zoffany's English reputation as a fashionable artist. He courted royal patronage from about 1763, gaining the peculiar honour of nomination by the King—rather than election by members—to the *Royal Academy in 1769.

In 1770 Queen Charlotte commissioned Zoffany to paint the Tribuna of the Uffizi, which contained the art collection of the Grand Duke of Tuscany, reputed to be the finest in Europe at the time. Zoffany arrived in Florence in 1772 and enjoyed favour from the imperial family, undertaking commissions from them and other patrons while supposedly working at the Queen's pleasure. He returned to Britain in 1779 only to meet disappointment. The vogue for his work was over and the completed *Tribuna* was sharply criticized by artists and royalty. The King and Queen were said to be baffled by the inclusion of many English connoisseurs in the setting and 'shocked by the impropriety of the whole thing'. Nevertheless, Zoffany continued to work, producing

Charles Townley's Library in Park Street (1781–3), which perhaps best represents his approach to the neoclassical style. In 1783 he resolved to make his fortune in India, succeeding in this ambition and painting the portraits of many notable colonials such as *Mr and Mrs Warren Hastings* (1783–7).

KF

zoology. Originally denoting the study of medical remedies obtained from animals, the word 'zoology', meaning the science of animal life, was first defined in Bailey's 1726 dictionary and popularized by Thomas *Pennant's *British Zoology* (1766).

General zoological interest and specialist knowledge was not confined to the élite, but was widespread across the general populace. During the late eighteenth century in particular, a love for the exotic and an escalating interest in improving domestic breeds made the subject ubiquitous. Menageries, circuses, and exhibitions reached a large audience, merging seamlessly into the raree shows staged all over the country.

Naturalists were mostly concerned with collecting and classifying—the central scientific motif of the age since collecting was perceived as a vital part of colonization and edification. Although government-sponsored materials were deposited in the new museums and institutions of the era, the *British Museum did not become a great centralized depot until Victorian times. Competition with proliferating alternatives prevented any easy supremacy; and some wealthy individuals like Sir Ashton Lever (1729–88) established their own museums or menageries.

109. Detail from *The Tribuna of the Uffizi*, 1780, by Johan Zoffany. Queen Charlotte was said to feel 'shocked by the impropriety of the whole thing'.

The system of classification which dominated zoological classification was that elaborated by the Swedish naturalist Carolus Linnaeus (1707–78) in his *Systema naturae* (1735), a system founded on the belief that all living beings were perfectly adapted to their circumstances in life. Fortified by traditional *Anglican natural theology, such concepts became deeply significant in Britain, exemplified by Gilbert White's (1720–93) *Natural History of Selborne* (1788) and William *Paley's *Natural Theology* (1802). Classification schemes consequently endorsed the idea that animals were divinely created and entirely distinct from human beings, and that species had been fixed since the Creation. Despite arguments to the contrary from the French naturalist Georges-Louis Buffon (1707–88), and others, most British thinkers clung to the idea of fixity, especially in the years after the *French Revolution.

For some, however, animals represented change and progress. Abraham Trembley's (1710–84) experiments on the hydra polyp, for example, which confused the boundaries between animals and plants, encouraged evolutionary thinkers like Erasmus *Darwin. Similar concepts lay behind the surge of interest in animal instincts, spontaneous generation, comparative anatomy, and the fossil record. Links between animals and humans were widely discussed, and human origins were sought among the great apes or in primitive cultures. These views easily interlaced with contemporary reform movements and progressive social doctrines. A number of radicals, such as William *Lawrence, adopted animal and human evolution as a politicized, secular alternative to natural theology, though perhaps few were outright atheists.

In Britain, zoology emerged as a professional discipline with the foundation of the Zoological Society of London (1826). The Society's rising young anatomists sought a professional niche and soon made it a centre for assessing material received from overseas. The gardens in Regent's Park were first opened to the public in 1828. Though there had been professors of natural history in the old universities for some time, the first chair in zoology in the country was awarded to Robert *Grant in 1827 at the new University College in London.   JBR

ILLUSTRATION
ACKNOWLEDGEMENTS

Page

7   By courtesy of the National Portrait Gallery, London
18   © British Museum
20   © British Museum
27   Courtesy of the Trustees of the Tate Gallery London
31   © British Museum
38   © British Museum
49   By courtesy of the National Portrait Gallery, London
55   Private Collection
60   Bristol Record Office, Accession no. 38169
70   By kind permission of the Metropolitan Police Museum
98   © British Museum
103 British Library 12835b.82
112–13 © British Museum
120 B1976.7.58 MORLAND, George (1762/3–1804) The Squire's Door, 1790 Oil on canvas 15 5/16 × 12 7/8 in (39.0 × 32.7 cm) Yale Center for British Art, Paul Mellon Collection
121 National Galleries of Scotland
126 © British Museum
128 Reproduced from *The Novels of Jane Austen, Vol IV, Emma*. Clarendon Press 1923
135 The Science Museum/Science & Society Picture Library
144 Board of Trustees of the National Museums & Galleries on Merseyside (Museum of Liverpool Life)
154 Rural History Centre, University of Reading
163 British Library C70612
169 The Whitworth Art Gallery, The University of Manchester
172 Bath & North East Somerset Library and Archive Service (Bath Central Library)
176 Wellcome Institute Library London
185 By Courtesy of the Trustees of the Wedgwood Museum, Barlaston, Stoke-on-Trent, Staffordshire, England
193 Courtesy of the Trustees of the Tate Gallery London
196 © British Museum
199 © British Museum
211 © British Museum
212 National Gallery of Victoria, Melbourne
218 By kind permission of the National Trust for Scotland, Brodick Castle Collection
221 Private Collection
225 © British Museum
227 By permission of the Syndics of Cambridge University Library
237 British Library 1261.S.23
239 British Library C119f1
251 © British Museum

Page

255 The Royal Collection © Her Majesty Queen Elizabeth II
259 V & A Picture Library
262 By courtesy of the Trustees of Sir John Soane's Museum
268–9 By courtesy of the Trustees of Sir John Soane's Museum
271t Bodleian Library
284 Maidstone Museum and Art Gallery/Bridgeman Art Library
288 © British Museum
309 University College London
315 By courtesy of the National Portrait Gallery, London
323 By permission of the Master and Fellows of Darwin College Cambridge
333 © British Museum
348 National Library of Australia
349 Private Collection
359 Private Collection
363 British Library 7306b.13 (1)
375 Private Collection
400 British Library C119f1
410 By permission of the Syndics of Cambridge University Library
417 Reproduced by permission of the National Gallery of Australia, Canberra
437 Crawford Municipal Art Gallery, Cork
441 The Royal Collection © Her Majesty Queen Elizabeth II
449 © British Museum
463 British Library 12835b.82
465 V & A Picture Library
478 Private Collection
483 © British Museum
489 Rex Nan Kivell Collection, National Library of Australia
493 Private Collection
503 Edgar Jones
504 Reproduced with permission from Marina Warner: *From the Beast to the Blonde*, Chatto & Windus 1994
508 By courtesy of the National Portrait Gallery, London
517 The National Trust Waddesdon Manor and The Courtauld Institute of Art
523 © British Museum
532 By courtesy of the National Portrait Gallery, London
533 © British Museum
539 © British Museum
552 Reproduced by kind permission of the President and Council of the Royal College of Surgeons of England
555 © British Museum